Oil Paintings in Public Ownership in South Yorkshire: Sheffield

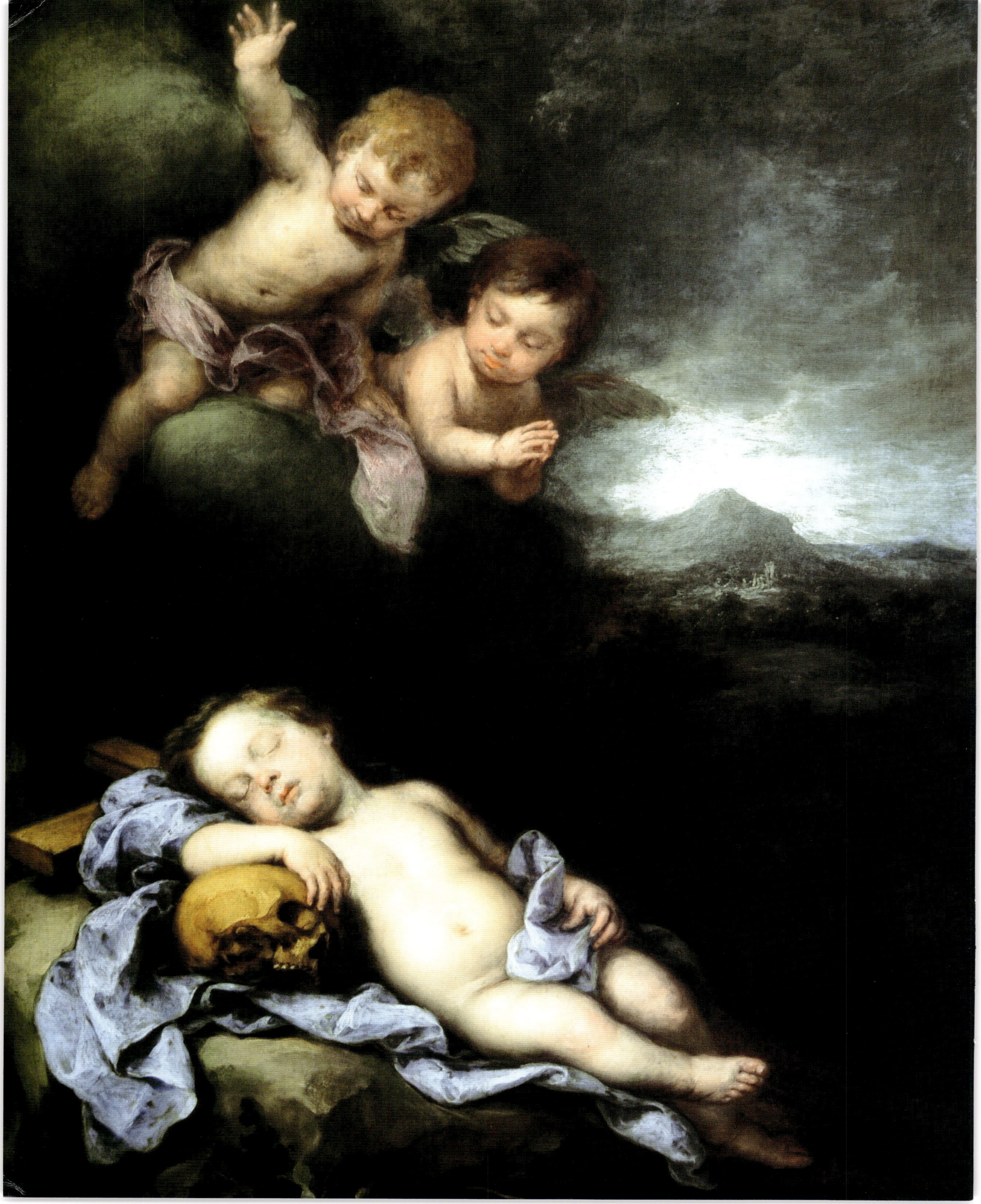

The *Oil Paintings in Public Ownership* series of catalogues is an extraordinary work in progress. Published by The Public Catalogue Foundation, it is the result of the determined efforts of a small team of administrative staff, researchers and photographers spread across the United Kingdom.

Our national collection of oil paintings in public ownership is probably one of the finest anywhere in the world. It is held not just by our museums and galleries but is also to be found in hospitals, universities and other civic buildings throughout the United Kingdom. A large proportion of these paintings are not on display and many have never before been reproduced.

This series of books for the first time allows the public to see an entire photographic record of these works – a collection likely to number some 200,000 in total. In doing so, these volumes provide a unique insight into our nation's artistic and cultural history.

As Patron of The Public Catalogue Foundation, my visits to collections across the country have highlighted to me not only the desire of curators to publicise their paintings, but also the limited resources at their disposal. The Foundation's work goes a long way towards helping to create access to these collections, while at the same time giving the British public the opportunity to see and enjoy *all* the paintings that they own.

I wish The Public Catalogue Foundation every success in its continuing endeavours.

Camilla

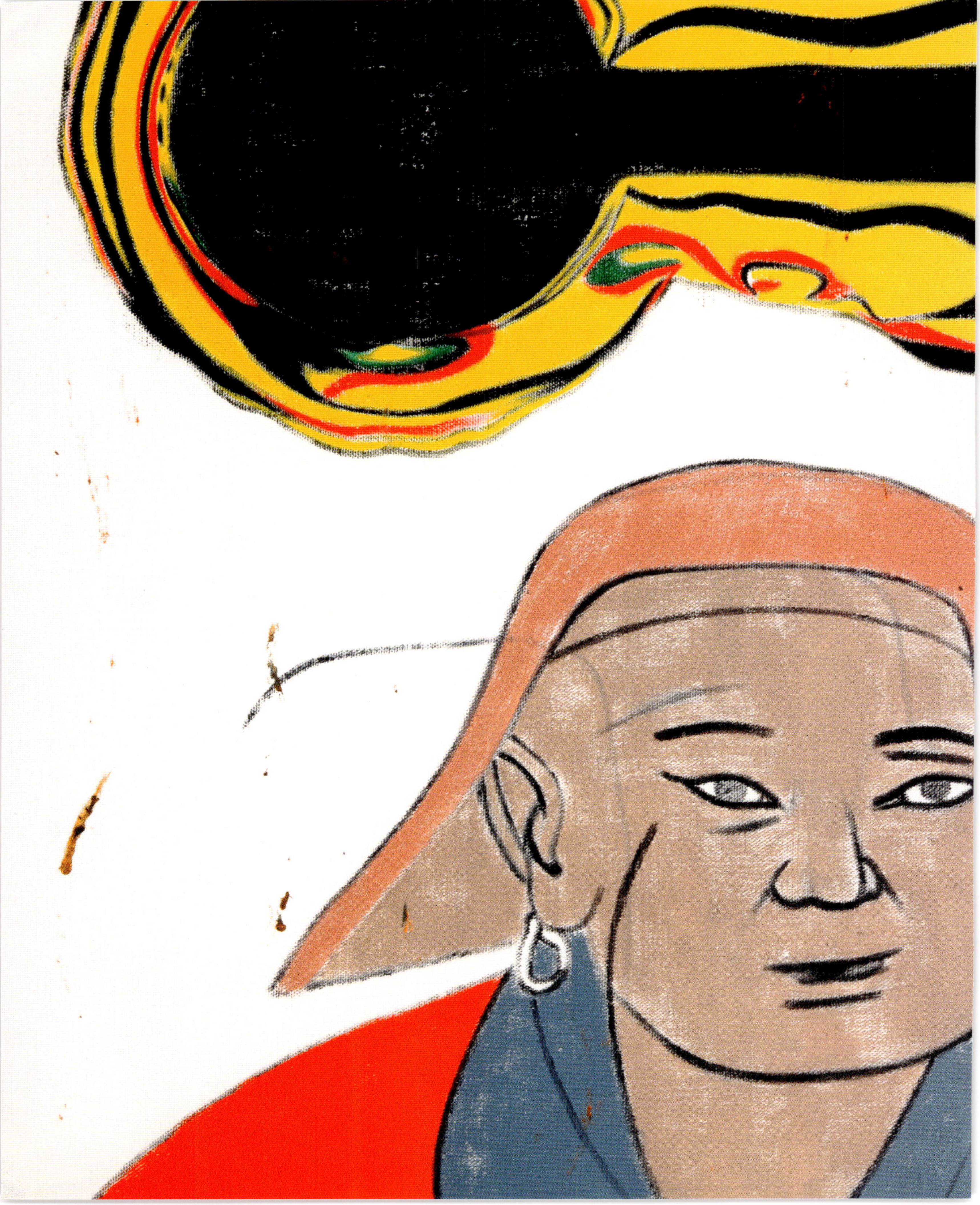

Oil Paintings in Public Ownership in South Yorkshire: Sheffield

Master Patron: Lord Roy Hattersley, PC

Coordinator: Pam Woolliscroft

Photographer: Norman Taylor

The Public Catalogue Foundation

Patron HRH The Duchess of Cornwall

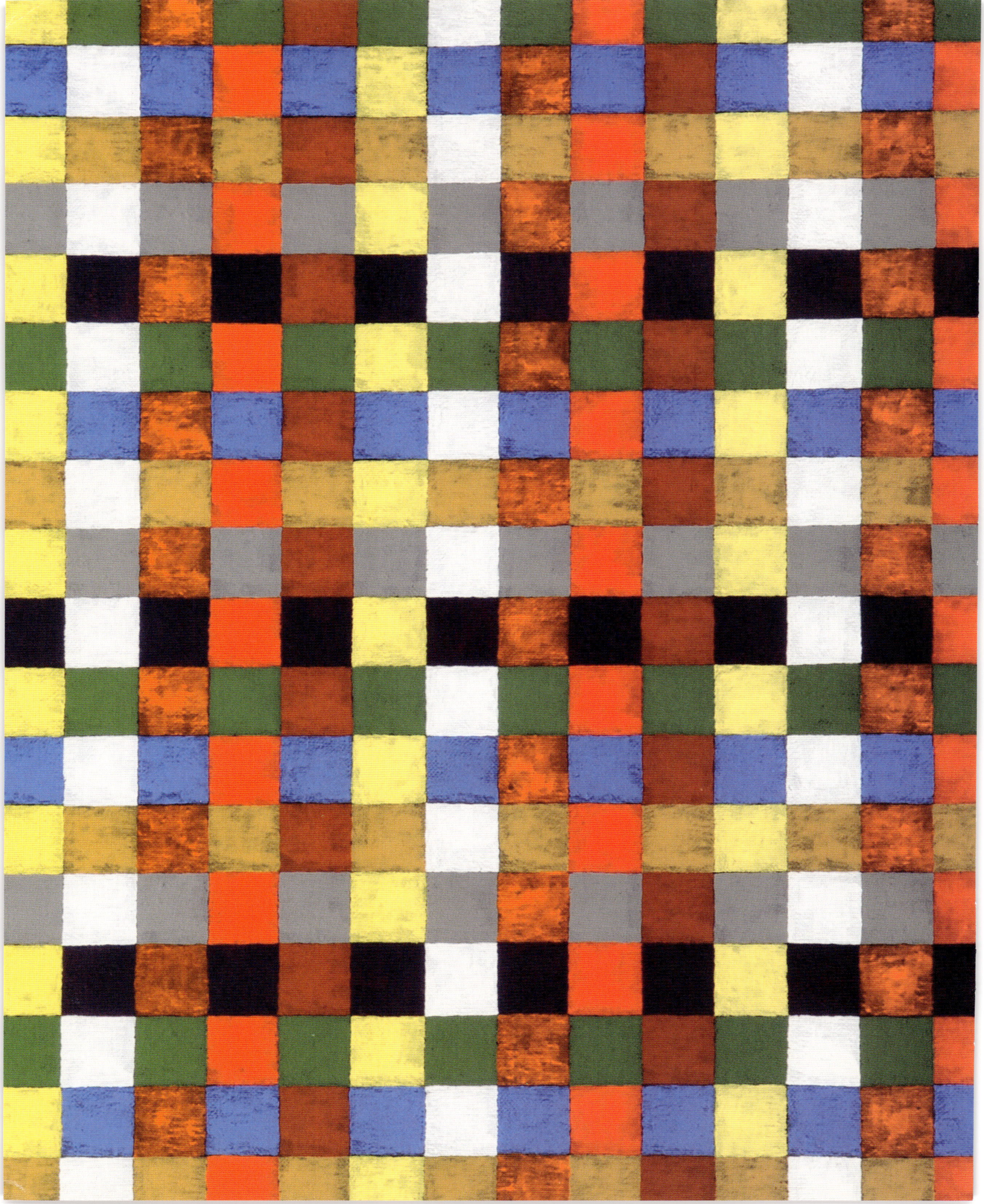

Contents

iii Statement by HRH The Duchess of Cornwall
ix Foreword by the Founder of The Public Catalogue Foundation
xi The Public Catalogue Foundation: People Involved
xii Financial Supporters
xiii Catalogue Scope and Organisation
xiv Key to Painting Information

THE PAINTINGS

3 Bradfield Parish Council
3 Fire & Police Museum at Sheffield
4 Museums Sheffield:
Graves Gallery
Millennium Gallery
Weston Park
255 Sheffield Central Library
258 Sheffield Hallam University
264 Sheffield Industrial Museums Trust:
Abbeydale Industrial Hamlet
Kelham Island Museum
268 Sheffield Libraries Archives and Information: Sheffield Archives
268 Sheffield Magistrates' Court
269 Sheffield Teaching Hospitals NHS Foundation Trust
274 Sheffield Town Hall
275 South Yorkshire Fire and Rescue Training Centre
275 Stocksbridge Town Council
276 The Children's Hospital
290 The Ken Hawley Collection Trust*
290 Traditional Heritage Museum, University of Sheffield
291 University of Sheffield:
Turner Glass Museum
University of Sheffield, Heritage Collection

307 Paintings Without Reproductions
309 Further Information
331 Collection Addresses
333 Index
343 Acknowledgements
344 Supporters

* The Ken Hawley Collection Trust is managed by Sheffield Industrial Museums Trust

Facing page: Brighton, Bob, b.1936, *Yellow Blue 2* (detail), c.2009, Sheffield Central Library, (p. 258)

Image opposite HRH The Duchess of Cornwall's statement: Murillo, Bartolomé Esteban, 1618–1682, *The Infant Christ Asleep on the Cross* (detail), Museums Sheffield, (p. 150)
Image opposite title page: Kitaj, R. B., 1932–2007, *The Rival Poet* (detail), 1965, Museums Sheffield, (p. 112)

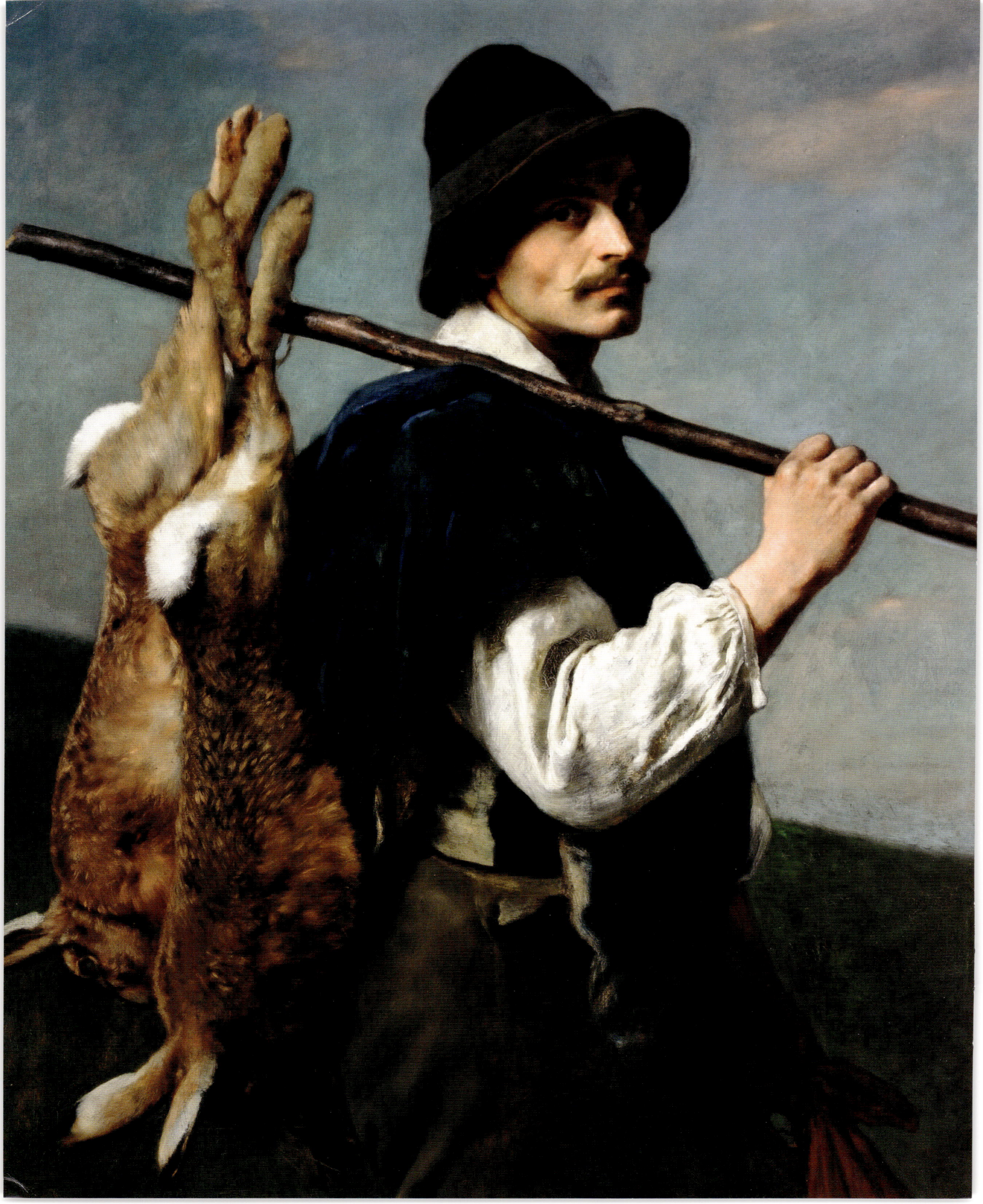

Foreword

Finding a Master Patron for the Sheffield catalogue proved surprisingly difficult. The right answer, as is ever the case, was staring me in the face but I couldn't see it. In my early years as a diplomat in New York, I worked for Roy Hattersley (as he then was) in a junior role at a General Assembly. We remade contact when he attended the launch of our catalogue of the Imperial War Museum. I knew that Yorkshire was his territory but I had failed miserably to remember his much more important relationship with Sheffield. Nor did I know his mother's.

Enid Hattersley, who died just at the turn of the century was one of those devoted Socialists who recognised the good and fought for it – so much more difficult than fighting against Evil. She embodied that belief, as do I, that people embrace culture to their own and to society's wider benefit if they are given the fullest access to books, art, music and drama. With her colleagues on the Sheffield Council, she helped Sheffield become the modern post-war industrial city it became but, more specifically, she spent twenty years on its Libraries and Arts Committee chairing it from 1968 to 1980. Described as kindly and formidably persistent, Enid Hattersley oversaw the recruitment of a number of talented directors of the Sheffield galleries, including Frank Constantine, whose tenure during the 1960s and 1970s resulted in the strength of Museums Sheffield's Modern British paintings. Innovations pioneered by her include a loan programme, permitting people to borrow available paintings from the City's galleries at a nominal fee.

It would be unfair on her memory not to recall as well her work over many years in regional arts organisations and in 1979 as chairman of the Yorkshire Museum Service. As such, she managed to persuade Kirklees Council not to sell some of the finest works from its collection including, a Francis Bacon and a Henry Moore. *Thou shouldst be living at this hour!*

So Lord Hattersley (as he has since become) happily became our Master Patron. One way or another this didn't prove especially onerous which was fortunate as he broke his leg shortly after accepting while out walking his dog, Buster. But for all his support and encouragement, all of us at the Foundation are enormously grateful.

As the foregoing will suggest, Museums Sheffield's collection, which is fully described in Liz Waring's introduction, is of exceptional quality. Apart from distinguished patrons, the city benefitted hugely from Sir John Rothenstein's long tenure at both the Graves and Mappin Galleries prior to moving to the Tate Gallery. The city has been very fortunate.

The Foundation's thanks go to all those who made this important volume happen: to the Museums Sheffield team, and especially Liz Waring, Curator of Visual Art, and Kim Streets, Director of Learning & Knowledge; to the coordinator, Pam Woolliscroft and to the photographer, Norman Taylor. To our team in Maiden Lane, especially Daniel Whibley and all the others there who collated and edited the data; and my particular thanks to Sophie Kullmann at the Printed Catalogue Division.

Fred Hohler, Founder

Facing page: Scholderer, Otto, 1834–1902, *Man and Hares* (detail), 1880, Museums Sheffield, (p. 192)

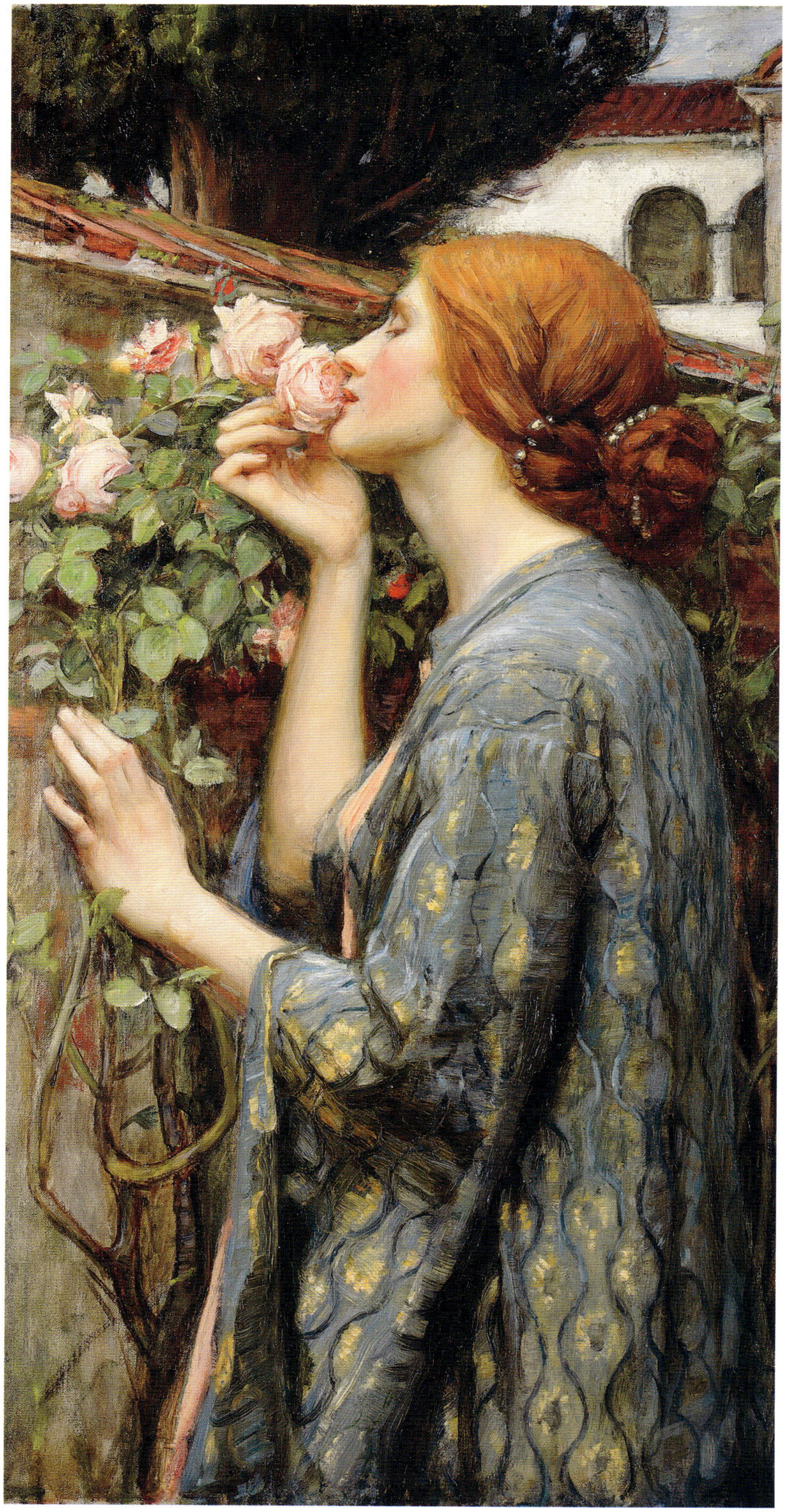

The Public Catalogue Foundation: People Involved

Financial Supporters

The Public Catalogue Foundation would like to express its profound appreciation to Museums Sheffield who have made the publication of this catalogue possible.

Catalogue Scope and Organisation

Medium and Support
The principal focus of this series is oil paintings. However, tempera and acrylic are also included as well as mixed media, where oil is the predominant constituent. Paintings on all forms of support (e.g. canvas, panel, etc.) are included as long as the support is portable. The principal exclusions are miniatures, hatchments or other purely heraldic paintings and wall paintings *in situ*.

Public Ownership
Public ownership has been taken to mean any paintings that are directly owned by the public purse, made accessible to the public by means of public subsidy or generally perceived to be in public ownership. The term 'public' refers to both central government and local government. Paintings held by national museums, local authority museums, English Heritage and independent museums, where there is at least some form of public subsidy, are included. Paintings held in civic buildings such as local government offices, town halls, guildhalls, public libraries, universities, hospitals, crematoria, fire stations and police stations are also included.

Geographical Boundaries of Catalogues
The geographical boundary of each county is the 'ceremonial county' boundary. This county definition includes all unitary authorities. Counties that have a particularly large number of paintings are divided between two or more catalogues on a geographical basis.

Criteria for Inclusion
As long as paintings meet the requirements above, all paintings are included irrespective of their condition and perceived quality. However, painting reproductions can only be included with the agreement of the participating collections and, where appropriate, the relevant copyright owner. It is rare that a collection forbids the inclusion of its paintings. Where this is the case and it is possible to obtain a list of paintings, this list is given in the Paintings Without Reproductions section. Where copyright consent is refused, the paintings are also listed in the Paintings Without Reproductions section. All paintings in collections' stacks and stores are included, as well as those on display. Paintings which have been lent to other institutions, whether for short-term exhibition or long-term loan, are listed under the owner collection. In addition, paintings on long-term loan are also included under the borrowing institution when they are likely to remain there for at least another five years from the date of publication of this catalogue. Information relating to owners and borrowers is listed in the Further Information section.

Layout
Collections are grouped together under their home town. These locations are listed in alphabetical order. In some cases collections that are spread over a number of locations are included under a single owner collection. A number of collections, principally the larger ones, are preceded by curatorial forewords. Within each collection paintings are listed in order of artist surname. Where there is more than one painting by the same artist, the paintings are listed chronologically, according to their execution date.

The few paintings that are not accompanied by photographs are listed in the Paintings Without Reproductions section.

There is additional reference material in the Further Information section at the back of the catalogue. This gives the full names of artists, titles and media if it has not been possible to include these in full in the main section. It also provides acquisition credit lines and information about loans in and out, as well as copyright and photographic credits for each painting. Finally, there is an index of artists' surnames.

Key to Painting Information

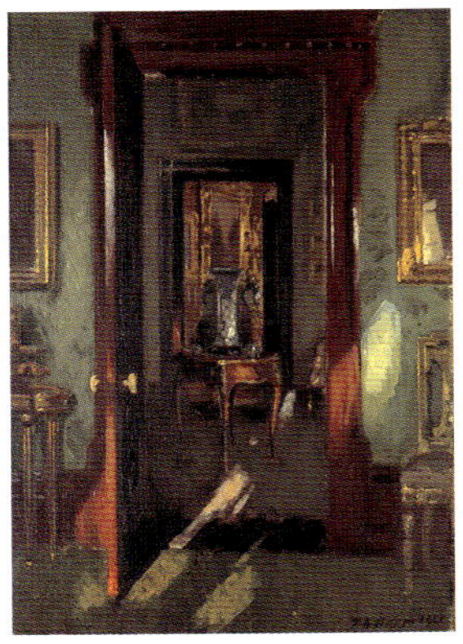

Almost all paintings are reproduced in the catalogue. Where this is not the case they are listed in the Paintings Without Reproductions section. Where paintings are missing or have been stolen, the best possible photograph on record has been reproduced. In some cases this may be black and white. Paintings that have been stolen are highlighted with a red border. Some paintings are shown with conservation tissue attached to parts of the painting surface.

Adam, Patrick William 1854–1929
Interior, Rutland Lodge: Vista through Open Doors 1920
oil on canvas 67.3 × 45.7
LEEAG.PA.1925.0671.LACF

Artist name This is shown with the surname first. Where the artist is listed on the Getty Union List of Artist Names (ULAN), ULAN's preferred presentation of the name is given. In a number of cases the name may not be a firm attribution and this is made clear. Where the artist name is not known, a school may be given instead. Where the school is not known, the painter name is listed as *unknown artist*. If the artist name is too long for the space, as much of the name is given as possible followed by (…). This indicates the full name is given at the rear of the catalogue in the Further Information section.

Painting title A painting title followed by *(?)* indicates that the title is in doubt. Where the alternative title to the painting is considered to be better known than the original, the alternative title is given in parentheses. Where the collection has not given a painting a title, the publisher does so instead and marks this with an asterisk. If the title is too long for the space, as much of the title is given as possible followed by *(…)* and the full title is given in the Further Information section.

Execution date In some cases the precise year of execution may not be known for certain. Instead an approximate date will be given or no date at all.

Artist dates Where known, the years of birth and death of the artist are given. In some cases one or both dates may not be known with certainty, and this is marked. No date indicates that even an approximate date is not known. Where only the period in which the artist was active is known, these dates are given and preceded with the word *active*.

Medium and support Where the precise material used in the support is known, this is given.

Dimensions All measurements refer to the unframed painting and are given in cm with up to one decimal point. In all cases the height is shown before the width. An (E) indicates where a painting has not been measured and its size has been calculated by sight only. If the painting is circular, the single dimension is the diameter. If the painting is oval, the dimensions are height and width.

Collection inventory number In the case of paintings owned by museums, this number will always be the accession number. In all other cases it will be a unique inventory number of the owner institution. (P) indicates that a painting is a private loan. Details can be found in the Further Information section. Accession numbers preceded by 'PCF' indicate that the collection did not have an accession number at the time of catalogue production and therefore the number given has been temporarily allocated by The Public Catalogue Foundation. The symbol indicates that the reproduction is based on a Bridgeman Art Library transparency (go to www.bridgemanart.com) or that Bridgeman administers the copyright for that artist.

Facing page: Neiland, Brendan, b.1941, *Effervescence* (detail), 2007, University of Sheffield, (p. 299)

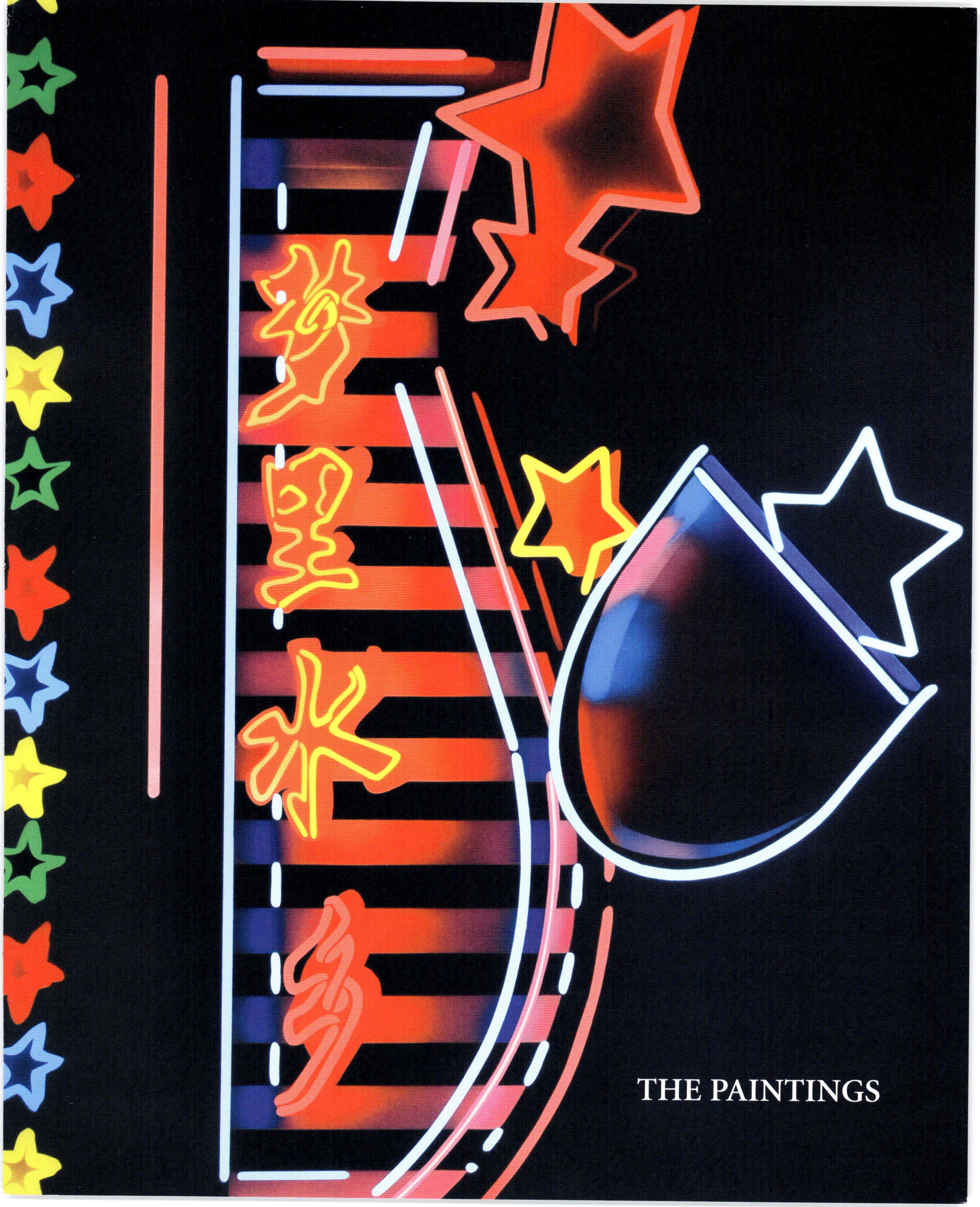

THE PAINTINGS

Bradfield Parish Council

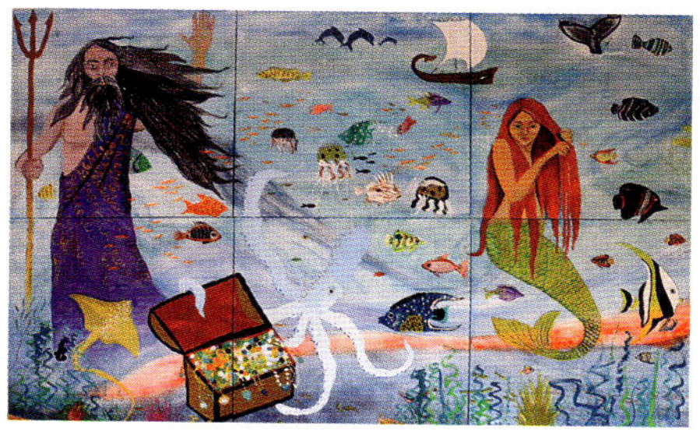

Members of the Rural Youth Project
Under the Sea (polyptych) 2008
acrylic on canvas 208 x 308
PCF1

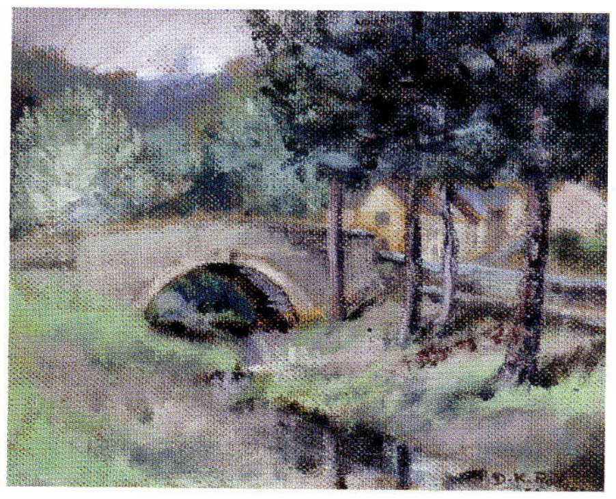

Rodgers, D. K.
Lower Bradfield, Sheffield
oil on board 24 x 29.5
PCF2

Fire & Police Museum at Sheffield

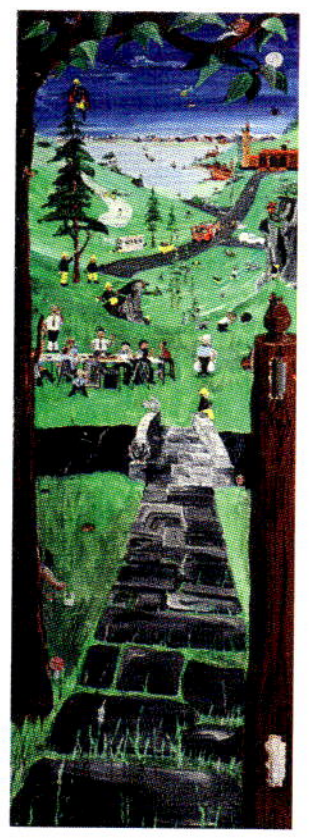

Brown, Chris active since c.1989
The Story of a Day at Ringinglow Fire Station c.1989
oil on door 196 x 68
PCF6

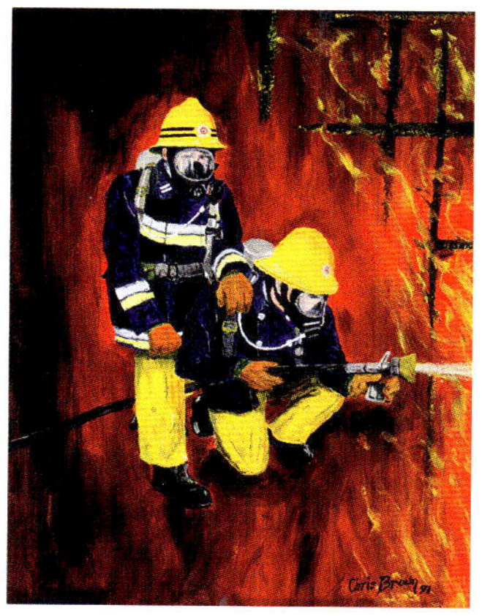

Brown, Chris active since c.1989
Firefighters Entering a Burning Building 1991
acrylic on board 52 x 39
PCF3

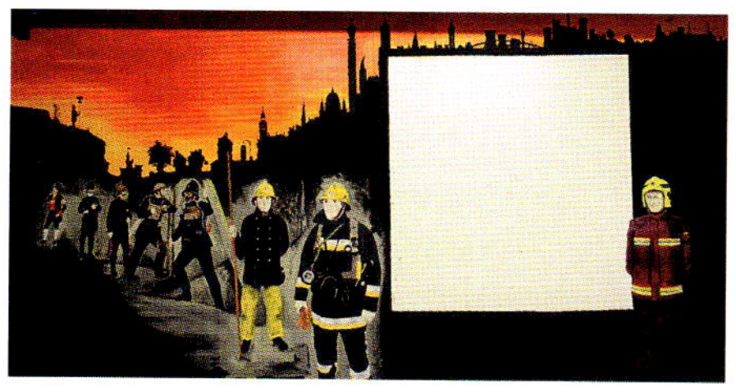

Brown, Chris active since c.1989
The Timeline of Firefighting (unfinished) (polyptych) 1993–2011
acrylic on plasterboard 300 x 570
PCF4

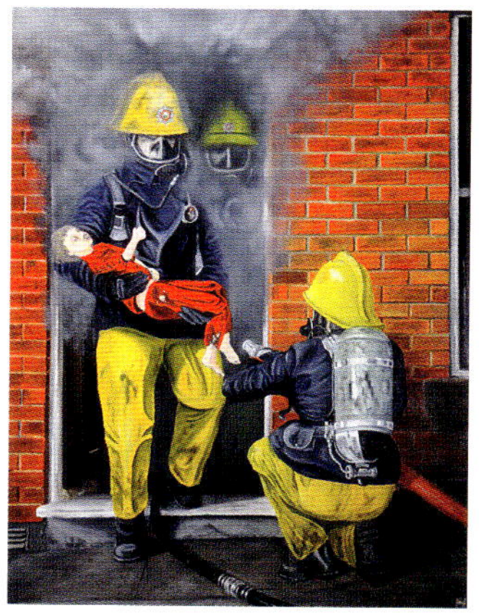

Howard, Reg
Street Fire Rescue
oil on canvas 126 x 96
PCF1

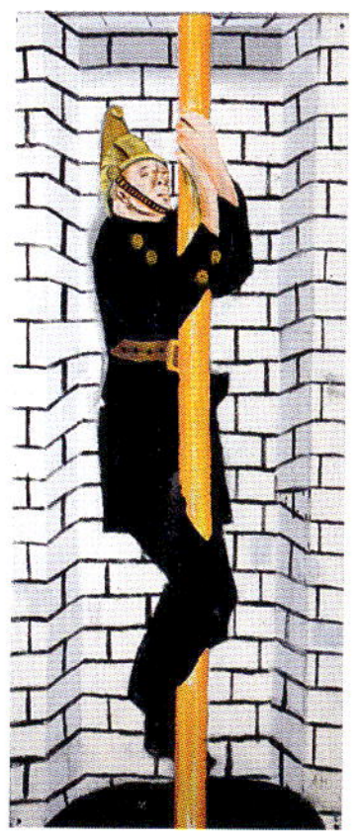

Muller, Axel
Division Street Fire Station Pole Drop
oil on board 160 x 80
PCF2

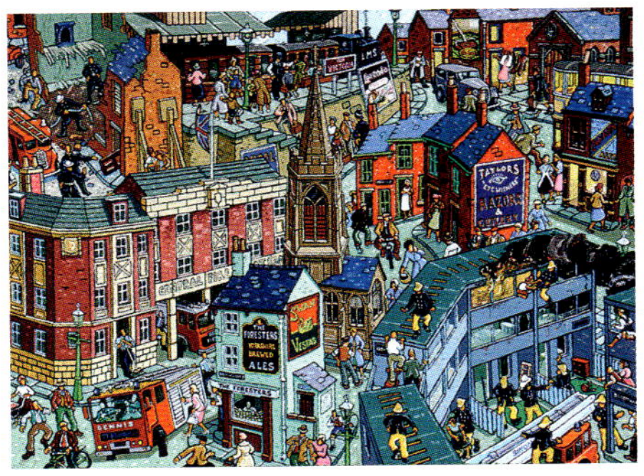

Scarborough, Joe b.1938
Fire 1985
oil on canvas 77 x 102
PCF5

Museums Sheffield

Museums Sheffield was established in April 1998 to take over the management of non-industrial museums and art galleries from the City Council. It is responsible for three sites: Graves Gallery, Millennium Gallery, and Weston Park. A range of collections are displayed across the venues which encompass Archaeology, Decorative Art, Geology, Natural History, Social History and Visual Art.

The Visual Art Collection comprises mainly British and European art from the sixteenth century to the present day. It contains over 6,000 items including paintings, sculptures and works on paper, of which the most well-represented is Modern British Art. As a whole, the Collection is extremely diverse and reflects the personal interests of directors and curators over the years. Nevertheless, the tastes of two main benefactors prevail as it is their artworks which constitute the foundations of the Collection.

John Newton Mappin (1800–1883) was a wealthy local brewer. When he died, he bequeathed £15,000 and his collection of 153 paintings to his nephews, J. Y. Cowlishaw, Frederick Thorpe Mappin and F. A. Colley. They were instructed to give the paintings to the city five years after his death, and that the paintings should be housed in a dedicated art gallery. The Mappin Gallery opened in 1887 as the first public art gallery in Sheffield. Frederick Thorpe Mappin was also an avid art collector, and gave a number of his own paintings to The Mappin Gallery over the following years.

The Mappin Gallery proved hugely popular and attracted around 350,000 visitors anually for 15 years. It provided one of the only cultural experiences in the city at that time and was accessible to everyone. It opened on a Sunday to give people who worked during the week a chance to visit, and more importantly, admission was free. Mappin's Deed of Trust specifically stated that the Gallery was to be used for the 'exhibition of pictures and works of art to be open to the public in perpetuity and without any change.'

John Newton Mappin's taste was for the historical and genre painters of his day, and he mainly purchased work by popular and established Victorian artists. He often acquired contemporary paintings from the Royal Academy summer exhibitions and also from studio sales of deceased artists such as Sir Edwin Henry Landseer. Over a period of 15 years he spent approximately £60,000 on paintings, which would be the equivalent of around two million pounds today. Mappin's favourite artist was the Scottish painter John Pettie, who painted the first work he ever bought, *The Drumhead Court Martial.*

Sir Frederick Thorpe Mappin said of his uncle's collection, 'These pictures have been selected by my deceased relative with great care, with much skill, at great cost, and their possession he greatly prized.'

John George Graves (1866–1945) was also a key patron. He ran one of the country's first mail-order companies, employing over 3,000 staff. In 1929 he gave £30,000 to aid the construction of a new library with the condition that a gallery would be built on the top floor. The Graves Gallery opened in 1934.

Graves collected a wider range of artworks than Mappin, ranging from sixteenth-century portraiture, to Victorian artists, such as Sir Edward Burne-Jones. He also collected works by the Spanish seventeenth-century artist Bartolomé Esteban Murillo, as well as pieces by his own contemporary Roger Eliot Fry.

Graves first began collecting art in 1899, and during his lifetime he amassed over 3,000 pictures: 700 of which he gave to the city of Sheffield. Two of the first works he purchased were James Collinson's *The Landlady* and *At the Bazaar*, a pair of Victorian paintings which now form part of Museums Sheffield Collection.

The Graves Gallery's first Director was Sir John Rothenstein, CBE (1901–1992), who also took control of the Mappin Gallery and oversaw its extension in 1937. This enabled both the Mappin and Graves collections to be shown alongside each other across two sites, providing the opportunity to hang the paintings in a more comprehensive way, for example, by period or by theme.

John Rothenstein left in 1938 to become Director of the Tate Gallery. During his time in Sheffield, he sought to augment the Collection with loans of national importance and a series of temporary exhibitions. His initial attempts to develop the Collection were fruitful. He purchased oil paintings and watercolours by contemporary artists such as Stanley Spencer, Edward Bawden and Percy Wyndham Lewis, which now form the cornerstones of the Modern British Collection. Unfortunately, it was not long before the purchase fund was withdrawn, and it was through organisations such as the Sheffield Art Collections Fund (Sheffield Society for the Encouragement of Art), the Contemporary Art Society and The National Art Collections Fund (The Art Fund) that the collection developed over the following decades.

After the Second World War, subsequent directors continued to add to the art collections, but it was under the enlightened leadership of Frank Constantine in the 1960s and 1970s that many of the most significant works were purchased. During this period, the Modern British Collection acquired new works by key artists such as Frank Helmuth Auerbach, David Bomberg, Patrick Caulfield and Christopher Nevinson.

Subsequent directors continued to collect until the 1980s, when economic decline in Sheffield meant that the purchase fund was withdrawn once more. From this point onwards, collection development again relied on the generosity of local and national organisations, and as a result there was limited growth, particularly during the 1990s.

Since Museums Sheffield took over the care of the Collection in 1998, the acquisition programme has been reinvigorated. The Contemporary Art

Society has continued to play an essential part in the development of the Collection with significant gifts across a range of media such as Stephen Farthing's *Room in Samur,* Helen Chadwick's sculpture *Ego geometria sum* and Michal Rovner's *One Person Game Against Nature.* While over the past five years the J. G. Graves Charitable Trust has provided funding in order for Museums Sheffield to refresh its collecting, the additional contributions from the Museums, Libraries and Archives Council/Victoria and Albert Museum Purchase Grant Fund and The Art Fund have enabled the acquisition of significant contemporary works such as Marc Quinn's sculpture, *Kiss.*

Museums Sheffield intends to develop the collections further through contemporary commissions and acquisitions, ensuring that they continue to have relevance for, and connect to, our audiences.

Liz Waring, Curator of Visual Art

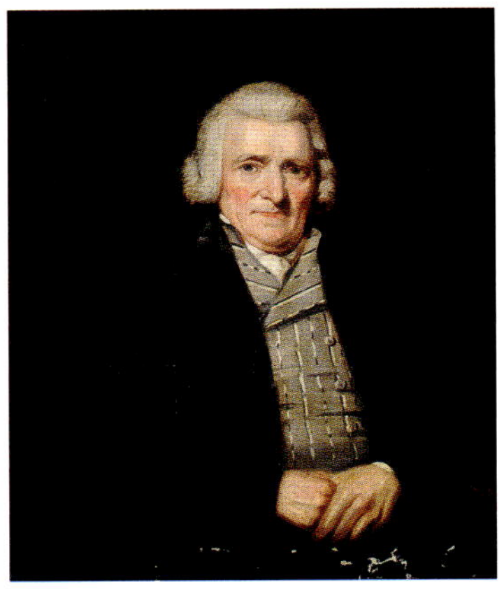

Abbott, Lemuel Francis 1760–1803
William Traies of Crediton (father of the artist) 1780–1800
oil on canvas 76.4 x 63.8
VIS.34

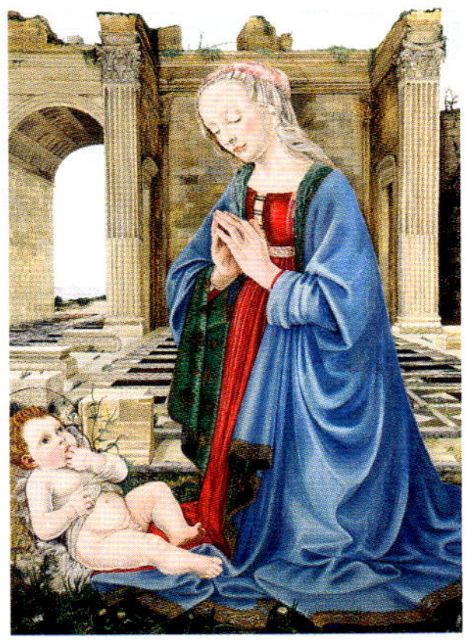

Abrahams, Philippa b.1947
The Virgin Adoring the Infant Christ (after Andrea del Verrocchio) 2000
tempera on gold panel 110 x 79
CGSG03600

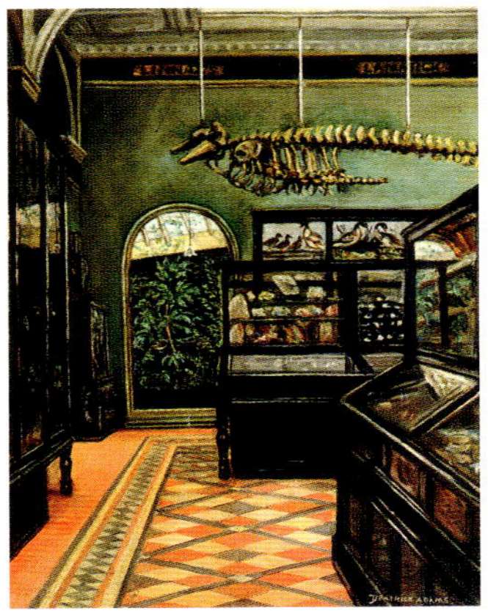

Adams, Beatrice b.1877
View of the Science Gallery at Weston Park Museum, Sheffield
oil on canvas 43 x 32.8
K1921.21

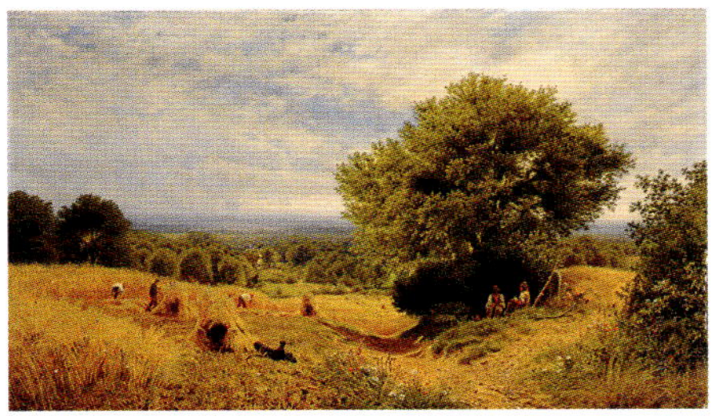

Adams, John Clayton 1840–1906
Harvest Time 1873
oil on canvas 76.1 x 127.7
VIS.1468

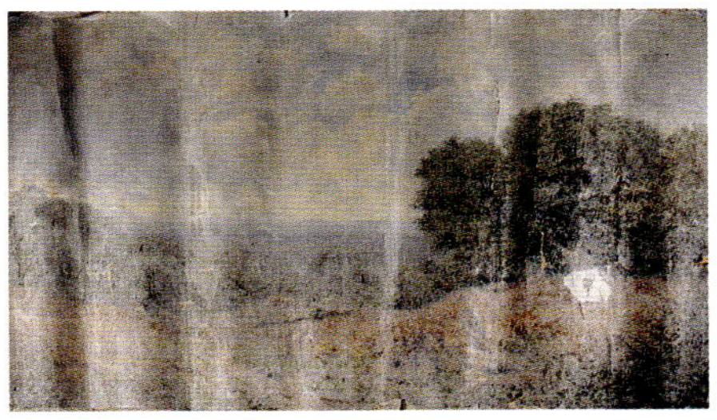

Adams, John Clayton 1840–1906
Harvest Time 1879
oil on canvas 122 x 180
VIS.1609

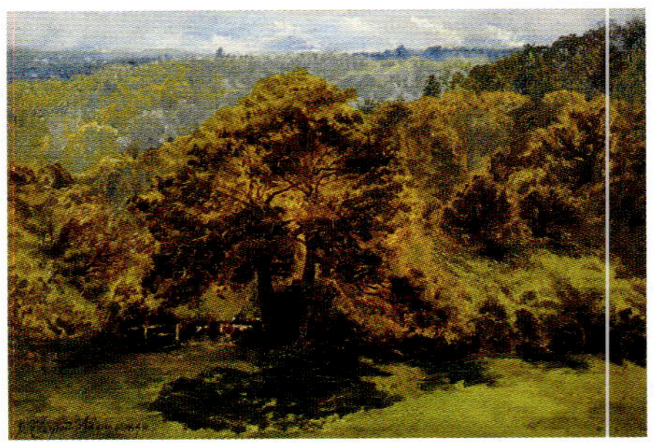

Adams, John Clayton 1840–1906
In the Surrey Woods 1895
oil on canvas 35 x 48.5
VIS.1247

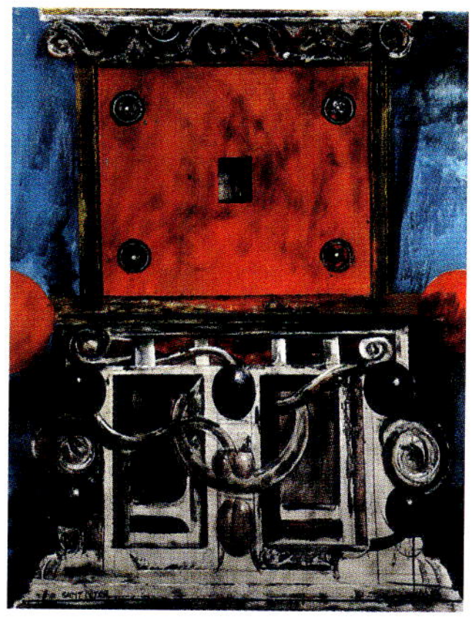

Adams, Norman 1927–2005
St Peter 1962
oil on canvas 129.3 x 96.6
VIS.3937

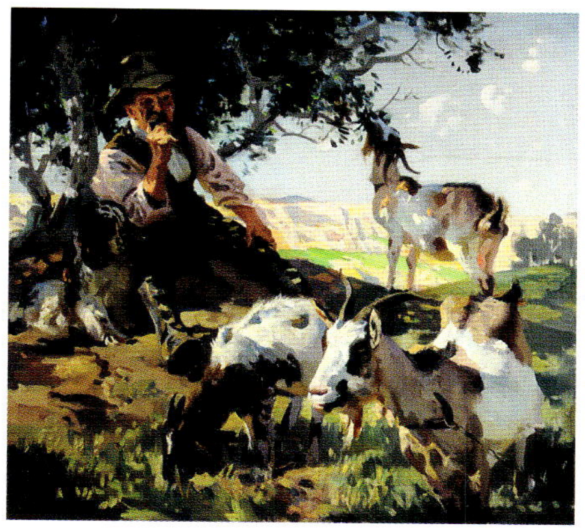

Adamson, Dorothy 1894–1934
Sunday
oil on canvas 85.5 x 93.4
VIS.320

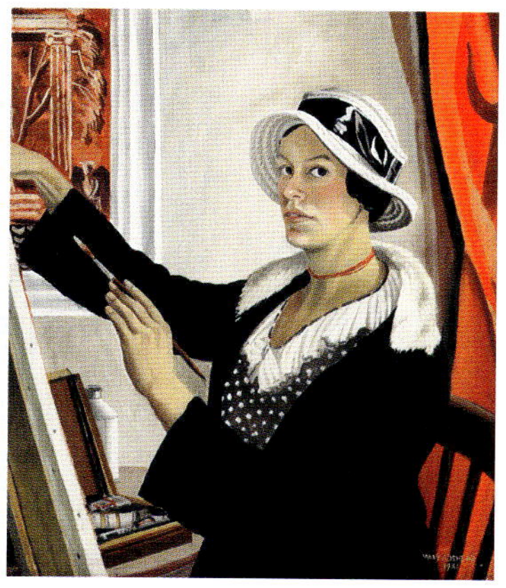

Adshead, Mary 1904–1995
Self Portrait 1931
oil on canvas 59.8 x 49.8
VIS.5306

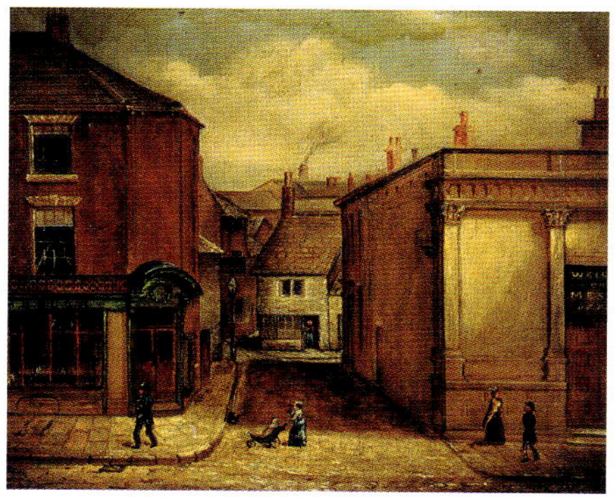

Aldam, Thomas
Balm Green, Sheffield 1858
oil on panel 24 x 29
1972.595

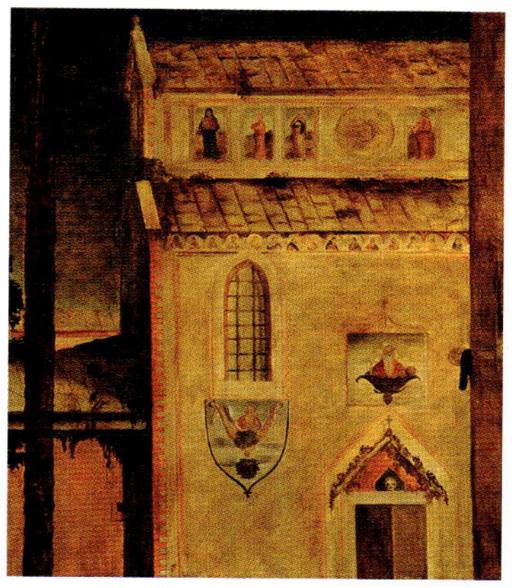

Alessandri, Angelo 1854–1931
St Jerome Leading the Tame Lion into the Monastery (detail) (after Vittore Carpaccio) 1879
oil on canvas 68 x 57.8
CGSG00262

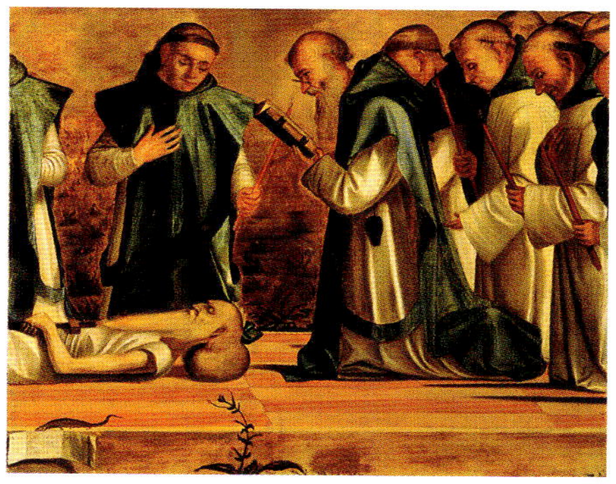

Alessandri, Angelo 1854–1931
The Obsequies of St Jerome (detail) (after Vittore Carpaccio) 1885
oil on canvas 55.8 x 68.5
CGSG00263

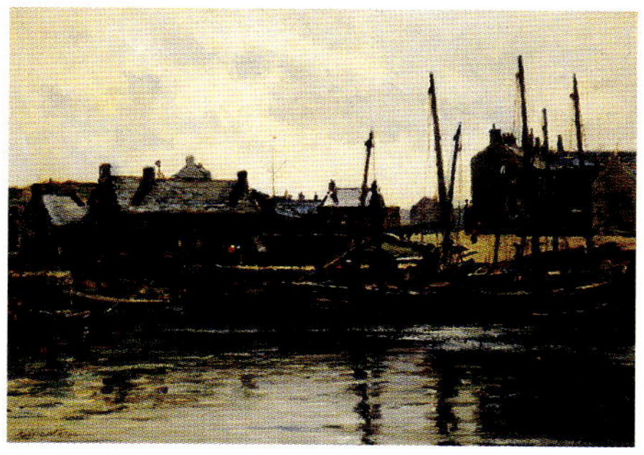

Allan, Robert Weir 1852–1942
The Old Harbour, Portsoy, Scotland
oil on canvas 36.8 x 52
VIS.572

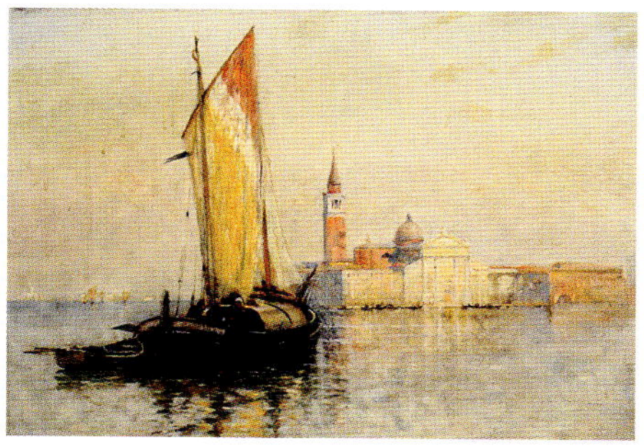

Allan, Robert Weir 1852–1942
Venice
oil on panel 36.4 x 51.5
VIS.765

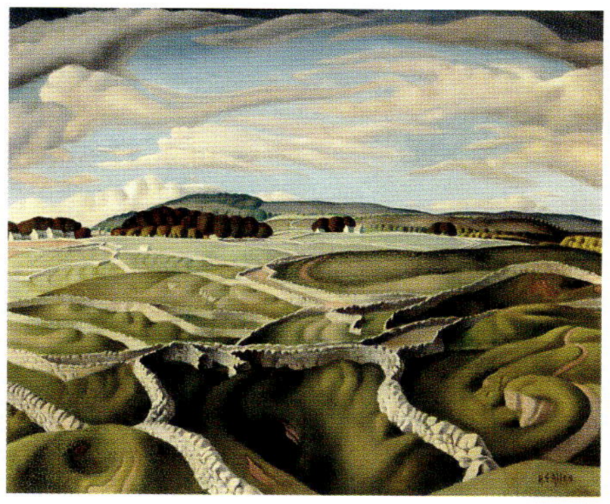

Allen, Harry Epworth 1894–1958
Derbyshire Walls
tempera on canvas 47.5 x 58
VIS.3140

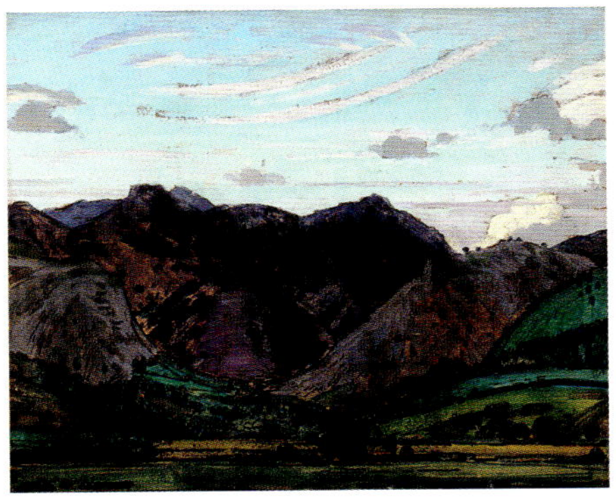

Allinson, Adrian Paul 1890–1959
Moel Hebog, North Wales 1919
oil on board 32 x 39.4
VIS.4519

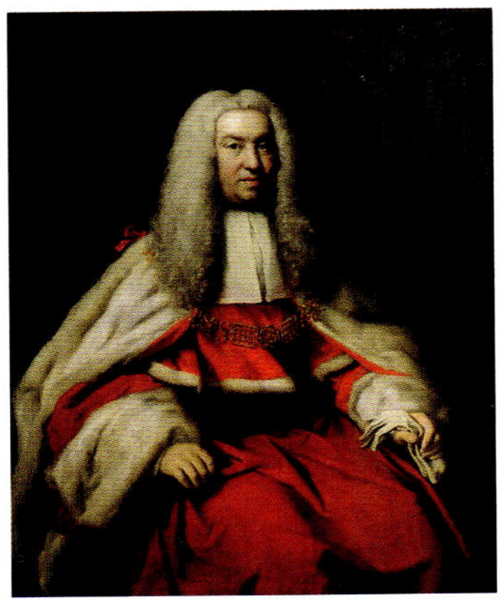

Amigoni, Jacopo c.1682–1752
Sir Thomas Reeve (1673–1737) 1730–1736
oil on canvas 124 x 100
VIS.3020

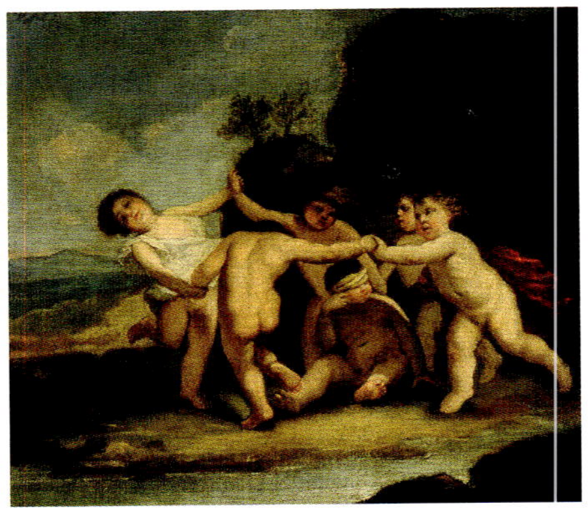

Amigoni, Jacopo (attributed to)
c.1682–1752
Cupids at Play 1730–1735
oil on canvas 41.6 x 46.4
VIS.275

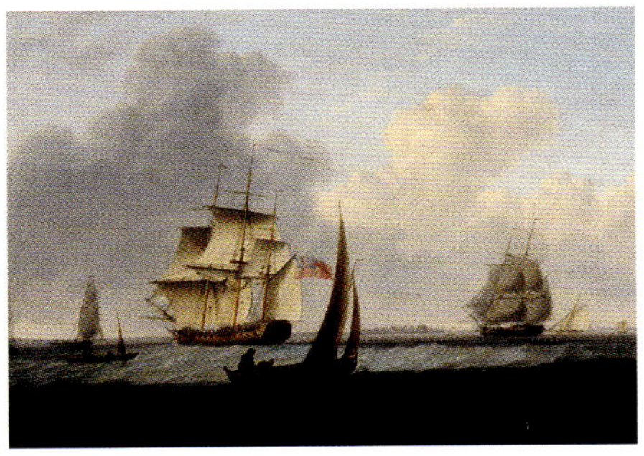

Anderson, William 1757–1837
Sea Piece
oil on panel 26.6 x 37.2
VIS.243

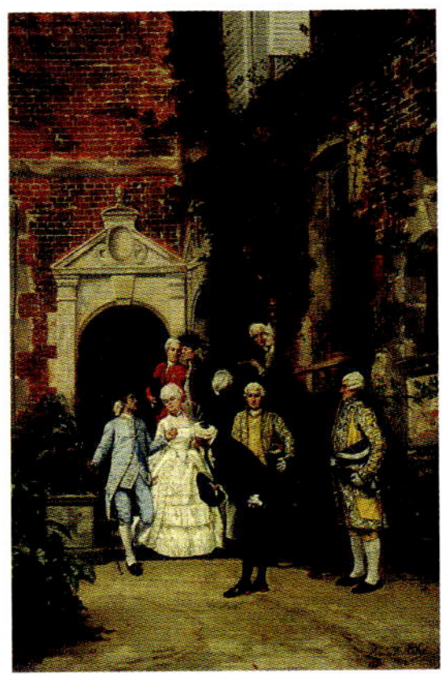

André, Edmond 1837–1877
The Introduction 1872
oil on canvas 45.6 x 29.6
VIS.1571

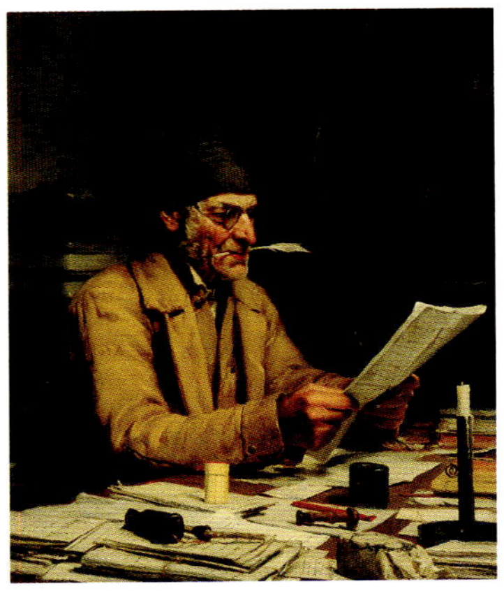

Anker, Albert 1831–1910
The Public Notary 1876
oil on canvas 58.4 x 48.6
VIS.1362

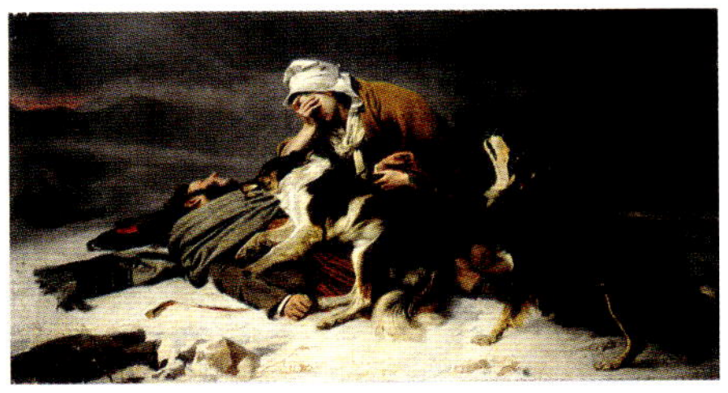

Ansdell, Richard 1815–1885
The Lost Shepherd 1860
oil on canvas 152.3 x 280.5
VIS.1680

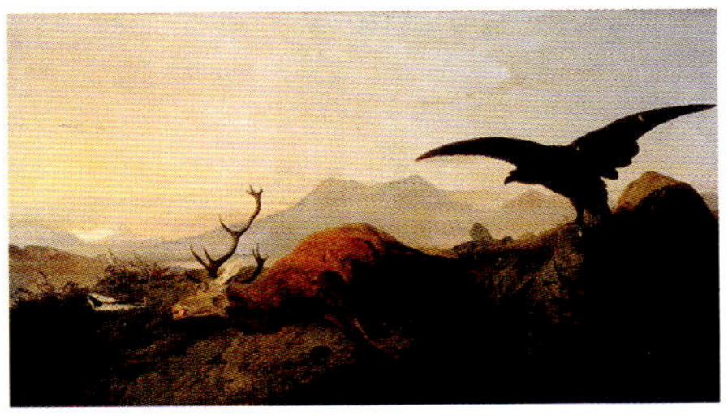

Ansdell, Richard 1815–1885
Dead Stag
oil on canvas 61 x 107.4
VIS.1487

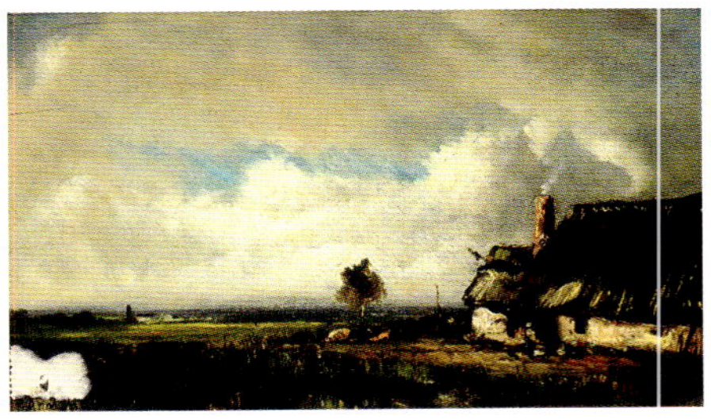

Armandi, Polermo b.1842
Stormy Weather
oil on panel 11.6 x 20
VIS.1043

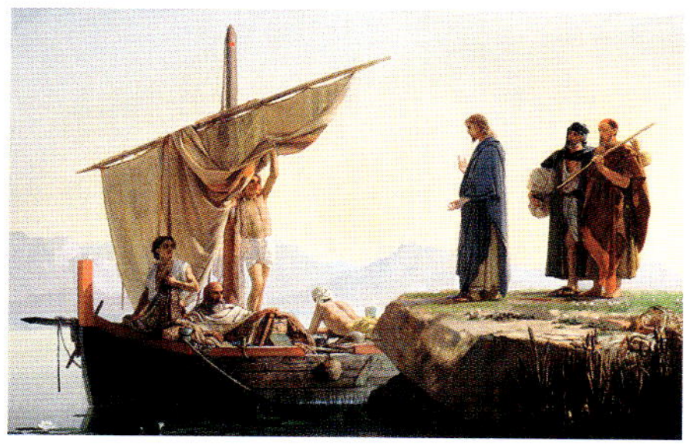

Armitage, Edward 1817–1896
Christ Calling the Apostles James and John
1869
oil on canvas 70.5 x 105.8
VIS.1520

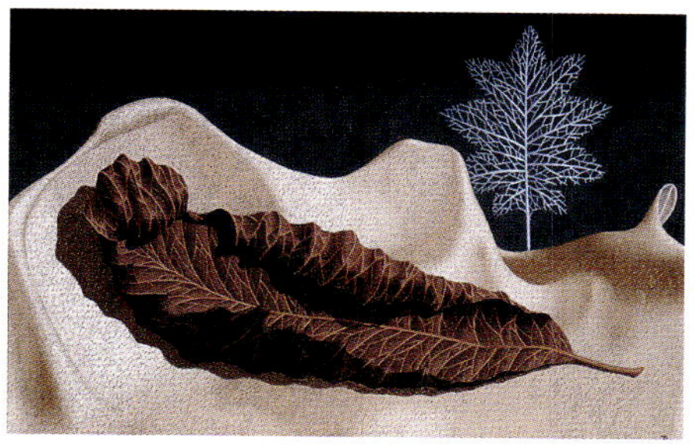

Armstrong, John 1893–1973
Nocturne 1947
tempera on board 61.9 x 87.2
VIS.3300

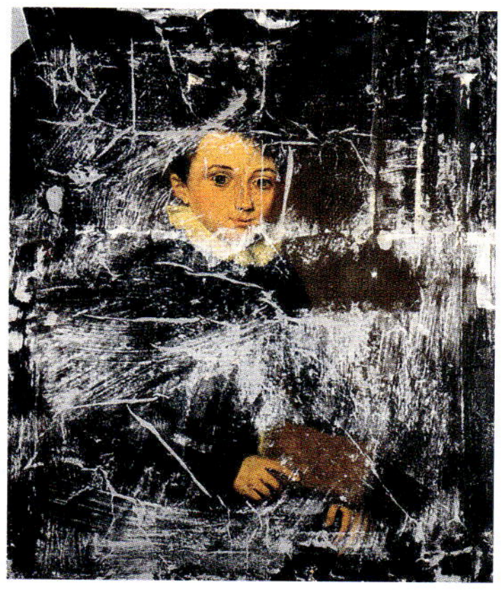

Arrowsmith, Thomas 1772–1830
Portrait of a Boy (probably George Woolhouse)
oil on canvas 75 x 62
1969.1

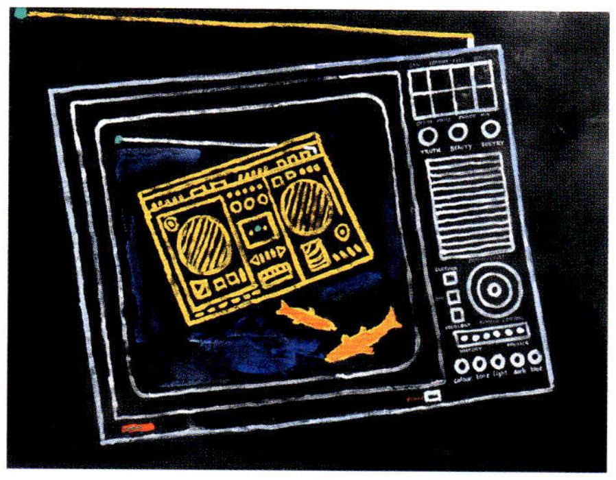

Atkinson, Conrad b.1940
Goldfish
acrylic on cotton duck 81.4 x 101.4
VIS.5225

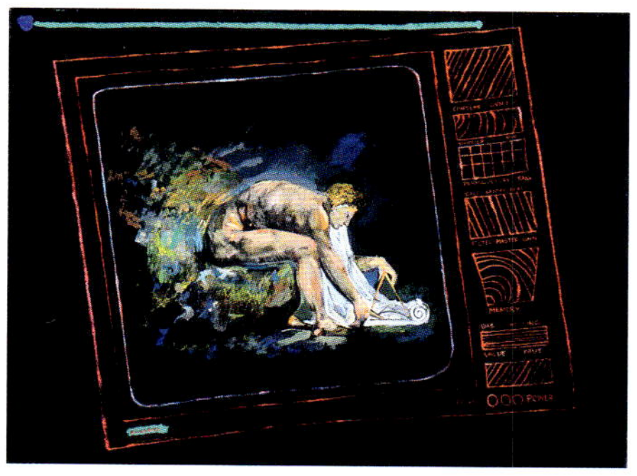

Atkinson, Conrad b.1940
Measures
acrylic on cotton duck 76.4 x 100.3
VIS.5226

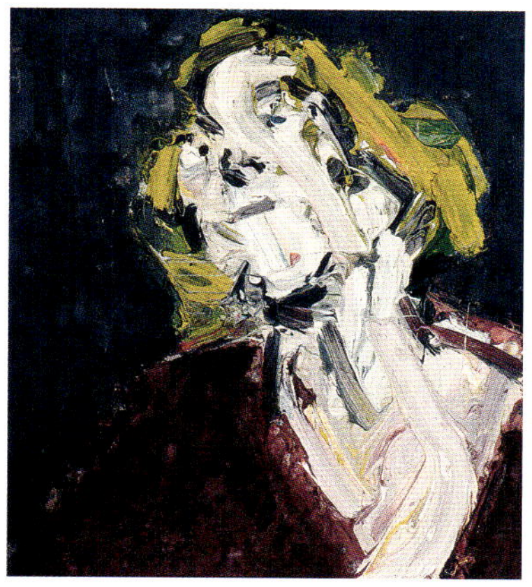

Auerbach, Frank Helmuth b.1931
Head of J. Y. M. 1973
oil on board 41 x 36
VIS.4033

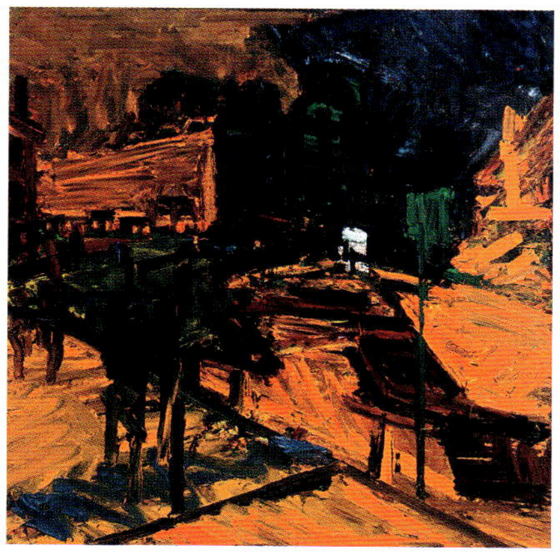

Auerbach, Frank Helmuth b.1931
Looking towards Mornington Crescent Station, Night 1973
oil on board 125.7 x 125.5
VIS.4053

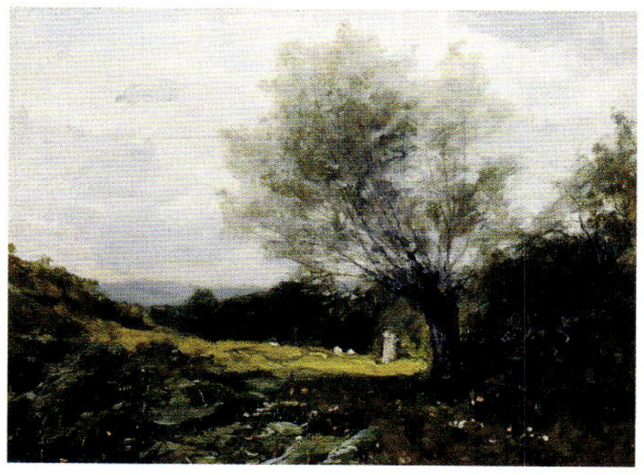

Aumonier, James 1832–1911
A Bypath
oil on canvas 28.9 x 39.3
VIS.641

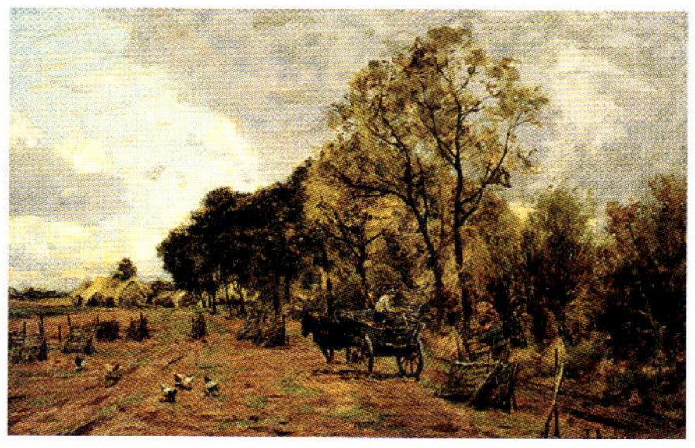

Aumonier, James 1832–1911
A Cambridgeshire Farm
oil on canvas 58.4 x 90.1
VIS.1285

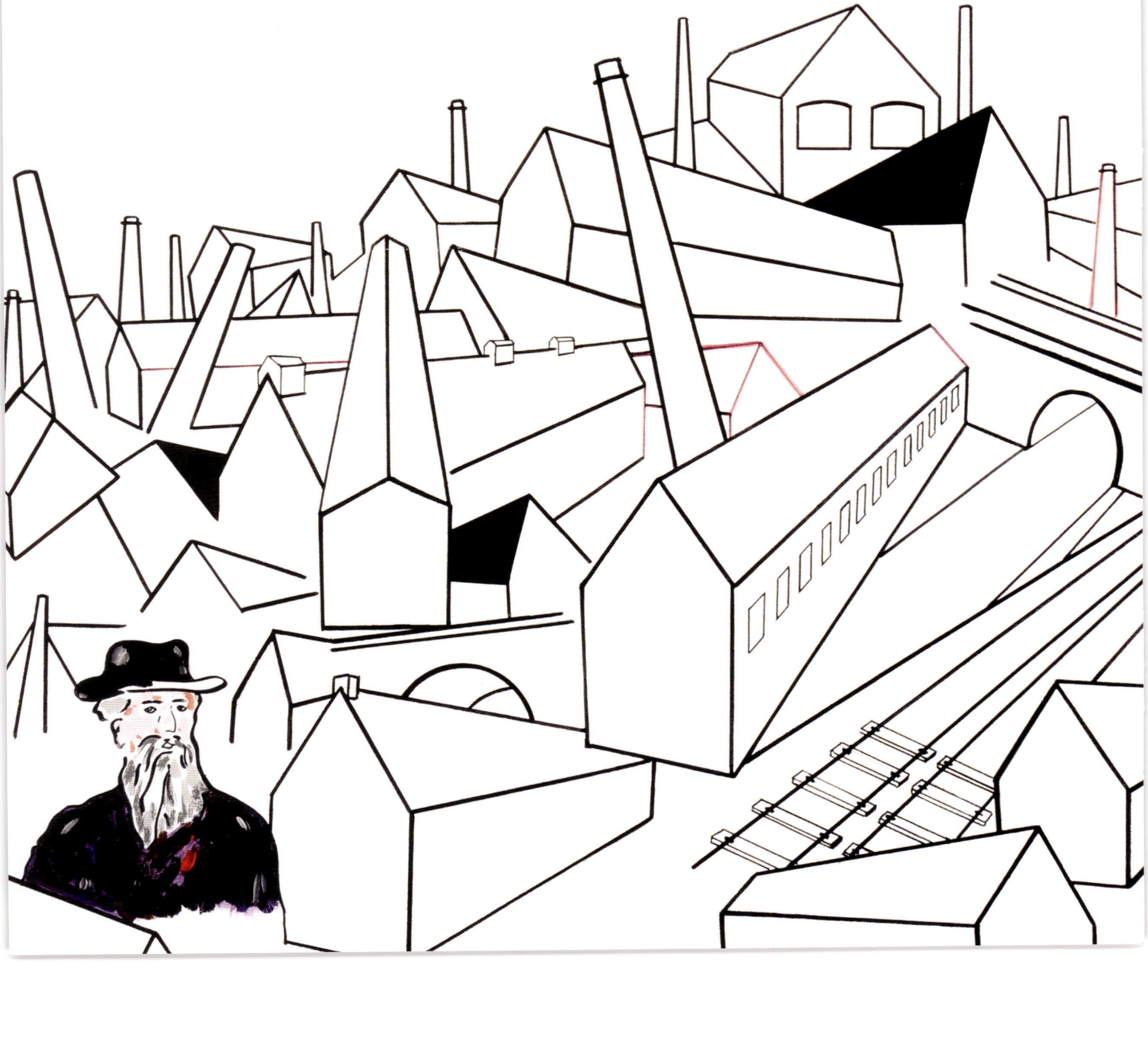

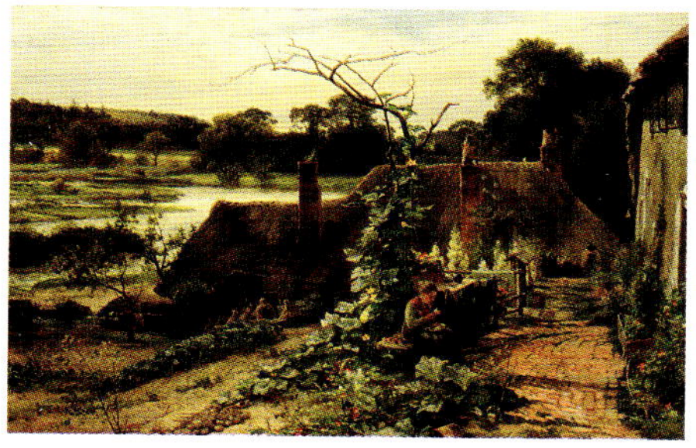

Aumonier, James 1832–1911
An English Cottage Home
oil on canvas 54.6 x 83.8
VIS.1423

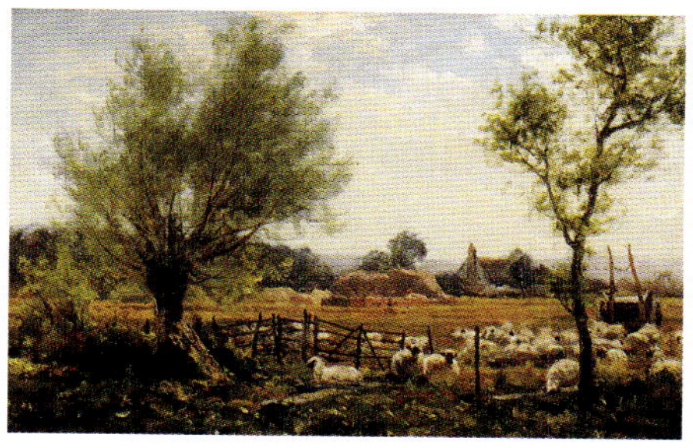

Aumonier, James 1832–1911
An Oxfordshire Sheep Farm
oil on canvas 25.3 x 39.3
VIS.542

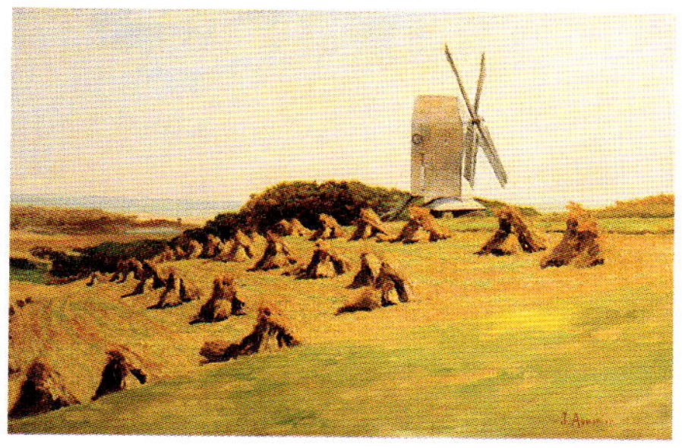

Aumonier, James 1832–1911
Lancing Mill, Sussex
oil on canvas 59.5 x 96
VIS.615

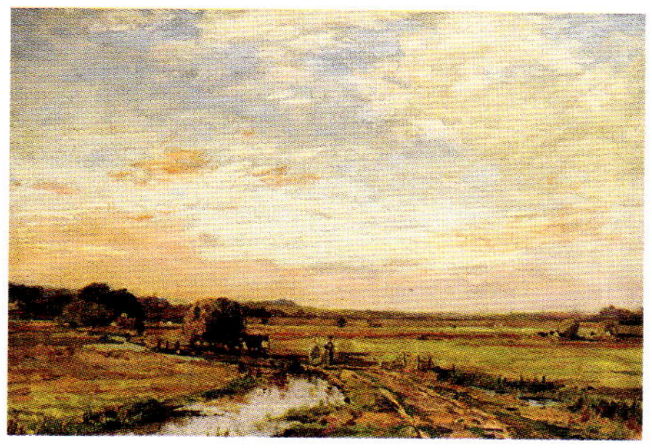

Aumonier, James 1832–1911
Sussex Hayfields
oil on canvas 55.8 x 71.8
VIS.1333

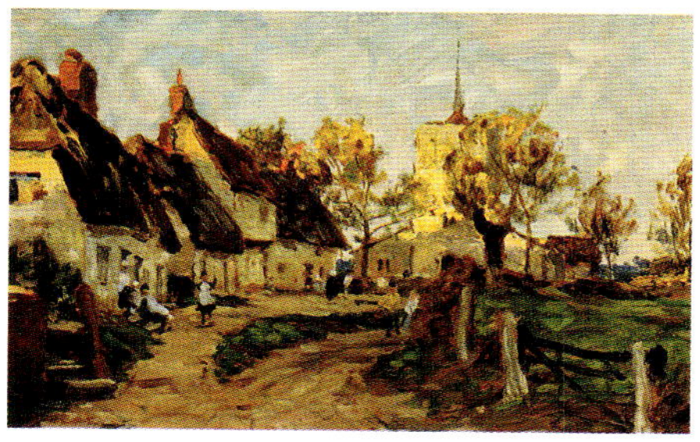

Aumonier, James 1832–1911
Village Street, Wendens Ambo, Essex
oil on panel 30 x 45.6
VIS.768

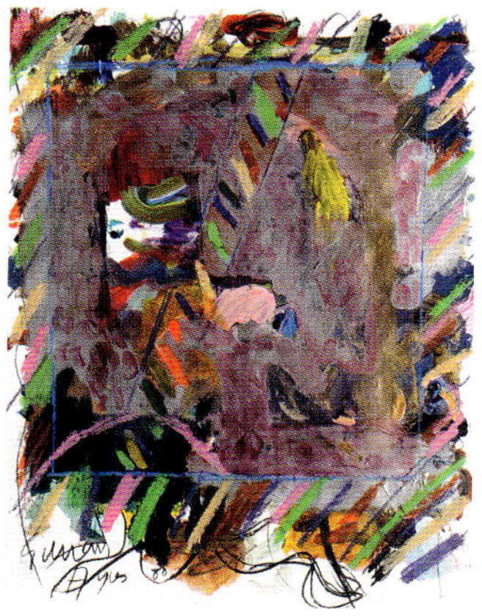

Ayres, Gillian b.1930
Untitled 1980 1980
oil & crayon on paper 75.8 x 56.5
VIS.4918

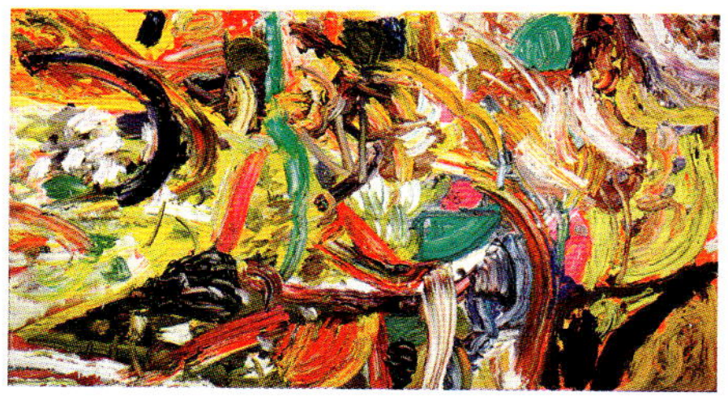

Ayres, Gillian b.1930
Belt of Straw and Ivy Leaves
oil on canvas 168 x 310.4
VIS.LI.974 (P)

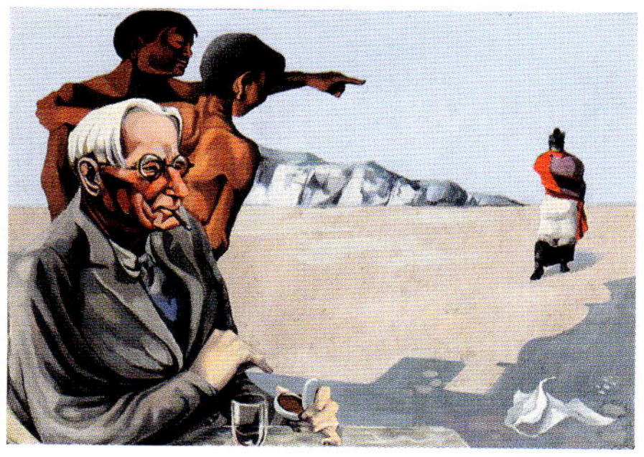

Ayrton, Michael 1921–1975
Norman Douglas (1868–1952) 1948
oil on metal 24.4 x 34.5
VIS.4144

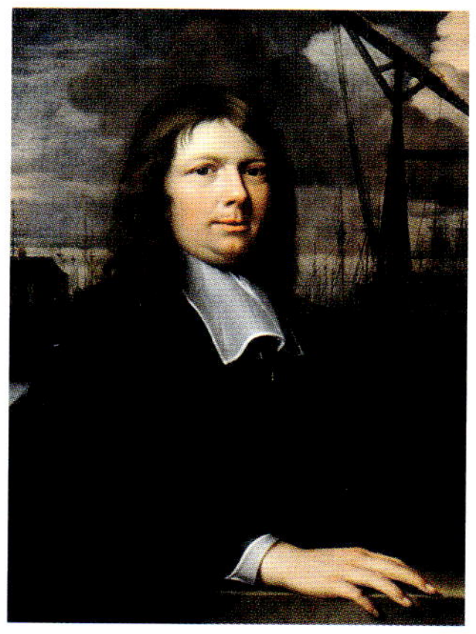

Backhuysen, Ludolf I 1630–1708
Self Portrait
oil on canvas 107.3 x 85.1
VIS.5384

Facing page: Morris, Stephen, b.1935, *Untitled* (detail), c.1992, Museums Sheffield, (p. 146)

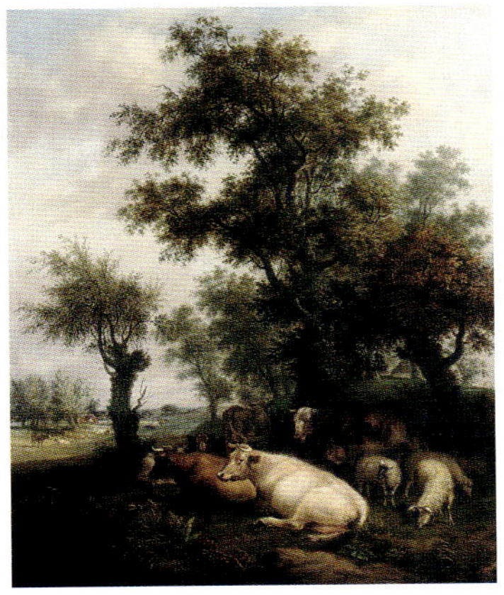

Baker, Thomas 1809–1869
Cattle Group
oil on canvas 74.1 x 61.4
VIS.306

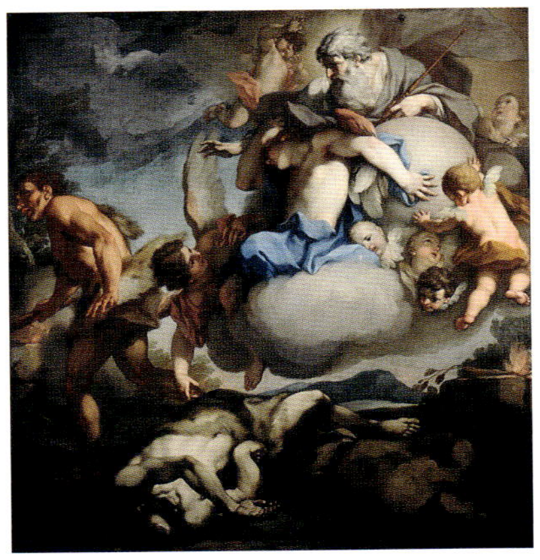

Balestra, Antonio 1666–1740
Cain and Abel 1733
oil on canvas 171.4 x 160.3
VIS.2766

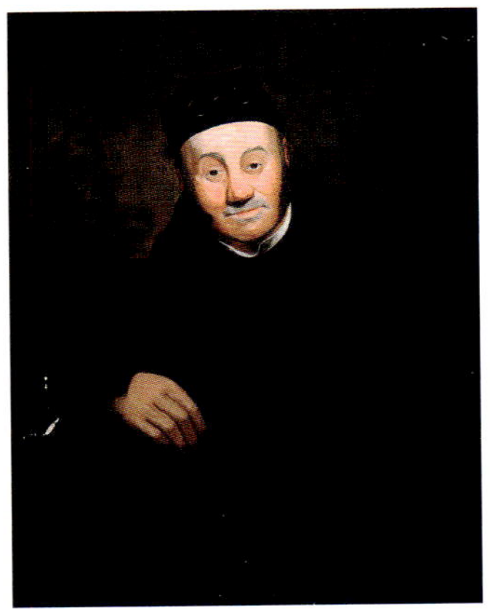

Banks, James
John Skinner 1830
oil on canvas 81.5 x 70.5
1962.98

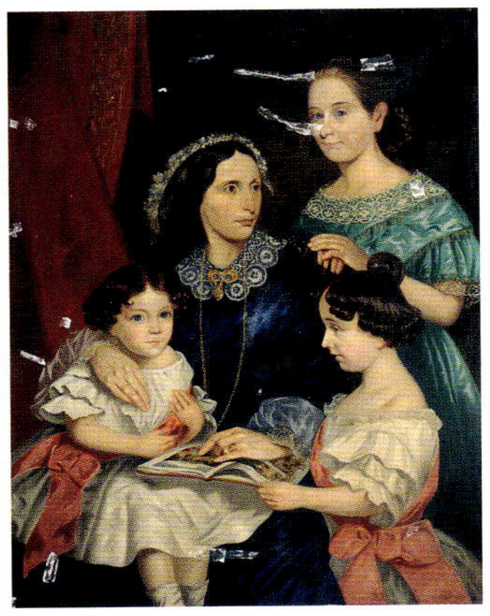

Banks, Thomas Joseph 1828–1896
Mrs Sarah Bateman with Her Three Daughters
1860
oil on canvas 110.5 x 85
1961.183

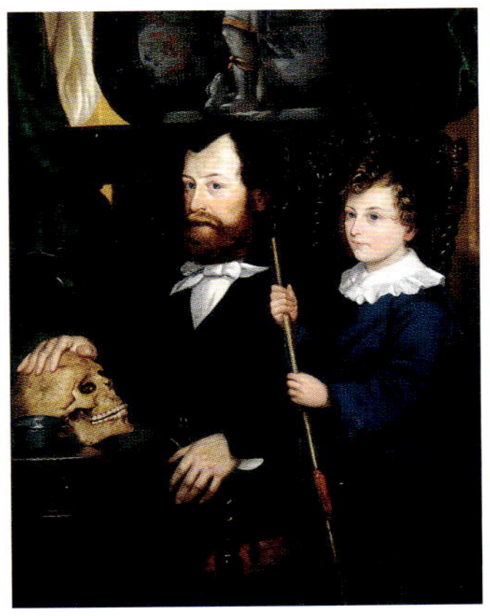

Banks, Thomas Joseph 1828–1896
Thomas Bateman (1821–1861), and His Son
1860
oil on canvas 110.5 x 85.5
1961.182

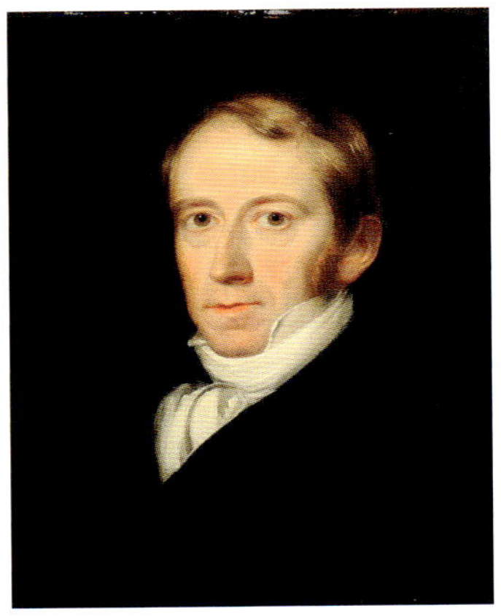

Barber, Thomas 1771–1843
James Montgomery (1771–1854)
oil on canvas on board 50.8 x 40.7
VIS.1880

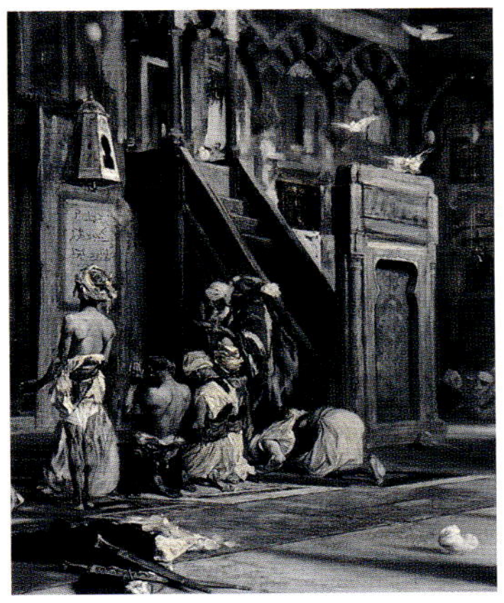

Bargue, Charles (attributed to) 1826–1883
Arabs at Prayer 1855–1865
oil on canvas 60.9 x 50.2
VIS.1252

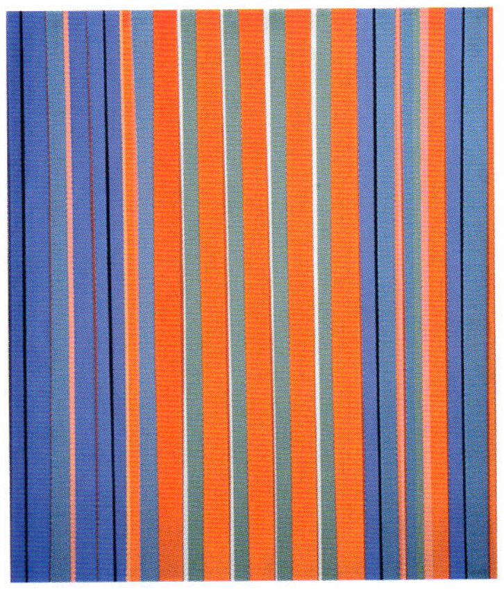

Barker, Allen b.1937
Painting 1972
oil on canvas 73.6 x 61
VIS.3911

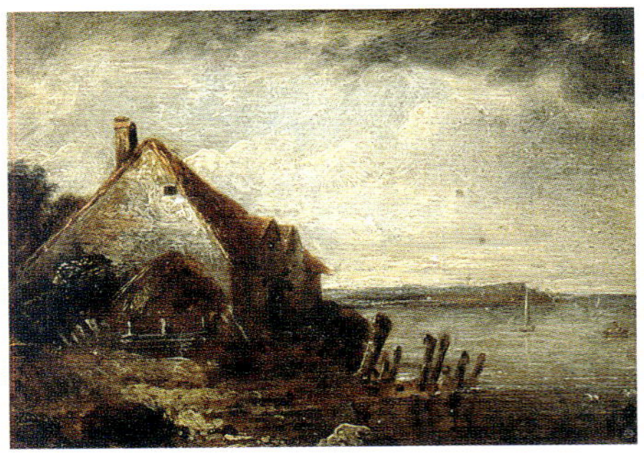

Barker, Benjamin II 1776–1838
Coast Scene
oil on panel 10.8 x 15.4
VIS.59

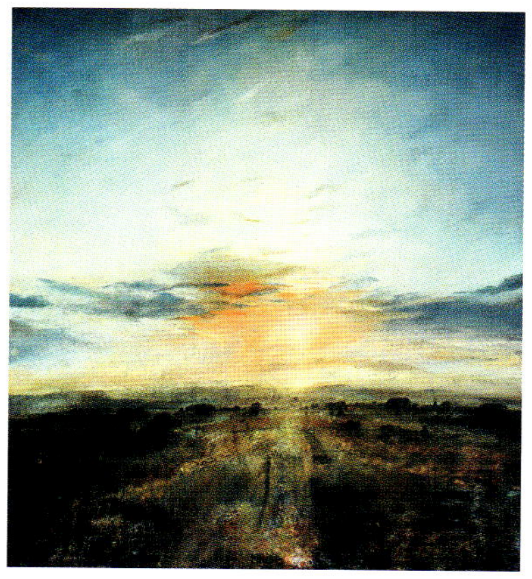

Barker, David Walker b.1947
Seascape
oil on canvas 136.7 x 121
VIS.4539

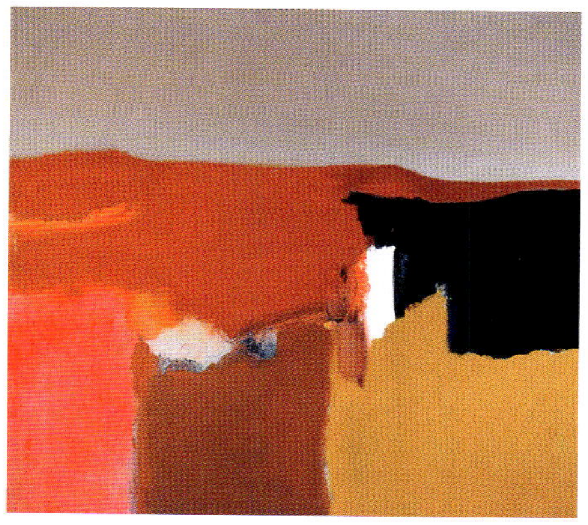

Barker, Kit 1916–1988
Tan Hill 1963
oil on canvas 102 x 110.6
VIS.LI.62 (P)

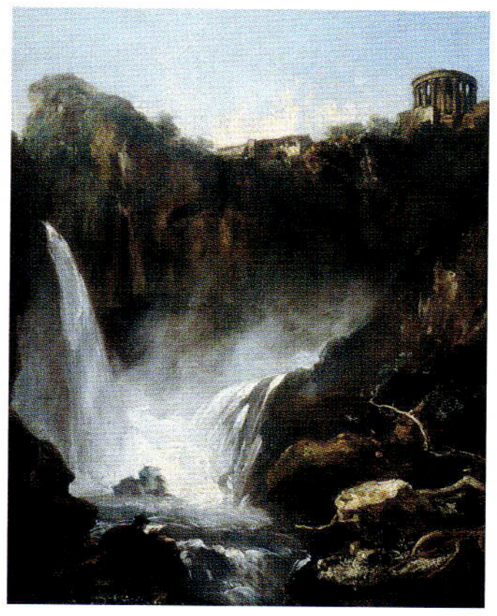

Barker, Thomas 1769–1847
The Falls of Tivoli, Italy 1836
oil on canvas 89.9 x 69.8
VIS.2200

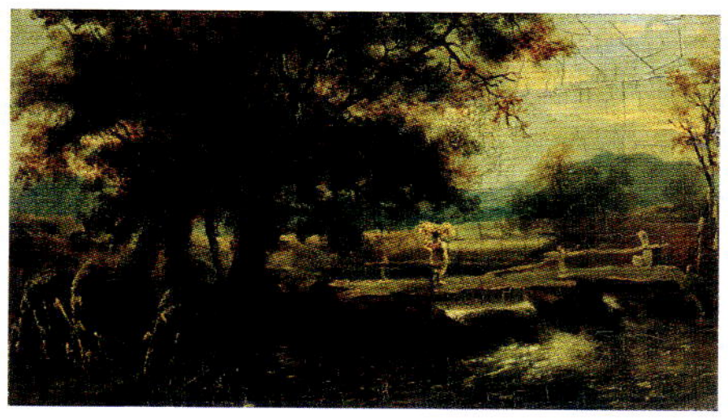

Barker, Thomas 1769–1847
Landscape with a River
oil on panel 45.5 x 65.8
VIS.1248

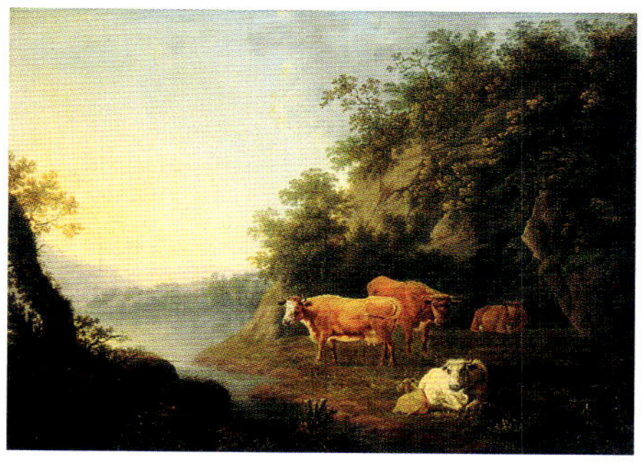

Barker, Thomas 1769–1847
Landscape with Cattle
oil on canvas 47.2 x 63.8
VIS.328

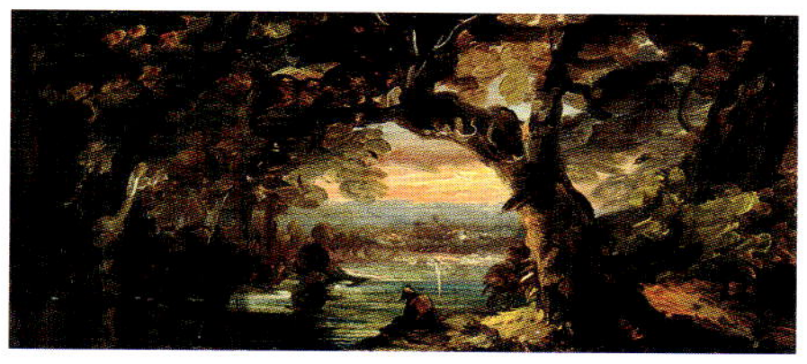

Barker, Thomas 1769–1847
The Pool
oil on panel 11.7 x 25.7
VIS.558

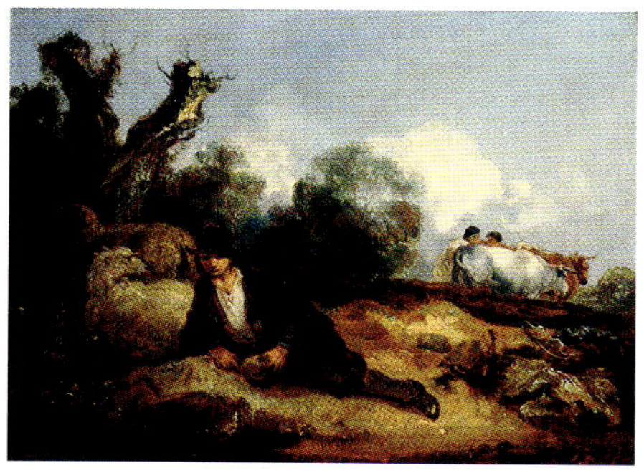

Barker, Thomas 1769–1847
The Shepherd
oil on canvas 29.5 x 39.7
VIS.266

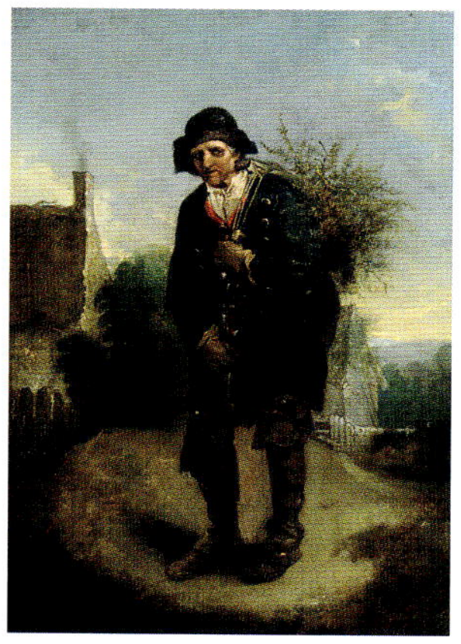

Barker, Thomas 1769–1847
The Woodman
oil on canvas 55.8 x 39
VIS.289

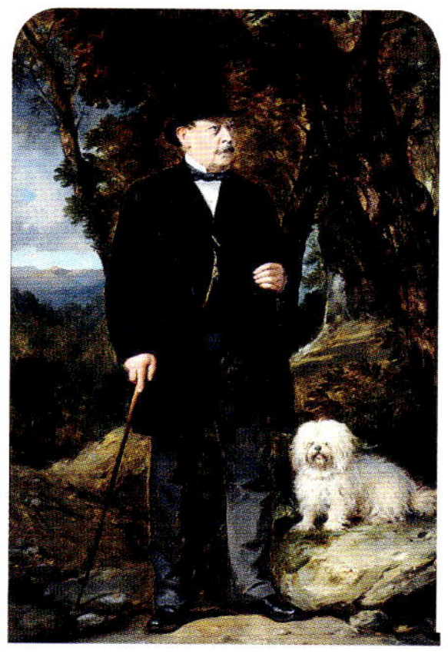

Barker, Thomas Jones 1815–1882
John Newton Mappin (1800–1883) 1877
oil on canvas 140.8 x 93
VIS.1664

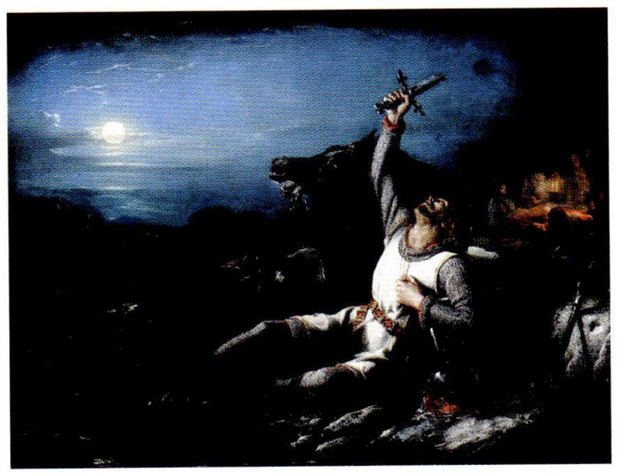

Barker, Thomas Jones 1815–1882
The Faithful Knight
oil on canvas on plywood 108 x 126
VIS.1298

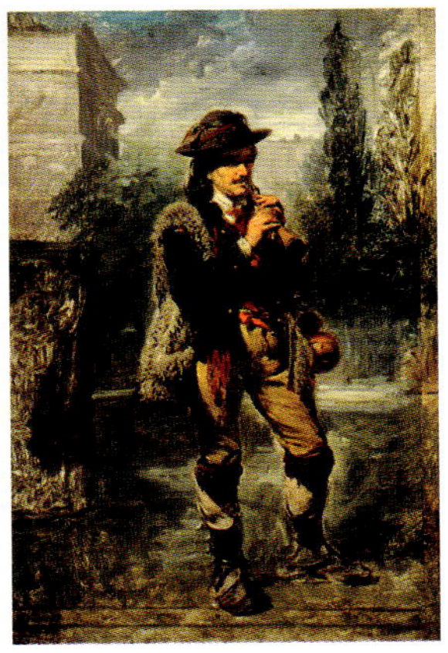

Barnes, Edward Charles 1830–1890
Savoyard with a Clarionet
oil on canvas 74.5 x 49.3
VIS.1551

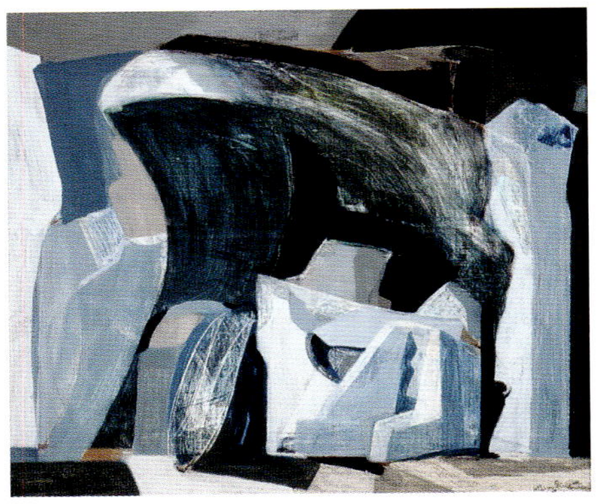

Barns-Graham, Wilhelmina 1912–2004
Glacier Painting, Green and Brown 1951
oil on canvas 54.5 x 64.2
VIS.4359

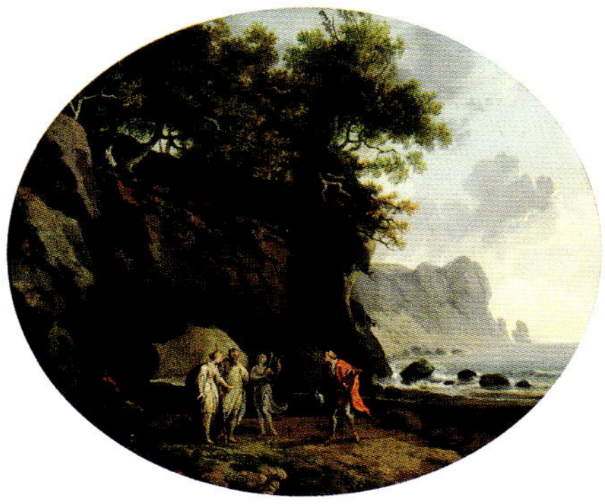

Barret, George the elder 1728/1732–1784
Scene from 'The Tempest' (from the play by William Shakespeare)
oil on panel 28.2 x 33
VIS.251

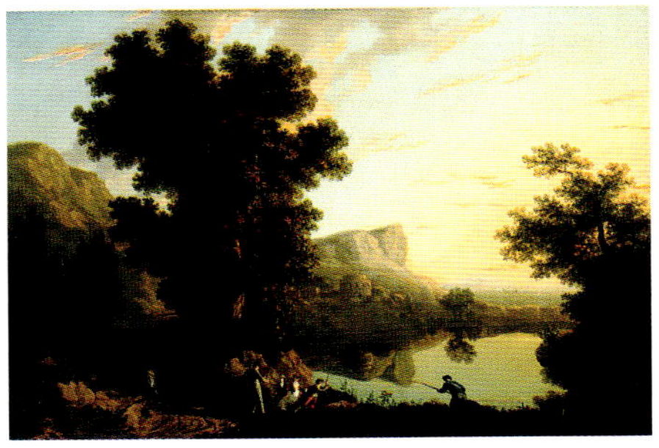

Barret, George the elder (attributed to) 1728/1732–1784
Landscape with a Lake
oil on canvas 56.9 x 82.4
VIS.135

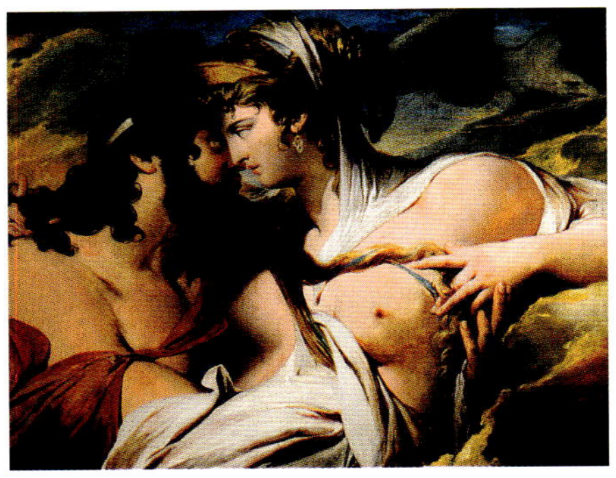

Barry, James 1741–1806
Jupiter Beguiled by Juno on Mount Ida
1790–1799
oil on canvas 130.2 x 155.4
VIS.2742

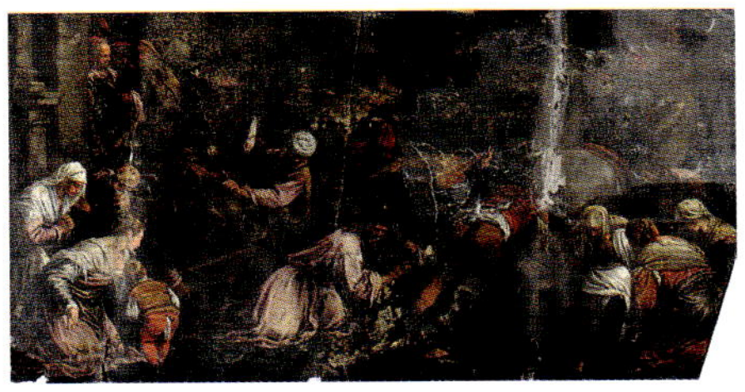

Bassano, Leandro (school of) 1557–1622
The Road to Calvary
oil on canvas 98.2 x 176.5
VIS.3134

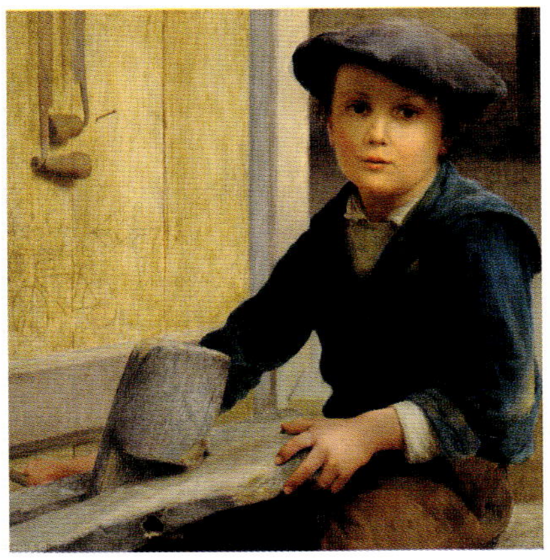

Bastien-Lepage, Émile 1854–1938
The Young Craftsman 1901
oil on panel 60.4 x 59.3
VIS.935

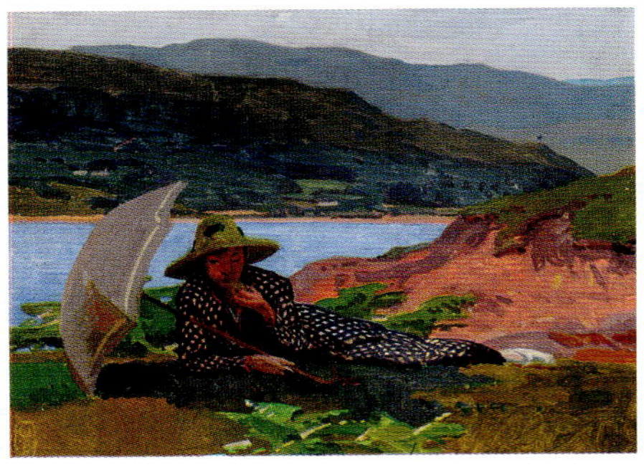

Bayes, Walter 1869–1956
The Lemon 1912
oil on canvas 26.7 x 36.6
VIS.3891

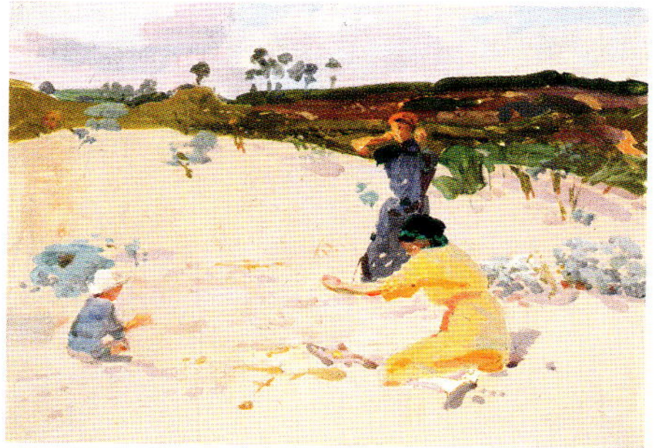

Bayes, Walter 1869–1956
On the Beach c.1915
oil on panel 27 x 38.1
VIS.2631

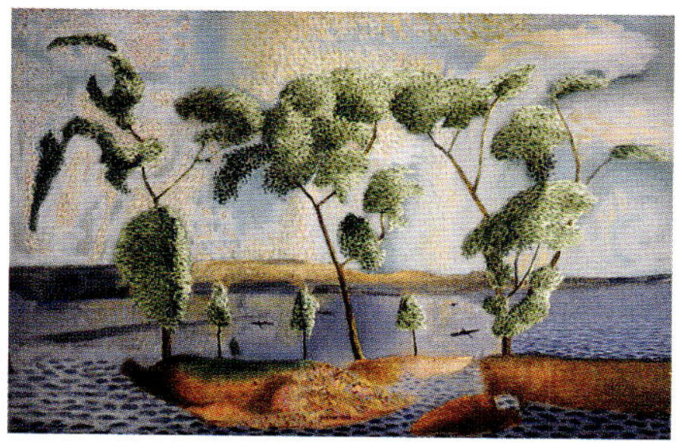

Baynes, John active 1935–1943
Trees on an Island 1935
oil on canvas 49.4 x 74.7
VIS.2952

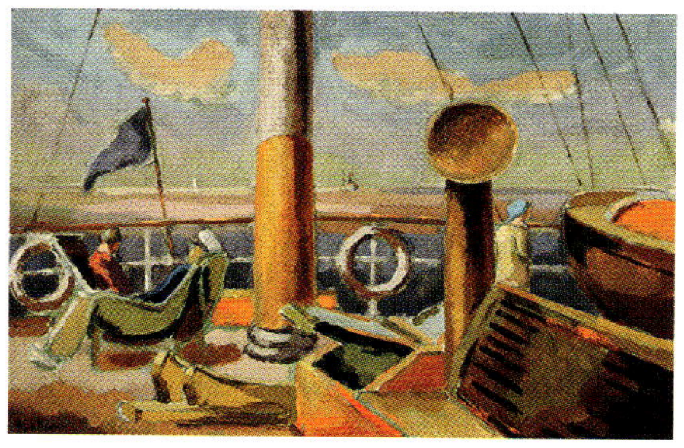

Baynes, Keith 1887–1977
In the Baltic
oil on canvas 50 x 75.3
VIS.1801

Bazler, Fred b.1934
Four on Four 1967
acrylic on canvas 183.5 x 183.2
VIS.4956

Bazler, Fred b.1934
Two on Six 1967
acrylic on canvas 183.2 x 183.1
VIS.4957

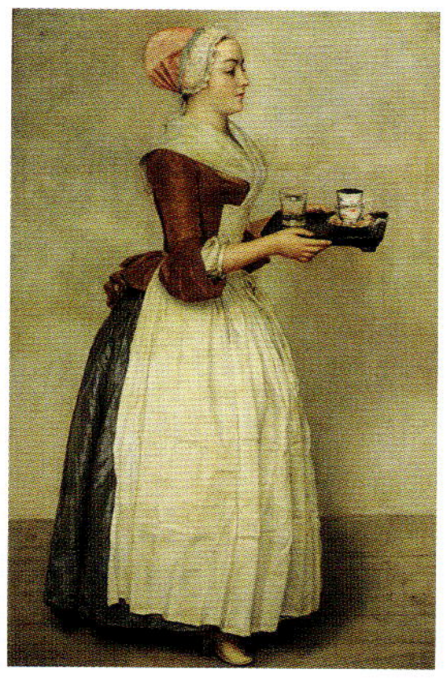

Beaune, M.
The Chocolate Maiden (after Jean-Etienne Liotard)
oil on canvas 83.5 x 53.6
VIS.785

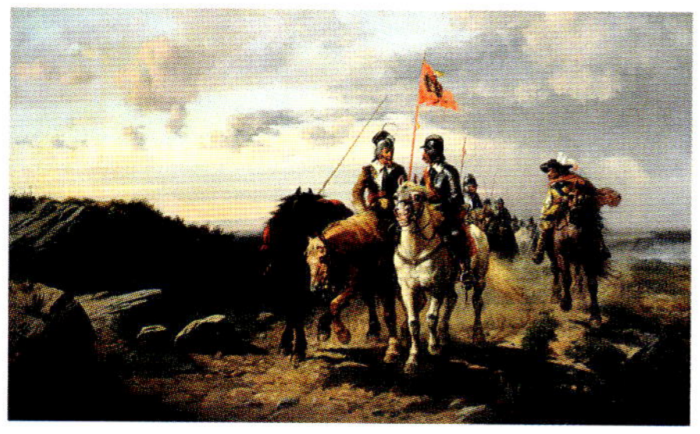

Beavis, Richard 1824–1896
Scene from 'The Lay of the Last Minstrel' (from the poem by Walter Scott) 1864–1870
oil on canvas 74.5 x 121.4
VIS.1662

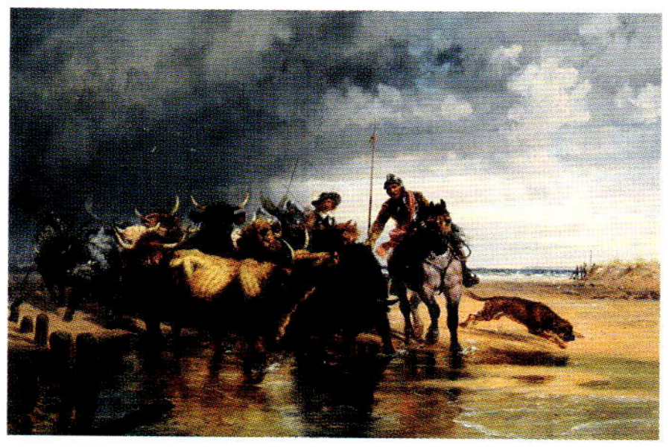

Beavis, Richard 1824–1896
Cattle Raid 1870
oil on canvas 76.5 x 110.2
VIS.1584

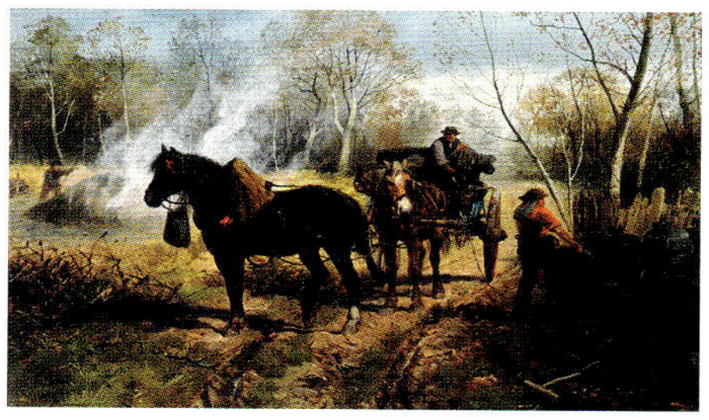

Beavis, Richard 1824–1896
The Charcoal Burners 1874
oil on canvas 29.7 x 50.3
VIS.1496

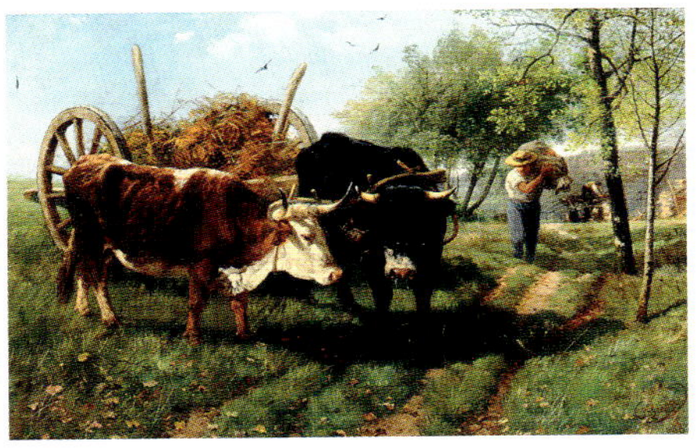

Beavis, Richard 1824–1896
Carting Bracken 1878
oil on canvas 40 x 60.3
VIS.788

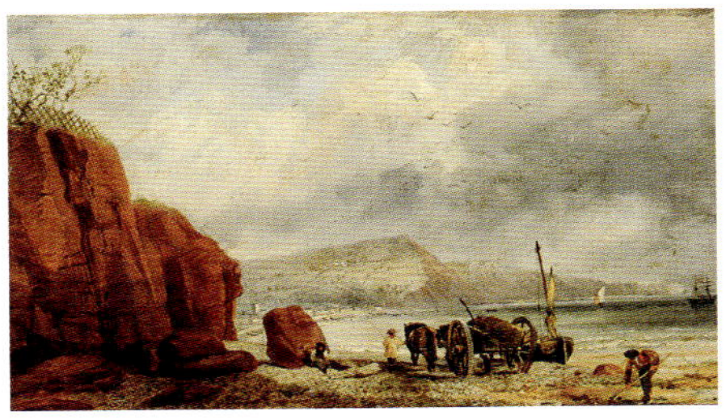

Beavis, Richard 1824–1896
Coast Scene near Sidmouth, Devon
oil on millboard 16.6 x 29.4
VIS.1069

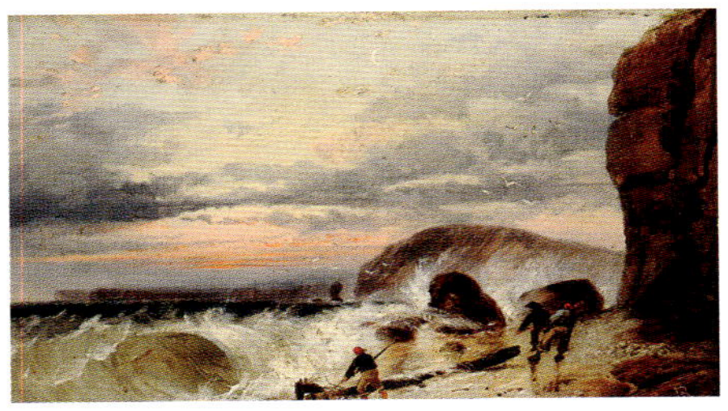

Beavis, Richard 1824–1896
Near Sidmouth, Devon
oil on panel 16.6 x 29.5
VIS.1008

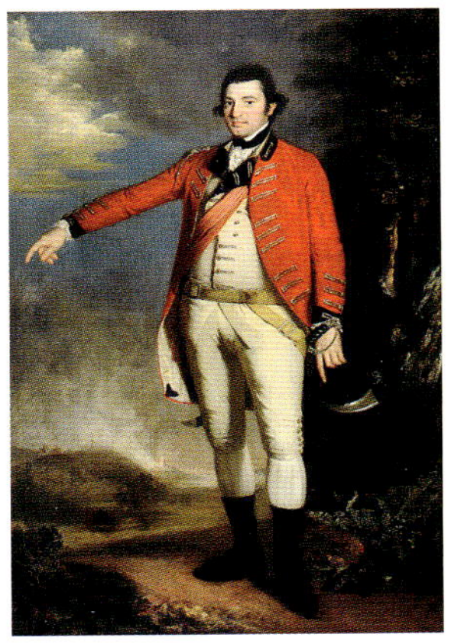

Beechey, William 1753–1839
Colonel Milner of Totley Hall 1790–1800
oil on canvas 204 x 137.9
VIS.1681

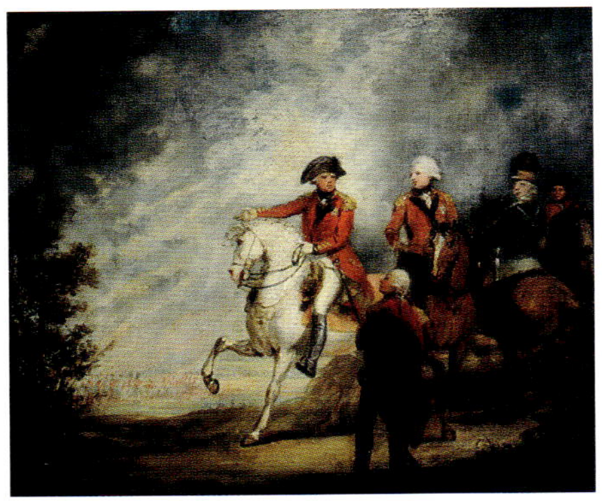

Beechey, William 1753–1839
George III (1738–1820), Reviewing His Troops
oil on canvas 49.3 x 57.1
VIS.2297

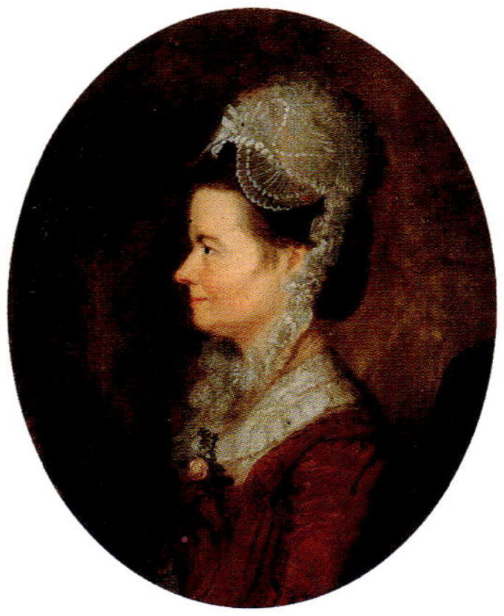

Beechey, William 1753–1839
Mrs Goldsmith
oil on panel 25.1 x 19.9
VIS.3032

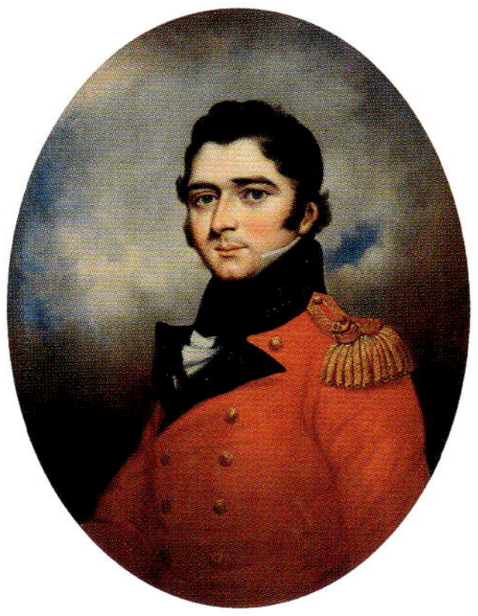

Beechey, William 1753–1839
Portrait of an Officer
oil on canvas 87 x 65.8
VIS.142

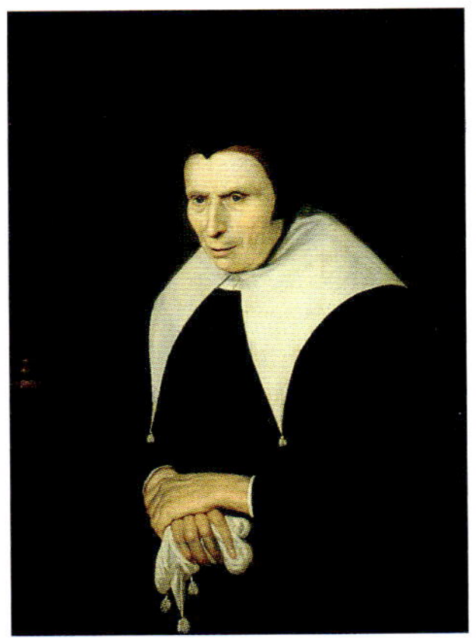

Beeldemaker, Adriaen Cornelisz.
1618–1709
Portrait of an Old Woman 1676
oil on canvas 81.4 x 58.9
VIS.42

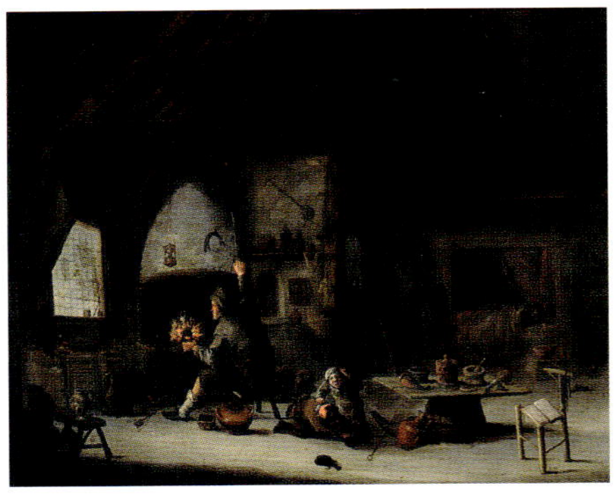

Beelt, Cornelis 1640–1702
The Tinker's Shop 1670–1690
oil on canvas 52.6 x 64.7
VIS.2274

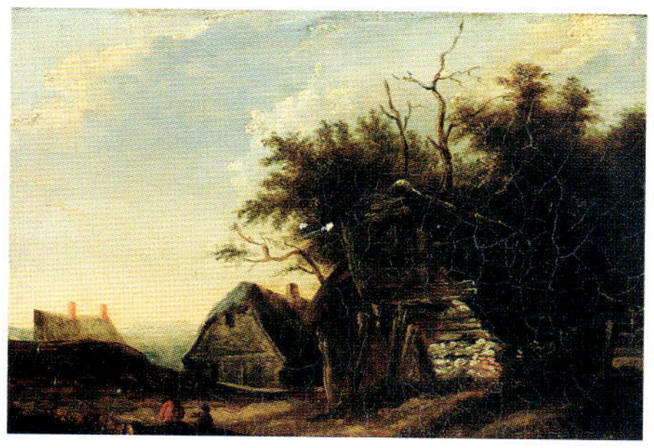

Beeton, J.
Landscape mid-19th C
oil on panel 28 x 39.4
VIS.1383

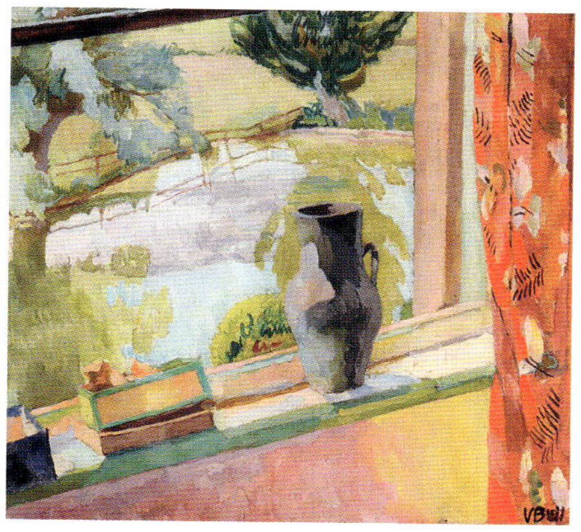

Bell, Vanessa 1879–1961
View of the Pond at Charleston, East Sussex
c.1919
oil on canvas 79.8 x 84
VIS.4155

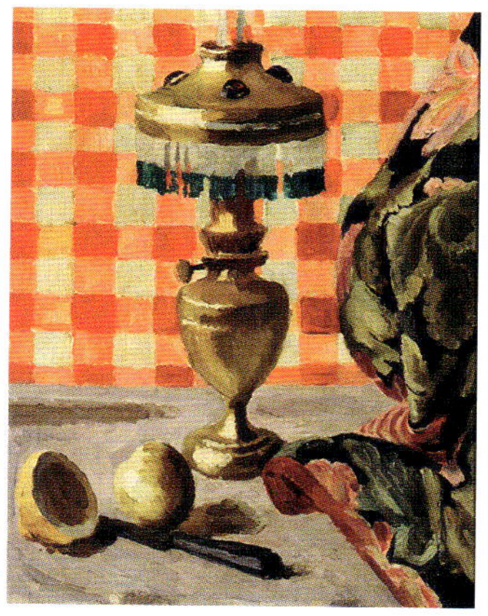

Bell, Vanessa 1879–1961
Still Life
oil on canvas 45 x 35
VIS.5424

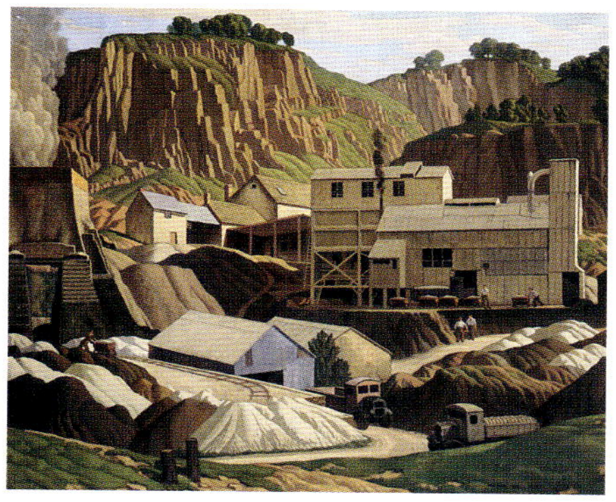

Bell, Walter b.1904
Derbyshire Quarry 1937
oil on canvas 62.1 x 74.8
VIS.2193

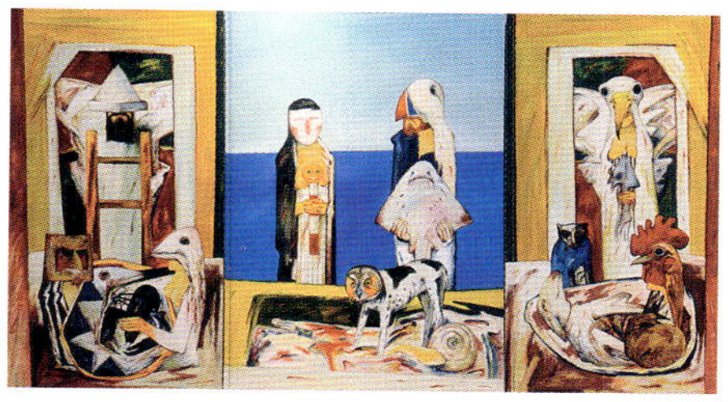

Bellany, John b.1942
Celtic Feast (triptych) 1974
oil on canvas 193.2 x 103; 194 x 137;
193.5 x 103.5
VIS.4938

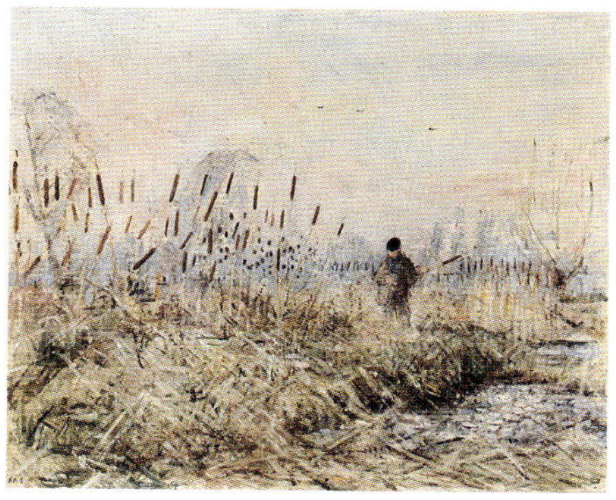

Bellingham-Smith, Elinor 1906–1988
Bullrushes
oil on canvas 62.7 x 75.4
VIS.3717

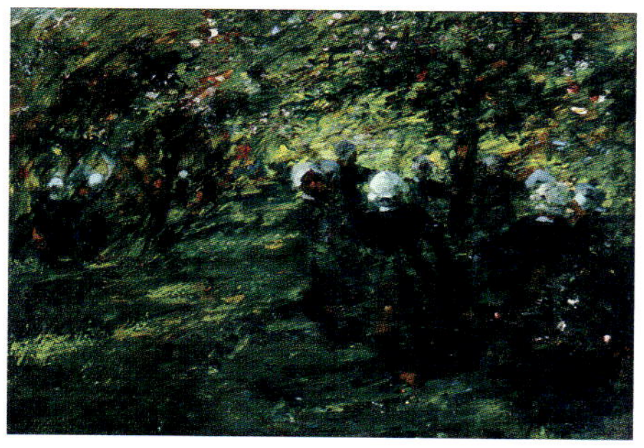

Bellingham-Smith, Hugh 1866–1922
Children in an Orchard
oil on canvas 24 x 34.3
VIS.1018

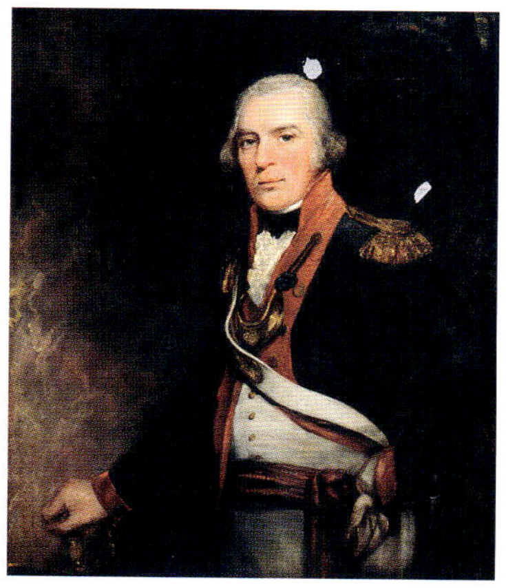

Bembridge, John Conrad c.1822–1857
Colonel Athorpe (d.1806) 1840
oil on canvas 109.7 x 91.8
VIS.3216

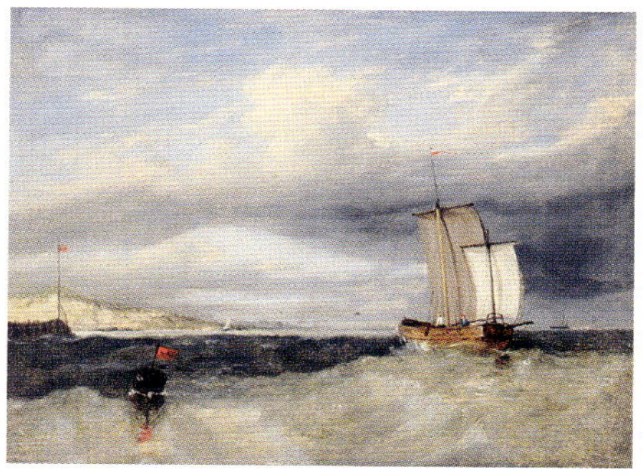

Bentley, Charles 1808–1854
Seascape
oil on panel 18.1 x 24.6
VIS.577

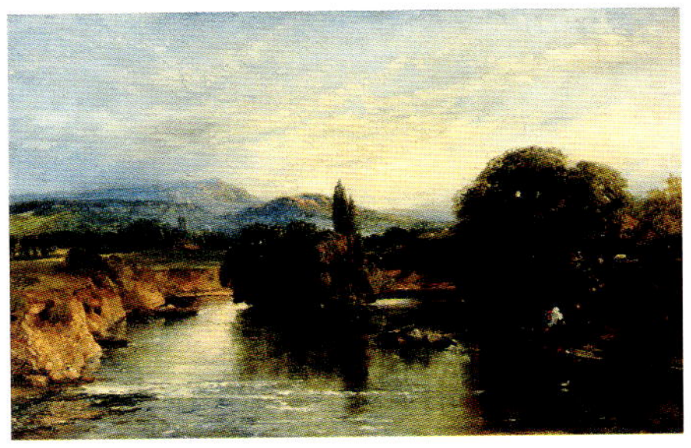

Bentley, Joseph Clayton 1809–1851
River Aire, near Appleby, Yorkshire
oil on canvas 28.5 x 44
VIS.1493

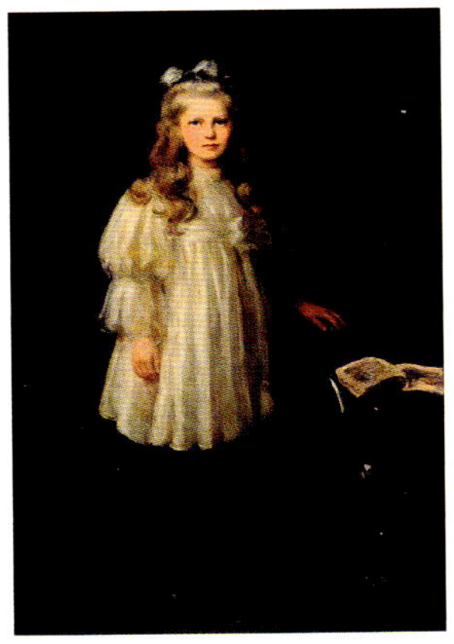

Bentley, Joseph Herbert 1866–1934
Miss Atkin
oil on canvas 152.2 x 101.5
VIS.3148

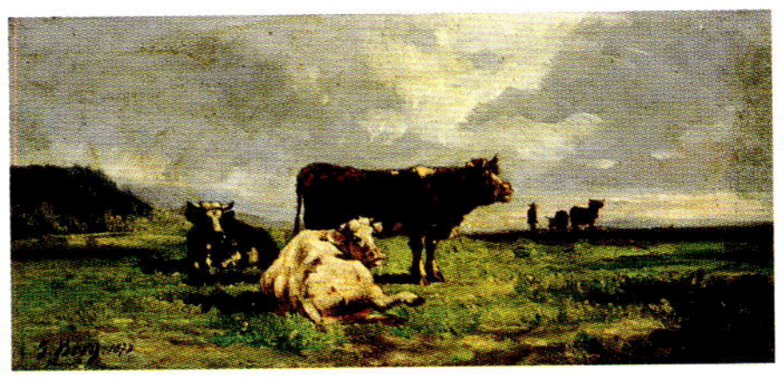

Berg, Gunnar 1864–1894
Cattle in a Landscape 1878
oil on panel 18.9 x 39
VIS.1078

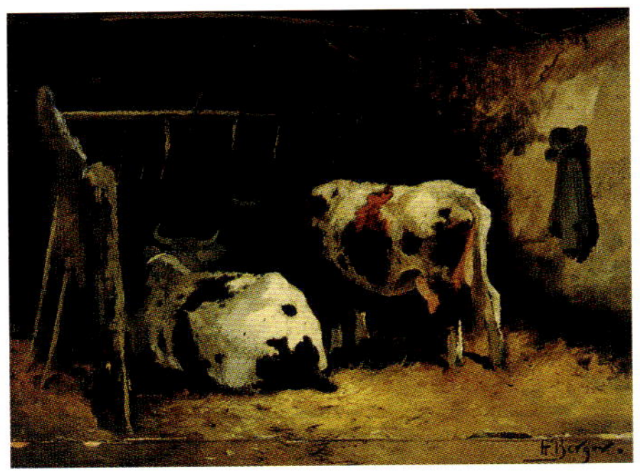

Bergen, Hans
Cattle in a Stall
oil on canvas on millboard 33 x 43.3
VIS.613

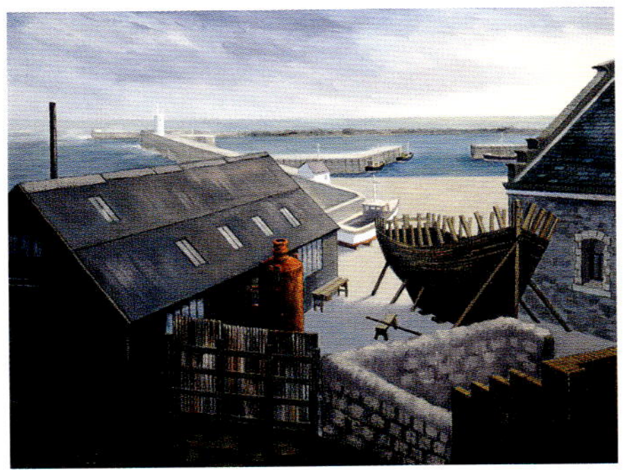

Bevan, Norman b.1900
Seahouses Harbour, Northumberland
oil on canvas 42.2 x 54.3
VIS.5425

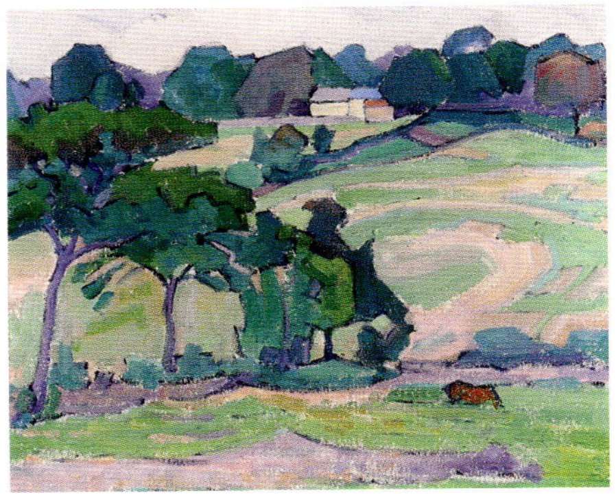

Bevan, Robert Polhill 1865–1925
Farm Landscape
oil on canvas 35.5 x 43.5
VIS.3347

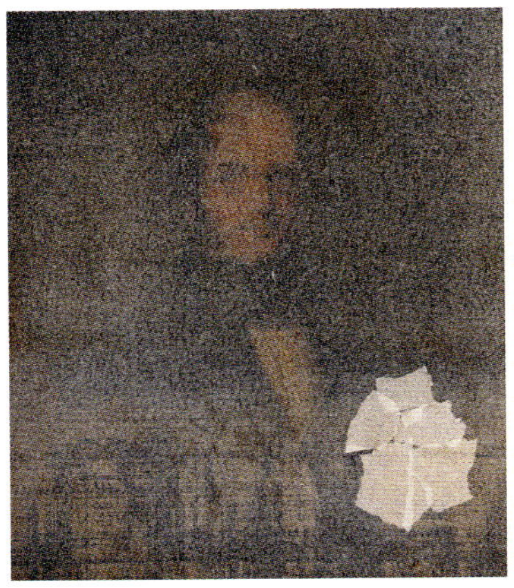

Birch, John 1807–1857
Sir Arnold Knight (1789–1871), MD
oil on canvas 76 x 63.5
K1936.23

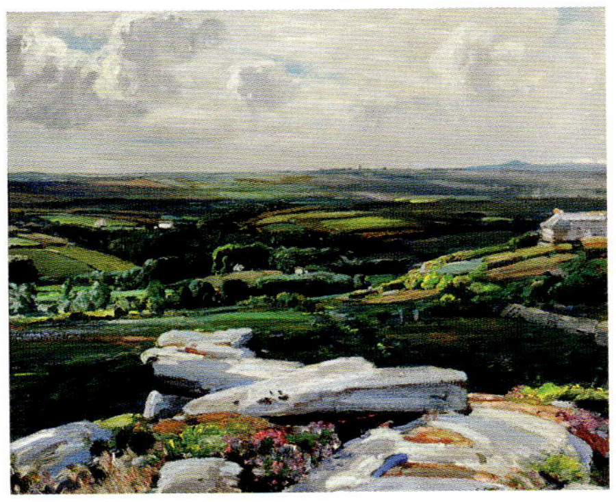

Birch, Samuel John Lamorna 1869–1955
Trewoofe from the Cairn, Cornwall c.1930
oil on canvas 60.1 x 72.8
VIS.134

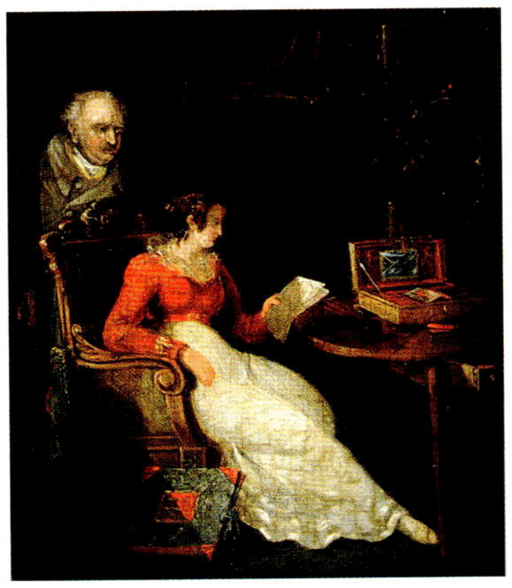

Bird, Edward 1772–1819
The Discovered Correspondence
oil on panel 22.8 x 18.8
VIS.335

Facing page: Redpath, Anne, 1895–1965, *Altar in Lisbon* (detail), Museums Sheffield, (p. 178)

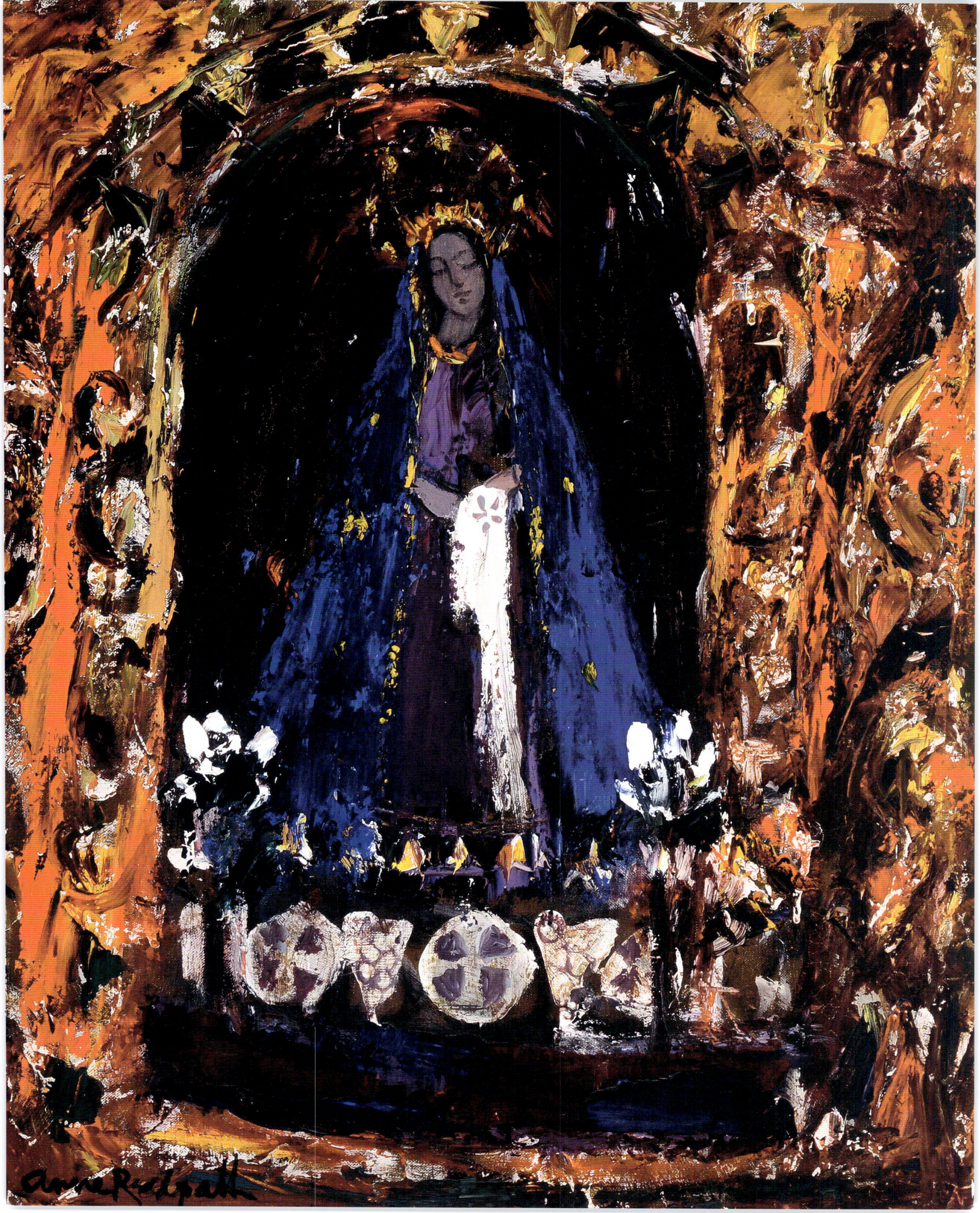
Anne Redpath

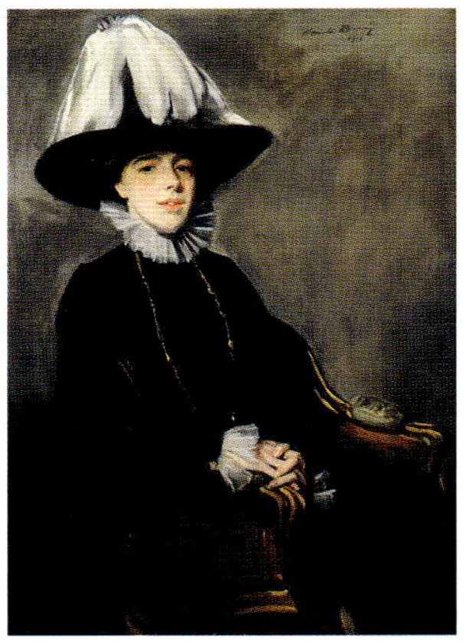

Birley, Oswald Hornby Joseph 1880–1952
The Spanish Plume 1912
oil on canvas 123 x 86.4
VIS.3017

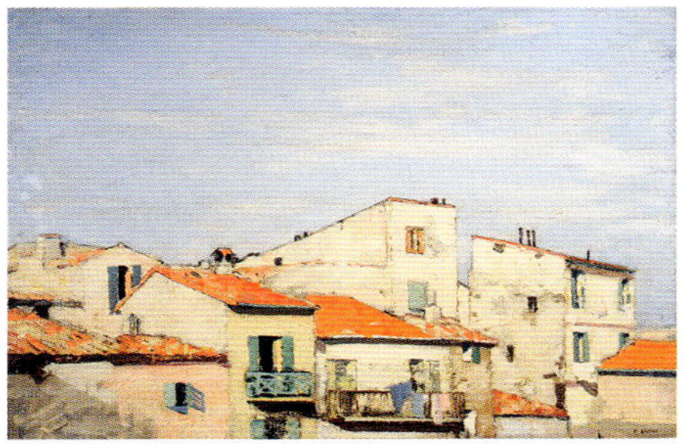

Bishop, Henry 1868–1939
Houses in Provence, France
oil on canvas 48.6 x 71.3
VIS.990

Bishop, Henry 1868–1939
Market Place, Concarneau, France
oil on canvas 42.4 x 59.7
VIS.682

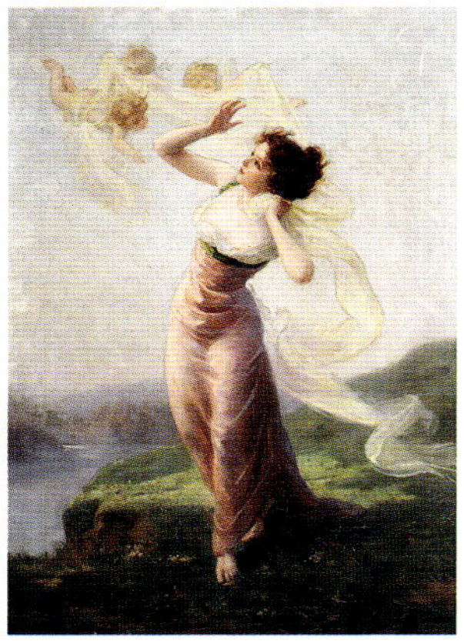

Bisson, Edouard 1856–1939
A Springtime Idyll 1896
oil on canvas 122.7 x 87.3
VIS.1286

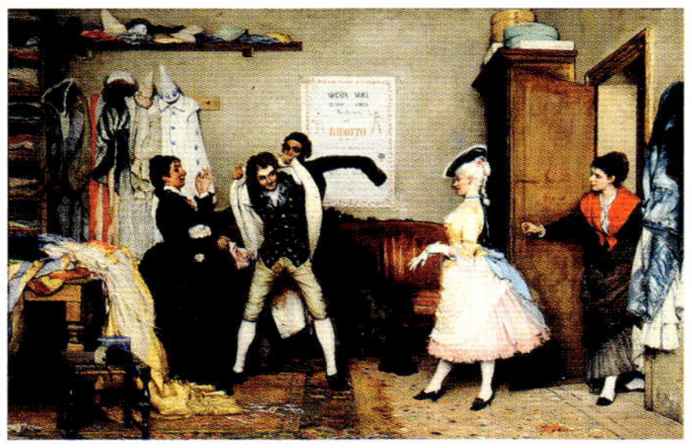

Blaas, Eugen von 1843–1931
Dressing for the Masquerade 1860–1885
oil on panel 69.8 x 106.8
VIS.1485

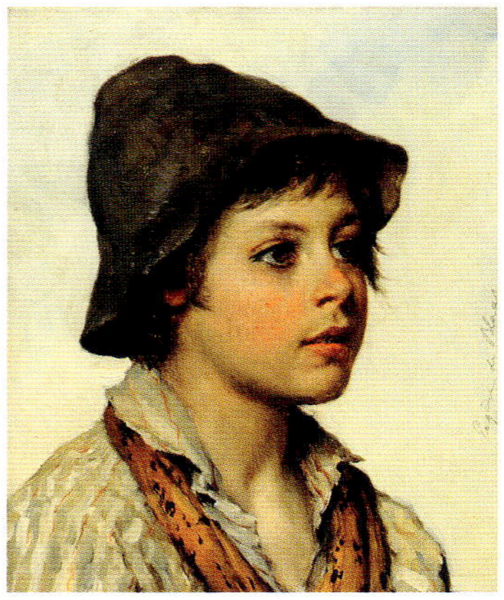

Blaas, Eugen von 1843–1931
Portrait of a Boy 1880–1900
oil on panel 25.5 x 20.9
VIS.1241

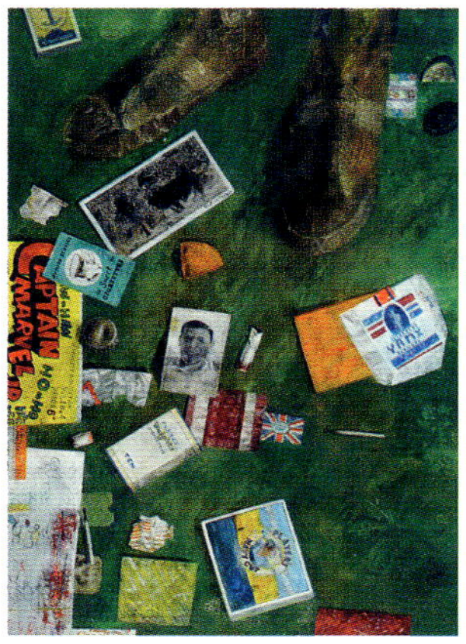

Blake, Peter b.1932
Footsteps 1955
oil on board 66.8 x 56.3
VIS.4727

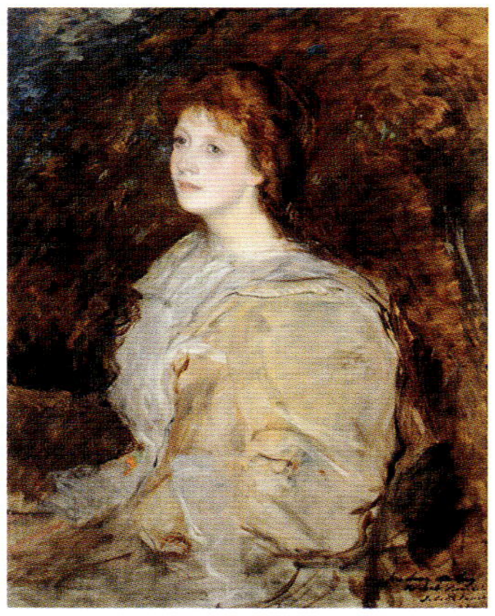

Blanche, Jacques-Emile 1861–1942
Mabel Beardsley (1871–1916) 1895
oil on canvas 90.4 x 71.6
VIS.2992

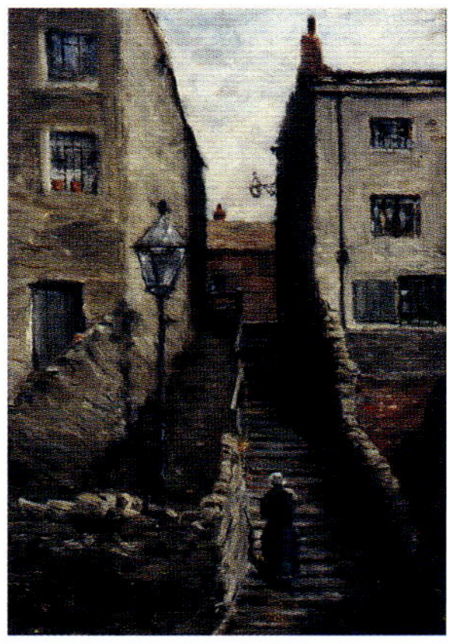

Boden, William 1840–1920
Long Steps, Bernard Street, Sheffield 1903
oil on canvas 34.4 x 24.5
K1905.59

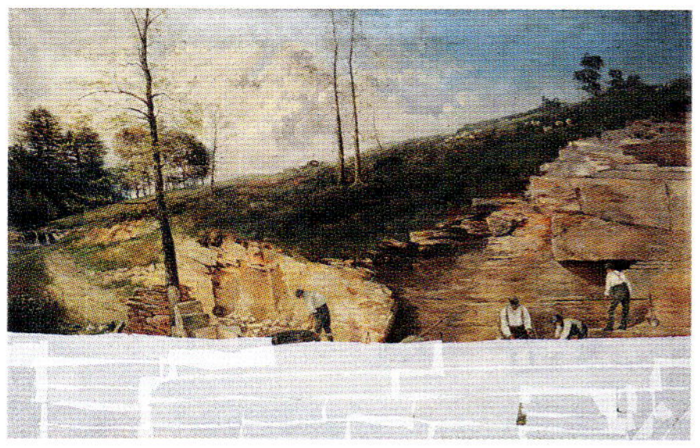

Boden, William 1840–1920
Wagwood Stone Quarries, Dore, Derbyshire
oil on canvas 102.4 x 152.8
K1922.5

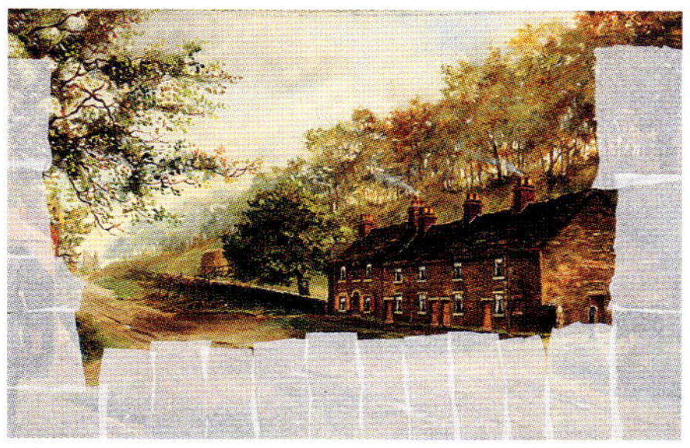

Boler, Albert Edward 1864–1939
Banner Cross 1890
oil on canvas 50.2 x 76.5
1963.98

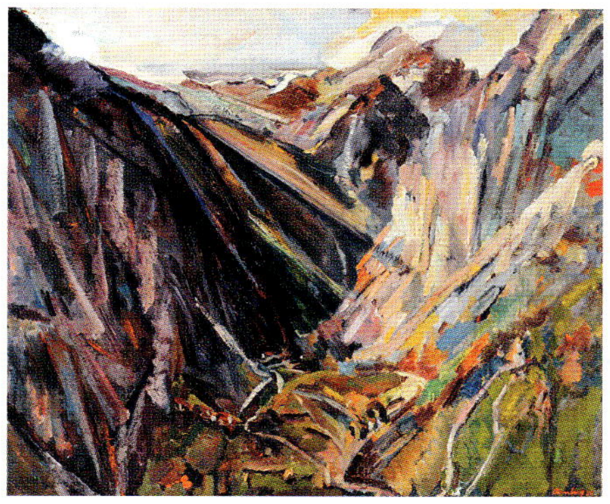

Bomberg, David 1890–1957
Valley of La Hermida: Picos de Europa, Asturias, Spain 1935
oil on canvas 109.2 x 126
VIS.2839

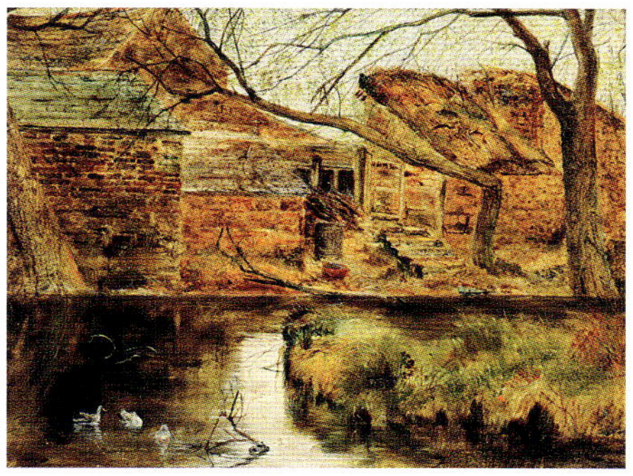

Bond, William Joseph Julius Caesar 1833–1926
The Duck Pond
oil on panel 15.4 x 20.1
VIS.238

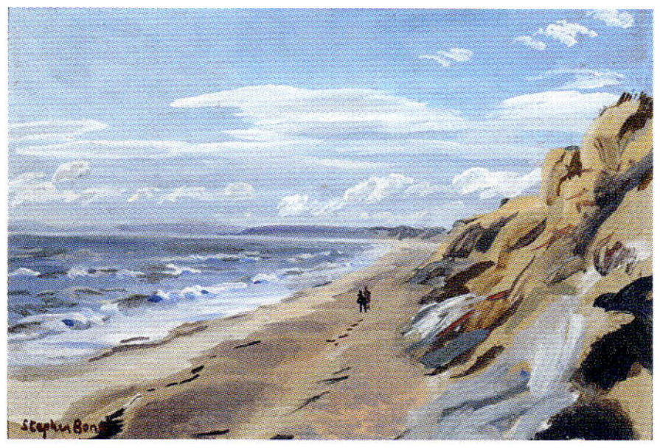

Bone, Stephen 1904–1958
Christchurch Bay, Dorset
oil on board 23.3 x 33.8
VIS.2032

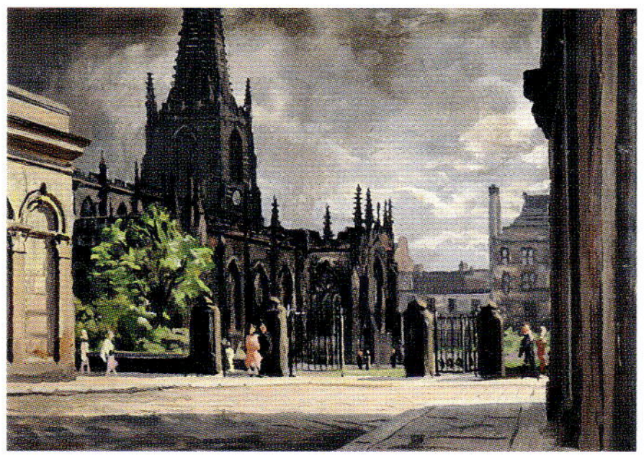

Bone, Stephen 1904–1958
Sheffield Cathedral
oil on board 28.4 x 38.7
VIS.5438

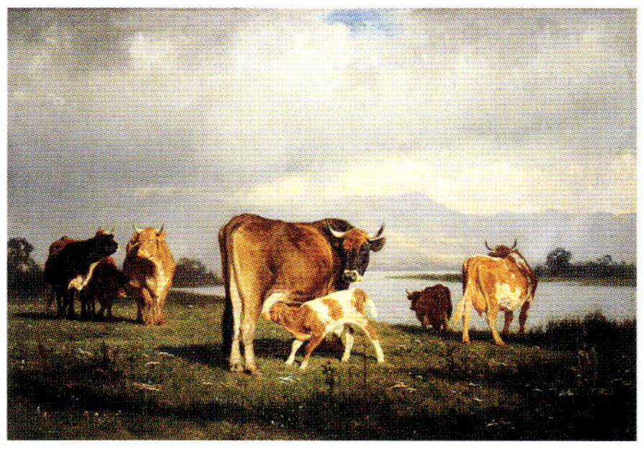

Bonheur, Auguste-François 1824–1884
Cattle 1860–1870
oil on canvas 101.3 x 140.4
VIS.1596

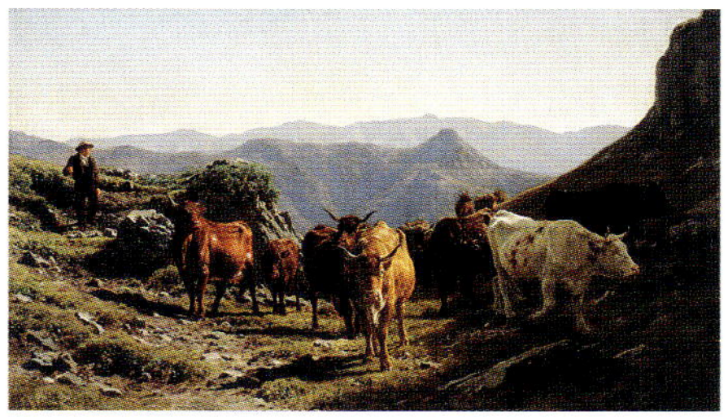

Bonheur, Auguste-François 1824–1884
Landscape with Cattle
oil on canvas 101 x 171.5
VIS.1454

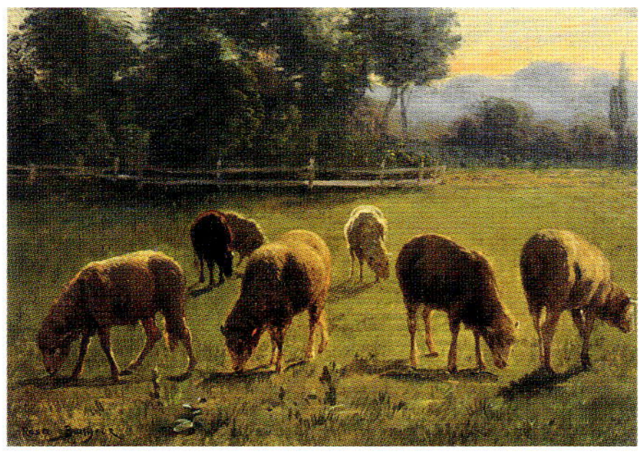

Bonheur, Rosa 1822–1899
Sheep in a Landscape
oil on canvas 24.8 x 35
VIS.1017

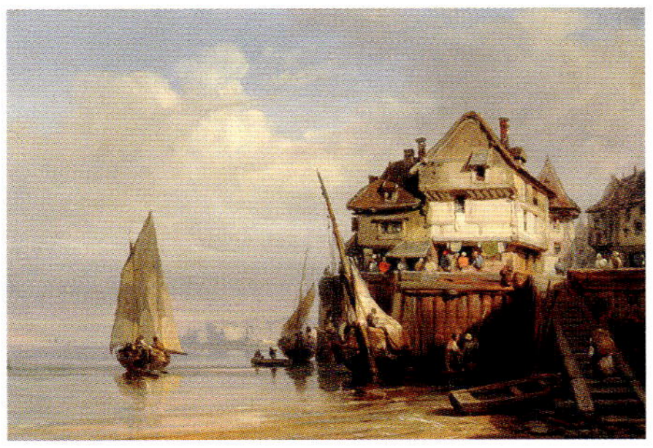

Bonington, Richard Parkes 1802–1828
Old Cherbourg, France
oil on panel 21.8 x 31.2
VIS.337

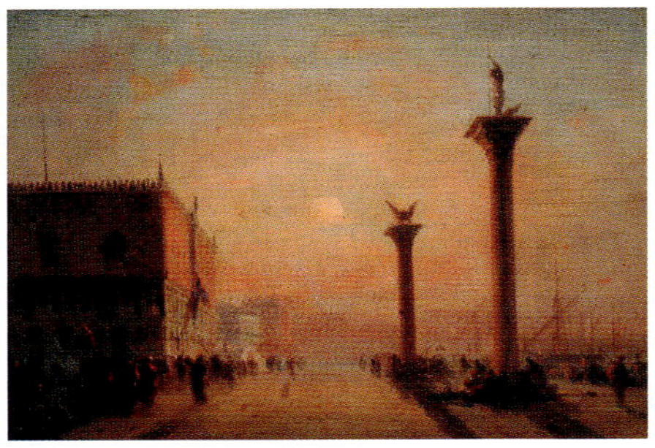

Bonington, Richard Parkes 1802–1828
The Piazzetta, Venice
oil on panel 15.2 x 20.5
VIS.58

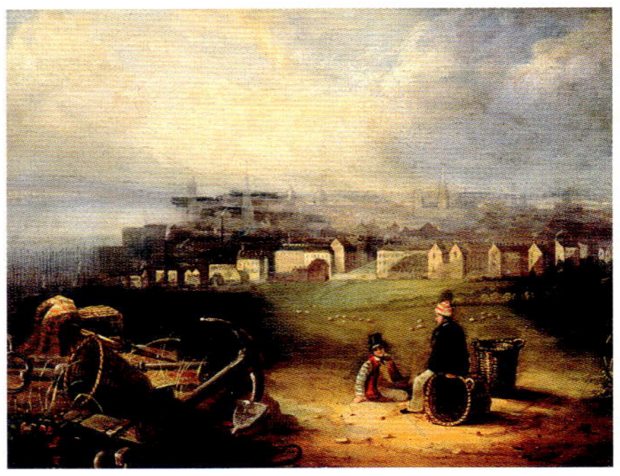

Bonington, Richard Parkes 1802–1828
View of the City of Lyons, France
oil on panel 21.5 x 28
VIS.1083

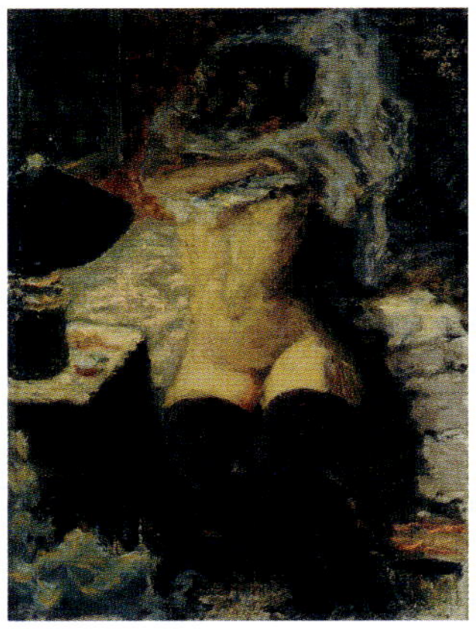

Bonnard, Pierre 1867–1947
Nu aux bas noires 1900
oil on panel 52.6 x 38.6
VIS.LI.843 (P)

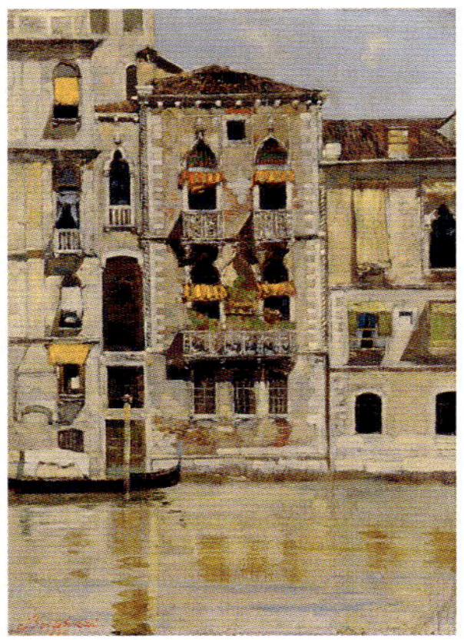

Bortoluzzi, Camillo 1868–1933
Venetian Houses 1888
oil on canvas 34.8 x 24.6
VIS.604

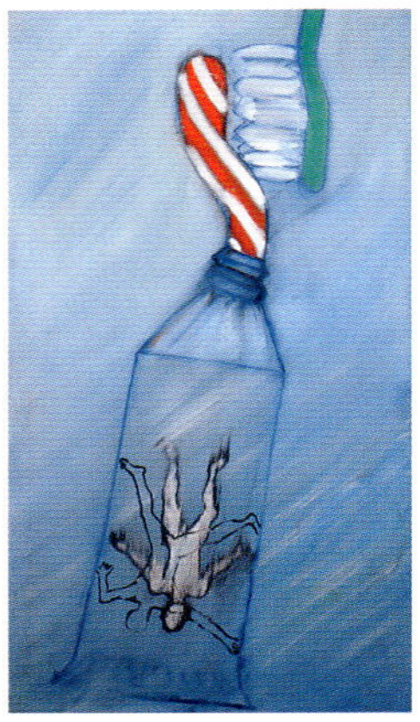

Boshier, Derek b.1937
First Toothpaste Painting 1962
oil on canvas 138 x 77.6
VIS.4585

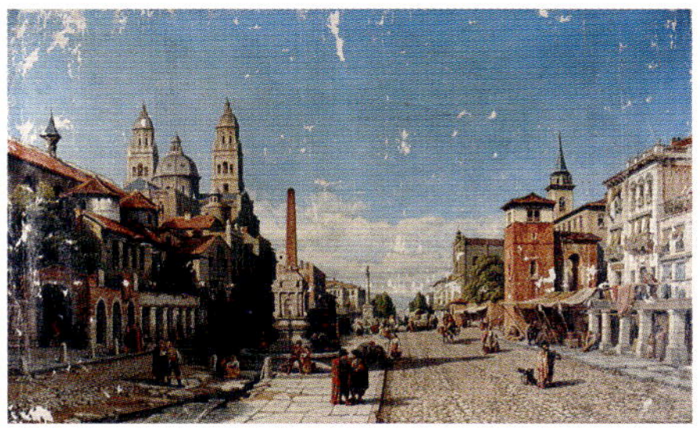

Bossuet, François Antoine 1798–1889
Place de la Constitution à Jaen, Espagne 1880
oil on canvas 97 x 150.5
VIS.2605

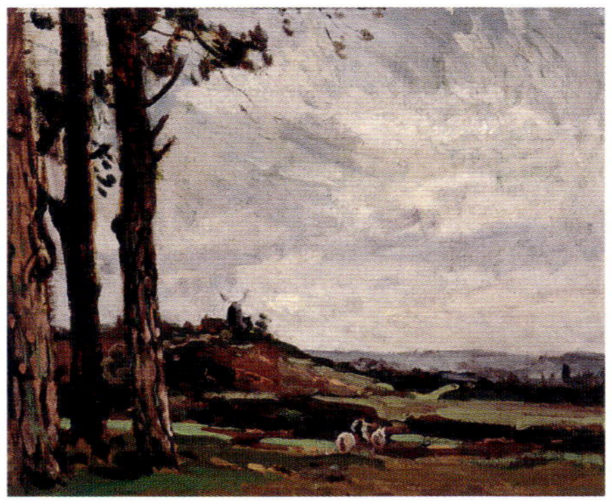

Bottomley, Albert Ernest 1873–1950
March Morning
oil on canvas 49.8 x 59.7
VIS.1324

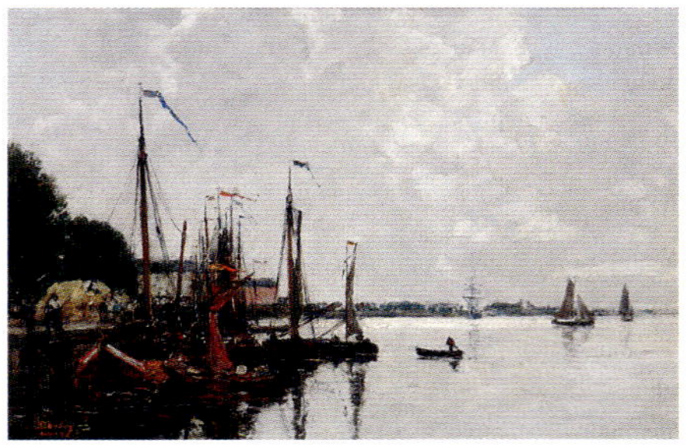

Boudin, Eugène Louis 1824–1898
The Quay at Antwerp, Belgium 1865–1870
oil on panel 49.3 x 64
VIS.180

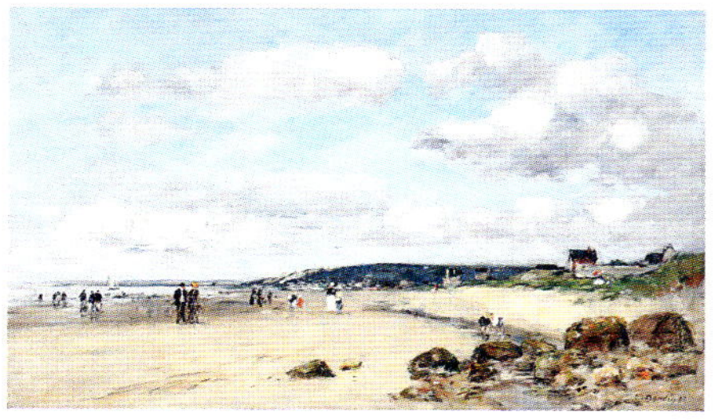

Boudin, Eugène Louis 1824–1898
Plage en Normandie, France 1890
oil on canvas 67.8 x 97.4
VIS.LI.900 (P)

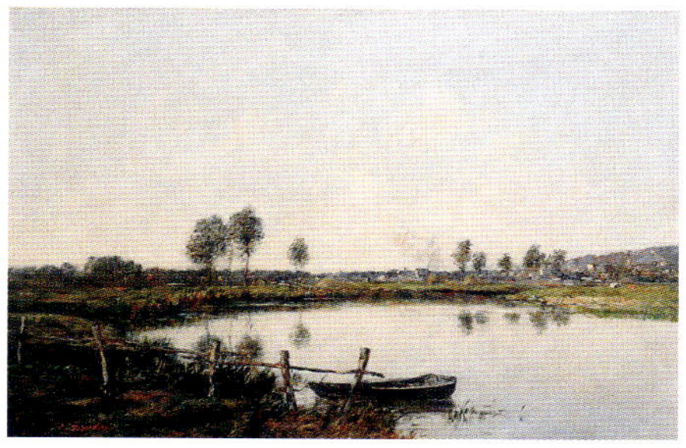

Boudin, Eugène Louis 1824–1898
The Water Meadows at Deauville, France
oil on canvas 49 x 72.5
VIS.352

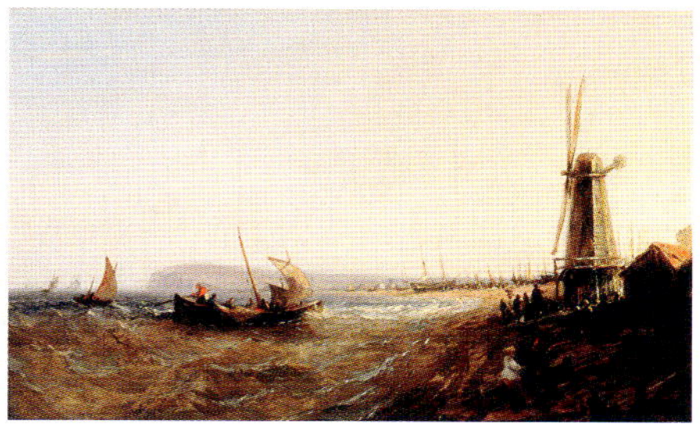

Bough, Samuel 1822–1878
Coast Scene 1856
oil on panel 26.5 x 42.9
VIS.698

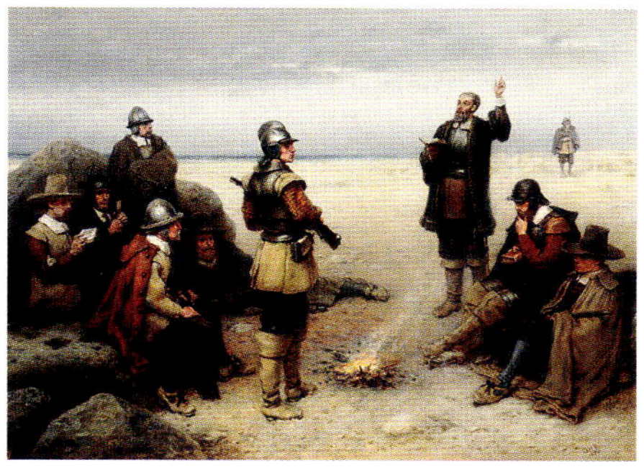

Boughton, George Henry 1833–1905
The Landing of the Pilgrim Fathers 1869
oil on canvas 74.8 x 99.8
VIS.1429

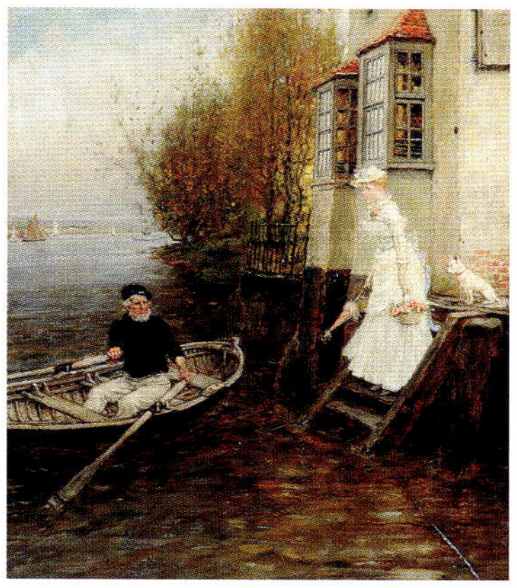

Boughton, George Henry 1833–1905
The Ferry, a Dainty Fare 1890
oil on panel 56.7 x 47.9
VIS.529

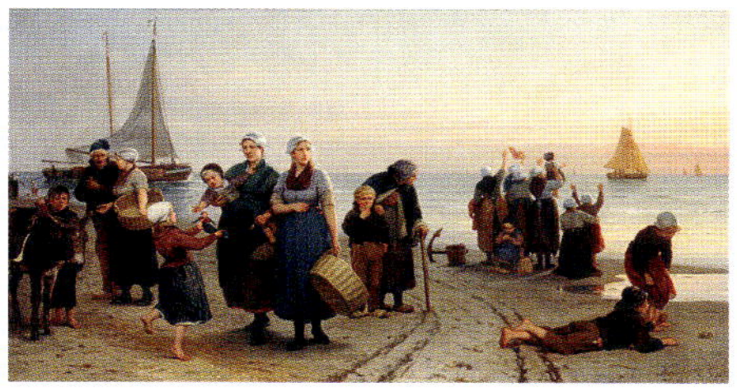

Bource, Henri Jacques 1826–1899
On the Beach, Scheveningen, Holland 1872
oil on canvas 81.5 x 149
VIS.1591

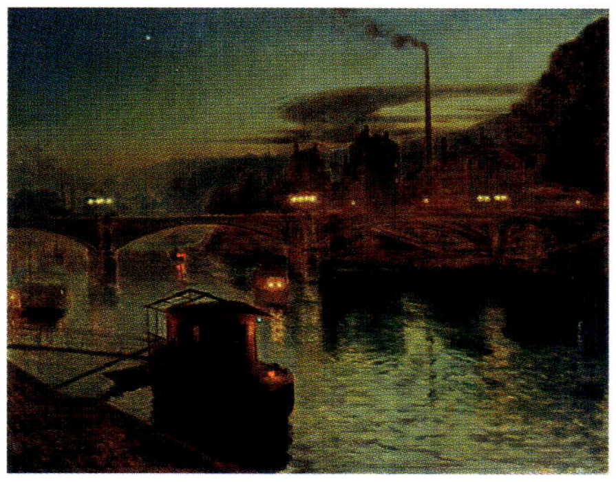

Bouvet, Henri Marius Camille 1859–1945
River Scene, Evening
oil on canvas 63.2 x 81.2
VIS.693

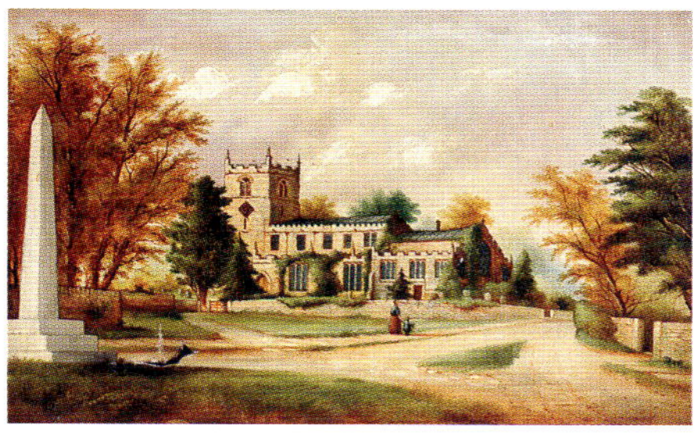

Bower, Reuben 1828–1912
St James's Church, Norton, Sheffield
before 1881
oil on canvas 65 x 102.6
2009.264

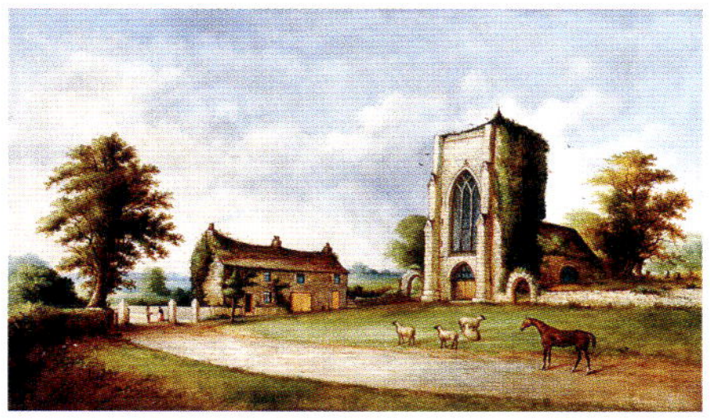

Bower, Reuben 1828–1912
Beauchief Abbey, Derbyshire 1884
oil on canvas 74.4 x 124.3
K1955.13

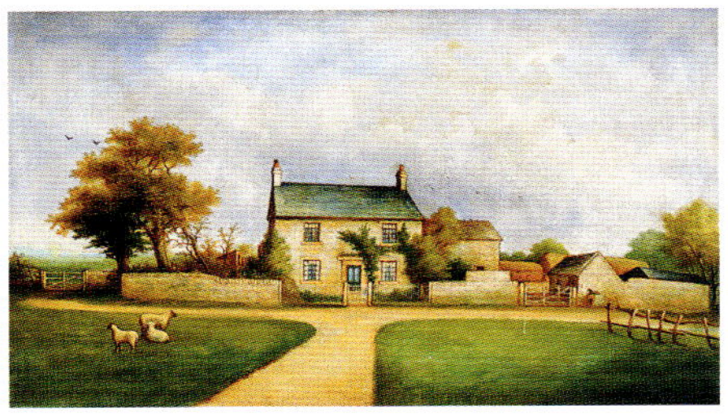

Bower, Reuben 1828–1912
Cottage at Backmoor, Norton, Sheffield
oil on canvas 56.6 x 96.5
2009.263

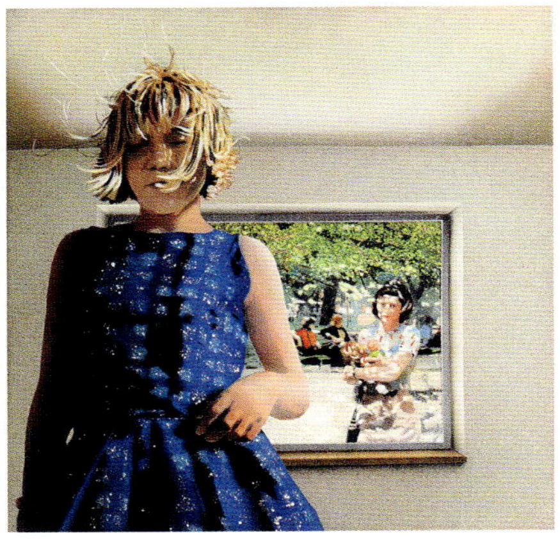

Boyd, Fionnuala b.1944 & **Evans, Leslie** b.1945
Evidence Wind 1974
acrylic on canvas 39.7 x 39.7
VIS.4135

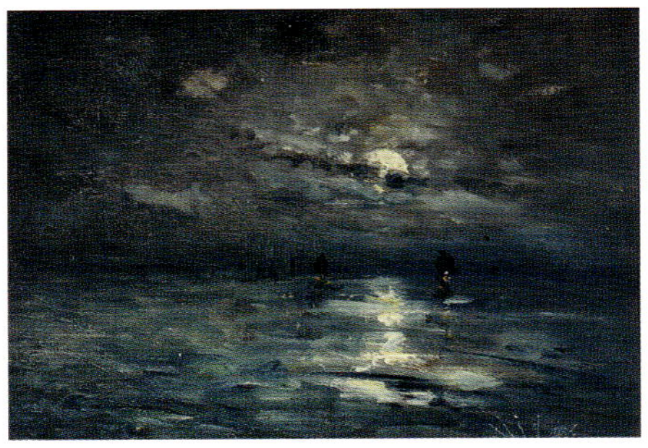

Boyle, George A. 1826–1899
Moonrise at Sea 1914
oil on millboard 24.5 x 34.7
VIS.1090

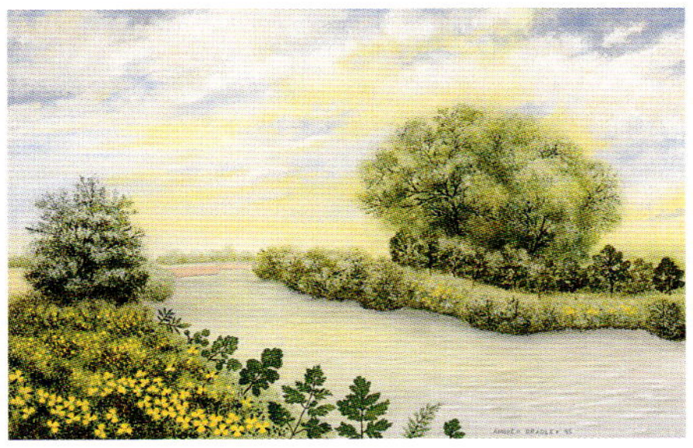

Bradley, Andrea 1970–2009
The River Rother 1995
oil on canvas 50.3 x 76.2
1996.219

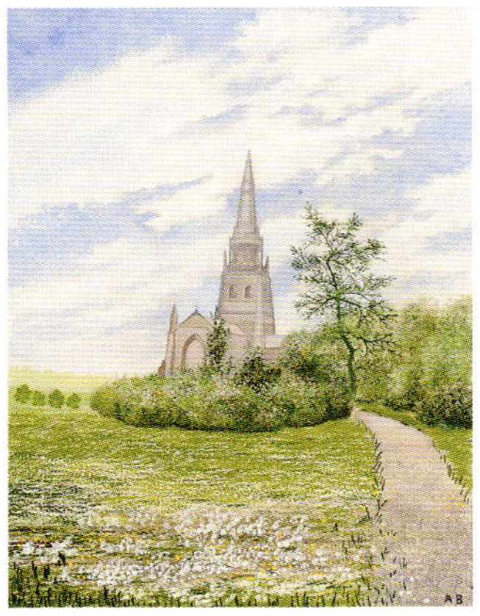

Bradley, Andrea 1970–2009
Clumber Park and Church, Nottinghamshire 1996
oil on canvas 60.4 x 45.1
1996.218

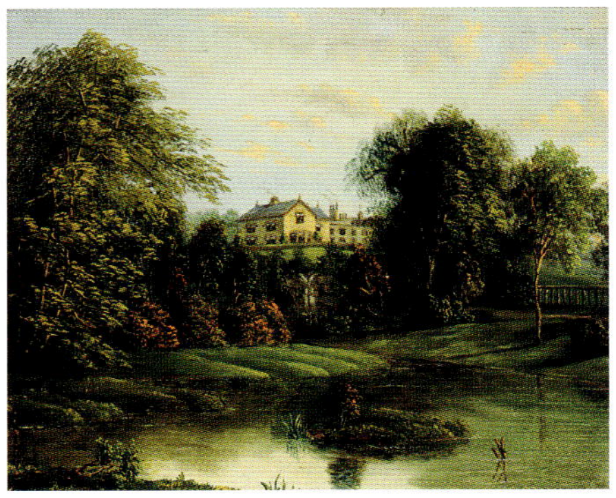

Brammall, J. H. active c.1860–1880
Endcliffe Hall, Sheffield c.1860
oil on panel 24.2 x 28.5
K1958.12

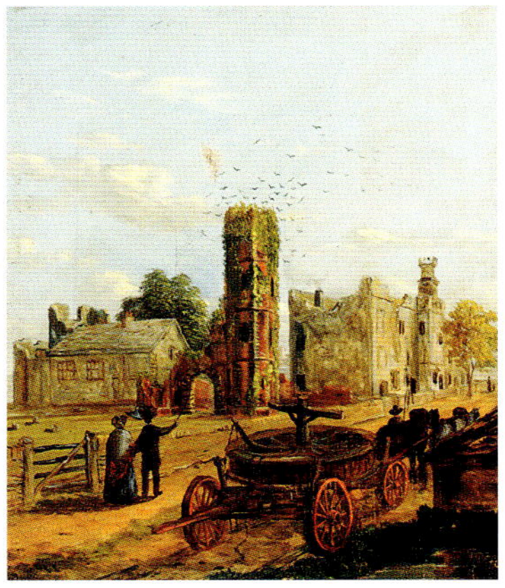

Brammall, J. H. active c.1860–1880
Manor Lodge, Sheffield c.1860
oil on canvas 24.5 x 21
K1958.11

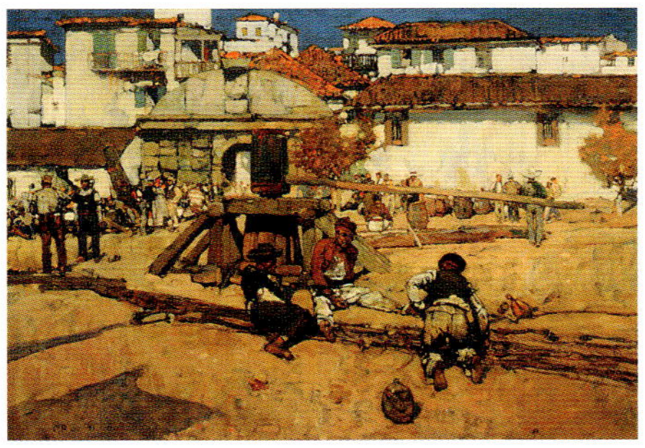

Brangwyn, Frank 1867–1956
Fishermen at Funchal, Madeira, Portugal 1891
oil on canvas 72.3 x 102.3
VIS.LI.758 (P)

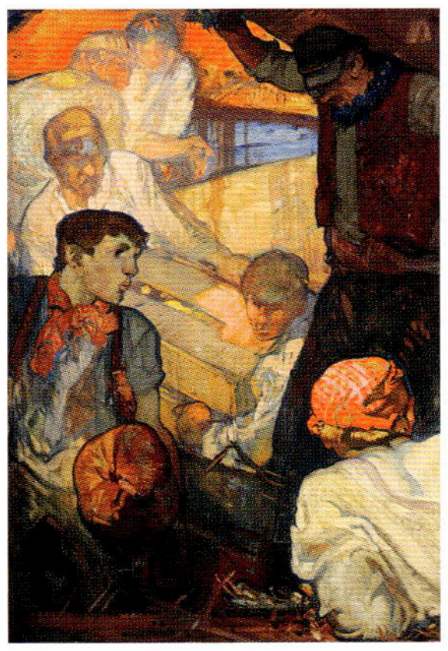

Brangwyn, Frank 1867–1956
Loading the Boat
oil on canvas 191.6 x 129.9
VIS.4345

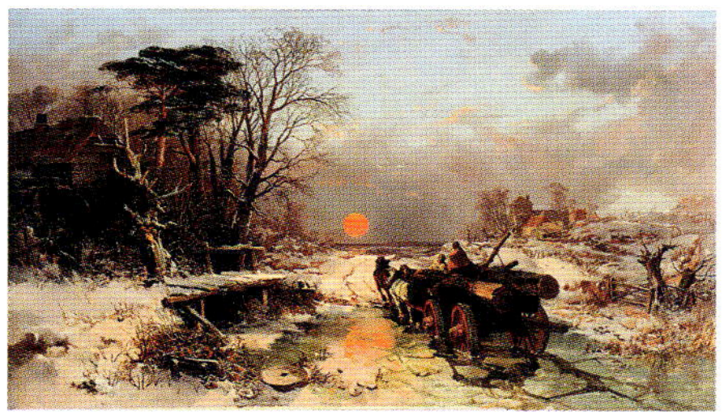

Branwhite, Charles 1817–1880
Winter Scene 1851
oil on canvas 81.6 x 137.4
VIS.1440

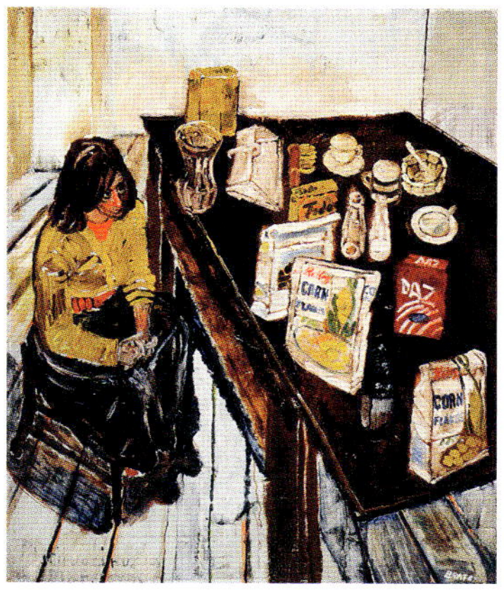

Bratby, John Randall 1928–1992
Jean and Table Top (Girl in a Yellow Jumper) 1953–1954
oil on board 122.1 x 101.2
VIS.4712

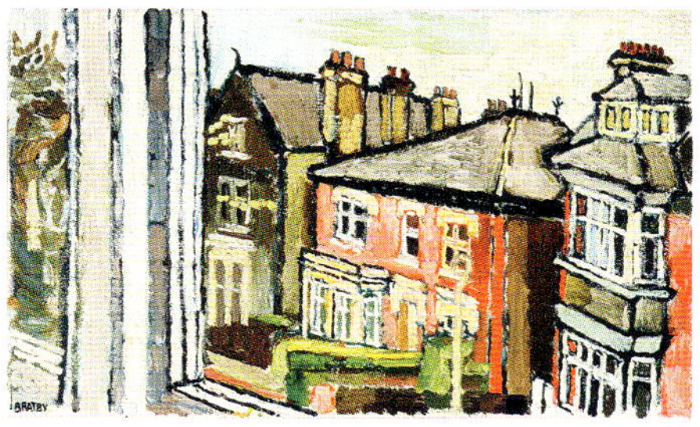

Bratby, John Randall 1928–1992
Hardy Road in November, II 1963
oil on canvas 20.3 x 33
VIS.4339

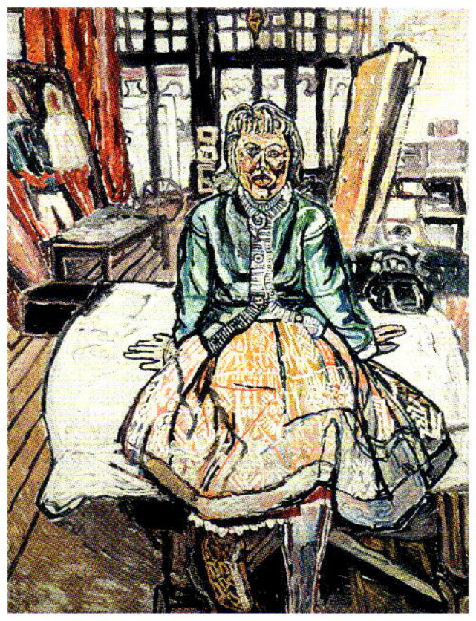

Bratby, John Randall 1928–1992
Antonia Fraser (b.1932)
oil on canvas 168.7 x 122.4
VIS.5208

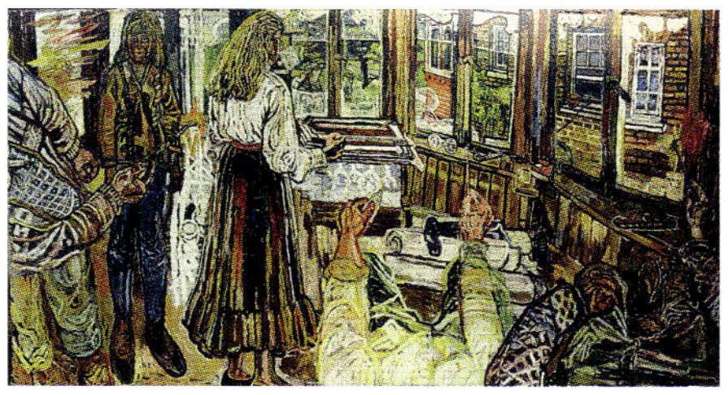

Bratby, John Randall 1928–1992
The Artist Painting a Picture
oil on board 201.5 x 367.2
VIS.5209

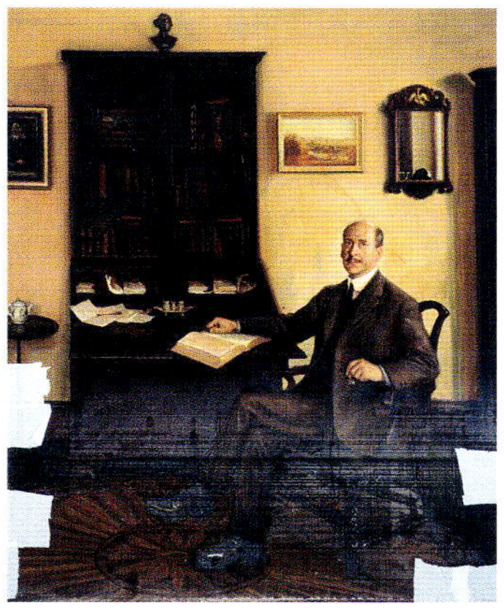

Brealey, William Ramsden 1889–1949
Frederick Bradbury 1914
oil on canvas 114.5 x 88.6
SH414

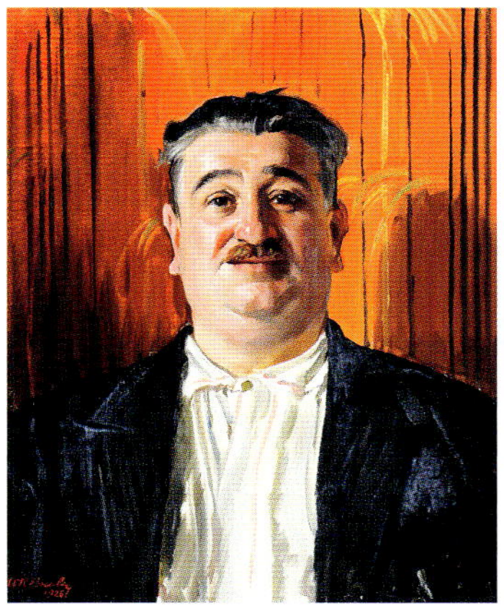

Brealey, William Ramsden 1889–1949
The Waiter, Dieppe 1926
oil on canvas 88 x 77.5
VIS.2021

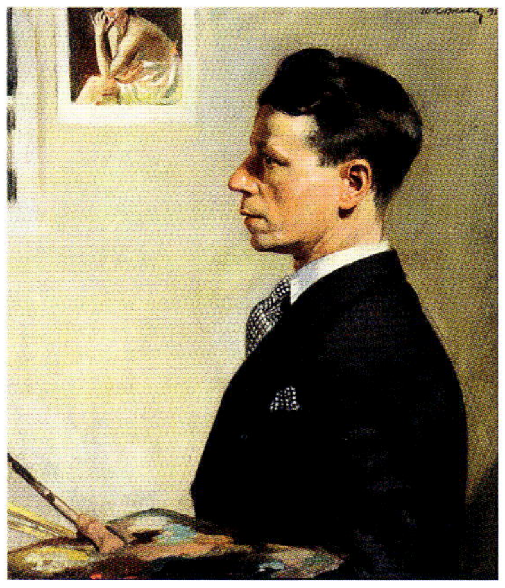

Brealey, William Ramsden 1889–1949
Self Portrait 1928
oil on canvas 78 x 68.5
VIS.1897

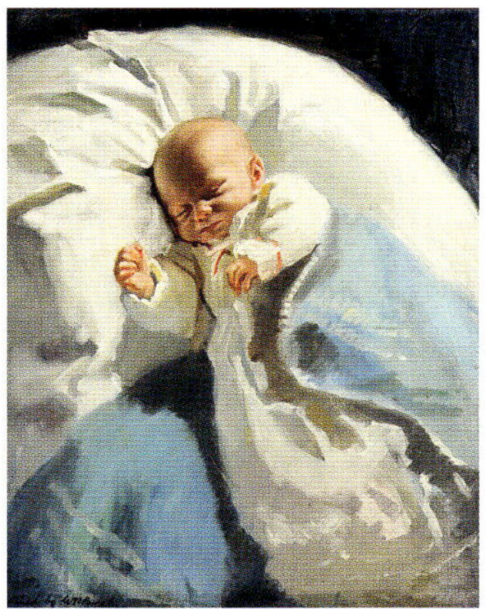

Brealey, William Ramsden 1889–1949
Portrait of a Baby
oil on millboard 59 x 46.7
VIS.2022

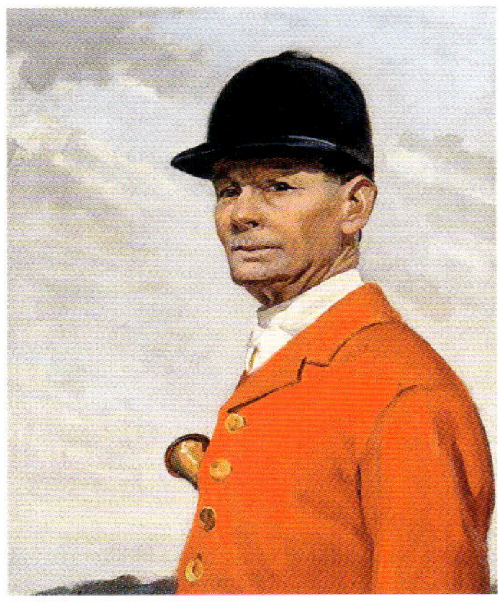

Brealey, William Ramsden 1889–1949
The Huntsman
oil on canvas 71.8 x 58.9
VIS.2017

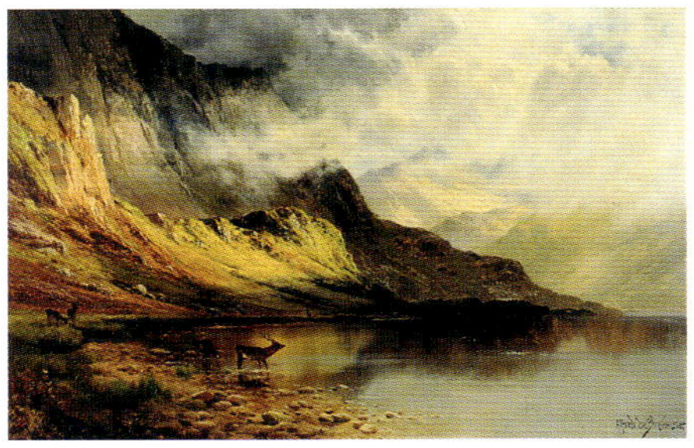

Breanski, Alfred de 1852–1928
A Glint of Sunshine, Glen Ogle, Scotland
oil on canvas 59.7 x 90.2
VIS.4590

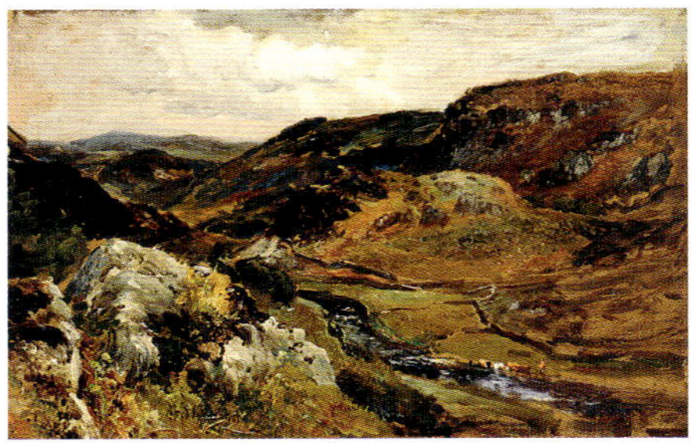

Breanski, Alfred de 1852–1928
Moorland
oil on panel 30.4 x 46
VIS.782

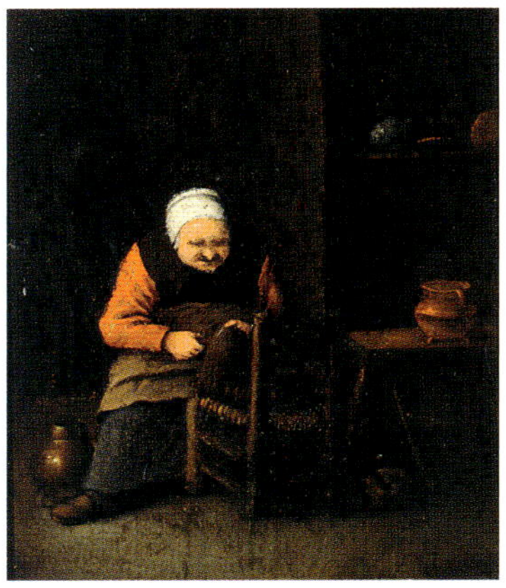

Brekelenkam, Quiringh van (attributed to)
after 1622–1669 or after
Old Woman 1645–1650
oil on panel 11.5 x 9.5
VIS.25

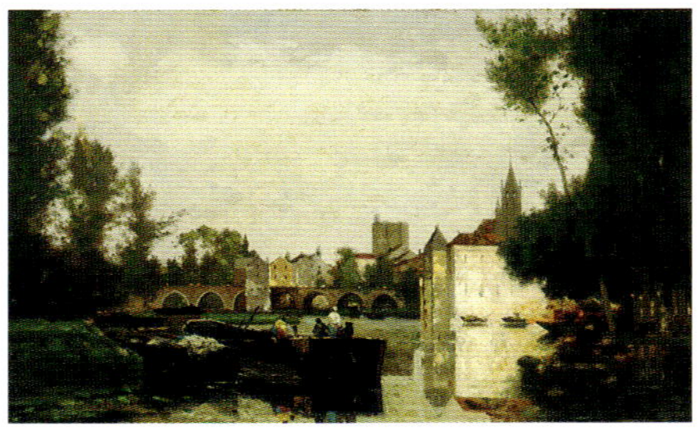

Brest, Germain Fabius 1823–1900
A Town on a French River 1840–1845
oil on canvas 31.2 x 49.1
VIS.1289

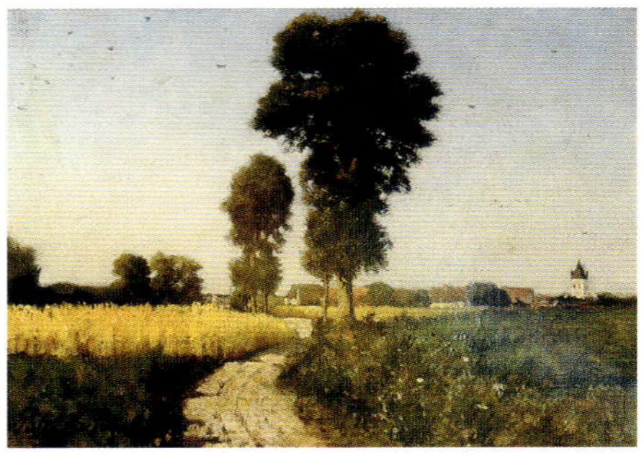

Breton, Jules Adolphe Aimé Louis
1827–1906
Landscape, Courrières, France 1854
oil on panel 22.8 x 32
VIS.707

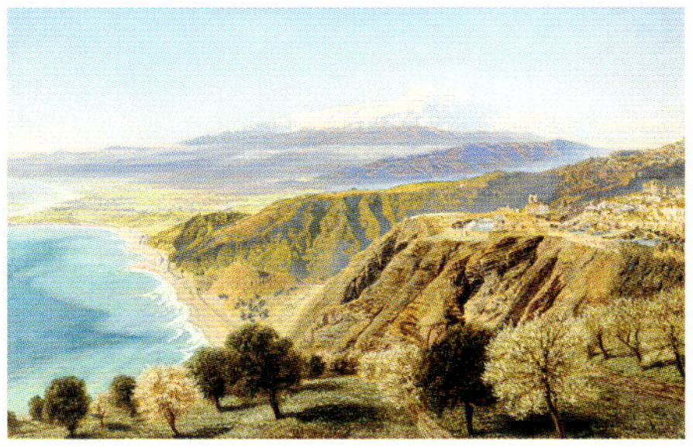

Brett, John 1830–1902
Mount Etna from Taormina, Sicily c.1870
oil on canvas 111.5 x 153.2
VIS.1

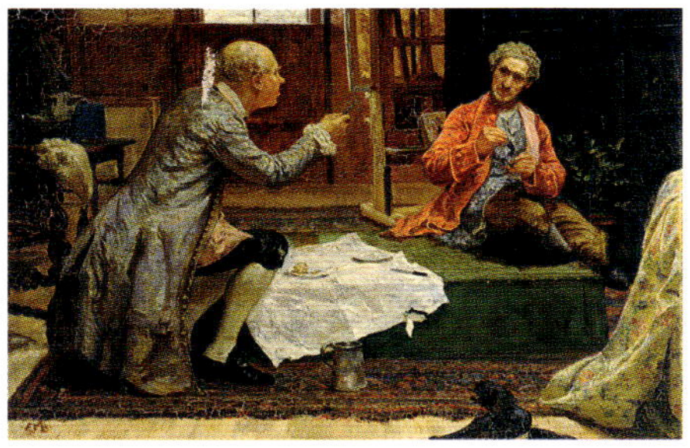

Brewtnall, Edward Frederick 1846–1902
The Model's Luncheon c.1872
oil on canvas 49.5 x 75
VIS.1521

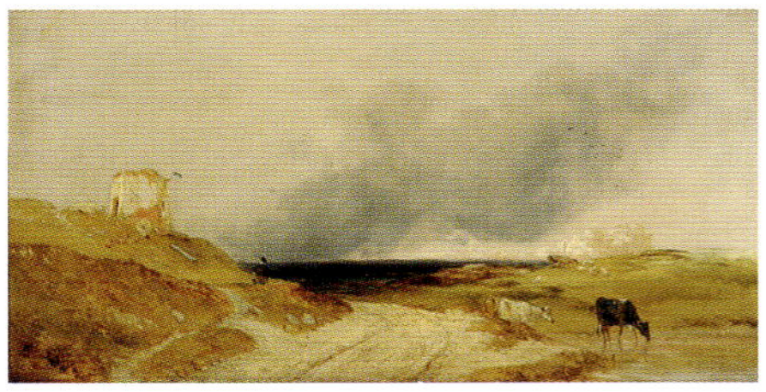

Bright, Henry 1814–1873
A Moorland View 1837
oil on canvas 30.8 x 60.8
VIS.171

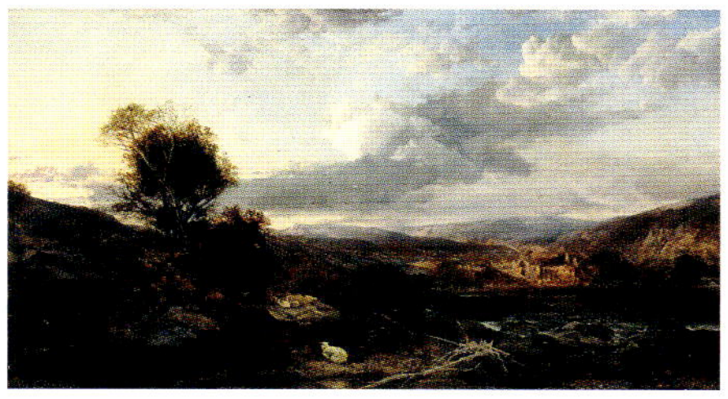

Bright, Henry 1814–1873
Mountainous Landscape with a Ruin
oil on canvas 45 x 80
VIS.2846

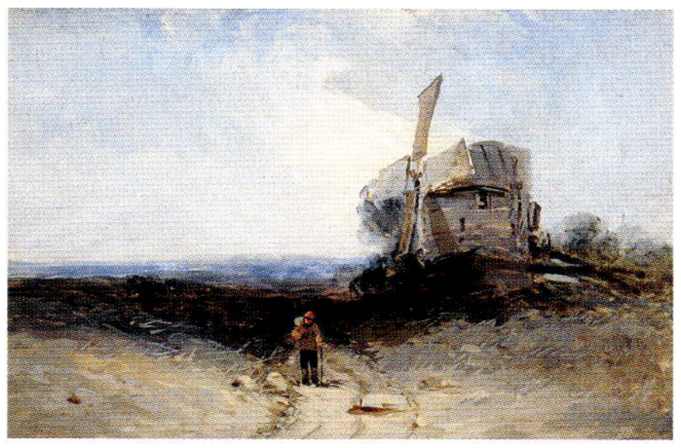

Bright, Henry 1814–1873
The Mill
oil on panel 19.3 x 29.3
VIS.237

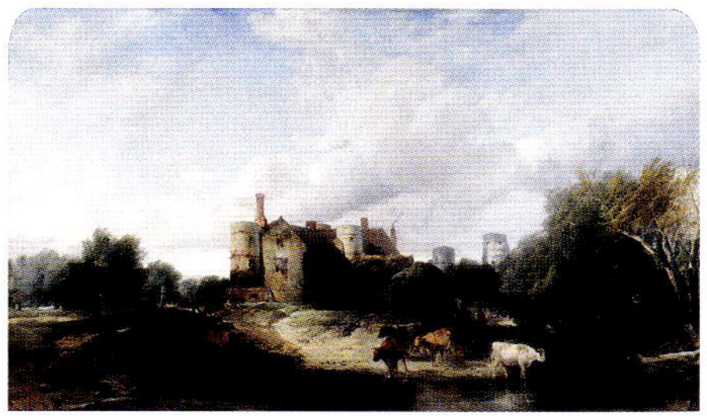

Bright, Henry 1814–1873
The Old Hall, Lincolnshire
oil on canvas 79.4 x 132.4
VIS.1438

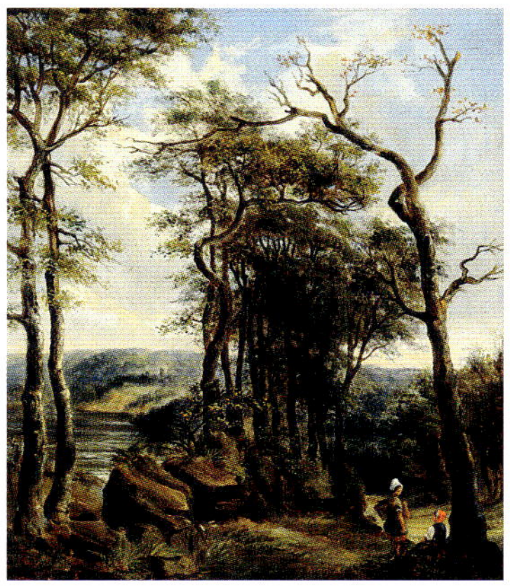

Bright, Henry 1814–1873
Woody Landscape
oil on canvas 34.5 x 28.8
VIS.540

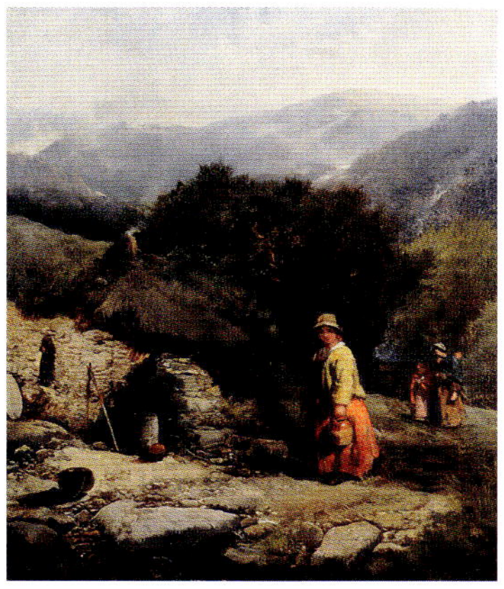

Bright, Henry 1814–1873 & **Hill**
Landscape with Figures
oil on canvas 48.8 x 40.7
VIS.1499

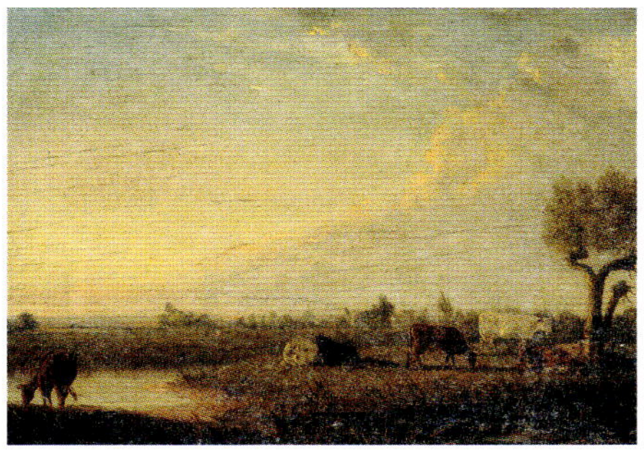

Bristow, Edmund 1787–1876
Landscape with Cattle 1827
oil on panel 25.5 x 34.7
VIS.583

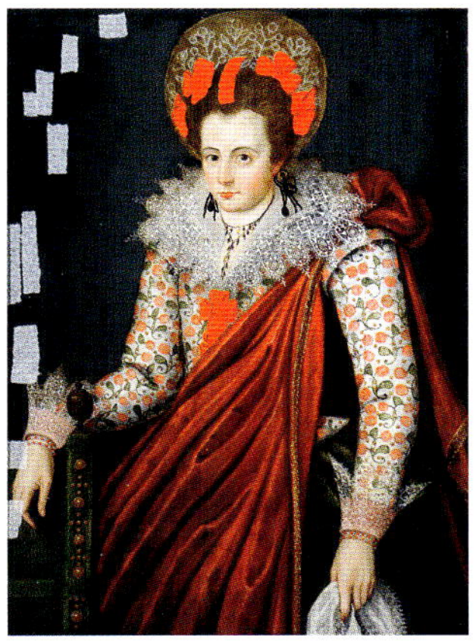

British (English) School 17th C
An Unknown Lady (possibly Lady Jane Grey, 1537–1554)
oil on panel 105.2 x 76.1
VIS.38

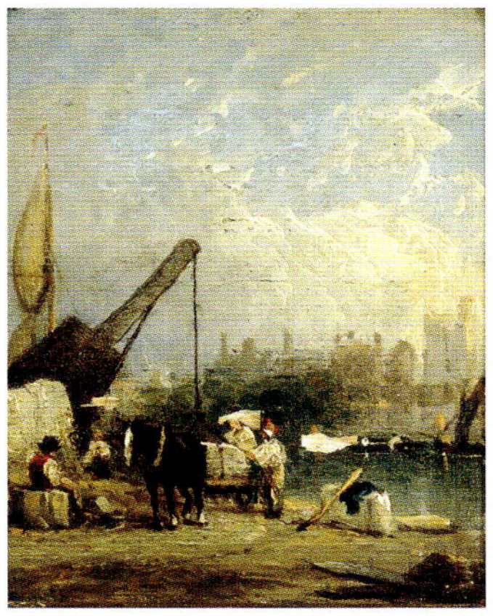

British (Norwich) School
At Norwich, Norfolk
oil on panel 16.5 x 13.4
VIS.61

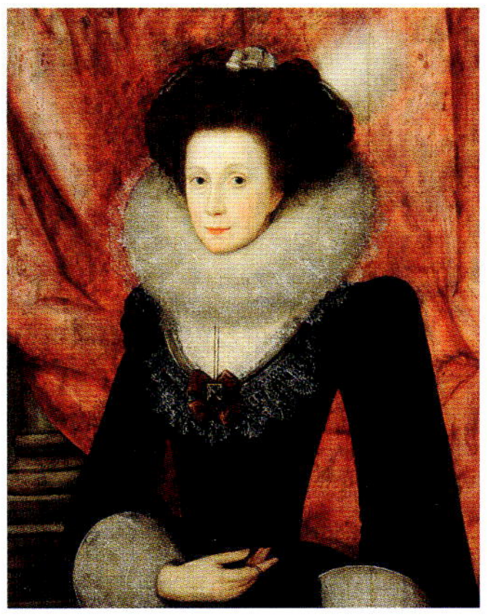

British School 17th C
Portrait of a Lady
oil on panel 80.2 x 64.2
VIS.56

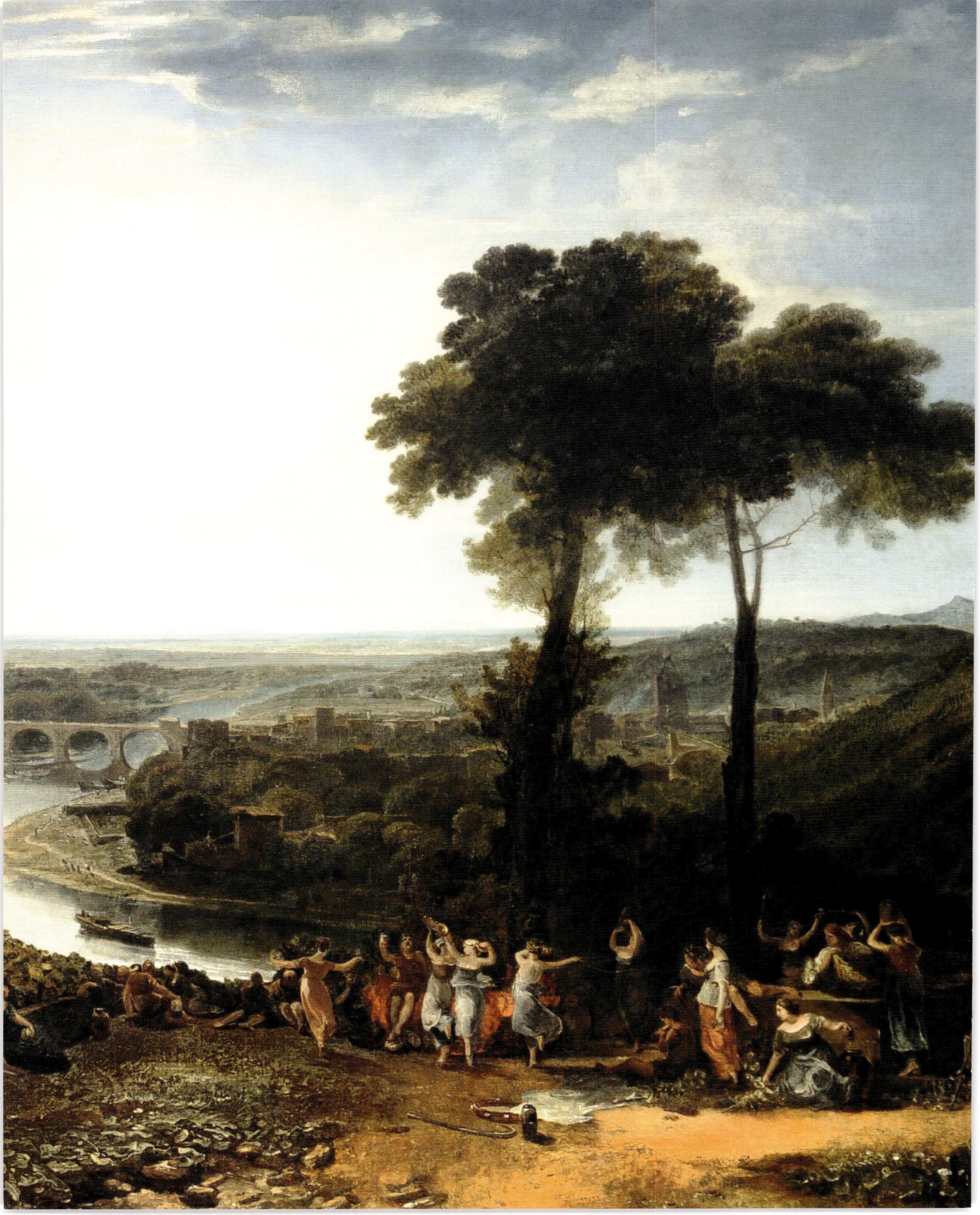

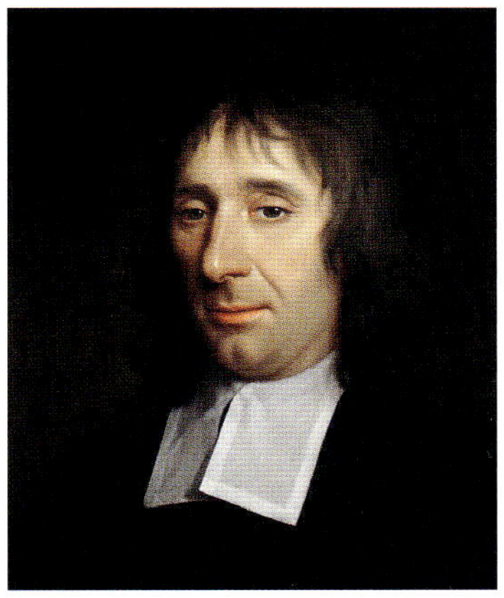

British School 17th C
William Mompesson (1639–1709), Rector of Eyam
oil on panel 46.5 x 37.8
VIS.3238

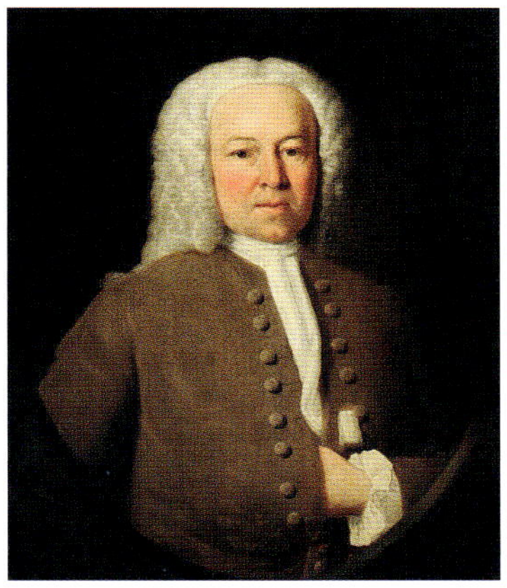

British School 18th C
Mr Batty, a Sheffield Solicitor
oil on canvas 76 x 63.3
VIS.2023

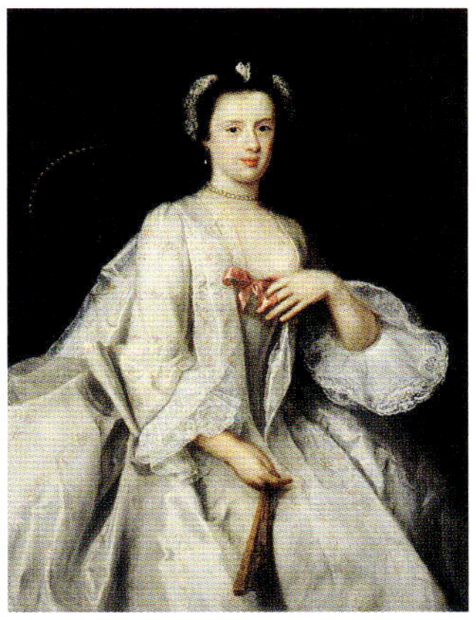

British School 18th C
Portrait of a Lady
oil on canvas 112 x 83.4
VIS.2238

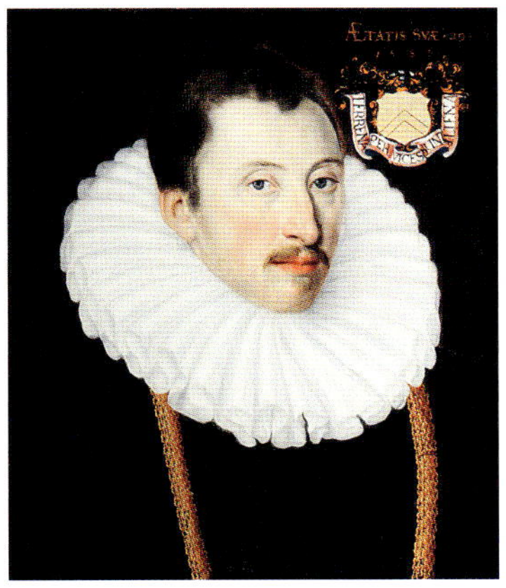

British School (attributed to)
Portrait of a Man, Aged 29 1584
oil on panel 73.6 x 62.5
VIS.1297

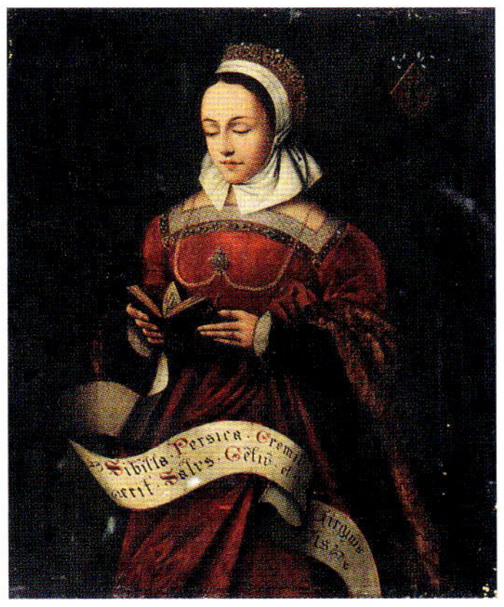

British School (attributed to) 19th C
Persian Sibyl
oil on panel 71 x 57
VIS.77

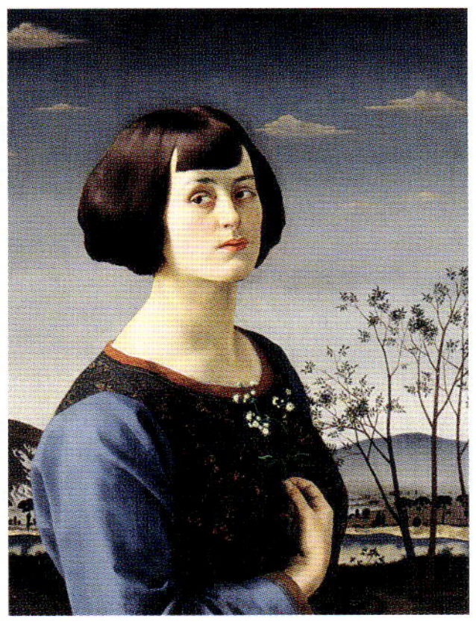

Brockhurst, Gerald Leslie 1890–1978
Ranunculus c.1914
oil on panel 79.5 x 66
VIS.531

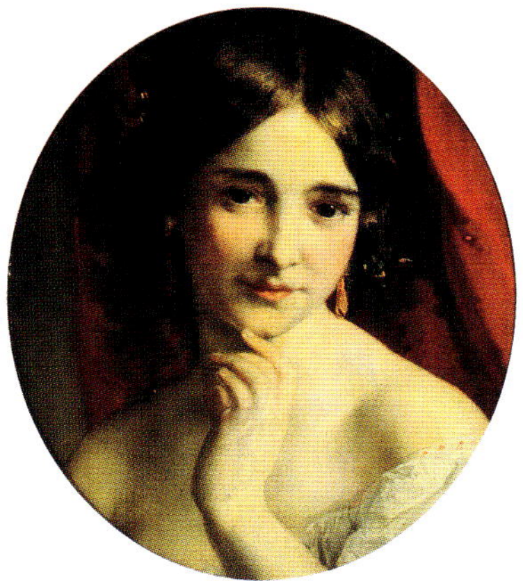

Brocky, Charles (attributed to) 1807–1855
Head of a Girl with Roses 1840–1845
oil on canvas 40.5 x 34.9
VIS.1390

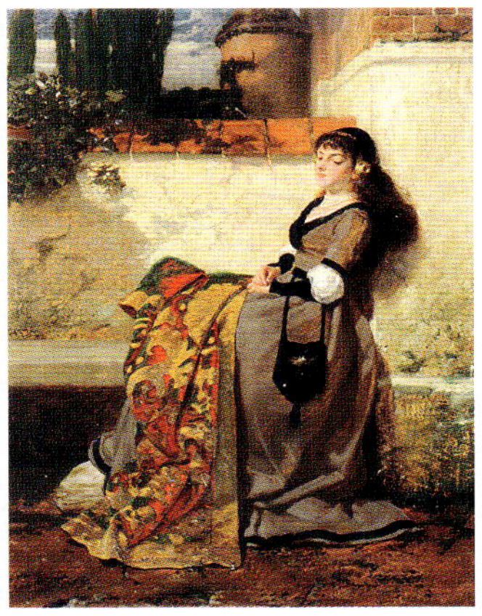

Bromley, Valentine Walter 1848–1877
Girl Resting 1871
oil on canvas 91.7 x 70.7
VIS.1342

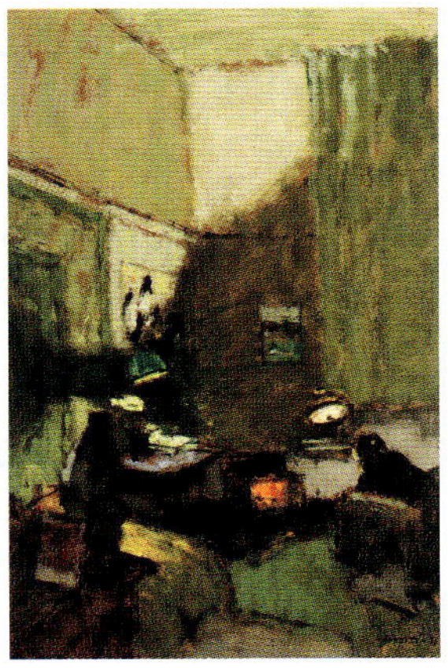

Brooker, William 1918–1983
Interior by Lamplight 1956
oil on board 45 x 29.8
VIS.4711

Facing page: Turner, Joseph Mallord William, 1775–1851, *The Festival of the Opening of the Vintage at Mâcon, France* (detail), c.1803, Museums Sheffield, (p. 215)

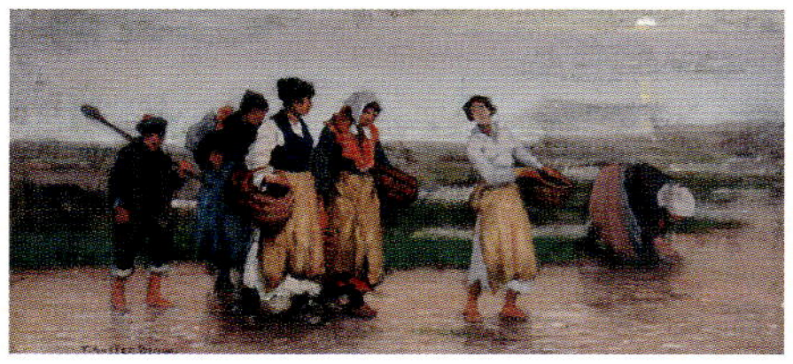

Brown, Thomas Austen 1859–1924
Fisherfolk
oil on canvas 26.8 x 57.9
VIS.764

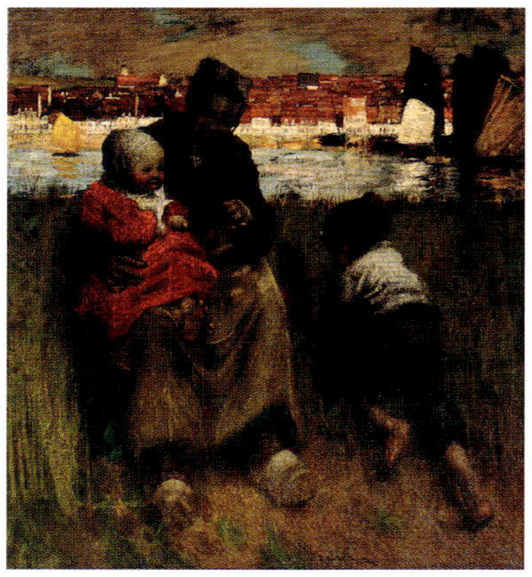

Brown, Thomas Austen 1859–1924
Sunshine and Shadow
oil on canvas 152.7 x 133.9
VIS.589

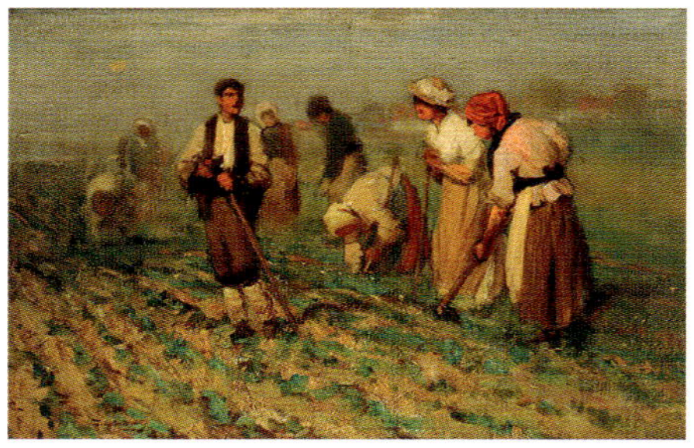

Brown, Thomas Austen 1859–1924
Turnip Hoeing
oil on canvas 50 x 75.2
VIS.679

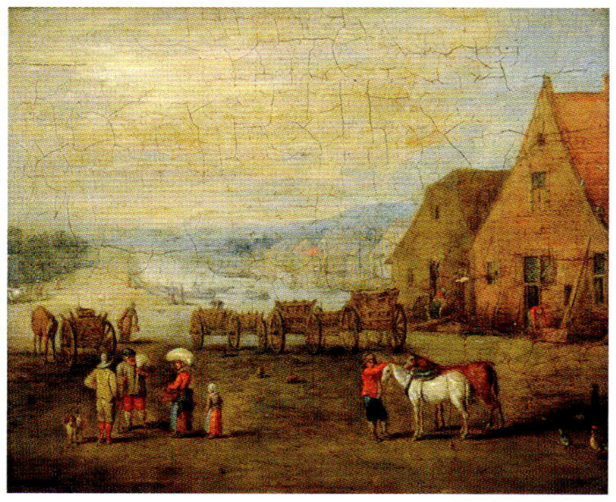

Brueghel, Jan the elder (attributed to)
1568–1625
A Village 1608
oil on panel 13.7 x 16.6
VIS.81

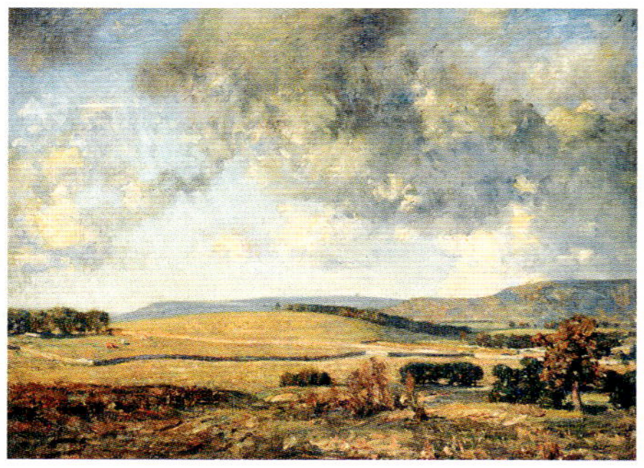

Brundrit, Reginald Grange 1883–1960
Clouds from the West
oil on canvas 75.3 x 100.5
VIS.2938

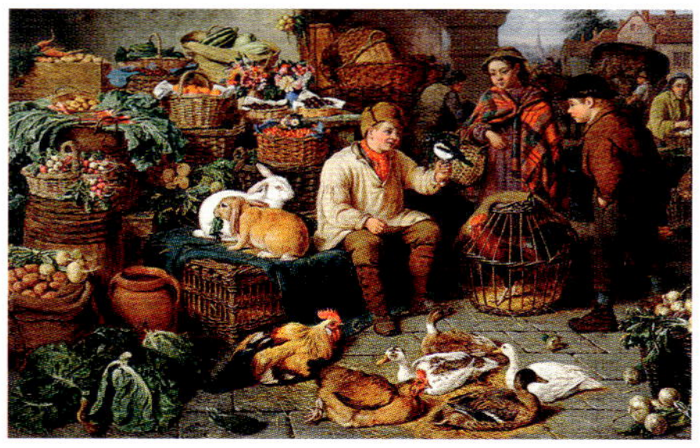

Bryant, Henry Charles 1836–1915
Market Scene 1878
oil on canvas 49.5 x 75.1
VIS.1513

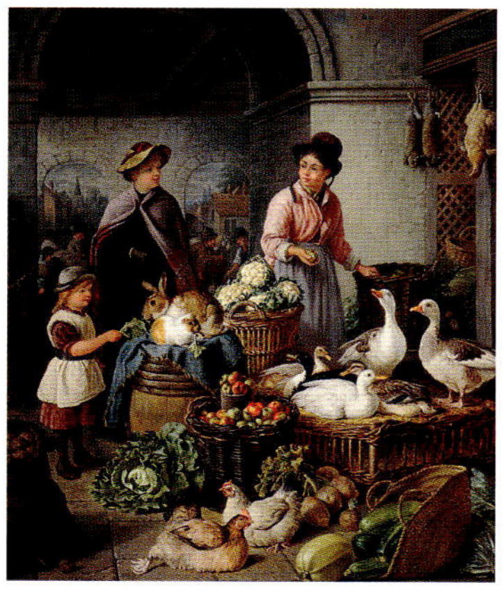

Bryant, Henry Charles 1836–1915
Portsmouth Market 1883
oil on canvas 74.6 x 61.7
VIS.1509

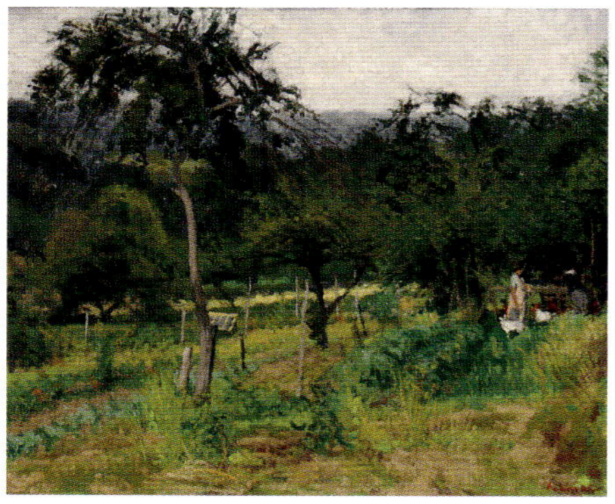

Buhler, Robert A. 1916–1989
The Orchard 1945
oil on canvas 49.5 x 59.5
VIS.3600

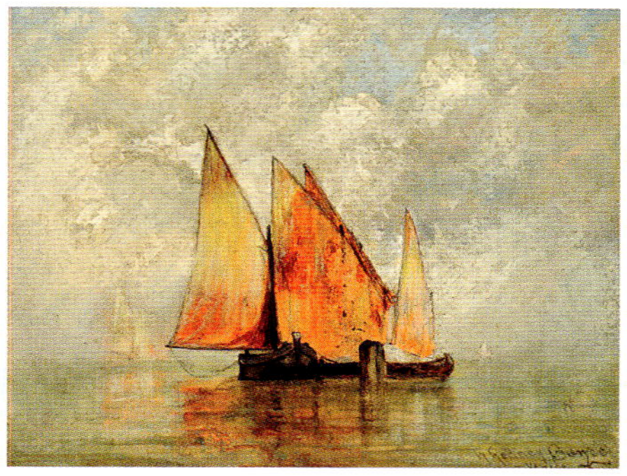

Bunce, William Gedney 1840–1916
A Hot Day on the Lagoons, Venice 1875
oil on millboard 50 x 64
VIS.1232

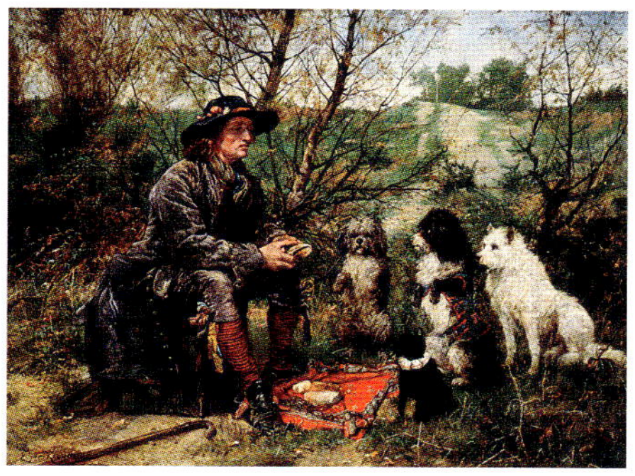

Bundy, Edgar 1862–1922
Man Eating Lunch
oil on canvas 68.8 x 89.2
VIS.2739

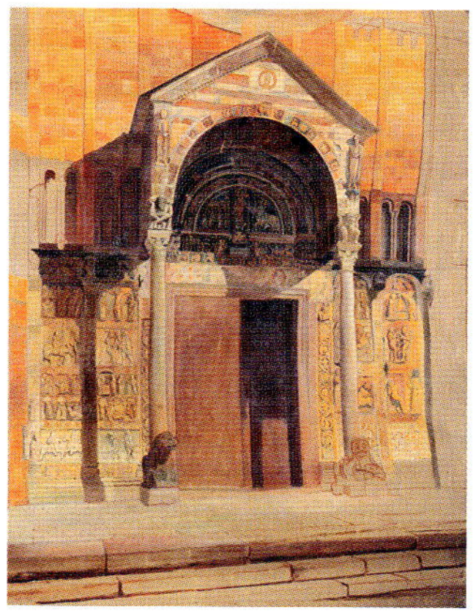

Bunney, John Wharlton 1828–1882
Exterior of a Church, Ravenna, Italy
1850–1882
oil on canvas 109 x 84 (E)
CGSGB943b

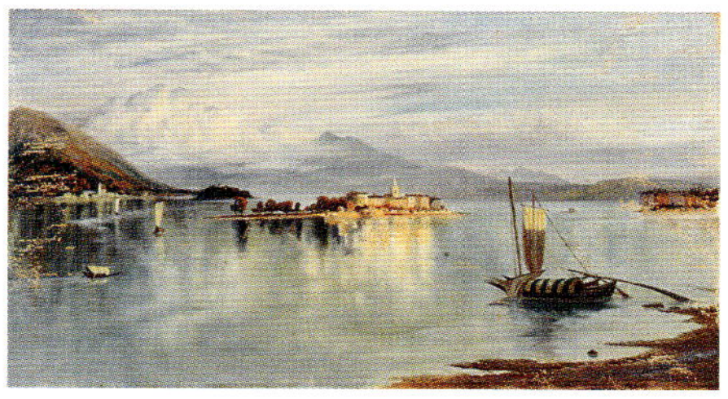

Bunney, John Wharlton 1828–1882
Lake with Islands and a Mountain Backdrop
1850–1882
oil on canvas 28 x 44.5
CGSGB785

Bunney, John Wharlton 1828–1882
Study of Tree Branches 1850–1882
oil on canvas 36.7 x 49
CGSGB316

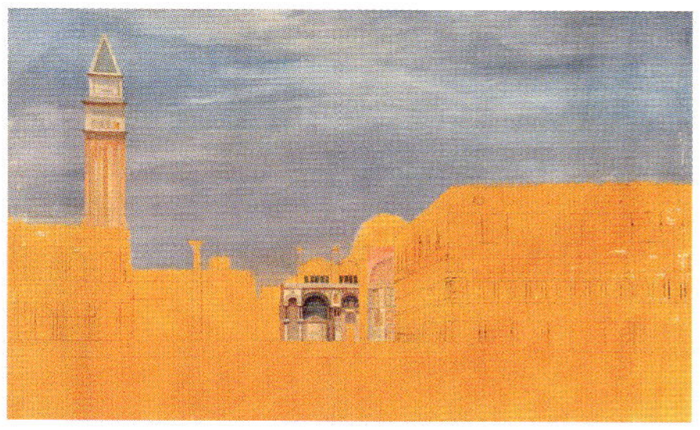

Bunney, John Wharlton 1828–1882
The Piazzetta of San Marco, Venice
(unfinished)
1850–1882
oil on canvas 64.5 x 99.5 (E)
CGSGB942

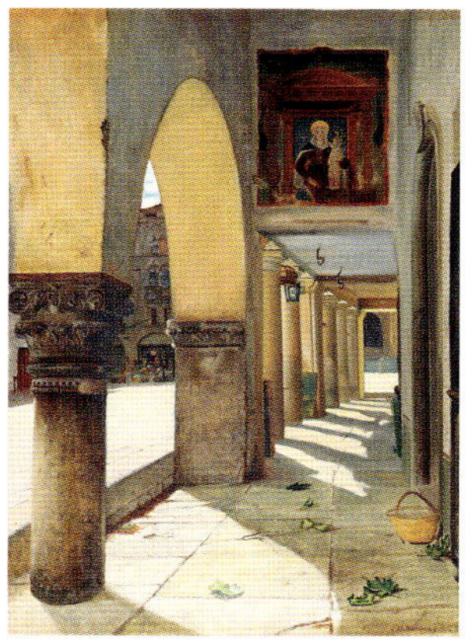

Bunney, John Wharlton 1828–1882
Colonnaded Street Scene, Serravalle, Italy
1860–1875
oil on canvas 53 x 37.2
CGSGB407

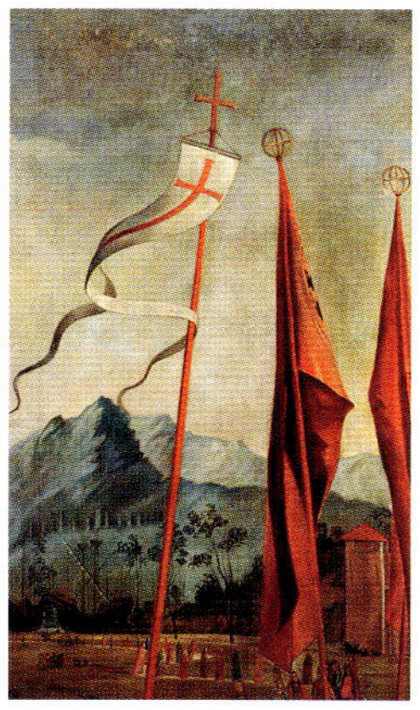

Bunney, John Wharlton 1828–1882
St Ursula's Banners, St Ursula Receiving the Pope's Benediction (detail) (after Vittore Carpaccio) 1860–1877
oil on canvas 83 x 13.5
CGSG00744

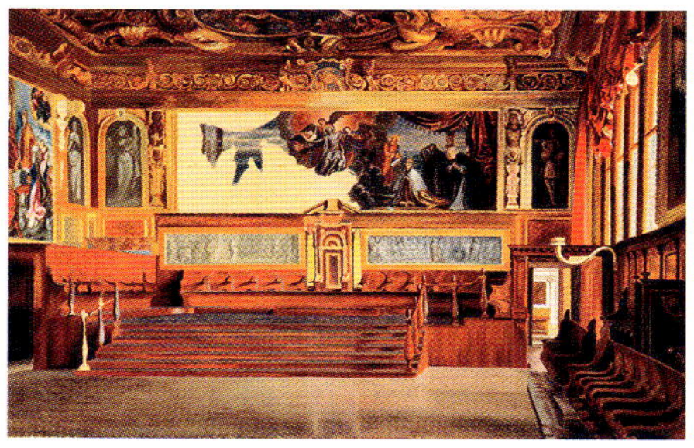

Bunney, John Wharlton 1828–1882
Interior of the Sala del Senato, Doge's Palace, Venice 1860–1882
oil on canvas 43 x 65.5
CGSGB186a

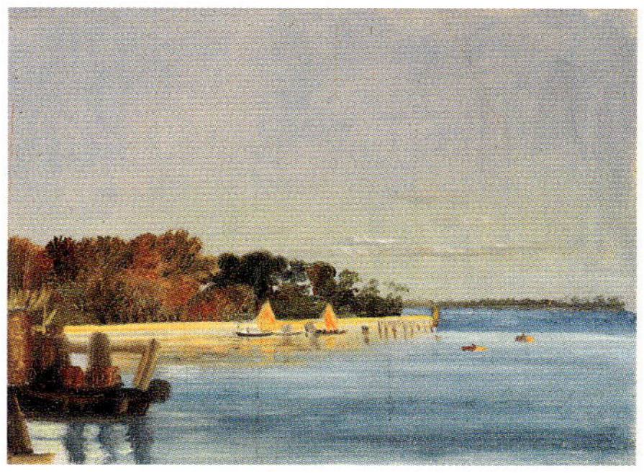

Bunney, John Wharlton 1828–1882
Outside the Public Gardens, Sant'Elena, Venice
1860–1882
oil on canvas 19.5 x 26
CGSGB646

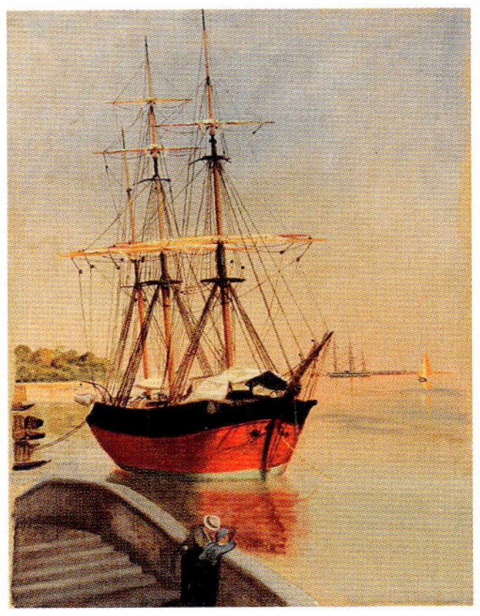

Bunney, John Wharlton 1828–1882
Sailing Ship by the Ponte Veneta Marina, Venice 1860–1882
oil on canvas 37.2 x 28
CGSGB647

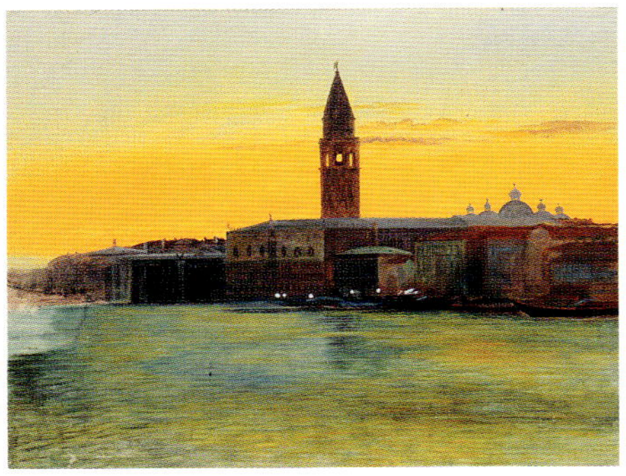

Bunney, John Wharlton 1828–1882
View of the Piazzetta di San Marco from San Giorgio, Venice 1860–1882
oil on wooden board 27 x 34.5
CGSGB730

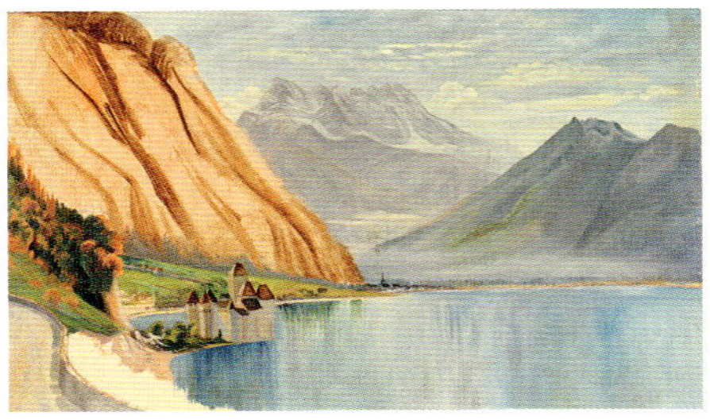

Bunney, John Wharlton 1828–1882
Lake Geneva and the Castle of Chillon, Switzerland c.1865
oil on canvas 27 x 44
CGSGB648

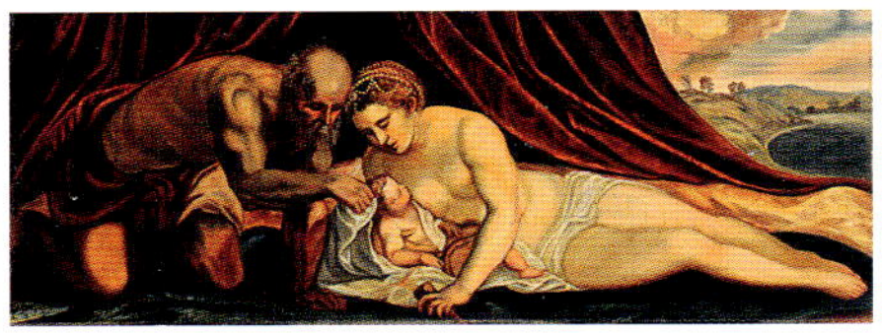

Bunney, John Wharlton 1828–1882
Venus, Vulcan and Cupid (after Jacopo Tintoretto) 1868
oil on canvas 22.2 x 52
CGSGB212

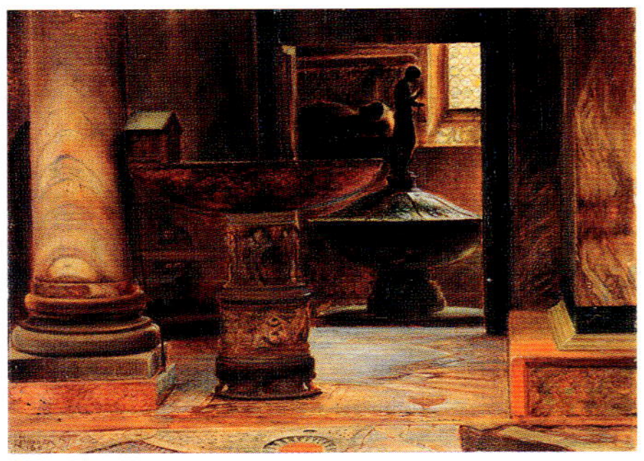

Bunney, John Wharlton 1828–1882
Interior of San Marco, with the Baptistery, Venice 1875
oil on canvas 28.5 x 38.2
CGSGB446

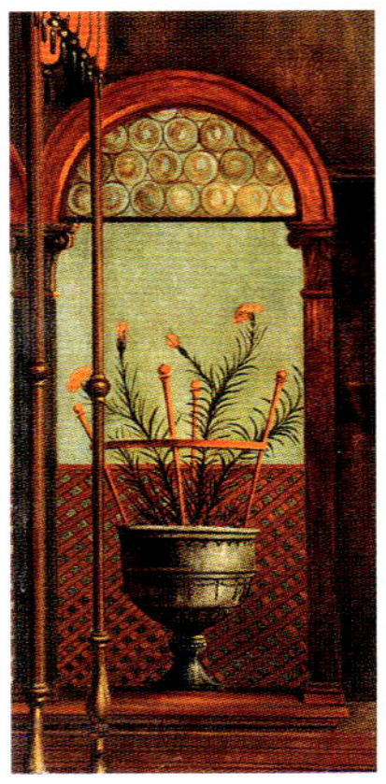

Bunney, John Wharlton 1828–1882
The Vision of St Ursula (detail) (after Vittore Carpaccio) 1876–1877
oil on canvas 87.5 x 42
CGSG00264

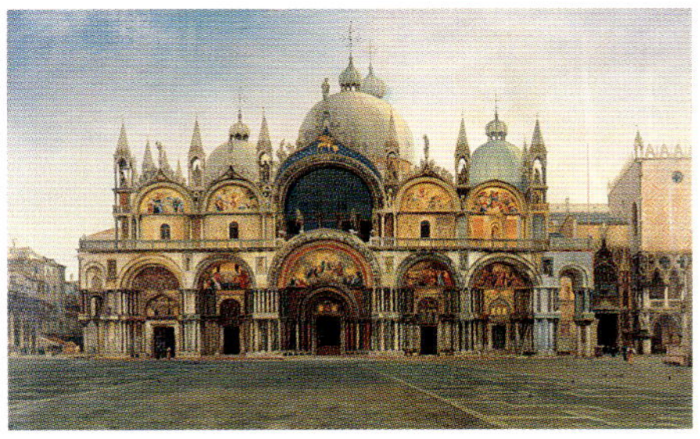

Bunney, John Wharlton 1828–1882
Western Facade of the Basilica of San Marco, Venice 1877–1882
oil on canvas 144.7 x 226
CGSG00780

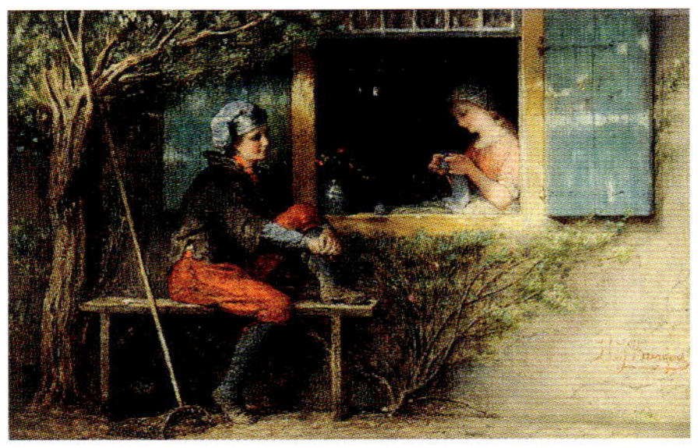

Burgers, Hendricus-Jacobus 1834–1899
Dutch Courtship
oil on panel 20 x 31.1
VIS.1964

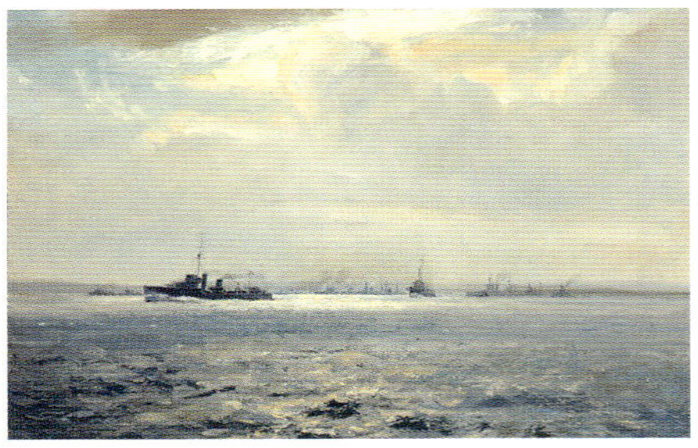

Burgess, Arthur James Wetherall 1879–1957
Destroyers on Scapa Flow
oil on canvas 49.9 x 75.1
VIS.199

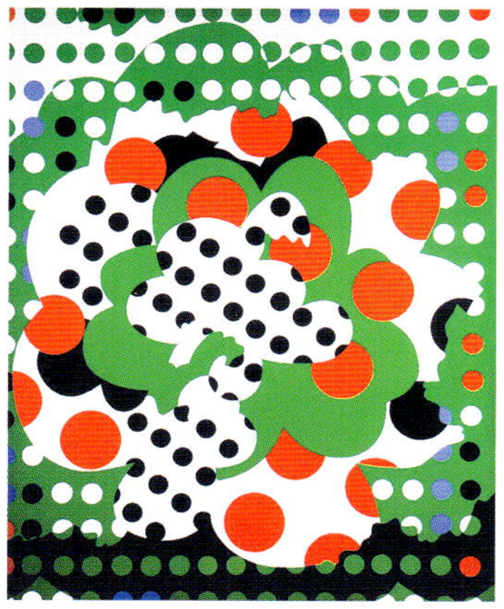

Burgin, Victor b.1941
Escalator
oil on canvas 228.7 x 180.3
VIS.2780

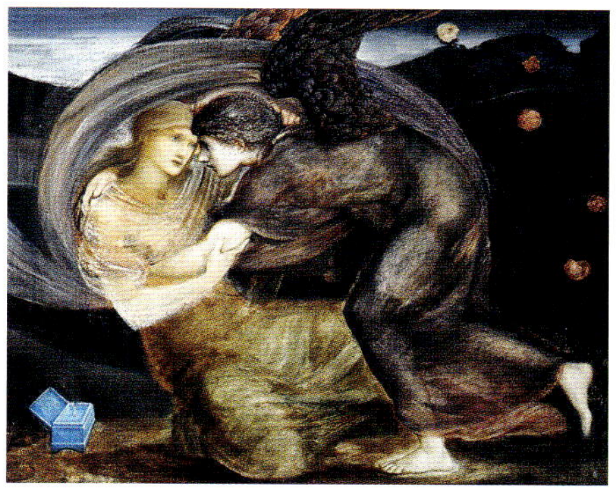

Burne-Jones, Edward 1833–1898
Cupid Delivering Psyche 1870
oil on canvas 99.5 x 115.3
VIS.3833

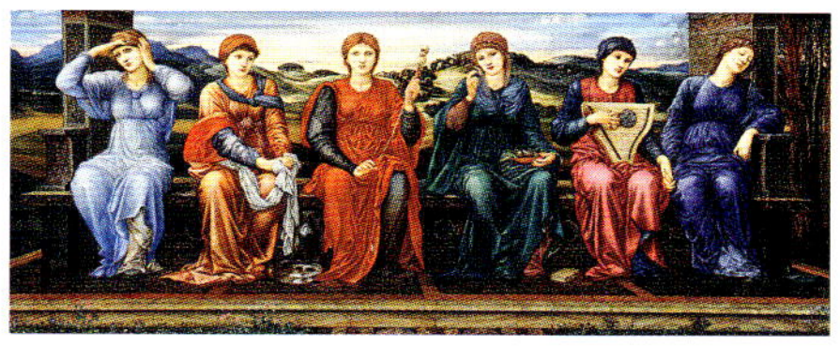

Burne-Jones, Edward 1833–1898
The Hours 1882
oil on canvas 118.7 x 227.8
VIS.13

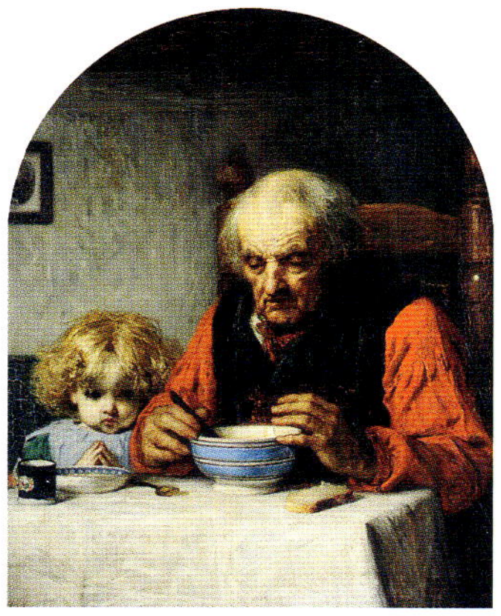

Burr, Alexander Hohenlohe 1835–1898
Grace before Meat 1871
oil on canvas 72.2 x 58.1
VIS.1947

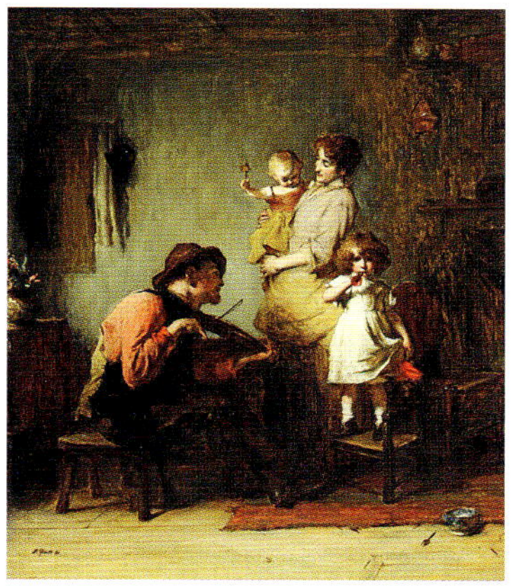

Burr, Alexander Hohenlohe 1835–1898
The Musical Party 1881
oil on canvas 42.5 x 35.7
VIS.1392

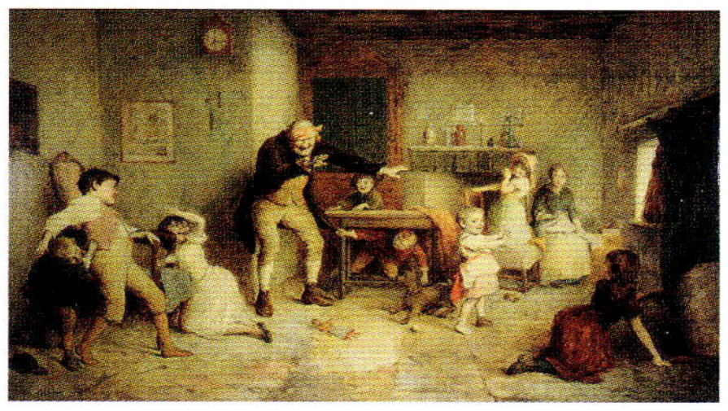

Burr, Alexander Hohenlohe 1835–1898
Blind Man's Buff
oil on canvas 79.8 x 135.8
VIS.798

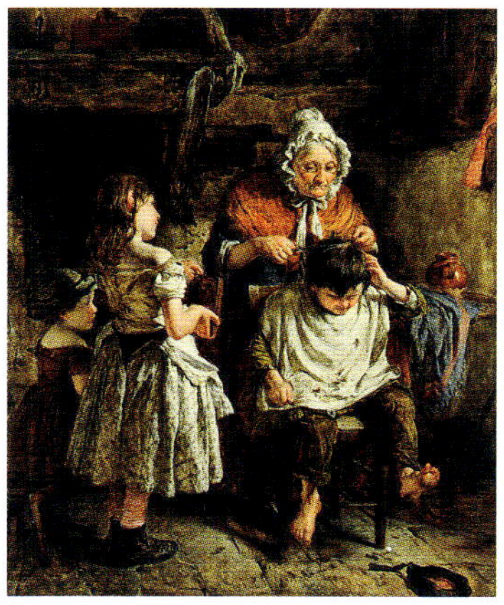

Burr, Alexander Hohenlohe 1835–1898
The Rustic Crop
oil on canvas 44 x 35.8
VIS.1404

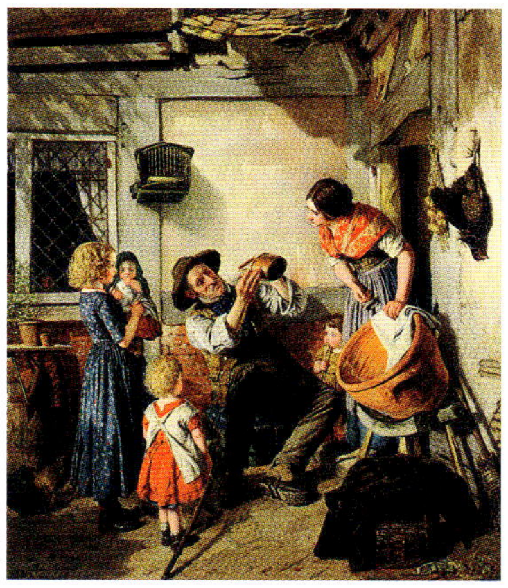

Burr, John P. 1831–1893
The Travelling Tinker 1863
oil on canvas 85 x 72.2
VIS.1427

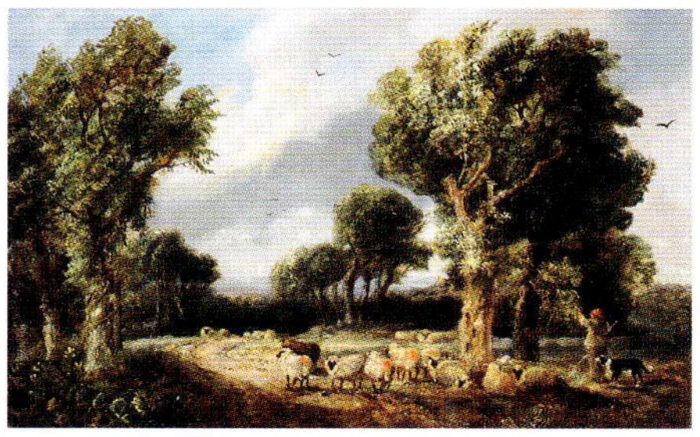

Burr, John P. 1831–1893
A Flock of Sheep
oil on canvas 51.2 x 78
VIS.2716

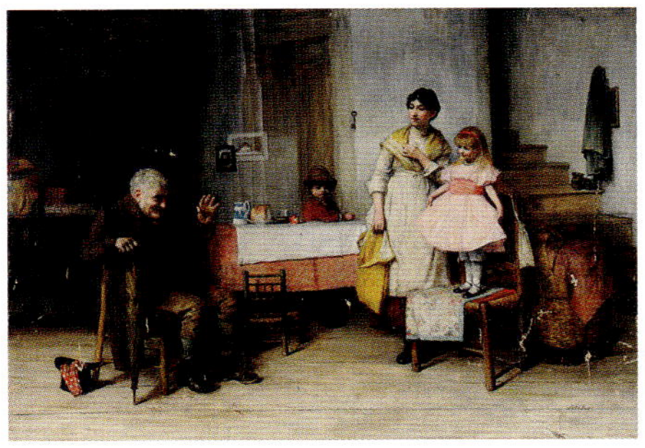

Burr, John P. 1831–1893
The New Dress
oil on canvas 68.7 x 76.8
VIS.2530

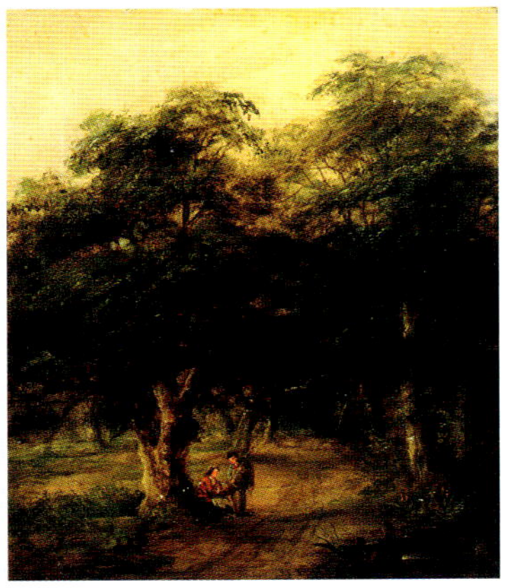

Burrows, Robert 1810–1893
A Wooded Glade
oil on canvas 29.3 x 24.5
VIS.331

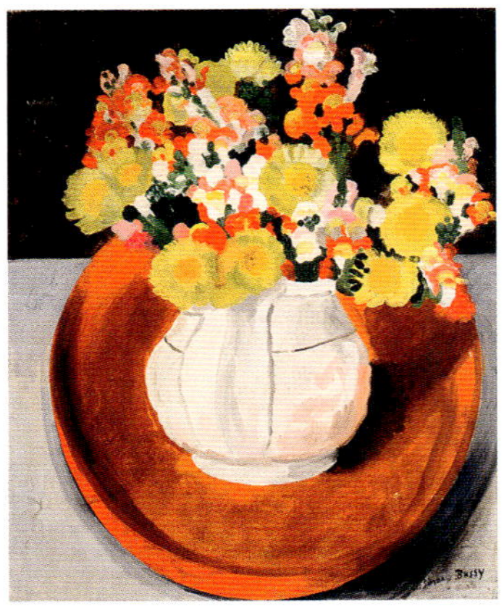

Bussy, Simon 1870–1954
Mixed Flowers in a White Jug
oil on canvas 59.6 x 48.7
VIS.4515

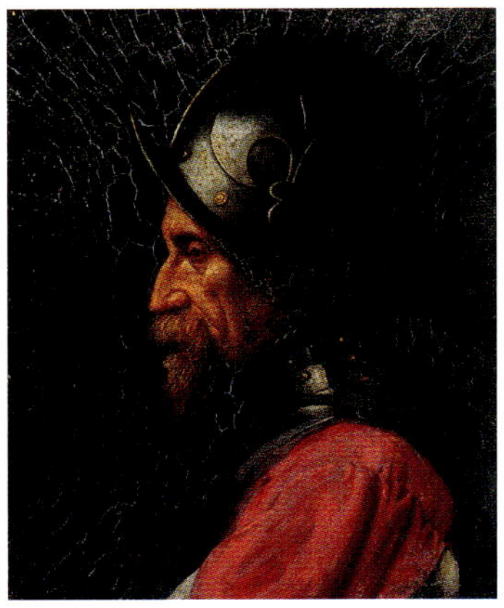

Butler, J. active 19th C
Cromwellian Soldier
oil on canvas 51.8 x 41.8
VIS.1503

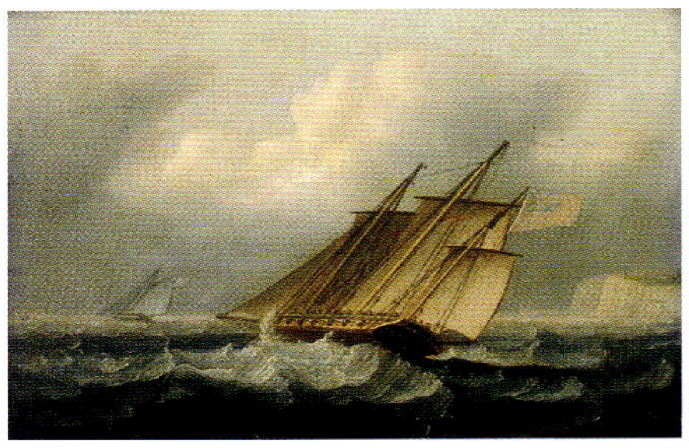

Buttersworth, Thomas 1768–1842
The Squall
oil on canvas 15 x 22.5
VIS.580

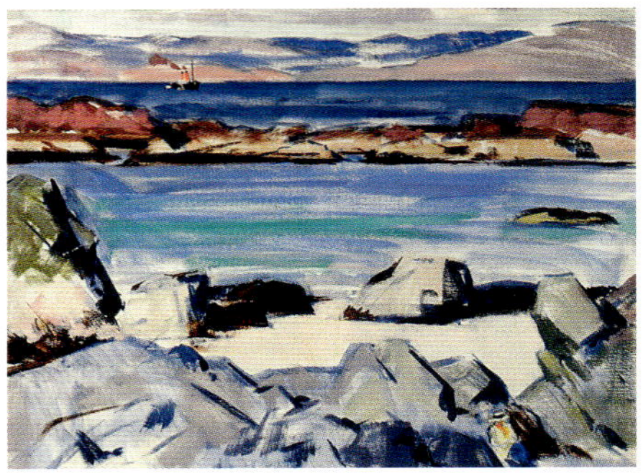

Cadell, Francis Campbell Boileau
1883–1937
Iona, Scotland c.1925
oil on canvas 63.7 x 79.2
VIS.4212

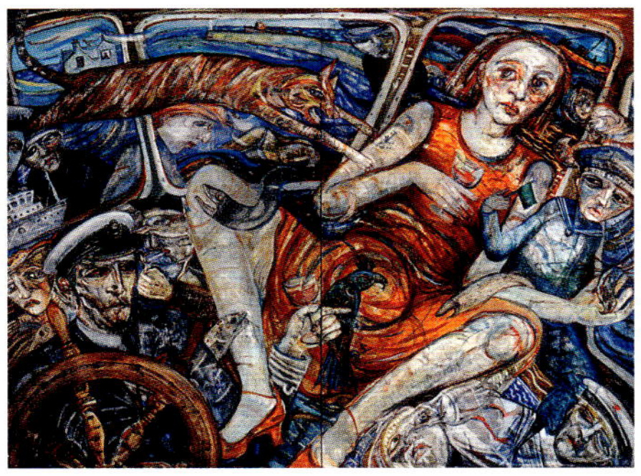

Cairns, Joyce W. b.1947
Martini Rose with the Captain of the 'Stirling Teal'
oil on board 181.4 x 243.1
VIS.5414

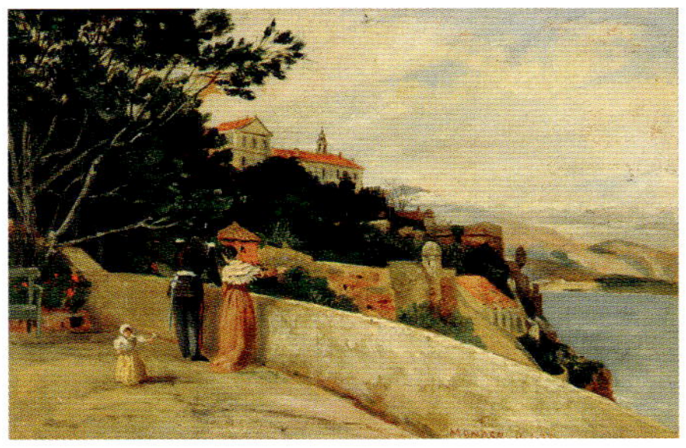

Caldecott, Randolph 1846–1886
Monaco 1877
oil on panel 14.9 x 22.3
VIS.582

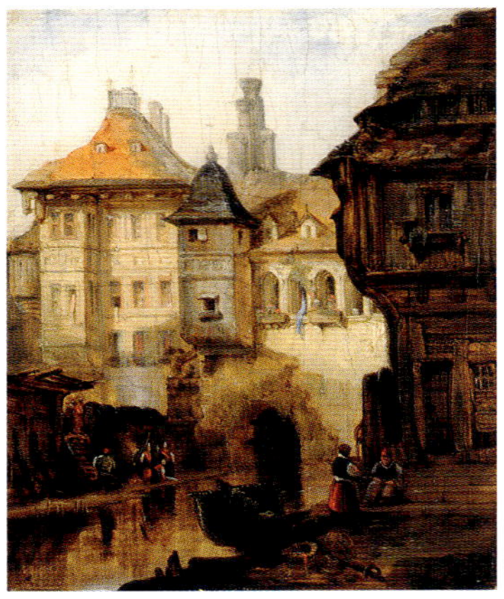

Callow, William (attributed to) 1812–1908
A Street in Bruges, Belgium
oil on canvas 29.6 x 24.8
VIS.1597

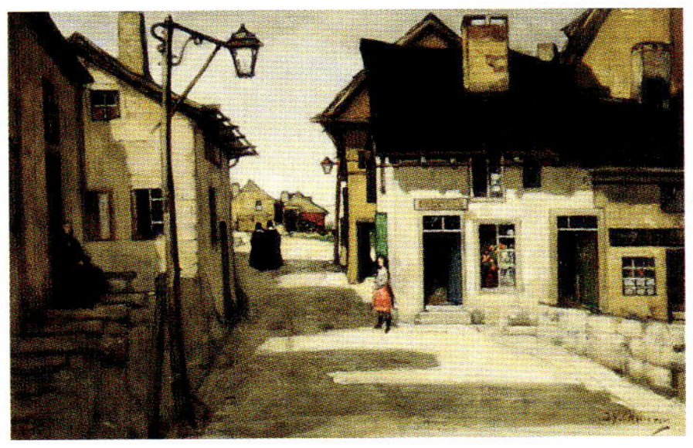

Cameron, David Young 1865–1945
La Roche, Belgium
oil on canvas 49.5 x 75.2
VIS.187

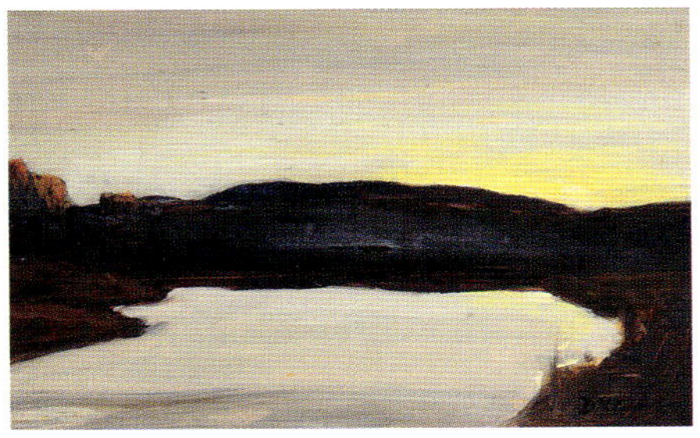

Cameron, David Young 1865–1945
Sunset on the Firth
oil on panel 14.5 x 22.7
VIS.5005

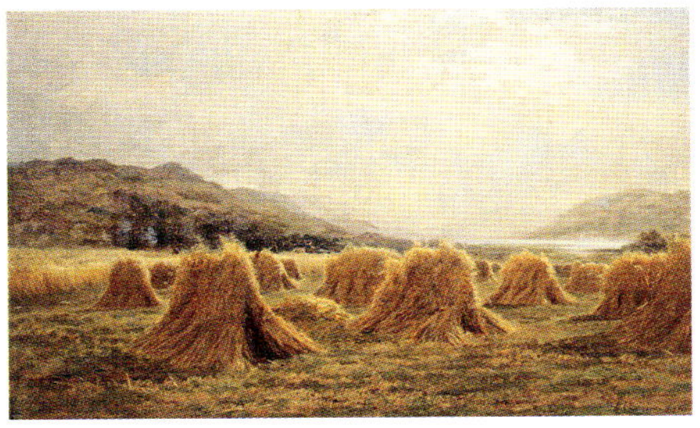

Cameron, Duncan 1837–1916
Harvest Time near St Fillans, Perthshire, Scotland 1877
oil on canvas 59.8 x 95.5
VIS.1459

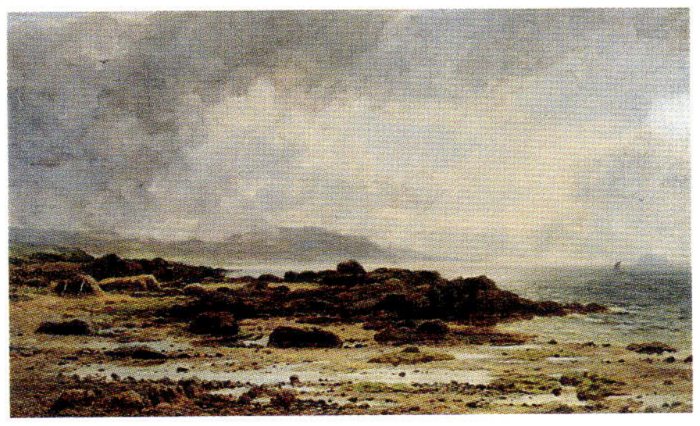

Cameron, Duncan 1837–1916
Largo Bay, Scotland 1877
oil on canvas 59.6 x 94.9
VIS.1458

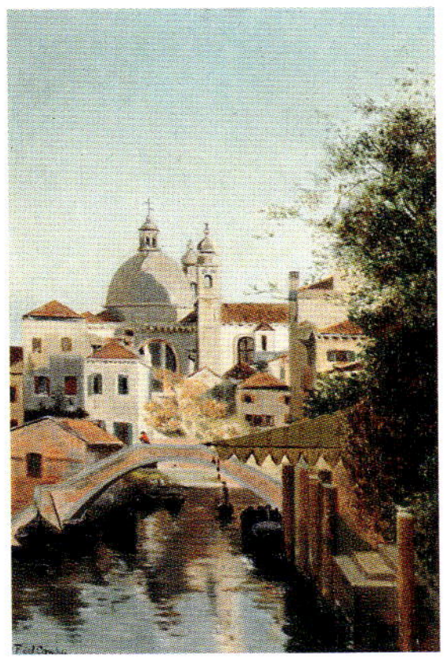

Campo, Federico del 1837–1923
Canal with a Bridge 1875–1880
oil on panel 29.8 x 19.4
VIS.643

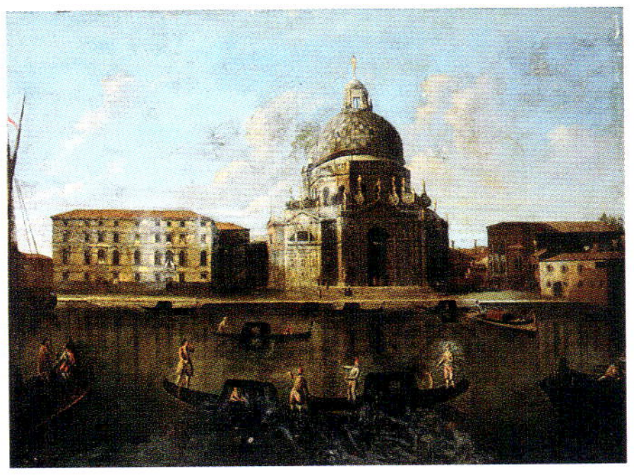

Canaletto (school of) 1697–1768
Santa Maria della Salute, Venice 1750–1780
oil on canvas 91.5 x 117
VIS.1314

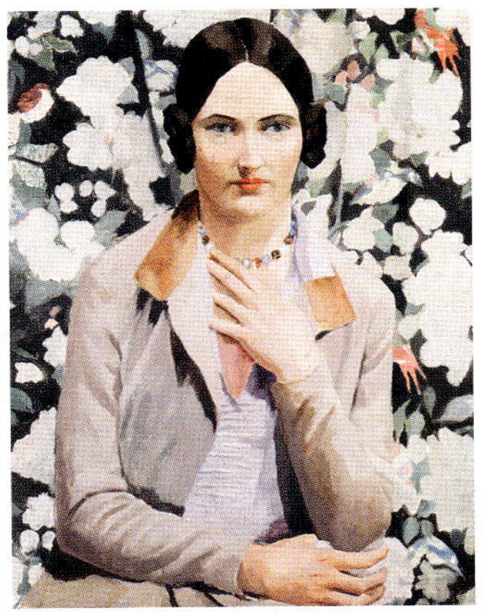

Carline, Richard 1896–1980
Kate (Katherine Foster) 1925
oil on canvas 64.7 x 49.5
VIS.5186

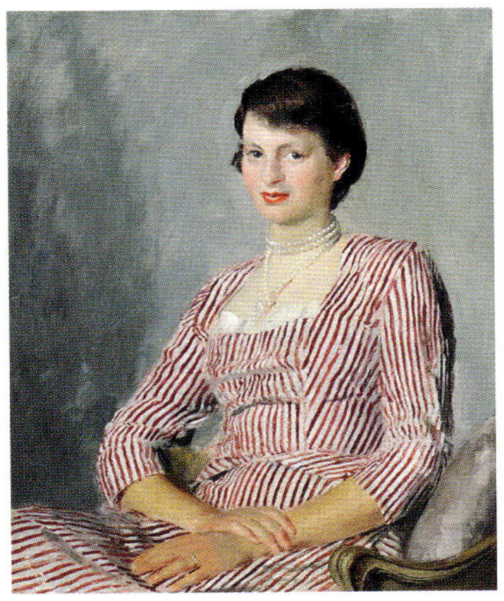

Carr, Henry Marvell 1894–1970
Henry Rushbury's Daughter
oil on canvas 75 x 62.4
VIS.3012

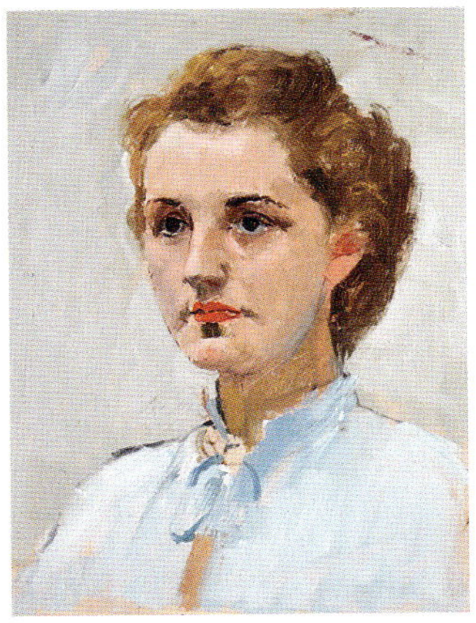

Carr, Henry Marvell 1894–1970
Portrait of a Girl
oil on canvas 45.1 x 34.2
VIS.3011

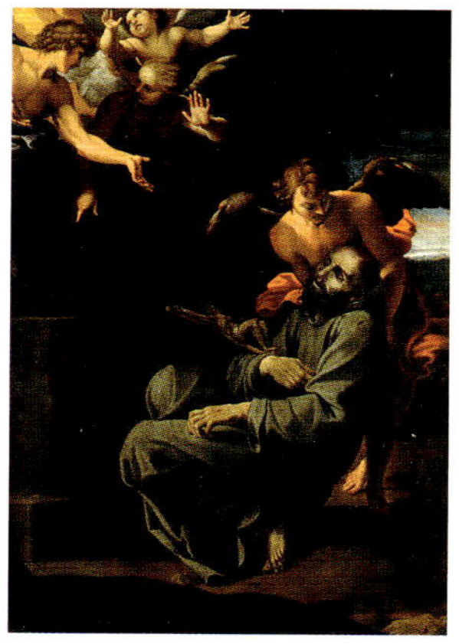

Carracci, Annibale (after) 1560–1609
The Death of St Francis (The Ecstasy of St Francis) 1590–1600
oil on panel 47.3 x 32.7
VIS.3137

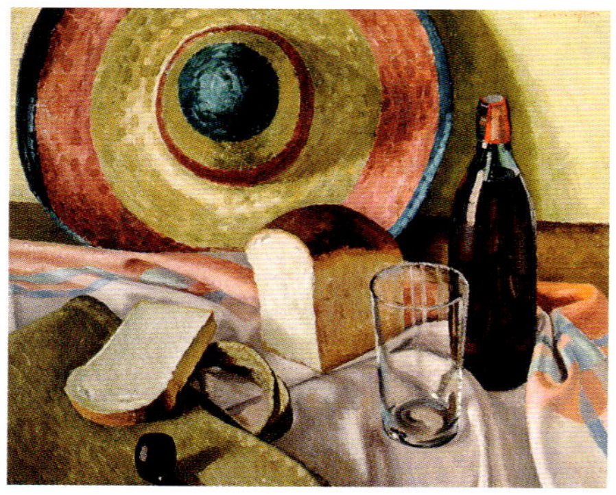

Carrington, Donald P. b.1907
Still Life
oil on canvas 49.5 x 59.8
VIS.1883

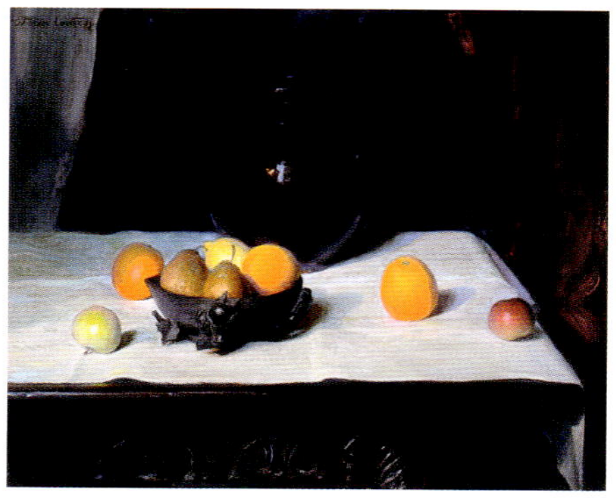

Carter, William 1863–1939
Still Life 1937
oil on canvas 62 x 75
VIS.1857

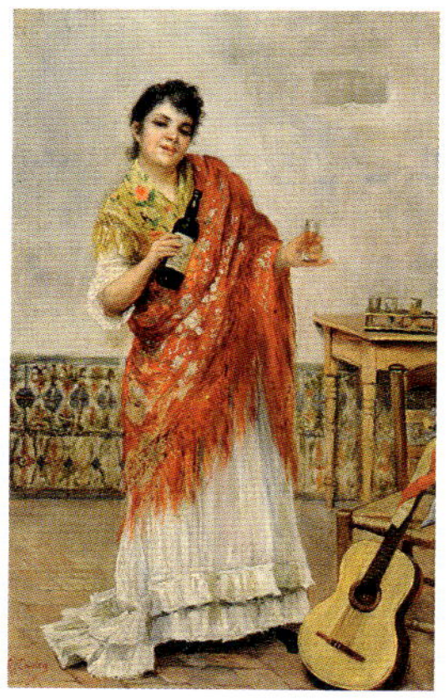

Castro, Manuel active before 1795–1805
A Spanish Music Girl
oil on panel 27.1 x 16.5
VIS.1046

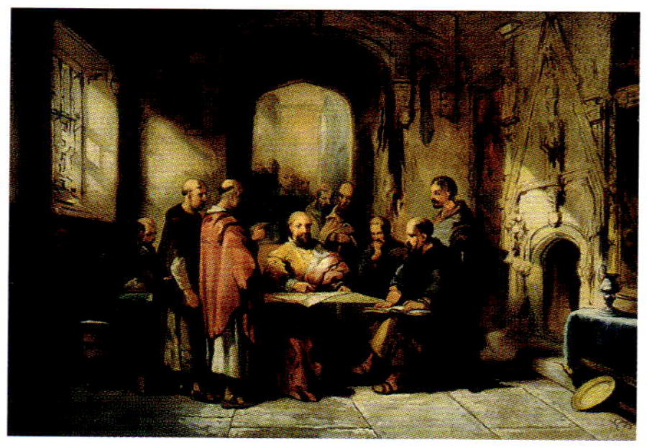

Cattermole, George 1800–1868
A Conference at the Monastery
oil on canvas 37.3 x 52.6
VIS.277

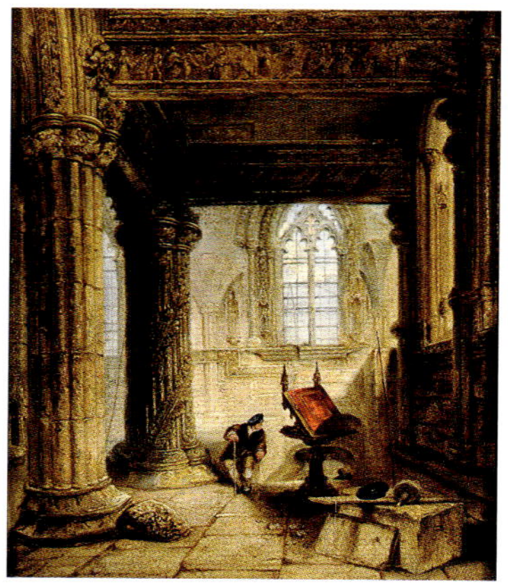

Cattermole, George 1800–1868
Rosslyn Chapel, Scotland
oil on canvas 26.8 x 22.1
VIS.550

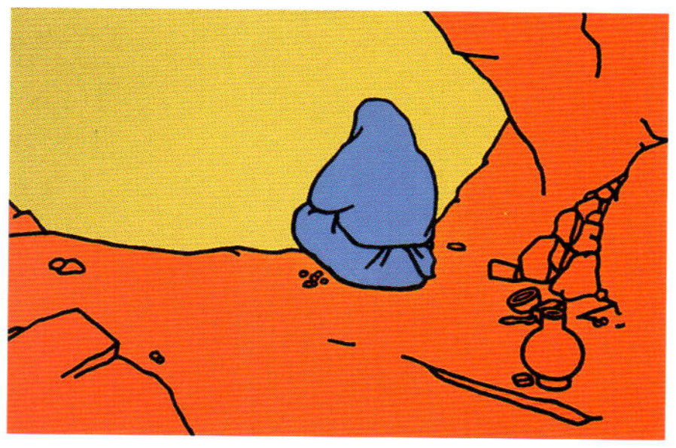

Caulfield, Patrick 1936–2005
The Hermit 1966
acrylic on board 68.9 x 97.6
VIS.4589

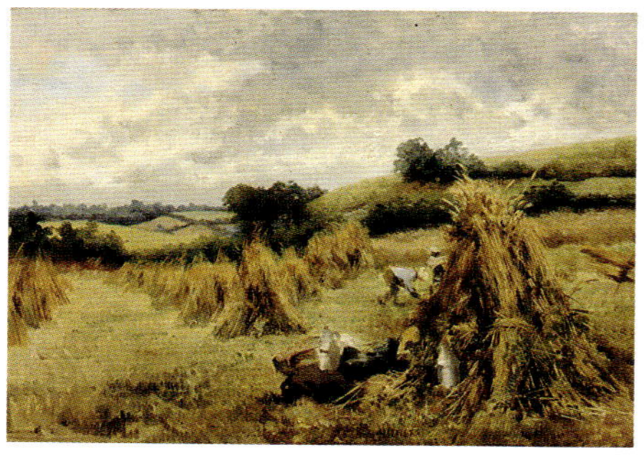

Cazin, Jean-Charles 1841–1901
Harvest Time
oil on canvas 33.4 x 47.6
VIS.587

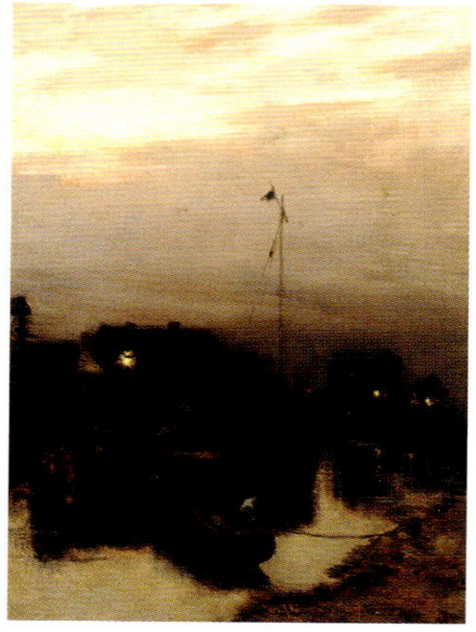

Cazin, Marie 1844–1924
The Harbour Lights 1880–1885
oil on panel 31.1 x 22.8
VIS.683

Facing page: Waplington, Paul Anthony, b.1938, *Dressing Billets* (detail), 1983, University of Sheffield, (p. 304)

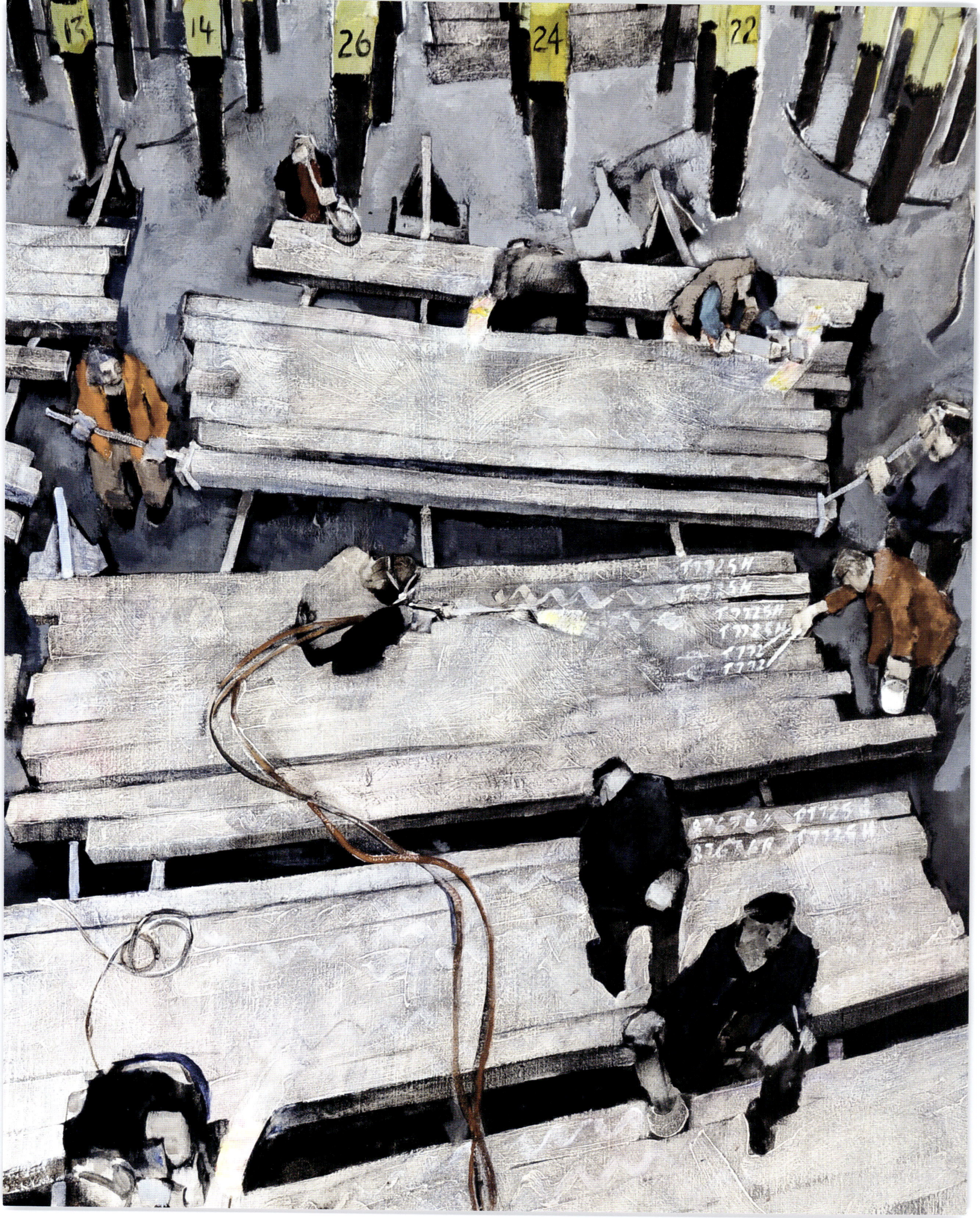
13
14
26
24
22

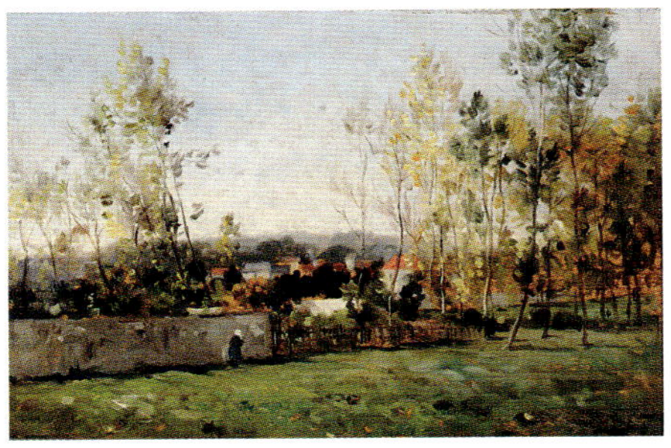

Cazin, Marie (attributed to) 1844–1924
Outskirts of Abbeville, France
oil on panel 22.7 x 33.7
VIS.514

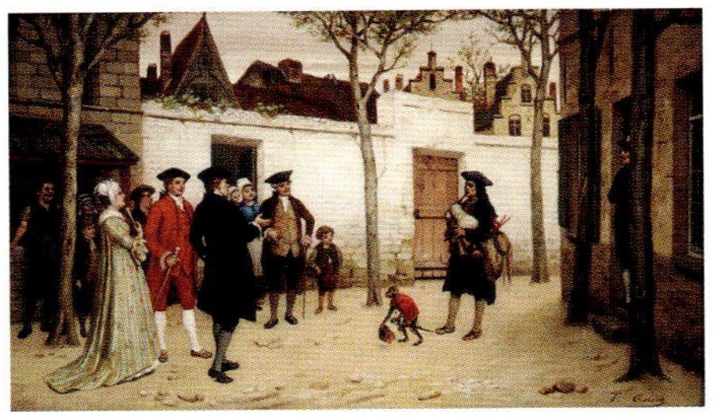

Ceriez, Theodore 1832–1904
A Savoyard in the Time of Louis XV c.1880
oil on panel 21.9 x 36.1
VIS.1601

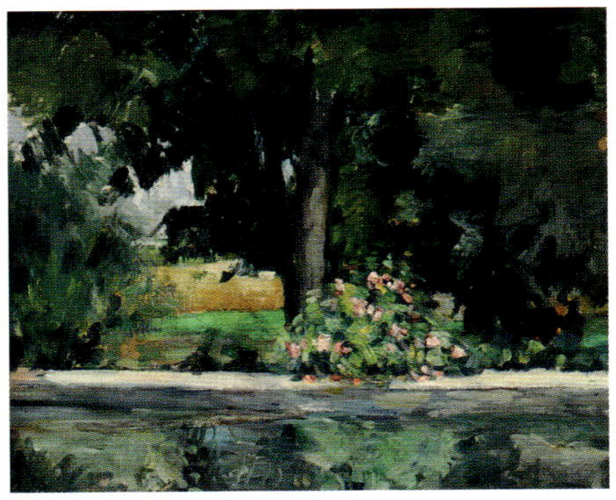

Cézanne, Paul 1839–1906
Bassin du Jas de Bouffan c.1874
oil on canvas 64 x 73.5
VIS.2580

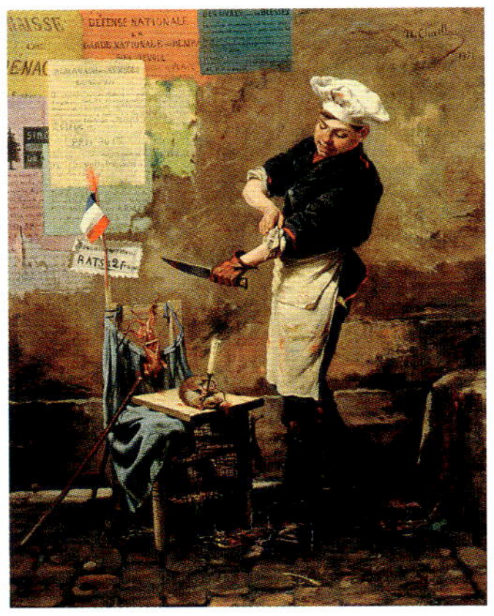

Chaillou, Narcisse 1837–1896
A Rat Seller during the Siege of Paris 1871
oil on canvas 59.3 x 46.5
VIS.1395

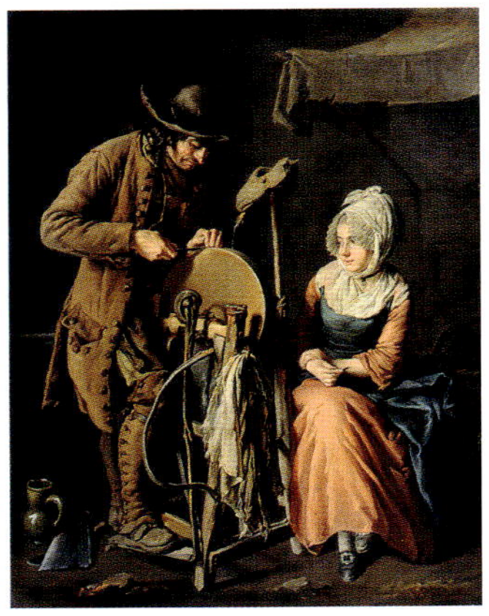

Chaillou, Narcisse (attributed to)
1837–1896
The Knife Grinder 1875–1880
oil on canvas 76 x 58.2
VIS.1555

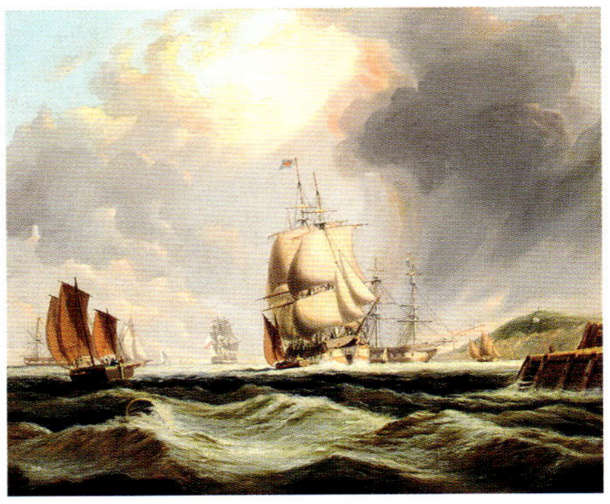

Chambers, George 1803–1840
Sailing Ships 1826–1836
oil on canvas 56.4 x 65.3
VIS.347

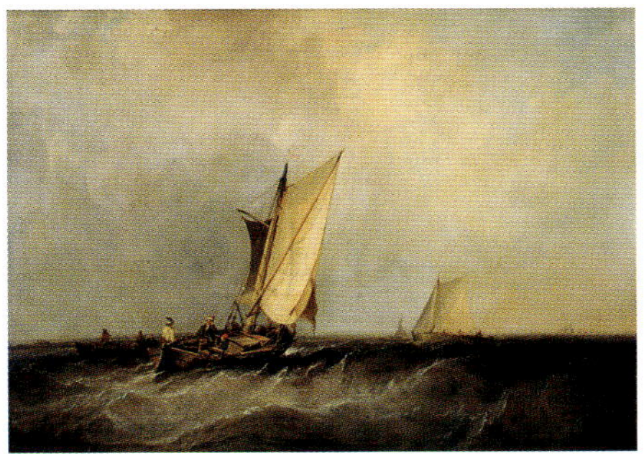

Chambers, George 1803–1840
Sea Piece 1834
oil on canvas 59.5 x 82.5
VIS.1606

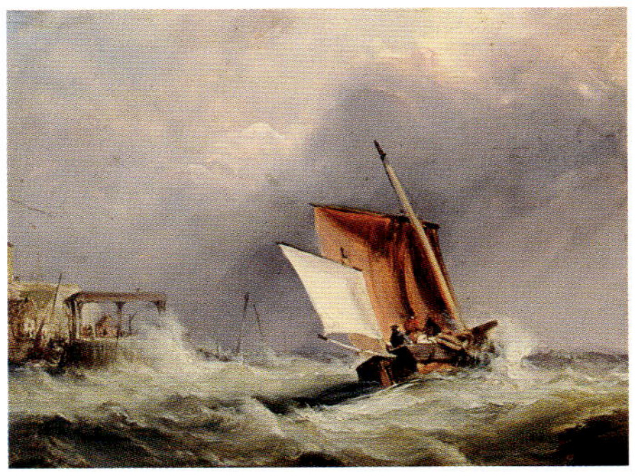

Chambers, George 1803–1840
Coast Scene
oil on canvas 23.9 x 31.5
VIS.288

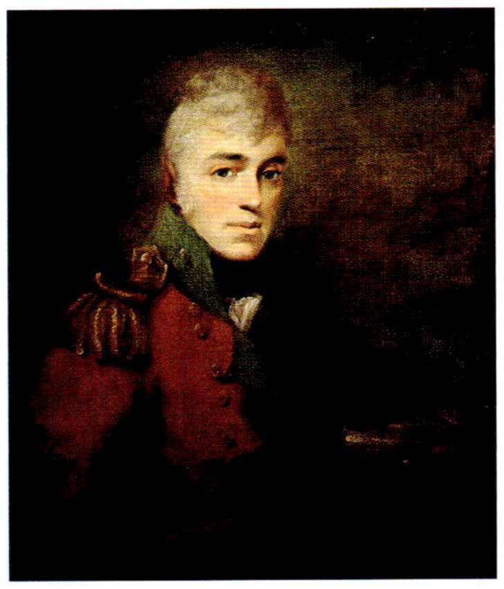

Chantrey, Francis Leggatt 1781–1842
Captain Thomas Asline Ward (1781–1871)
oil on canvas 74.7 x 62.2
VIS.2134

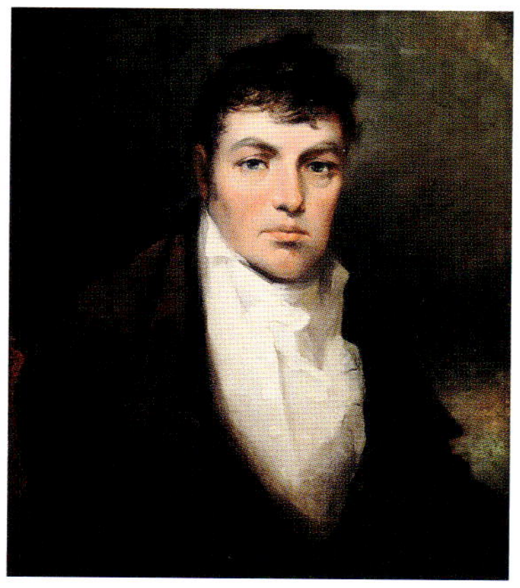

Chantrey, Francis Leggatt 1781–1842
Ebenezer Rhodes (1762–1839)
oil on canvas 62.1 x 52.2
VIS.2720

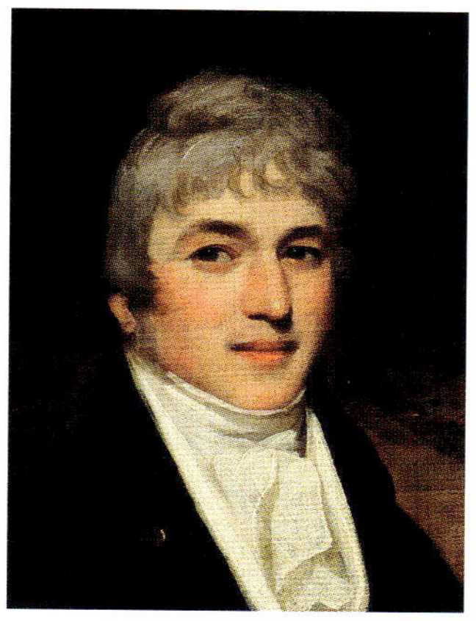

Chantrey, Francis Leggatt 1781–1842
John B. Morton, Esq.
oil on canvas 40.7 x 30.2
VIS.2132

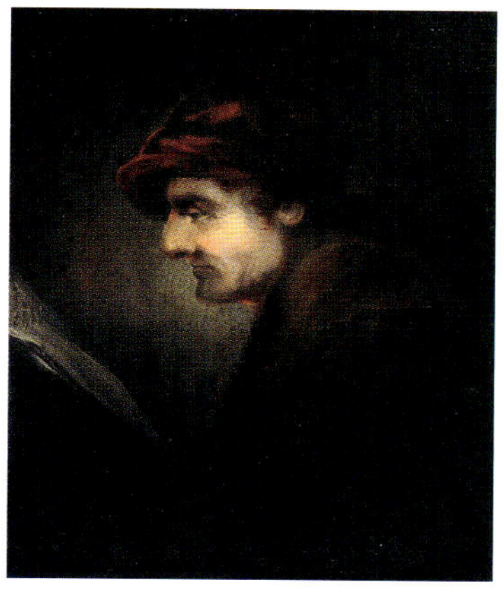

Chantrey, Francis Leggatt 1781–1842
John Fox of Dore
oil on canvas 60.3 x 50
VIS.2729

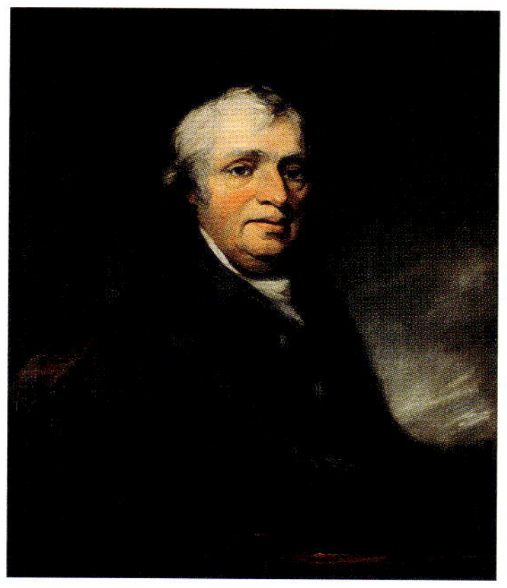

Chantrey, Francis Leggatt 1781–1842
John Porter (1736–1812)
oil on canvas 74.5 x 61.3
VIS.2136

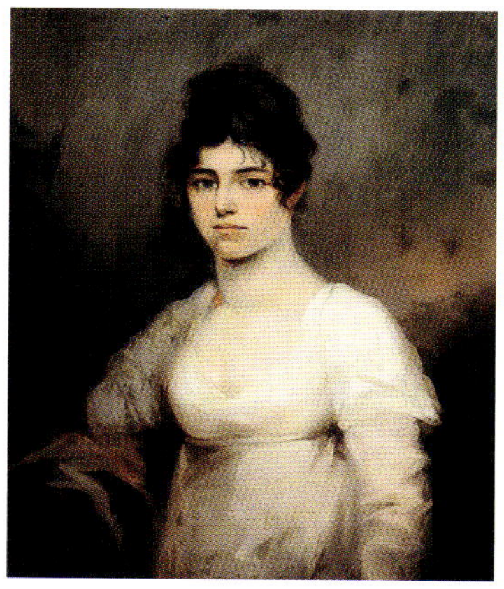

Chantrey, Francis Leggatt 1781–1842
Miss Bramall (b.1784)
oil on canvas 75 x 60.6
VIS.2714

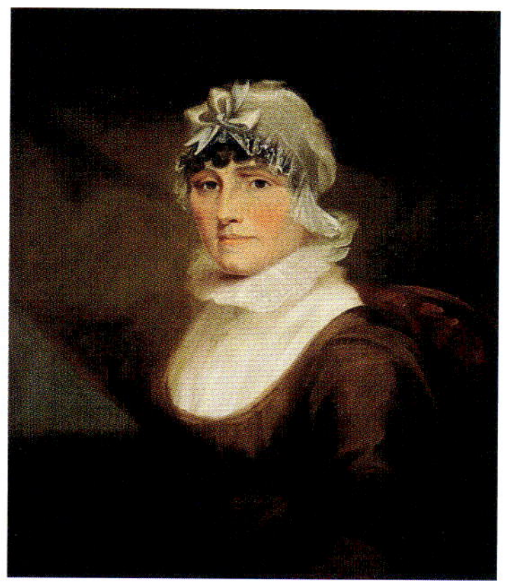

Chantrey, Francis Leggatt 1781–1842
Portrait of a Lady (Miss Bramall)
oil on canvas 74.4 x 61.5
VIS.3195

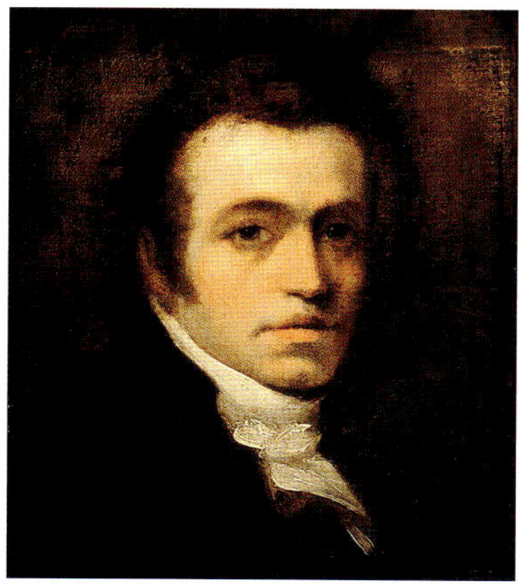

Chantrey, Francis Leggatt 1781–1842
Self Portrait
oil on canvas 39.5 x 34.6
VIS.2133

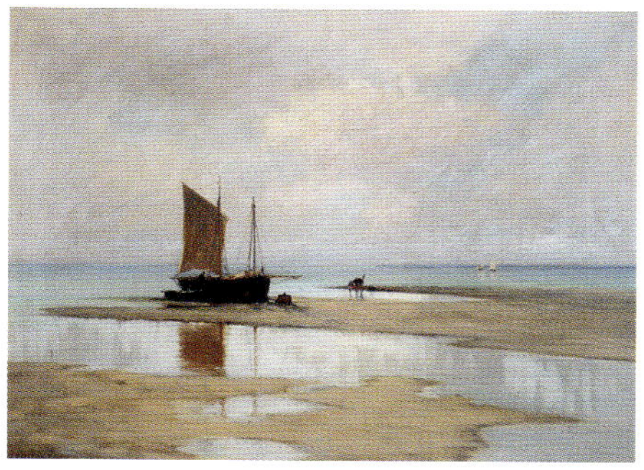

Chapman, Carlton Theodore 1860–1925
Coast Scene
oil on canvas 44 x 59.8
VIS.2416

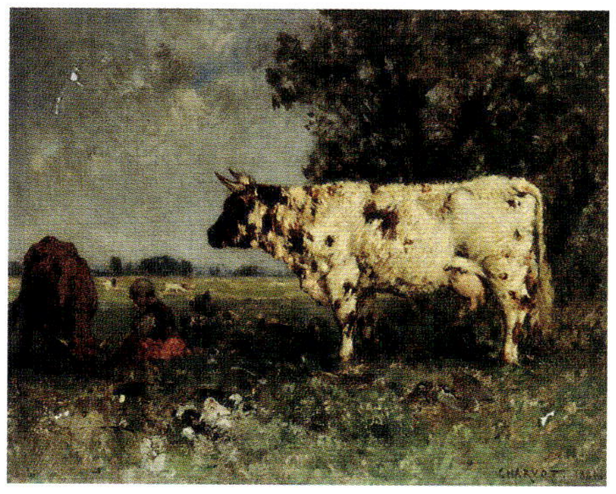

Charvot, Eugène (attributed to) 1847–1924
Landscape with Cattle 1881
oil on canvas 31.2 x 39.1
VIS.1216

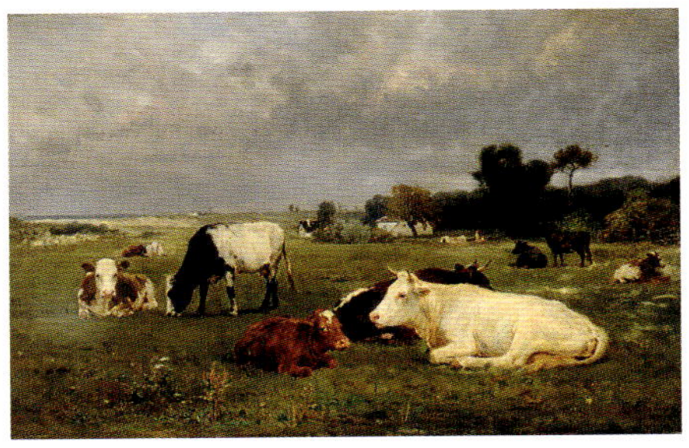

Chialiva, Luigi 1842–1914
Landscape with Cattle 1873
oil on panel 30 x 46.3
VIS.1384

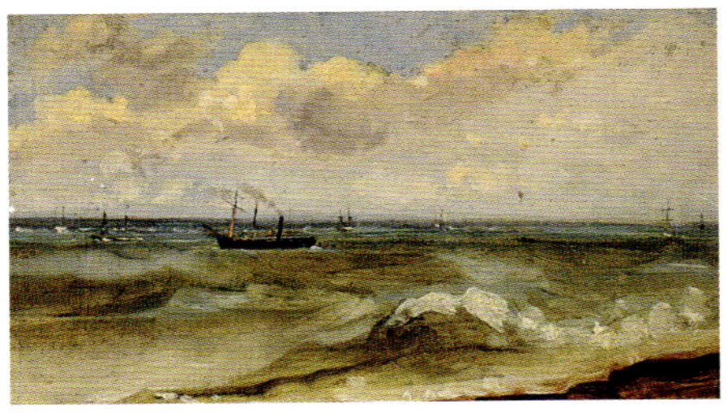

Churchyard, Thomas 1798–1865
Seascape
oil on millboard 11.3 x 19.4
VIS.2302

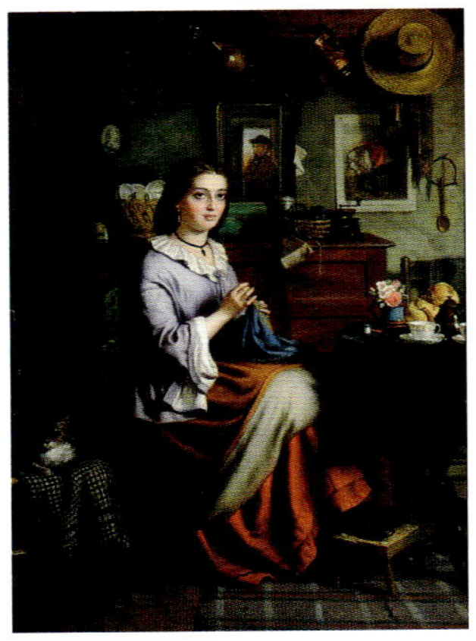

Clark, Joseph 1834–1926
The Labourer's Welcome
oil on canvas 76.4 x 54.6
VIS.10

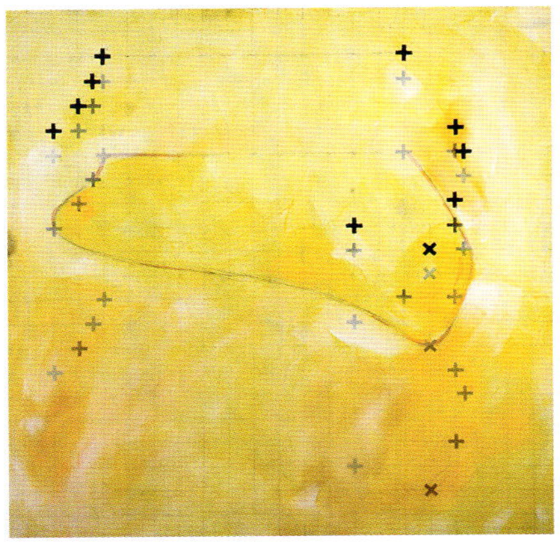

Clarke, Brian b.1953
Site Plan 1978
acrylic on canvas 168.2 x 167.3
VIS.4572

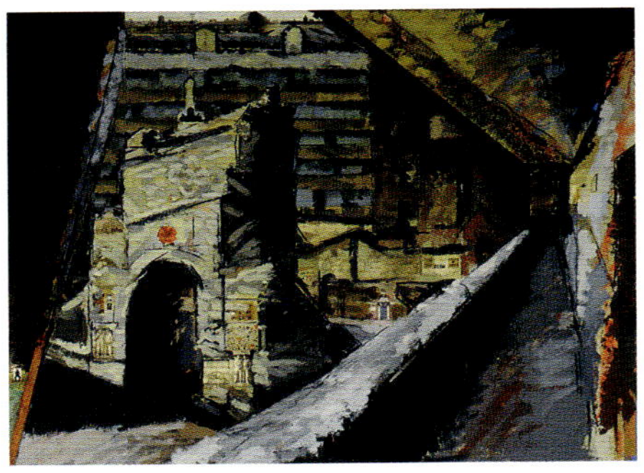

Clarke, Pete b.1951
Ways of Living: Inside Looking Out, a Monument 1984
oil & collage on canvas on panel
183.5 x 243.8
VIS.5170

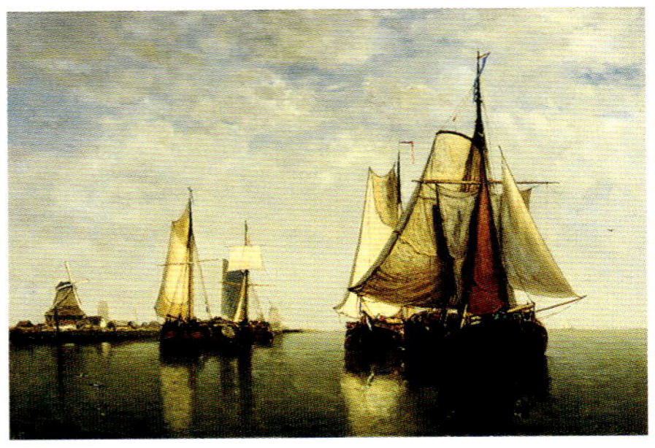

Clays, Paul Jean 1819–1900
The Calm 1870
oil on panel 59.4 x 83.2
VIS.1565

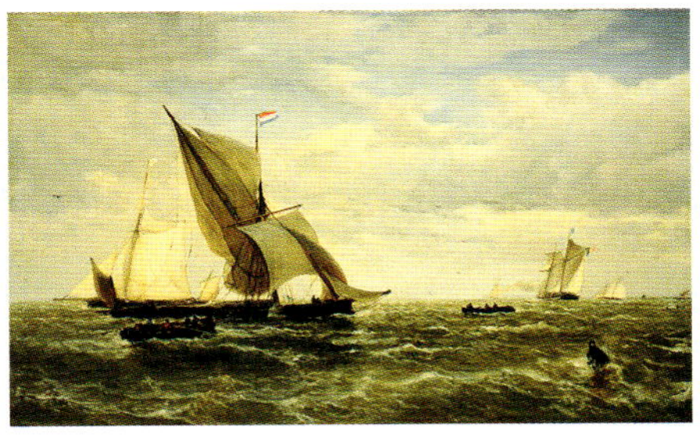

Clays, Paul Jean 1819–1900
The Storm 1870–1875
oil on panel 77.1 x 122.3
VIS.1442

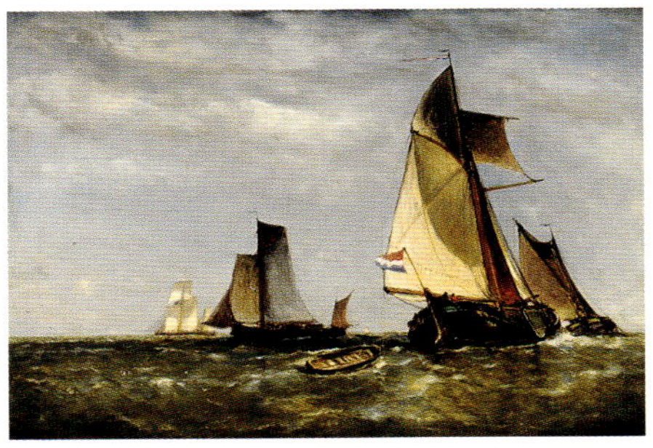

Clays, Paul Jean 1819–1900
Dutch Fishing Boats 1872
oil on panel 59.2 x 84.6
VIS.1415

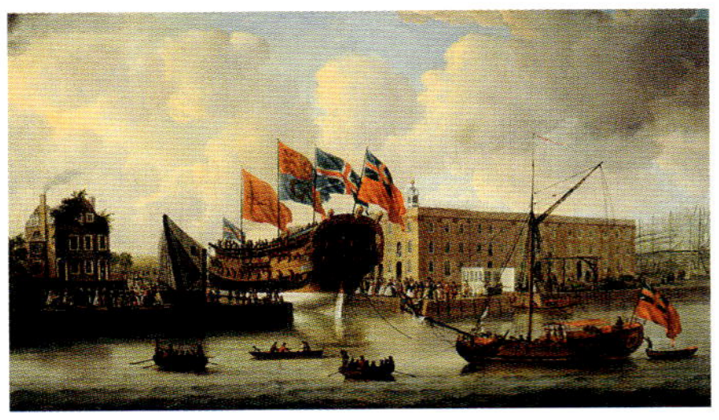

Cleveley, John c.1712–1777
Deptford Dockyard
oil on canvas 89 x 149.3
VIS.3144

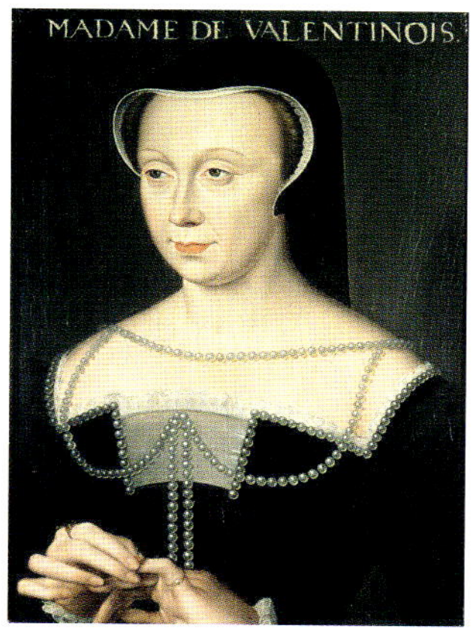

Clouet, François (school of) c.1515–1572
Diane de Poitiers (1499–1566), Duchess of Valentinois after 1547
oil on panel 46.6 x 37
VIS.43

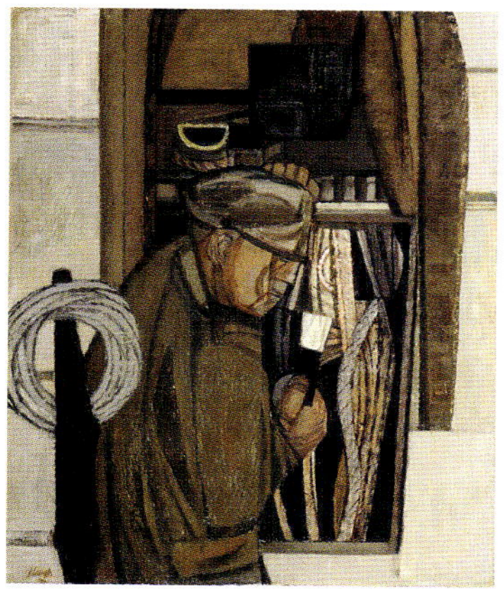

Clough, Prunella 1919–1999
Telephone Engineer II 1952
oil on canvas 65 x 54.4
VIS.4588

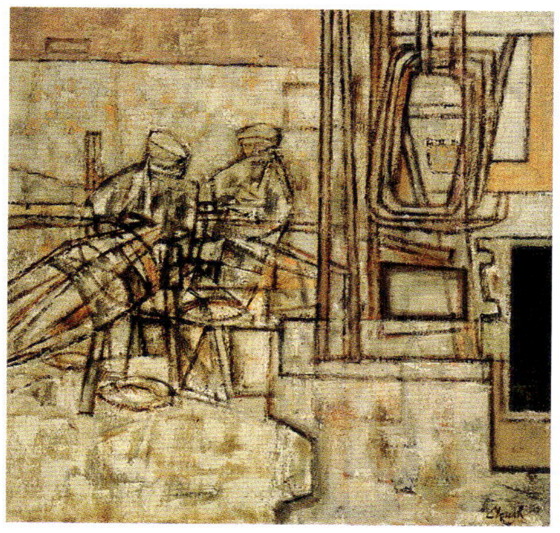

Clough, Prunella 1919–1999
Building Site 1956
oil on canvas 61.6 x 63.9
VIS.4269

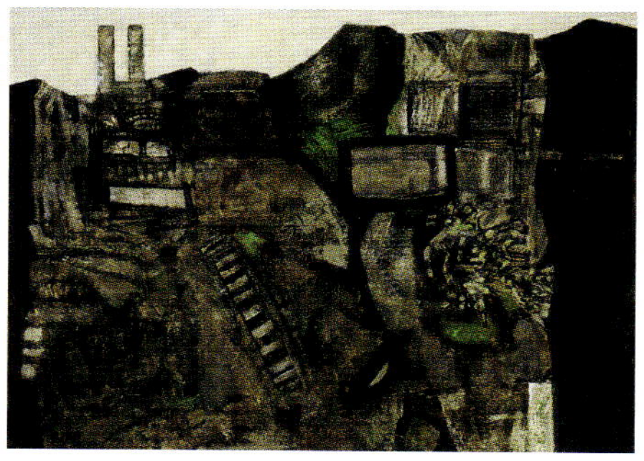

Clough, Prunella 1919–1999
Landscape in a Mining Area 1956
oil on canvas 57.6 x 77.8
VIS.3848

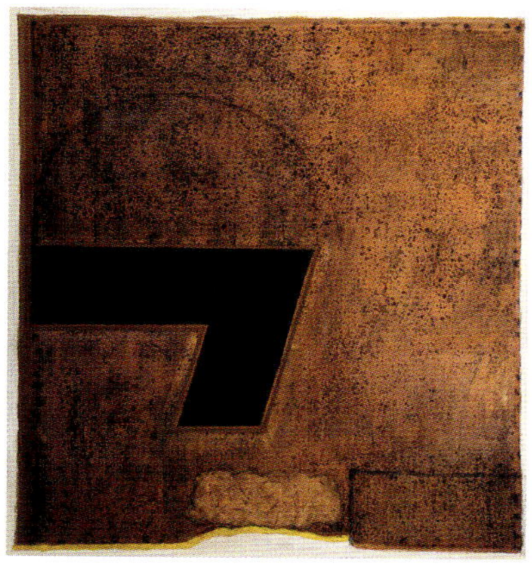

Clough, Prunella 1919–1999
Discovered Check 1968–1969
oil on canvas 114.5 x 105.1
VIS.4013

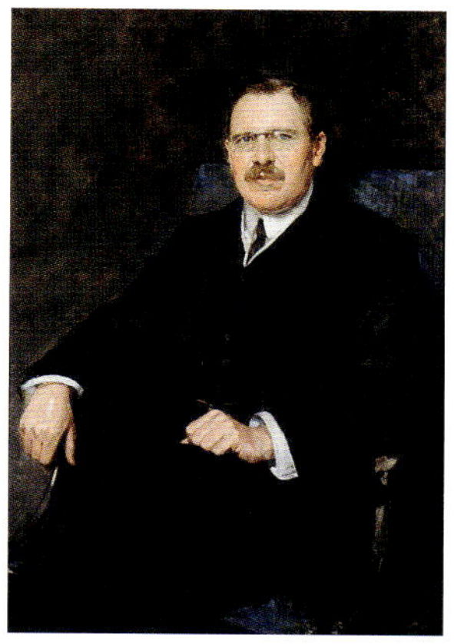

Cluysenaar, André 1872–1939
Arthur Balfour (1848–1930) 1919
oil on canvas 116.5 x 79.4
VIS.4166

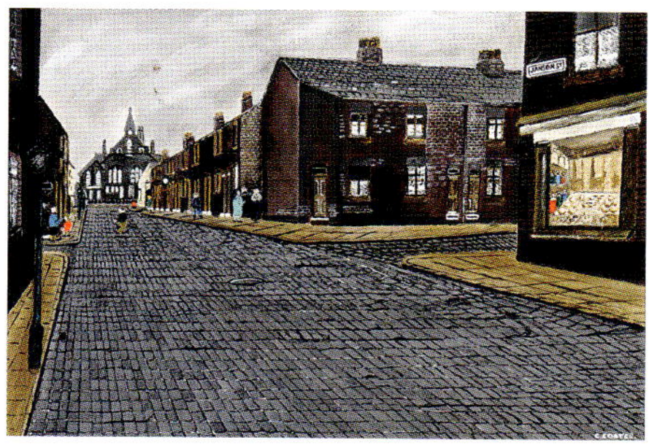

Coates, Colin 1908–1991
Jansen Street, Sheffield c.1950
oil on canvas 34.2 x 49
1974.77

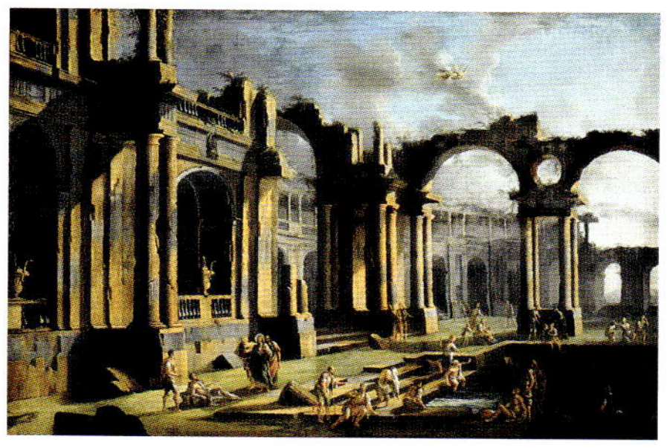

Coccorante, Leonardo (school of)
1680–1750
The Pool of Bethesda 1730–1750
oil on canvas 125.2 x 178
VIS.2417

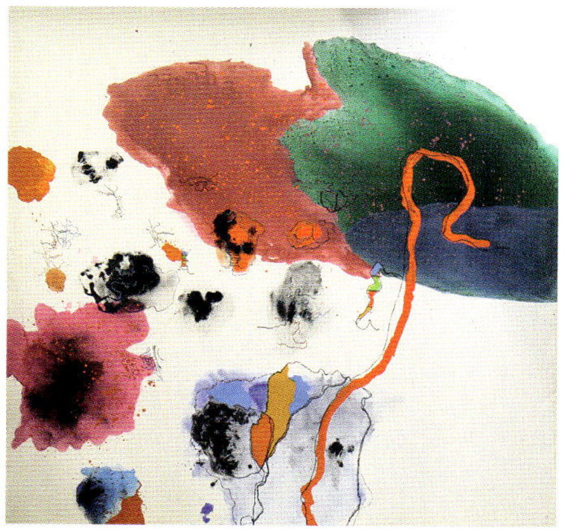

Cohen, Harold b.1928
As If 1965
acrylic on canvas 258.2 x 254 (E)
VIS.4199

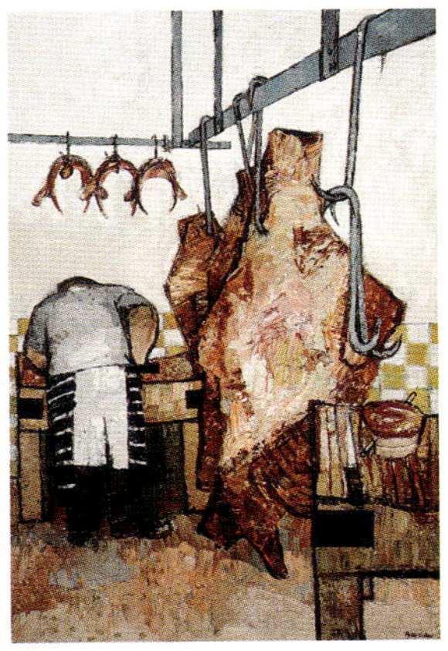

Coker, Peter 1926–2004
Butcher's Shop No.1 1955
oil on board 185 x 120.2
VIS.3990

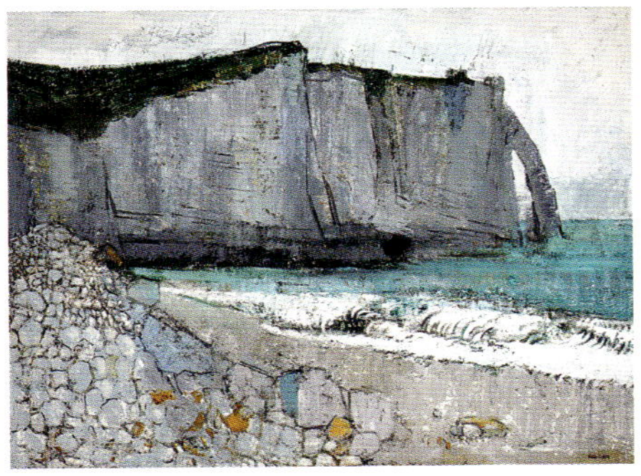

Coker, Peter 1926–2004
Cliff at Étretat, France 1955
oil on canvas 144.5 x 192
VIS.5211

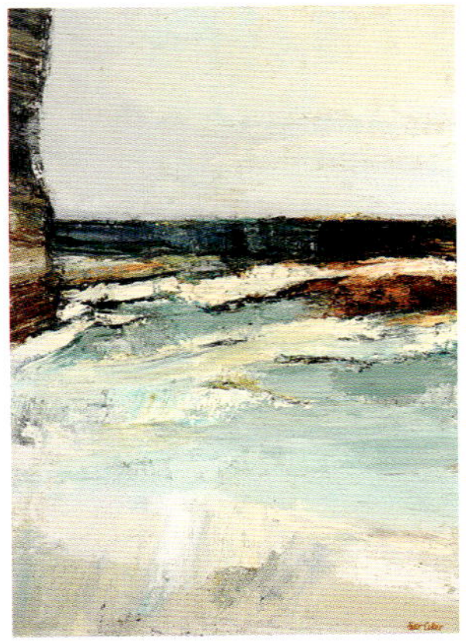

Coker, Peter 1926–2004
Seascape
oil on canvas 83 x 58.4
VIS.5443

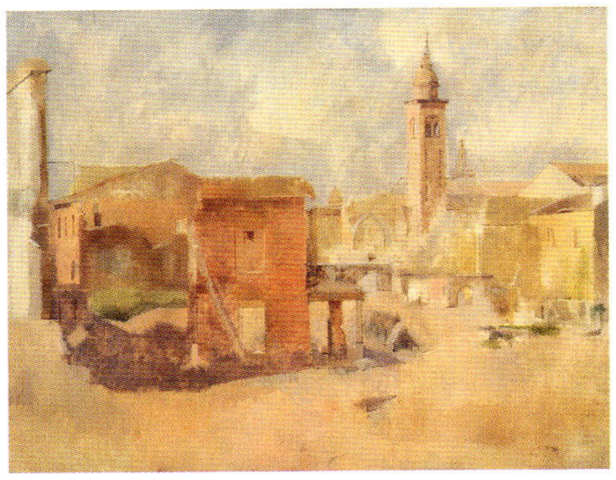

Coldstream, William Menzies 1908–1987
Rimini, Italy
oil on canvas 70.5 x 90.2
VIS.1848

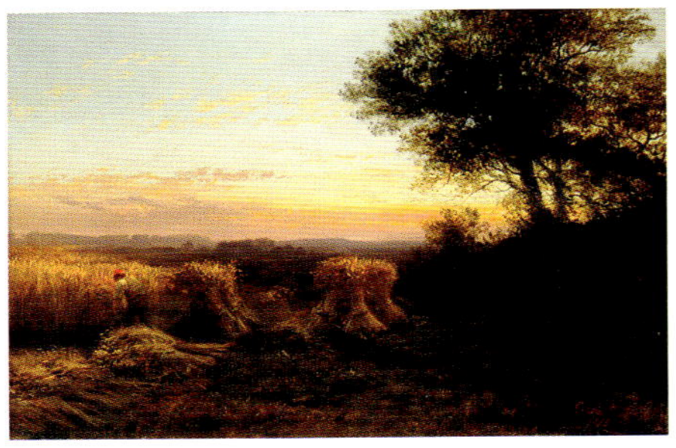

Cole, George 1810–1883
Landscape 1873
oil on canvas 38.2 x 56
VIS.1396

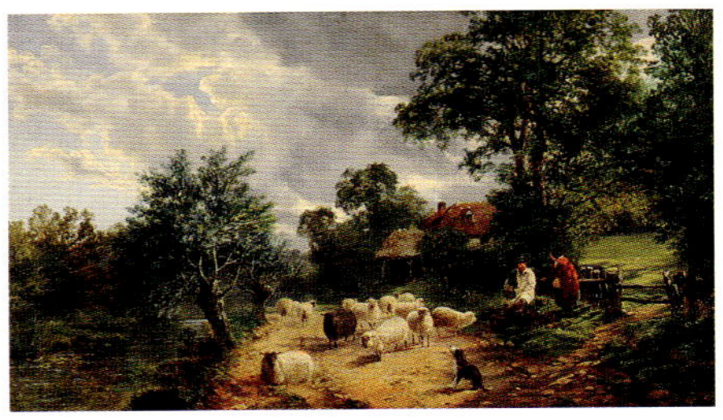

Cole, George Vicat 1833–1893
Landscape with Sheep and Figures 1855
oil on canvas 29 x 49.4
VIS.2725

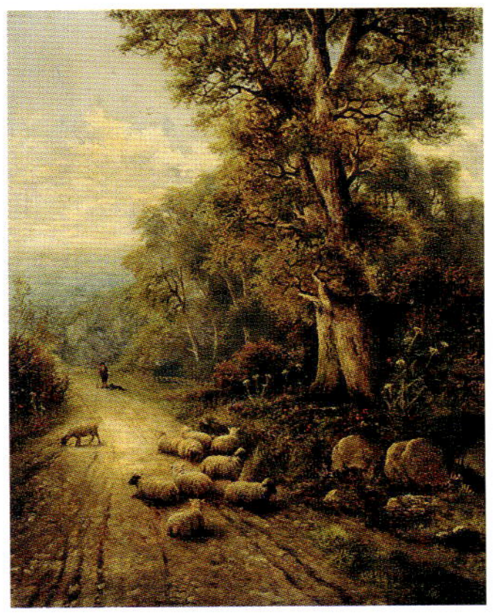

Cole, George Vicat 1833–1893
Landscape with Sheep 1870
oil on canvas on board 90.3 x 69.9
VIS.1341

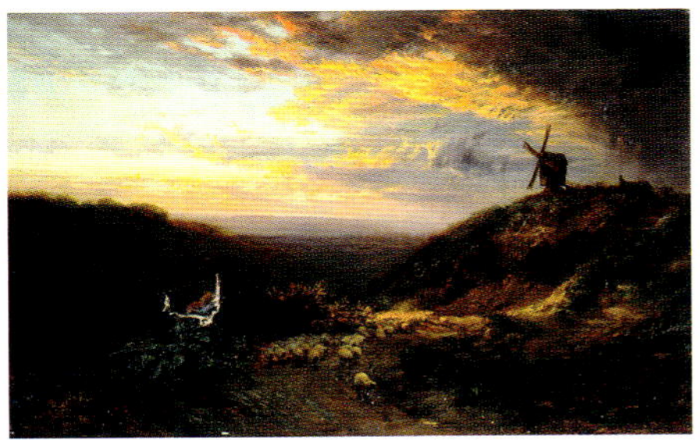

Cole, George Vicat 1833–1893
Near Petersfield, Hampshire 1870
oil on canvas 66 x 118
VIS.196

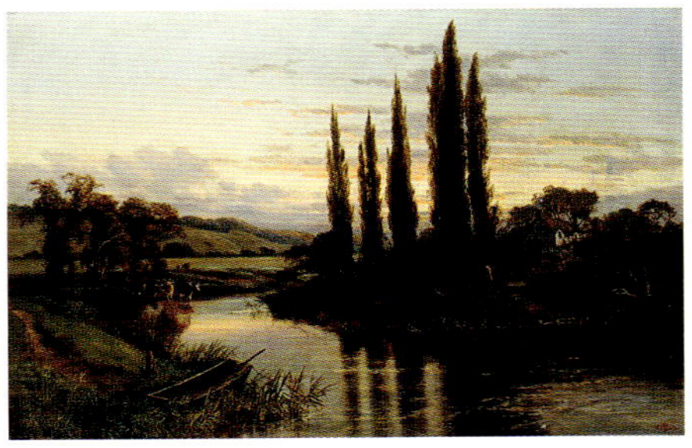

Cole, George Vicat 1833–1893
On the Thames 1883
oil on canvas 59.5 x 90.2
VIS.2872

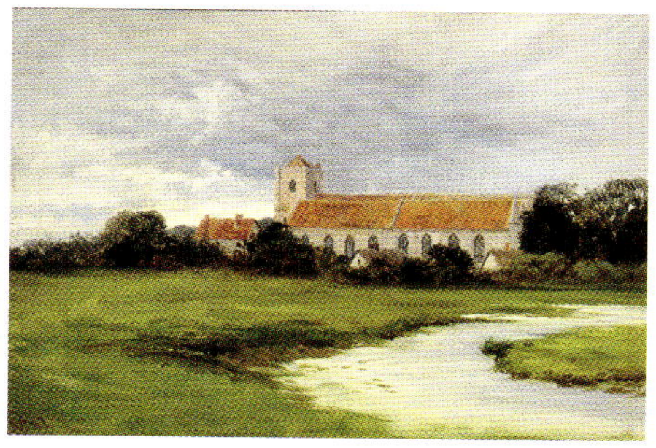

Cole, George Vicat 1833–1893
Dorchester Abbey, Oxfordshire 1887
oil on millboard 33.5 x 48.9
VIS.1215

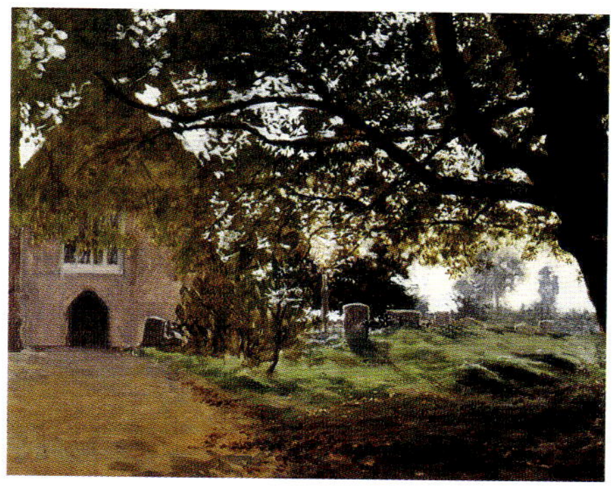

Cole, George Vicat 1833–1893
Churchyard, Dorchester Abbey, Oxfordshire
oil on canvas 44 x 54
VIS.769

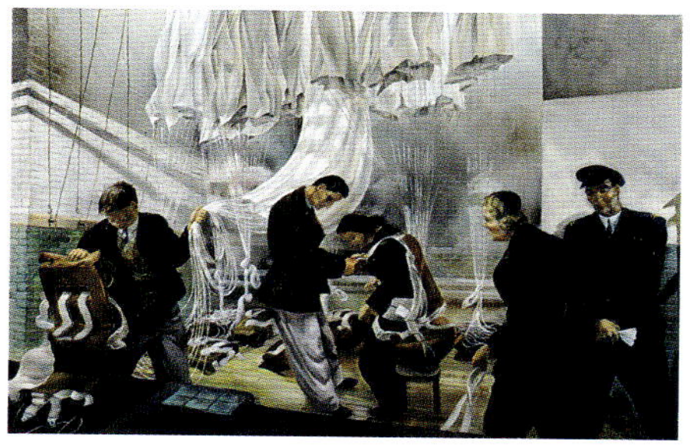

Cole, Leslie 1910–1976
Air Transport Auxiliary 1943
oil on canvas 59.9 x 90.4
VIS.1808

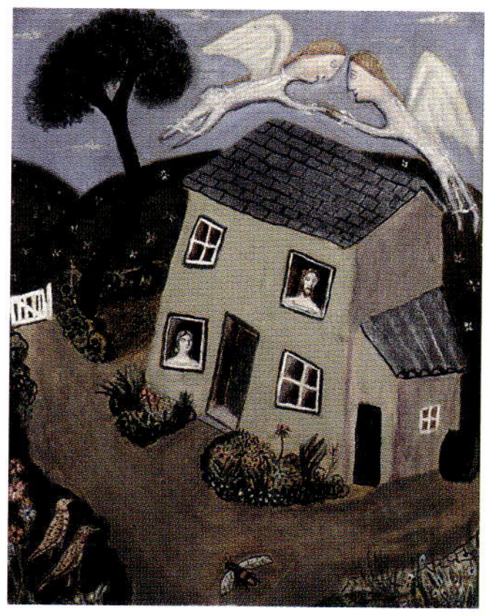

Collins, Cecil 1908–1989
The Artist's House 1932
oil on canvas 41.1 x 31.8
VIS.5328

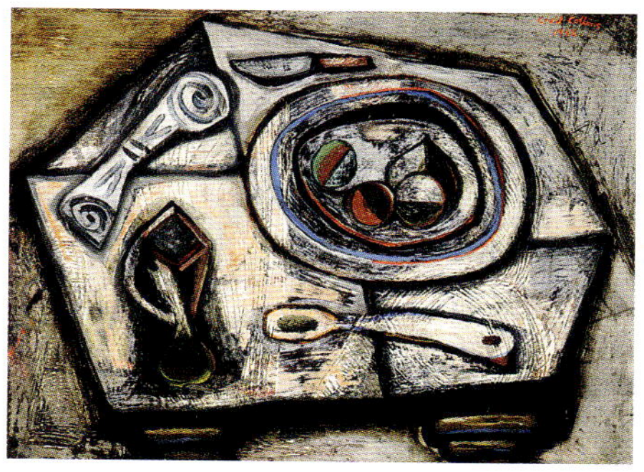

Collins, Cecil 1908–1989
Still Life 1938
oil on board 37.3 x 49.8
VIS.5327

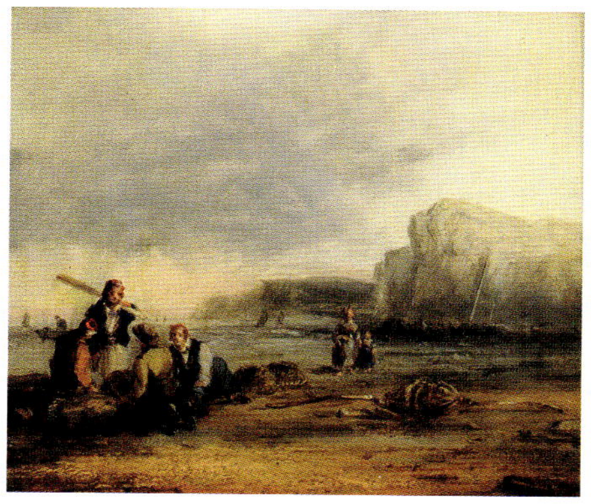

Collins, William 1788–1847
Cromer Sands, Norfolk
oil on panel 14.5 x 17
VIS.901

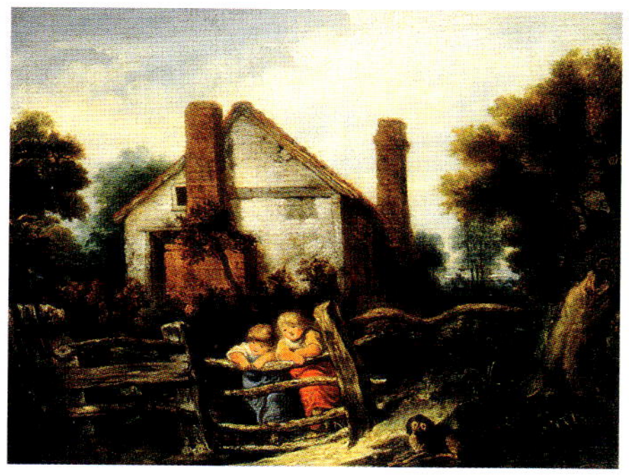

Collins, William 1788–1847
English Cottage Scene
oil on canvas 40 x 52.3
VIS.150

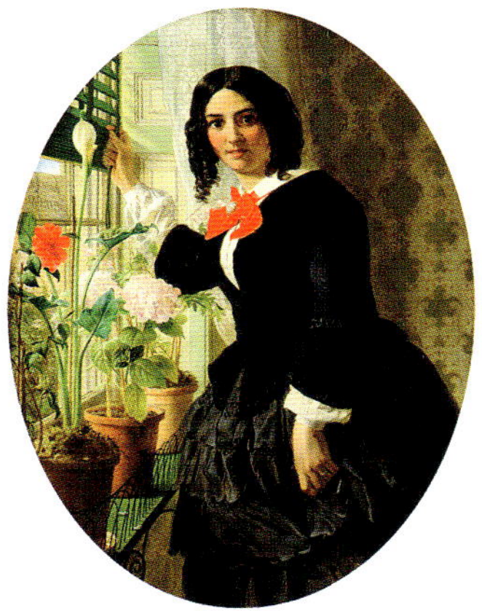

Collinson, James 1825–1881
The Landlady 1856
oil on canvas 84.7 x 69.7
VIS.14

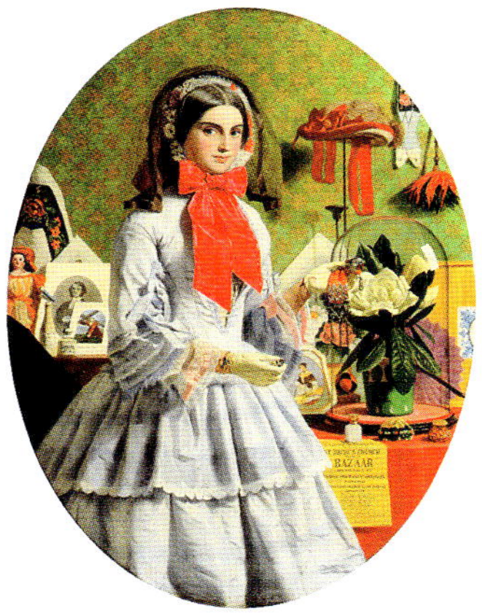

Collinson, James 1825–1881
At the Bazaar 1857
oil on panel 84.4 x 70.9
VIS.11

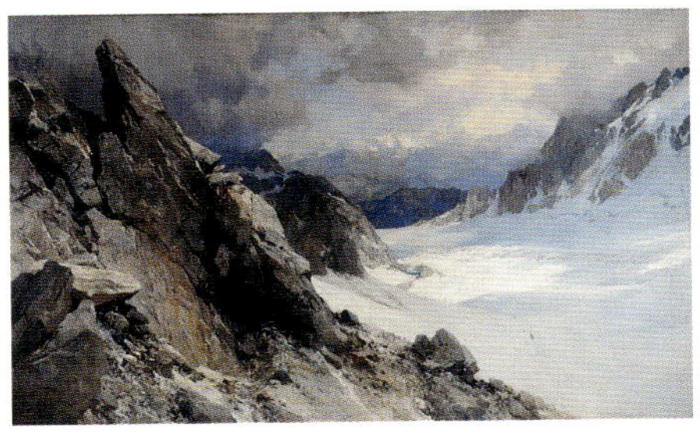

Compton, Edward Theodore 1849–1921
Snow Scene on the Col d'Orny, Valais, Switzerland 1914
oil on canvas 100.8 x 160.9
VIS.2000

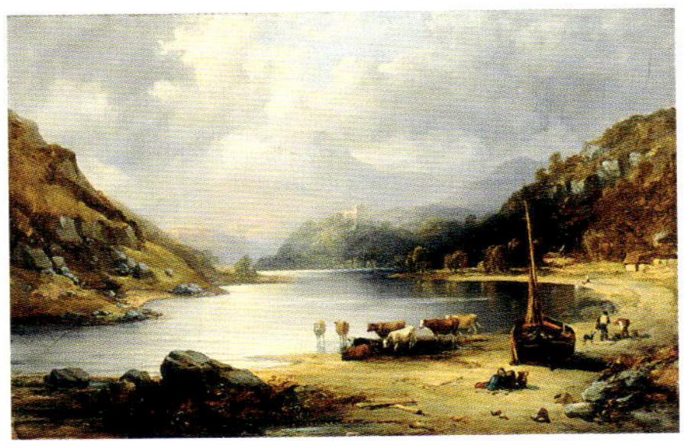

Compton, Edward Theodore 1849–1921
Loch Ness, Scotland
oil on canvas 60.9 x 91.3
VIS.790

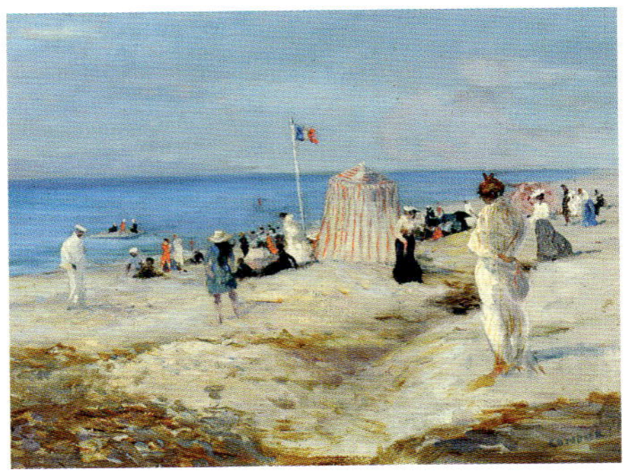

Conder, Charles 1868–1909
French Beach Scene, Dieppe
oil on canvas 33.5 x 43.2
VIS.8

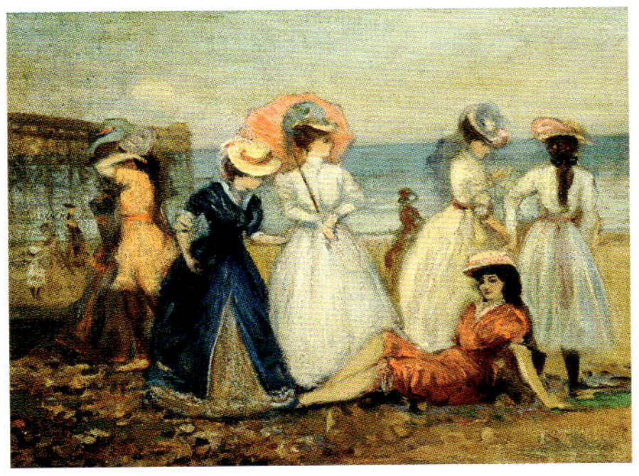

Conder, Charles 1868–1909
On the Seashore
oil on canvas 68 x 89.1
VIS.2037

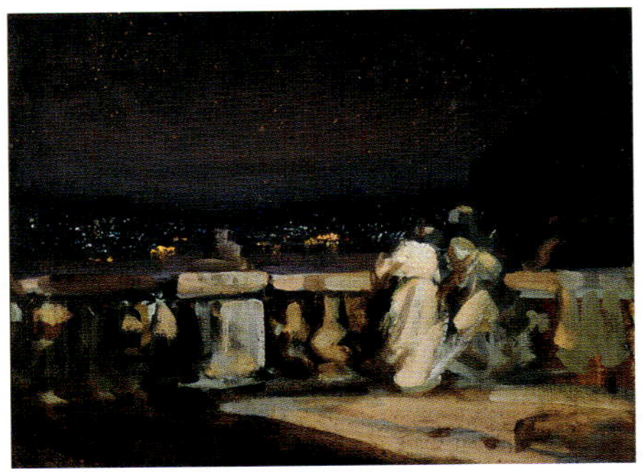

Conder, Charles 1868–1909
Watching the Fireworks at Saint-Cloud, France
oil on canvas 46.5 x 60.7
VIS.125

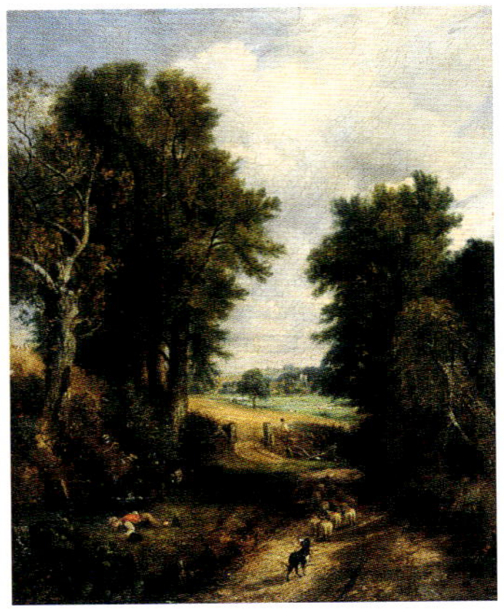

Constable, John (after) 1776–1837
Cornfield (Country Lane)
oil on canvas 93.5 x 75
VIS.1435

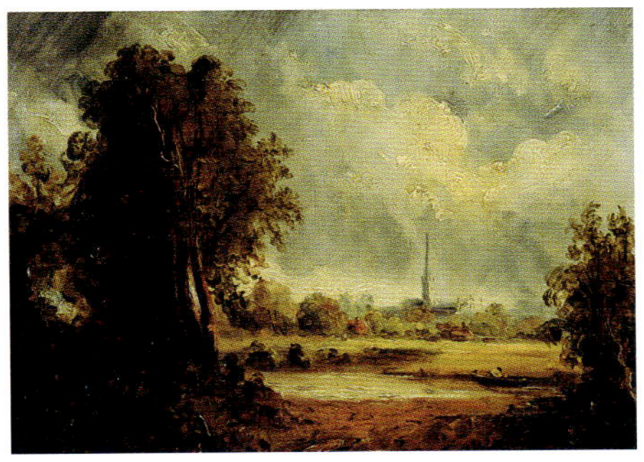

Constable, John (attributed to) 1776–1837
Salisbury Cathedral, Wiltshire 1821
oil on canvas 28 x 39
VIS.424

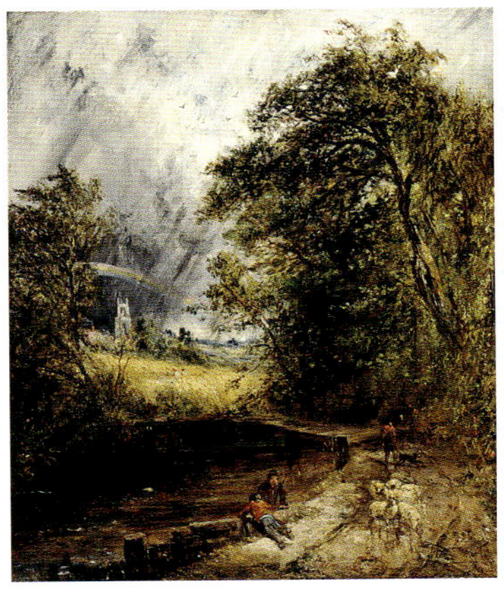

Constable, John (attributed to) 1776–1837
Landscape 1829
oil on canvas 74.3 x 60.8
VIS.1568

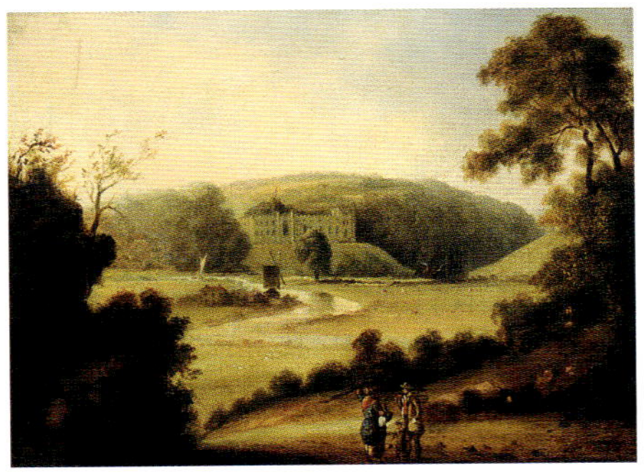

Constable, John (attributed to) 1776–1837
Arundel Castle, West Sussex
oil on canvas 29.7 x 39.9
VIS.1246

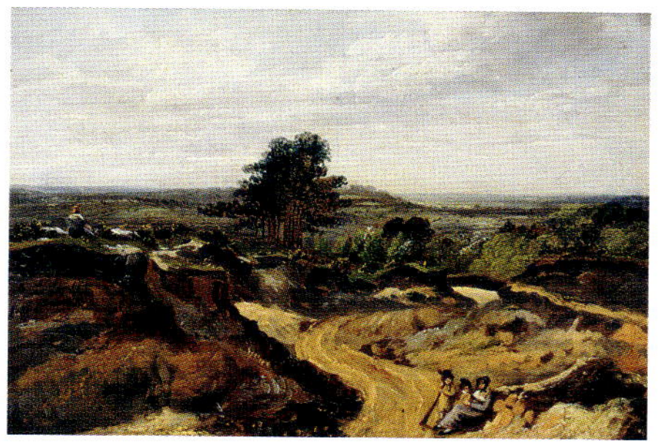

Constable, John (attributed to) 1776–1837
Hampstead, London
oil on panel 23 x 34.1
VIS.654

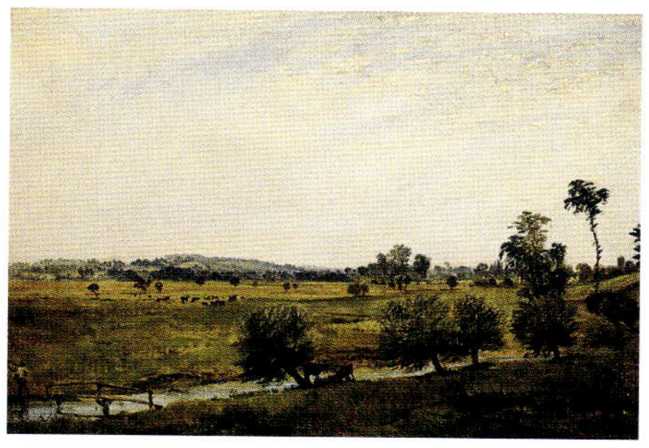

Constable, John (attributed to) 1776–1837
The Water Meadows, Salisbury, Wiltshire
oil on panel 23.8 x 34
VIS.343

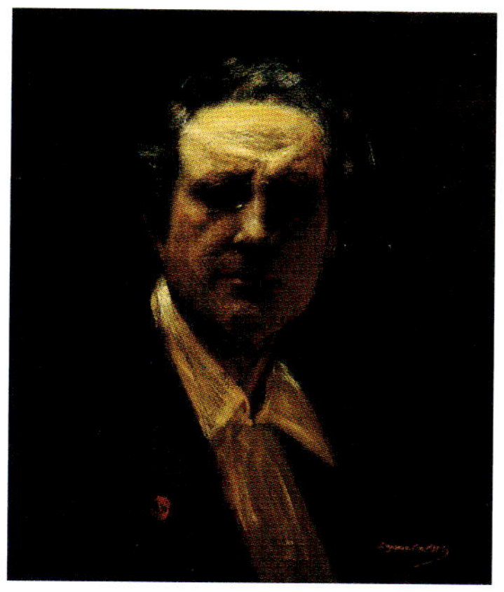

Constant, Jean Joseph Benjamin 1845–1902
Portrait of the Artist 1870–1890
oil on canvas 54 x 44.4
VIS.242

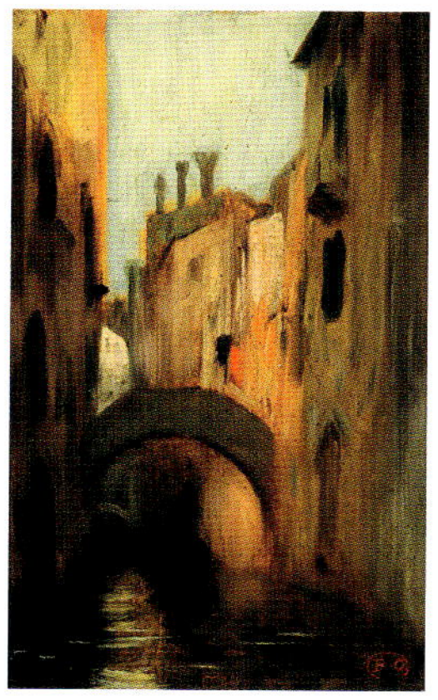

Constant, Jean Joseph Benjamin 1845–1902
Venetian Scene 1875–1880
oil on panel 22.4 x 13.7
VIS.1970

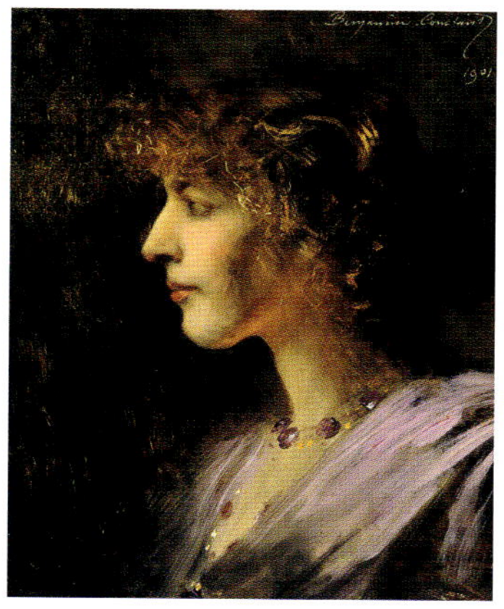

Constant, Jean Joseph Benjamin 1845–1902
Portrait 1901
oil on panel 39.8 x 31.8
VIS.1965

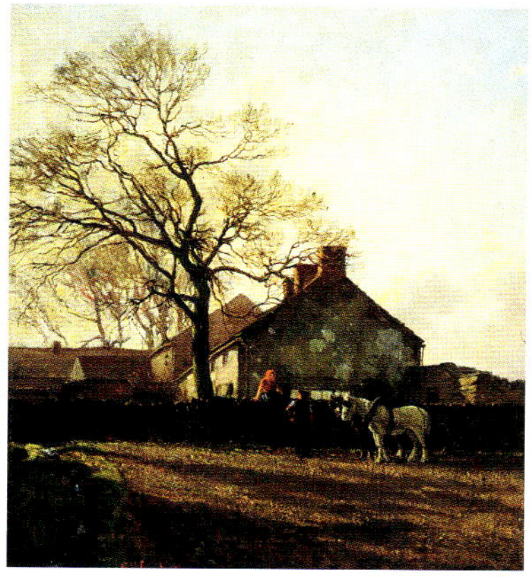

Constantine, George Hamilton 1875–1968
March Afternoon
oil on canvas 46.2 x 41
VIS.1877

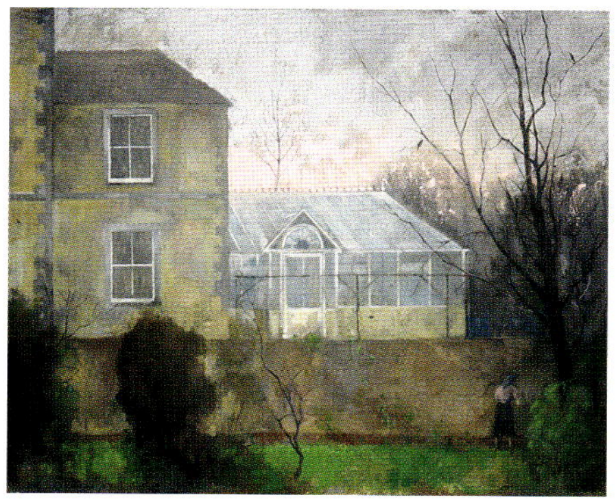

Constantine, Harry Francis b.1919
A Winter Garden (Brocco Bank, Sheffield)
1953
oil on canvas 49.5 x 59.7
VIS.5020

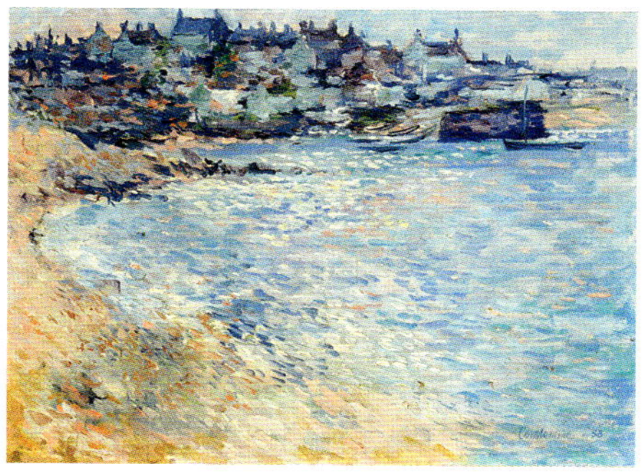

Constantine, Harry Francis b.1919
Cemaes Bay, Anglesey, Wales 1958
oil on panel 28.9 x 39.2
VIS.5021

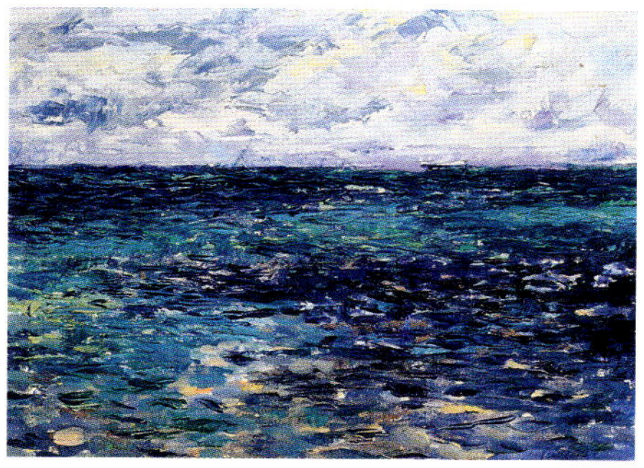

Constantine, Harry Francis b.1919
Sun, Sea and Cloud, Irish Sea from Anglesey, Wales
oil on board 28.3 x 38.8
VIS.5426

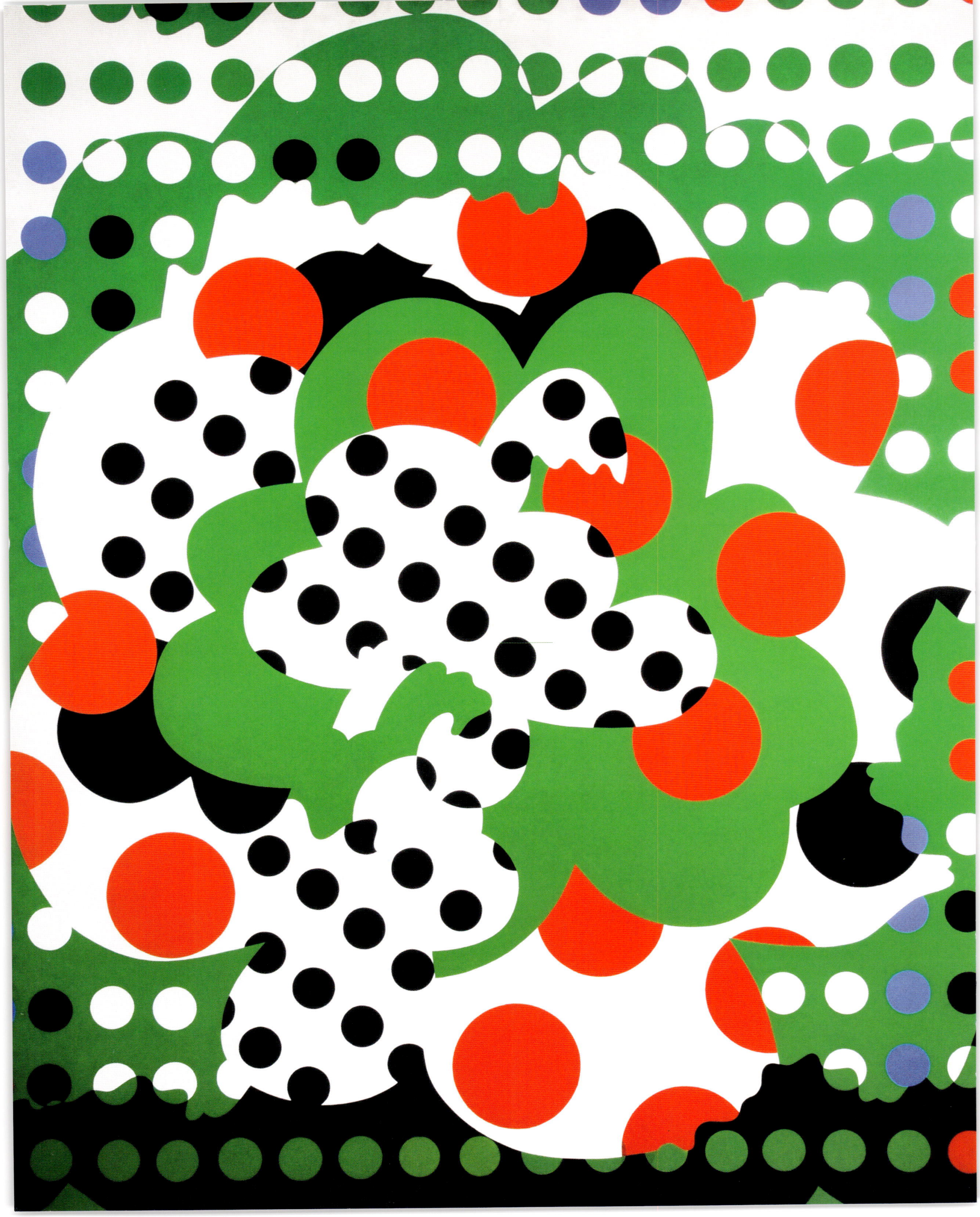

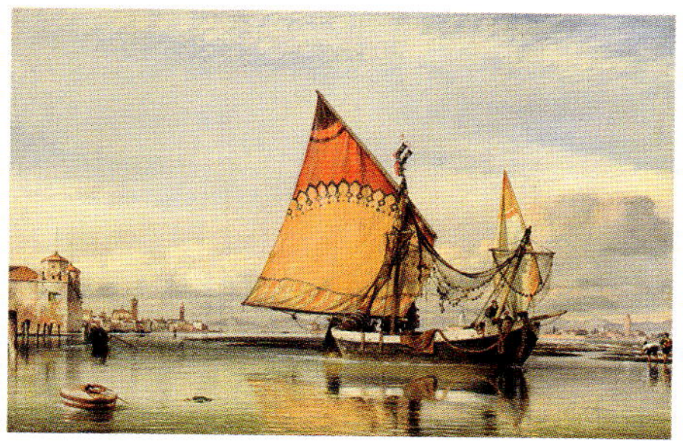

Cooke, Edward William 1811–1880
Venetian Fishing Craft off the Adriatic Shore of the Lido 1857
oil on panel 29.2 x 43.1
VIS.1407

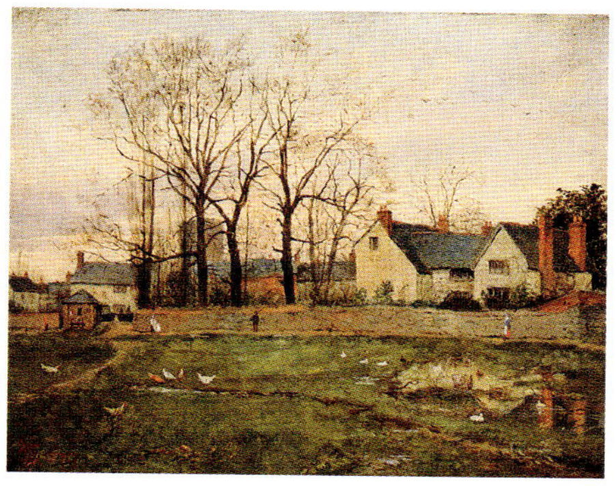

Cooke, Edward William 1811–1880
A Village Scene 1879
oil on panel 19.7 x 24.8
VIS.689

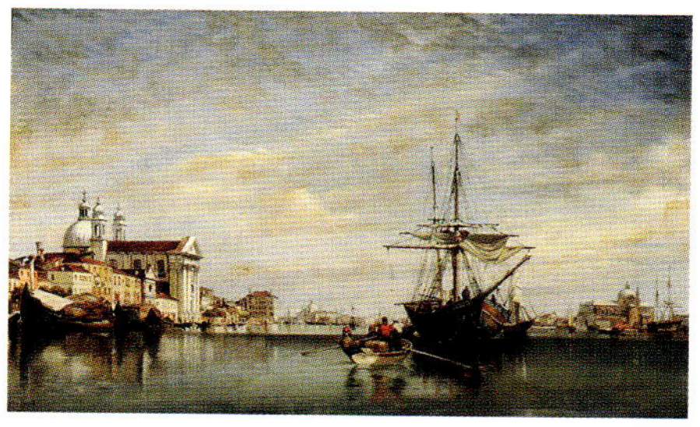

Cooke, Edward William 1811–1880
Venice
oil on canvas 47.8 x 76.4
VIS.370

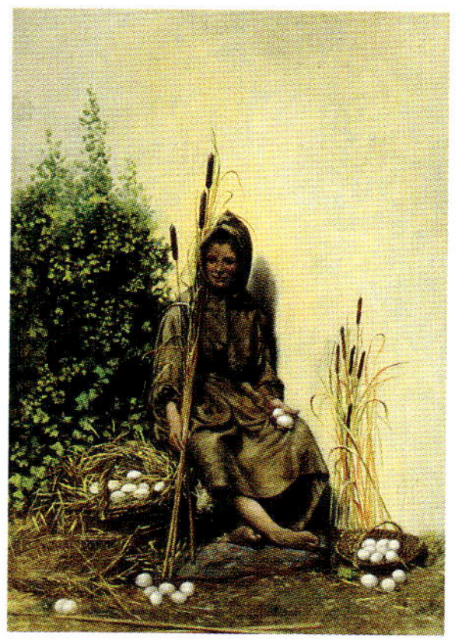

Cookesley, Margaret Deborah 1844–1927
The Egg Seller 1891
oil on canvas 47.5 x 32.4
VIS.786

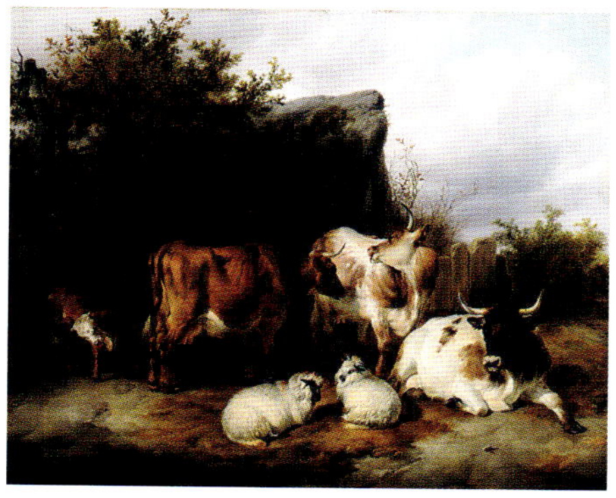

Cooper, Thomas Sidney 1803–1902
Cattle and Sheep 1840
oil on canvas 63 x 76
VIS.321

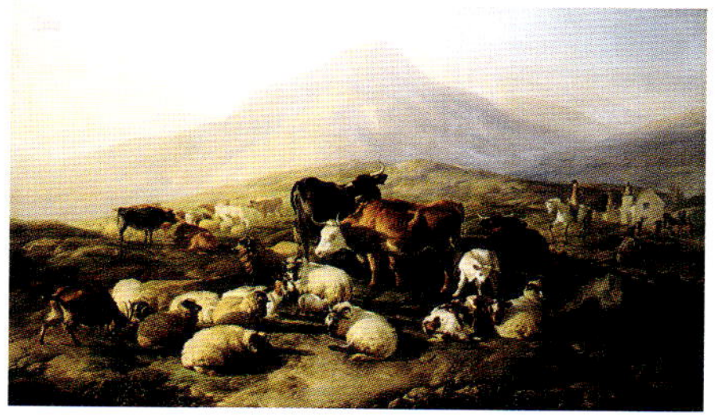

Cooper, Thomas Sidney 1803–1902
The Halt on the Hills 1847
oil on canvas 148 x 239.5
VIS.1482

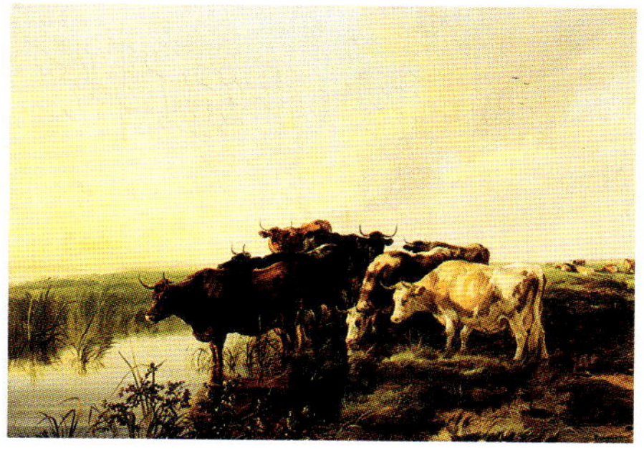

Cooper, Thomas Sidney 1803–1902
In the Whitehall Meadows, Canterbury, Kent 1854
oil on canvas 63.7 x 88.9
VIS.1545

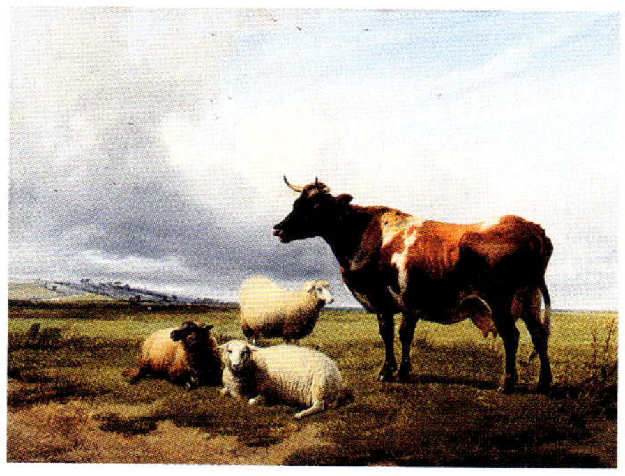

Cooper, Thomas Sidney 1803–1902
Morning, Canterbury Meadows, Kent 1869
oil on millboard 29.8 x 38
VIS.2407

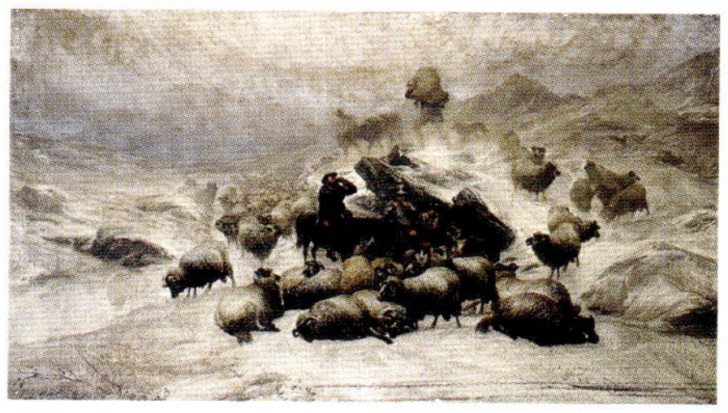

Cooper, Thomas Sidney 1803–1902
Amongst the Fells, East Cumberland 1871
oil on canvas 121.5 x 213.4
VIS.1456

Facing page: Burgin, Victor, b.1941, *Escalator* (detail), Museums Sheffield, (p. 33)

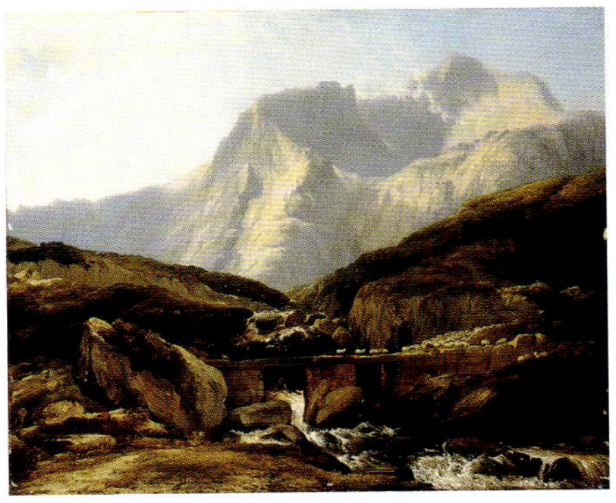

Cooper, Thomas Sidney 1803–1902 & **Lee, Frederick Richard** 1798–1879
Landscape, Sheep Crossing a Bridge 1849
oil on canvas 64.8 x 77.5
VIS.1577

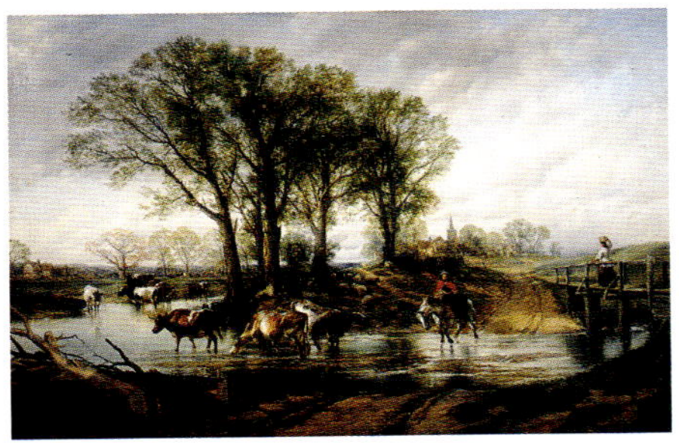

Cooper, Thomas Sidney 1803–1902, **Creswick, Thomas** 1811–1869 & **Frith, William Powell** 1819–1909
Landscape with Cattle
oil on canvas 123.8 x 182.8
VIS.1477

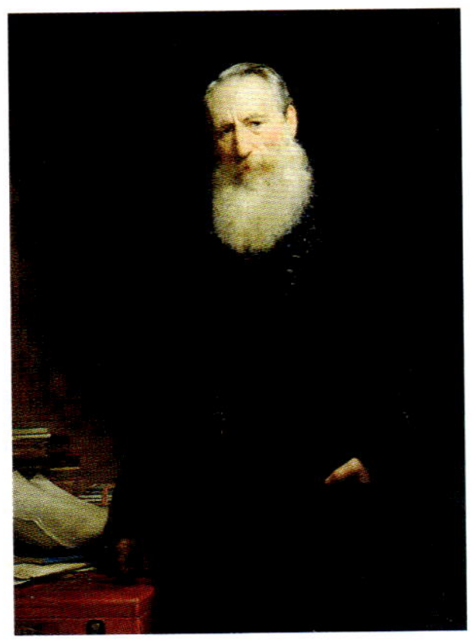

Cope, Arthur Stockdale 1857–1940
The Right Honourable Anthony John Mundella (1825–1897), MP 1894
oil on canvas 126.9 x 89.6
VIS.LI.820 (P)

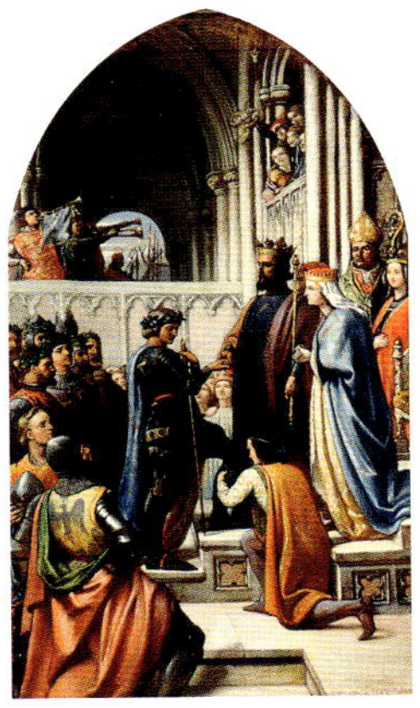

Cope, Charles West 1811–1890
Edward III Conferring the Order of the Garter on Edward the Black Prince 1847
oil on canvas 81.5 x 46.7
VIS.3799

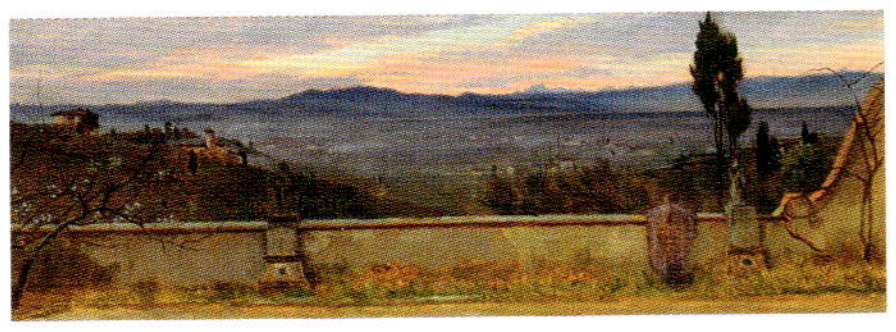

Corbet, Matthew Ridley 1850–1902
Landscape Study for 'Val d'Arno, Italy, Evening' 1897
oil on canvas 11.3 x 31.3
VIS.4232

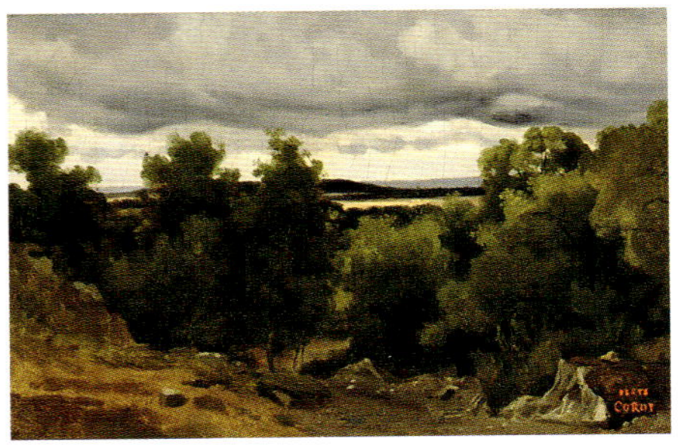

Corot, Jean-Baptiste-Camille 1796–1875
Au Petit Chaville 1835–1840
oil on canvas 20.9 x 31.5
VIS.1665

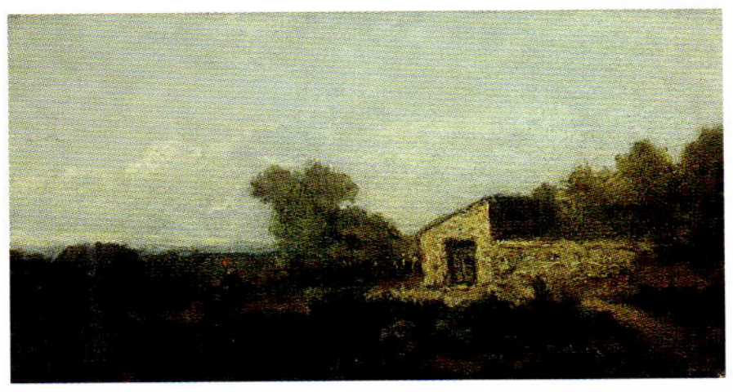

Corot, Jean-Baptiste-Camille (attributed to) 1796–1875
Landscape and Farm Buildings 1860–1870
oil on panel 16.5 x 32.3
VIS.1076

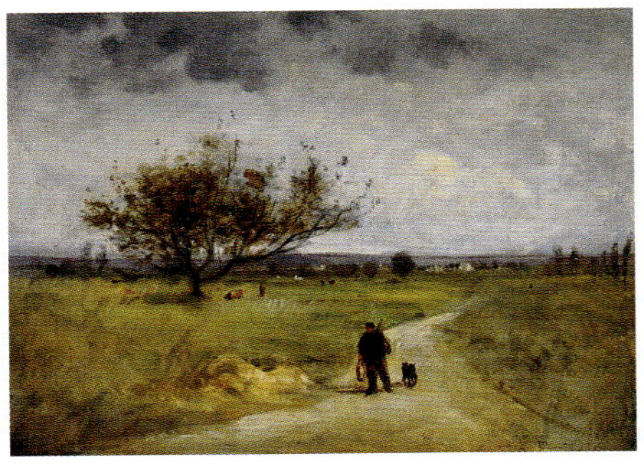

Corot, Jean-Baptiste-Camille (attributed to) 1796–1875
Landscape
oil on canvas 29 x 39.5
VIS.534

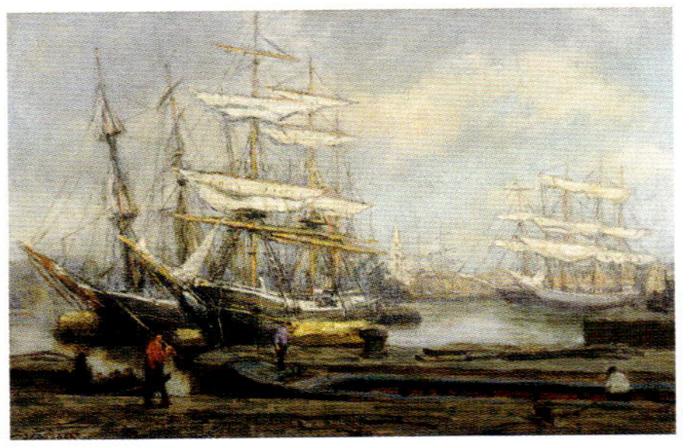

Cossaar, Jacobus Cornelis Wyand 1874–1966
Rotterdam Boats
oil on canvas 39.8 x 59.7
VIS.623

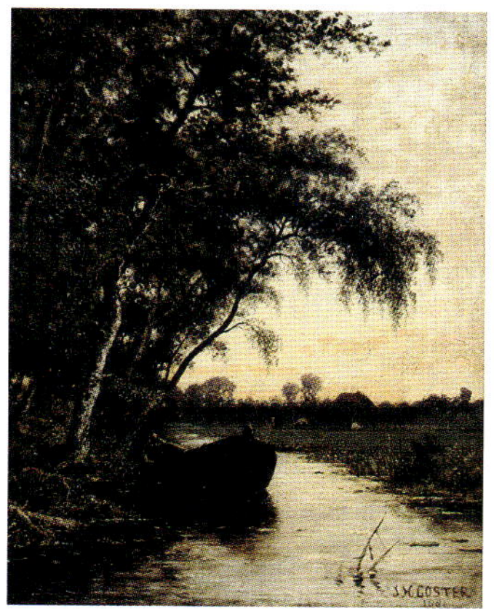

Coster, Jan Herman 1846–1920
River Scene 1881
oil on canvas 39.8 x 31.5
VIS.1358

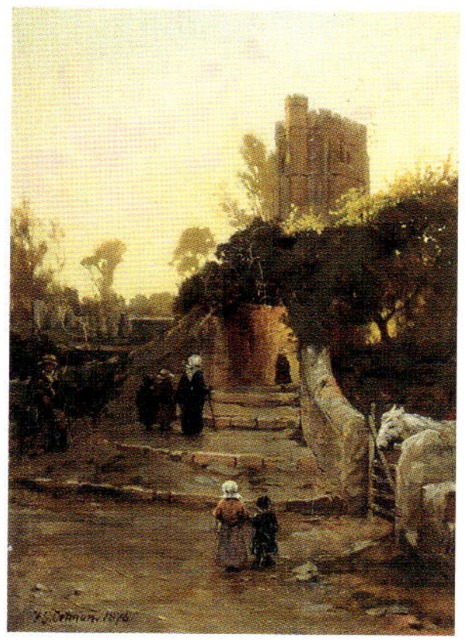

Cotman, Frederick George 1850–1920
Sunday Morning 1876
oil on canvas 34.3 x 23.8
VIS.1211

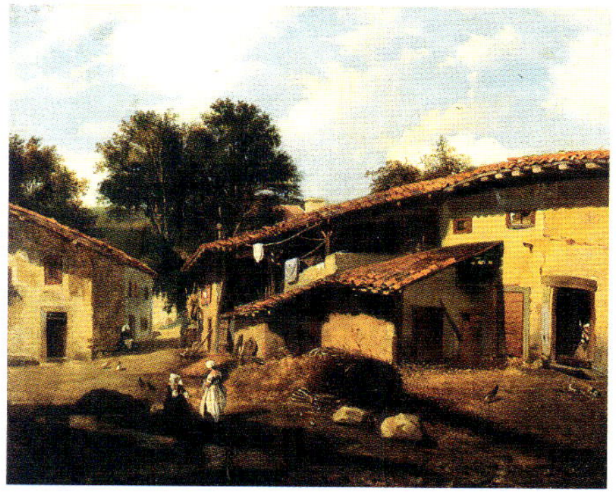

Cotman, John Sell 1782–1842
Village in Normandy, France, Noon
1817–1820
oil on canvas 53.2 x 63.2
VIS.325

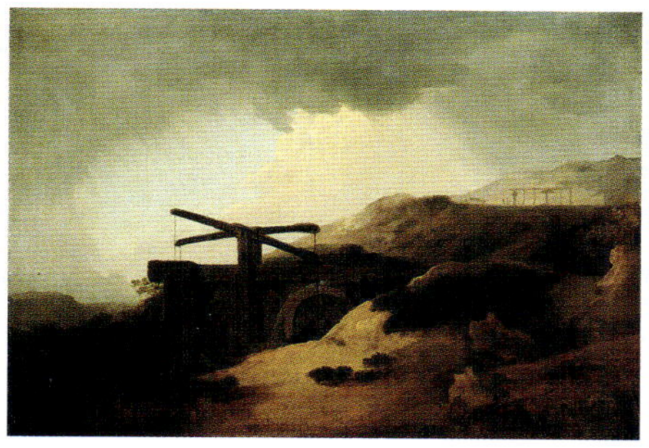

Cotman, John Sell (attributed to)
1782–1842
Consett Iron Works, Durham 1800–1810
oil on canvas 35.7 x 50.5
VIS.292

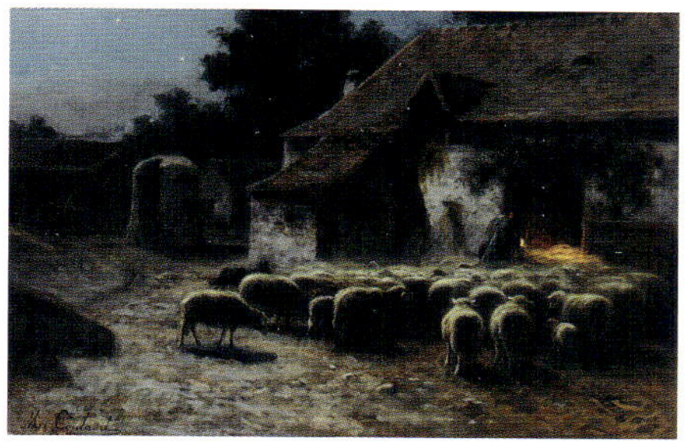

Coulaud, Martin d.1906
Returning to the Fold
oil on canvas 48 x 71.5
VIS.1340

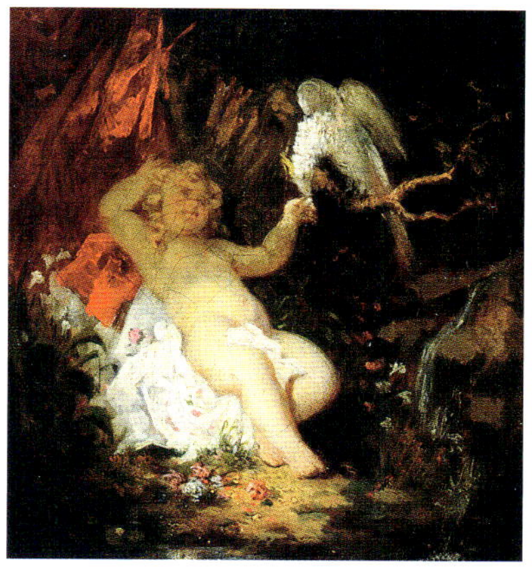

Courbet, Gustave 1819–1877
Boy with a Parrot
oil on canvas 27.7 x 25.2
VIS.295

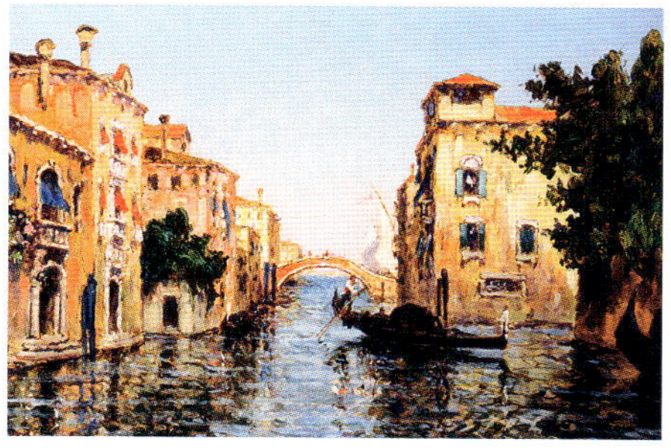

Cousin, Charles-Louis-Auguste 1807–1887
A Venetian Byway
oil on canvas 36.6 x 54.2
VIS.2894

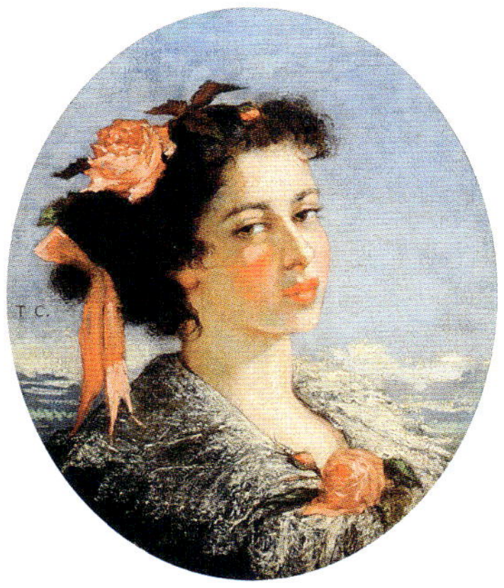

Couture, Thomas (attributed to) 1815–1879
A Portrait Study
oil on canvas 48.7 x 41
VIS.1219

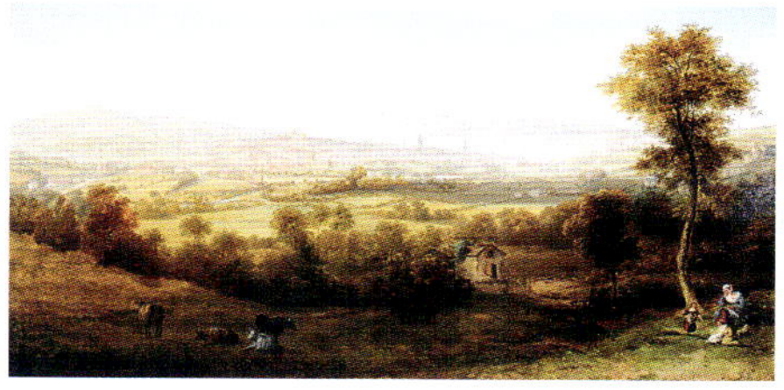

Cowen, William 1791–1864
View of Sheffield from Meersbrook 1836
oil on canvas 91.2 x 181.2
K86.27

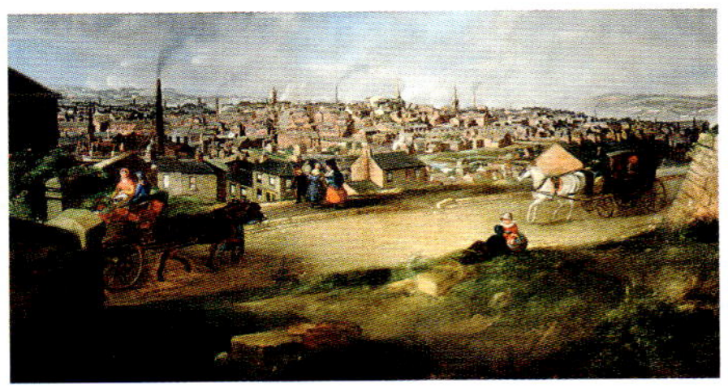

Cowen, William 1791–1864
View of Sheffield from Shrewsbury Road c.1838
oil on canvas 101 x 183
K1952.1

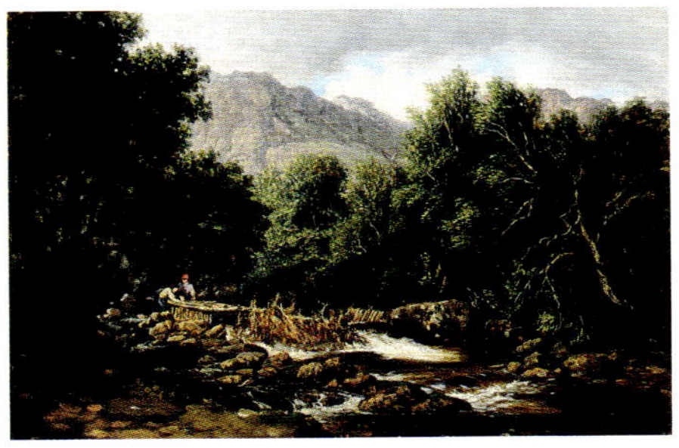

Cox, David the elder 1783–1859
On the Lledr, North Wales 1841–1846
oil on canvas 34.8 x 50.8
VIS.2270

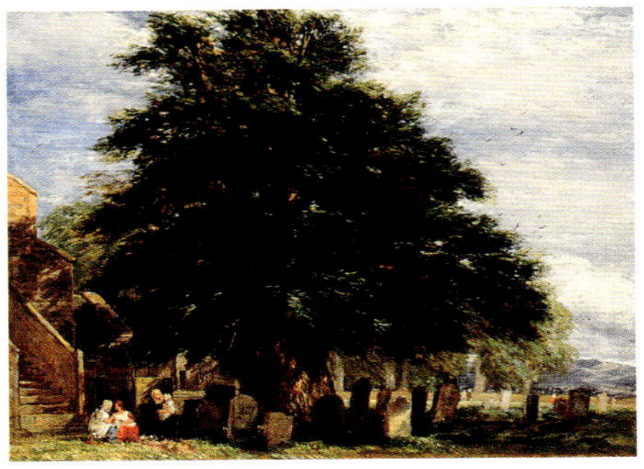

Cox, David the elder 1783–1859
Darley Churchyard, Derbyshire 1850
oil on canvas 45.1 x 60.9
VIS.311

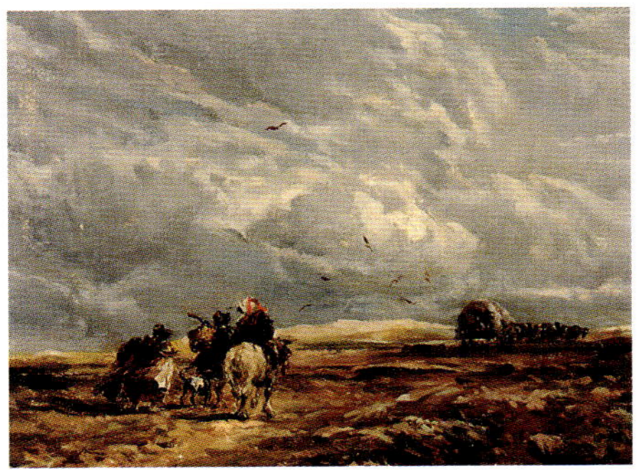

Cox, David the elder 1783–1859
Crossing the Heath
oil on canvas 17 x 22.3
VIS.551

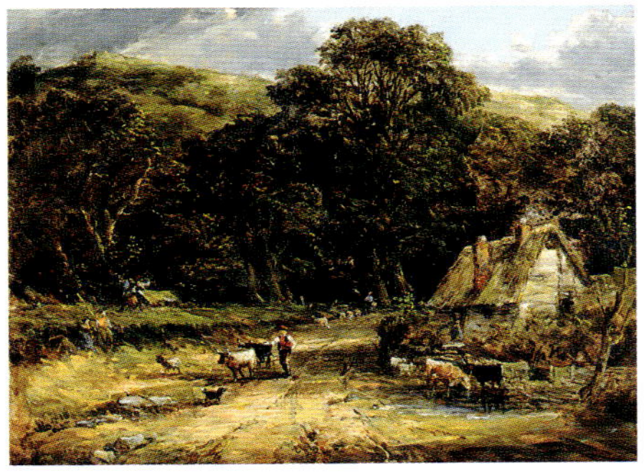

Cox, David the elder 1783–1859
Landscape
oil on canvas 35.9 x 46.6
VIS.1540

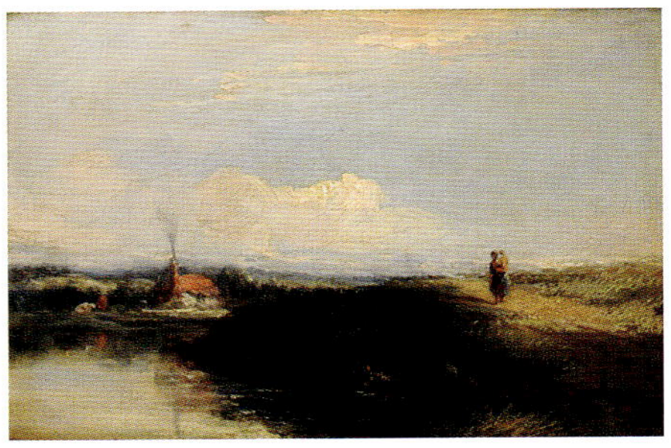

Cox, David the elder 1783–1859
Riverside Path
oil on canvas 19.7 x 30
VIS.185

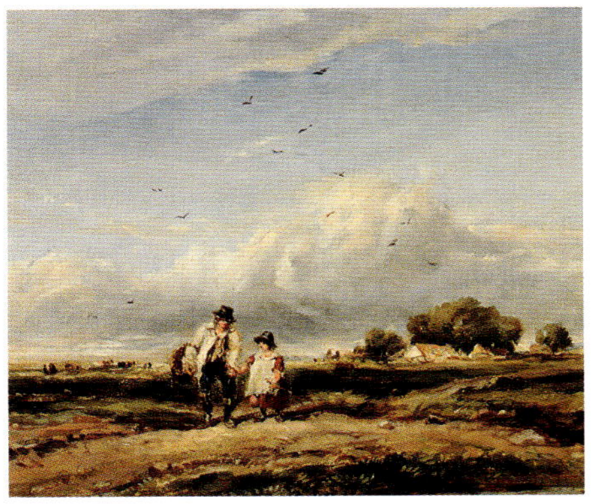

Cox, David the elder 1783–1859
The Wayfarers
oil on canvas 18.8 x 21.7
VIS.541

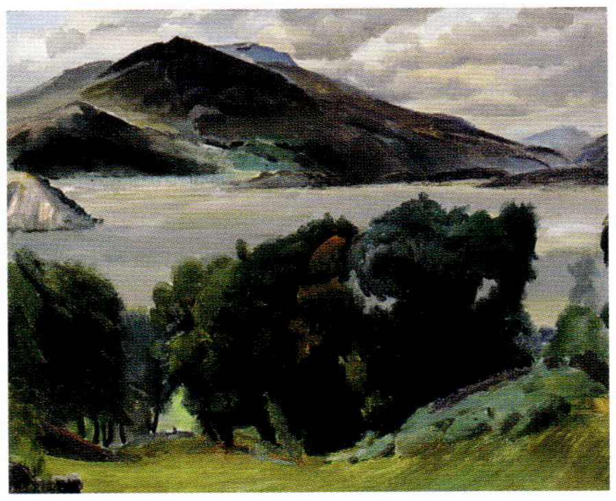

Coxon, Raymond James 1896–1997
Near Portmadoc, Wales
oil on canvas 62.5 x 75.1
VIS.2943

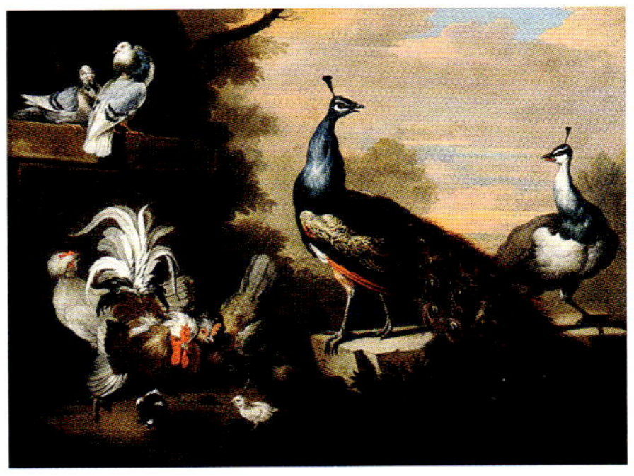

Cradock, Marmaduke (after) c.1660–1717
Peacocks and Poultry
oil on canvas 105 x 137
VIS.1993

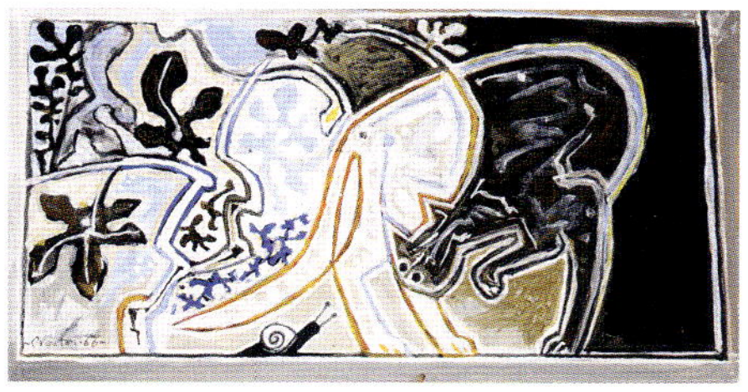

Craxton, John 1922–2009
Cat and Snail 1966
tempera on board 20.9 x 39
VIS.4290

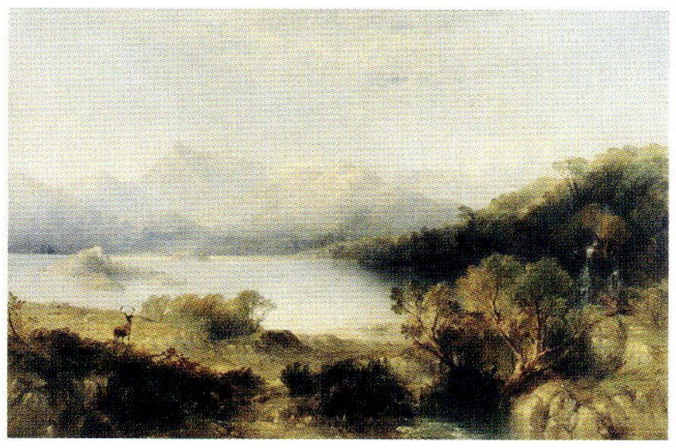

Creswick, Thomas 1811–1869
Glengarriff, County Cork, Ireland 1837
oil on canvas 64.2 x 94.3
VIS.1425

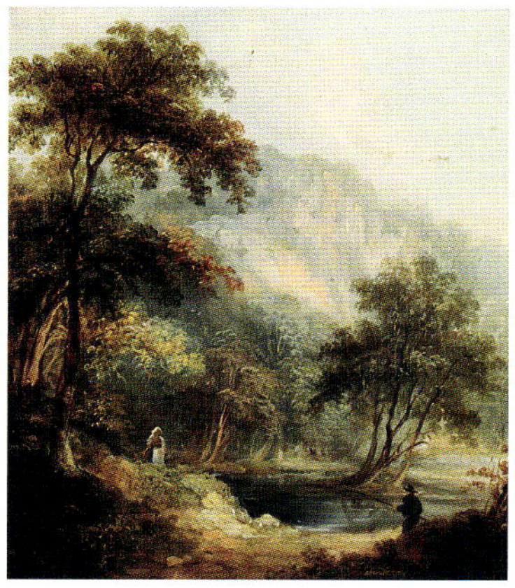

Creswick, Thomas 1811–1869
High Tor, Matlock, Derbyshire 1841
oil on millboard 25.4 x 21.6
VIS.103

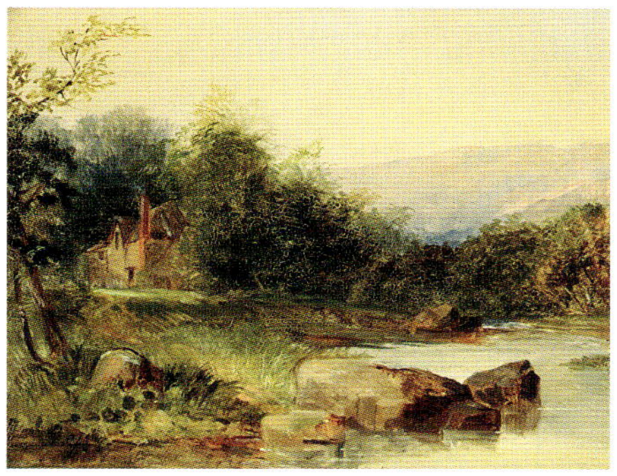

Creswick, Thomas 1811–1869
Landscape, River Scene 1860
oil on millboard 19.1 x 24
VIS.1958

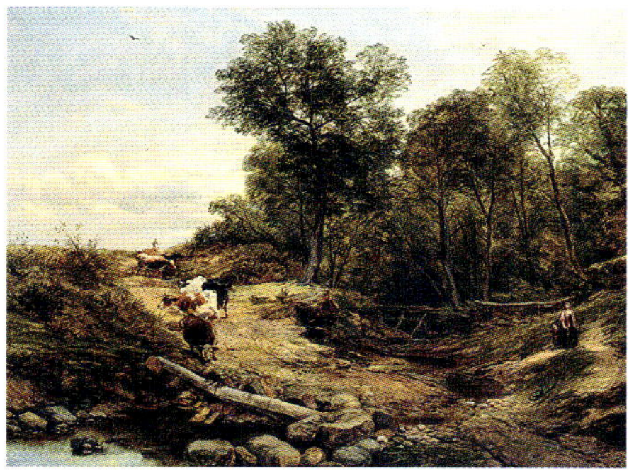

Creswick, Thomas 1811–1869
A Mill Stream in Eskdale, Cumbria 1865
oil on canvas 71 x 94
VIS.1552

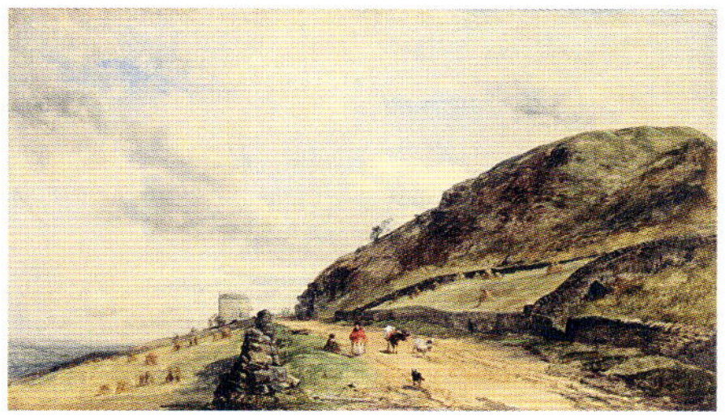

Creswick, Thomas 1811–1869
A Road near Sheffield
oil on canvas 21 x 35.5
VIS.102

Creswick, Thomas 1811–1869
A Welsh Landscape
oil on canvas 29.4
VIS.549

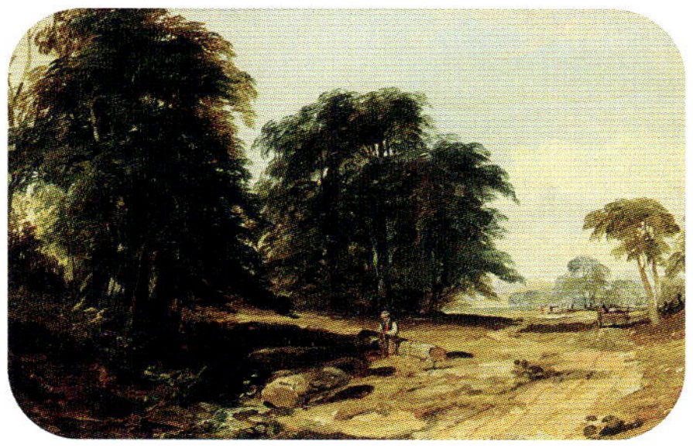

Creswick, Thomas 1811–1869
Across the Common
oil on panel 29.3 x 45.7
VIS.92

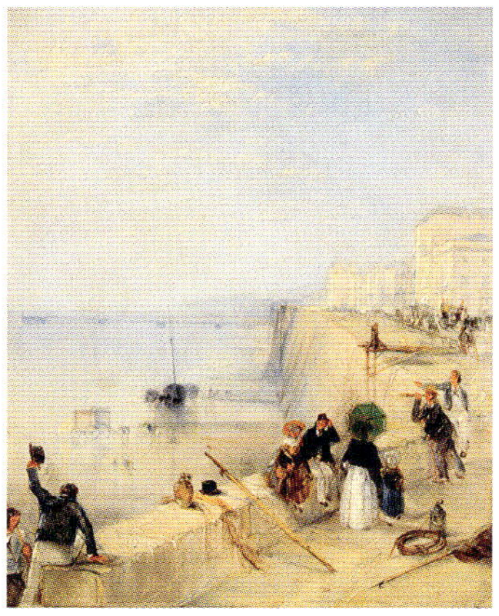

Creswick, Thomas 1811–1869
Brighton Pier, East Sussex
oil on panel 20.7 x 16.9
VIS.2928

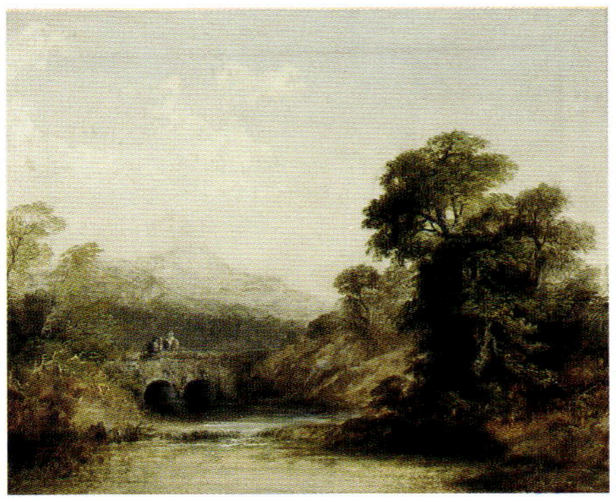

Creswick, Thomas 1811–1869
Cumberland
oil on canvas 23.5 x 28.5
VIS.113

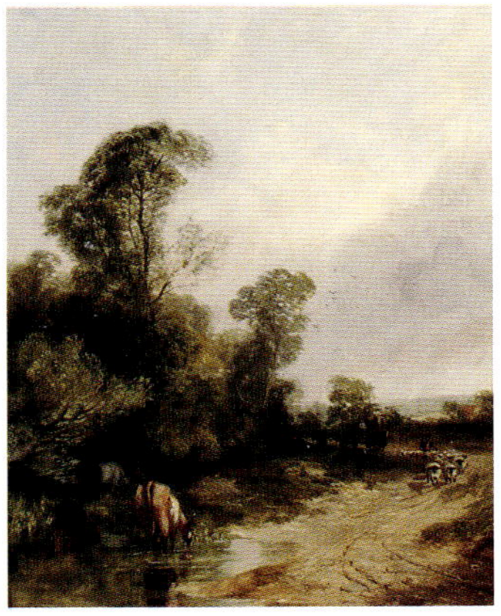

Creswick, Thomas 1811–1869
Hillsborough, Sheffield
oil on panel 24.2 x 19.2
VIS.107

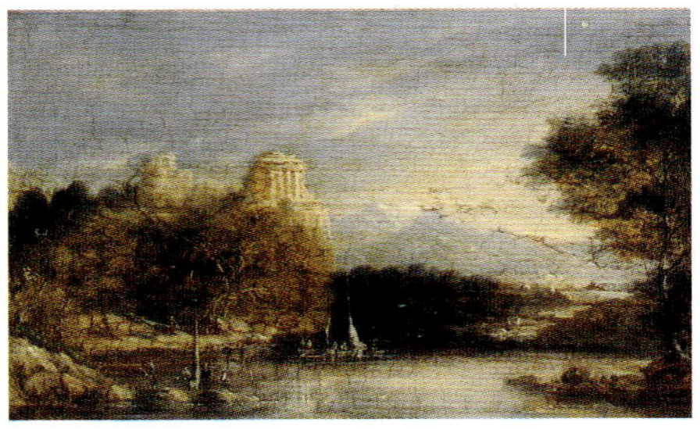

Creswick, Thomas 1811–1869
Italian Landscape
oil on panel 24.2 x 38.6
VIS.99

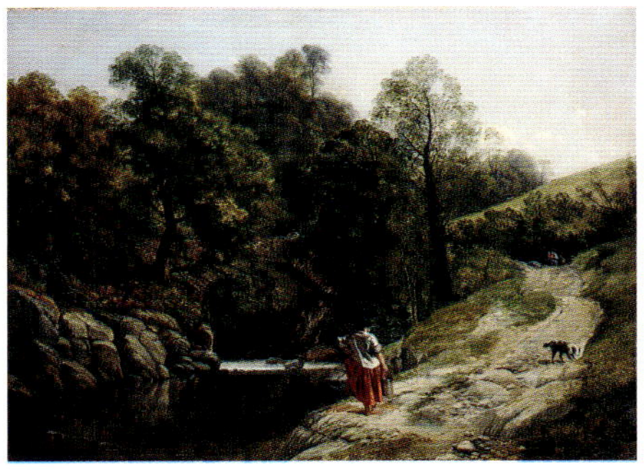

Creswick, Thomas 1811–1869
Landscape
oil on canvas 53 x 70.6
VIS.1560

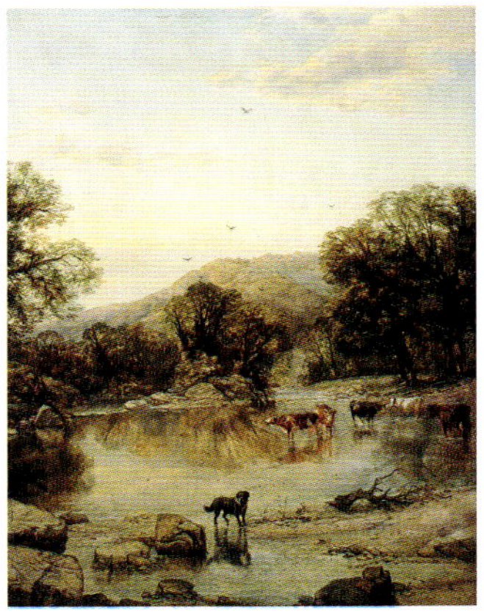

Creswick, Thomas 1811–1869
Landscape with Cattle
oil on canvas 122 x 91.3
VIS.1315

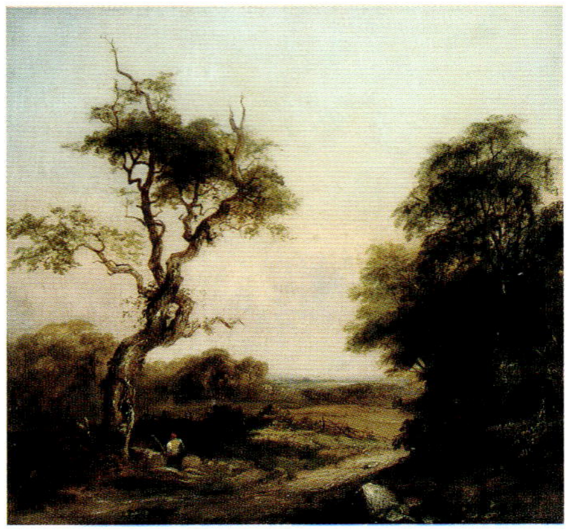

Creswick, Thomas 1811–1869
Landscape with Trees
oil on canvas 35.5 x 36.5
VIS.98

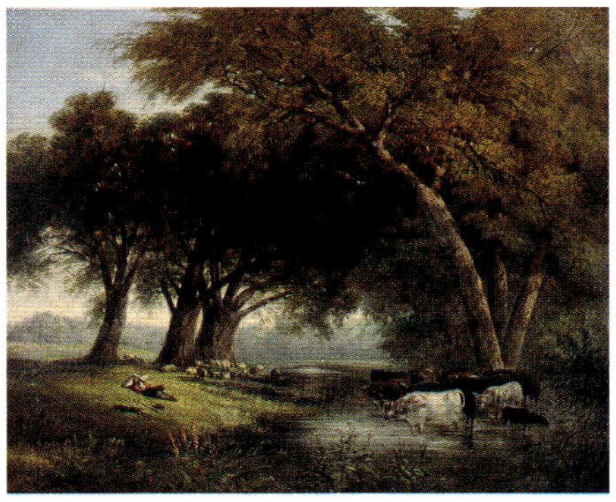

Creswick, Thomas 1811–1869
Near Ashover, Derbyshire
oil on panel 61.6 x 74.2
VIS.96

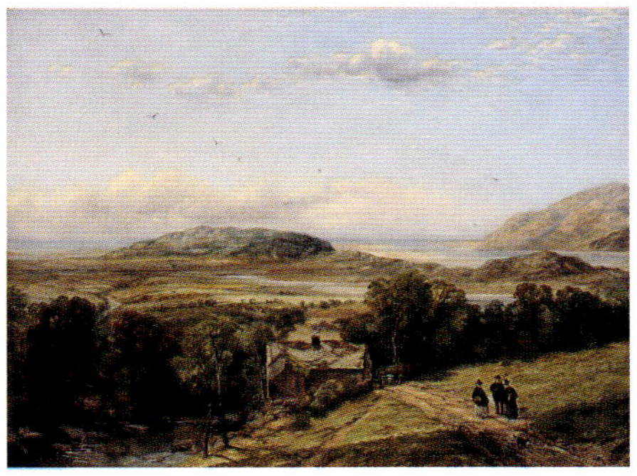

Creswick, Thomas 1811–1869
Near Barmouth, Wales
oil on canvas 52.5 x 70.2
VIS.109

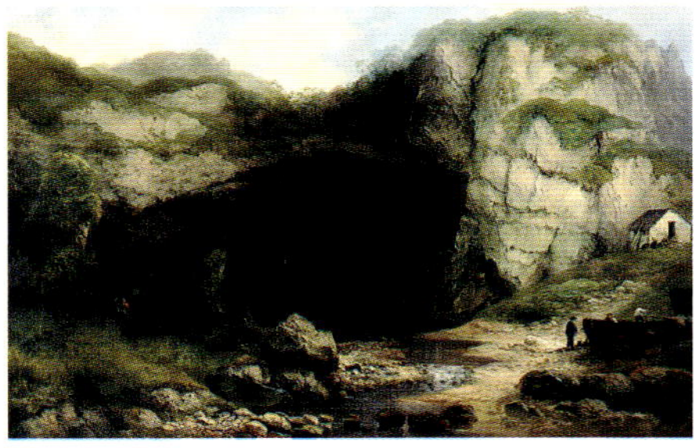

Creswick, Thomas 1811–1869
Smoo Cave, Sutherland, Scotland
oil on canvas 59.7 x 90
VIS.97

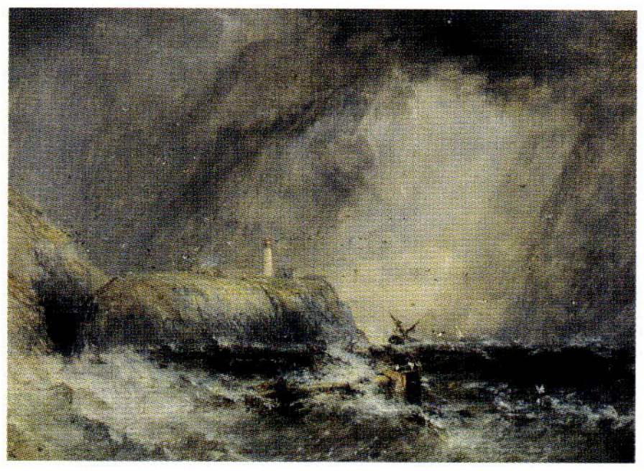

Creswick, Thomas 1811–1869
South Stack Lighthouse, Holyhead, Wales
oil on canvas 29.4 x 39.8
VIS.1544

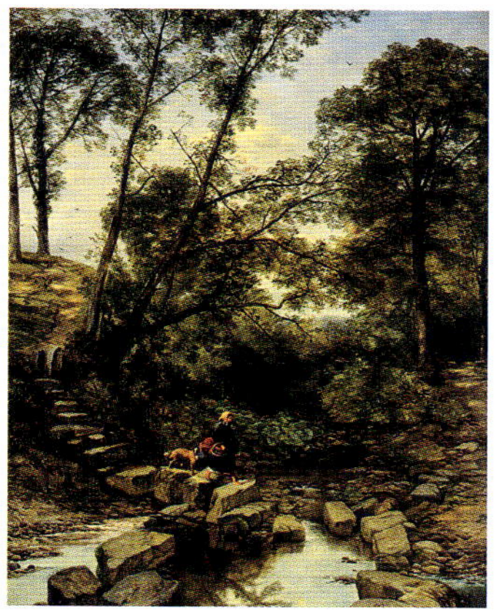

Creswick, Thomas 1811–1869
Stepping Stones
oil on canvas 91.8 x 71
VIS.1996

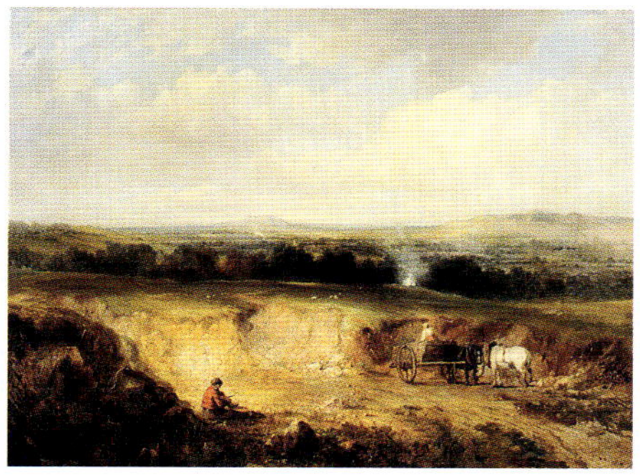

Creswick, Thomas 1811–1869
Surrey Sandhills
oil on canvas 69.7 x 91.5
VIS.1661

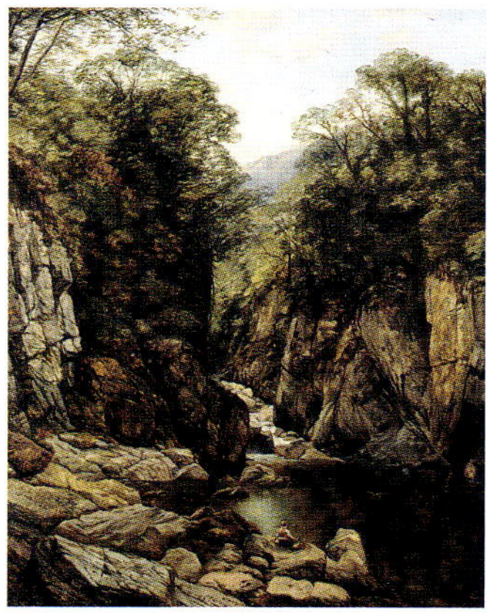

Creswick, Thomas 1811–1869
The Fairy Glen, Betws-y-Coed, Wales
oil on canvas 90.6 x 70.2
VIS.114

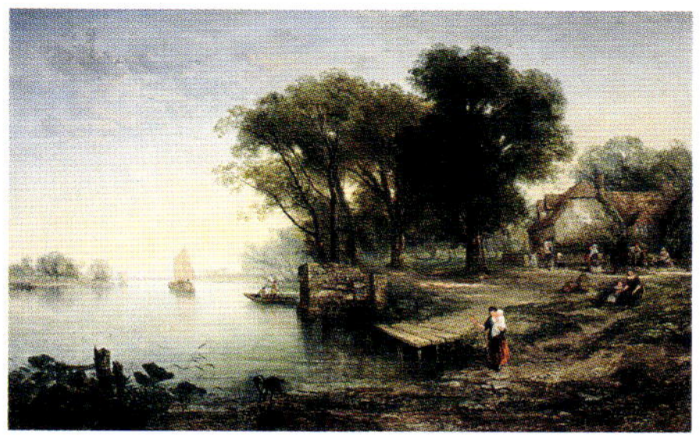

Creswick, Thomas 1811–1869
The Ferry
oil on canvas 120.7 x 182.8
VIS.105

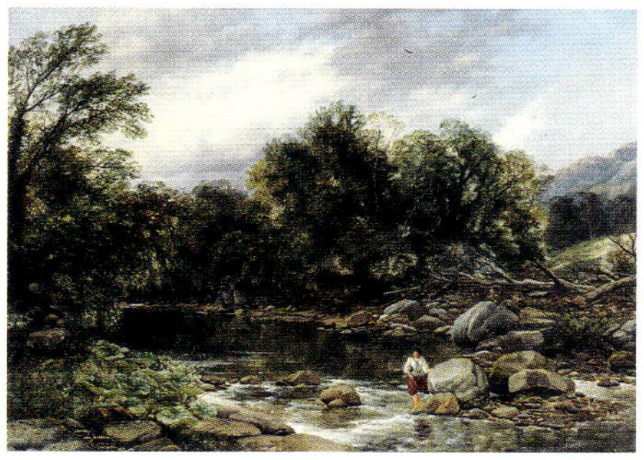

Creswick, Thomas 1811–1869
The Ford
oil on canvas 50.2 x 67.1
VIS.2718

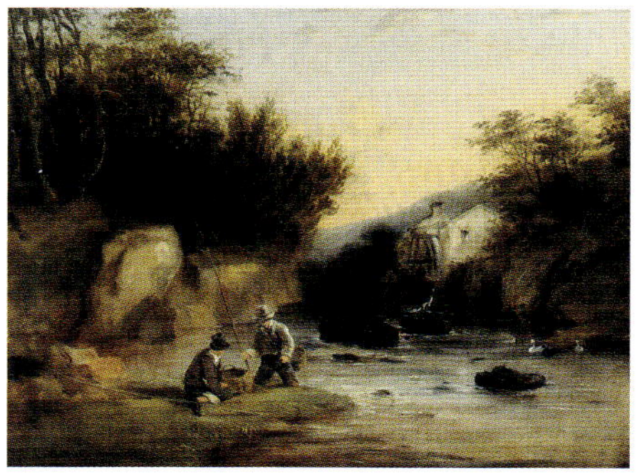

Creswick, Thomas 1811–1869
The Millstream
oil on canvas 29.4 x 38.5
VIS.93

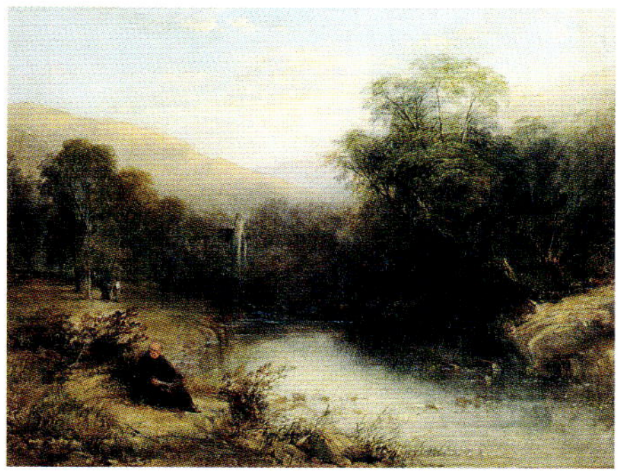

Creswick, Thomas 1811–1869
The Priory
oil on panel 34.7 x 43.4
VIS.115

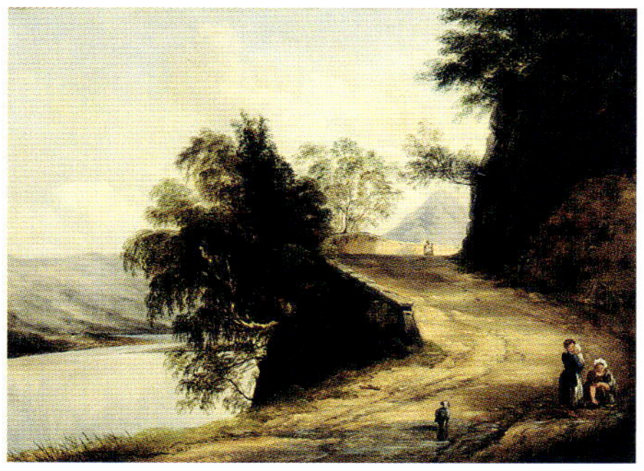

Creswick, Thomas 1811–1869
The River Road
oil on canvas 28.5 x 38.5
VIS.2740

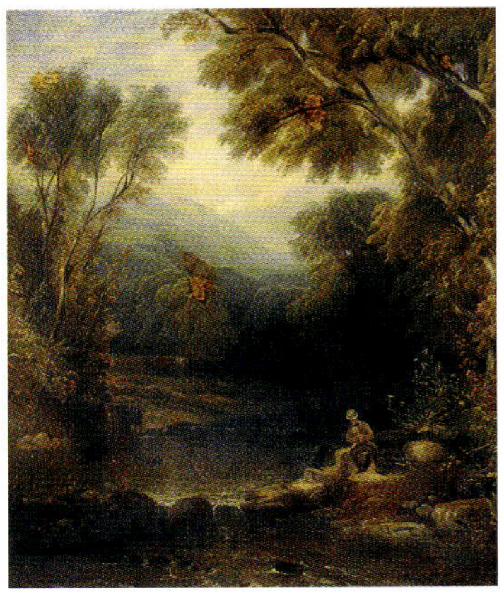

Creswick, Thomas 1811–1869
The Trout Stream
oil on canvas 74 x 61.8
VIS.94

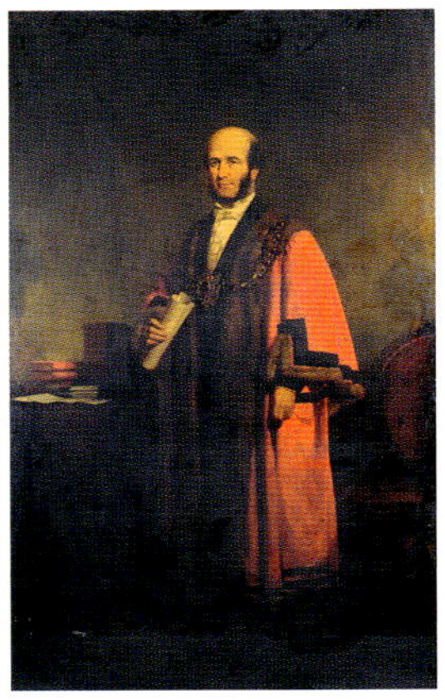

Crighton, Hugh Ford 1824–1886
Thomas Moore (1809–1880), Mayor of Sheffield (1868–1871) 1868–1871
oil on canvas 239.4 x 147.5
VIS.LI.835 (P)

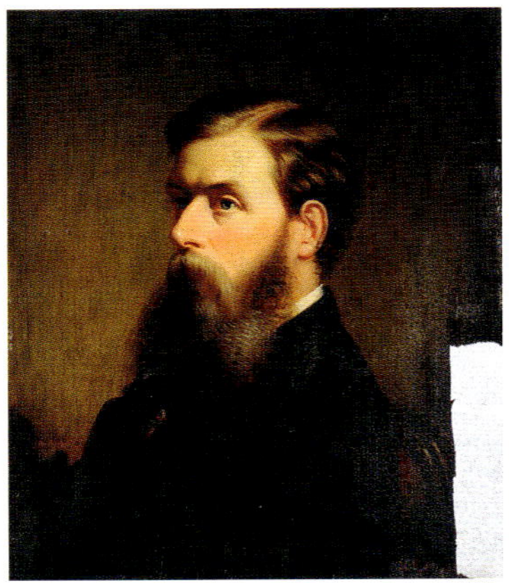

Crighton, Hugh Ford 1824–1886
Henry Seebohm (1832–1895) 1869
oil on canvas 61.3 x 50.8
K1945.1

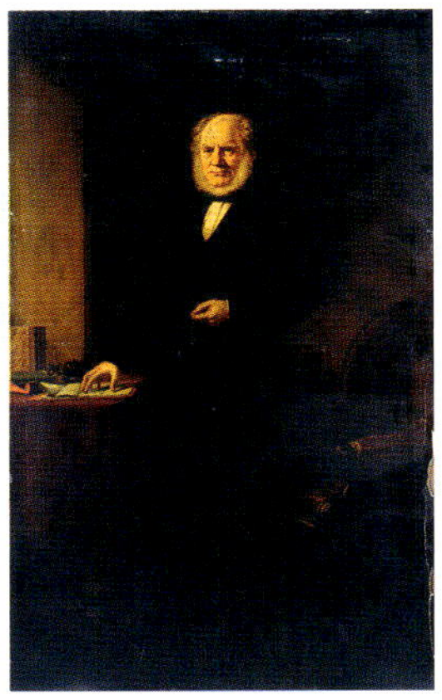

Crighton, Hugh Ford 1824–1886
Thomas Jessop (1804–1887), JP, Mayor of Sheffield (1863–1864) 1875
oil on canvas 240.9 x 148
VIS.LI.830 (P)

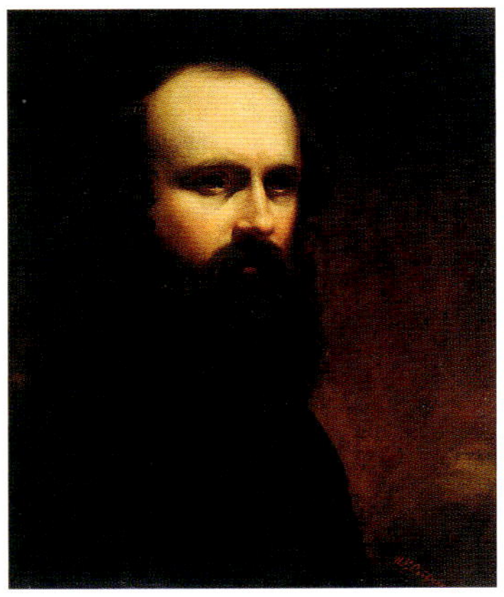

Crighton, Hugh Ford 1824–1886
Self Portrait
oil on canvas 57.4 x 48
K1910.1

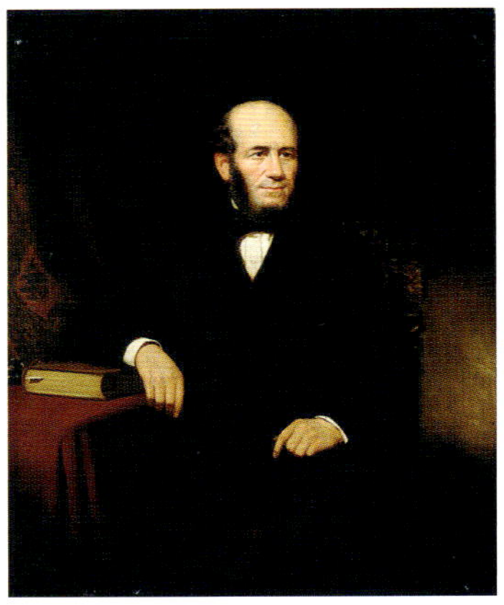

Crighton, Hugh Ford 1824–1886
Thomas Moore (1809–1880), Mayor of Sheffield (1868–1871)
oil on canvas 127.4 x 102.2
VIS.LI.824 (P)

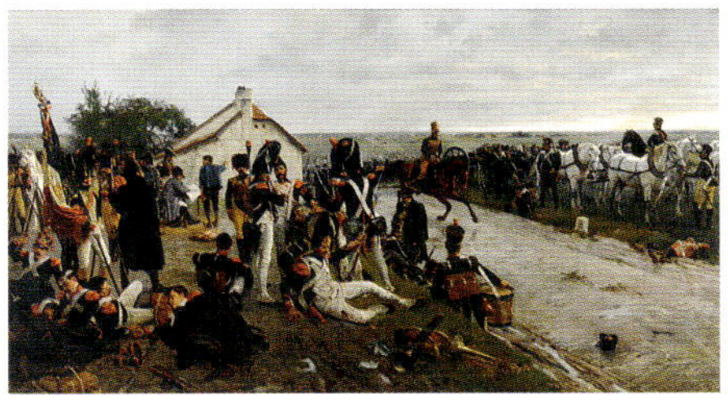

Crofts, Ernest 1847–1911
The Morning of the Battle of Waterloo 1876
oil on canvas 99.3 x 177.8
VIS.1615

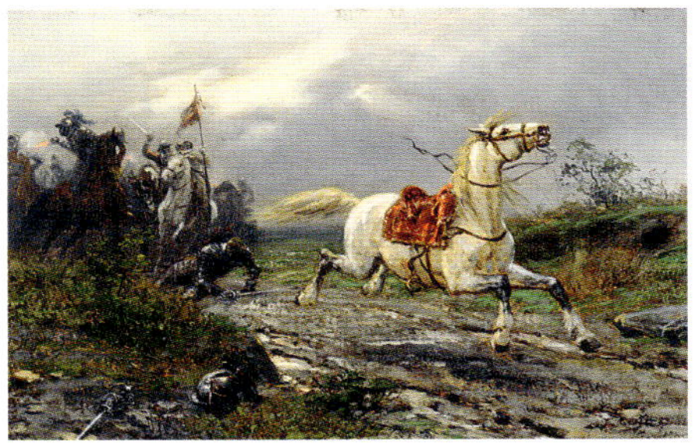

Crofts, Ernest 1847–1911
The Empty Saddle 1882
oil on canvas 22.3 x 34.1
VIS.1387

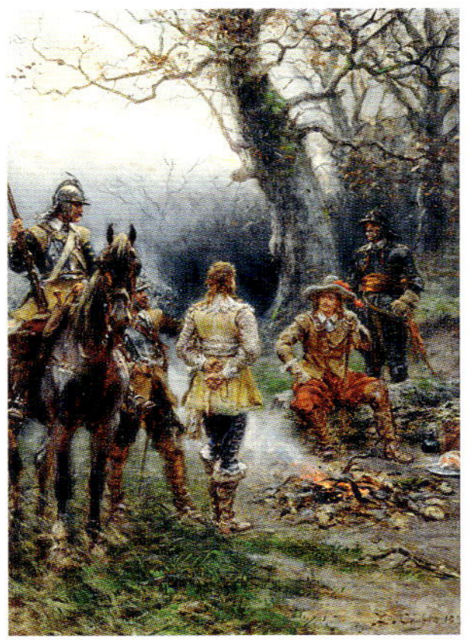

Crofts, Ernest 1847–1911
Cromwell Questioning a Prisoner 1895
oil on canvas 43.8 x 31.4
VIS.1961

Facing page: Müller, Alfredo, 1869–1940, *Ruins* (detail), 1913, Museums Sheffield, (p. 147)

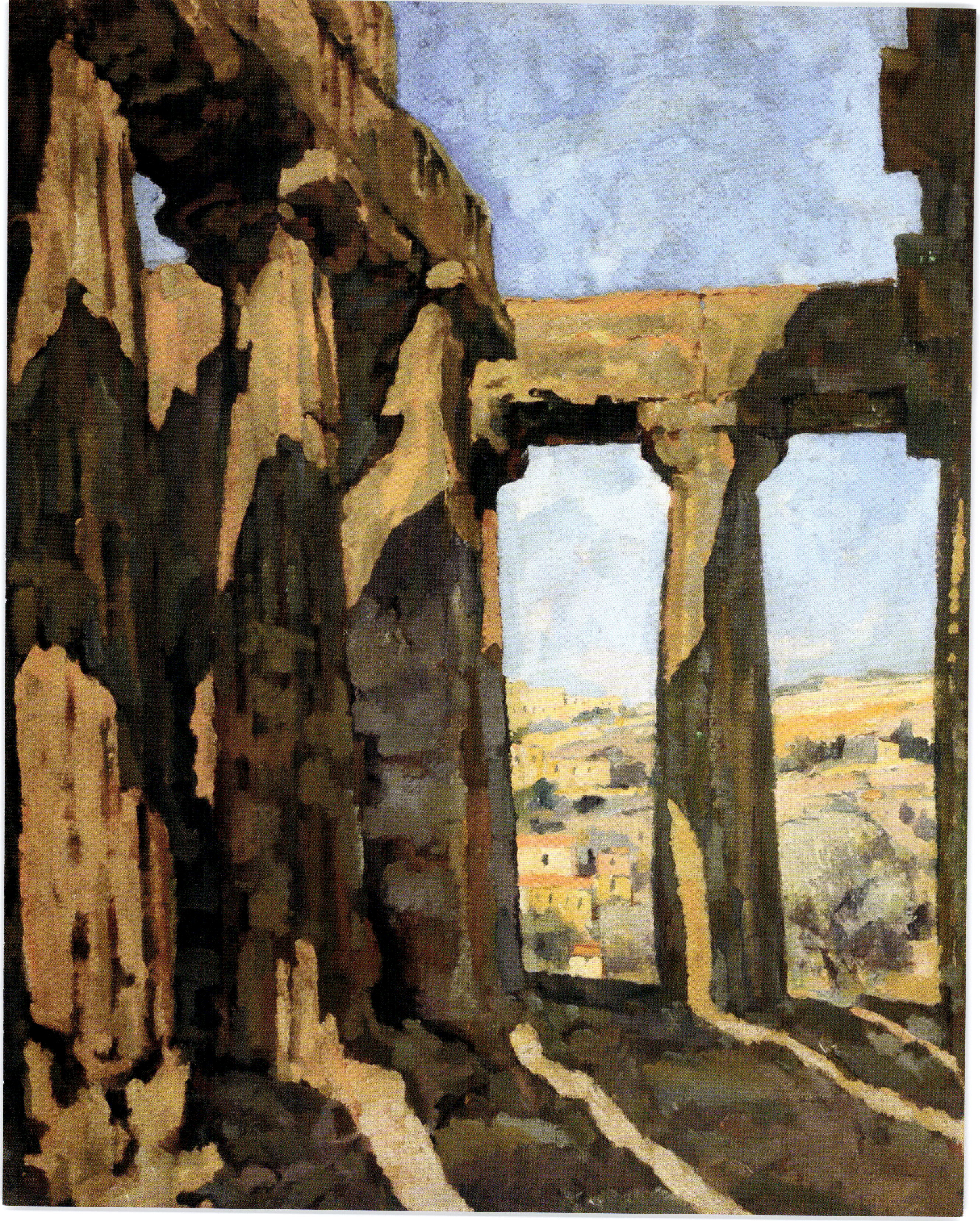

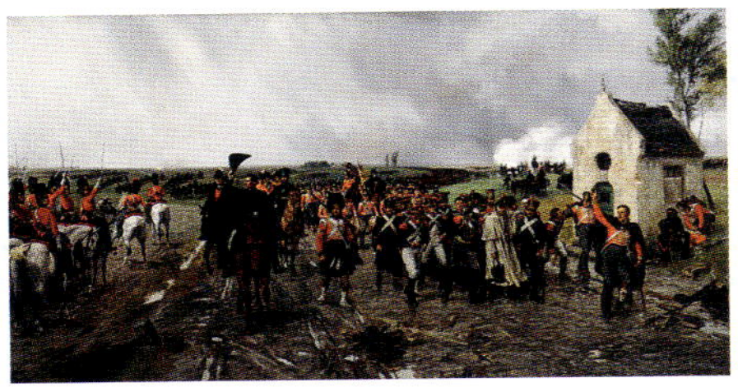

Crofts, Ernest 1847–1911
Wellington's March from Quatre Bras to Waterloo
oil on canvas 104 x 194
VIS.1614

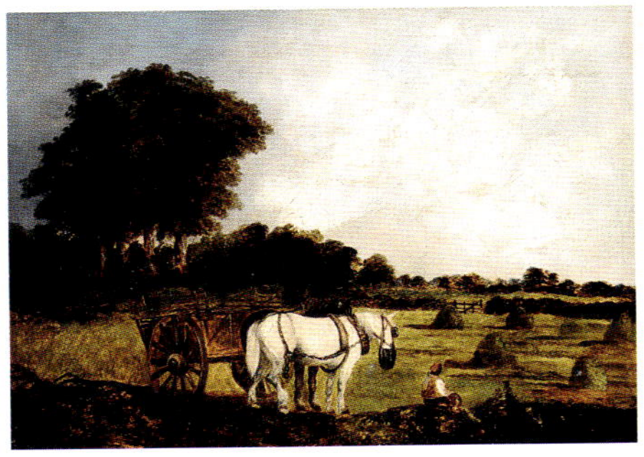

Crome, John 1768–1821
A Harvest
oil on canvas 50.5 x 68.8
VIS.516

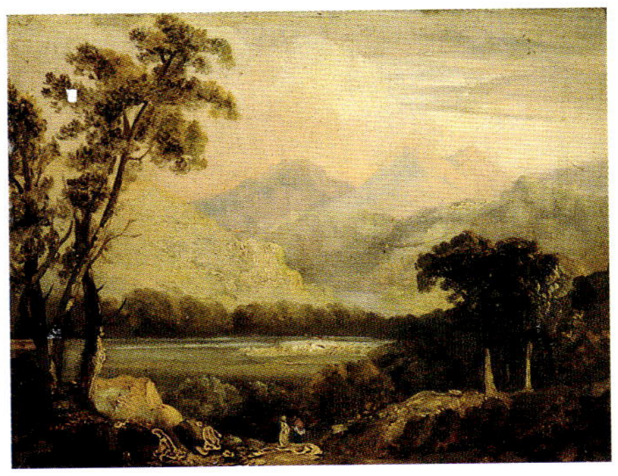

Crome, John 1768–1821
Landscape with a River
oil on millboard 21 x 27.2
VIS.1067

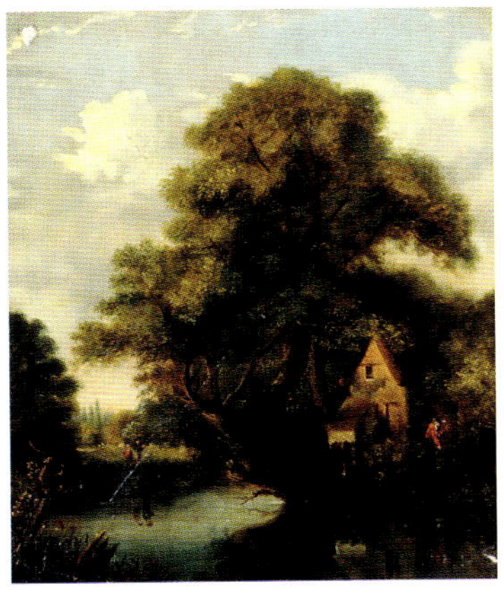

Crome, John 1768–1821
Near St Martin, Norfolk
oil on canvas 73.9 x 61.1
VIS.1852

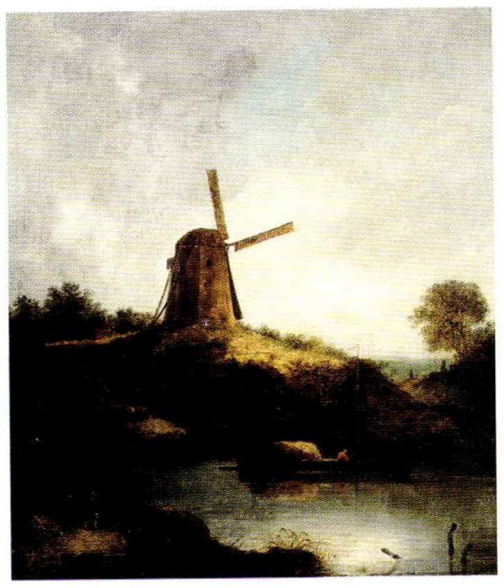

Crome, John 1768–1821
The Windmill
oil on canvas 74.4 x 61.5
VIS.1522

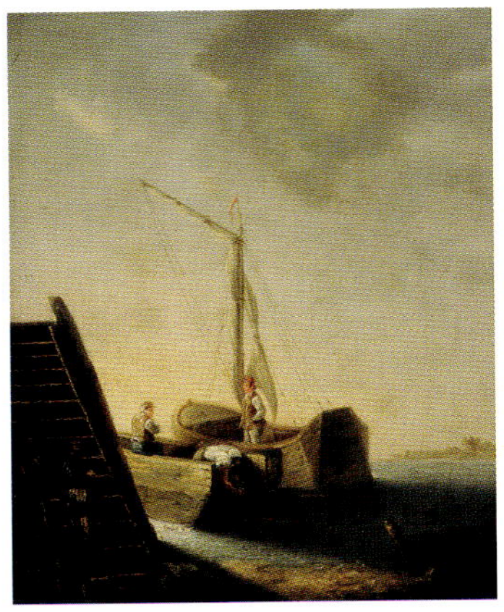

Crome, John Berney 1794–1842
Barges by a Jetty
oil on canvas 45.6 x 36.9
VIS.240

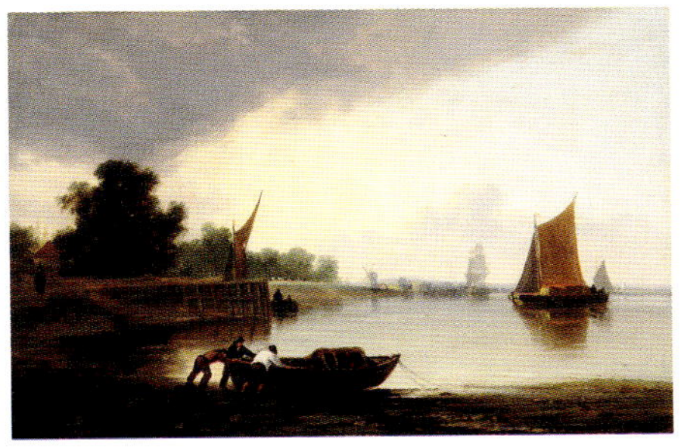

Crome, John Berney 1794–1842
On the Yare, Norfolk
oil on panel 29.7 x 44.8
VIS.324

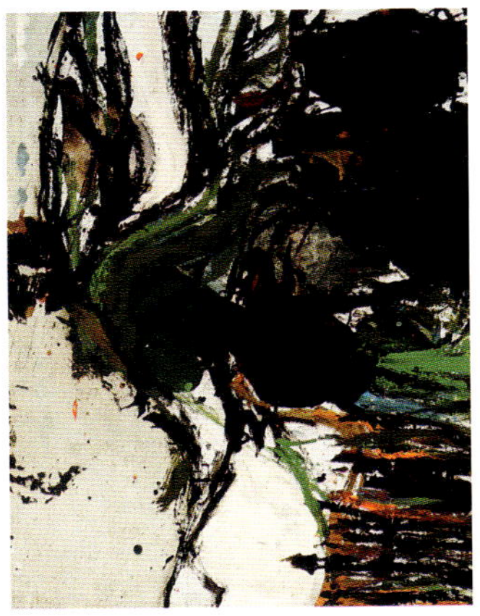

Crozier, William 1930–2011
Putney Heath, London c.1958
oil on woodboard 60.2 x 45.5
VIS.3318

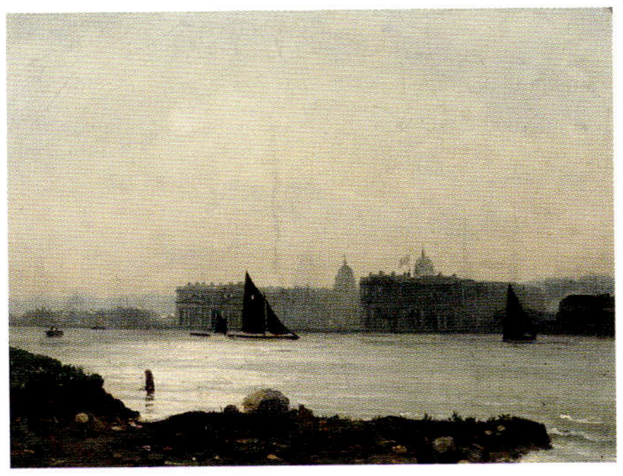

Danby, Francis 1793–1861
A Misty Spring Morning
oil on canvas 20 x 26.2
VIS.1037

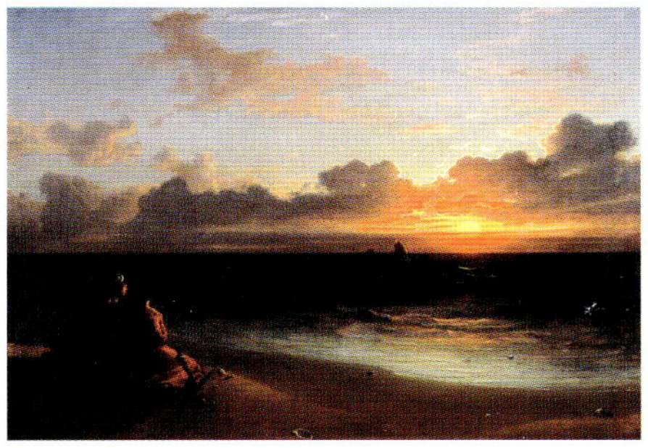

Danby, Francis 1793–1861
Sunset
oil on canvas 73.5 x 103.8
VIS.2583

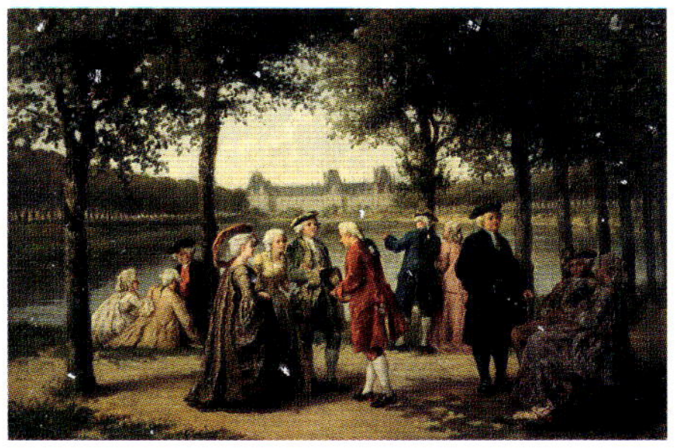

Dansaert, Léon Marie Constant 1830–1909
The Promenade of Versailles in the Time of Louis XV
oil on panel 40 x 58.7
VIS.1397

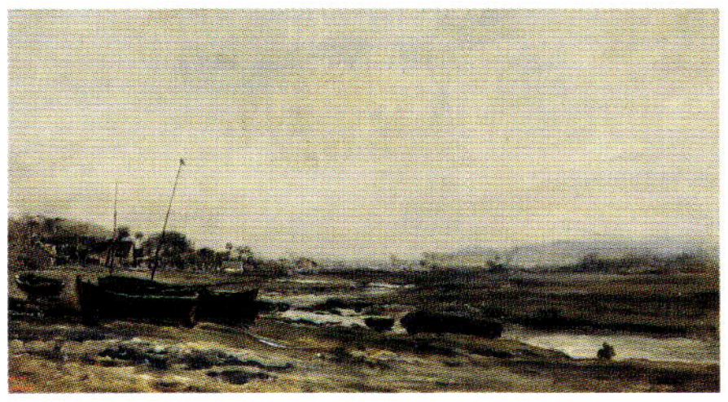

Daubigny, Charles-François 1817–1878
Fishing Boats by a Stream 1870–1878
oil on panel 37.1 x 65.4
VIS.332

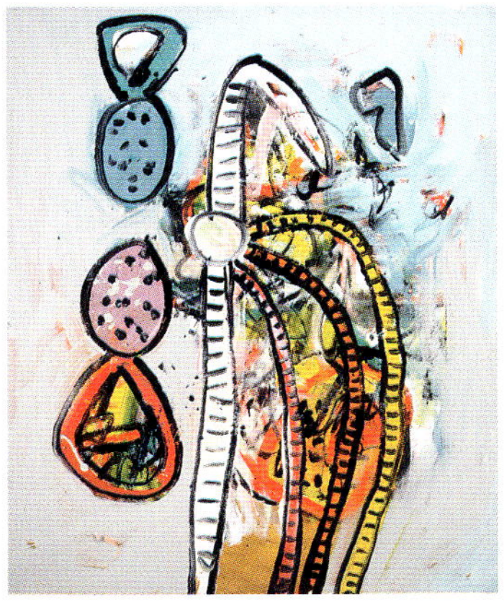

Davie, Alan b.1920
Tree into Animal No.1 1962
oil on canvas 152.7 x 121.7
VIS.4701

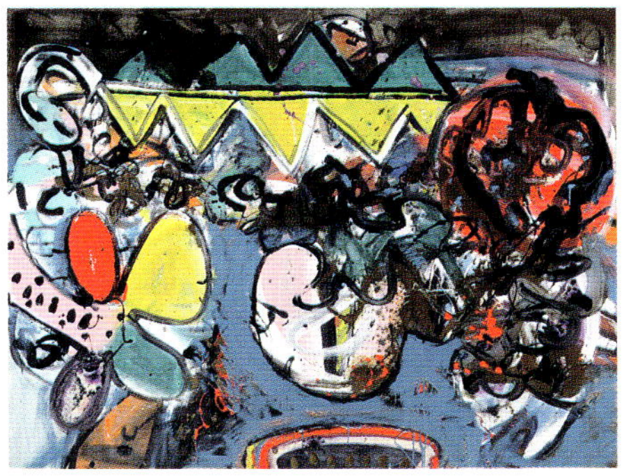

Davie, Alan b.1920
Prize for a Serpent
oil on canvas 122 x 152.7
VIS.5304

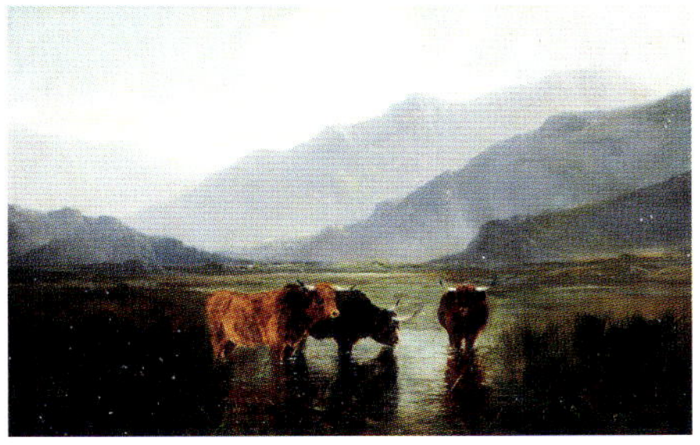

Davis, Henry William Banks 1833–1914
Landscape with Cattle 1872
oil on canvas 58.2 x 88.5
VIS.2419

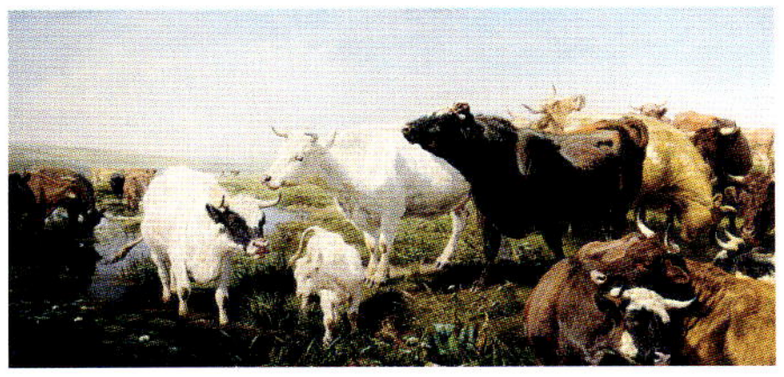

Davis, Henry William Banks 1833–1914
A Summer Afternoon c.1873
oil on canvas 117 x 237
VIS.1481

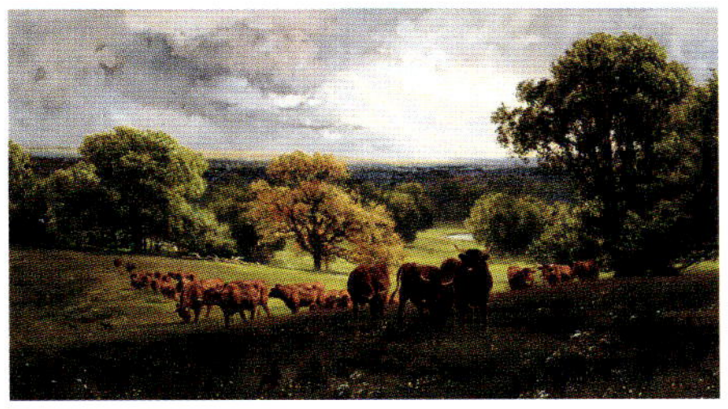

Davis, Henry William Banks 1833–1914
Landscape in Wiltshire 1875
oil on canvas 36.5 x 64.7
VIS.1375

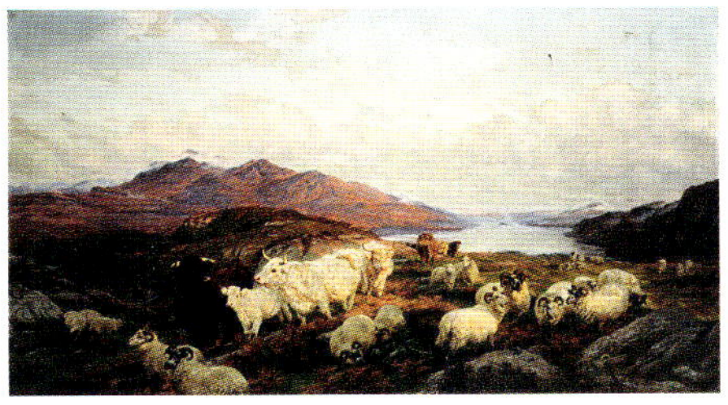

Davis, Henry William Banks 1833–1914
Landscape with Cattle and Sheep
oil on canvas 123 x 214.1
VIS.1457

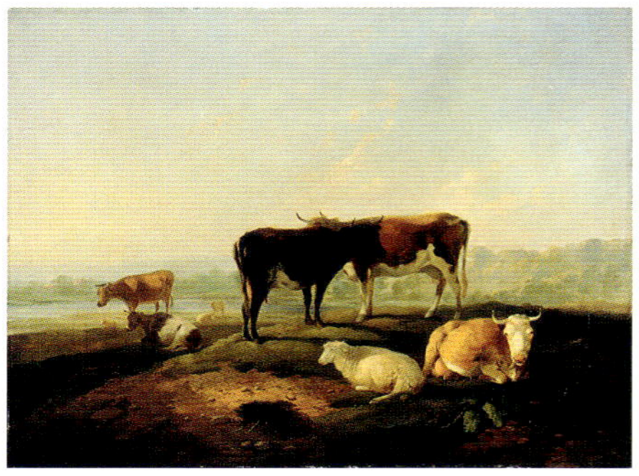

Davis, Richard Barrett 1782–1854
Cattle 1848
oil on panel 70.6 x 91.3
VIS.313

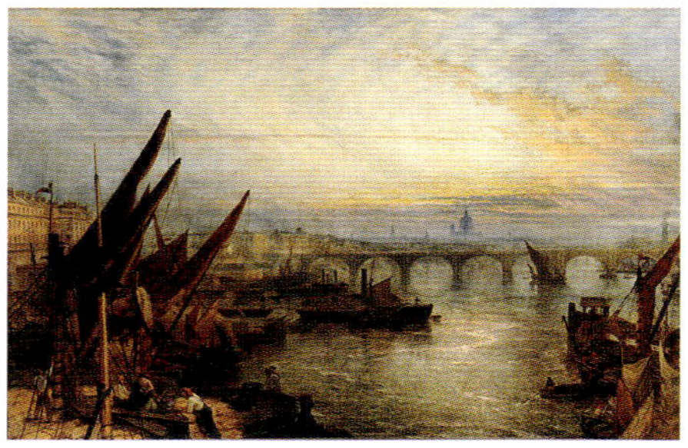

Dawson, Henry 1811–1878
View on the Thames Looking towards St Paul's, London 1852
oil on canvas 120 x 181
VIS.1612

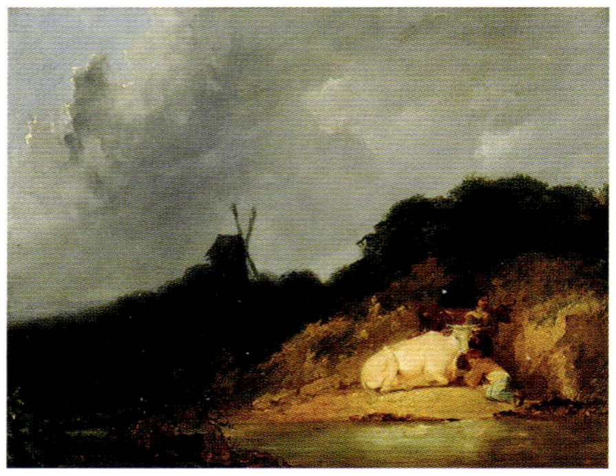

Dawson, Henry 1811–1878
Cattle Sheltering
oil on canvas 34.1 x 43.9
VIS.645

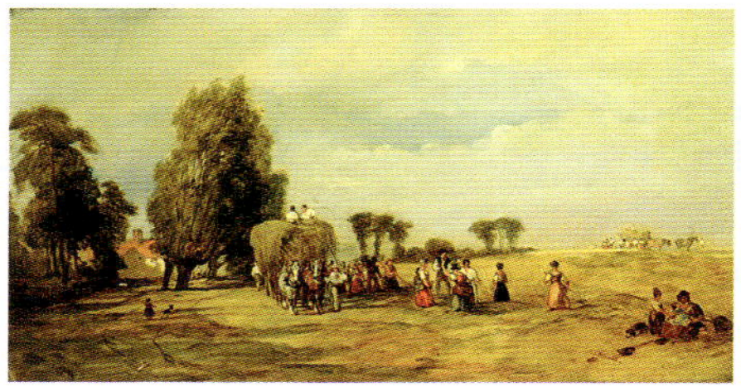

Dawson, Henry 1811–1878
The Last Load
oil on millboard 22.5 x 42.8
VIS.376

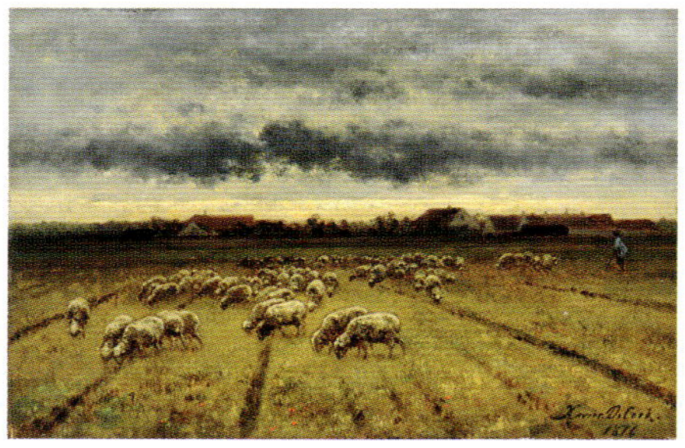

De Cock, Xavier 1818–1896
Evening 1876
oil on panel 29.5 x 43.6
VIS.795

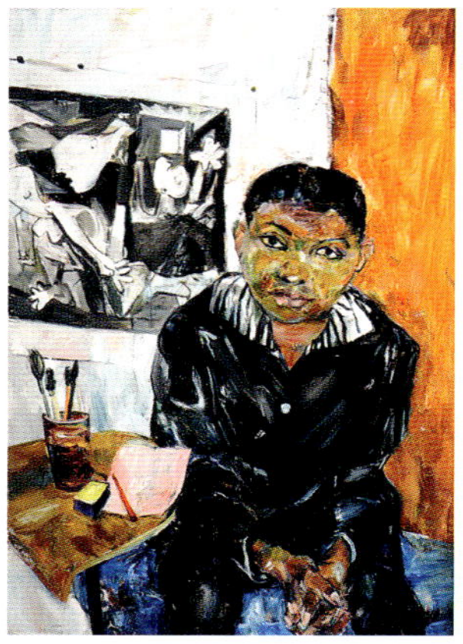

de Francia, Peter 1921–2012
Portrait of an African Girl 1957
oil on canvas 178 x 131
VIS.5195

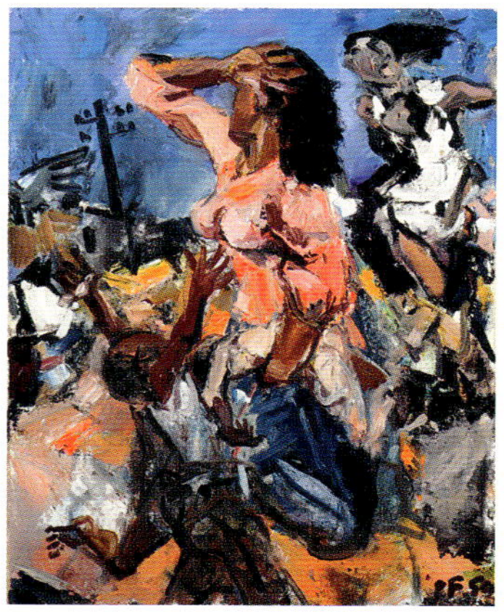

de Francia, Peter 1921–2012
Figure Study for 'The Bombing of Sakiet' 1959
oil on canvas 48.6 x 37.9
VIS.5419

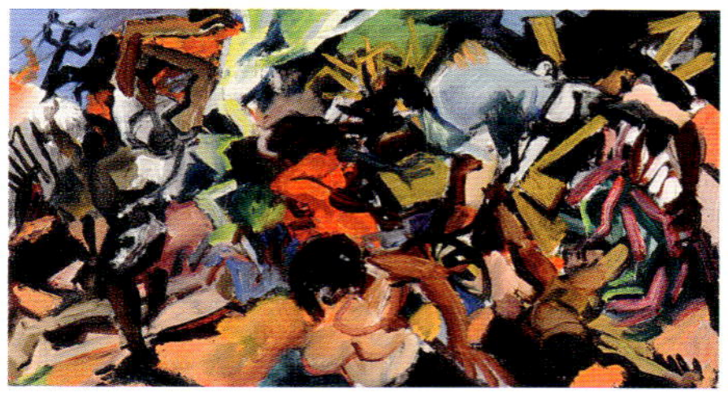

de Francia, Peter 1921–2012
Oil Sketch for 'The Bombing of Sakiet' 1959
oil on paper on canvas 24.4 x 45
VIS.5420

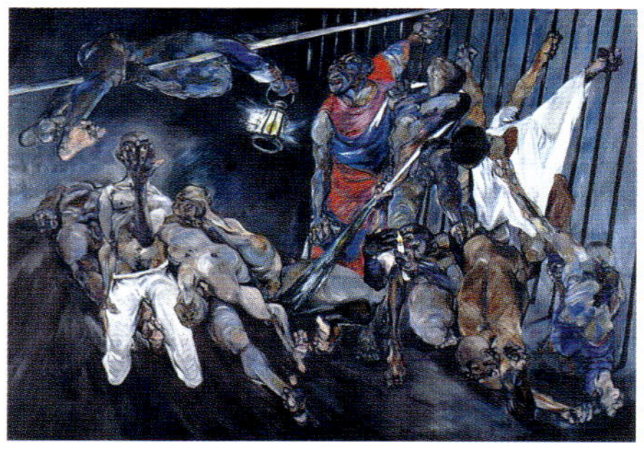

de Francia, Peter 1921–2012
African Prison
oil on canvas 27.4 x 39.2
VIS.5197

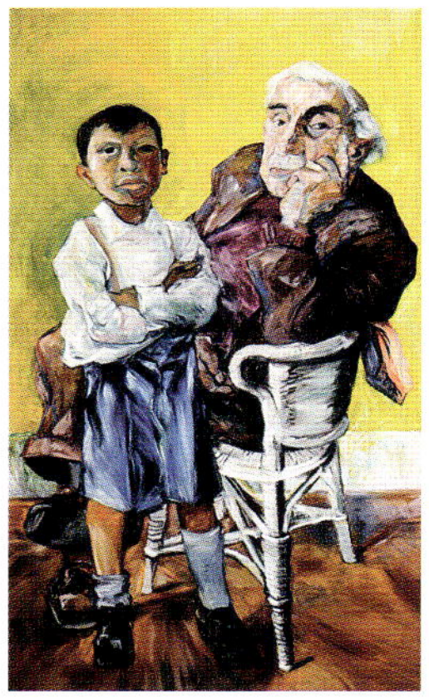

de Francia, Peter 1921–2012
Old Man and a Boy
oil on canvas 152.4 x 91.6
VIS.5196

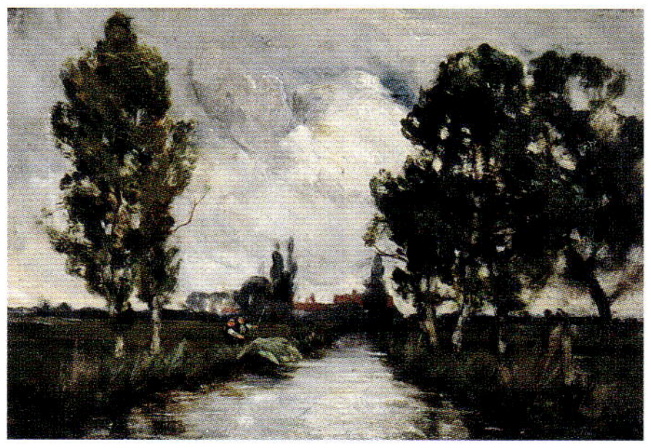

de Groot, Adelaide Milton 1876–1967
The Dutch Canal
oil on canvas 24.4 x 34.5
VIS.1045

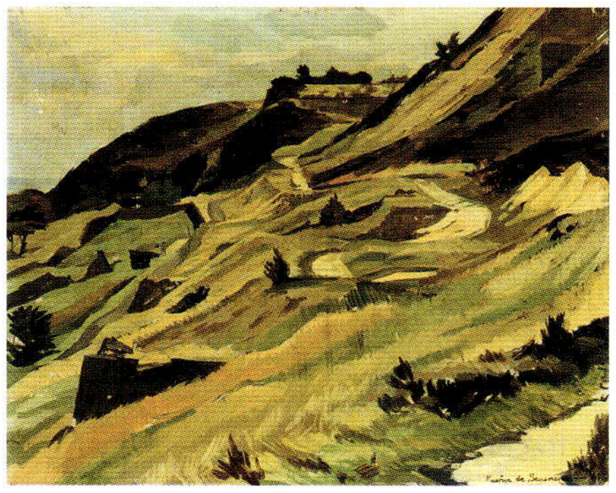

De Sausmarez, Lionel Maurice 1915–1969
Lodge Moor, Sheffield, in the Evening 1941
oil on board 34 x 36.7
VIS.4937

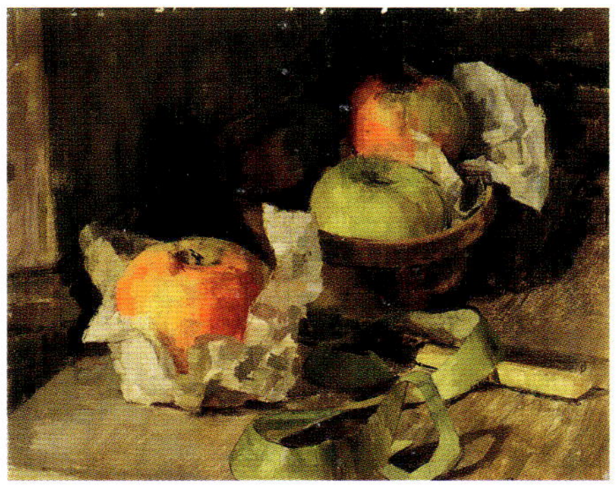

De Sausmarez, Lionel Maurice 1915–1969
Apples, Apple Peel and a Knife on a Table (recto)
oil on panel 21.9 x 26.9
VIS.4710

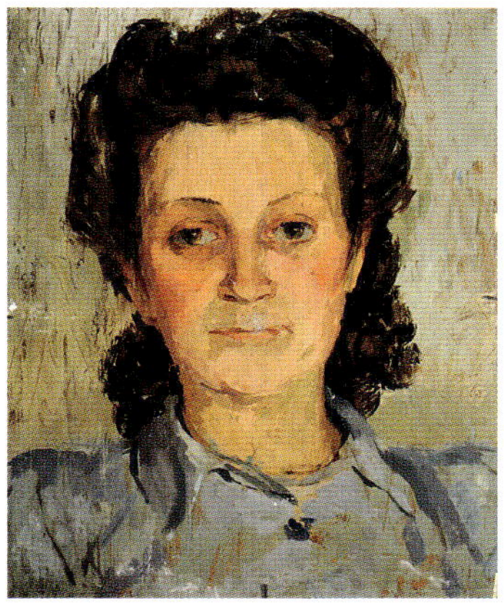

De Sausmarez, Lionel Maurice 1915–1969
*Portrait of an Unknown Woman** (verso)
oil on panel 26.9 x 21.9
VIS.4710

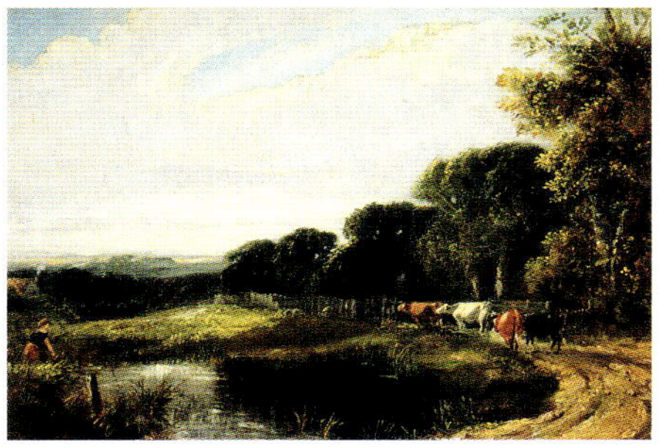

De Wint, Peter 1784–1849
The Wayside Pool
oil on canvas 31.5 x 45.1
VIS.363

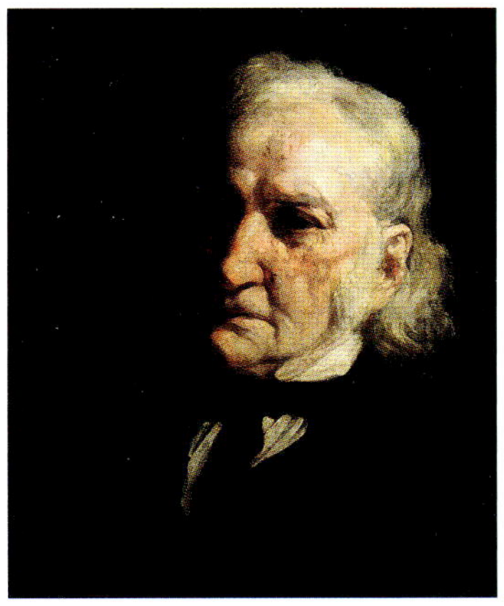

De Wint, Peter 1784–1849
William Hilton Senior
oil on canvas 53.5 x 43.6
VIS.17

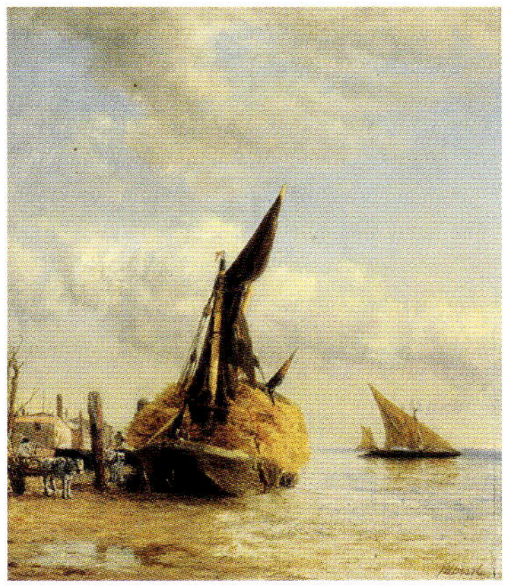

Dearle, John Henry 1860–1932
A Straw Barge
oil on canvas 27.1 x 22.7
VIS.509

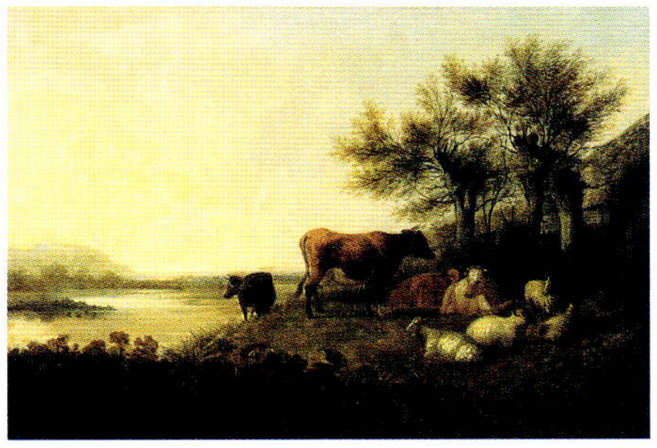

Dearman, John active 1824–1857
Landscape with Cattle 1856
oil on canvas 36.5 x 53
VIS.755

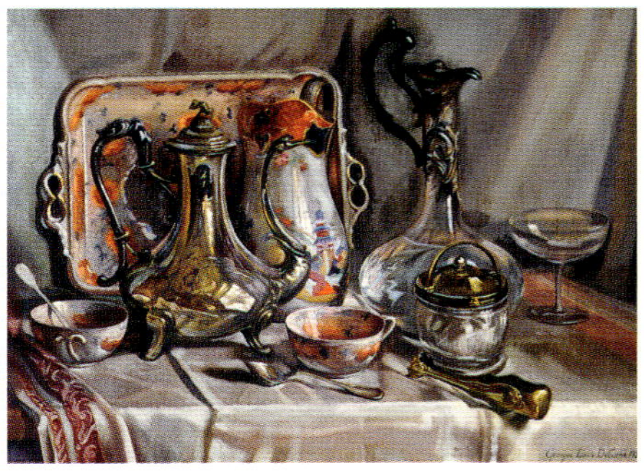

Debuche, Georges L. active 1925–1928
The Silver Coffee Service 1928
oil on panel 48.4 x 64.4
VIS.1254

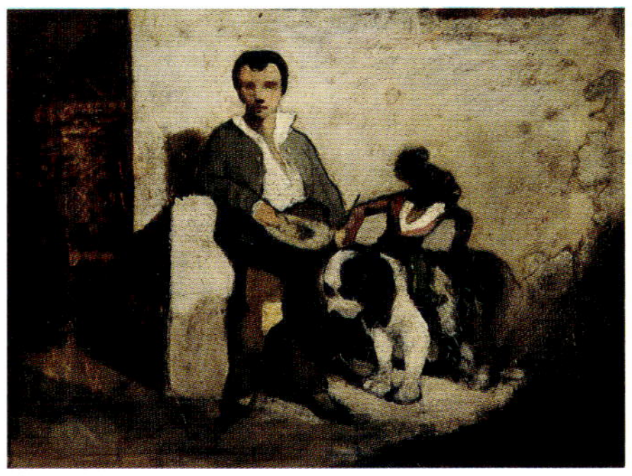

Decamps, Alexandre-Gabriel 1803–1860
The Blind Beggar
oil on canvas 52.2 x 61.3
VIS.254

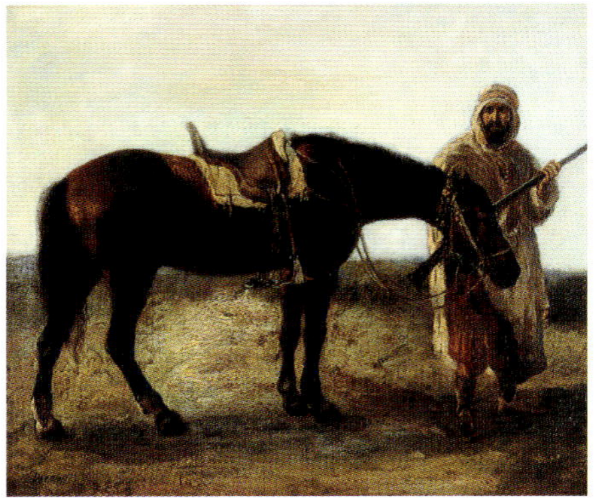

Decamps, Alexandre-Gabriel (attributed to)
1803–1860
An Arab and His Steed 1840–1845
oil on panel 43 x 49
VIS.536

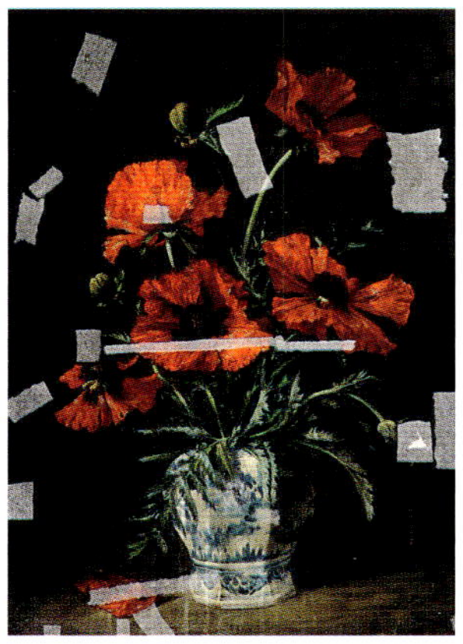

Delamotte, A.
Oriental Poppies 1875
oil on canvas 98.5 x 67.9
VIS.1337

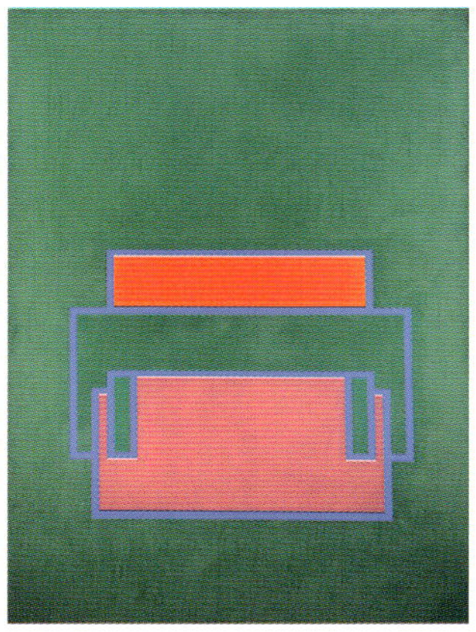

Denny, Robyn b.1930
Rising I 1969–1970
acrylic on canvas 162.9 x 119.9
VIS.3850

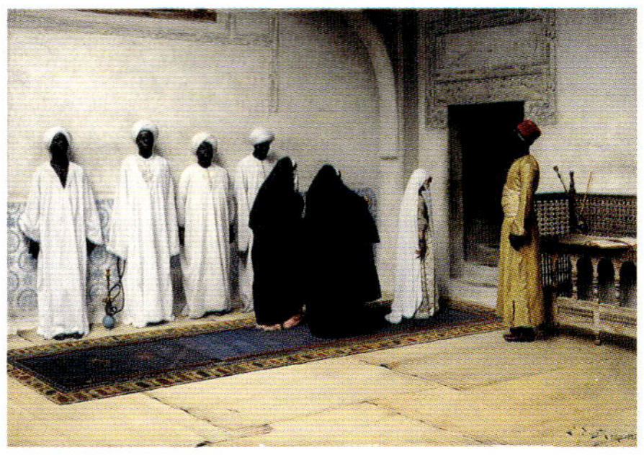

Deutsch, Ludwig 1855–1935
The Sultan's Daughter 1888
oil on panel 91.5 x 126.1
VIS.716

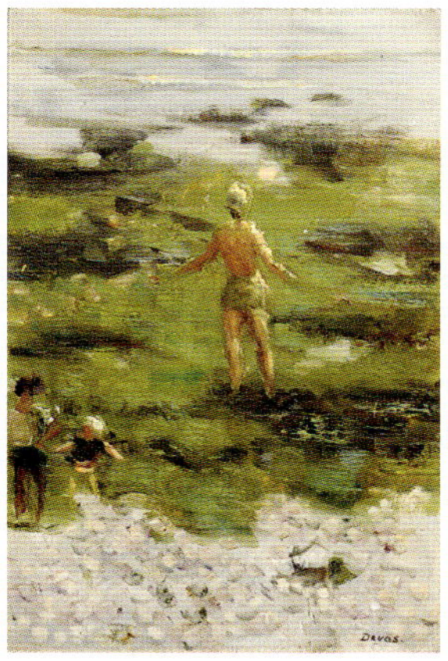

Devas, Anthony 1911–1958
St Margaret's Bay, Kent
oil on canvas 32.7 x 21.2
VIS.5292

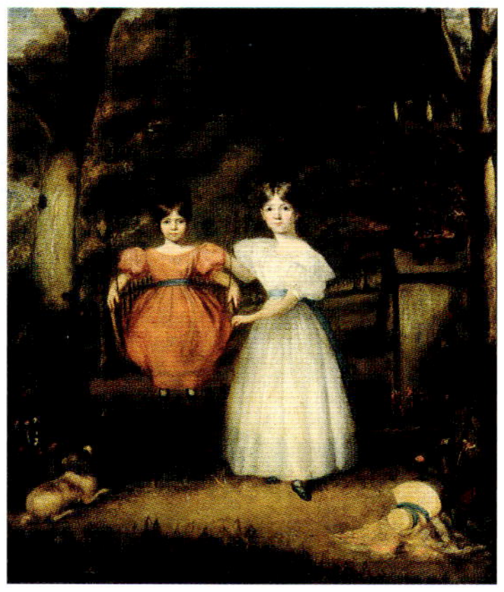

Devis, Arthur William 1762–1822
The Swing
oil on canvas 76.7 x 63.7
VIS.16

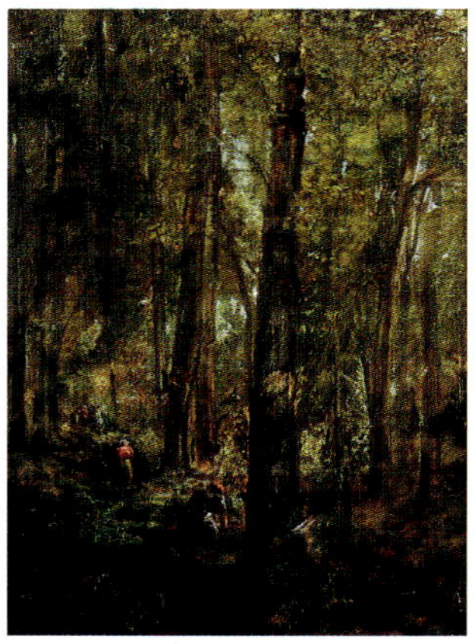

Diaz de la Peña, Narcisse Virgile (attributed to) 1808–1876
A Wood Scene
oil on canvas 54.6 x 39.3
VIS.839

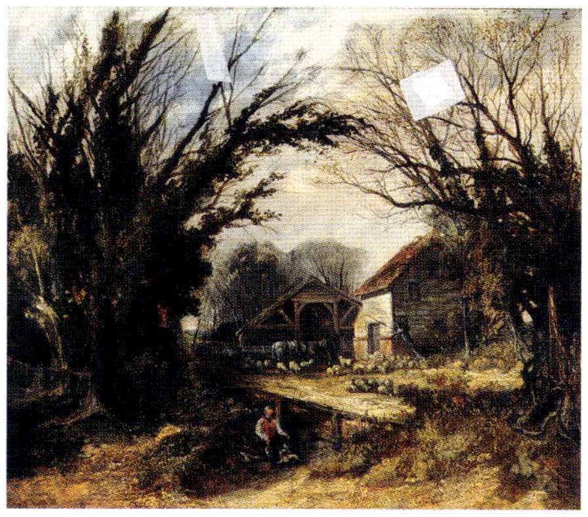

Dibdin, Thomas Colman 1810–1893
Landscape
oil on canvas 60.2 x 66.6
VIS.3476

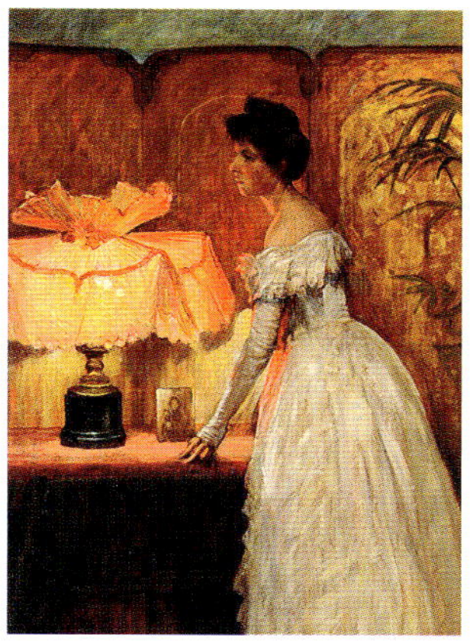

Dicksee, Frank 1853–1928
Interior with a Lady 1891
oil on panel 33.8 x 24.4
VIS.1204

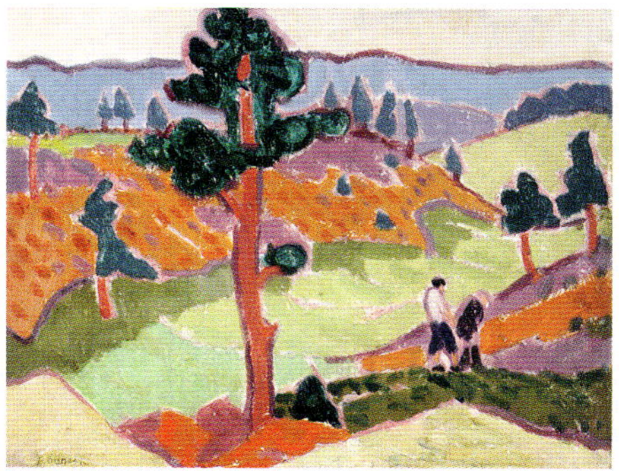

Dismorr, Jessica 1885–1939
Landscape with Figures
oil on panel 32.5 x 41
VIS.5252

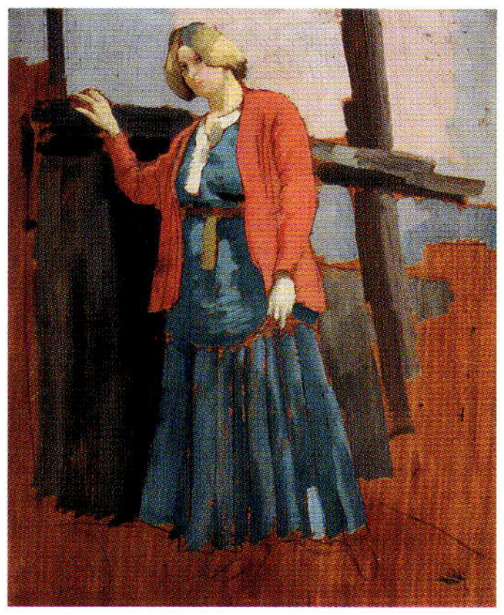

Dobson, Frank 1888–1963
Portrait of the Artist's Wife
oil on panel 39.3 x 31.1
VIS.4032

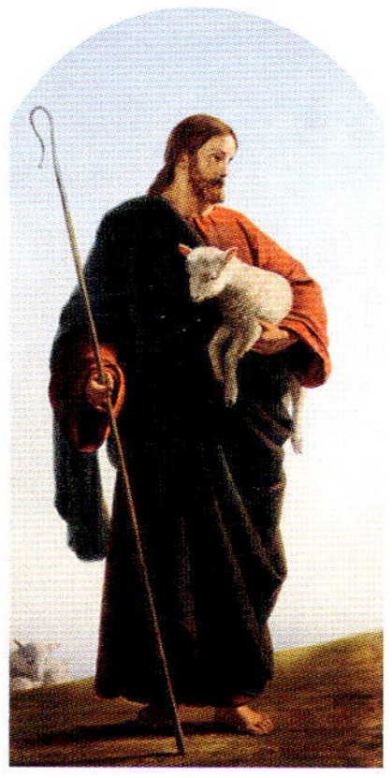

Dobson, William Charles Thomas
1817–1898
The Good Shepherd 1868
oil on canvas 116.6 x 57.9
VIS.1617

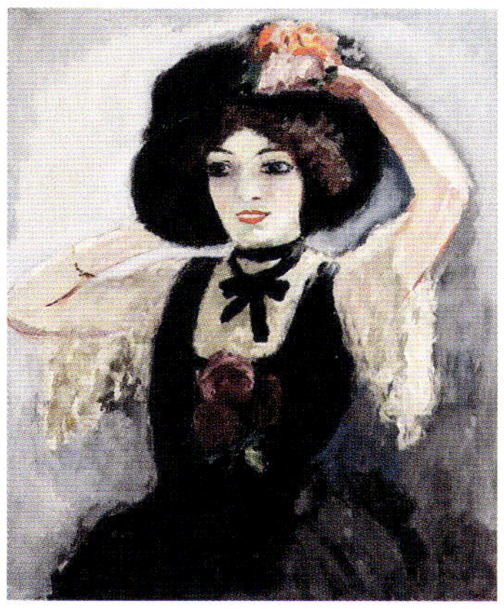

Dongen, Kees van 1877–1968
Kiki de Montparnasse (1901–1953) c.1909
oil on canvas 98.7 x 79.7
VIS.LI.897 (P)

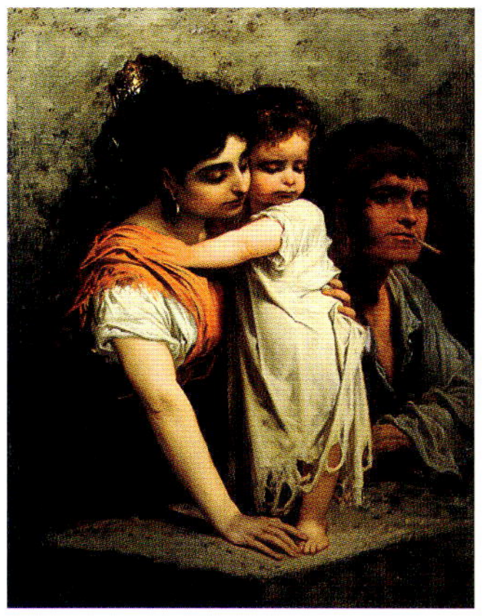

Doré, Gustave 1832–1883
Three Figures 1860–1870
oil on canvas 116 x 88.7
VIS.1449

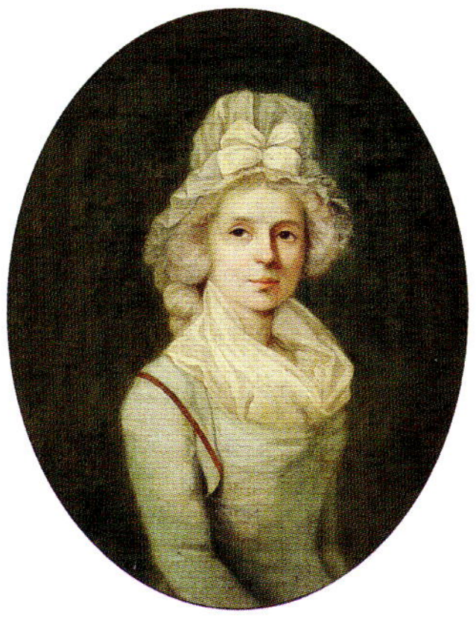

Downman, John 1750–1824
Lady in a Grey Dress
oil on canvas 27.2 x 20.5
VIS.88

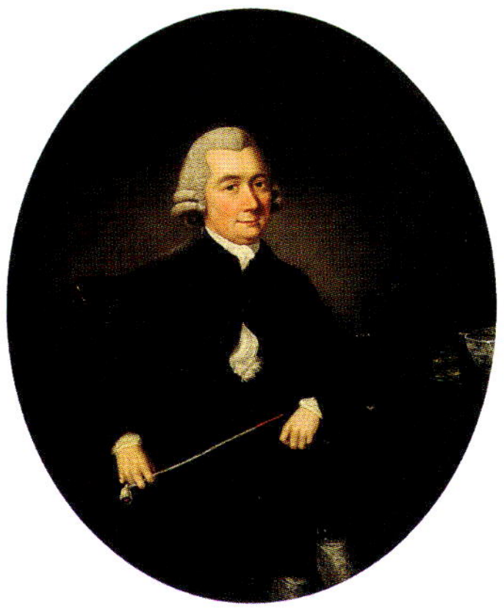

Downman, John 1750–1824
Portrait of a Gentleman
oil on canvas 43.6 x 35.7
VIS.35

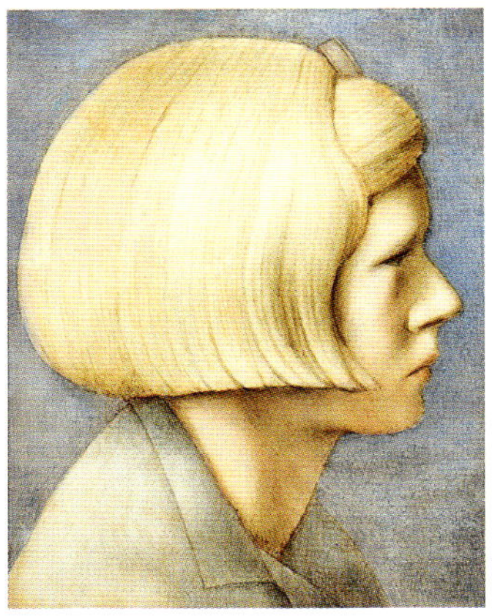

Downton, John 1906–1991
Joan Harris
tempera on panel 24.5 x 19.1
VIS.5293

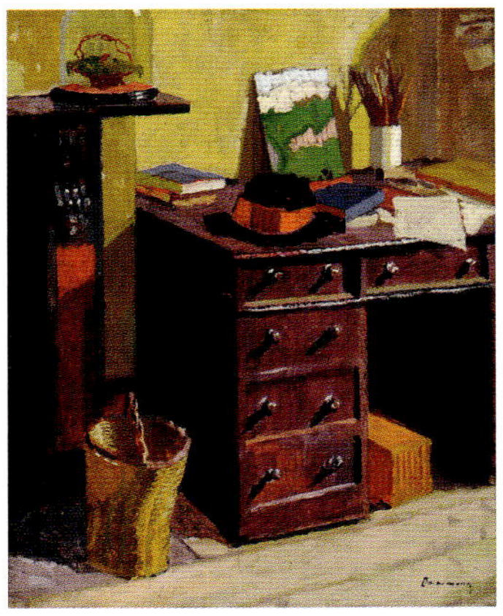

Drummond, Malcolm 1880–1945
The Artist's Desk c.1915
oil on canvas 49.3 x 39.6
VIS.4134

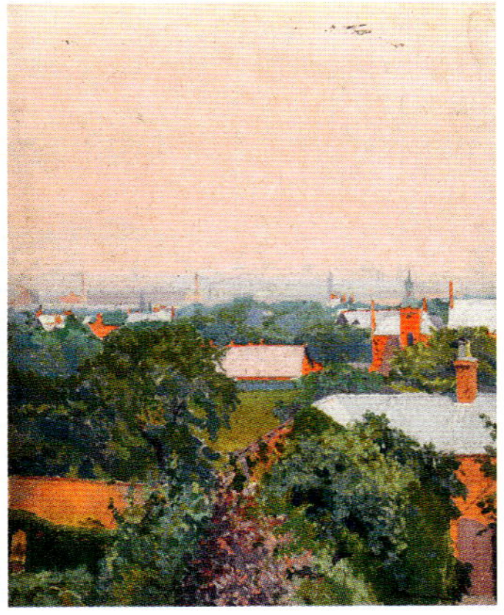

Drummond, Malcolm 1880–1945
Near Beaconsfield, Buckinghamshire
oil on board 66.5 x 56.8
VIS.3898

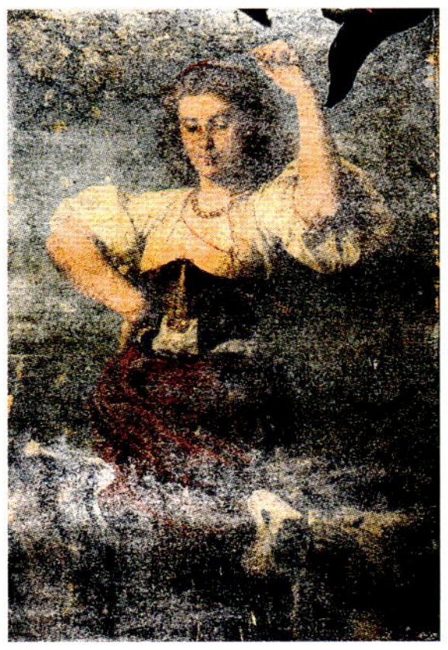

Dubufe, Guillaume 1853–1909
Spring Time in Italy
oil on canvas 131.8 x 91.5
VIS.2606

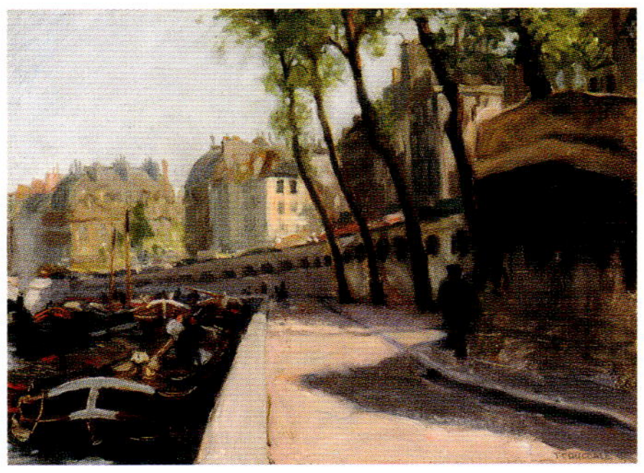

Dugdale, Thomas Cantrell 1880–1952
Un quai à Paris 1903
oil on board 24.8 x 33.1
VIS.4226

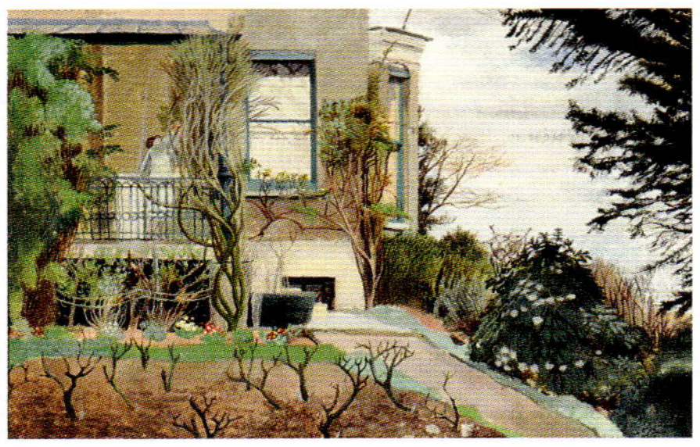

Dunbar, Evelyn Mary 1906–1960
The Garden
oil on millboard 21 x 32.6
VIS.2776

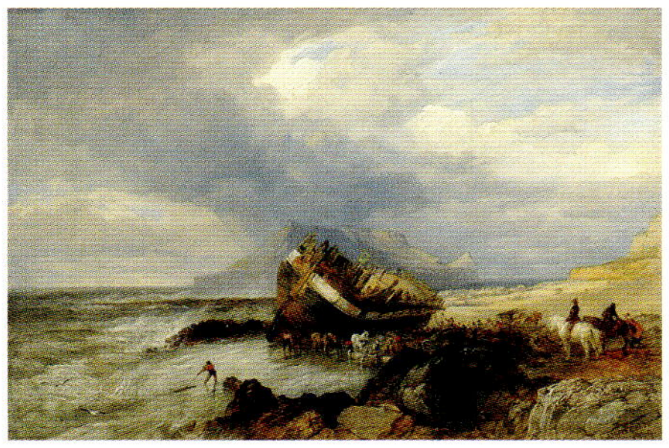

Duncan, Edward 1803–1882
The Wreck 1849
oil on canvas 32.5 x 49
VIS.1377

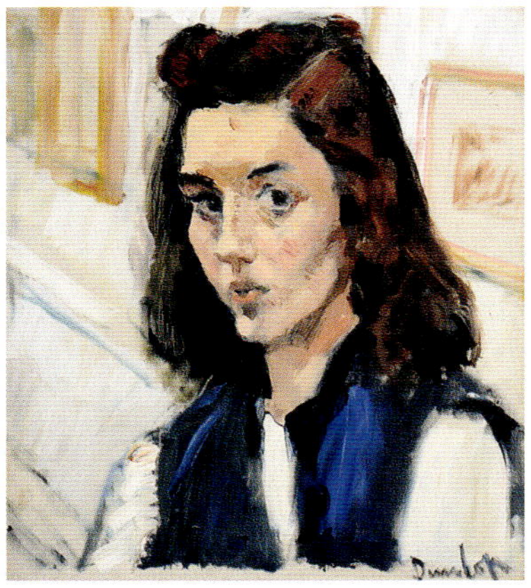

Dunlop, Ronald Ossory 1894–1973
Portrait
oil on canvas 48 x 43
VIS.1839

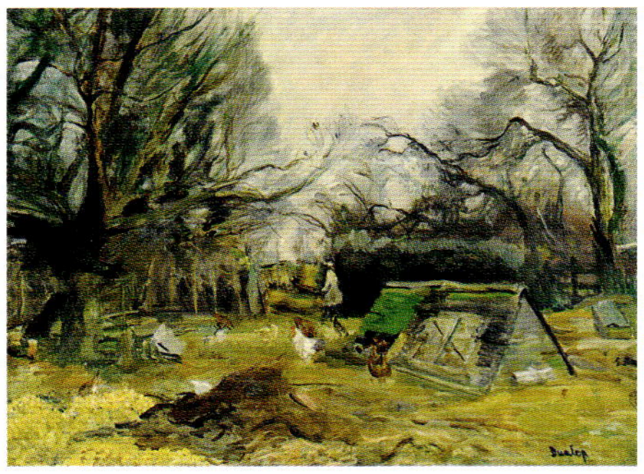

Dunlop, Ronald Ossory 1894–1973
The Untidy Farmyard
oil on canvas 75.4 x 100.7
VIS.2981

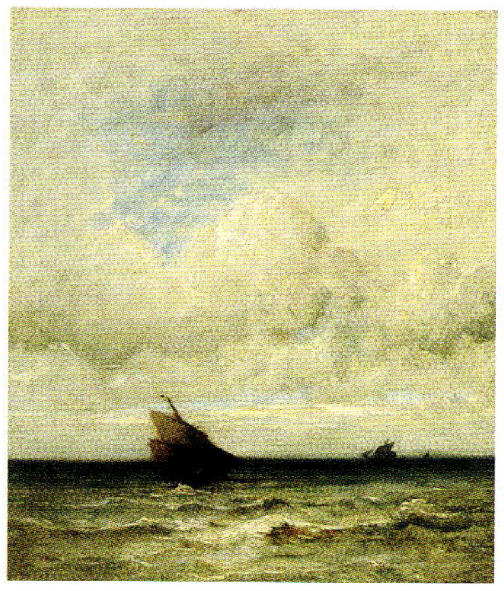

Dupré, Jules 1811–1889
A Stiff Breeze 1870–1889
oil on canvas 46 x 37.5
VIS.350

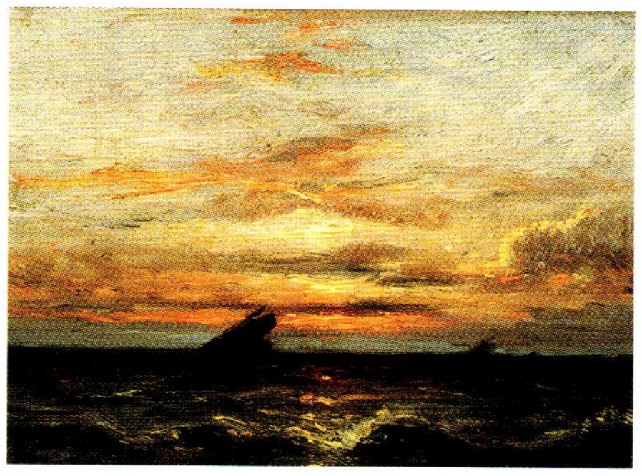

Dupré, Jules 1811–1889
Coucher du soleil 1879–1889
oil on canvas 15.6 x 20.9
VIS.2042

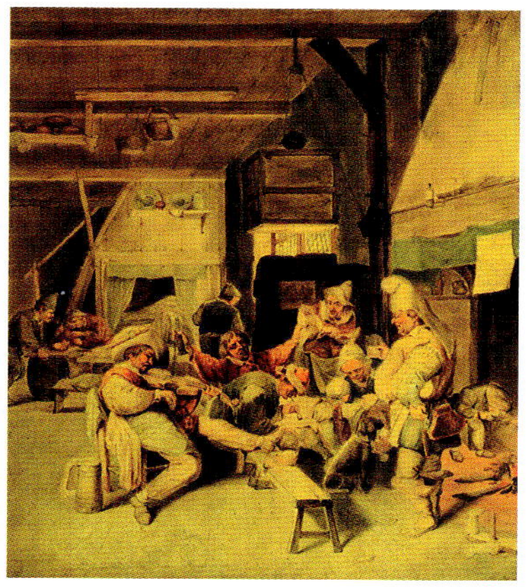

Dusart, Cornelis 1660–1704
A Merrymaking 1685
oil on panel 26 x 23.3
VIS.31

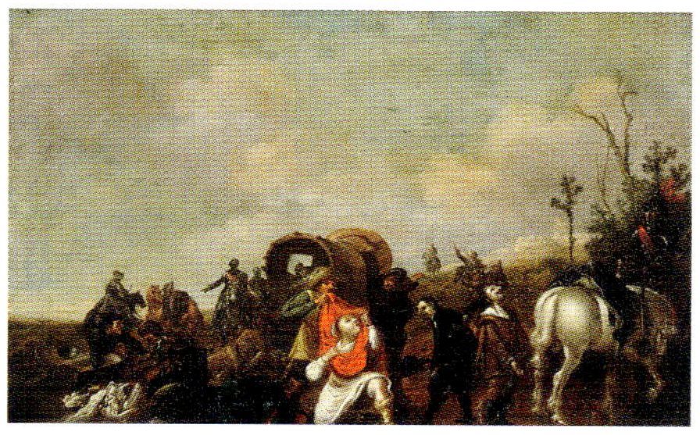

Dutch School
Soldiers Attacking Villagers 1635
oil on panel 23 x 36.8
VIS.1058

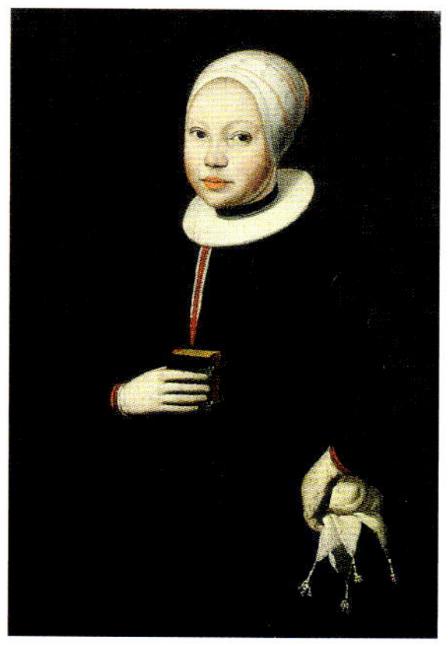

Dutch School 17th C
Portrait
oil on panel 58.3 x 38.8
VIS.345

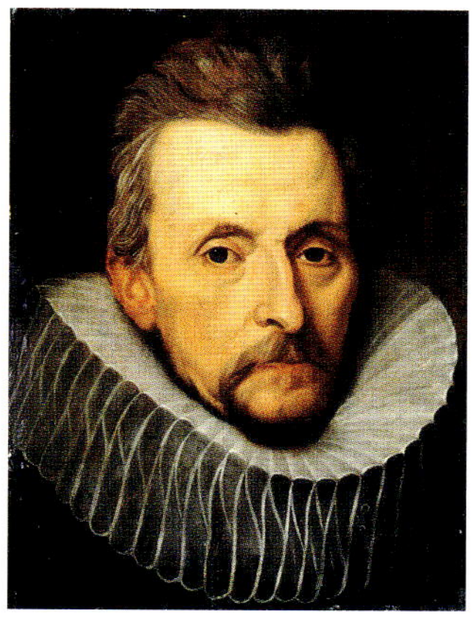

Dutch School 17th C
Portrait of a Gentleman
oil on panel 39.8 x 29.7
VIS.48

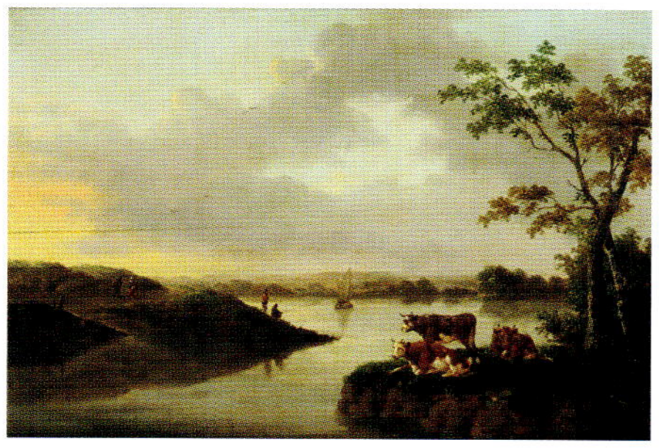

Dutch School 17th C
River Scene
oil on panel 34.2 x 50
VIS.333

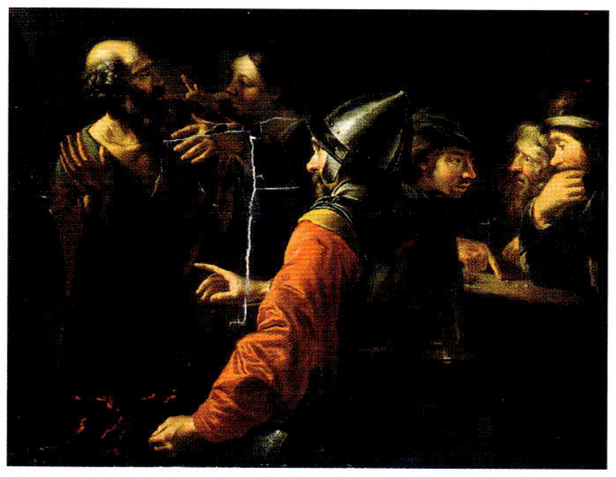

Dutch School 17th C
The Denial of Christ
oil on canvas 75.8 x 137.5
VIS.3133

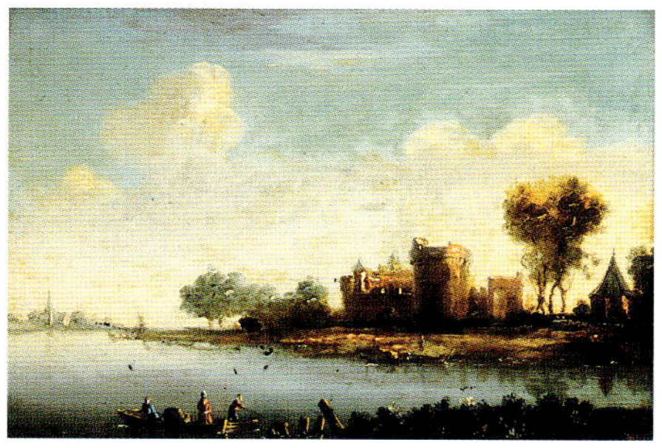

Dutch School 17th C
View of a Waterway
oil on canvas 16.7 x 24.3
VIS.1007

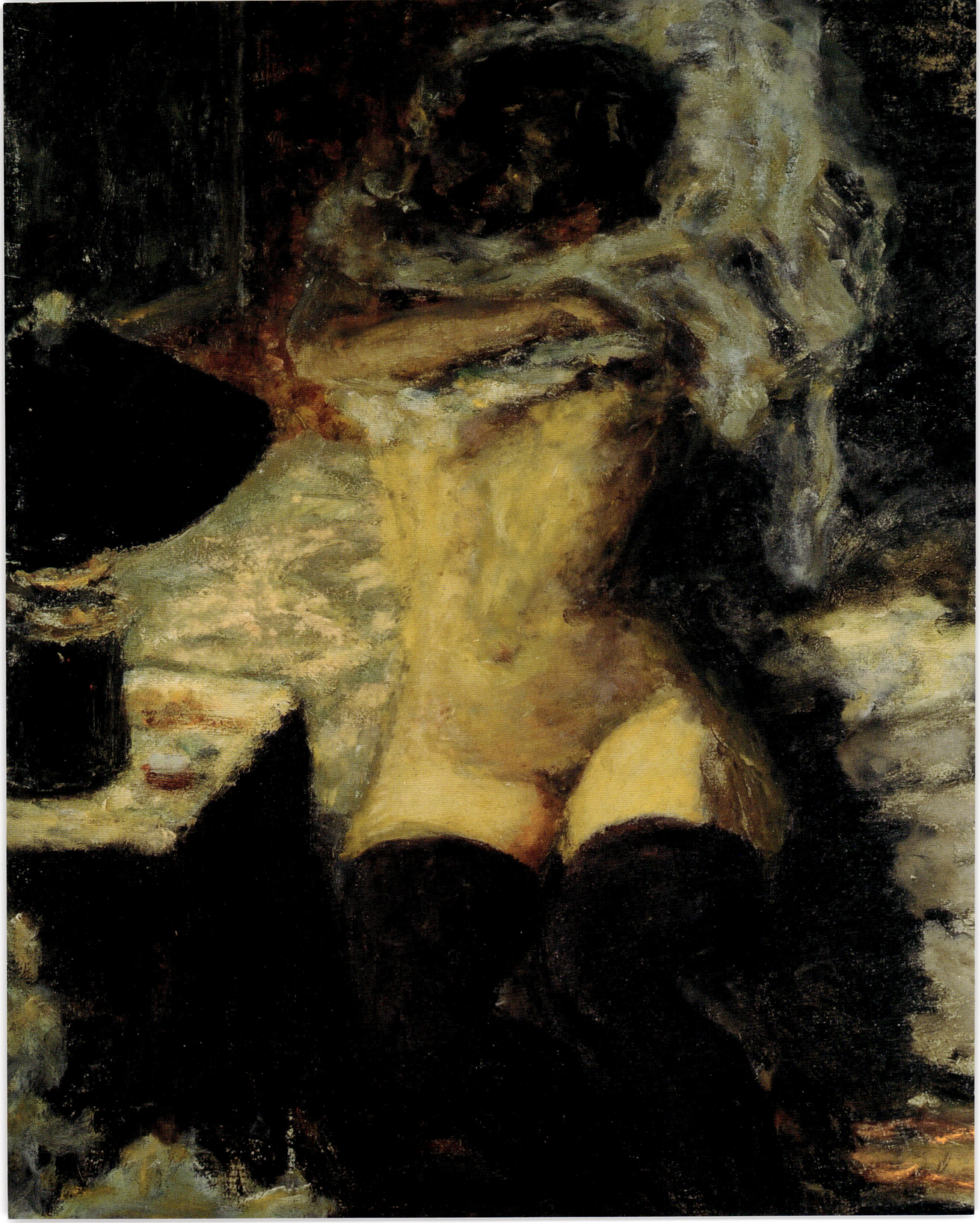

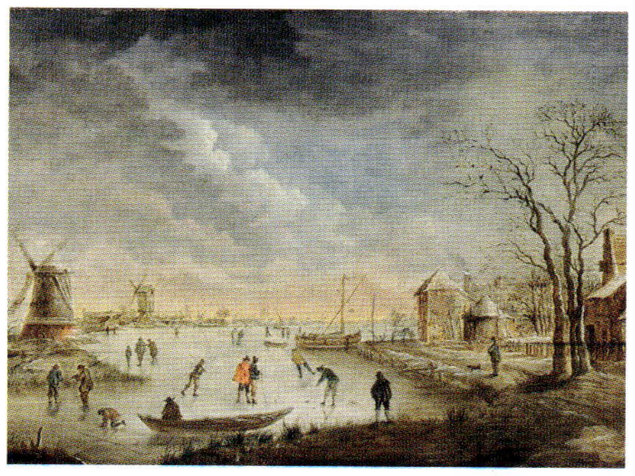

Dutch School 18th C
Skating in Holland
oil on panel 67.2 x 78
VIS.1402

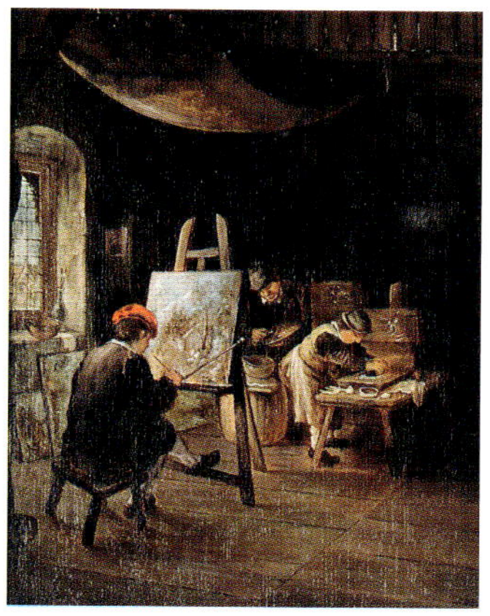

Dutch School 18th C
The Artist's Studio
oil on canvas 17.7 x 14.1
VIS.235

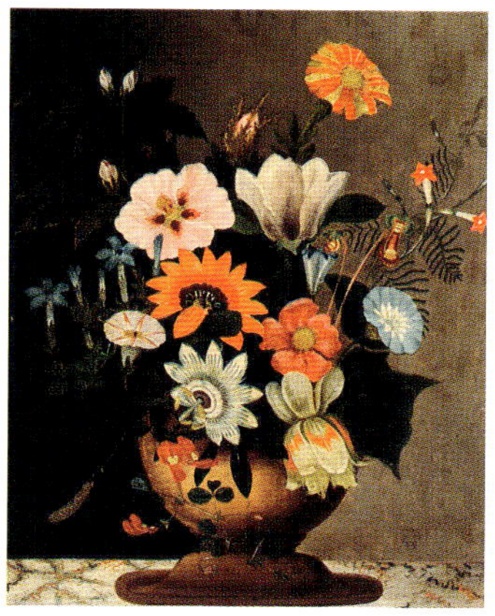

Dutch School
Flower Piece
oil on panel 48.1 x 36.5
VIS.166

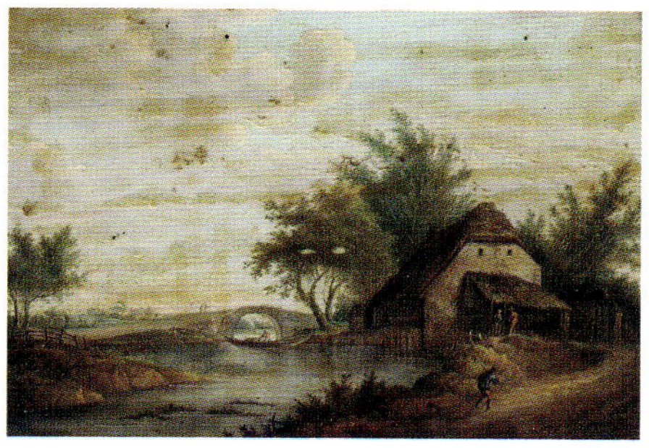

Dutch School
River Scene
oil on copper 14.2 x 20.1
VIS.231

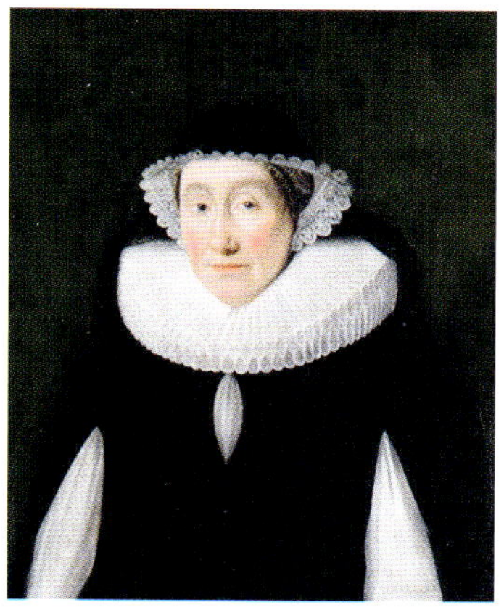

Dutch School (attributed to)
Lady in a Ruff c.1630
oil on panel 65.8 x 54.3
VIS.264

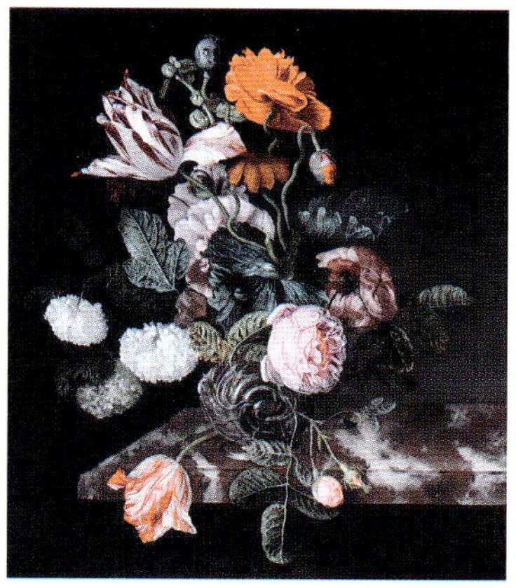

Dutch School (attributed to) 18th C
Flowers in a Vase
oil on canvas 65.1 x 55.4
VIS.37

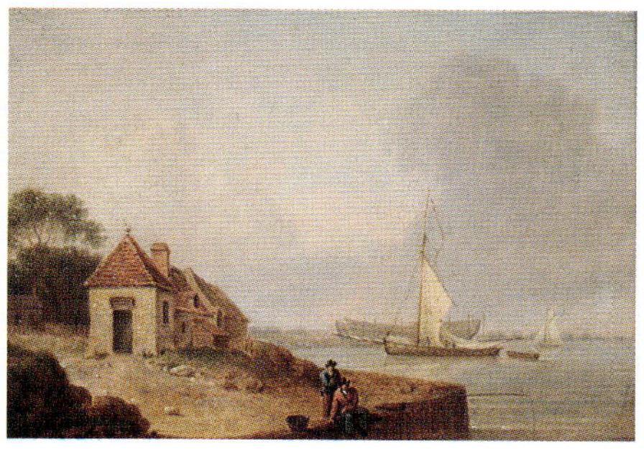

Dutch School (attributed to) 18th C
Harbour Scene
oil on panel 12 x 18
VIS.82

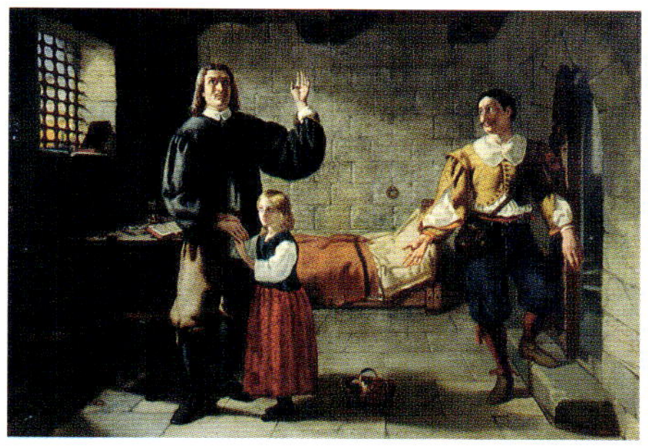

Duval, John 1816–1892
John Bunyan in Bedford Gaol 1844
oil on canvas 49 x 69.5
VIS.133

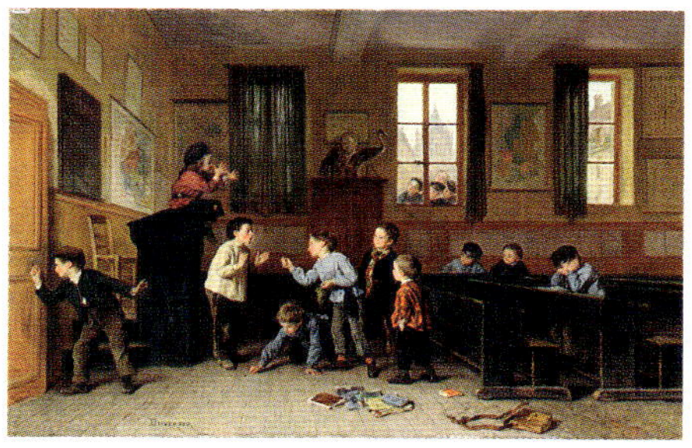

Duverger, Théophile Emmanuel 1821–1901
When the Cat's Away the Mice Will Play
1850–1860
oil on panel 45.8 x 69.9
VIS.1575

Facing page: Bonnard, Pierre, 1867–1947, *Nil aux bas noires* (detail), 1900, Museums Sheffield, (p. 22)

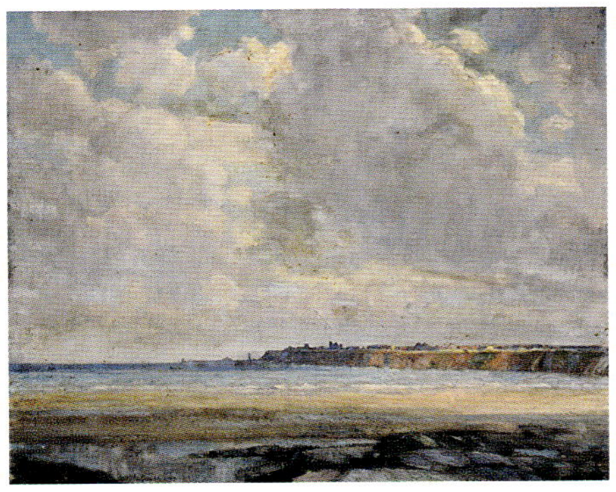

Eadon, Willis 1870–1945
Shore Scene
oil on canvas 63.8 x 76.1
VIS.3273

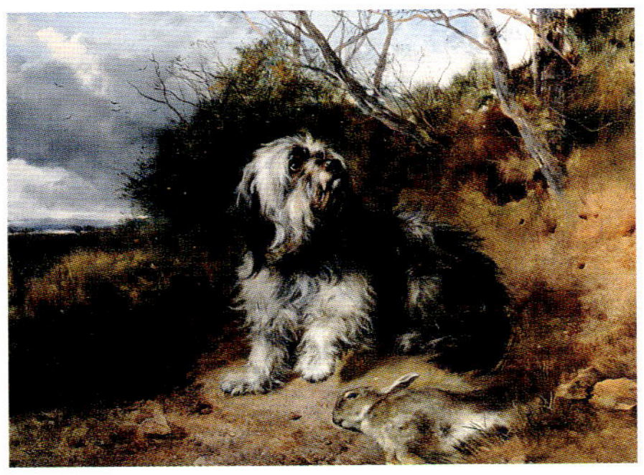

Earl, Thomas 1810–1876
Dog and Rabbit 1862
oil on canvas 76 x 101
VIS.1517

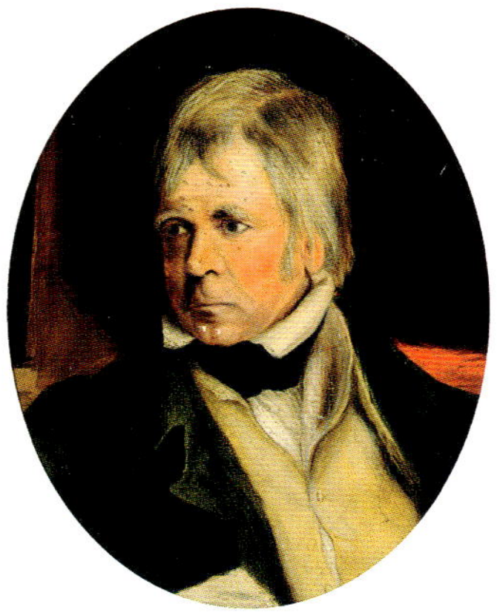

Eatwell, W. active 1862
Sir Walter Scott (1771–1832), Bt
oil on canvas on panel 19.8 x 15.8
VIS.226

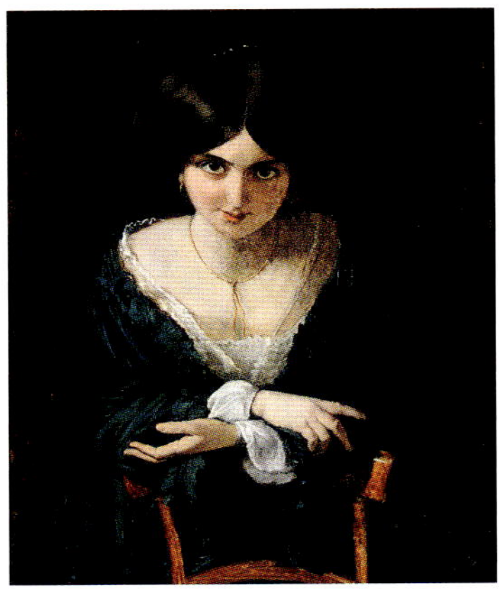

Egg, Augustus Leopold 1816–1863
Lady in a Green Dress
oil on canvas 29.4 x 24.2
VIS.6

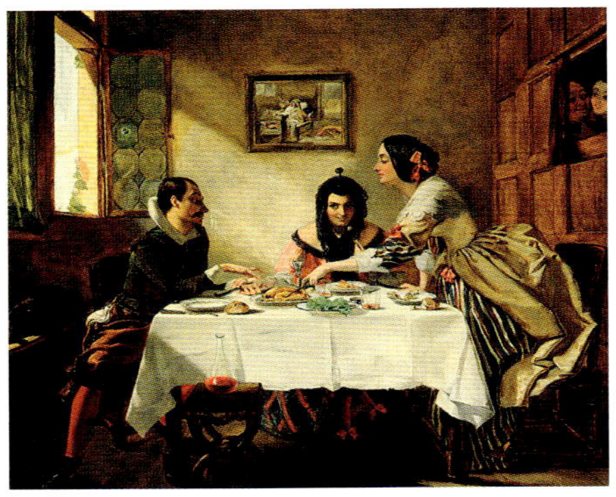

Egg, Augustus Leopold 1816–1863
Le diable boiteux
oil on canvas 37.4 x 44.9
VIS.1542

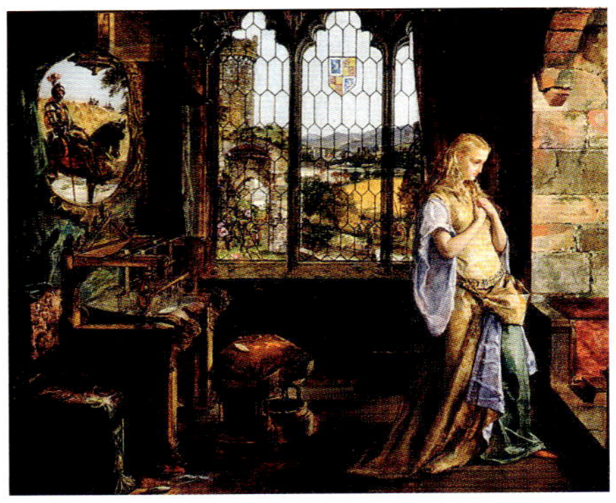

Egley, William Maw 1826–1916
The Lady of Shalott 1858
oil on canvas 88 x 100.7
VIS.630

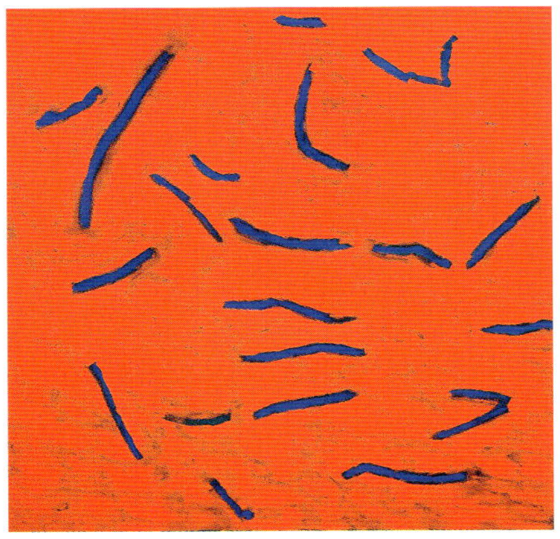

Elliott, John b.1953
Not Quite Social
oil on canvas 71 x 71.3
VIS.4952

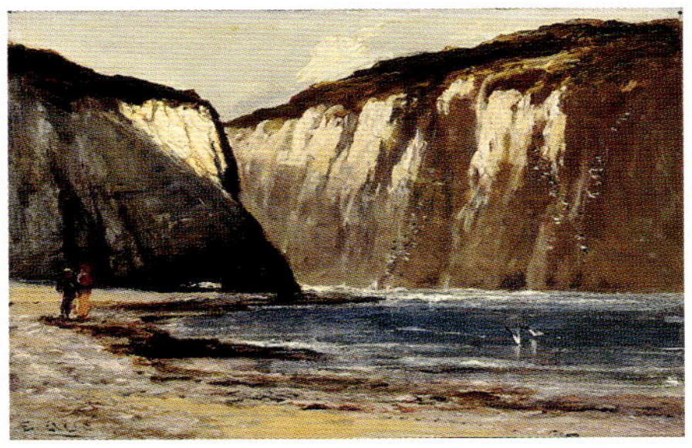

Ellis, Edwin 1841–1895
Cliffs and Sea
oil on panel 30.2 x 45.8
VIS.651

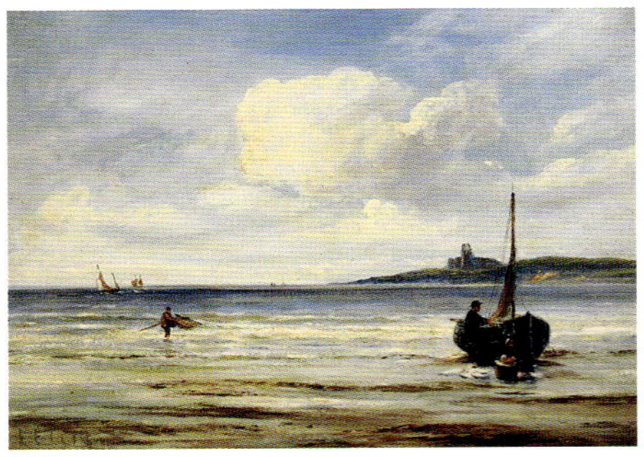

Ellis, Edwin 1841–1895
Coast View
oil on millboard 44 x 61.8
VIS.625

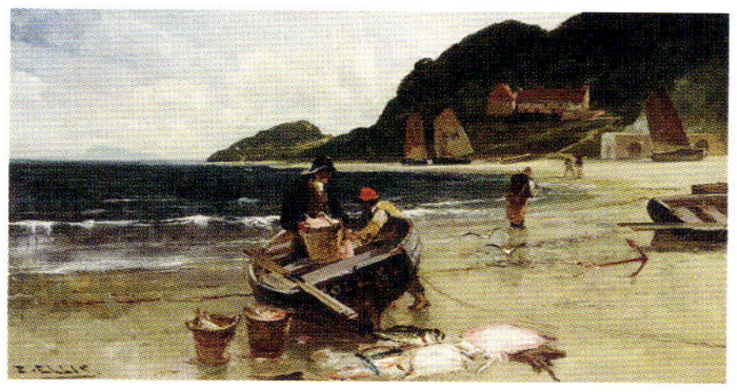

Ellis, Edwin 1841–1895
Landing the Catch
oil on canvas 44.5 x 81.9
VIS.145

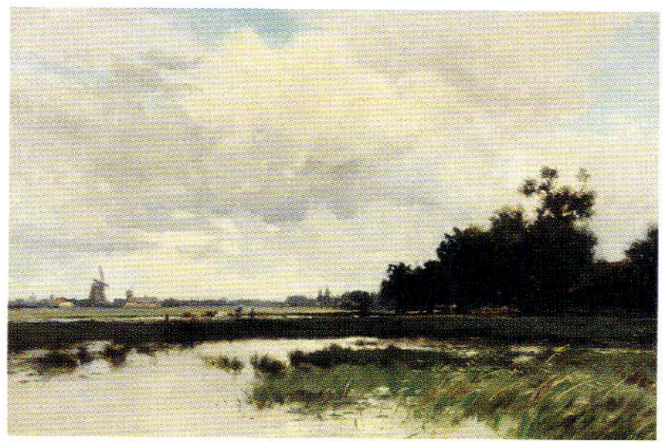

Ellis, Edwin 1841–1895
Landscape and a River
oil on canvas 37.9 x 54.7
VIS.208

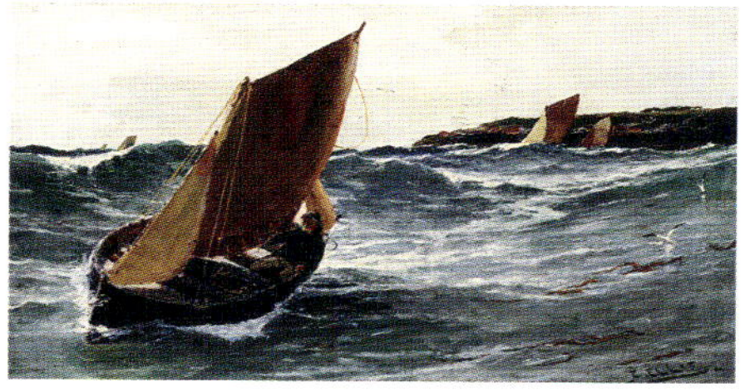

Ellis, Edwin 1841–1895
Over the Harbour Bar
oil on canvas 45 x 83.1
VIS.1553

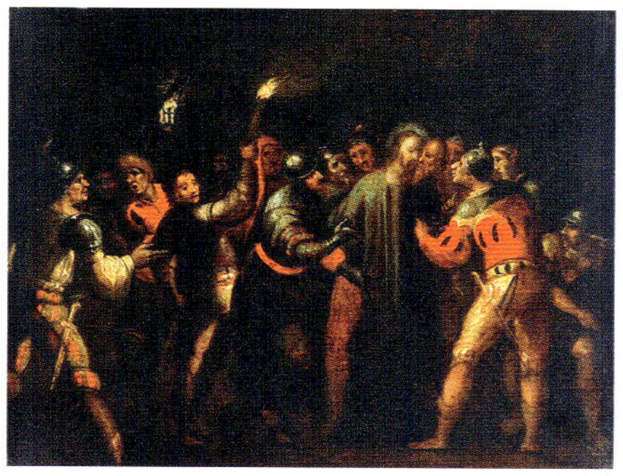

Elsheimer, Adam (attributed to) 1578–1610
The Betrayal of Christ
oil on panel 28.8 x 32.8
VIS.296

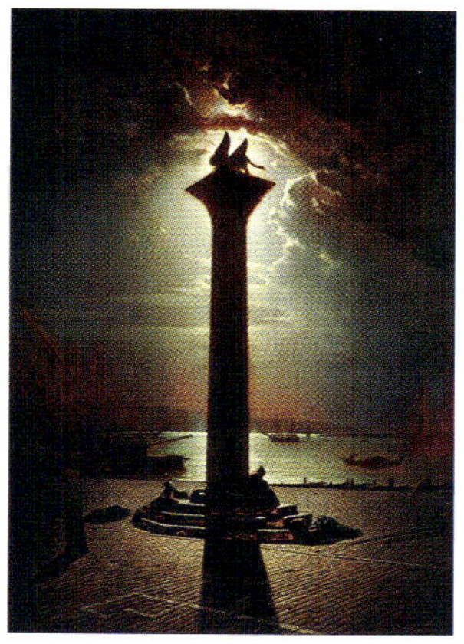

Eluke, Julius active 20th C
The Lion of St Mark, Venice
oil on canvas 73.7 x 51
VIS.209

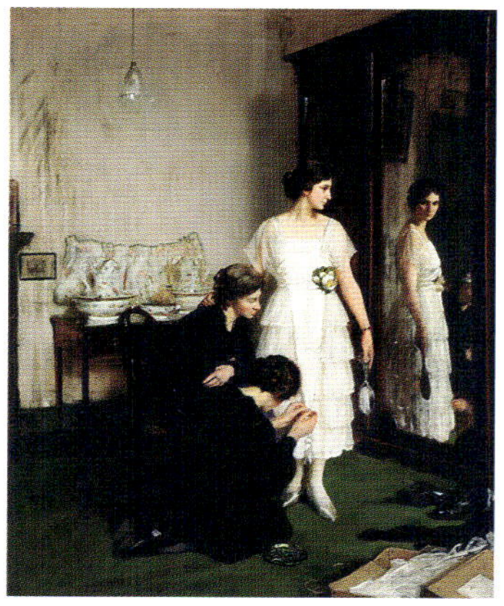

Elwell, Frederick William 1870–1958
The New Frock 1919
oil on canvas 125.6 x 100
VIS.565

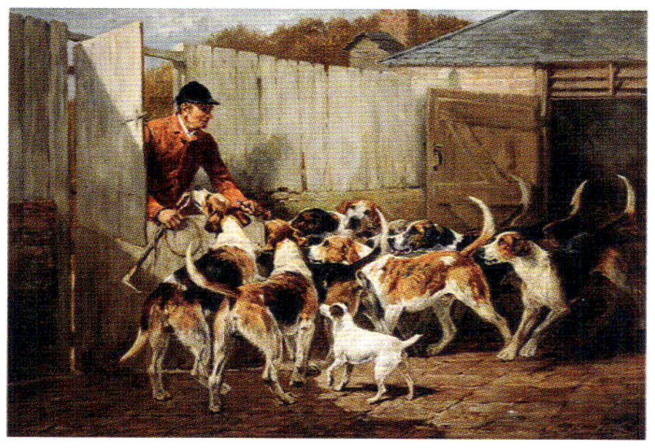

Emms, John 1843–1912
Hunting Scene 1897
oil on canvas 65.3 x 92.3
VIS.3229

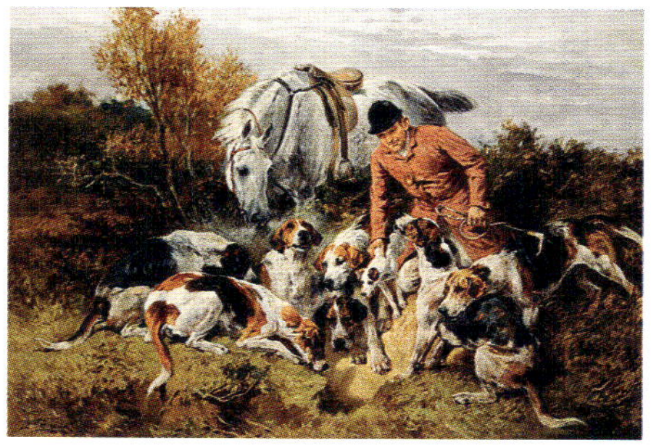

Emms, John 1843–1912
Run to Earth
oil on canvas 65.1 x 91.7
VIS.2607

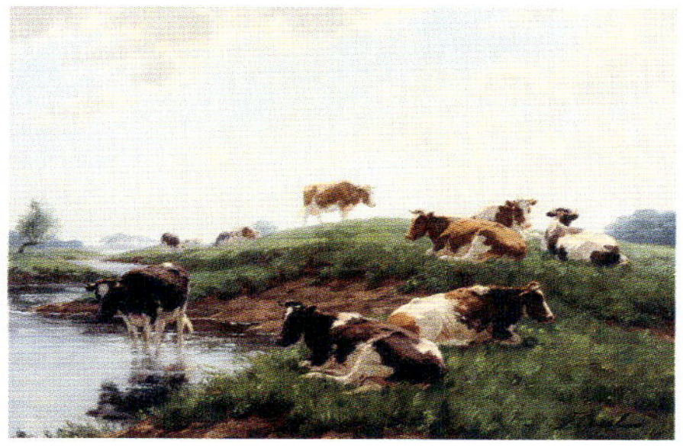

Engel, Fritz Franz c.1878–1956
Summer Day 1941
oil on canvas 60.5 x 90.5
VIS.3288

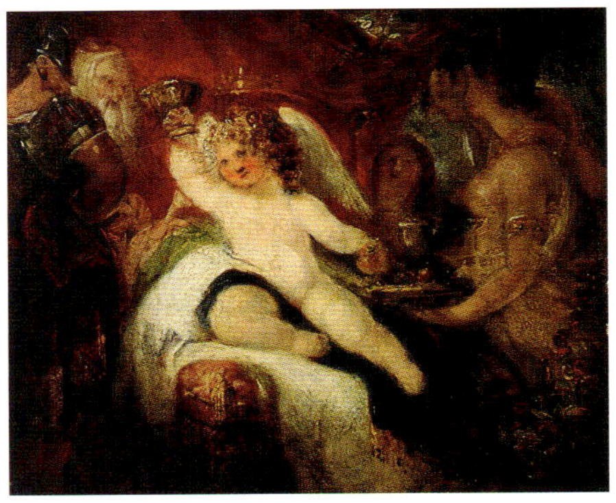

Etty, William 1787–1849
Classical Subject
oil on canvas 24.7 x 29.7
VIS.2980

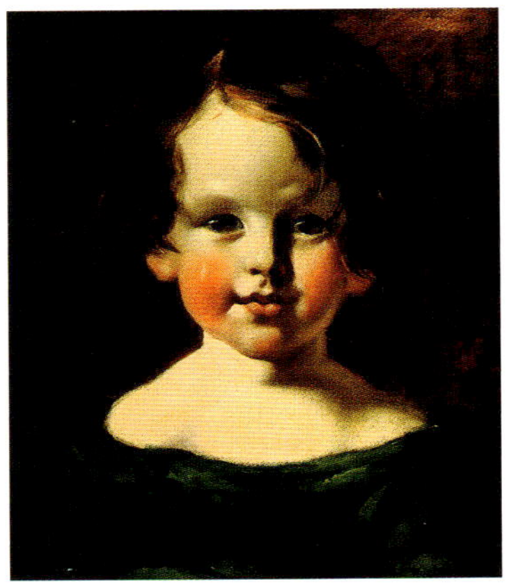

Etty, William 1787–1849
Head of a Girl
oil on canvas 34.6 x 29.2
VIS.273

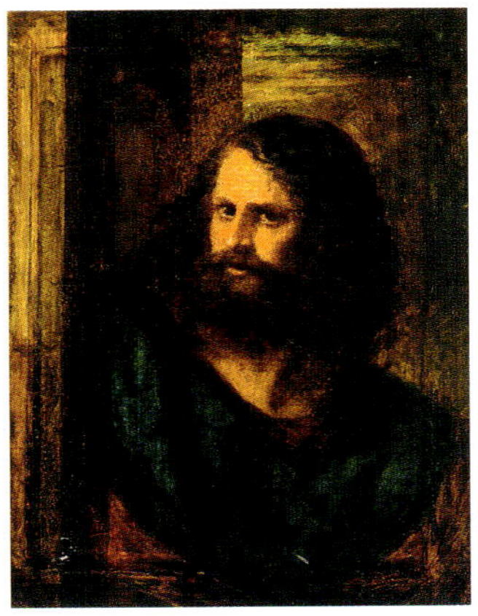

Etty, William 1787–1849
Judas Iscariot
oil on board 41.9 x 31.6
VIS.257

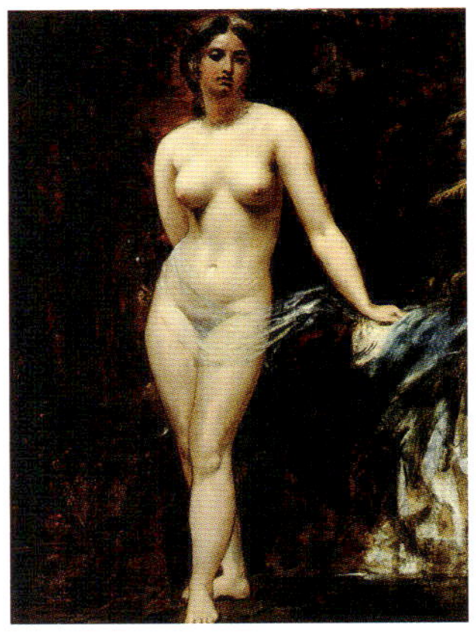

Etty, William 1787–1849
Nude
oil on panel 68 x 49.8
VIS.359

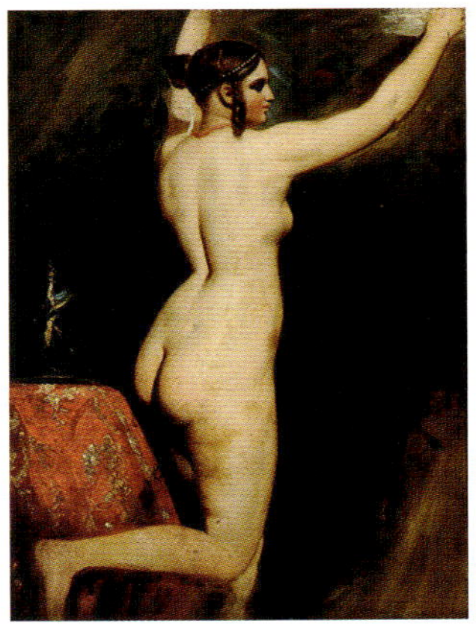

Etty, William 1787–1849
Nude
oil on canvas 59.6 x 43.5
VIS.2299

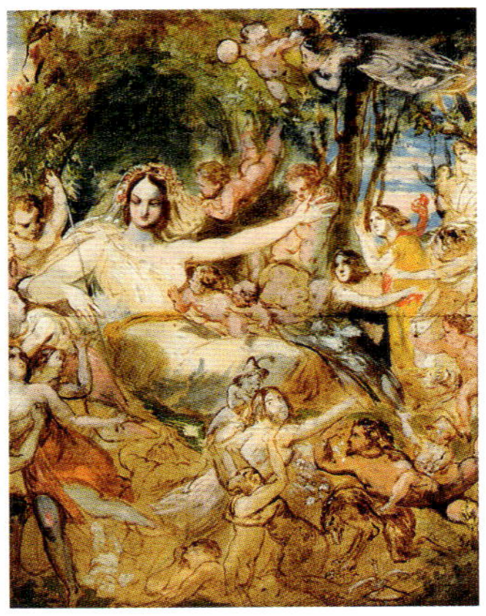

Etty, William 1787–1849
Titania and the Fairies
oil on paper 21 x 16.3
VIS.500

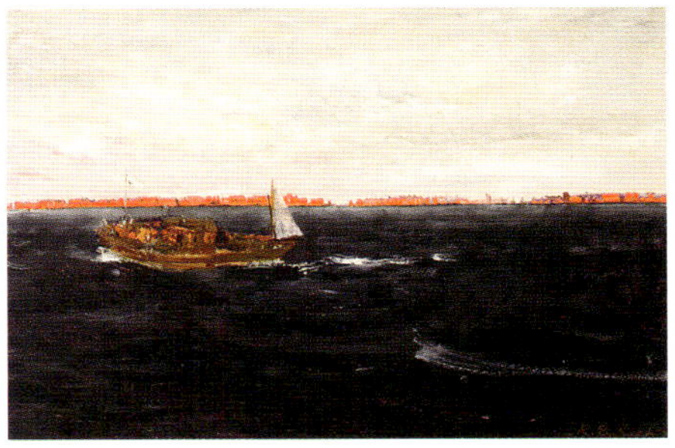

Eurich, Richard Ernst 1903–1992
Crab Boat 1971
oil on panel 24.9 x 37.5
VIS.4015

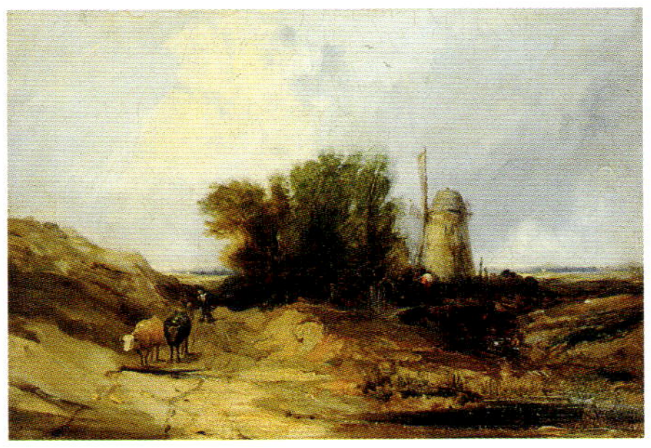

Eyre, James 1802–1838
A Windmill in Derbyshire
oil on canvas 29.3 x 42
VIS.614

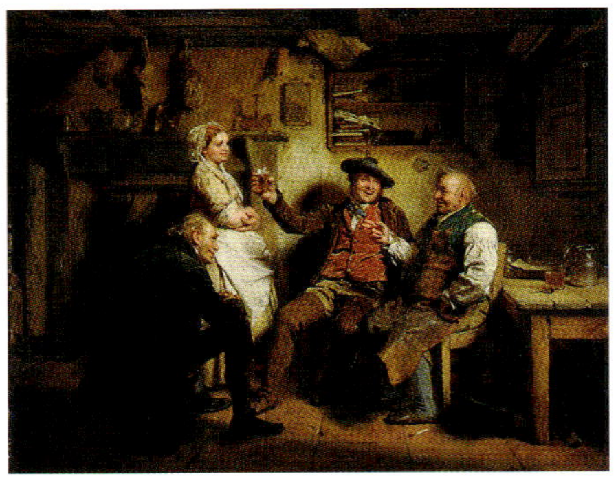

Faed, John 1820–1902
Highland Interior with Figures
oil on canvas 32.8 x 41.2
VIS.1497

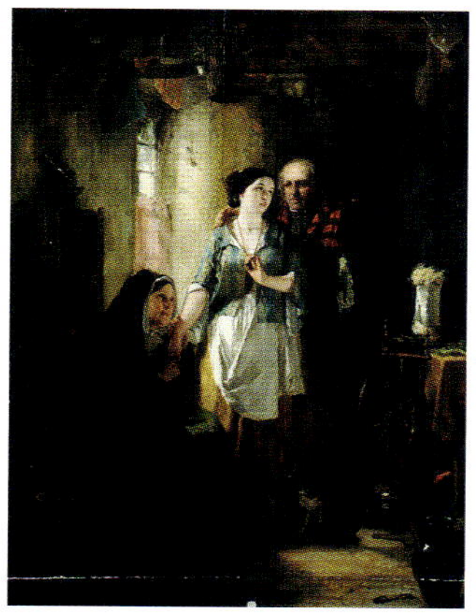

Faed, Thomas 1826–1900
Auld Robin Gray 1850
oil on panel 97 x 72.2
VIS.1624

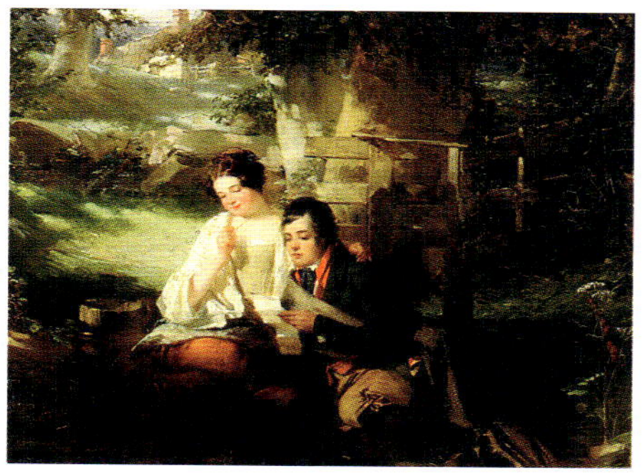

Faed, Thomas 1826–1900
Robert Burns and Highland Mary 1852
oil on panel 19.9 x 26.7
VIS.1475

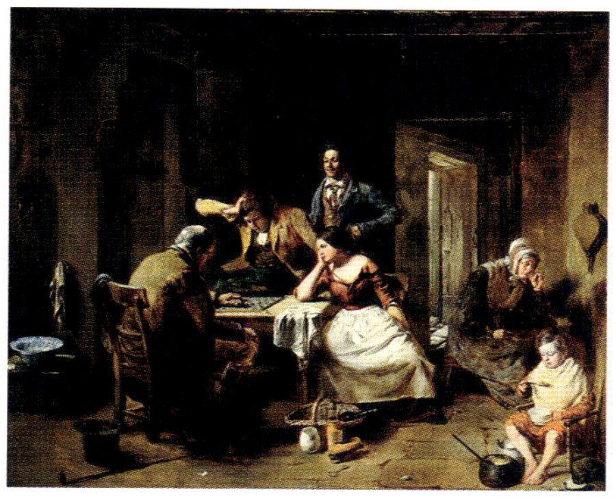

Faed, Thomas 1826–1900
A Game of Draughts
oil on panel 49.5 x 59.6
VIS.1570

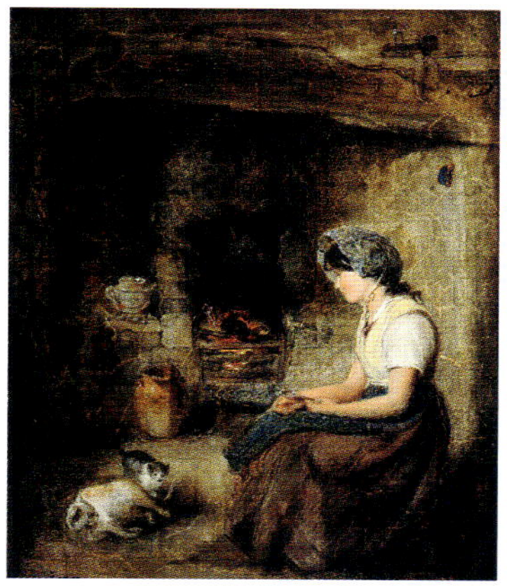

Faed, Thomas 1826–1900
Cottage Interior
oil on canvas 35.9 x 29.5
VIS.302

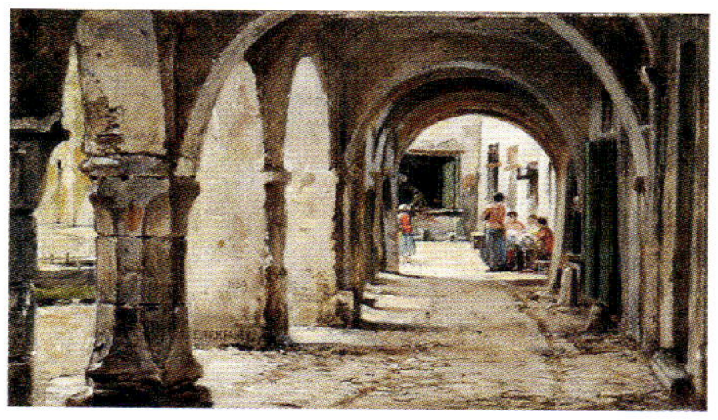

Fahey, Edward Henry 1844–1907
The Via Massala, Rapallo, Italy 1889
oil on panel 13.3 x 22.5
VIS.1080

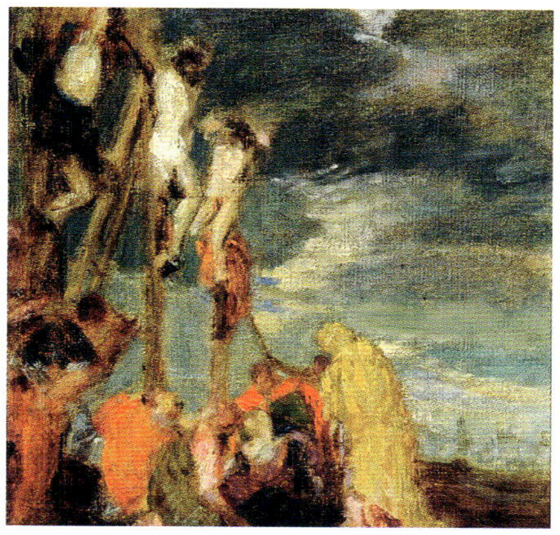

Fantin-Latour, Henri 1836–1904
The Crucifixion 1854
oil on canvas 22.5 x 22.5
VIS.179

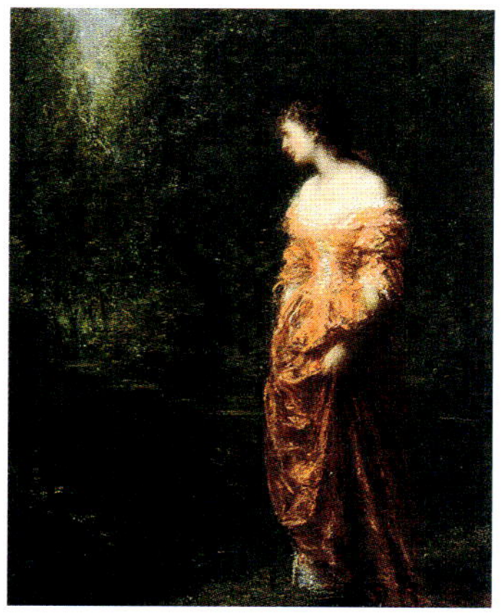

Fantin-Latour, Henri (attributed to)
1836–1904
The Trysting Place
oil on canvas 25.7 x 20.4
VIS.164

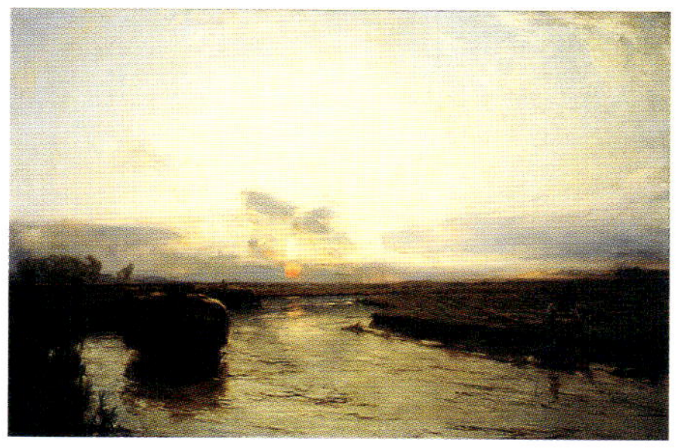

Farquharson, David 1839–1907
Eventide 1906
oil on canvas 122.3 x 183.7
VIS.1471

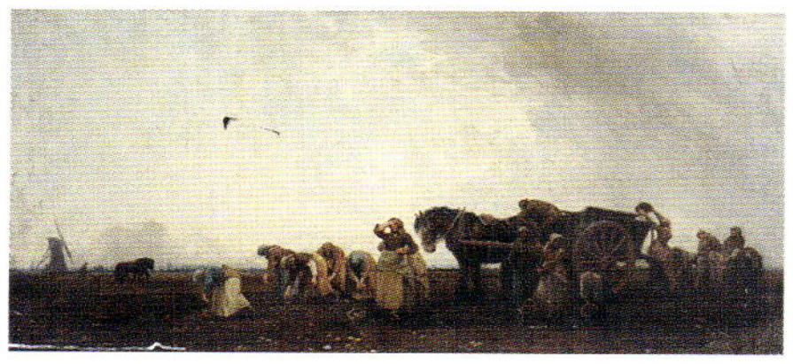

Farren, Robert Dennis 1832–1912
Potato Picking in Cambridgeshire 1877
oil on canvas 63.7 x 137.7
VIS.574

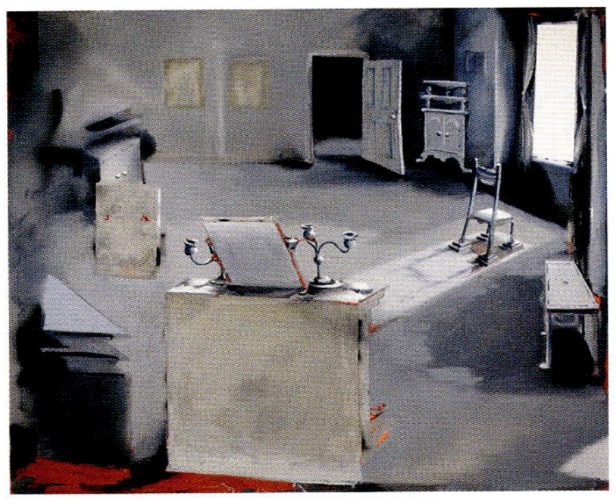

Farthing, Stephen b.1950
Room in Samur 1990
oil on canvas 173.4 x 206.4
VIS.5300

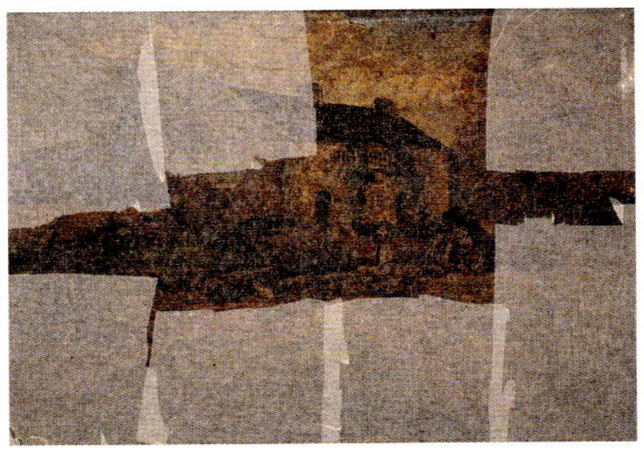

Fawley, J. F.
*Rural Cottage** 1890–1900
oil on canvas 25.5 x 35.5
1978.925

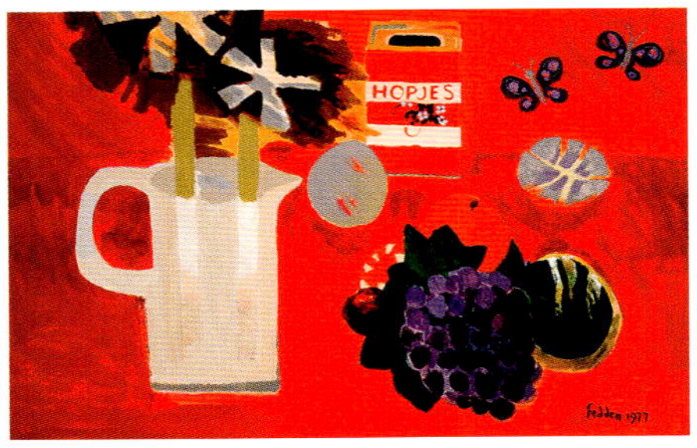

Fedden, Mary b.1915
Red Still Life 1977
oil on board 47.5 x 73
VIS.5427

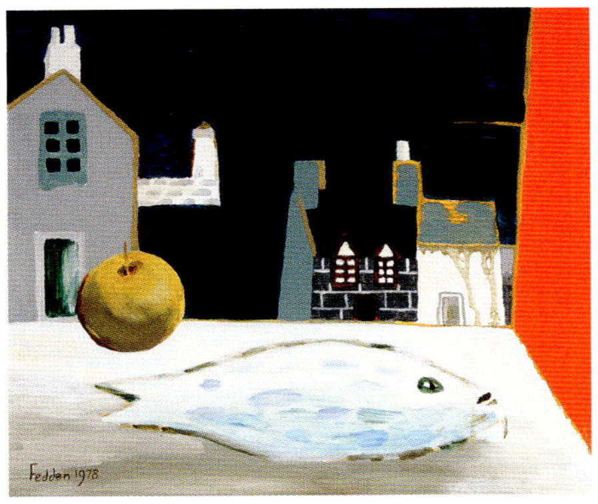

Fedden, Mary b.1915
Shetland Still Life 1978
oil on panel 46.5 x 53.5
VIS.5445

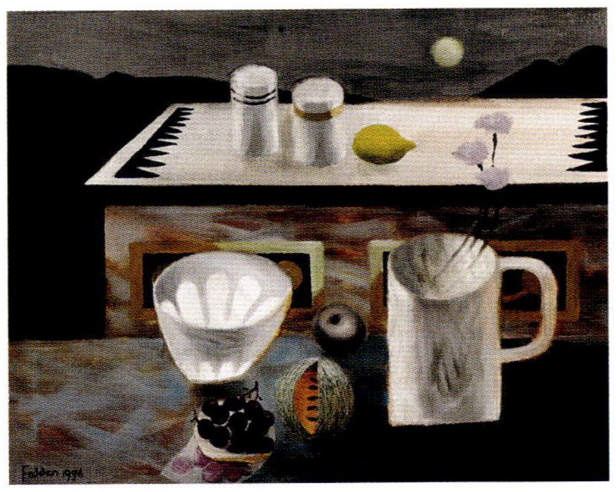

Fedden, Mary b.1915
Three Mauve Flowers 1996
oil on canvas 57.5 x 69.8
VIS.5253

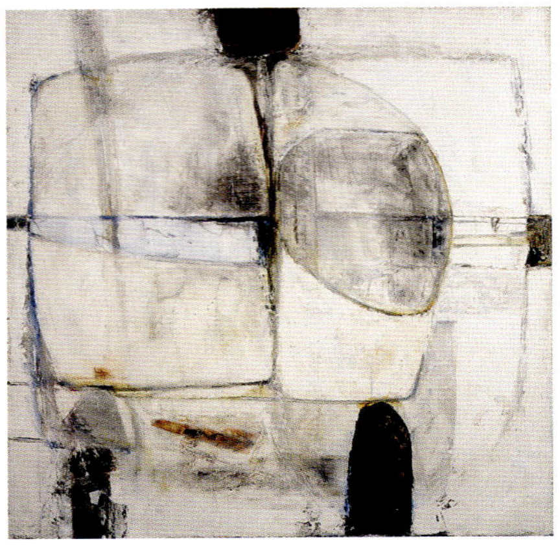

Feiler, Paul b.1918
Strata Brown and Grey
oil on canvas 93 x 93
VIS.LI.137 (P)

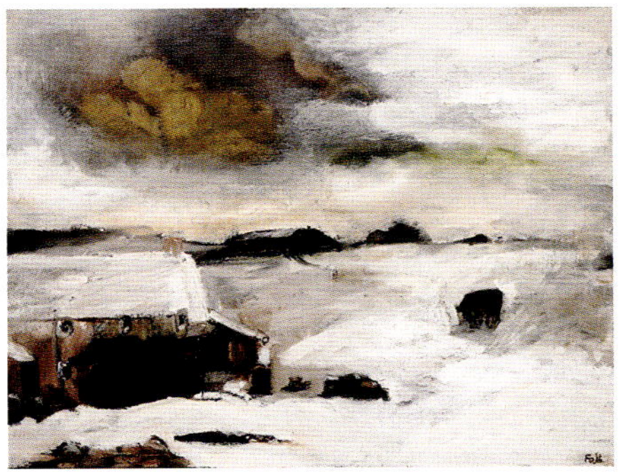

Fell, Sheila Mary 1931–1979
Snowscape, Cumbria 1977
oil on canvas 71.6 x 91.6
VIS.4294

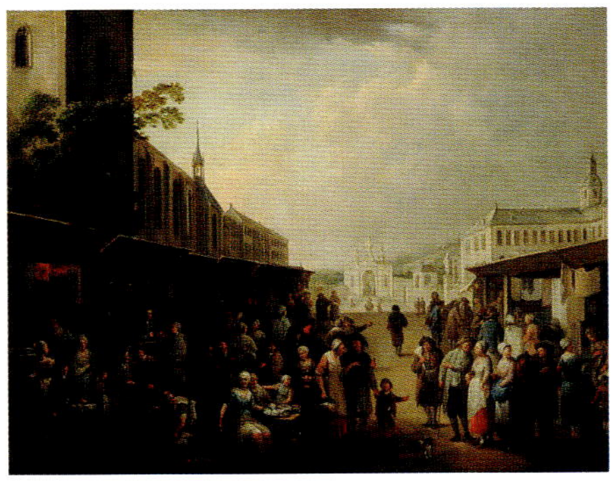

Ferg, Franz de Paula 1689–1740
A Street Scene 1720–1725
oil on copper 28.5 x 36.3
VIS.1879

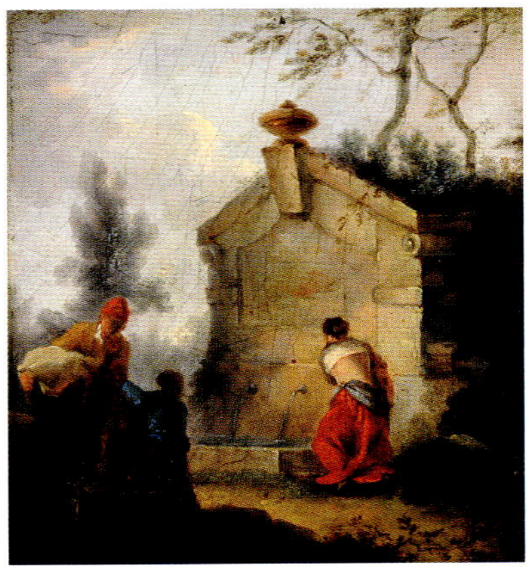

Ferg, Franz de Paula 1689–1740
The Fountain 1720–1725
oil on panel 17.4 x 16.4
VIS.90

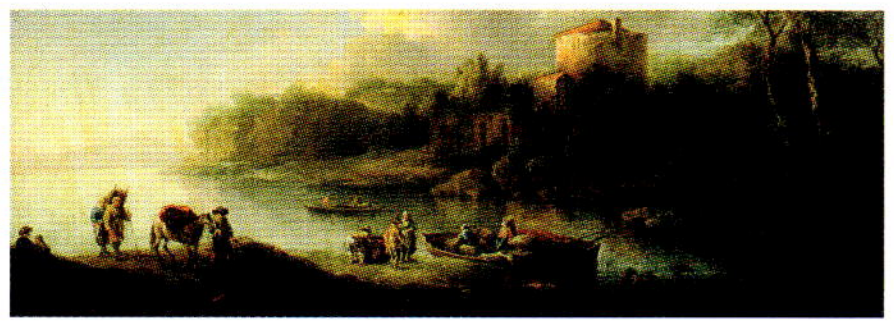

Ferg, Franz de Paula (attributed to)
1689–1740
The Ferryboat 1715–1720
oil on canvas 26.2 x 70.8
VIS.526

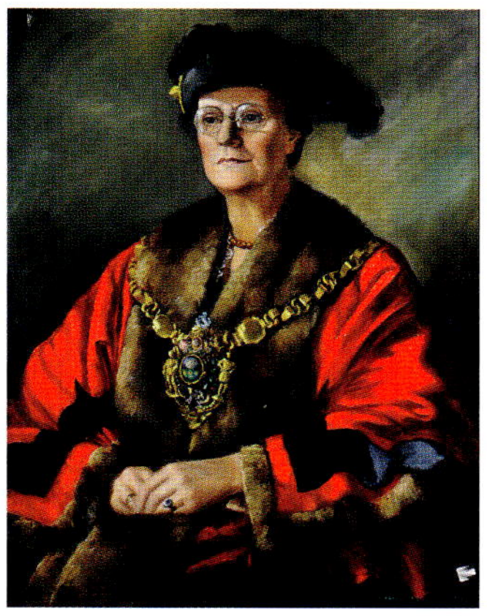

Fieldhouse, Florence 1898–1974
Alderman Mrs A. E. Longden (d.1952), First Lady Lord Mayor of Sheffield 1937
oil on canvas 89.4 x 69.2
VIS.4171

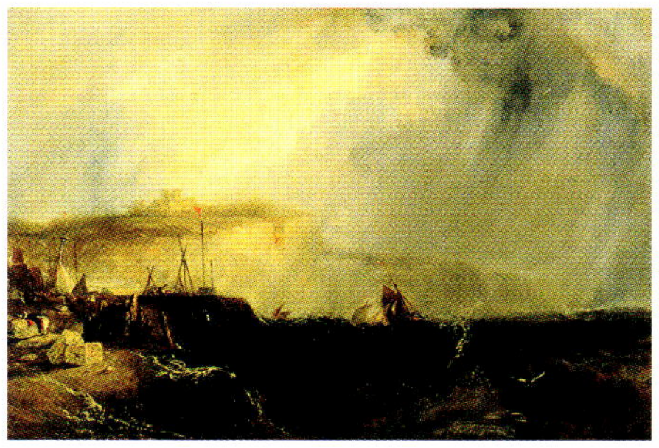

Fielding, Anthony V. C. 1787–1855
A Rough Sea off Dover, Kent 1826
oil on canvas 58.9 x 85.3
VIS.1602

Fielding, Anthony V. C. 1787–1855
Ben Venue, Scotland
oil on panel 24.5 x 35.3
VIS.372

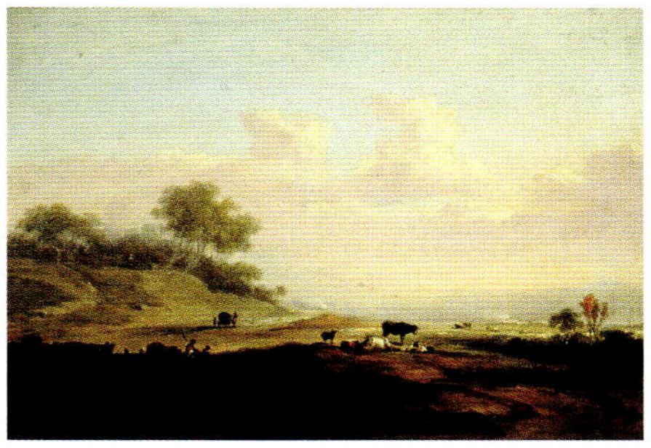

Fielding, Anthony V. C. 1787–1855
Landscape
oil on board 27 x 37.8
VIS.256

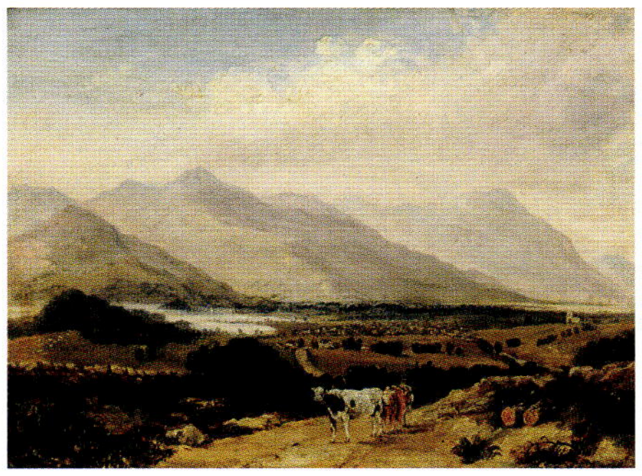

Fielding, Anthony V. C. 1787–1855
Landscape with Cattle
oil on canvas 32.2 x 42.8
VIS.642

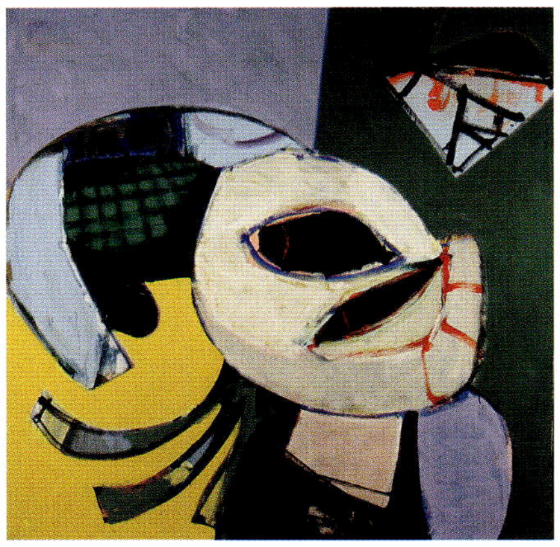

Fielding, Brian 1933–1987
Baltic Angel
oil on canvas 153 x 152.5
VIS.5299

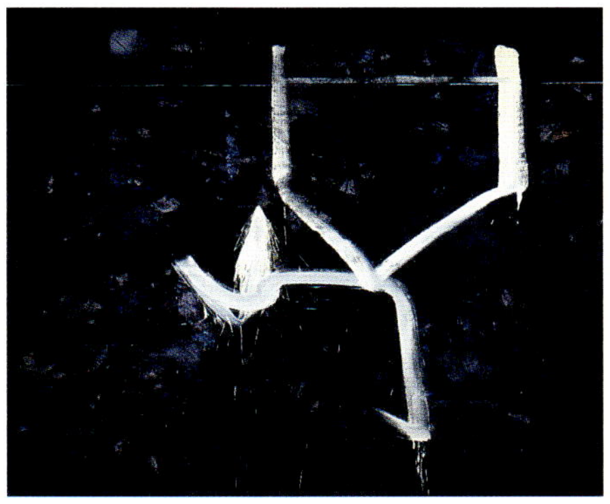

Fielding, Brian 1933–1987
Ink City
oil on canvas 191 x 235
VIS.5417

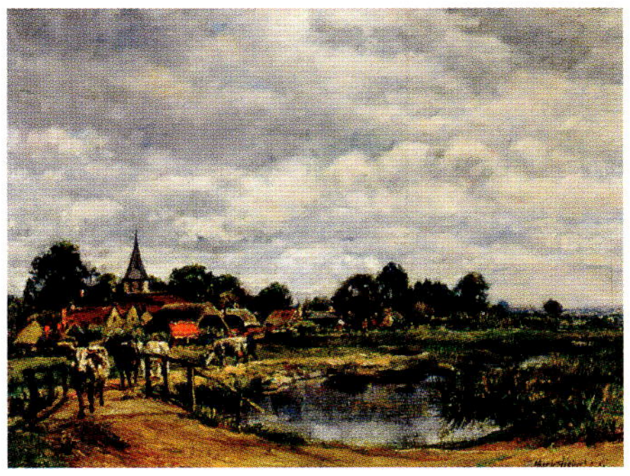

Fisher, Mark 1841–1923
A Grey Day
oil on canvas 34.3 x 44.9
VIS.117

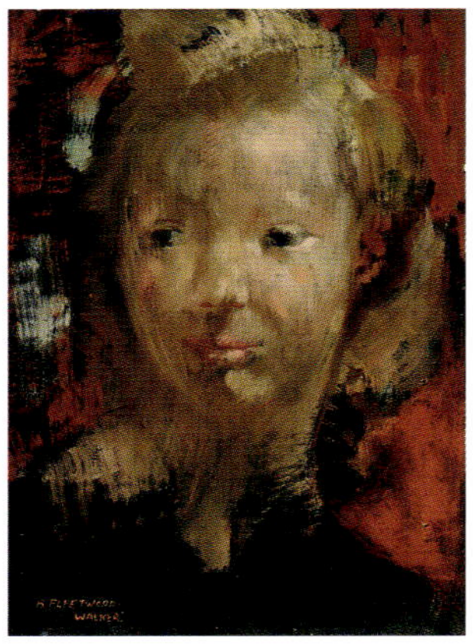

Fleetwood-Walker, Bernard 1893–1965
Head of a Girl
oil on board 34.4 x 24.4
VIS.1920

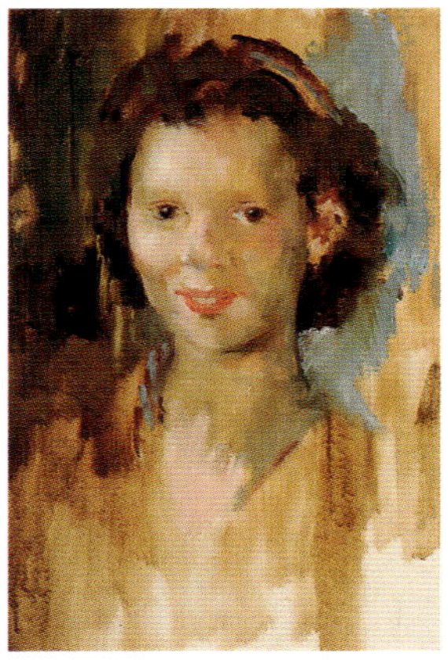

Fleetwood-Walker, Bernard 1893–1965
Miss Bryan
oil on canvas 46 x 32
VIS.2949

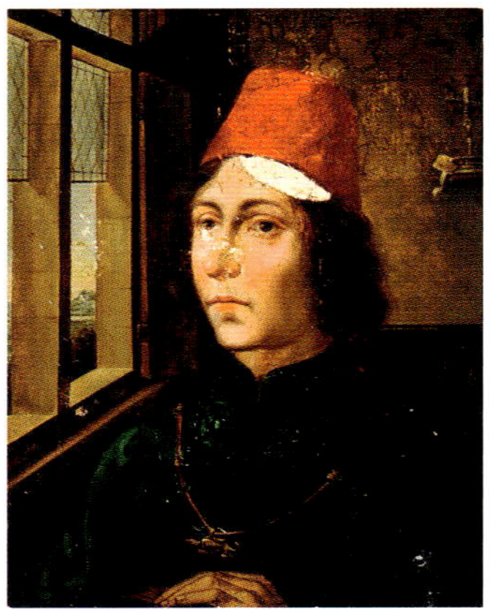

Flemish School 15th C
Man with a Red Cap
oil on panel 27.3 x 21.3
VIS.91

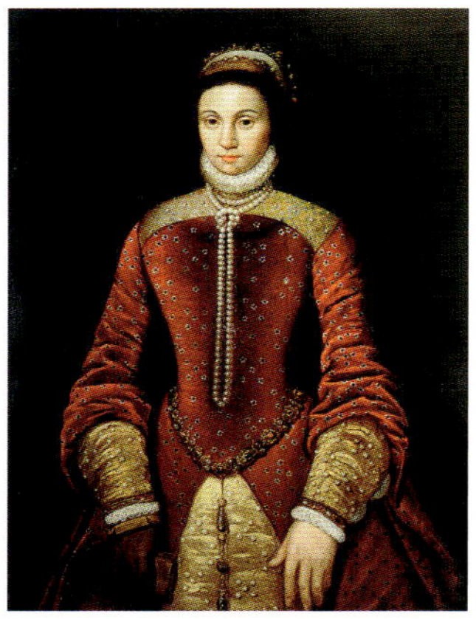

Flemish School 16th C
Mary Tudor (1516–1558)
oil on panel 89.8 x 66.8
VIS.50

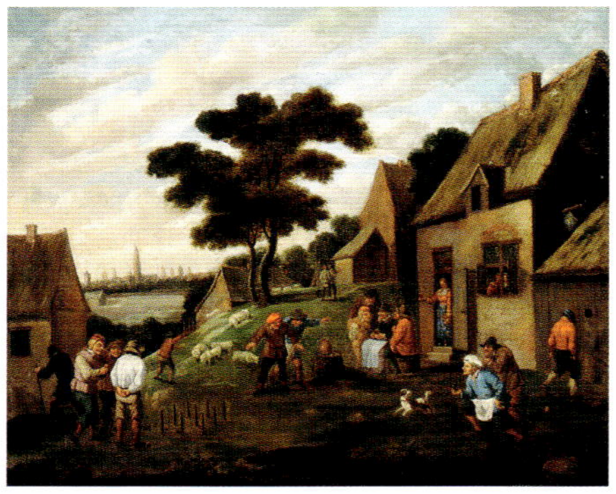

Flemish School 19th C
Peasants (Skittle Alley)
oil on canvas 62.9 x 75.5
VIS.259

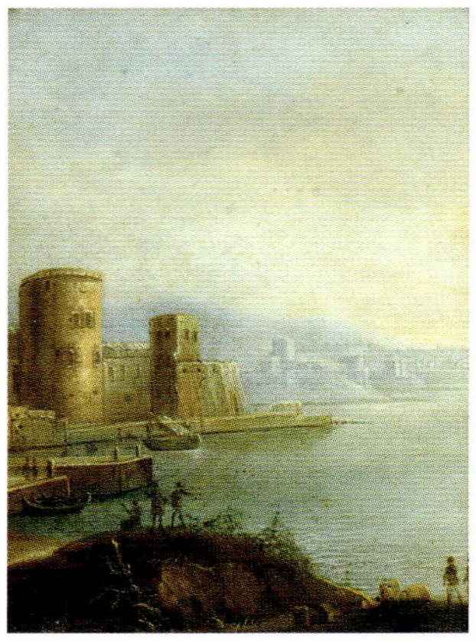

Flemish School (attributed to) 16th C
Fortress
oil on copper 19.5 x 14.7
VIS.579

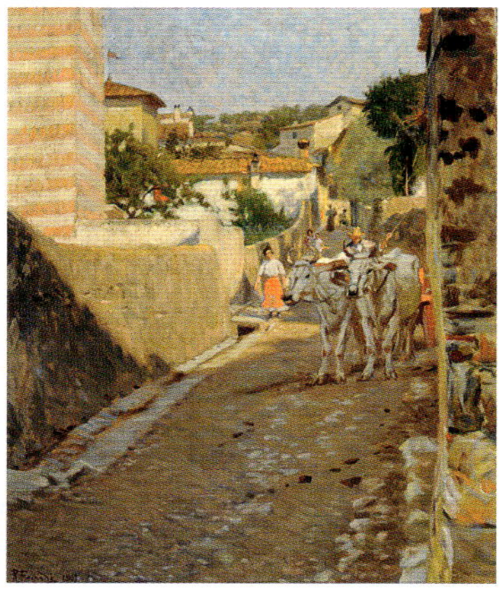

Focardi, Ruggero 1864–1934
A Spanish Street Scene 1913
oil on canvas 76.2 x 63.2
VIS.342

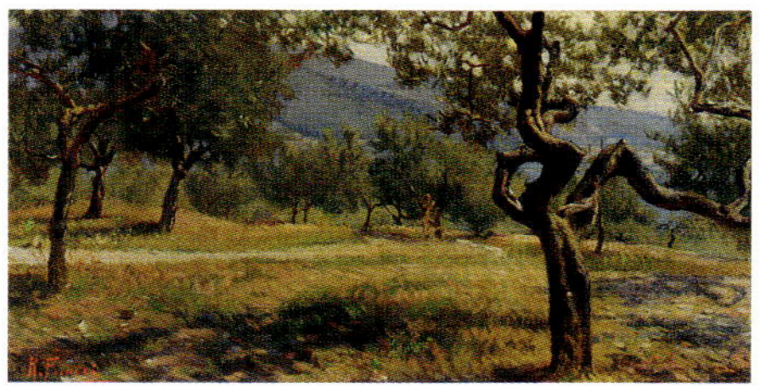

Focardi, Ruggero 1864–1934
The Olive Grove
oil on canvas 30 x 59
VIS.2953

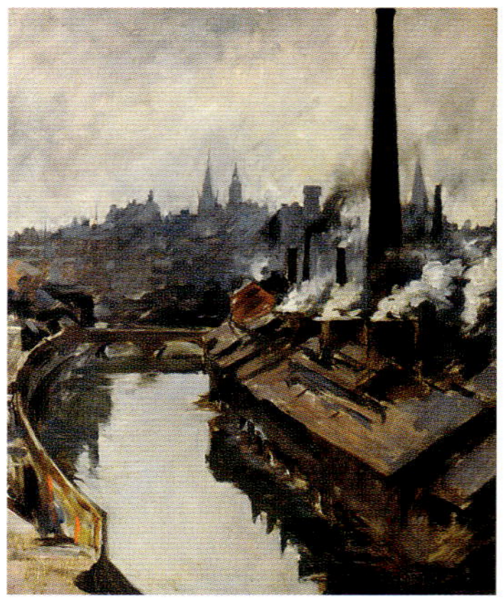

Forbes, Stanhope Alexander 1857–1947
Sheffield, River and Smoking Chimneys 1915
oil on canvas 58.3 x 48.3
VIS.4656

Facing page: Scarborough, Joe, b.1938, *Steel and Steelworkers* (detail), 1993, Sheffield Hallam University, (p. 260)

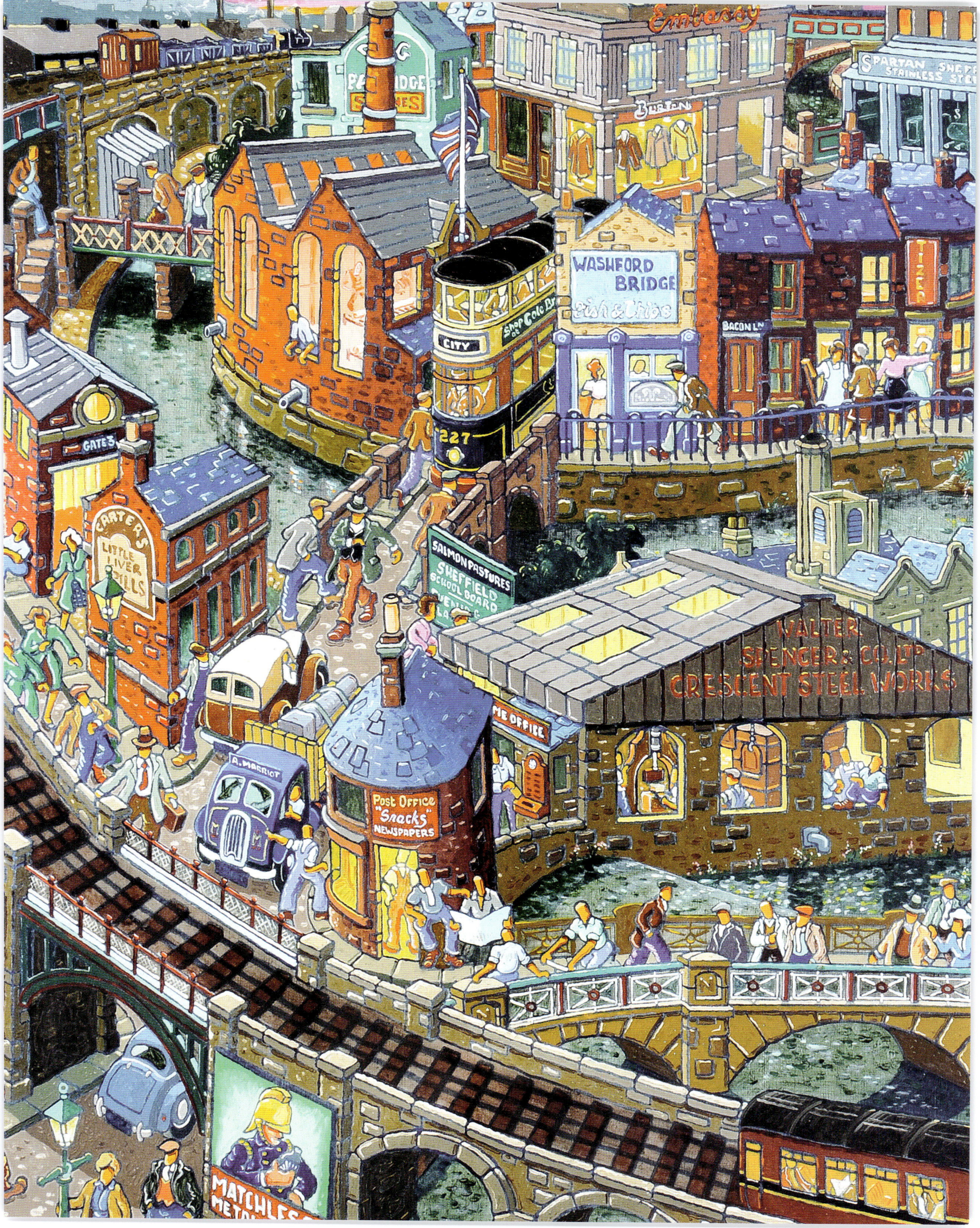
Embassy
BURTON
WASHFORD BRIDGE
Fish & Chips
BACON LN
CITY
227
GATE 3
CARTER'S LITTLE LIVER PILLS
SALMON PASTURES
SHEFFIELD SCHOOL BOARD
WALTER SPENCER & CO LTD
CRESCENT STEEL WORKS
A. MARRIOT
Post Office
"Snacks"
NEWSPAPERS

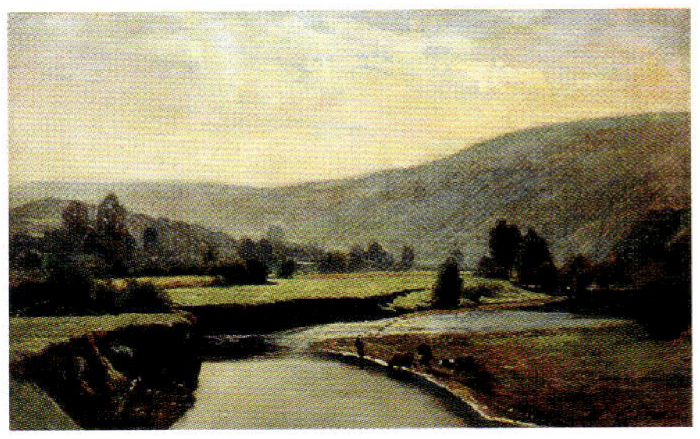

Formois, Théodore 1814–1871
In the Belgian Ardennes
oil on canvas 33 x 49
VIS.375

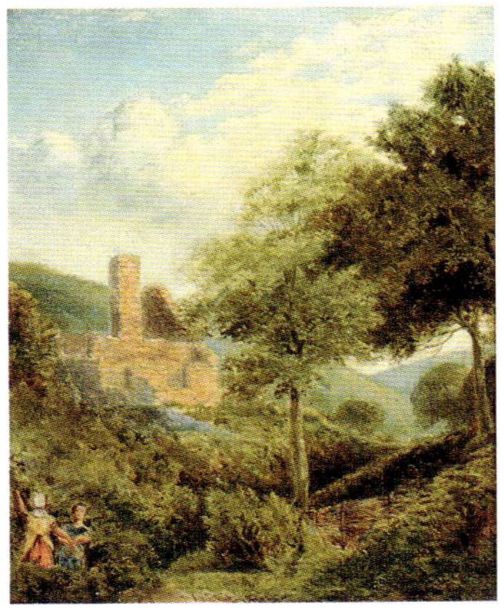

Foster, Myles Birket 1825–1899
The Ruined Mill
oil on panel 22.2 x 18.3
VIS.336

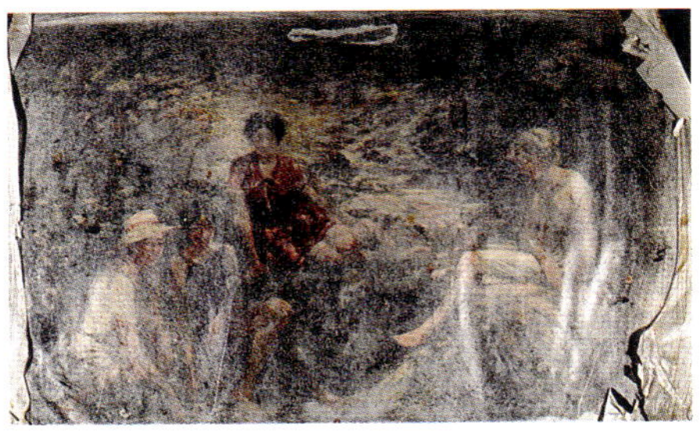

Fowler, Robert 1853–1926
Halcyon Weather
oil on canvas 118.8 x 174.5
VIS.2538

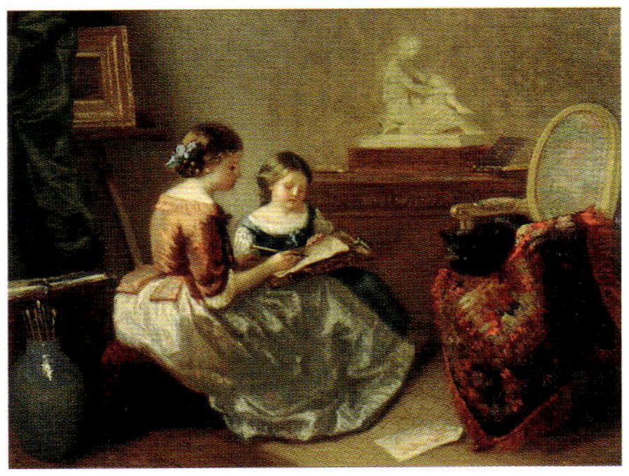

Fragonard, Jean-Honoré (attributed to)
1732–1806
The Sketching Lesson
oil on canvas 25 x 33
VIS.1205

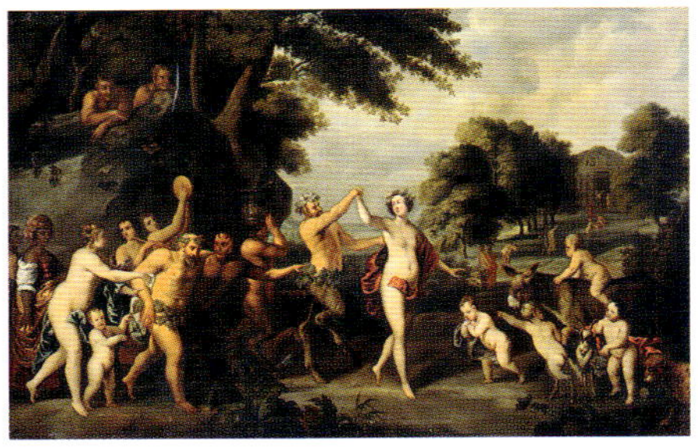

Franco-Flemish School
The Triumph of Bacchus
oil on canvas 125 x 191.2
VIS.2770

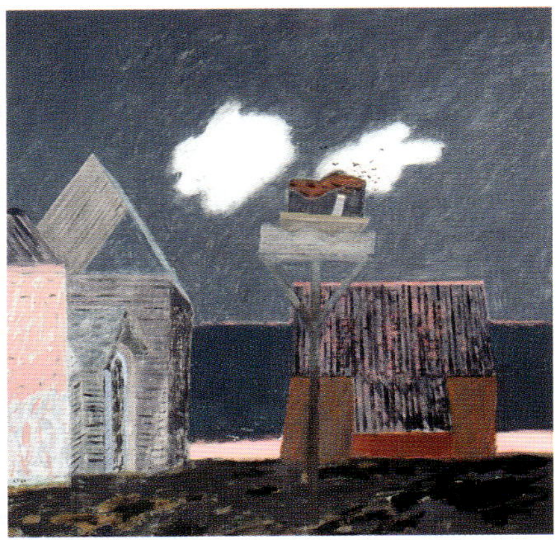

Fraser, Alexander b.1940
Pink Beach 1969
oil on panel 90.5 x 90.5
VIS.3692

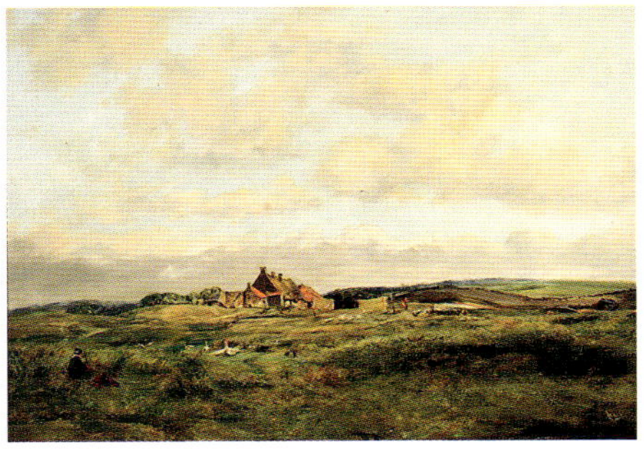

Fraser, Alexander George 1786–1865
The Goose Girl
oil on canvas 63.8 x 90.5
VIS.1278

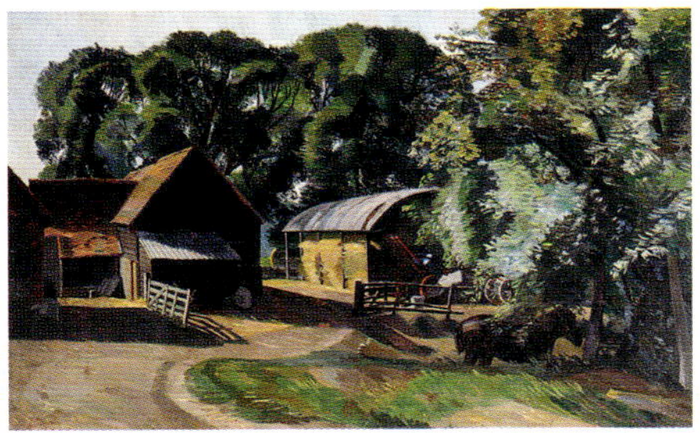

Freedman, Barnett 1901–1958
The Farmyard 1933
oil on canvas 52.9 x 83.1
VIS.1853

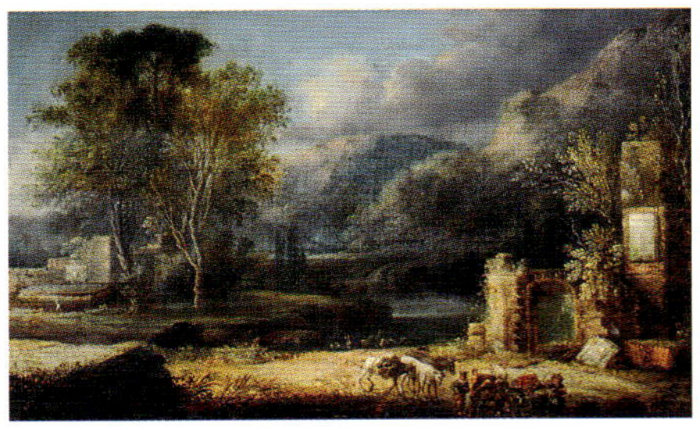

French School 18th C
Classical Landscape
oil on canvas 34 x 54.5
VIS.2617

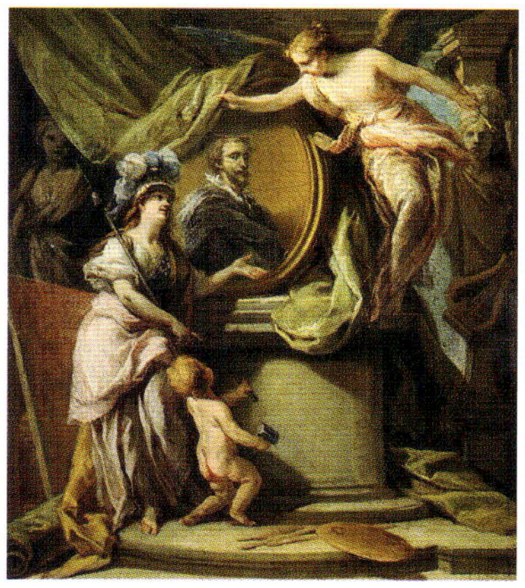

French School 18th C
The Arts
oil on canvas 44.4 x 36.6
VIS.2774

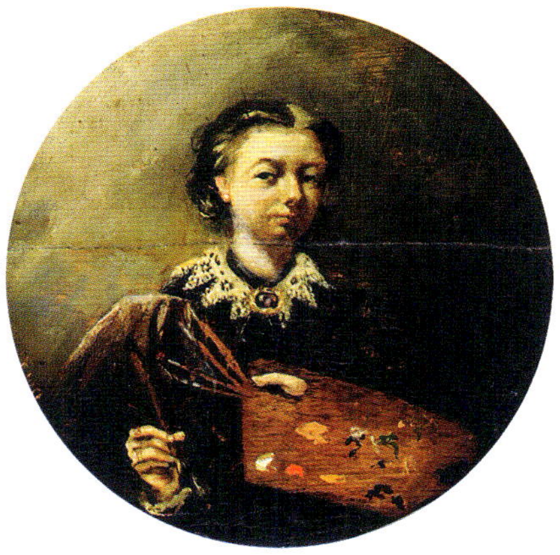

French School
Self Portrait 1854
oil on panel 12
VIS.230

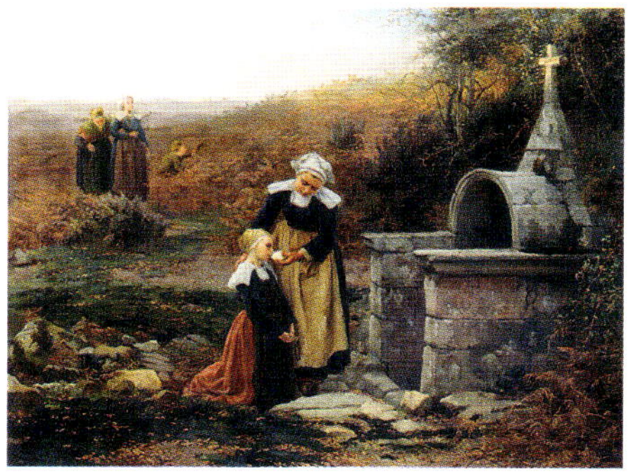

French School
The Holy Well 1878
oil on canvas 83.5 x 111
VIS.340

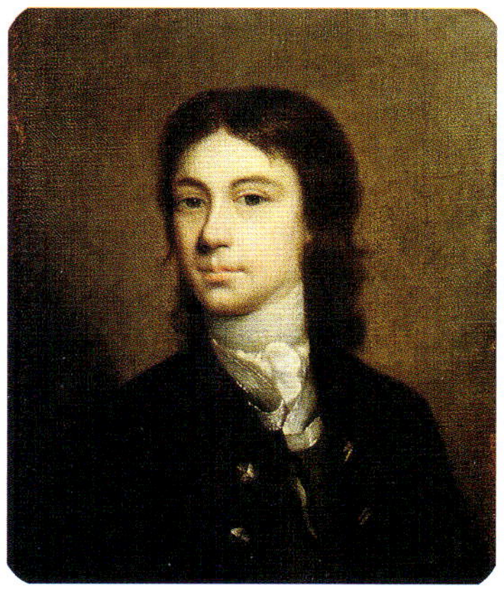

French School (attributed to) 18th C
Maximilien François Marie Isidore de Robespierre (1758–1794)
oil on canvas 49.6 x 41.1
VIS.40

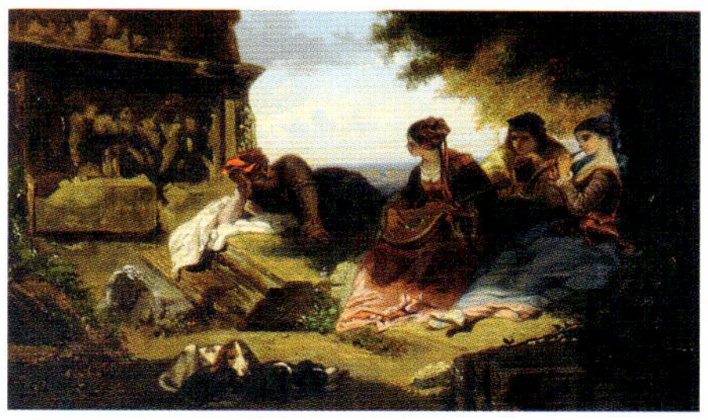

French School (attributed to) 19th C
A Musical Party
oil on panel 24.4 x 41.1
VIS.544

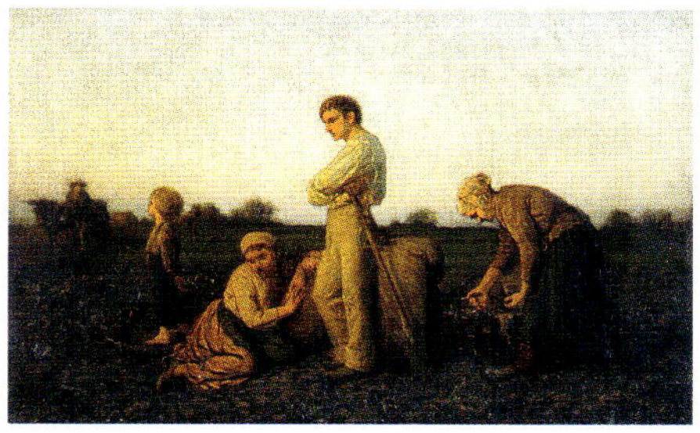

French School (attributed to) 19th C
Peasants in a Field at Rest
oil on canvas 26 x 40.9
VIS.952

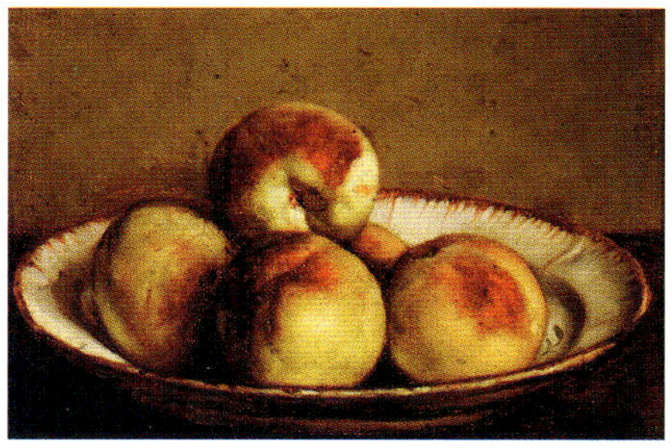

French School (attributed to) 19th C
Still Life, Peaches on a Dish
oil on canvas 17.4 x 26.2
VIS.53

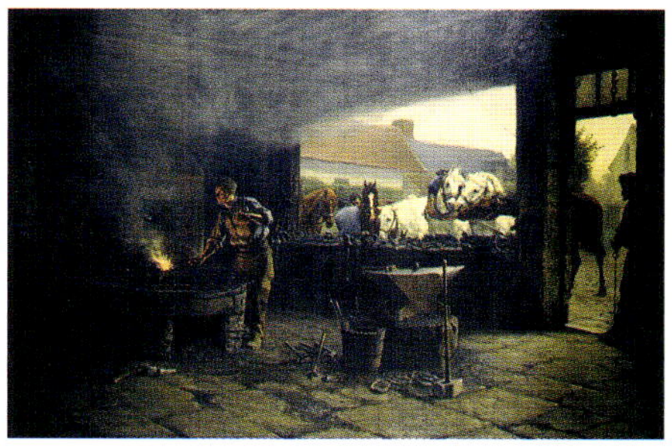

Frère, Charles Édouard 1837–1894
Shoeing Forge 1886
oil on canvas 126.6 x 191
VIS.1478

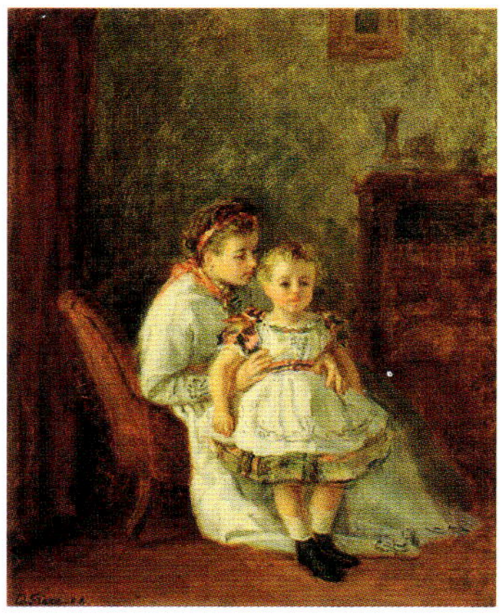

Frère, Pierre Edouard 1819–1886
Waiting for Visitors 1868
oil on panel 26.6 x 21.5
VIS.676

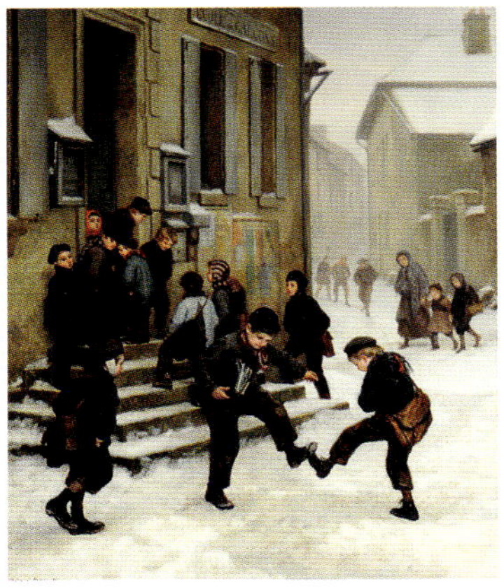

Frère, Pierre Edouard 1819–1886
In front of the School 1881
oil on panel 53.8 x 45
VIS.1364

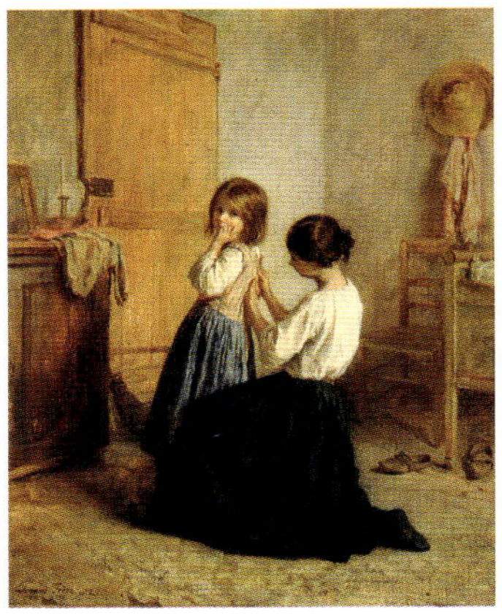

Frère, Pierre Edouard 1819–1886
Sewing on a Button 1882
oil on canvas 40.5 x 32.1
VIS.1393

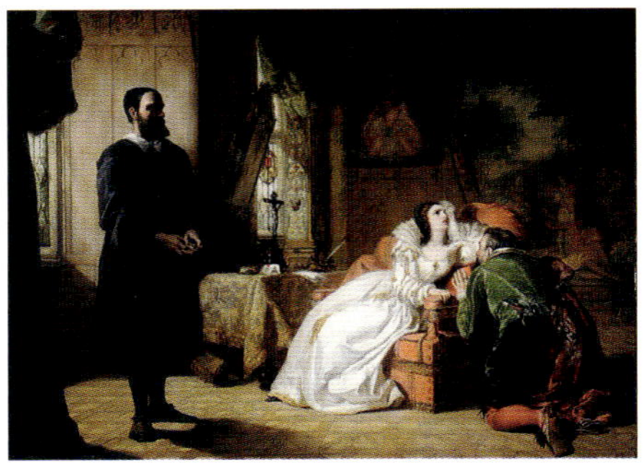

Frith, William Powell 1819–1909
John Knox Reproving Mary Queen of Scots 1844
oil on canvas 72.3 x 97.2
VIS.1564

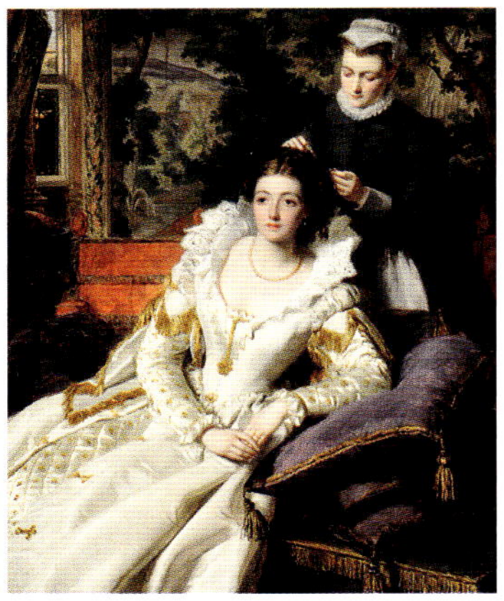

Frith, William Powell 1819–1909
The Toilet 1870
oil on canvas 78.9 x 64.5
VIS.1510

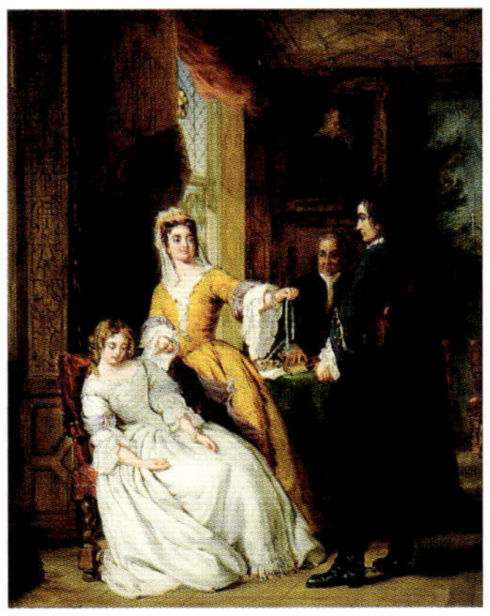

Frith, William Powell 1819–1909
The Bride of Lammermoor (from the novel by Walker Scott)
oil on canvas 44.8 x 34.6
VIS.2941

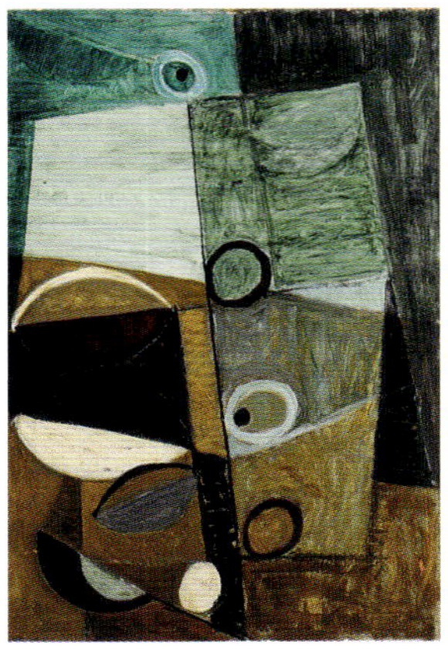

Frost, Terry 1915–2003
Green and Maroon Movement c.1952
oil on panel 75.5 x 50.8
VIS.5347

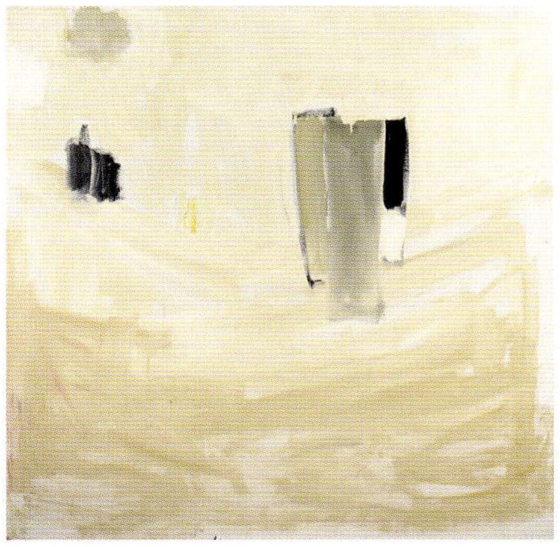

Frost, Terry 1915–2003
Abstract Painting
oil on canvas 121 x 121
VIS.LI.810 (P)

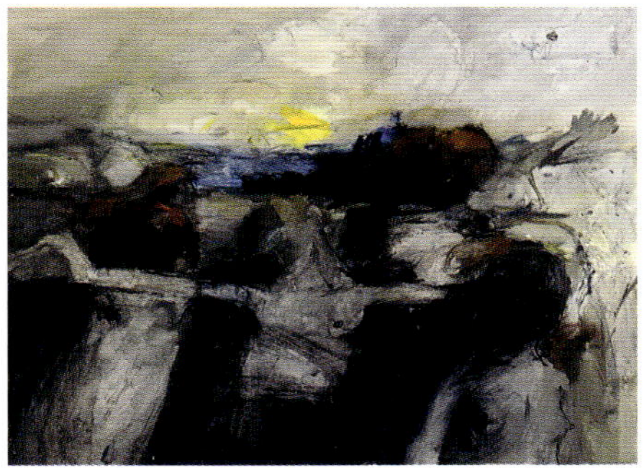

Fry, Anthony b.1927
Dancing Figures No.9 1959
oil on canvas 73.6 x 98.7
VIS.3428

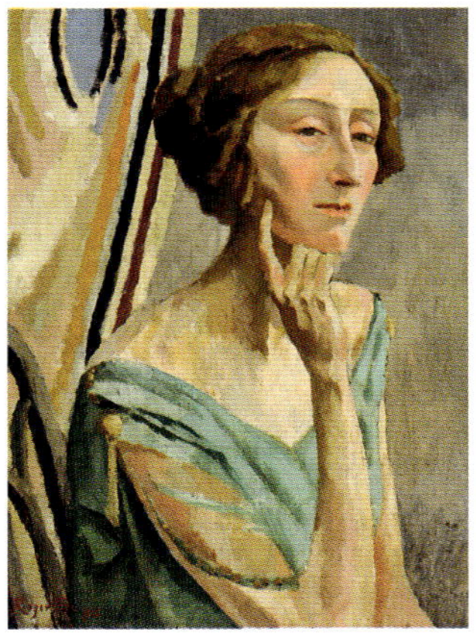

Fry, Roger Eliot 1866–1934
Edith Sitwell (1887–1964) 1918
oil on canvas 72 x 58
VIS.213

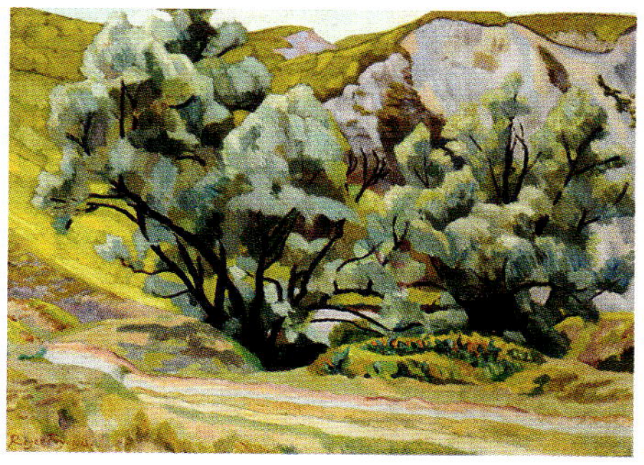

Fry, Roger Eliot 1866–1934
Quarry, Bo Peep Farm, Sussex 1918
oil on canvas 70.7 x 90.5
VIS.647

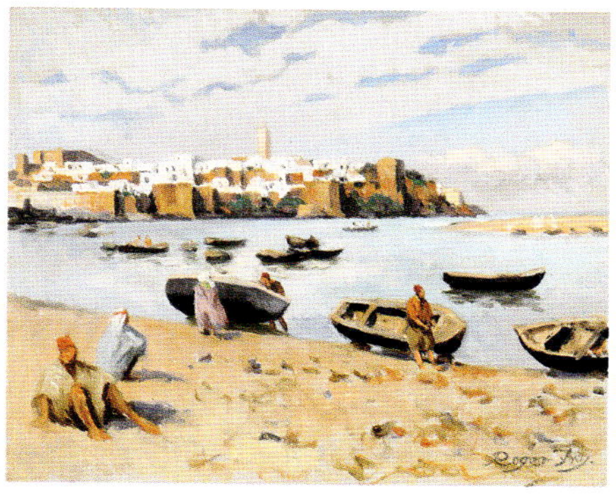

Fry, Roger Eliot 1866–1934
Rabat, Morocco
oil on board 32 x 40.4
VIS.1863

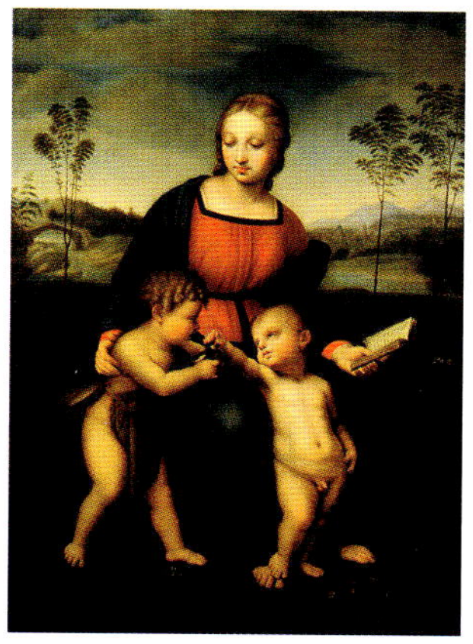

Fumi, Tebaldo active 1870–1880
Madonna del Cardelino (after Raphael) 1873
oil on canvas 136 x 105.5
CGSG00748

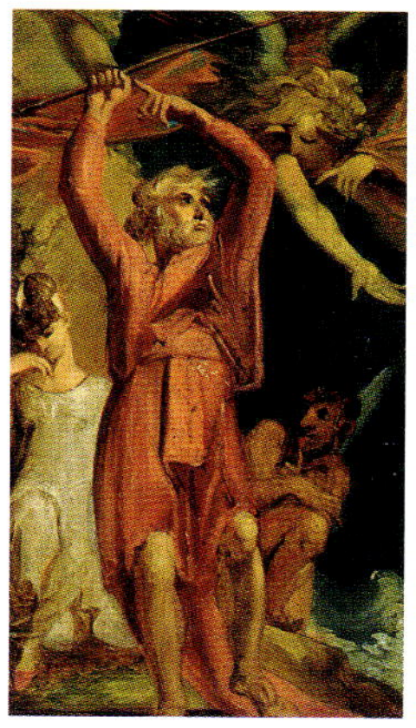

Fuseli, Henry 1741–1825
The Tempest
oil on millboard 21.3 x 11.8
VIS.2215

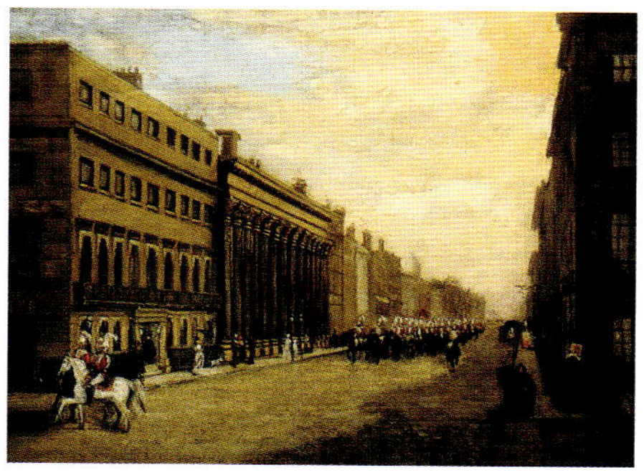

Fuseli, Henry (attributed to) 1741–1825
Albermarle Street, London
oil on cardboard 24 x 31.8
VIS.575

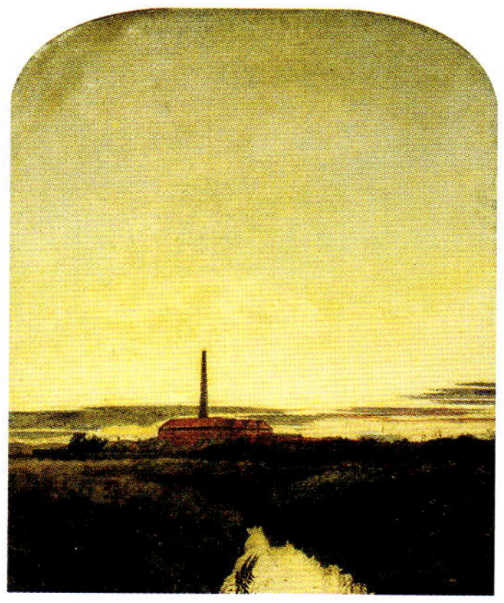

Fyfe, William Baxter Collier 1836–1882
Landscape in West Ireland
oil on panel 40.8 x 32.6
VIS.1255

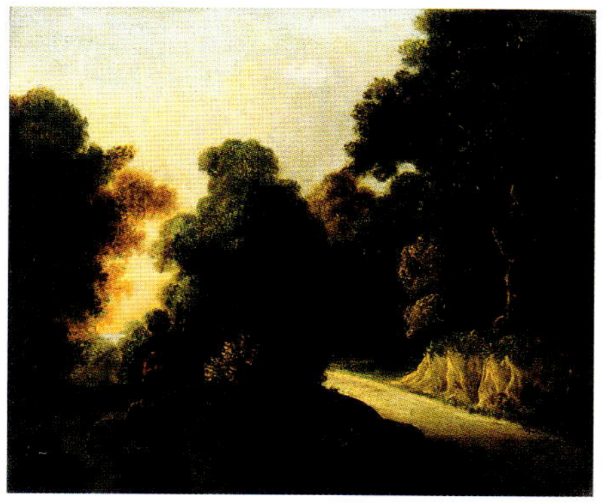

Gainsborough, Thomas (attributed to)
1727–1788
Landscape
oil on canvas 29.6 x 35
VIS.189

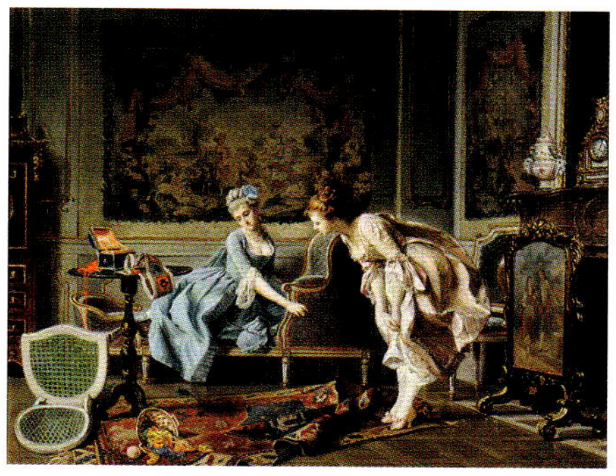

Garay Arévalo, Manuel 1844–1911
The Mouse
oil on canvas 35.8 x 44.7
VIS.2433

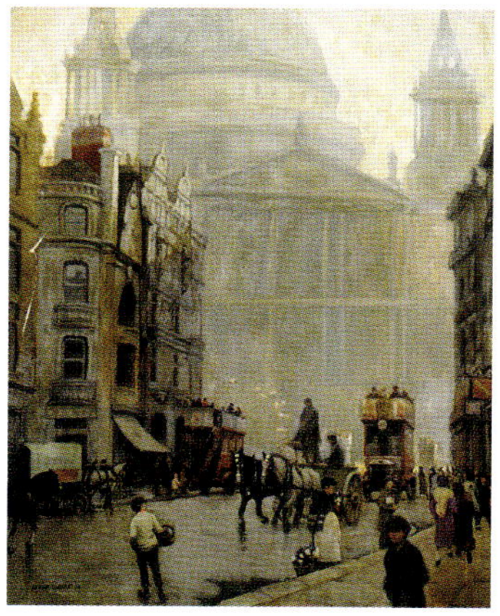

Garstin, Norman 1847–1926
Wren's Monument (St Paul's Cathedral, London) 1921
oil on canvas 127 x 101.5
VIS.2608

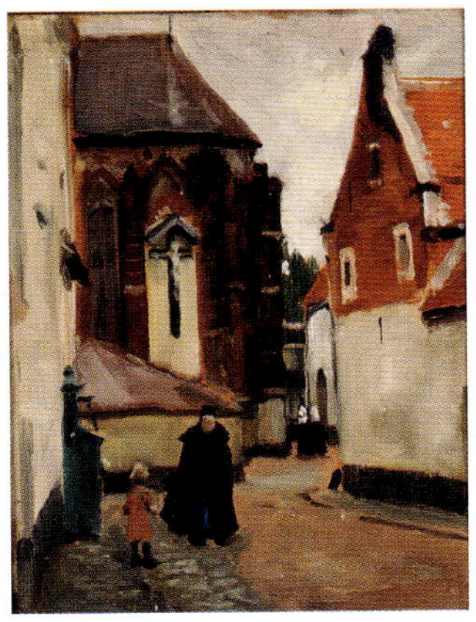

Garstin, Norman 1847–1926
Béguinage Church
oil on panel 26.1 x 19.9
VIS.4917

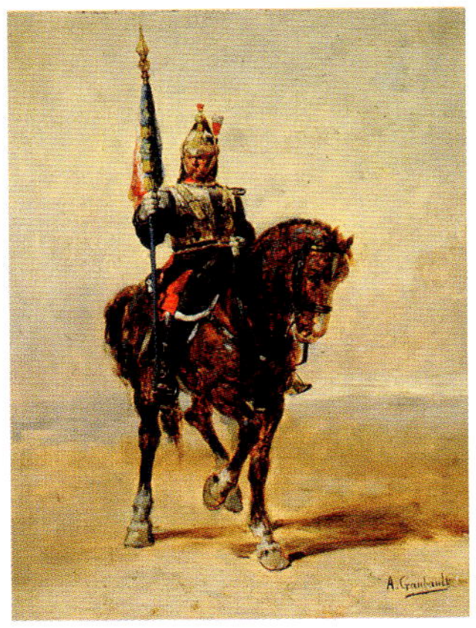

Gaubault, Alfred Émile d.1895
A French Guardsman
oil on canvas 34 x 25.5
VIS.1019

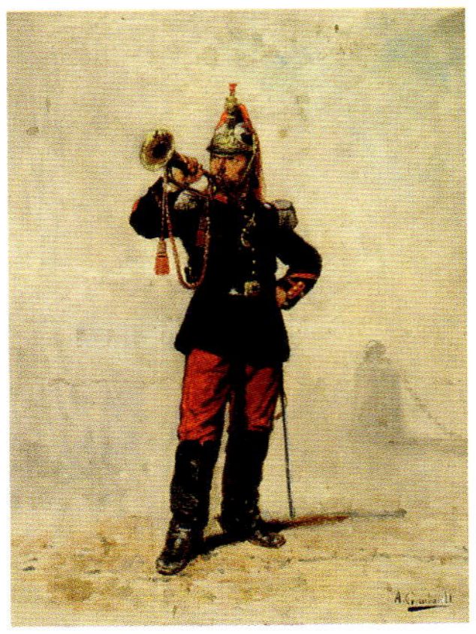

Gaubault, Alfred Émile d.1895
A French Guardsman
oil on canvas 34.1 x 25.5
VIS.1056

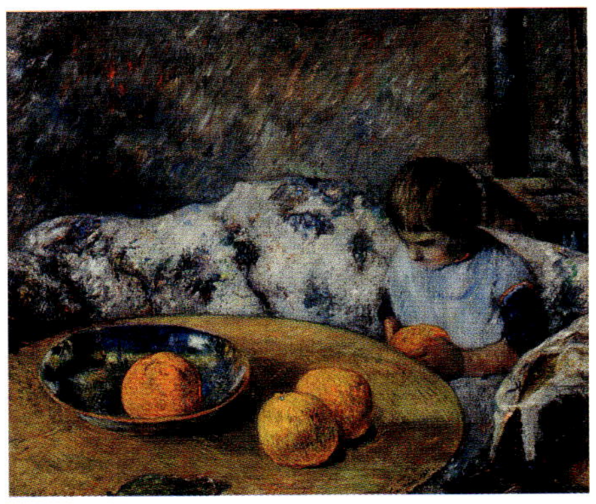

Gauguin, Paul 1848–1903
Interieur avec Aline Gauguin 1881
oil on canvas 52.4 x 60.3
VIS.LI.901 (P)

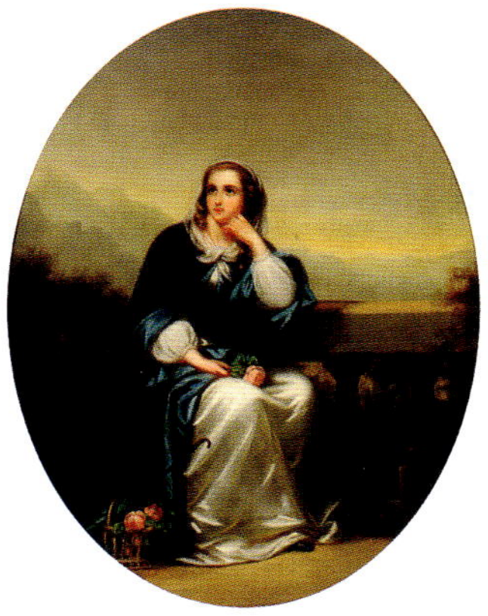

Geefs, Fanny 1807–1883
Meditation
oil on panel 37.2 x 28.7
VIS.1089

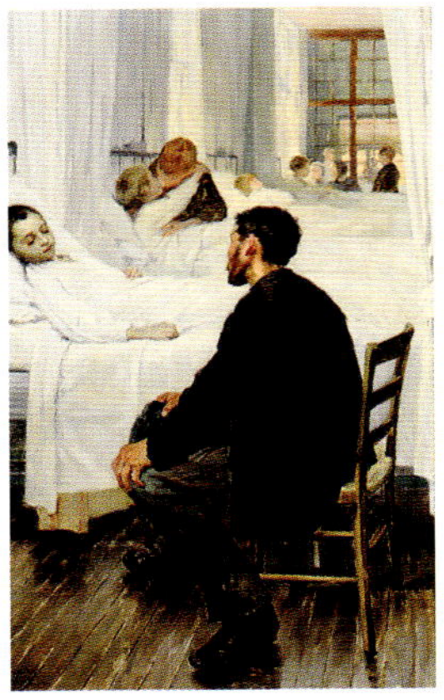

Geoffroy, Jean Jules Henry 1853–1924
Visiting Day
oil on canvas 83.4 x 43.3
VIS.779

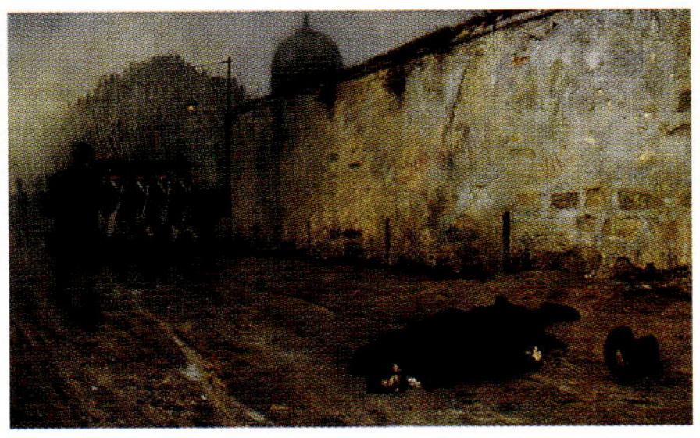

Gérome, Jean-Léon 1824–1904
The Execution of Marshal Ney 1855–1865
oil on canvas 65.2 x 104.2
VIS.1844

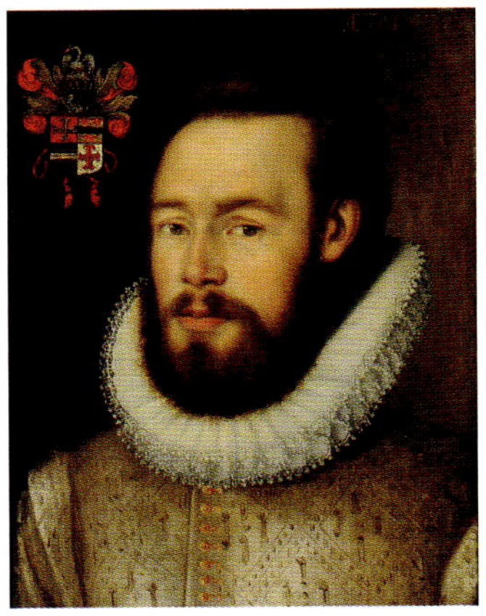

Gheeraerts, Marcus the elder (attributed to)
c.1520–before 1604
Lord Hunsdon (1526–1596)
oil on panel 41.2 x 31.9
VIS.78

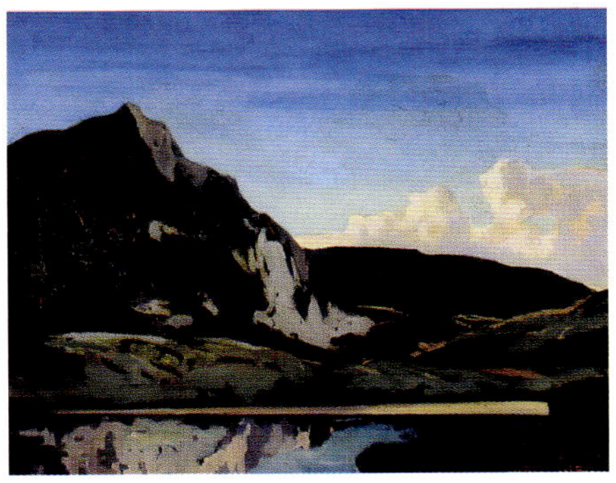

Gibbs, Lewis T.
Evening Stillness
oil on canvas 38.1 x 48.4
VIS.362

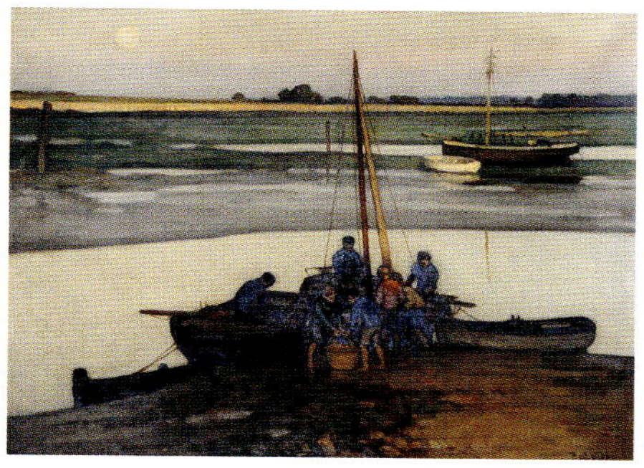

Gibbs, Percy William 1894–1937
Landing the Catch
oil on canvas 76.1 x 92.8
VIS.758

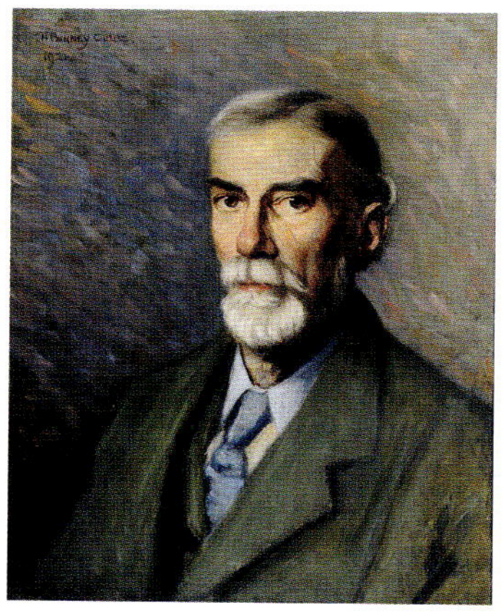

Gibbs, Thomas Binney 1870–1947
Edward Carpenter (1844–1929) 1921
oil on canvas 59 x 49.5
K1949.8

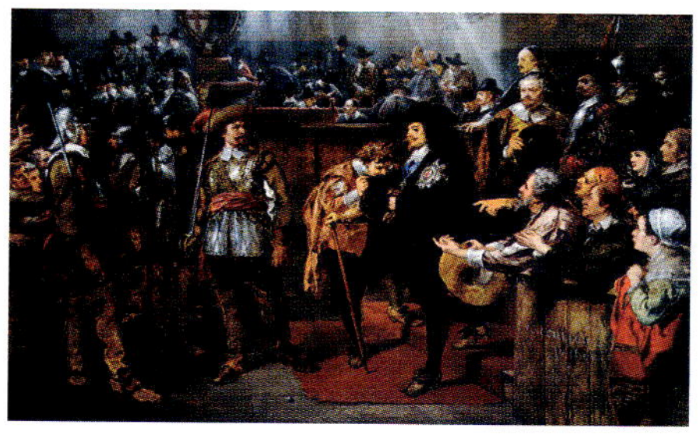

Gilbert, John 1817–1897
Charles I Leaving Westminster after His Death Sentence Had Been Passed 1872
oil on canvas 120 x 182.2
VIS.1473

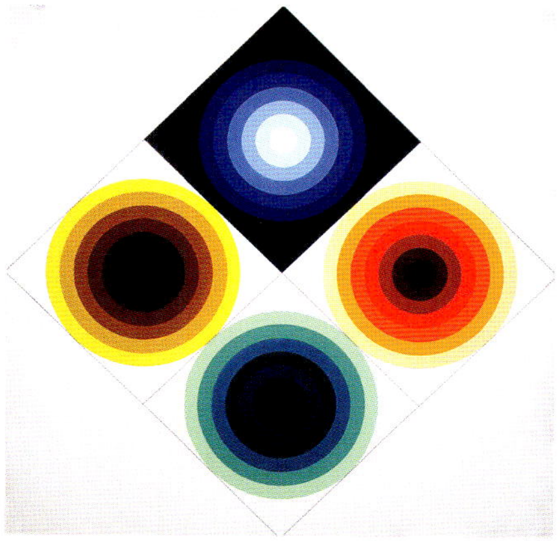

Giles, Frank Lynton 1910–2003
The Elements 1961
acrylic on board 122.2 x 122.4
VIS.4939

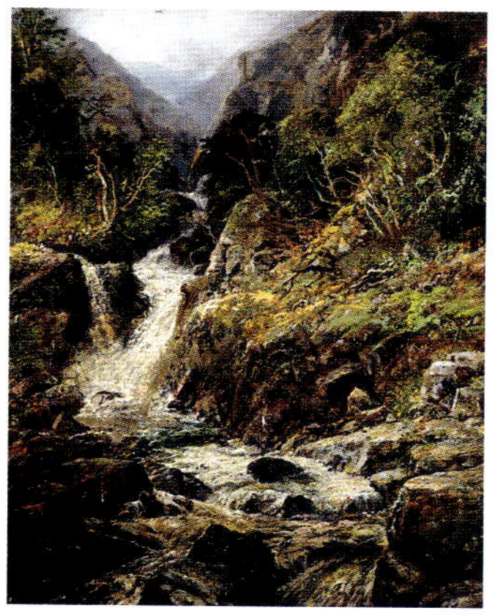

Gill, Edmund Marriner 1820–1894
A Welsh Mountain Torrent
oil on canvas 91.8 x 70.1
VIS.1277

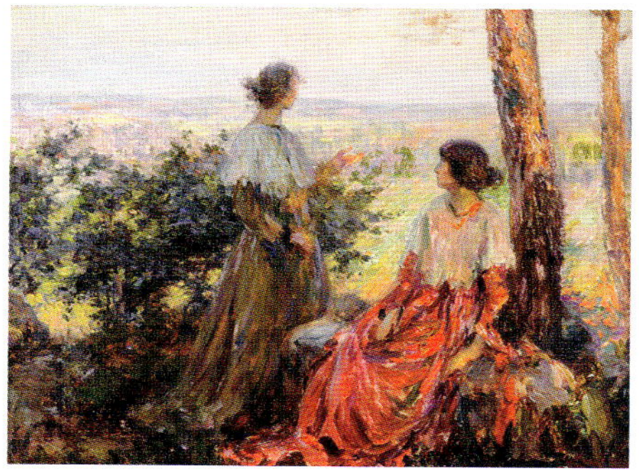

Gillet, Numa François 1868–1940
Summer Sunshine
oil on canvas 31 x 40
VIS.2933

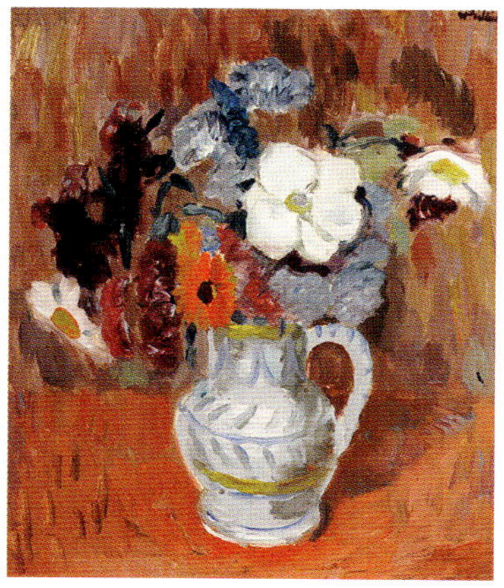

Gillies, William George 1898–1973
Flowers in a Vase
oil on board 49.4 x 41.9
VIS.5428

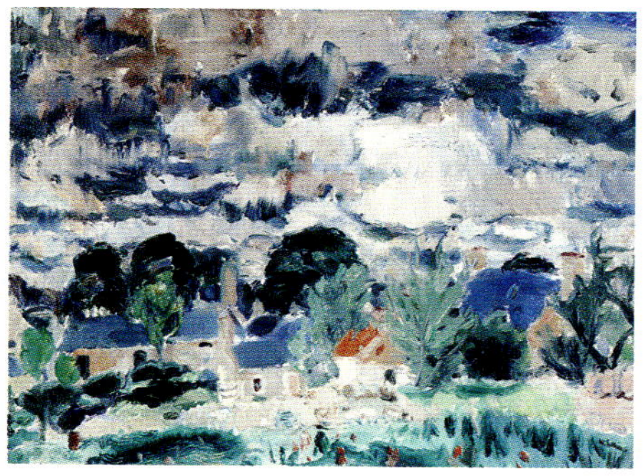

Gillies, William George 1898–1973
Temple, Midlothian, Scotland
oil on canvas 44.7 x 60
VIS.3268

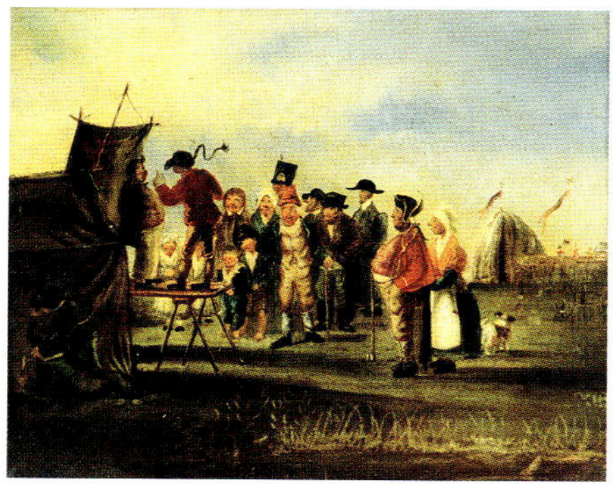

Gillray, James 1757–1815
A Country Fair
oil on panel 19 x 24.4
VIS.298

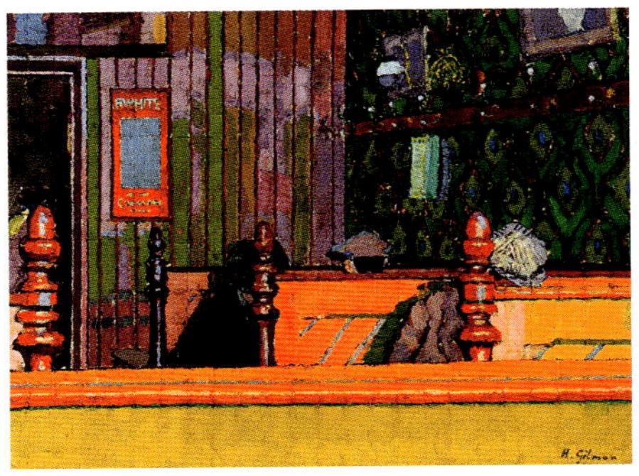

Gilman, Harold 1876–1919
Eating House c.1914
oil on canvas 72.7 x 91.4
VIS.2779

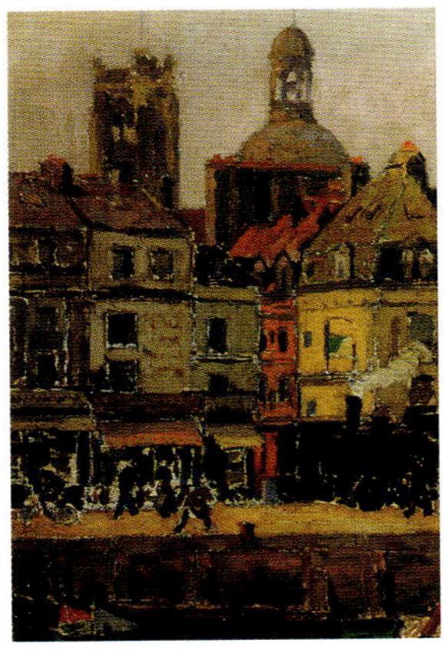

Ginner, Charles 1878–1952
Le quai Duquesne, Dieppe, France
oil on board 24.5 x 16.5
VIS.4228

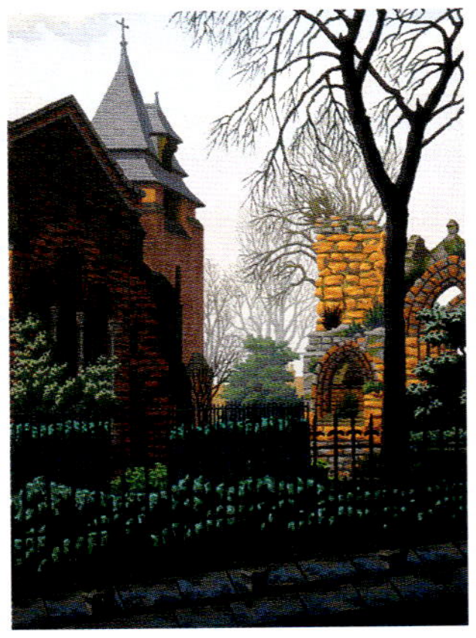

Ginner, Charles 1878–1952
St John's Church, Chester
oil on canvas 67.4 x 49.5
VIS.2987

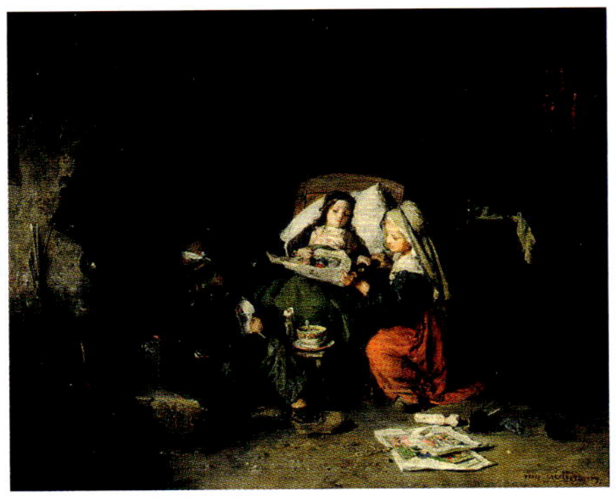

Girardet, Léopold-Henri 1848–1904
The Sick Child 1897
oil on canvas 84.1 x 99.8
VIS.1600

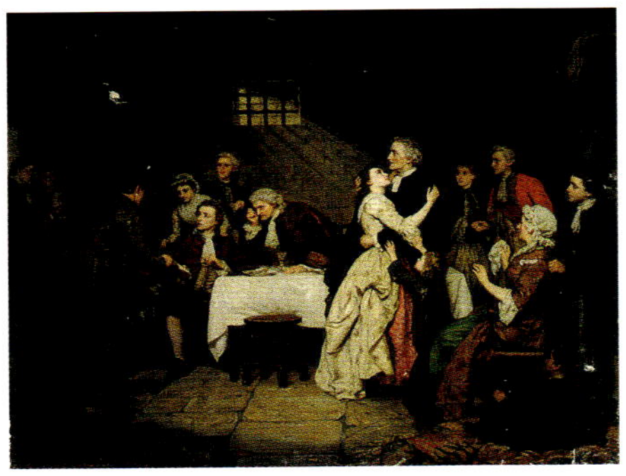

Girardot, Ernest Gustave 1840–1904
Scene from 'The Vicar of Wakefield' (from the novel by Oliver Goldsmith) 1883
oil on canvas 102.6 x 130.1
VIS.1686

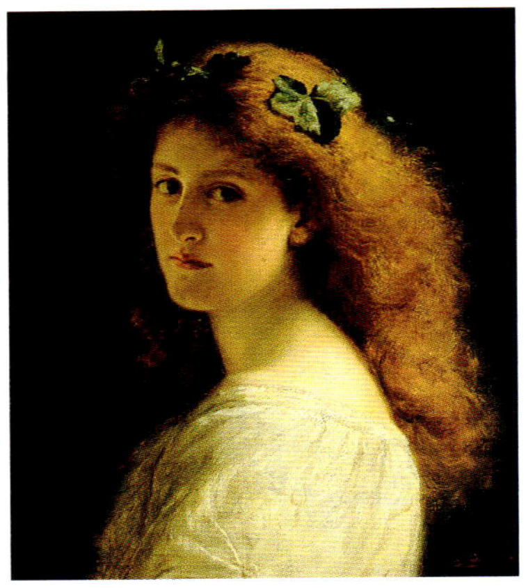

Gogin, Charles 1844–1931
Ivy Leaves 1877
oil on canvas 51 x 44.4
VIS.1394

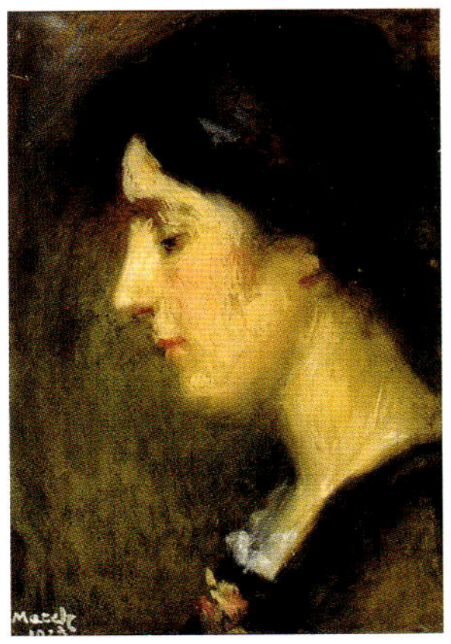

Gogin, Charles 1844–1931
A Profile 1923
oil on cardboard 41.2 x 28.6
VIS.2358

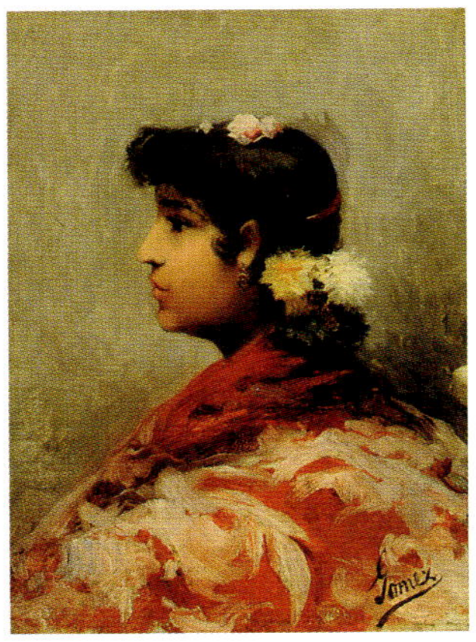

Gomez
Portrait
oil on canvas 25.6 x 19.2
VIS.1099

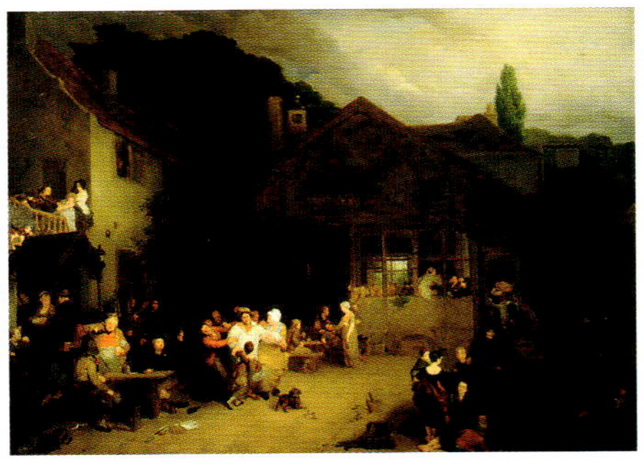

Goodall, Frederick 1822–1904
The Village Holiday (after David Wilkie) 1843
oil on canvas 95.2 x 127.1
VIS.1443

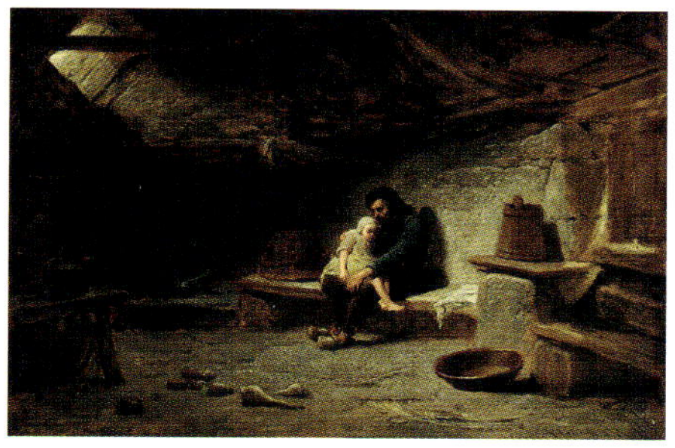

Goodall, Frederick 1822–1904
The Sick Child 1856
oil on panel 34 x 50
VIS.1376

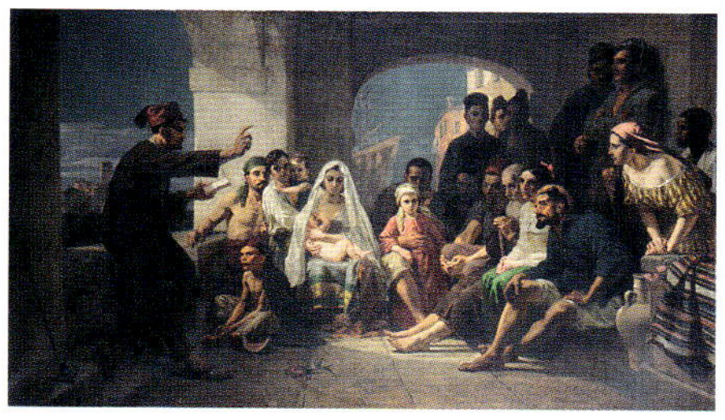

Goodall, Frederick 1822–1904
Felice Ballarin Reciting Tasso to the People of Chioggia 1858
oil on canvas 145.5 x 244
VIS.1472

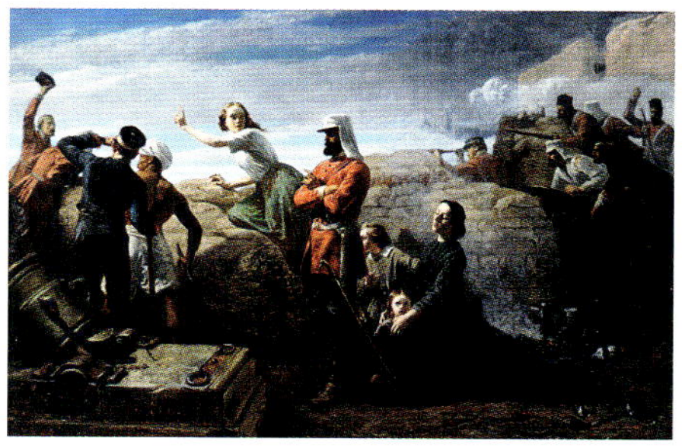

Goodall, Frederick 1822–1904
The Relief of Lucknow (Jessie's Dream) 1858
oil on canvas 120 x 165.8
VIS.1586

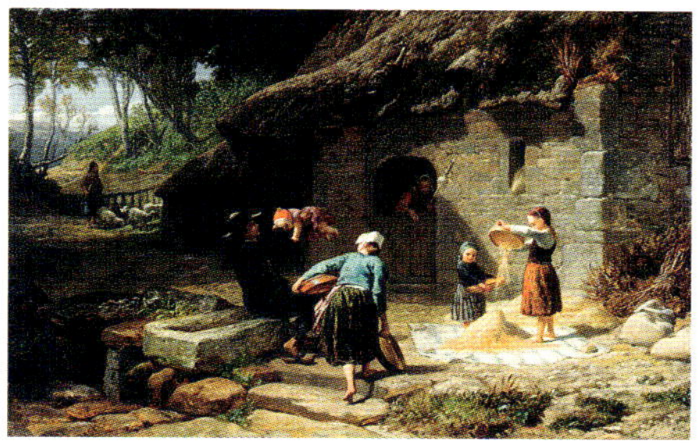

Goodall, Frederick 1822–1904
Winnowing Corn in Brittany, France 1858
oil on panel 34.8 x 52.4
VIS.1414

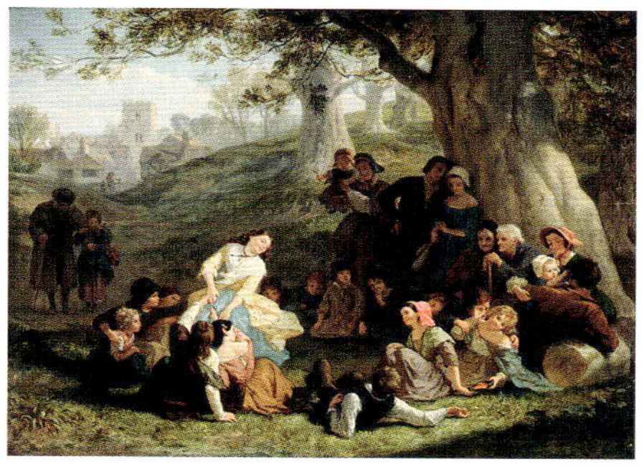

Goodall, Frederick 1822–1904
Hunt the Slipper 1860
oil on panel 44.8 x 59.8
VIS.1536

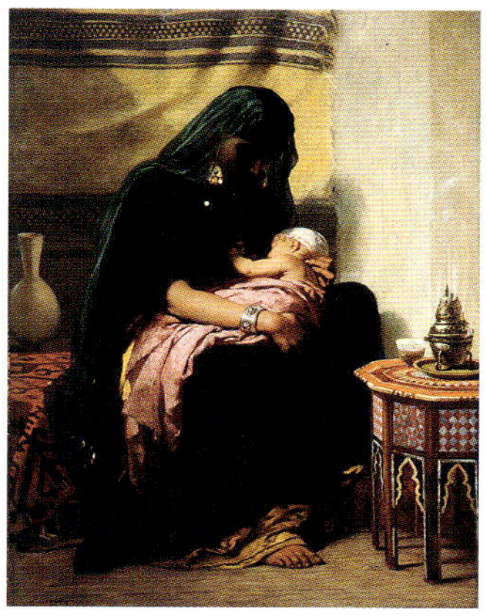

Goodall, Frederick 1822–1904
The First Born 1861
oil on canvas 129.8 x 98.5
VIS.1583

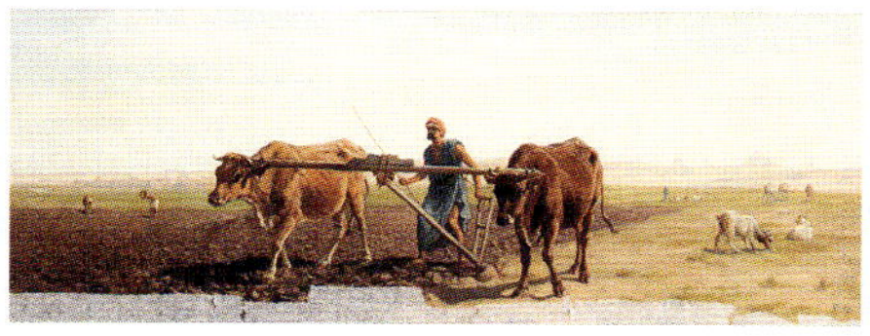

Goodall, Frederick 1822–1904
Agriculture in the Valley of the Nile 1874
oil on canvas 28.8 x 74.6
VIS.1408

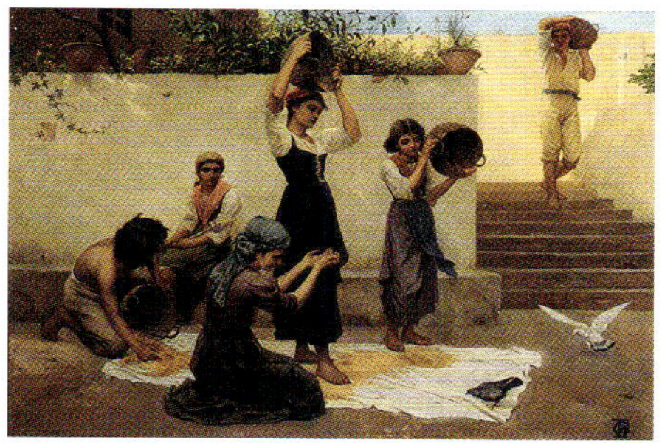

Goodall, Howard 1850–1874
Capri Girls Winnowing Corn 1865–1874
oil on canvas 84.4 x 121.6
VIS.1431

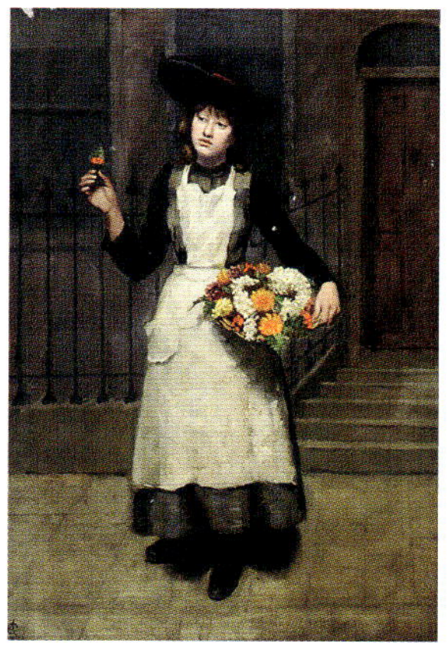

Goodwin, Albert 1845–1932
London Flower Girl 1892
oil on canvas 89.7 x 59.3
VIS.594

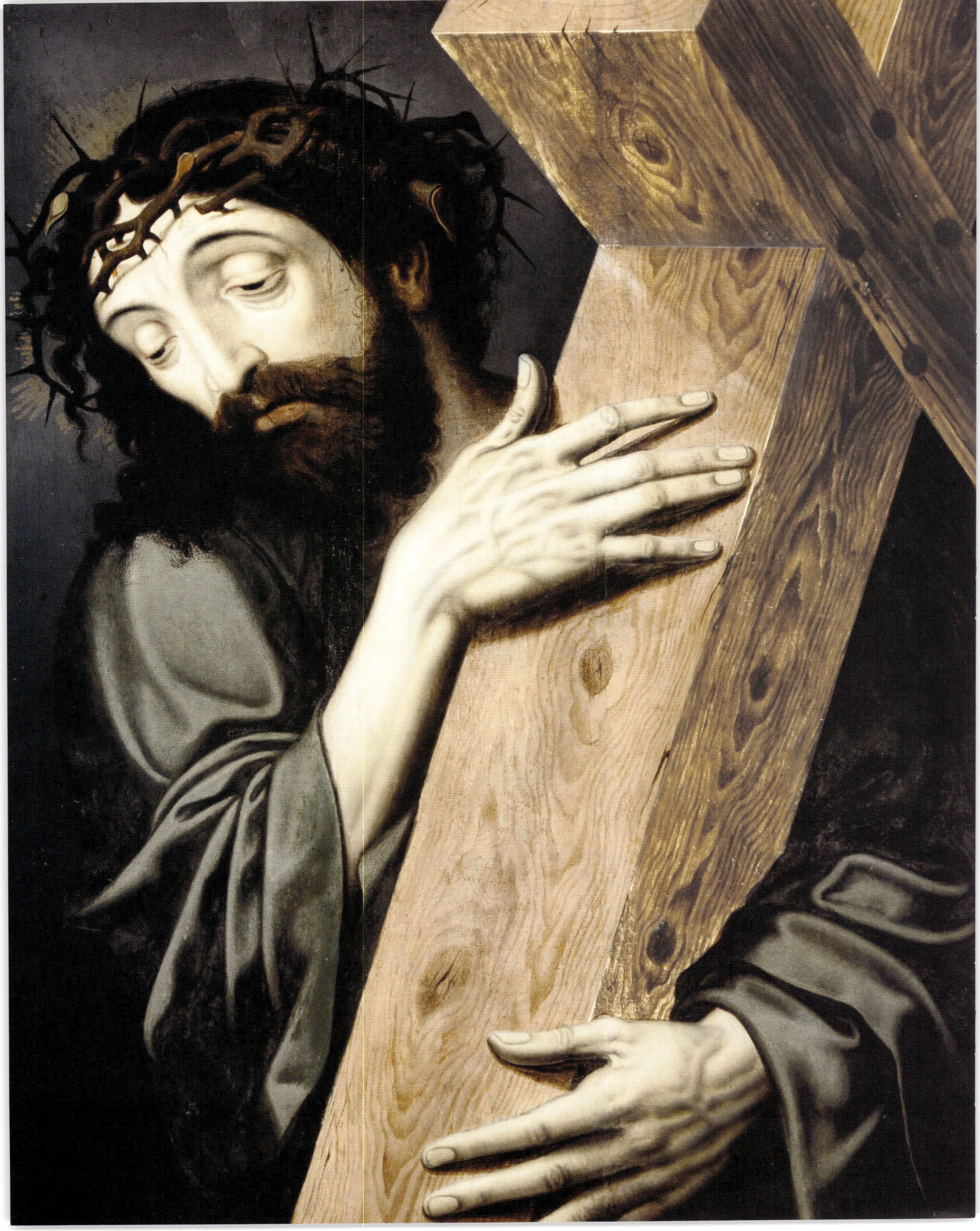

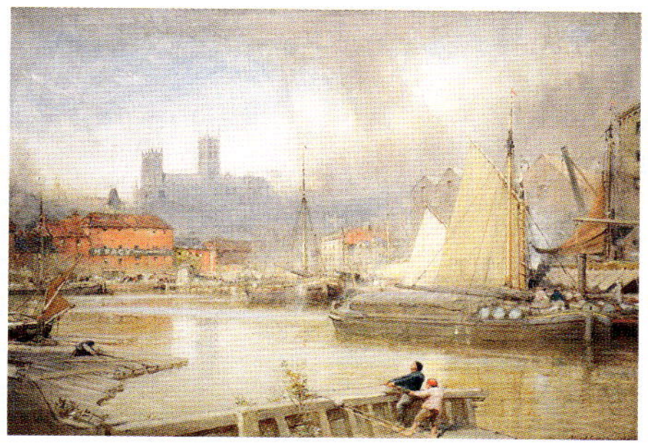

Goodwin, Albert 1845–1932
Lincoln 1902
oil on canvas 89 x 126
VIS.568

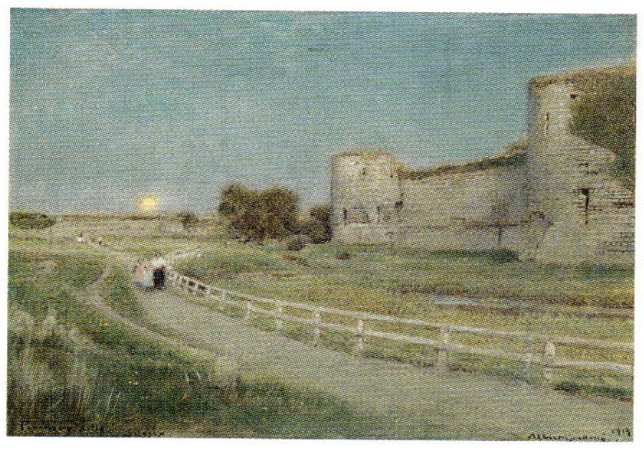

Goodwin, Albert 1845–1932
Pevensey Castle, East Sussex 1919
oil on paper on board 26 x 37
VIS.1951

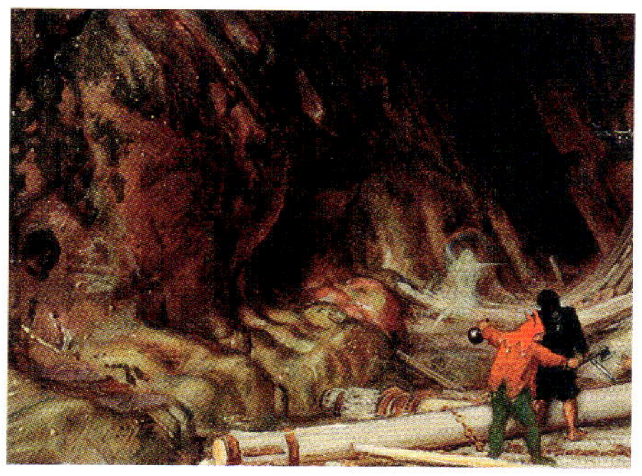

Goodwin, Albert 1845–1932
Scene from 'The Tempest' (from the play by William Shakespeare) 1920
oil on panel 24.4 x 32.8
VIS.207

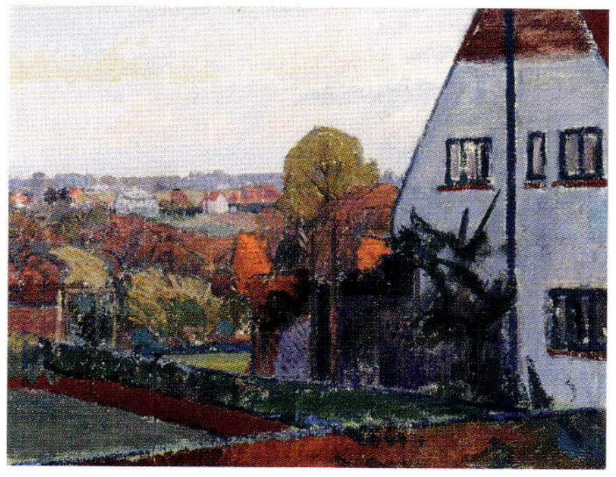

Gore, Spencer 1878–1914
Harold Gilman's House at Letchworth, Hertfordshire
oil on canvas 39.2 x 49.5
VIS.4472

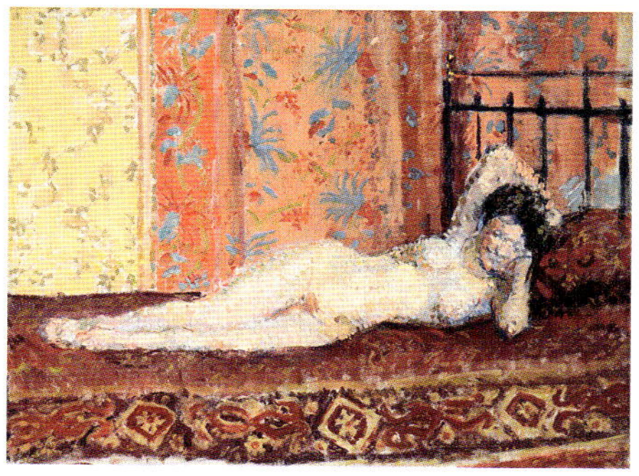

Gore, Spencer 1878–1914
Reclining Nude
oil on canvas 44.8 x 59.5
VIS.1884

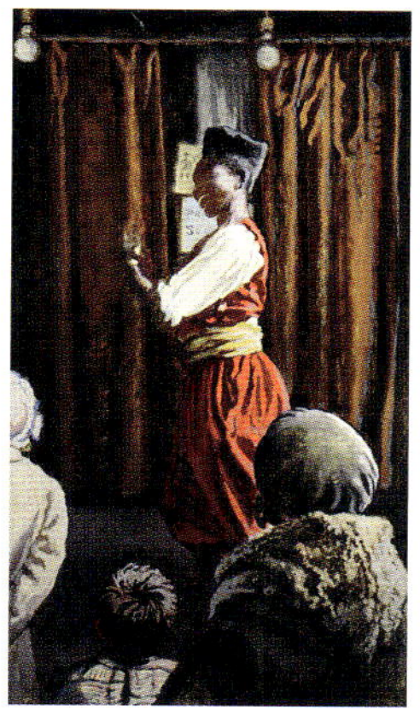

Gosse, Laura Sylvia 1881–1968
Dancing Negro
oil on canvas 110.9 x 62.2
VIS.153

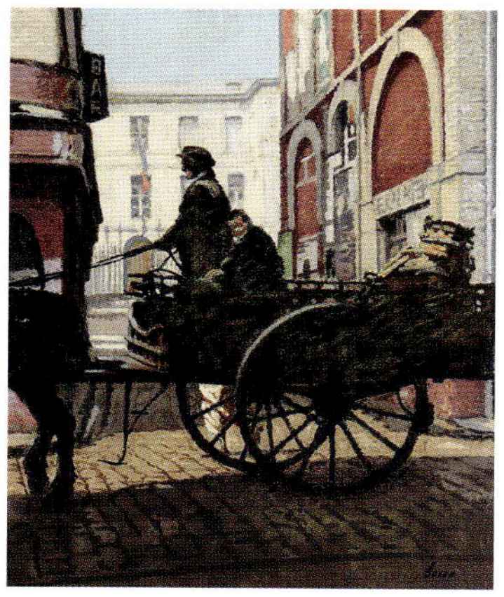

Gosse, Laura Sylvia 1881–1968
Homeward Bound, la rue St Remi, Dieppe, France
oil on canvas 73.5 x 63.4
VIS.151

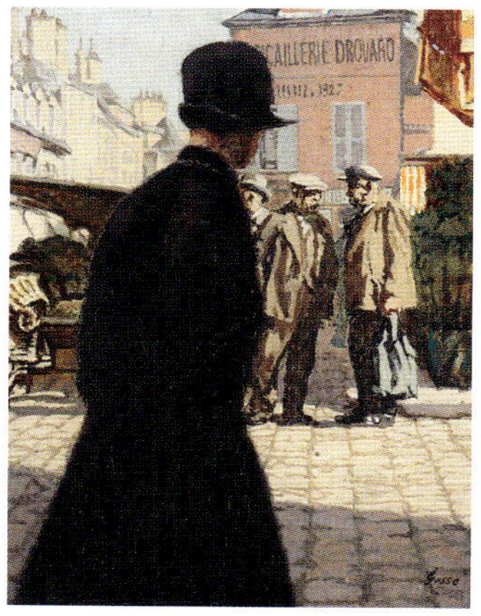

Gosse, Laura Sylvia 1881–1968
Les rentiers
oil on canvas 44.5 x 34.3
VIS.210

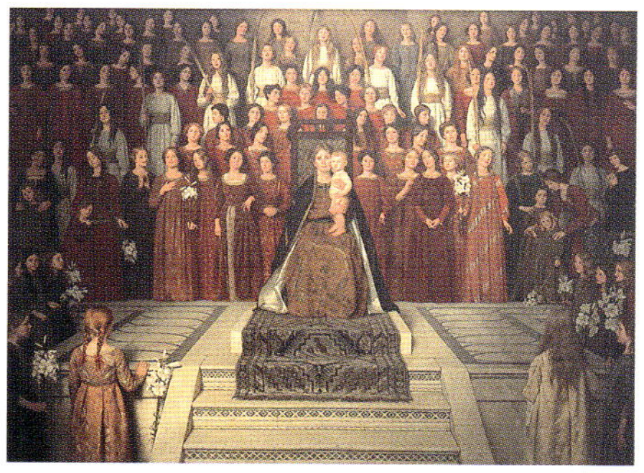

Gotch, Thomas Cooper 1854–1931
The Mother Enthroned
oil on canvas 214 x 285
VIS.4524

Facing page: Morales, Luis de (school of), c.1509–c.1586, *Christ Carrying the Cross* (detail), Museums Sheffield, (p. 143)

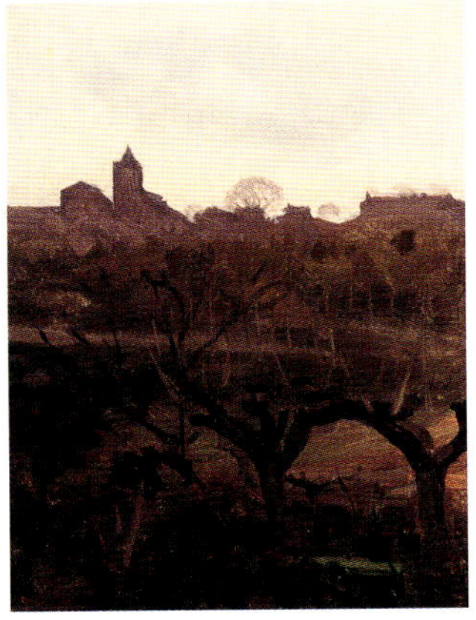

Gotch, Thomas Cooper 1854–1931
Winter Sketch, Provence, France
oil on board 26.5 x 19.4
VIS.4319

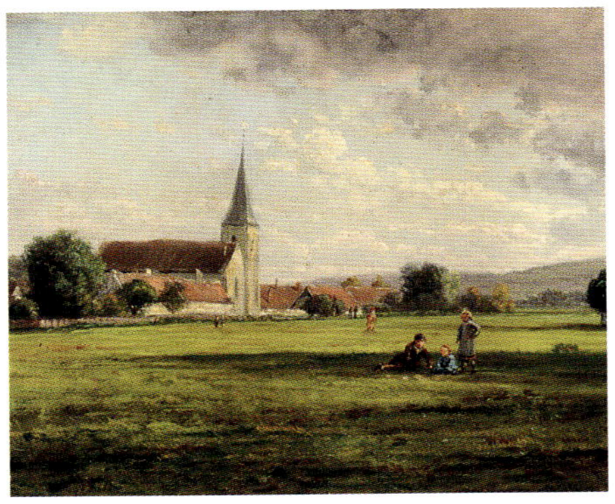

Goupil, Jules Adolphe 1839–1883
Landscape with a Church 1854
oil on panel 23.6 x 28.9
VIS.1009

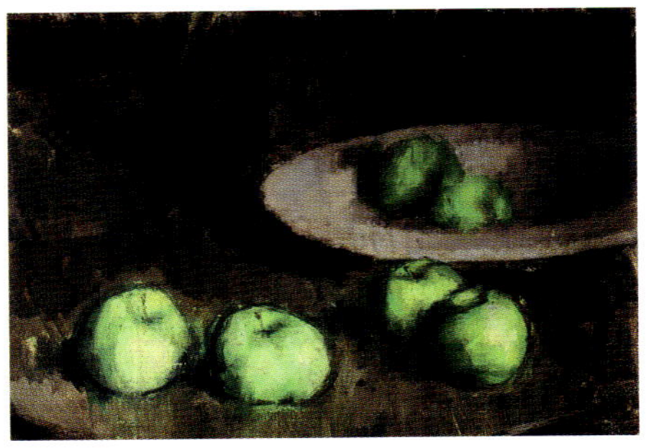

Gowing, Lawrence 1918–1991
Apples
oil on canvas 24.2 x 34.5
VIS.3299

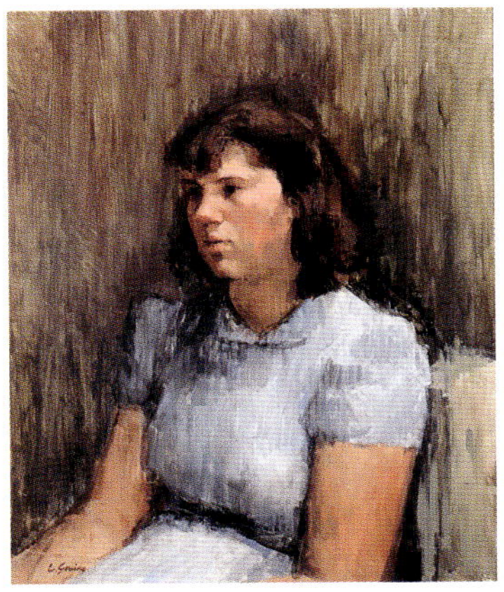

Gowing, Lawrence 1918–1991
Barbara Saxon
oil on canvas 59.5 x 49.5
VIS.5222

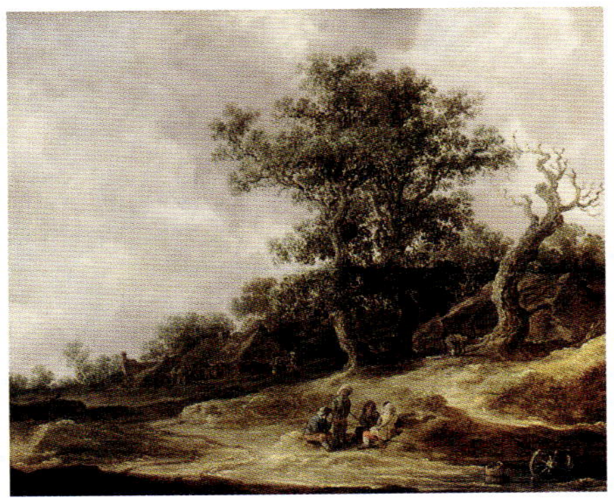

Goyen, Jan van 1596–1656
Landscape with Cottages on the Dunes 1633
oil on panel 50.3 x 58.7
VIS.3100

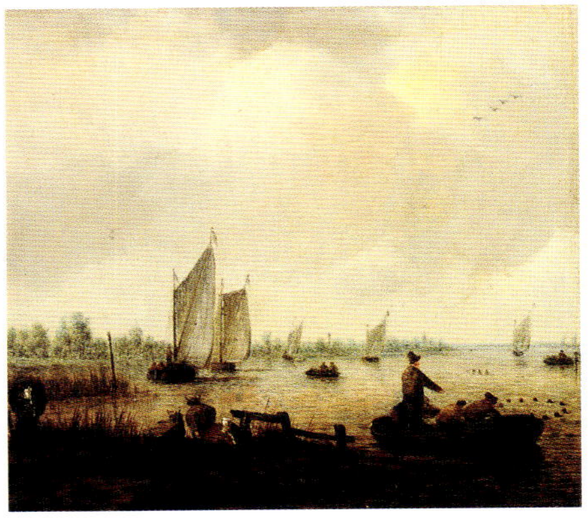

Goyen, Jan van (school of) 1596–1656
River Scene with Boats 1640–1650
oil on panel 16.4 x 17.8
VIS.297

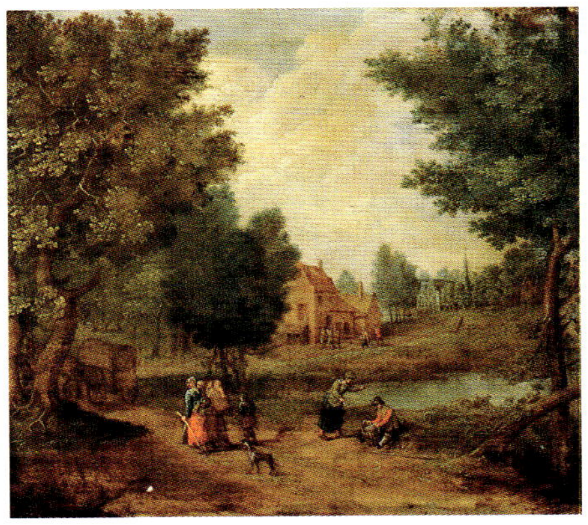

Goyen, Jan van (style of) 1596–1656
Landscape
oil on panel 18.5 x 20.6
VIS.63

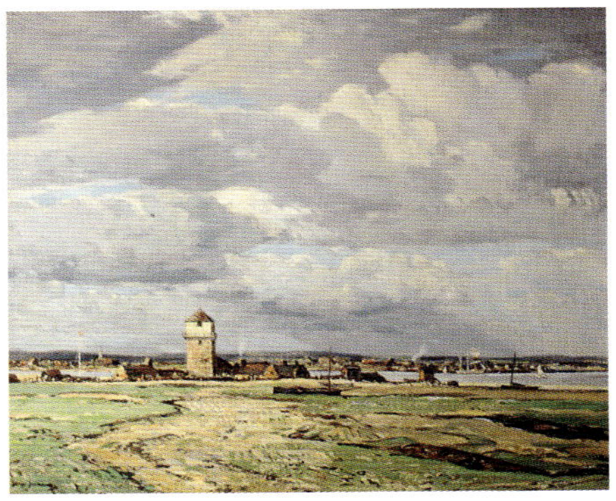

Graham, George 1881–1949
The Look Out, Winchelsea, East Sussex
oil on canvas on plywood 49 x 58.5
VIS.158

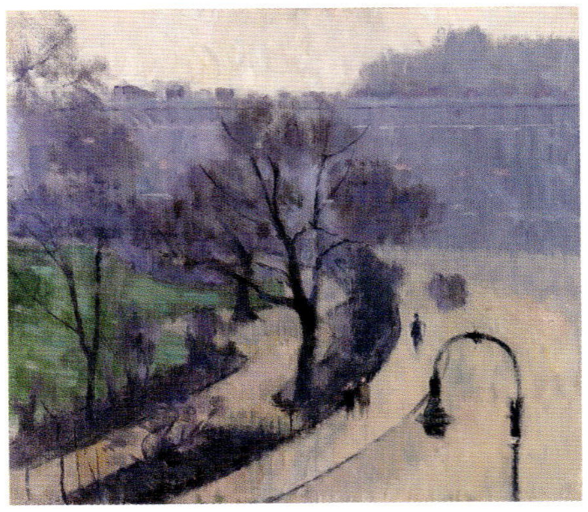

Graham Bell, Frank 1910–1943
Brunswick Square, London 1940
oil on canvas 34.7 x 39.8
VIS.5190

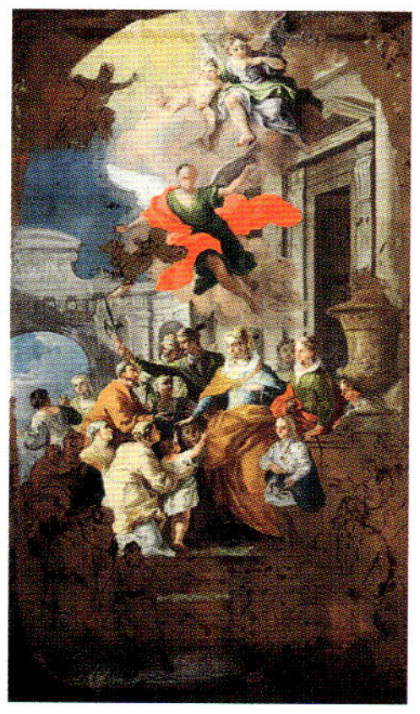

Gran, Daniel 1694–1757
The Charity of St Elizabeth of Hungary
1720–1736
oil on canvas 96.5 x 55
VIS.3270

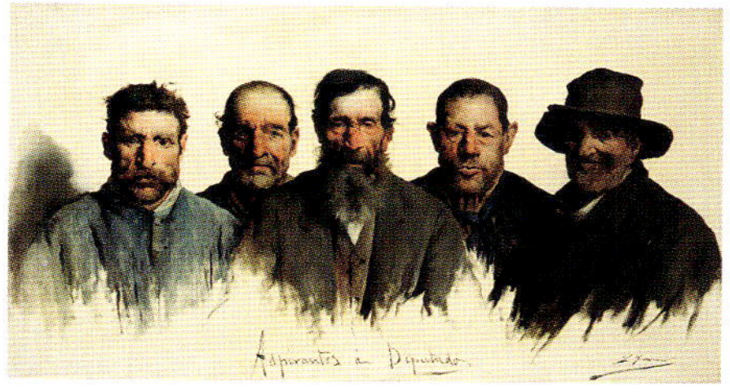

Graner, Luis 1863–1929
The Losing Candidates
oil on canvas 56.3 x 102.5 (E)
VIS.776

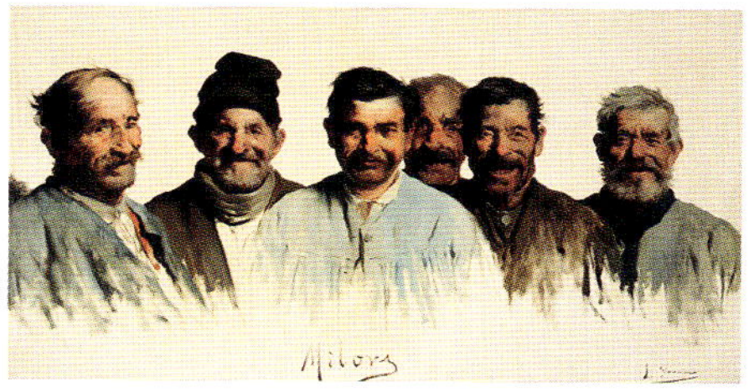

Graner, Luis 1863–1929
The Winning Candidates
oil on panel 57 x 102.4 (E)
VIS.775

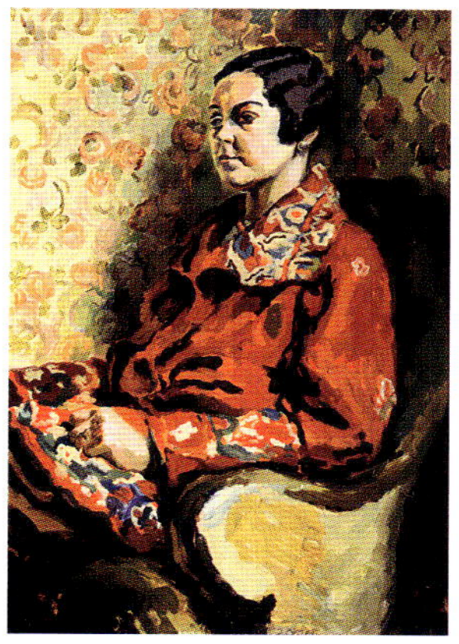

Grant, Duncan 1885–1978
Bea Howe c.1925
oil on board 85 x 53
VIS.4295

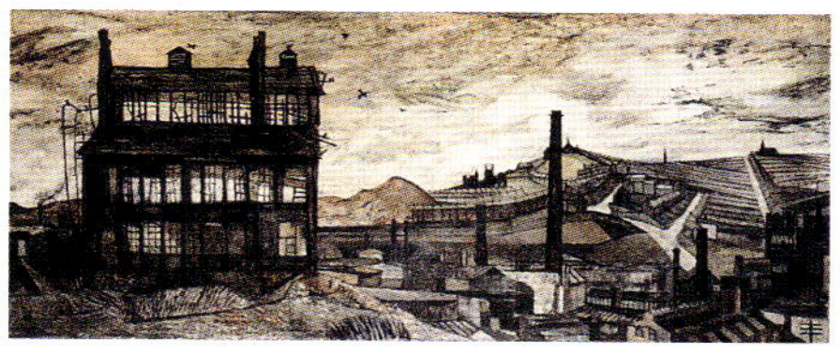

Greaves, Derrick b.1927
Sheffield 1953
oil on canvas 93.6 x 210.5
VIS.4586

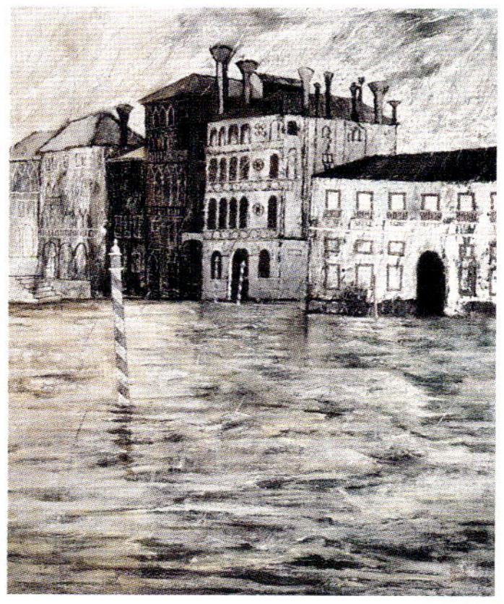

Greaves, Derrick b.1927
Venice in the Rain 1953
oil on canvas 142.4 x 117
VIS.3145

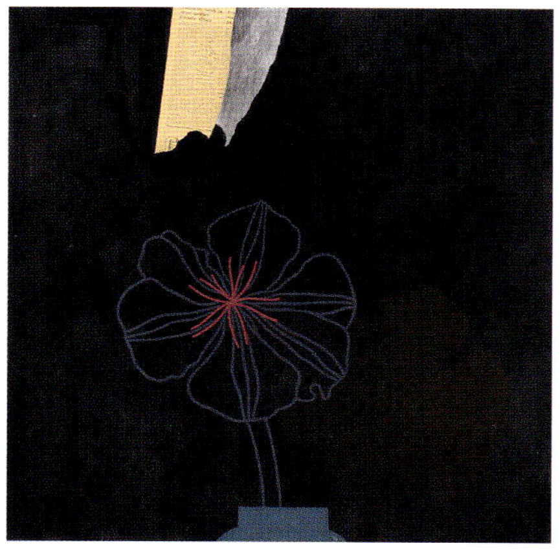

Greaves, Derrick b.1927
Flower and Collage 1968–1969
acrylic & collage on canvas on panel
120 x 120
VIS.3847

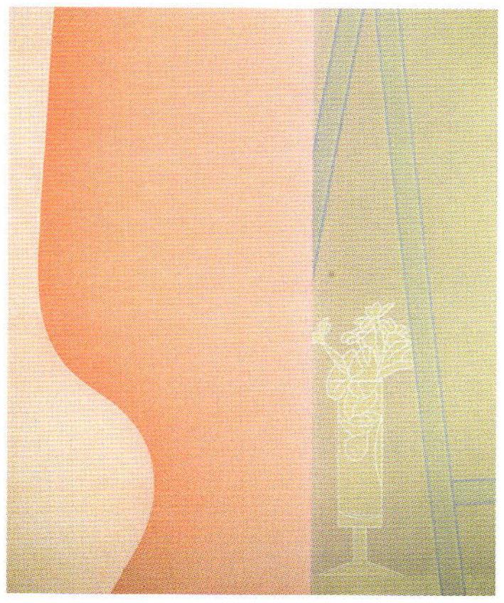

Greaves, Derrick b.1927
In the Studio 2, Flowers in the Studio 1973
acrylic on canvas 144 x 118
VIS.4708

Greaves, Walter 1846–1930
Nocturne, Battersea Reach, London
oil on canvas 29.4 x 46
VIS.4054

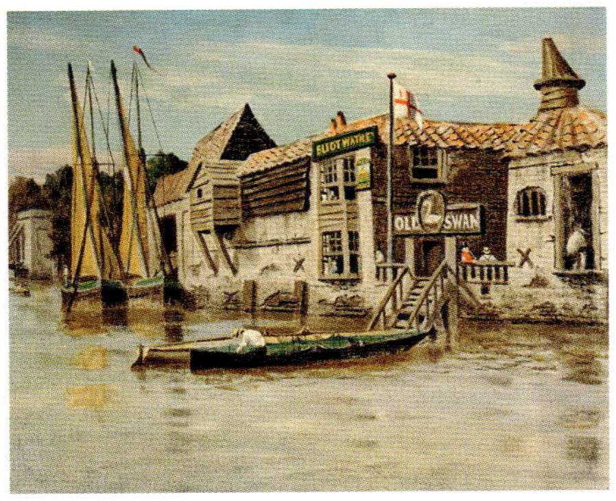

Greaves, Walter 1846–1930
The Thames at Chelsea, London
oil on canvas 48.9 x 59.1
VIS.2036

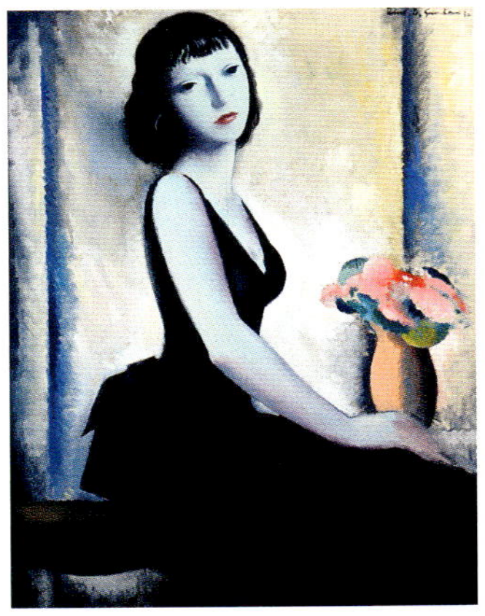

Greenham, Robert Duckworth 1906–1976
Mary 1932
oil on canvas 78 x 62.5
VIS.5004

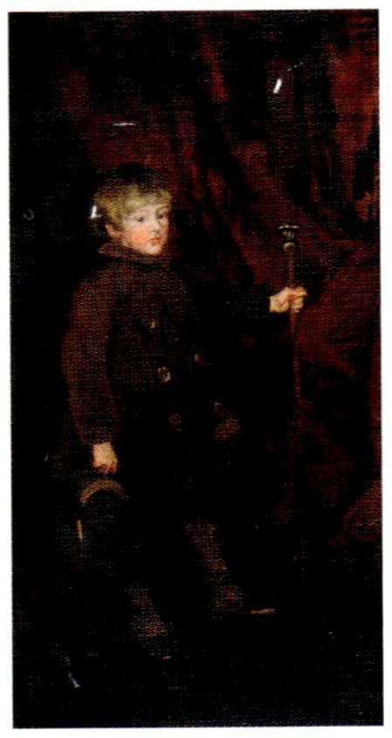

Greiffenhagen, Maurice 1862–1931
Portrait of a Boy
oil on canvas 148.5 x 76.7
VIS.2613

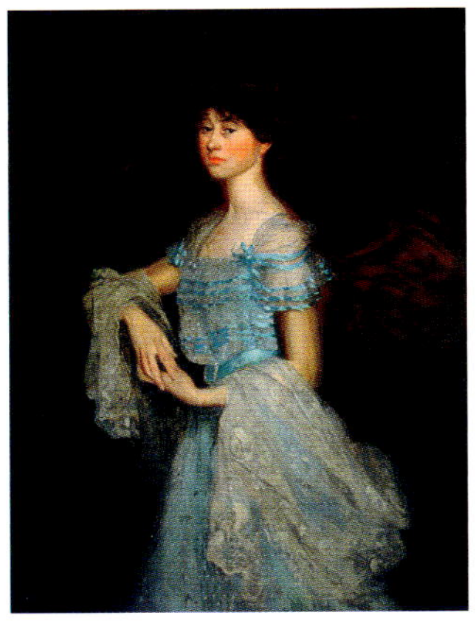

Greiffenhagen, Maurice 1862–1931
Portrait of a Lady
oil on canvas 124 x 92.5
VIS.2273

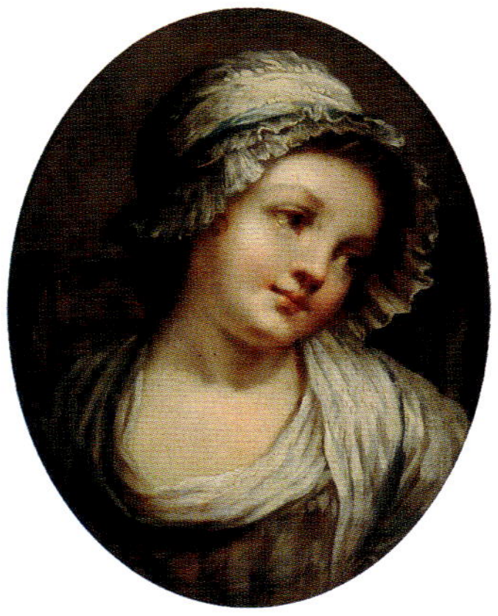

Greuze, Jean-Baptiste 1725–1805
Portrait of a Girl
oil on canvas 41.8 x 33.6
VIS.1073

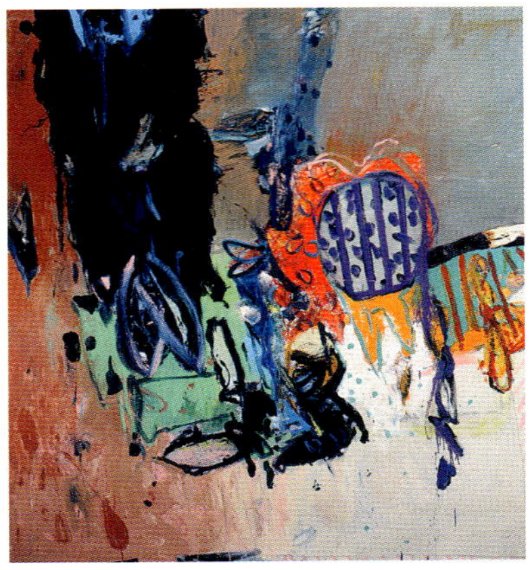

Griffin, Paul b.1955
Strange Time
oil on canvas 193.5 x 176
VIS.4963

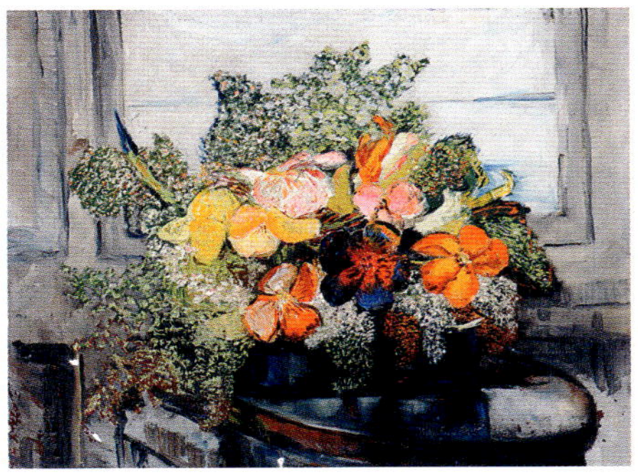

Grimm, Stanley 1891–1966
Flower Piece
oil on canvas 50.2 x 66.3
VIS.713

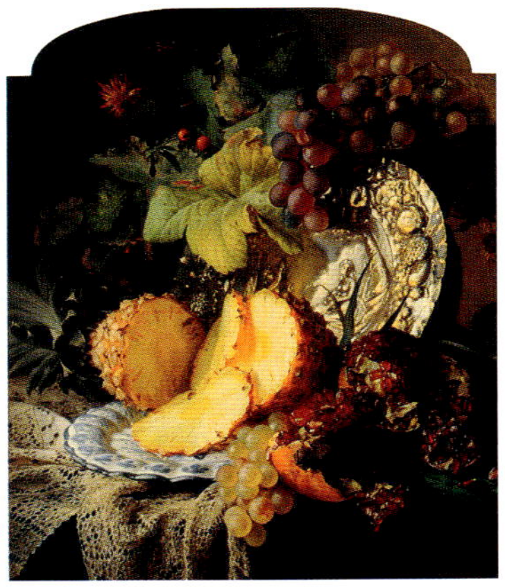

Grönland, Theude 1817–1876
Fruit 1855
oil on canvas 54 x 45.2
VIS.155

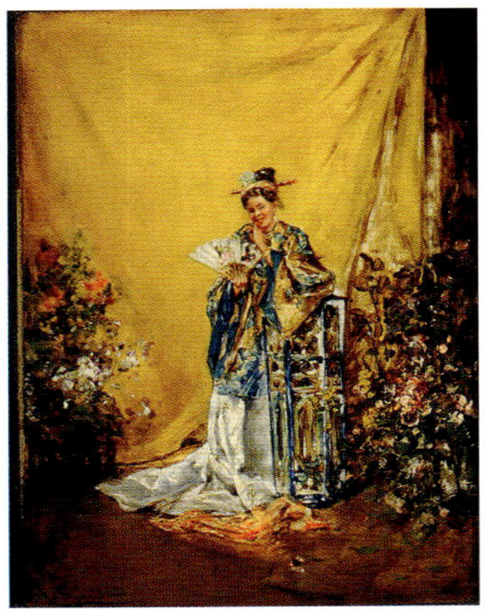

Guise, A.
A Japanese Girl
oil on panel 17 x 12.7
VIS.1081

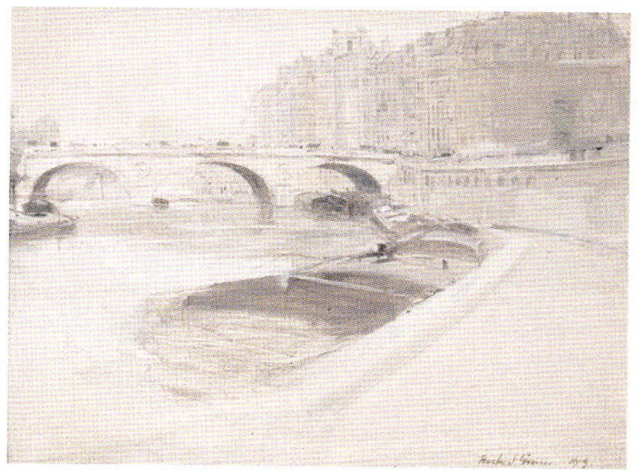

Gunn, Herbert James 1893–1964
Le pont de Napoléon, Paris 1913
oil on panel 21.6 x 29.3
VIS.3995

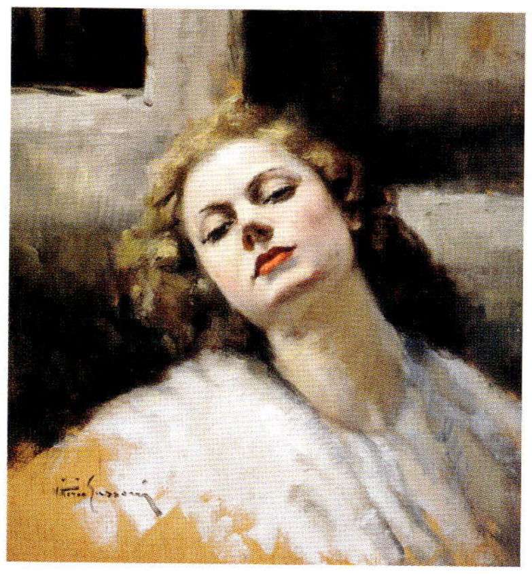

Gussoni, Vittorio 1893–1968
Lady's Head c.1935
oil on board 53.1 x 48.1
VIS.1323

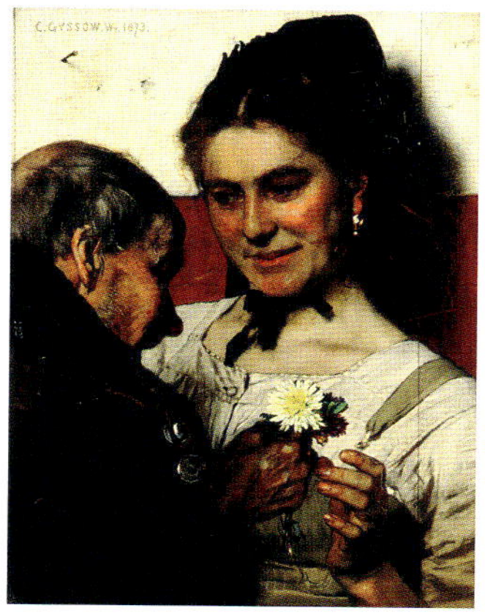

Gussow, Carl 1843–1907
Autumn Flowers 1873
oil on panel 56.5 x 44
VIS.1366

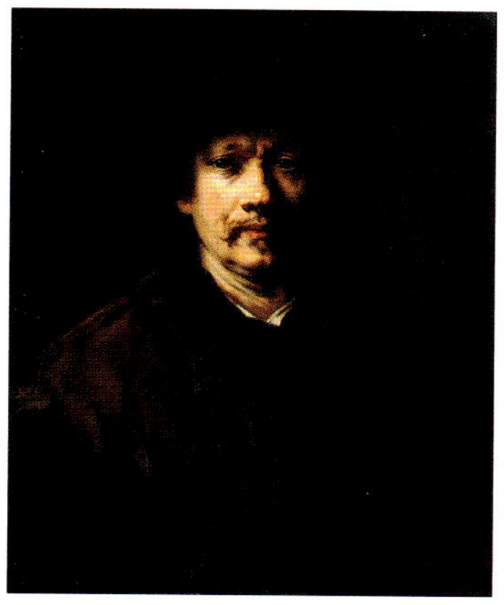

Guttman, J. b.1869
Self Portrait (after Rembrandt van Rijn) c.1890
oil on canvas 75.2 x 59.9
VIS.1530

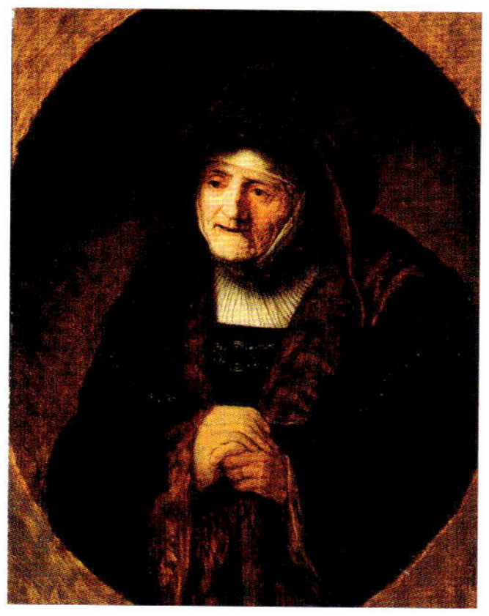

Guttman, J. b.1869
Rembrandt's Mother (after Rembrandt van Rijn) c.1890
oil on panel 75 x 56.7
VIS.1529

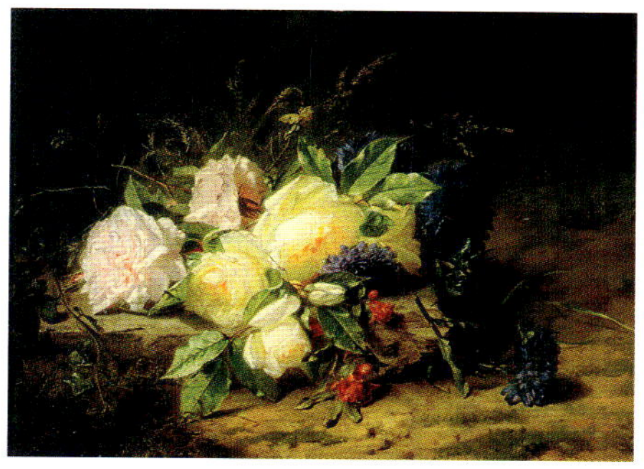

Haanen, Adriana Johanna 1814–1895
Flowers
oil on board 41.2 x 55.2
VIS.1576

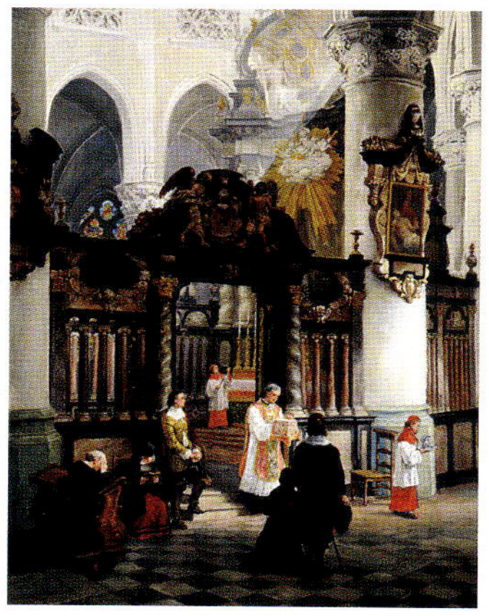

Haghe, Louis 1806–1885
The Church of St Jacques, Antwerp, Belgium 1882
oil on canvas 91.9 x 71.8
VIS.1437

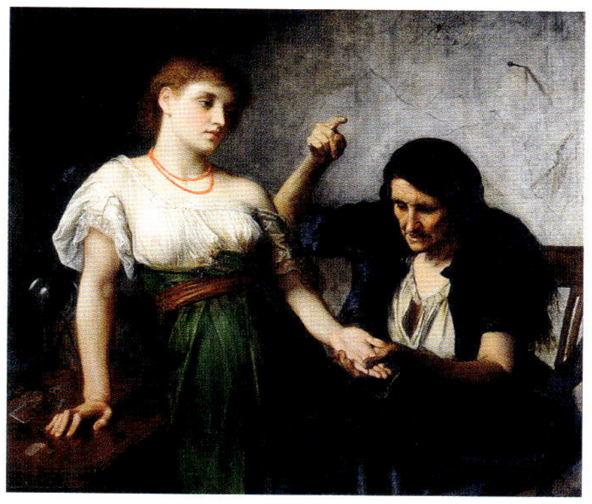

Hallé, Charles Edward 1846–1919
The Fortune Teller
oil on canvas 107 x 122.5
VIS.1451

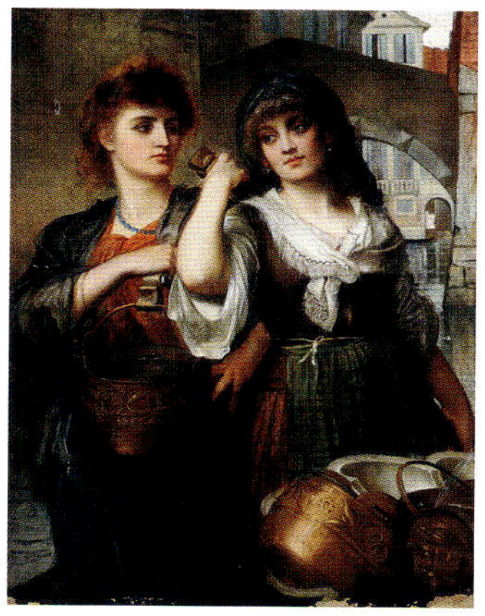

Hallé, Charles Edward 1846–1919
The Rivals
oil on canvas 107.3 x 83.5
VIS.1488

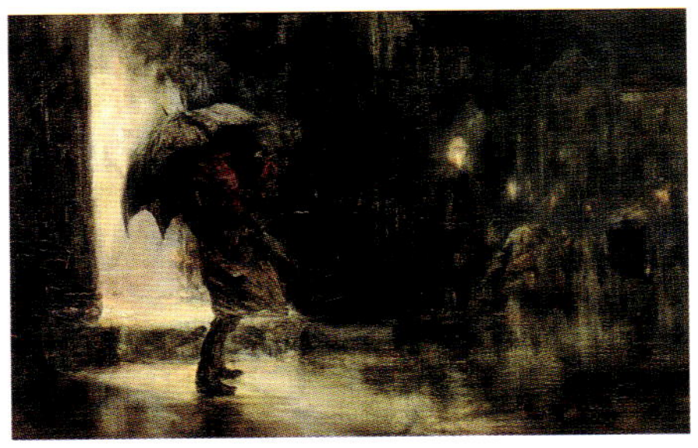

Halswelle, Keeley 1832–1891
A Rainy Night
oil on canvas 28.5 x 44
VIS.703

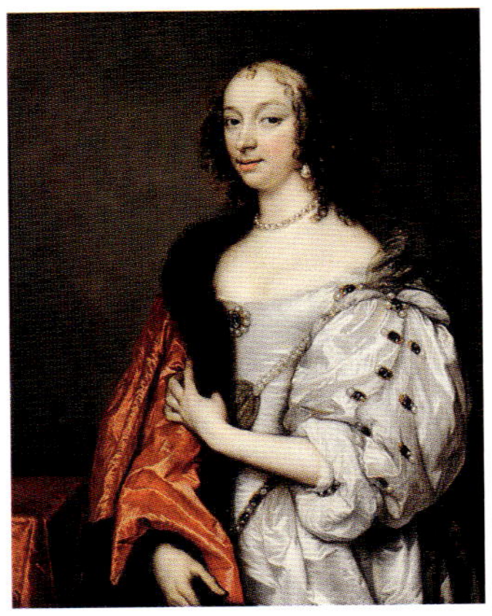

Hanneman, Adriaen c.1601–1671
Portrait of a Lady 1655
oil on canvas 97.7 x 77.6
VIS.2996

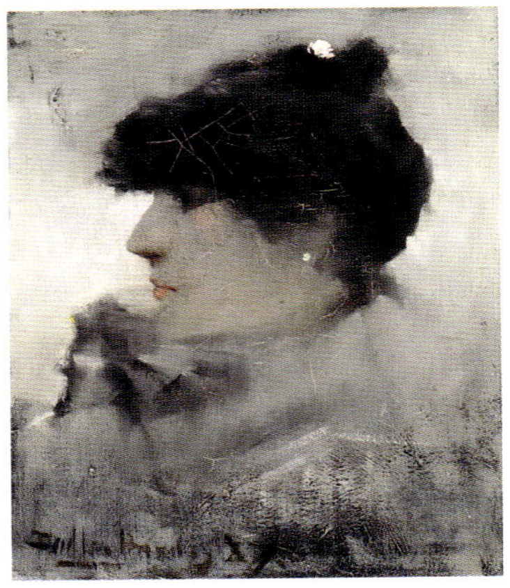

Hardy, Dudley 1866–1922
Madame Sarah Bernhardt (1844–1923) 1887
oil on canvas 33.1 x 27.9
VIS.165

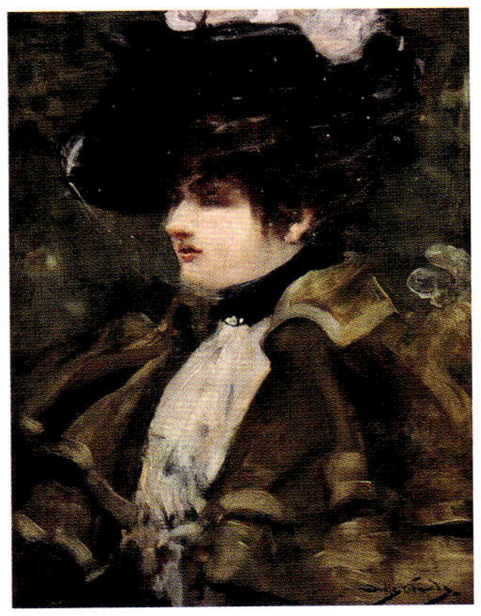

Hardy, Dudley 1866–1922
Madame Sarah Bernhardt (1844–1923)
oil on canvas 59.7 x 44.9
VIS.1684

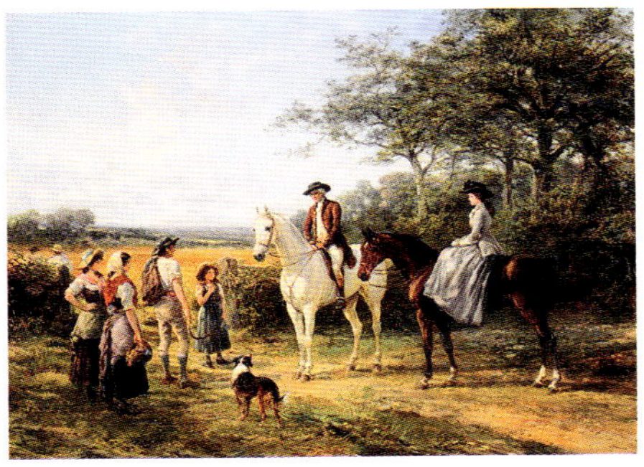

Hardy, Heywood 1842–1933
Country Scene 1905
oil on canvas 65.5 x 87.2
VIS.3864

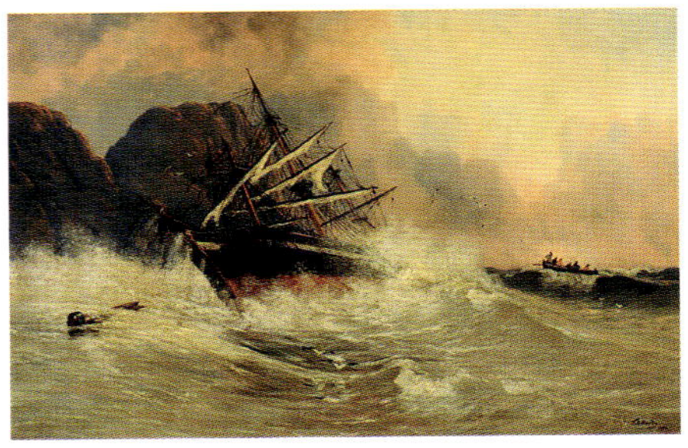

Hardy, Thomas Bush 1842–1897
Sea Piece 1880
oil on canvas 49.1 x 74.8
VIS.1266

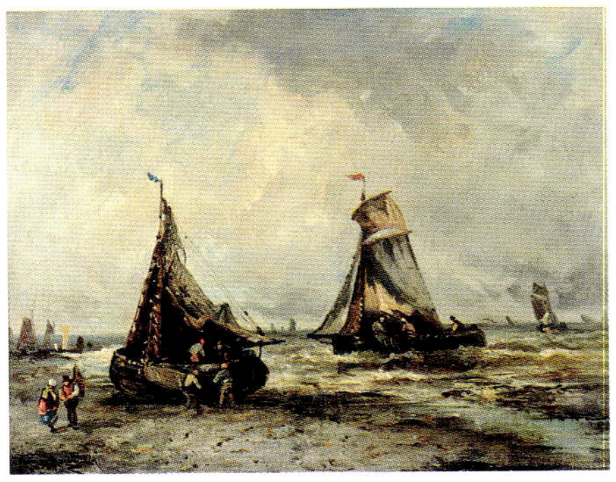

Hardy, Thomas Bush 1842–1897
Seascape 1887
oil on canvas 45.6 x 51
VIS.1256

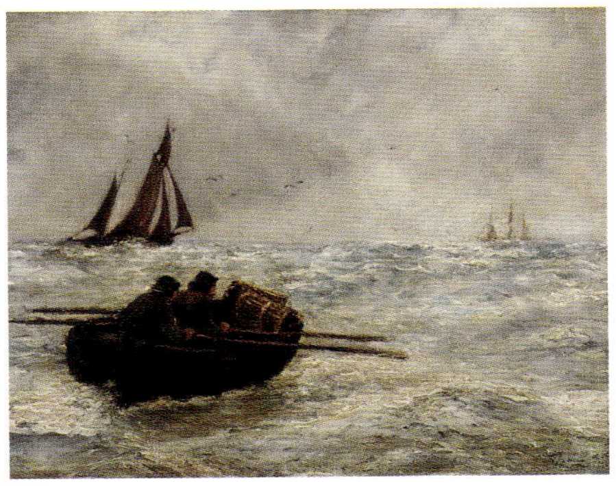

Hardy, Thomas Bush 1842–1897
Sea Piece
oil on millboard 27.5 x 35.1
VIS.1015

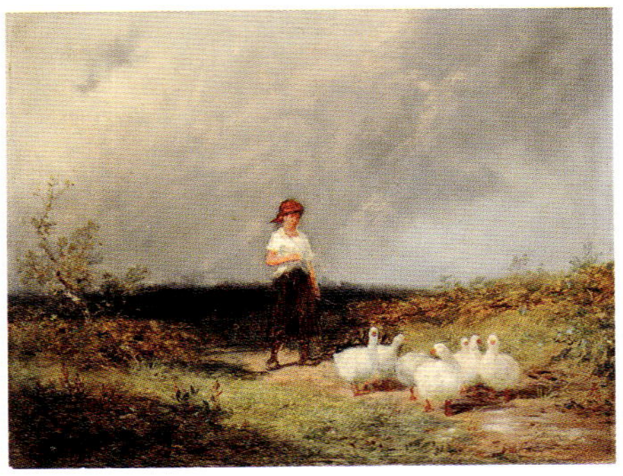

Hargitt, Edward 1835–1895
The Goose Girl 1879
oil on panel 17.8 x 23
VIS.1102

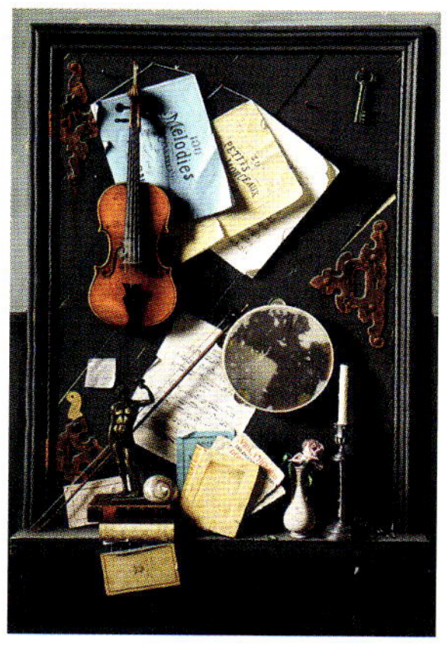

Harnett, William Michael 1848–1892
The Old Cupboard Door 1889
oil on canvas 153.6 x 101.8
VIS.2738

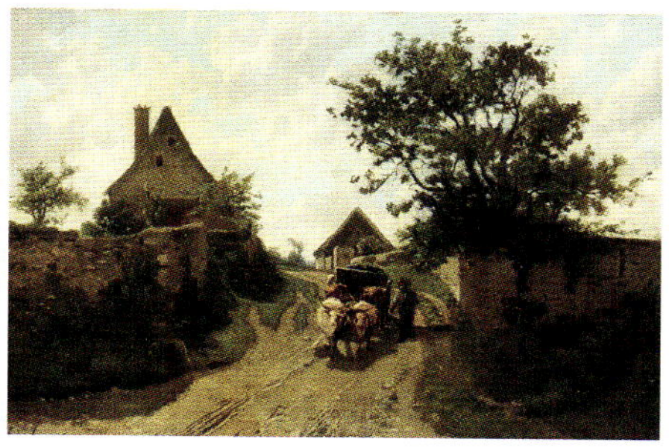

Harpignies, Henri-Joseph 1819–1916
Farmhouses, St Aubin, Jersey 1860–1865
oil on canvas 29.2 x 43
VIS.354

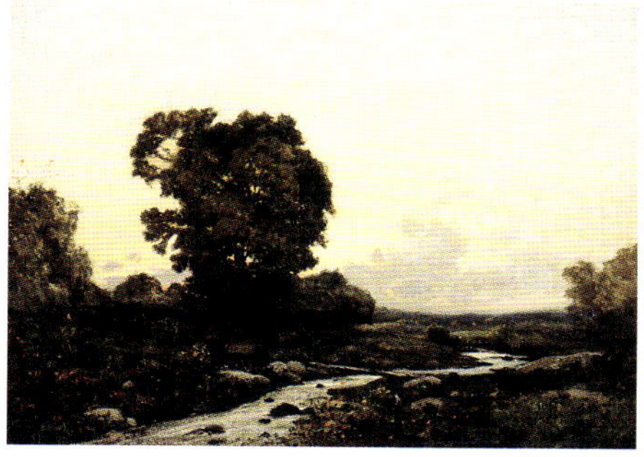

Harpignies, Henri-Joseph 1819–1916
Sunset
oil on canvas 52.1 x 70.2
VIS.356

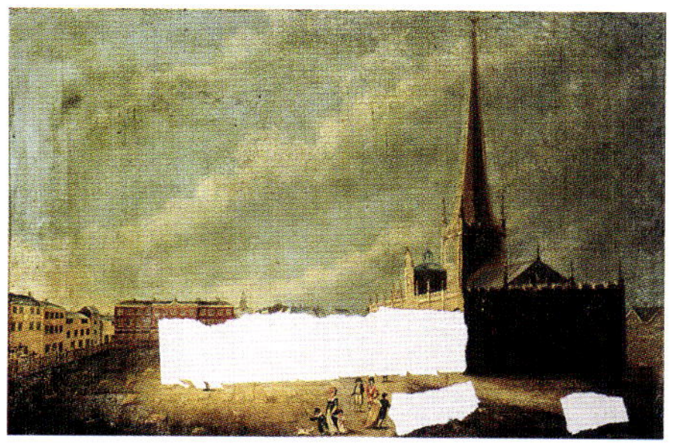

Harris, Thomas 1787–1817
St Paul's Parish Church of Sheffield
oil on canvas 60.6 x 95.5
VIS.800

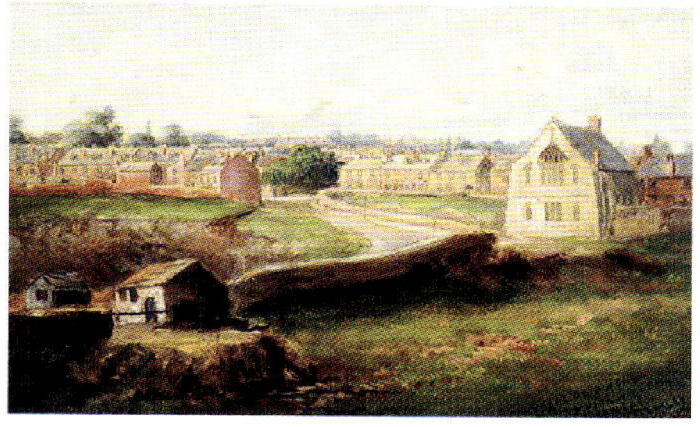

Hattersley, George Pearson 1858–1937
Site of Crookes Valley Road (Great Dam Road from Mushroom Lane, Western Park, Sheffield) 1882
oil on canvas 29.9 x 42.5
K1929.2

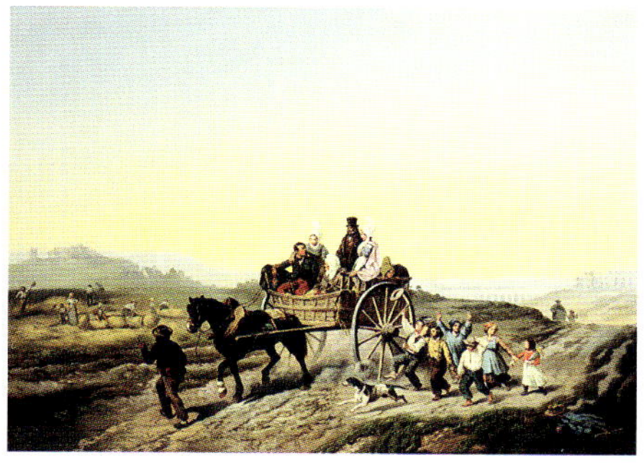

Hauve, A. van
The Soldier's Return 1850–1870
oil on canvas 74 x 104
VIS.327

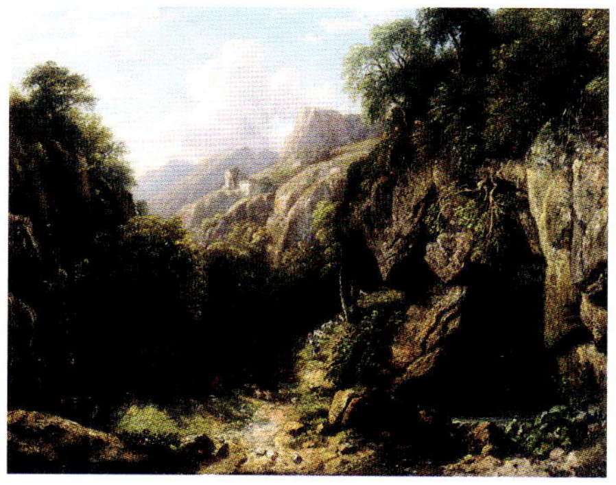

Havell, William 1782–1857
Mountain Pass near Subiaco, Roman States 1851
oil on canvas 57.5 x 72.7
VIS.1550

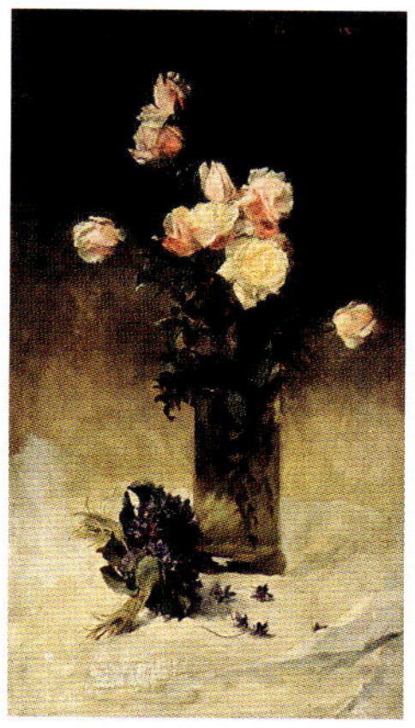

Havers, Alice 1850–1890
Roses in a Vase c.1887
oil on canvas 76.5 x 42.5
VIS.995

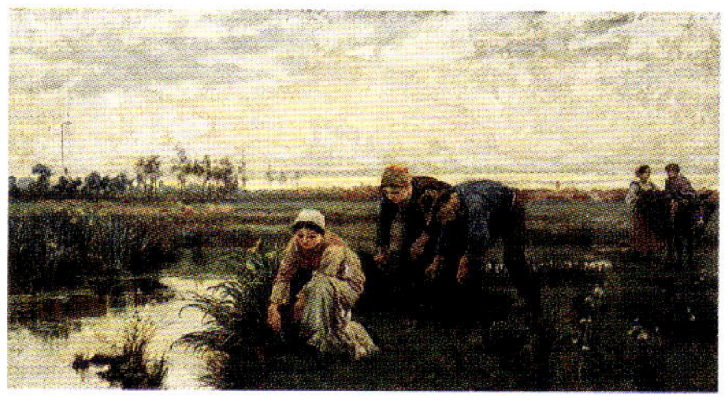

Havers, Alice 1850–1890
Rush Cutters
oil on canvas 71.6 x 128.3
VIS.1490

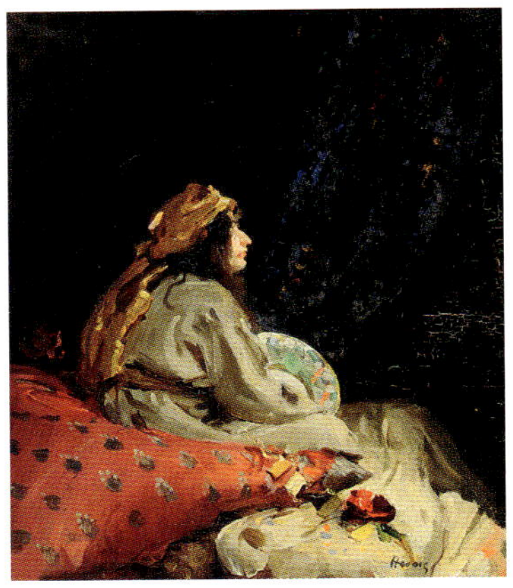

Havers, Val 1873–1912
A Turkish Lady
oil on canvas 36.2 x 30.6
VIS.1094

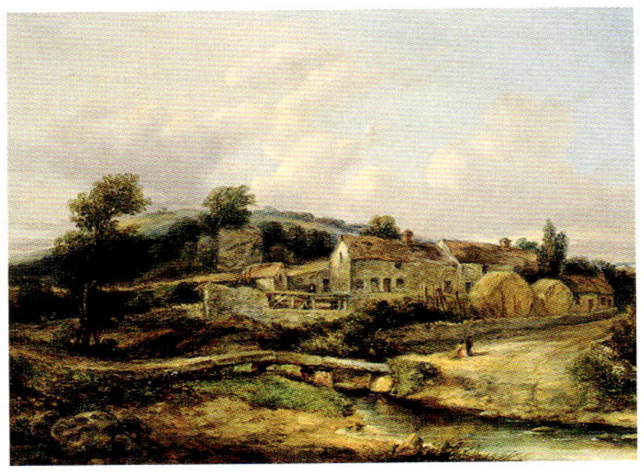

Hawkesworth, Joseph Hallam 1827–1908
Landscape
oil on canvas 44.5 x 59.6
VIS.2851

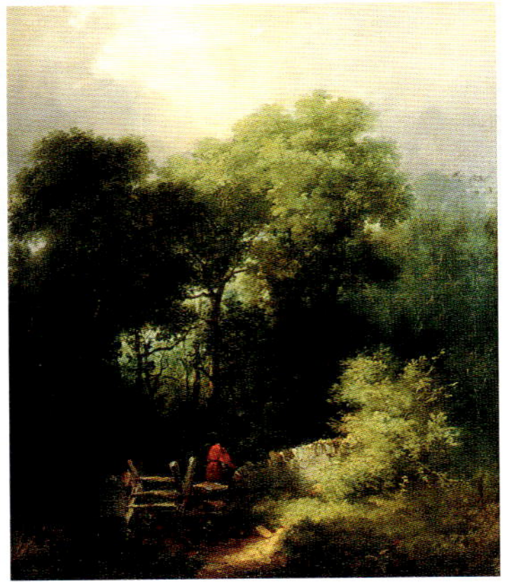

Hawkesworth, Joseph Hallam 1827–1908
Old Endcliffe Woods, Sheffield
oil on panel 45.4 x 37.6
VIS.371

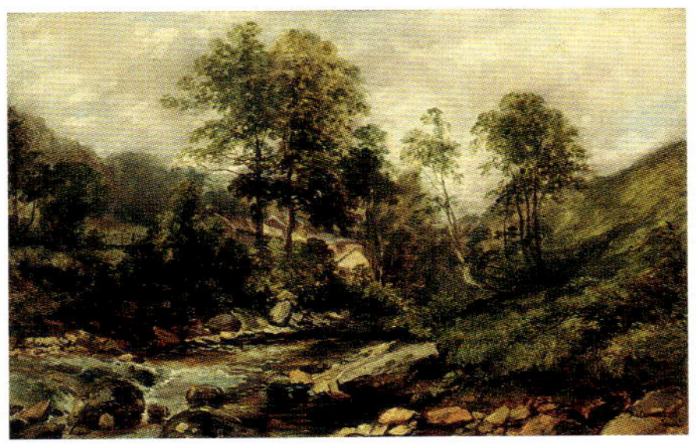

Hawkesworth, Joseph Hallam 1827–1908
Rivelin Valley, Sheffield
oil on canvas 33.7 x 52
VIS.2362

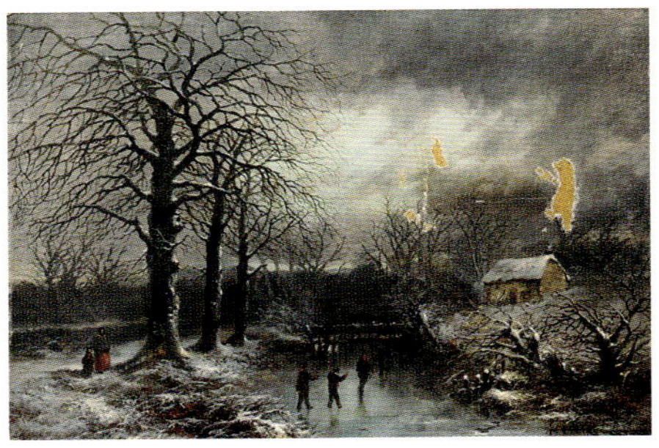

Hawkesworth, Joseph Hallam 1827–1908
Winter Scene
oil on canvas 54.6 x 77.2
VIS.3093

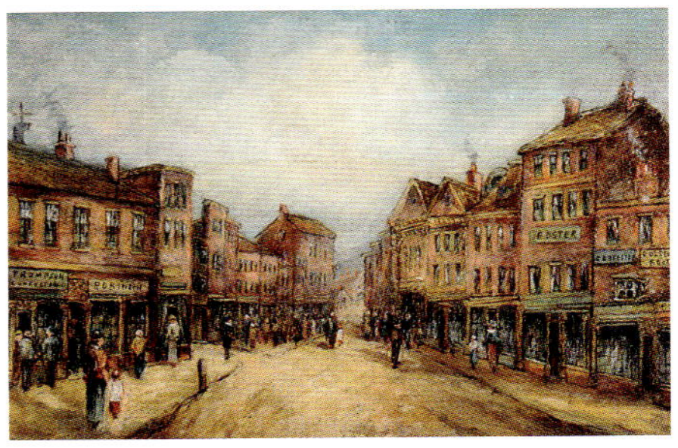

Hawkesworth, Joseph Hallam 1827–1908 or **Pickford, Ralph Randolphus (attributed to)** 1834–1911
High Street, Sheffield 1850
oil on board 13.5 x 22
1973.469

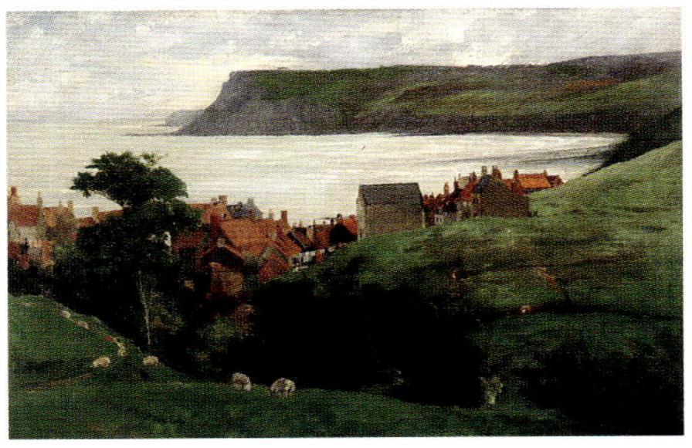

Hawksley, Arthur 1842–1915
Robin Hood's Bay, North Yorkshire
oil on canvas on board 38.3 x 58.8
VIS.2873

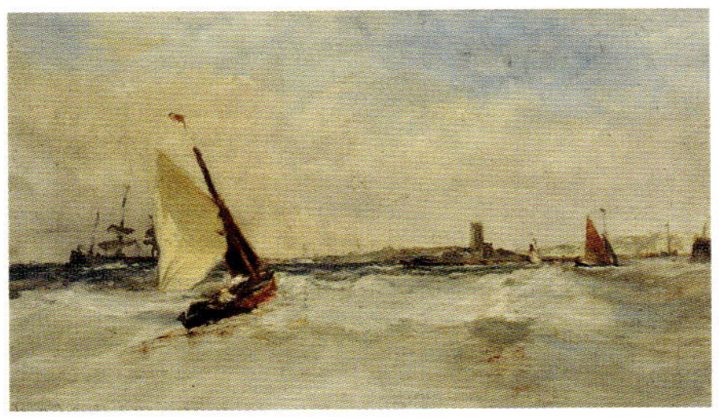

Hayes, Edwin 1819–1904
Port Rush 1845–1865
oil on canvas 29 x 49
VIS.781

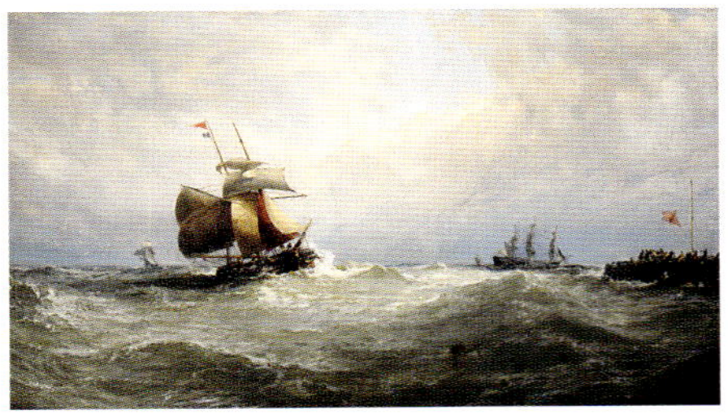

Hayes, Edwin 1819–1904
Sea Piece 1879
oil on canvas 70.9 x 122.1
VIS.1489

Facing page: de Francia, Peter, 1921–2012, *Old Man and a Boy* (detail), Museums Sheffield, (p. 59)

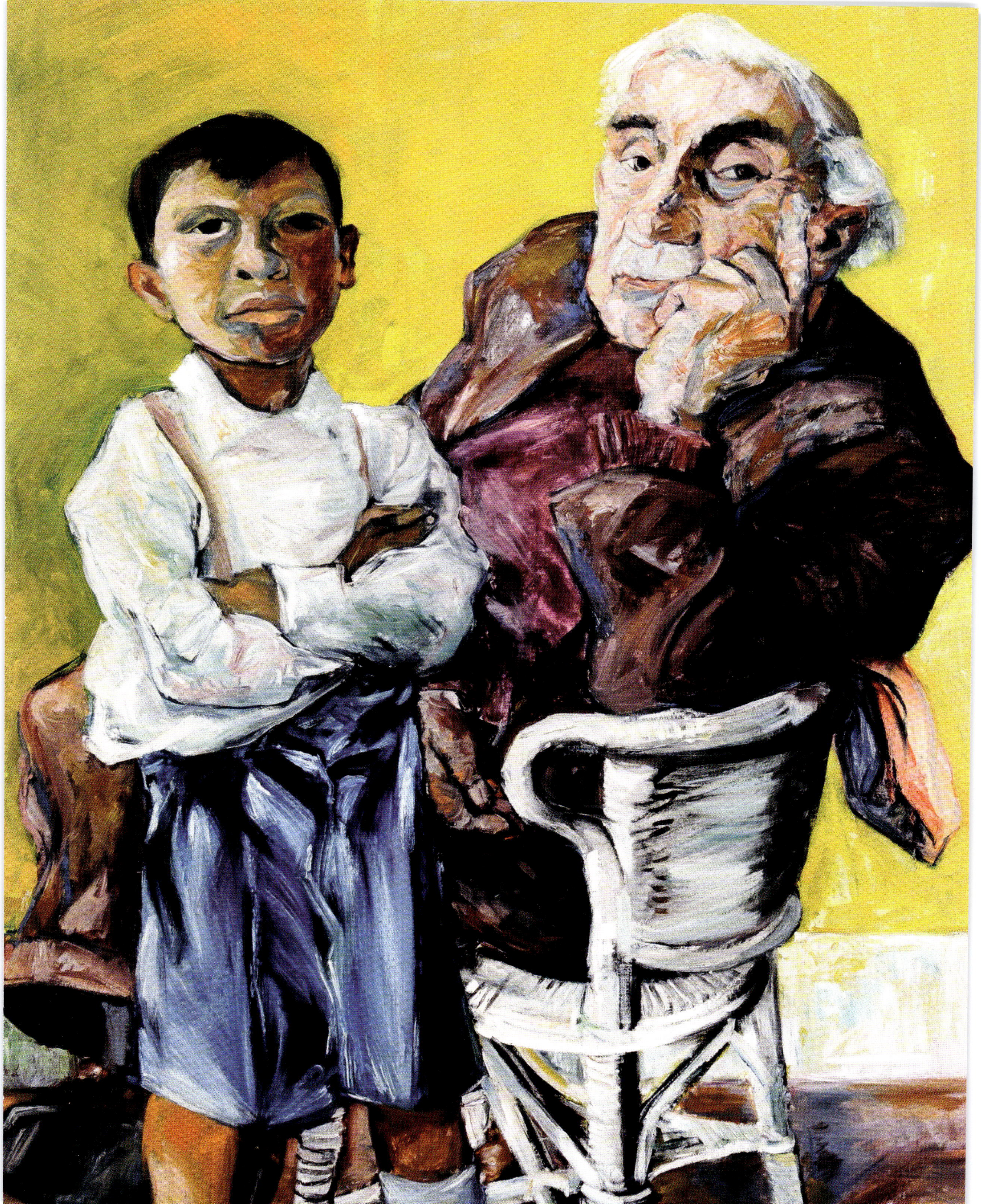

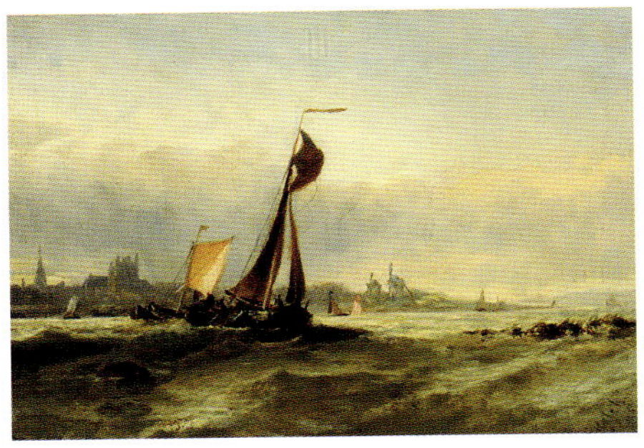

Hayes, Edwin 1819–1904
Seascape 1895
oil on canvas 24.2 x 34.5
VIS.619

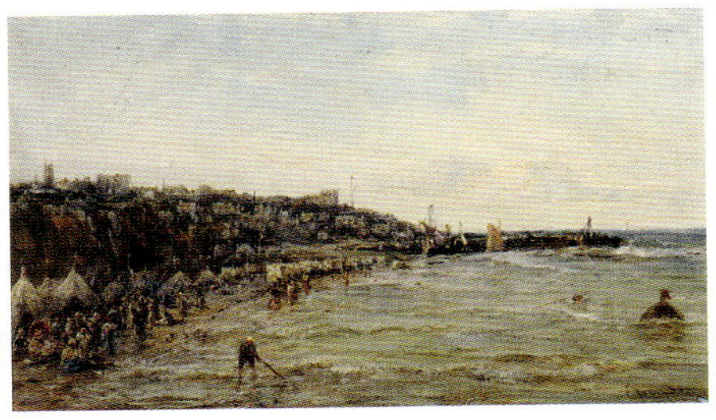

Hayes, Edwin 1819–1904
Broadstairs Harbour, Kent
oil on canvas 29.8 x 49
VIS.1212

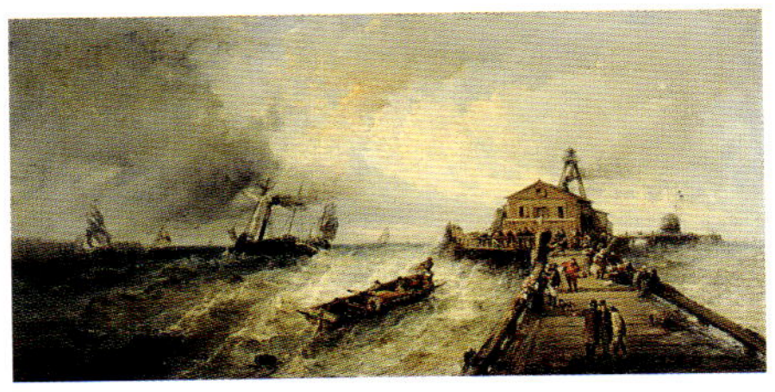

Hayes, Edwin 1819–1904
Shipping Making for a Harbour in a Rough Sea
oil on canvas 60 x 116
VIS.1325

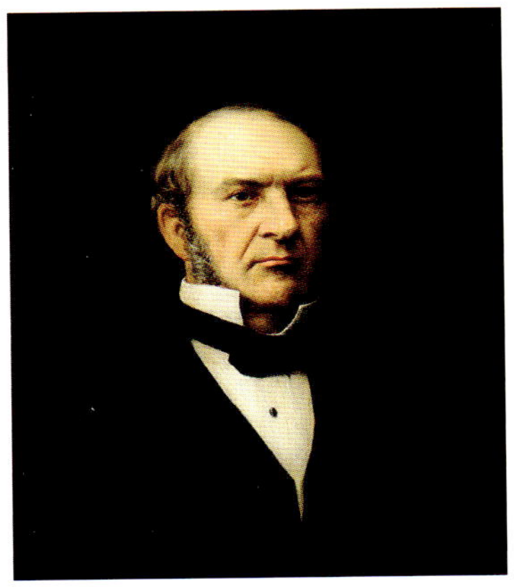

Head, B. G. active 1867–1890
William Gladstone (1809–1898)
oil on canvas 61.1 x 51
VIS.2040

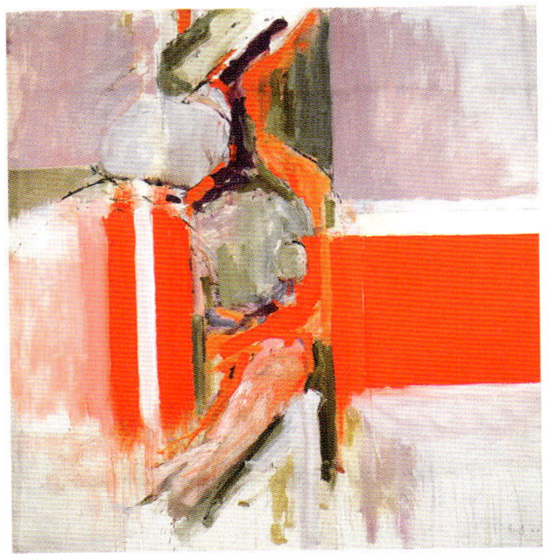

Heath, Adrian 1920–1992
Divided 1963
oil on canvas 183.3 x 173.2
VIS.3828

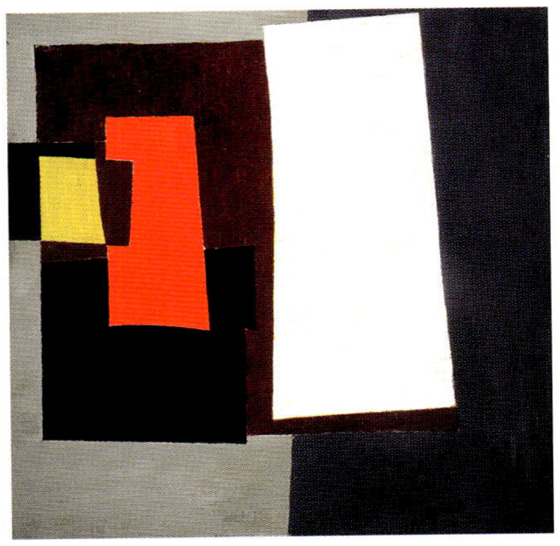

Heath, Adrian 1920–1992
Divided Form
oil on canvas 76.7 x 76.3
VIS.3829

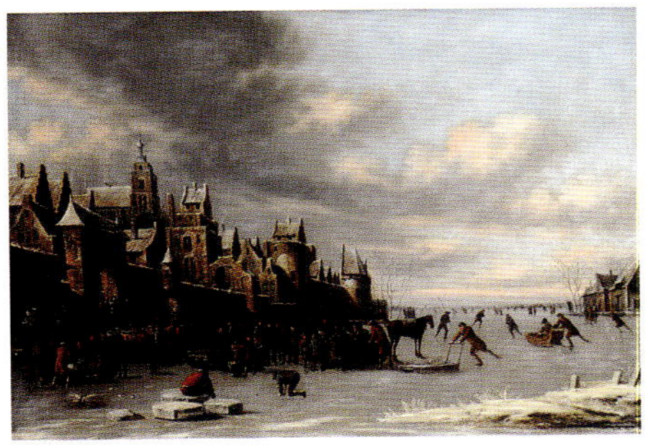

Heeremans, Thomas c.1640–1697
Winter Landscape 1691
oil on panel 61.3 x 67
VIS.3026

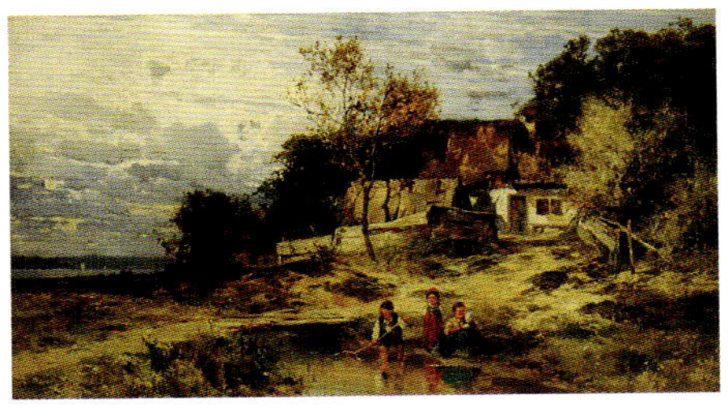

Heinish, Karl Adam 1847–1923
Cottages 1878
oil on canvas 21.9 x 37.1
VIS.796

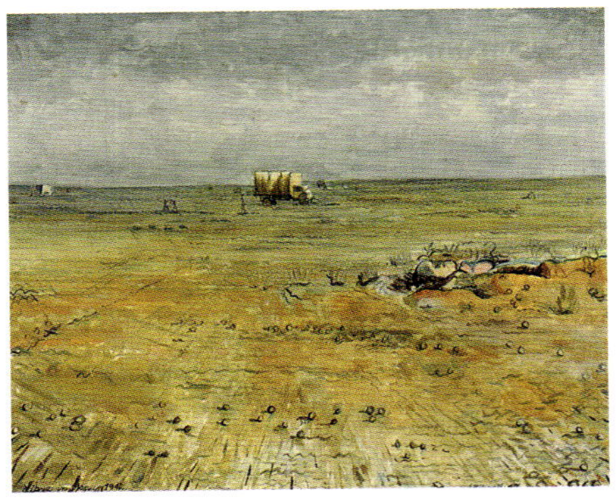

Hellewell, Jack 1920–2000
Libya in January 1942
oil on canvas 49.5 x 59.5
VIS.5449 (P)

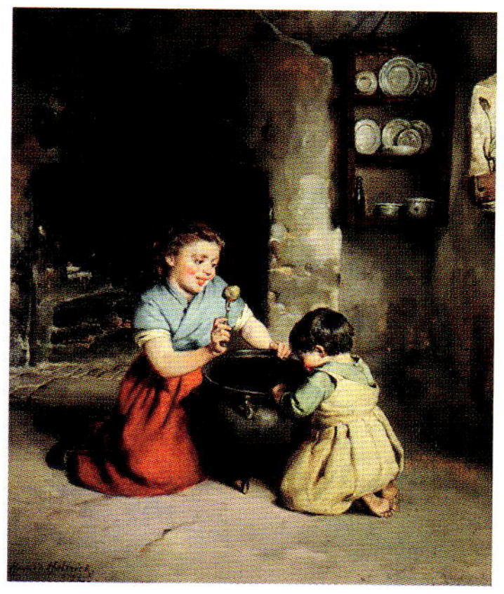

Helmick, Howard 1845–1907
A Frugal Meal 1872
oil on panel 38.7 x 31.9
VIS.2367

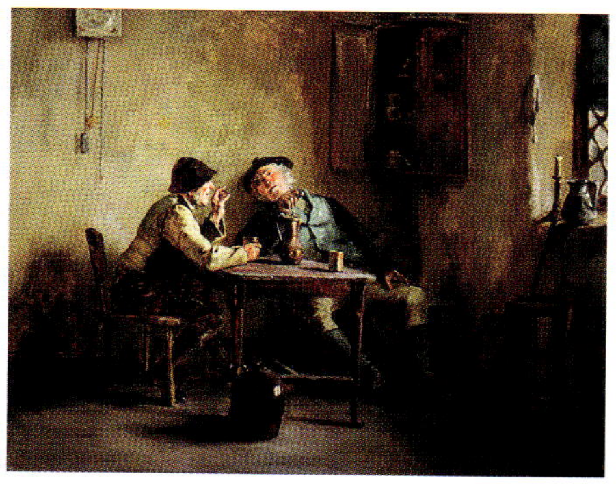

Helmick, Howard 1845–1907
The Gossips 1877
oil on canvas 44.2 x 54.5
VIS.2927

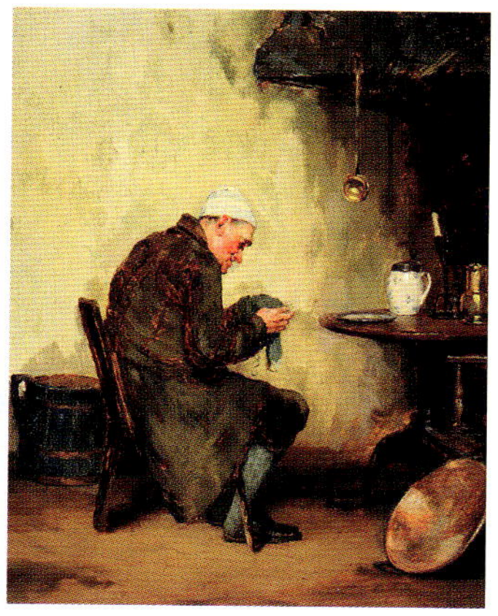

Helmick, Howard 1845–1907
A Stitch in Time Saves Nine 1880
oil on panel 24.3 x 19.3
VIS.1960

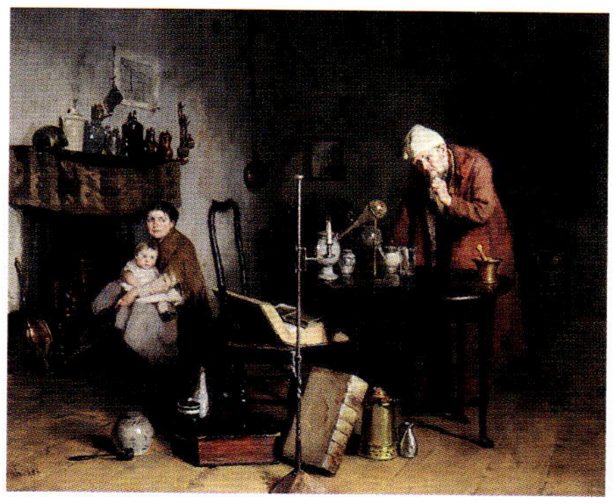

Helmick, Howard 1845–1907
The Alchemist 1883
oil on canvas 49.6 x 59.8
VIS.2722

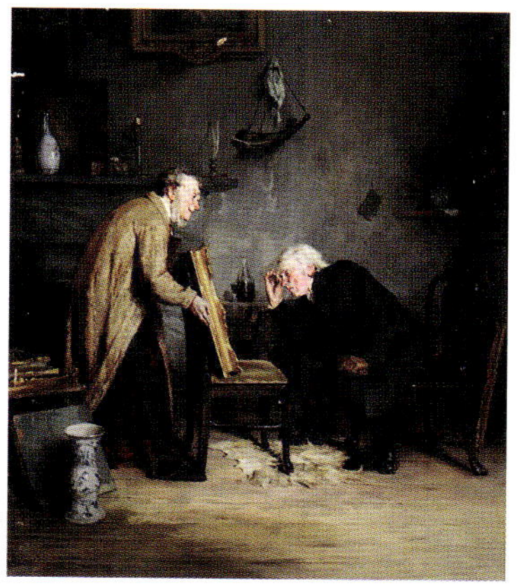

Helmick, Howard 1845–1907
The Connoisseurs
oil on canvas 67.6 x 57.1
VIS.2406

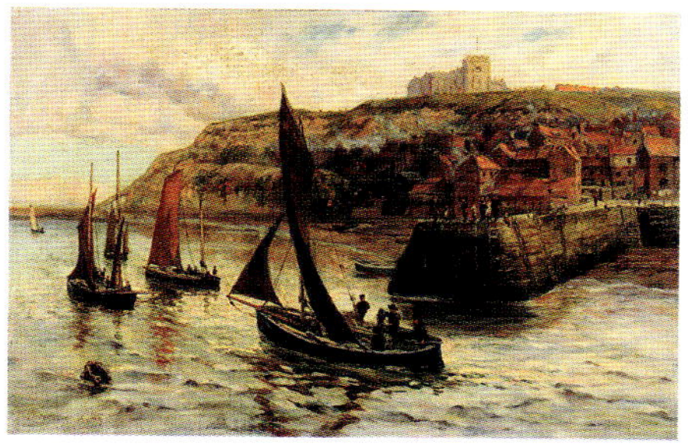

Hemy, Charles Napier 1841–1917
Whitby, North Yorkshire 1876
oil on canvas 50.9 x 76.2
VIS.1343

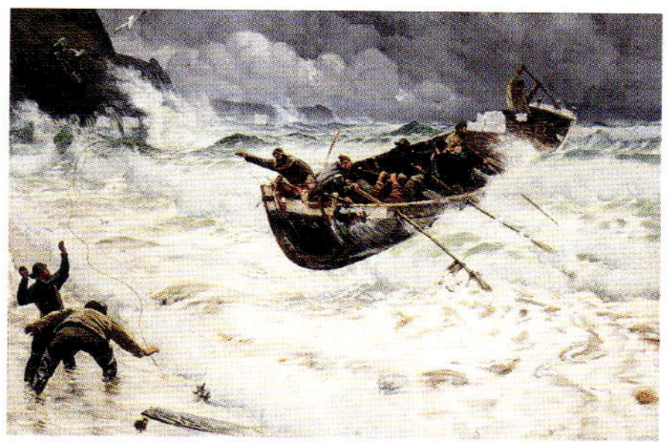

Hemy, Charles Napier 1841–1917
How the Boat Came Home 1886
oil on canvas 120.8 x 181
VIS.1476

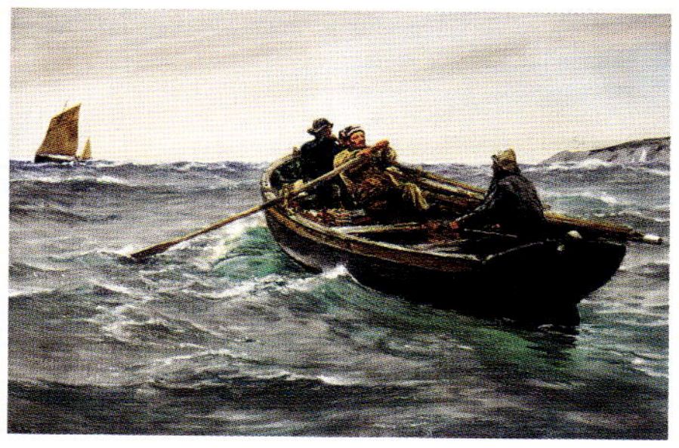

Hemy, Charles Napier 1841–1917
A Pull to Windward, Falmouth, Cornwall 1913
oil on canvas 60.4 x 89
VIS.3178

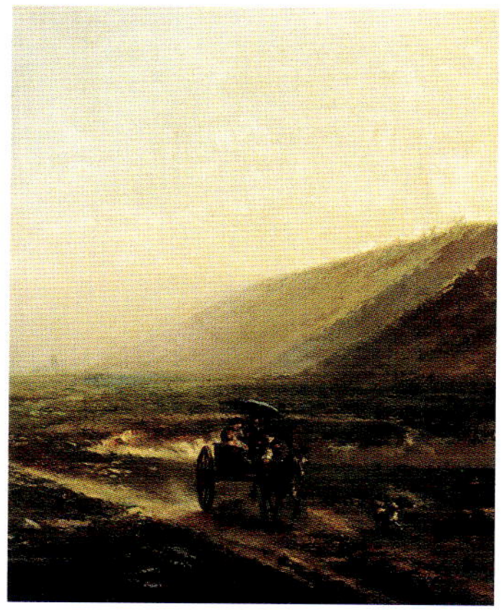

Henry, Émile (attributed to) 1844–1920
Travellers on a Showery Day 1860–1870
oil on canvas 64 x 49
VIS.586

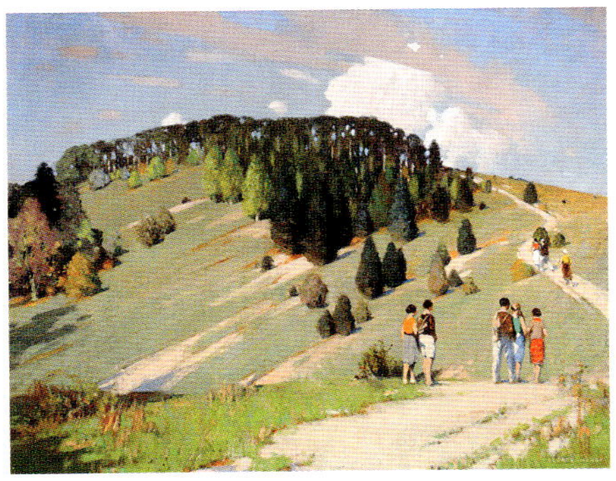

Henry, George 1858–1943
Hikers at Goodwood Downs, West Sussex
oil on canvas 99.2 x 127.3
VIS.2782

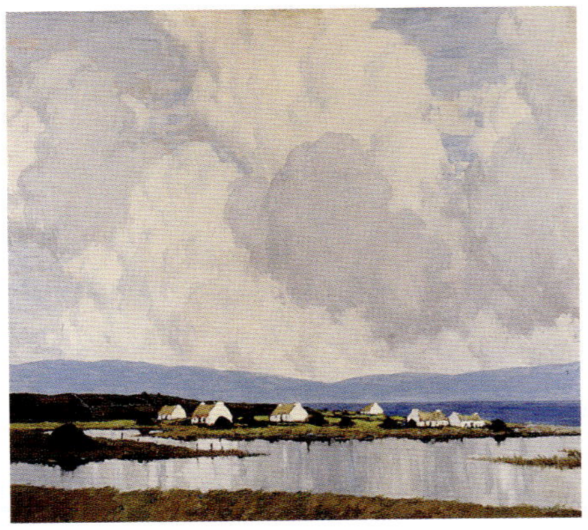

Henry, Paul 1876–1958
The Village by the Lake
oil on panel 84.7 x 90.8
VIS.5254

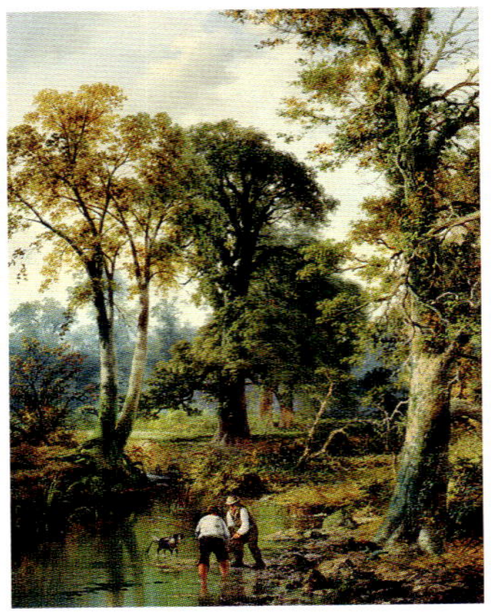

Henshaw, Frederick Henry 1807–1891
In the Forest of Arden, Warwickshire
oil on canvas 89.4 x 69.8
VIS.581

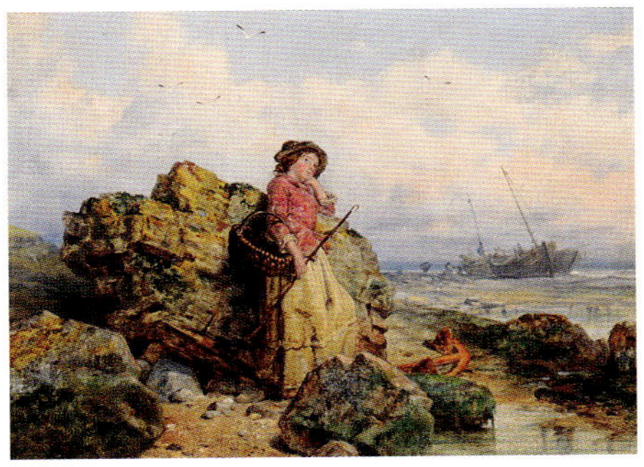

Henzell, Isaac 1815–1876
The Crab Catcher
oil on canvas 29.5 x 39.3
VIS.1385

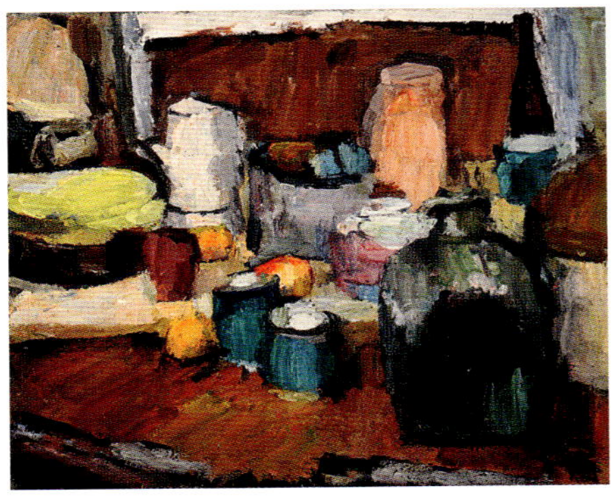

Hepher, David b.1935
Still Life 1963
oil on panel 109.4 x 131
VIS.4120

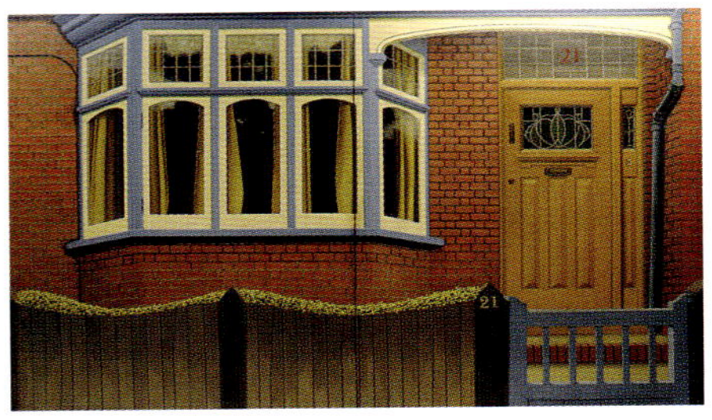

Hepher, David b.1935
No.21 (diptych) 1971
oil on canvas 208.2 x 172.7; 208.4 x 172.8
VIS.3938 & VIS.4240

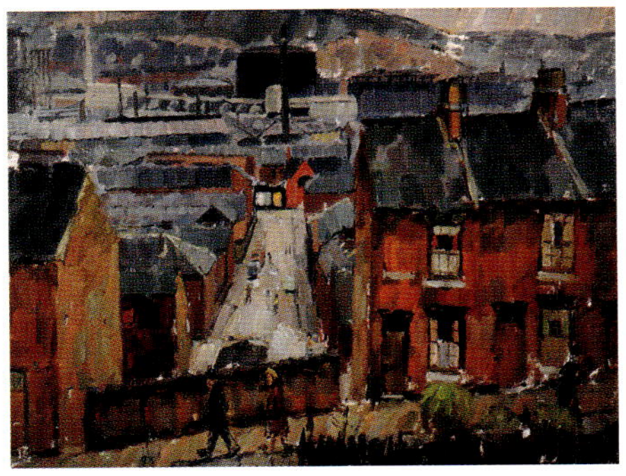

Hepher, David b.1935
Upperthorpe, Sheffield
oil on canvas 68.2 x 87.6
VIS.4542

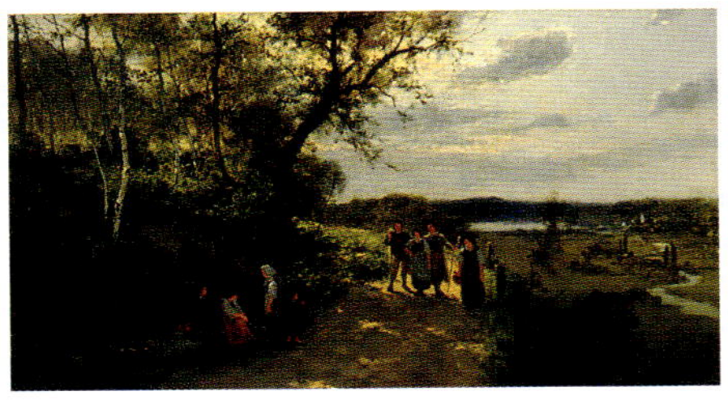

Her, Theodor 1838–1892
Landscape with Figures 1875–1880
oil on canvas 21.4 x 37.5 (E)
VIS.1229

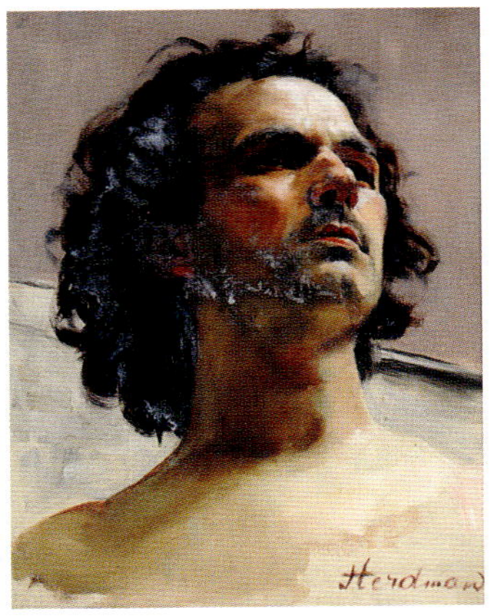

Herdman, Robert Duddingstone 1863–1922
Head of a Man
oil on canvas 39.9 x 31.4
VIS.1249

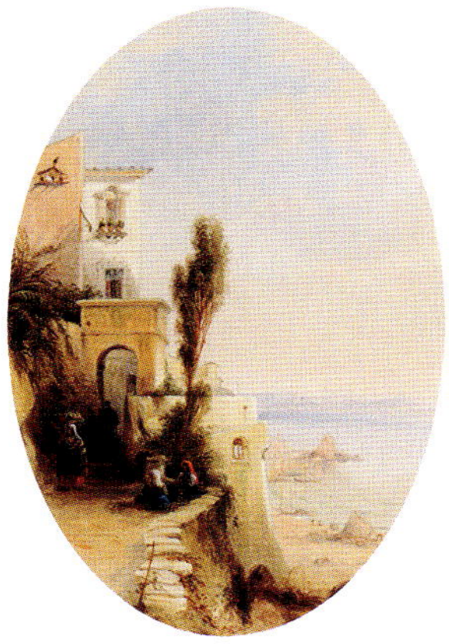

Hering, George Edwards 1805–1879
On Lake Como, Italy
oil on panel 19.7 x 13.5
VIS.1142

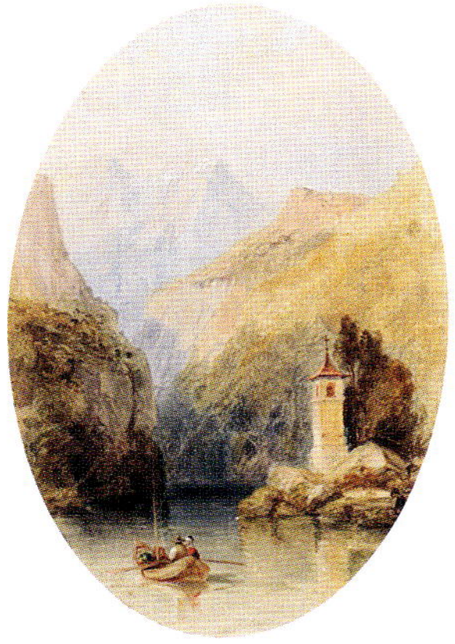

Hering, George Edwards 1805–1879
William Tell's Chapel on the Lake of Lucerne, Switzerland
oil on board 19.5 x 13.8
VIS.1141

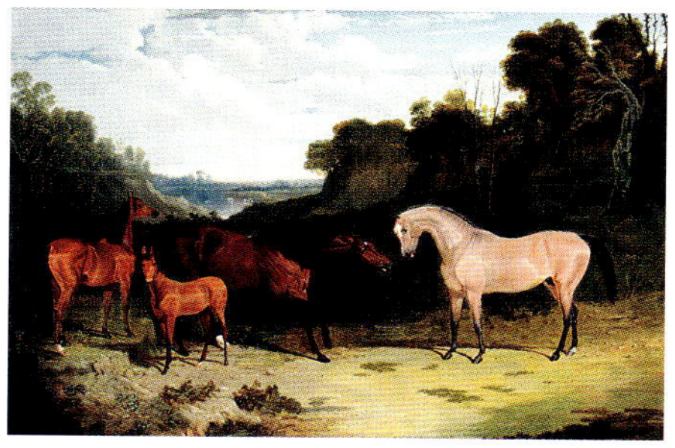

Herring, John Frederick I 1795–1865
Horses in a Landscape 1827
oil on canvas 70.5 x 103.5
VIS.2271

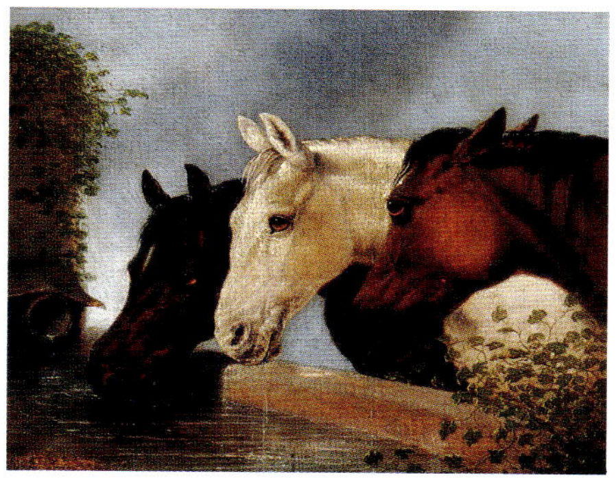

Herring, John Frederick I 1795–1865
The Good Templars
oil on canvas 19.5 x 24.6
VIS.1100

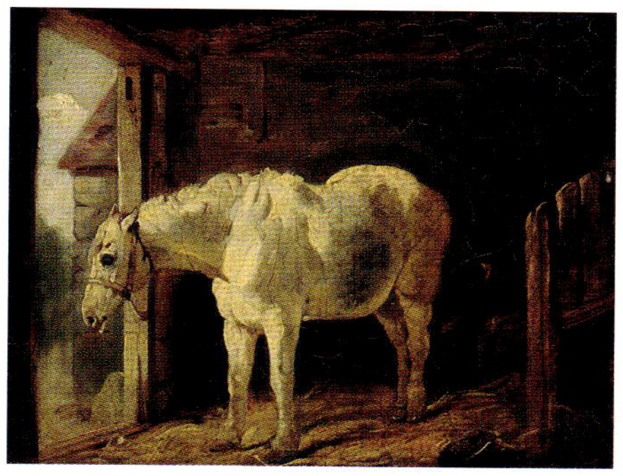

Herring, John Frederick I 1795–1865
The White Horse
oil on canvas 26.7 x 34
VIS.188

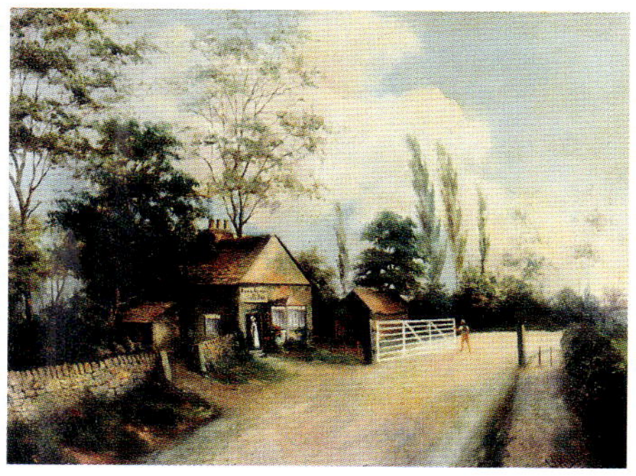

Highfield, William 1870–1957
Broadfield Toll-Bar, Sheffield c.1900
oil on canvas 44 x 59
K1956.5

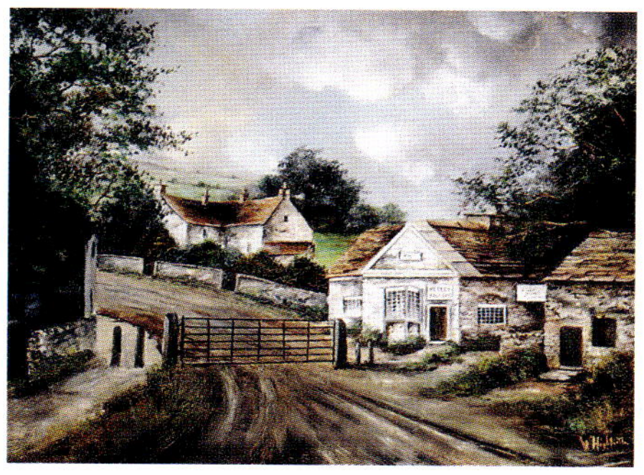

Highfield, William 1870–1957
Heeley Toll-Bar, Sheffield c.1900
oil on canvas 43.5 x 59
K1956.4

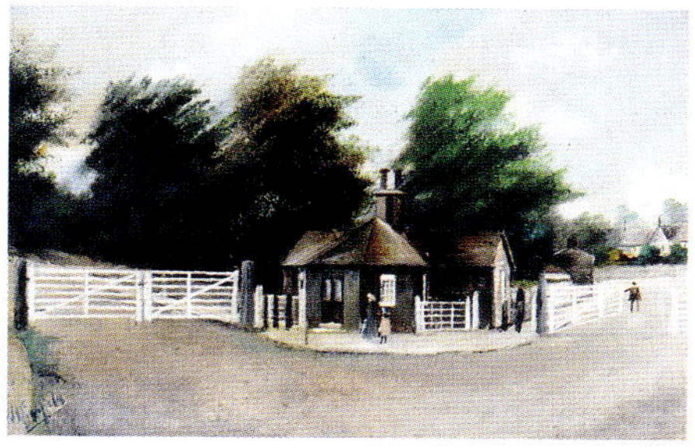

Highfield, William 1870–1957
Pitsmoor Toll-Bar, Sheffield c.1900
oil on canvas 31.5 x 44
1981.716

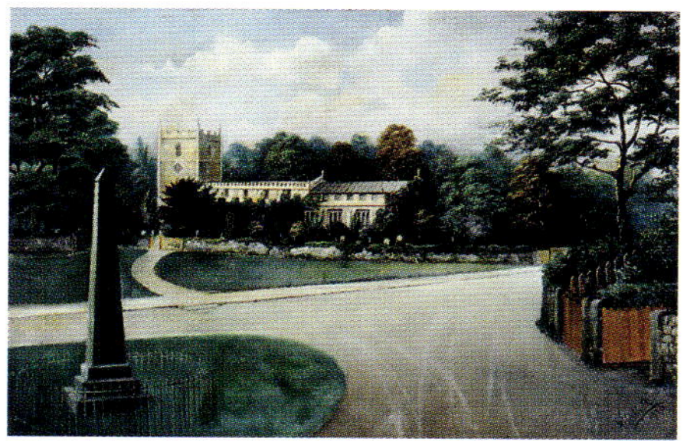

Highfield, William 1870–1957
Norton Church, Sheffield 1923
oil on canvas 49.3 x 74
K1957.5

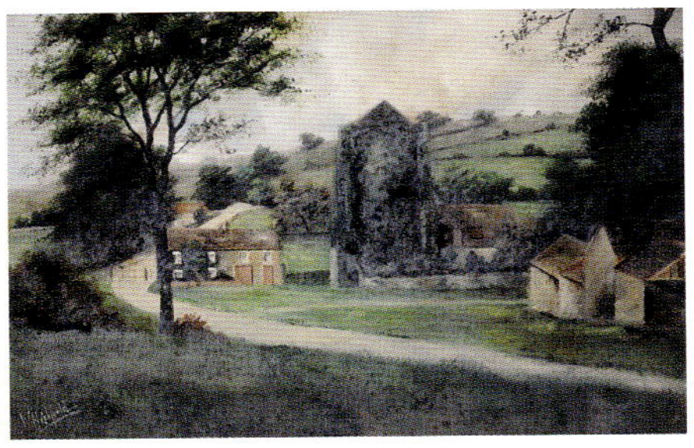

Highfield, William 1870–1957
Beauchief Abbey, Sheffield
oil on canvas 39.1 x 59.2
VIS.3941

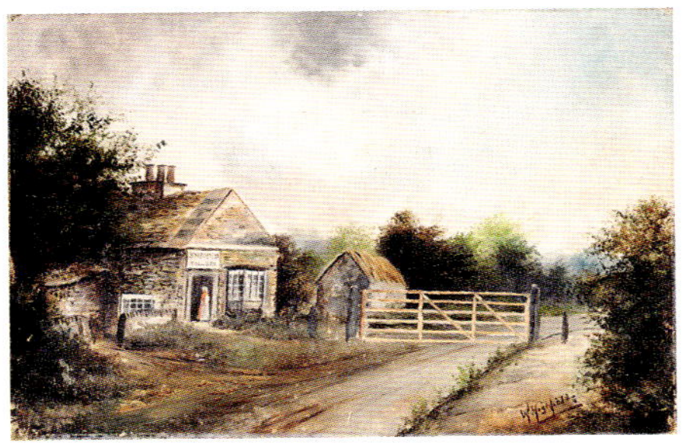

Highfield, William 1870–1957
Broadfield Road Toll-Bar, Sheffield
oil on canvas 30.6 x 45.9
VIS.3943

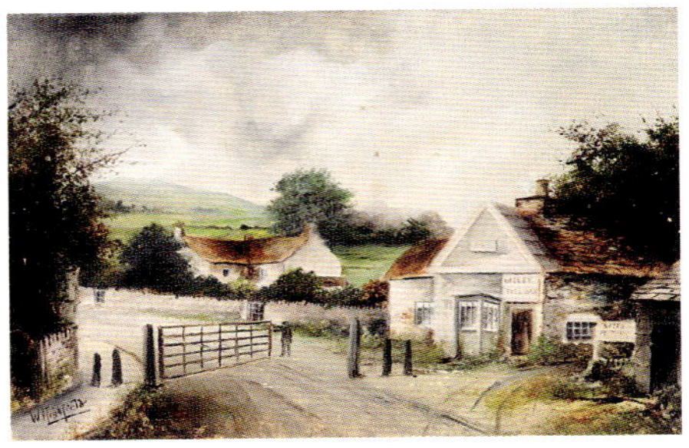

Highfield, William 1870–1957
Heeley Toll-Bar, Sheffield
oil on canvas 35.6 x 46
VIS.3942

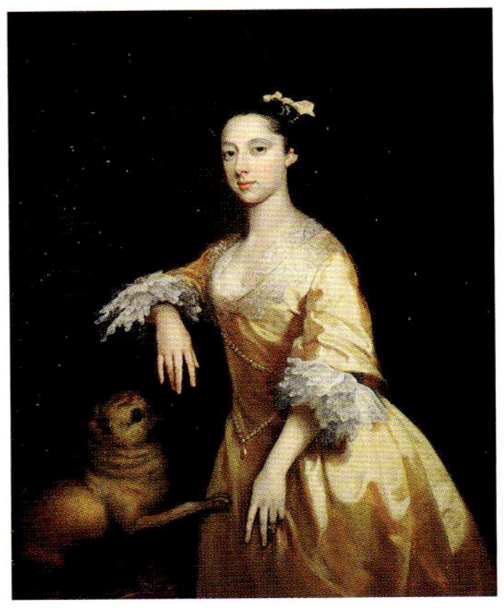

Highmore, Joseph 1692–1780
Portrait of a Lady with a Pug Dog 1738
oil on canvas 125.5 x 100.1
VIS.2994

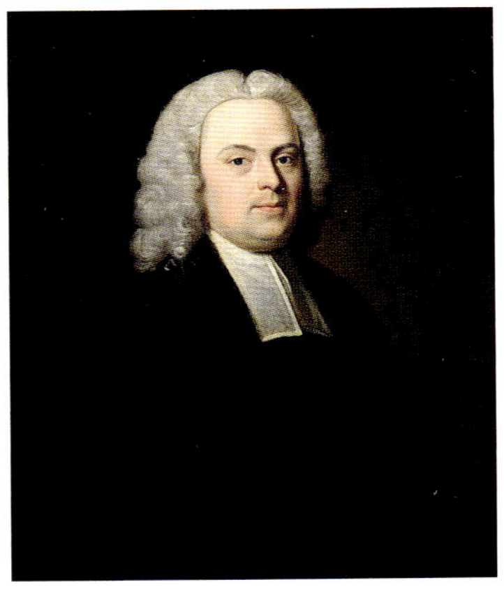

Highmore, Joseph 1692–1780
Portrait of a Divine, Laurence Degge
oil on canvas 74.8 x 61.3
VIS.3030

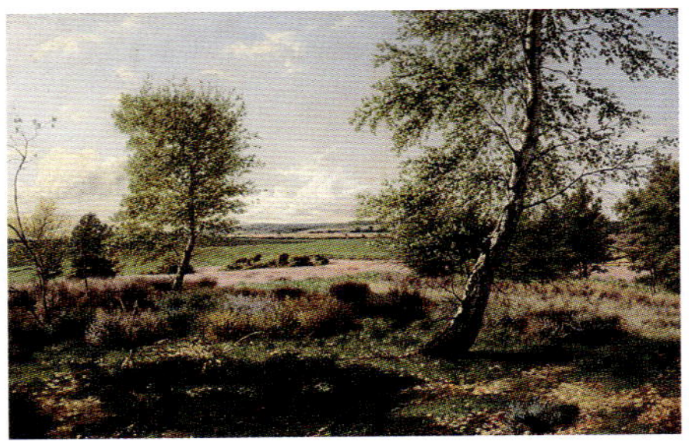

Hill, Arthur c.1829–1894
A Study of Beeches 1858
oil on canvas 39.5 x 60.3
VIS.2937

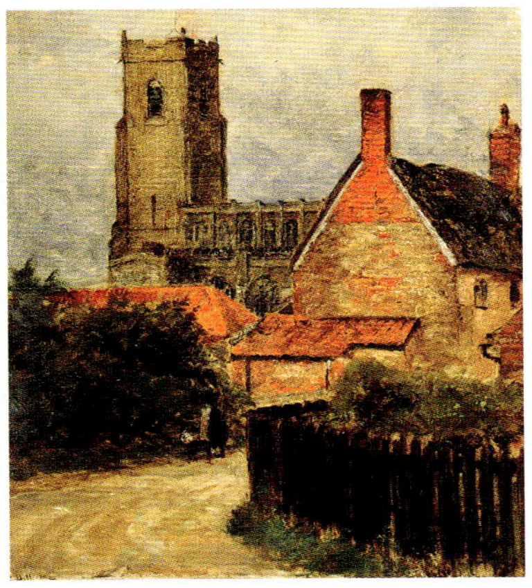

Hill, James Stevens 1854–1921
Landscape with a Church
oil on canvas 44 x 39.8
VIS.1220

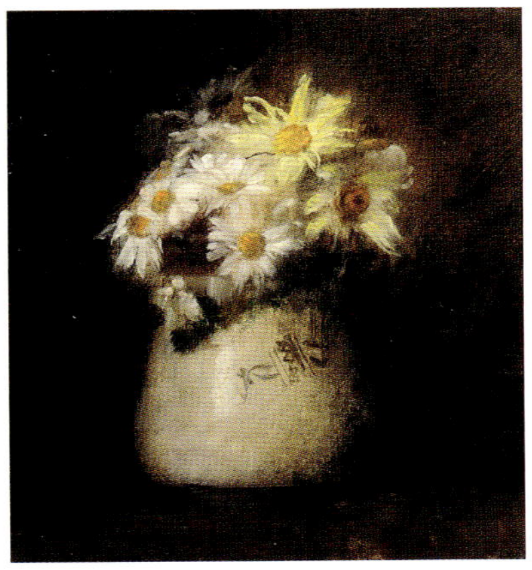

Hill, James Stevens 1854–1921
Marguerites in a Vase
oil on canvas 30 x 27.5
VIS.1207

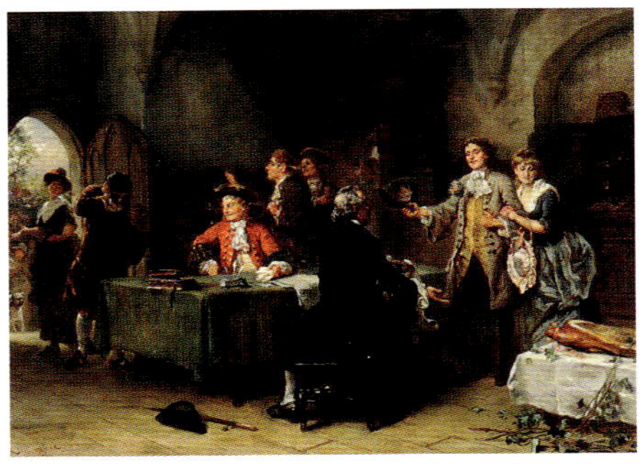

Hillingford, Robert Alexander 1825–1904
The Dunmow Flitch
oil on canvas 44.4 x 59.7
VIS.1967

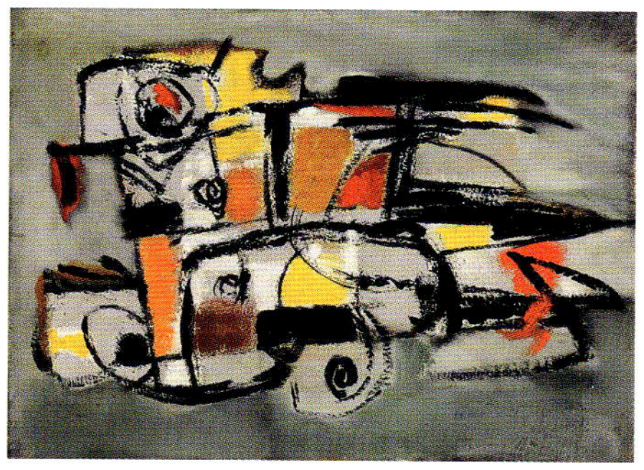

Hilton, Roger 1911–1975
Composition
oil on canvas 46 x 61
VIS.5440

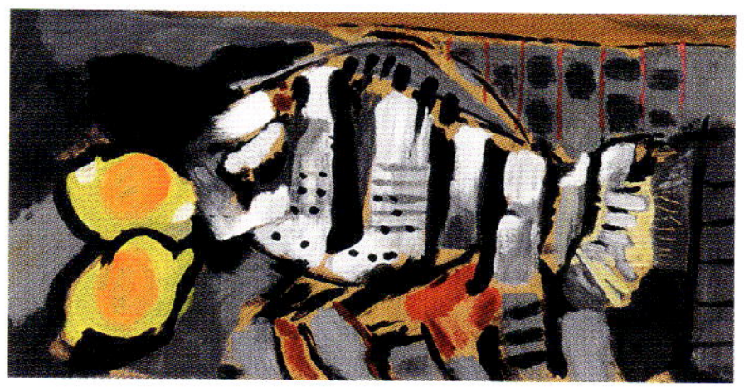

Hilton, Roger 1911–1975
Fish and Two Lemons
oil on board 21.7 x 41.3
VIS.5429

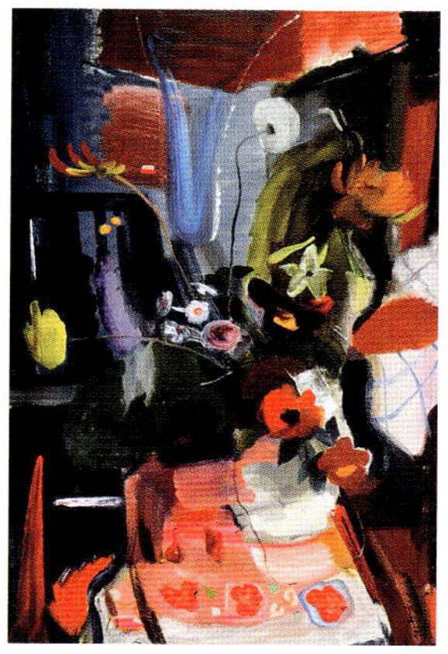

Hitchens, Ivon 1893–1979
Flower Piece 1943
oil on canvas 103.2 x 68.9
VIS.4158

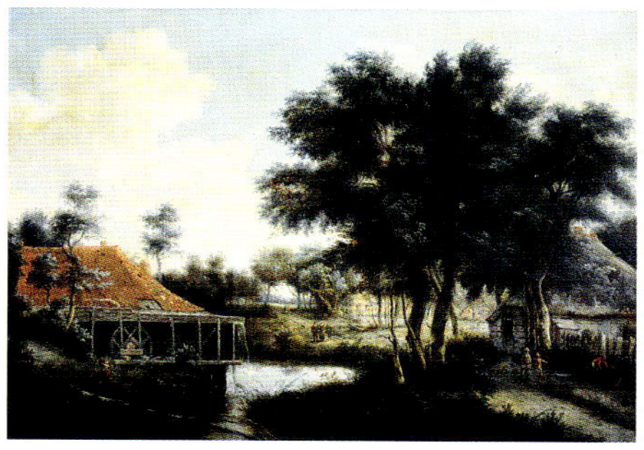

Hobbema, Meindert (after) 1638–1709
The Watermill
oil on panel 75 x 107.8
VIS.455

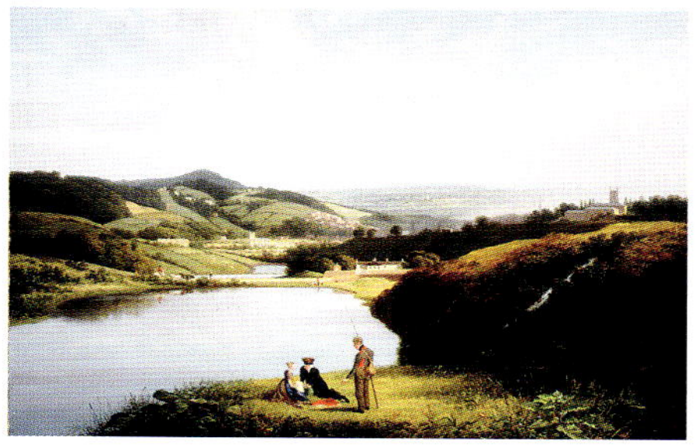

Hofland, Thomas Christopher 1777–1843
Sheffield from Crookes c.1826
oil on canvas 108 x 140
1972.151

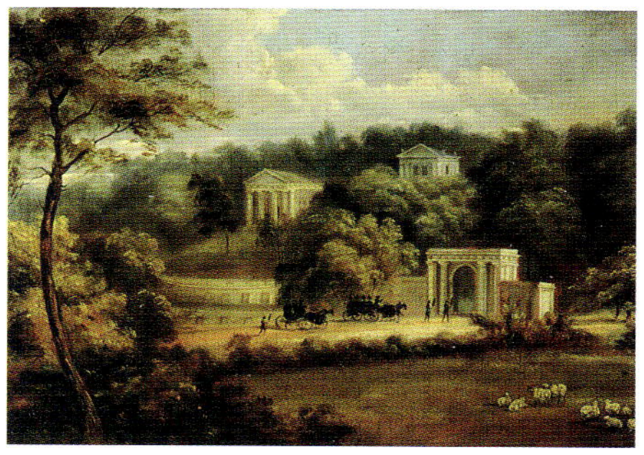

Hofland, Thomas Christopher 1777–1843
Sheffield General Cemetery 1840
oil on canvas 24.2 x 34.2
K1903.4

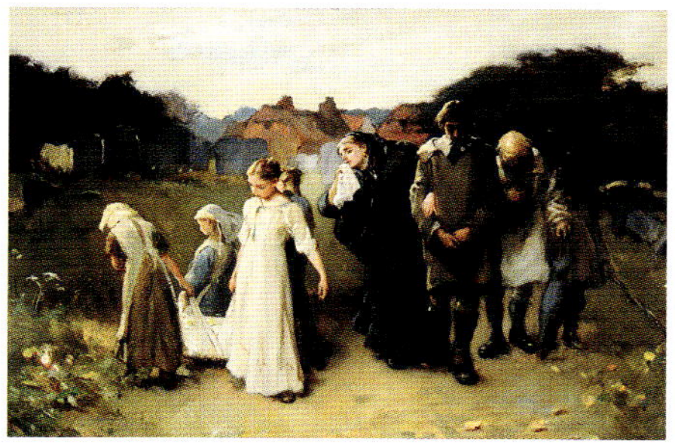

Holl, Frank 1845–1888
Her First Born 1877
oil on panel 33.1 x 48.2
VIS.5128

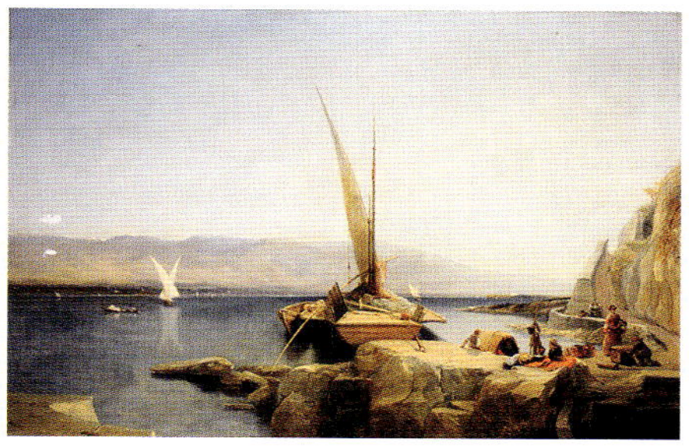

Holland, James 1799–1870
Head of Lake Geneva, Switzerland 1844
oil on canvas 91.6 x 138.2
VIS.121

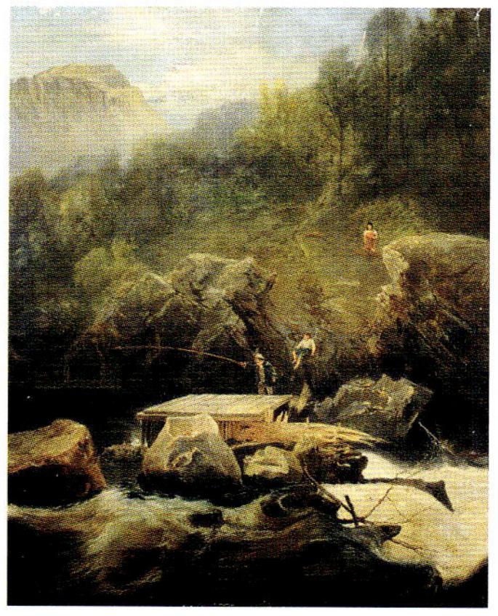

Holland, James 1799–1870
A Highland River Scene with a Salmon Trap
oil on canvas 126.3 x 101.4
VIS.1528

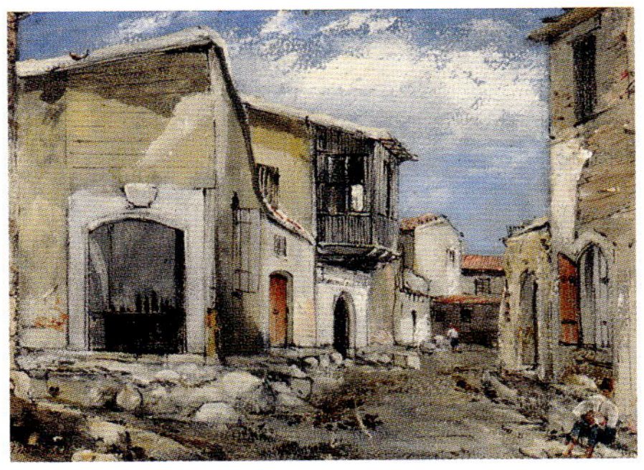

Holland, James 1799–1870
Italian Village
oil on paper 18.9 x 25.4
VIS.751

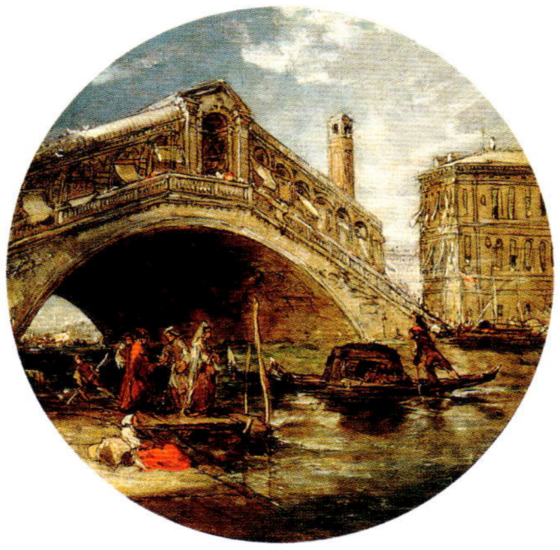

Holland, James 1799–1870
The Rialto, Venice
oil on panel 29.1
VIS.1598

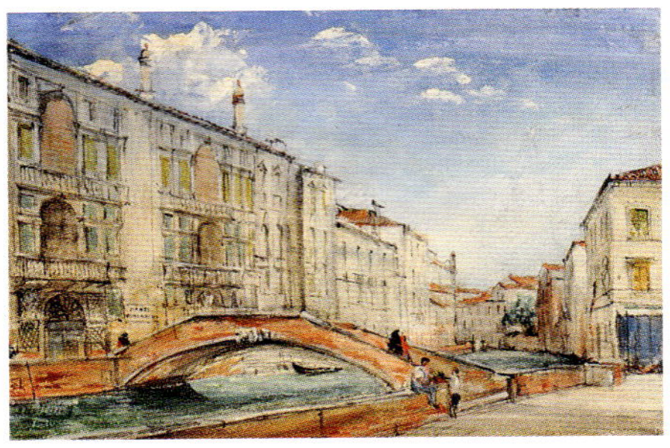

Holland, James 1799–1870
Venice
oil on paper 17.8 x 26.5
VIS.1345

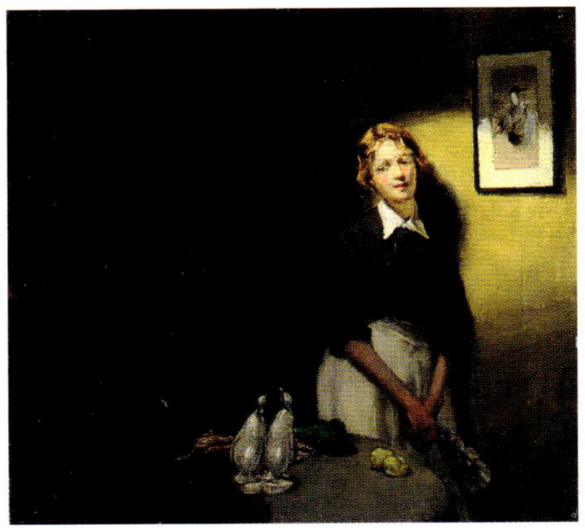

Hollingsworth, Ruth b. 1880
Daydreams
oil on canvas 35.7 x 38
VIS.982

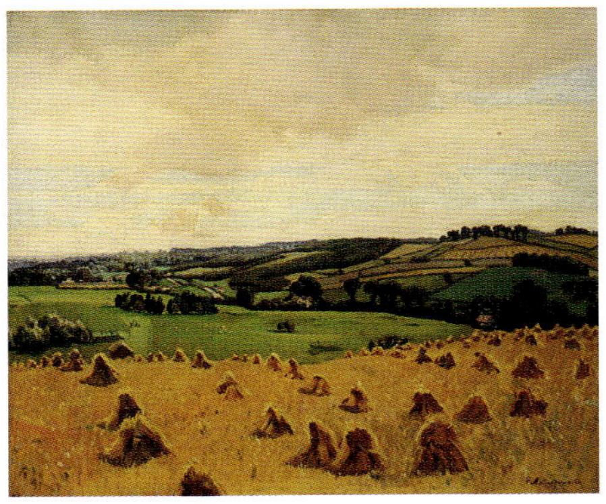

Hollingsworth, Ruth b. 1880
Landscape
oil on canvas 61.8 x 72.7
VIS.128

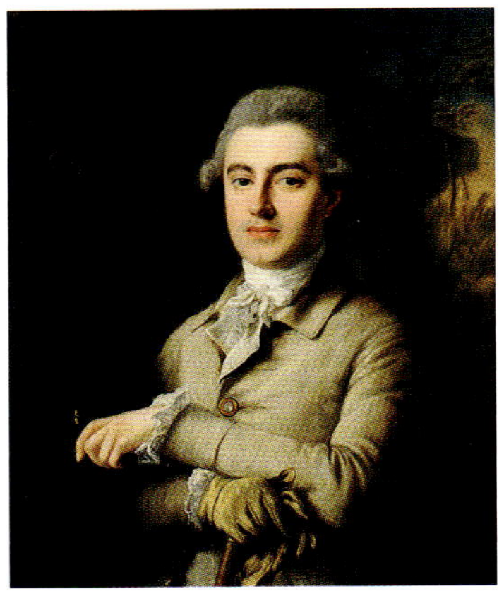

Hone, Nathaniel I 1718–1784
The Honourable David Murray (1748–1794), MP for Peebleshire 1779
oil on canvas 73.9 x 61.1
VIS.3947

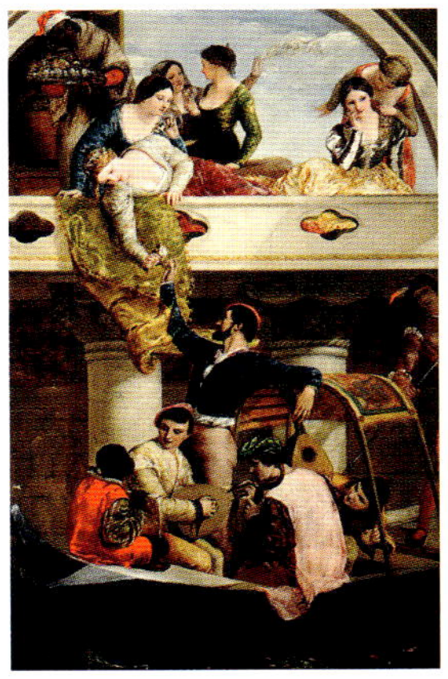

Hook, James Clarke 1819–1907
A Dream of Venice 1850
oil on canvas 124.7 x 80.5
VIS.1453

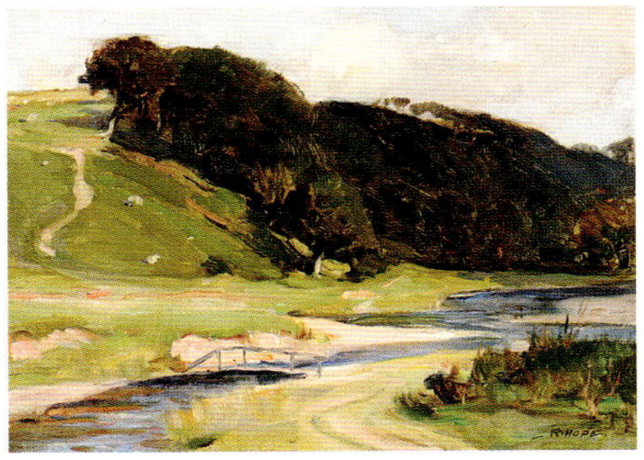

Hope, Robert 1869–1936
Stream in Galloway, Scotland
oil on board 24.5 x 33.8
VIS.4476

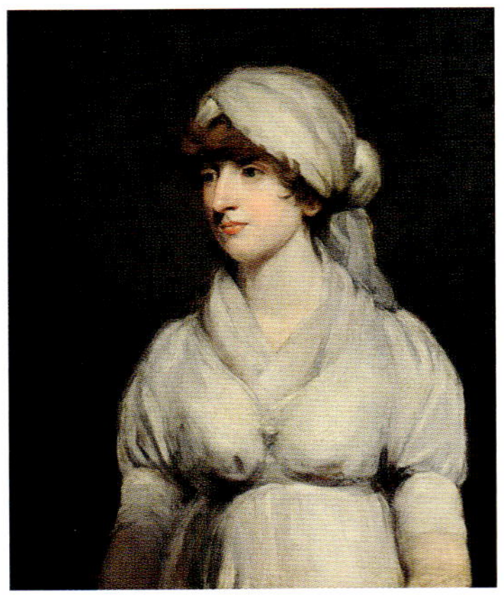

Hoppner, John 1758–1810
Mary Anne Sykes
oil on canvas 75 x 62.1
VIS.3021

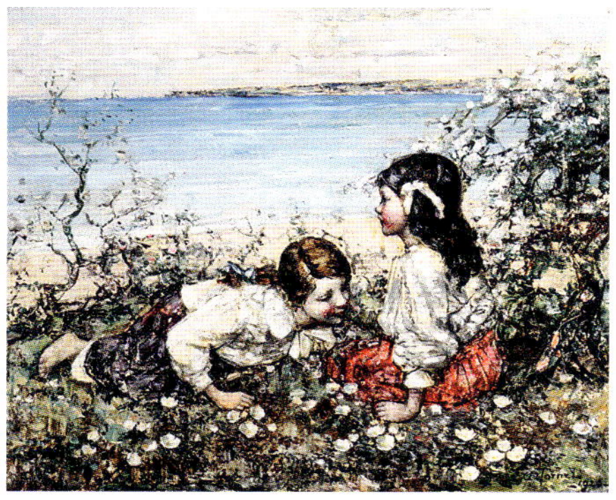

Hornel, Edward Atkinson 1864–1933
Children by the Sea 1920
oil on canvas 49.7 x 59.8
VIS.441

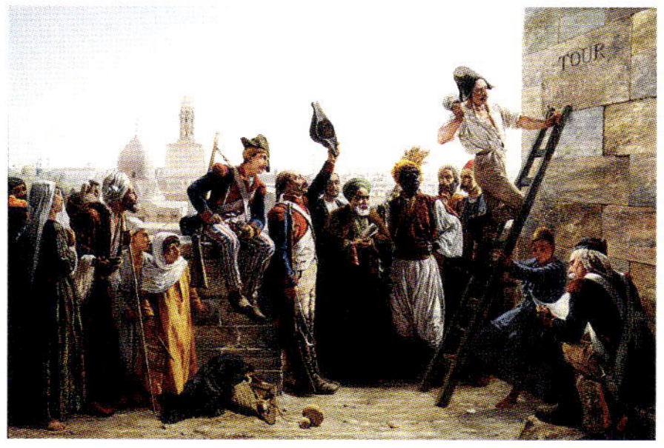

Horsley, Walter Charles 1855–1934
The French in Cairo c.1884
oil on canvas 135.2 x 195
VIS.1479

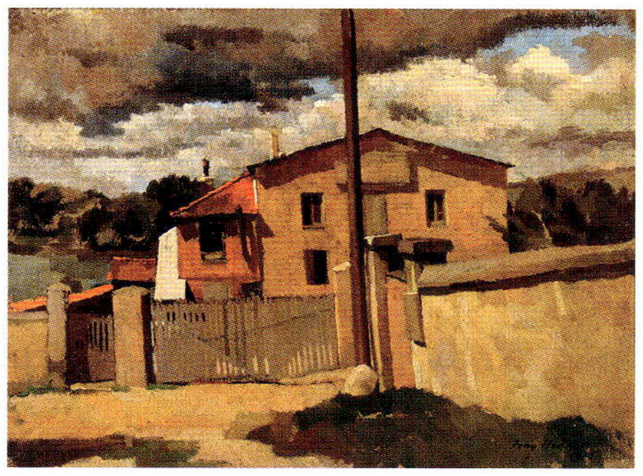

Horton, Percy Frederick 1897–1970
House on the Seine 1925
oil on board 27.4 x 36
VIS.5187

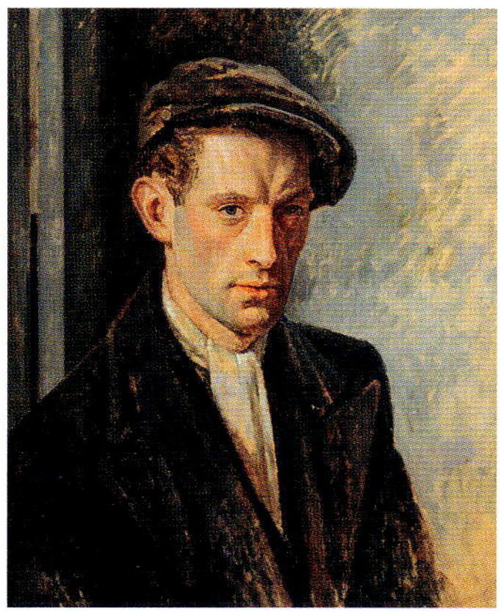

Horton, Percy Frederick 1897–1970
Unemployed Man c.1929
oil on panel 44.3 x 36.1
VIS.2290

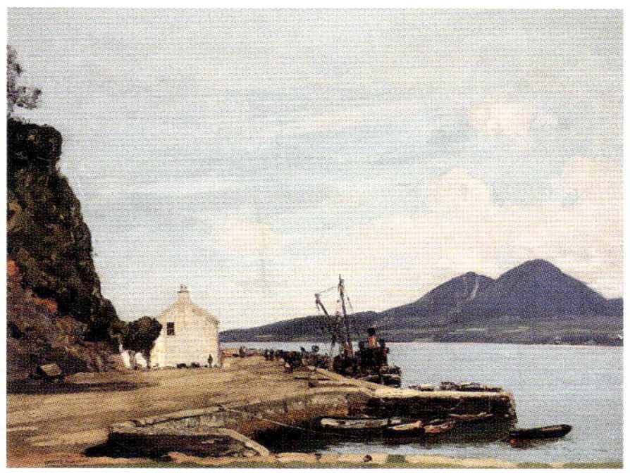

Houston, George 1869–1947
Port Askaig, Islay, Scotland
oil on canvas 69.3 x 89
VIS.2604

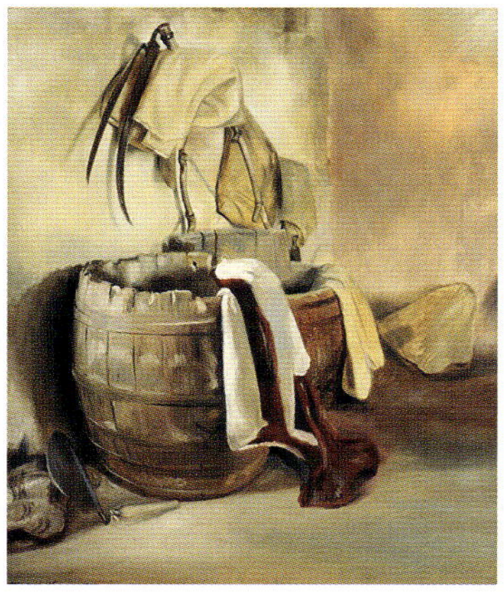

Houthuesen, Albert Anthony 1903–1979
Grain Barrels 1933
oil on canvas 75.3 x 62.4
VIS.1855

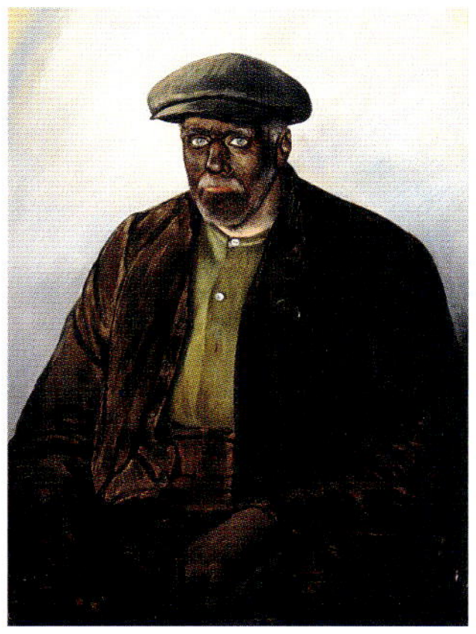

Houthuesen, Albert Anthony 1903–1979
The Collier 1933
oil on canvas 67.3 x 49.3
VIS.1858

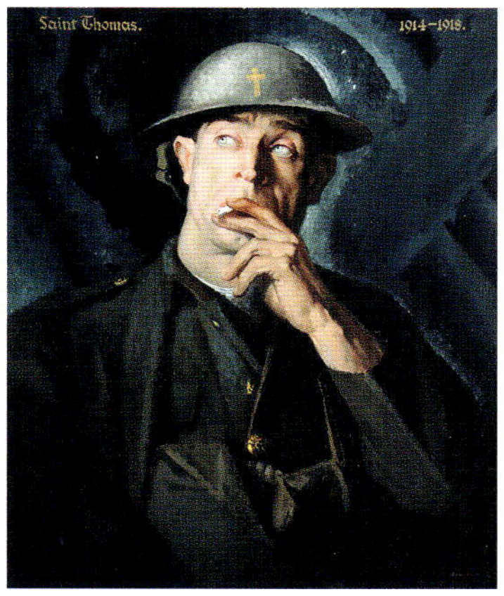

Hoyland, Henry George 1895–1948
'Saint Thomas, 1914–1918'
oil on canvas 75 x 62.4
VIS.780

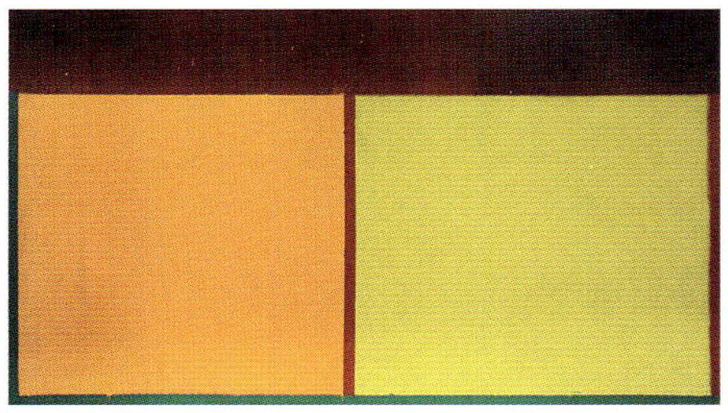

Hoyland, John 1934–2011
12.1.1969 1969
acrylic on cotton 197 x 365.3
VIS.3862

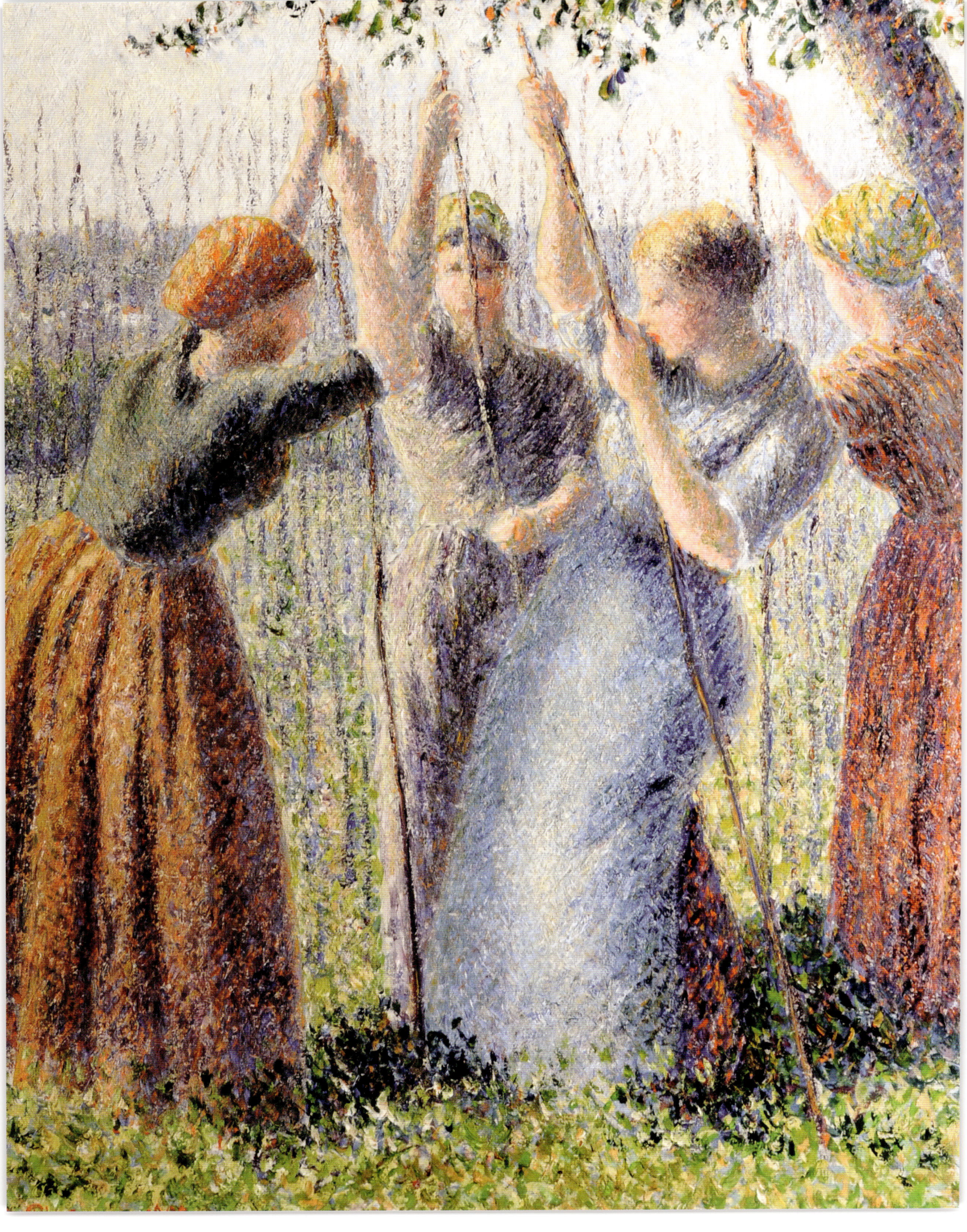

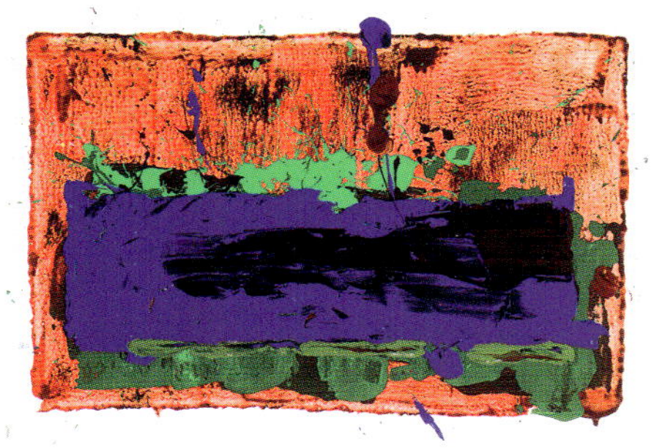

Hoyland, John 1934–2011
Composition XVIII
acrylic on paper 50.2 x 72.2
VIS.5146

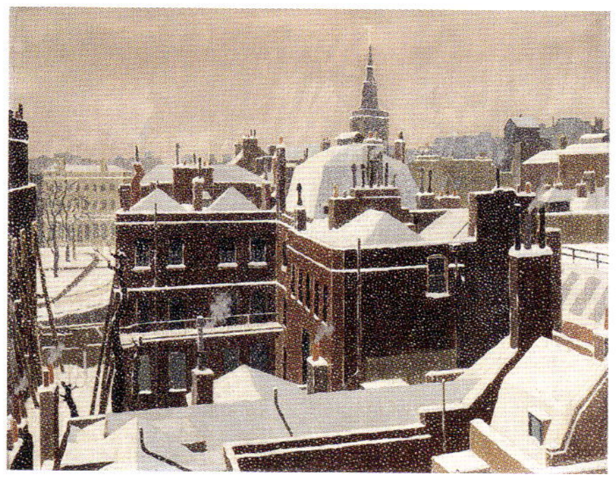

Hubbard, Eric Hesketh 1892–1957
A London Winter View
oil on canvas 46 x 56.8
VIS.670

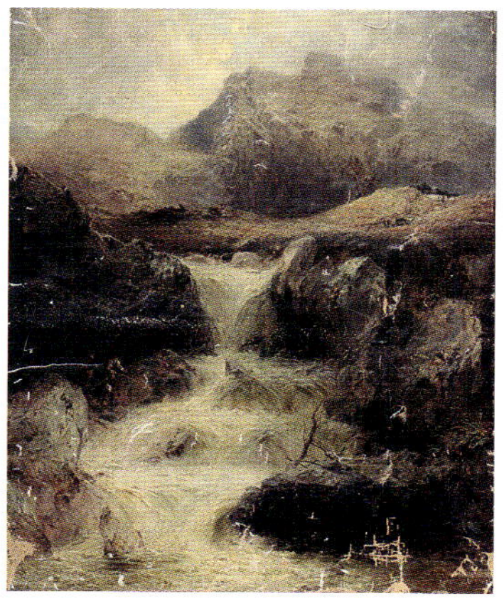

Hudson, Robert 1852–1884
After Rain of the Tummell, Perthshire, Scotland
1878
oil on canvas 128.9 x 110.2
VIS.2535

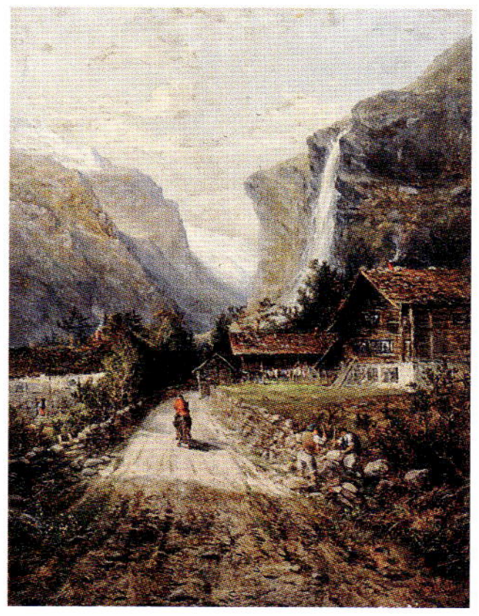

Hudson, Robert 1852–1884
Mountain Scene 1882
oil on canvas 61.1 x 45.8
VIS.2383

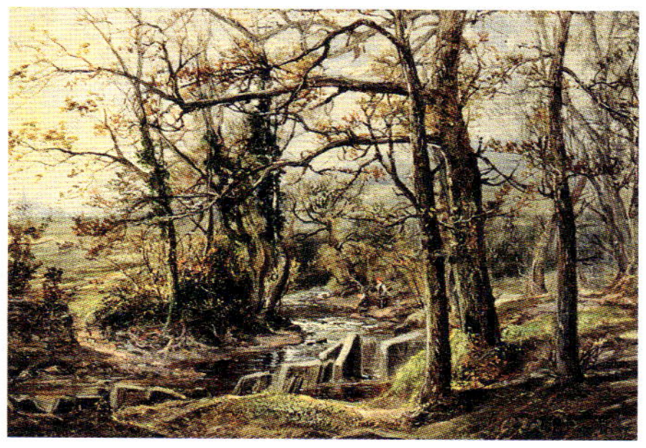

Hudson, Robert 1852–1884
Brook Scene, Endcliffe Woods, Sheffield
oil on board 23.8 x 33.3
VIS.2874

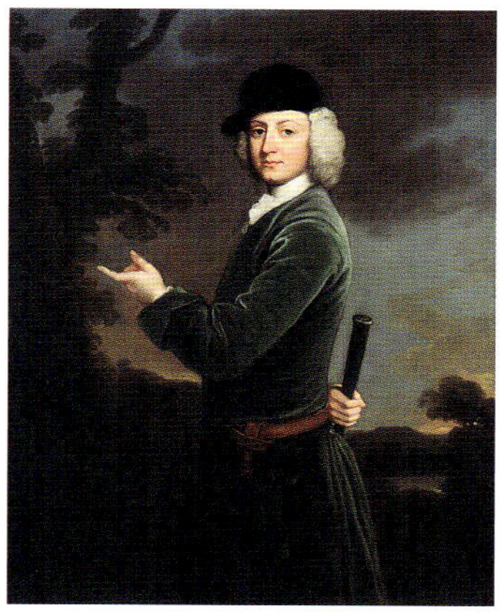

Hudson, Thomas 1701–1779
Dormer Fynes
oil on canvas 124 x 99.5
VIS.329

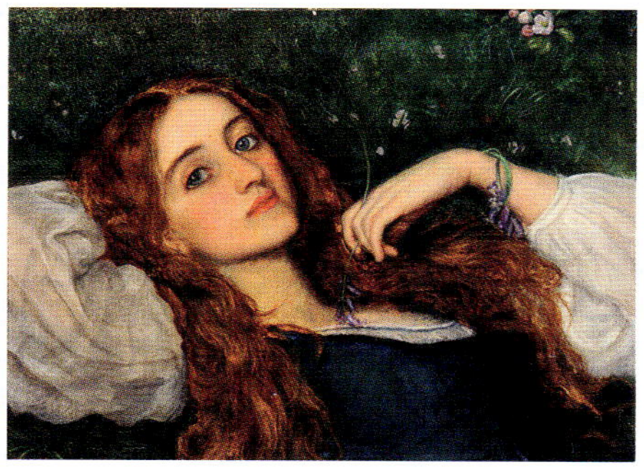

Hughes, Arthur 1832–1915
In the Grass
oil on board 26.5 x 35.6
VIS.3

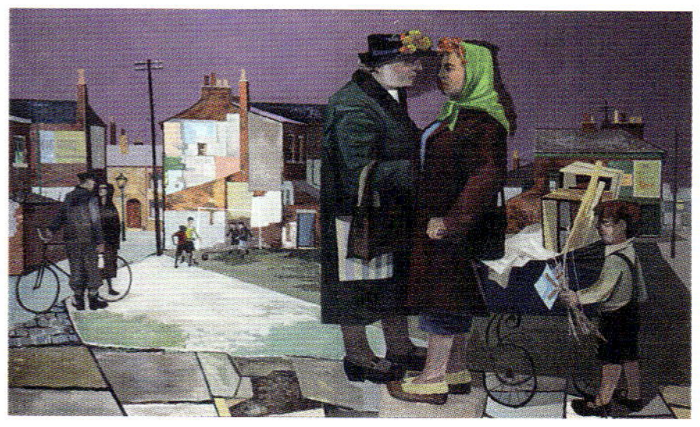

Hughes, Malcolm Edward 1920–1997
Street Gossip
oil on board 120.5 x 192.4
VIS.5423

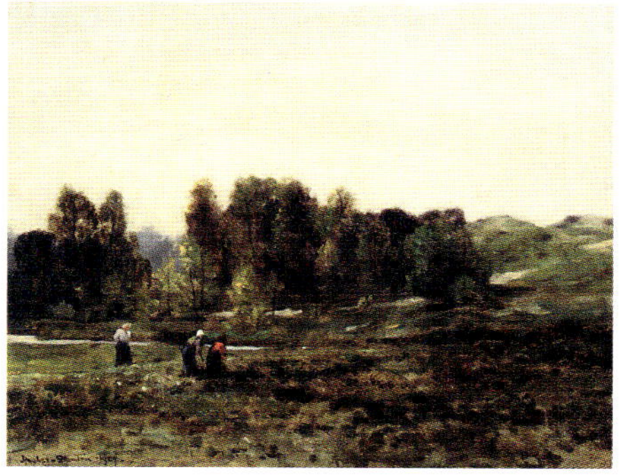

Hughes-Stanton, Herbert Edwin Pelham
1870–1937
Peat Gatherers 1909
oil on canvas 34.5 x 43
VIS.548

Facing page: Pissarro, Camille, 1831–1903, *Paysannes plantant des rammes* (detail), 1891, Museums Sheffield, (p. 169)

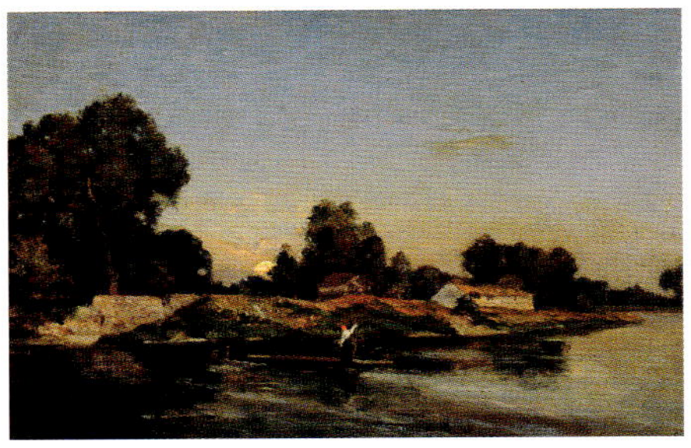

Hughes-Stanton, Herbert Edwin Pelham 1870–1937
Moonrise
oil on canvas 29 x 44.5
VIS.766

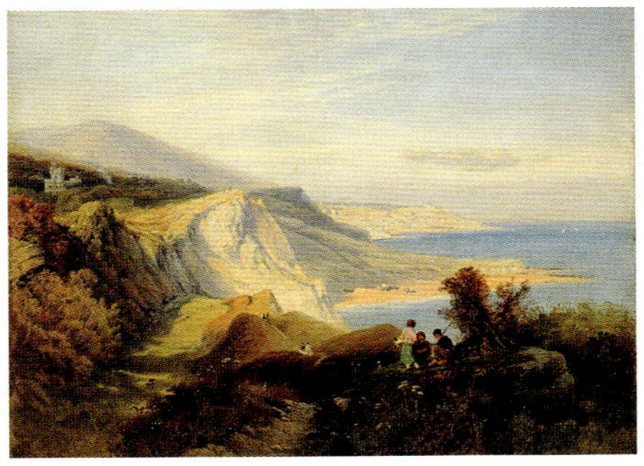

Hulme, Frederick William 1816–1884
Ventnor from St Lawrence, Isle of Wight 1858
oil on canvas 54.4 x 72.5
VIS.622

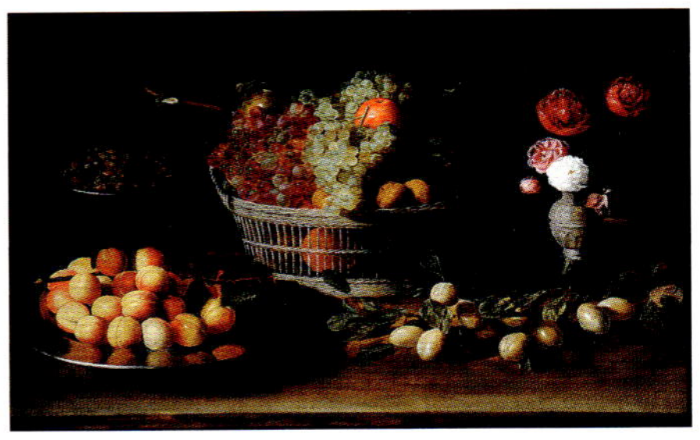

Hulsdonck, Jacob van (attributed to) 1582–1647
Still Life c.1630
oil on panel 64.9 x 101.5
VIS.270

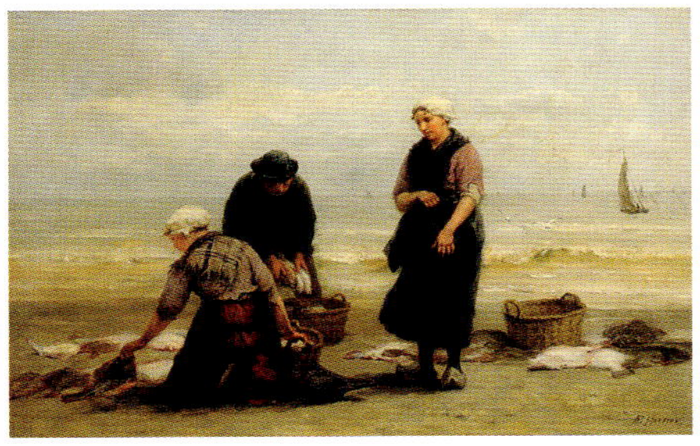

Hume, Edith 1843–1906
Packing Fish
oil on canvas 39 x 59.3
VIS.1623

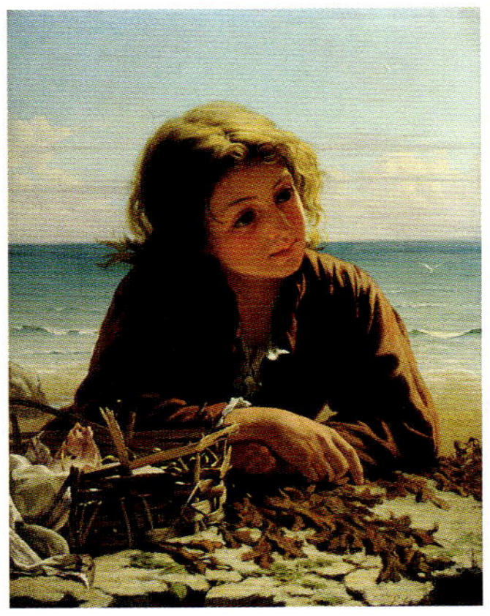

Humphrey, Edward J. active 1872–1890
Resting
oil on canvas 62.2 x 48.2
VIS.1515

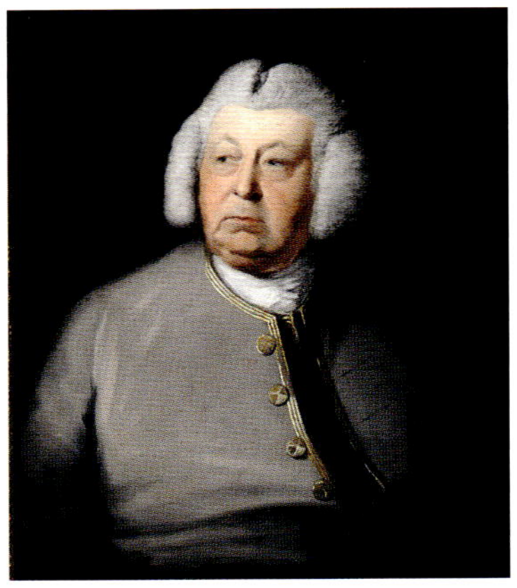

Humphry, Ozias 1742–1810
Francis Austen, Esq., of Sevenoaks c.1780
oil on canvas 90.7 x 78.2
VIS.74

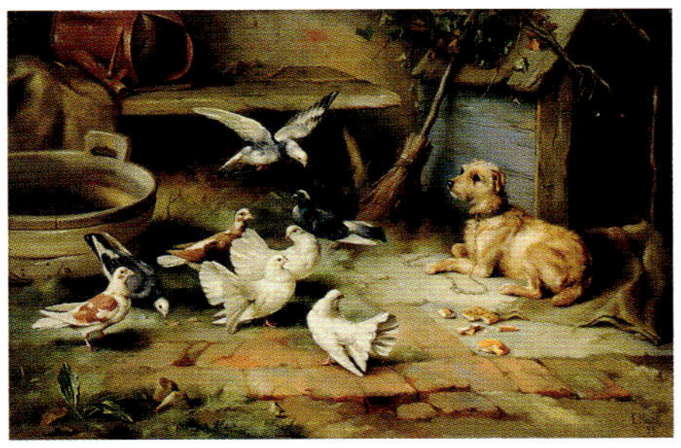

Hunt, Edgar 1876–1953
Dog and Pigeons 1898
oil on canvas 51 x 76.2
VIS.195

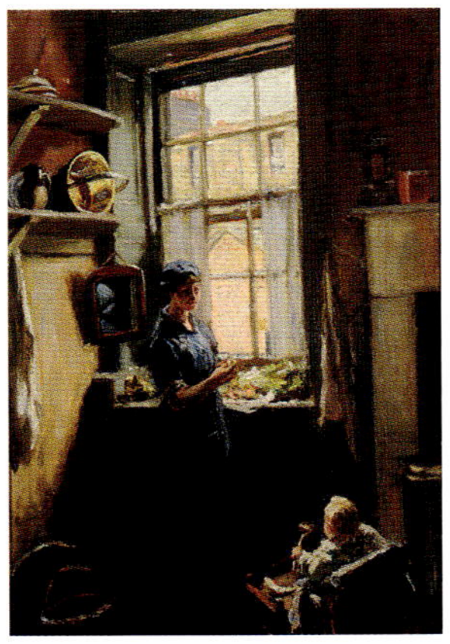

Hunt, Thomas 1854–1929
Home Sunshine
oil on canvas 59.5 x 40.5
VIS.1322

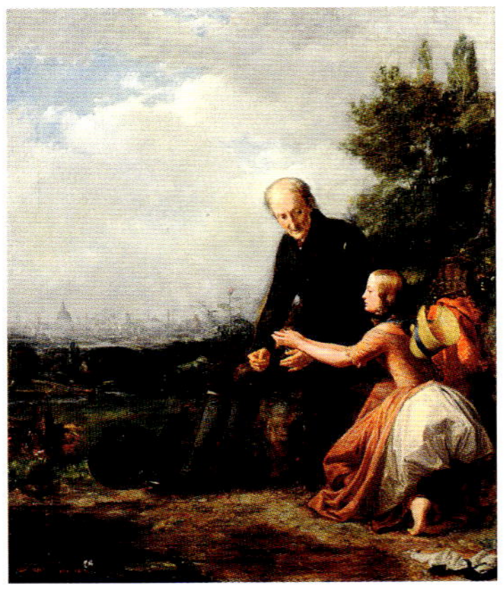

Hunt, William Holman 1827–1910
Little Nell and Her Grandfather 1845
oil on canvas 111.1 x 99
VIS.21

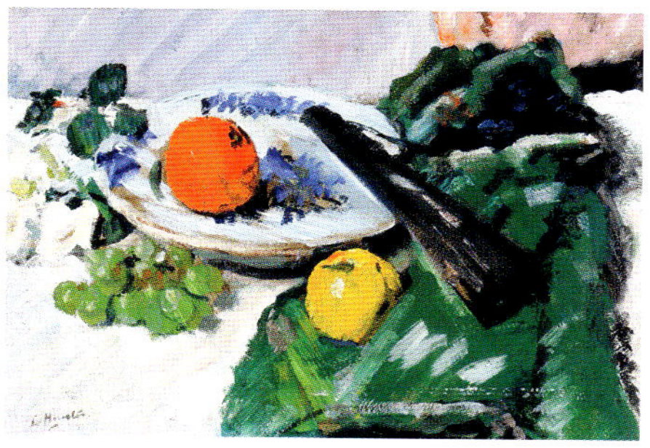

Hunter, George Leslie 1877–1931
Still Life with Fruit and a Black Fan
oil on canvas 37.9 x 54.2
VIS.4143

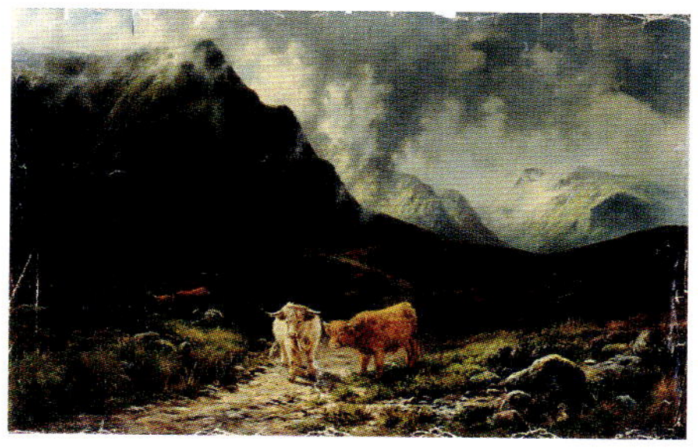

Hurt, Louis Bosworth 1856–1929
At the Head of Glen Etive, Scotland 1882
oil on canvas 60.5 x 82
VIS.2525

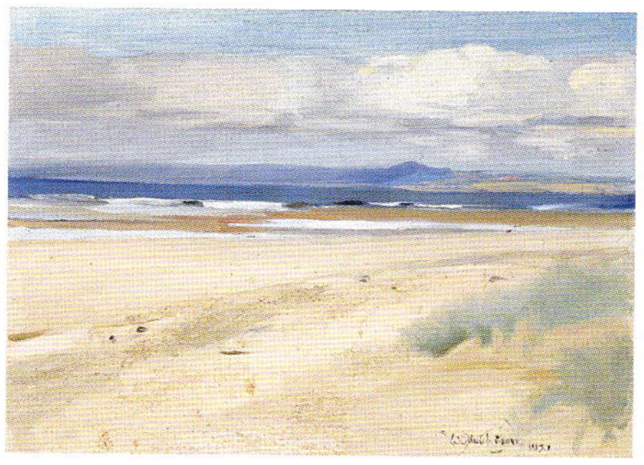

Hutchison, William Oliphant 1889–1970
The Hills of Fife, Scotland 1921
oil on panel 21.5 x 29.4
VIS.4475

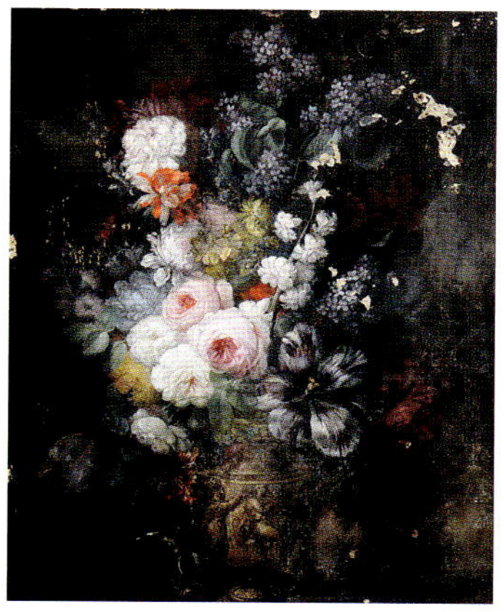

Huysum, Jacob van 1686–1740
Flowers in a Sculptured Vase
oil on canvas 71.2 x 57
VIS.39

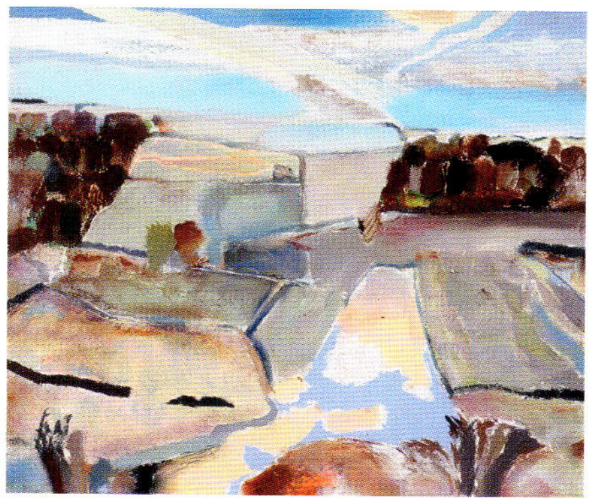

Hyatt, Derek James b.1931
Woodpecker Woods, Autumn 1984
oil on board 24.8 x 28.5
VIS.5439

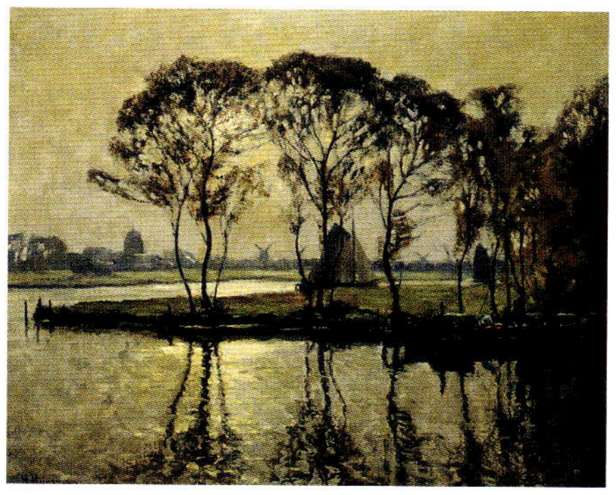

Hyneman, Herman N. 1859–1907
River Scene
oil on canvas 49.1 x 59.1
VIS.341

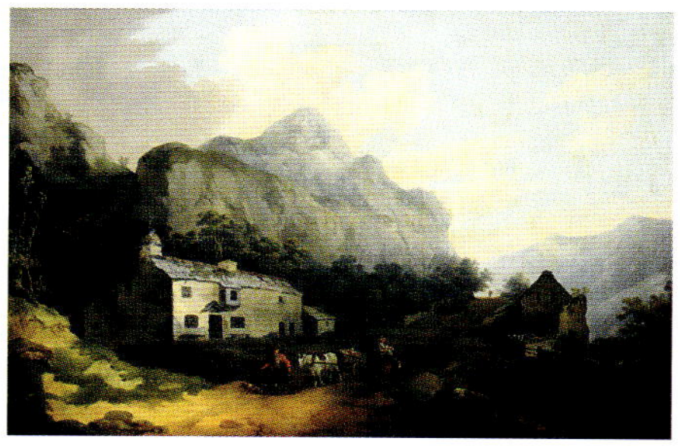

Ibbetson, Julius Caesar 1759–1817
Mountain Landscape c.1800
oil on canvas 68.3 x 103.8
VIS.2219

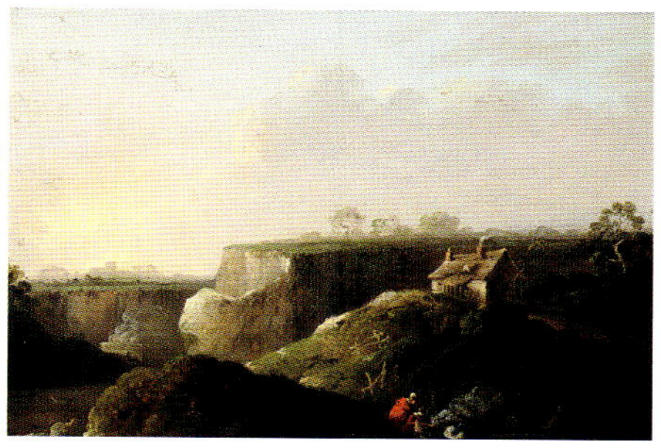

Ibbetson, Julius Caesar 1759–1817
A View in North Wales
oil on canvas 23 x 34.1
VIS.104

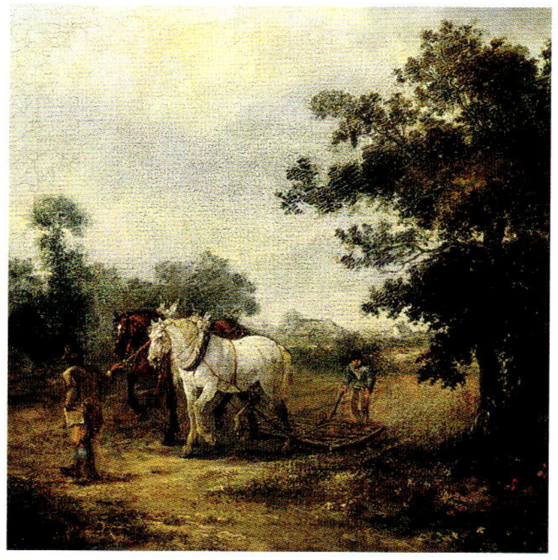

Ibbetson, Julius Caesar 1759–1817
The Harrow
oil on panel 24.6 x 24
VIS.366

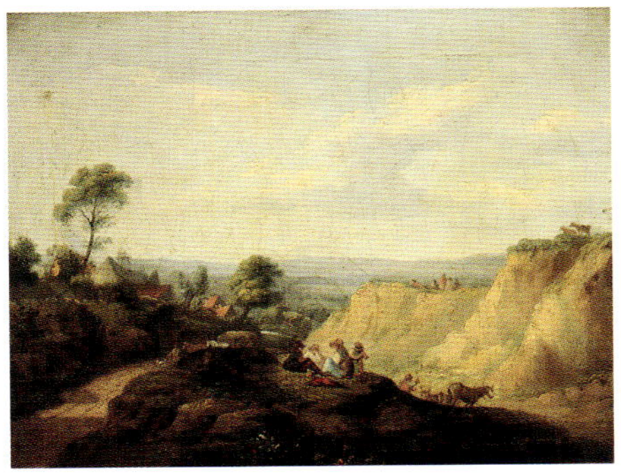

Ibbetson, Julius Caesar 1759–1817
Welsh Landscape
oil on canvas 24.3 x 31.3
VIS.281

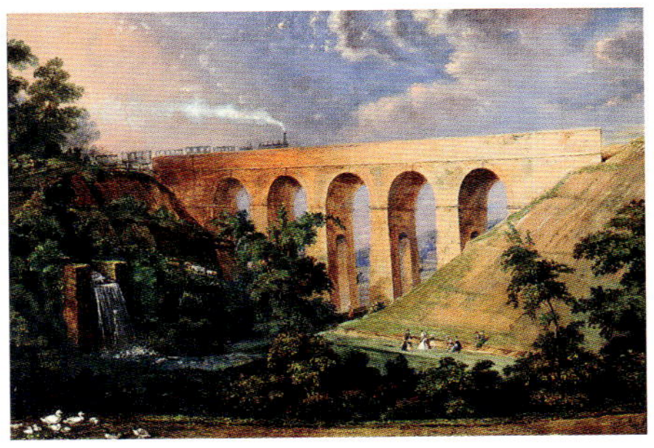

Ibbitt, William 1804–1869
Wardsend Arches, Sheffield c.1855
oil on canvas 50.7 x 73.2
K1911.37

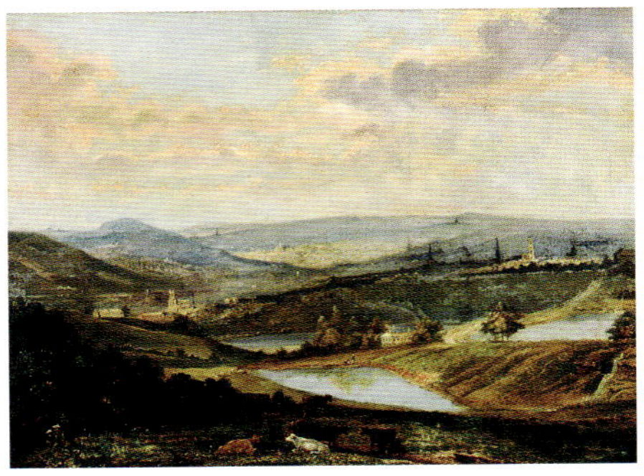

Ibbitt, William 1804–1869
Sheffield from Crookesmoor 1856
oil on canvas 44.6 x 59.7
K1931.52

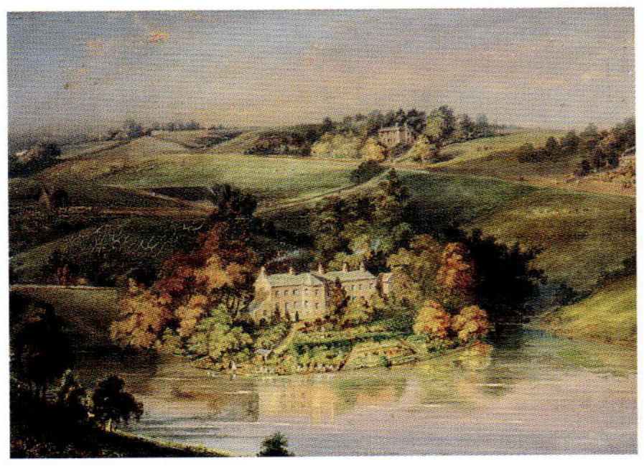

Ibbitt, William 1804–1869
Dam House, Crookesmoor, Sheffield 1858
oil on canvas 37 x 49
K1903.36

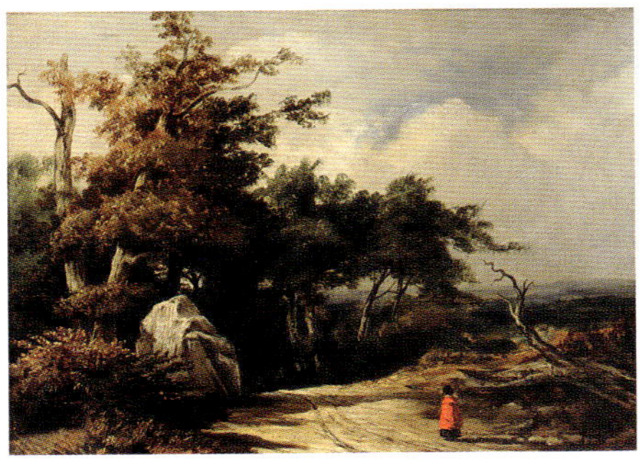

Ifold, Frederick 1821–1904
In Northern France
oil on millboard 21 x 28.9
VIS.1033

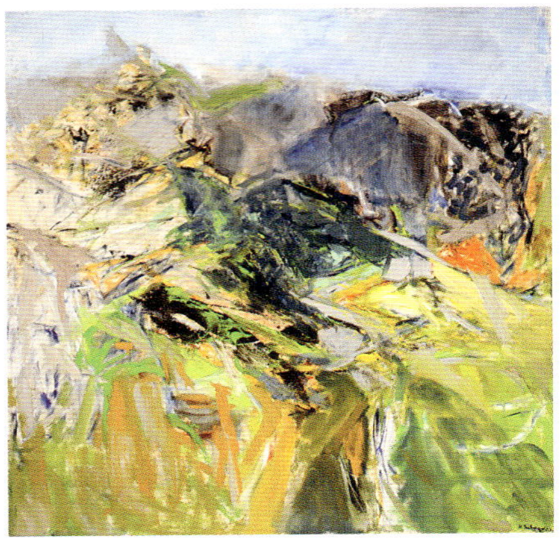

Inlander, Henry 1925–1983
Mountains in Tuscany, Italy 1961
oil on canvas 99.9 x 99.6
VIS.3969

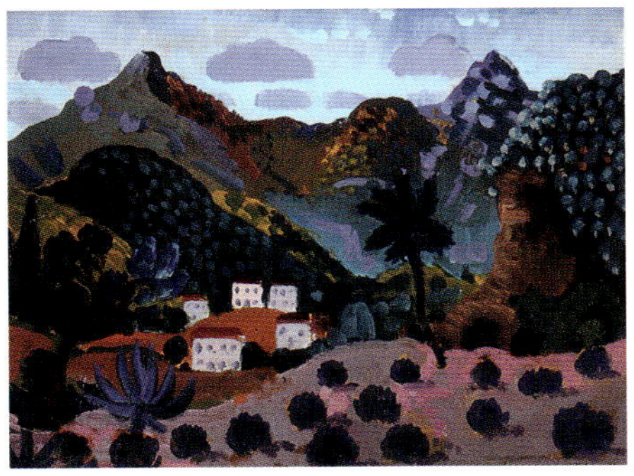

Innes, James Dickson 1887–1914
Mediterranean Coast Scene (Landscape Pyrenees) 1911
oil on panel 28.9 x 39.3
VIS.2575

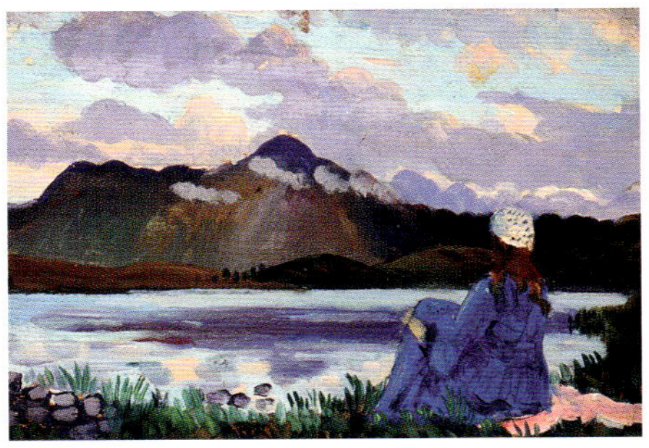

Innes, James Dickson 1887–1914
Landscape with a Figure, Arenig, Wales c.1911
oil on board 20.9 x 31.2
VIS.2574

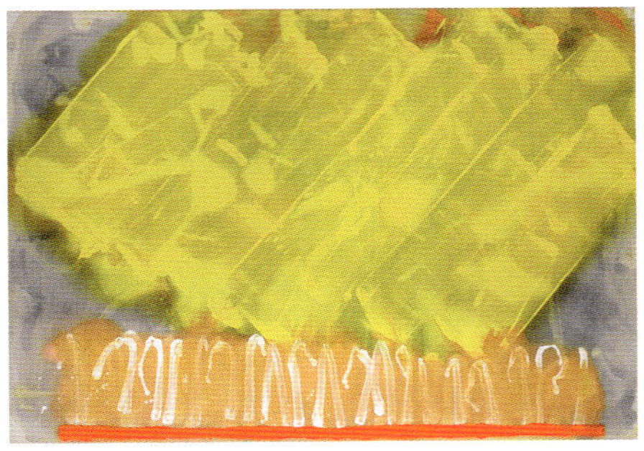

Irvin, Albert b.1922
Cathay 1979
acrylic on canvas 285 x 333
VIS.5416

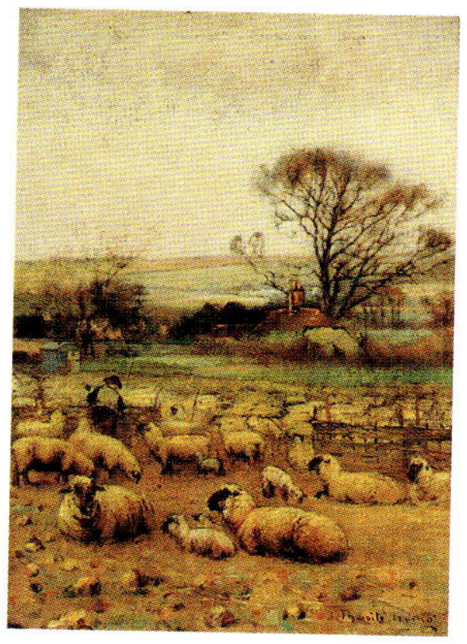

Irving, J. Thwaite active 1888–1909
Lambing Time
oil on canvas 34 x 23.7
VIS.1240

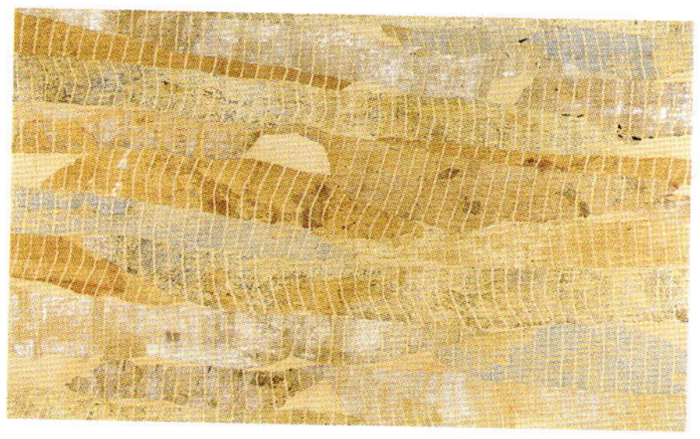

Irwin, Gwyther 1931–2008
Daymer, 1961 1961
oil on canvas 90.6 x 143.8
VIS.4915

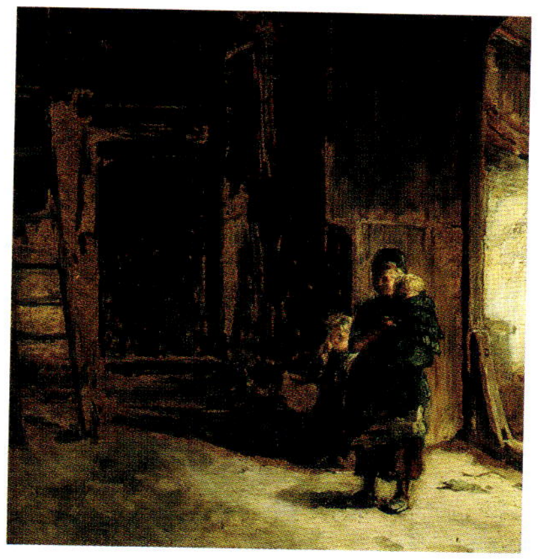

Israëls, Jozef (attributed to) 1824–1911
Peasant Children 1860–1880
oil on millboard 52.3 x 48.5
VIS.513

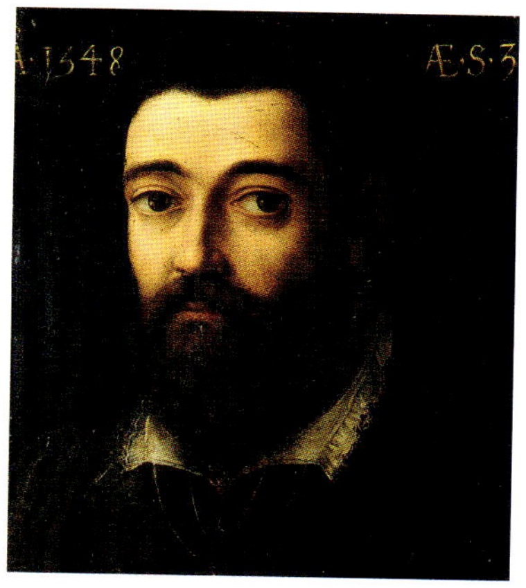

Italian School
Portrait of a Gentleman 1548
oil on panel 30.2 x 27
VIS.52

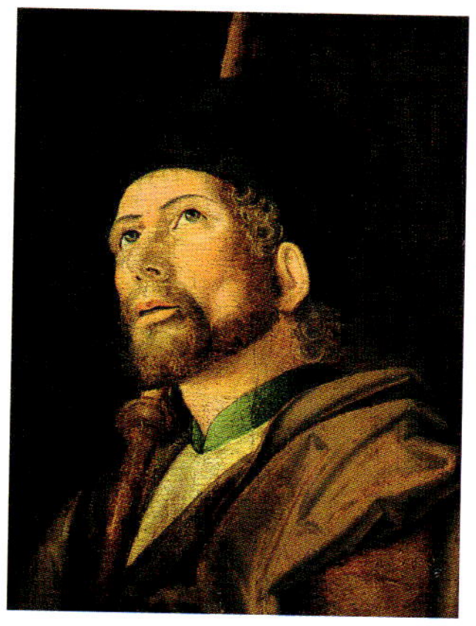

Italian School 16th C
San Rocco
oil on panel 41 x 30.6
VIS.1310

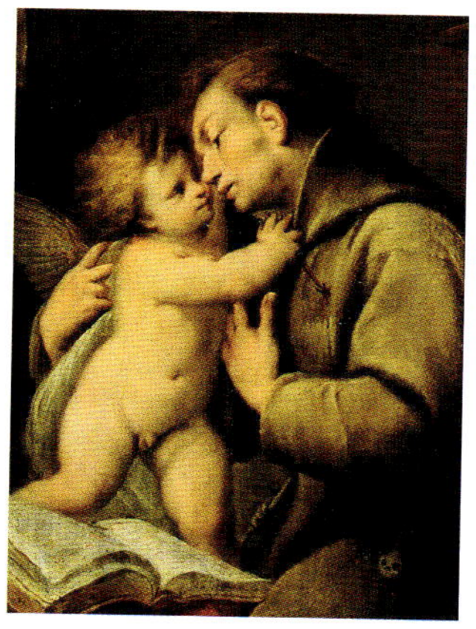

Italian School 17th C
Cupid and Monk
oil on panel 42.5 x 30.7
VIS.24

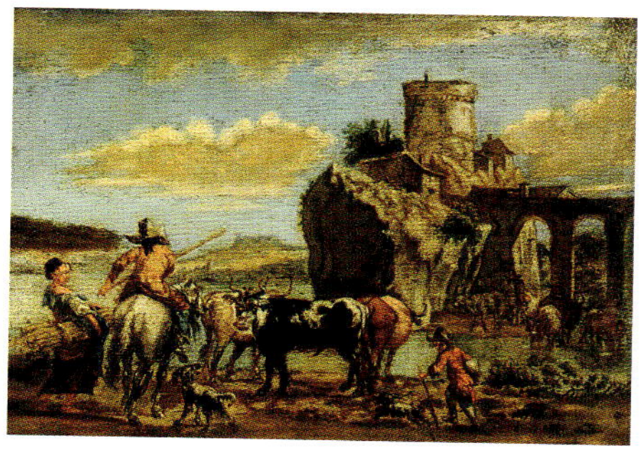

Italian School 18th C
Cattle Drovers
oil on panel 40.3 x 50.8
VIS.258

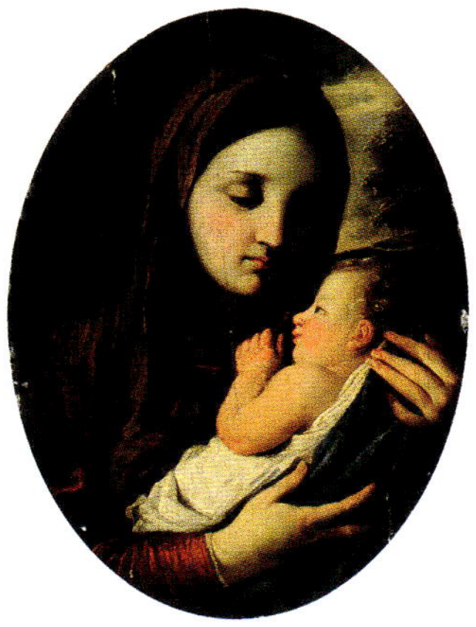

Italian School 18th C
Madonna and Child
oil on panel 65 x 48.8
VIS.487

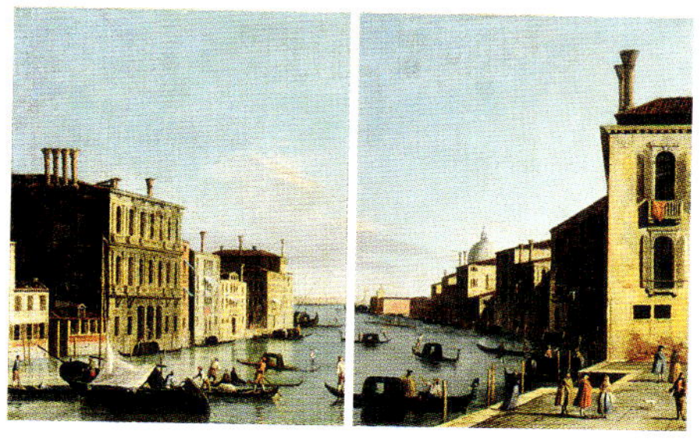

Italian School 18th C
The Grand Canal, Venice (diptych)
oil on canvas 53.5 x 43; 53.5 x 43
VIS.2741A & VIS.2741B

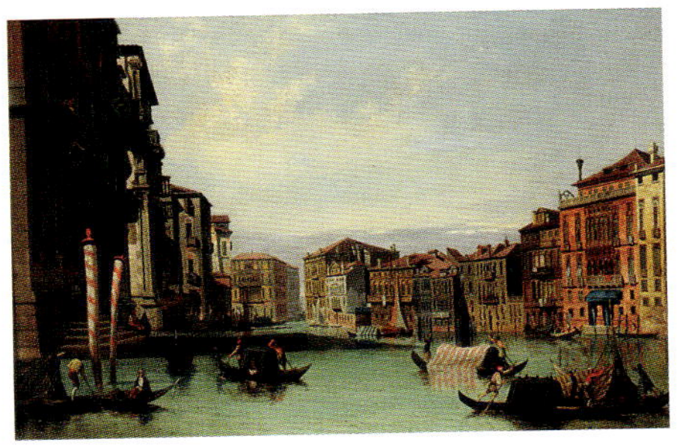

Italian School 18th C
Venetian Canal
oil on canvas 36.9 x 54.6
VIS.1335

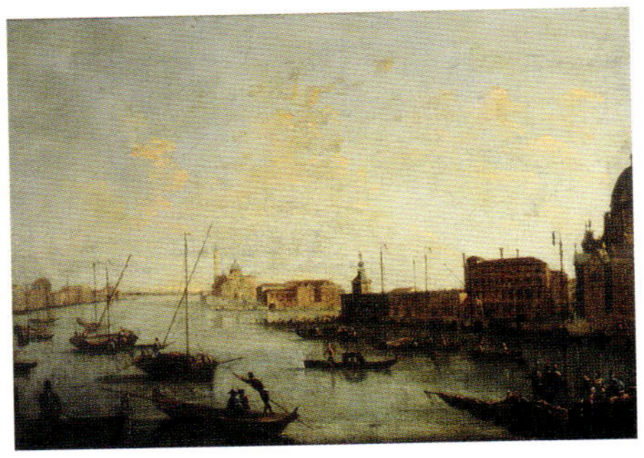

Italian School 19th C
The Grand Canal, Venice
oil on canvas 60.1 x 84.7
VIS.840

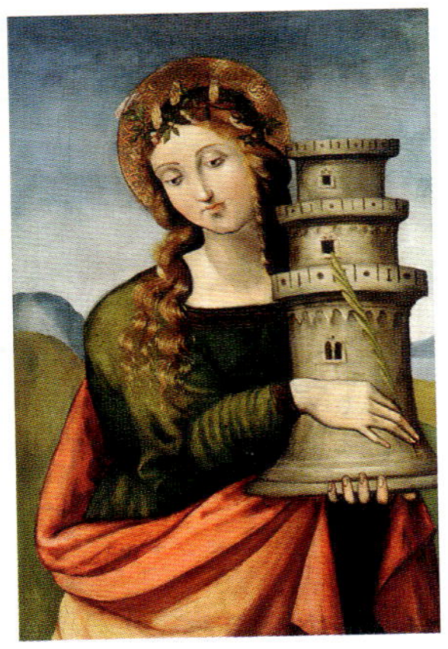

Italian School (attributed to) 15th C
St Barbara
tempera on panel 68.5 x 46.2
VIS.2730

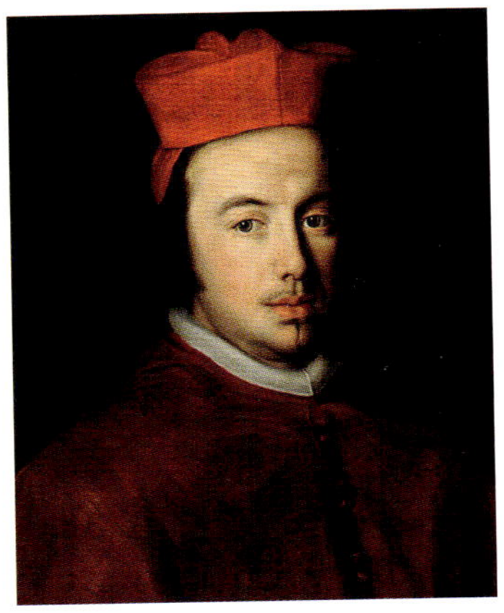

Italian School (attributed to) 18th C
Portrait of a Cardinal
oil on canvas 58.8 x 46.5
VIS.33

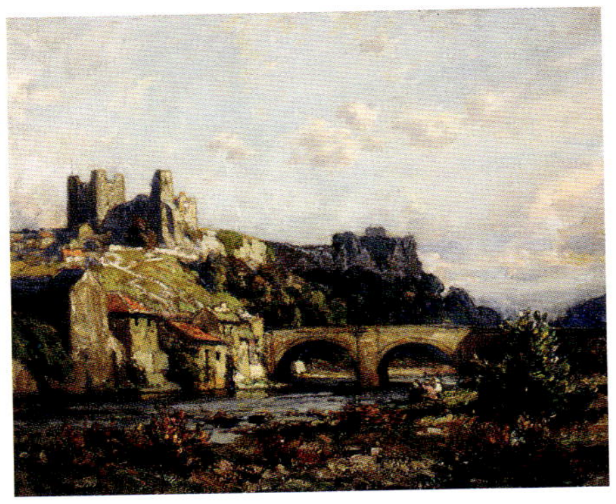

Jack, Richard 1866–1952
Richmond Castle, North Yorkshire 1911
oil on canvas 61.7 x 74.9
VIS.2320

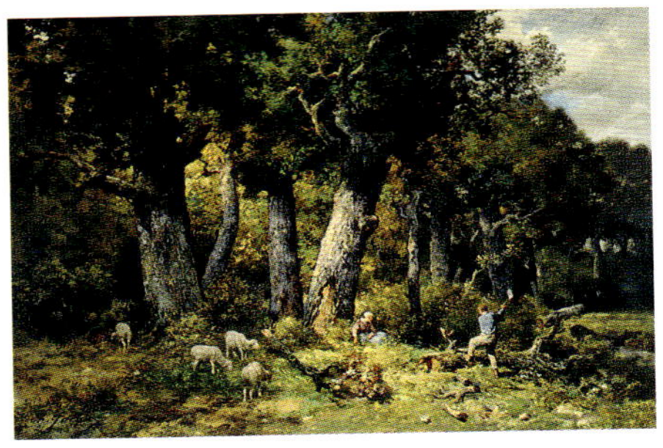

Jacque, Charles Émile 1813–1894
Forest Scene 1850–1860
oil on canvas 65.7 x 96.4
VIS.1538

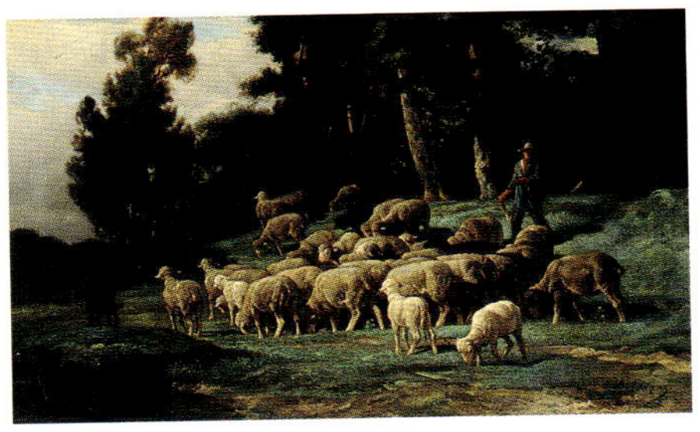

Jacque, Charles Émile 1813–1894
The Flock 1855–1860
oil on canvas 42.8 x 67
VIS.1420

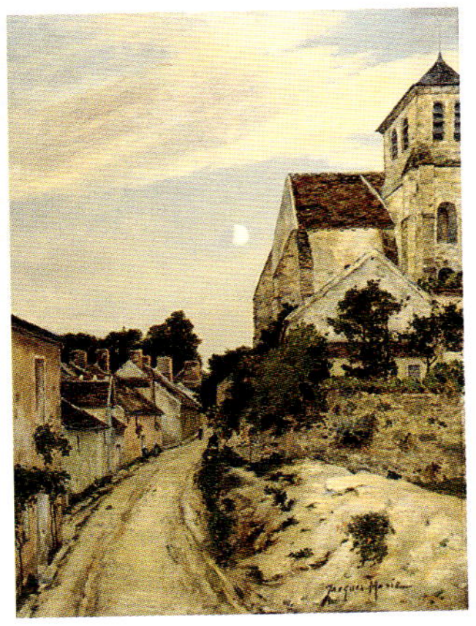

Jacques, Marie b.1868
Moonlight
oil on canvas 83.2 x 64.3
VIS.783

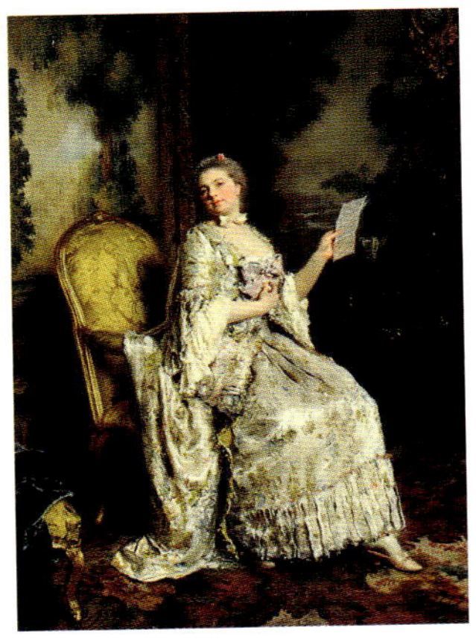

Jacquet, Gustave Jean 1846–1909
Good News 1880–1885
oil on panel 57 x 48.6
VIS.1962

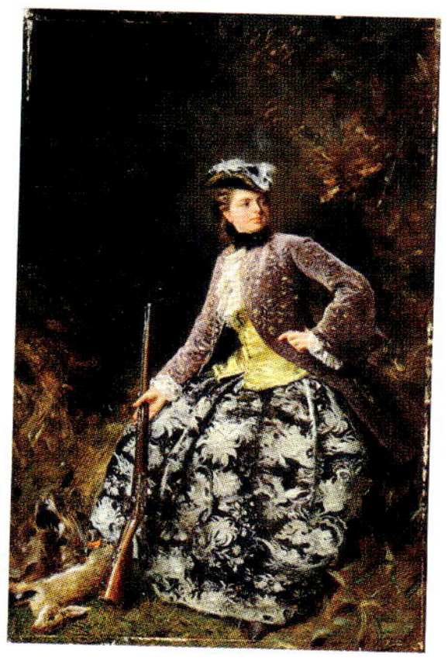

Jacquet, Gustave Jean 1846–1909
Sport 1885–1890
oil on panel 32.9 x 21.4
VIS.1963

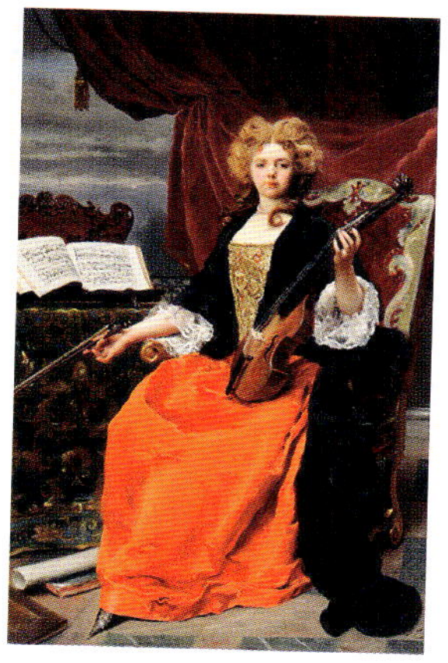

Jacquet, Gustave Jean 1846–1909
Music
oil on panel 32 x 21.5
VIS.2923

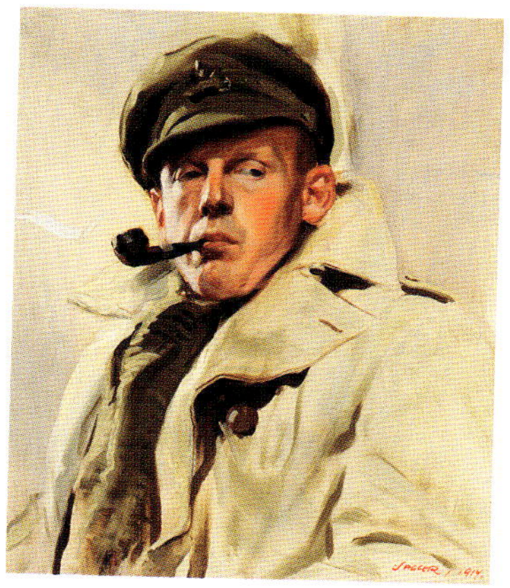

Jagger, David 1891–1958
Charles Jagger (1885–1934) 1917
oil on canvas 60.1 x 49.6
VIS.1998

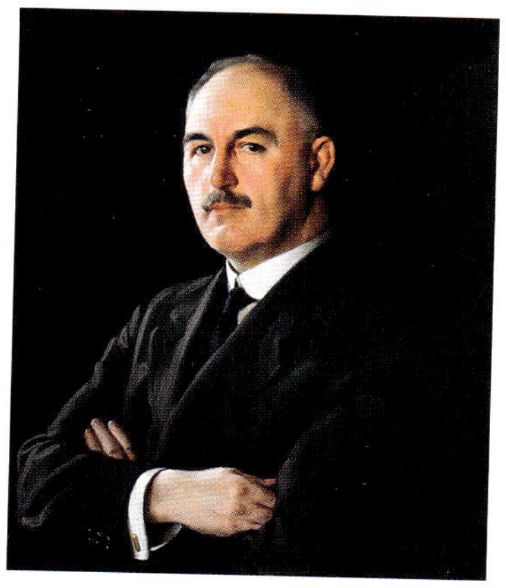

Jagger, David 1891–1958
Dr John George Graves (1866–1945)
oil on canvas 76 x 62.2
VIS.3214

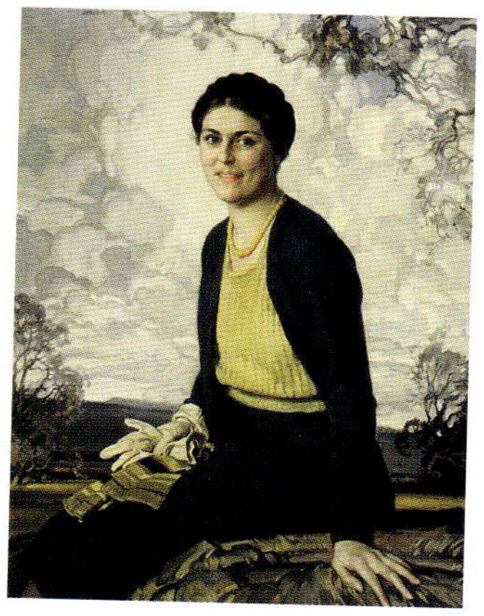

Jagger, David 1891–1958
Portrait of a Lady
oil on canvas 115.1 x 86.5
VIS.5251

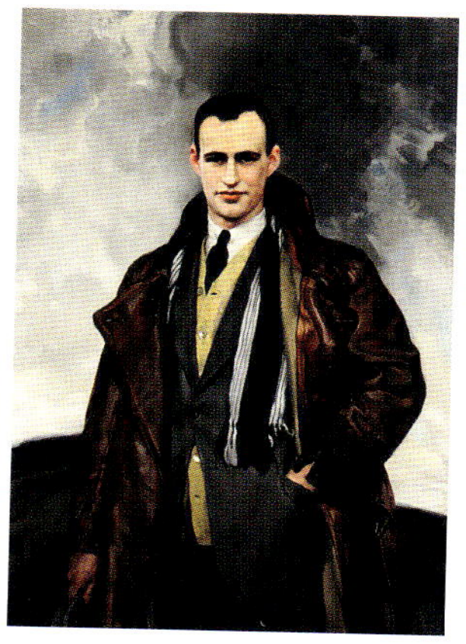

Jagger, David 1891–1958
Portrait of a Man
oil on canvas 127.6 x 88.4
VIS.1668

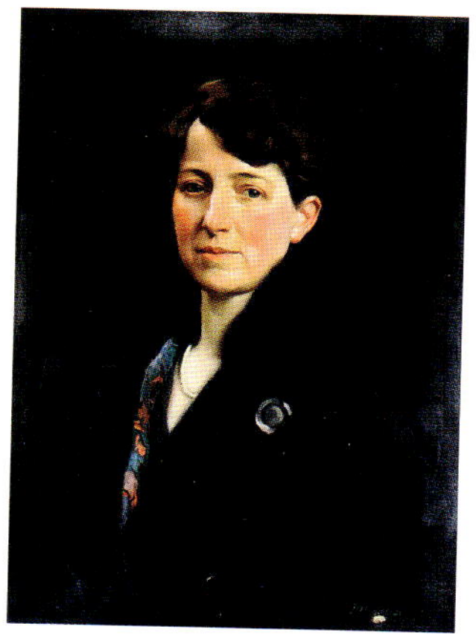

Jagger, David 1891–1958
The Late Cyrus Jones
oil on canvas 69 x 50.2
VIS.4223

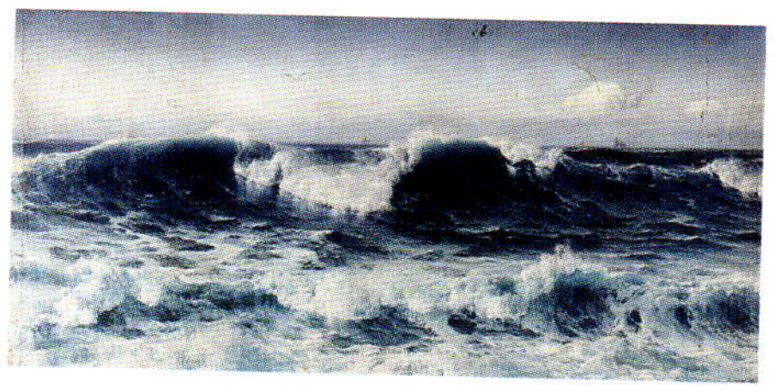

James, David 1834–1897
A Cornish Breaker 1896
oil on canvas 67.4 x 130.4
VIS.2523

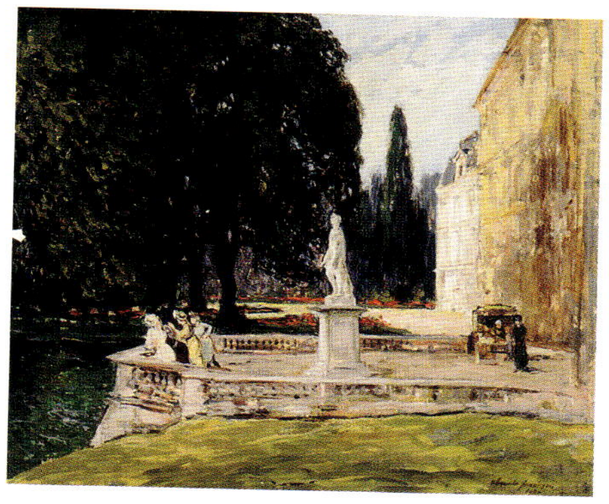

Jamieson, Alexander 1873–1937
Fontainebleau, France 1920
oil on millboard 50 x 60.3
VIS.2374

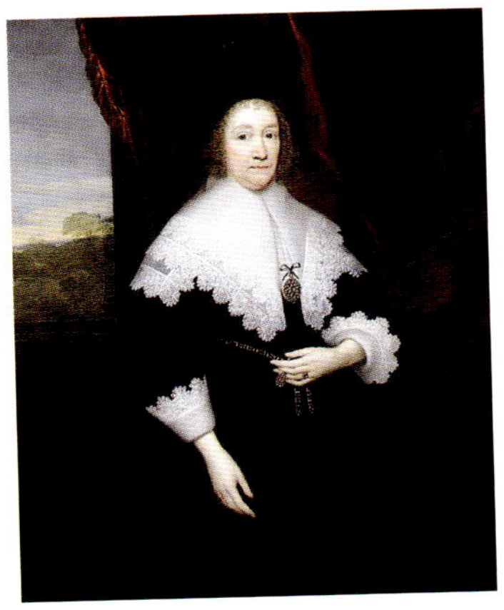

Janssens van Ceulen, Cornelis 1593–1661
Lady Coventry 1630–1639
oil on canvas 155.3 x 129.7
VIS.3718

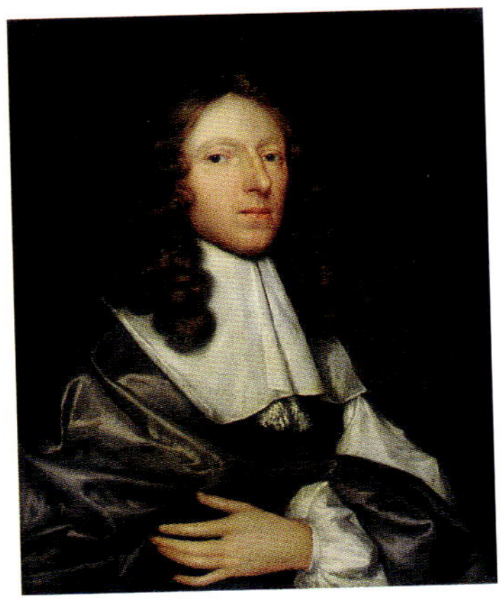

Janssens van Ceulen, Cornelis (attributed to)
1593–1661
Portrait of a Gentleman
oil on canvas 71 x 57.5
VIS.72

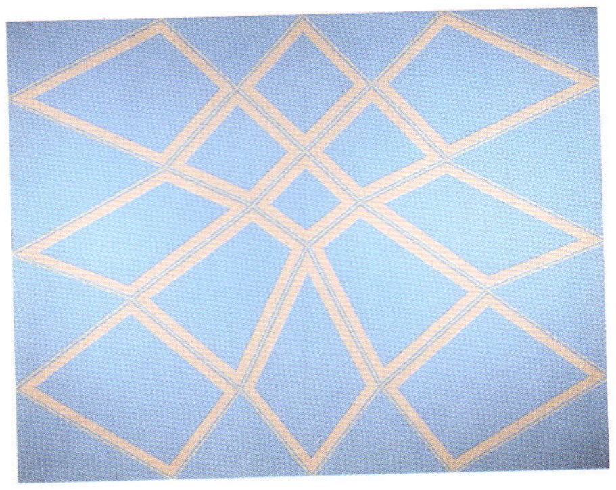

Jaray, Tess b.1937
Minuet 1966
oil on canvas 180 x 228
VIS.3893

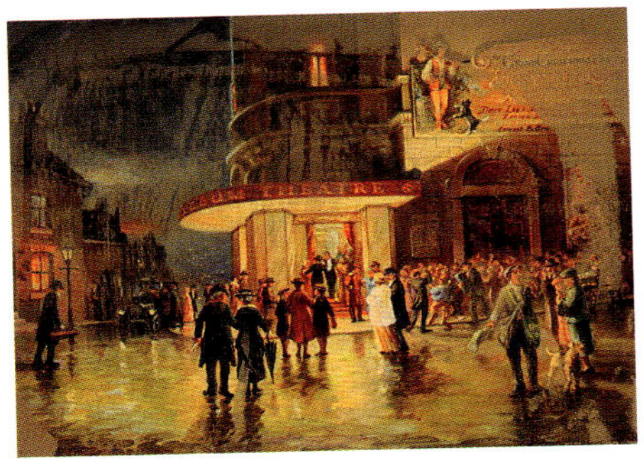

Jennings, Roberta Louise b.1919
Christmas Eve, 1932 (First Night of the Pantomime at the Lyceum Theatre, Sheffield) 2003–2004
oil on canvas 32.4 x 44.5
2004.91

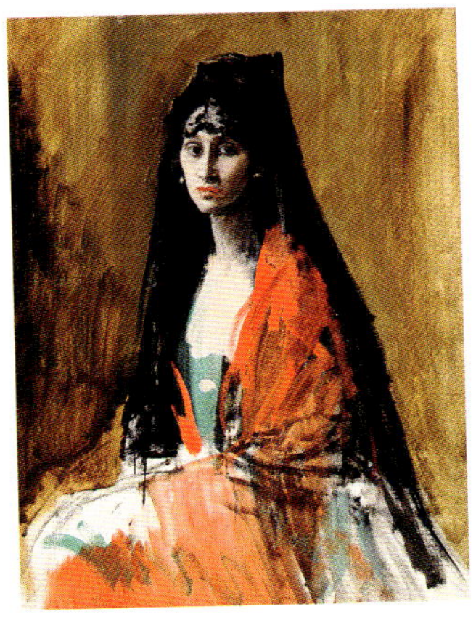

John, Augustus Edwin 1878–1961
Señora Gandarillas c.1916
oil on canvas 101.6 x 76.2
VIS.3840

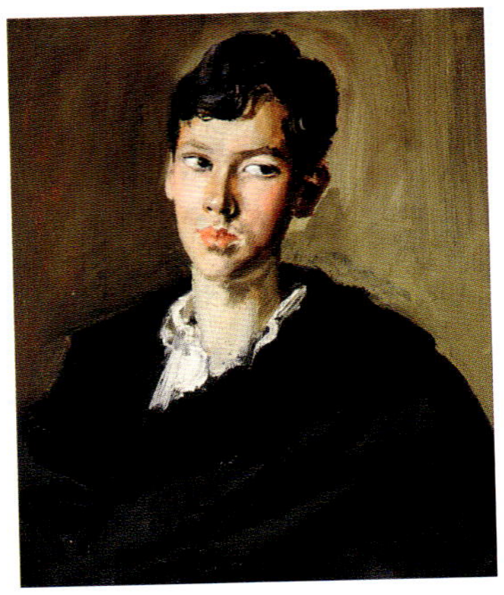

John, Augustus Edwin 1878–1961
Robin John
oil on canvas 55 x 44.8
VIS.3635

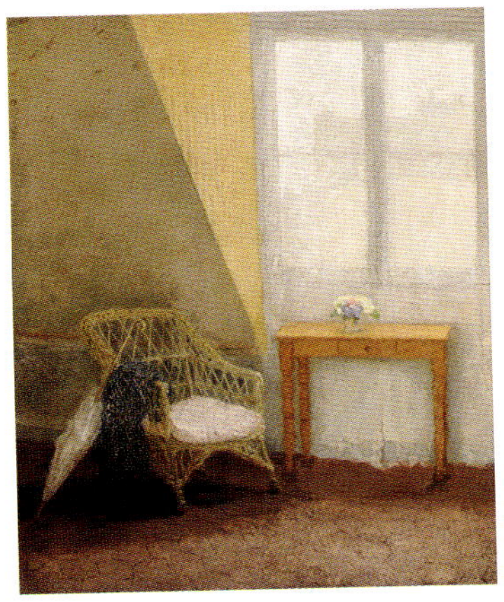

John, Gwen 1876–1939
A Corner of the Artist's Room in Paris
1907–1909
oil on canvas 31.7 x 26.7
VIS.2576

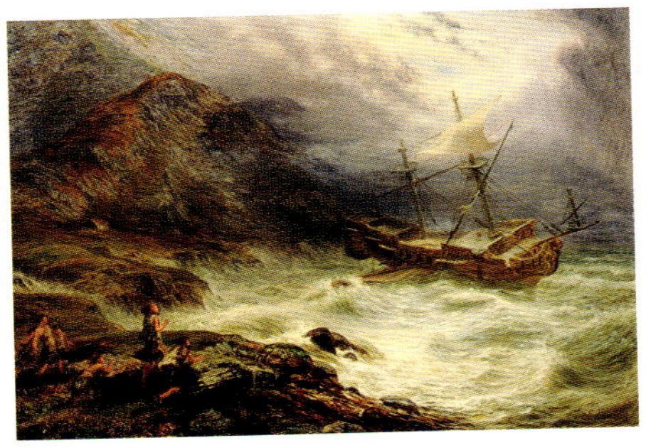

Johnson, Charles Edward 1832–1913
The Last of the Spanish Armada 1869
oil on canvas 57.4 x 82.4
VIS.1422

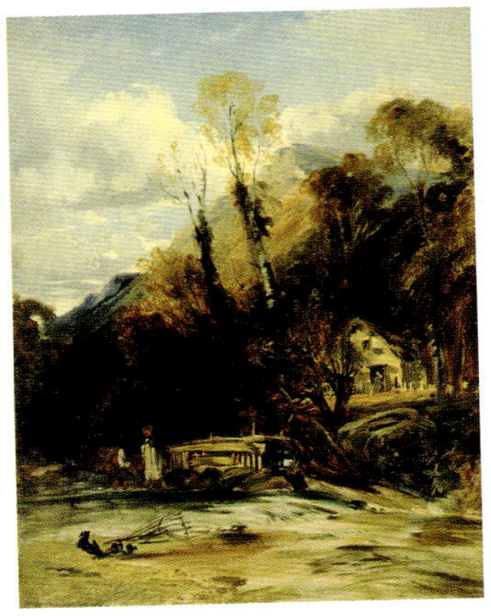

Johnson, Harry John 1826–1884
The Salmon Trap
oil on canvas 49.9 x 38.1
VIS.1525

Facing page: Dutch School (attributed to), 18th C, *Flowers in a Vase* (detail), Museums Sheffield, (p. 65)

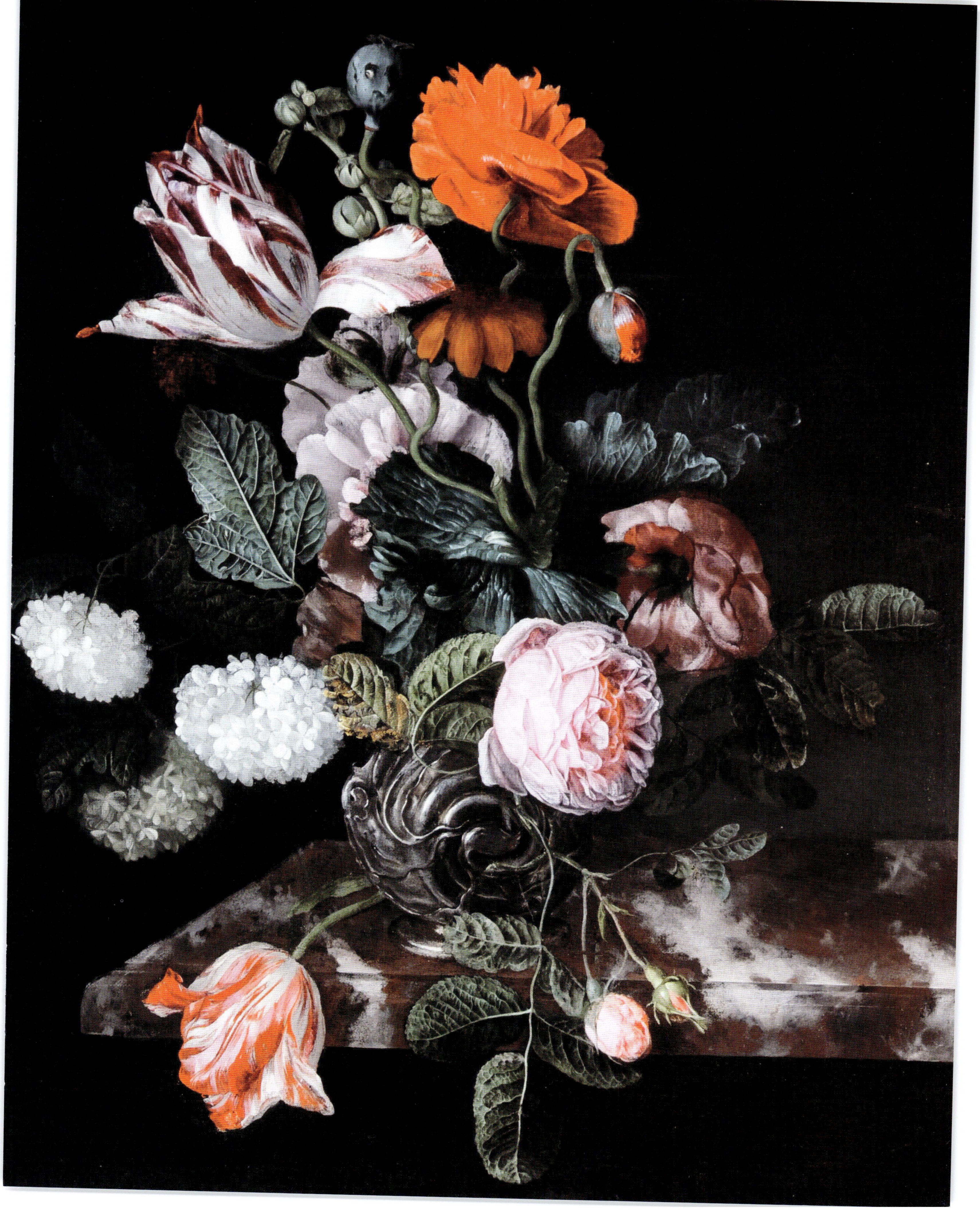

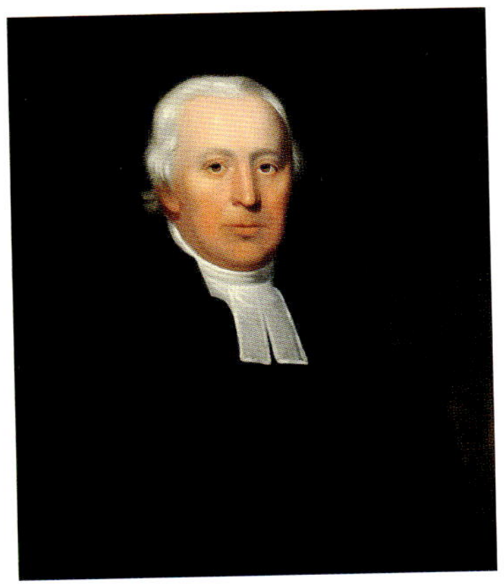

Johnson, Valentine active 1777–1799
Reverend Alexander McKenzie (1755–1816), Curate of St Paul's, Sheffield
oil on canvas 75.2 x 61.8
VIS.3141

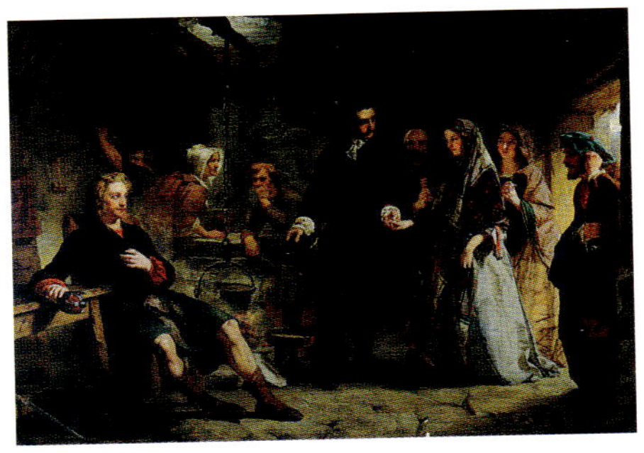

Johnston, Alexander 1815–1891
Flora MacDonald's Introduction to Bonnie Prince Charlie
oil on canvas 107.8 x 151.1
VIS.1447

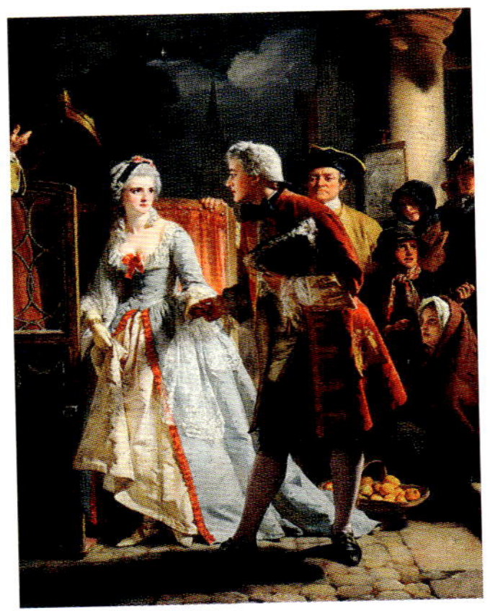

Johnston, Alexander 1815–1891
Robin Adair
oil on canvas 111.9 x 85.4
VIS.1439

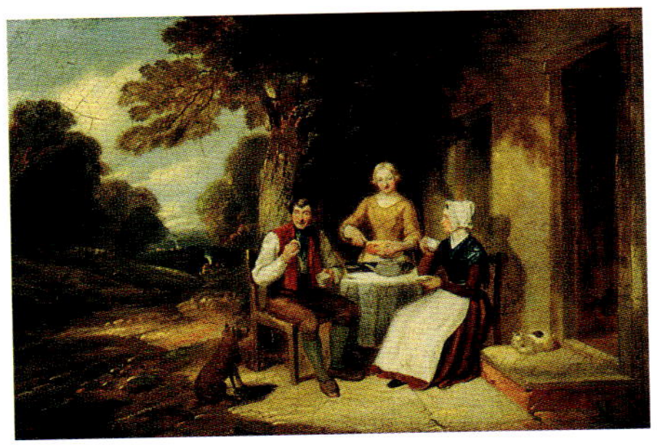

Johnston, Alexander 1815–1891
The Peaceful Cottagers
oil on canvas 25 x 36.7
VIS.688

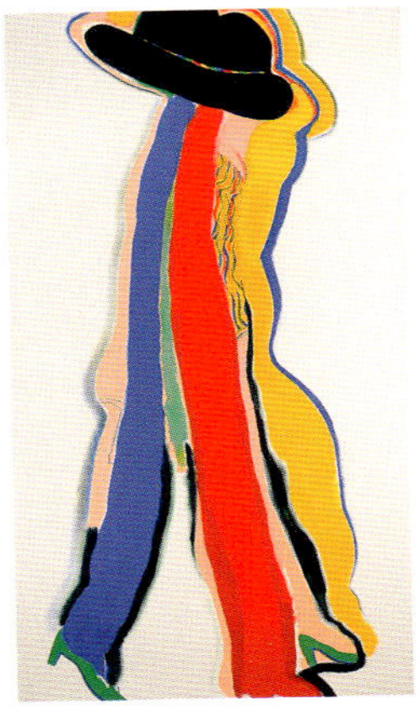

Jones, Allen b.1937
Black Hat c.1964
oil on canvas 213.3 x 121.9
VIS.4268

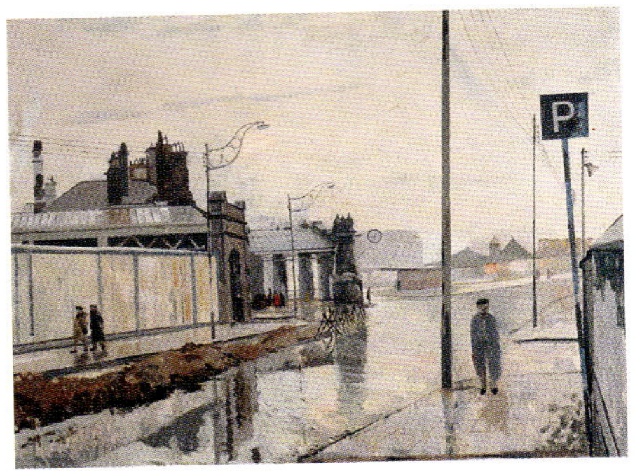

Jones, Stanley Robert b.1927
Hopeless Dawn, Sheffield
oil on canvas 66.7 x 87
VIS.5430

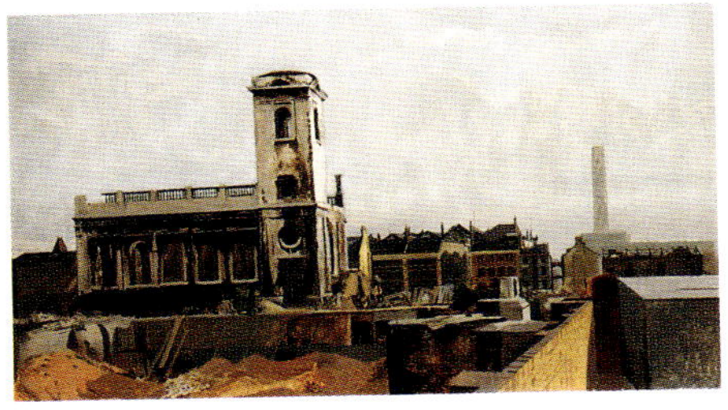

Jones, Stanley Robert b.1927
St Nicholas Cole Abbey, London
oil on canvas 45.6 x 61.7
VIS.5431

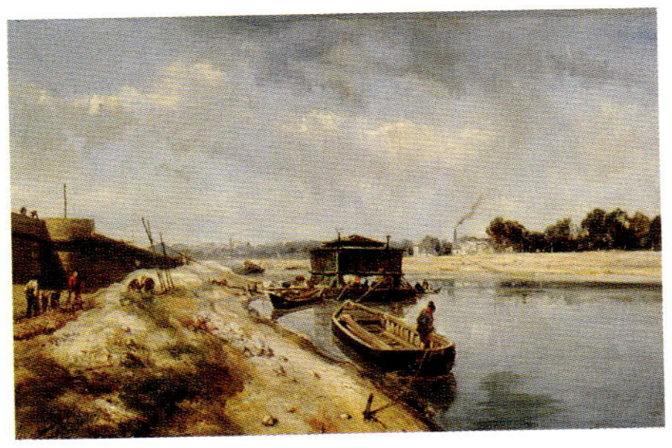

Jongkind, Johan Barthold 1819–1891
River Scene with Barges and Figures 1865–1870
oil on canvas 26.1 x 39.5
VIS.1533

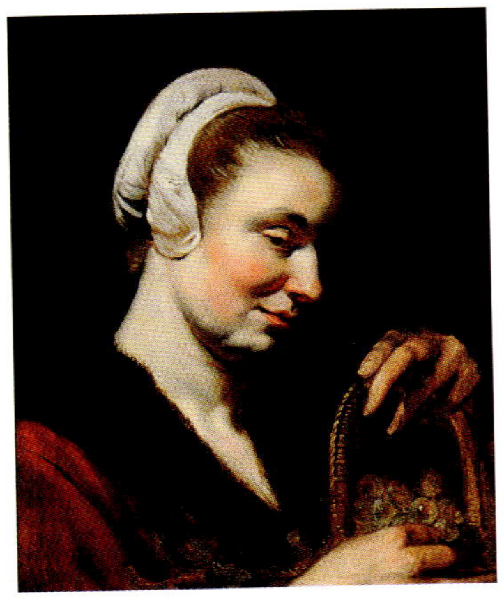

Jordaens, Jacob 1593–1678
Tasting
oil on panel 49.6 x 40.4
VIS.LI.718 (P)

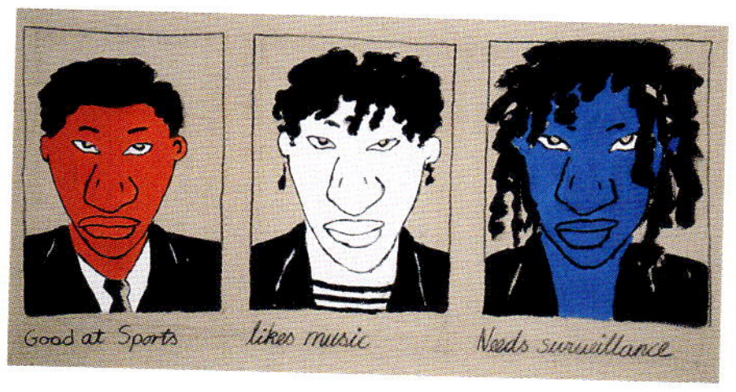

Joseph, Tam b.1947
School Report
acrylic on canvas 75.9 x 142
VIS.5202

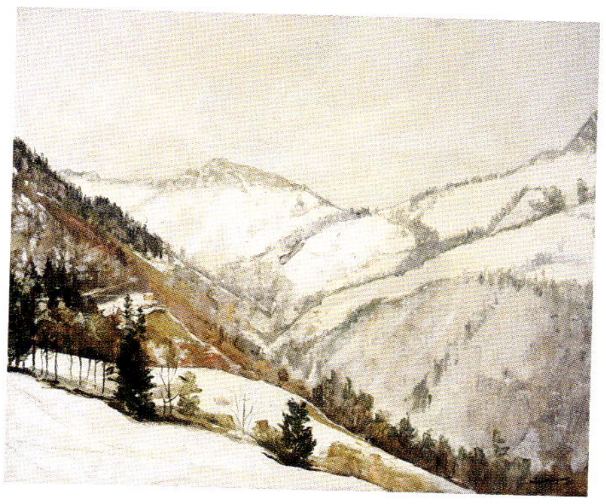

Jungman, Nico 1872–1935
Les Avants, Switzerland 1931
oil on canvas 63.7 x 76.6
VIS.2956

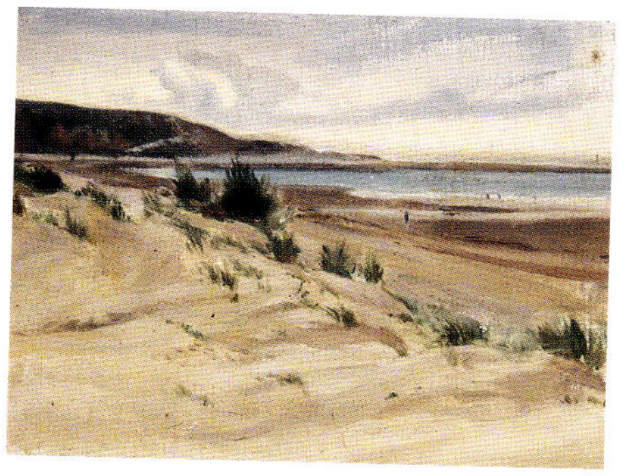

Kay, Ernest active 1907
Landscape
oil on canvas 27.7 x 36.1
VIS.2901

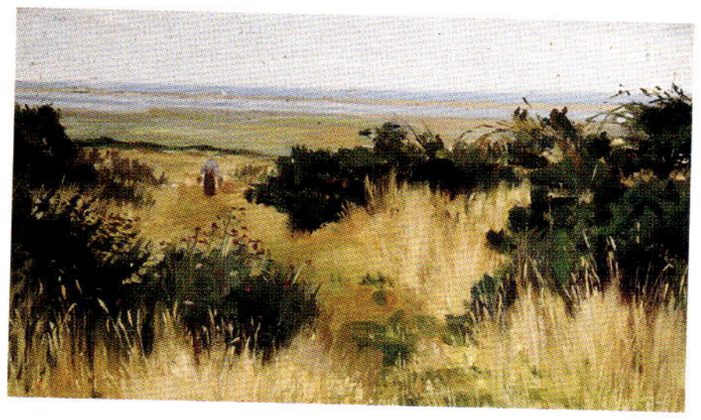

Kay, Ernest active 1907
Landscape
oil on canvas 22.4 x 37.1
VIS.2973

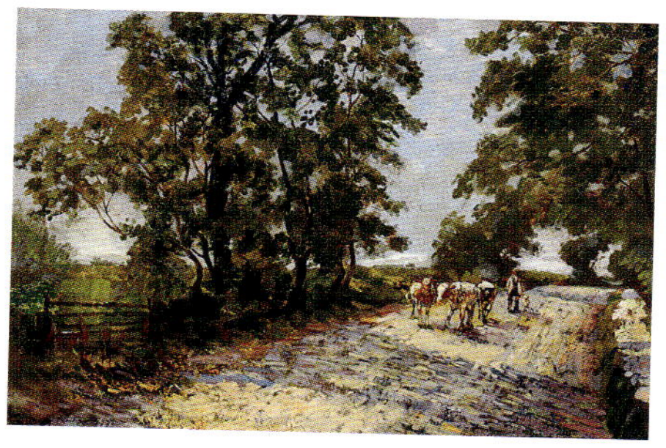

Keeling, William 1860–1930
A Derbyshire Road 1925
oil on canvas 68.2 x 100.4
VIS.2422

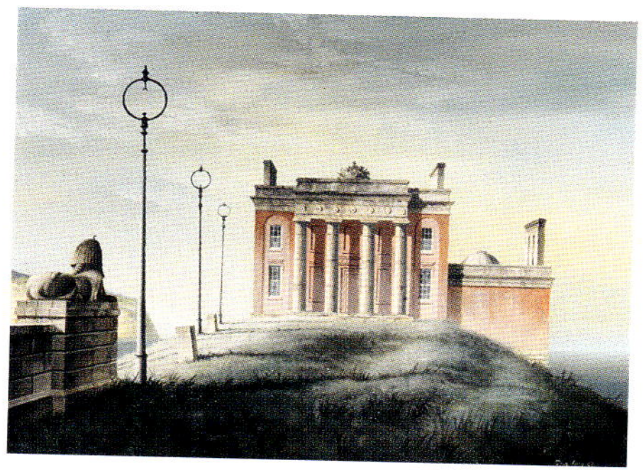

Kelly, Felix Runcie 1914–1994
Pink House on a Hill 1947
oil on board 33.9 x 44.7
VIS.4338

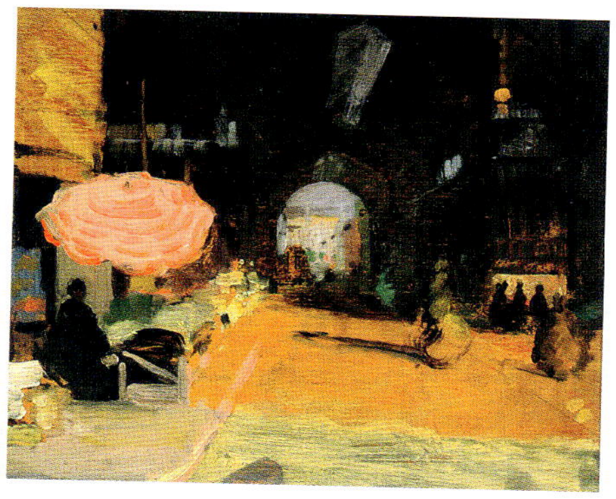

Kelly, Gerald Festus 1879–1972
Les Halles Centrales, Paris c.1907
oil on canvas 20.4 x 26
VIS.4318

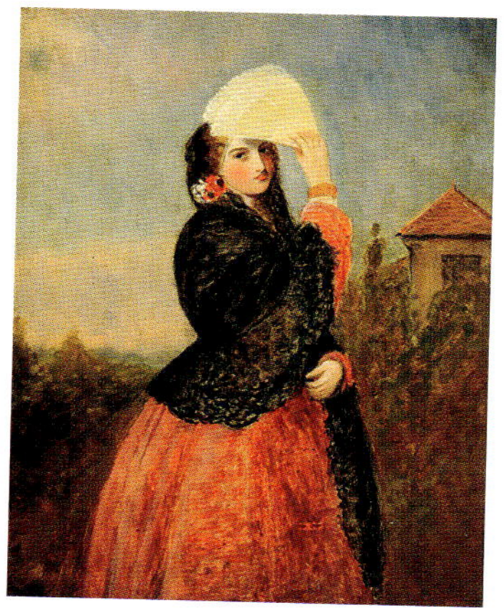

Kemm, Robert 1830–1895
A Spanish Lady
oil on panel 30.1 x 23.9
VIS.1044

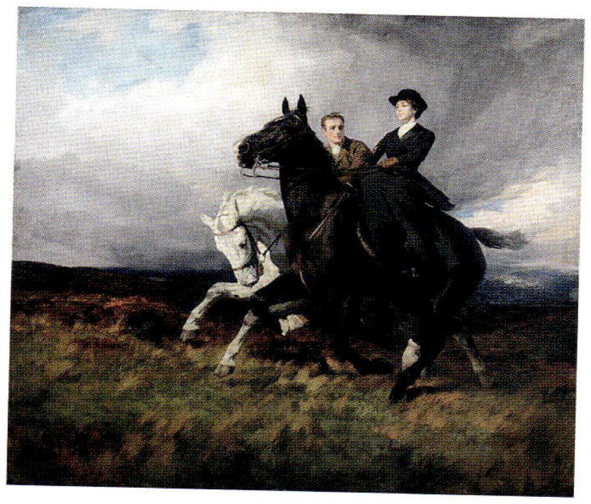

Kemp-Welch, Lucy 1869–1958
The Riders 1911
oil on canvas 230.7 x 264.4
VIS.3029

Kennedy, William Denholm 1813–1865
River Scene
oil on millboard 14.5 x 24.5
VIS.1072

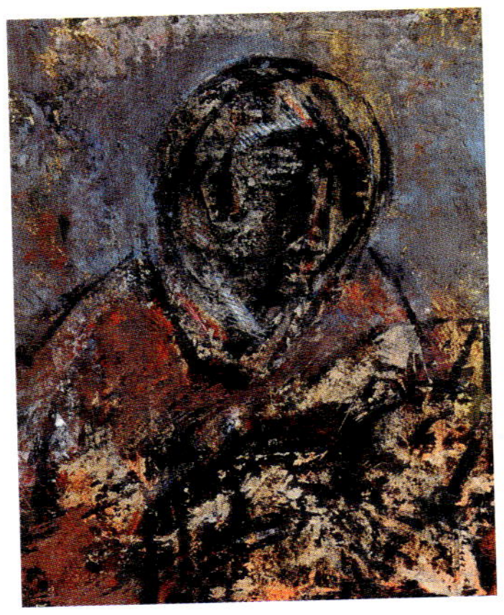

Kessell, Mary 1914–1977
Portrait of a Woman
oil on millboard 41.5 x 32.4
VIS.1898

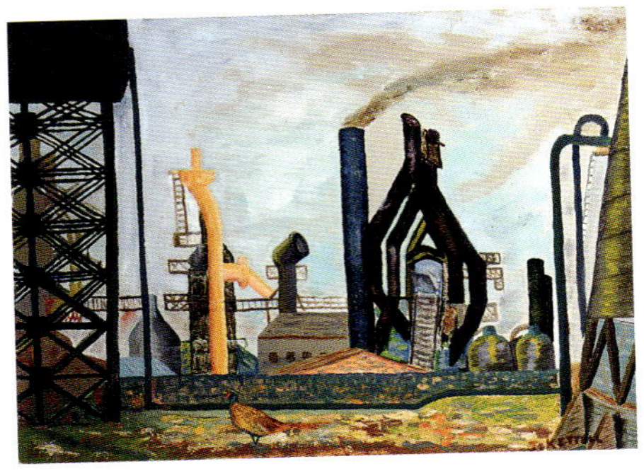

Kettell, Jack
Rebuilding a Blast Furnace
oil on canvas 50.8 x 68.8
1988.139

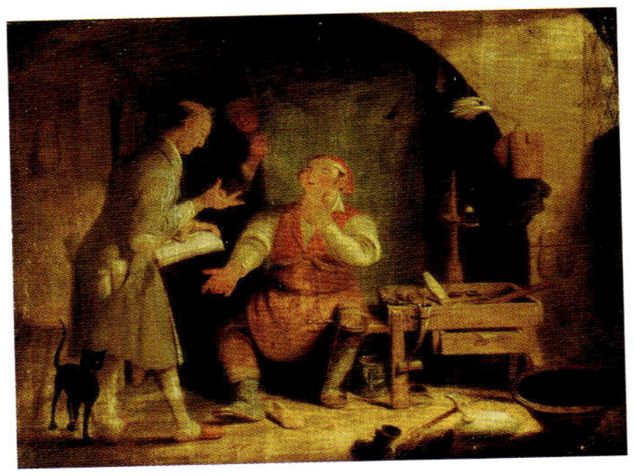

Kidd, William 1790–1863
A Scene from a Work by Walter Scott
oil on canvas 29.4 x 38.7
VIS.245

Kilgore, Constance b.1951
Haptic
acrylic, mixed media, pins & cotton on canvas
162.1 x 140.5
VIS.4930

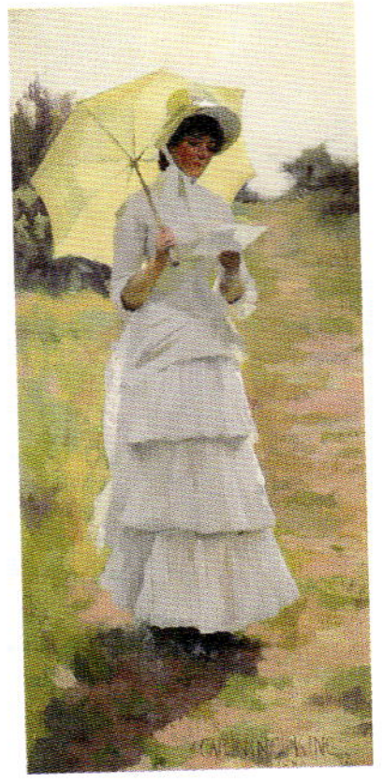

King, Gunning 1859–1940
The Letter 1884
oil on millboard 33.5 x 15.2
VIS.685

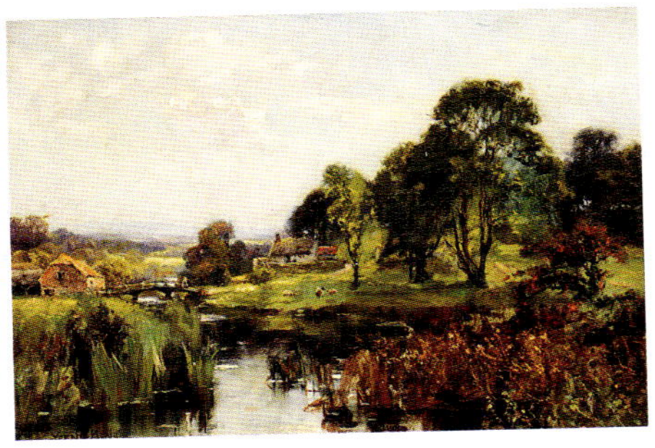

King, Henry John Yeend 1855–1924
Lathkill Dale, Derbyshire
oil on canvas 35 x 51.4
VIS.2785

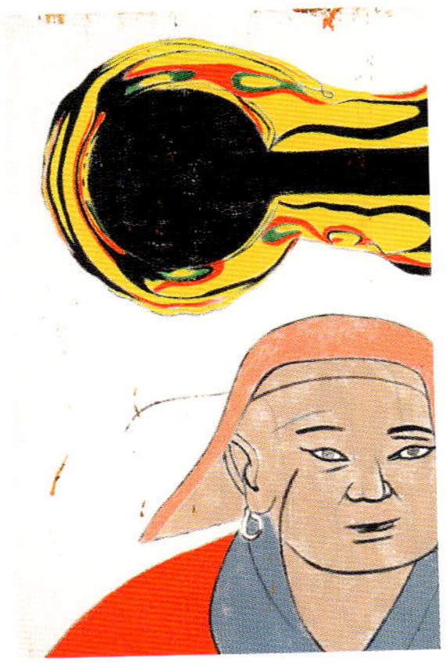

Kitaj, R. B. 1932–2007
The Rival Poet 1965
oil on canvas 75.4 x 55.8
VIS.3691

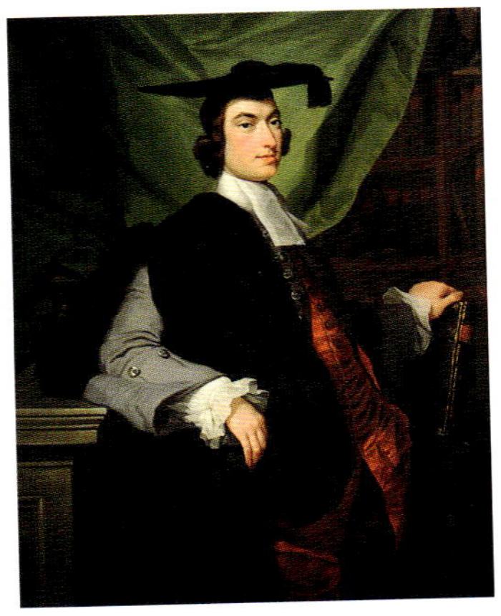

Knapton, George 1698–1778
Portrait of a Scholar 1753
oil on canvas 126.1 x 100.4
VIS.2272

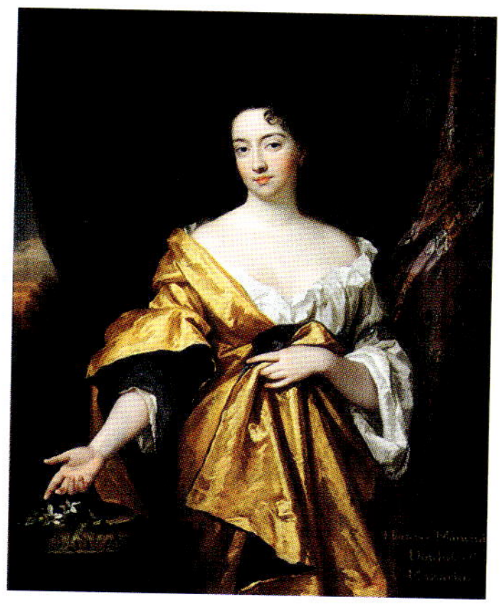

Kneller, Godfrey 1646–1723
Hortense Mancini (1646–1699), Duchess of Mazarin 1693
oil on canvas 147.4 x 122.7
VIS.3953

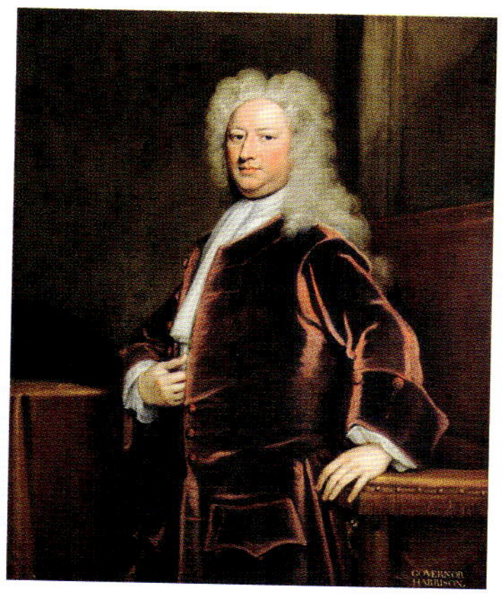

Kneller, Godfrey 1646–1723
Governor Harrison 1719
oil on canvas 123.5 x 100
VIS.3130

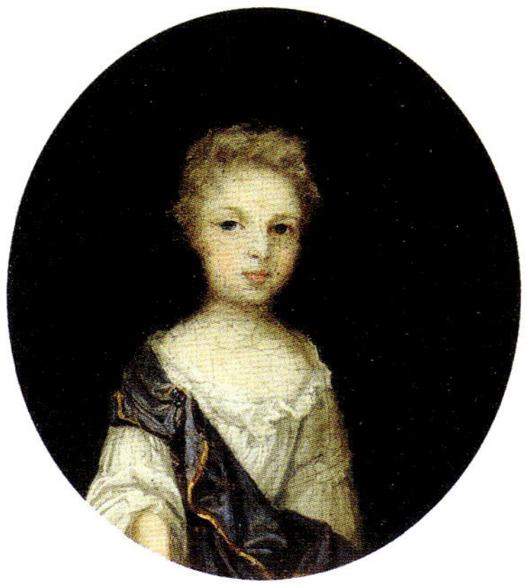

Kneller, Godfrey 1646–1723
Portrait
oil on canvas 12.5 x 10.8
VIS.249

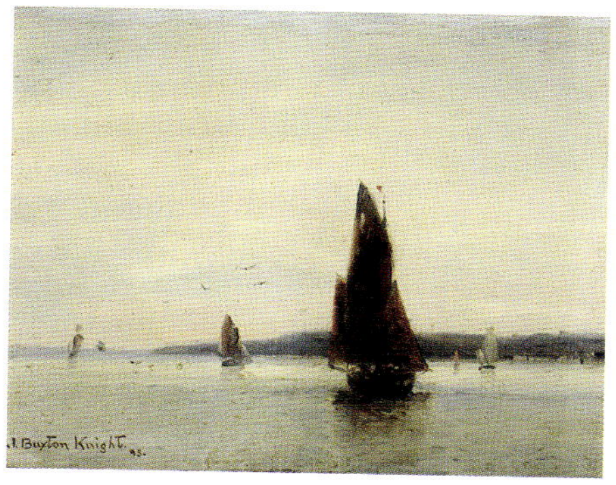

Knight, John William Buxton 1842/1843–1908
River Scene 1895
oil on panel 18.5 x 23.1
VIS.1918

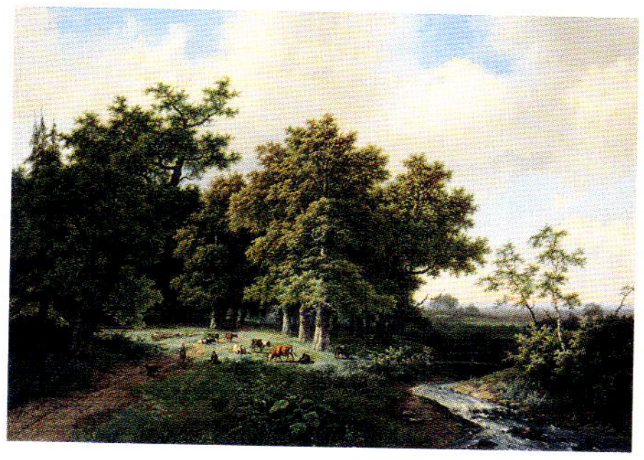

Koekkoek, Barend Cornelis 1803–1862
Landscape 1853
oil on canvas 77.3 x 106.1
VIS.1430

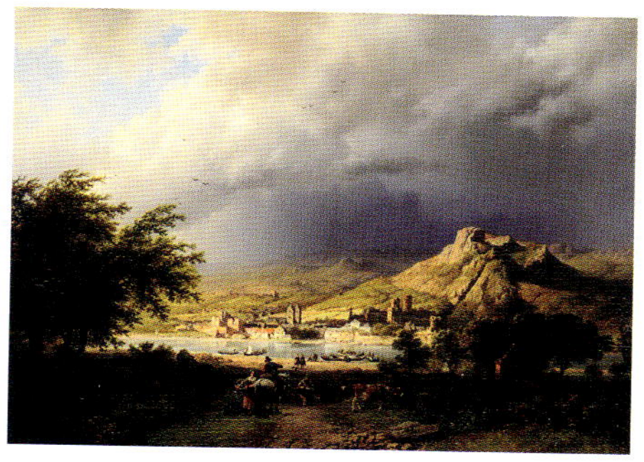

Koekkoek, Barend Cornelis 1803–1862
A Coming Storm 1855
oil on panel 47 x 65.5
VIS.1541

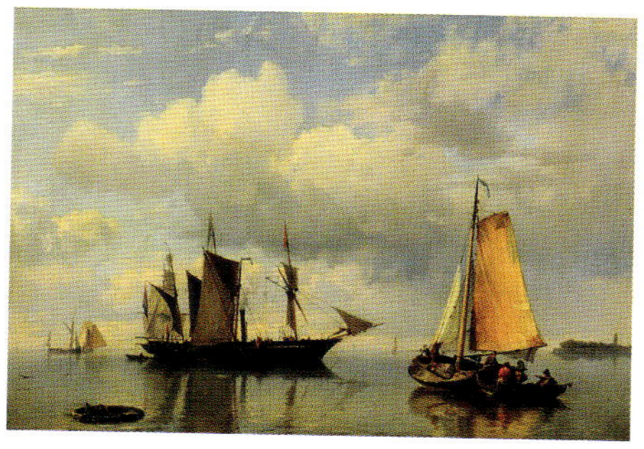

Koekkoek, Hermanus the elder 1815–1882
Ships at Sea 1858
oil on panel 72.5 x 88
VIS.1539

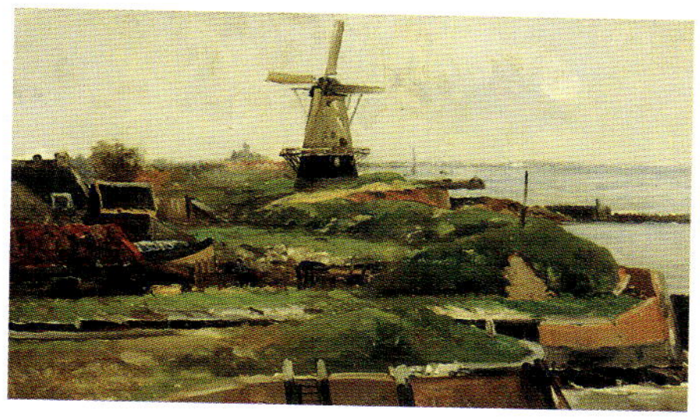

Koekkoek, Hermanus the younger 1836–1909
Flushing, Holland
oil on canvas 28.7 x 49
VIS.644

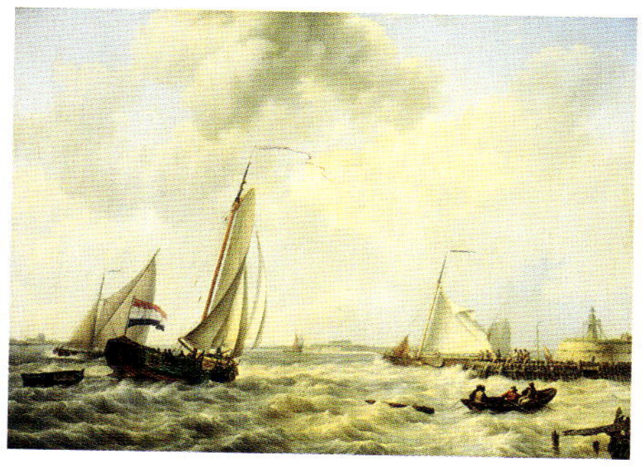

Koekkoek, Johannes Hermanus 1778–1851
Sea Piece 1790–1815
oil on canvas 53 x 72.1
VIS.1603

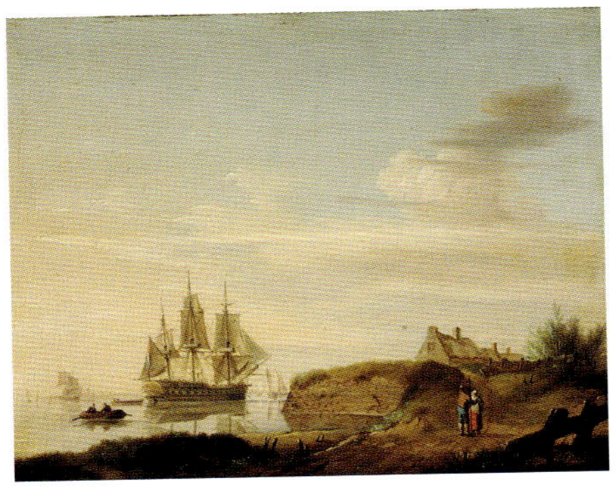

Koekkoek, Johannes Hermanus 1778–1851
Seascape 1811
oil on panel 23.8 x 29.8
VIS.1511

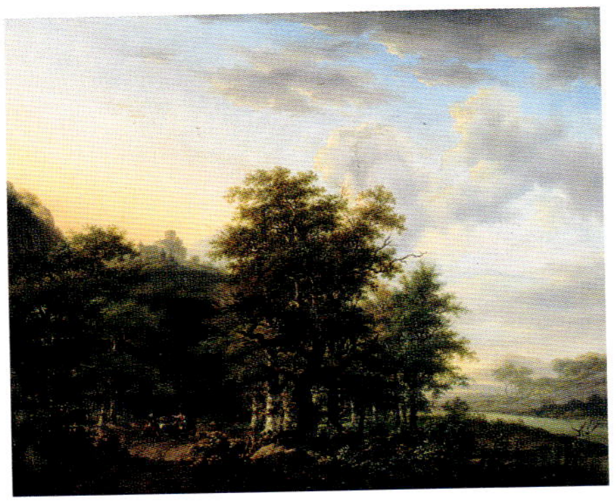

Koekkoek, Marinus Adrianus (attributed to) 1807–1870
Landscape 1830–1862
oil on canvas 69 x 83
VIS.1627

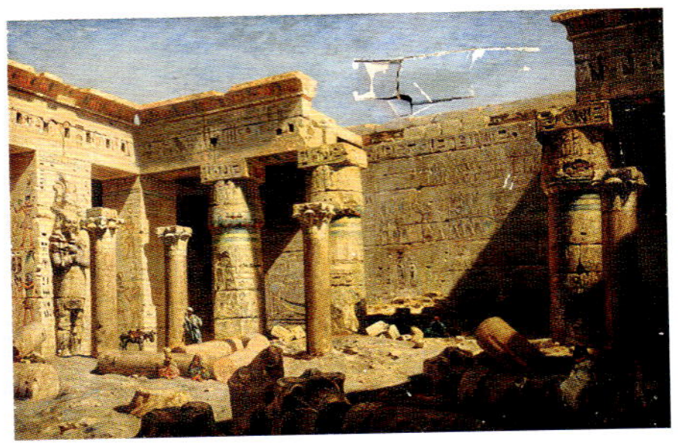

Koerner, Ernest Carl 1846–1927
Temple of the Medinet Habu, Upper Egypt 1879
oil on canvas 84.5 x 126.2
VIS.1293

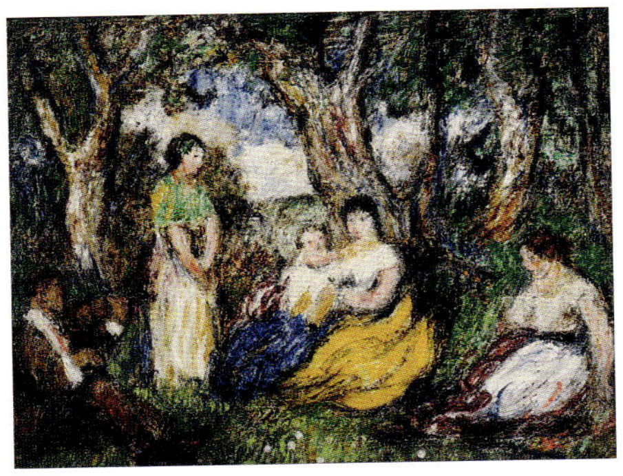

Kotasz, Károly 1872–1941
A Figure Group 1895–1900
oil on canvas 34.2 x 43.7
VIS.760

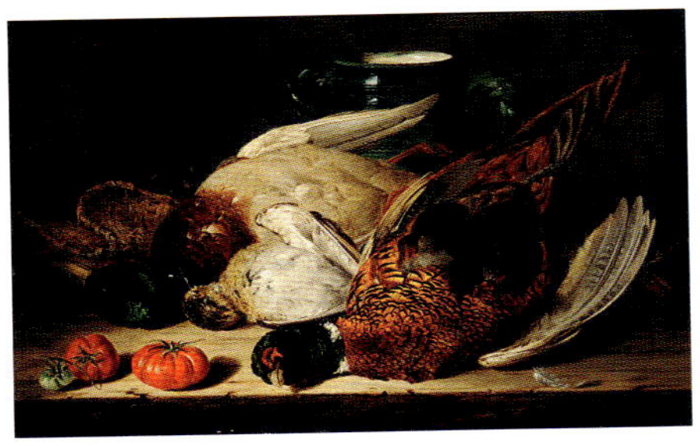

Ladell, Edward 1821–1886
Birds from Nature
oil on canvas 42.2 x 64.8
VIS.1972

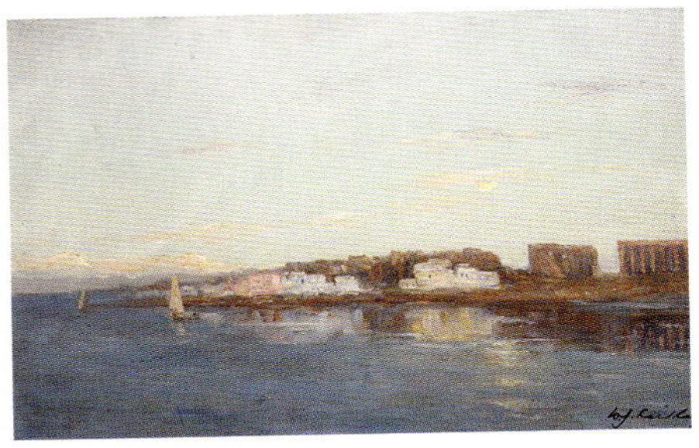

Laidlay, William James 1846–1912
On the Nile at Luxor, Egypt
oil on canvas 29.5 x 44.8
VIS.609

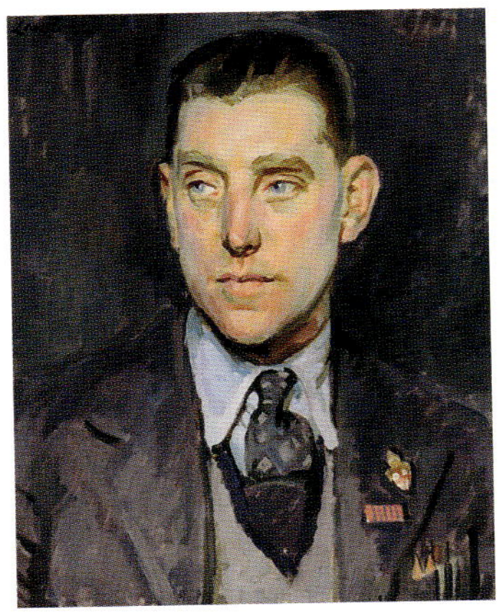

Lamb, Henry 1883–1960
Edward Hector Bent, GM 1942
oil on canvas 49.5 x 39.5
VIS.1929

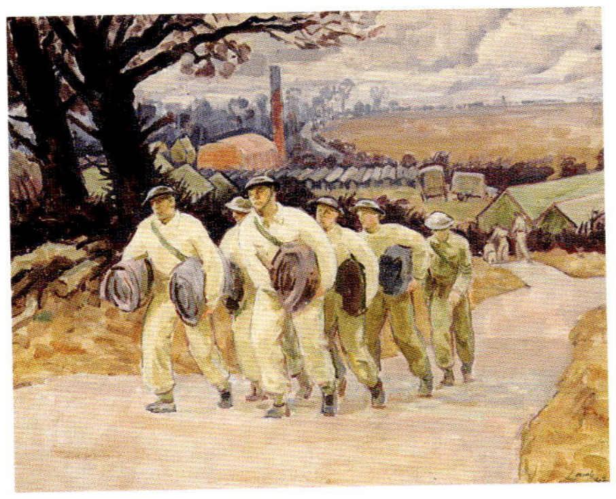

Lamb, Henry 1883–1960
The Night Watch, Canadian Heavy Gunners, 2nd A. A. Battery 1942
oil on canvas 44.7 x 54.7
VIS.1932

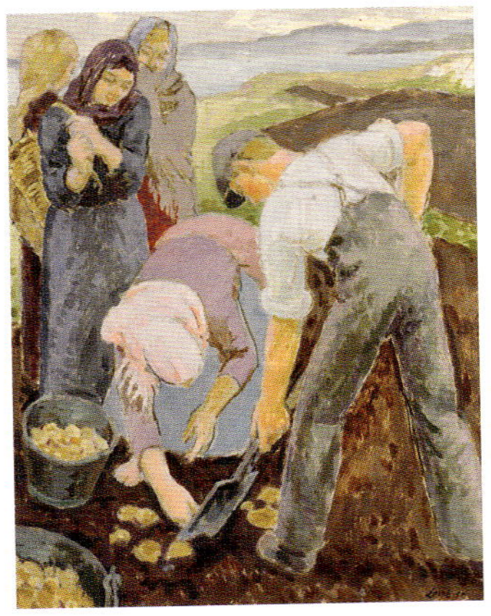

Lamb, Henry 1883–1960
Donegal Potato Pickers 1950
oil on panel 48.2 x 37.9
VIS.3974

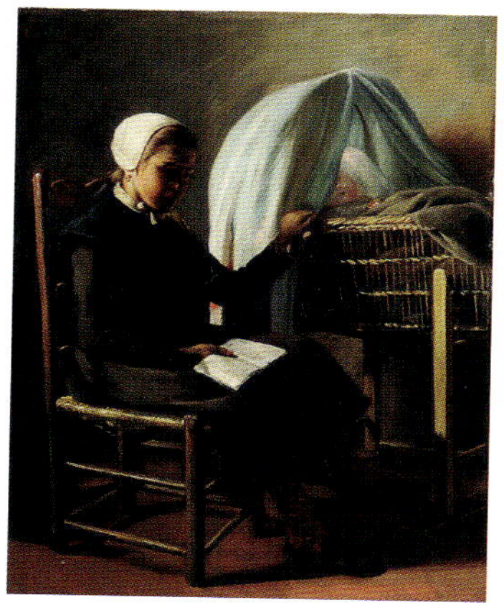

Lambeaux, Jules (attributed to) 1858–1890
Infant and Nurse 1870–1880
oil on canvas 45.6 x 37
VIS.519

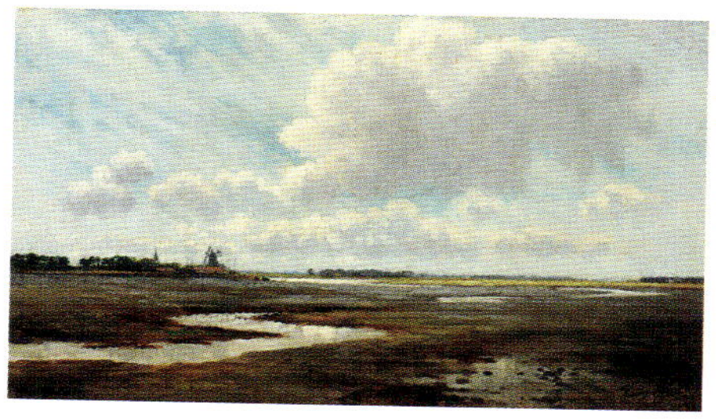

Lambert, Clement 1855–1925
A Marshland
oil on canvas 44.1 x 74.5
VIS.144

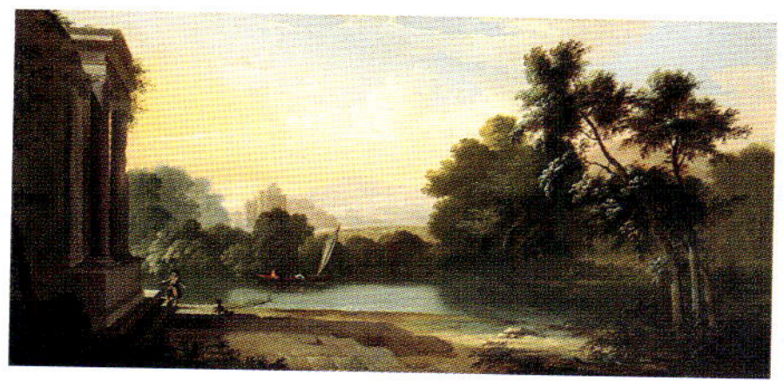

Lambert, Clement 1855–1925
Romantic Landscape
oil on canvas 74.5 x 150.6
VIS.2988

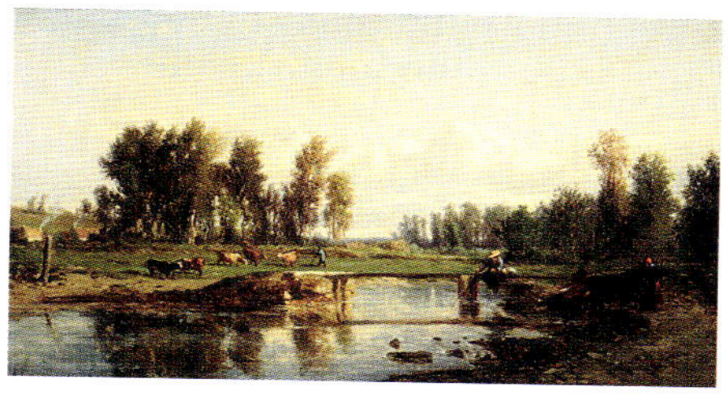

Lambinet, Emile Charles 1815–1877
Landscape 1866
oil on canvas 33.1 x 61.4
VIS.1373

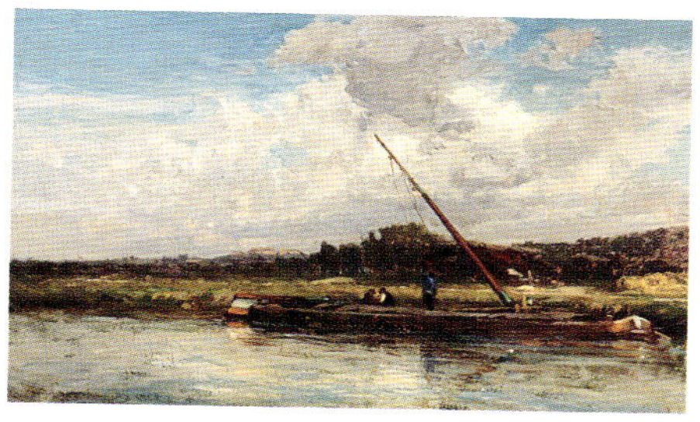

Lambinet, Emile Charles 1815–1877
River Scene with Barges 1868
oil on panel 30 x 50
VIS.567

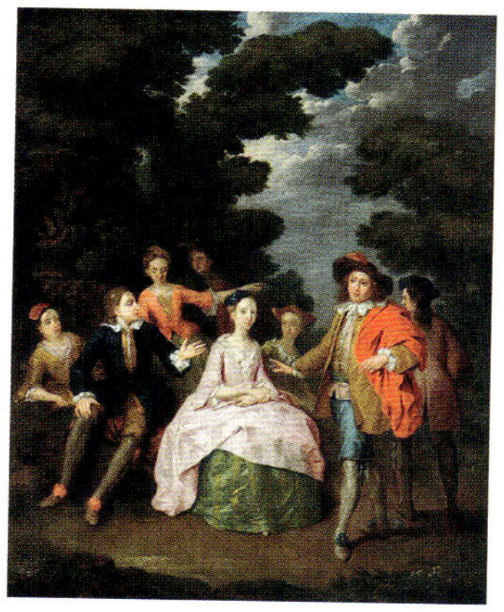

Lancret, Nicolas (attributed to) 1690–1743
Conversation Piece
oil on canvas 81.7 x 64.5
VIS.2471

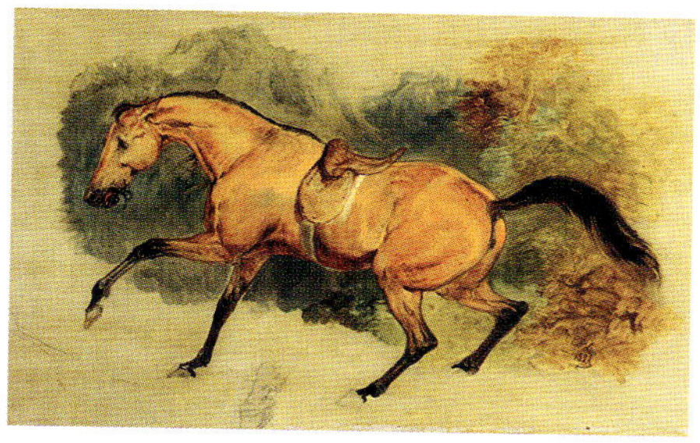

Landseer, Edwin Henry 1802–1873
Count d'Orsay's Charger 1822
oil on panel 25.8 x 40.5
VIS.1389

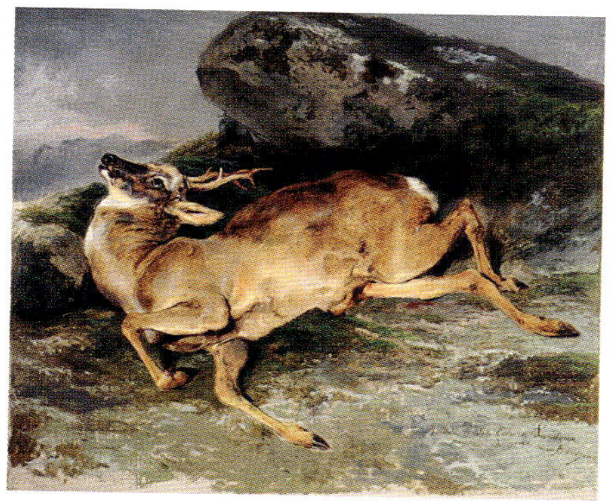

Landseer, Edwin Henry 1802–1873
A Stray Shot
oil on canvas 118.6 x 139.7
VIS.1619

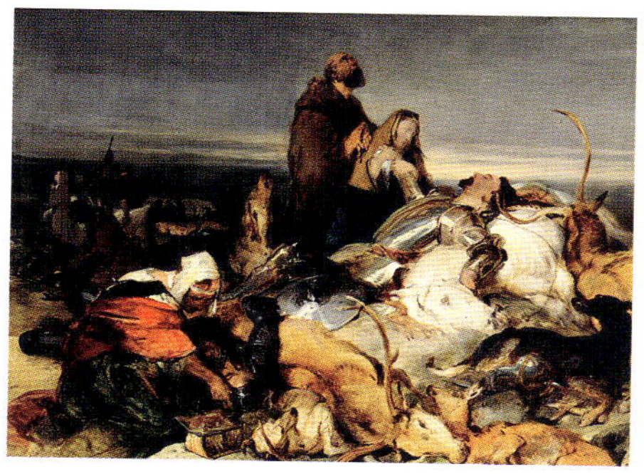

Landseer, Edwin Henry 1802–1873
Chevy Chase
oil on panel 44.4 x 60.4
VIS.1543

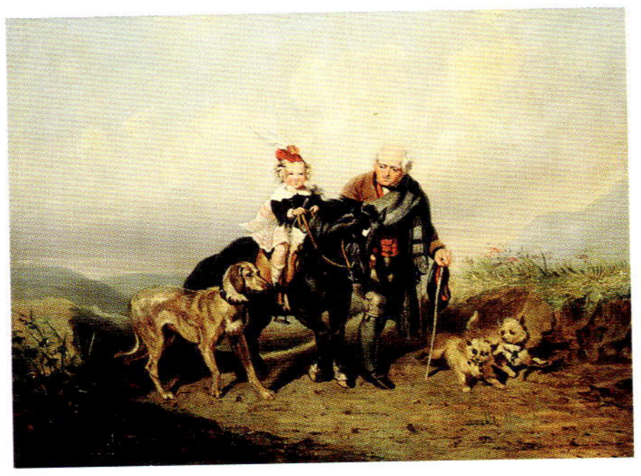

Landseer, Edwin Henry 1802–1873
The Young Laird
oil on canvas 45 x 59.5
VIS.276

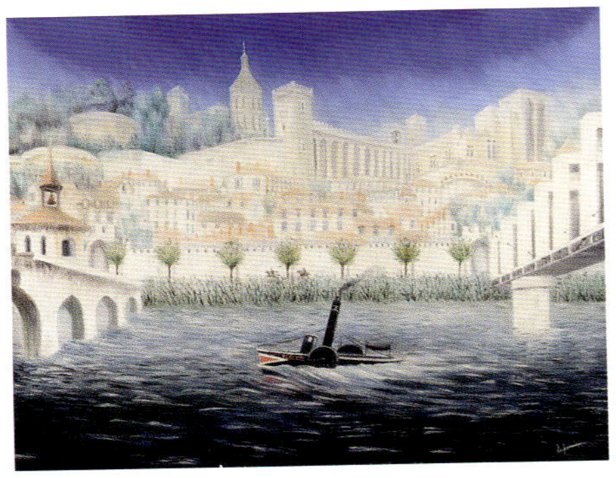

Lascaux, Elie 1888–1969
Avignon, France c.1930
oil on canvas 71 x 90
VIS.714

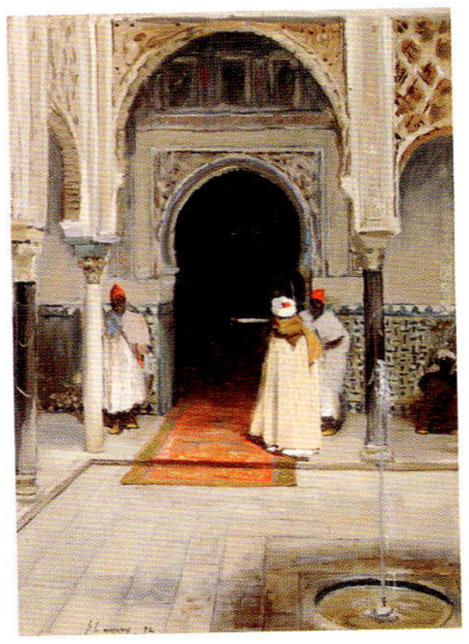

Lavery, John 1856–1941
Dar el Cadi, Interior of a Mosque 1892
oil on canvas 34.2 x 24.2
VIS.192

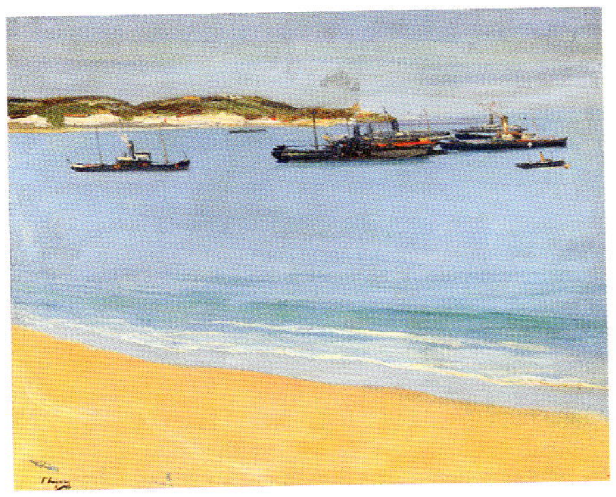

Lavery, John 1856–1941
The Harbour at St Jean de Luz, France: Early Morning 1917
oil on canvas 79.8 x 92.5
VIS.3374

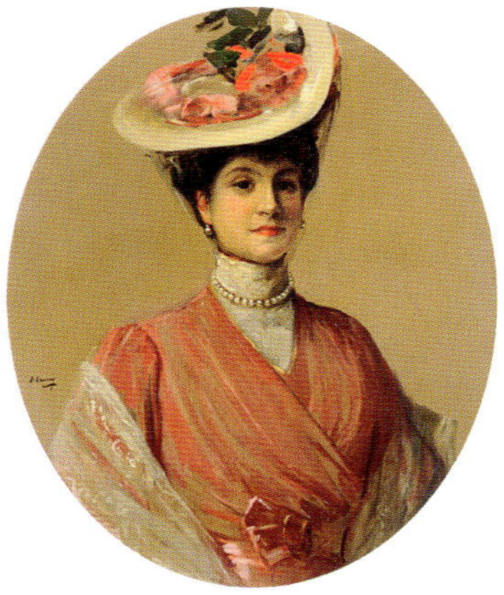

Lavery, John 1856–1941
Portrait of a Lady
oil on canvas 79 x 64
VIS.741

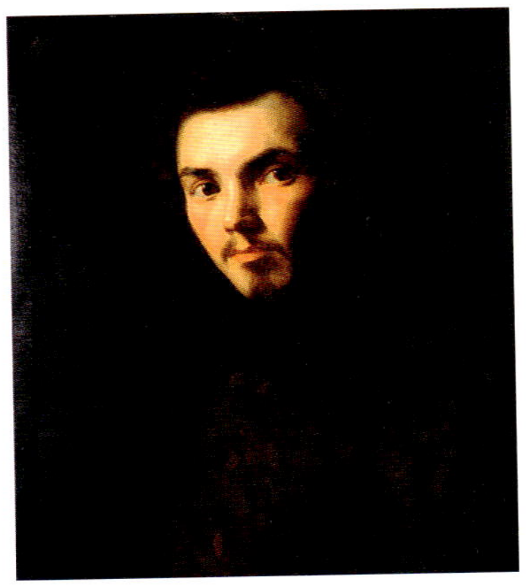

Lavoine, Louis Victor (attributed to) 1808–1861
Young Mitchell (1811–1865) 1833
oil on canvas 52.7 x 45.3
VIS.3197

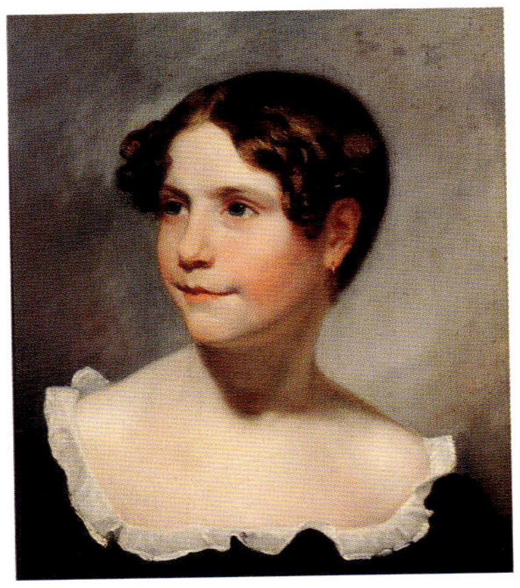

Lawrence, Thomas 1769–1830
Head of a Girl
oil on canvas 42 x 36.2
VIS.837

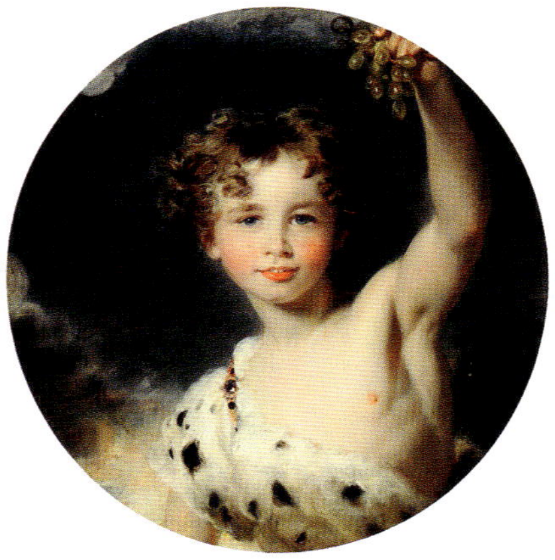

Lawrence, Thomas 1769–1830
Master Charles Hope
oil on canvas 62 x 61
VIS.LI.388 (P)

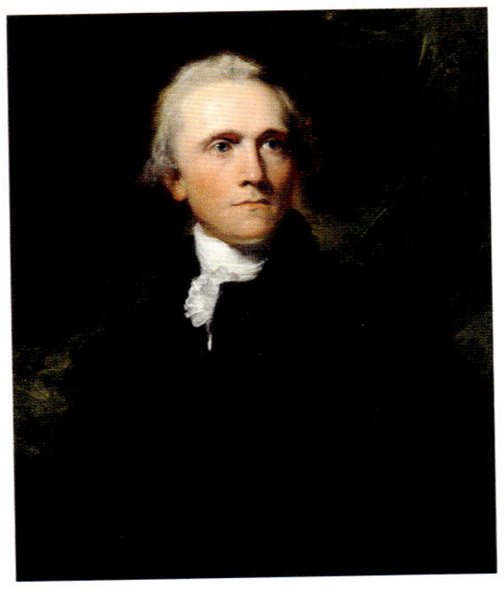

Lawrence, Thomas 1769–1830
Sir William Grant (1752–1832)
oil on canvas 94.1 x 81.4
VIS.3135

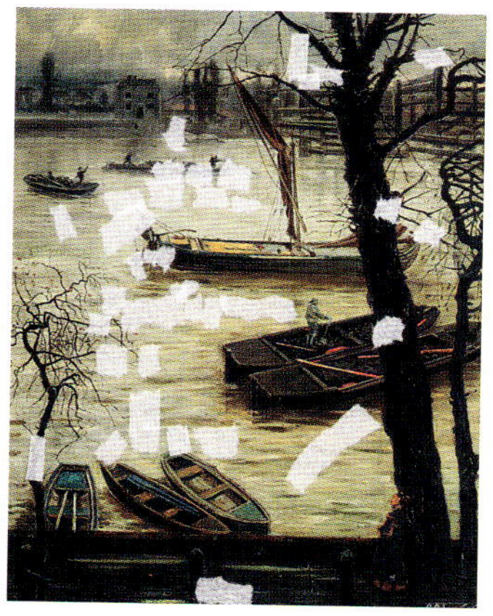

Lawson, Cecil Gordon 1851–1882
River Scene with Shipping
oil on canvas 49.6 x 39.4
VIS.1500

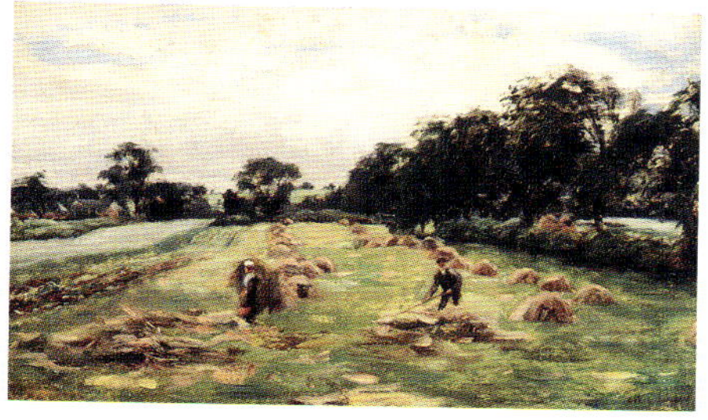

Lawson, Cecil Gordon 1851–1882
The Hayfield
oil on canvas 23.5 x 38.9
VIS.201

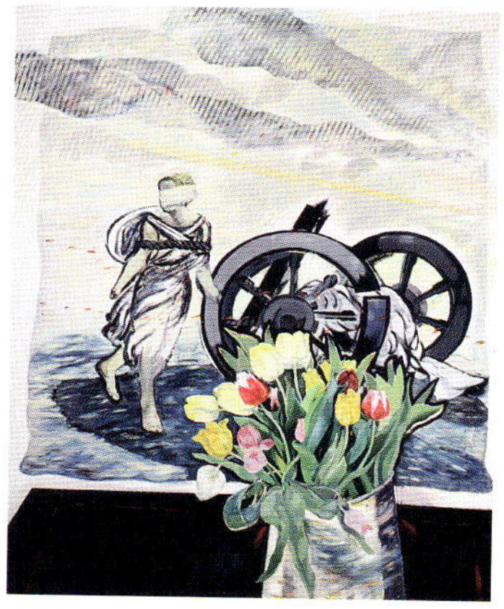

Lawson, Sonia b.1934
Frail Peace
oil on canvas 150.8 x 121.1
VIS.5137

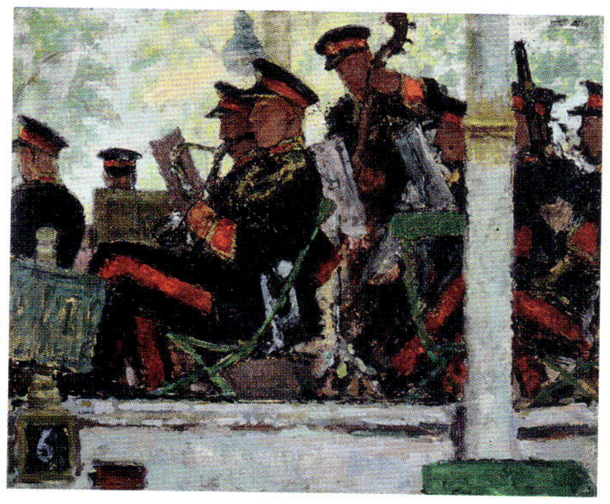

Le Bas, Edward 1904–1966
The Bandstand at Hyde Park, London
oil on board 54.5 x 64.1
VIS.4749

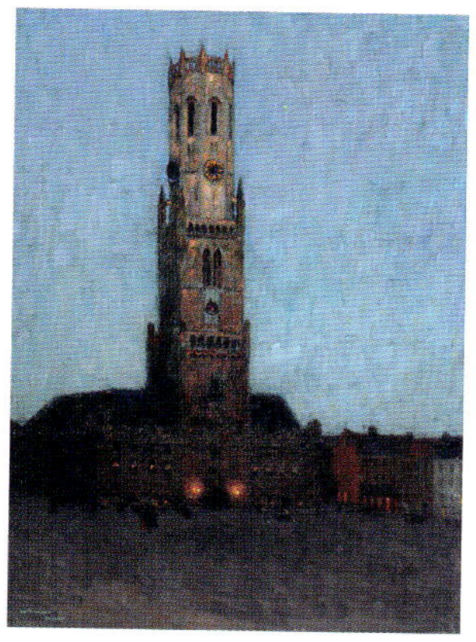

Le Sidaner, Henri Eugène 1862–1939
The Belfry at Bruges, Belgium 1898–1900
oil on canvas 81 x 56.7
VIS.186

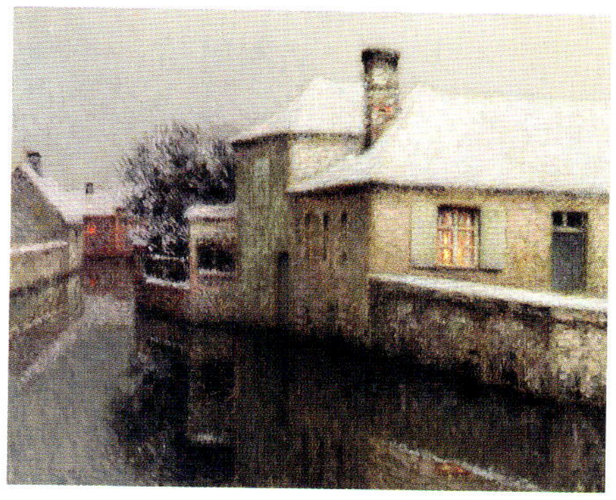

Le Sidaner, Henri Eugène 1862–1939
Nemours, Seine-et-Marne, France
oil on canvas 55.5 x 66
VIS.255

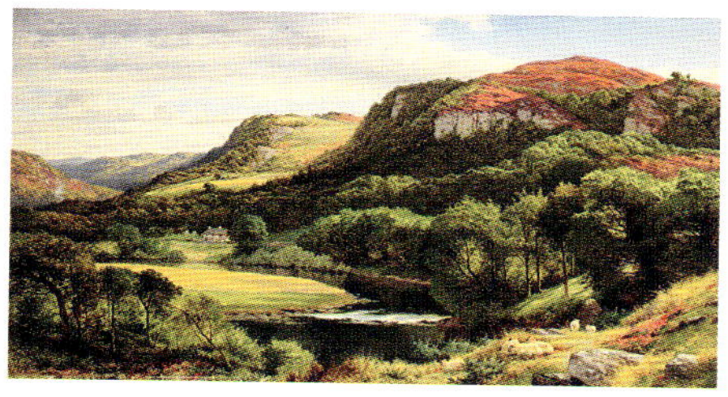

Leader, Benjamin Williams 1831–1923
The River Llugwy, Betws-y-Coed, Wales 1863
oil on canvas 48 x 88.8
VIS.996

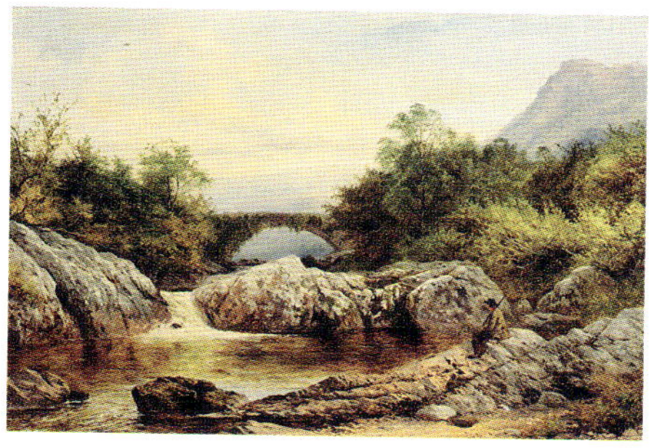

Leader, Benjamin Williams 1831–1923
The Lledr Bridge, near Betws-y-Coed, Wales
1865
oil on canvas 44.4 x 64.6
VIS.1505

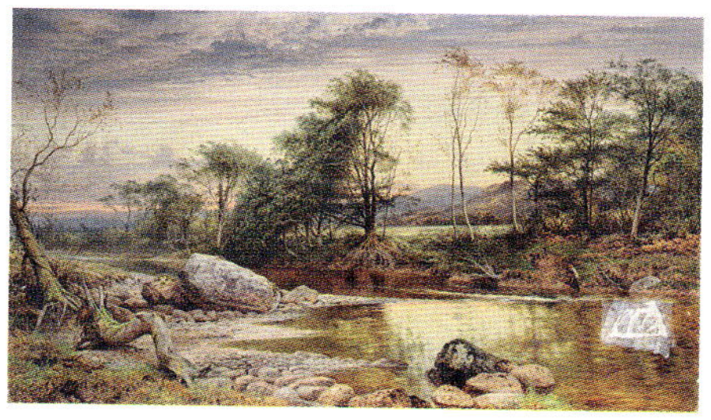

Leader, Benjamin Williams 1831–1923
The Close of Summer 1866
oil on canvas 91.3 x 152.6
VIS.1452

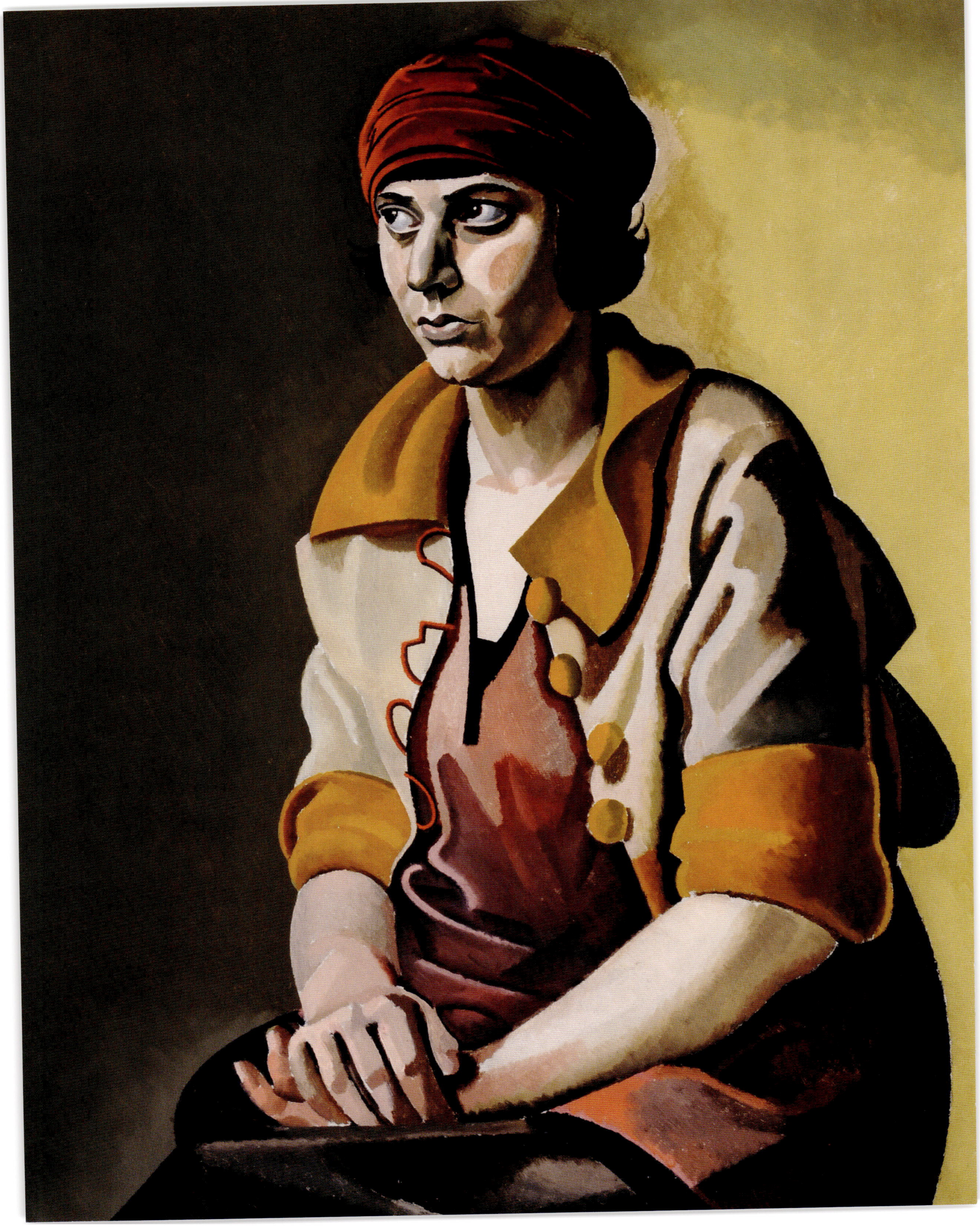

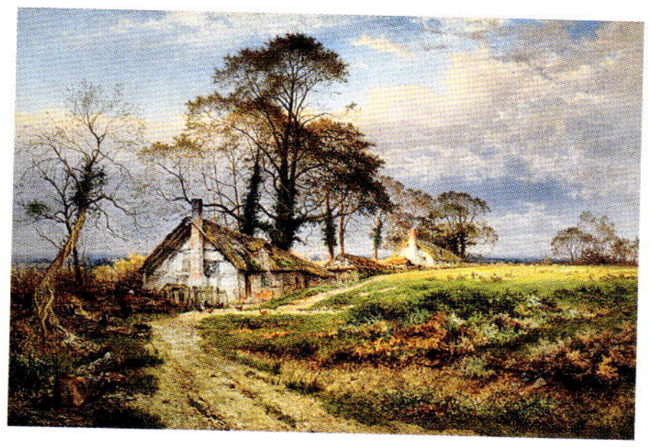

Leader, Benjamin Williams 1831–1923
The Last Gleam 1871
oil on canvas 102.5 x 147.3
VIS.1692

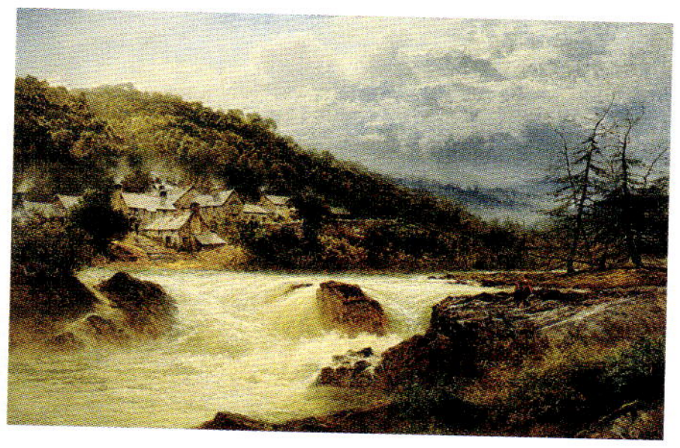

Leader, Benjamin Williams 1831–1923
Betws-y-Coed, Wales 1872
oil on canvas 89.9 x 136.1
VIS.1590

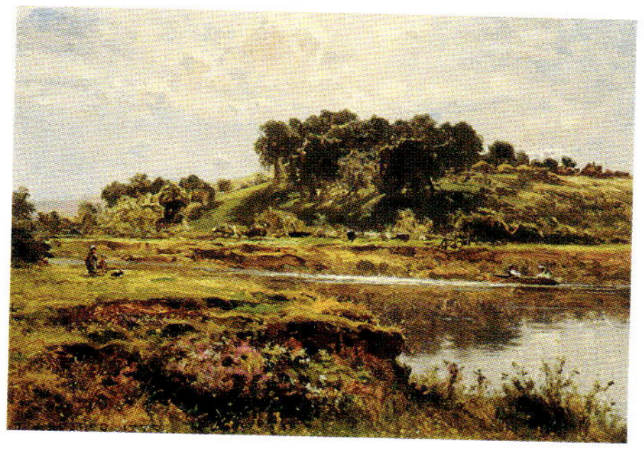

Leader, Benjamin Williams 1831–1923
On the Severn 1885
oil on panel 24.9 x 34.9
VIS.176

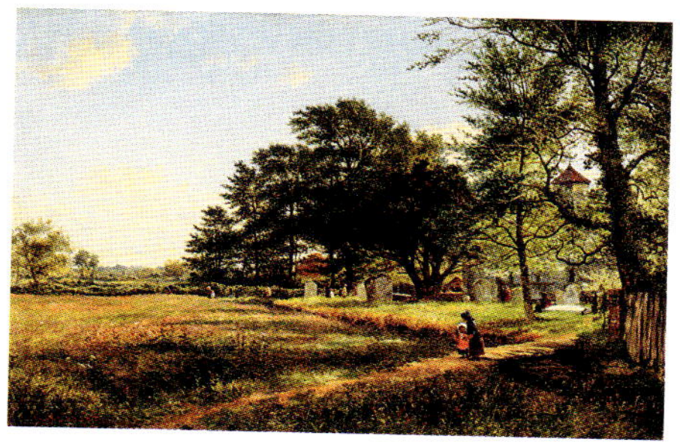

Leader, Benjamin Williams 1831–1923
A Country Churchyard 1886
oil on millboard 39.9 x 60.2
VIS.750

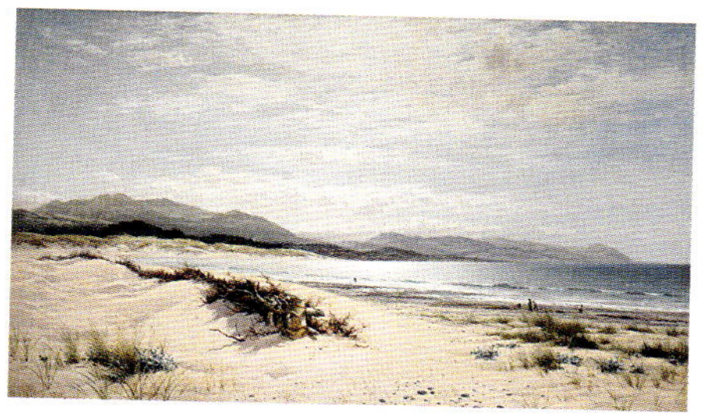

Leader, Benjamin Williams 1831–1923
Seascape, North Welsh Coast 1891
oil on canvas 90.1 x 151.1
VIS.1999

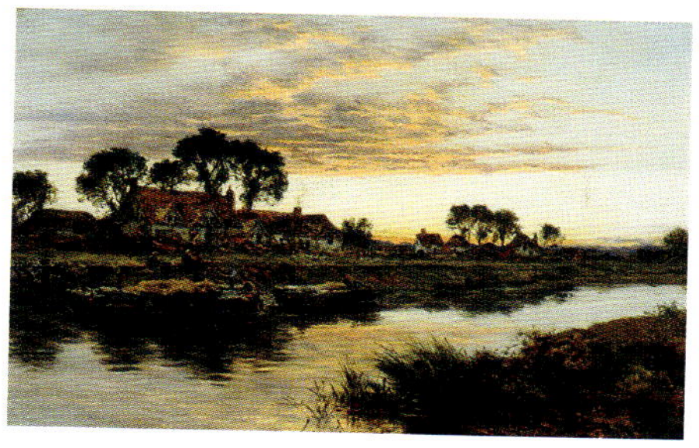

Leader, Benjamin Williams 1831–1923
On the Severn 1897
oil on canvas 28.3 x 43.7
VIS.2717

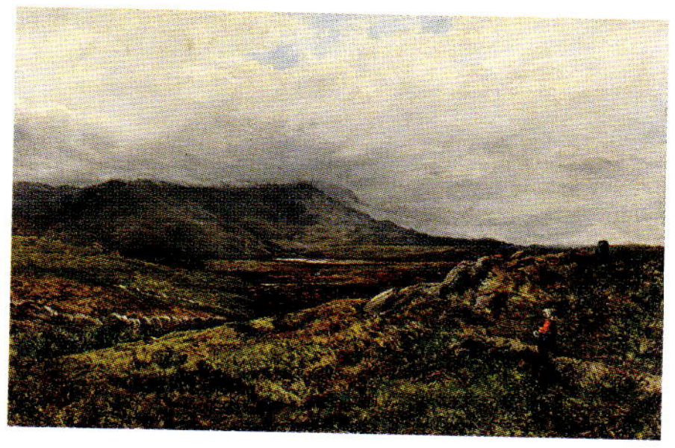

Leader, Benjamin Williams 1831–1923
Near Moel Siabod, Wales 1898
oil on canvas 28.8 x 44
VIS.793

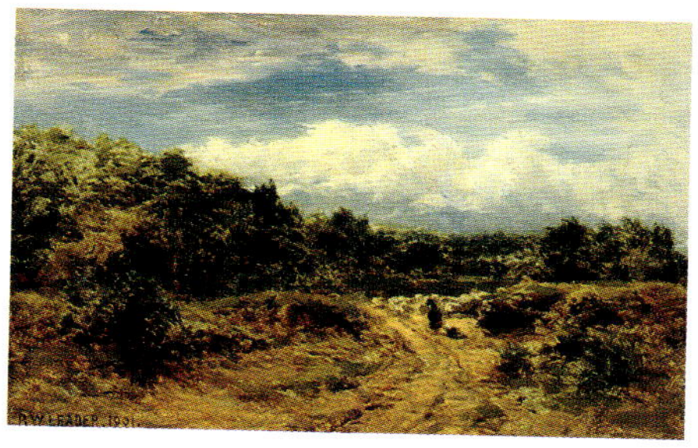

Leader, Benjamin Williams 1831–1923
Across the Common 1901
oil on canvas 34.9 x 71.9
VIS.763

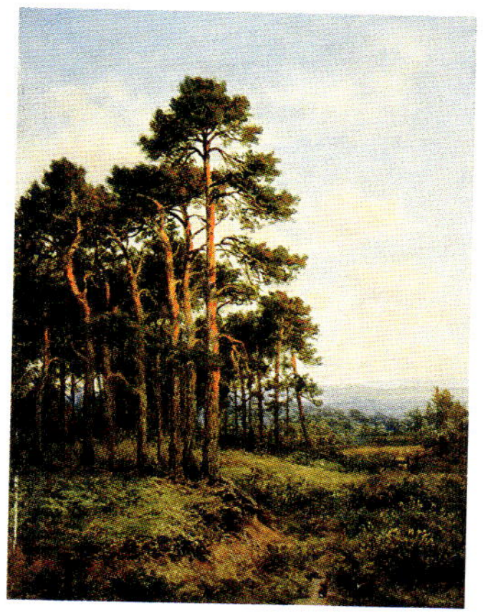

Leader, Benjamin Williams 1831–1923
Morning 1916
oil on board 43.4 x 32
VIS.2043

Facing page: Roberts, William Patrick, 1895–1980, *The Red Turban* (detail), c.1928, Museums Sheffield, (p. 183)

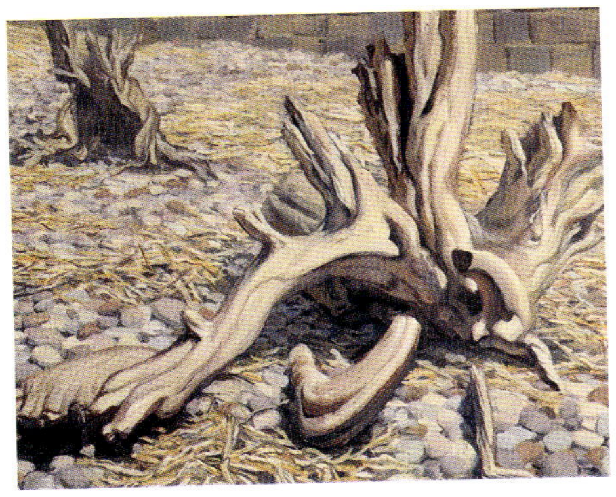

Leadley, W. E. 1903–1973
Driftwood 1960
oil on millboard 46.5 x 56.9
VIS.5432

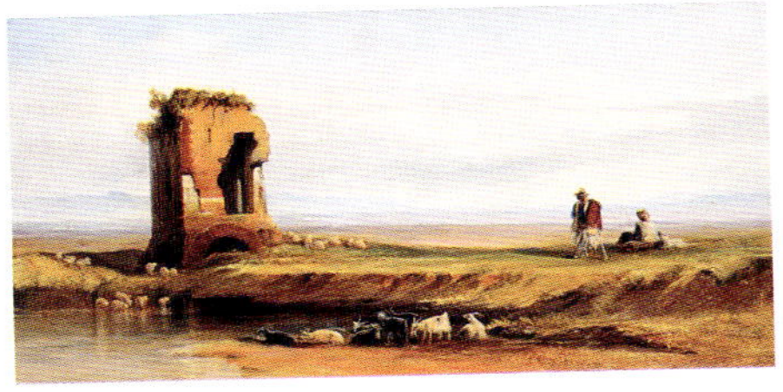

Lear, Edward 1812–1888
Buon Ricovero, in the Roman Campagna 1878
oil on canvas 23.4 x 46.4
VIS.3644

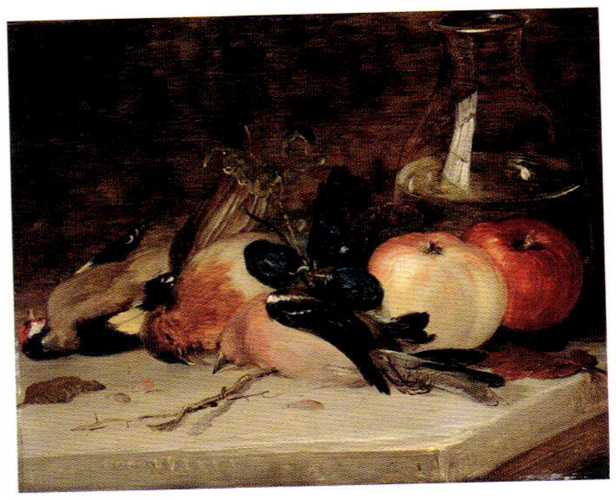

Lee, Frederick Richard 1798–1879
Birds and Fruit
oil on panel 24.4 x 29.6
VIS.1330

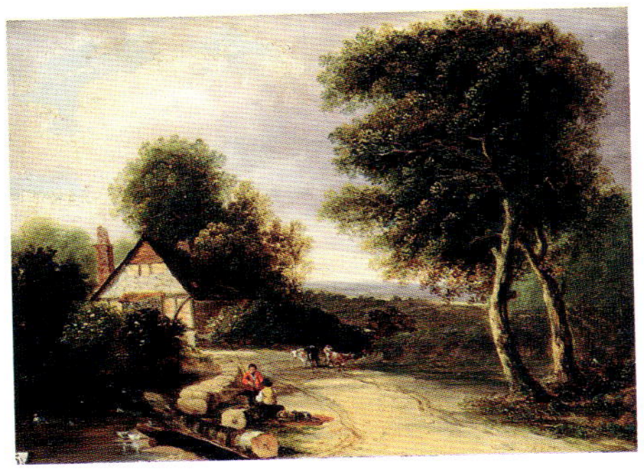

Lee, Frederick Richard 1798–1879
Landscape with a River
oil on canvas 44.4 x 59.8
VIS.1290

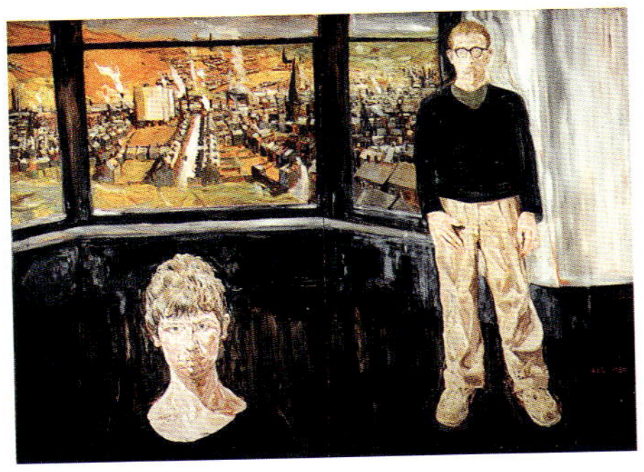

Lee, Terry b.1932
Self Portrait 1959
oil on board 182.8 x 242
VIS.2578

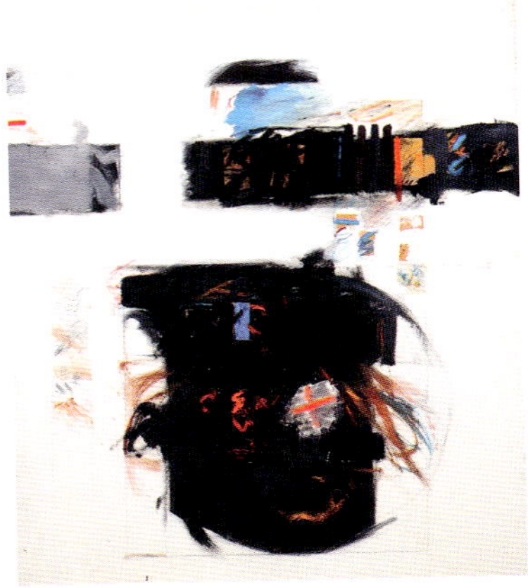

Lee, Terry b.1932
Ask for Whom 1966
oil & mixed media on canvas 106.5 x 91.5
VIS.3304

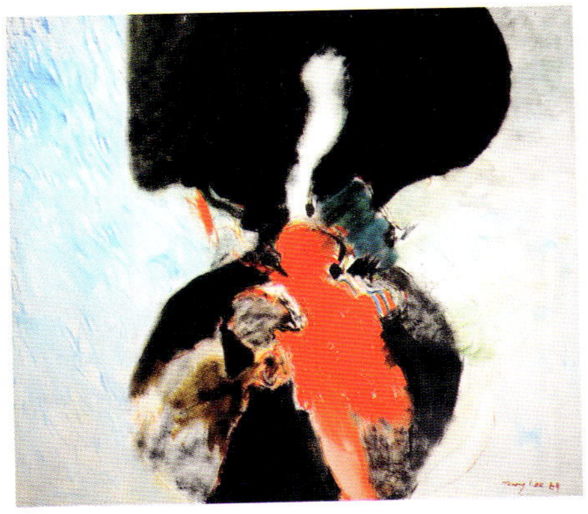

Lee, Terry b.1932
Adam's Tree 1967
oil on canvas 122.4 x 137.4
VIS.LI.30 (P)

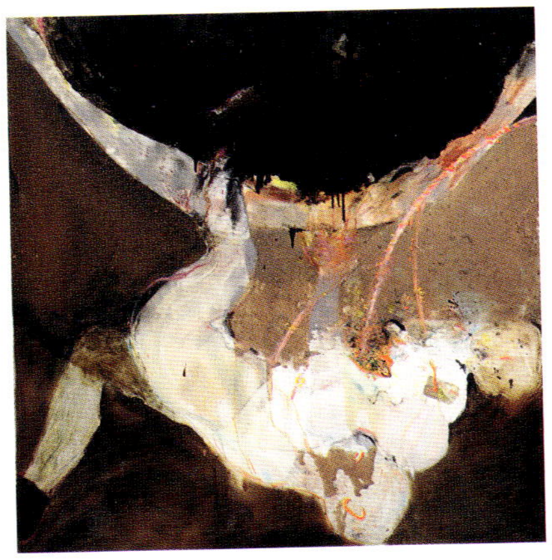

Lee, Terry b.1932
The Swinger 1967
oil on canvas 126.9 x 121.4
VIS.3343

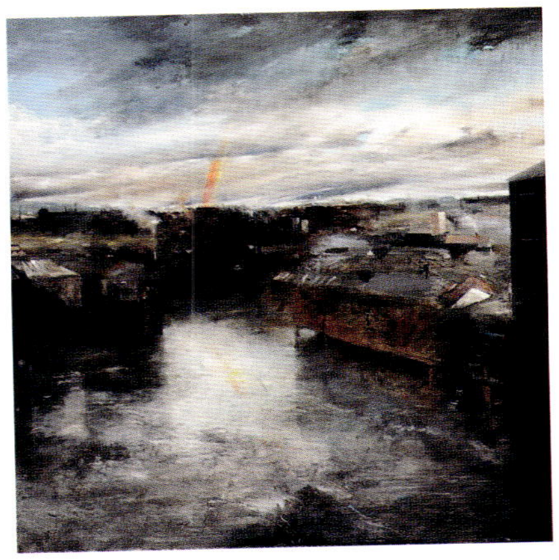

Lee, Terry b.1932
Sheffield River
oil on canvas 106.6 x 105.4
VIS.4746

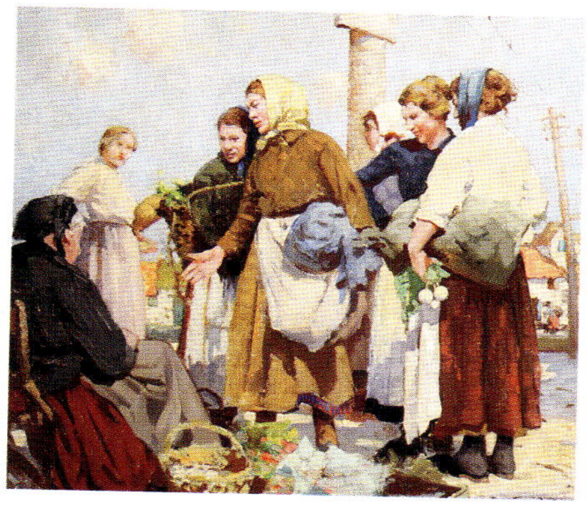

Lee-Hankey, William 1869–1952
A French Market Place
oil on canvas 59.2 x 66.9
VIS.147

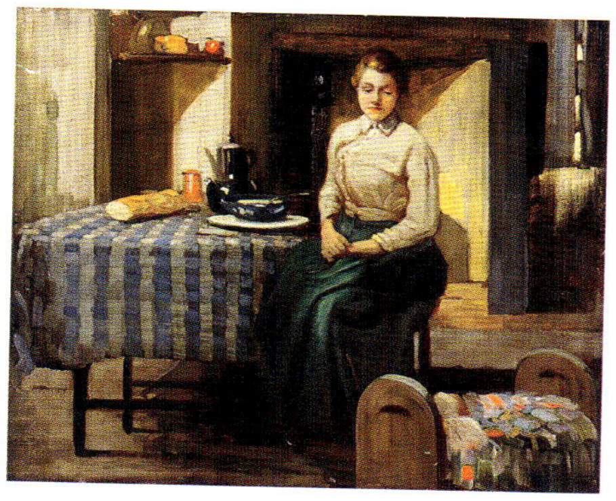

Lee-Hankey, William 1869–1952
Anxious Thoughts
oil on canvas 64.6 x 77.4
VIS.1273

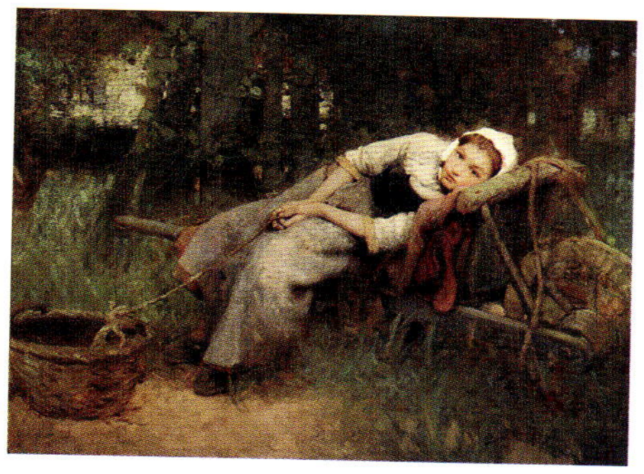

Lee-Hankey, William 1869–1952
'In the silent woody places by the home that gave me birth'
oil on canvas 133.4 x 173.8
VIS.591

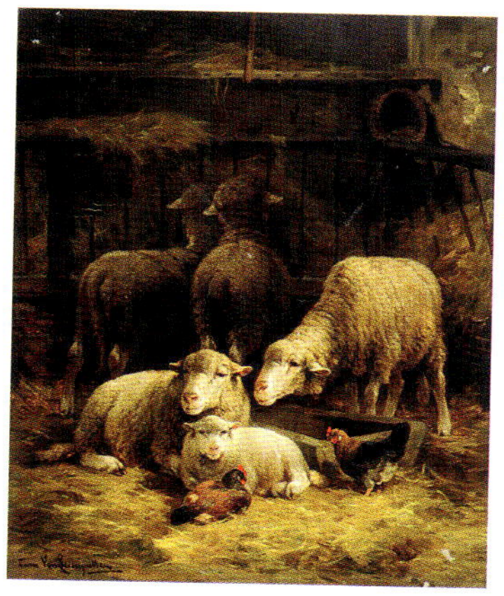

Leemputten, Cornelis van 1841–1902
Sheep and Poultry 1875–1880
oil on canvas 54.5 x 44.7
VIS.1363

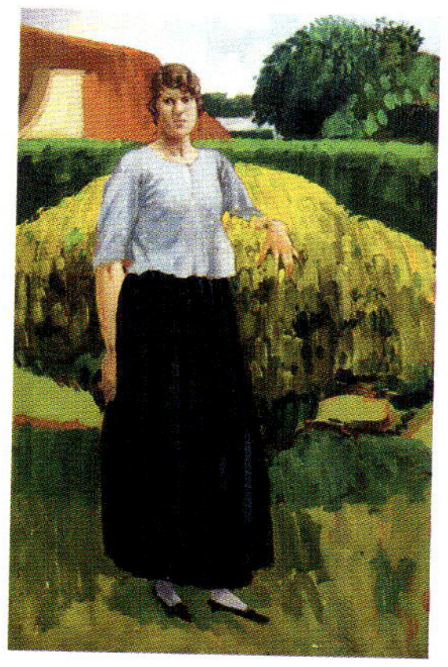

Lees, Derwent 1885–1931
A Girl Standing by a Hay Cart
oil on panel 49.5 x 31.7
VIS.3373

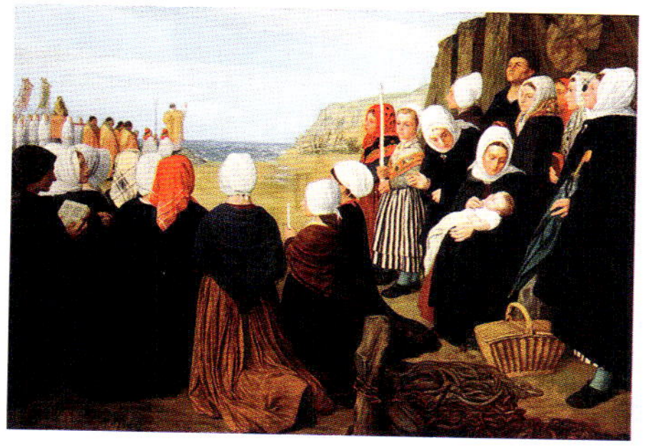

Legros, Alphonse 1837–1911
Blessing the Sea 1872
oil on canvas 179.5 x 243.3
VIS.661

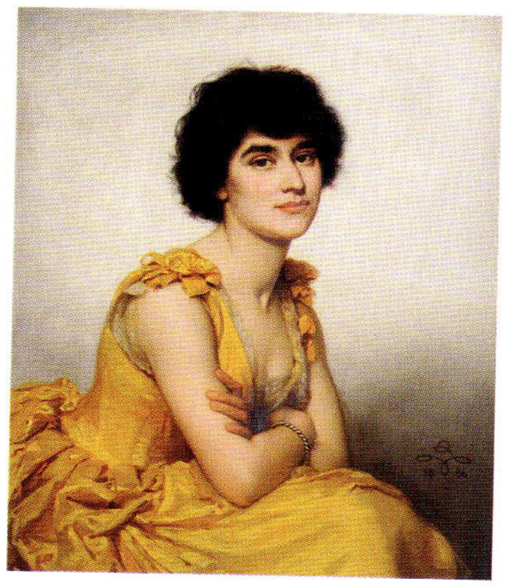

Lehmann, Rudolph 1819–1905
Portrait of a Lady 1886
oil on canvas 75.5 x 62
VIS.1274

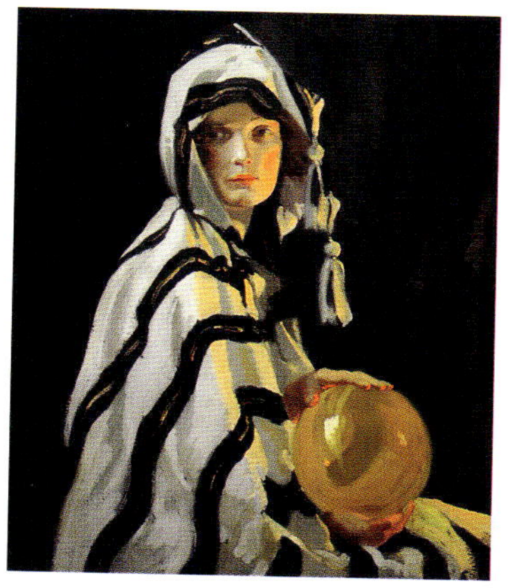

Leist, Frederick William 1878–1945
A Carnival Souvenir 1920
oil on canvas 73.4 x 62
VIS.1997

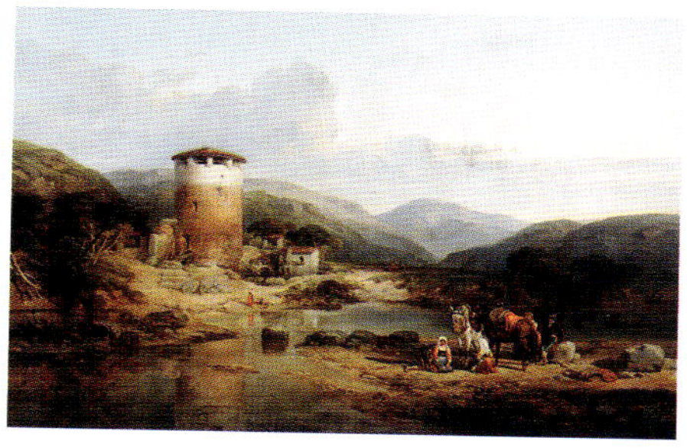

Leitch, William Leighton 1804–1883
View above the Capua, Southern Italy
oil on canvas 69.5 x 105.7
VIS.1486

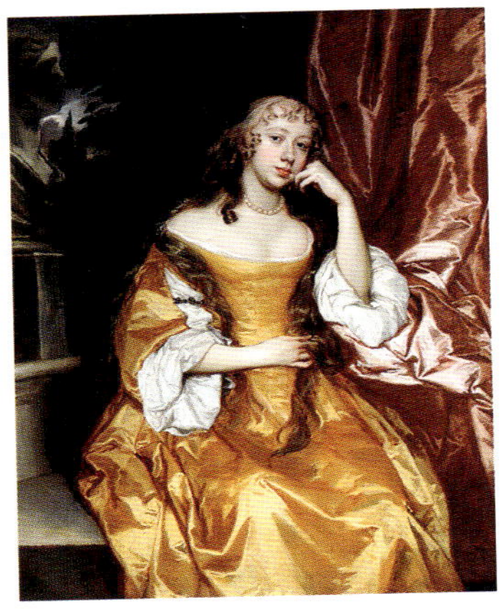

Lely, Peter 1618–1680
Margaret Brooke (c.1647–1667), Lady Denham c.1664
oil on canvas 148.4 x 124
VIS.3119

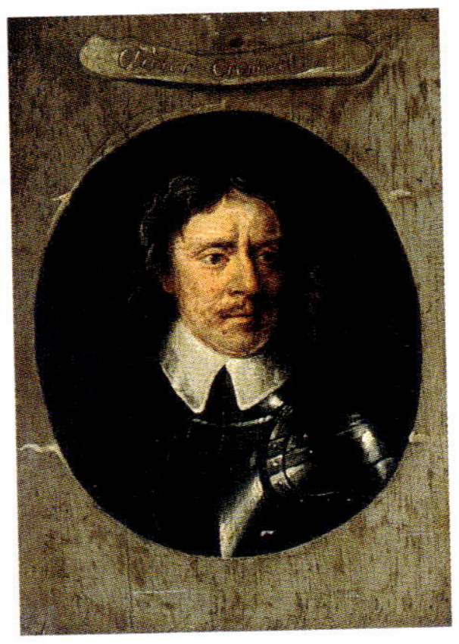

Lely, Peter (after) 1618–1680
Oliver Cromwell (1599–1658)
oil on panel 26.5 x 18.5
VIS.1635

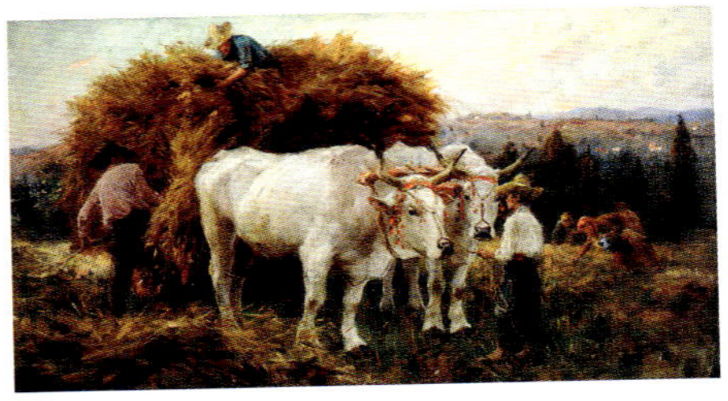

Lemon, Arthur 1850–1912
Harvest in Tuscany
oil on canvas 74.4 x 132.7
VIS.1676

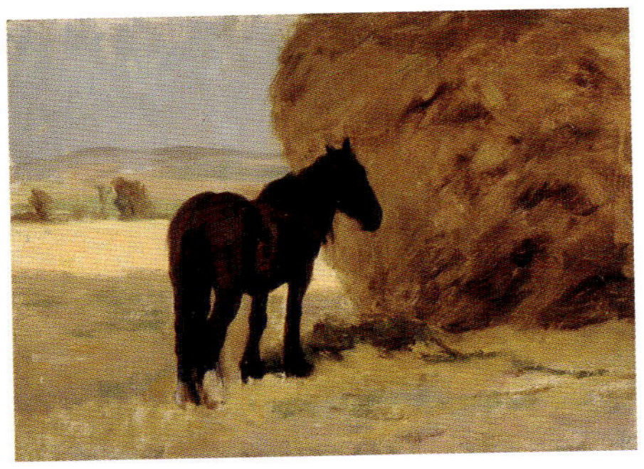

Lemon, Arthur 1850–1912
Landscape
oil on canvas 33.2 x 44.6
VIS.2364

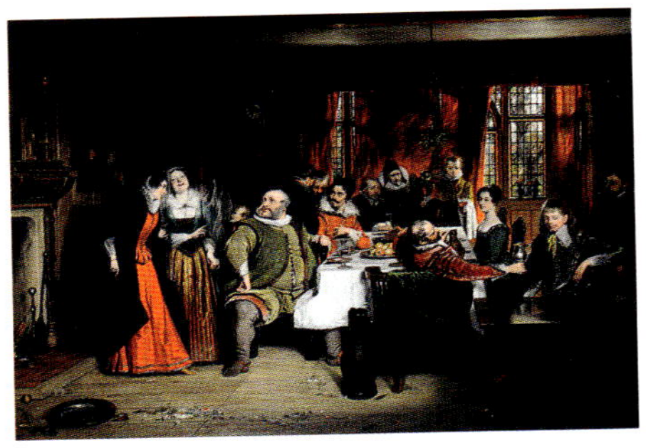

Leslie, Charles Robert 1794–1859
Scene from William Shakespeare's 'The Merry Wives of Windsor' 1830
oil on canvas 120.6 x 172.4
VIS.1549

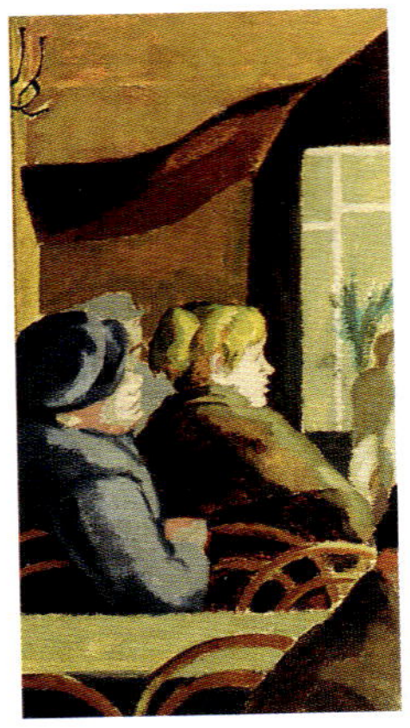

Lessore, Thérèse 1884–1945
Saturday Evening 1920
oil on canvas 55.4 x 29.9
VIS.1881

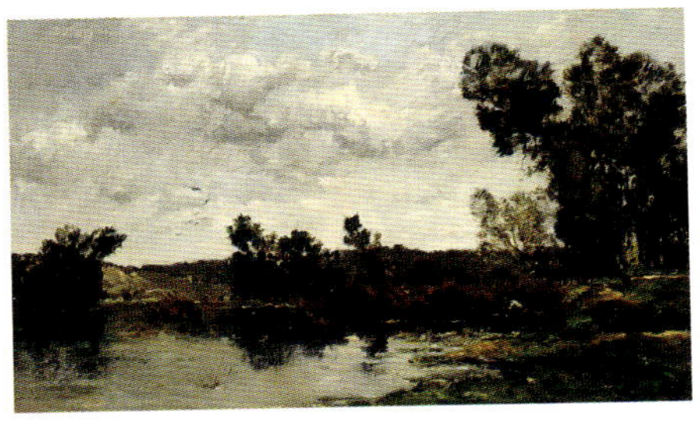

Levis, Maurice 1860–1940
On the River Yonne, France 1880–1900
oil on canvas 47 x 76.9
VIS.527

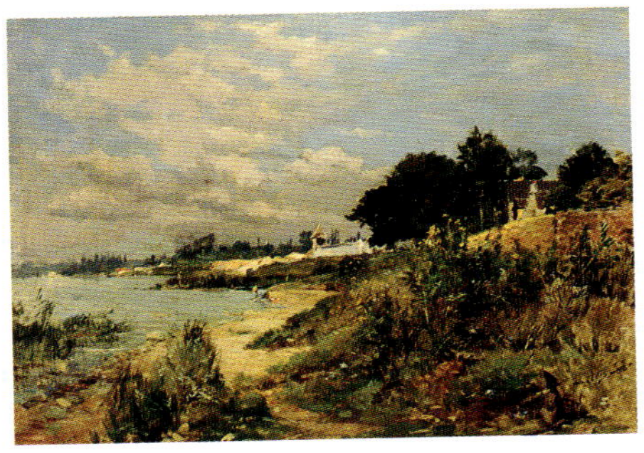

Levis, Maurice 1860–1940
At Boutigny, France 1888
oil on canvas 27.4 x 38.7
VIS.206

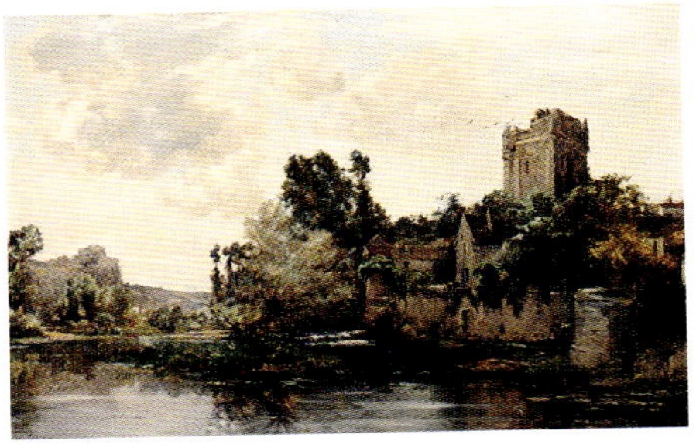

Levis, Maurice 1860–1940
Les vieux remparts 1890–1895
oil on canvas 59.7 x 91
VIS.1338

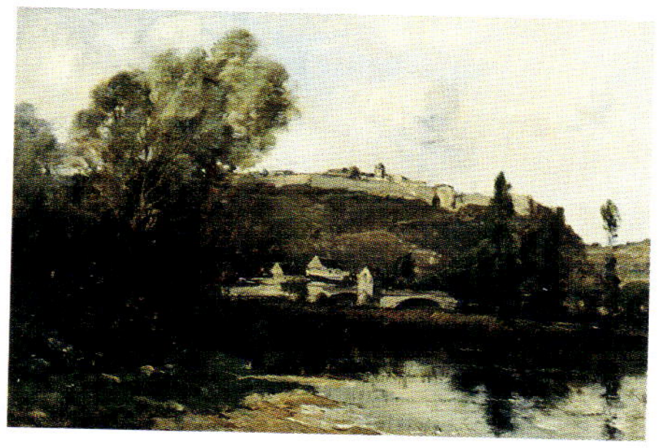

Levis, Maurice 1860–1940
The Old Ramparts, Mailly-le-Château, France
oil on canvas 36.6 x 53.8
VIS.1320

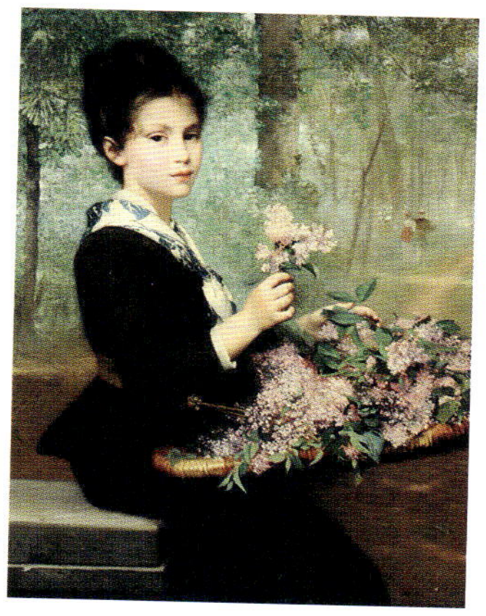

Levy, Émile 1826–1890
The First Lilac 1880–1885
oil on canvas 95.4 x 72.3
VIS.1279

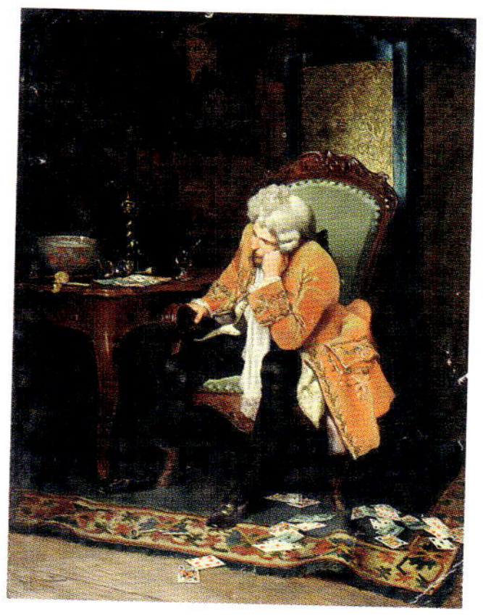

Lewin, Stephen Samuel 1848–1909
End of the Game 1888
oil on canvas 61 x 45.6
VIS.2526

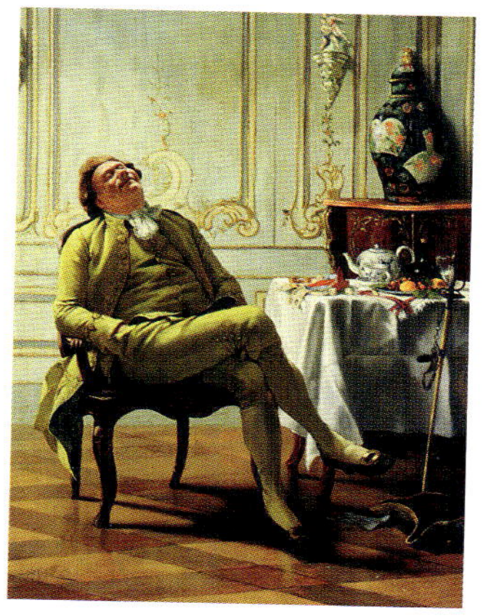

Lewin, Stephen Samuel 1848–1909
Forty Winks 1888
oil on canvas 61 x 45.6
VIS.2414

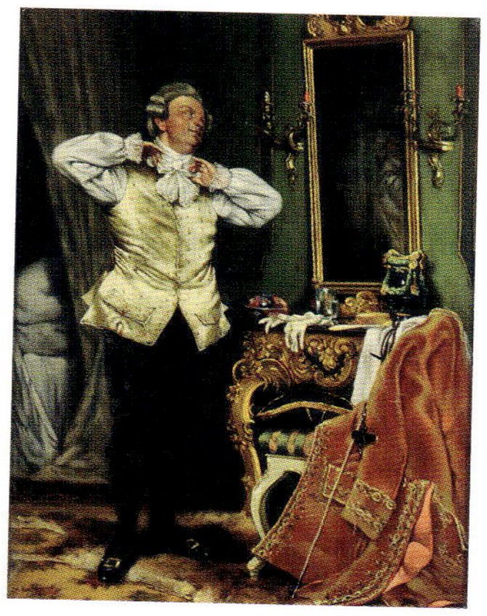

Lewin, Stephen Samuel 1848–1909
The Toilet 1889
oil on panel 31.5 x 23.6
VIS.1971

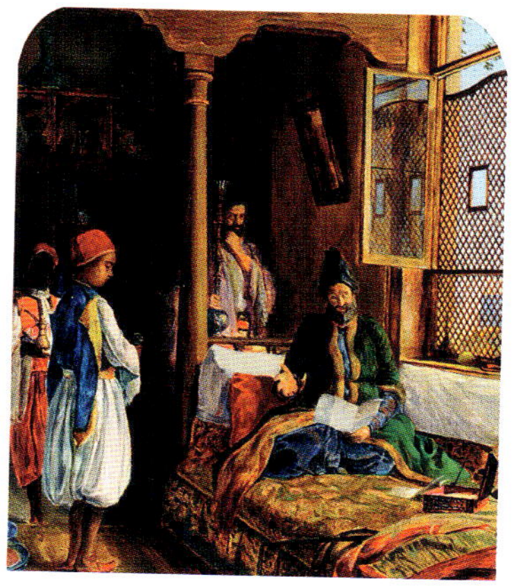

Lewis, John Frederick 1805–1876
Persian Interior
oil on board 29.1 x 24
VIS.4

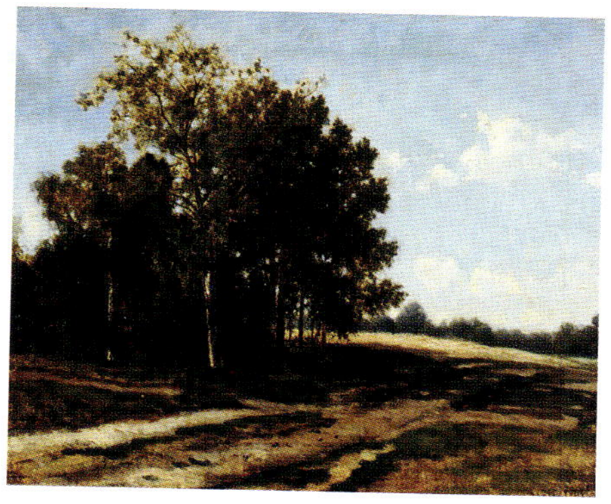

Lhermitte, Léon-Augustin (attributed to)
1844–1925
Landscape 1860–1900
oil on canvas 36.2 x 44
VIS.1317

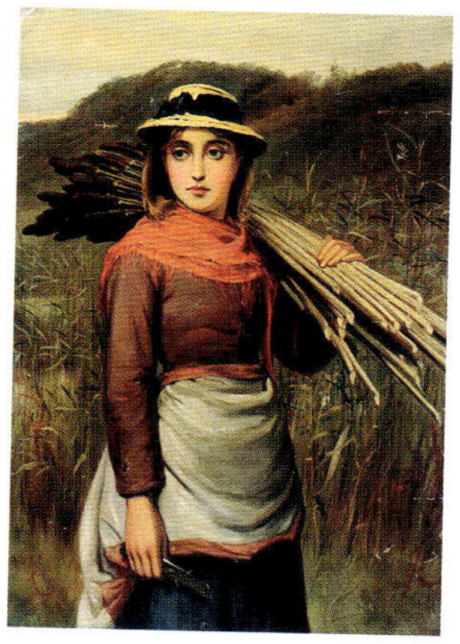

Lidderdale, Charles Sillem 1831–1895
Portrait with Bullrushes 1880
oil on canvas 109 x 81.3
VIS.2709

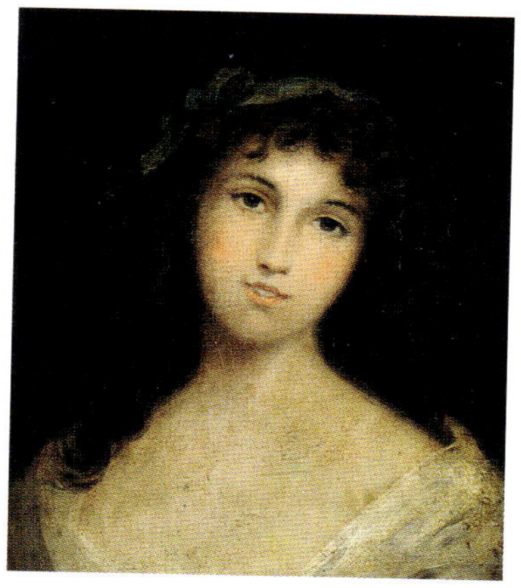

Lidderdale, Charles Sillem 1831–1895
Portrait of a Lady
oil on canvas 28 x 24
VIS.1024

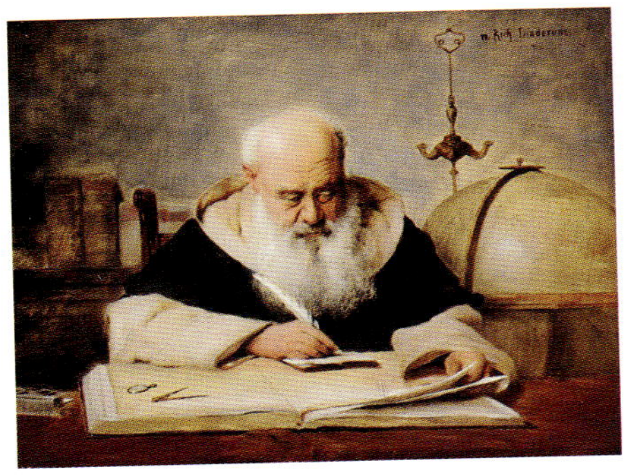

Linderum, Richard 1851–1926
The Scientist after 1866
oil on panel 18 x 24
VIS.234

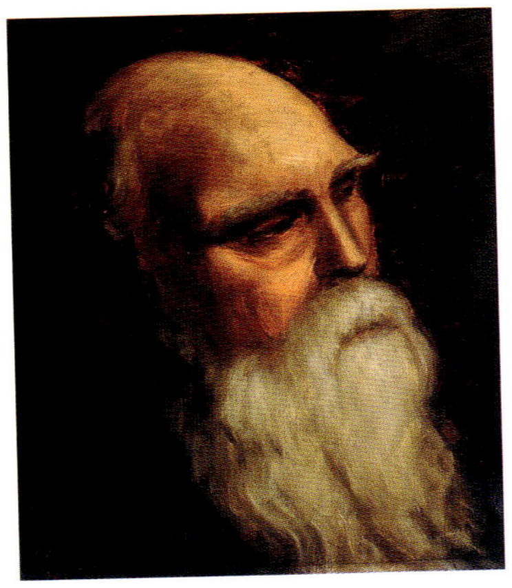

Lindley, W.
Reuben Hallam (1818–1908) 1888
oil on canvas 95.3 x 54.9
K1913.158

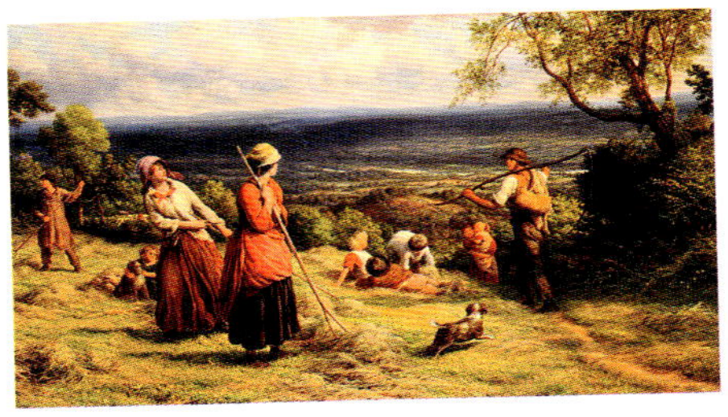

Linnell, James Thomas 1826–1905
The Haymakers 1862
oil on canvas 87.5 x 150
VIS.1592

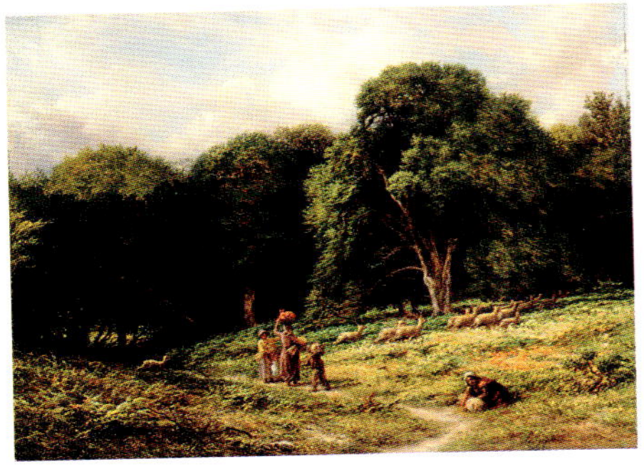

Linnell, James Thomas 1826–1905
Knole Park, Kent 1875
oil on canvas 40.4 x 53.8
VIS.566

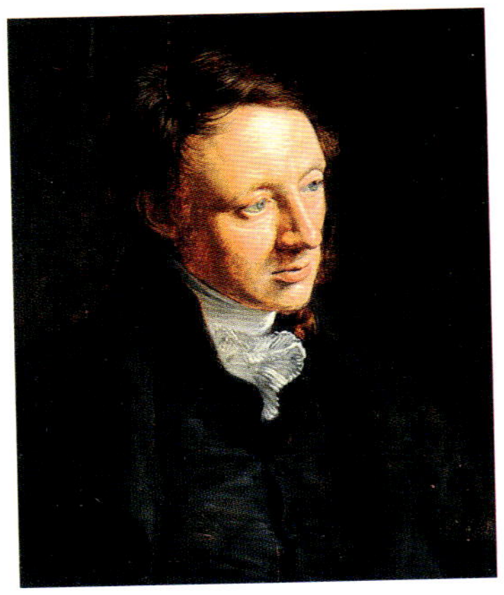

Linnell, John 1792–1882
Portrait of a Man (possibly W. J. White, the Engraver) 1816
oil on panel 19 x 15.8
VIS.32

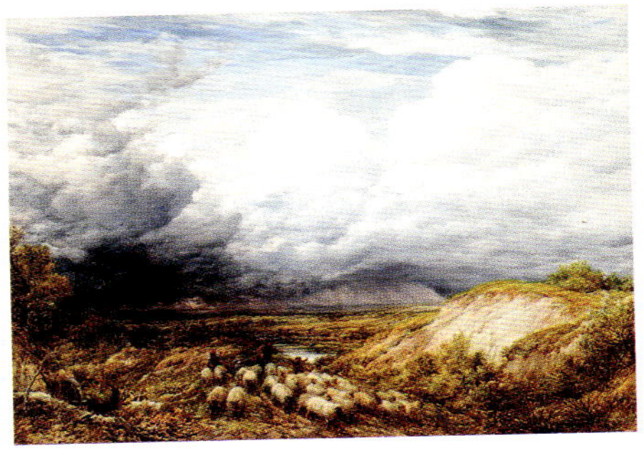

Linnell, John 1792–1882
Landscape with Sheep 1869
oil on canvas 70.1 x 97.8
VIS.1618

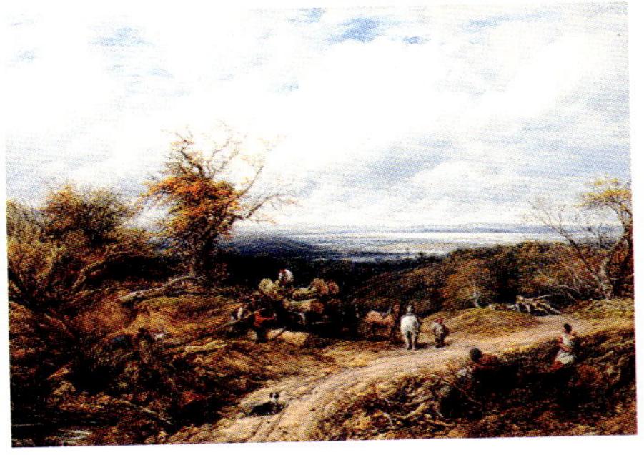

Linnell, John 1792–1882
The Timber Wagon 1871
oil on canvas 104.5 x 132.3
VIS.1418

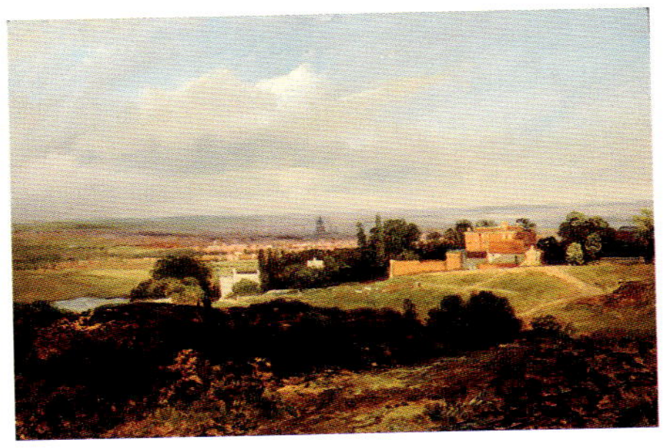

Linnell, John 1792–1882
A View of Hampstead Heath, London
oil on panel 23.5 x 35.1
VIS.351

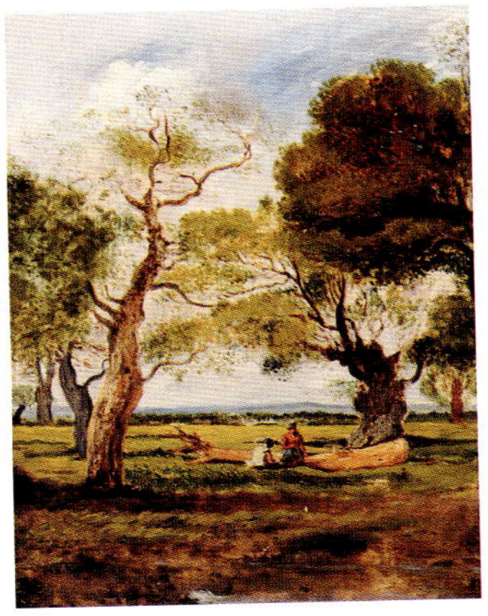

Linnell, John 1792–1882
In Windsor Forest, Berkshire
oil on panel 20.8 x 16.5
VIS.45

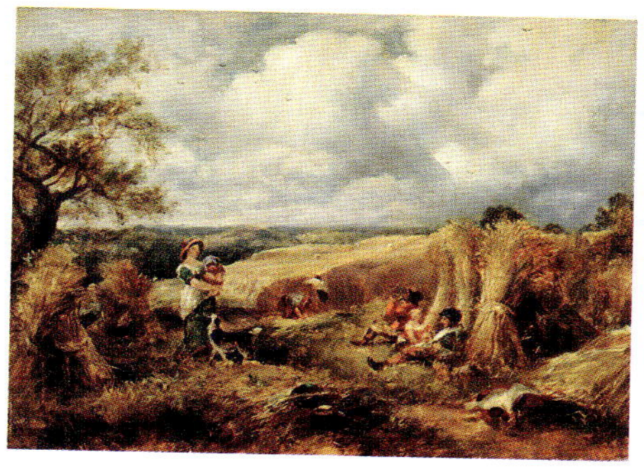

Linnell, John 1792–1882
Rest Time
oil on panel 33.4 x 44.8
VIS.267

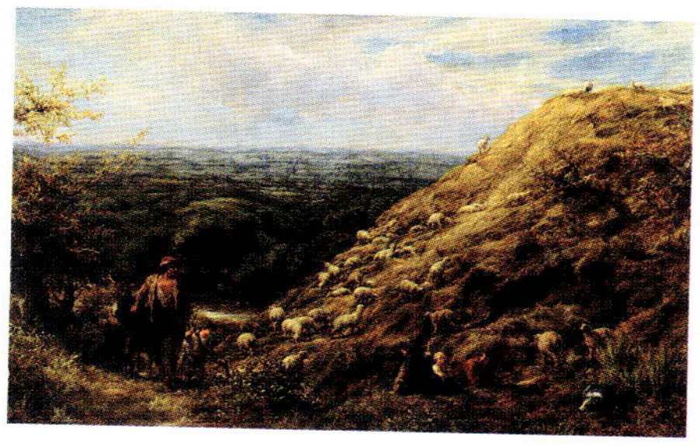

Linnell, William 1826–1906
'Where the nibbling flocks do stray' 1857
oil on canvas 101 x 156.4
VIS.1595

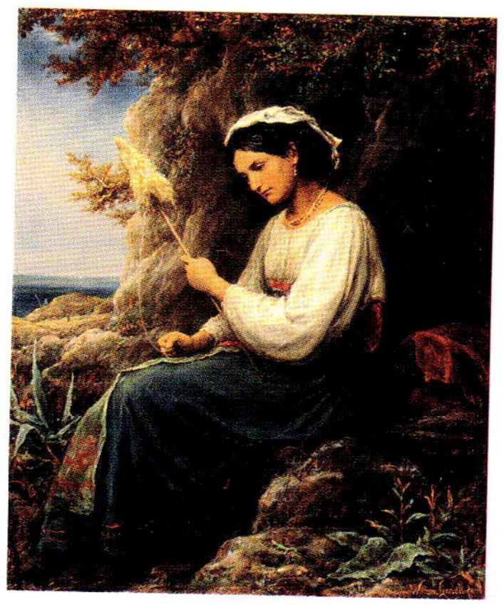

Linnell, William 1826–1906
The Distaff 1868
oil on canvas 41.6 x 33.3
VIS.1367

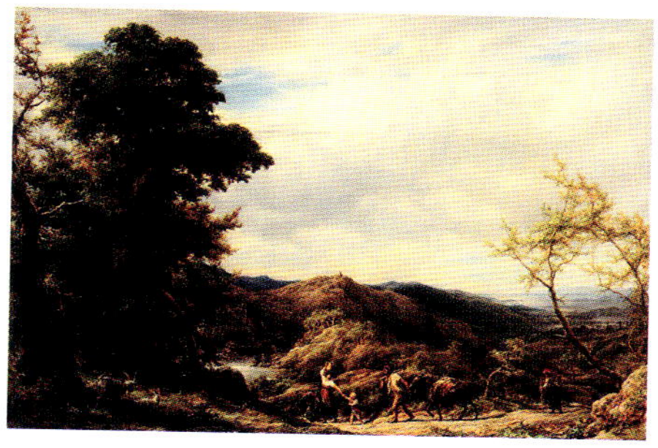

Linnell, William 1826–1906
In viaggio 1875
oil on canvas 68 x 98
VIS.1428

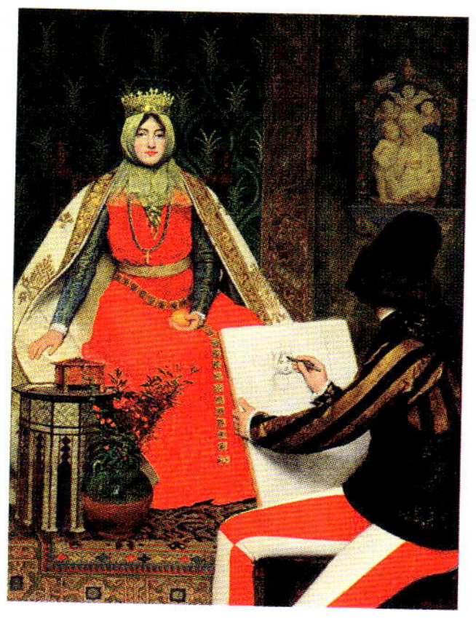

Linton, James Dromgole 1840–1916
Queen Elizabeth of Hungary and the Court Painter c.1910
oil on canvas 52.4 x 38.8
VIS.9

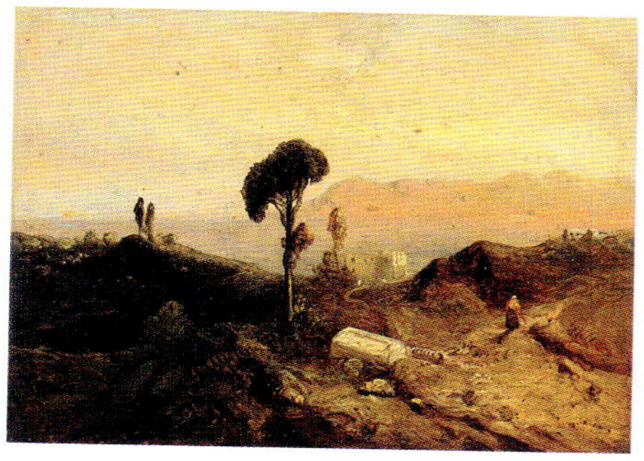

Linton, William 1791–1876
Italian Landscape
oil on canvas 20.5 x 28
VIS.1048

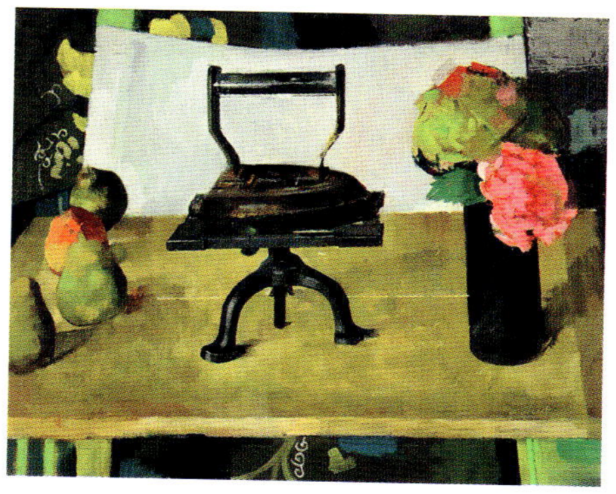

Lisle, Frank 1916–1986
Flat Iron
oil on canvas 39.6 x 49.4
VIS.4968

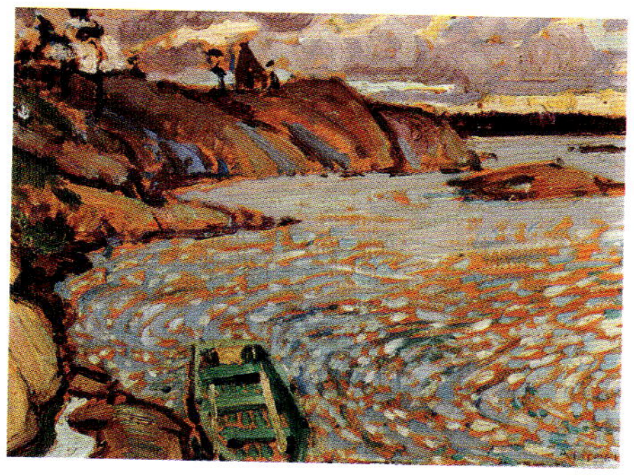

Lismer, Arthur 1885–1969
Little Seaboat
oil on panel 21.3 x 29.2
VIS.1708

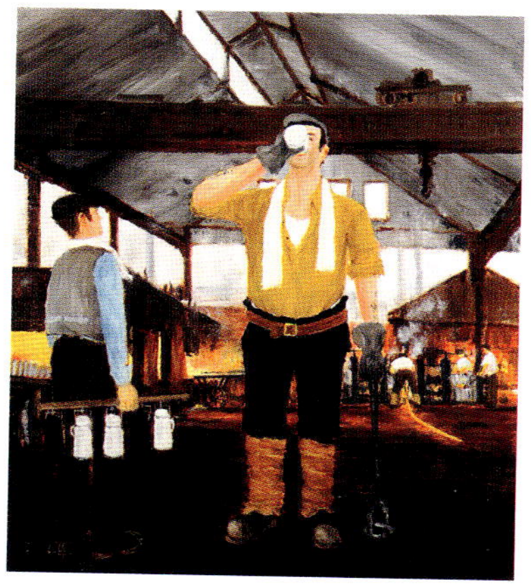

Little, Douglas Patrick active 1981–1985
The Philadelphian (Interior of a Strip Mill at Shalesmoor, Sheffield) 1981
oil on panel 39 x 34.5
1985.563

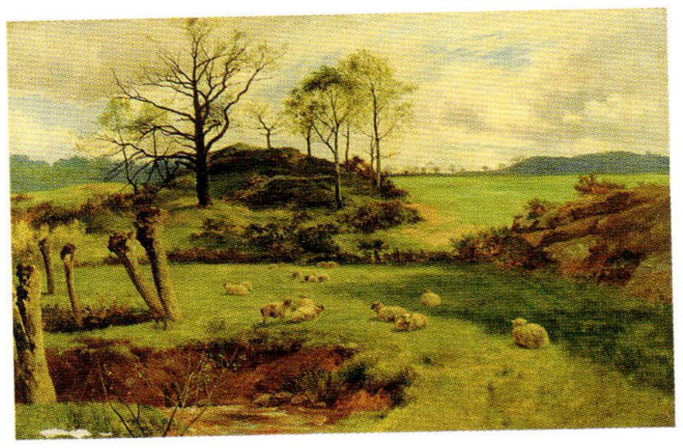

Lloyd, Stuart active 1875–1929
Sheep in Pasture 1887
oil on canvas 59.5 x 90
VIS.1339

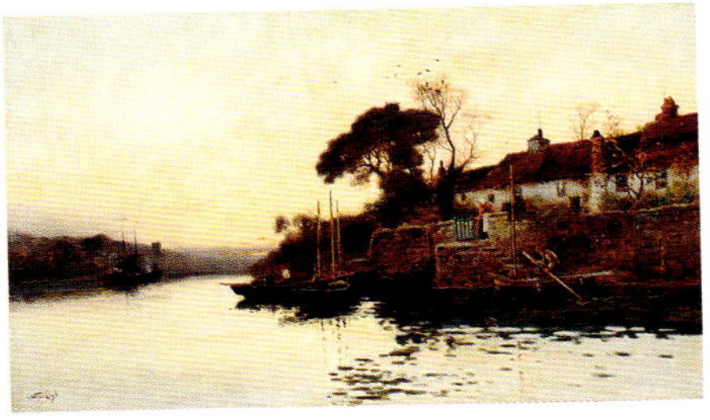

Lloyd, Stuart active 1875–1929
On the Stour
oil on canvas 76.9 x 127.2
VIS.617

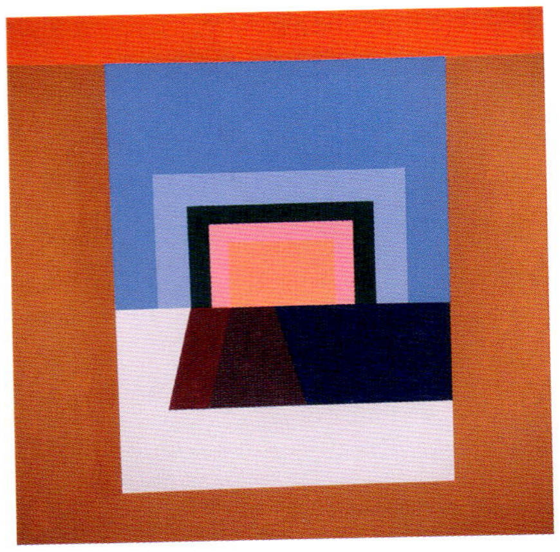

Lloyd-Jones, Peter 1940–2001
Early Theme 1968
oil on canvas 99.7 x 99.7
VIS.3720

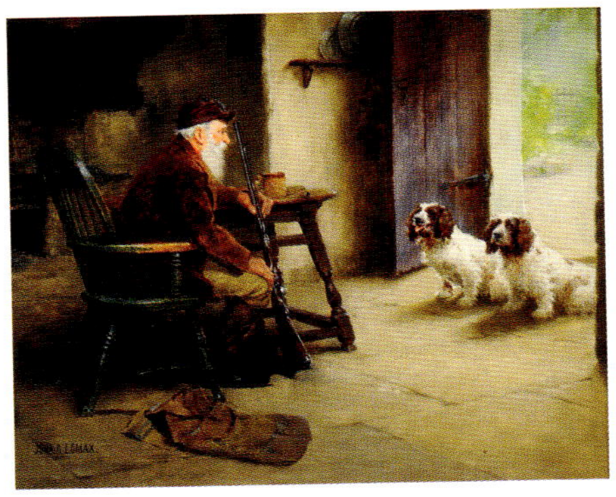

Lomax, John Arthur 1857–1923
Aren't You Ready?
oil on panel 24.5 x 29.2
VIS.1862

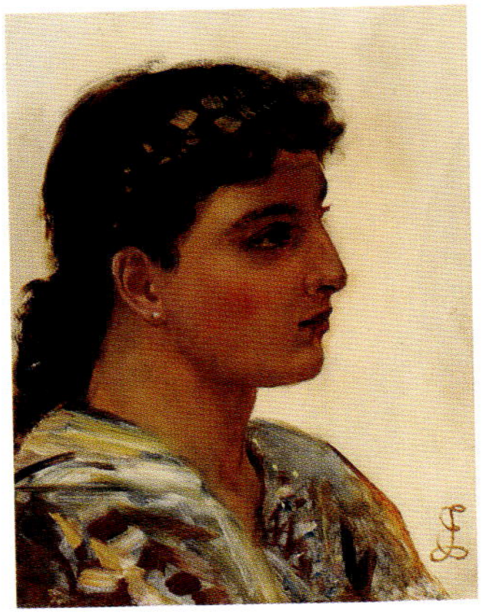

Long, Edwin 1829–1891
Princess Helen Randis Singh
oil on canvas 31.2 x 24.1
VIS.1239

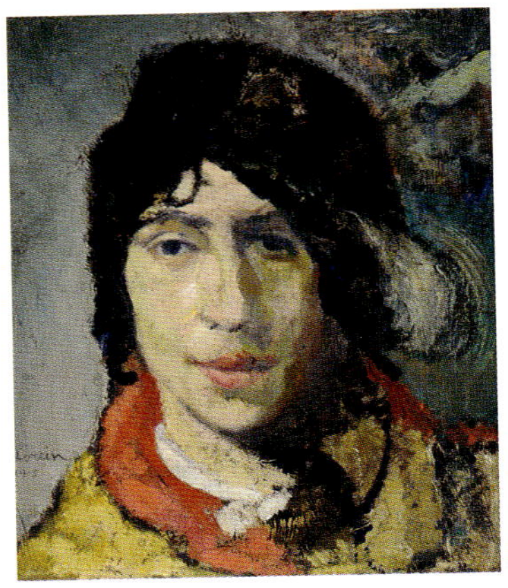

Lorein, Victor 1894–1954
Portrait of the Artist 1915
oil on canvas 34.9 x 30
VIS.726

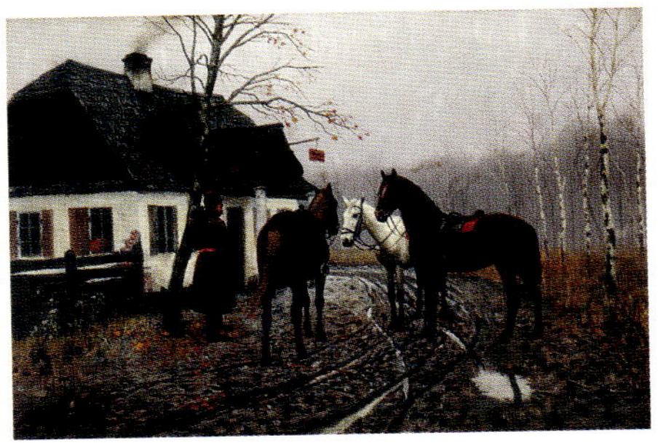

Los, Waldermar 1849–1888
The Outpost 1885
oil on canvas 31.5 x 46.7
VIS.673

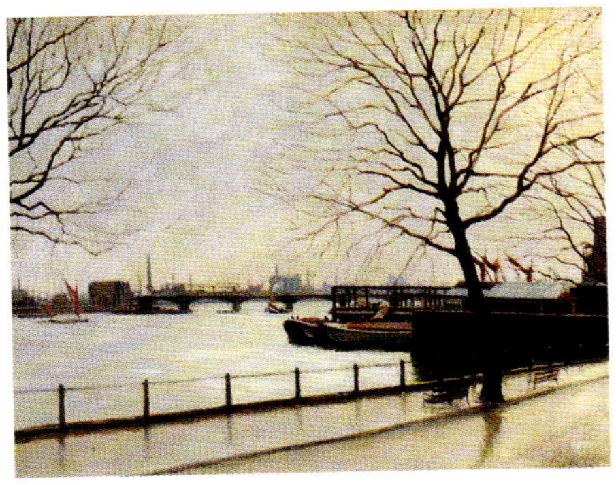

Lotz, H. J.
Battersea Reach, London
oil on canvas 59.7 x 74.4
VIS.660

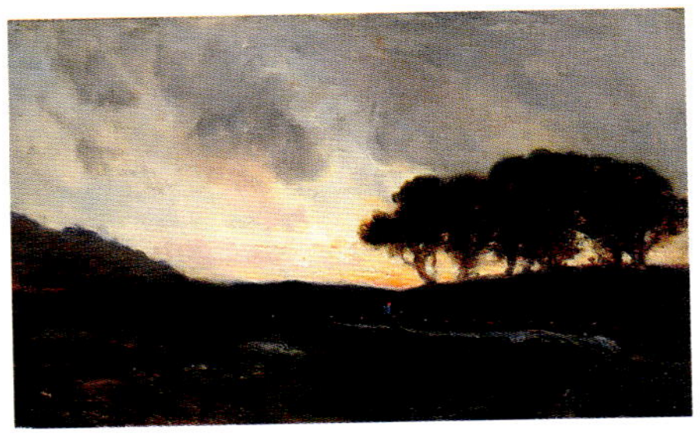

Loudin, H. D.
An Evening View
oil on canvas 24.5 x 39.9
VIS.1060

Facing page: Pope, Alexander, 1849–1924, *Still Life (Sporting Equipment)* (detail), Museums Sheffield, (p. 171)

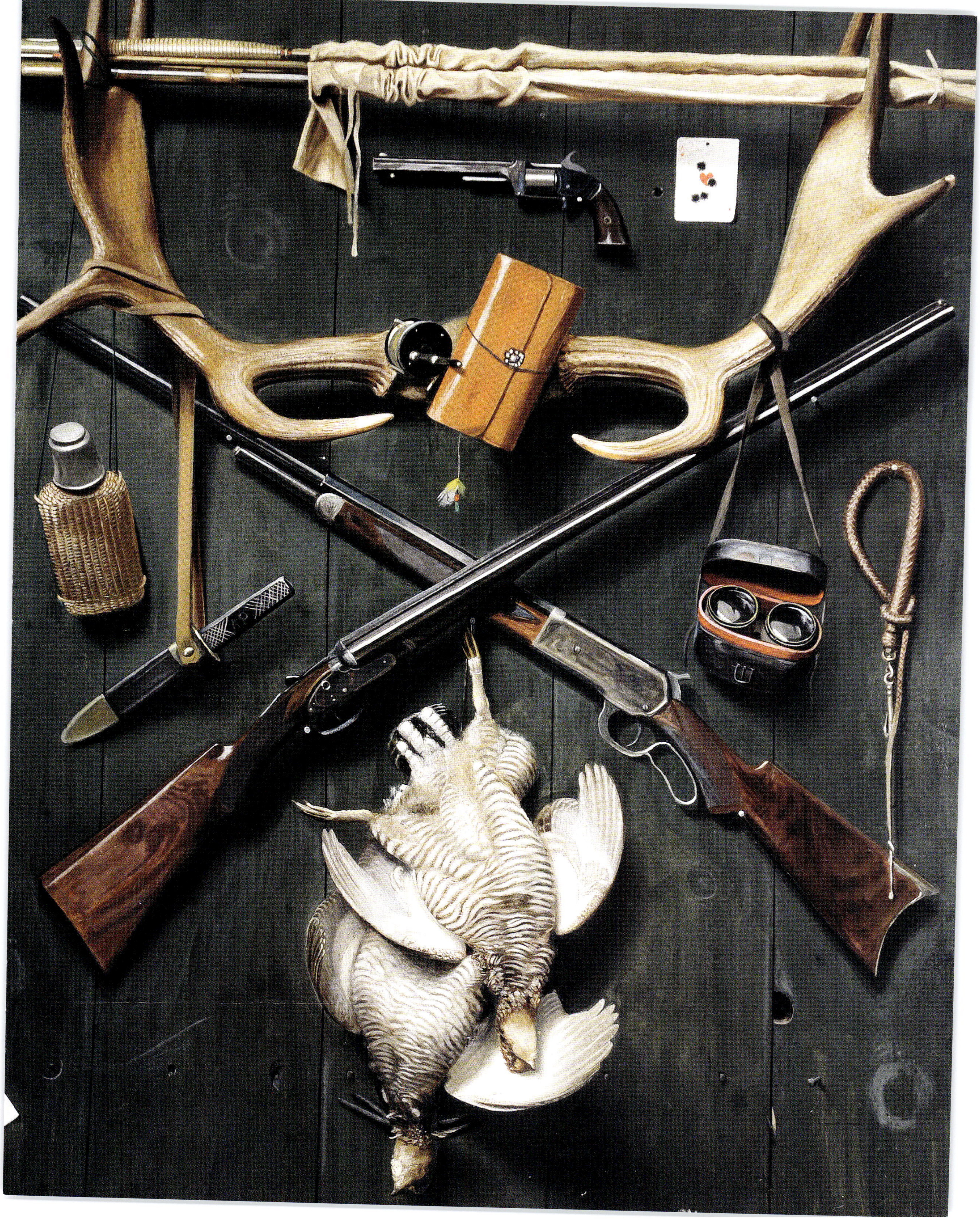

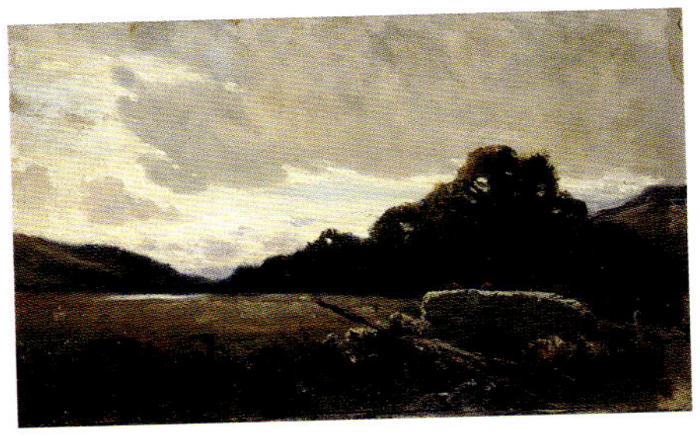

Loudin, H. D.
The Storm Cloud
oil on canvas 24.6 x 39.5
VIS.690

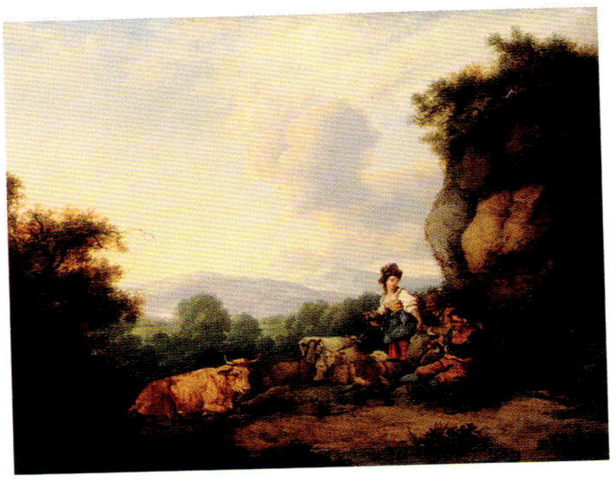

Loutherbourg, Philip James de 1740–1812
Landscape with Shepherds 1803
oil on canvas 58.9 x 74.2
VIS.841

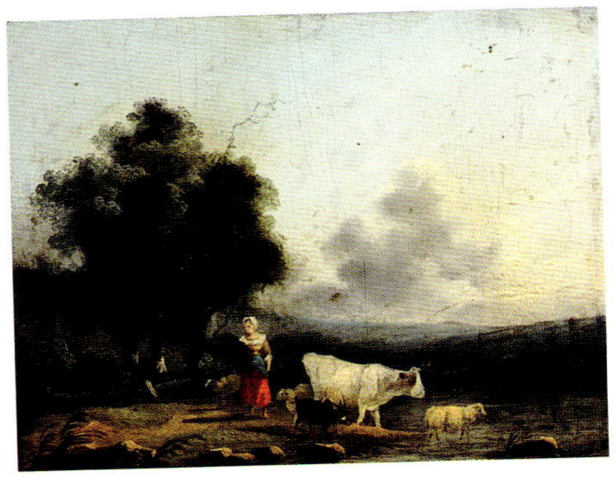

Loutherbourg, Philip James de 1740–1812
Landscape
oil on panel 12.5 x 16
VIS.62

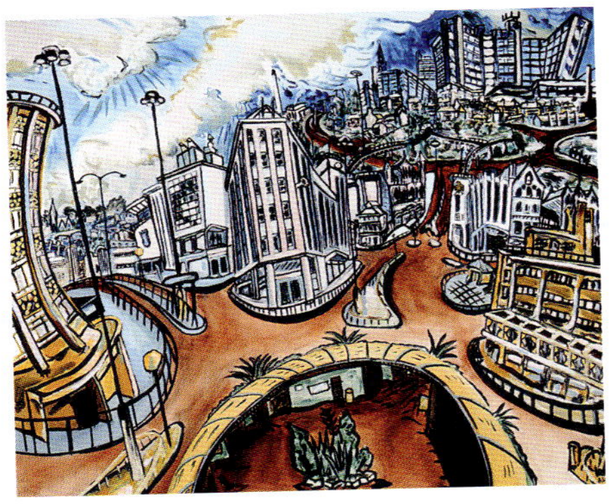

Lowe, Anthony b.1957
Hole in the Road, Sheffield 1986
oil on canvas 145.6 x 172.5
VIS.5415

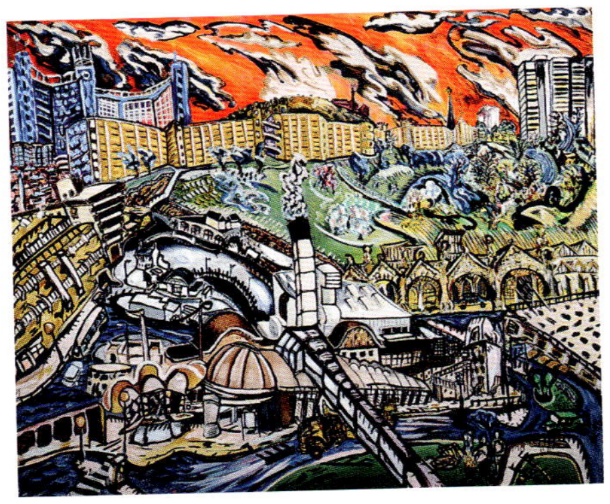

Lowe, Anthony b.1957
Pond Street Bus Station, Sheffield 1986
oil on canvas 146.1 x 172.8
VIS.5421

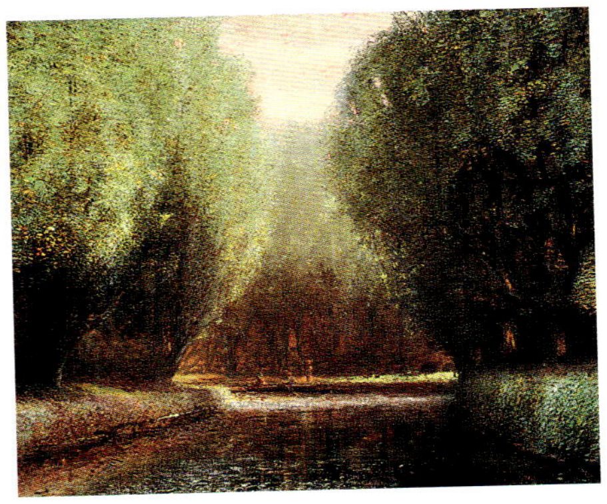

Lowe, Arthur 1866–1940
The Canal Bend
oil on panel 64.3 x 75.8
VIS.2375

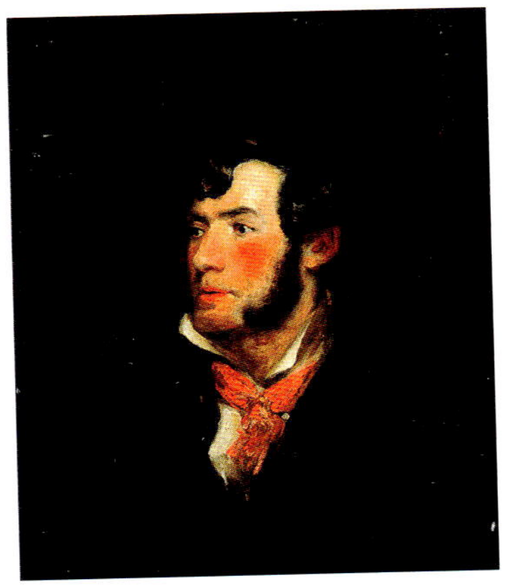

Lowe, David active 19th C
Portrait of a Man
oil on canvas 60.7 x 50.3
VIS.2721

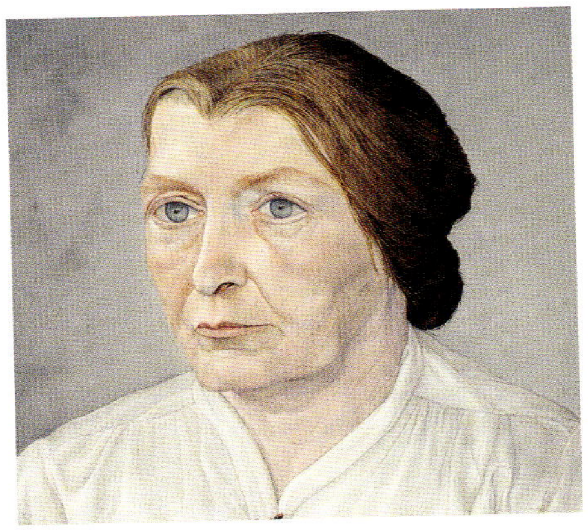

Lowinsky, Thomas Esmond 1892–1947
Miss Cicely Hamilton (1872–1952) 1926
oil on canvas 36 x 38.8
VIS.1861

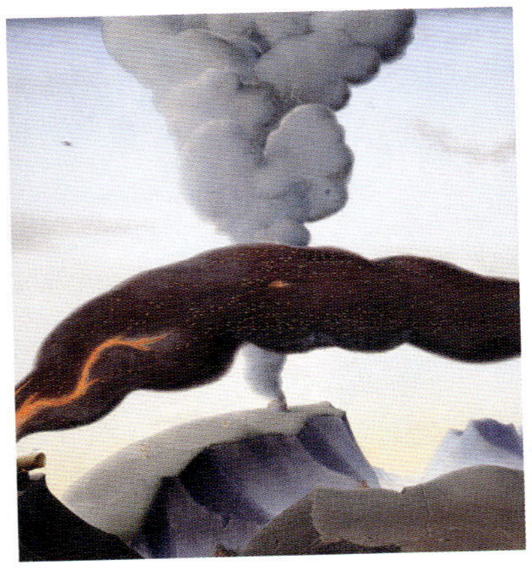

Lowinsky, Thomas Esmond 1892–1947
The Offering of Cain and Offering of Abel 1932
oil on canvas 52.2 x 49
VIS.1797

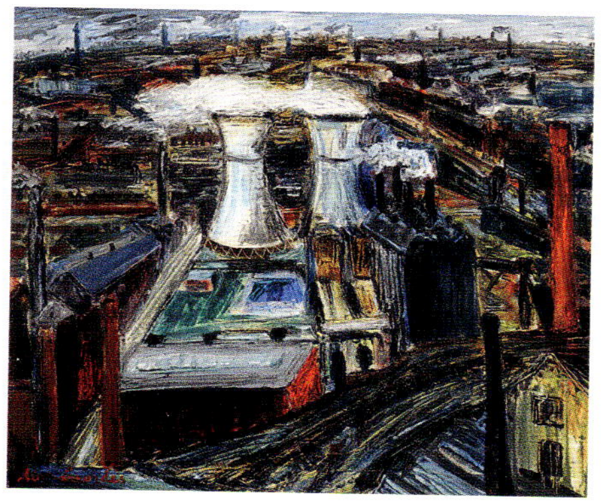

Lowndes, Alan 1921–1978
Halifax, West Yorkshire 1953
oil on canvas 59 x 68.9
VIS.5192

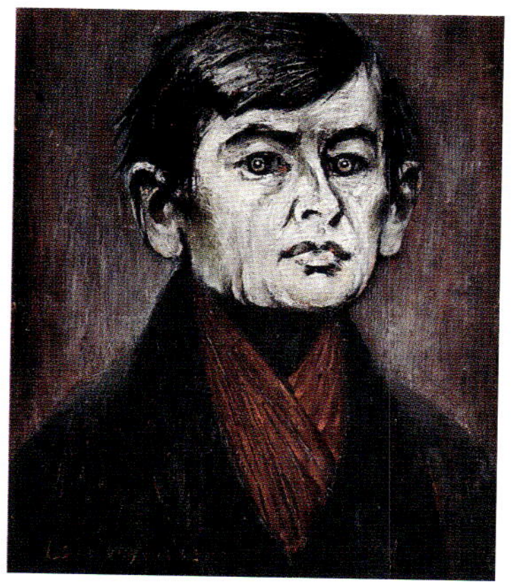

Lowry, Laurence Stephen 1887–1976
Fire Watcher (recto) 1943
oil on panel 65 x 56.5
VIS.2803

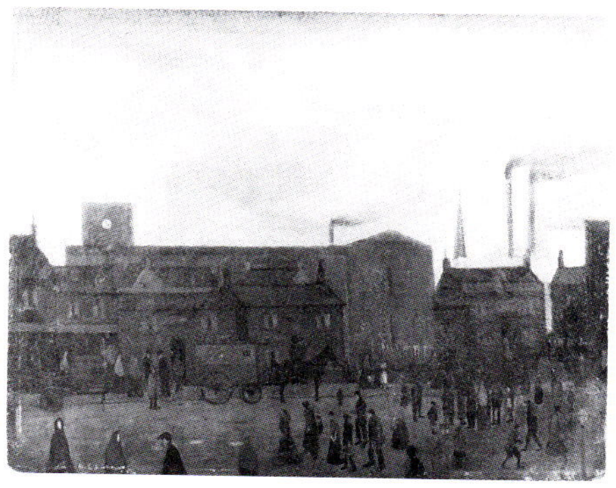

Lowry, Laurence Stephen 1887–1976
Street Scene (verso) c.1925
oil on panel 56.5 x 65
VIS.2803VERSO

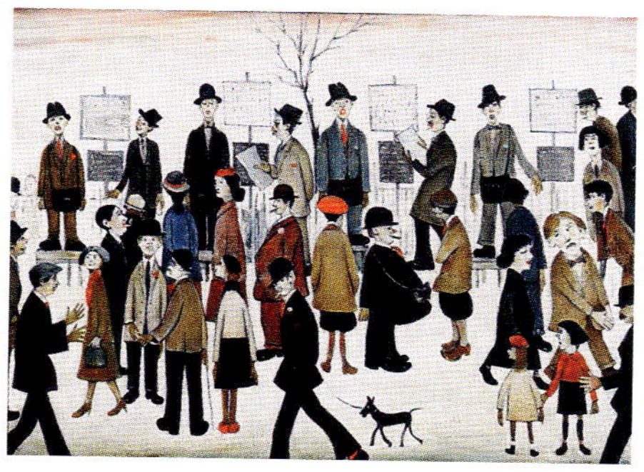

Lowry, Laurence Stephen 1887–1976
Northern Race Meeting c.1950
oil on canvas 75 x 100.6
VIS.LI.905 (P)

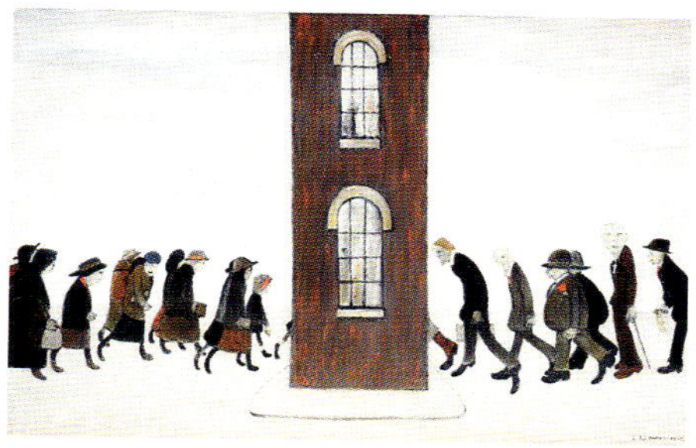

Lowry, Laurence Stephen 1887–1976
Meeting Point 1965
oil on canvas 64 x 89.6
VIS.LI.508 (P)

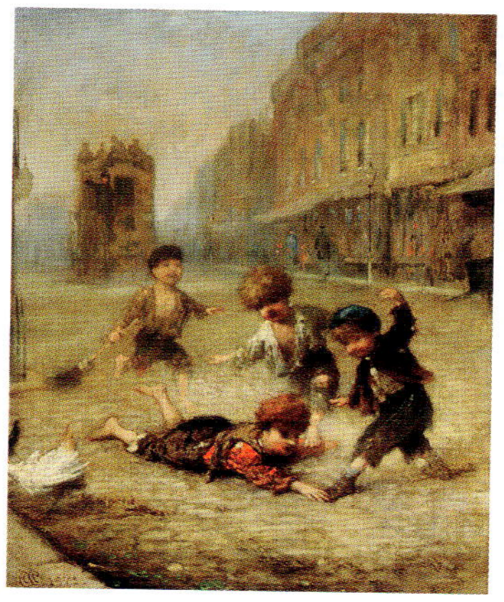

Ludovici, Albert 1852–1932
London Street Arabs Struggling for a Coin 1872
oil on canvas 33 x 27.5
VIS.140

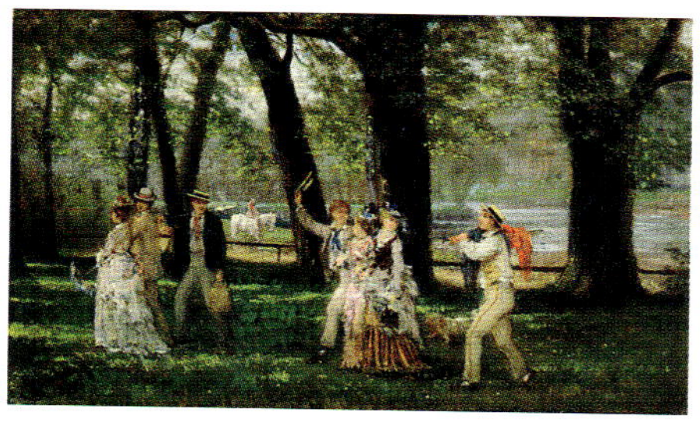

Ludovici, Albert 1852–1932
The Picnic Party 1875
oil on panel 26.8 x 44.3
VIS.669

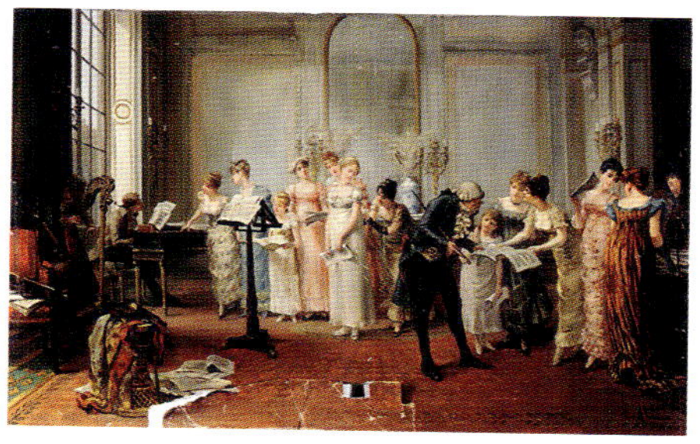

Ludovici, Albert 1852–1932
The Dancing Lesson
oil on canvas 78 x 118
VIS.4573

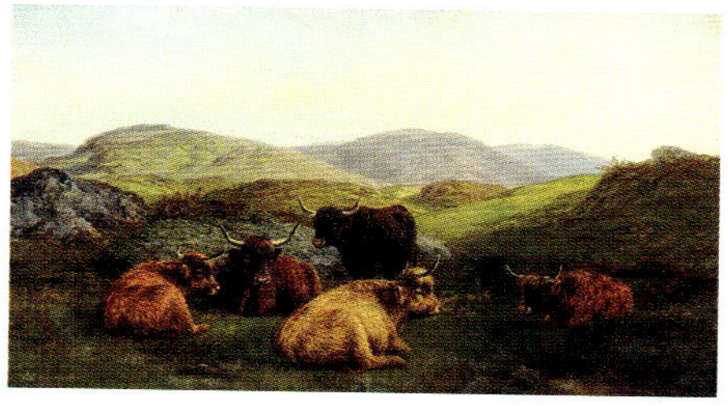

Luker, William 1828–1892
Aberfoyle, Highland Cattle
oil on paper 25 x 45
VIS.963

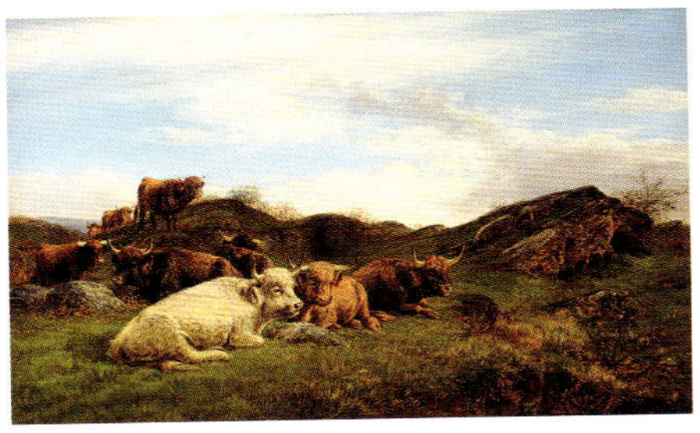

Luker, William 1828–1892
Highland Cattle
oil on canvas 49.8 x 80.4
VIS.628

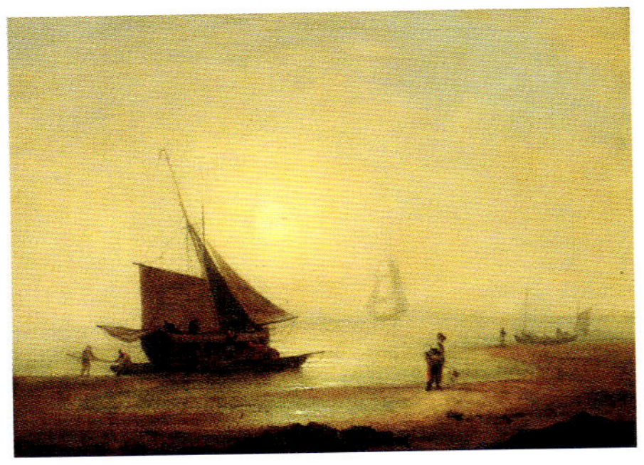

Luny, Thomas 1759–1837
Sea Piece
oil on canvas 21.9 x 29.6
VIS.1071

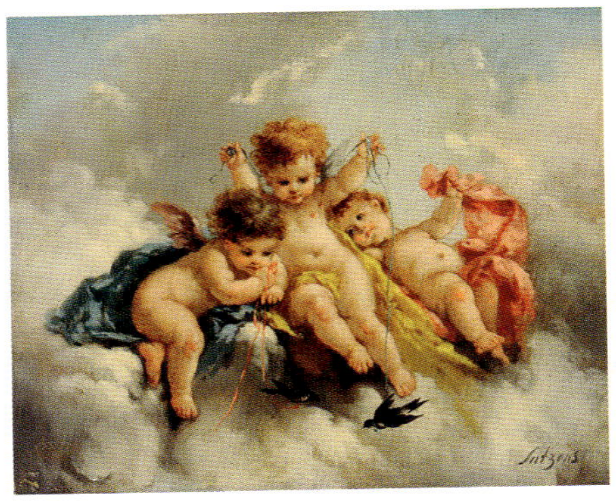

Lutzens
Cupid and Birds
oil on canvas 24.5 x 29.8
VIS.1380

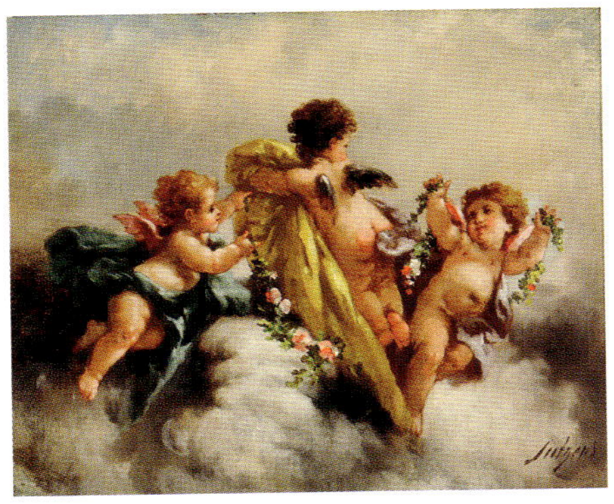

Lutzens
Cupids and Flowers
oil on canvas 24.5 x 29
VIS.1381

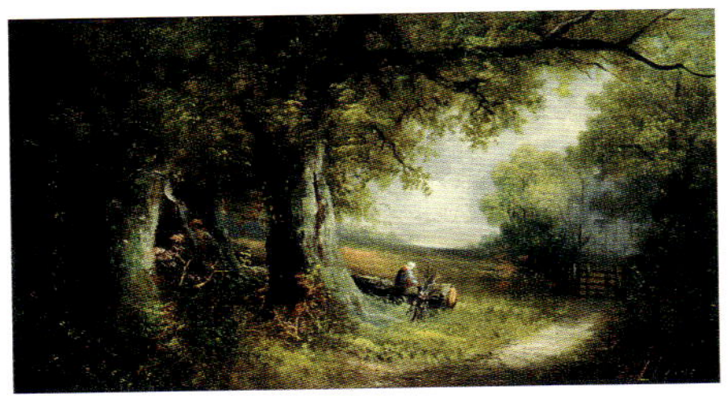

Lyons, L.
The Wood Gatherer
oil on canvas 31.8 x 57
VIS.2847

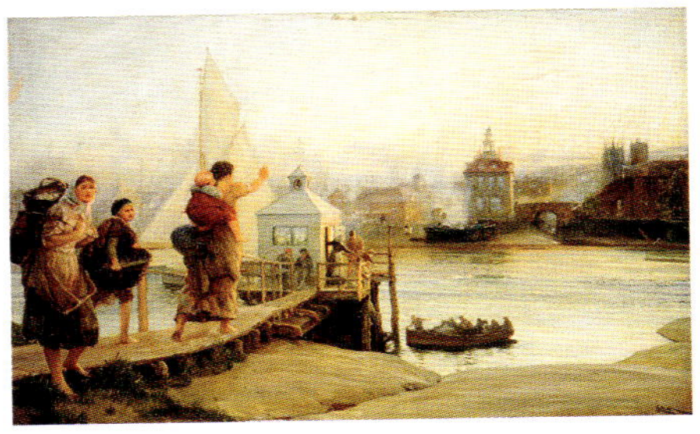

Macbeth, Robert Walker 1848–1910
Late for the Ferry, King's Lynn, Norfolk 1881
oil on canvas 36.5 x 58.4
VIS.198

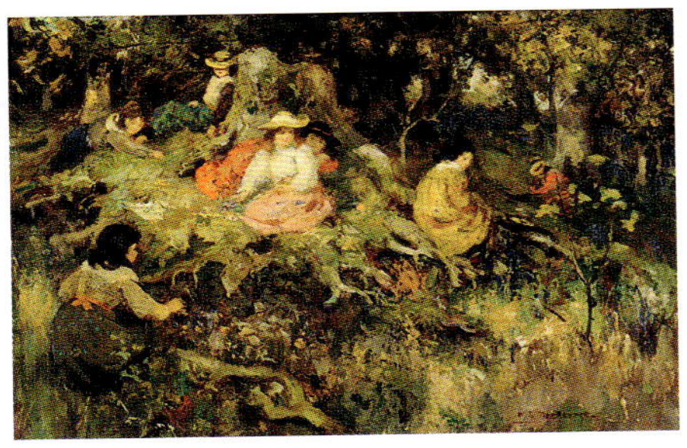

MacGeorge, William Stewart 1861–1931
A Children's Picnic
oil on panel 32.4 x 49.8
VIS.671

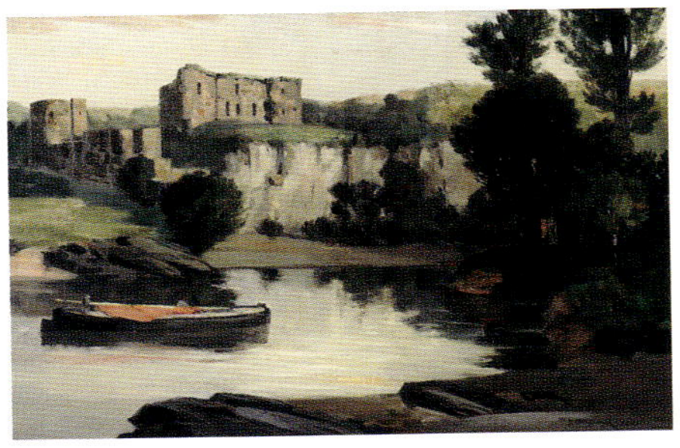

MacGregor, William York 1855–1923
Chepstow Castle, Wales 1906
oil on canvas 80.5 x 120.8
VIS.811

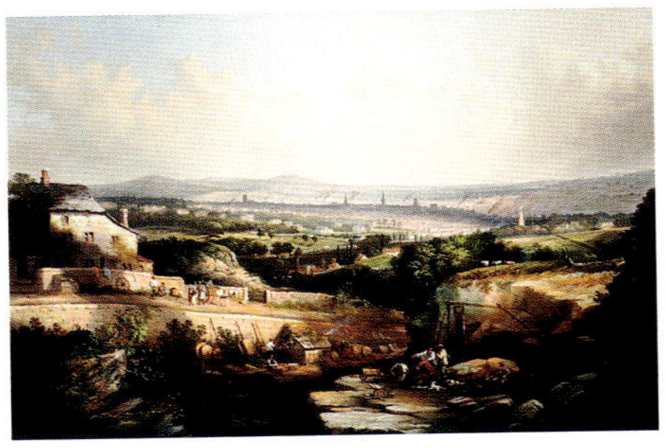

MacIntyre, James Crichton active 1867–c.1911
A View of Sheffield from Psalter Lane
oil on canvas 129.2 x 195.3
VIS.1678

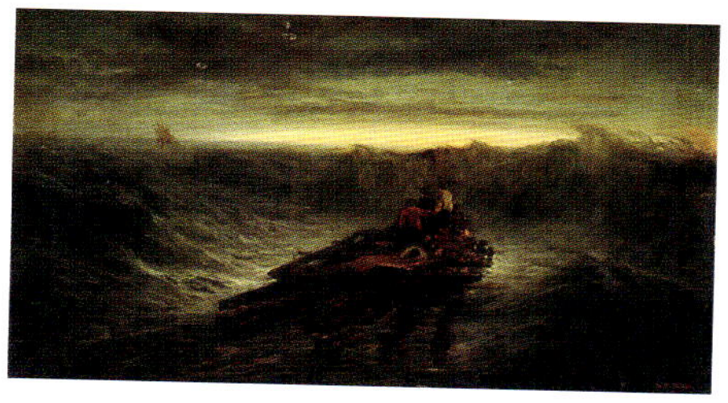

MacIntyre, Joseph Wrightson 1842–1897
A Gleam of Hope 1872
oil on canvas 42 x 75
VIS.4168

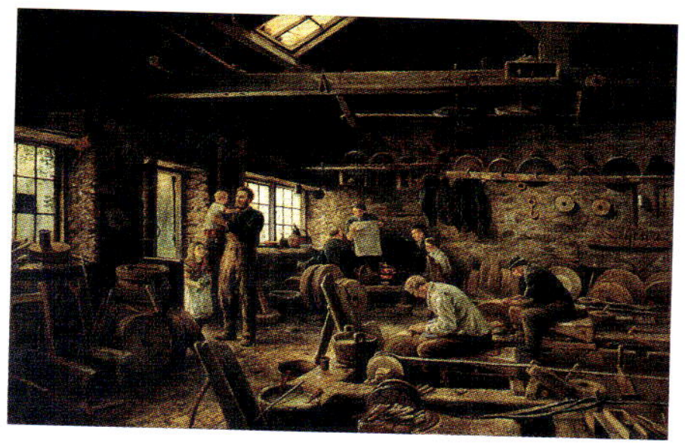

MacIntyre, Joseph Wrightson 1842–1897
Interior of Holme Head Wheel, Rivelin Valley, Sheffield 1879
oil on canvas 70 x 105.5
K1955.6

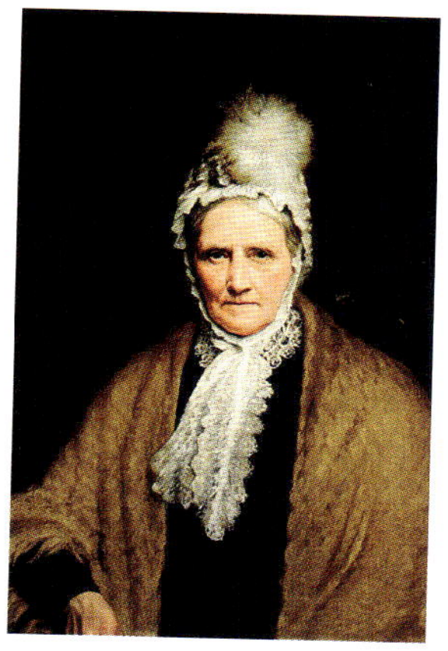

MacIntyre, Joseph Wrightson 1842–1897
Mary (Anne) Beal
oil on canvas 90.3 x 60.1
VIS.3242

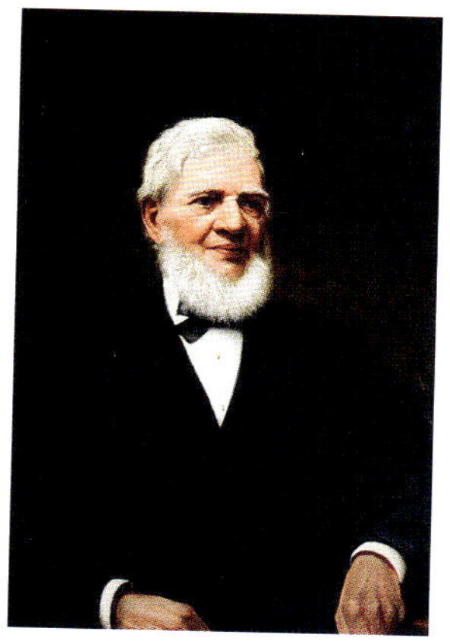

MacIntyre, Joseph Wrightson 1842–1897
Michael Beal
oil on canvas 89.5 x 59.3
VIS.3241

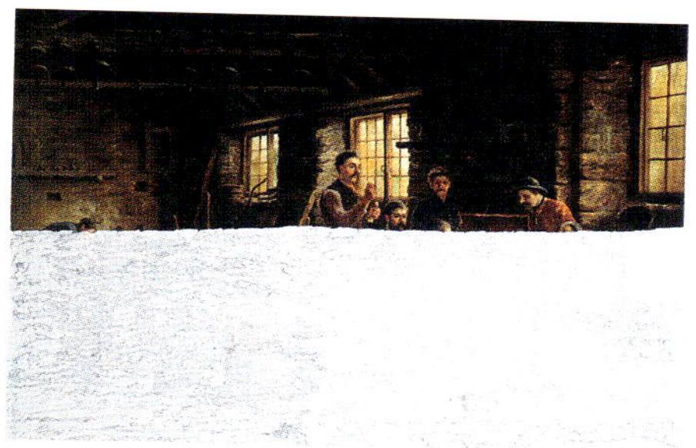

MacIntyre, Joseph Wrightson 1842–1897
Men Seated around a Fire in a Grinding Shop
oil on canvas 76.5 x 111.2
1960.28

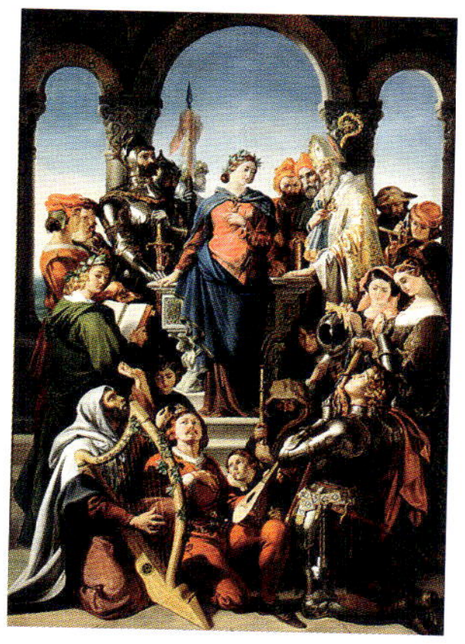

Maclise, Daniel 1806–1870
The Spirit of Chivalry c.1845
oil on canvas 125.8 x 84.8
VIS.1441

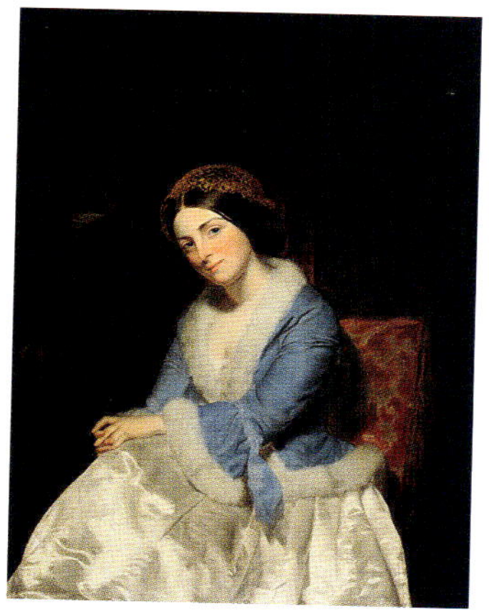

Maclise, Daniel 1806–1870
Yes or No?
oil on canvas 51.4 x 43.6
VIS.15

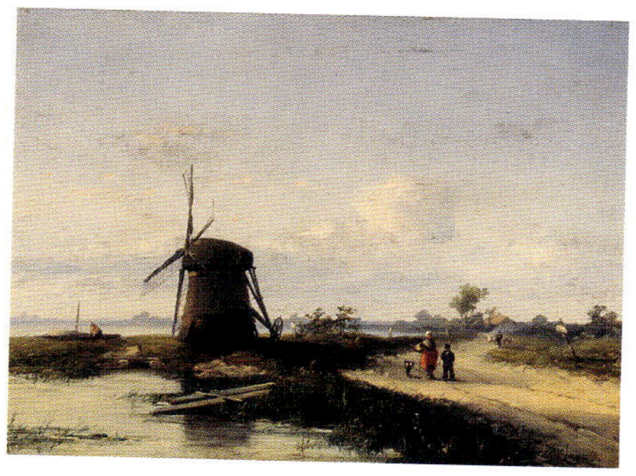

Madliner, W. J.
The Windmill 1843
oil on panel 28.2 x 37.2
VIS.1370

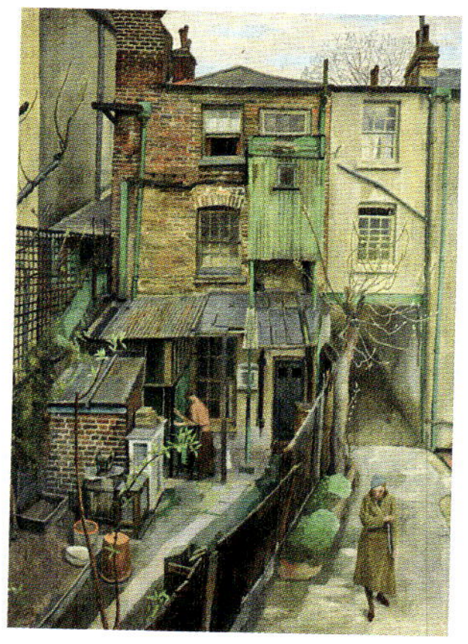

Mahoney, Charles 1903–1968
Hampstead Backs, London
oil on canvas 52.8 x 37.4
VIS.1927

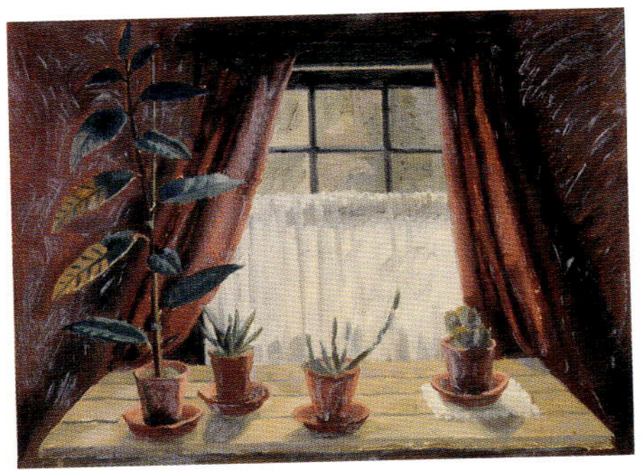

Mahoney, Charles 1903–1968
The Plant Table
oil on paper 25 x 33.4
VIS.2186

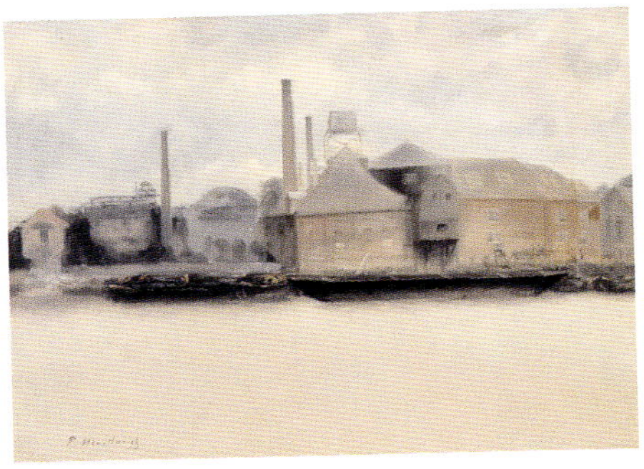

Maitland, Paul Fordyce 1863–1909
Battersea Reach, London
oil on canvas 39.3 x 54.4
VIS.129

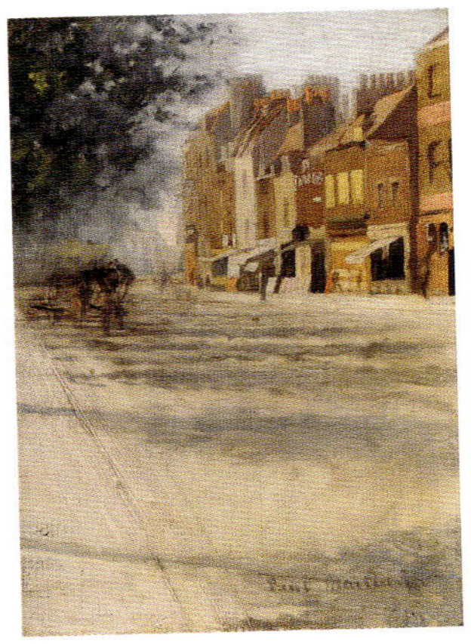

Maitland, Paul Fordyce 1863–1909
Cheyne Walk, Chelsea, London
oil on canvas 34.8 x 24.3
VIS.639

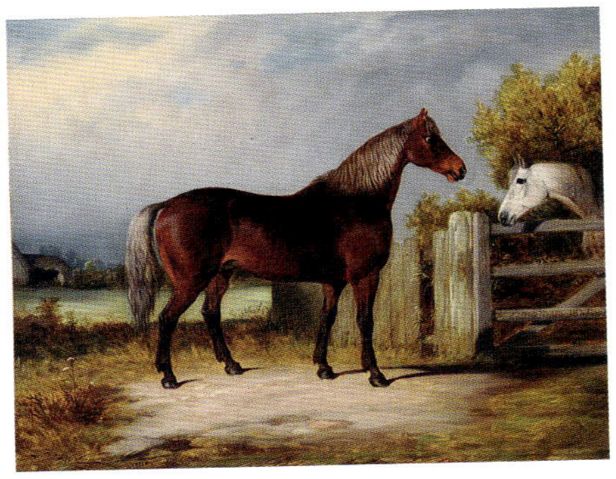

Malbon, William 1805–1877
'Samson', Sire of 'Sally' 1841
oil on canvas 52 x 64.9
VIS.3014

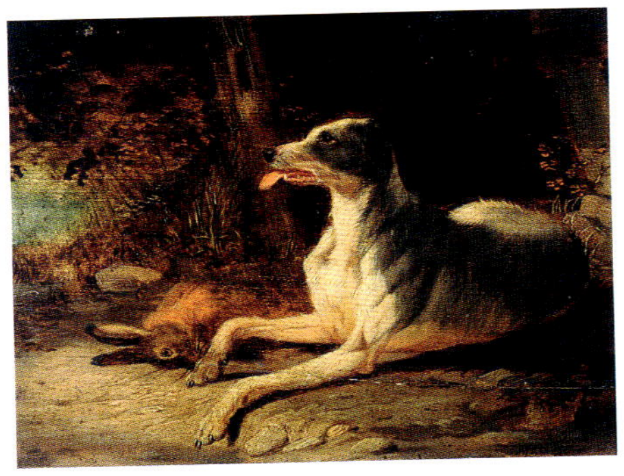

Malbon, William 1805–1877
Dog and Hare c.1850
oil on panel 17.5 x 22.8
VIS.3006

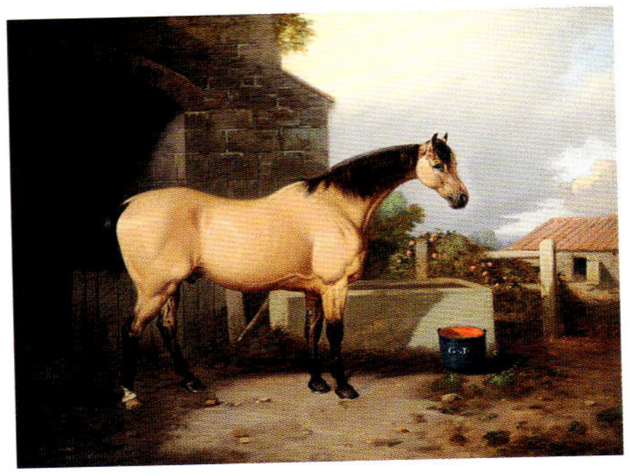

Malbon, William 1805–1877
Horse in a Stable Yard 1854
oil on canvas 69.8 x 90.5
VIS.3004

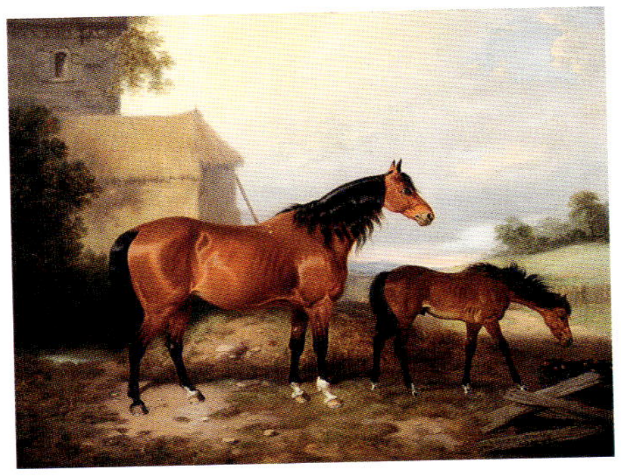

Malbon, William 1805–1877
Mare and Foal 1854
oil on canvas 70.4 x 90.7
VIS.3003

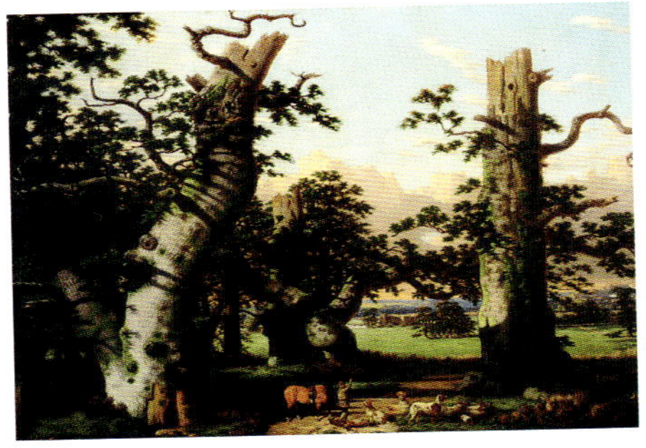

Malbon, William 1805–1877
The Sherwood Rangers 1869
oil on canvas 66.8 x 94.7
VIS.2209

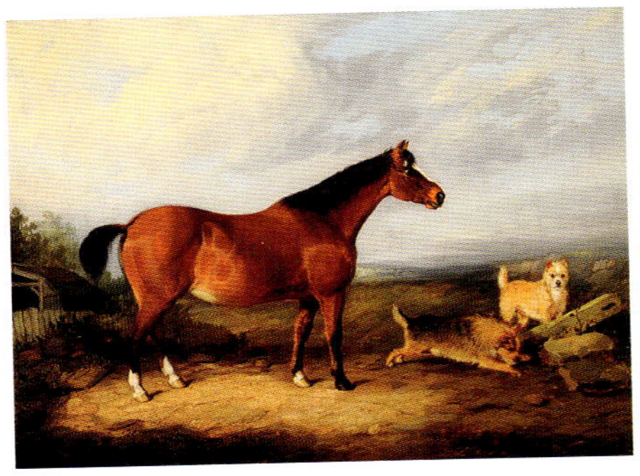

Malbon, William 1805–1877
'Sally'
oil on canvas 49.2 x 65.2
VIS.3013

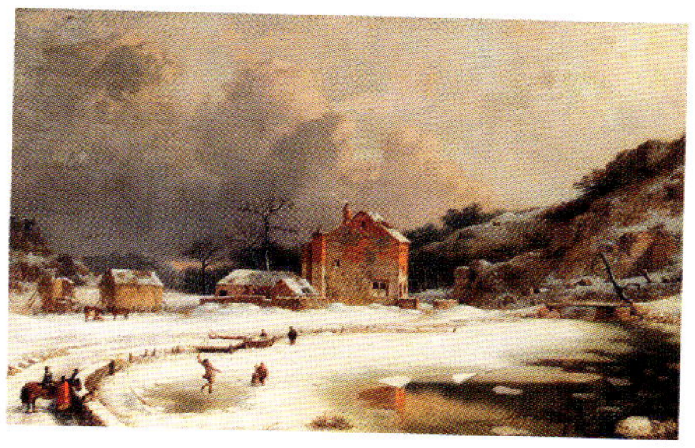

Malbon, William 1805–1877
Winter Scene
oil on panel 29.2 x 46.2
VIS.3010

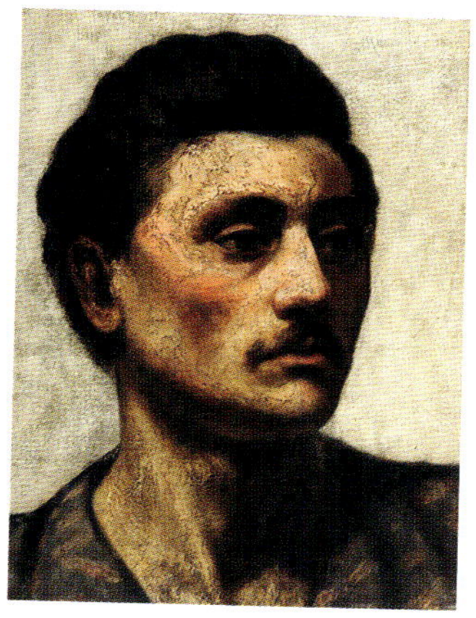

Mancini, Antonio 1852–1930
Portrait of a Man
oil on canvas 40.5 x 30.5
VIS.177

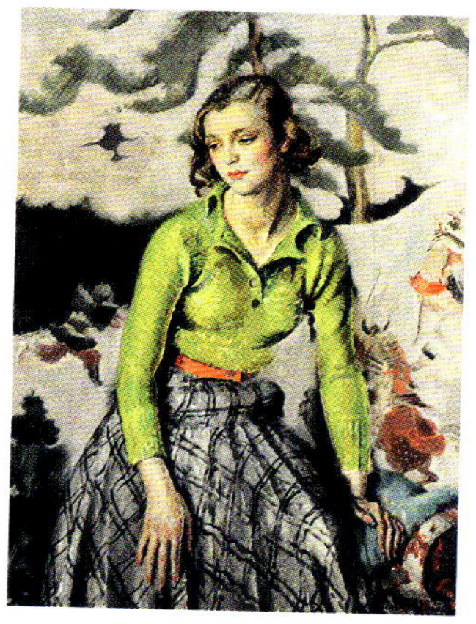

Mann, Cathleen 1896–1959
Portrait of a Lady 1931
oil on canvas 111.7 x 82.1
VIS.937

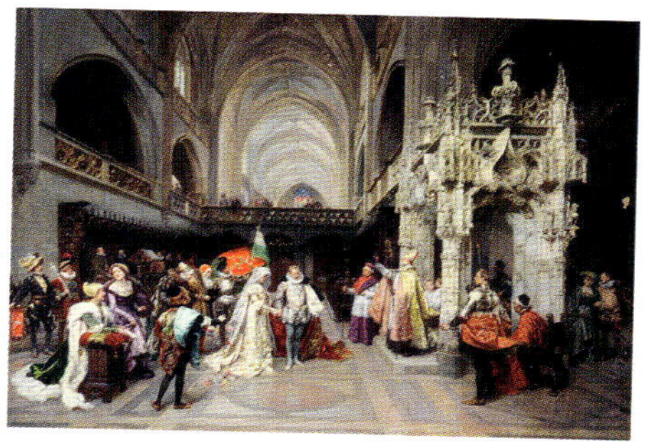

Marchetti, Ludovico 1853–1909
Ducal Wedding
oil on canvas 61.5 x 88.5
VIS.2781

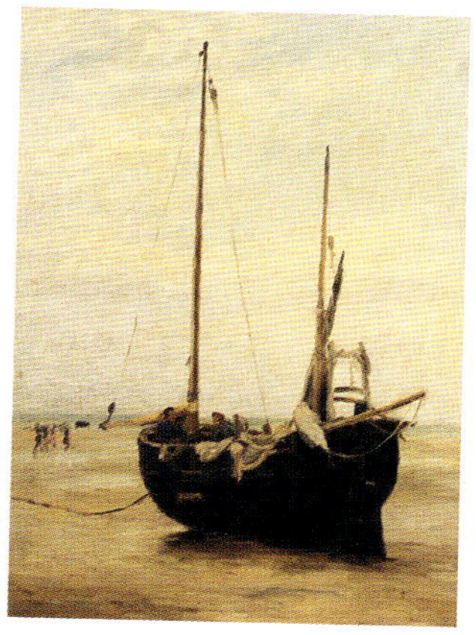

Maris, Jacob Henricus 1837–1899
Shore Scene
oil on canvas 37.2 x 26.7
VIS.1210

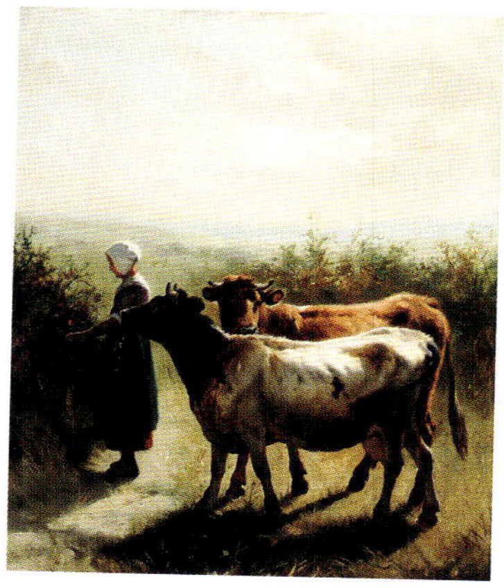

Maris, Willem 1844–1910
Cattle 1870–1880
oil on canvas 74.2 x 61.6
VIS.143

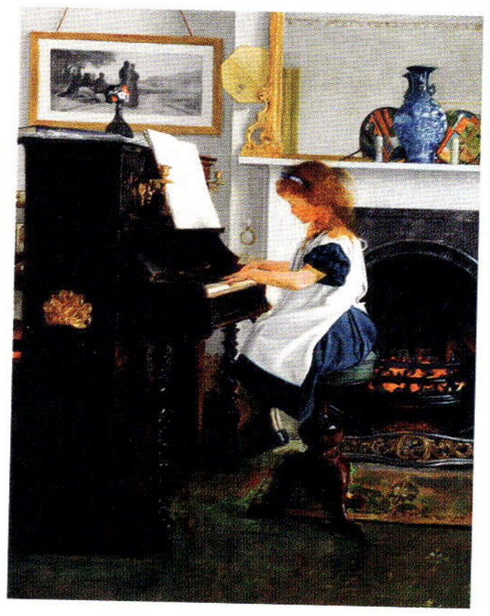

Marks, Henry Stacey 1829–1898
At the Piano
oil on canvas 67.3 x 52
VIS.557

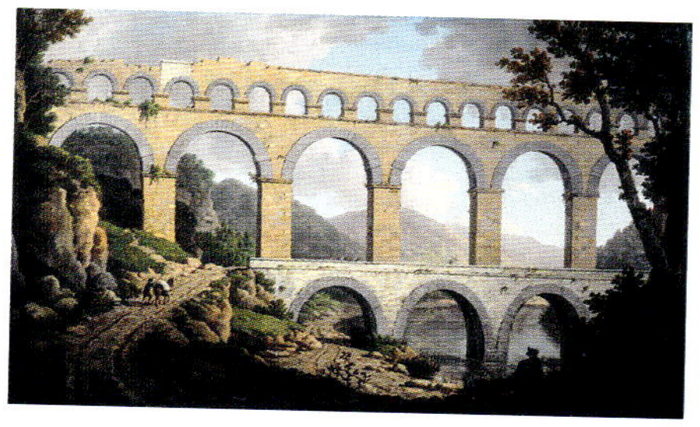

Marlow, William 1740–1813
Le pont du gard, Nimes, France
oil on canvas 94 x 142.7
VIS.2208

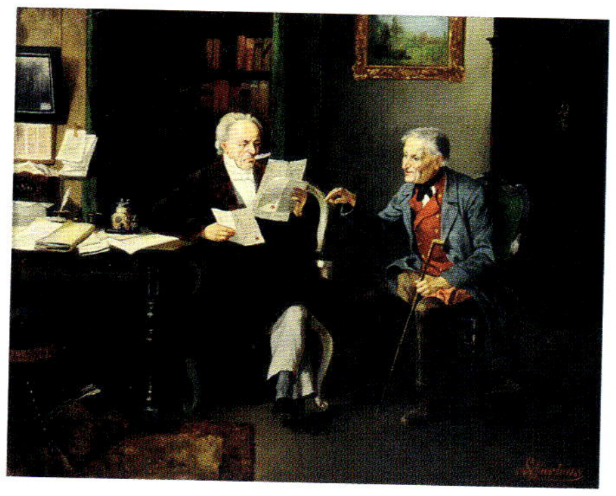

Marten, J. active 19th C
A Visit to the Lawyer
oil on canvas 54 x 66.6
VIS.702

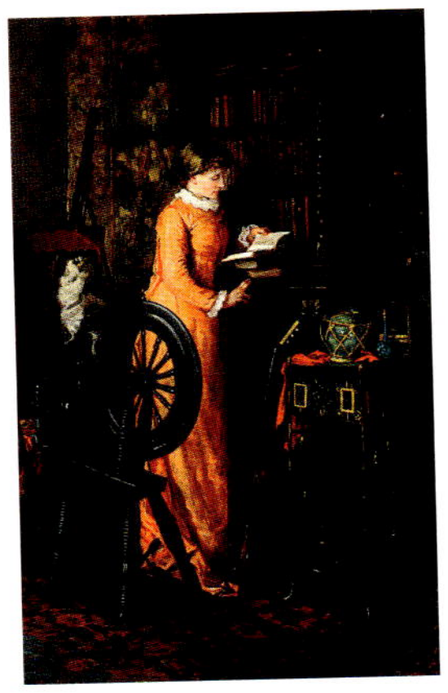

Martin, Florence b.c.1845
The Art Student 1879
oil on canvas 110.5 x 68
VIS.1466

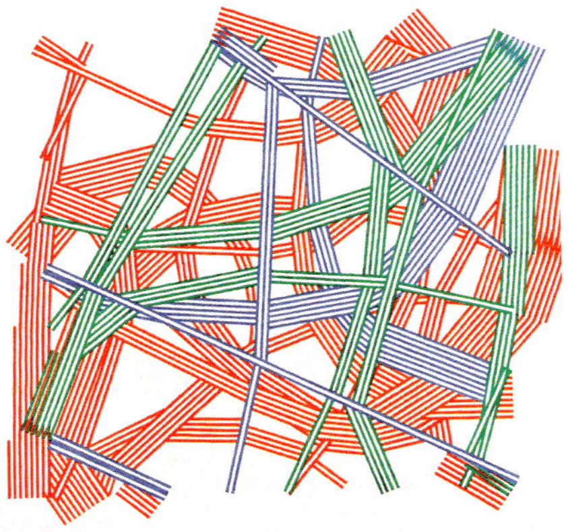

Martin, Kenneth 1905–1984
Chance, Order, Change, 24 History Painting A
1982
oil on canvas 91 x 91
VIS.5169

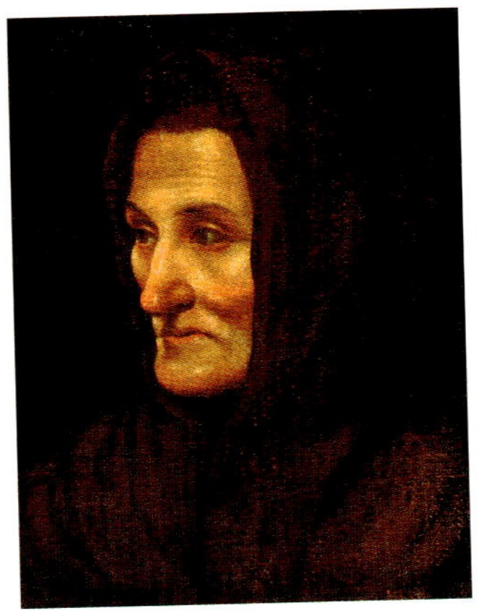

Masaccio (after) 1401–1428
Girolamo Savonarola (1452–1498)
oil on canvas 22.1 x 16.8
VIS.1010

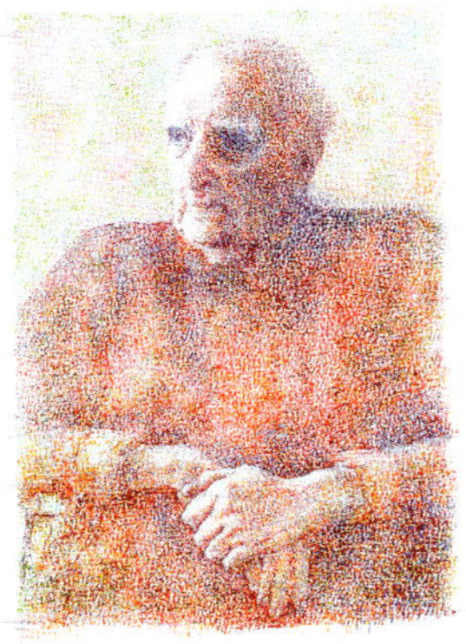

Masoero, Jeanne b.1937
Kenneth Martin (1905–1984) 1982–1983
acrylic on canvas 30.6 x 27.8
VIS.5448

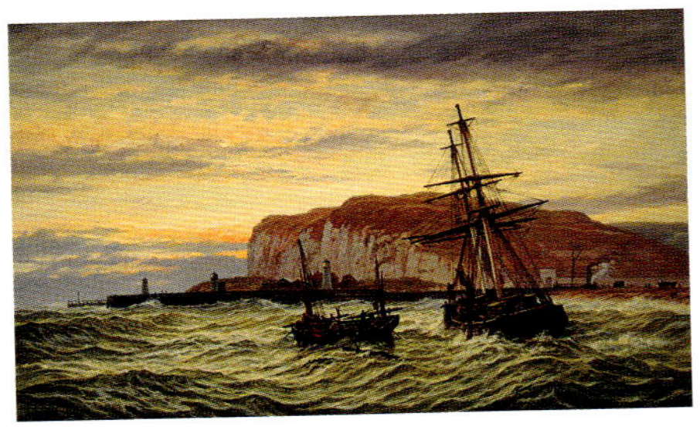

Mason, William Henry active 1858–1917
Coast Scene with Shipping 1877
oil on canvas 76.8 x 122.1
VIS.1467

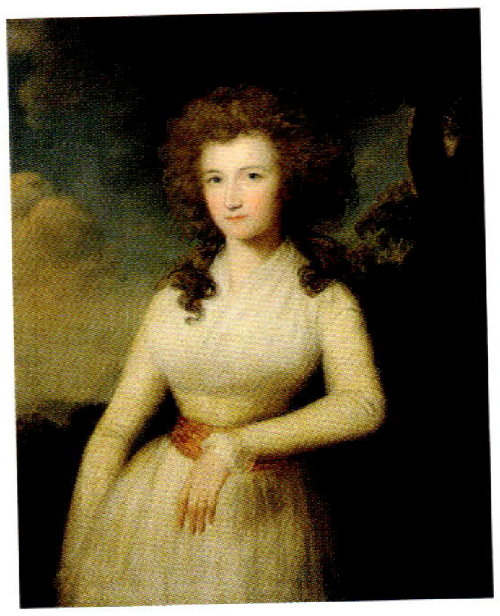

Masquerier, John James 1778–1855
Portrait of a Lady
oil on canvas 91.5 x 72.4
VIS.789

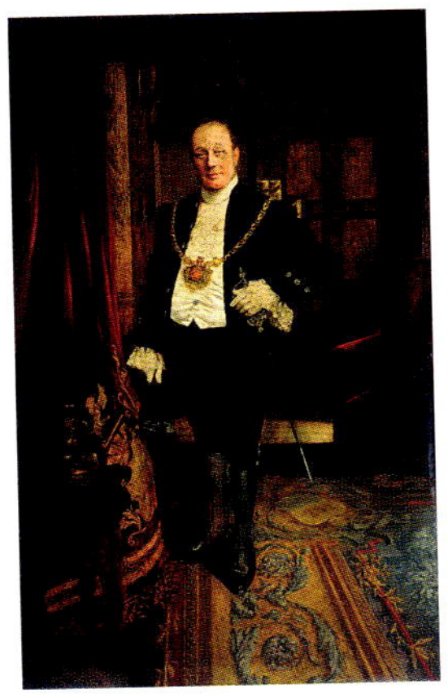

Mastin, John 1865–1932
Alderman George Senior (d.1915), JP, Lord Mayor of Sheffield (1901) 1902
oil on canvas 238.8 x 148
VIS.LI.834 (P)

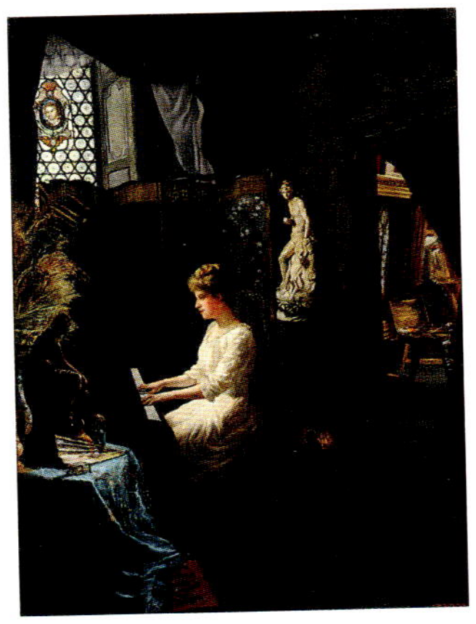

Matesdorf, Théodore (attributed to)
1849–1909
Interior 1888
oil on canvas 67.6 x 49.8
VIS.606

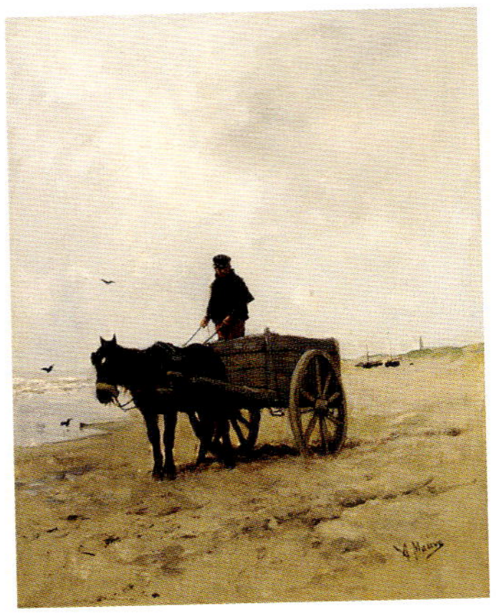

Mauve, Anton 1838–1888
On the Sea Shore 1865–1875
oil on canvas 40.8 x 32.5
VIS.1574

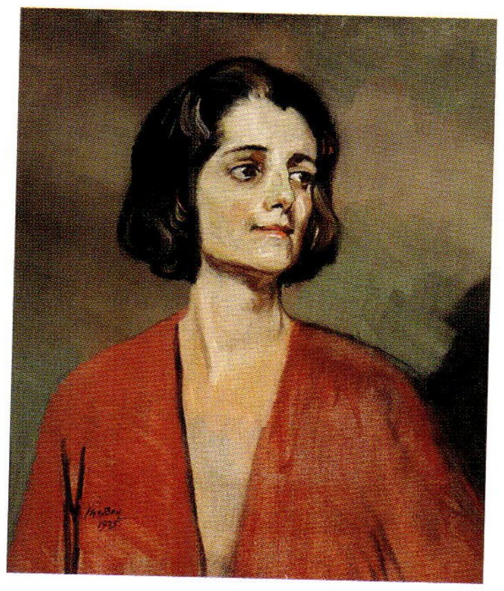

McBey, James 1883–1959
Lady in a Red Dress 1925
oil on canvas 60.5 x 49.7
VIS.629

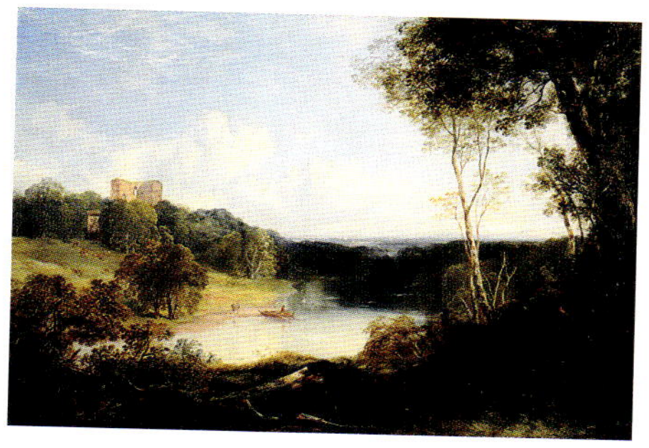

McCulloch, Horatio 1805–1867
Newark Castle Overlooking the Yarrow, Scotland
oil on canvas 62.1 x 90.3
VIS.2737

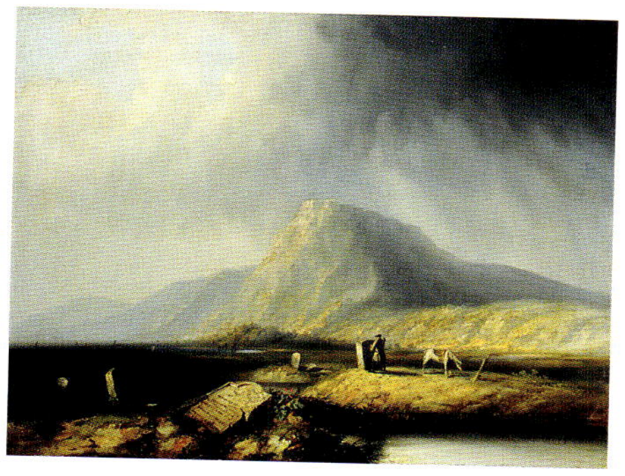

McCulloch, Horatio 1805–1867
Old Mortality Recutting the Tomb Stones of the Covenanters
oil on canvas 69.8 x 90.4
VIS.792

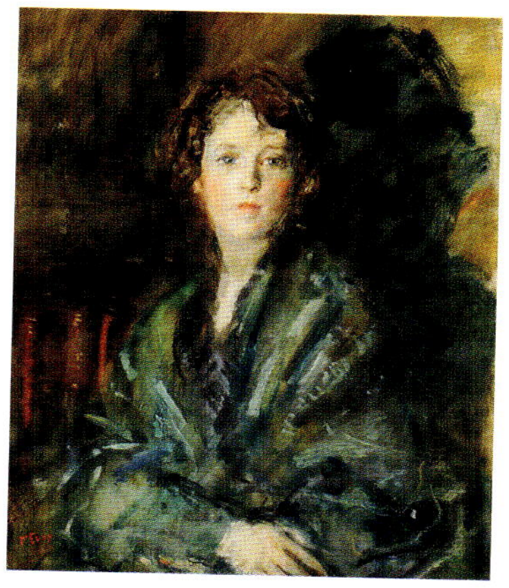

McEvoy, Ambrose 1878–1927
Miss Joan Claudia Johnson, in Green c.1920
oil on canvas 81 x 67.1
VIS.3475

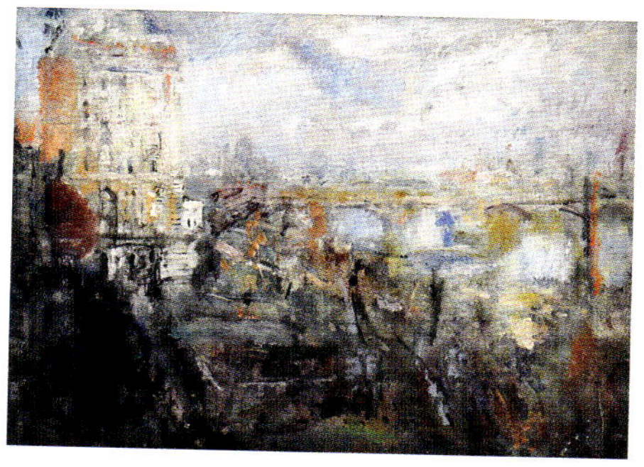

McEvoy, Ambrose 1878–1927
View from the Adelphi, London c.1920
oil on canvas 75.5 x 101
VIS.3464

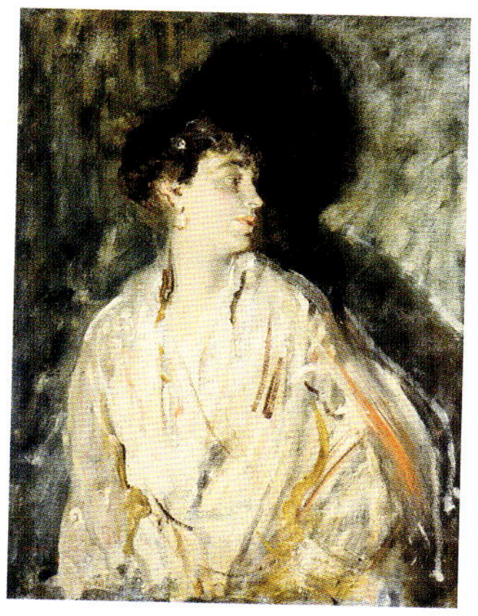

McEvoy, Ambrose 1878–1927
The Honourable Mrs Akers-Douglas
oil on canvas 100.5 x 75.3
VIS.LI.569 (P)

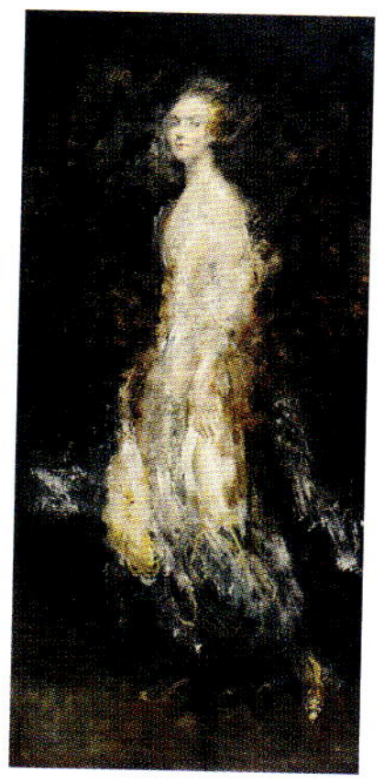

McEvoy, Ambrose 1878–1927
Viscountess Cranborne
oil on canvas 226.7 x 104.8
VIS.2769

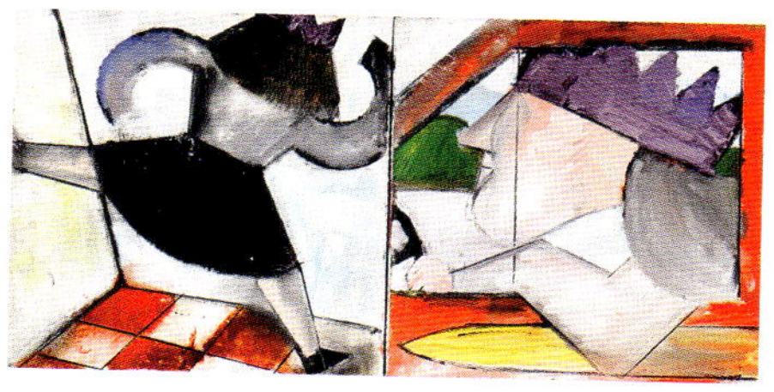

McFadyen, Jock b.1950
When Not Driving Fast Cars Queenie Loved to Dance
oil on canvas 45.9 x 92.5
VIS.4996

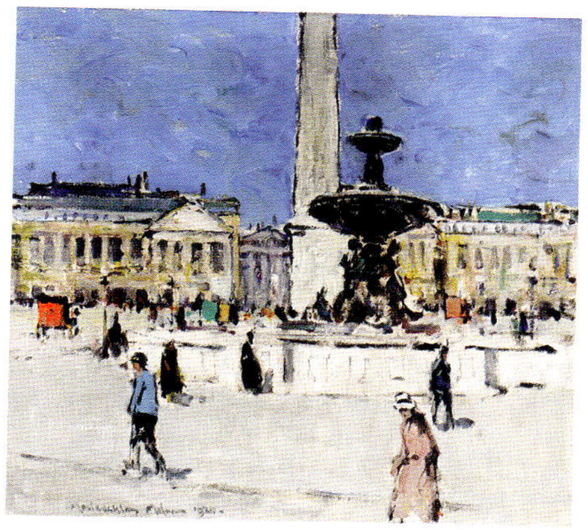

McLaughlin, John 1885–1957
Obelisque de Luxor, Paris 1924
oil on canvas 59.7 x 64.9
VIS.646

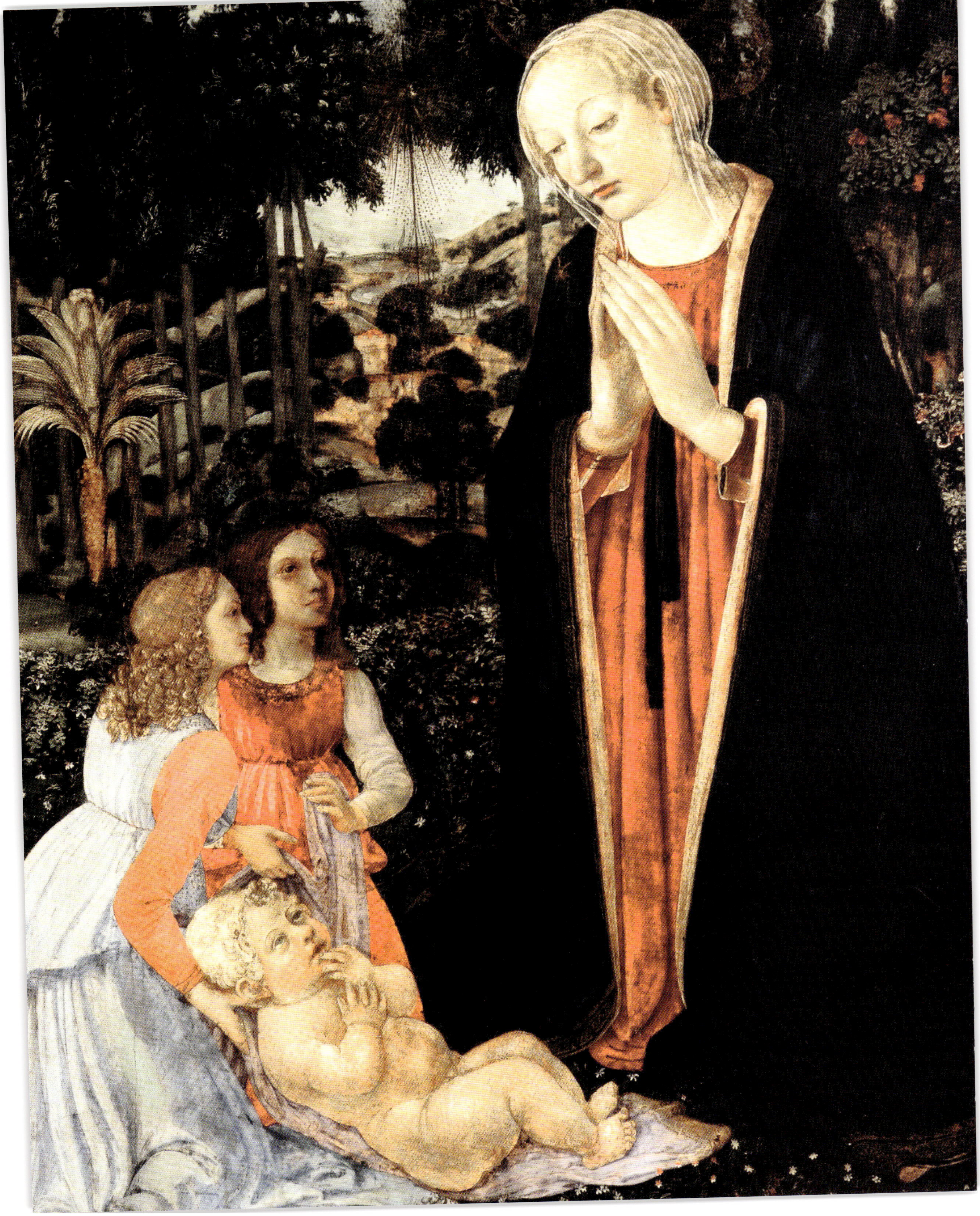

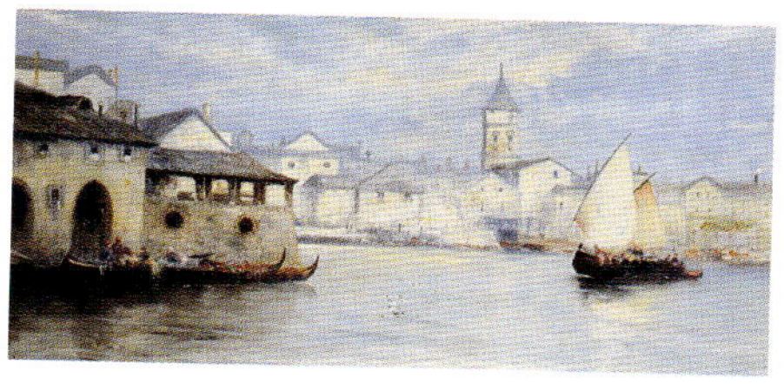

Meadows, Arthur Joseph 1843–1907
Venice 1890
oil on board 36 x 74.2
VIS.1354

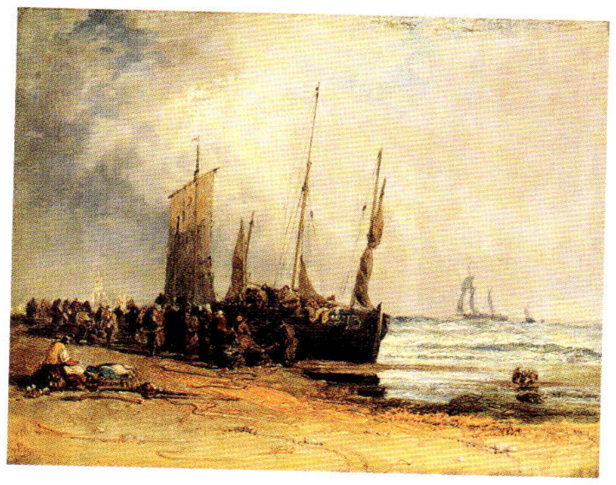

Meadows, Arthur Joseph 1843–1907
Seascape
oil on canvas 19.6 x 24.3
VIS.1075

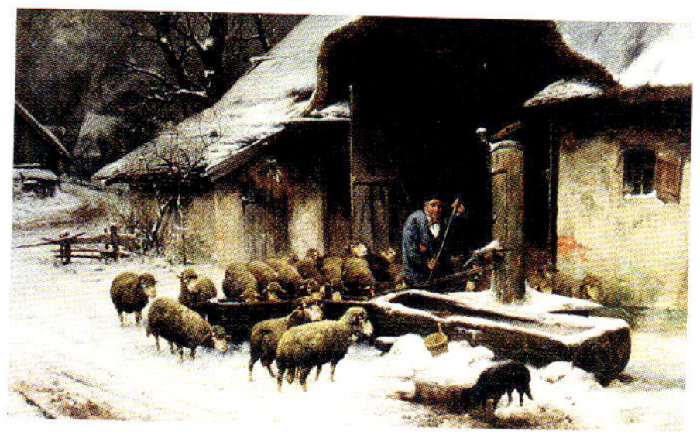

Meffsner, Ernst (attributed to)
active mid-19th C
Feeding Sheep 1850–1870
oil on canvas 64.1 x 101
VIS.1620

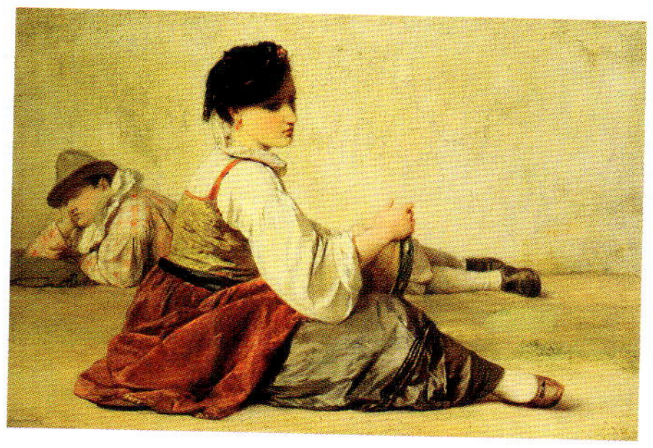

Meissonier, Jean Louis Ernest 1815–1891
Strolling Players
oil on canvas 66.8 x 95.7
VIS.517

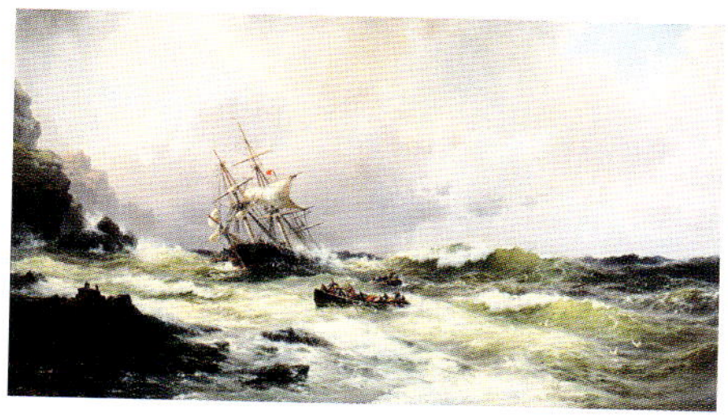

Melby, William 1824–1882
Seascape 1866
oil on canvas 87.8 x 151.5
VIS.1450

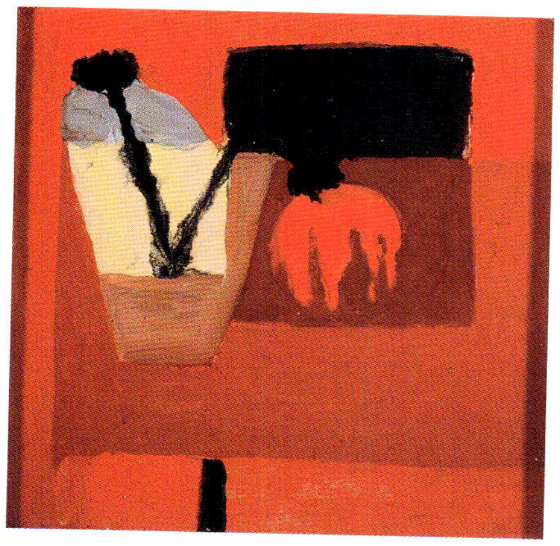

Mellis, Margaret 1914–2009
Red Flower 1958
oil on board 39.4 x 39.1
VIS.4951

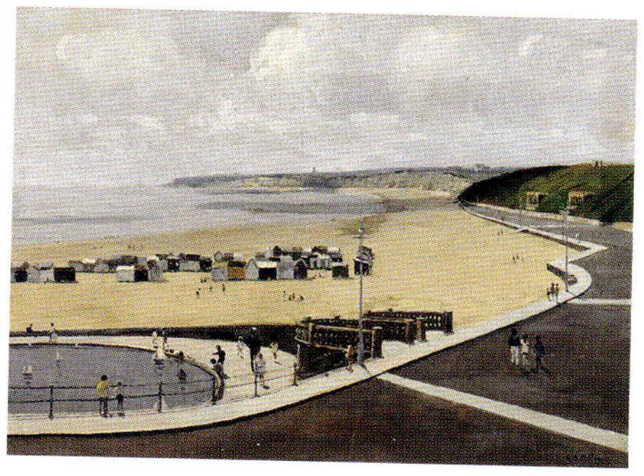

Mellon, Campbell Archibald 1876–1955
Foreshore at Gorleston, Norfolk
oil on canvas 44.1 x 59.5
VIS.991

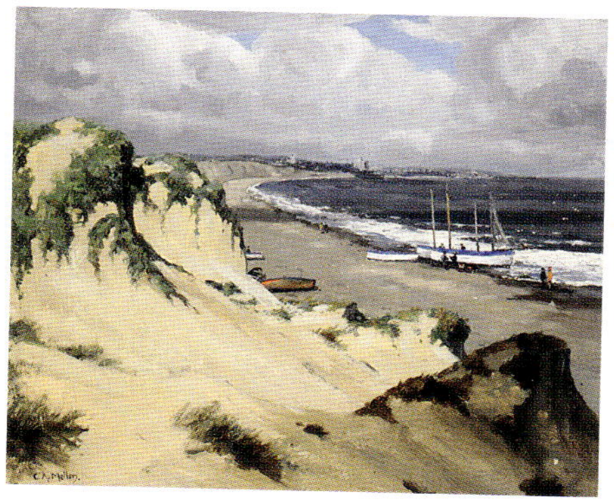

Mellon, Campbell Archibald 1876–1955
The Gap, Kessingland, Suffolk
oil on canvas 49 x 59.4
VIS.992

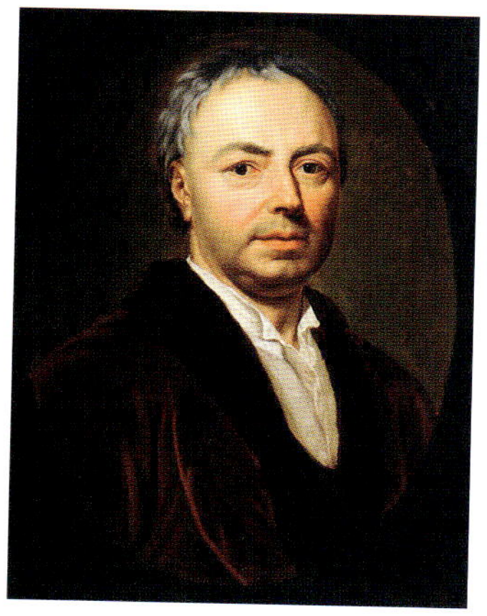

Mengs, Anton Raphael 1728–1779
Portrait of the Artist's Father
oil on canvas 60.8 x 46.7
VIS.69

Facing page: Rosselli, Cosimo, 1439–1507, *Virgin and Child with Angels* (detail), Museums Sheffield, (p. 184)

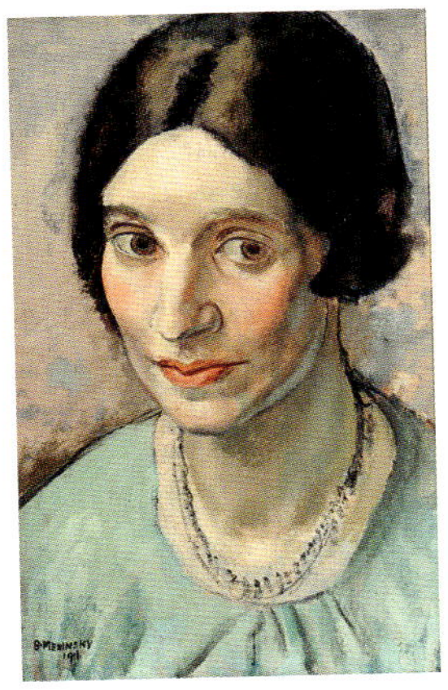

Meninsky, Bernard 1891–1950
Portrait of a Girl 1916
oil on canvas 64.2 x 49
VIS.174

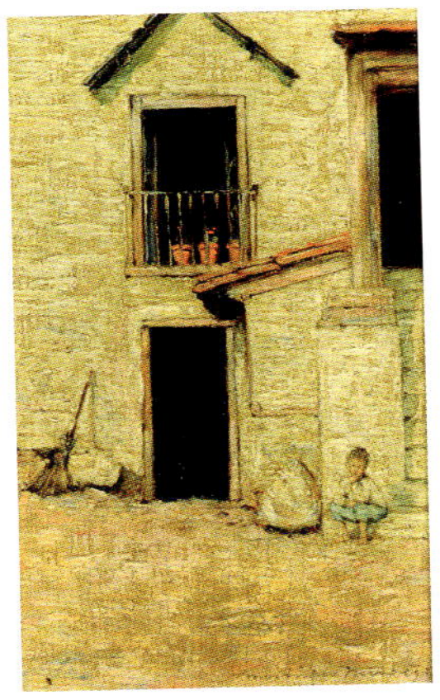

Menpes, Mortimer L. 1855–1938
A Courtyard
oil on canvas 15.5 x 9.4
VIS.956

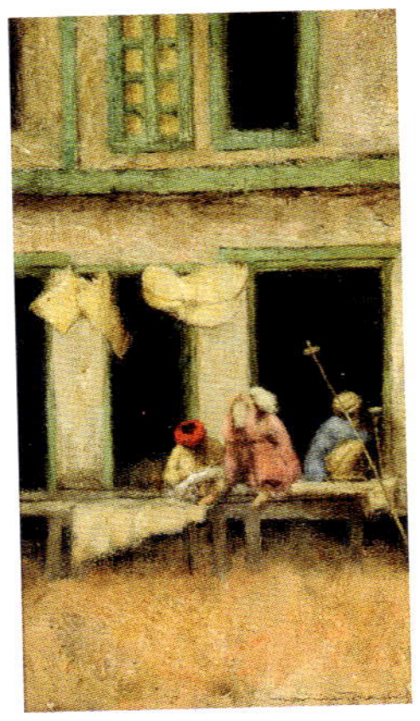

Menpes, Mortimer L. 1855–1938
All the Day's Work (Lahore)
oil on millboard 21.3 x 12.2
VIS.946

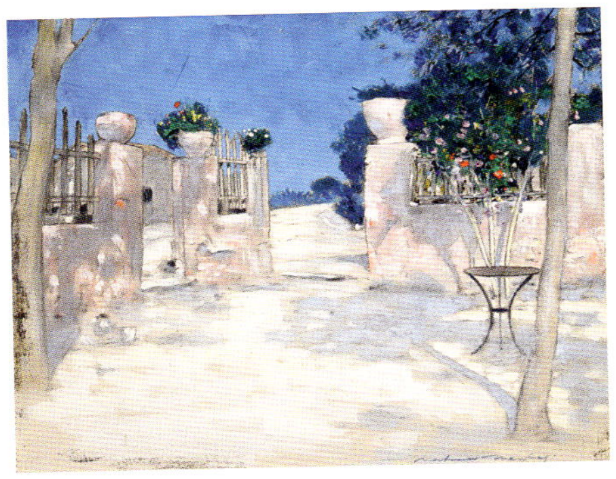

Menpes, Mortimer L. 1855–1938
Entrance to a Japanese Garden
oil on millboard 32 x 40.3
VIS.650

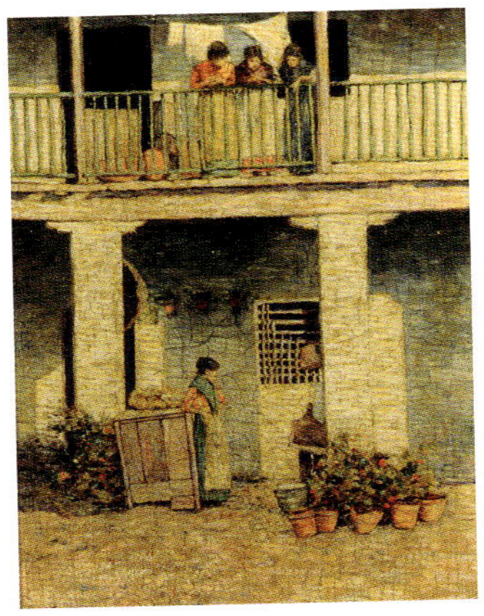

Menpes, Mortimer L. 1855–1938
On the Balcony
oil on board 15.7 x 12
VIS.655

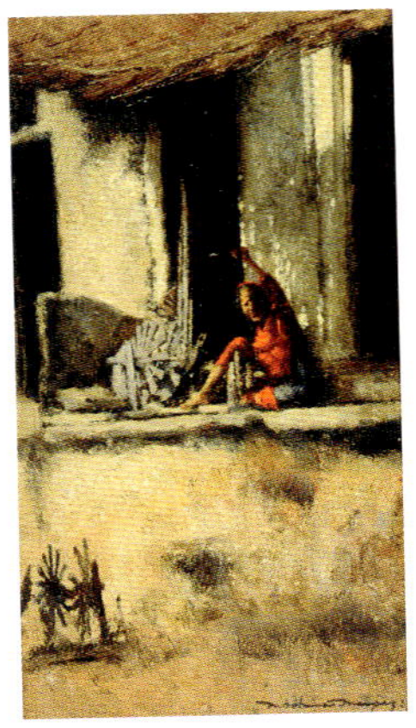

Menpes, Mortimer L. 1855–1938
Spinning (Ajmere)
oil on millboard 21.1 x 12.3
VIS.949

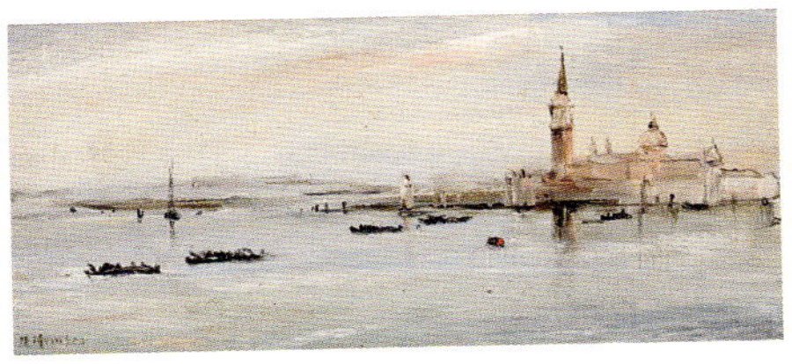

Menpes, Mortimer L. 1855–1938
Venice
oil on panel 12.1 x 27.4
VIS.1062

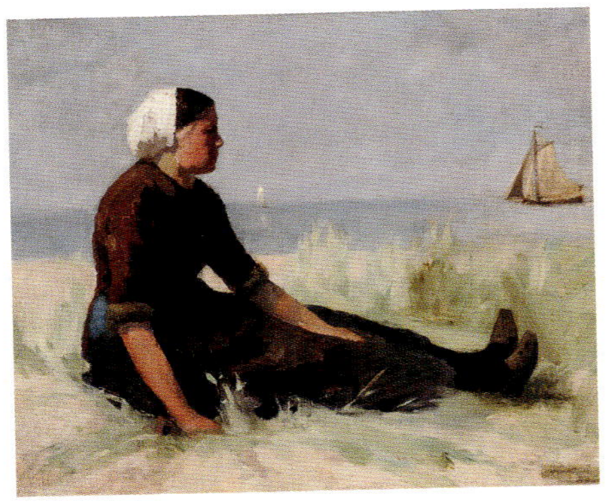

Mesdag, Hendrik Willem 1831–1915
A Fisher Girl 1887
oil on canvas 37 x 44.7
VIS.262

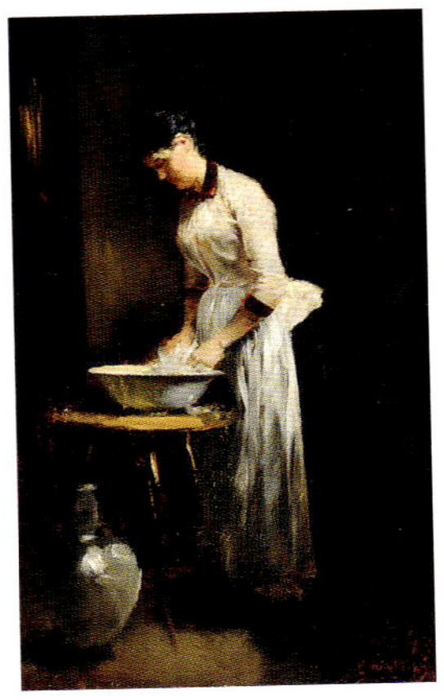

Mettling, Louis 1847–1904
The Washing 1880–1885
oil on panel 47 x 28.8
VIS.717

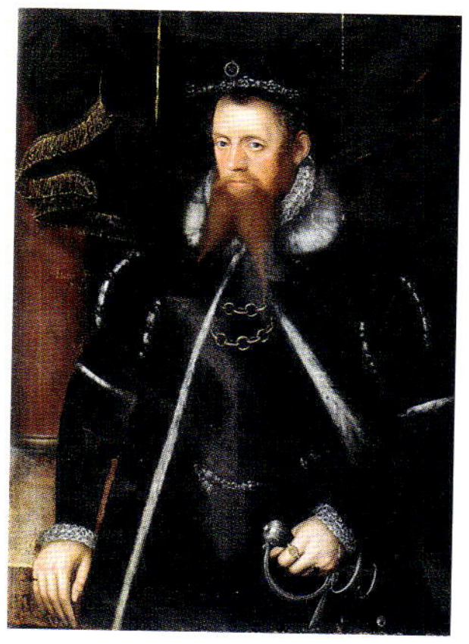

Meulen, Steven van der 1493–1563
Portrait of a Member of the Tichborne Family
oil on panel 101.3 x 76.3
VIS.649

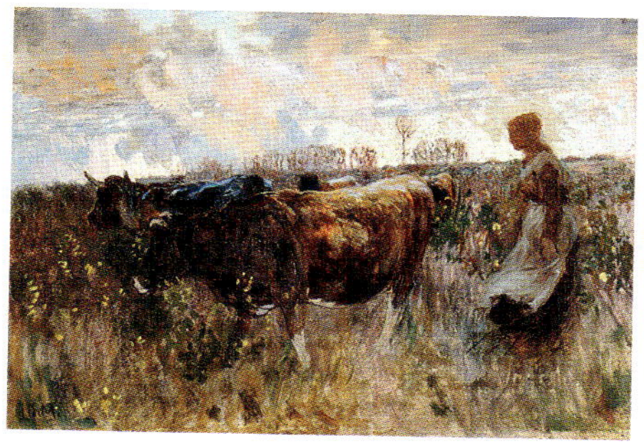

Meyerheim, Robert Gustav 1847–1920
A Pastoral 1870–1875
oil on canvas 23.3 x 33.5
VIS.770

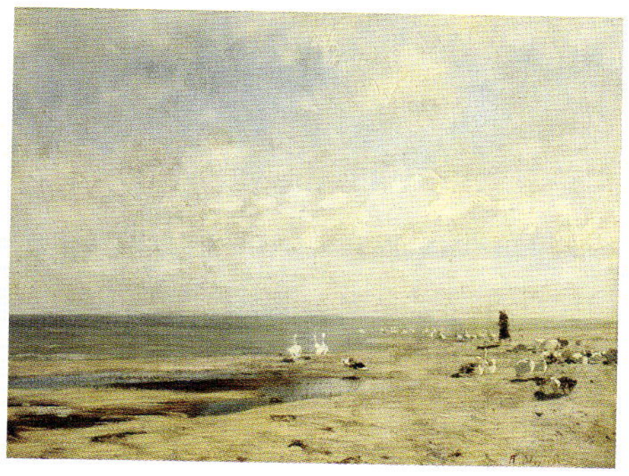

Meyerheim, Robert Gustav (attributed to)
1847–1920
The Goose Girl 1870–1875
oil on canvas 24.1 x 32.3
VIS.524

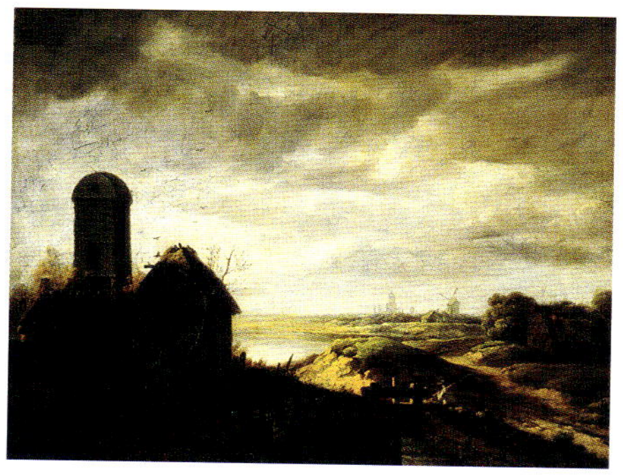

Michel, Georges 1763–1843
Landscape with Windmills 1790–1795
oil on panel 47.4 x 61.3
VIS.308

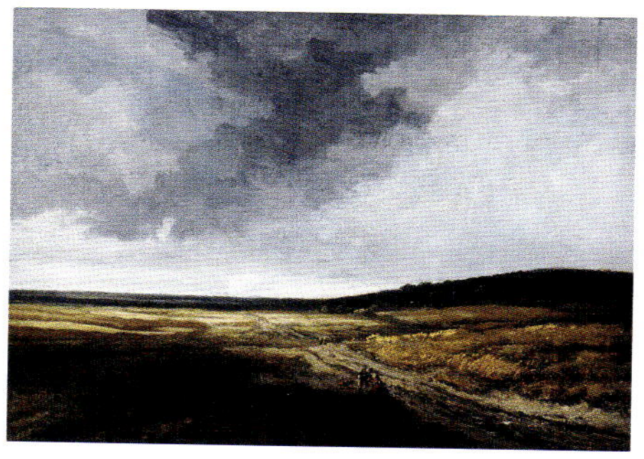

Michel, Georges 1763–1843
Stormy Landscape
oil on canvas 51.5 x 71.1
VIS.365

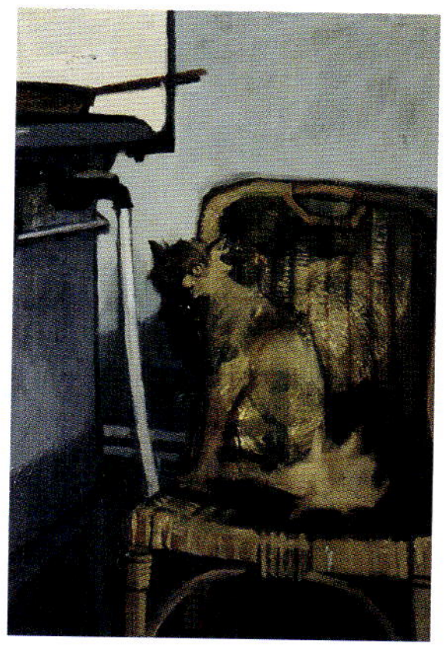

Middleditch, Edward 1923–1987
Cat on a Chair c.1952
oil on canvas 73.8 x 48.6
VIS.4680

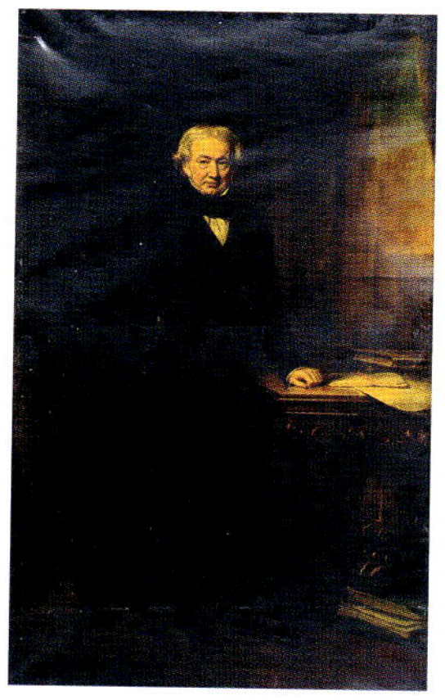

Middleton, James Godsell 1805–1874
George Hadfield (1787–1879)
oil on canvas 238.4 x 147.4
VIS.LI.832 (P)

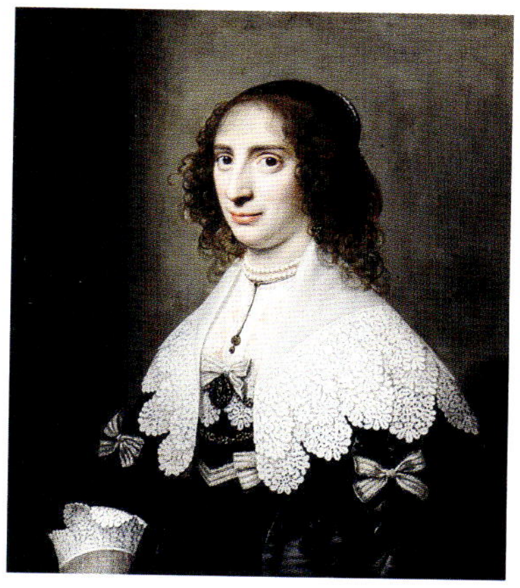

Miereveld, Michiel Jansz. van 1567–1641
Johanna de Witt 1638
oil on panel 67.6 x 58.1
VIS.842

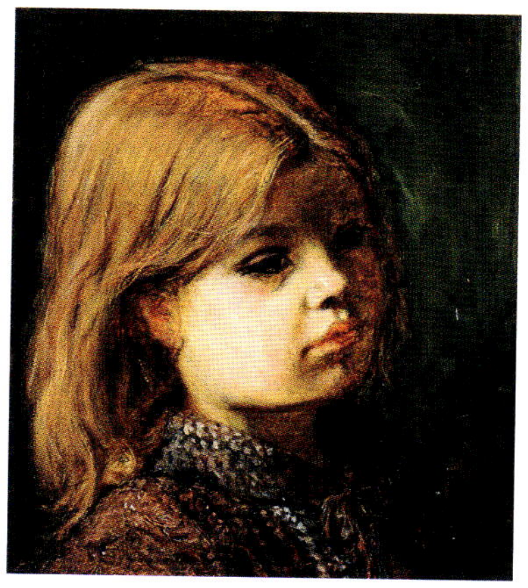

Millais, John Everett 1829–1896
Portrait of a Girl
oil on panel 19.5 x 17
VIS.3151

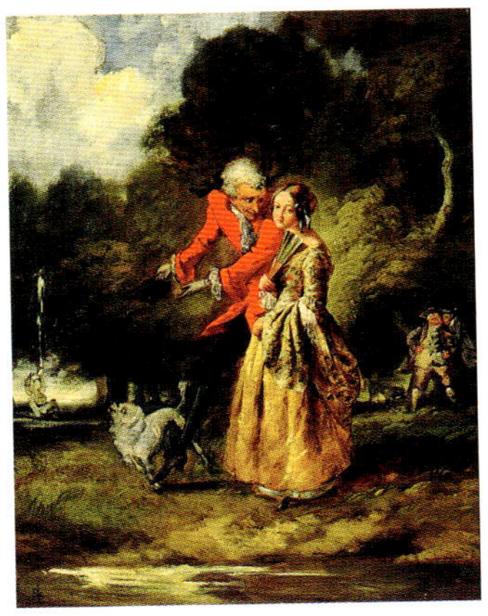

Millais, John Everett 1829–1896
The Proposal
oil on canvas 44.3 x 34.3
VIS.1532

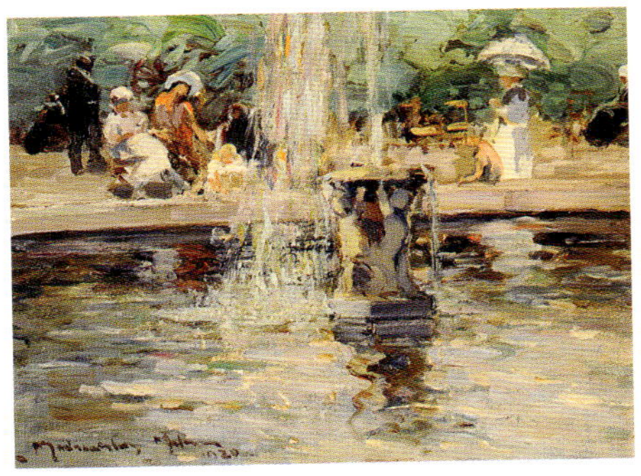

Milne, John Maclauchlan 1886–1957
La fontain 1929
oil on board 32.5 x 43.5
VIS.1032

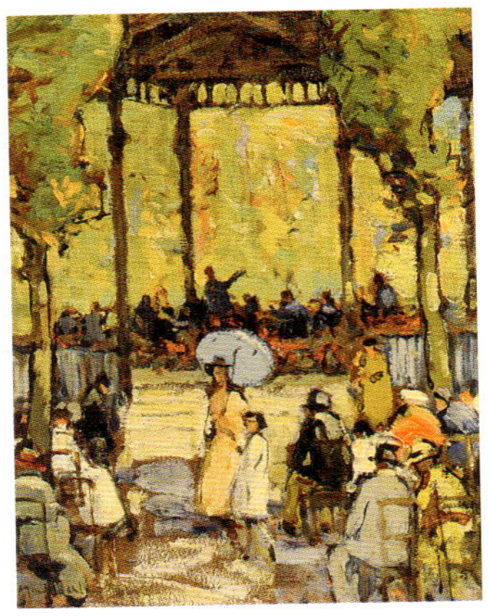

Milne, John Maclauchlan 1886–1957
Concert au Jardin du Luxembourg, Paris
oil on canvas 43.6 x 33.5
VIS.633

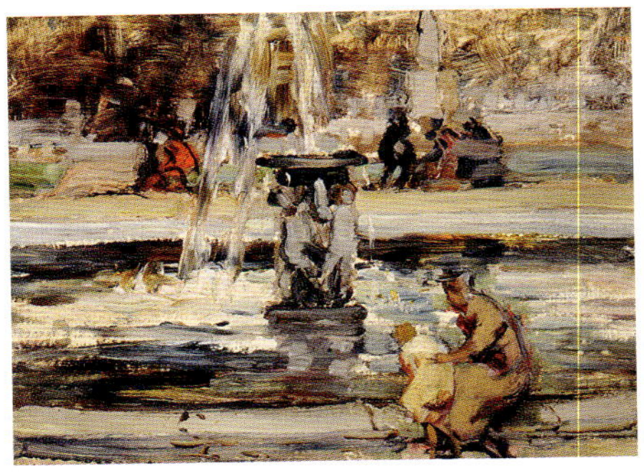

Milne, John Maclauchlan 1886–1957
La fontain
oil on board 24.4 x 32.7
VIS.979

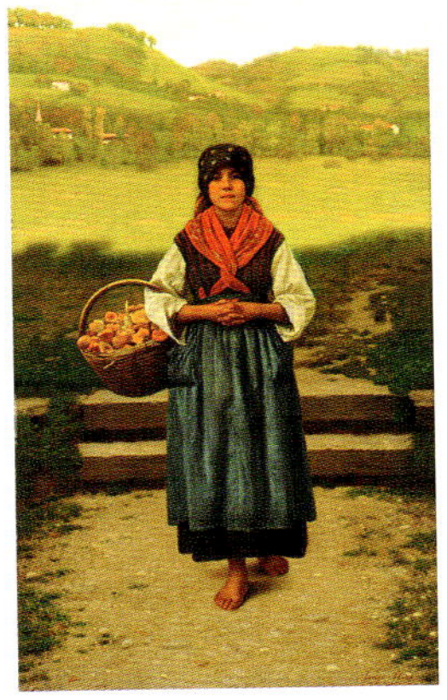

Mion, Luigi 1843–c.1920
Study of a Girl
oil on panel 78.4 x 45.7
VIS.197

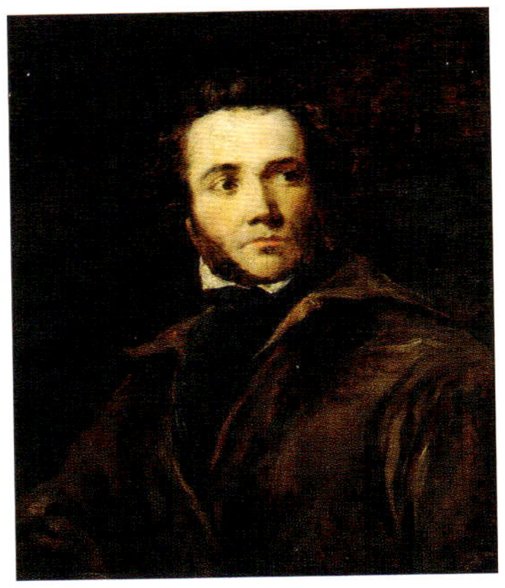

Mitchell, J. Young 1811–1865
Self Portrait
oil on canvas 59.5 x 49.8
VIS.2311

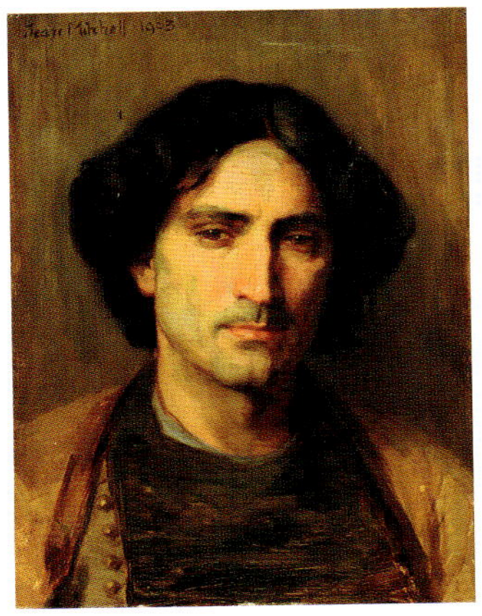

Mitchell, Jean 1861–1941
Portrait of a Man 1903
oil on canvas 45.7 x 35.8
VIS.3152

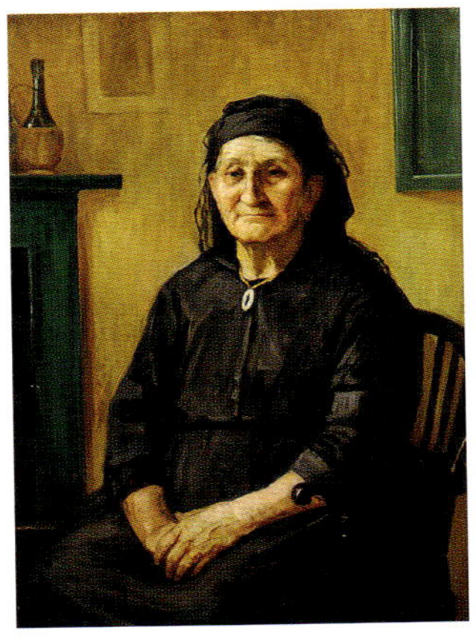

Mitchell, Jean 1861–1941
An Old Italian
oil on canvas 67.5 x 49.7
VIS.2723

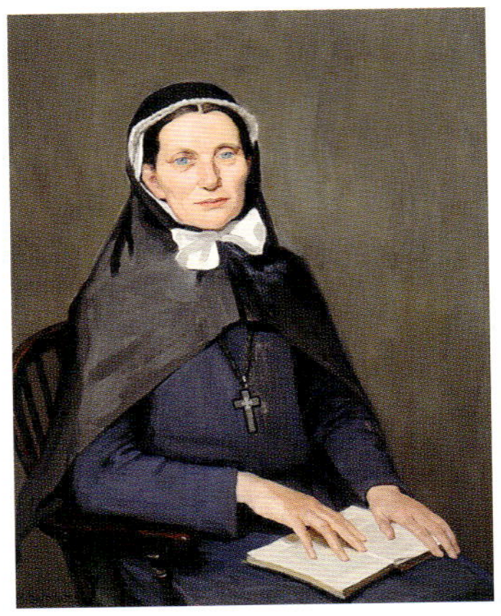

Mitchell, Jean 1861–1941
The Deaconess
oil on canvas 76.6 x 61.1
VIS.797

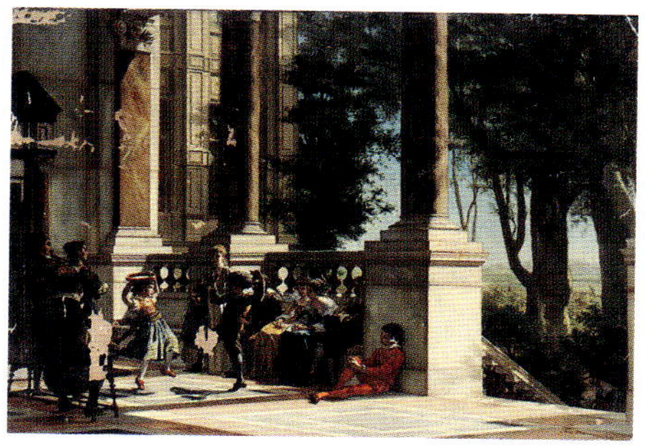

Moermans, Frans (attributed to)
active 1871–1878
Gypsies in a Spanish Château 1878
oil on canvas 71.1 x 91.1
VIS.2603

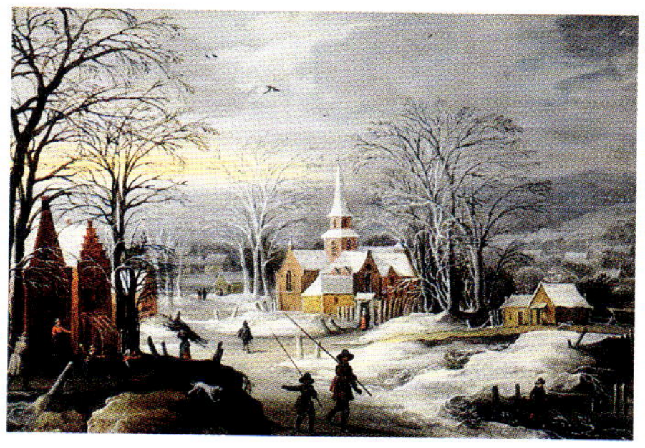

Momper, Joos de the younger (attributed to)
1564–1635
Winter Landscape with Buildings and Figures
oil on panel 55.8 x 79.5
VIS.3027

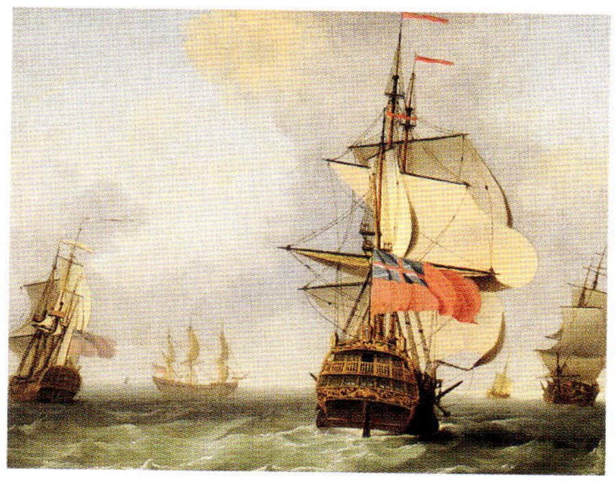

Monamy, Peter 1681–1749
Men o' War in a Choppy Sea 1703
oil on canvas 41.8 x 52.9
VIS.3711

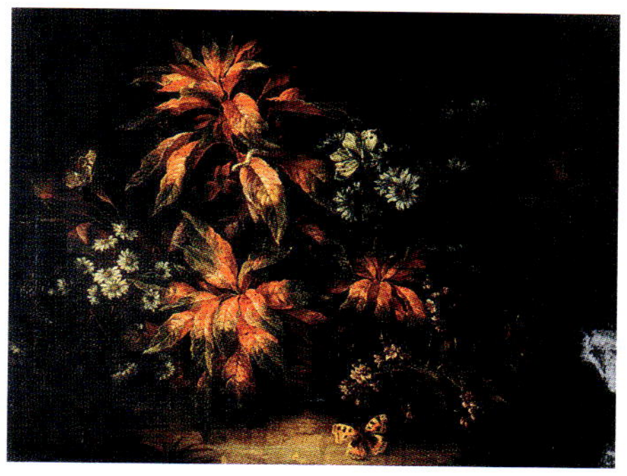

Monnoyer, Jean-Baptiste 1636–1699
Leaves and Flowers with a Butterfly
oil on canvas 44.7 x 57.7
VIS.253

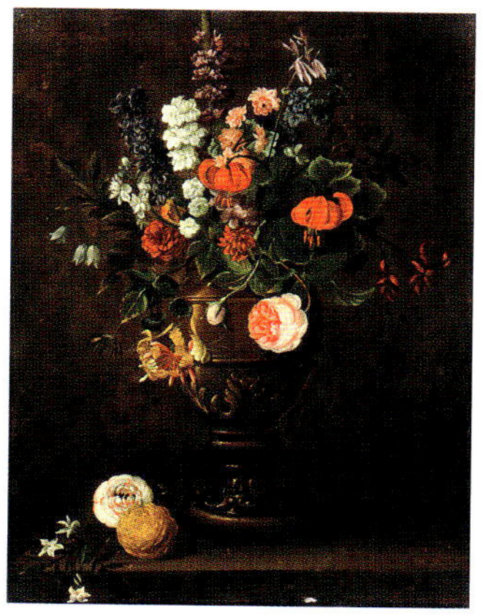

Monnoyer, Jean-Baptiste (attributed to)
1636–1699
Flower Piece
oil on canvas 66 x 49.5
VIS.68

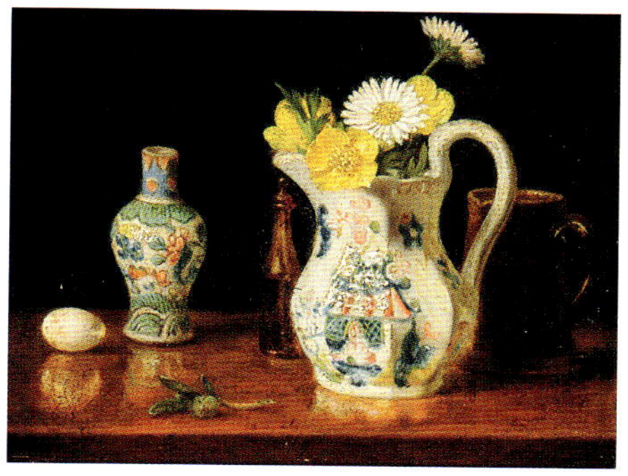

Monnoyer, Jean-Baptiste (attributed to)
1636–1699
Still Life
oil on panel 13.4 x 17
VIS.299

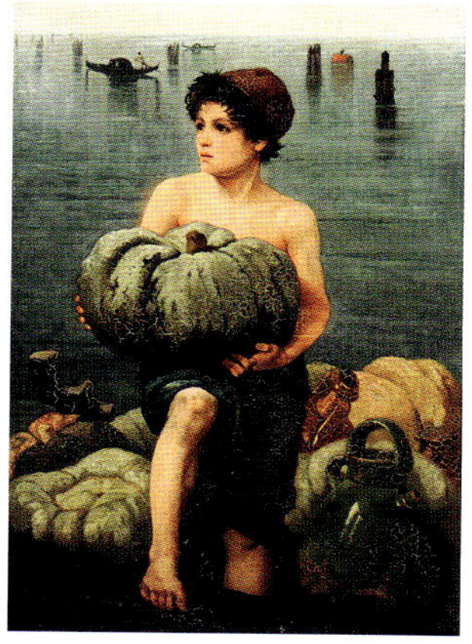

Montalba, Hilda 1846–1919
Boy Unloading a Venetian Market Boat 1880
oil on canvas 121.5 x 86.2
VIS.1594

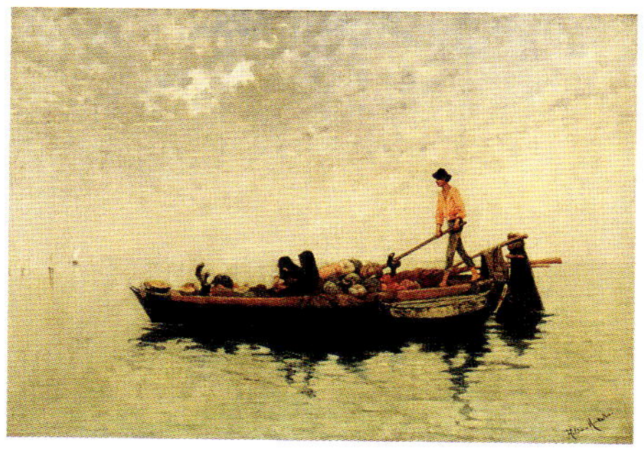

Montalba, Hilda 1846–1919
Venetian Boatman
oil on canvas 62.2 x 88.3
VIS.1346

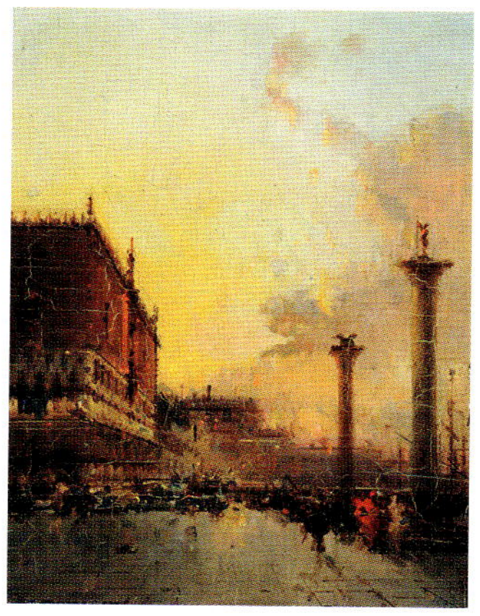

Monticelli, Adolphe Joseph Thomas
1824–1886
The Piazzetta, Venice 1850–1855
oil on panel 23.3 x 18.2
VIS.57

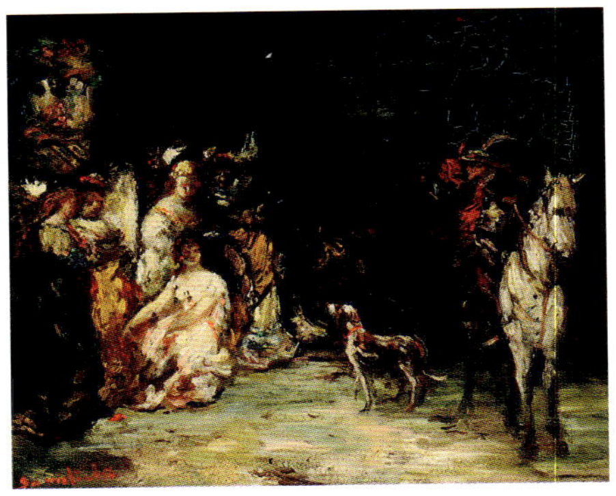

Monticelli, Adolphe Joseph Thomas
1824–1886
Figure Composition 1855–1860
oil on canvas 31.2 x 37.8
VIS.293

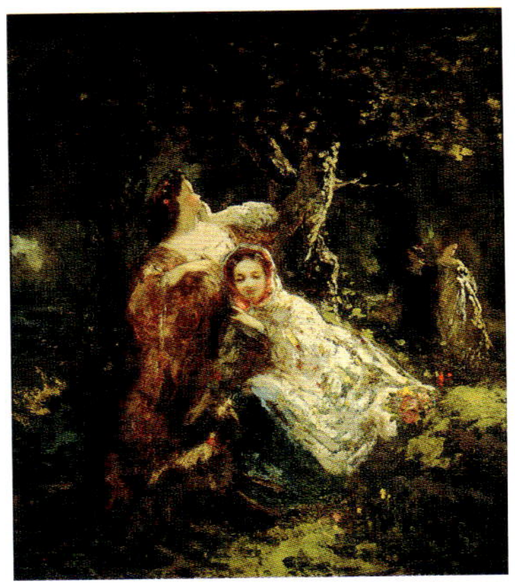

Monticelli, Adolphe Joseph Thomas
1824–1886
Echo in the Wood 1860–1865
oil on panel 54.2 x 45.2
VIS.300

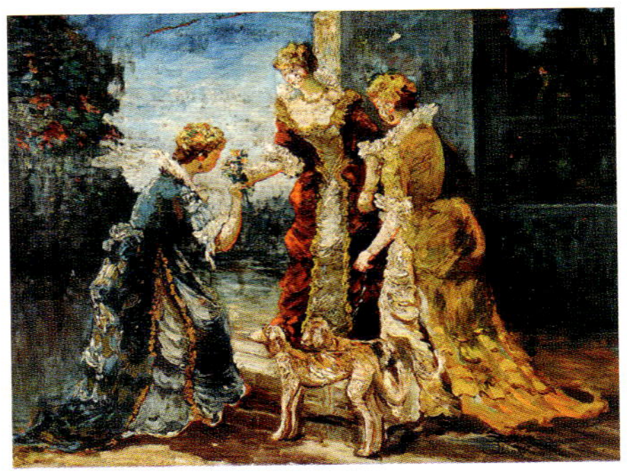

Monticelli, Adolphe Joseph Thomas (attributed to) 1824–1886
The Bouquet 1870–1886
oil on panel 40 x 52.7
VIS.294

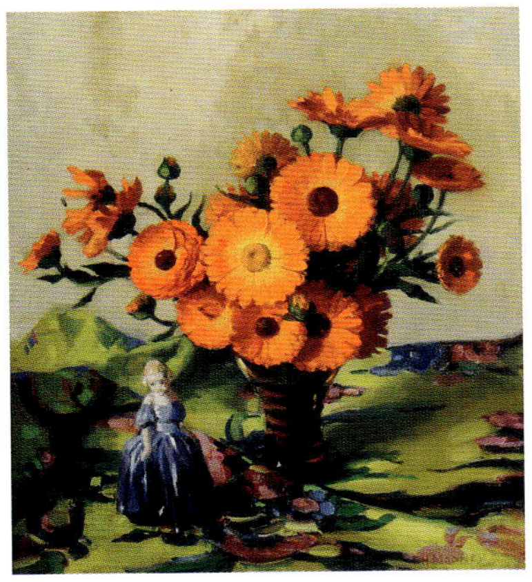

Mooney, Edward Hartley c.1878–1938
Marigolds
oil on canvas 44.2 x 39.2
VIS.784

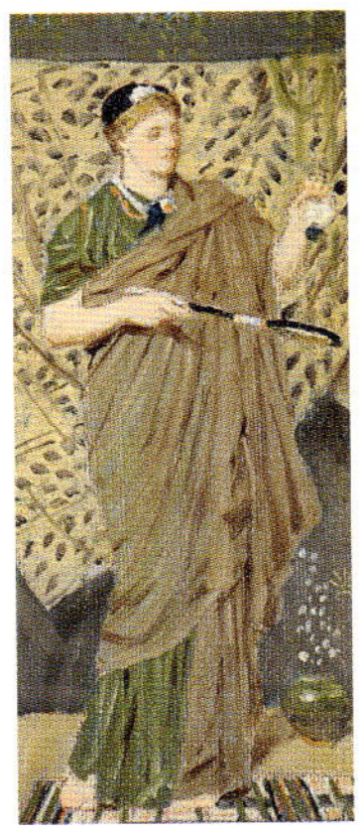

Moore, Albert Joseph 1841–1893
Battledore and Shuttlecock
oil on canvas on millboard 36 x 14.9
VIS.20

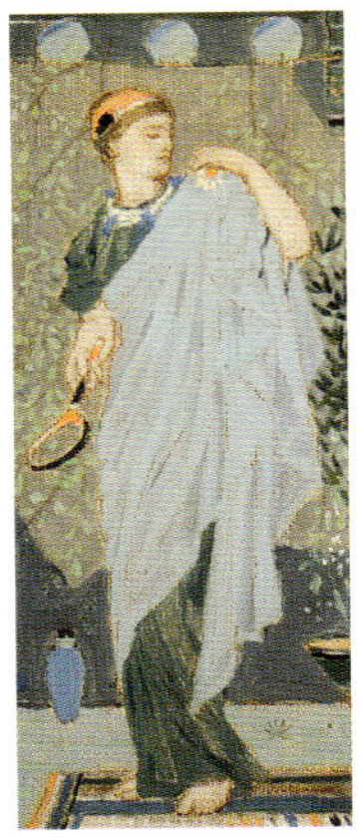

Moore, Albert Joseph 1841–1893
Battledore and Shuttlecock
oil on canvas on millboard 36.2 x 14.9
VIS.23

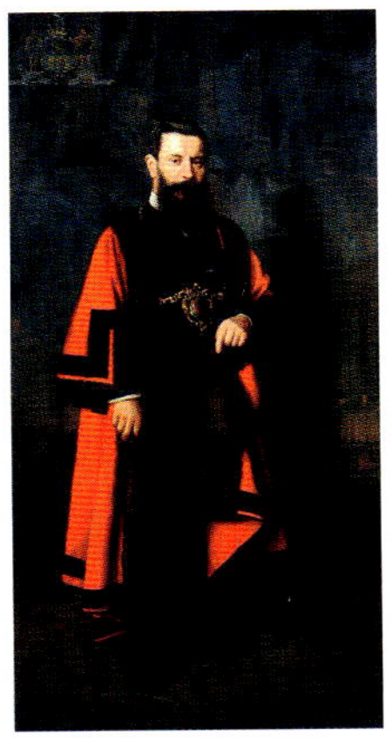

Moore, Ernest 1865–1940
Henry Fitzalan-Howard (1847–1917), 15th Duke of Norfolk, First Lord Mayor of Sheffield
c.1897
oil on canvas 223.2 x 116.4
VIS.LI.829 (P)

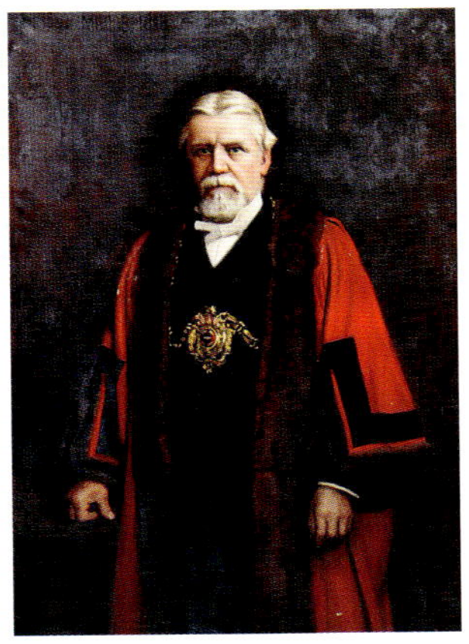

Moore, Ernest 1865–1940
Alderman William Johnson Clegg (1827–1895), JP, Mayor of Sheffield (1887–1888)
1898
oil on canvas 137.1 x 97.1
VIS.LI.819 (P)

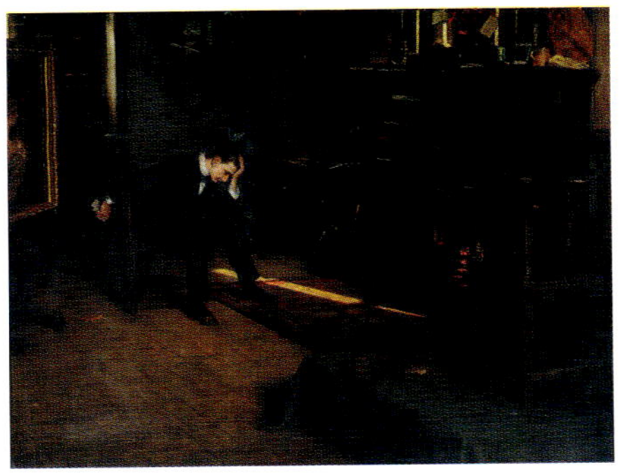

Moore, Ernest 1865–1940
Rejected 1898
oil on canvas 85.5 x 110.4
VIS.3099

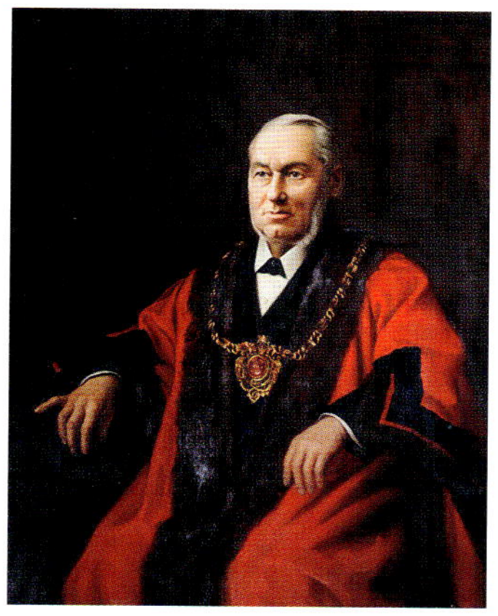

Moore, Ernest 1865–1940
Alderman Edward Saville Foster (d.1894), Mayor of Sheffield (1893–1894)
oil on canvas 127 x 101.5
VIS.LI.825 (P)

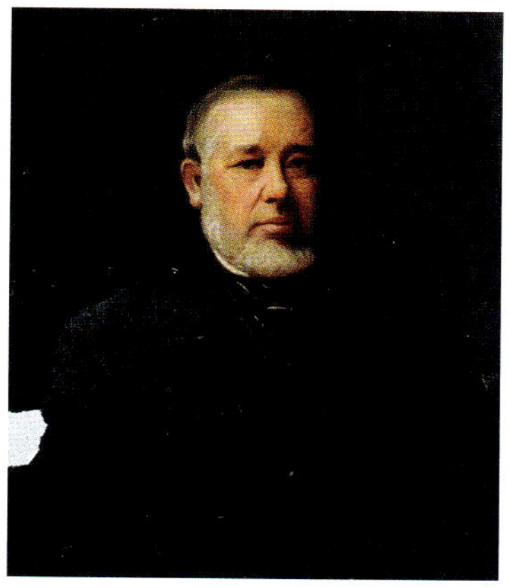

Moore, Ernest 1865–1940
Charles William Styring
oil on canvas 76.5 x 63.7
K1901.20

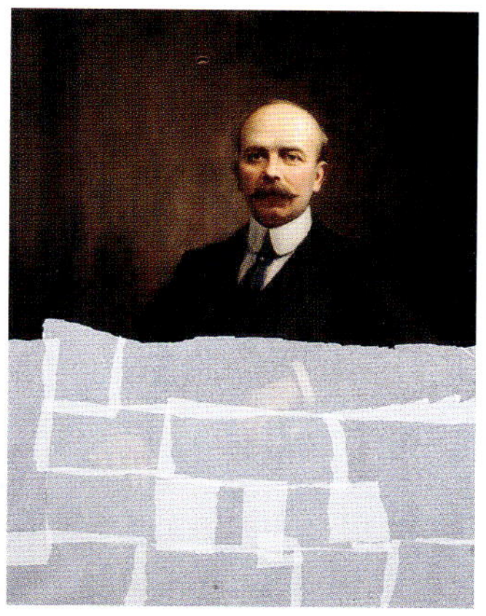

Moore, Ernest 1865–1940
Robert J. Wales
oil on canvas 112.9 x 86.6
SH411

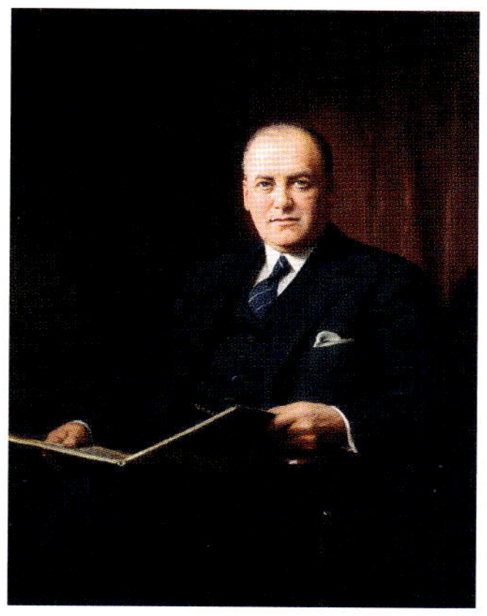

Moore, Ernest 1865–1940
William Ward
oil on canvas 112.5 x 86.6
SH410

Moore, Henry 1831–1895
Sea Shore 1879
oil on panel 38.1 x 27.8
VIS.3116

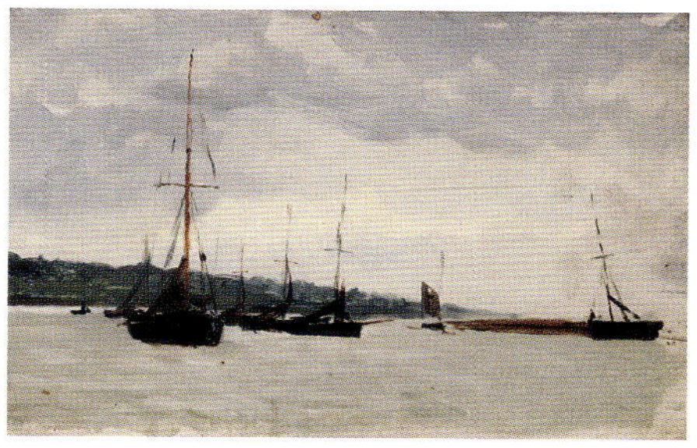

Moore, Henry 1831–1895
Sea Piece
oil on panel 18.5 x 28.8
VIS.1014

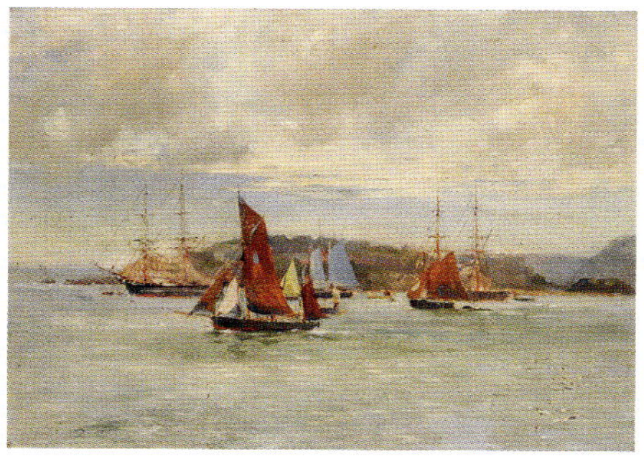

Moore, Henry 1831–1895
Shipping off the Coast
oil on panel 27.3 x 37.6
VIS.777

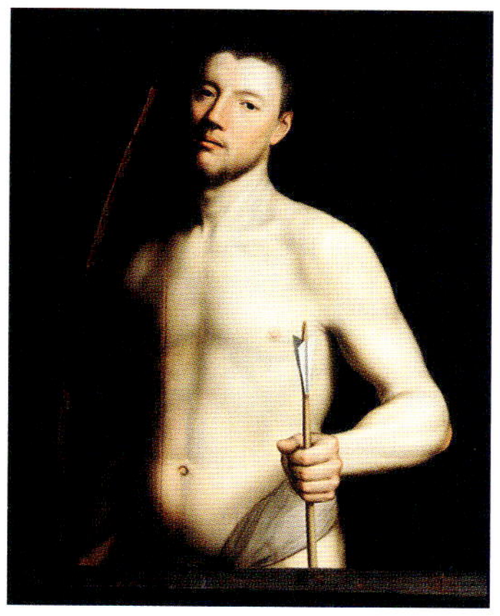

Mor, Antonis (attributed to) 1512–1516–c.1576
St Sebastian c.1550
oil on panel 90 x 73.7
VIS.2251

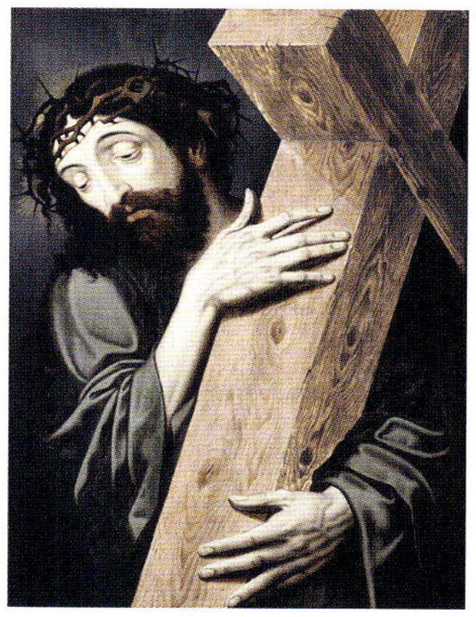

Morales, Luis de (school of) c.1509–c.1586
Christ Carrying the Cross
oil on panel 104 x 82.6
VIS.1837

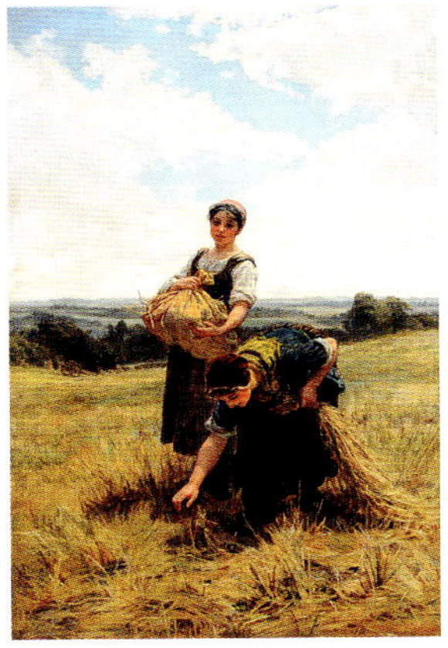

Morgan, Frederick 1856–1927
Gleaners 1880
oil on canvas 107.9 x 72.4
VIS.1581

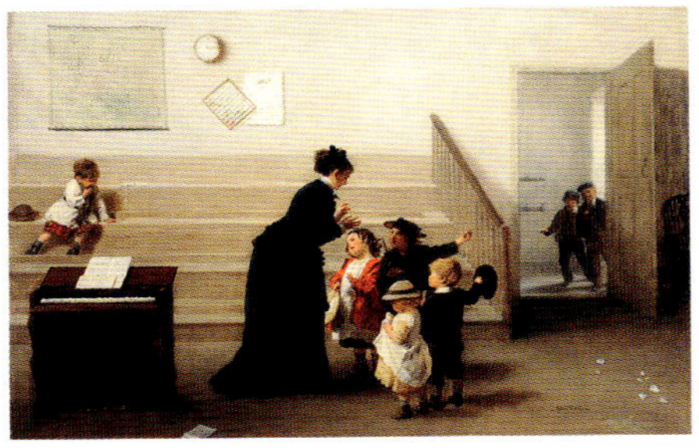

Morgan, John 1823–1886
Interior of a Village School
oil on canvas 59.7 x 91.5
VIS.1507

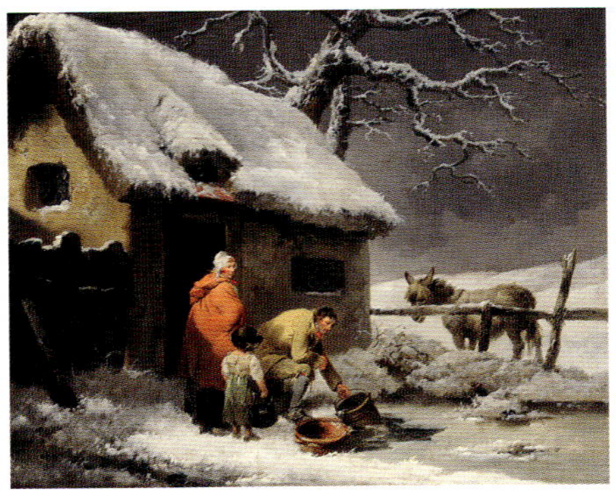

Morland, George 1763–1804
Breaking the Ice 1792
oil on canvas 60.5 x 73.7
VIS.2217

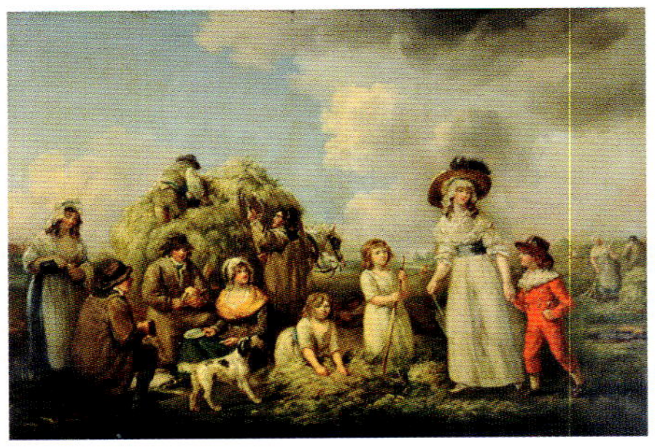

Morland, George 1763–1804
In the Hayfield 1797
oil on canvas 70 x 100
VIS.838

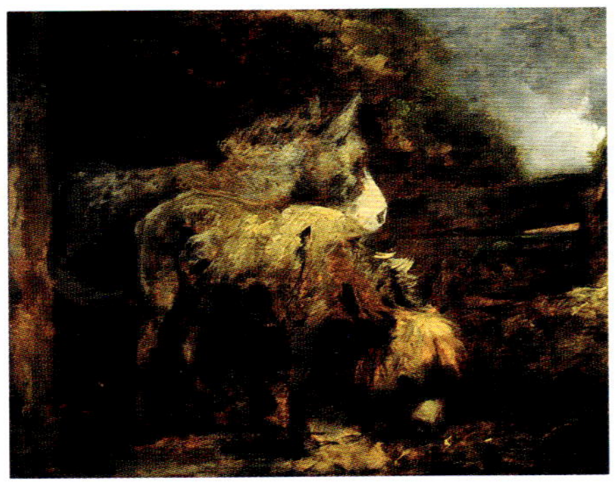

Morland, George 1763–1804
Donkeys
oil on panel 23 x 28.4
VIS.2211

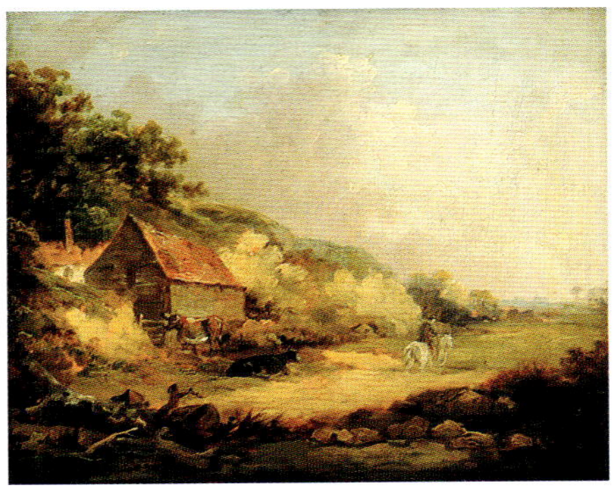

Morland, George 1763–1804
Landscape
oil on canvas 24.8 x 29.8
VIS.322

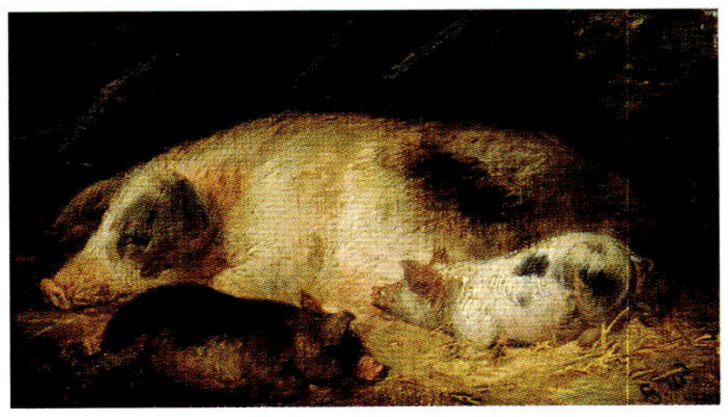

Morland, George 1763–1804
Pigs
oil on panel 12.2 x 21
VIS.46

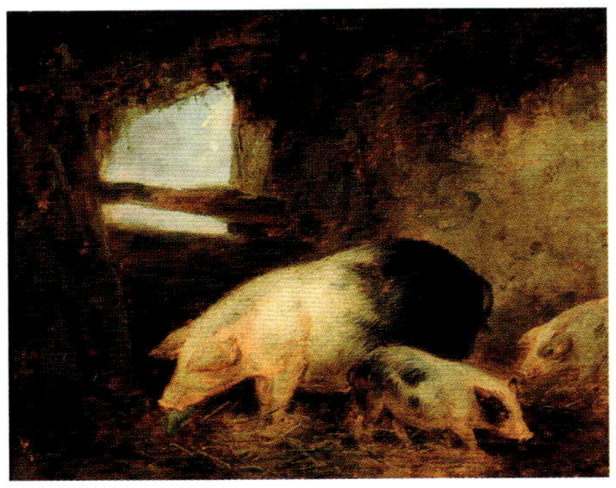

Morland, George 1763–1804
Pigs in a Sty
oil on panel 31 x 38.4
VIS.236

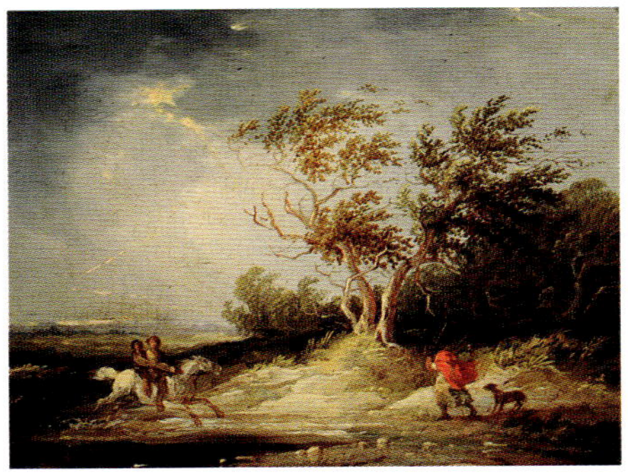

Morland, George 1763–1804
The Approaching Storm
oil on panel 14 x 18.1
VIS.36

Facing page: Lowry, Laurence Stephen, 1887–1976, *Fire Watcher* (recto) (detail), 1943, Museums Sheffield, (p. 129)

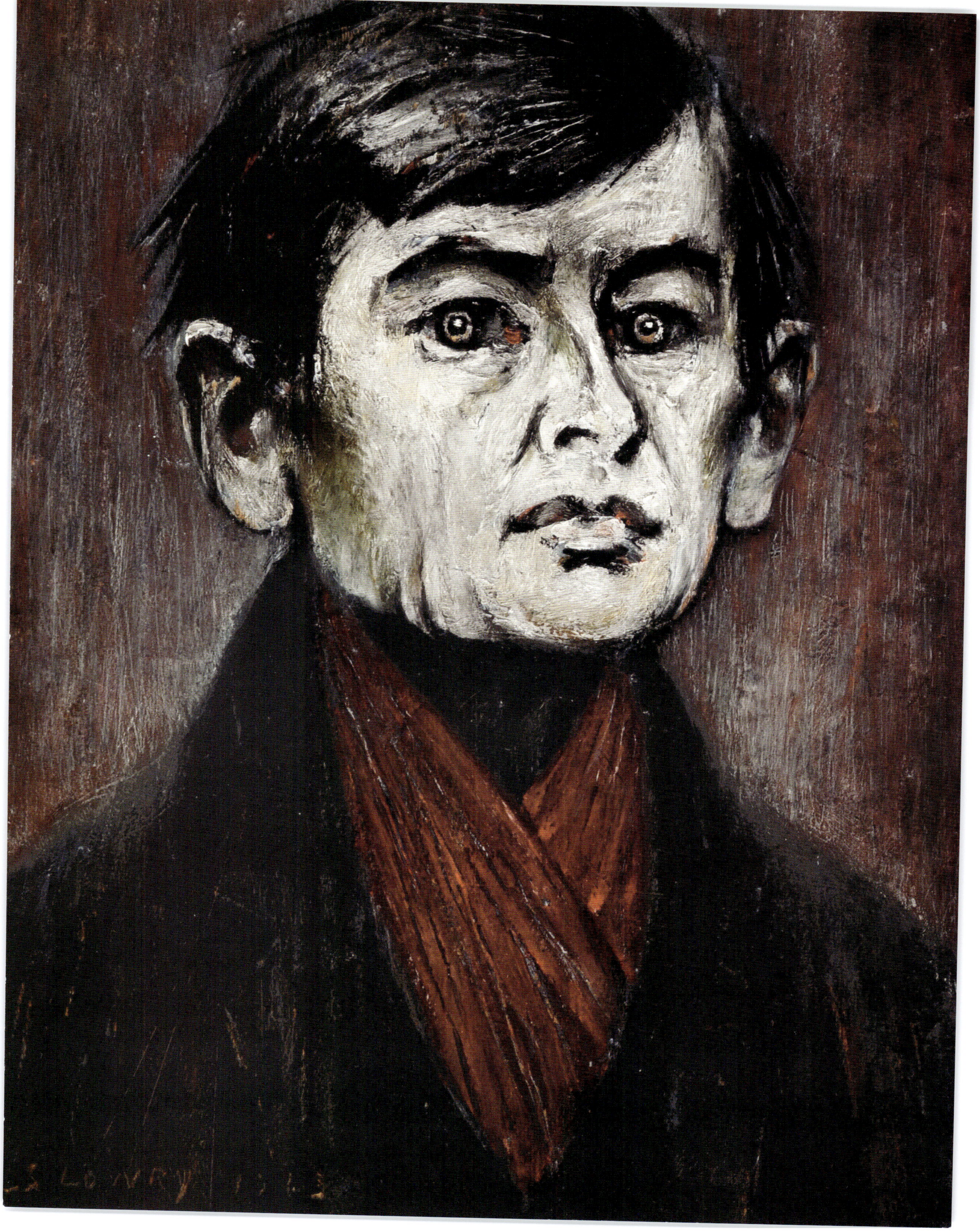

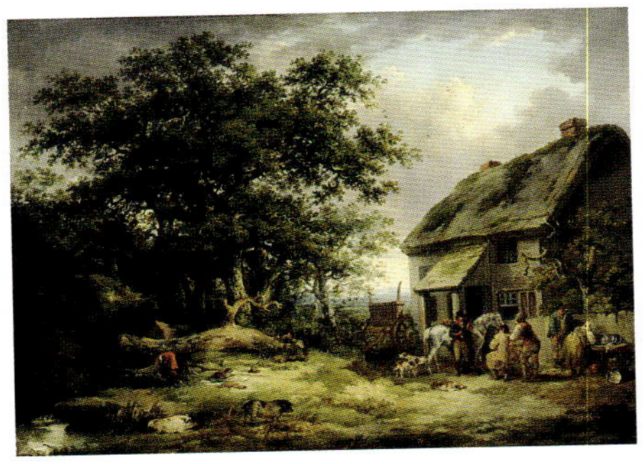

Morland, George 1763–1804
The Village Inn
oil on canvas 54.6 x 74.8
VIS.1579

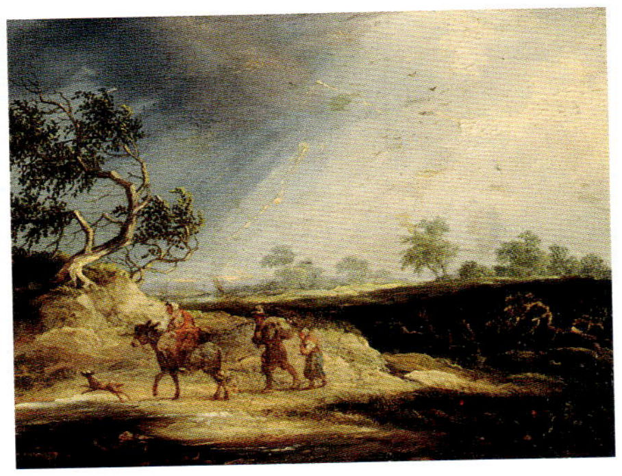

Morland, George 1763–1804
Travelling Gypsies
oil on canvas 14 x 18.3
VIS.41

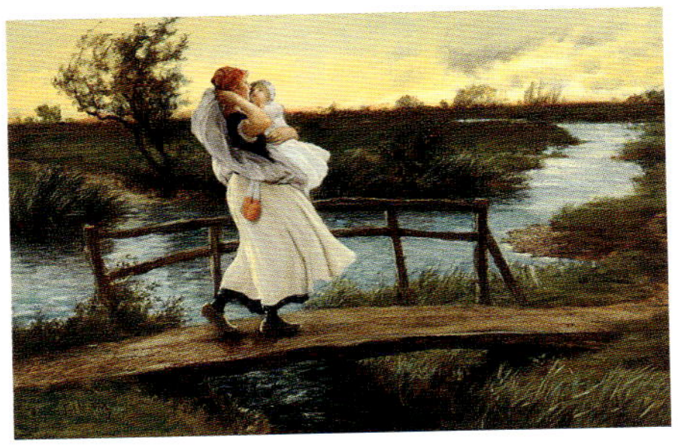

Morris, Philip Richard 1834–1902
March Winds
oil on millboard 49.9 x 75.1
VIS.344

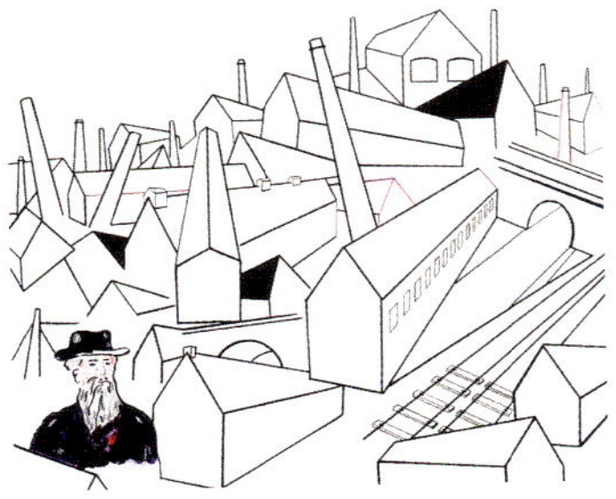

Morris, Stephen b.1935
Untitled c.1992
oil on canvas 106 x 87
CGSG00229

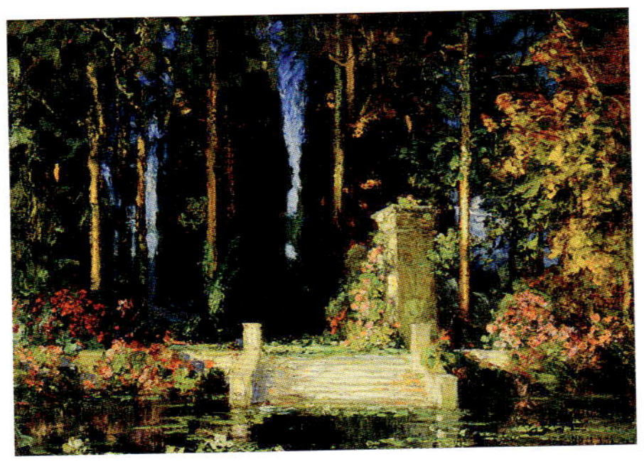

Mostyn, Thomas Edwin 1864–1930
The Enchanted Garden
oil on canvas 49.4 x 67.3
VIS.2728

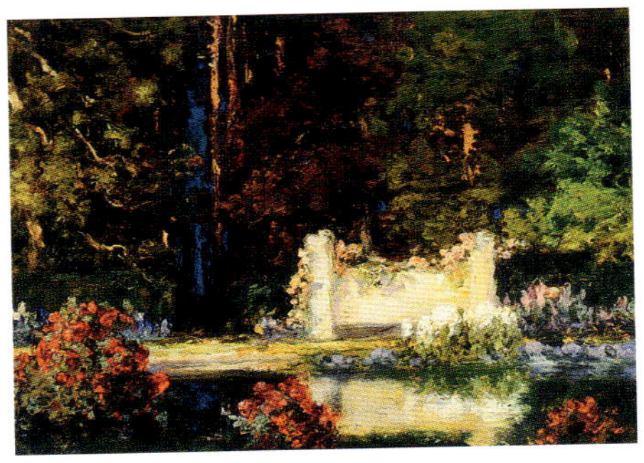

Mostyn, Thomas Edwin 1864–1930
The Garden of Memory
oil on canvas 48.9 x 67.4
VIS.715

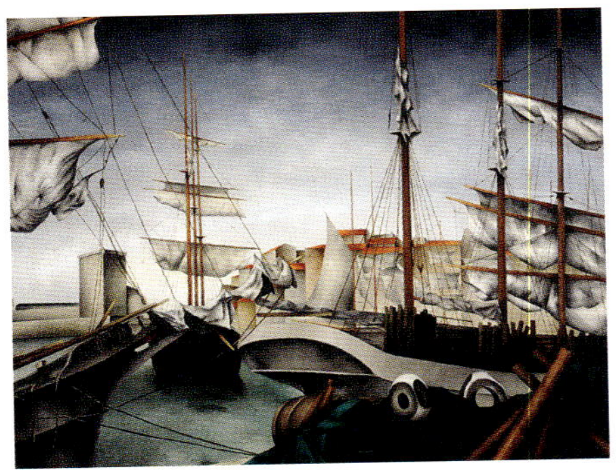

Mouillot, Marcel 1889–1972
Shipping in a Port
oil on canvas 69.8 x 88.7
VIS.710

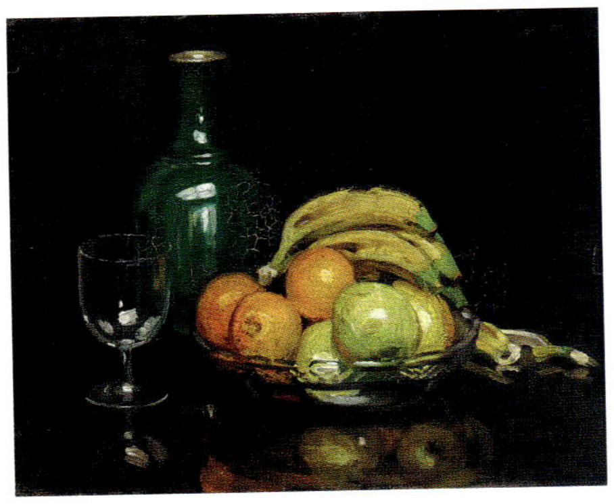

Mücke, Karl Anton Heinrich 1806–1891
Still Life 1840–1850
oil on canvas 40.5 x 48.6
VIS.260

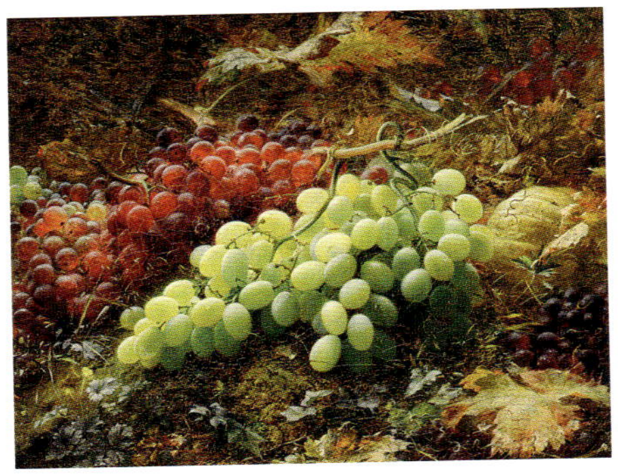

Muckley, William Jabez 1829–1905
Grapes 1869
oil on canvas 41.7 x 53.8
VIS.1534

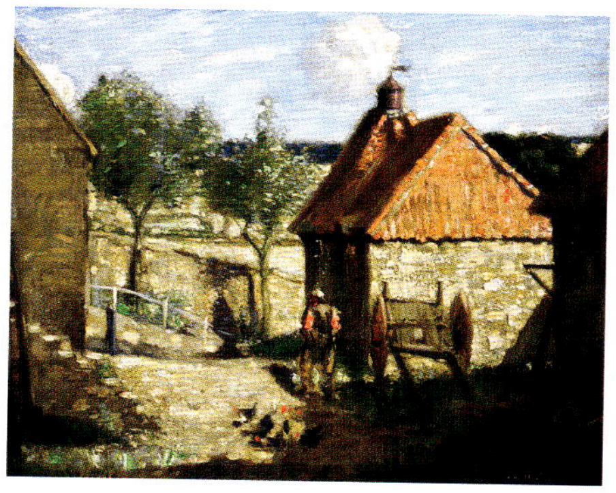

Muirhead, David 1867–1930
Farmyard
oil on canvas 61.9 x 74.6
VIS.3736

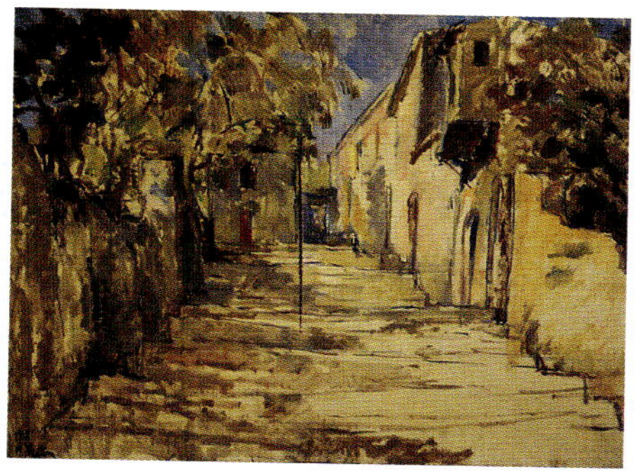

Müller, Alfredo 1869–1940
Landscape 1913
oil on canvas 67.2 x 88
VIS.1326

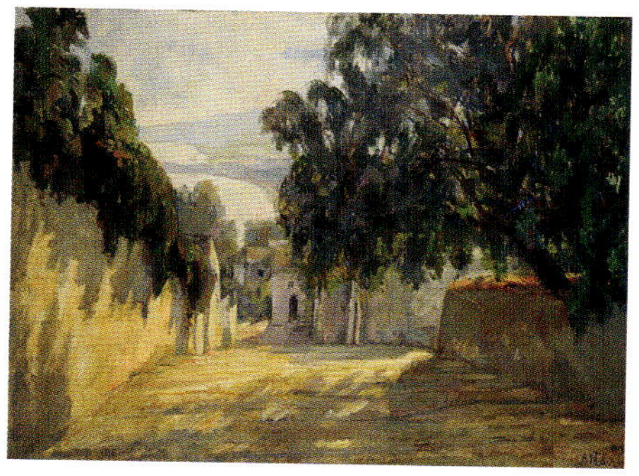

Müller, Alfredo 1869–1940
Landscape 1913
oil on canvas 68.5 x 88.5
VIS.1336

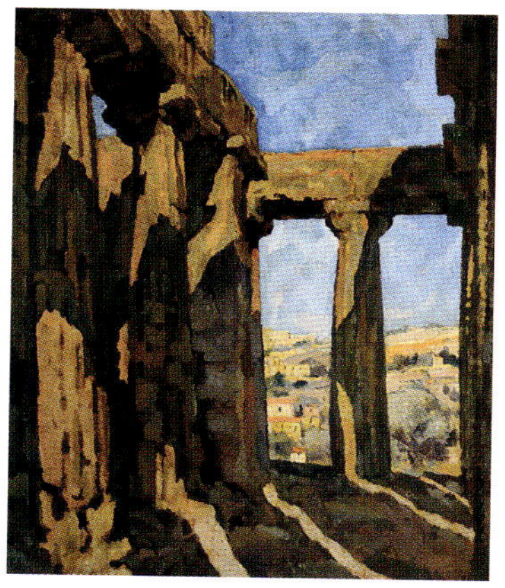

Müller, Alfredo 1869–1940
Ruins 1913
oil on canvas 80.6 x 70.1
VIS.1092

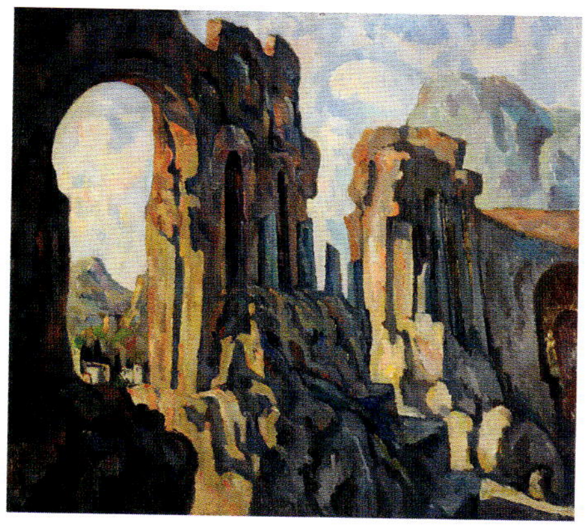

Müller, Alfredo 1869–1940
Sicily 1913
oil on canvas 84.3 x 90.7
VIS.1284

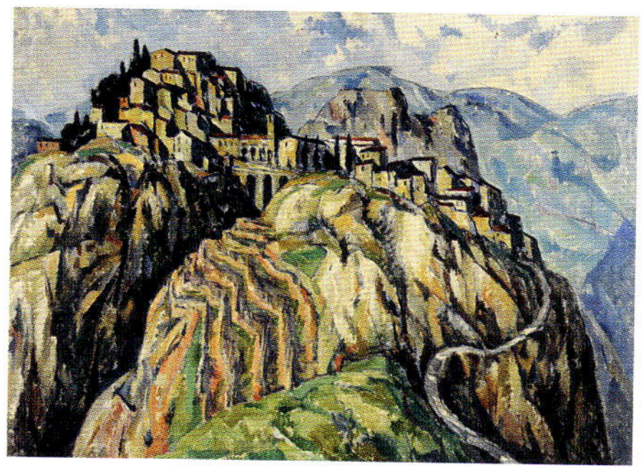

Müller, Alfredo 1869–1940
A Rocky Landscape 1914
oil on canvas 85 x 111
VIS.1093

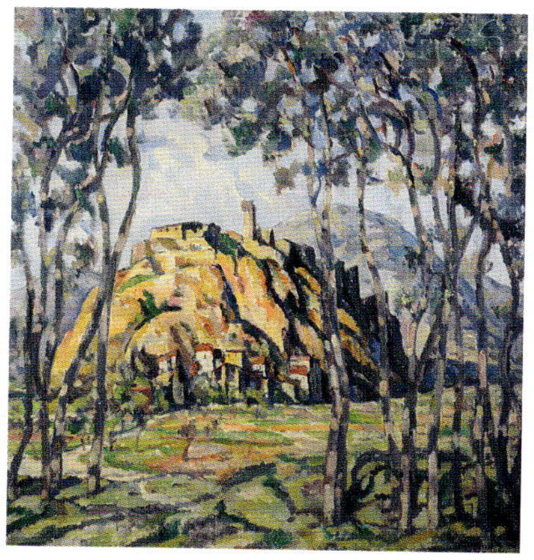

Müller, Alfredo 1869–1940
Landscape 1914
oil on canvas 90.8 x 84.5
VIS.1091

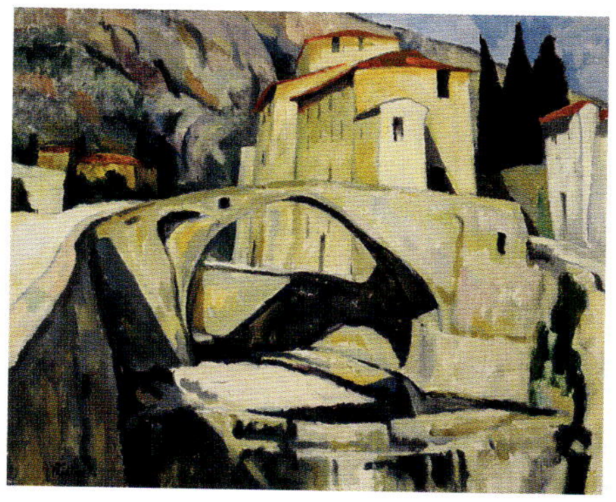

Müller, Alfredo 1869–1940
Old Bridge, Sicily 1914
oil on canvas 59 x 72
VIS.1282

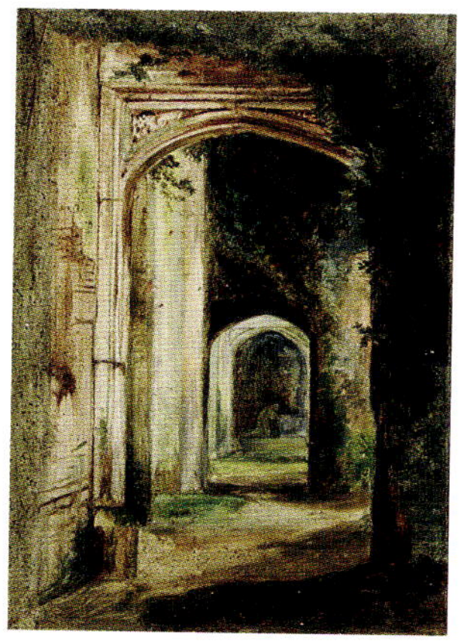

Müller, Alfredo 1869–1940
Study
oil on card 19.3 x 13.4
VIS.1101

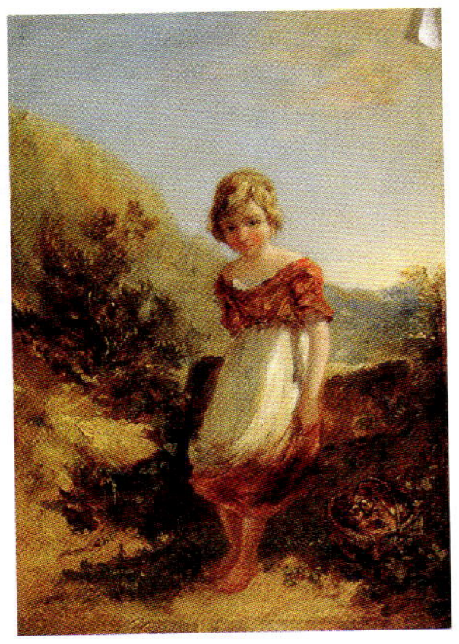

Muller, William James 1812–1845
Landscape with a Little Boy and a Basket 1832–1845
oil on canvas 35.8 x 24.9
VIS.1391

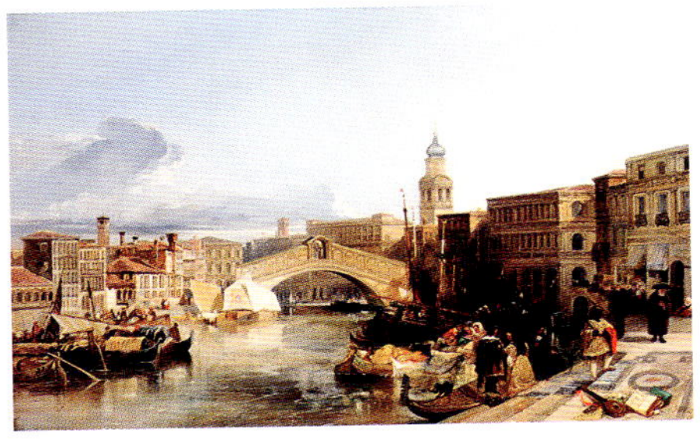

Muller, William James 1812–1845
Grand Canal, Venice 1835
oil on canvas 59.5 x 95.1
VIS.1462

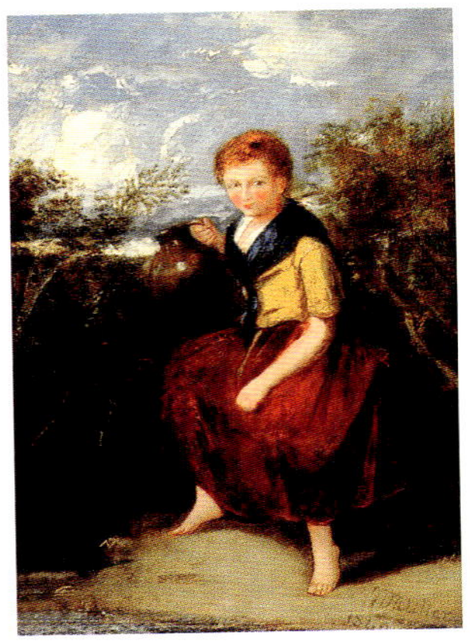

Muller, William James 1812–1845
A Peasant Girl 1840
oil on canvas 35.6 x 25.3
VIS.1040

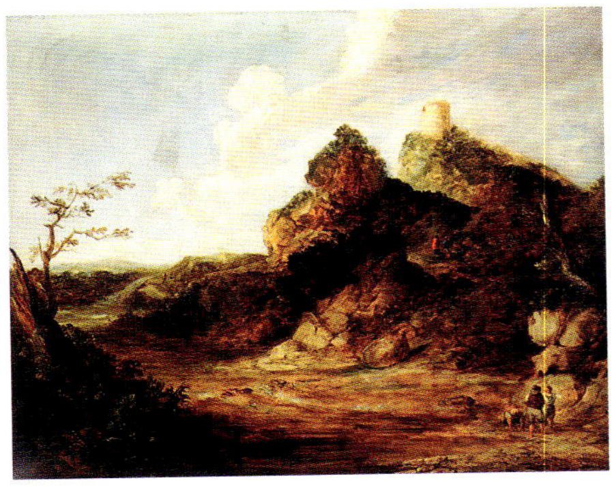

Muller, William James 1812–1845
Landscape 1843
oil on canvas 61.4 x 76.7
VIS.1361

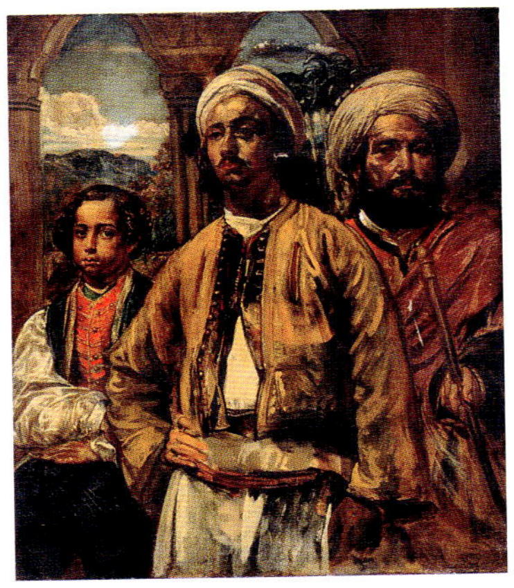

Muller, William James 1812–1845
A Moorish Nobleman and His Attendants
oil on canvas 60.8 x 50.6
VIS.3813

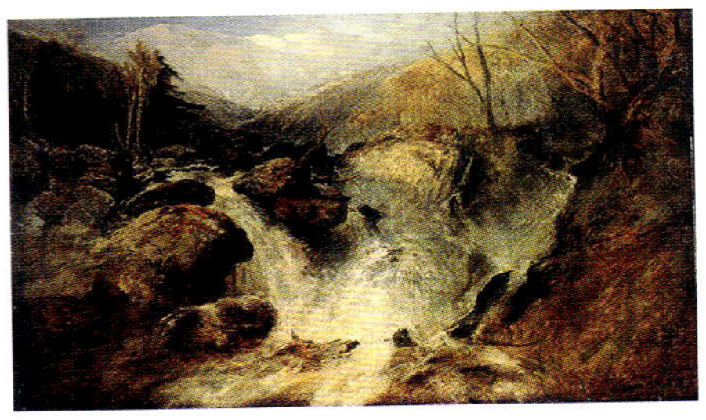

Muller, William James 1812–1845
A Mountain Waterfall in Snowdonia, Wales
oil on canvas 129.6 x 211.3
VIS.1480

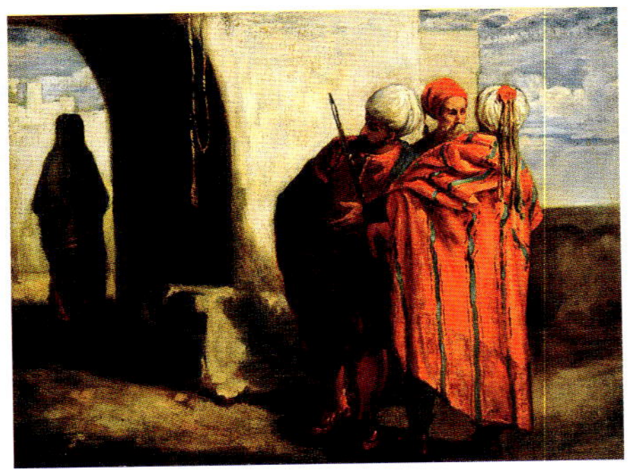

Muller, William James 1812–1845
A Persian Group
oil on canvas 55.4 x 72.6
VIS.284

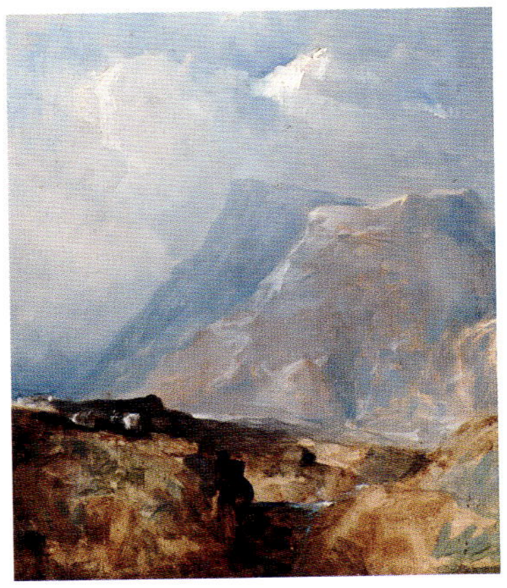

Muller, William James 1812–1845
A Sketch in Wales
oil on board 22.5 x 19.9
VIS.338

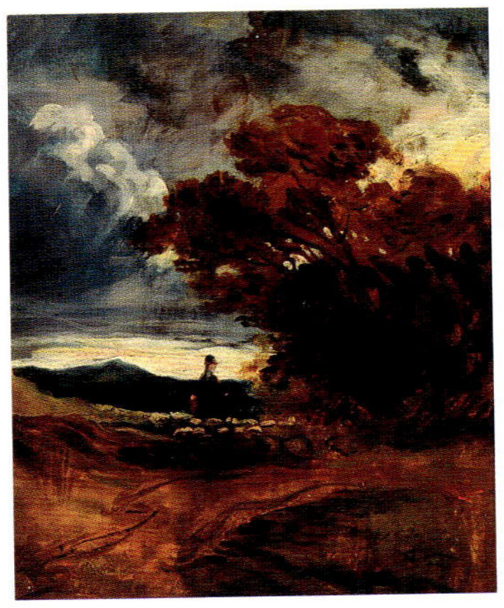

Muller, William James 1812–1845
Evening Sketch
oil on millboard 33.8 x 27.8
VIS.162

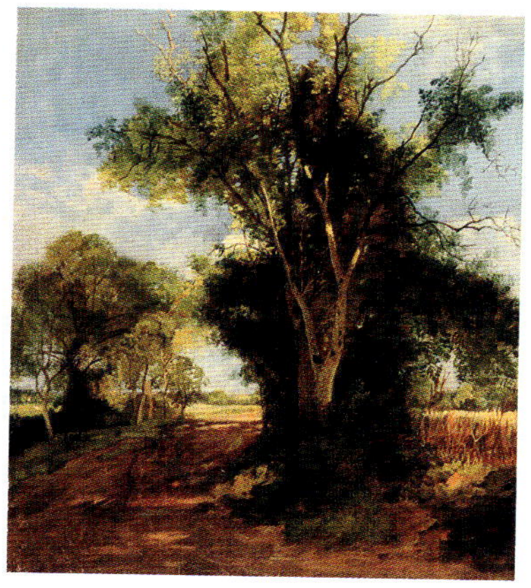

Muller, William James 1812–1845
Landscape
oil on board 30 x 26.4
VIS.1244

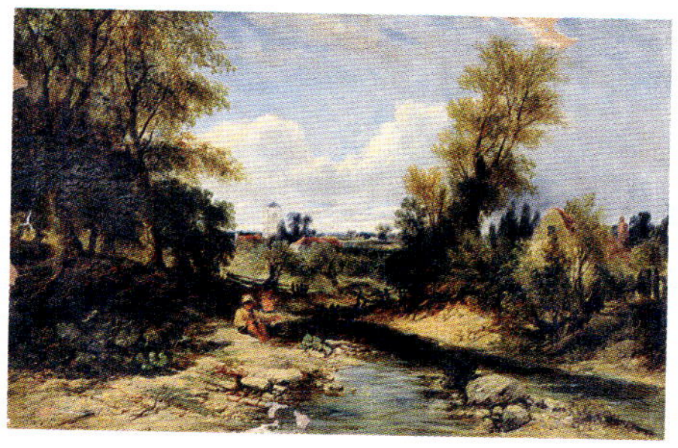

Muller, William James 1812–1845
Landscape
oil on canvas 60.5 x 90.5
VIS.1562

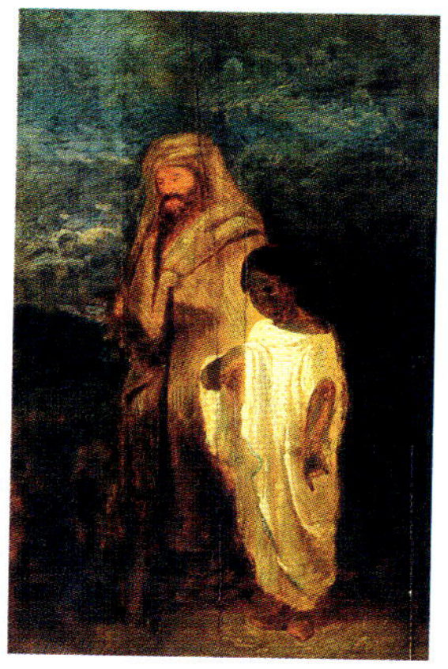

Muller, William James 1812–1845
Oriental and Girl
oil on panel 28.5 x 18
VIS.1369

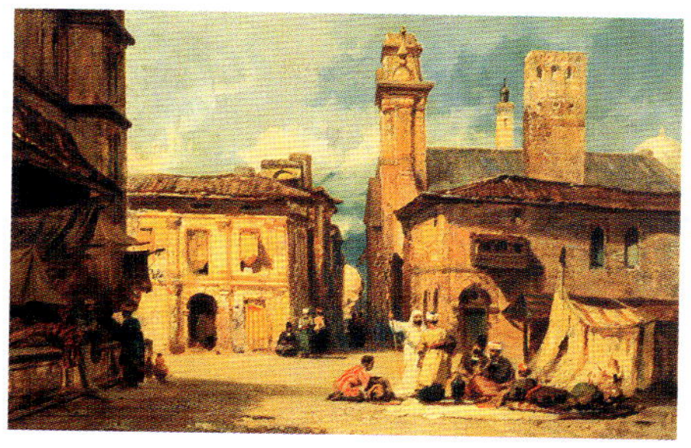

Muller, William James 1812–1845
Scene in Algiers
oil on canvas 59.2 x 89.7
VIS.1416

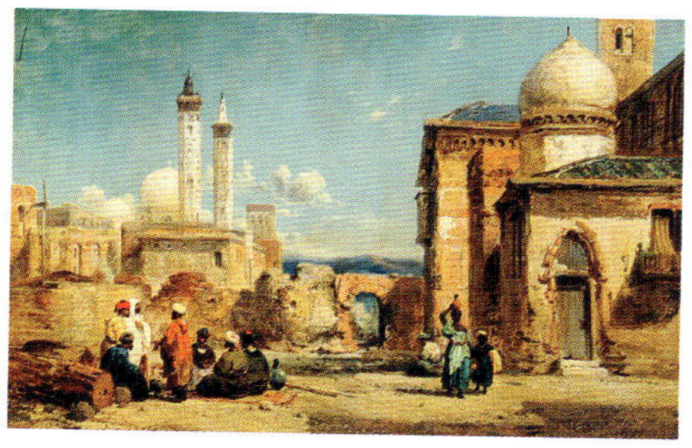

Muller, William James 1812–1845
Scene in Morocco
oil on canvas 59.5 x 90.6
VIS.1628

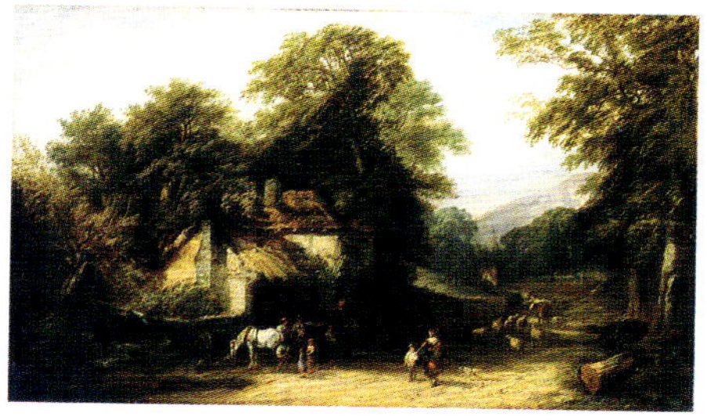

Muller, William James 1812–1845
The Village Smithy
oil on canvas 75.5 x 123.1
VIS.361

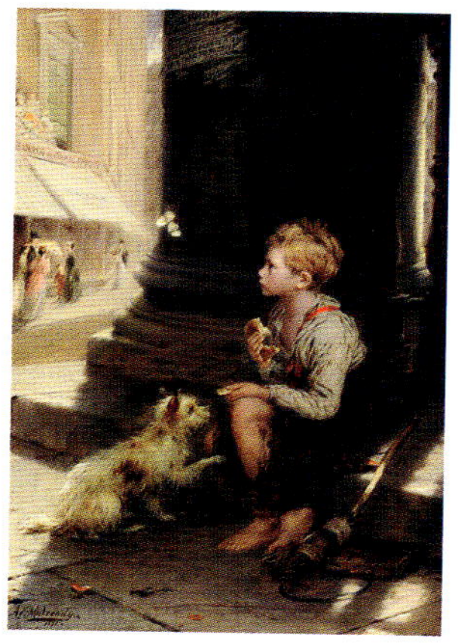

Mulready, Augustus Edwin 1844–1905
A Share of a Crust 1871
oil on canvas 33.3 x 23.1
VIS.1599

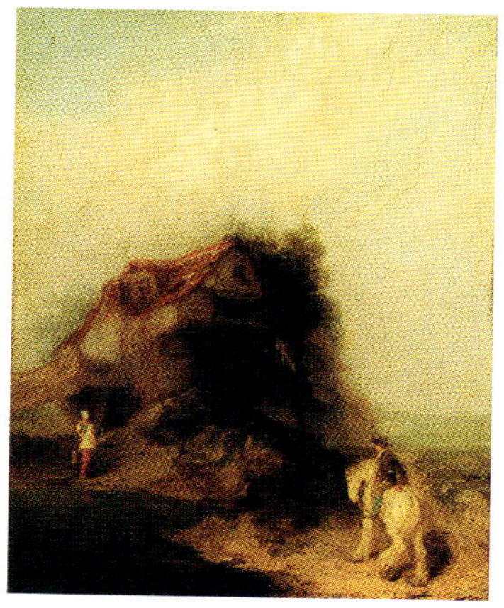

Mulready, William 1786–1863
Farmhouse with a White Horse
oil on canvas 30.5 x 24.8
VIS.653

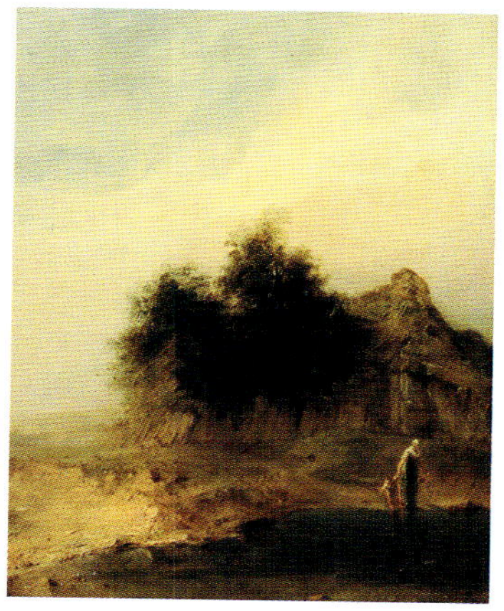

Mulready, William 1786–1863
The Cottage
oil on panel 30.3 x 24.9
VIS.2

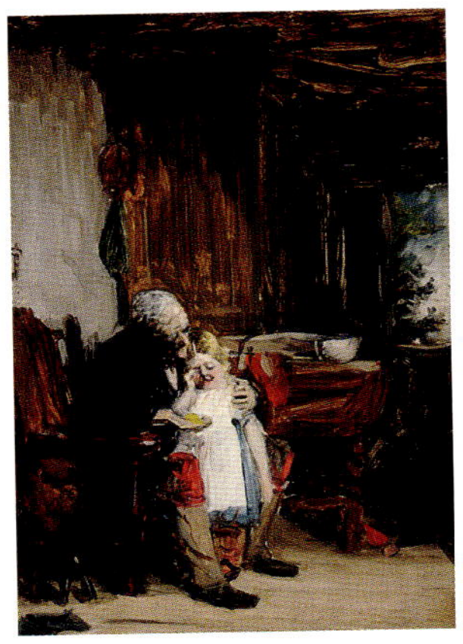

Mulready, William 1786–1863
The Dead Canary
oil on canvas 30.6 x 21.4
VIS.692

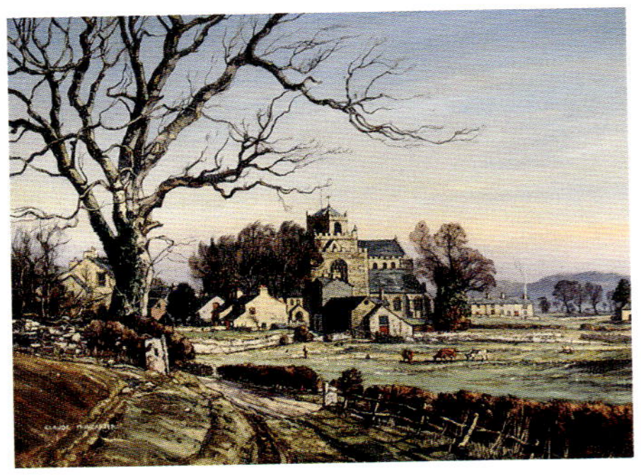

Muncaster, Claude 1903–1974
Winter's Morning, Cartmel Priory, Cumbria
oil on canvas 73.5 x 100.6
VIS.1847

Image removed due to copyright restrictions

Munnings, Alfred James 1878–1959
Goats on a Common 1903
oil on canvas 39.8 x 31.9
VIS.211

Image removed due to copyright restrictions

Munnings, Alfred James 1878–1959
Hop-Picking
oil on canvas 92.1 x 102.2
VIS.132

Image removed due to copyright restrictions

Munnings, Alfred James 1878–1959
The Grey Mare
oil on canvas 49.5 x 59.6
VIS.1885

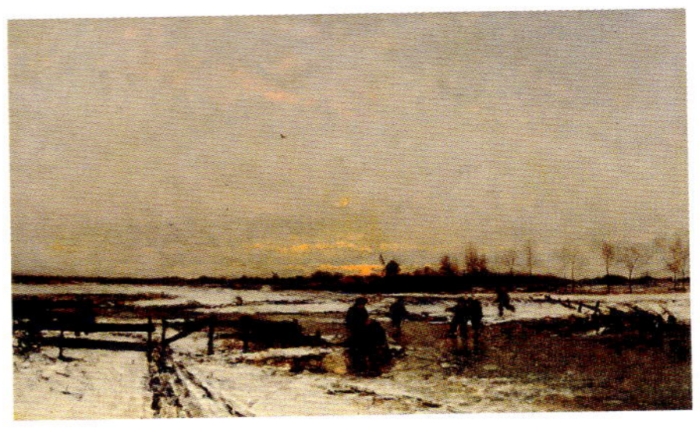

Munthe, Ludwig 1841–1896
Winter Scene
oil on canvas 51.8 x 82.8
VIS.1580

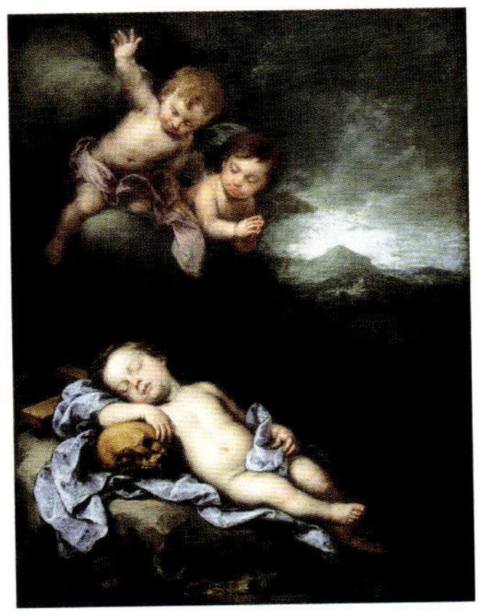

Murillo, Bartolomé Esteban 1618–1682
The Infant Christ Asleep on the Cross
oil on canvas 198.8 x 143.5
VIS.73

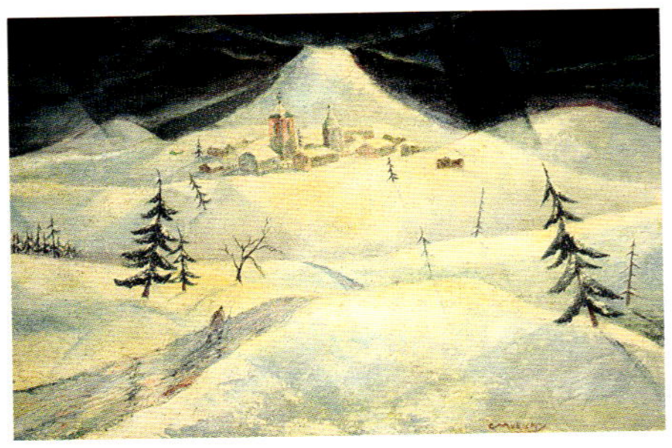

Murray, Charles 1894–1954
Russian Village, Winter c.1933
oil on canvas 59.2 x 89.3
VIS.1856

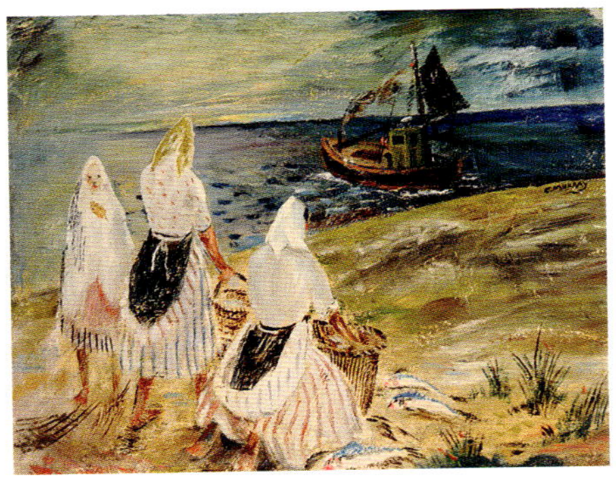

Murray, Charles 1894–1954
Scottish Fisherwomen
oil on plywood 27.8 x 35.5
VIS.5433

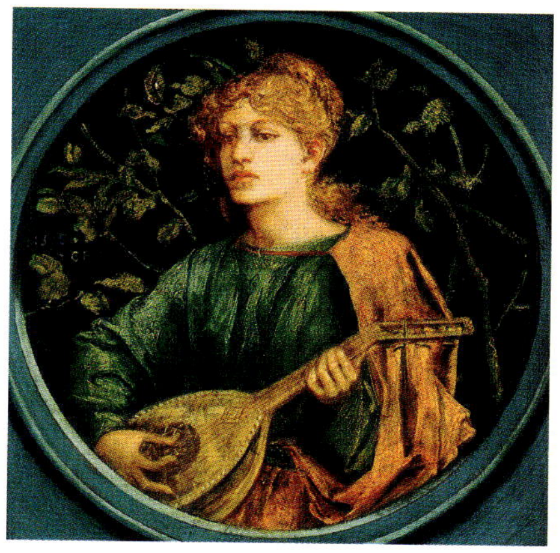

Murray, Charles Fairfax 1849–1919
Mandolin Player
oil on panel 23.5 x 23.5
VIS.22

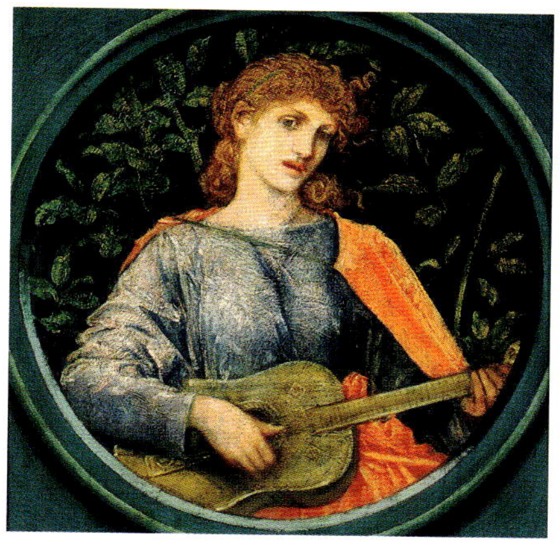

Murray, Charles Fairfax (attributed to) 1849–1919
Guitar Player
oil on panel 23.3 x 23.3
VIS.19

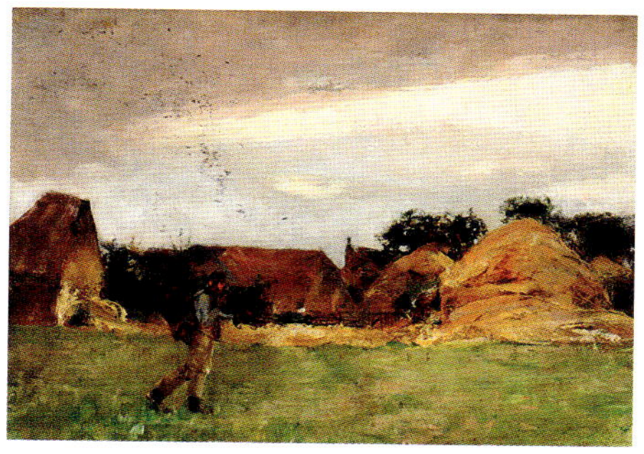

Murray, David 1849–1933
Homeward, Sunset 1890
oil on canvas 24.3 x 34.2
VIS.4474

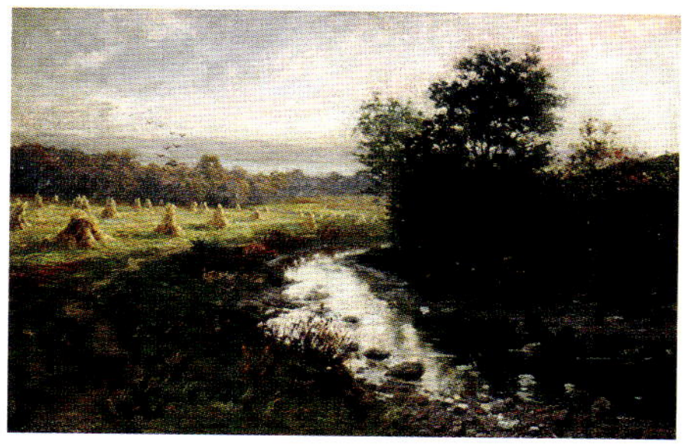

Murray, David 1849–1933
The Stream 1892
oil on canvas 49.3 x 74.7
VIS.204

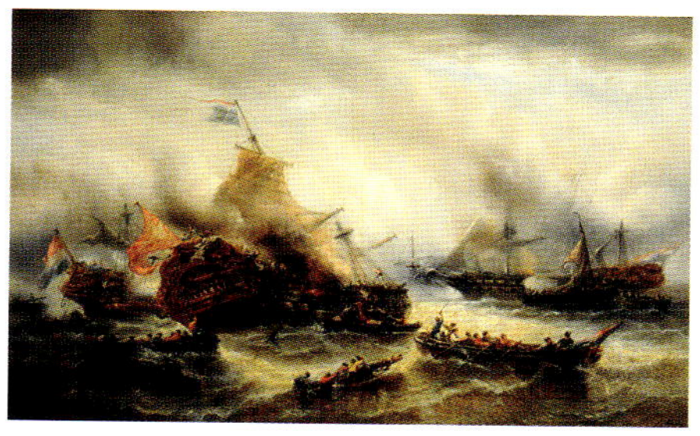

Musin, François Etienne 1820–1888
Sea Fight
oil on canvas 49.7 x 78.7
VIS.1523

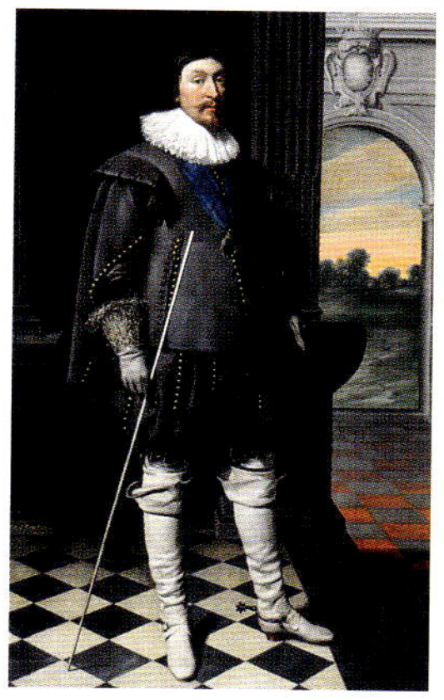

Mytens, Daniel I c.1590–1647
James Hamilton (1589–1625), 2nd Marquess of Hamilton and 4th Earl of Arran, KG, PC
1623
oil on canvas 258.3 x 174
VIS.3599

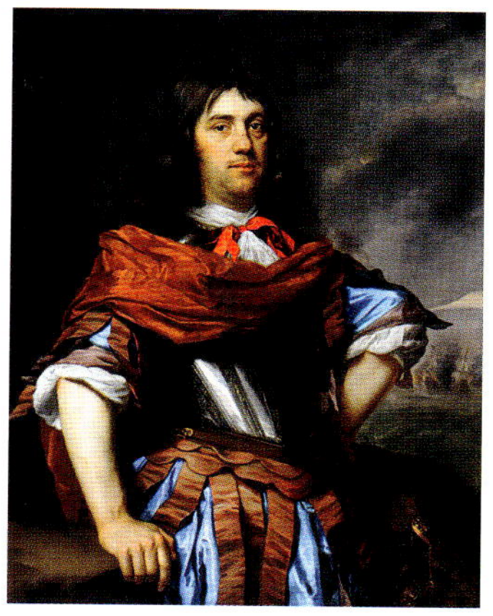

Mytens, Jan (attributed to) c.1614–1670
Admiral Cornelius Tromp (1629–1691) c.1668
oil on panel 109.3 x 84.8
VIS.89

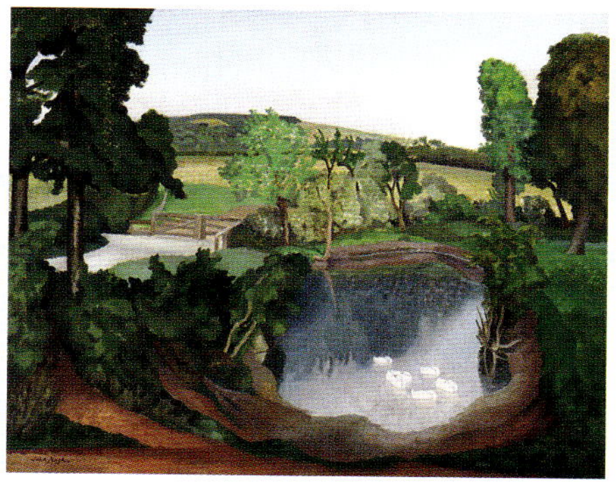

Nash, John Northcote 1893–1977
Ashby's Pond c.1937
oil on canvas 67.9 x 85
VIS.2947

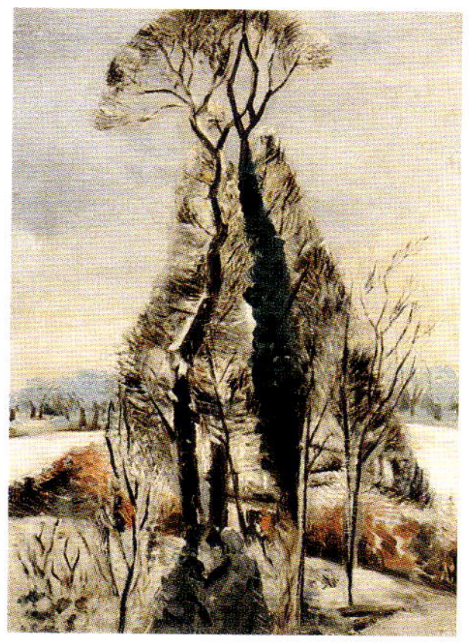

Nash, Paul 1889–1946
Iver Heath, Buckinghamshire, Snow
1927–1928
oil on canvas 82.5 x 64
VIS.4224

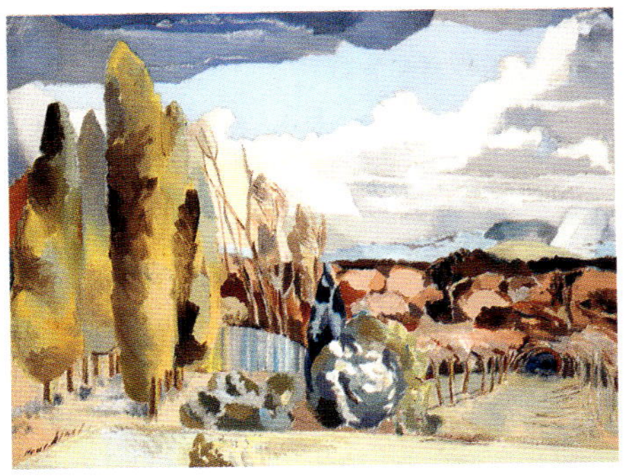

Nash, Paul 1889–1946
March Landscape 1944
oil on canvas 69.8 x 84.8
VIS.5184

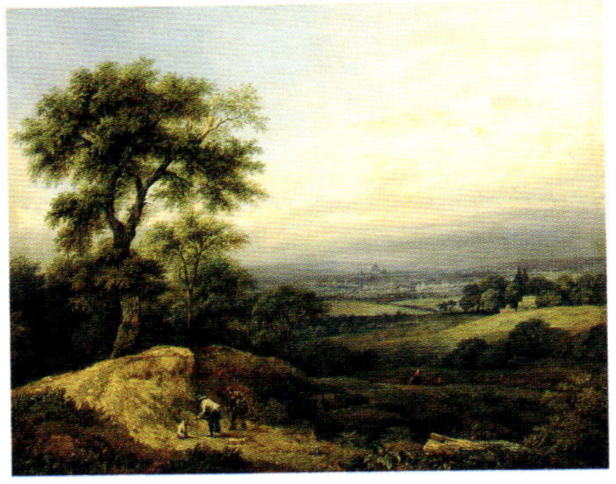

Nasmyth, Patrick 1787–1831
Landscape 1826
oil on canvas 62.3 x 75.6
VIS.1548

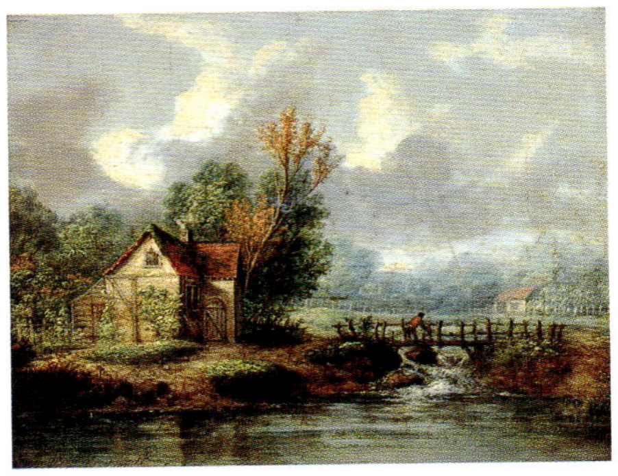

Nasmyth, Patrick 1787–1831
Landscape 1828
oil on panel 27.1 x 47.2
VIS.538

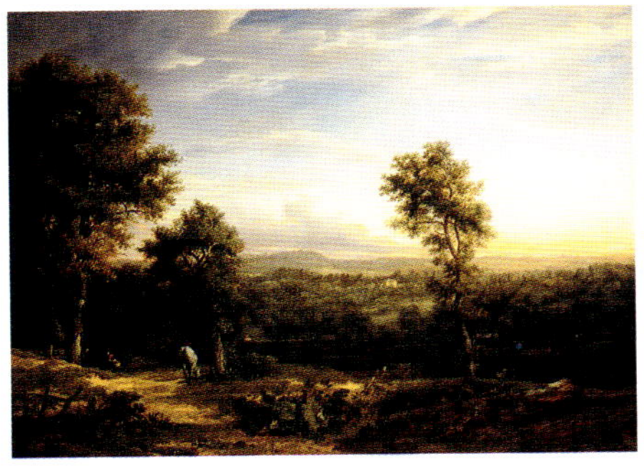

Nasmyth, Patrick 1787–1831
Landscape 1828
oil on canvas 45.6 x 60.9
VIS.1569

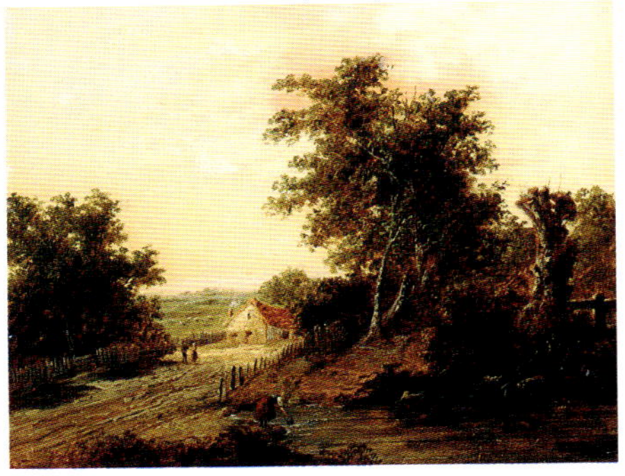

Nasmyth, Patrick 1787–1831
Landscape 1830
oil on panel 19.1 x 24.3
VIS.1098

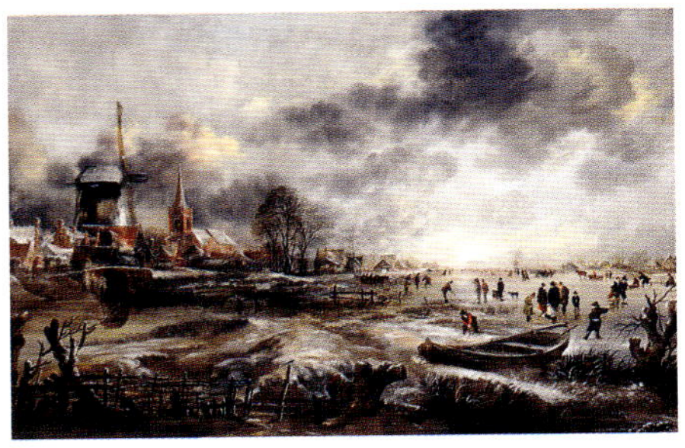

Neer, Aert van der 1603–1677
Frozen River Scene 1641–1660
oil on canvas 111 x 165.9
VIS.4676

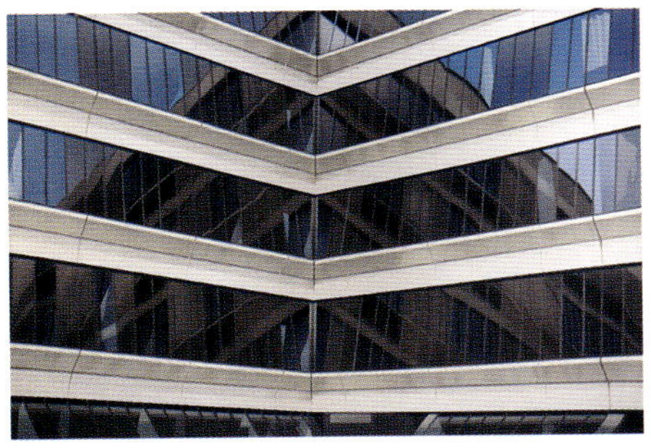

Neiland, Brendan b.1941
Corner 1975
acrylic on canvas 149.2 x 215.3
VIS.4203

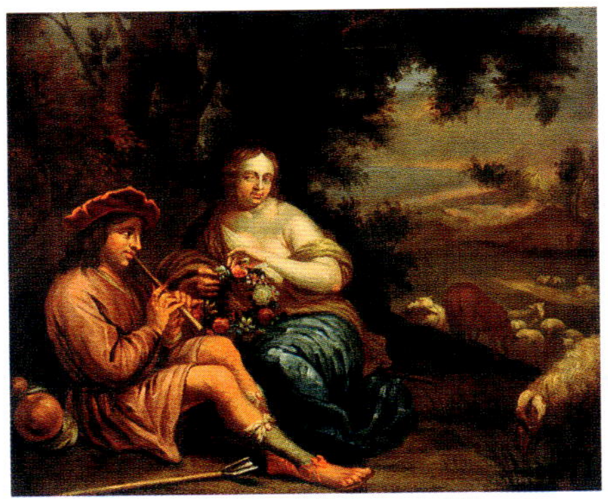

Netscher, Wilhelm Adrian 1791–1851
Landscape with Figures 1815
oil on canvas 28.9 x 34.5
VIS.1238

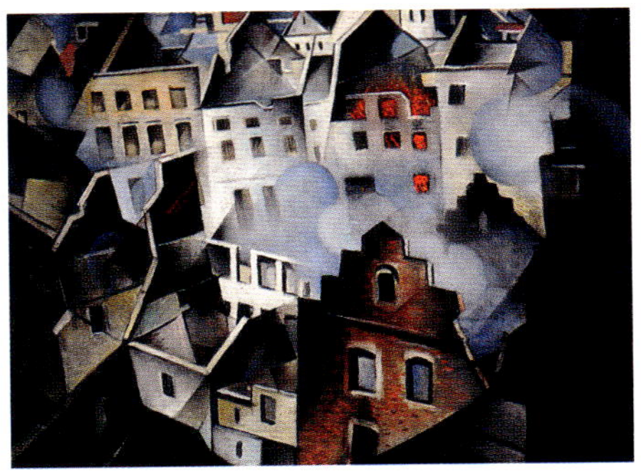

Nevinson, Christopher 1889–1946
Ypres after the First Bombardment 1916
oil on canvas 99.1 x 124.8
VIS.4347

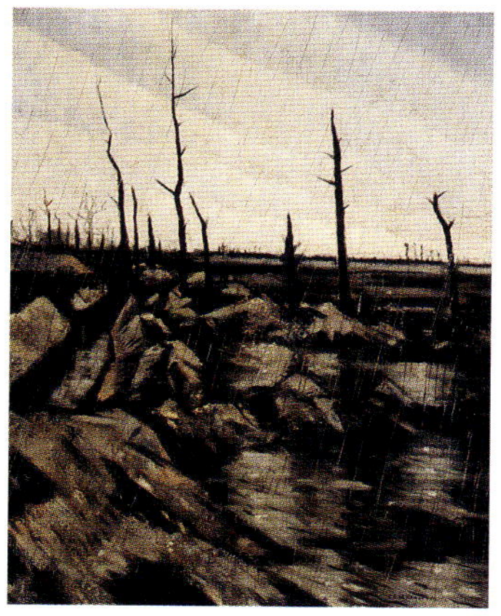

Nevinson, Christopher 1889–1946
Rain and Mud after the Battle 1917
oil on canvas 63.5 x 53.2
VIS.3781

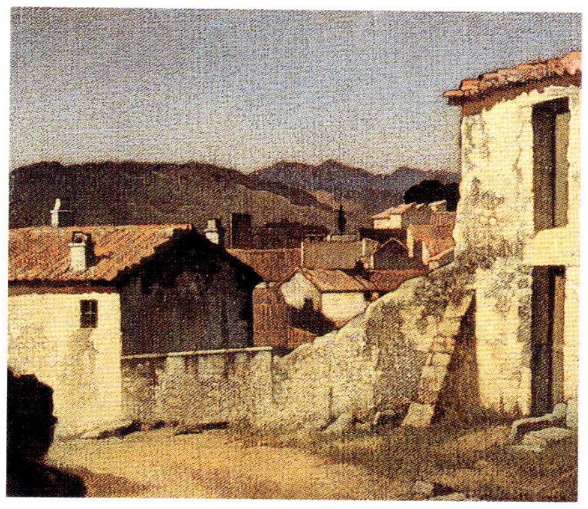

Nicholls, Bertram 1883–1974
View in Provence, France 1923
oil on canvas 33.8 x 38.9
VIS.2968

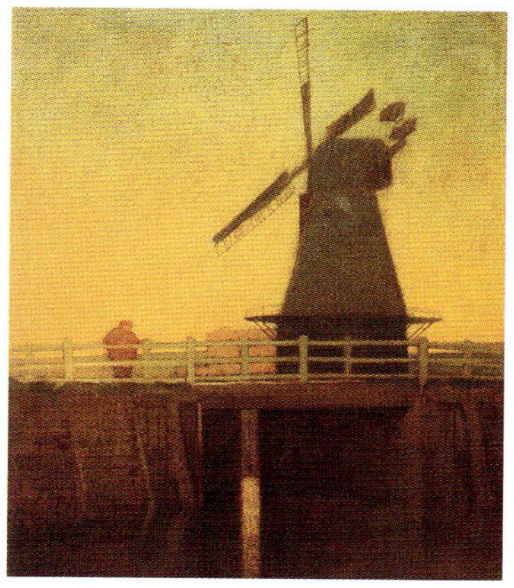

Nicholls, Bertram 1883–1974
The Windmill at Rye, East Sussex
oil on canvas 45.5 x 39.8
VIS.163

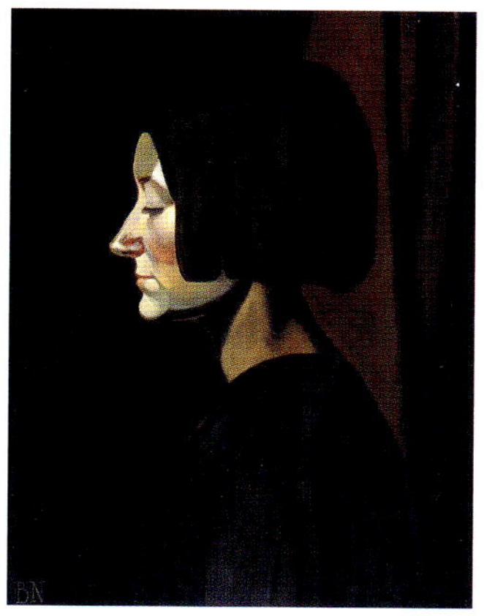

Nicholson, Ben 1894–1982
1917 (portrait of Edie)
oil on canvas 47 x 35.5
VIS.250

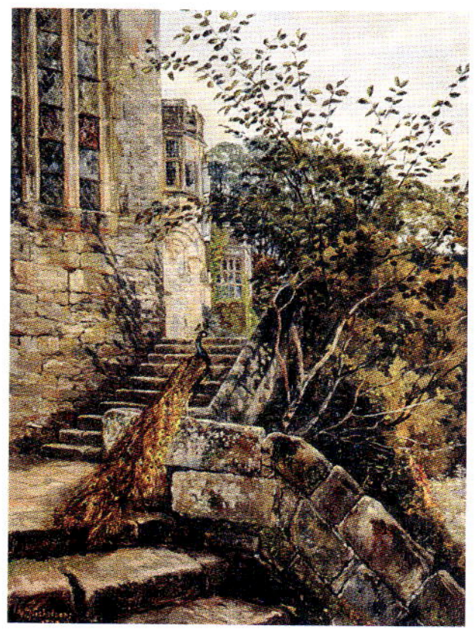

Nicholson, Walter 1830–1907
Old Chapel Steps, Haddon Hall, Derbyshire
1879
oil on canvas 50.1 x 36
VIS.1508

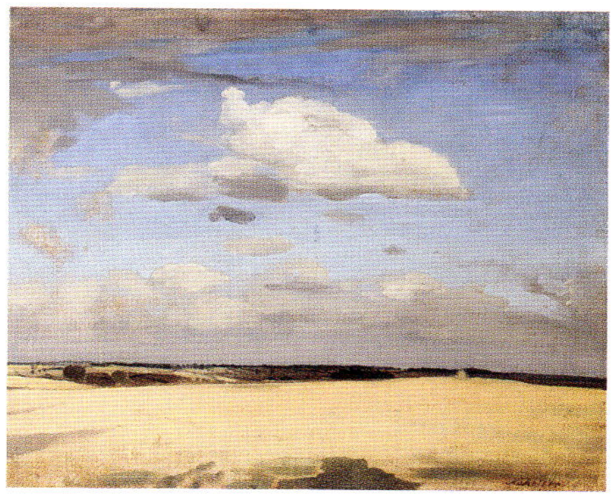

Nicholson, William 1872–1949
The Devil's Flight, Gloucestershire c.1911
oil on canvas 67.2 x 77.3
VIS.127

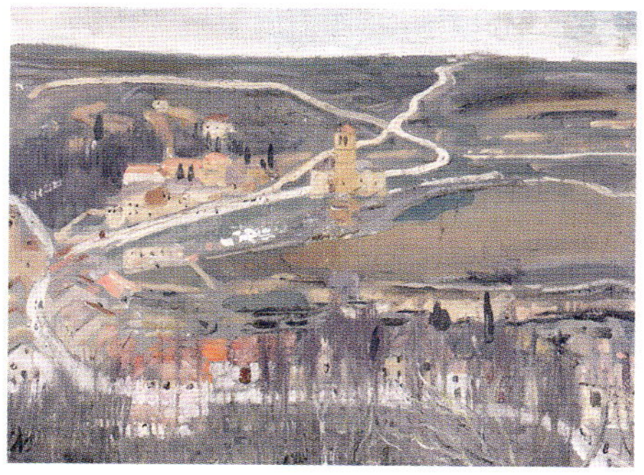

Nicholson, William 1872–1949
The Road to Zamarramala, Spain
oil on panel 29.3 x 39.3
VIS.4055

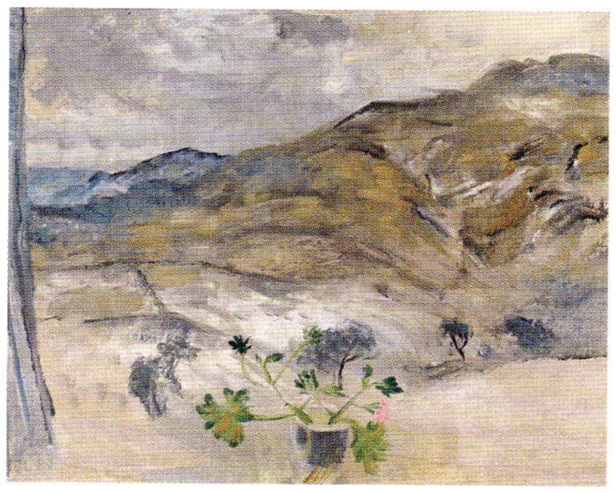

Nicholson, Winifred 1893–1981
Cockley Moor, Cumbria
oil on canvas 44.4 x 54.7
VIS.3814

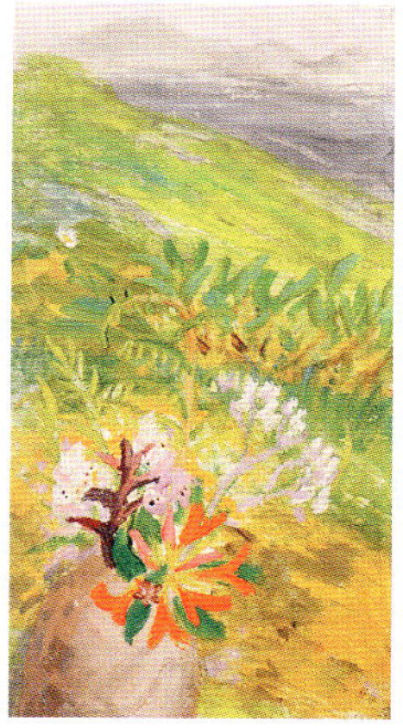

Nicholson, Winifred 1893–1981
Kathleen's Bunch II
oil on panel 48.5 x 26.1
VIS.3975

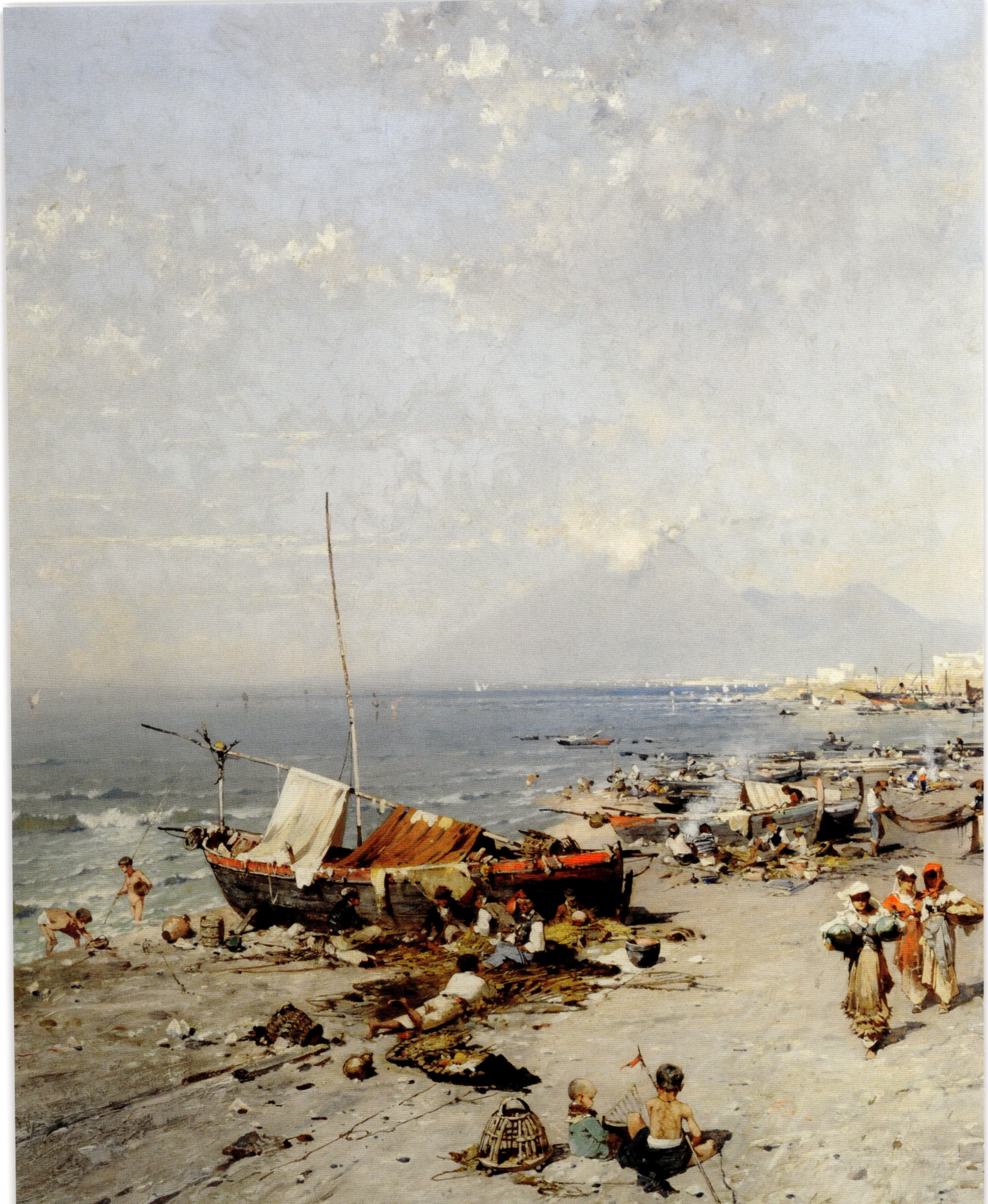

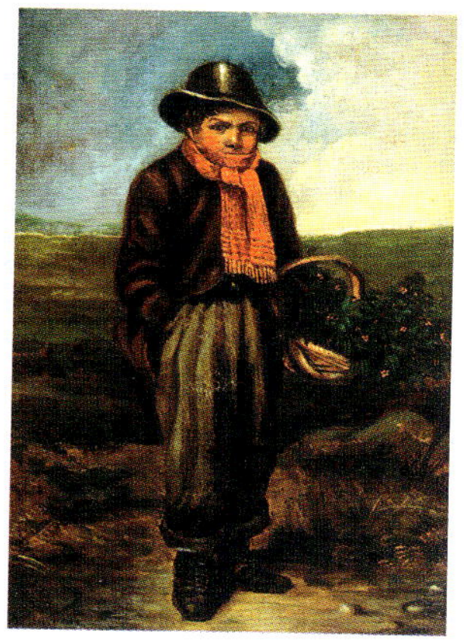

Nicol, Erskine 1825–1904
The Errand Boy 1849
oil on canvas 19 x 13.5
VIS.1011

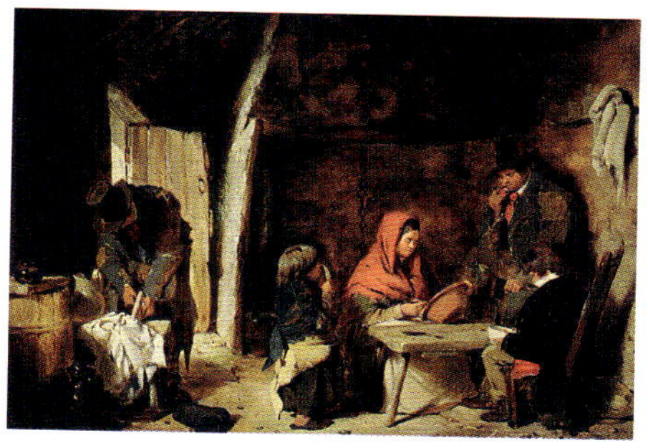

Nicol, Erskine 1825–1904
Scene in an Irish Cabin 1851
oil on canvas 36.2 x 51.3
VIS.1399

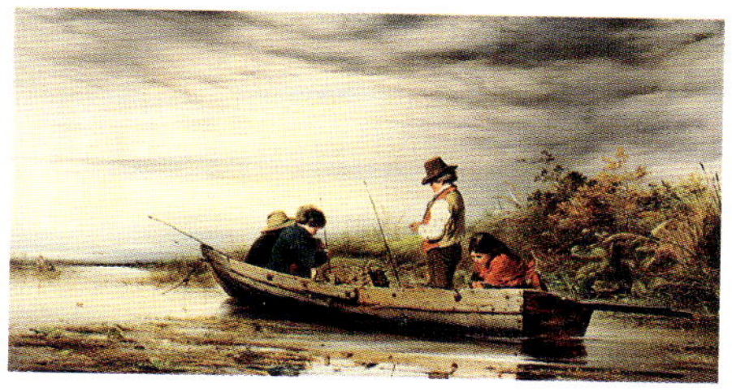

Nicol, Erskine 1825–1904
The Perch Fishers 1857
oil on canvas 57.4 x 106.1
VIS.1554

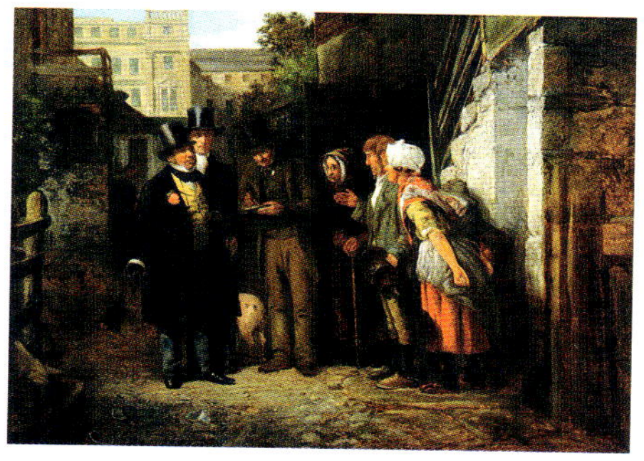

Nicol, Erskine 1825–1904
Notice to Quit 1862
oil on canvas 51 x 69.1
VIS.543

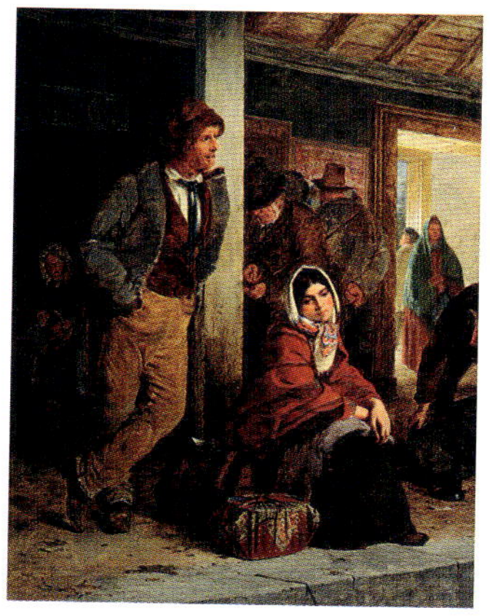

Nicol, Erskine 1825–1904
Irish Emigrants Waiting for the Train 1864
oil on canvas 71 x 55.3
VIS.1616

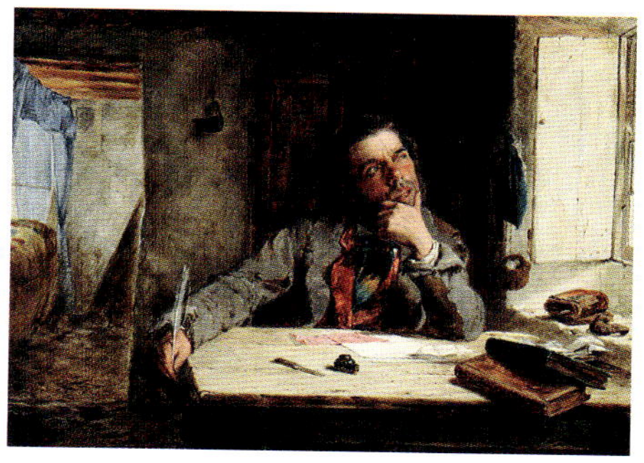

Nicol, Erskine 1825–1904
Collecting His Thoughts 1865
oil on canvas 35 x 47.1
VIS.1371

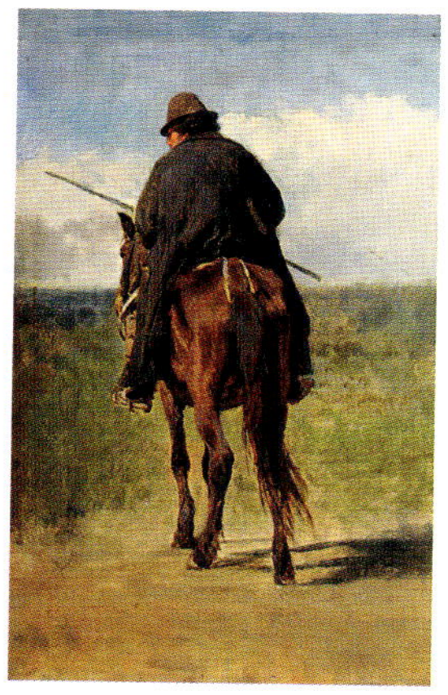

Nicol, Erskine 1825–1904
An Irish Peasant 1881–1904
oil on millboard 44.4 x 28.3
VIS.691

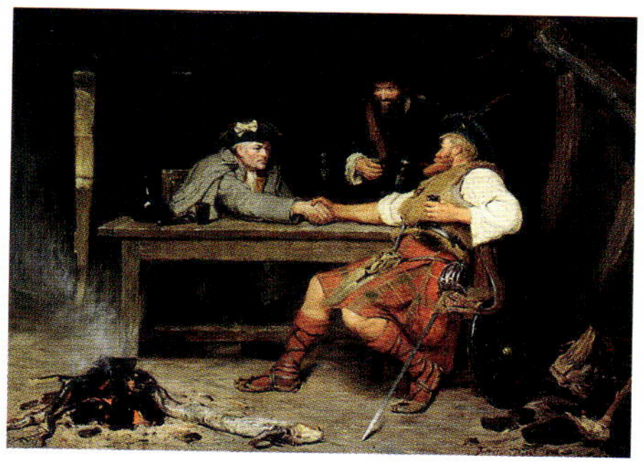

Nicol, John Watson 1856–1926
For Better, for Worse: Rob Roy and the Baillie
1886
oil on canvas 71.6 x 98.3
VIS.1426

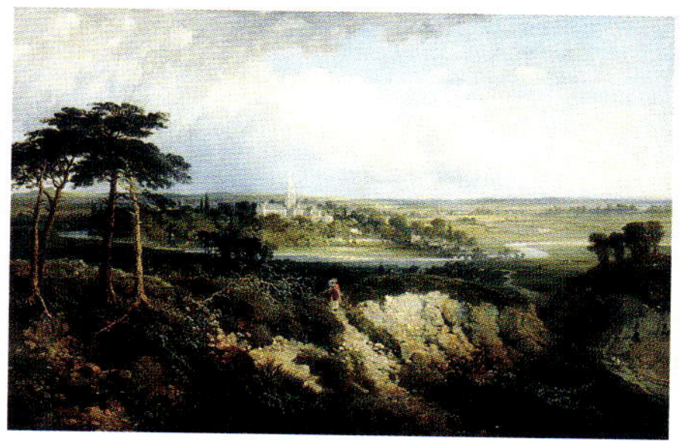

Niemann, Edmund John 1813–1876
Salisbury, Wiltshire 1859
oil on canvas 49 x 74.5
VIS.323

Facing page: Unterberger, Franz Richard, 1838–1902, *Rivera de Castellammare, Italy* (detail), 1870–1875, Museums Sheffield, (p. 231)

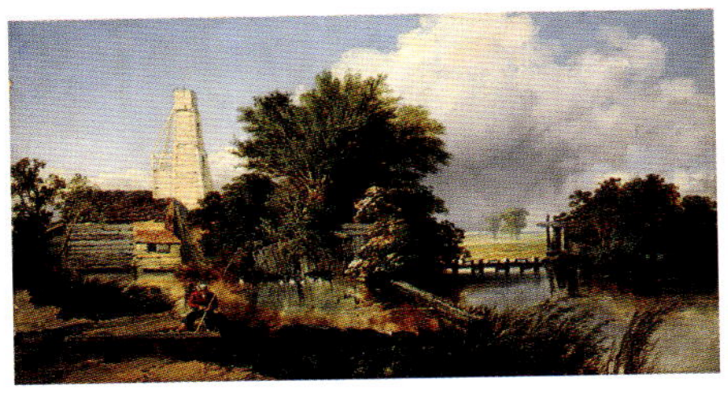
Niemann, Edmund John 1813–1876
View at Hertford 1859
oil on canvas 62.4 x 113.1
VIS.1526

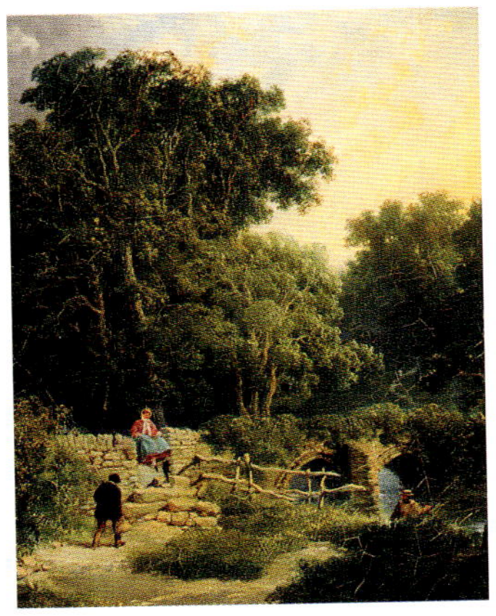
Niemann, Edmund John 1813–1876
A Wooded Glade 1862
oil on canvas 36.7 x 28.7
VIS.2743

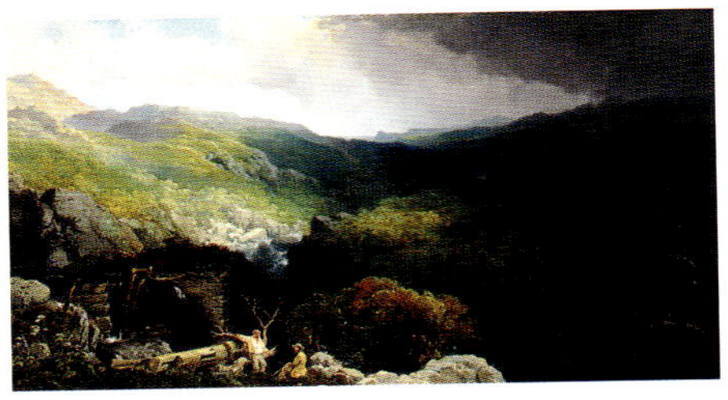
Niemann, Edmund John 1813–1876
Mountain Scene near Barmouth, Wales 1862
oil on canvas 63.8 x 114.7
VIS.118

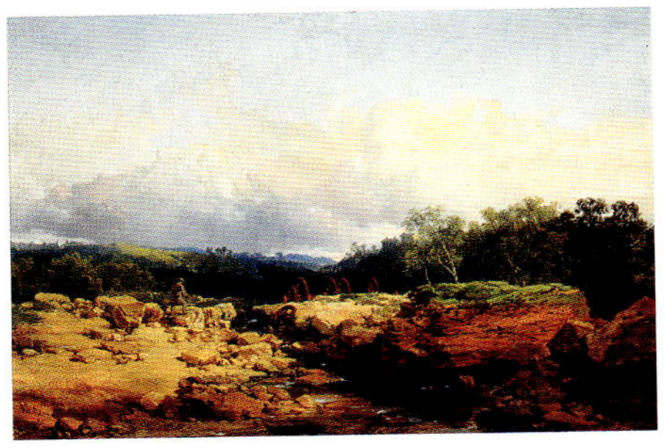
Niemann, Edmund John 1813–1876
The River Don after the Flood 1865
oil on canvas 33.5 x 49
K1955.4

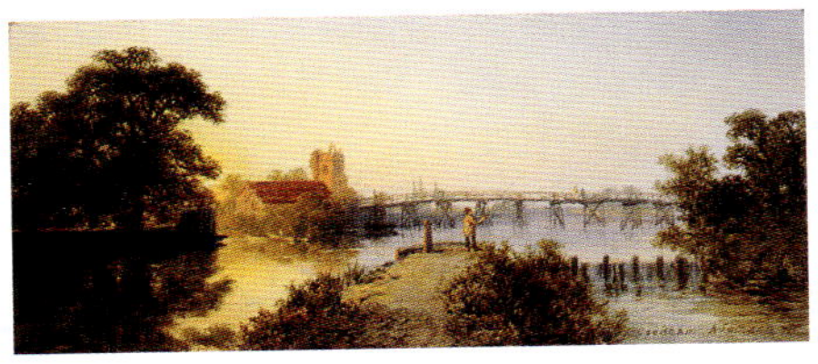
Niemann, Edmund John 1813–1876
Cookham on Thames, Berkshire 1878
oil on millboard 20.1 x 45.7
VIS.2775

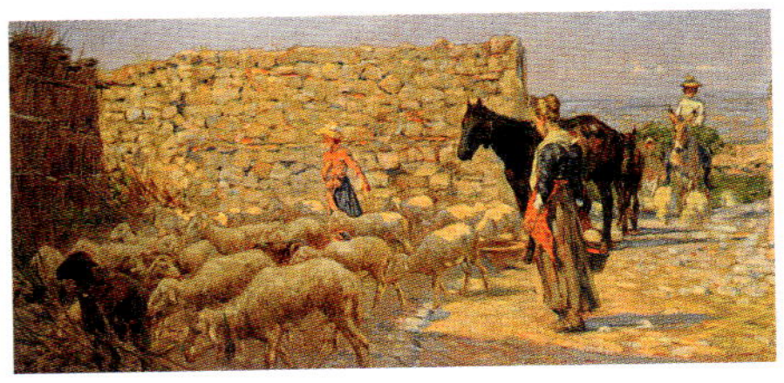
Niemann, Edmund John 1813–1876
Flock of Sheep 1905
oil on canvas 53 x 92.5
VIS.997

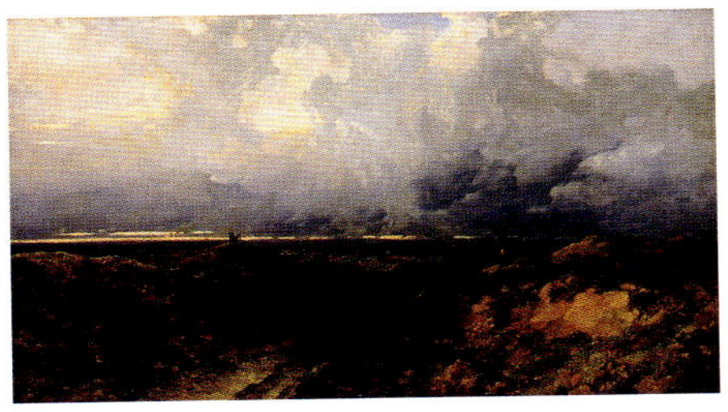
Niemann, Edmund John 1813–1876
A Storm on the Moors
oil on canvas 58.7 x 103.5
VIS.2746

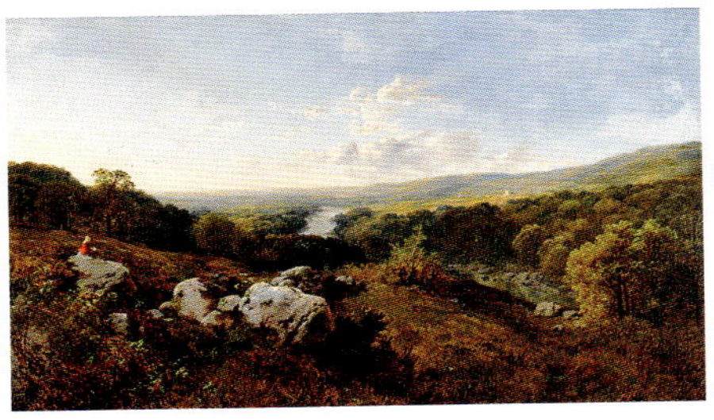
Niemann, Edmund John 1813–1876
In the Valley of the Nidd, Yorkshire
oil on canvas 74.2 x 125
VIS.1316

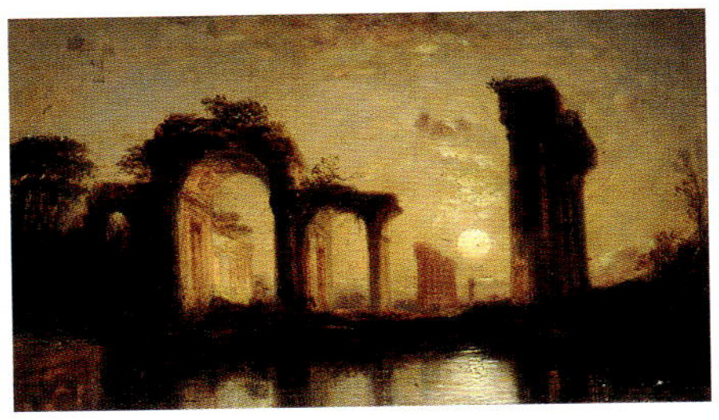
Niemann, Edmund John 1813–1876
Moonrise
oil on panel 13.7 x 23.8
VIS.278

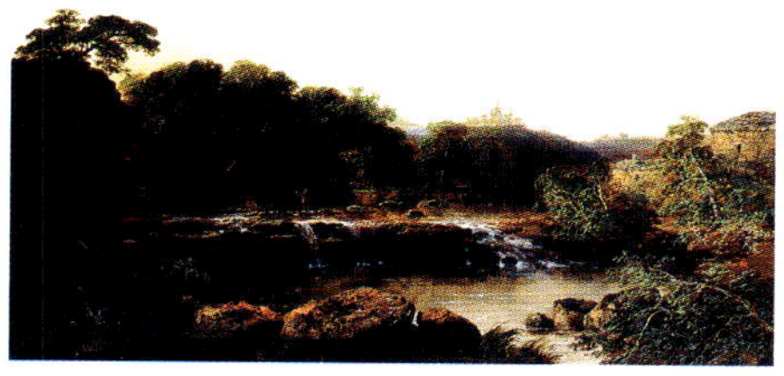

Niemann, Edmund John 1813–1876
Near Richmond, Yorkshire
oil on canvas 61.3 x 112.8
VIS.2734

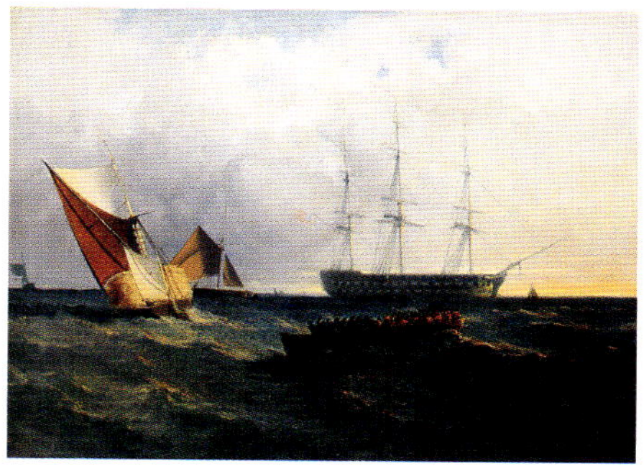

Niemann, Edmund John 1813–1876
The Guardship of the Nore
oil on canvas 44.6 x 59.7
VIS.1604

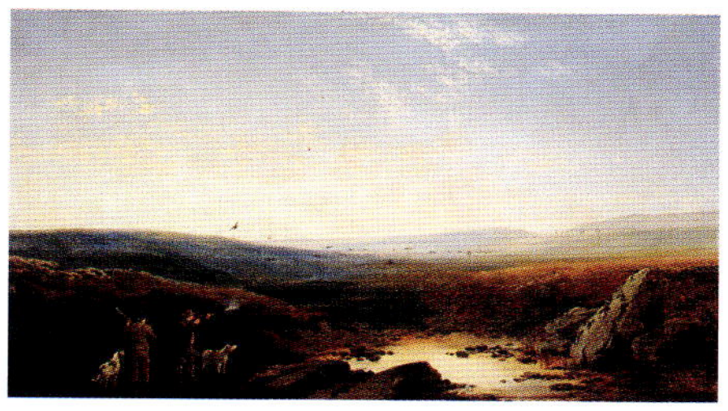

Niemann, Edmund John 1813–1876 & **Prades, Alfred F. de** active 1844–1883
Pateley Moor, North Yorkshire 1879
oil on canvas 54.7 x 95.4
VIS.593

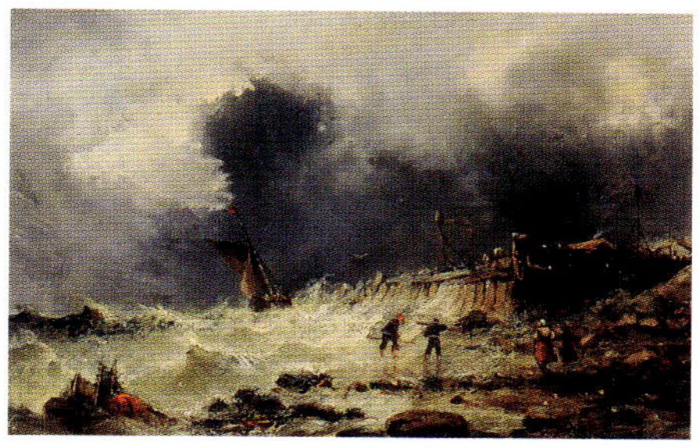

Niemann, Edmund John (school of) 1813–1876
Sailing Ship in a Storm
oil on millboard 29 x 44.5
VIS.2366

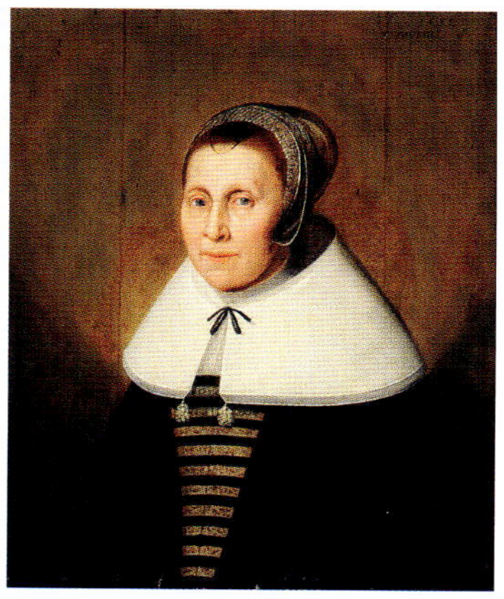

Nieuwal, Jan Rutgers active 1620–1661
Portrait of a Lady, Aged 58 1651
oil on panel 70 x 57
VIS.141

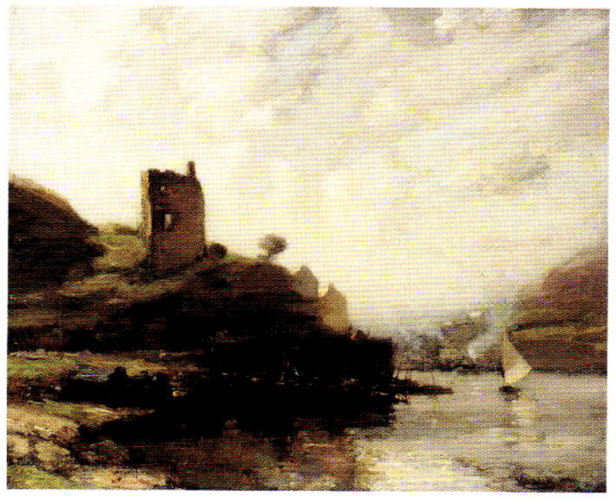

Noble, James Campbell 1846–1913
Tarbert, Scotland
oil on canvas 63.8 x 77
VIS.511

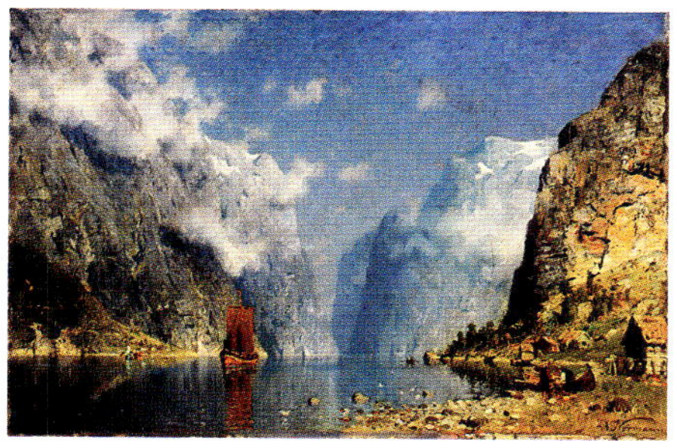

Normann, Adelsteen 1848–1918
Lake Scene
oil on canvas 68.5 x 120
VIS.111

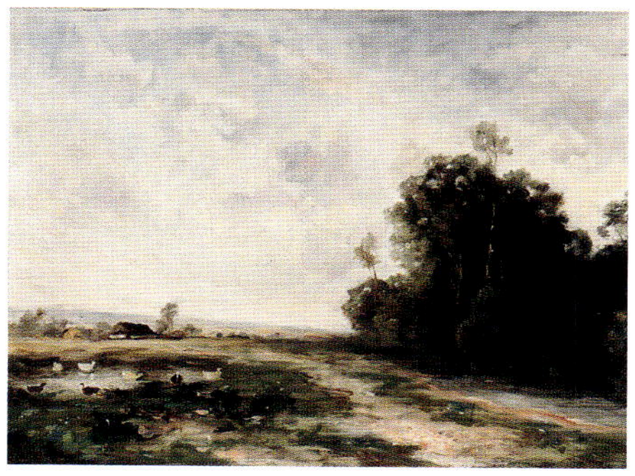

O'Briton (attributed to)
Landscape 1870–1880
oil on panel 45 x 59.9
VIS.1287

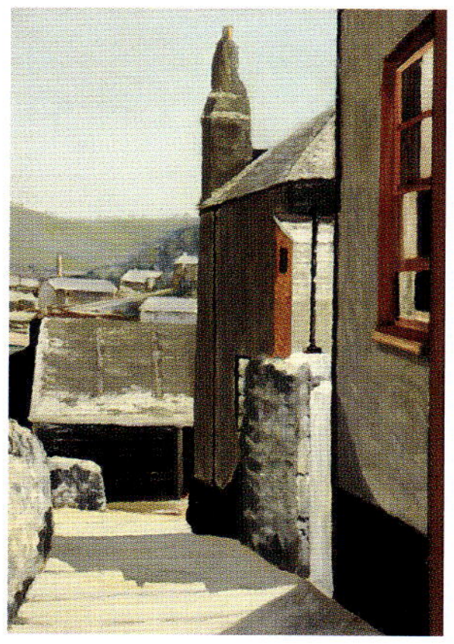

O'Connor, Aloysius Patrick
Overgang, Brixham, Devon
oil on canvas 60.6 x 39.4
VIS.648

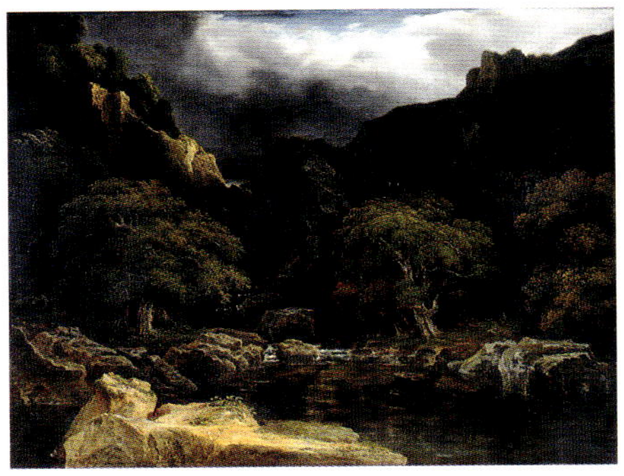

O'Connor, James Arthur 1792–1841
In the Dargle Country, Ireland 1829
oil on canvas 70 x 88.5
VIS.1546

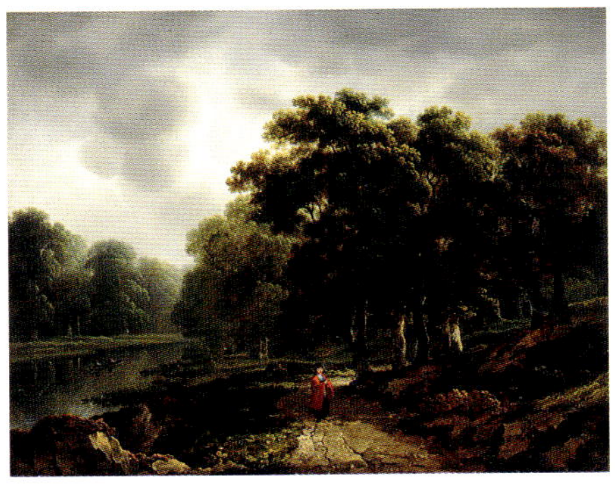

O'Connor, James Arthur 1792–1841
Landscape 1840
oil on canvas 35.2 x 43.7
VIS.1413

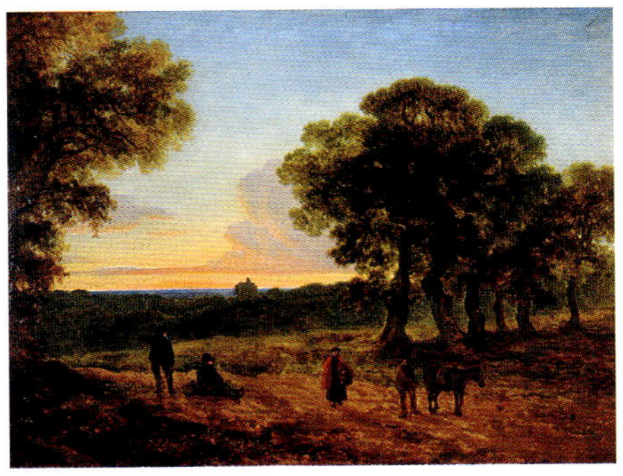

O'Connor, James Arthur 1792–1841
Evening
oil on panel 17.2 x 22.5
VIS.65

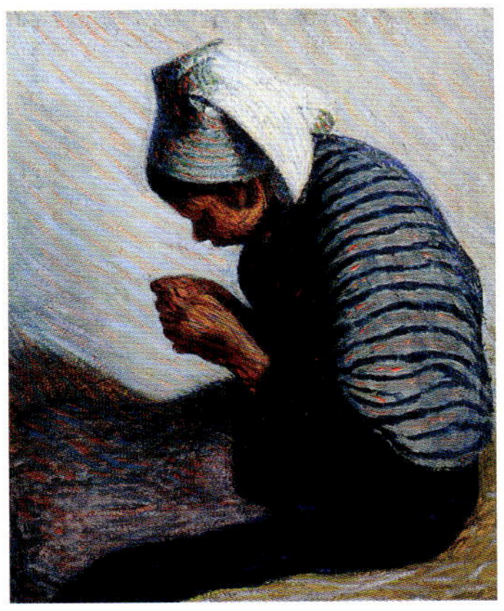

O'Conor, Roderic 1860–1940
Jeune paysanne Bretonne
oil on canvas 79.2 x 63.7
VIS.LI.1111 (P)

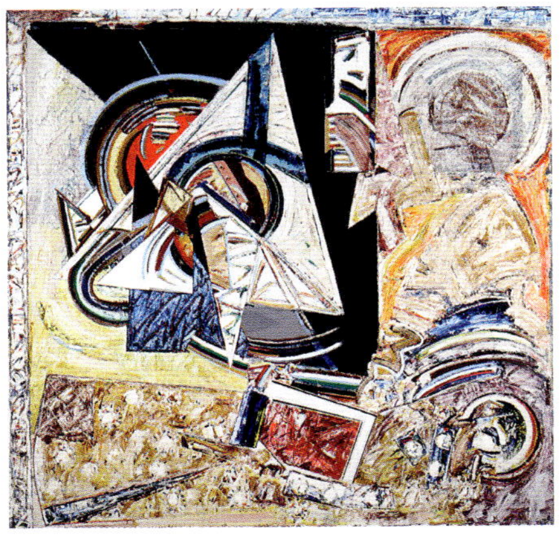

Oliver, Ken b.1948
The Visit 1981
acrylic, wax & collage on canvas 188 x 188
VIS.5104

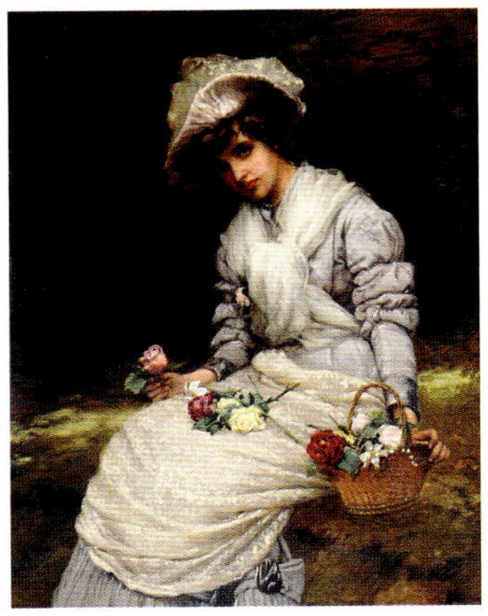

Oliver, William 1823–1901
Gathering ye Roses 1882
oil on canvas 90.1 x 69.7
VIS.2920

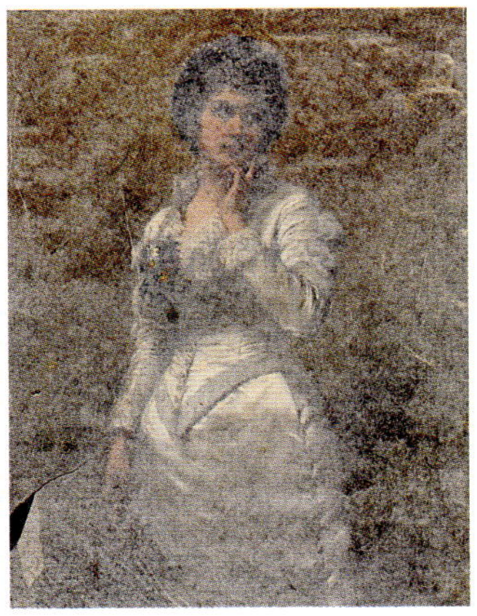

Oliver, William 1823–1901
Hark 1882
oil on canvas 60.5 x 45.4
VIS.2528

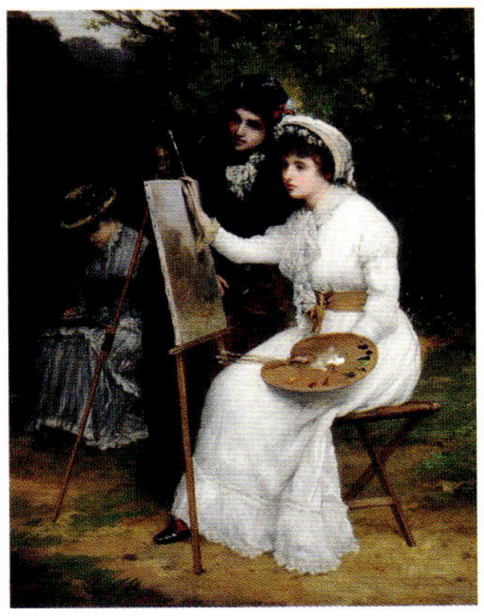

Oliver, William 1823–1901
Sketching from Nature 1882
oil on canvas 90 x 69.5
VIS.2925

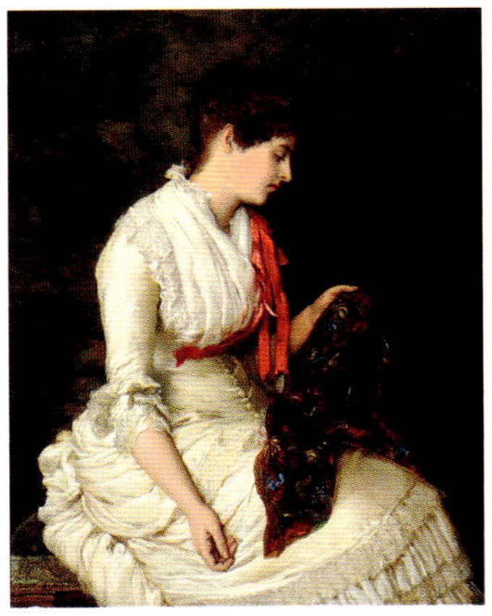

Oliver, William 1823–1901
Industry 1883
oil on canvas 92 x 71
VIS.2921

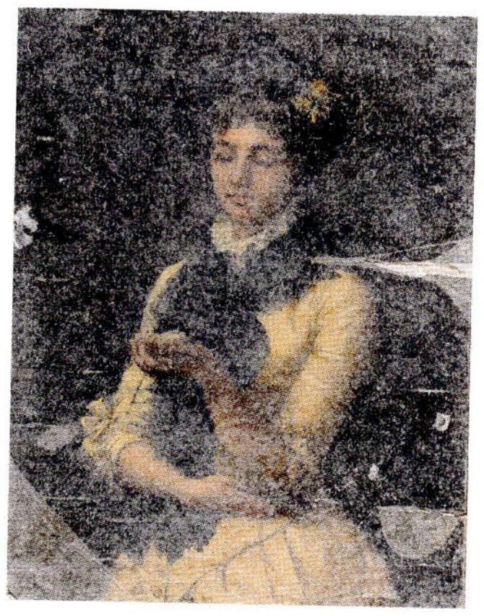

Oliver, William 1823–1901
Pity, Oh the Pity 1883
oil on canvas 60 x 45.4
VIS.2527

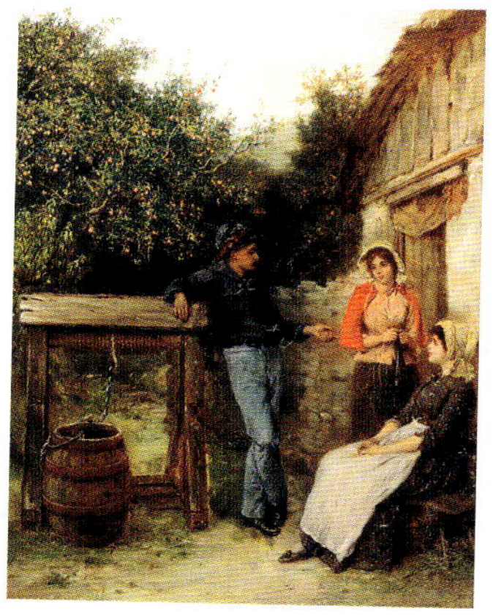

Oliver, William 1823–1901
At the Well 1885
oil on canvas 64.5 x 49.5
VIS.1952

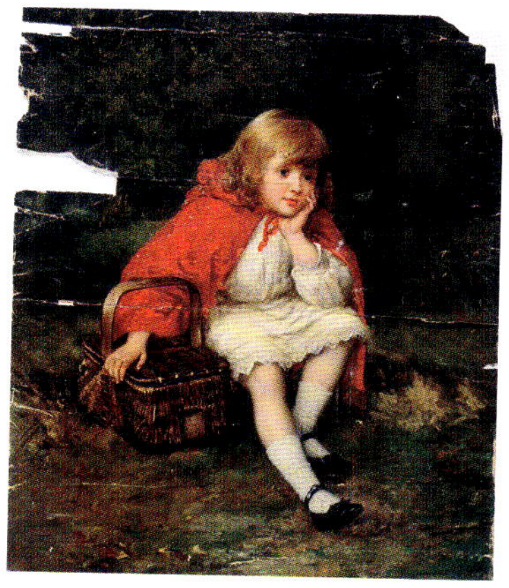

Oliver, William 1823–1901
Red Riding Hood (a portrait of the artist's granddaughter) 1886
oil on canvas 82.9 x 70 (E)
VIS.4574

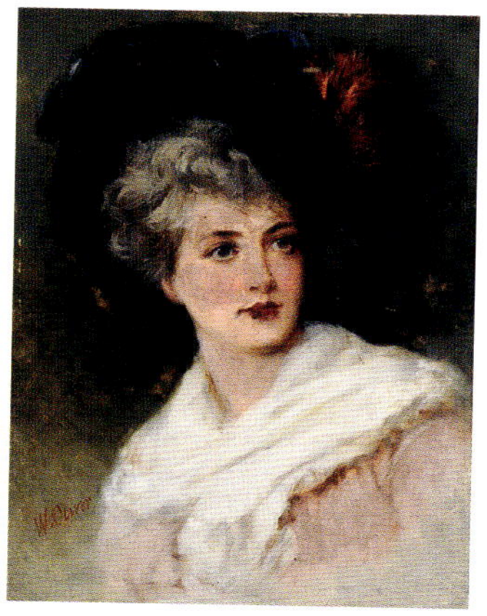

Oliver, William 1823–1901
A Lady
oil on panel 32.4 x 24.7
VIS.1969

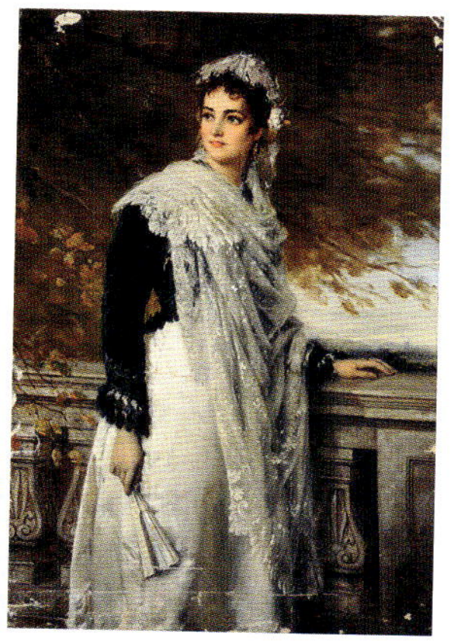

Oliver, William 1823–1901
A Spanish Lady
oil on canvas 91.5 x 61.4
VIS.2534

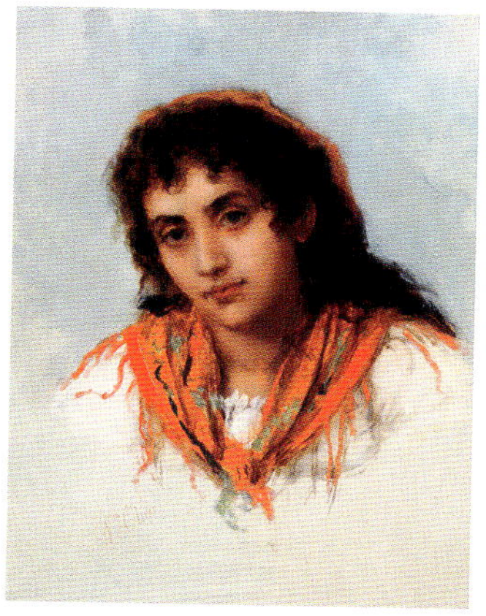

Oliver, William 1823–1901
The Gipsy
oil on panel 32.3 x 24.6
VIS.2360

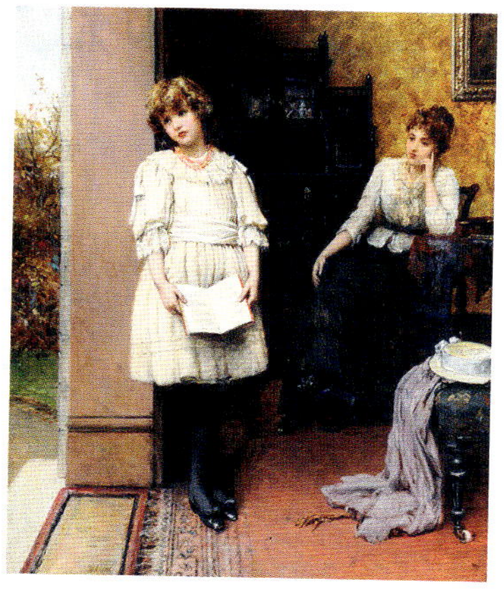

Oliver, William 1823–1901
The Lesson
oil on canvas 74.7 x 62.4
VIS.2421

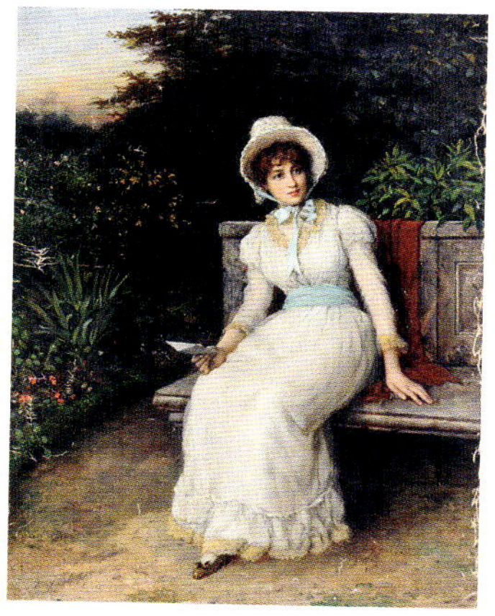

Oliver, William 1823–1901
The Letter
oil on canvas 91.4 x 70.6
VIS.2531

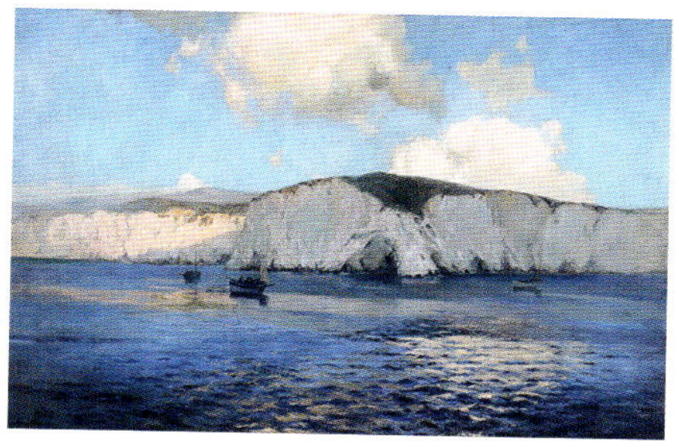

Olsson, Albert Julius 1864–1942
Off the Isle of Wight
oil on canvas 100.3 x 151.1
VIS.2966

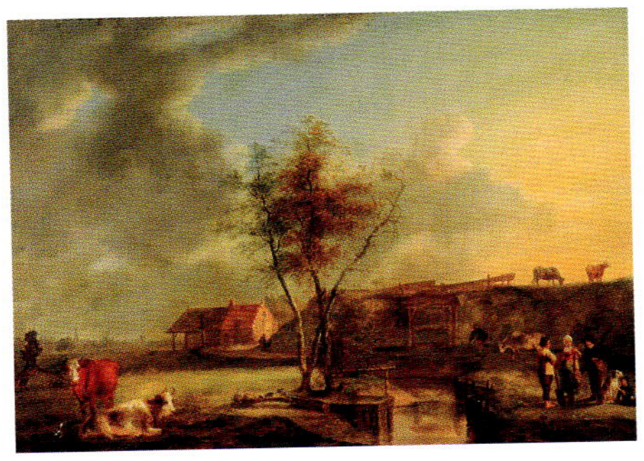

Ommeganck, Balthazar Paul 1755–1826
Canal Scene 1780–1800
oil on panel 27.2 x 37.4
VIS.374

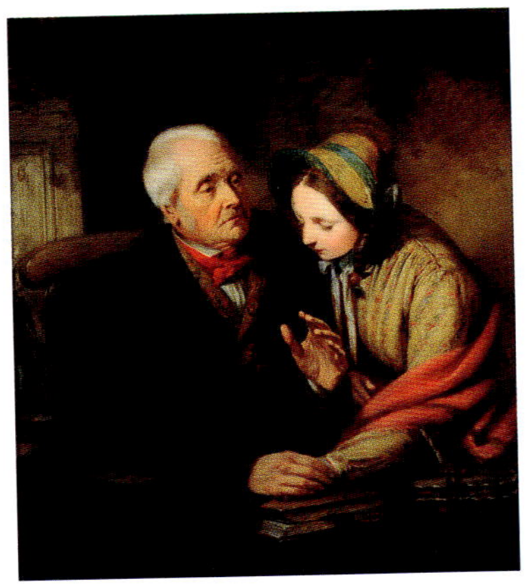

O'Neill, George Bernard 1828–1917
Grandfather's Advice
oil on panel 28.5 x 24.5
VIS.1388

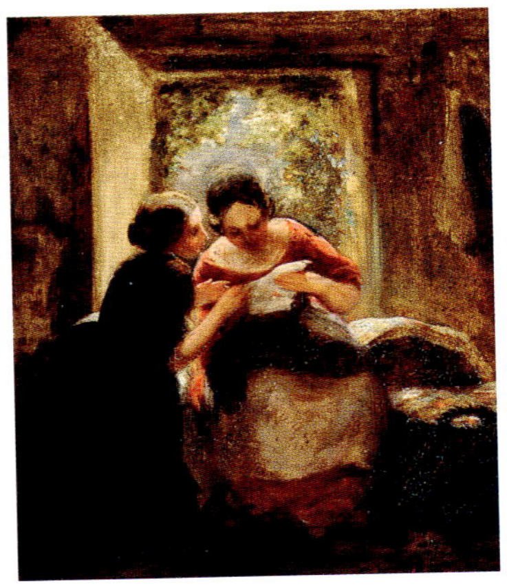

O'Neill, George Bernard 1828–1917
The Letter
oil on panel 12.6 x 10.2
VIS.561

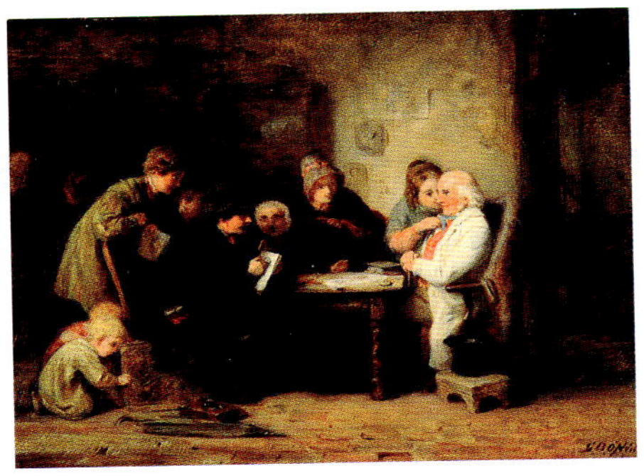

O'Neill, George Bernard 1828–1917
The Travelling Artist
oil on panel 15.9 x 21.5
VIS.200

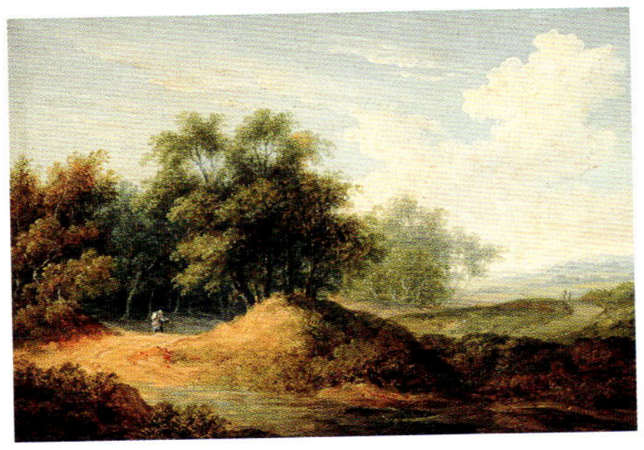

Oram, Edward d.1810
Landscape
oil on panel 17.3 x 24.8
VIS.512

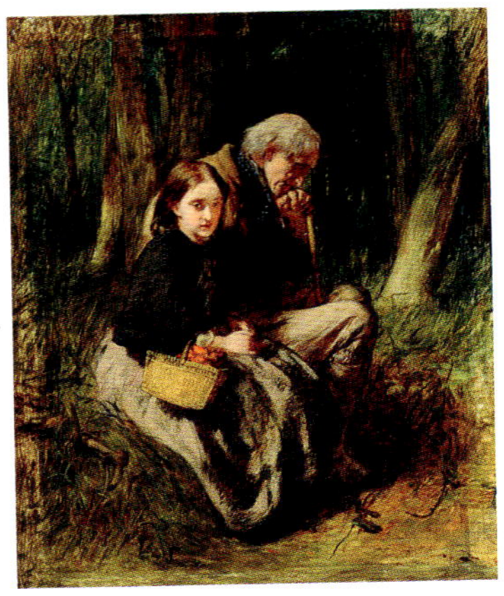

Orchardson, William Quiller 1832–1910
Little Nell and Her Grandfather in the Wood
c.1863
oil on canvas 55.4 x 45.6
VIS.1572

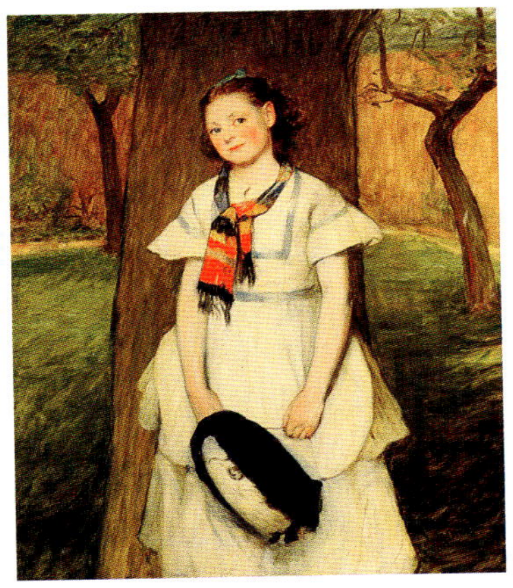

Orchardson, William Quiller 1832–1910
A Girl in a Muslin Dress 1871
oil on canvas 79.6 x 68.3
VIS.571

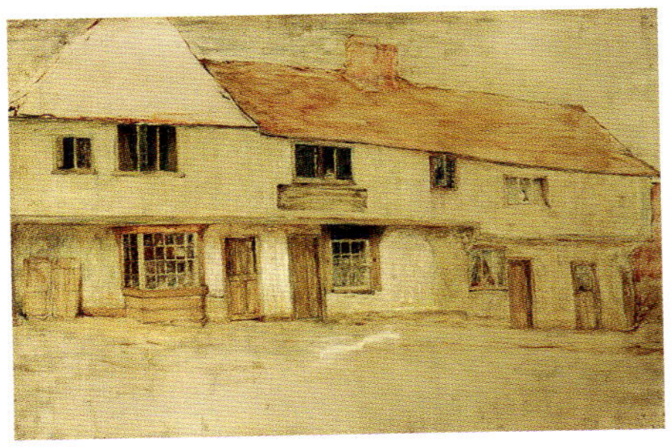

Orchardson, William Quiller 1832–1910
Cottages, Stanstead, Essex 1878
oil on canvas 50 x 75.2
VIS.556

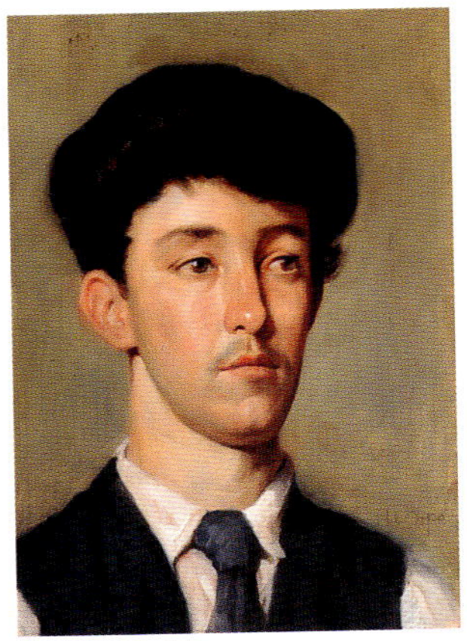

Orpen, William 1878–1931
Portrait of a Youth
oil on canvas 36.7 x 26.3
VIS.157

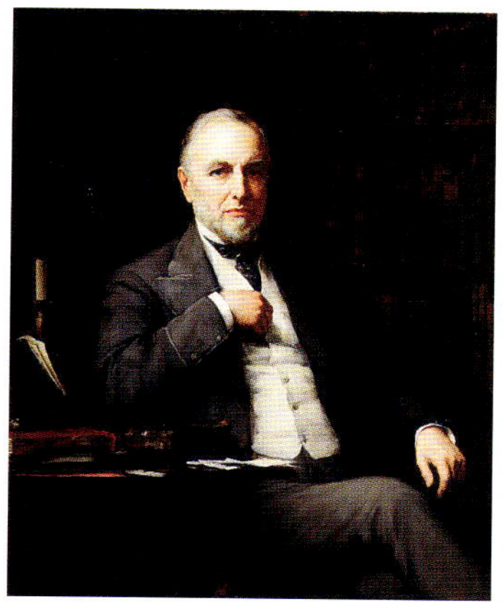

Ouless, Walter William 1848–1933
Sir Frederick Thorpe Mappin (1821–1910), Bt 1892
oil on canvas 127.5 x 102.2
VIS.1689

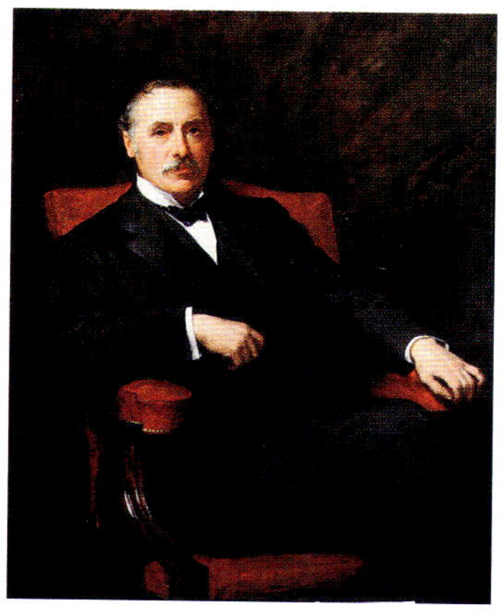

Ouless, Walter William 1848–1933
Alderman George Franklin (d.1916), JP, Lord Mayor of Sheffield (1897–1898) 1909
oil on canvas 127.5 x 102.8
VIS.LI.826 (P)

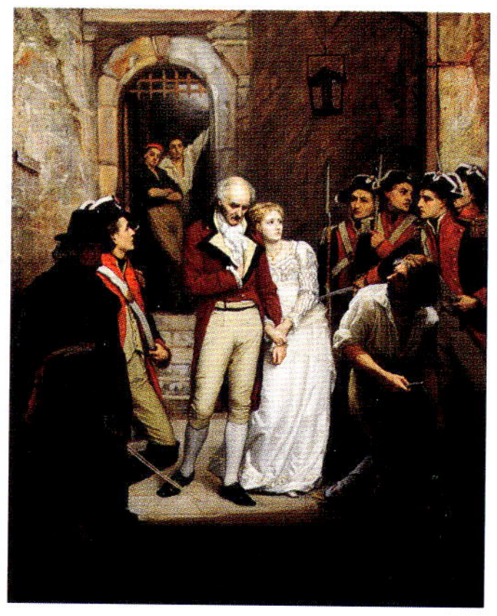

Ouless, Walter William 1848–1933
Scene from the French Revolution
oil on canvas 117.2 x 91.2
VIS.1632

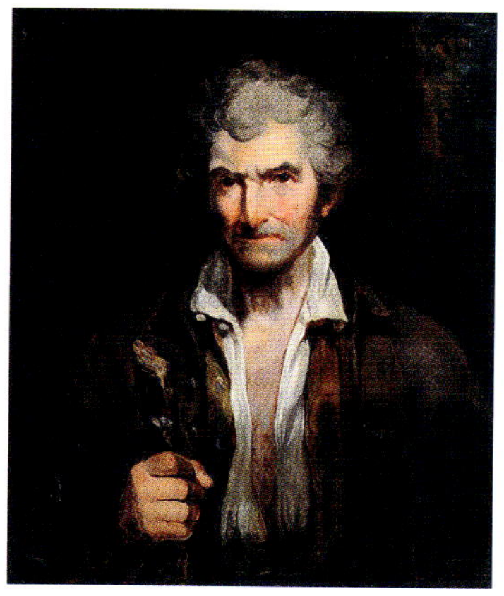

Owen, William 1769–1825
John Kemble in 'The Stranger' (an adaptation of August von Kotzebue's Menschenhaß und Reue')
oil on canvas 75.8 x 62
VIS.2744

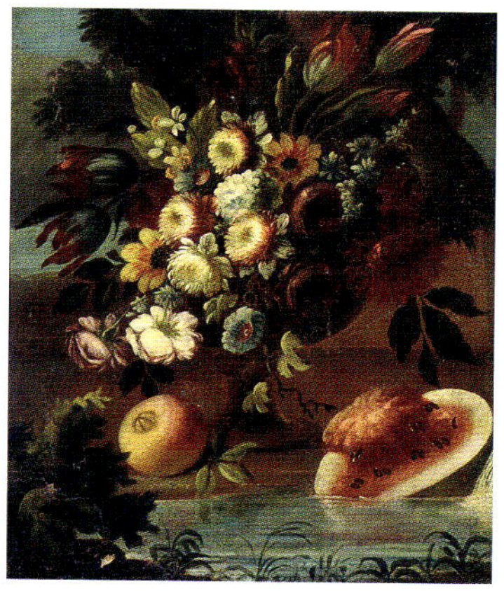

Pace del Campidoglio, Michele (attributed to) 1610–probably 1670
Flowers and Fruit 1650–1670
oil on canvas 70.4 x 57.1
VIS.2849

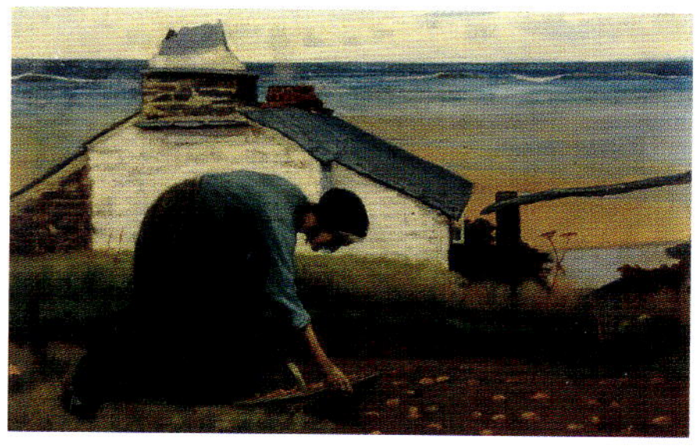

Padgett, William 1851–1904
The Old Wife's Work 1885
oil on panel 18.7 x 29.4
VIS.635

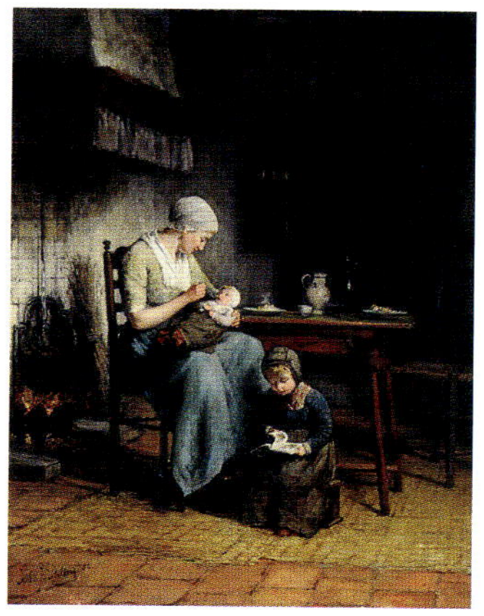

Palizzi, Filippo 1818–1899
Mother and Child 1884
oil on canvas 76.5 x 58.9
VIS.1563

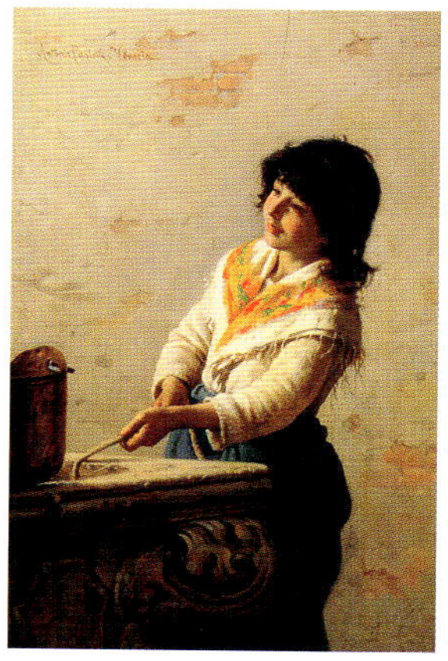

Paoletti, Antonio Ermolao 1834–1912
The Girl at the Well 1865–1870
oil on canvas 45 x 29.5
VIS.2922

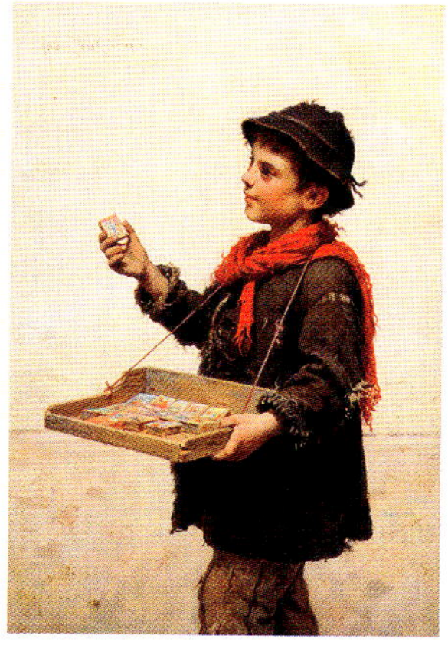

Paoletti, Antonio Ermolao 1834–1912
The Match Seller 1865–1870
oil on panel 45.7 x 30.6
VIS.1901

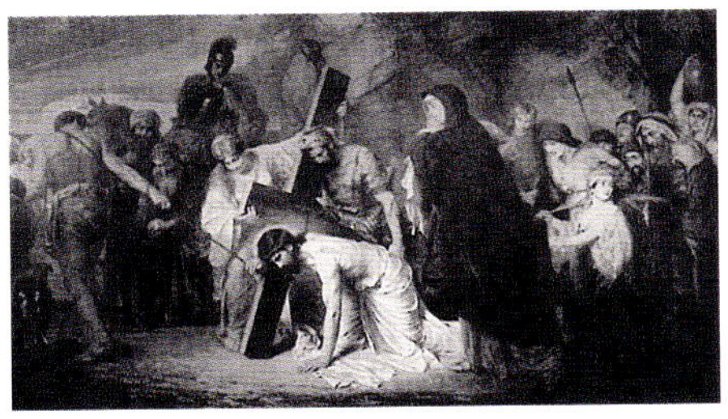

Papperitz, Friedrich Georg 1846–1918
The Procession to Calvary, Christ Falling under the Weight of the Cross 1883
oil on canvas 238.7 x 414
VIS.1607

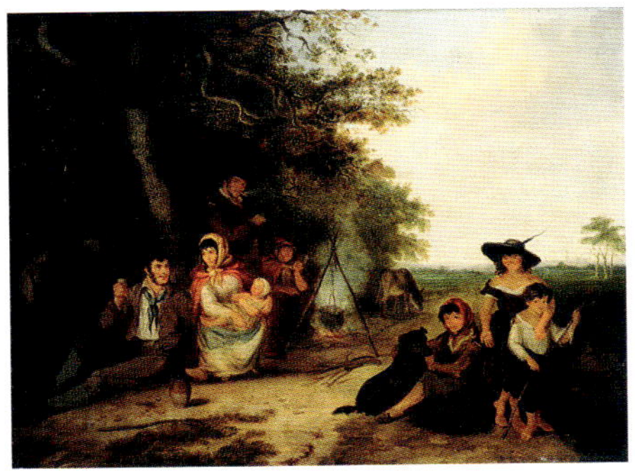

Park, Henry 1816–1871
Gipsy Encampment 1843
oil on canvas 70.7 x 91.8
VIS.1915

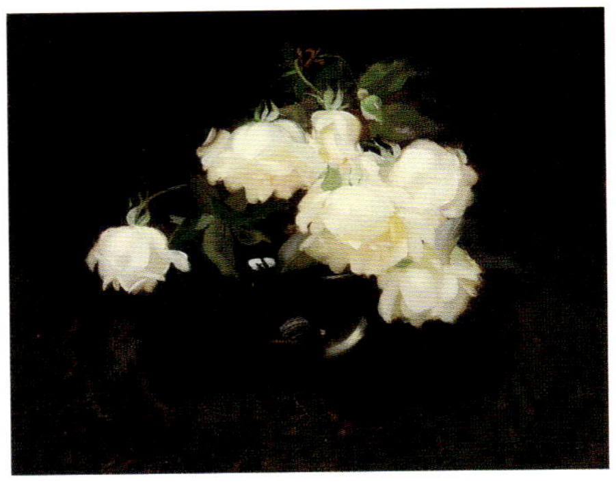

Park, Stuart 1862–1933
Roses
oil on canvas 39.6 x 49.8
VIS.425

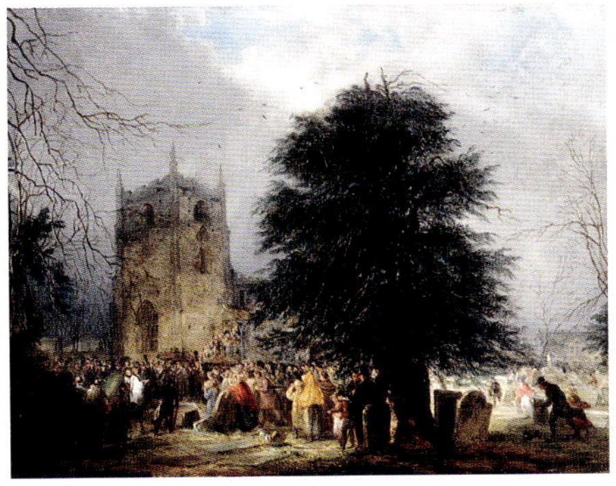

Parker, Henry Perlee 1795–1873
The Burial of Sir Francis Chantrey in Norton Churchyard, Sheffield 1841
oil on canvas 37.1 x 57.8
K1905.10

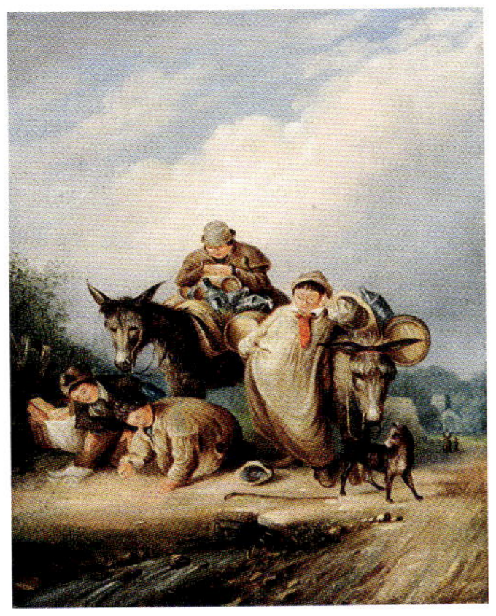

Parker, Henry Perlee 1795–1873
The Milk Boys
oil on canvas 46.2 x 36.4
K1929.10

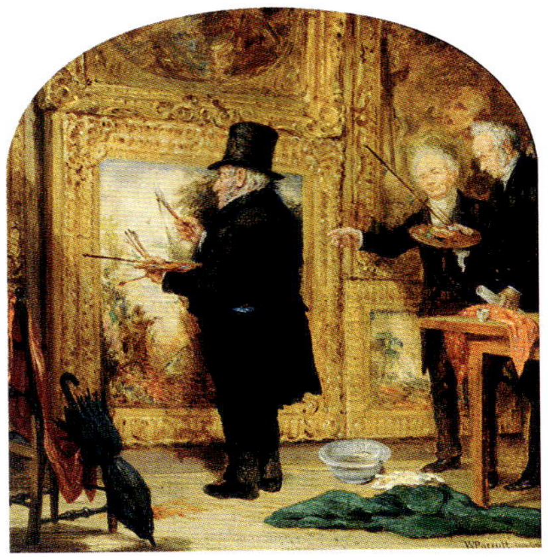

Parrott, William 1813–after 1891
Turner on Varnishing Day 1846
oil on panel 45 x 43.7
CGSG00741

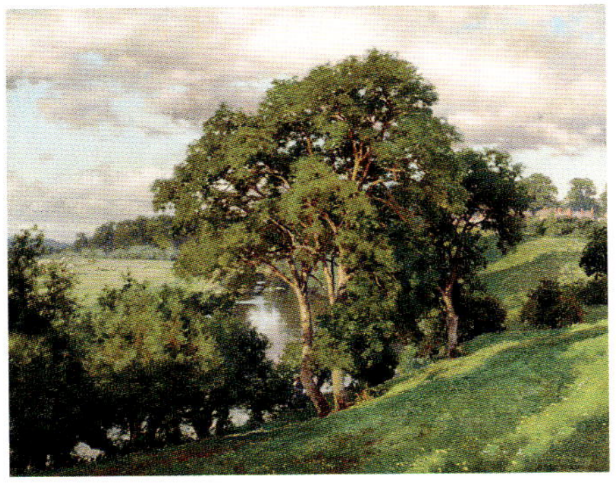

Parsons, Alfred William 1847–1920
Ash Trees at Cropthorne, Worcestershire
oil on canvas 42.2 x 52.4
VIS.989

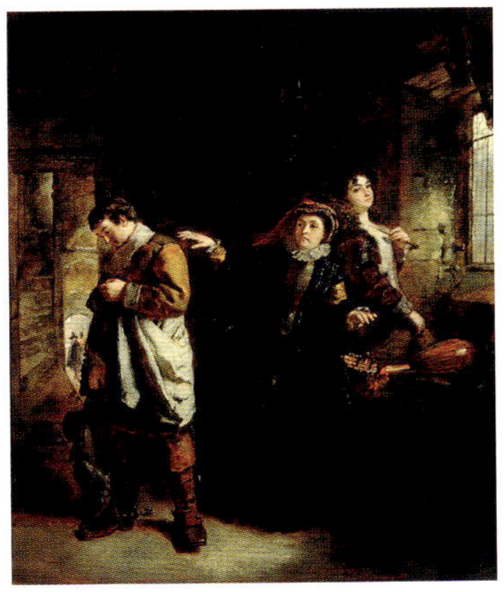

Pasmore, Daniel I c.1815–1893
Interior with Figures 1866
oil on canvas 42.5 x 34.6
VIS.1498

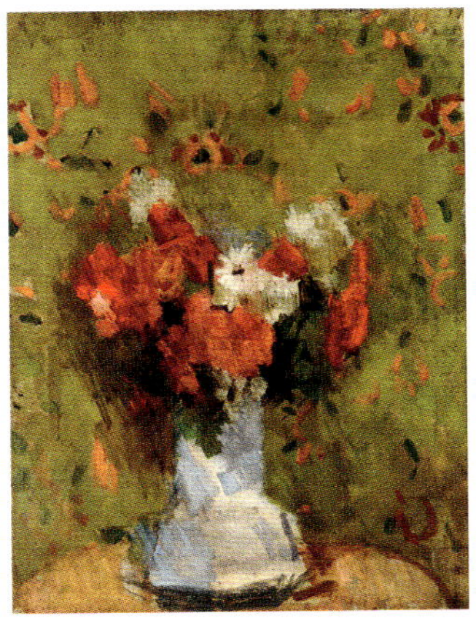

Pasmore, Victor 1908–1998
Vase of Flowers
oil on canvas 59.9 x 44.9
VIS.2582

Facing page: Roberts, David, 1796–1864, *The Piazza Navona at Rome* (detail), 1857, Museums Sheffield, (p. 182)

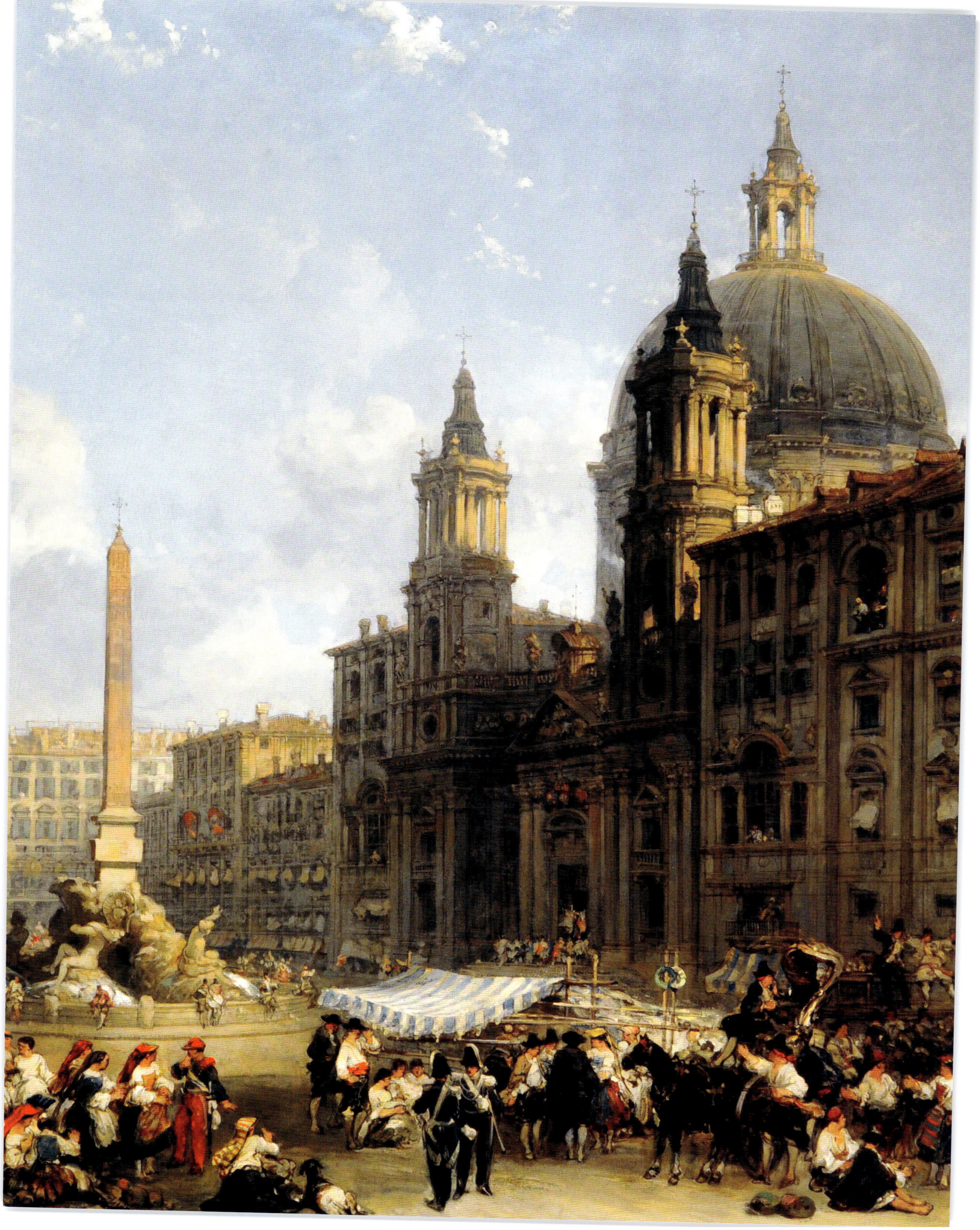

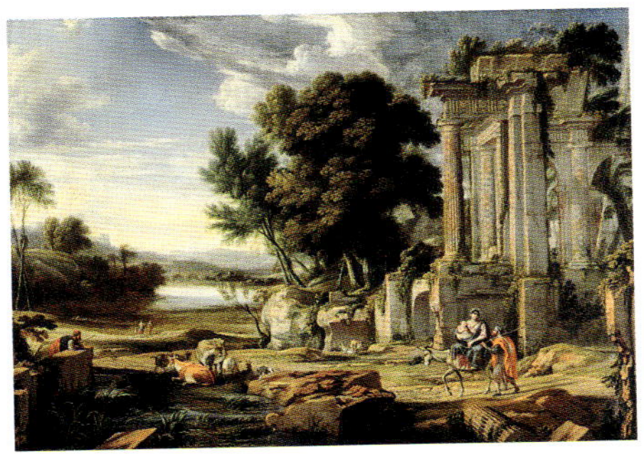

Patel, Pierre I c.1605–1676
The Flight into Egypt
oil on canvas 51.3 x 70.9
VIS.2235

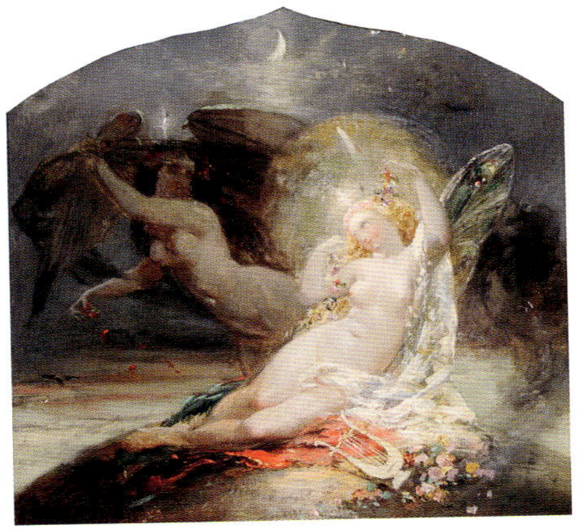

Paton, Joseph Noel 1821–1901
The Fairy Queen
oil on panel 23 x 23
VIS.4207

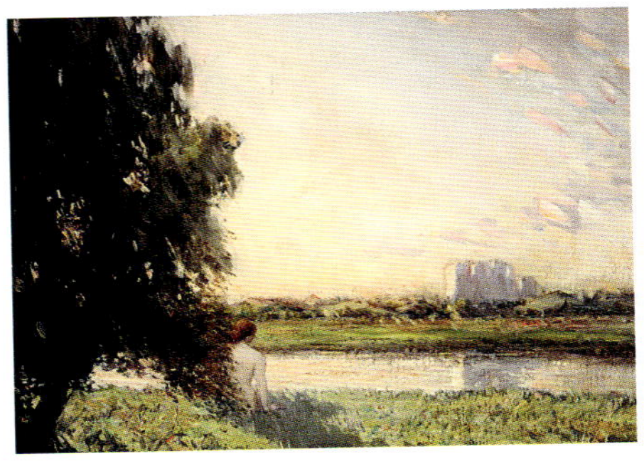

Paul, Paul 1865–1937
Landscape with a River
oil on board 22.4 x 31.1
VIS.1034

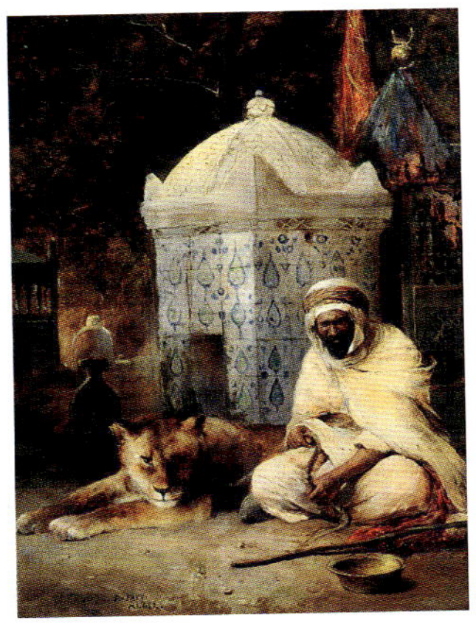

Pavy, Philippe b.1860
The Sacred Lion 1880–1889
oil on canvas 73.6 x 53.9
VIS.699

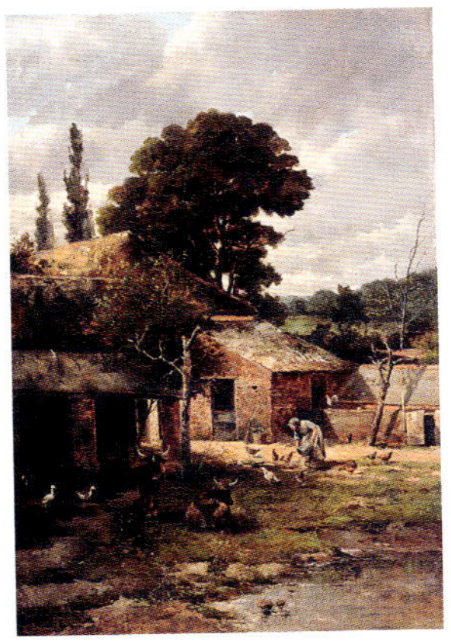

Pavy, Philippe b.1860
Farmyard Scene c.1890
oil on canvas 91.5 x 61.5
VIS.1675

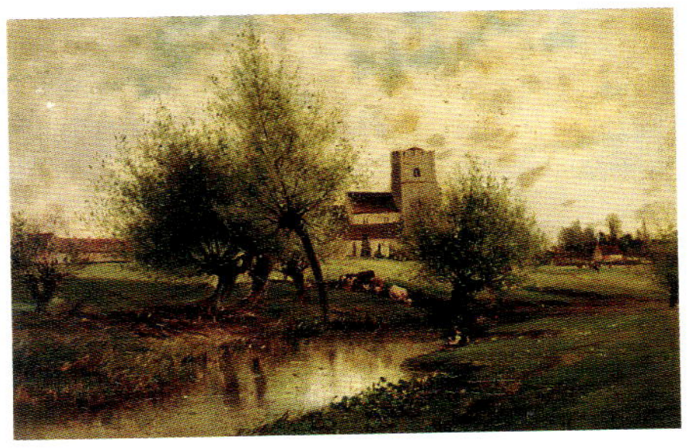

Peel, James 1811–1906
Landscape with a River 1877
oil on canvas 39.3 x 59.7
VIS.988

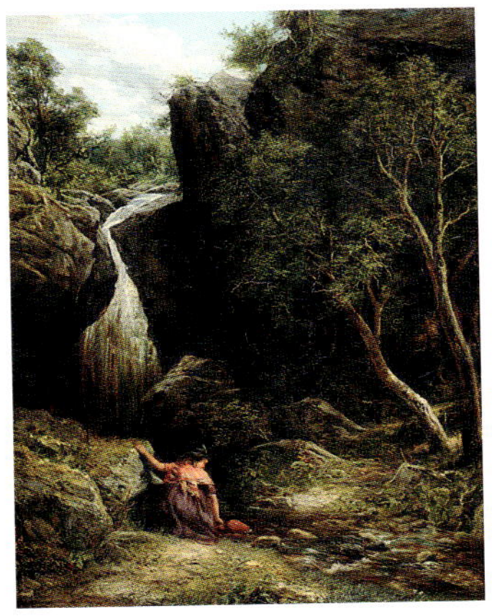

Peele, John Thomas 1822–1897
Landscape 1887
oil on canvas 92.7 x 72.4
VIS.1846

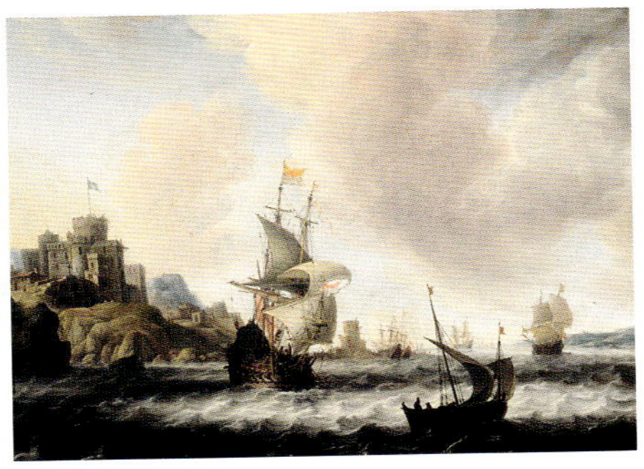

Peeters, Bonaventura I 1614–1652
Coast Scene with Shipping
oil on panel 87.6 x 119.8
VIS.L1.245 (P)

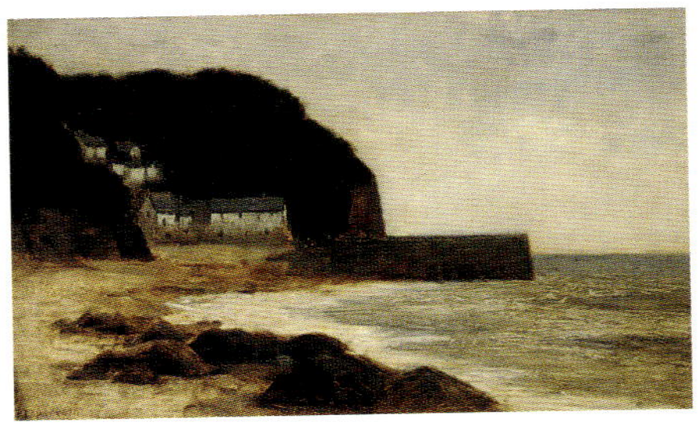

Peppercorn, Arthur Douglas 1847–1926
A Fishing Village
oil on panel 32.9 x 53.9
VIS.244

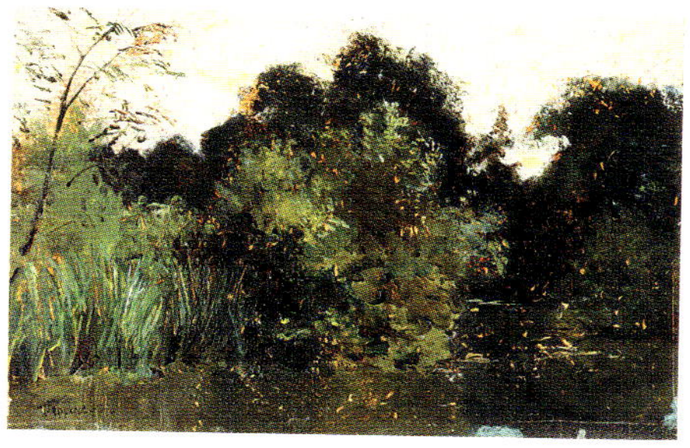

Peppercorn, Arthur Douglas 1847–1926
Landscape
oil on millboard 15.3 x 23.1
VIS.1105

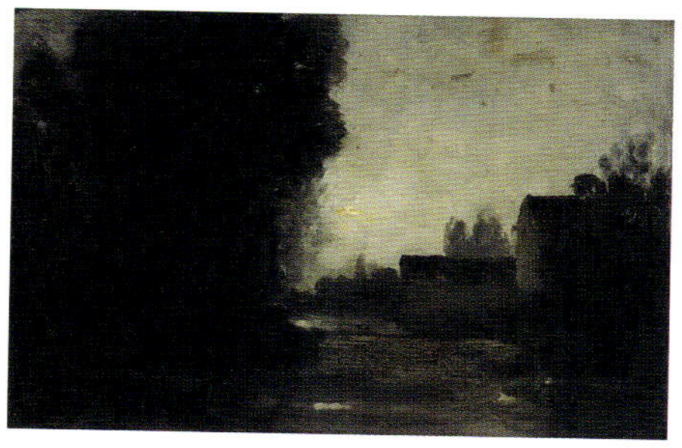

Peppercorn, Arthur Douglas 1847–1926
Moonlight
oil on canvas 38.8 x 58.5
VIS.701

Peppercorn, Arthur Douglas 1847–1926
River Scene
oil on canvas 17.4 x 44.5
VIS.378

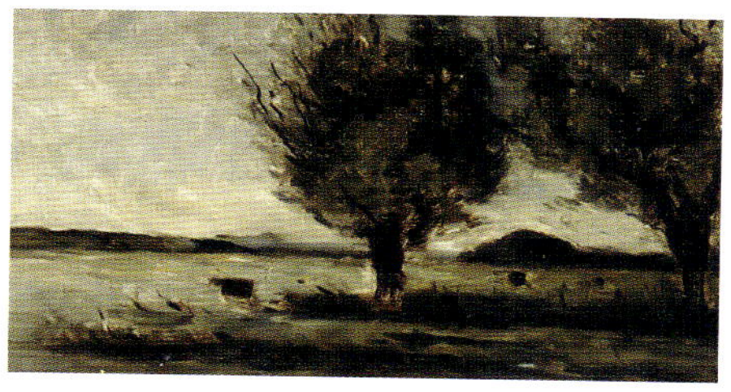

Peppercorn, Arthur Douglas 1847–1926
Two Pollards
oil on canvas 23.4 x 44
VIS.317

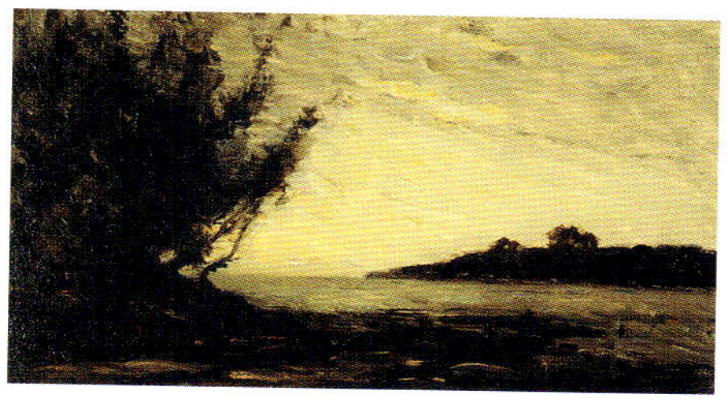

Peppercorn, Arthur Douglas 1847–1926
View near Portsmouth, Hampshire
oil on canvas 24.5 x 44.5
VIS.312

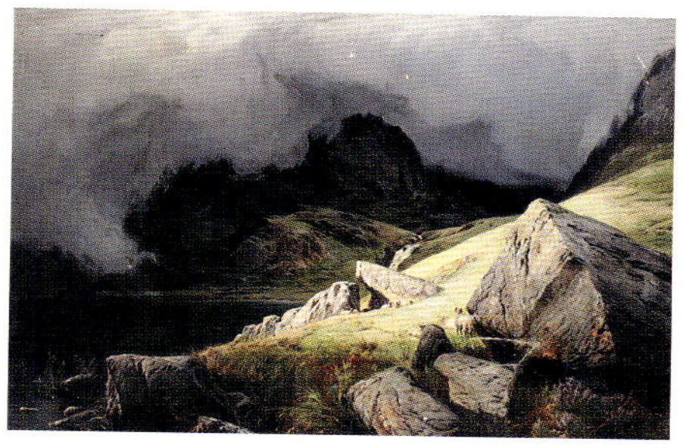

Percy, Sidney Richard 1821–1886
Coniston Lake, Cumbria 1875
oil on canvas 128.6 x 192.1
VIS.1474

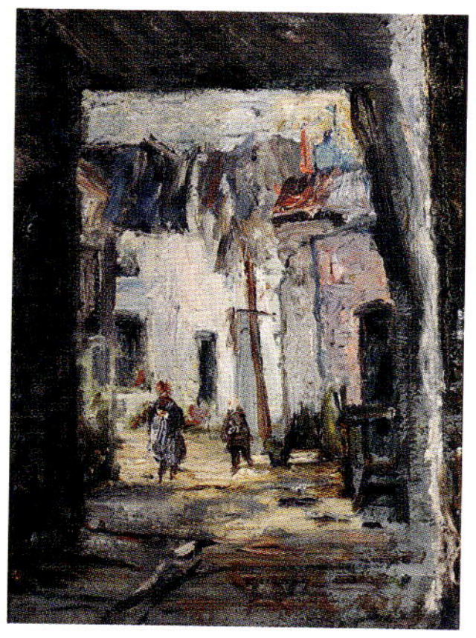

Perkins, J. M.
An Old Courtyard, Greenwich, London
oil on panel 29.5 x 21
VIS.1049

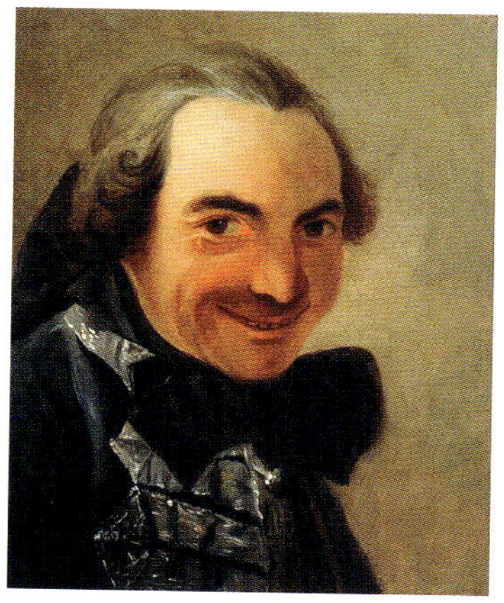

Perronneau, Jean-Baptiste (attributed to)
1715–1783
Portrait of an Actor
oil on canvas 37 x 30.5
VIS.64

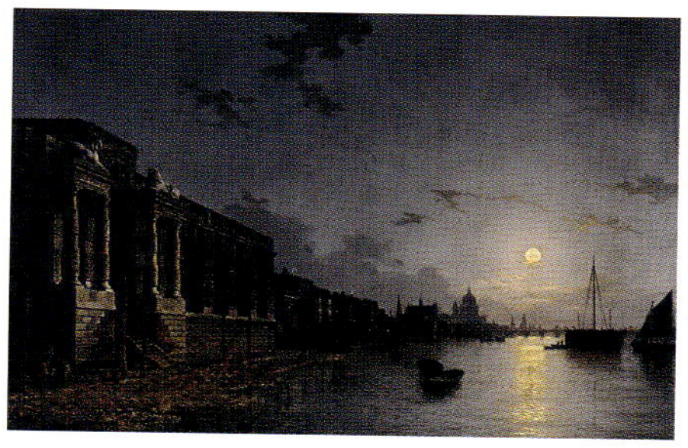

Pether, Henry c.1801–1880
A View of the Thames
oil on canvas 59.6 x 90.3
VIS.246

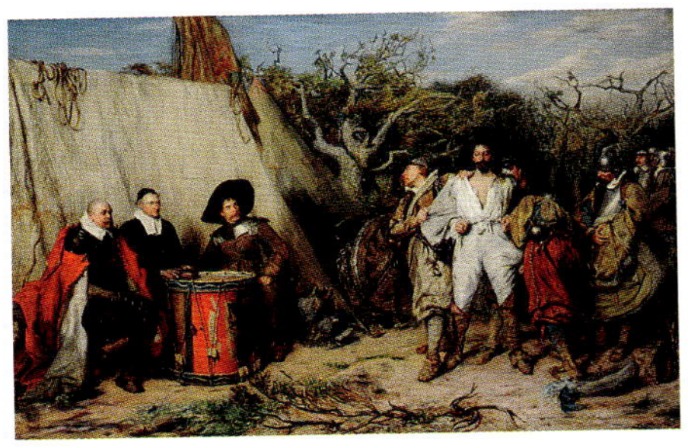

Pettie, John 1839–1893
The Drumhead Court Martial 1865
oil on canvas 68.2 x 103
VIS.1537

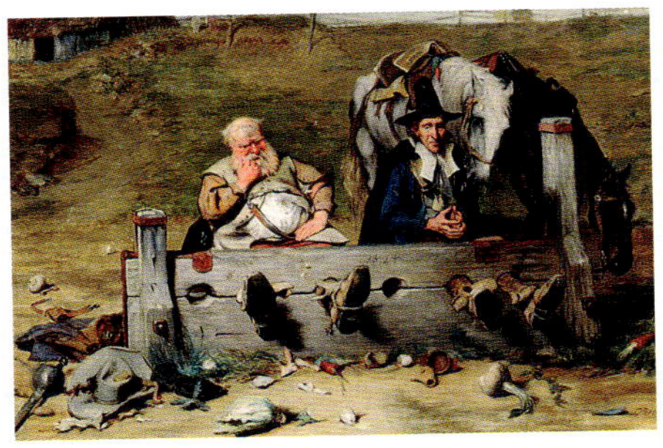

Pettie, John 1839–1893
Hudibras and Ralpho in the Stocks (from the poem by Samuel Butler) 1867
oil on canvas 39.3 x 57.2
VIS.1611

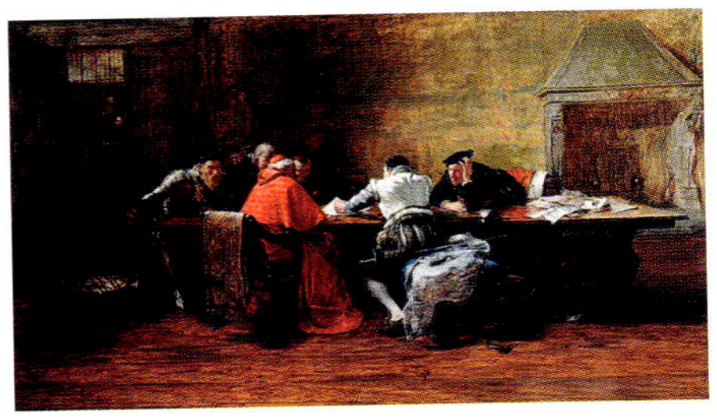

Pettie, John 1839–1893
Treason 1867
oil on canvas 81.4 x 137.2
VIS.1433

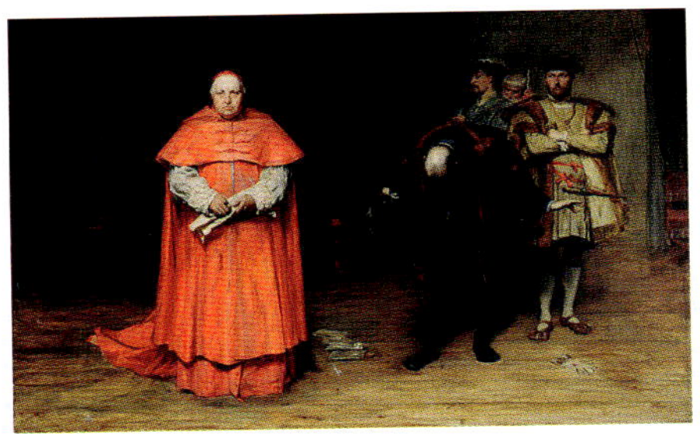

Pettie, John 1839–1893
The Disgrace of Cardinal Wolsey 1869
oil on canvas 100 x 155
VIS.1673

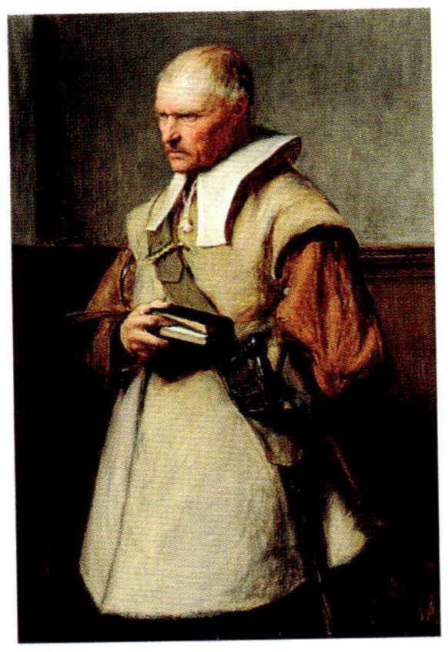

Pettie, John 1839–1893
The Puritan 1870
oil on canvas 66 x 43.8
VIS.1561

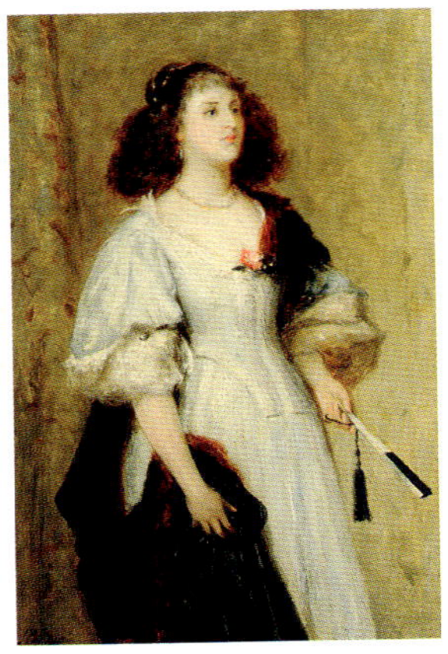

Pettie, John 1839–1893
A Lady of the Seventeenth Century 1877
oil on canvas 29.7 x 19.3
VIS.1535

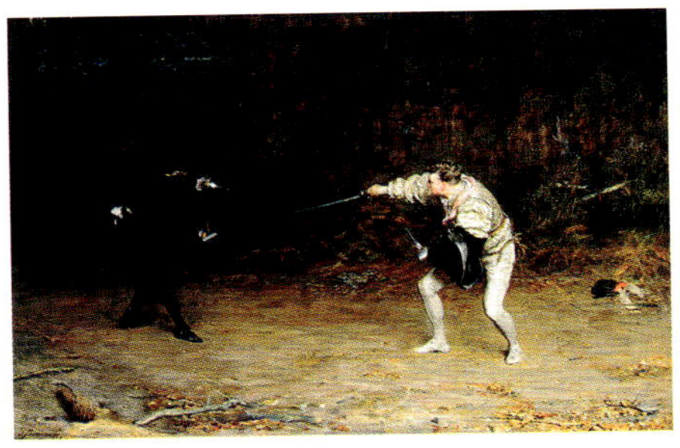

Pettie, John 1839–1893
To the Death 1877
oil on canvas 90.5 x 135.9
VIS.1445

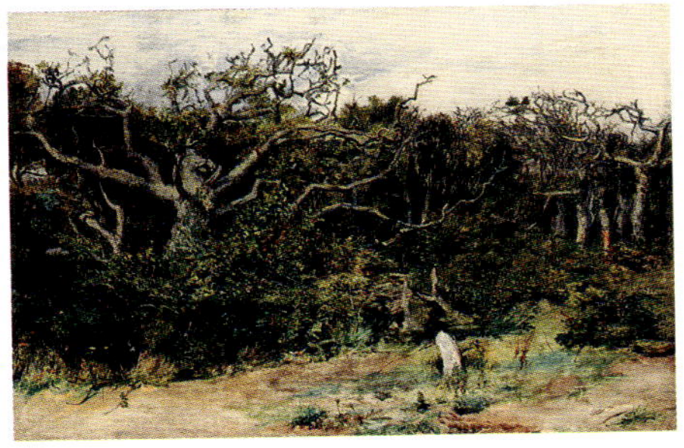

Pettie, John 1839–1893
The Edge of the Wood
oil on canvas 49.3 x 74.6
VIS.4969

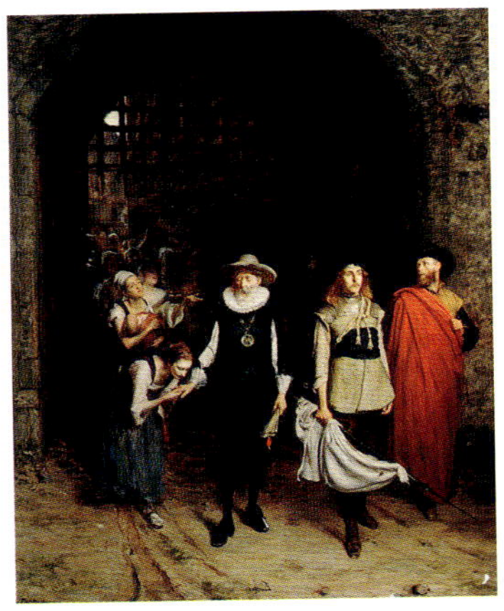

Pettie, John 1839–1893
The Flag of Truce
oil on canvas 133.2 x 104.2
VIS.1446

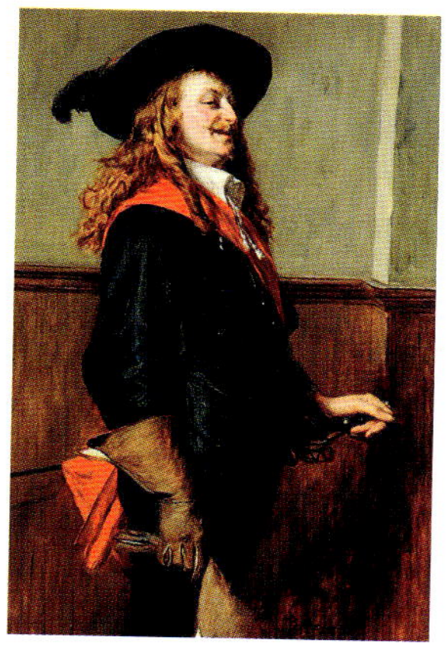

Pettie, John 1839–1893
The Royalist
oil on canvas 67.7 x 45.5
VIS.1557

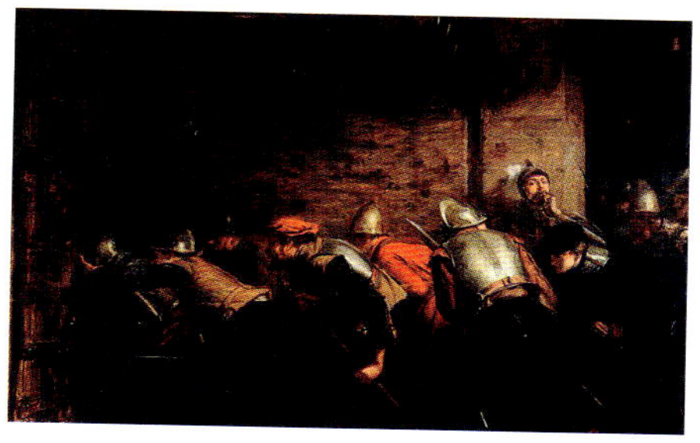

Pettie, John 1839–1893
The Sally
oil on canvas 80.8 x 125.5
VIS.1436

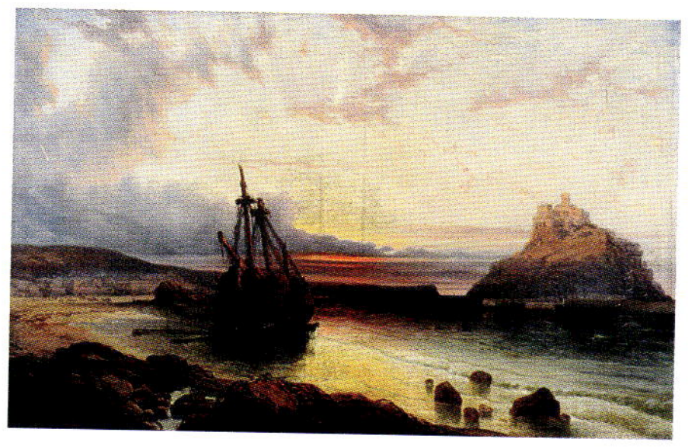

Pettit, Joseph Paul 1812–1882
Mont St Michel, France 1857
oil on canvas 61.2 x 91.5
VIS.626

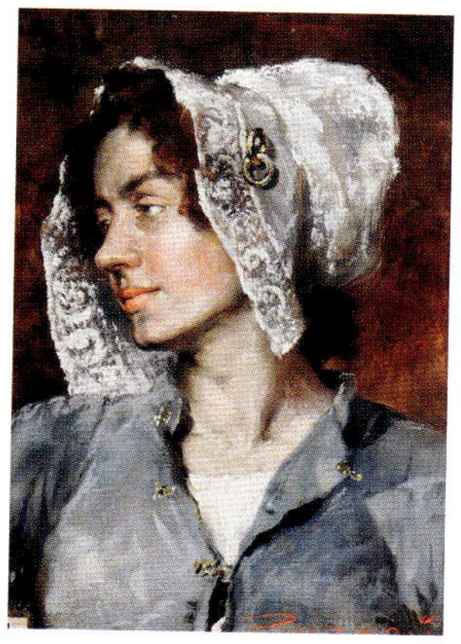

Pezzoia
Portrait of an Italian Girl
oil on millboard 50.2 x 34.5
VIS.1250

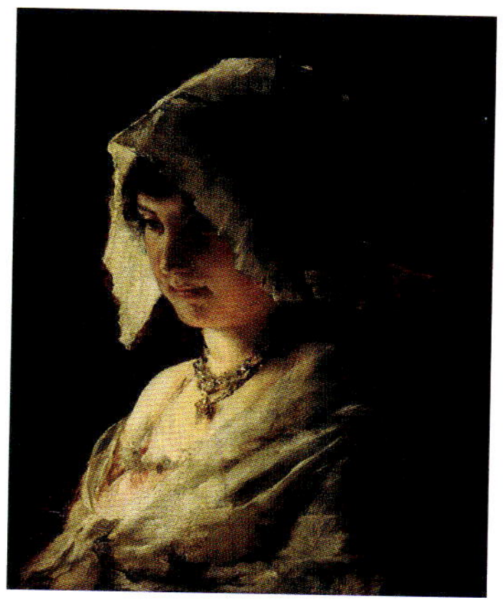

Philips, Hermann August 1844–1927
Reverie
oil on panel 50.5 x 40.8
VIS.778

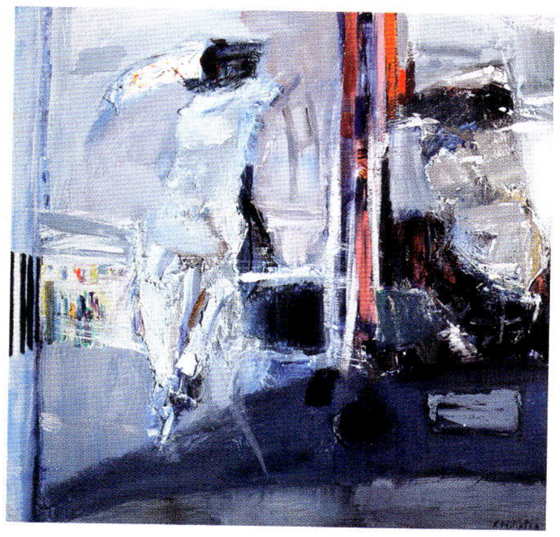

Philipson, Robin 1916–1992
Dancing Odalisque
oil on canvas 74.7 x 74.7
VIS.2587

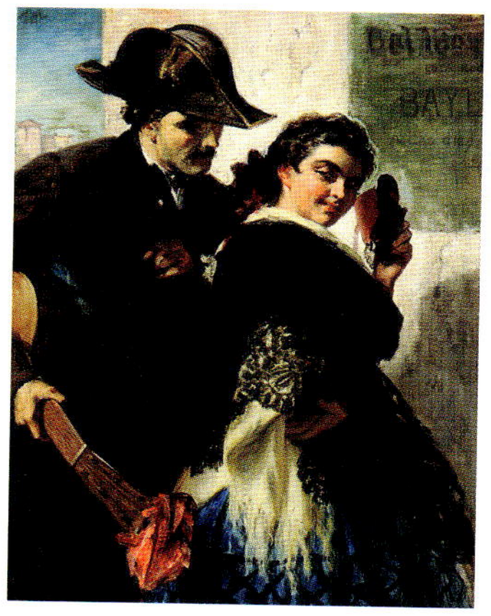

Phillip, John 1817–1867
Carnival Time, Seville, Spain 1860
oil on canvas 72.8 x 56.1
VIS.1547

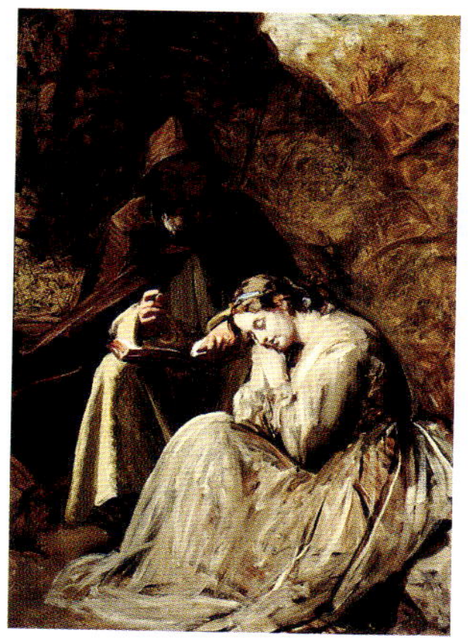

Phillip, John 1817–1867
The Fair Maid of Perth
oil on canvas 121.6 x 86.2
VIS.1633

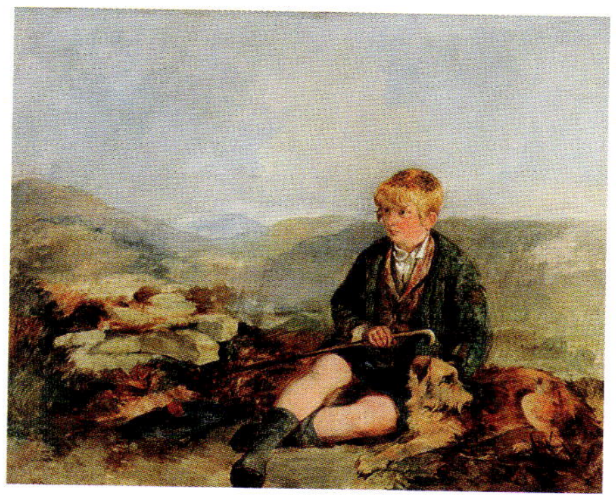

Phillip, John 1817–1867
The Highland Gillie
oil on panel 40.7 x 50
VIS.1398

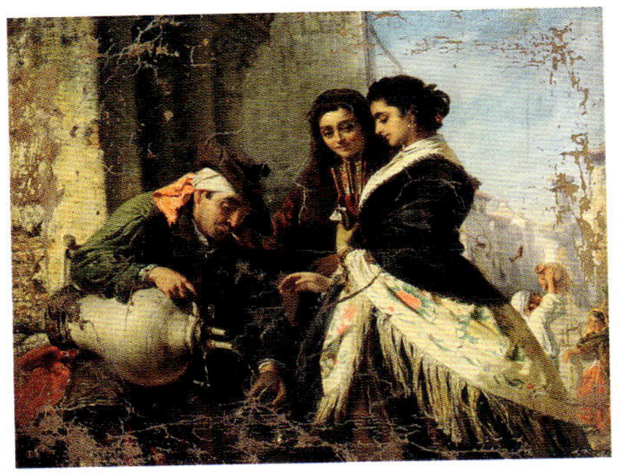

Phillip, John 1817–1867
The Water Drinkers
oil on canvas 53.6 x 67.3
VIS.1621

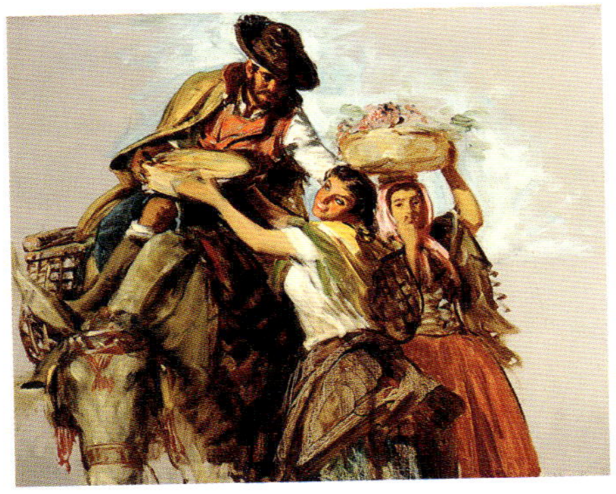

Phillip, John 1817–1867
Vintage of Seville
oil on canvas 75.1 x 90.8
VIS.2733

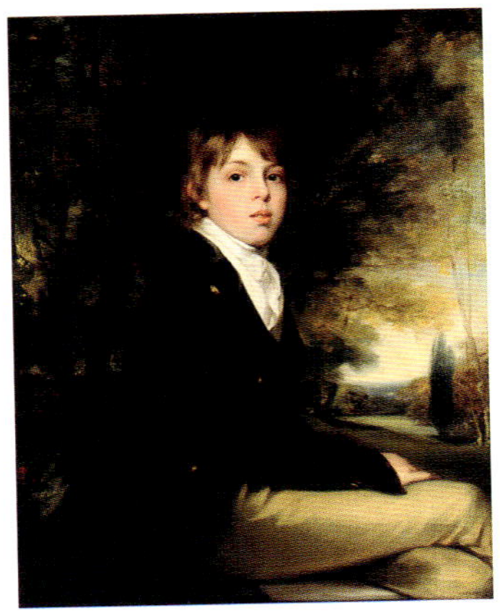

Phillips, Thomas 1770–1845
Master Millward 1798
oil on canvas 90 x 70.1
VIS.2288

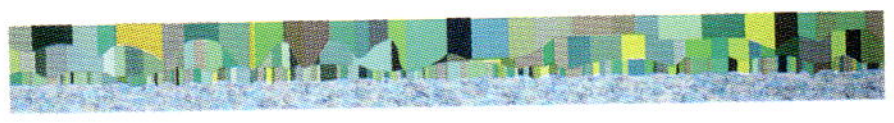

Phillips, Tom b.1937
Synthetic English Landscape No.3 1971
acrylic on canvas 30.8 x 202.5
VIS.3970

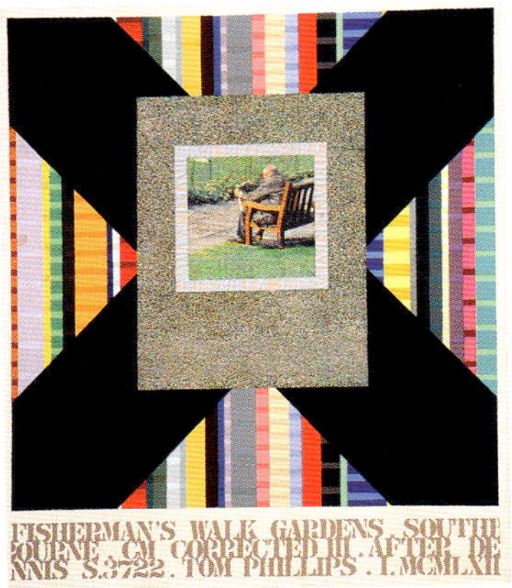

Phillips, Tom b.1937
Fisherman's Walk Gardens 1971–1973
acrylic on canvas 60.5 x 51.1
VIS.4006

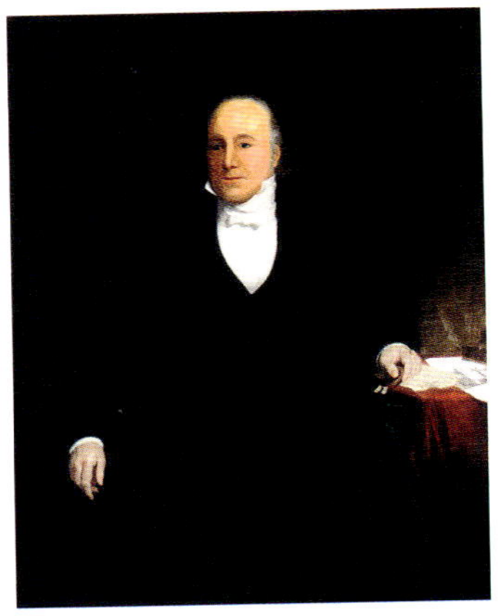

Pickersgill, Henry William 1782–1875
Reverend Joseph Hunter (1783–1861)
oil on canvas 138.4 x 107.5
VIS.3240

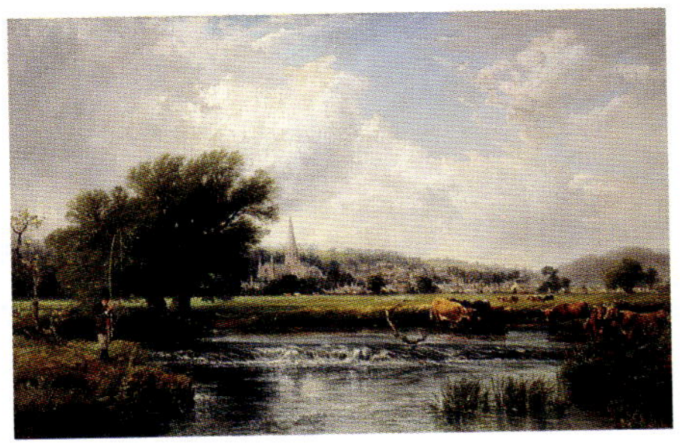

Pigott, William Henry c.1810–1901
Bakewell Meadows, Derbyshire 1880
oil on canvas 49.1 x 74.3
VIS.515

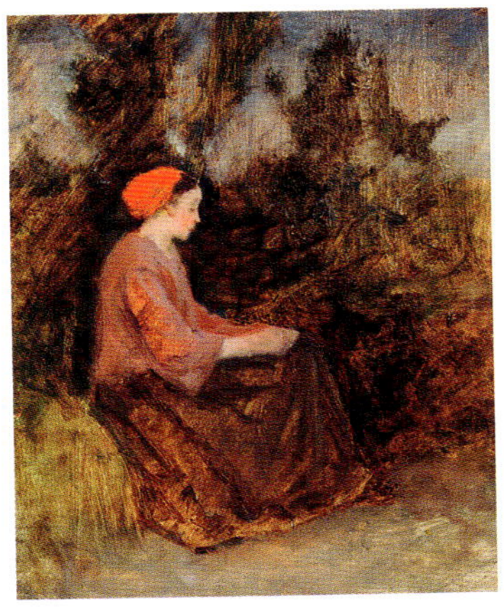

Pinwell, George John 1842–1875
Portrait
oil on canvas on card 24.4 x 20
VIS.1038

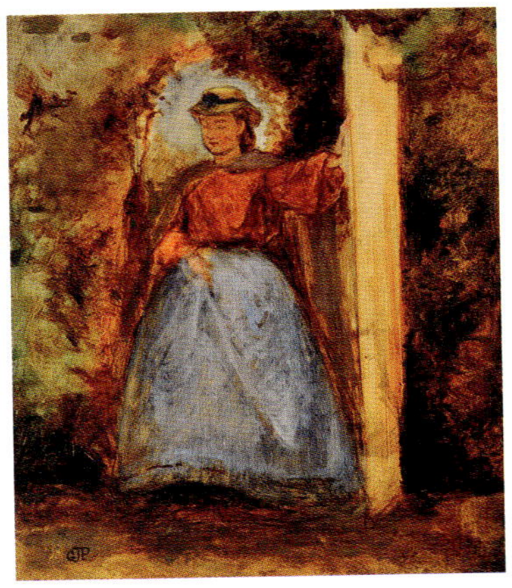

Pinwell, George John 1842–1875
The Garden Gate
oil on canvas 34.7 x 29
VIS.7

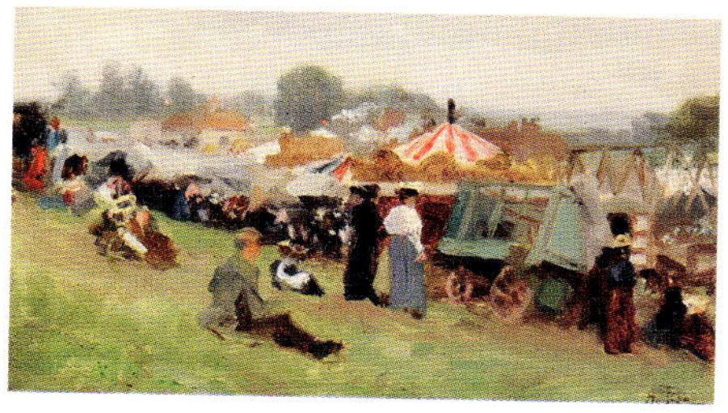

Pisa, Alberto 1864–1931
Hampstead Heath, London
oil on board 13 x 23
VIS.233

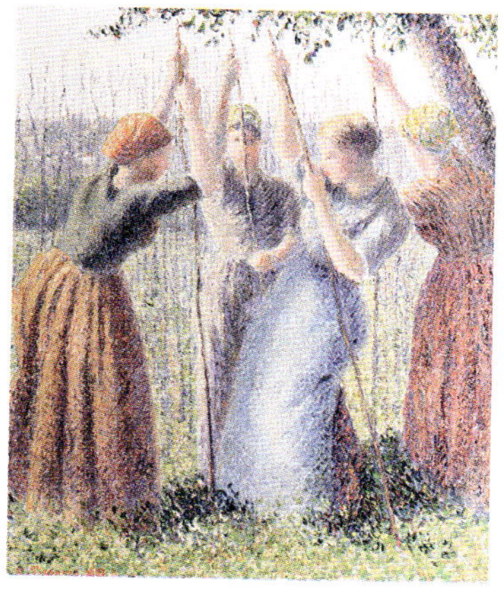

Pissarro, Camille 1831–1903
Paysannes plantant des rammes 1891
oil on canvas 74 x 65
VIS.LI.898 (P)

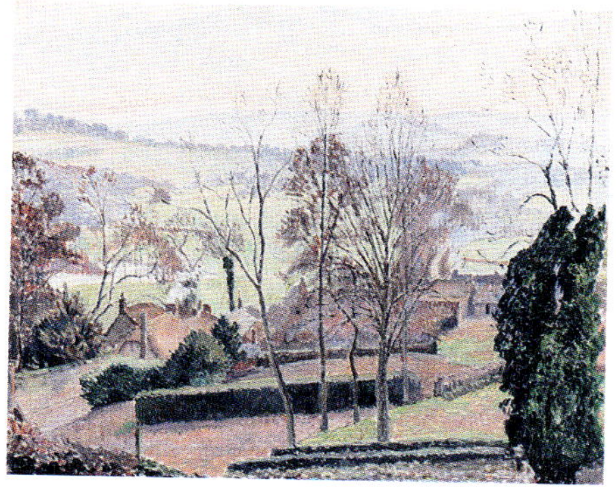

Pissarro, Lucien 1863–1944
A February Morning, East Knoyle, Wiltshire
1917
oil on canvas 52 x 63.5
VIS.3102

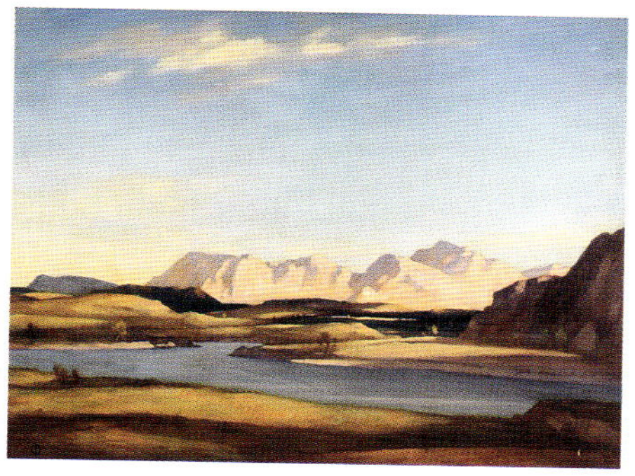

Pittman, Osmund 1874–1968
Loch Crocach, Scotland
oil on canvas 80.5 x 110
VIS.120

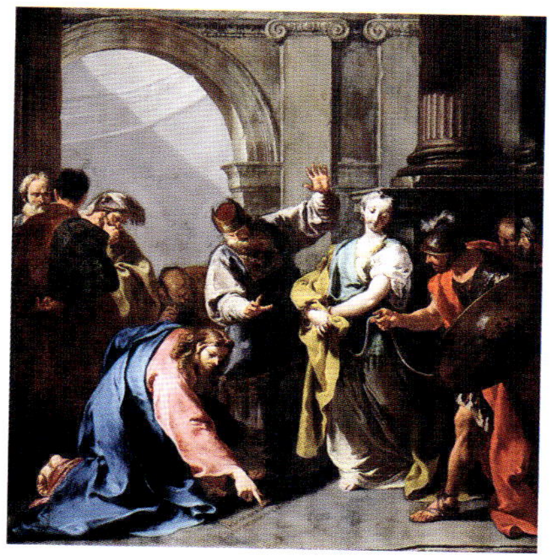

Pittoni, Giovanni Battista the younger
1687–1767
The Adulteress before Christ 1730–1740
oil on canvas 172 x 160
VIS.2612

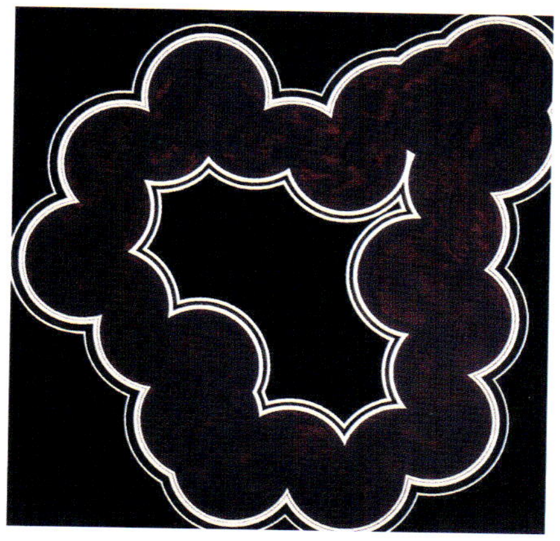

Plummer, Robin b.1931
Blackberry 1966
oil on canvas 125.3 x 125.3
VIS.3345

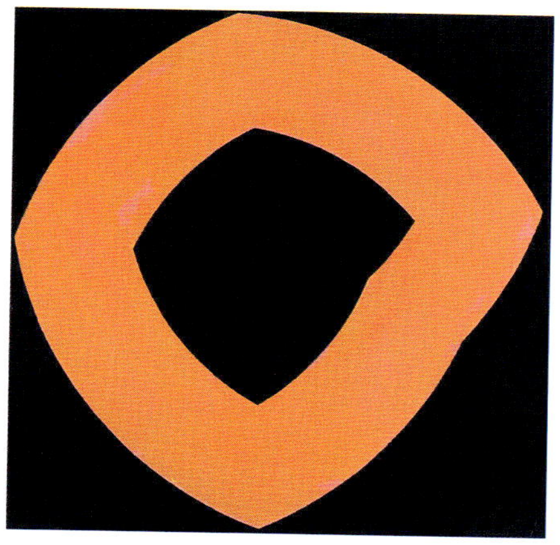

Plummer, Robin b.1931
Squash
acrylic on canvas 91.7 x 91.7
VIS.3348

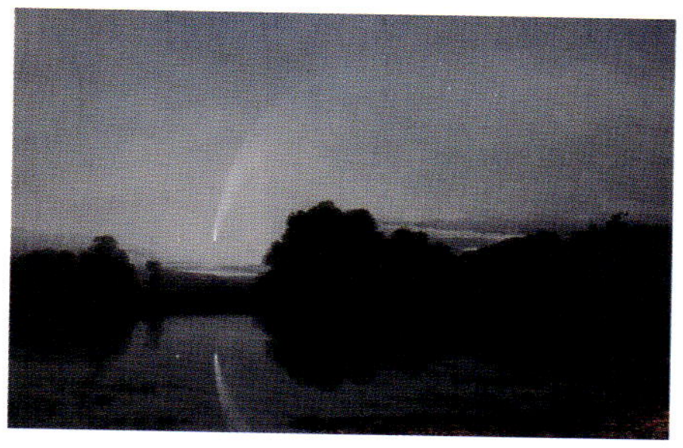

Poole, James 1803–1886
Donati's Comet 1858
oil on canvas 58.5 x 89.5
K1908.66

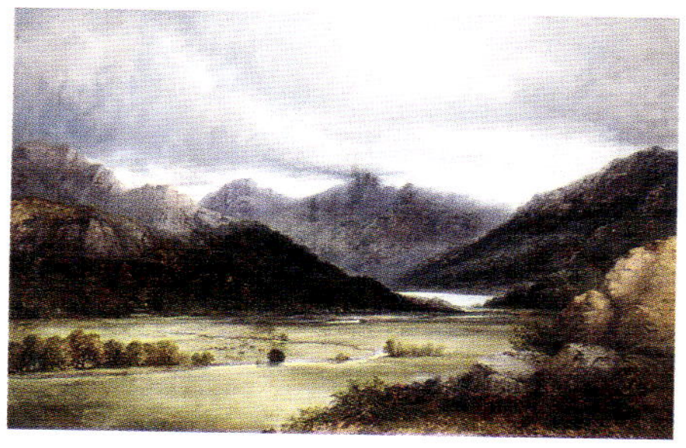

Poole, James 1803–1886
Clogwyn Mawr, near Capel Curig, Wales
oil on canvas 70.3 x 107
VIS.1682

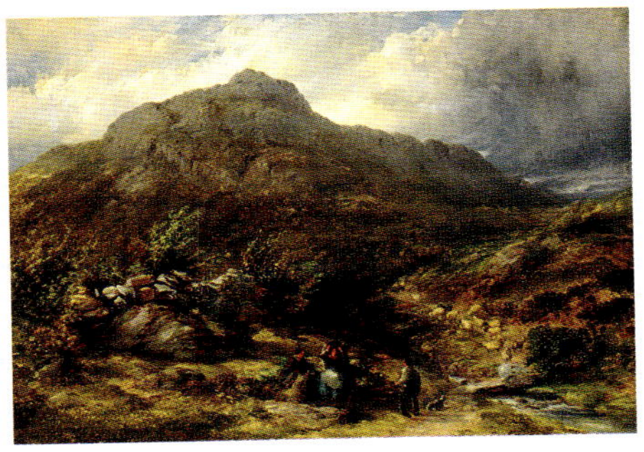

Poole, James 1803–1886
Clogwyn Mawr, near Capel Curig, Wales
oil on canvas 63.8 x 89.4
VIS.2868

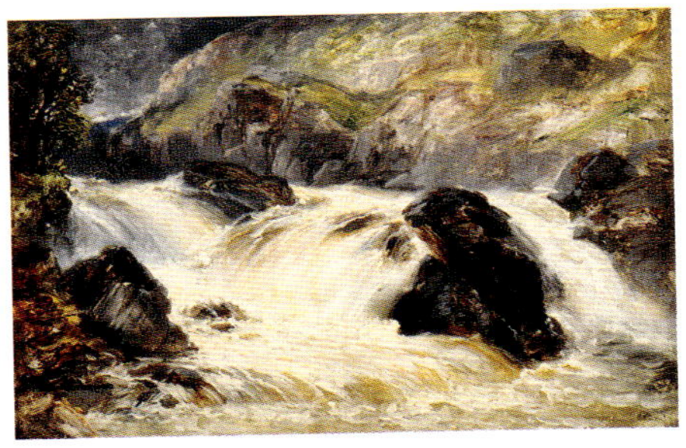

Poole, James 1803–1886
Falls near Pont-y-Cefn, North Wales
oil on canvas 34.4 x 51.7
VIS.2807

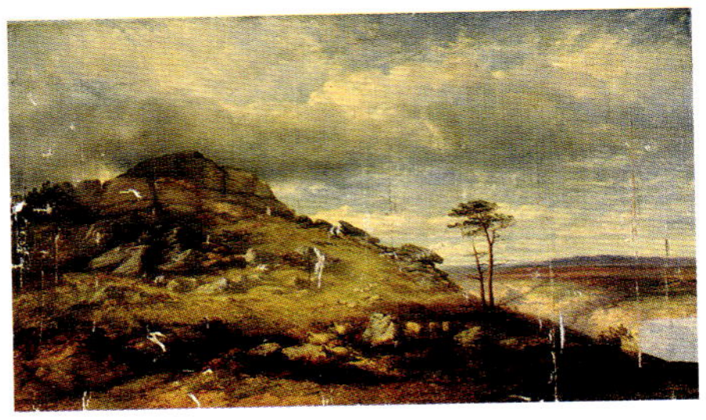

Poole, James 1803–1886
Landscape
oil on canvas 63.2 x 106.3
VIS.2532

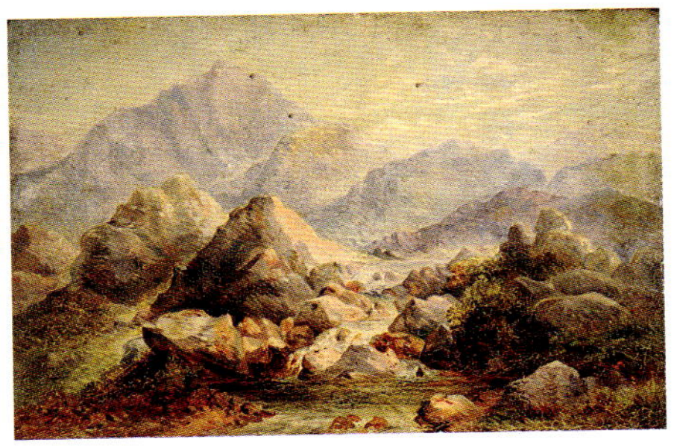

Poole, James 1803–1886
Landscape
oil on canvas 35.7 x 53.1
VIS.2732

Poole, James 1803–1886
Landscape with Gypsies
oil on canvas 100 x 134
VIS.2536

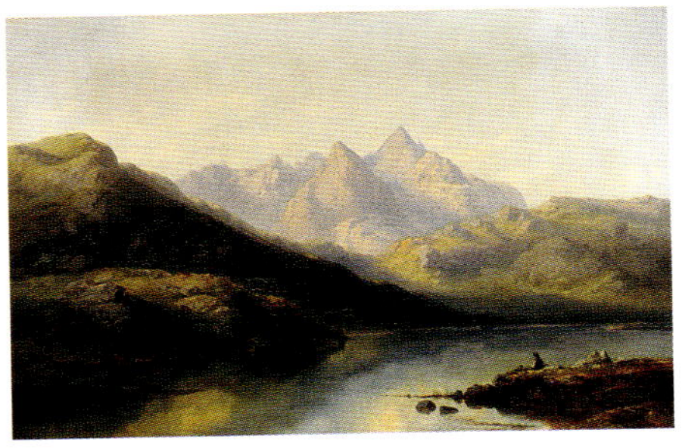

Poole, James 1803–1886
Mountain Landscape
oil on canvas 49.4 x 75.4
VIS.2343

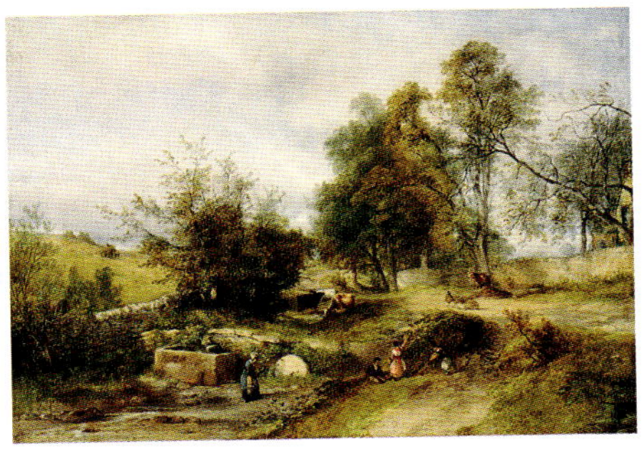

Poole, James 1803–1886
Off Machon Bank, Sheffield
oil on canvas 53.1 x 74.7
VIS.3213

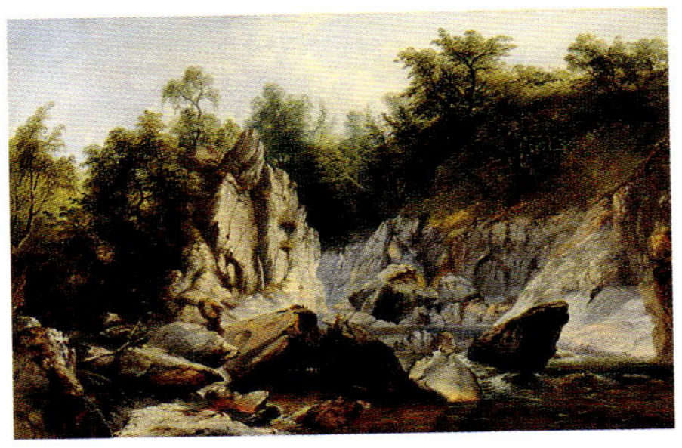

Poole, James 1803–1886
On the Conway, Betws-y-Coed, North Wales
oil on canvas 49.6 x 75
VIS.2344

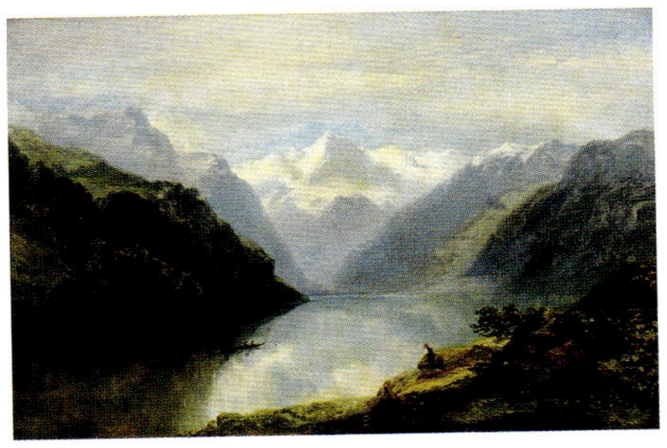

Poole, James 1803–1886
The Head of Lake Lucerne, Switzerland
oil on canvas 38 x 56.5
VIS.2870

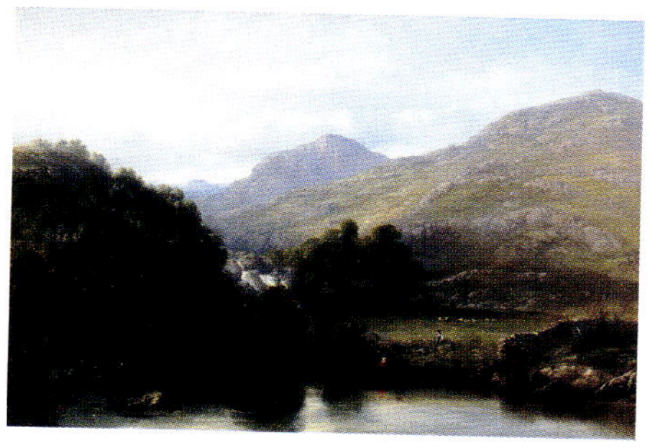

Poole, James 1803–1886
View on the River Llugwy, North Wales
oil on canvas 45.2 x 65.4
VIS.1504

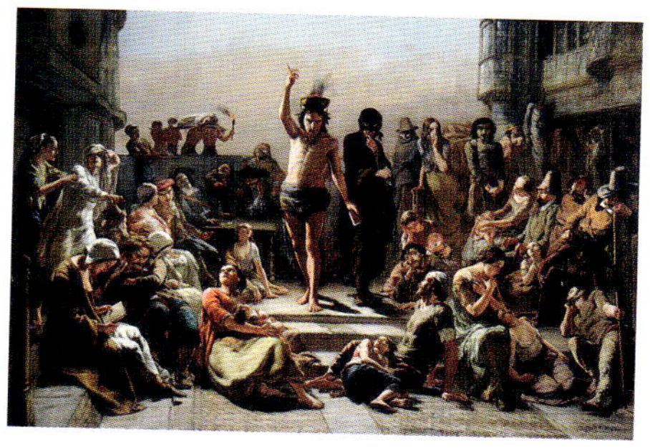

Poole, Paul Falconer 1807–1879
Solomon Eagle 1843
oil on canvas 173.2 x 241
VIS.1483

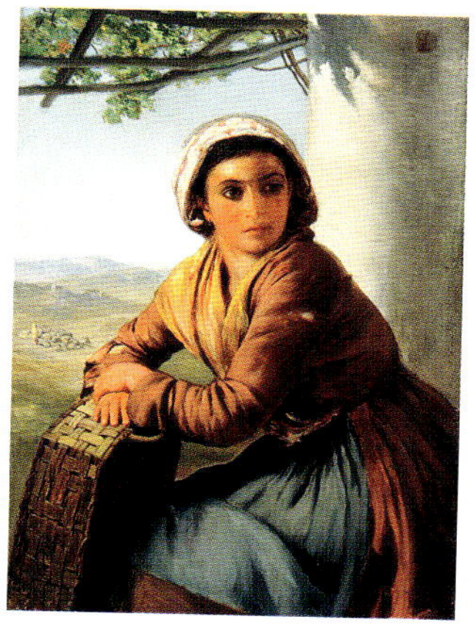

Poole, Paul Falconer 1807–1879
A Capri Girl 1865
oil on canvas 45.7 x 33.2
VIS.1406

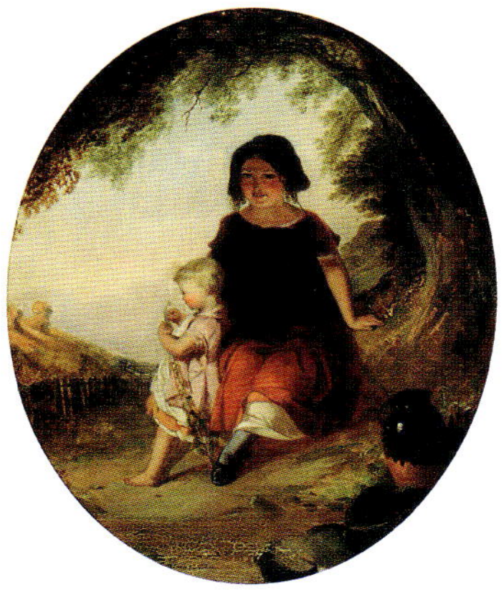

Poole, Paul Falconer 1807–1879
Gypsy Children
oil on canvas 33.7 x 28.3
VIS.248

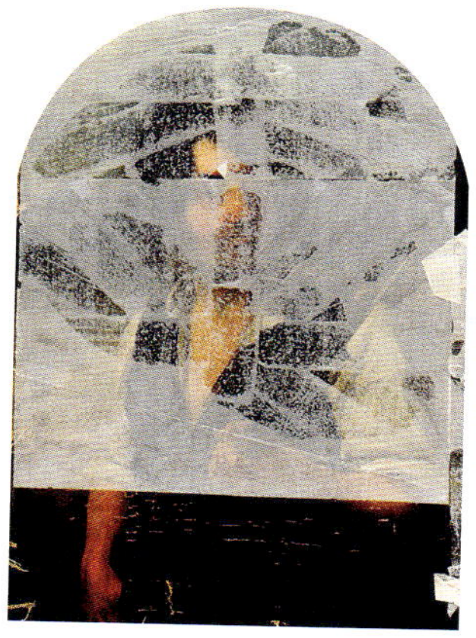

Poole, William c.1798–1888
'Let 'em Come'
oil on canvas 90.8 x 67.6
VIS.2533

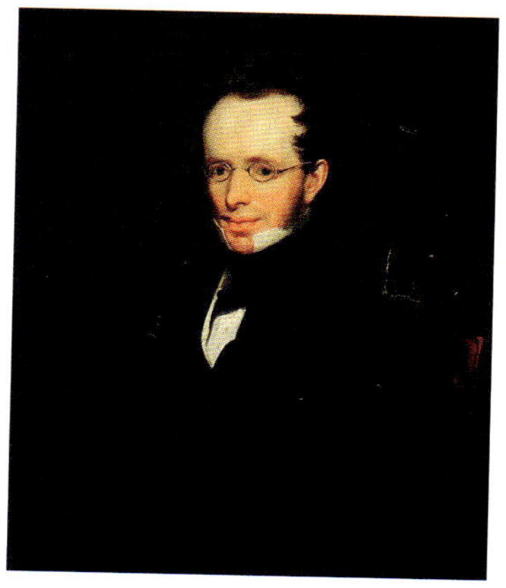

Poole, William c.1798–1888
Samuel Bailey (1791–1870), Poet and Philosopher
oil on canvas 73.5 x 61
K1936.22

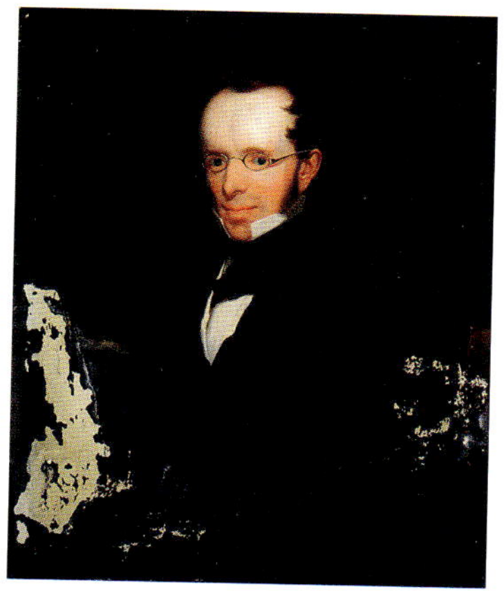

Poole, William c.1798–1888
Samuel Bailey (1791–1870), Poet and Philosopher
oil on canvas 76.2 x 63.1
VIS.LI.817 (P)

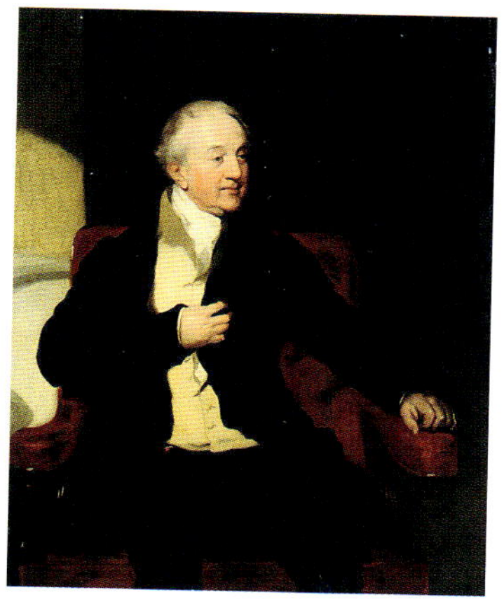

Poole, William c.1798–1888
William Wentworth-Fitzwilliam (1748–1833), 4th Earl Fitzwilliam
oil on canvas 127.1 x 101.7
VIS.LI.821 (P)

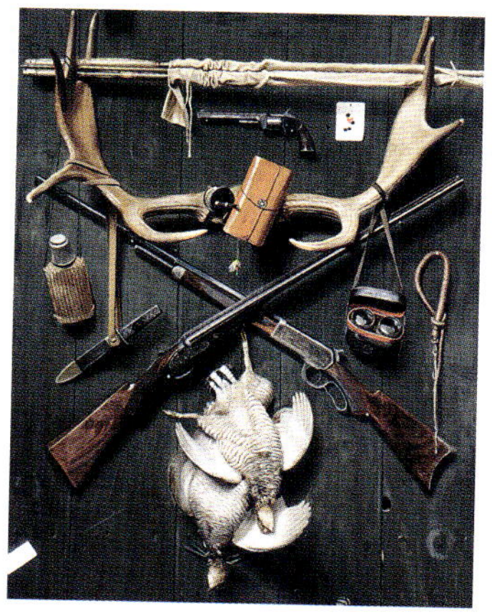

Pope, Alexander 1849–1924
Still Life (Sporting Equipment)
oil on canvas 133.9 x 103.3
VIS.2611

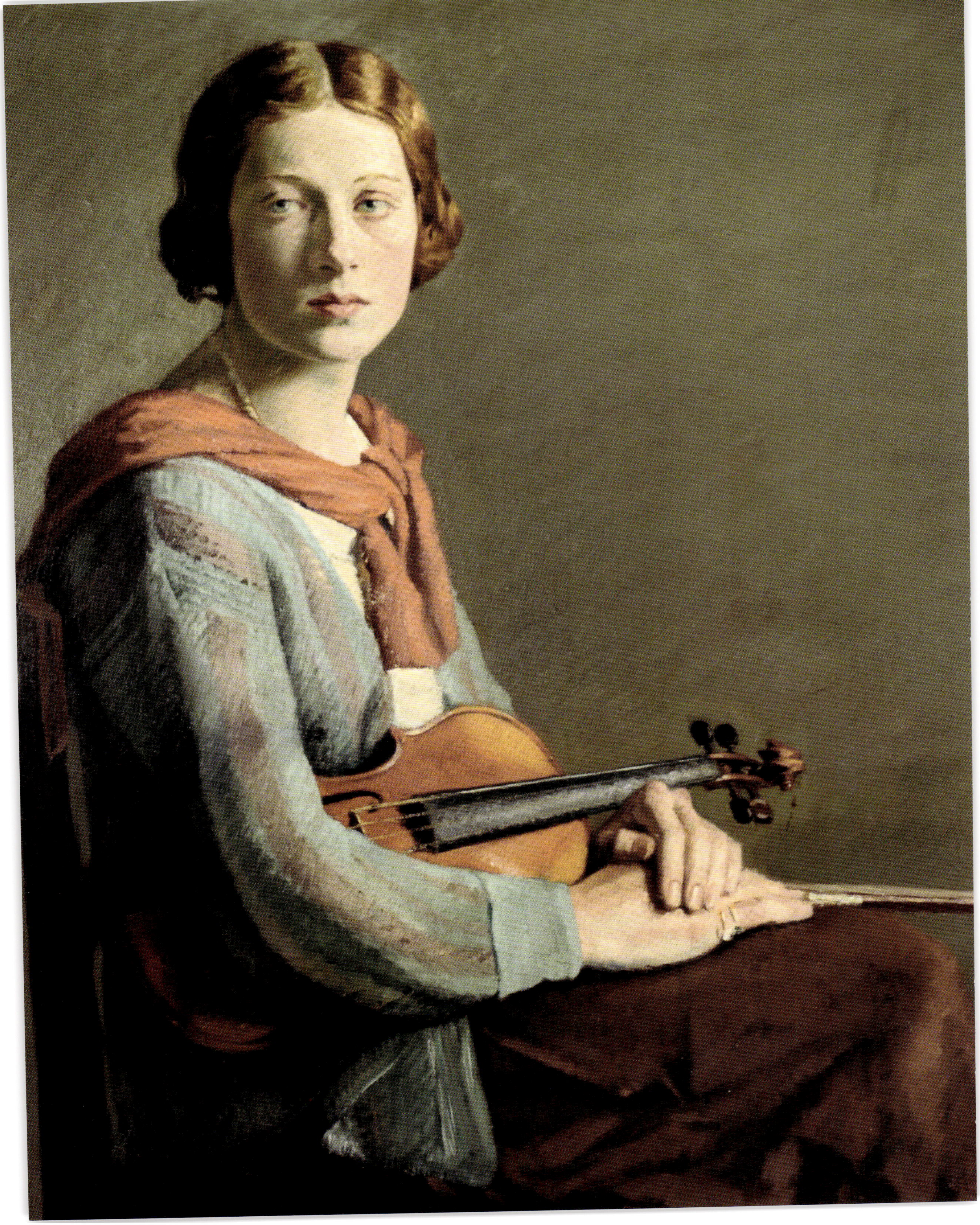

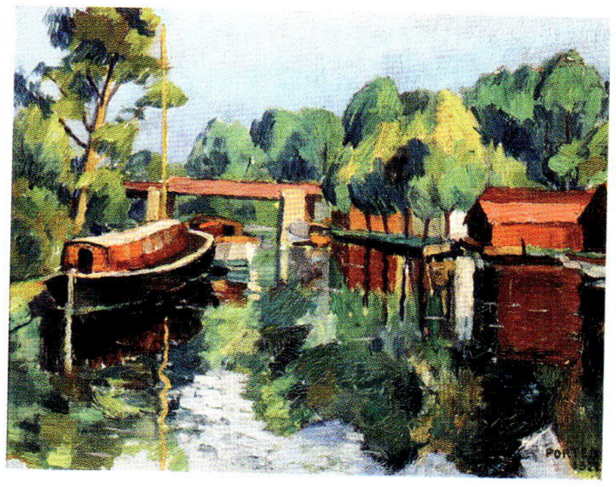

Porter, Frederick James 1883–1944
River Scene 1922
oil on canvas 31.9 x 39.9
VIS.4004

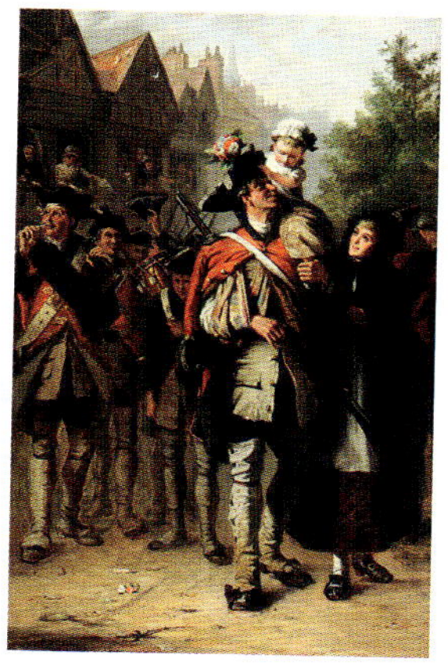

Pott, Laslett John 1837–1898
The Return of the Victors 1869
oil on canvas 108.5 x 71
VIS.1663

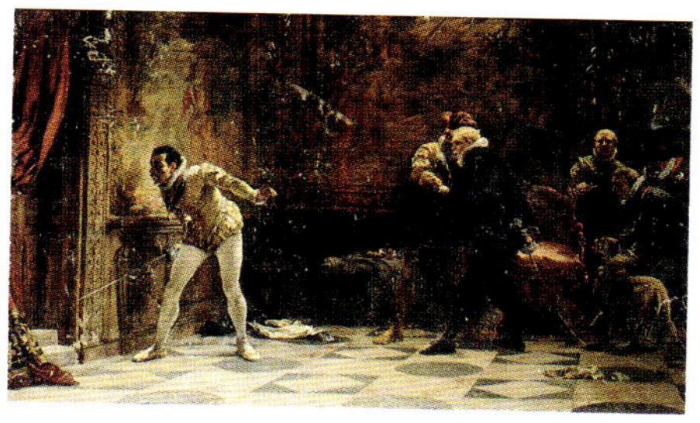

Pott, Laslett John 1837–1898
Waiting for the King's Favourite 1877
oil on canvas 92 x 153.2
VIS.2610

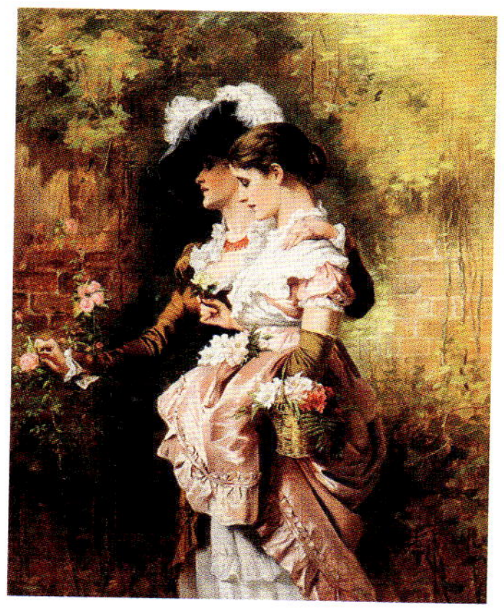

Pott, Laslett John 1837–1898
The Sisters 1879
oil on canvas 72 x 57.2
VIS.2792

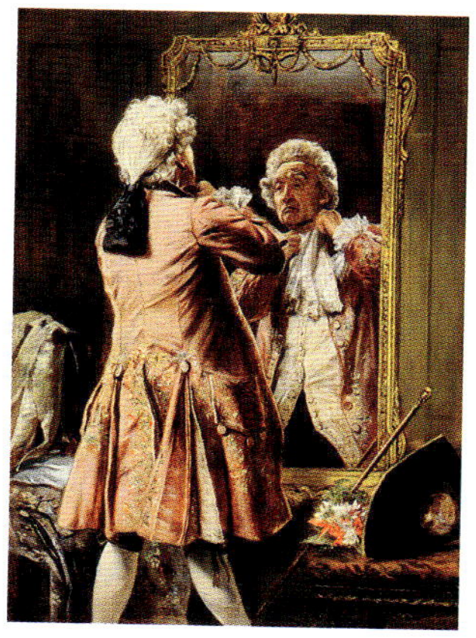

Pott, Laslett John 1837–1898
Sir Peter Teazle
oil on canvas 55.5 x 40
VIS.2415

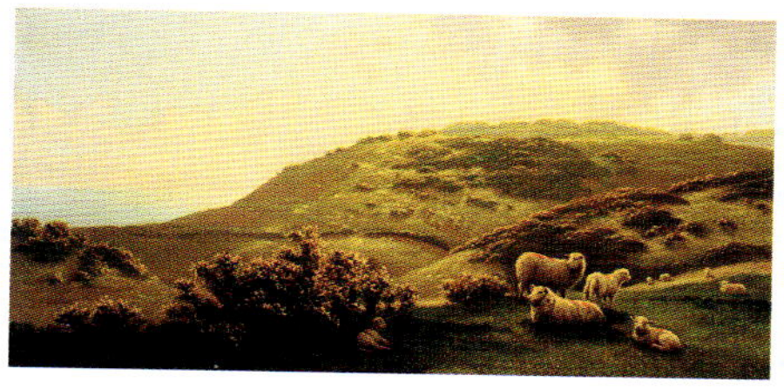

Potten, Christopher Nerry 1849–1934
Landscape
oil on canvas 46.2 x 91.3
VIS.1332

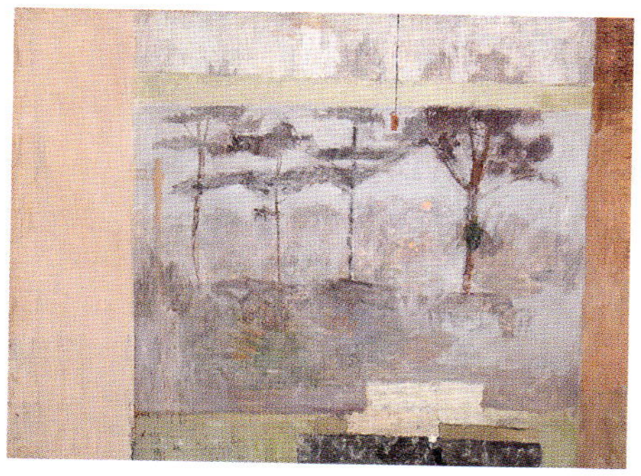

Potter, Mary 1900–1981
End of Daylight 1954
oil on canvas 74.2 x 99.6
VIS.2584

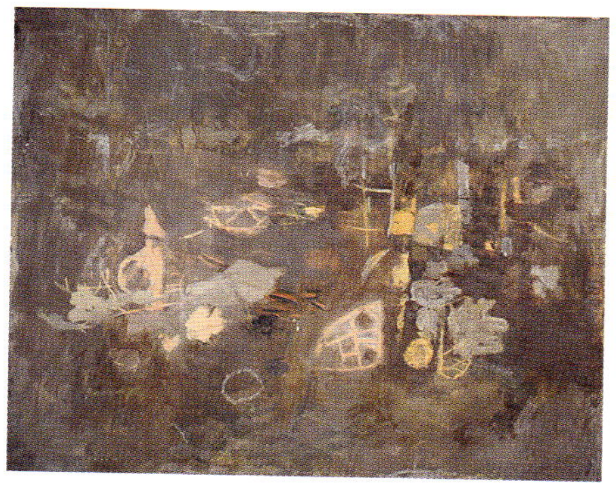

Potter, Mary 1900–1981
Evening Light on the Trees
oil on canvas 101.5 x 126.5
VIS.5198

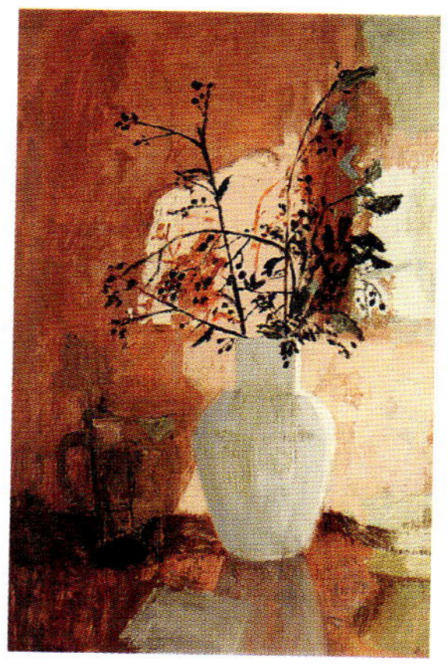

Potter, Mary 1900–1981
Still Life with a Vase
oil on canvas 59.6 x 39.4
VIS.4481

Facing page: Rothenstein, William, 1872–1945, *The Violinist* (detail), University of Sheffield, (p. 300)

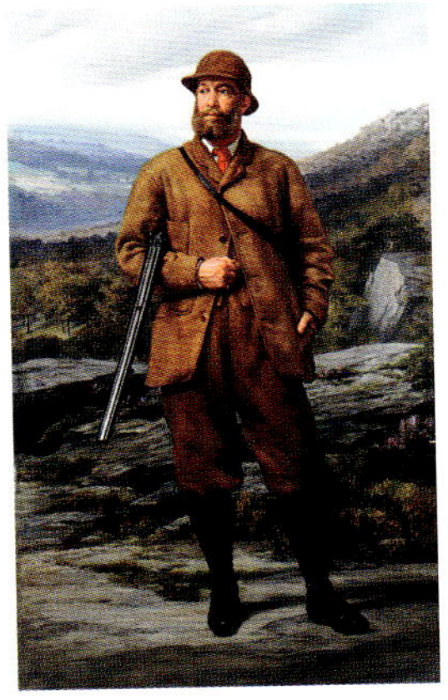

Poynter, Edward John 1836–1919
Edward Montagu Stuart Granville Montagu-Stuart-Wortley-Mackenzie (1827–1899), 1st Earl of Wharncliffe 1881
oil on canvas 222.5 x 134.8
VIS.5422

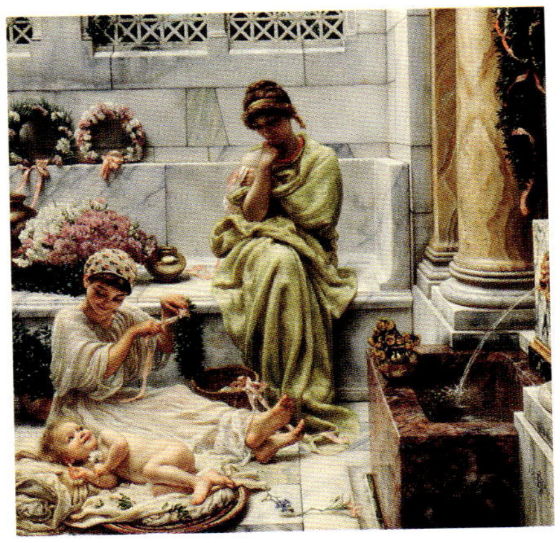

Poynter, Edward John 1836–1919
Corner of the Market Place 1887
oil on canvas 54.1 x 54
VIS.LI.757 (P)

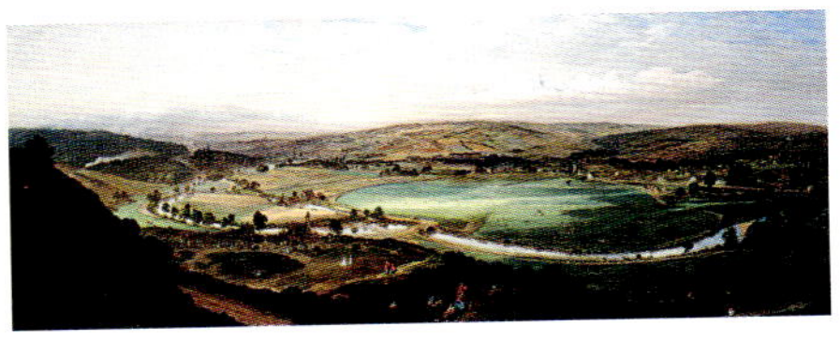

Price, Edward 1800–1885
Sheffield and the Valley of the Don 1863
oil on canvas 58.2 x 149.5
K1948.1

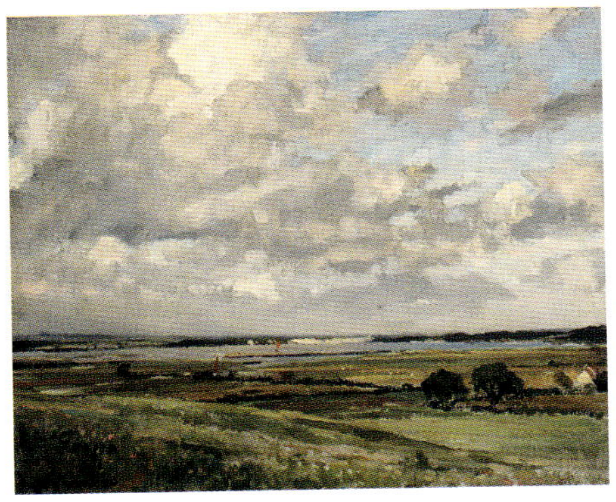

Priestman, Bertram 1868–1951
Wareham Channel, Dorset 1910
oil on canvas 62 x 74.5
VIS.149

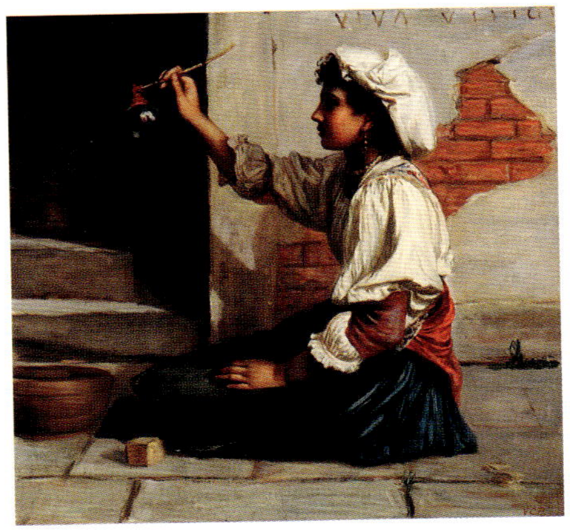

Prinsep, Valentine Cameron 1838–1904
Girl Blowing Soap Bubbles
oil on canvas 49.5 x 47.8
VIS.1365

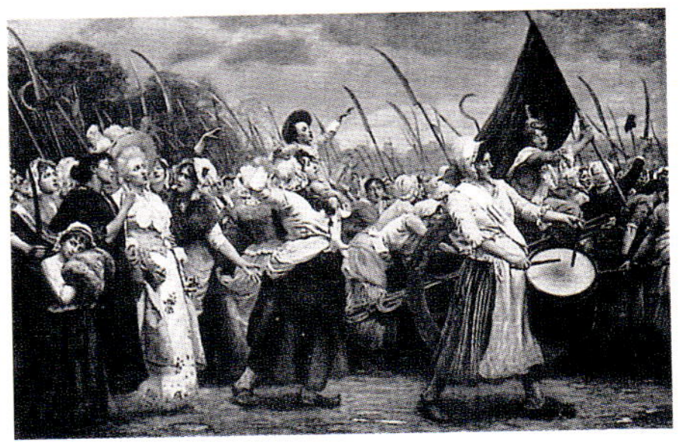

Prinsep, Valentine Cameron 1838–1904
To Versailles, an Incident in the French Revolution
oil on canvas 240 x 357
VIS.1610

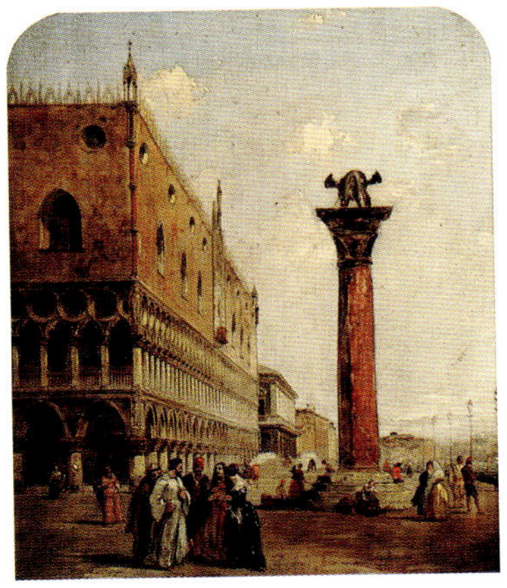

Pritchett, Edward active c.1828–1879
The Piazzetta, Venice
oil on canvas 29.1 x 24
VIS.718

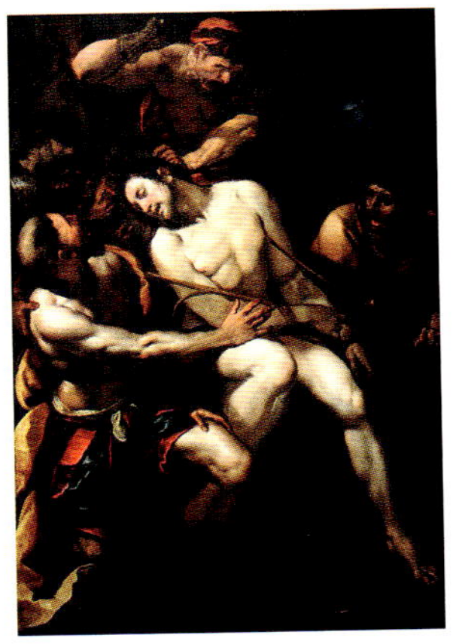

Procaccini, Giulio Cesare 1574–1625
The Mocking of Christ c.1617
oil on canvas 236.8 x 166.9
VIS.2459

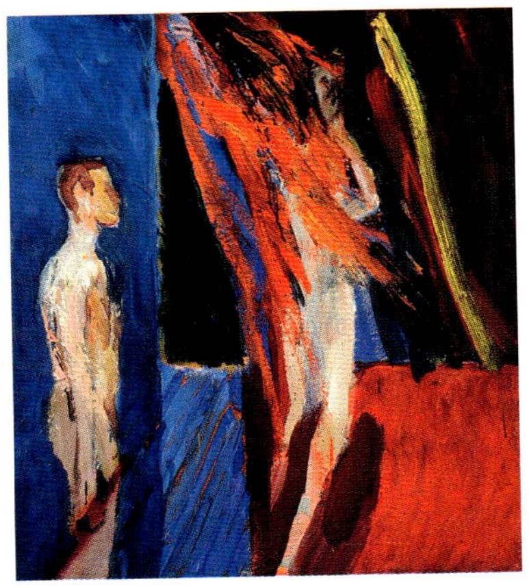

Procktor, Patrick 1936–2003
Figures, Red and Blue 1963
oil on canvas 64 x 56.5
VIS.LI.2 (P)

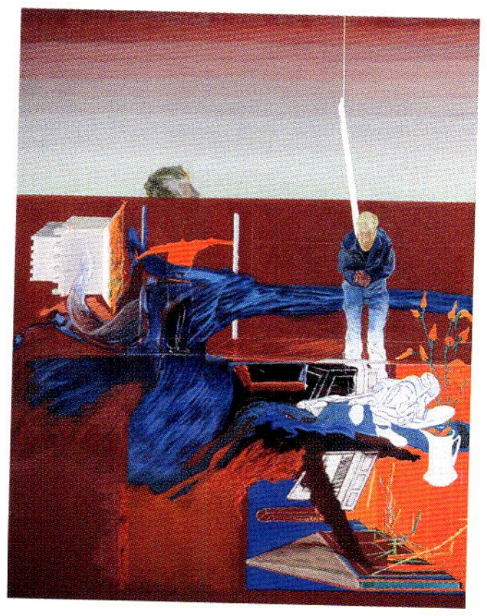

Procktor, Patrick 1936–2003
Beneath the Surface 1964
oil on canvas 194.9 x 147.2
VIS.4050

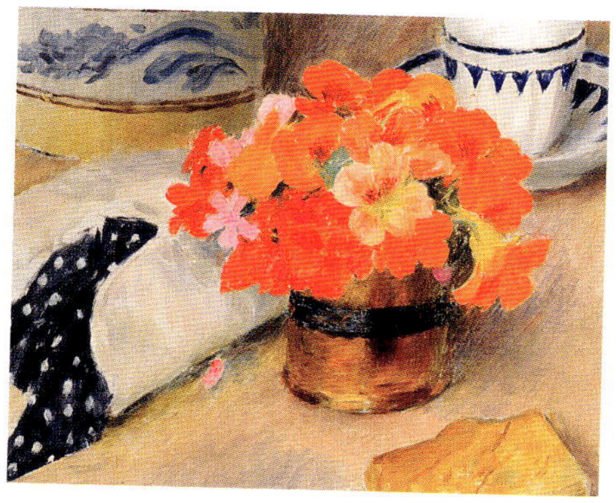

Procter, Dod 1892–1972
Nasturtiums
oil on plywood 23.3 x 28.4
VIS.5434

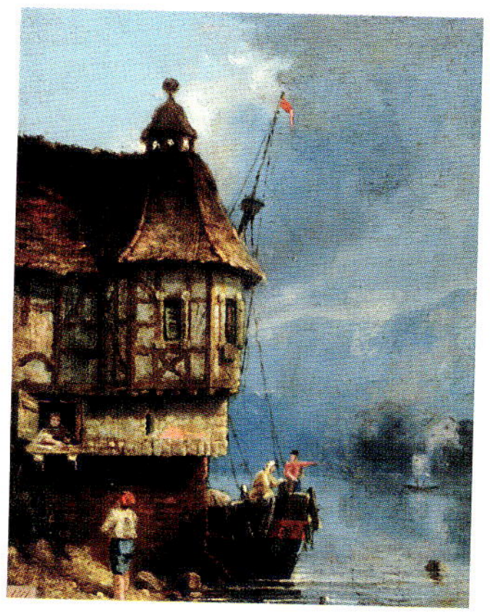

Prout, Samuel 1783–1852
River Scene
oil on millboard 24 x 19
VIS.958

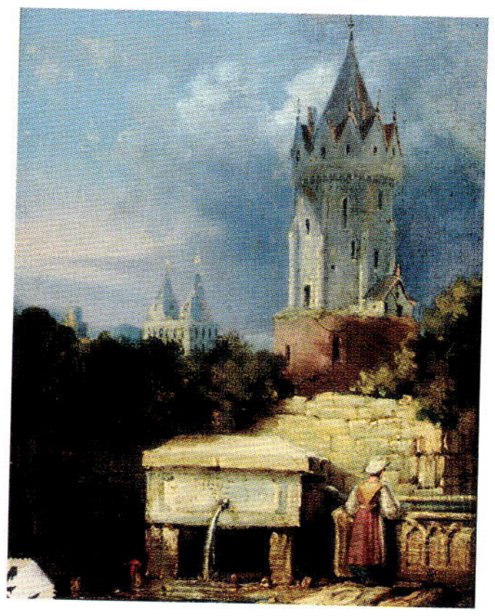

Prout, Samuel 1783–1852
The Fountain
oil on panel 23.7 x 18.5
VIS.966

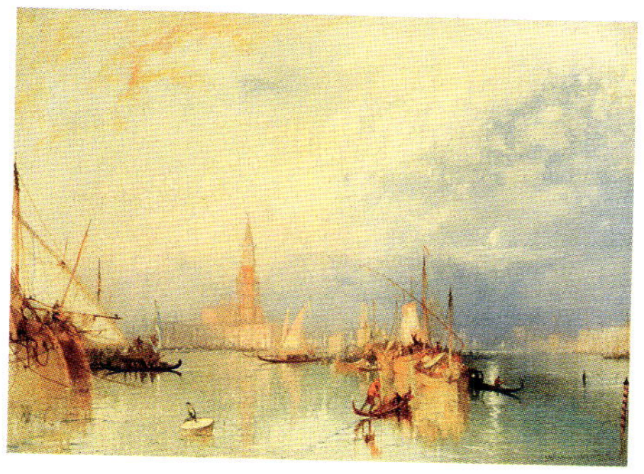

Pyne, James Baker 1800–1870
Marine Piece 1847
oil on canvas 44.5 x 60
VIS.1573

Pyne, James Baker 1800–1870
Marine Piece 1849
oil on canvas 47 x 64.9
VIS.1625

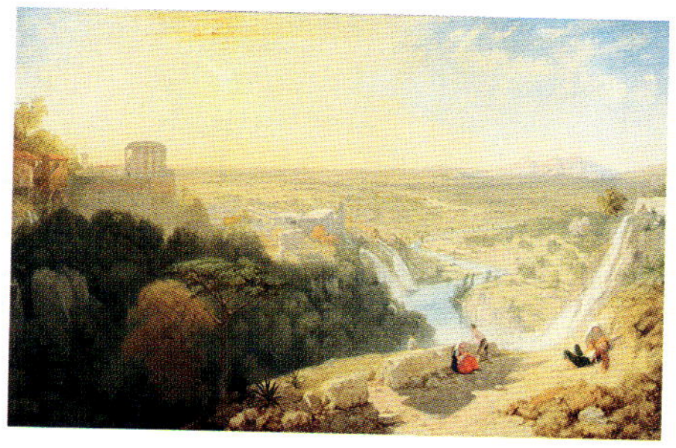

Pyne, James Baker 1800–1870
Rome from Tivoli, Italy 1868
oil on canvas 65.9 x 98.2
VIS.525

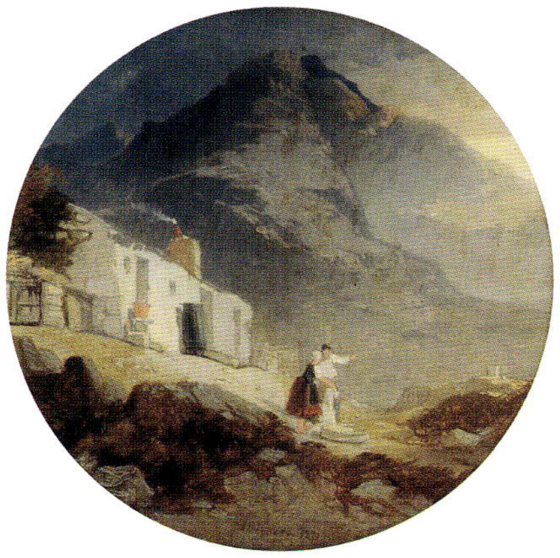

Pyne, James Baker 1800–1870
Moel Hebog, North Wales
oil on canvas 21
VIS.1082

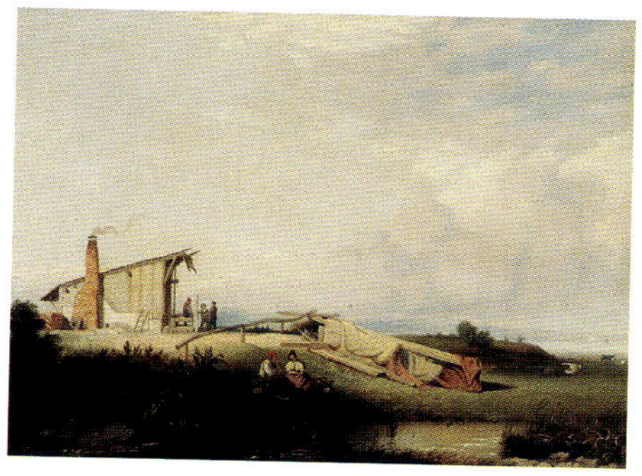

Pyne, James Baker 1800–1870
Near Eastbourne, East Sussex, with a View of Pevensey Bay
oil on canvas 44.4 x 59.5
VIS.316

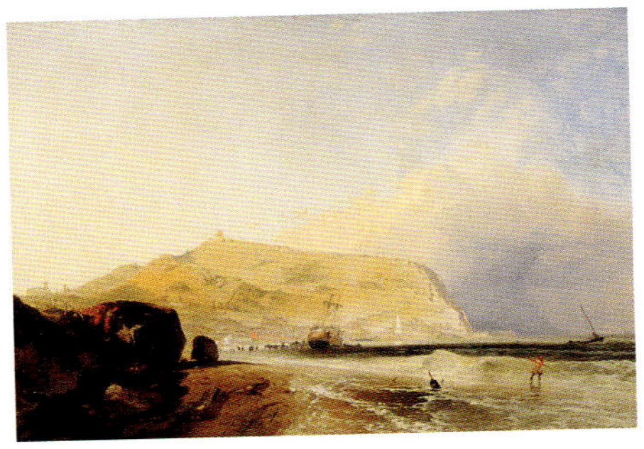

Pyne, James Baker 1800–1870
Scarborough, North Yorkshire
oil on canvas 93.4 x 134.2
VIS.662

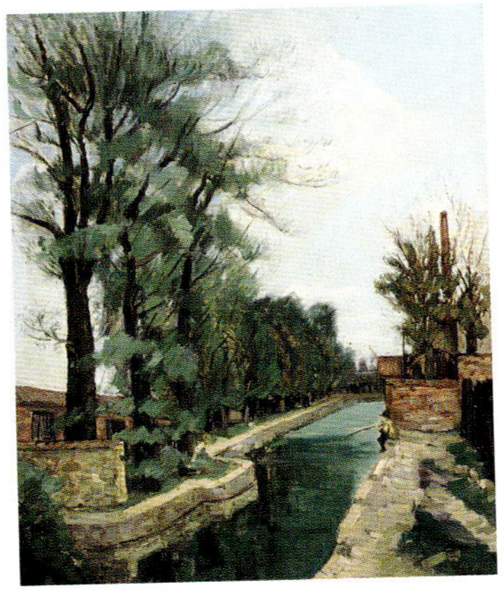

Quizet, Alphonse 1885–1955
The Canal at La Villette, Paris
oil on canvas 71.5 x 58.3
VIS.772

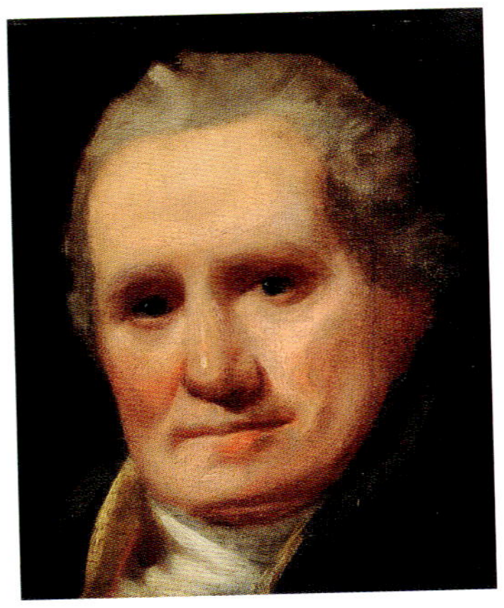

Raeburn, Henry 1756–1823
Head of a Man
oil on panel 31.9 x 25.7
VIS.290

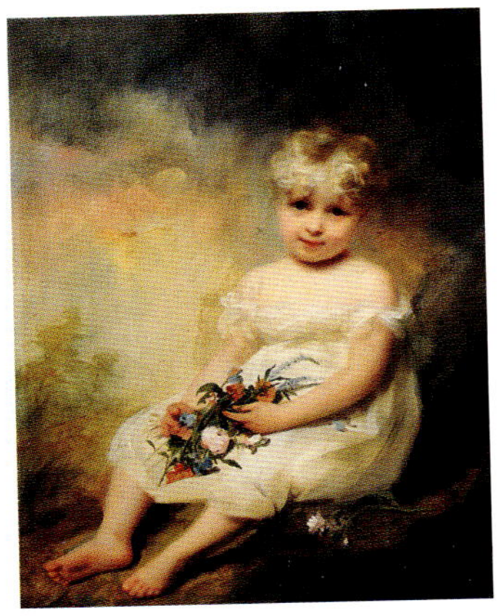

Raeburn, Henry 1756–1823
Lady Mary Lyon, Daughter of the Earl of Strathmore
oil on canvas 88.5 x 68.4
VIS.26

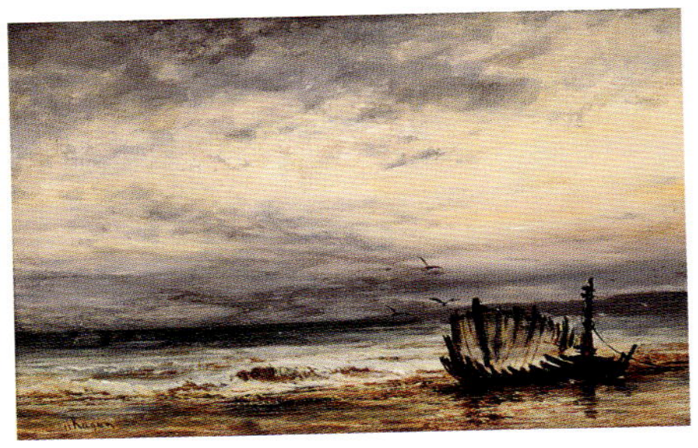

Ragon, Adolphe 1847–1924
Coast Scene
oil on board 18.8 x 29.6
VIS.239

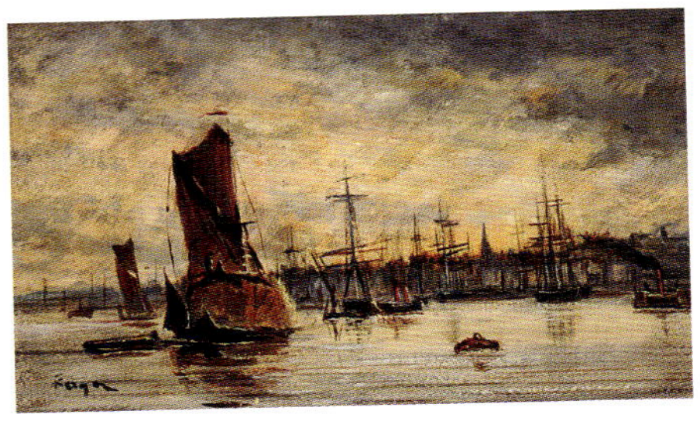

Ragon, Adolphe 1847–1924
Gravesend, Kent
oil on millboard 13.9 x 22.9
VIS.228

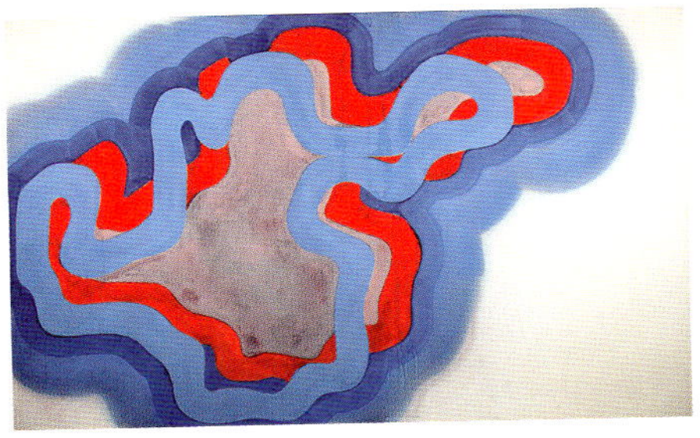

Rainer, Richard b.1933
Fecundity
oil on canvas 152.3 x 243.5
VIS.3721

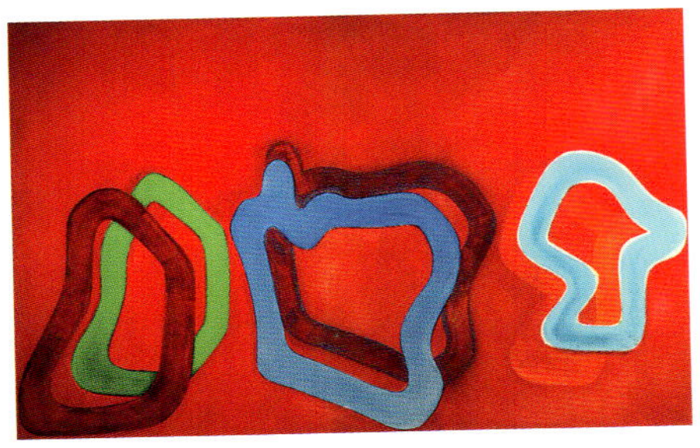

Rainer, Richard b.1933
Fecundity II
oil on canvas 152.5 x 244
VIS.4547

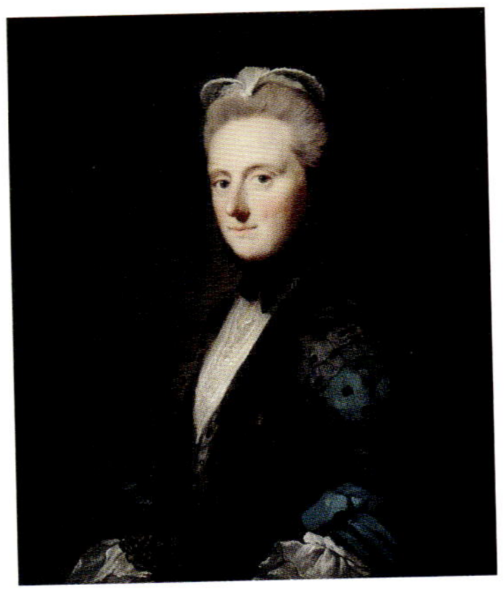

Ramsay, Allan 1713–1784
The Honourable Mrs Clarges (daughter of the 1st Viscount Barrington)
oil on canvas 75 x 62
VIS.3946

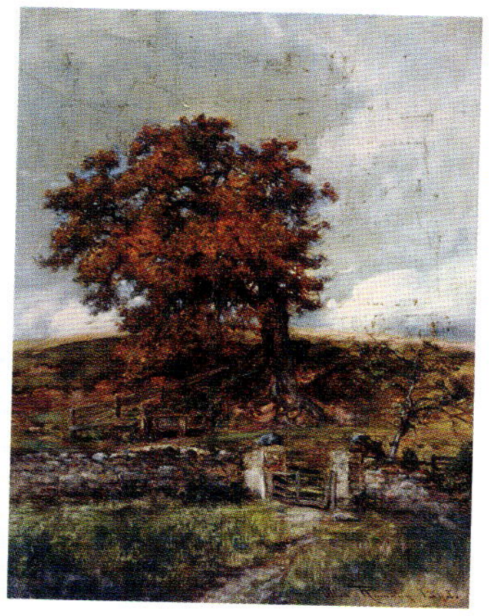

Ramsay, Allan 1852–1912
The Old Green Tree and the Gateway at Edzell Castle, Scotland 1898
oil on canvas 44.7 x 34.6
VIS.1234

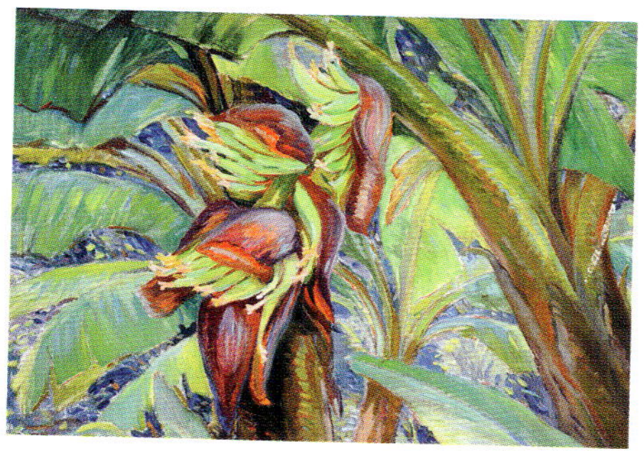

Ramsay, Patricia 1886–1974
Banana Tree
oil on board 52 x 72.8
VIS.1806

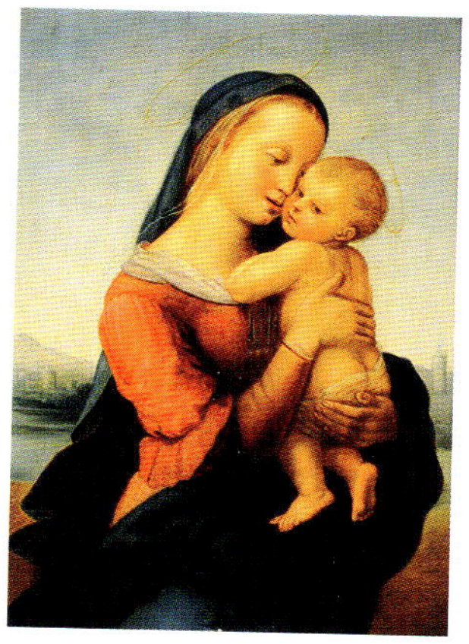

Raphael (after) 1483–1520
Madonna and Child
oil on panel 25.5 x 18.4
VIS.1085

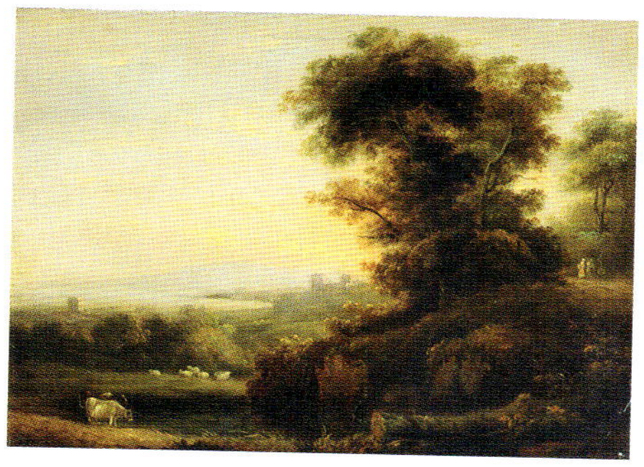

Rathbone, John 1750–1807
Evening
oil on canvas 21.6 x 29.2
VIS.357

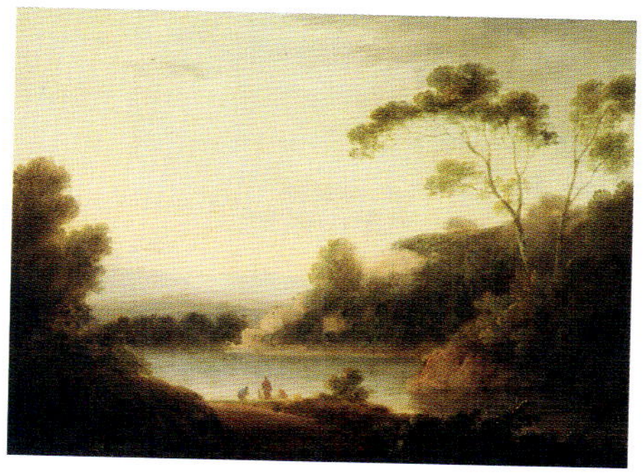

Rathbone, John 1750–1807
Morning
oil on canvas 21.8 x 29.2
VIS.110

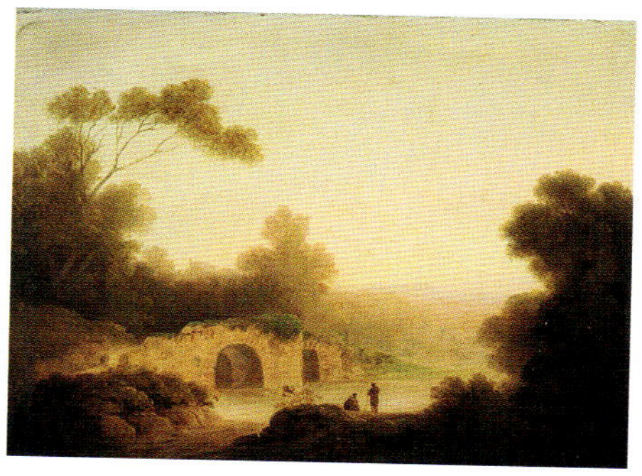

Rathbone, John 1750–1807
Sunset
oil on board 21.2 x 29.5
VIS.522

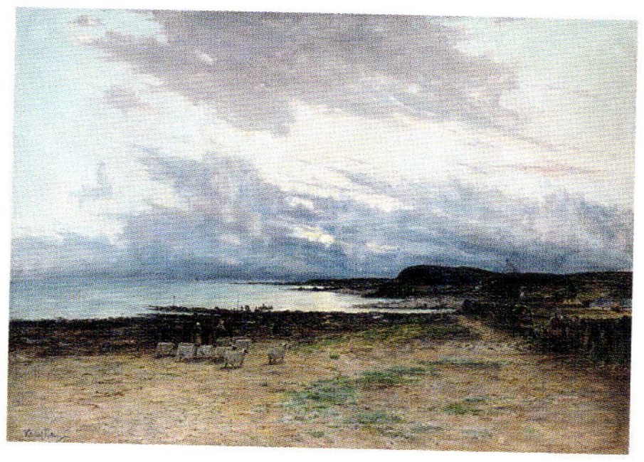

Rattray, Alexander William Wellwood
1849–1902
Black Water Bay, Isle of Arran, Scotland
oil on canvas 111.3 x 152.6
VIS.205

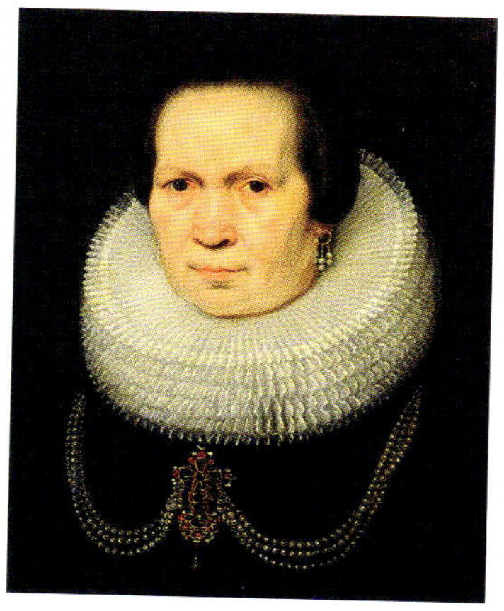

Ravesteyn, Jan Anthonisz. van (attributed to)
c.1570–1657
Portrait of a Lady
oil on panel 47.1 x 37.2
VIS.304

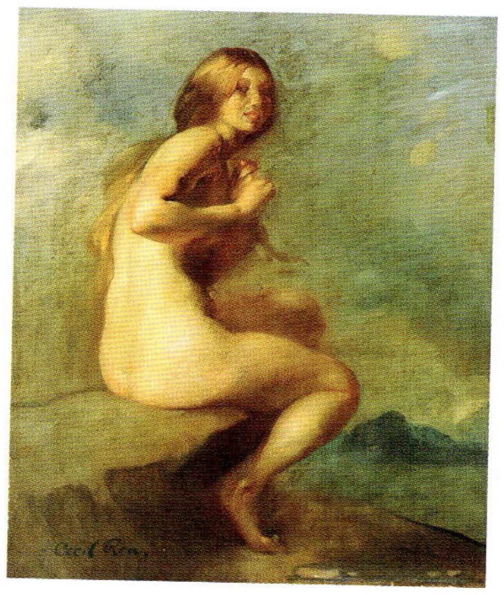

Rea, Cecil William 1860–1935
Nude
oil on canvas 60.9 x 50.9
VIS.1911

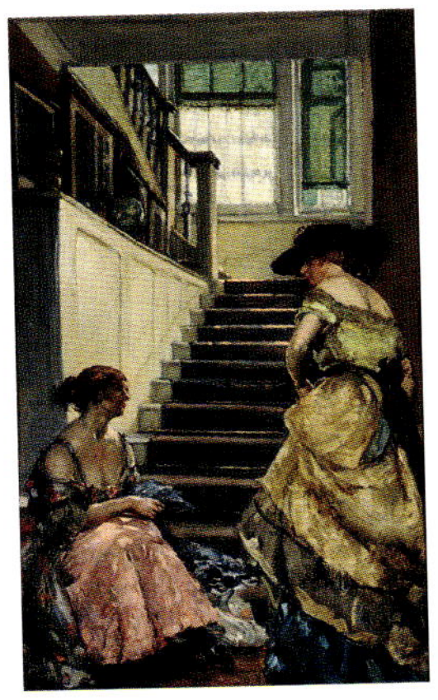

Rea, Constance 1891–1935
Interior with Figures
oil on canvas 59.1 x 35.2
VIS.1209

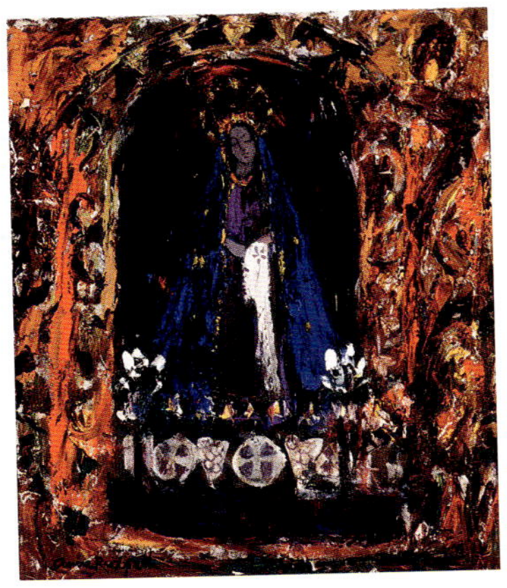

Redpath, Anne 1895–1965
Altar in Lisbon
oil on canvas 60.2 x 50.2
VIS.2577

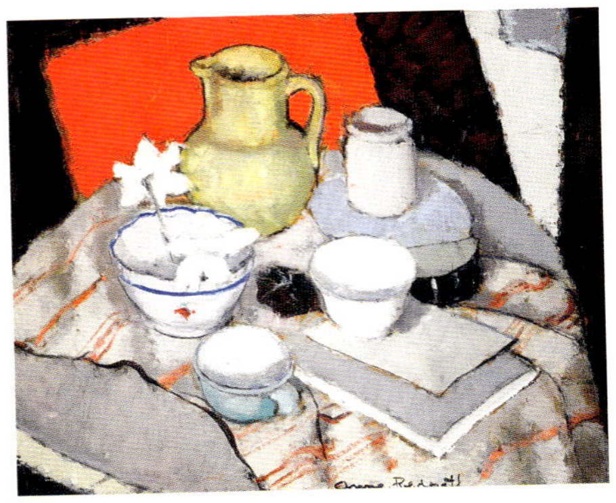

Redpath, Anne 1895–1965
Still Life on a Table
oil on board 49.4 x 59.7
VIS.4346

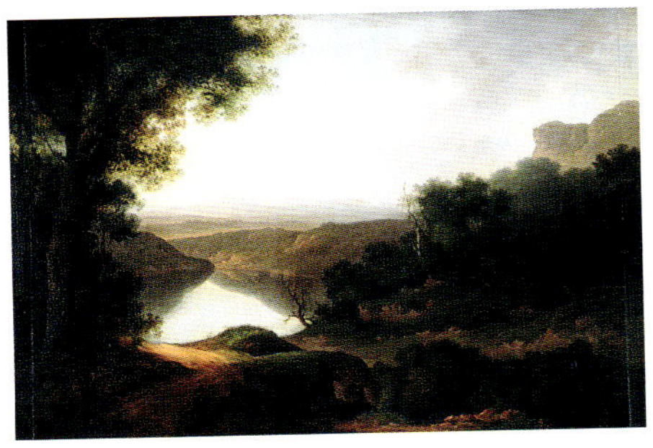

Reinagle, George Philip c.1802–1835
A Lake Scene
oil on panel 41.6 x 59
VIS.148

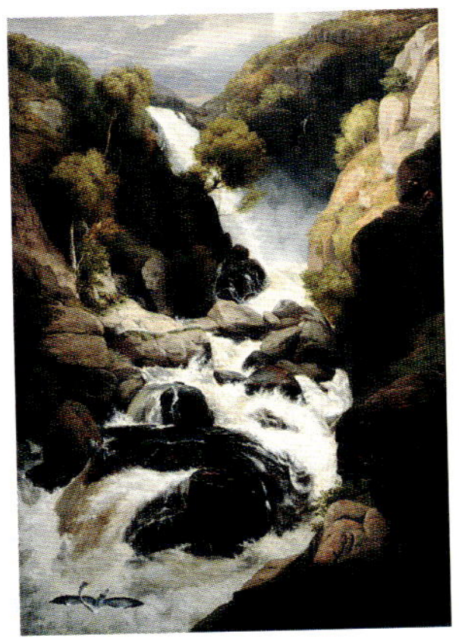

Reinagle, Philip 1749–1833
The Heron Shoot
oil on canvas 150.8 x 100.5
VIS.3222

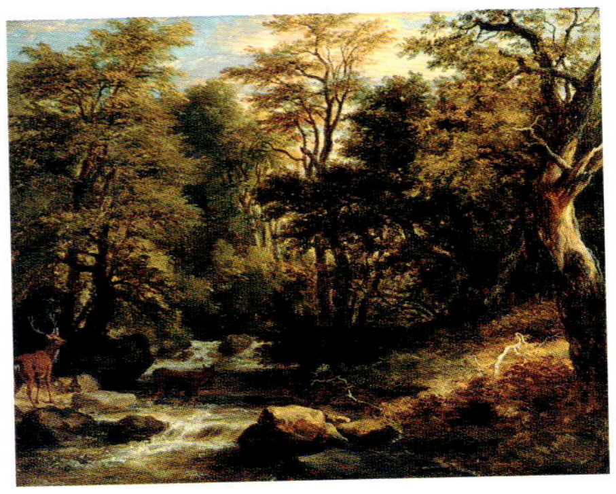

Reinagle, Ramsay Richard 1775–1862
Forest, Gowbarrow Park, Ullswater, Cumbria
1842
oil on canvas 36.4 x 44.7
VIS.360

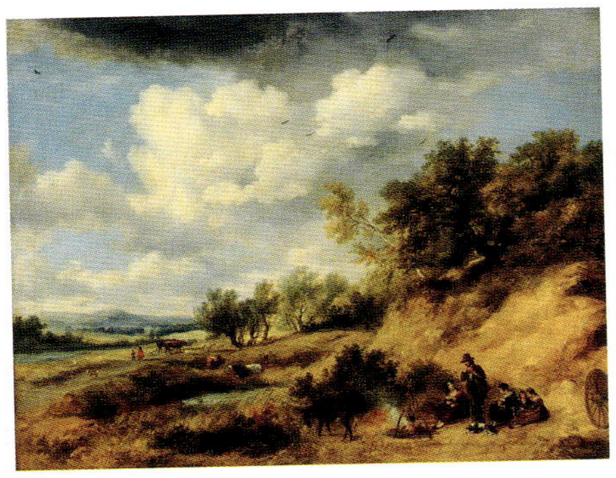

Reinagle, Ramsay Richard 1775–1862
Gypsy Encampment 1842
oil on canvas 36.2 x 46.9
VIS.537

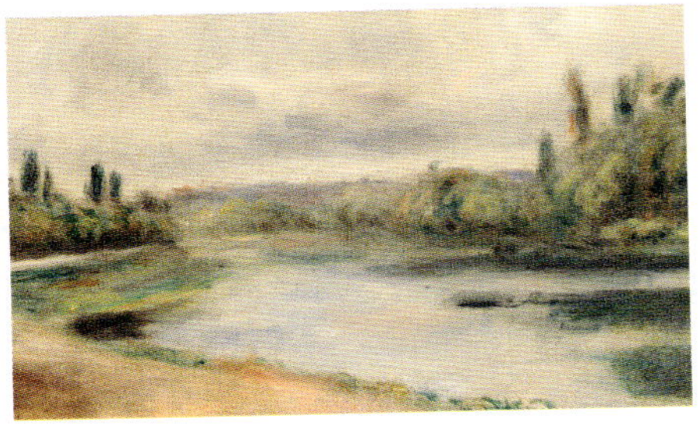

Renoir, Pierre-Auguste 1841–1919
La rivière
oil on canvas 17.9 x 30.1
VIS.LI.896 (P)

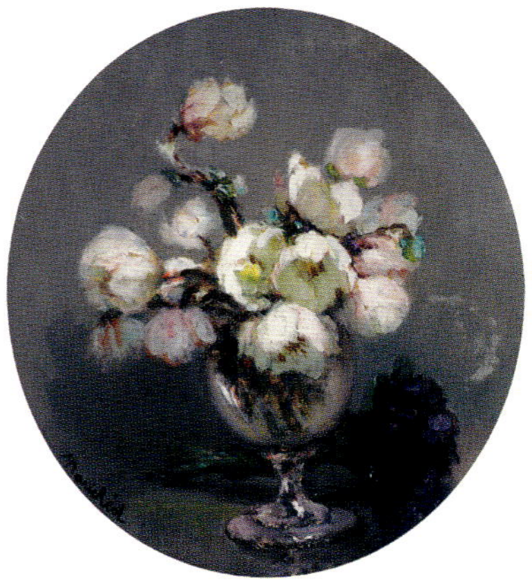

Réol, Marie Marguerite 1880–1963
Christmas Roses
oil on panel 38.9 x 34.5
VIS.1328

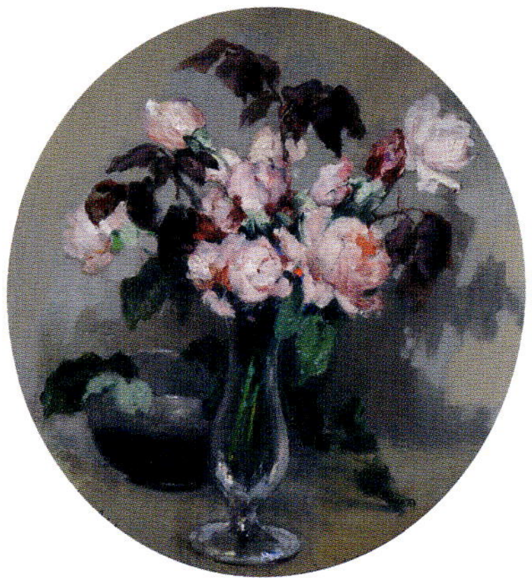

Réol, Marie Marguerite 1880–1963
Winter Roses
oil on panel 39 x 34.5
VIS.1327

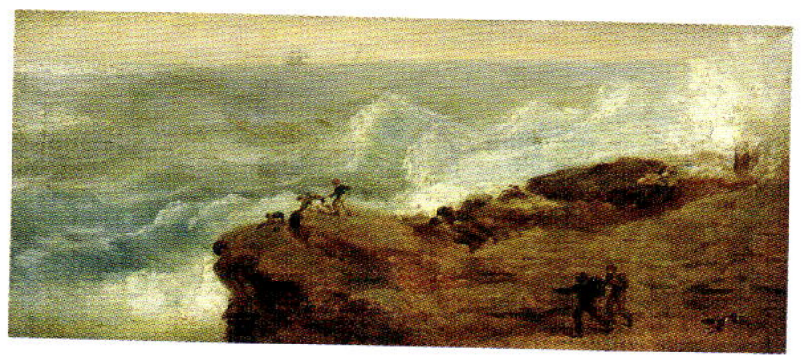

Reynolds, Joshua (attributed to) 1723–1792
A Storm on the Coast near Plympton, Devon
oil on canvas 27 x 62.3
VIS.307

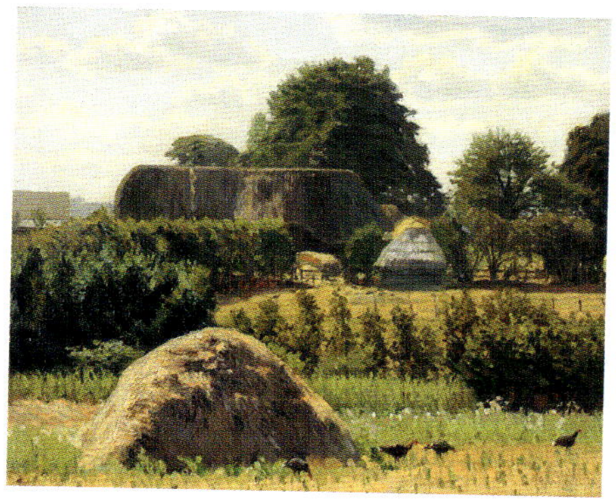

Rhoades, Geoffrey 1898–1980
Noon's Farm, Oxenwood, Wiltshire
oil on canvas 50 x 59.7
VIS.1800

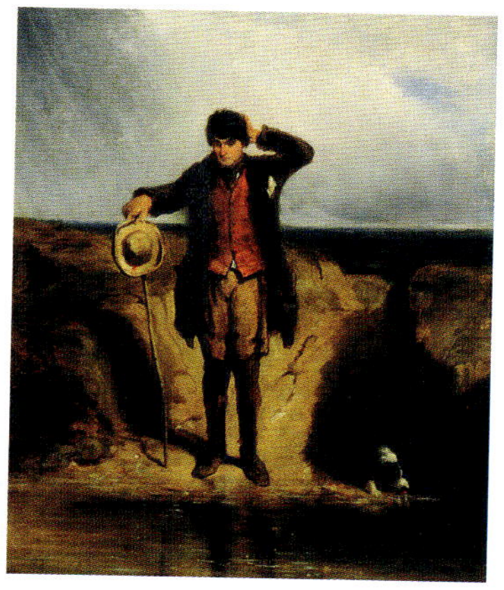

Rhodes, M. active 19th C
Bothered
oil on canvas 58 x 48
VIS.1524

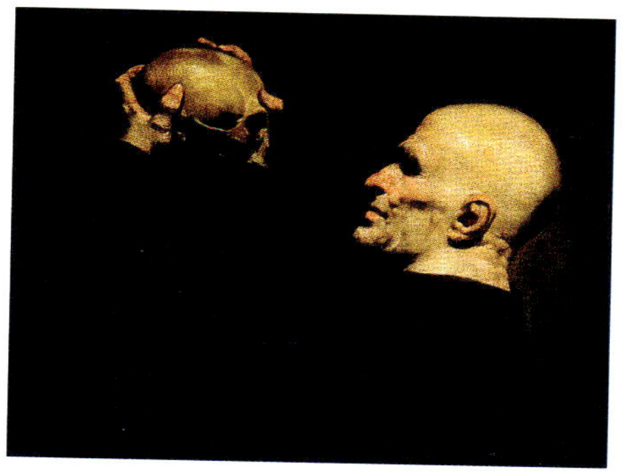

Ribera, Jusepe de 1591–1652
Man with a Skull 1630–1640
oil on canvas 68 x 87
VIS.291

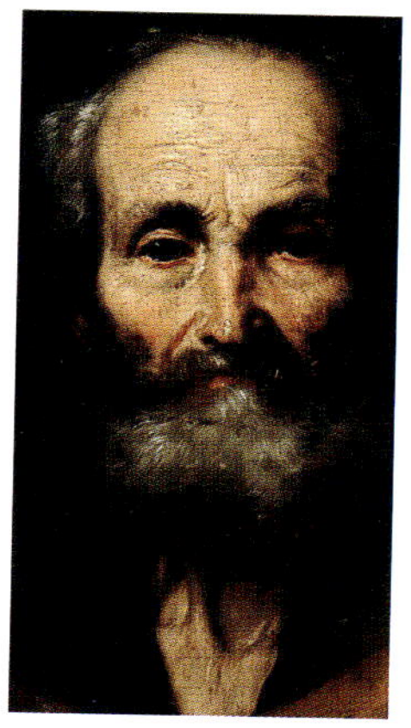

Ribera, Jusepe de (attributed to) 1591–1652
Head of an Apostle 1630–1640
oil on canvas 42 x 23
VIS.2293

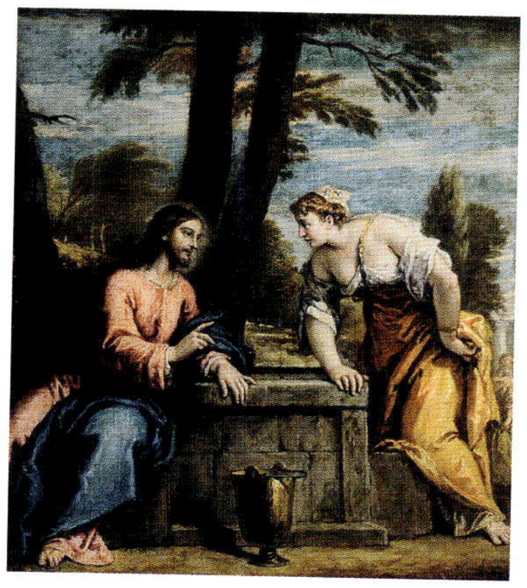

Ricci, Sebastiano 1659–1734
Christ and the Woman of Samaria
oil on canvas 71.3 x 61.6
VIS.2232

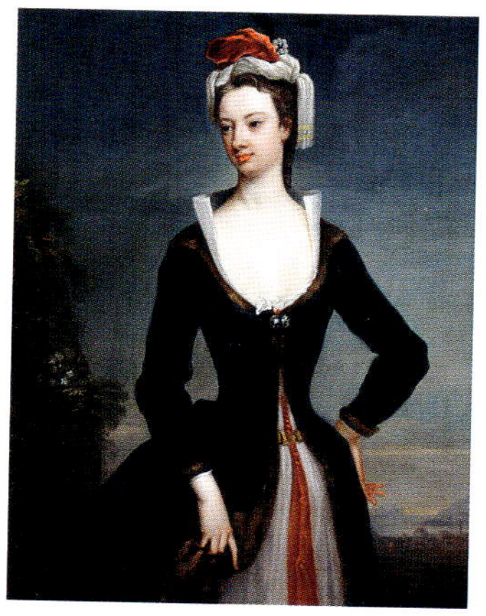

Richardson, Jonathan the elder
1664/1665–1745
Lady Mary Wortley Montagu (1689–1762)
c.1718
oil on canvas 136.7 x 108.8
VIS.4279

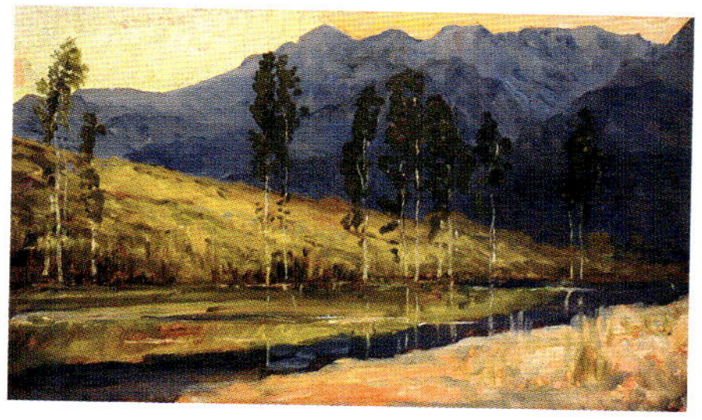

Richmond, William Blake 1842–1921
Valley of the Eurotas, Pastoral, Greece
oil on panel 26.7 x 44.7
VIS.4234

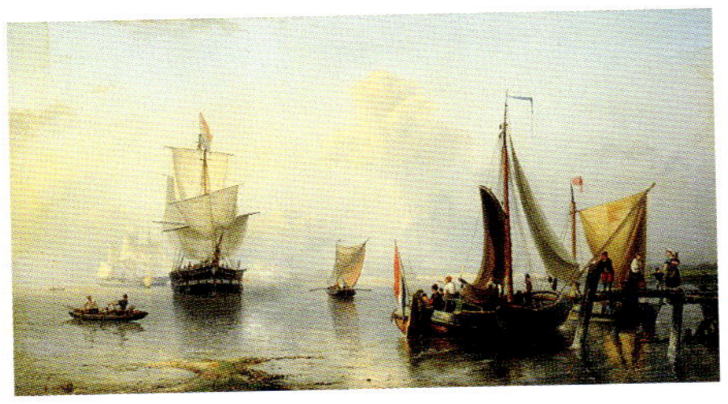

Riegen, Nicholaas 1827–1889
French Shipping
oil on canvas 37 x 66.4
VIS.518

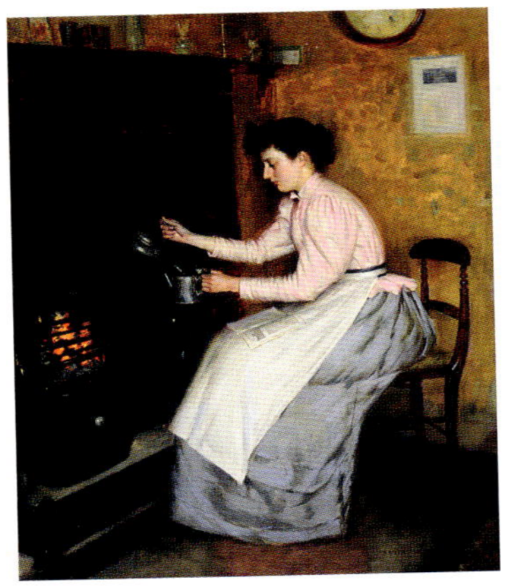

Rigg, Ernest Higgins 1868–1947
Quiet Hour 1895
oil on canvas 76.2 x 63.8
VIS.578

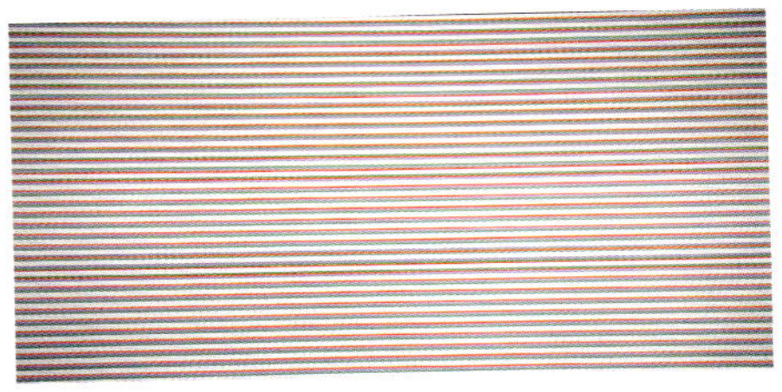

Riley, Bridget b.1931
Rise I 1968
acrylic on cotton 188.3 x 377.2
VIS.5163

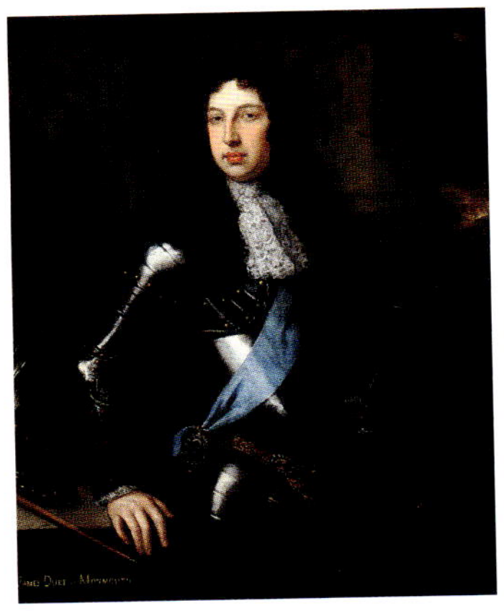

Riley, John 1646–1691
James Scott (1649–1685), 1st Duke of Monmouth
oil on canvas 123 x 97.2
VIS.3101

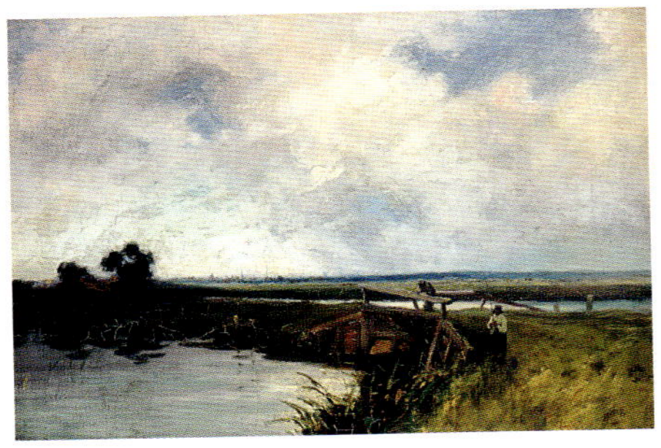

Rivers, Leopold 1852–1905
Landscape with a Bridge
oil on canvas 42.3 x 60.8
VIS.627

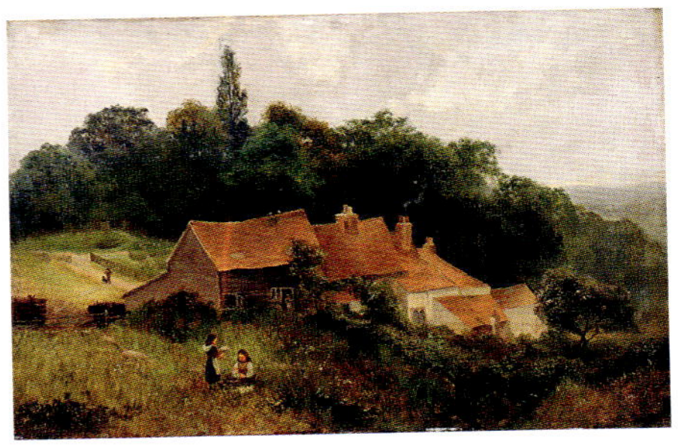

Rivers, Leopold 1852–1905
Landscape with Cottages
oil on canvas on millboard 50.4 x 75
VIS.1265

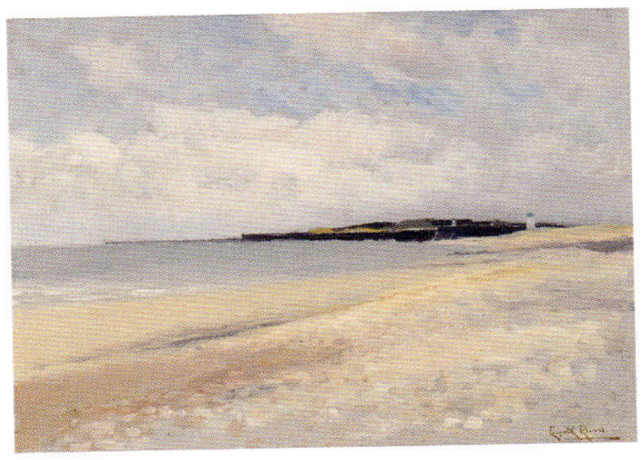

Rivers, Leopold 1852–1905
Littlehampton, Sussex
oil on panel 24.3 x 34.2
VIS.999

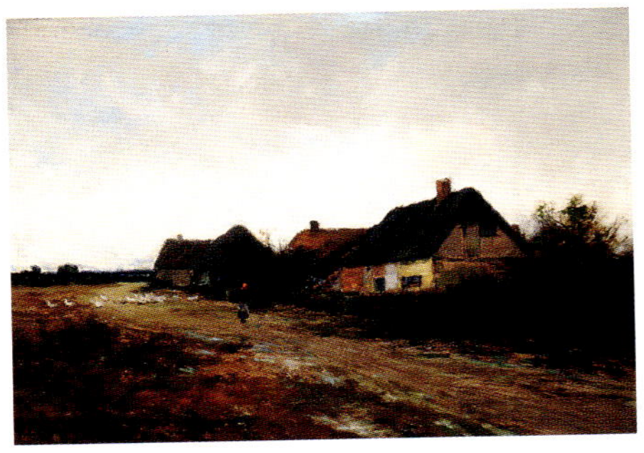

Rivers, Leopold 1852–1905
Near Newbury, Berkshire
oil on panel 23.7 x 34.3
VIS.1041

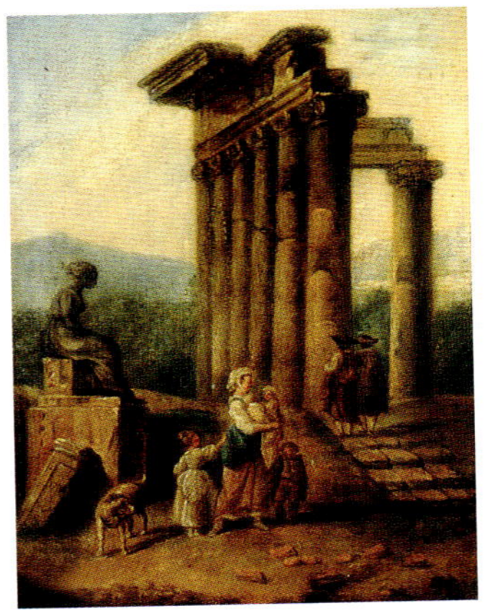

Robert, Hubert 1733–1808
Landscape with Ruins
oil on canvas 22.8 x 17.8
VIS.1042

Facing page: Ricci, Sebastiano, 1659–1734, *Christ and the Woman of Samaria* (detail), Museums Sheffield, (p. 179)

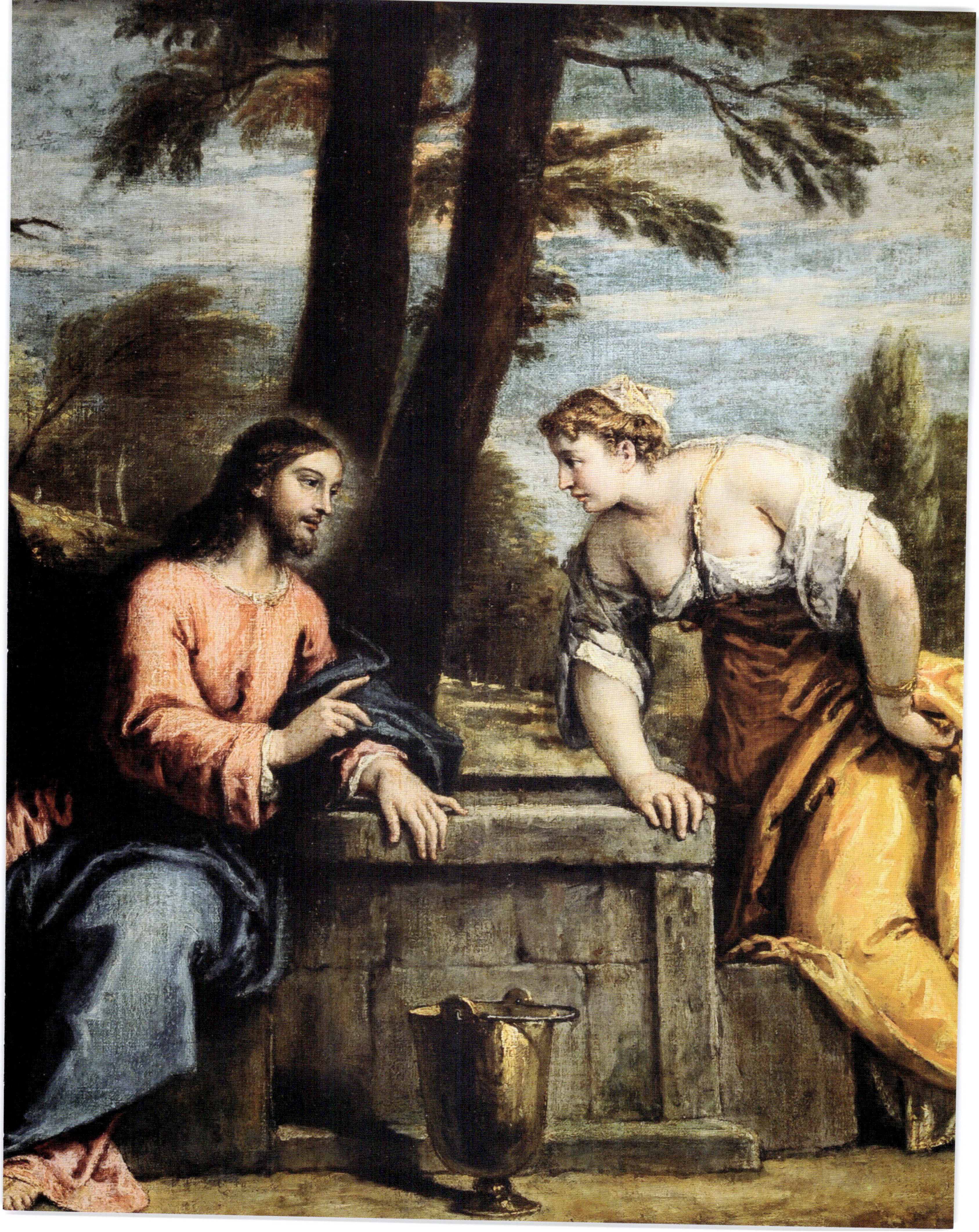

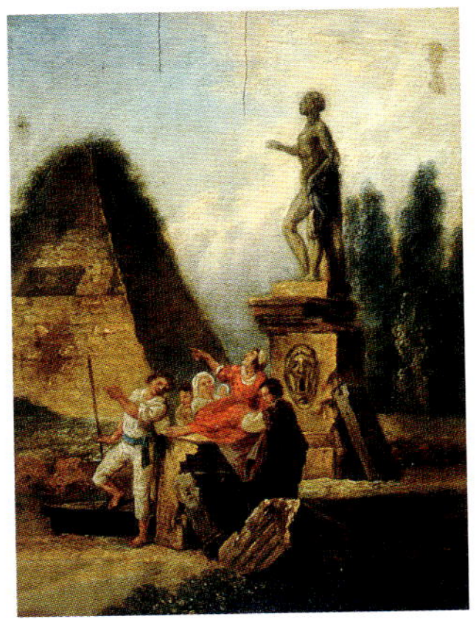

Robert, Hubert 1733–1808
Pyramid of Cestius, Rome
oil on panel 24.4 x 18.4
VIS.1077

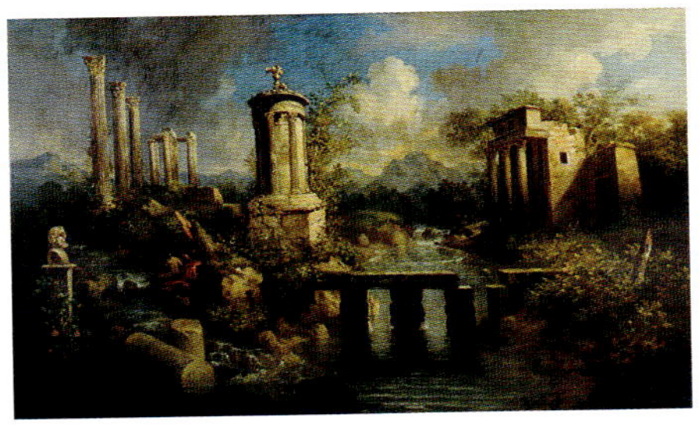

Robert, Hubert (attributed to) 1733–1808
Classical Landscape
oil on canvas 82 x 133.3
VIS.535

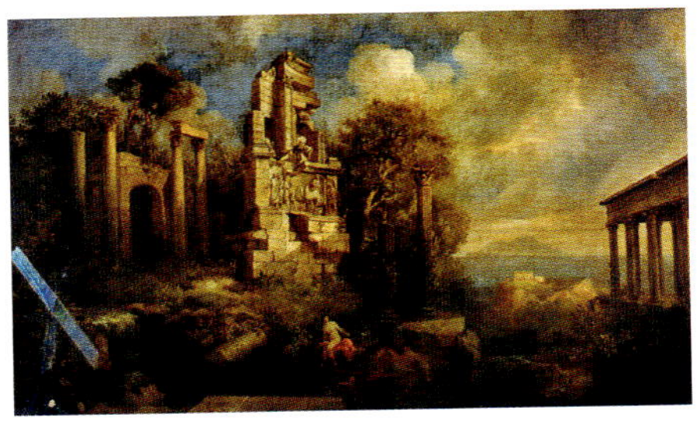

Robert, Hubert (attributed to) 1733–1808
Classical Landscape
oil on canvas 81.1 x 133.3
VIS.555

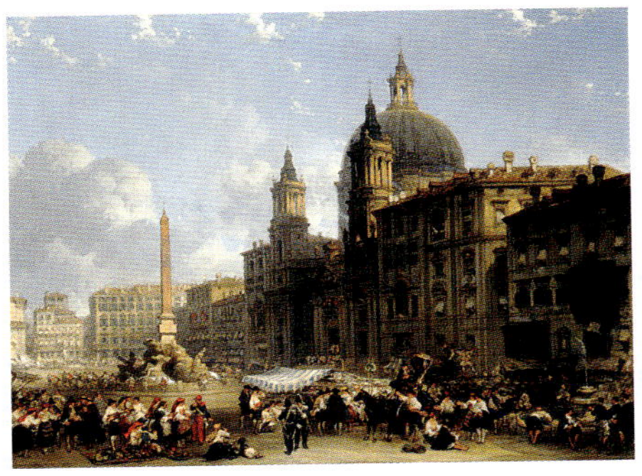

Roberts, David 1796–1864
The Piazza Navona at Rome 1857
oil on canvas 127.5 x 156.7
VIS.1419

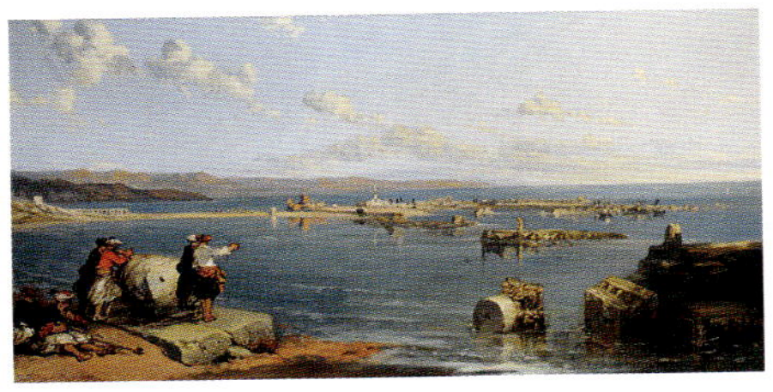

Roberts, David 1796–1864
The Ruins of Tyre, Lebanon 1858
oil on canvas 57.5 x 113.2
VIS.377

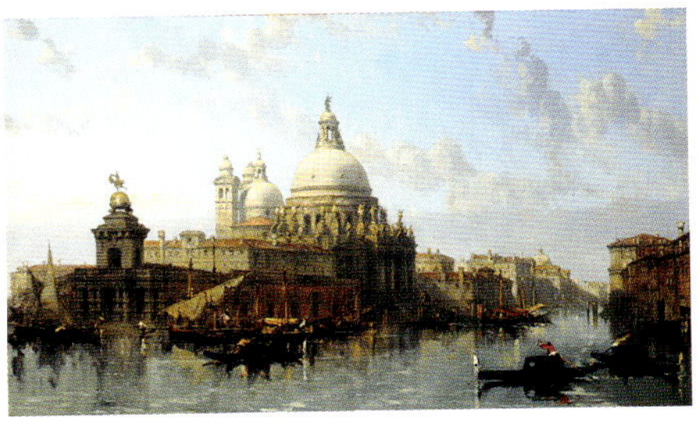

Roberts, David 1796–1864
Church of Santa Maria della Salute, Venice
1862
oil on canvas 67.5 x 113
VIS.1559

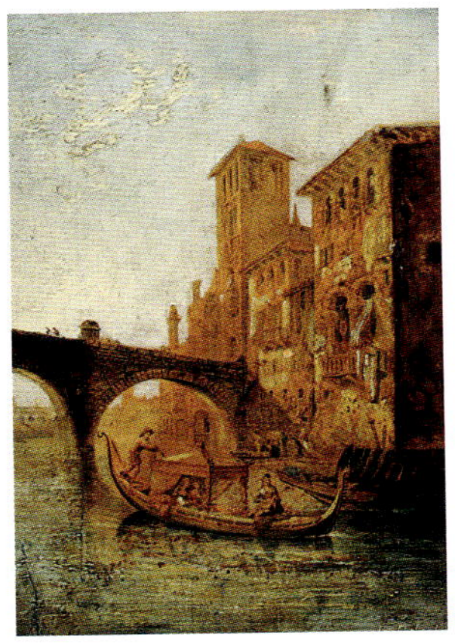

Roberts, David 1796–1864
Canal Scene, Venice
oil on panel 20 x 14
VIS.1302

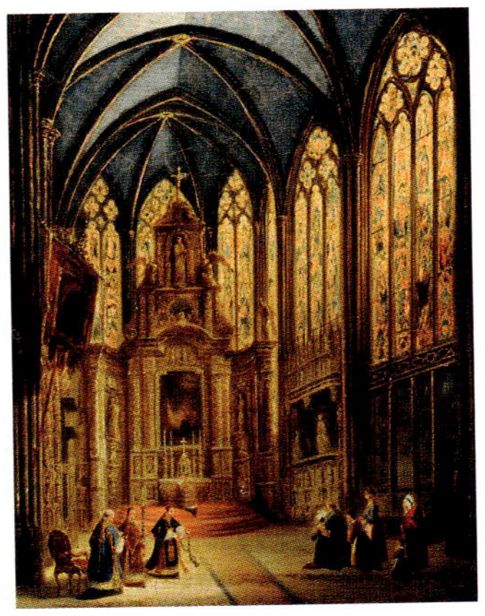

Roberts, David 1796–1864
Cathedral, France
oil on panel 29.7 x 22.8
VIS.44

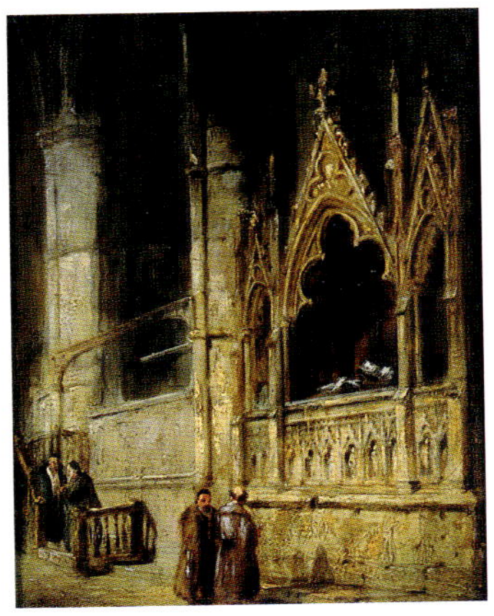

Roberts, David 1796–1864
Cathedral Interior
oil on panel 17.4 x 13.7
VIS.83

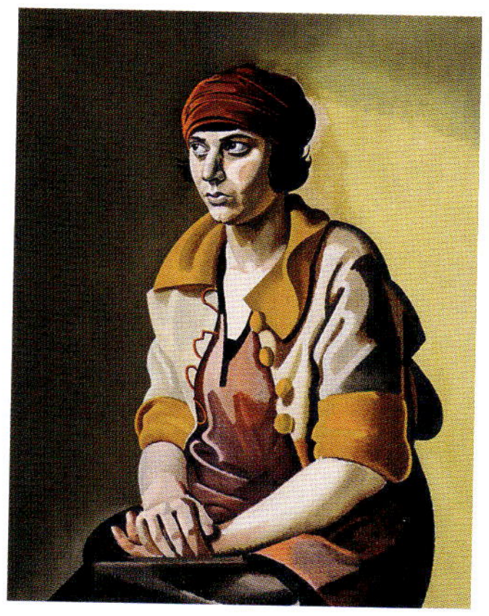

Roberts, William Patrick 1895–1980
The Red Turban c.1928
oil on canvas 103 x 82.8
VIS.1968

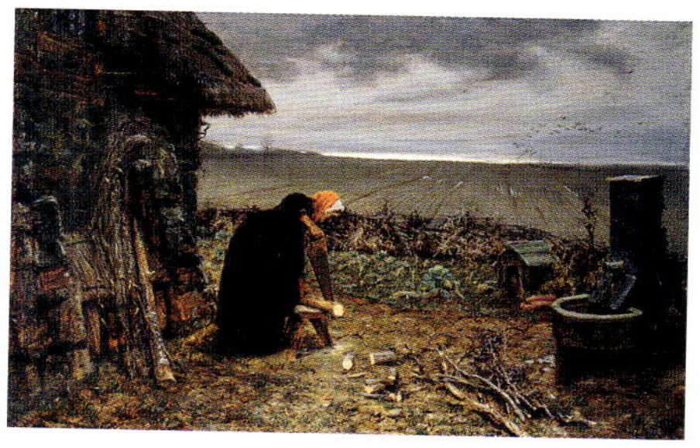

Robertson, Henry Robert 1839–1921
Winter
oil on canvas 97.9 x 151.6
VIS.1593

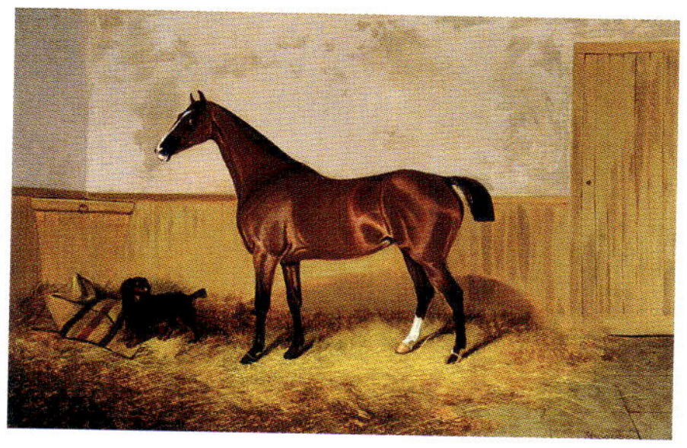

Roe, Colin Graeme 1857–1910
Study of a Horse 1890
oil on canvas 49.5 x 75
VIS.3034

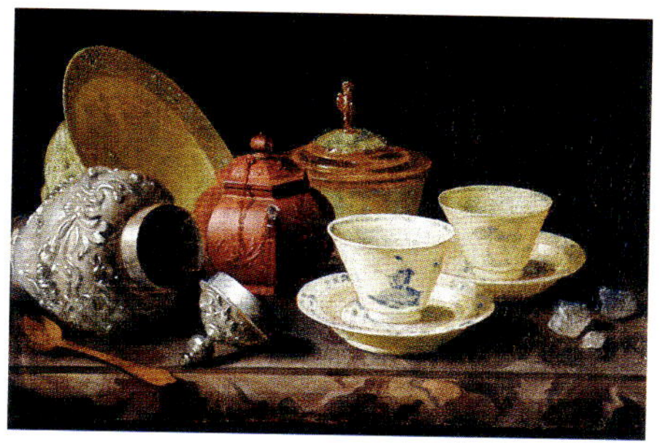

Roestraten, Pieter Gerritsz. van
1629/1630–1700
Still Life with Tea Cups 1670–1685
oil on canvas 24.8 x 36.6
VIS.305

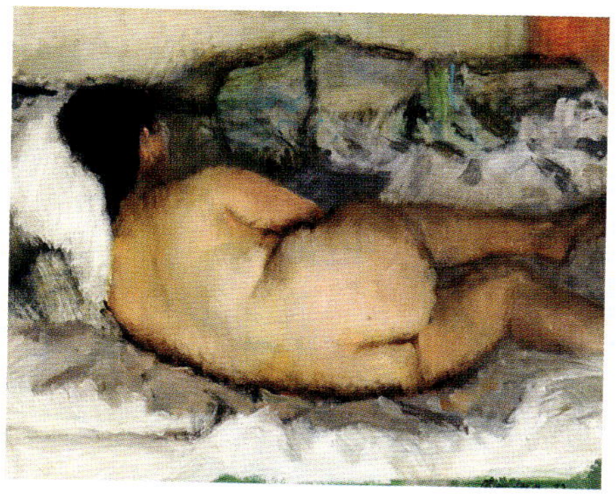

Rogers, Claude 1907–1979
Nude 1938
oil on canvas 47.9 x 58.3
VIS.2044

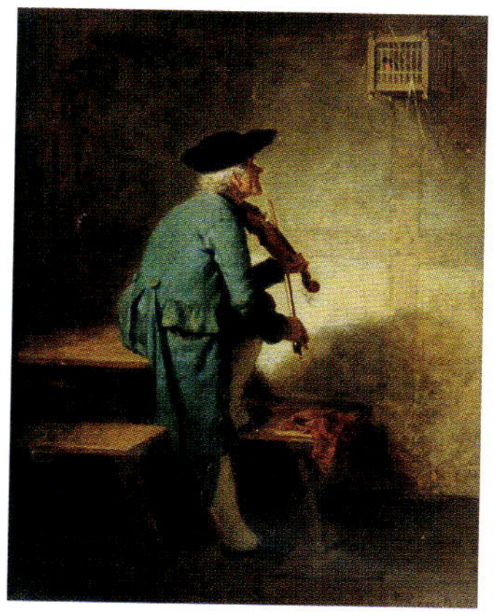

Rögge, Wilhelm 1829–1908
The Frenchman Playing to His Bird 1872
oil on canvas 43.8 x 33.9
VIS.1403

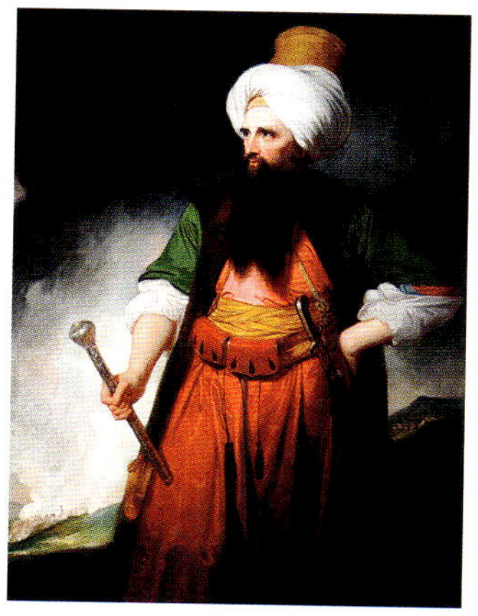

Romney, George 1734–1802
Edward Wortley Montagu (1713–1776), MP
c.1775
oil on canvas 146.5 x 112
VIS.5383

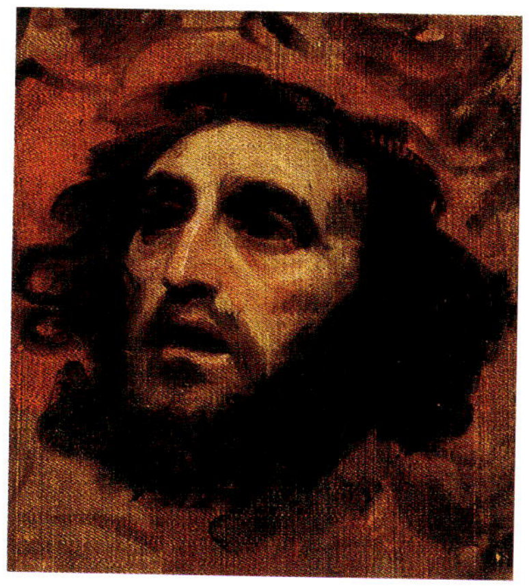

Romney, George 1734–1802
Head of an Apostle
oil on canvas 27.8 x 24.7
VIS.2166

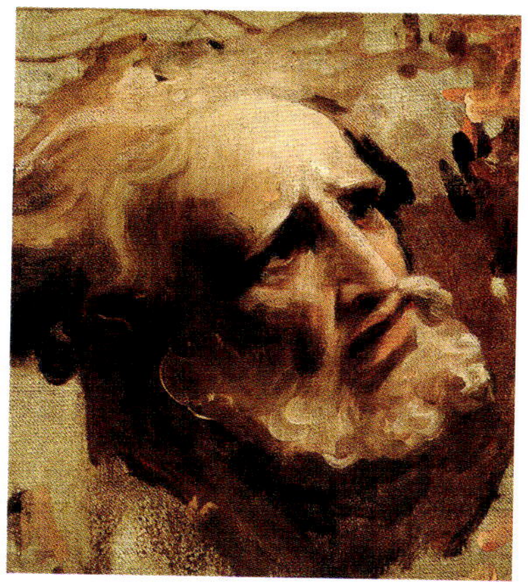

Romney, George 1734–1802
Head of an Apostle
oil on canvas 27.9 x 24.8
VIS.2223

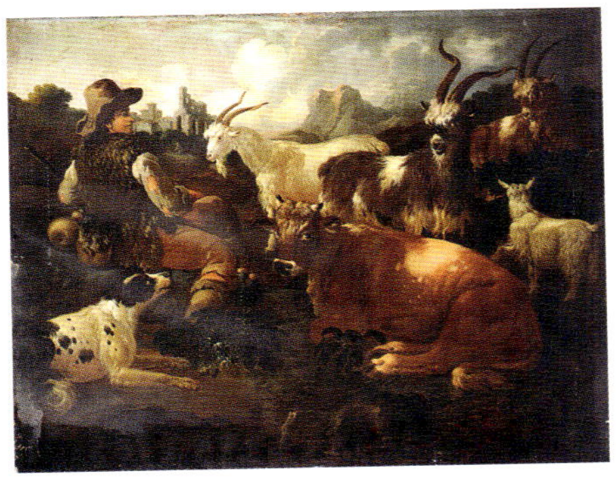

Roos, Philipp Peter 1657–1706
Landscape with Goats and Cattle
oil on canvas 166 x 209.4
VIS.3097

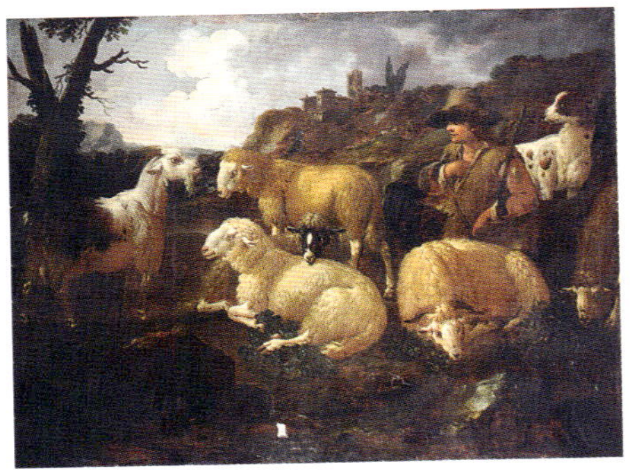

Roos, Philipp Peter 1657–1706
Landscape with Sheep
oil on canvas 171 x 218.3
VIS.3098

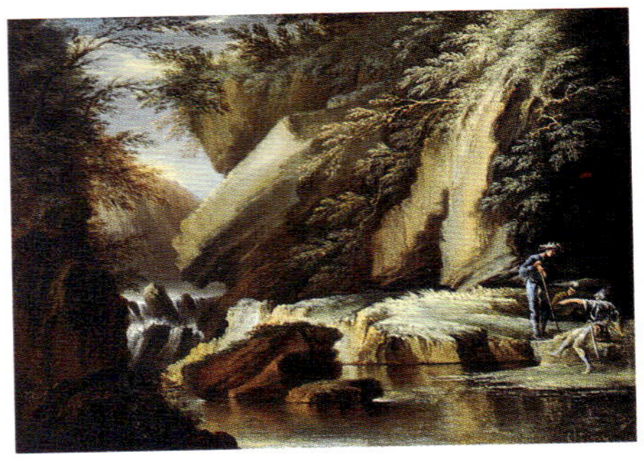

Rosa, Salvator (attributed to) 1615–1673
Figures by a Mountain Stream
oil on canvas 45.5 x 63
VIS.2241

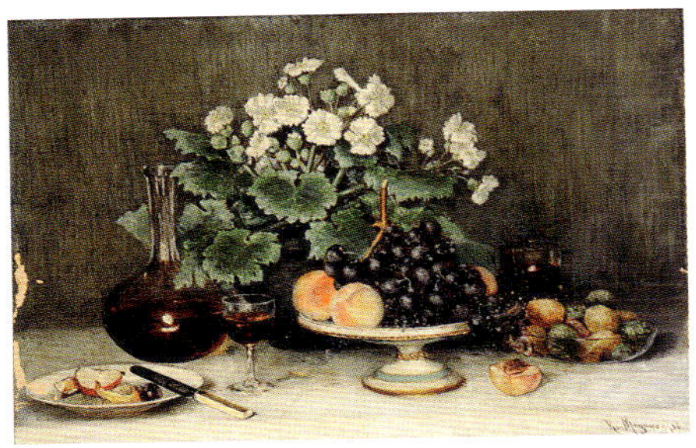

Rose, Magnus 1859–1900
Flowers and Fruit 1886
oil on canvas 49.5 x 75
VIS.1400

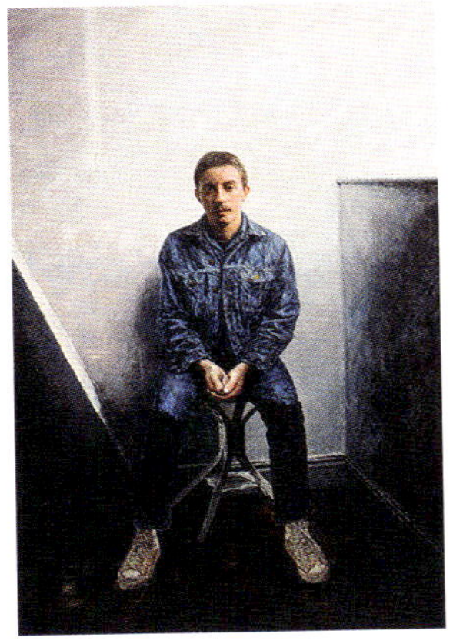

Rose, Martin H. b.1946
Martin Harris, an Art Student
oil & acrylic on canvas 186.6 x 119
VIS.5006

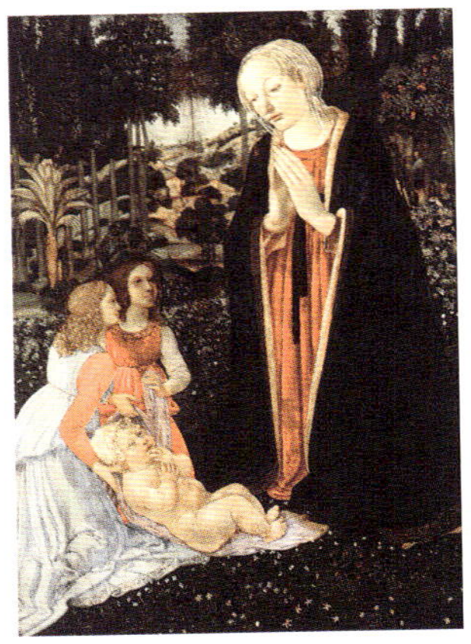

Rosselli, Cosimo 1439–1507
Virgin and Child with Angels
oil on panel 101.6 x 72.3
CGSG00770

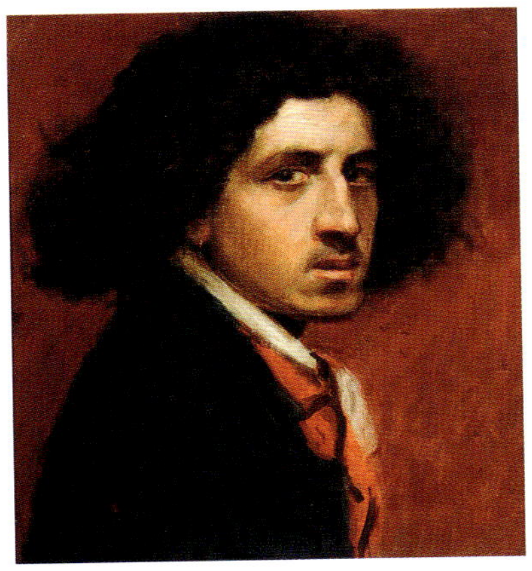

Rossetti, Dante Gabriel 1828–1882
Portrait of a Musician
oil on canvas 42.4 x 37.9
VIS.12

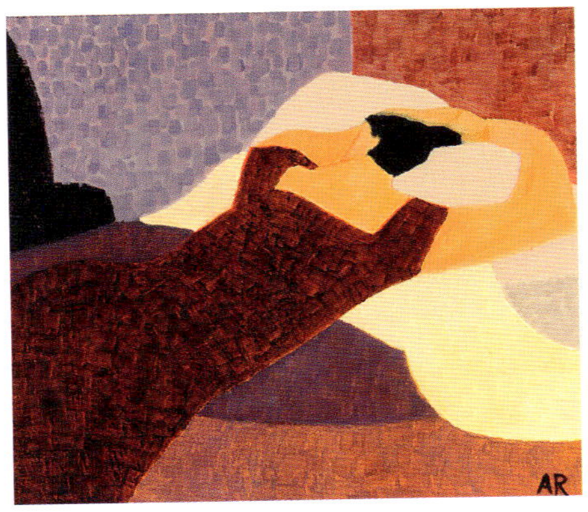

Rothenstein, Anne b.1949
Figure on a Bed
oil on panel 33.8 x 38.9
VIS.5242

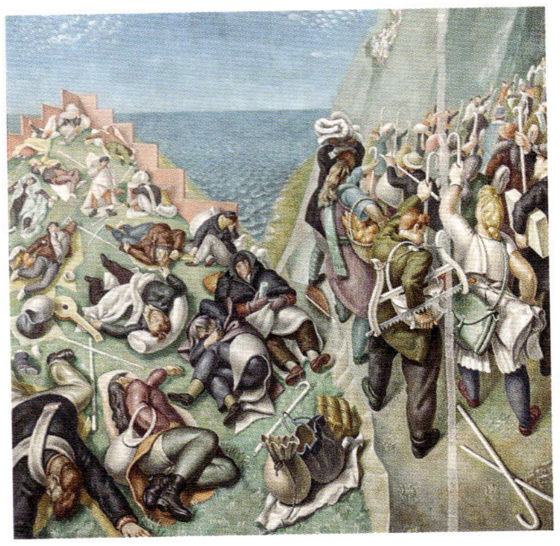

Rothenstein, Michael 1908–1993
Journey to the Promised Land 1938
oil & tempera on canvas 120.9 x 120.9
VIS.4192

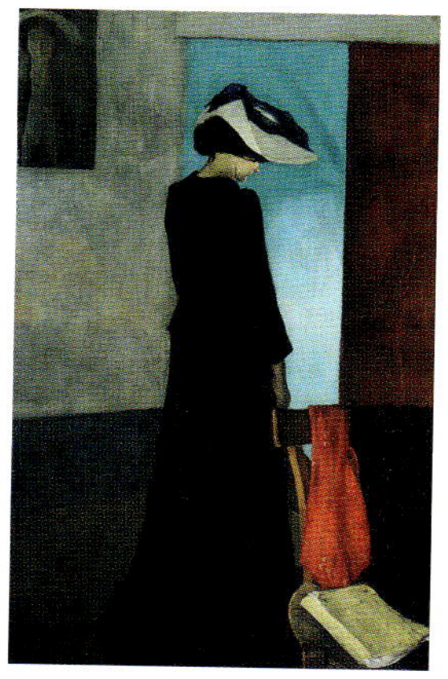

Rothenstein, William 1872–1945
Interior (Lady with a Hat) 1891
oil on canvas 90.7 x 57.5
VIS.5418

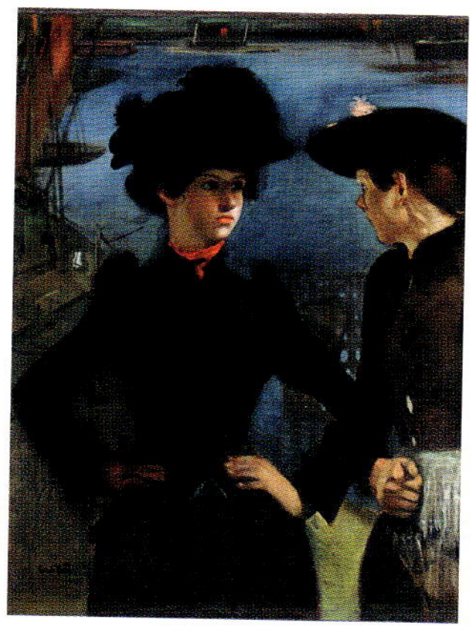

Rothenstein, William 1872–1945
Coster Girls 1894
oil on canvas 97.9 x 72
VIS.2771

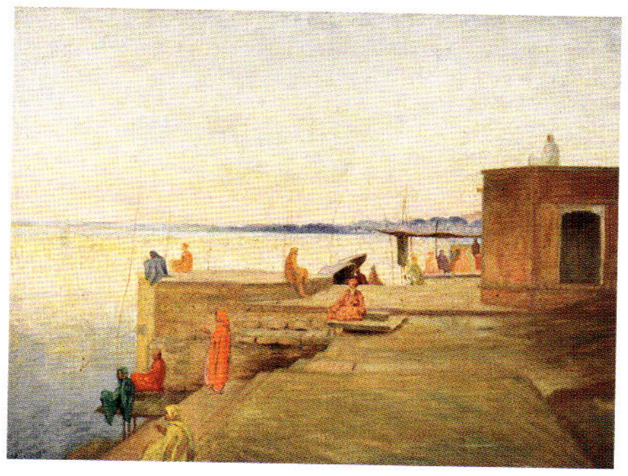

Rothenstein, William 1872–1945
Evening in Benares, India 1912
oil on canvas 69.5 x 90.2 (E)
VIS.3154

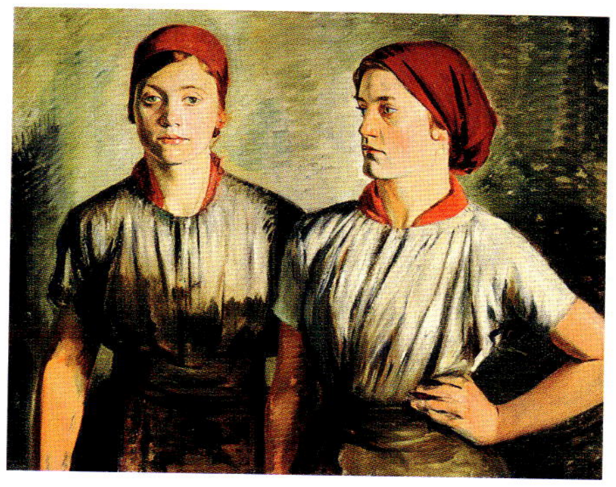

Rothenstein, William 1872–1945
Buffer Girls 1919
oil on canvas 69.2 x 90 (E)
VIS.2303

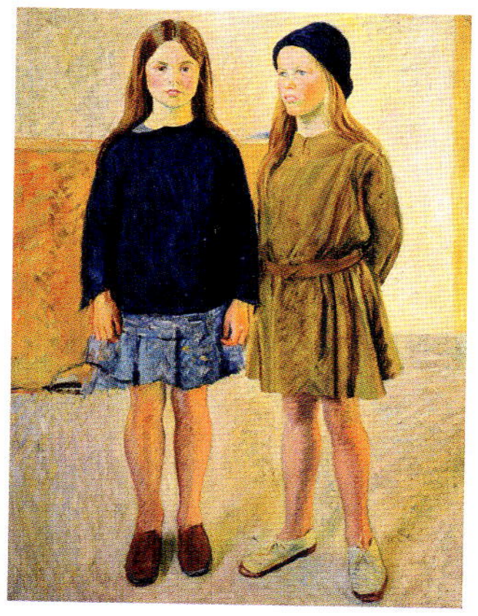

Rothenstein, William 1872–1945
Rachael and Betty
oil on canvas 100.5 x 75.4
VIS.4014

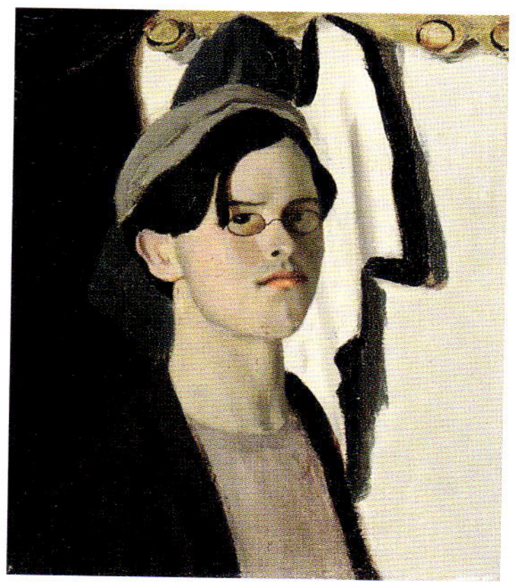

Rothenstein, William 1872–1945
Self Portrait
oil on canvas 27.5 x 23.6
VIS.3182

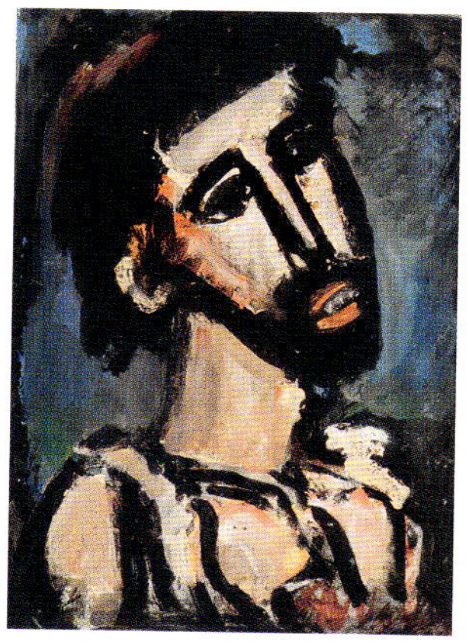

Rouault, Georges 1871–1958
Head of Christ
oil on canvas 72.5 x 50.6
VIS.LI.904 (P)

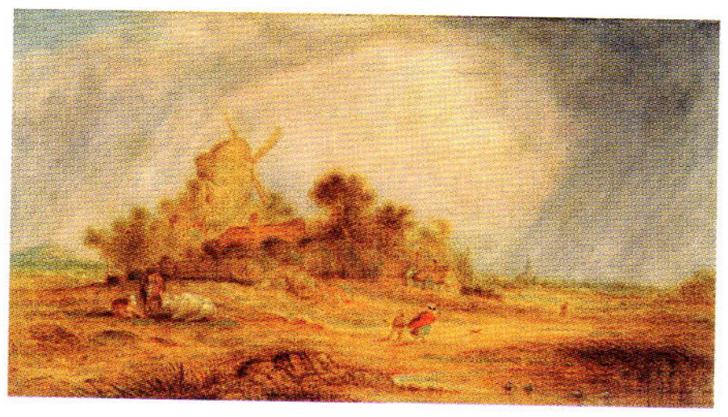

Rousseau, Théodore (attributed to)
1812–1867
Pastoral Scene 1850–1855
oil on panel 27 x 47.2
VIS.71

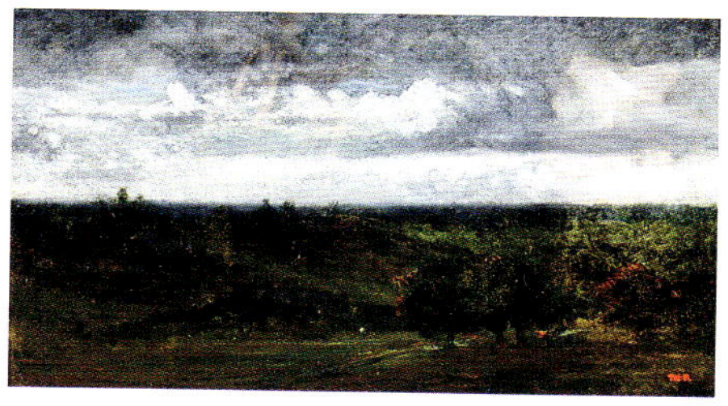

Rousseau, Théodore (attributed to)
1812–1867
Landscape
oil on panel 15 x 26.9
VIS.30

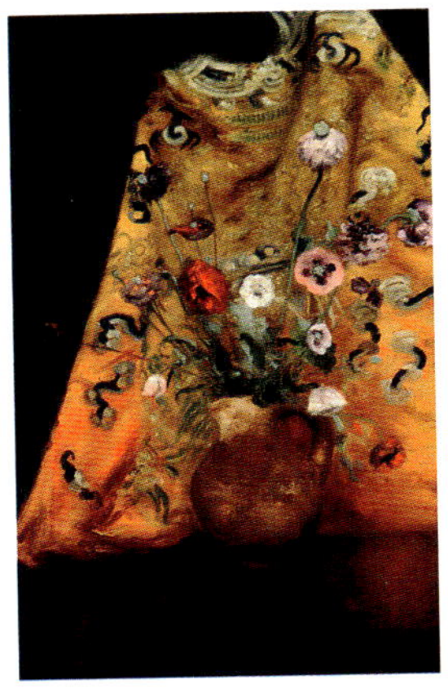

Roussel, Théodore Casimir 1847–1926
Flowers
oil on canvas 79.9 x 49.3
VIS.203

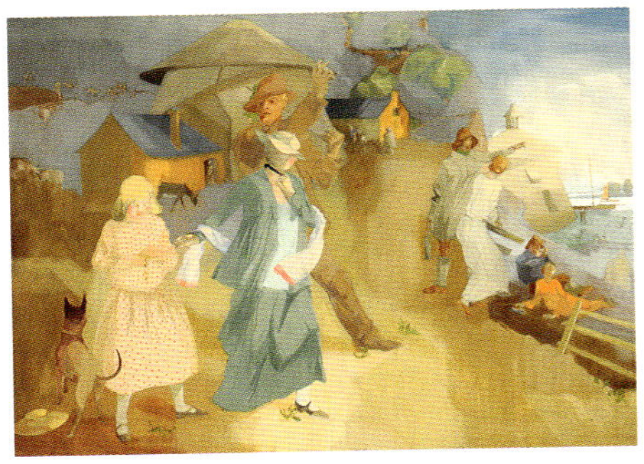

Rowles, Marjorie Kathleen
active 1923–1929
The Coming Thunderstorm
oil on canvas 61.4 x 84.3
VIS.1942

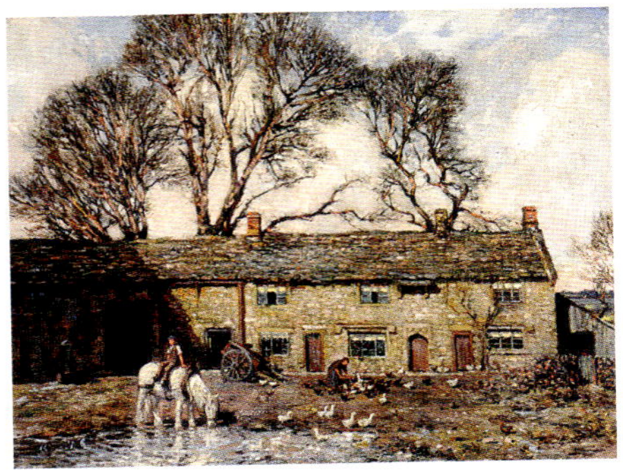

Royle, Stanley 1888–1961
The Farmyard 1914
oil on canvas 69.5 x 79.8
VIS.4738

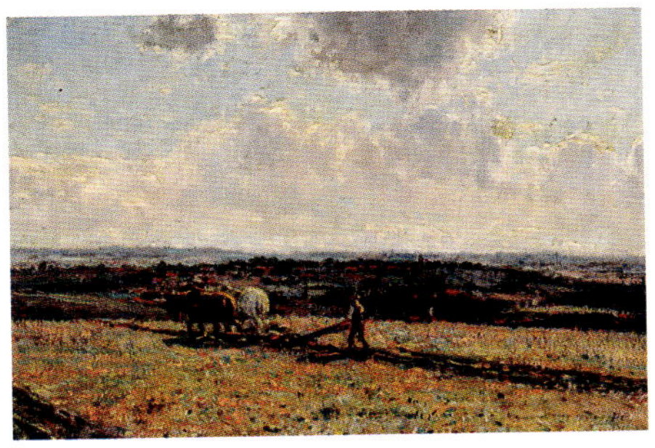

Royle, Stanley 1888–1961
Ploughing 1915
oil on canvas 33.9 x 49.5
VIS.2866

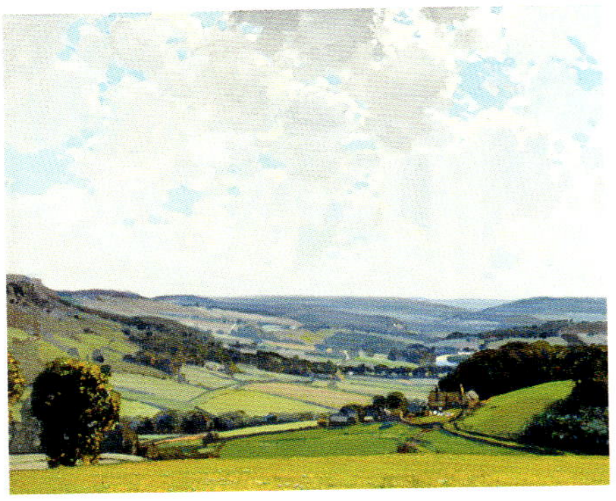

Royle, Stanley 1888–1961
Landscape 1920
oil on canvas 61.7 x 73.8
VIS.5444

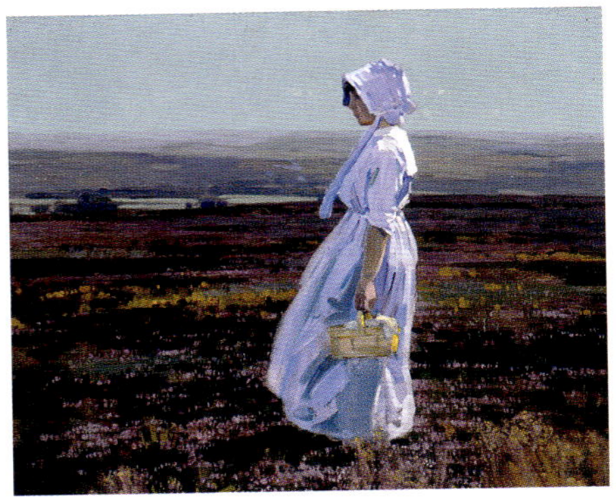

Royle, Stanley 1888–1961
Morning on the Derbyshire Moors 1920
oil on canvas 80 x 92.5
VIS.2963

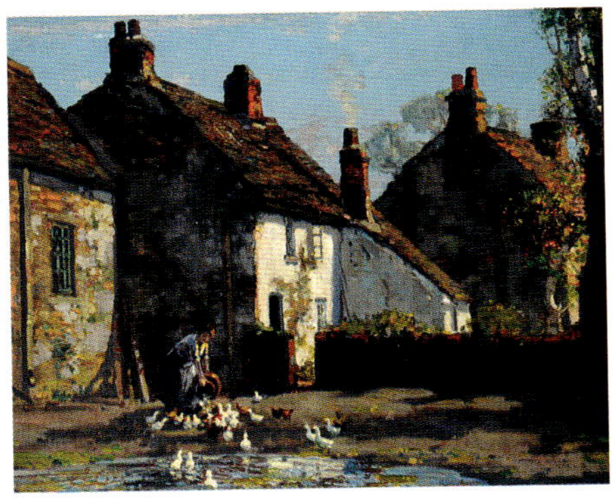

Royle, Stanley 1888–1961
Bents Green, Sheffield 1923
oil on canvas 63.8 x 75.8
VIS.2886

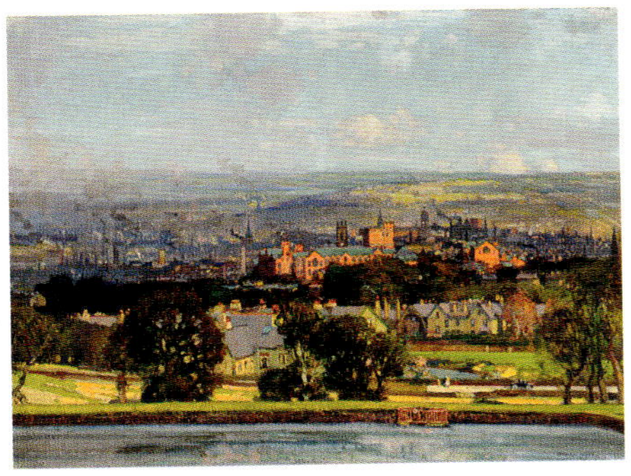

Royle, Stanley 1888–1961
Sheffield from Crookes 1923
oil on canvas 68.7 x 89.7
VIS.1894

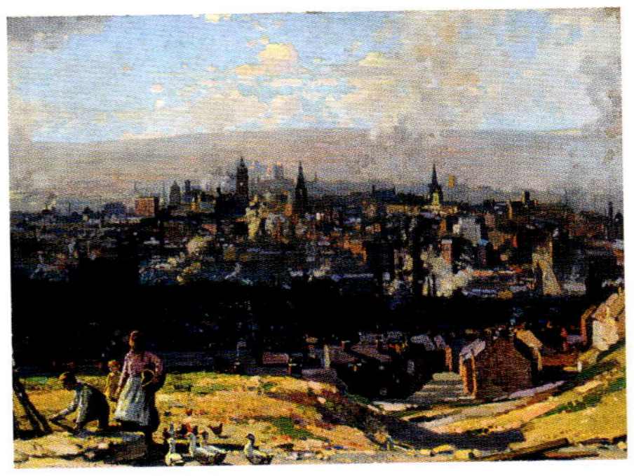

Royle, Stanley 1888–1961
Sheffield from the Park 1923
oil on canvas 69 x 89.9
VIS.3007

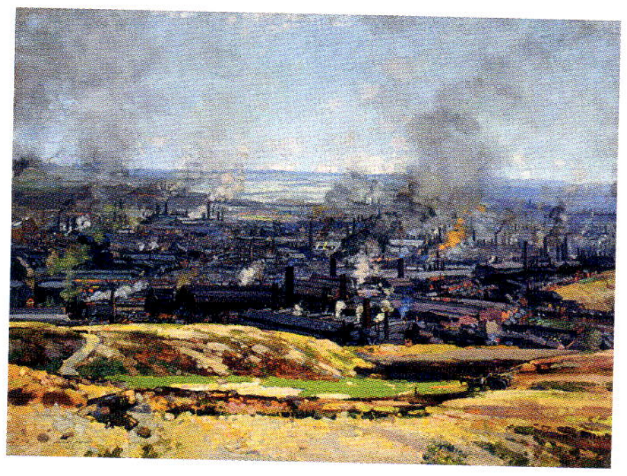

Royle, Stanley 1888–1961
Sheffield from Wincobank Wood 1923
oil on canvas 70.2 x 90.2
VIS.1893

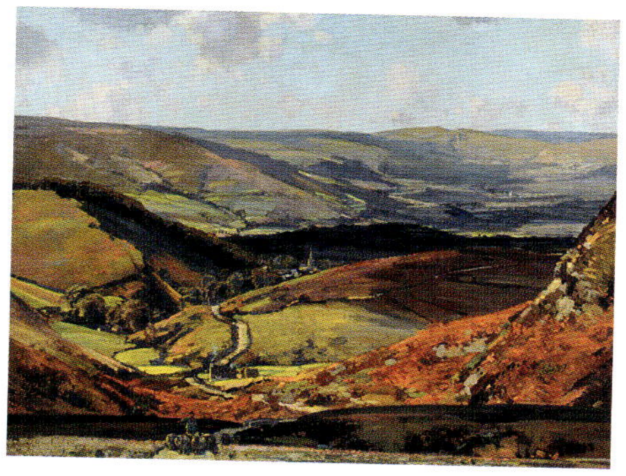

Royle, Stanley 1888–1961
View from the Cupola, Derbyshire 1924
oil on canvas 110.2 x 141.2
VIS.1292

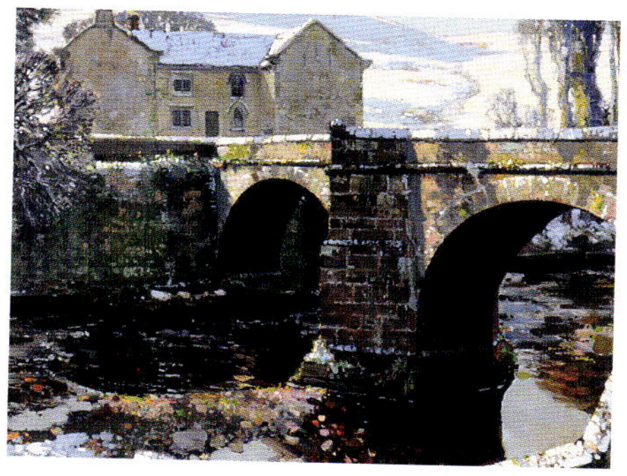

Royle, Stanley 1888–1961
Packhorse Bridge, Derwent, Derbyshire 1925
oil on canvas 69.5 x 89.9
VIS.112

Royle, Stanley 1888–1961
Bluebell Wood c.1930
oil on canvas 33.8 x 43.2
VIS.3274

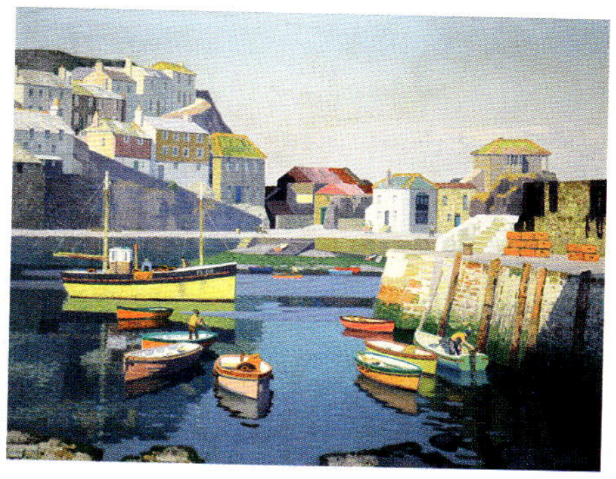

Royle, Stanley 1888–1961
Mevagissey, Cornwall 1960
oil on canvas 100.7 x 126.1
VIS.3816

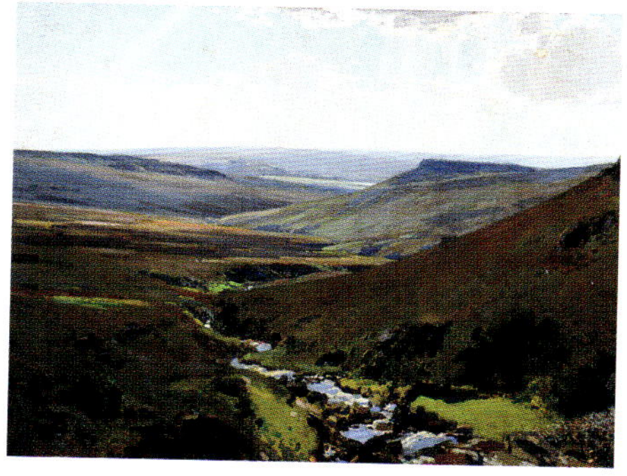

Royle, Stanley 1888–1961
Burbage Brook, Derbyshire
oil on canvas 119.5 x 150
VIS.3245

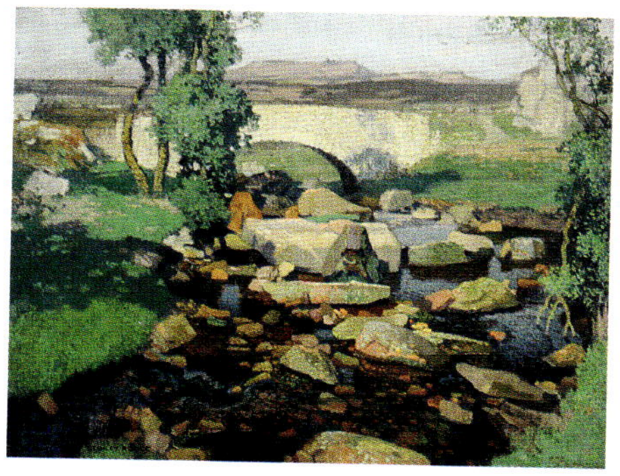

Royle, Stanley 1888–1961
Burbage Brook, Derbyshire (recto)
oil on canvas 69.5 x 90.3
VIS.5435

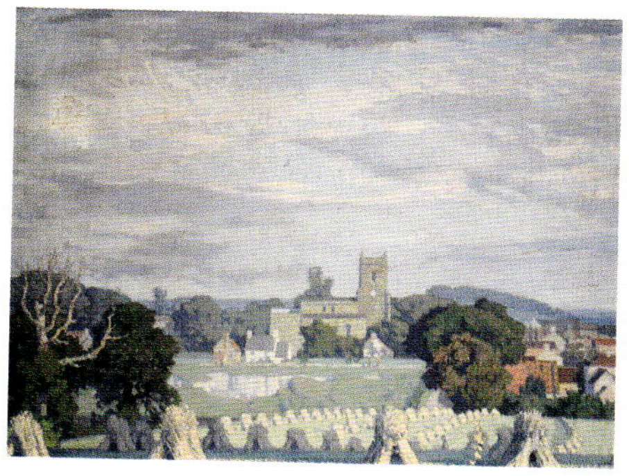

Royle, Stanley 1888–1961
*Landscape with a Church and Corn Stooks** (verso)
oil on canvas 69.5 x 90.3
VIS.5435

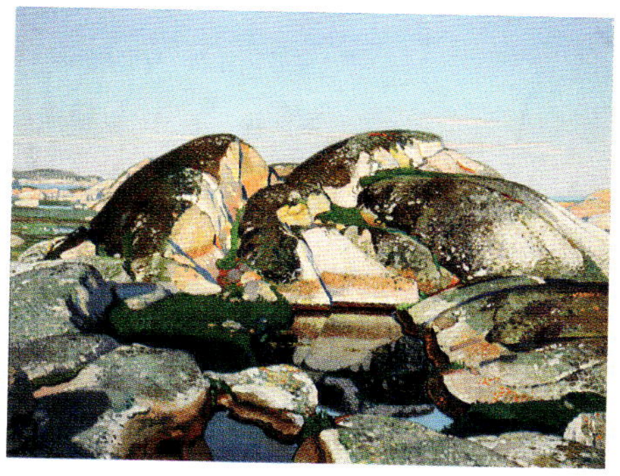

Royle, Stanley 1888–1961
Rock Formation, Nova Scotia, Canada
oil on canvas 70 x 89.7
VIS.5393

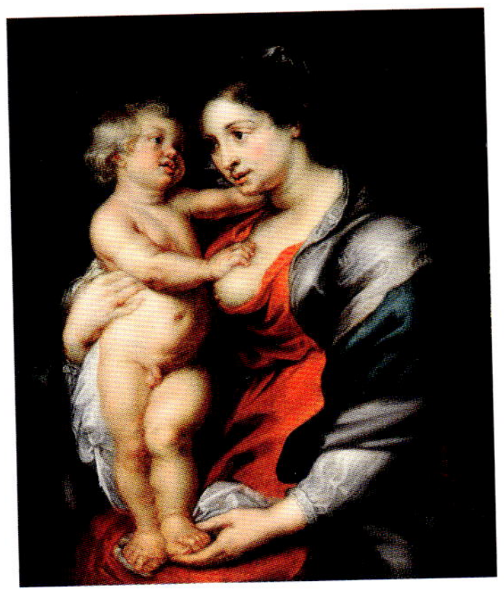

Rubens, Peter Paul (studio of) 1577–1640
Virgin and Child 1628–1640
oil on panel 59.3 x 47.7
VIS.106

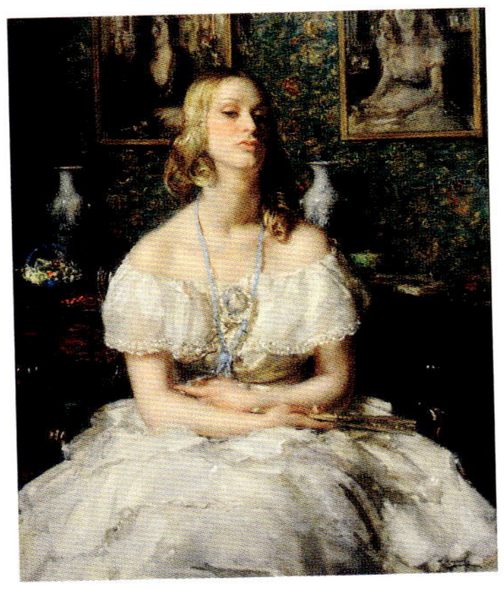

Russell, Walter Westley 1867–1949
Girl in a Muslin Dress
oil on canvas 90.2 x 72
VIS.1916

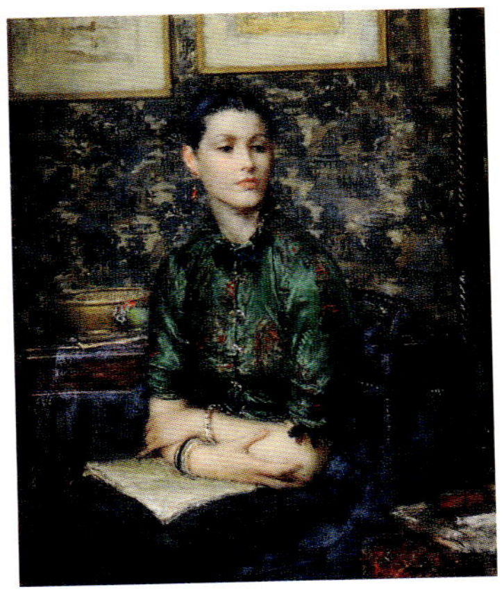

Russell, Walter Westley 1867–1949
Marion
oil on canvas 59.5 x 49.7
VIS.1799

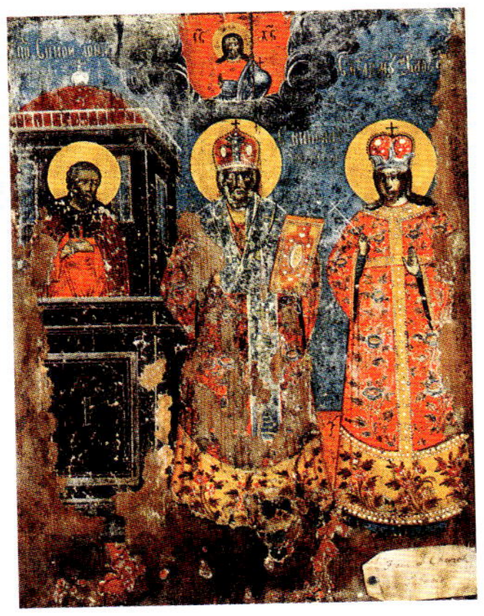

Russian School
Russian Painted Icon
oil on board 57.6 x 43
J89.27

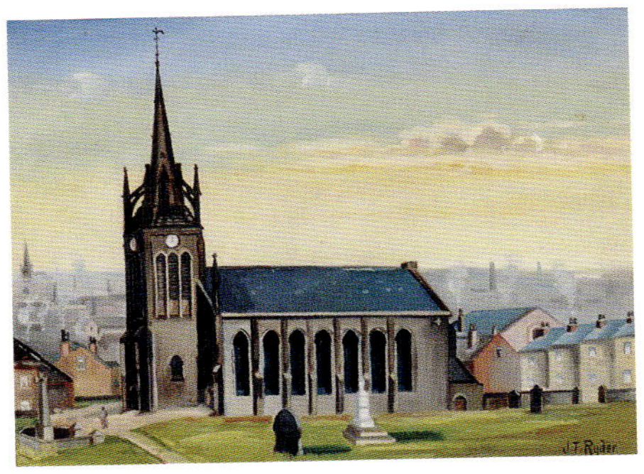

Ryder, J. T. active c.1933–c.1960
St John's Church, Sheffield c.1933
oil on canvas 45.5 x 55.4
2009.1

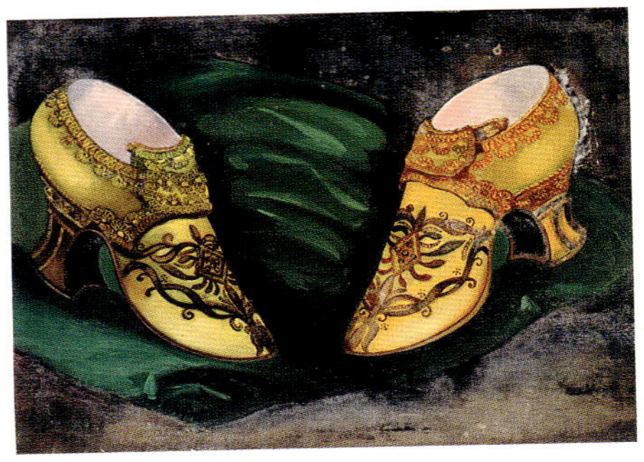

Ryder, J. T. active c.1933–c.1960
Mary Queen of Scots' Shoes
oil on canvas on board 30 x 40.1
1979.455

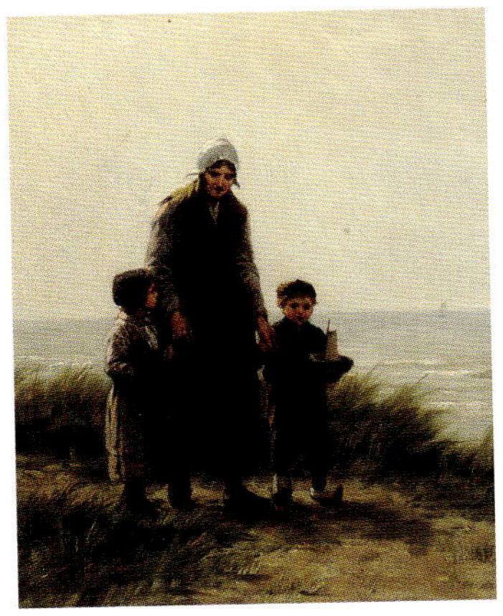

Sadée, Philip Lodewijk Jacob Frederik
1837–1904
Figure Piece 1860–1870
oil on panel 22 x 17.5
VIS.1382

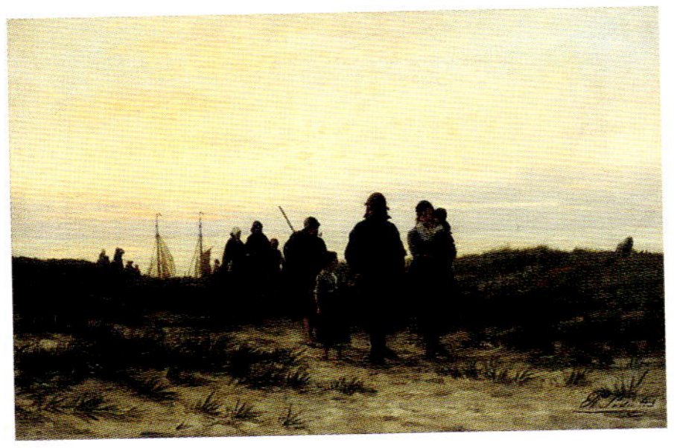

Sadée, Philip Lodewijk Jacob Frederik (attributed to) 1837–1904
The End of the Day 1860–1870
oil on canvas 49.1 x 73.5
VIS.1368

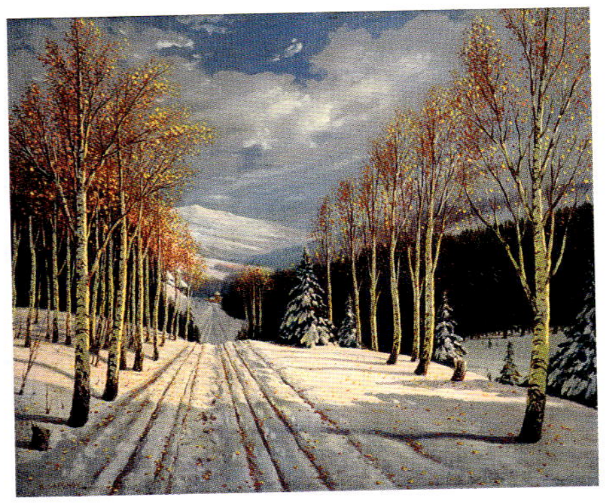

Safonov, N.
Woodland Path
oil on canvas 50.3 x 60.3
VIS.1329

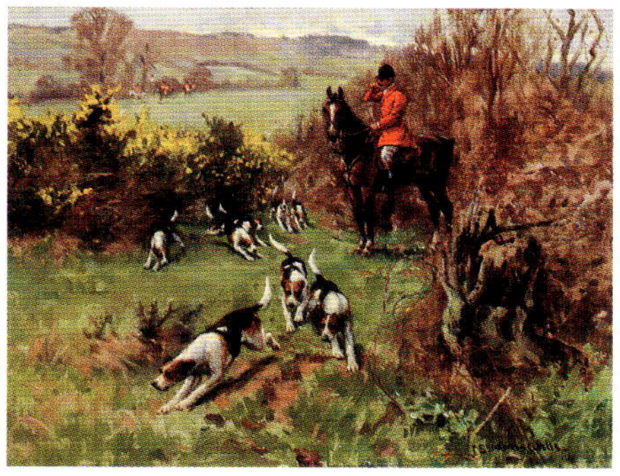

Sanderson-Wells, John 1872–1955
Hunting Scene
oil on millboard 19.7 x 25.7
VIS.1331

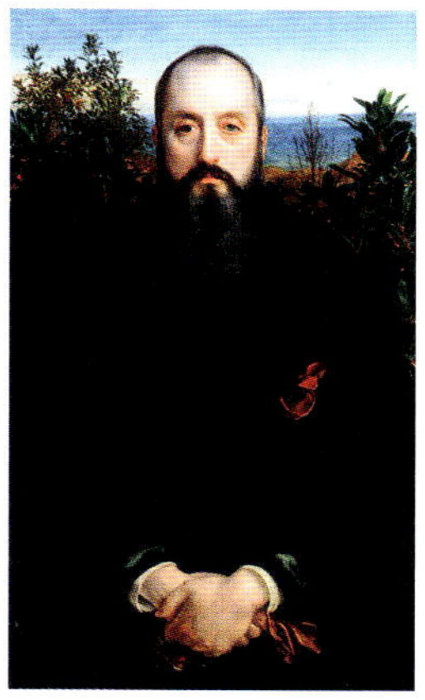

Sandys, Frederick 1829–1904
William H. Clabburn 1870
oil on canvas 111.8 x 65.8
VIS.5

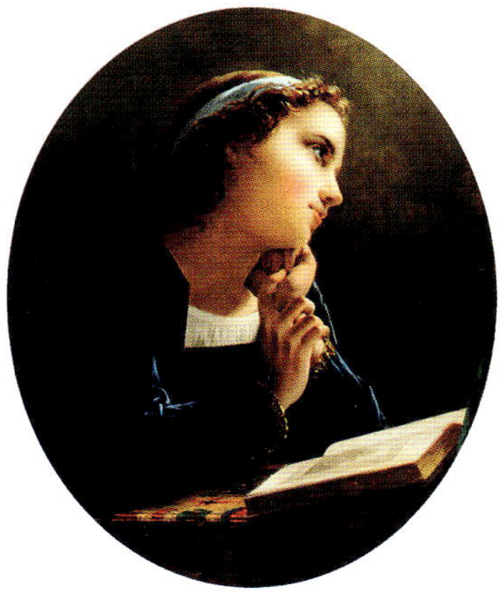

Sant, James 1820–1916
Meditation
oil on canvas 70.5 x 58.2
VIS.282

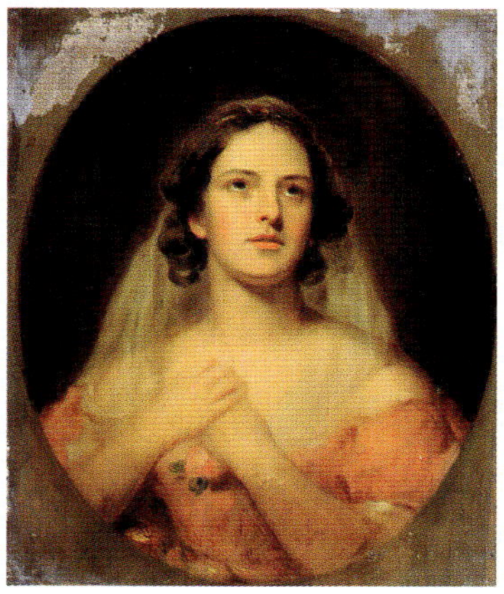

Sant, James 1820–1916
The Bride
oil on canvas 73 x 60
VIS.605

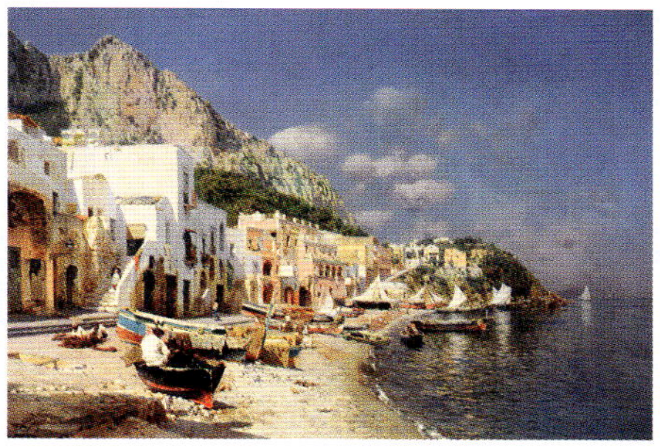

Santoro, Rubens 1859–1942
Capri, Italy
oil on canvas 44.3 x 63
VIS.2957

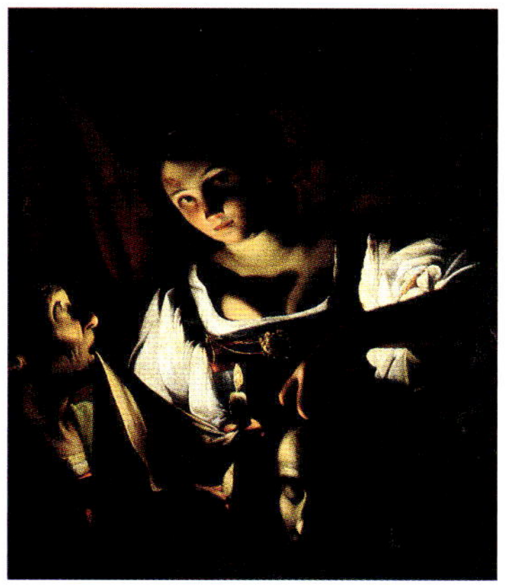

Saraceni, Carlo (after) 1579–1620
Judith with the Head of Holofernes 1610–1620
oil on canvas 89.7 x 74.4
VIS.3778

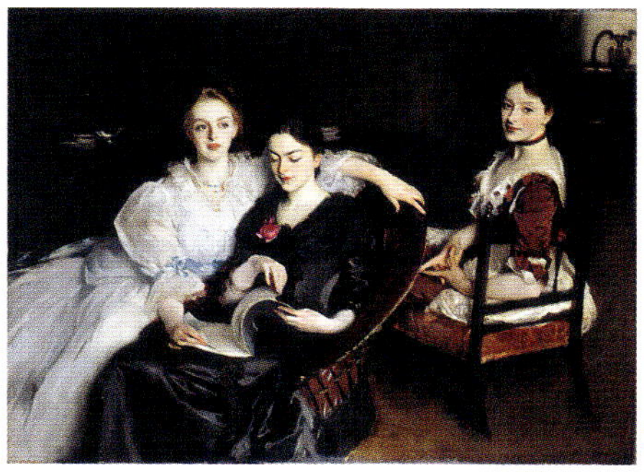

Sargent, John Singer 1856–1925
The Misses Vickers 1884
oil on canvas 166.6 x 212.2
VIS.2601

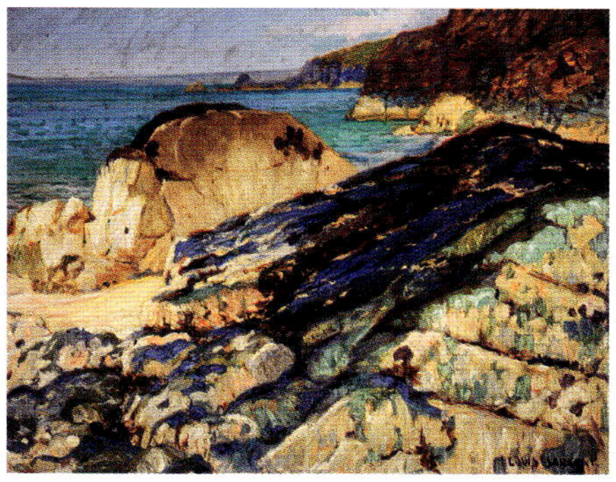

Sargent, Louis Augustus b.1881
Atlantic Shore, Cornwall
oil on canvas 81 x 100.7
VIS.2602

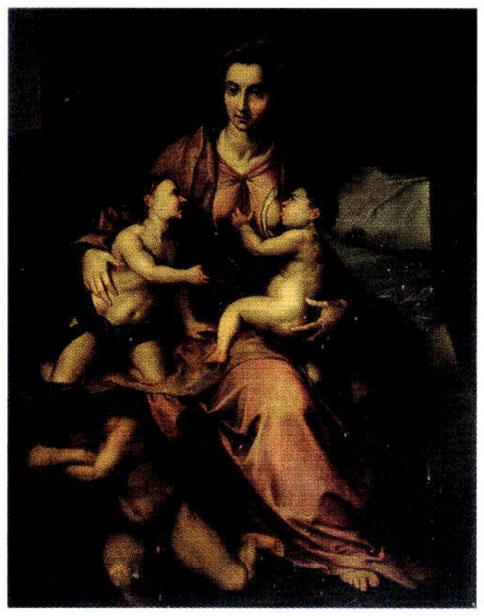

Sarto, Andrea del (after) 1486–1530
Figure of Charity
oil on canvas 107 x 82
VIS.1845

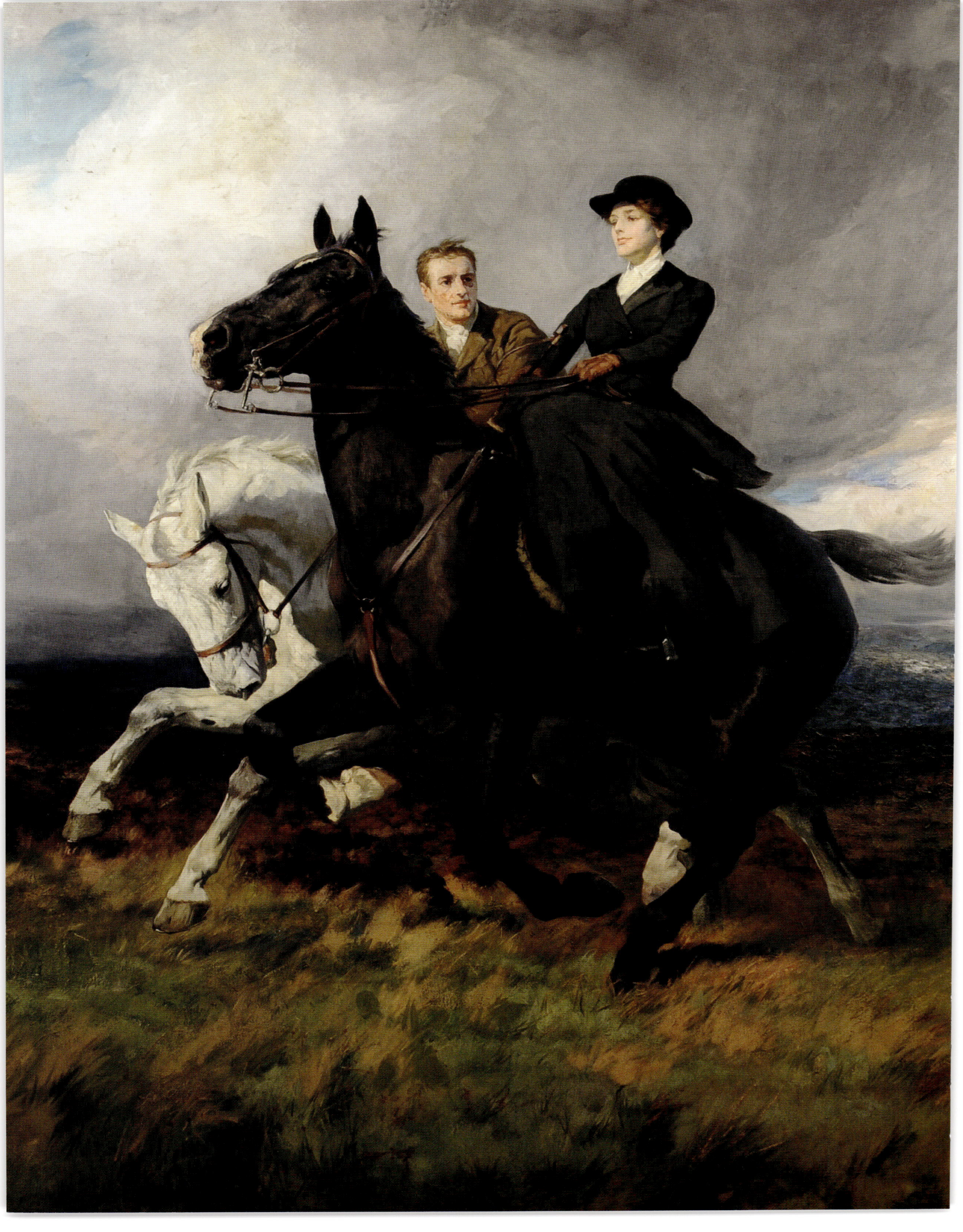

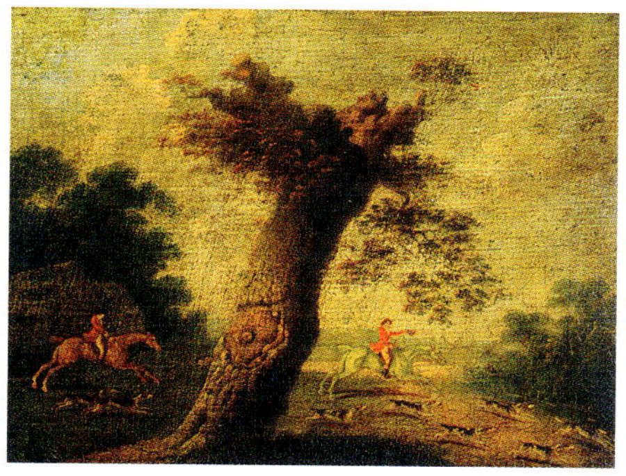

Sartorius, John Nost 1759–1828
Fox Hunting
oil on canvas 29.3 x 37.8
VIS.539

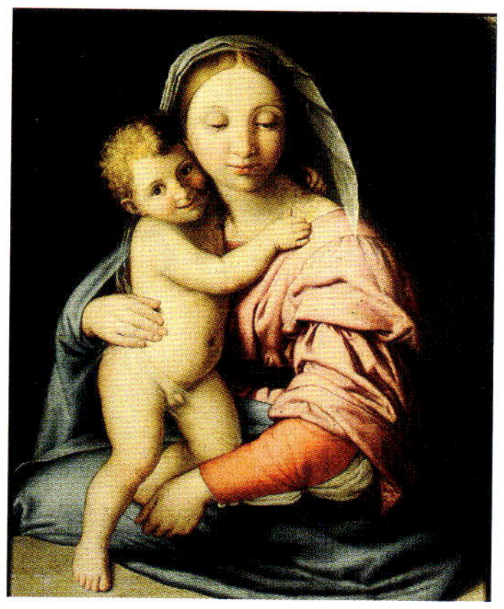

Sassoferrato (attributed to) 1609–1685
Madonna and Child
oil on canvas 45.6 x 35.9
VIS.523

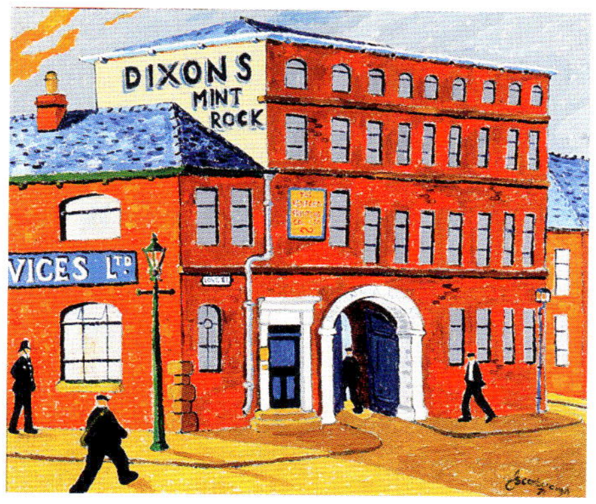

Scarborough, Joe b.1938
Britannia Works on Love Street (recto) 1971
oil on canvas 52.6 x 61.9
2008.360a

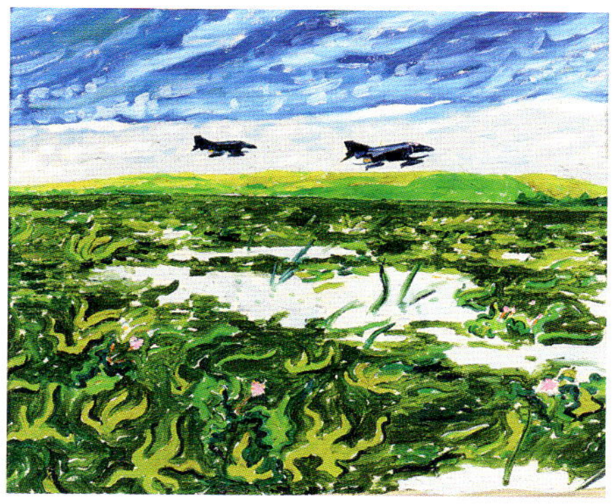

Scarborough, Joe b.1938
*Landscape with Fighter Planes** (verso) c.1971
oil on canvas 52.6 x 61.9
2008.360b

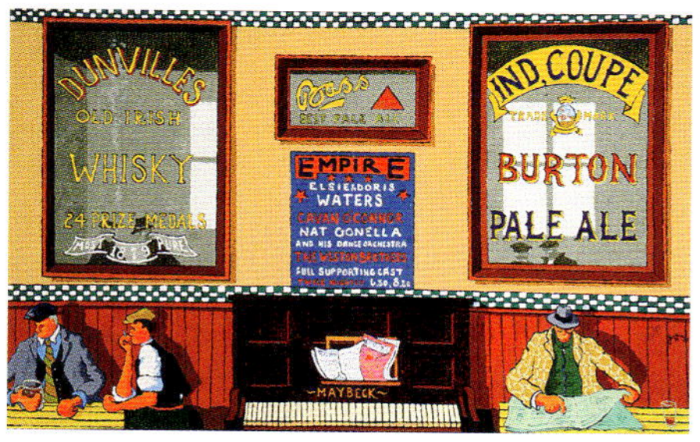

Scarborough, Joe b.1938
Pub Interior 1974
oil on canvas 77.1 x 121.5
VIS.4167

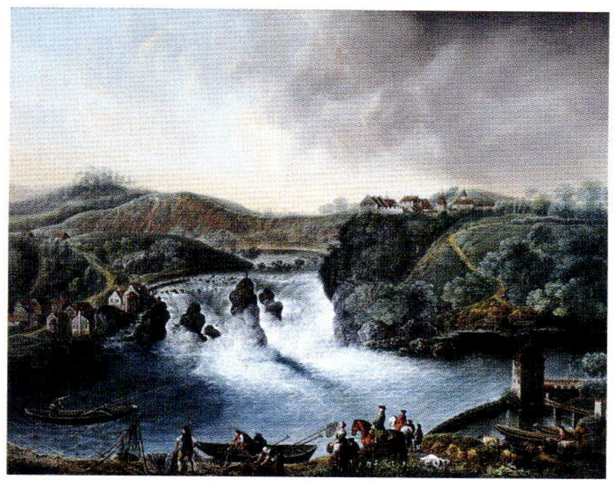

Schalch, Johann Jacob 1723–1789
Schaffhausen Falls, Switzerland 1740–1750
oil on canvas 81.7 x 95.8
VIS.314

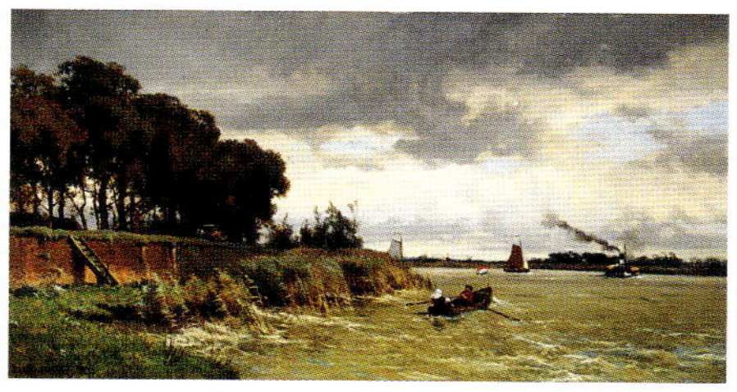

Schampheleer, Edmond de 1824–1899
River Scene with a Steam Boat 1875
oil on canvas 54.2 x 100.2
VIS.1463

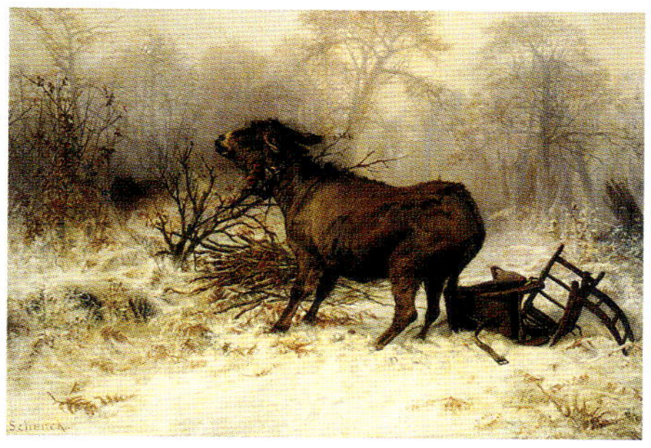

Schenck, August Friedrich Albrecht
1828–1901
Donkey Surprised by a Wolf 1860–1870
oil on canvas 69.8 x 102
VIS.1519

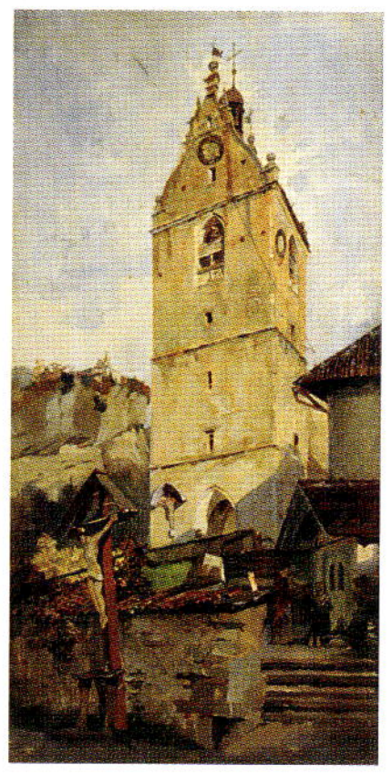

Schieler, Robert
Village Church
oil on panel 29.3 x 14.8
VIS.283

Facing page: Kemp-Welch, Lucy, 1869–1958, *The Riders* (detail), 1911, Museums Sheffield, (p. 111)

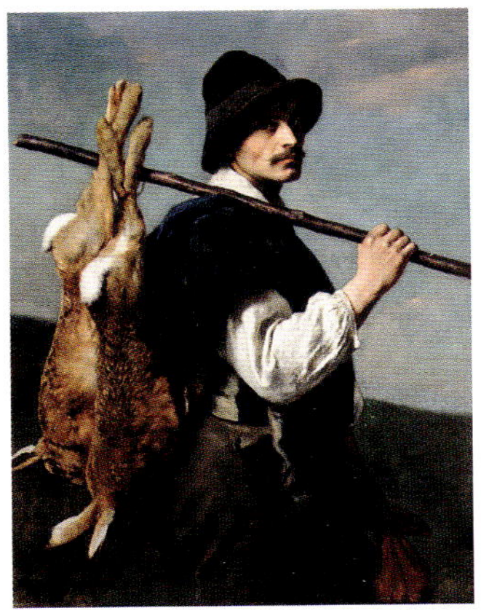

Scholderer, Otto 1834–1902
Man and Hares 1880
oil on canvas 107 x 81
VIS.1444

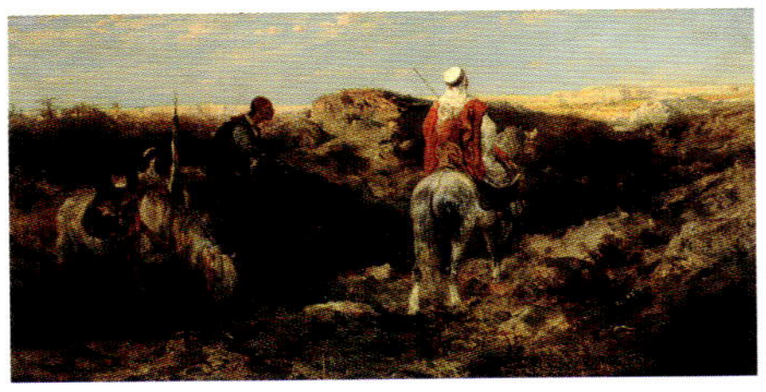

Schreyer, Christian Adolf 1828–1899
The Approach to Cairo c.1887
oil on canvas 55.8 x 108.2
VIS.1629

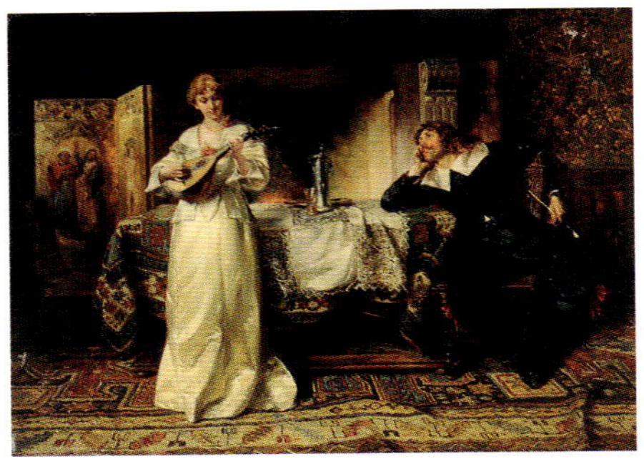

Schröder, Albert Friedrich 1854–1939
The Love Song 1886
oil on panel 59 x 71
VIS.2001

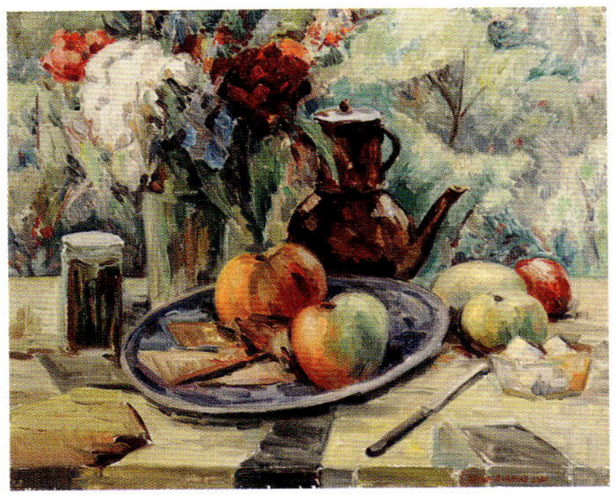

Seabrooke, Elliott 1886–1950
The Coffee Pot 1930
oil on board 49.8 x 60
VIS.1882

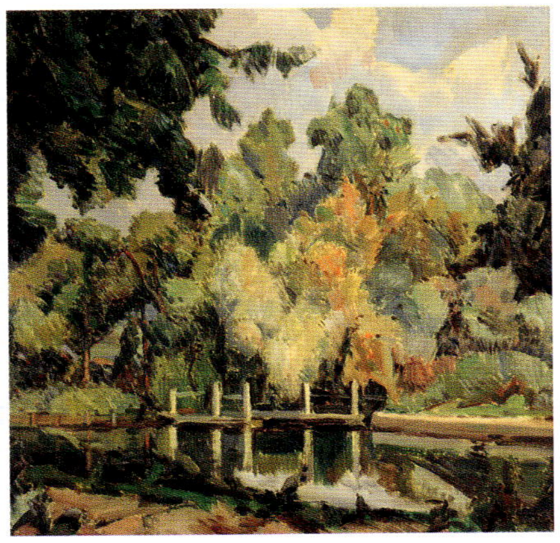

Seabrooke, Elliott 1886–1950
Landscape
oil on canvas 58.5 x 58.5
VIS.2768

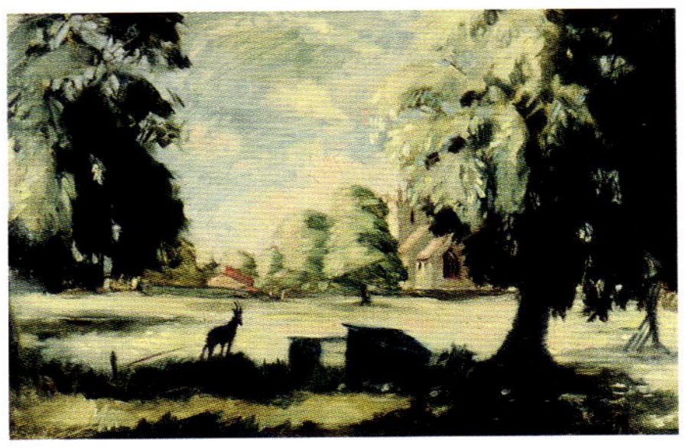

Seddon, Richard 1915–2002
Suffolk Village
oil on canvas 49 x 73.6
VIS.3138

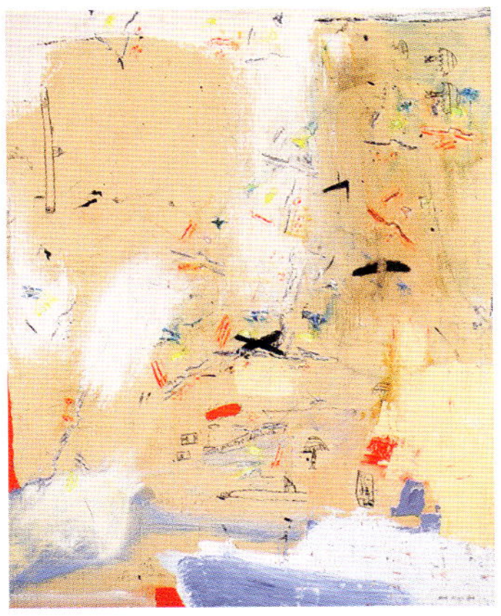

Selden, Roger b.1945
Composition 1978
oil & mixed media on canvas 100.3 x 79.8
VIS.5012

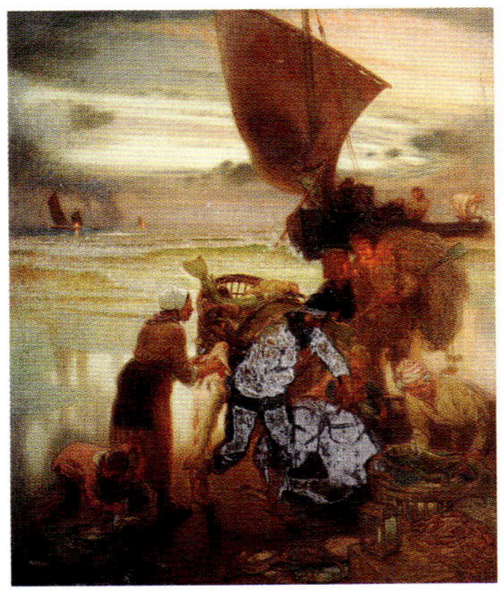

Shackleton, William 1872–1933
Shore Scene
oil on canvas 81.8 x 67.4
VIS.2379

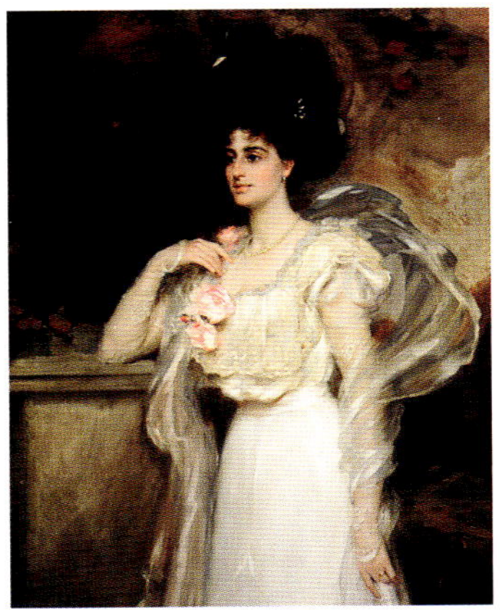

Shannon, James Jebusa 1862–1923
Portrait of a Lady
oil on canvas 123.4 x 98.2
VIS.3033

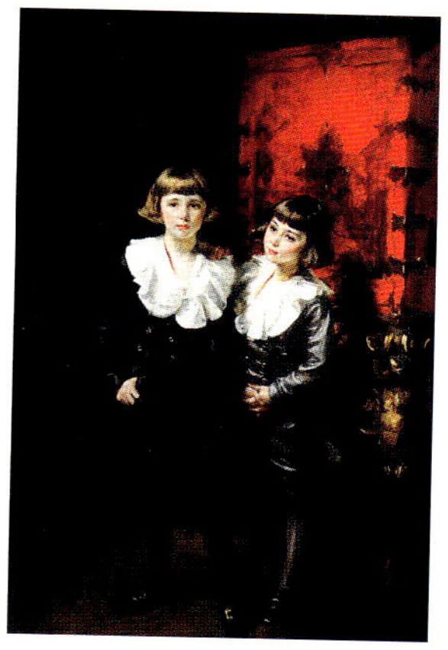

Shannon, James Jebusa 1862–1923
The Children of Douglas Vickers
oil on canvas 179.2 x 115.2
VIS.4707

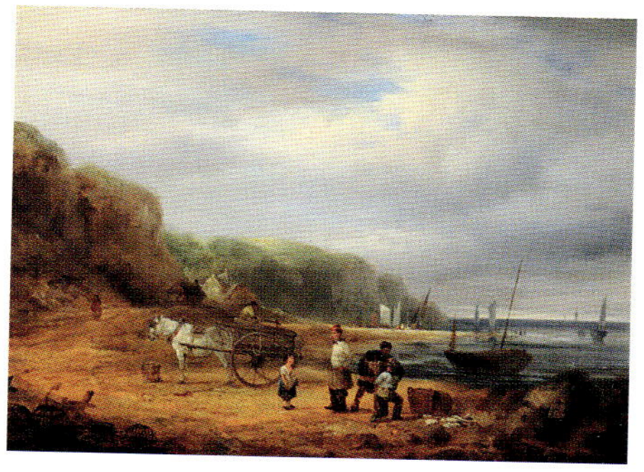

Shayer, William 1788–1879
Coast Scene 1822
oil on board 28.3 x 38.4
VIS.241

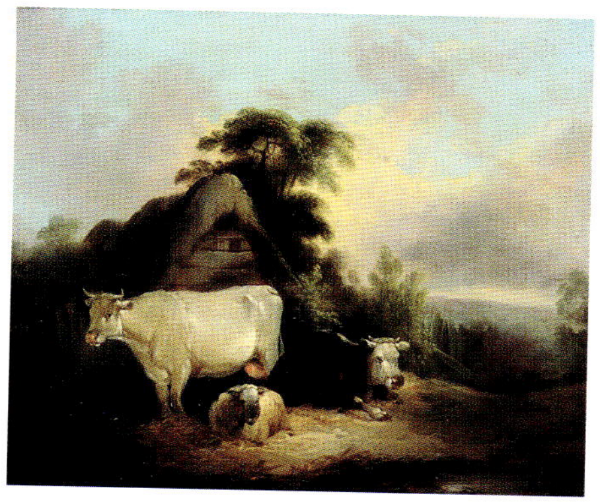

Shayer, William 1788–1879
The White Cow 1840
oil on panel 29.5 x 35
VIS.263

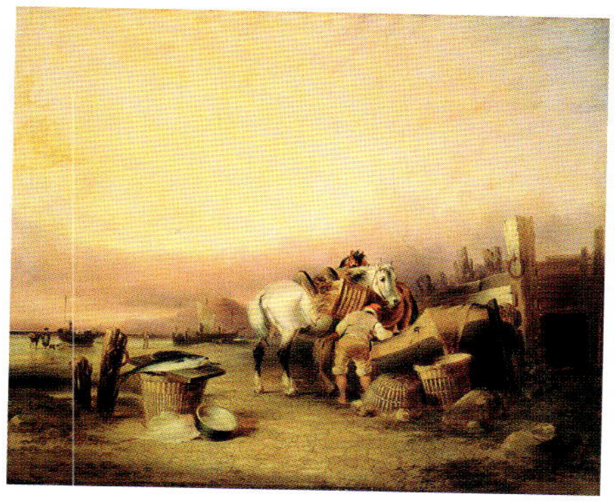

Shayer, William 1788–1879
Shore Scene 1841
oil on canvas 62.1 x 74.7
VIS.1272

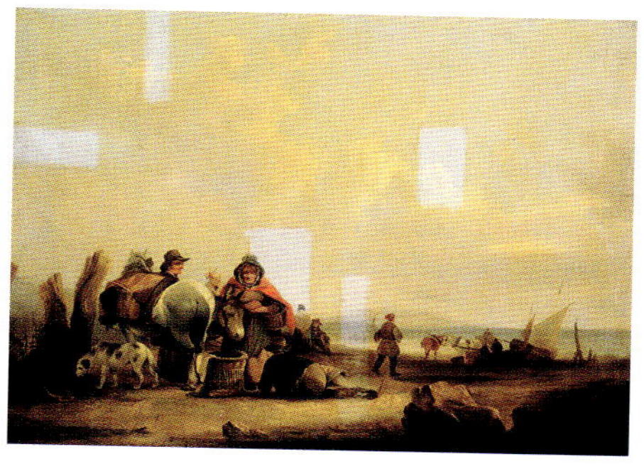

Shayer, William 1788–1879
Coast Scene
oil on canvas 63.8 x 87.8
VIS.677

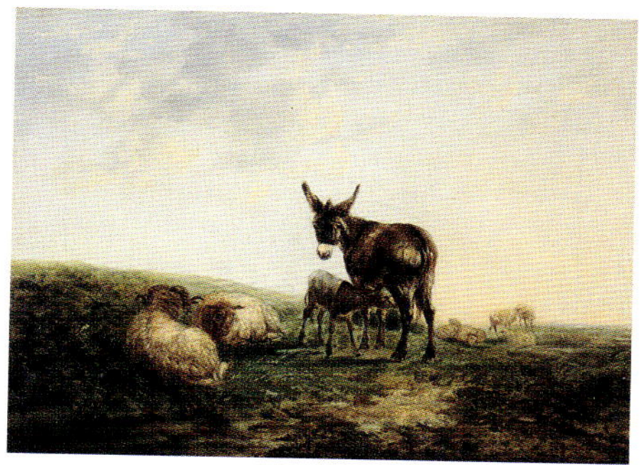

Shayer, William 1788–1879
Donkey and Sheep
oil on canvas 29 x 38
VIS.601

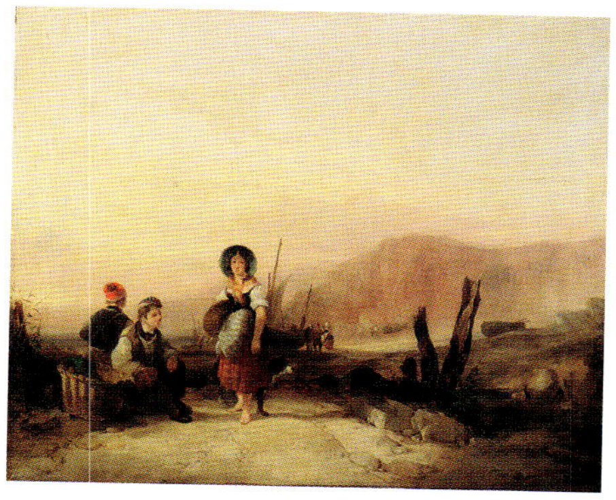

Shayer, William 1788–1879
Fisherman's Children near Blackgang, Isle of Wight
oil on canvas 50.5 x 60.8
VIS.1264

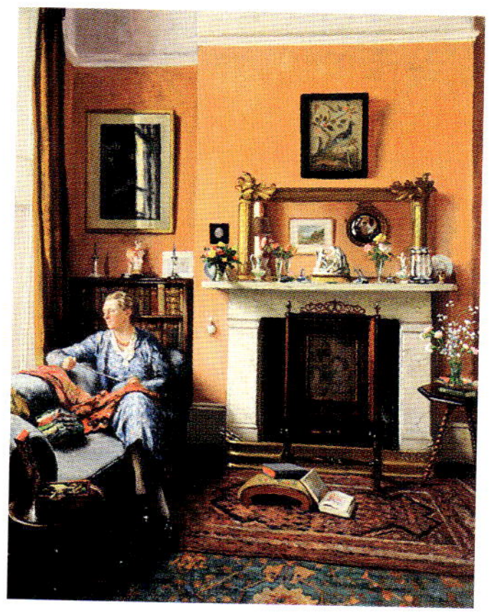

Shepherd, F. H. S. 1877–1948
Drawing Room Interior
oil on canvas 90.4 x 70.2
VIS.2024

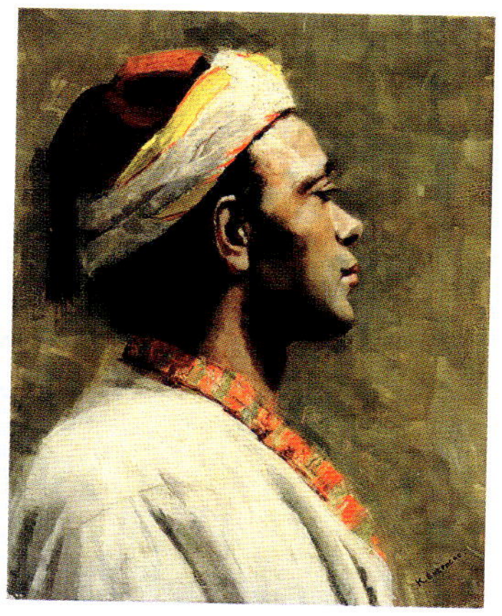

Shepherd, Kate active 1888–1916
Portrait of an Arab
oil on canvas 50.8 x 40.7
VIS.1253

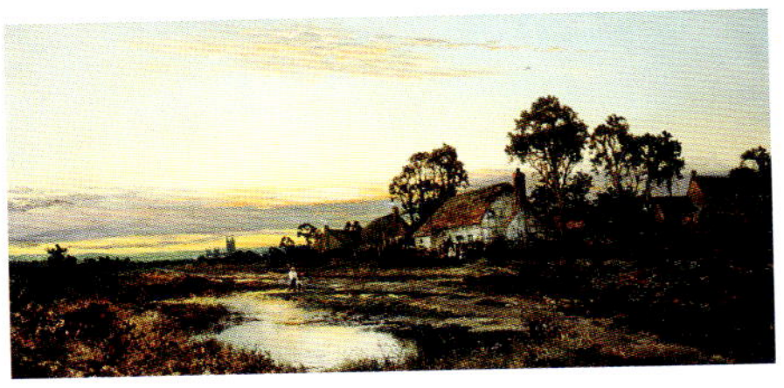

Sherrin, Daniel 1869–1940
Sunset near Canterbury, Kent
oil on canvas 51 x 100.2
VIS.2524

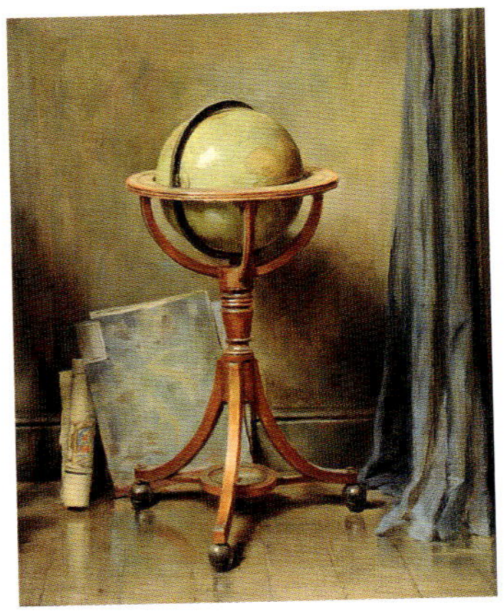

Sichel, Ernest Leopold 1862–1941
Globe and Maps
oil on canvas 49 x 39
VIS.2190

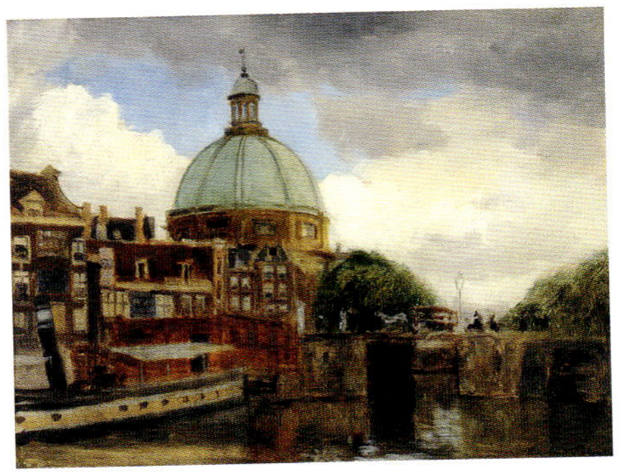

Sickert, Bernard 1863–1932
The Lutheran Church, Amsterdam 1900
oil on panel 30.8 x 39
VIS.152

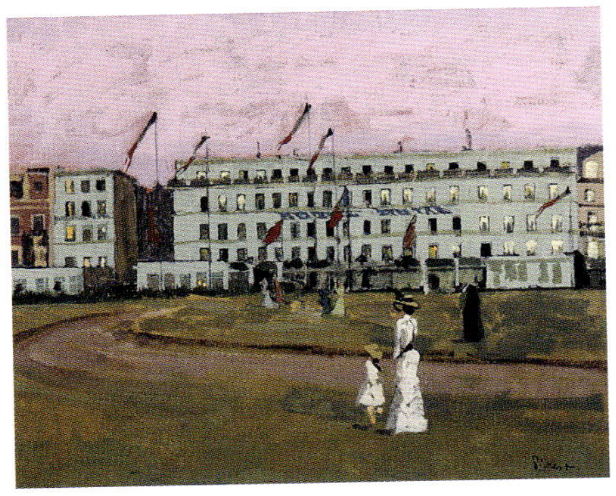

Sickert, Walter Richard 1860–1942
L'Hotel Royal, Dieppe, France 1894
oil on canvas 66.8 x 78.8
VIS.5185

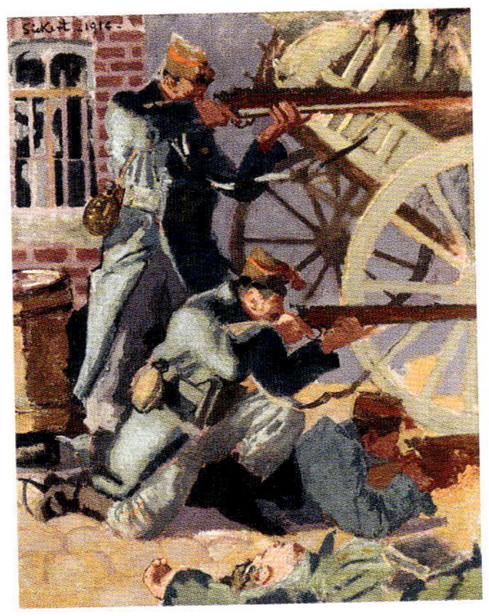

Sickert, Walter Richard 1860–1942
Soldiers of King Albert at the Ready 1914
oil on canvas 211.5 x 166.4
VIS.3530

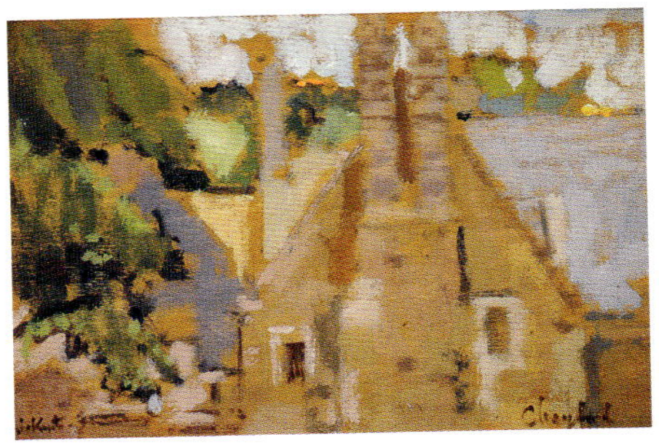

Sickert, Walter Richard 1860–1942
Chagford, Devon c.1915
oil on panel 15.4 x 23.2
VIS.190

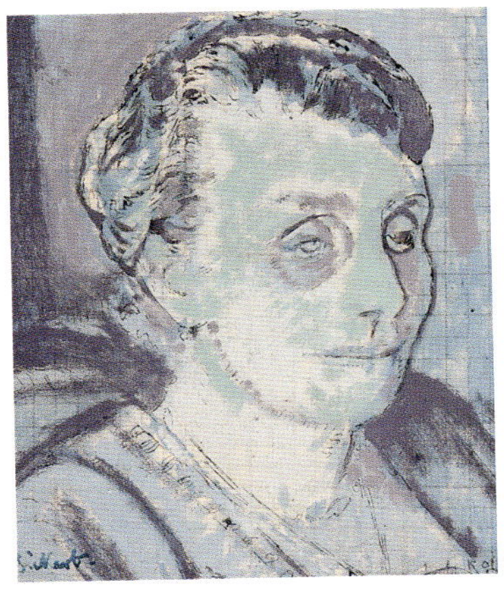

Sickert, Walter Richard 1860–1942
Portrait of a Woman 1935
oil on canvas 49.5 x 44
VIS.172

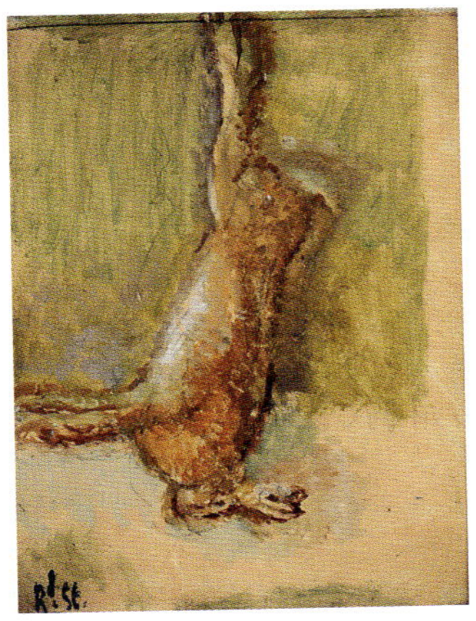

Sickert, Walter Richard 1860–1942
A Dead Hare
oil on panel 23.4 x 18.5
VIS.227

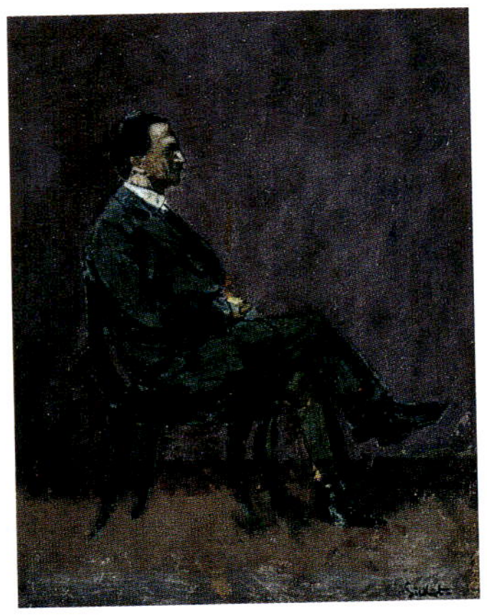

Sickert, Walter Richard 1860–1942
Fred Winter
oil on canvas 45.5 x 33.4
VIS.3376

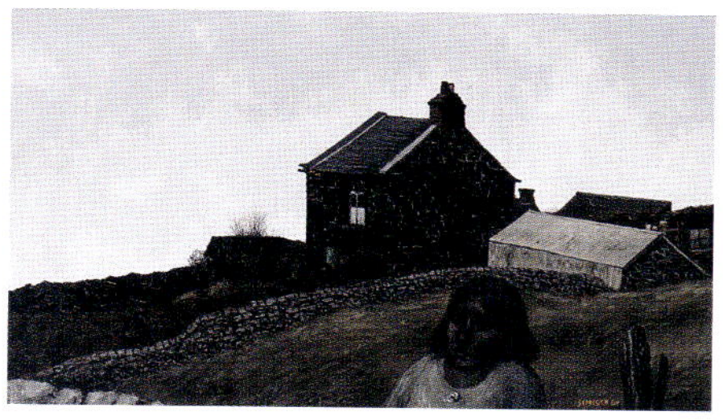

Simcock, Jack b.1929
Cottage and Woman (Biddulph, near Stoke-on-Trent, Staffordshire) 1964
oil on panel 44 x 74.6
VIS.3427

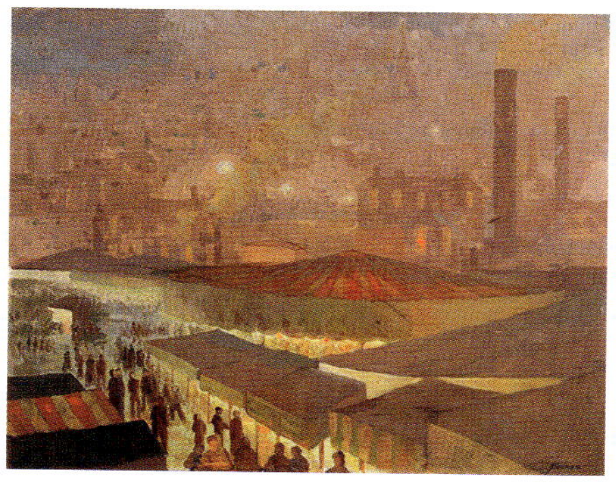

Simmons, John 1871–1944
Sheffield Fair
oil on canvas 40 x 49.9
VIS.2951

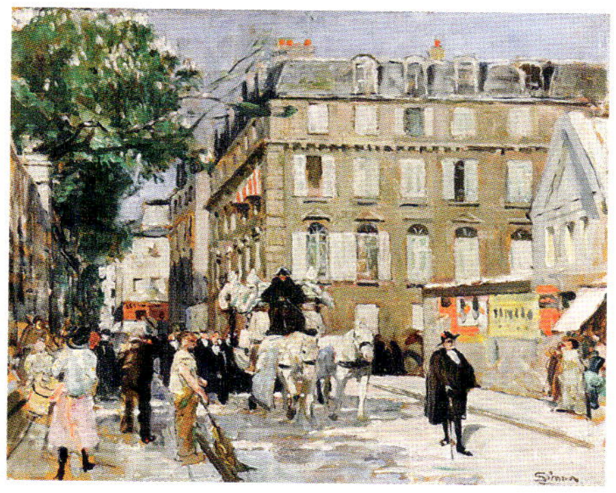

Simon, Lucien 1861–1945
A Parisian Funeral
oil on canvas 59.7 x 73.3
VIS.757

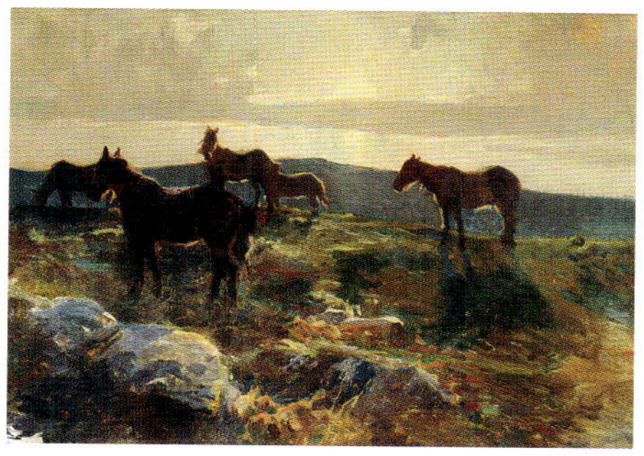

Simpson, Charles Walter 1885–1971
Dartmoor Ponies
oil on millboard 50.7 x 70.5
VIS.2019

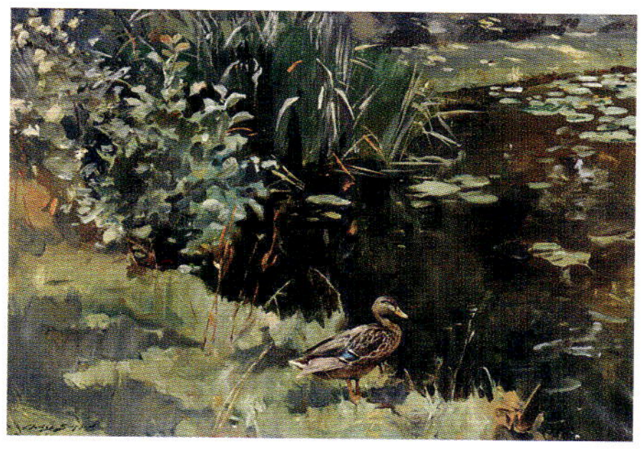

Simpson, Charles Walter 1885–1971
Mallard Drake
oil on canvas 62 x 87
VIS.2934

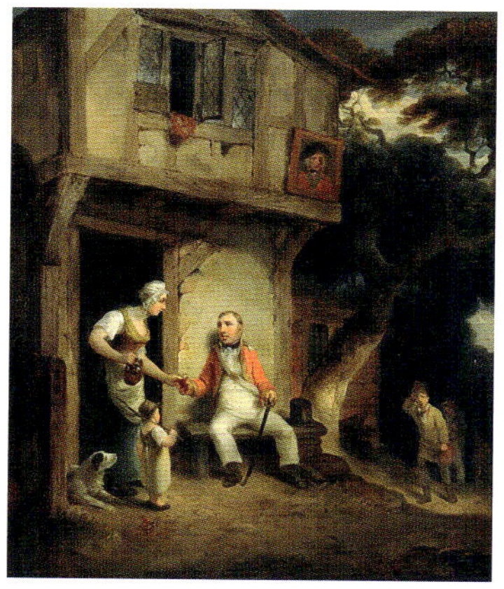

Singleton, Henry 1766–1839
The Tired Soldier
oil on panel 32.4 x 26.6
VIS.47

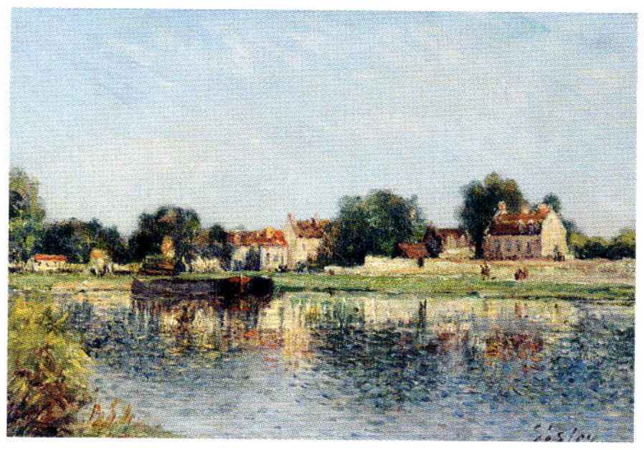

Sisley, Alfred 1839–1899
Le barrage à Saint-Mammes, France
oil on canvas 52.2 x 65
VIS.LI.903 (P)

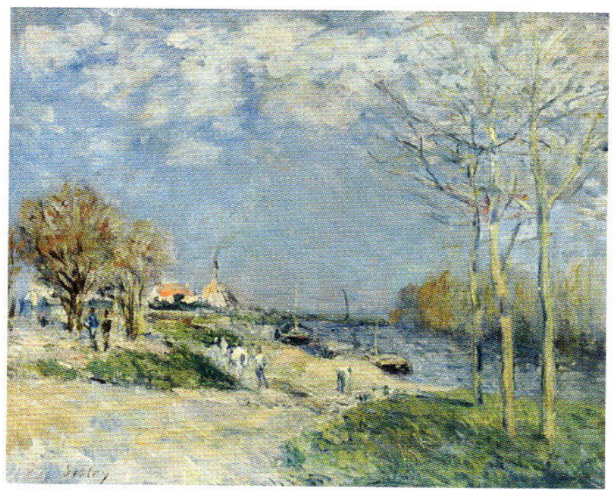

Sisley, Alfred 1839–1899
The Banks of the River Seine around Louveciennes, France
oil on canvas 65 x 76
VIS.LI.842 (P)

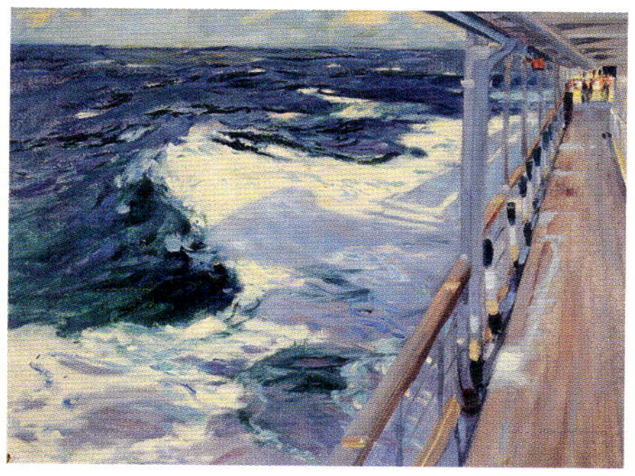

Smart, Robert Borlase 1881–1947
In the Bay of Biscay
oil on canvas 44.8 x 59.7
VIS.1321

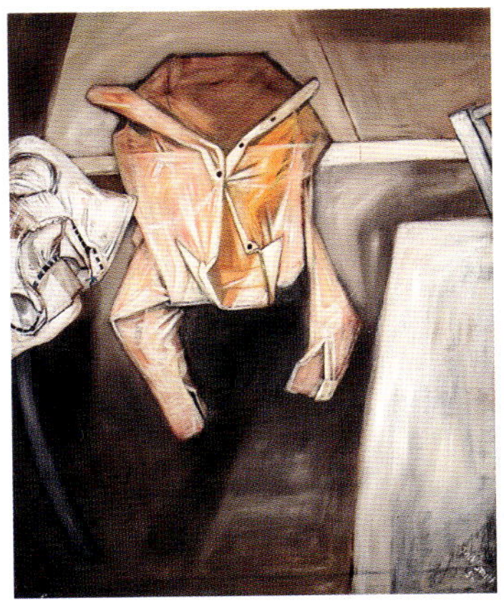

Smith, Jack 1928–2011
The Pink Shirt 1956
oil on panel 150.8 x 121.3
VIS.3174

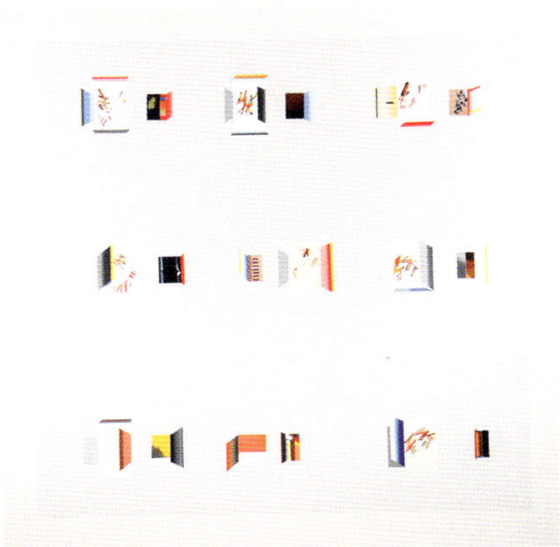

Smith, Jack 1928–2011
Sounds on Grey 1972
oil on board 104.6 x 104.1
VIS.4160

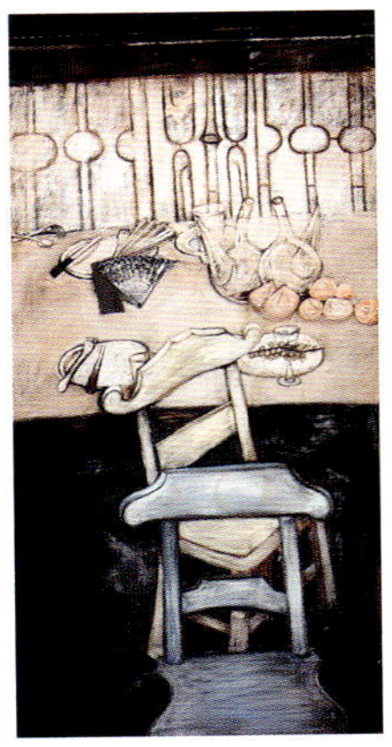

Smith, Jack 1928–2011
Spanish Still Life
oil on board 243.4 x 122.7
VIS.3796

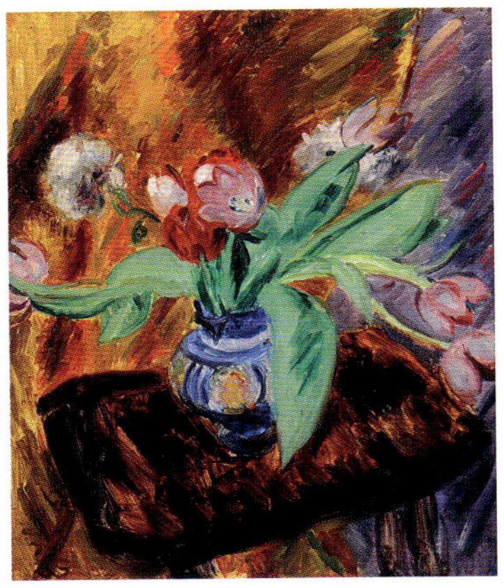

Smith, Matthew Arnold Bracey 1879–1959
Tulips
oil on canvas 75.5 x 62.7
VIS.3005

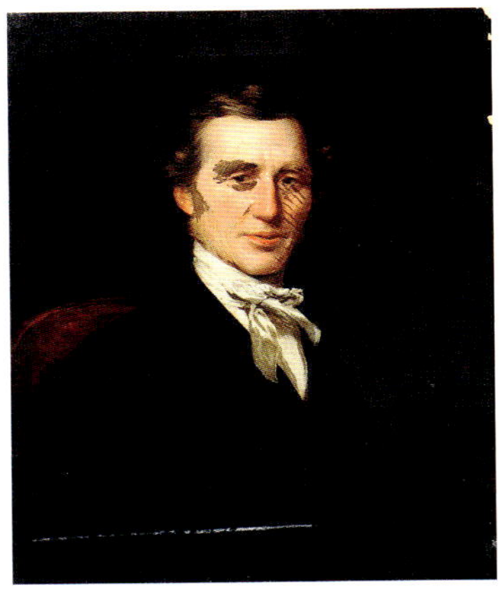

Smith, Richard 1818–1890
John Holland 1852
oil on canvas 76.2 x 63.7
VIS.LI.816 (P)

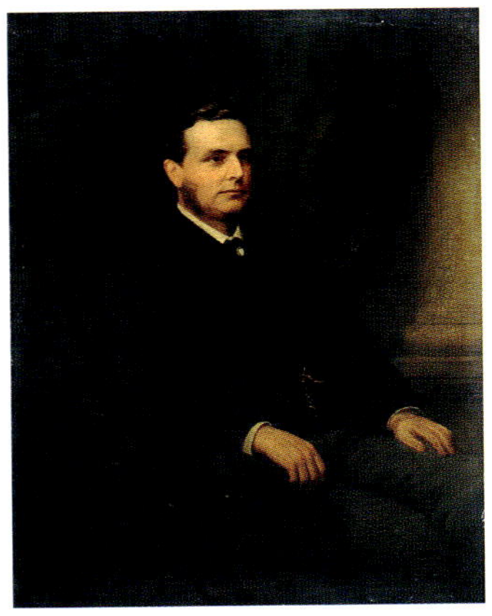

Smith, Richard 1818–1890
Arthur Thomas, Capital Church Burgess of Sheffield 1885
oil on canvas 132 x 102.2
VIS.LI.823 (P)

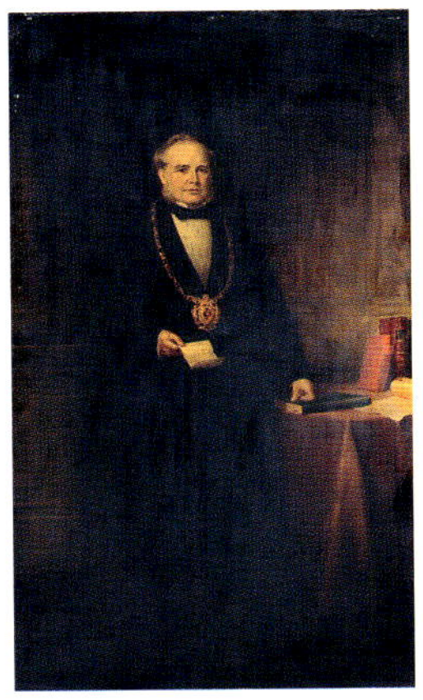

Smith, Richard 1818–1890
John Brown (1816–1896), Mayor of Sheffield (1861–1863)
oil on canvas 248.7 x 147
VIS.LI.831 (P)

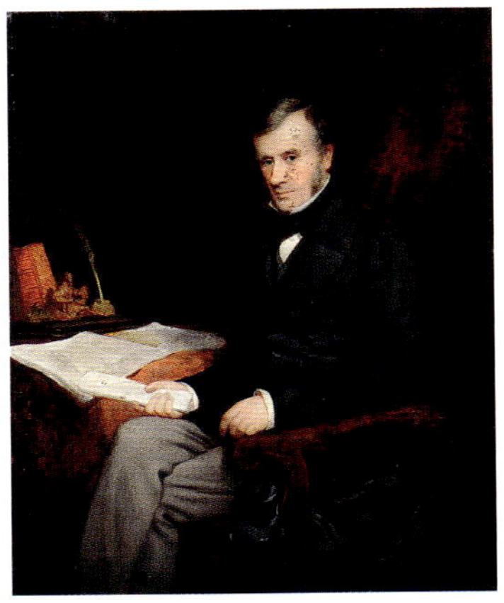

Smith, Richard 1818–1890
William Smith
oil on canvas 126.8 x 102.1
VIS.LI.822 (P)

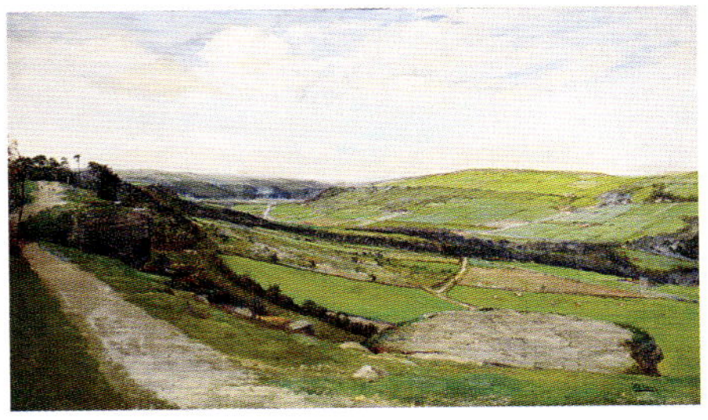

Smith, W. E.
Rivelin Valley, Sheffield
oil on canvas 90.1 x 151.3
VIS.3278

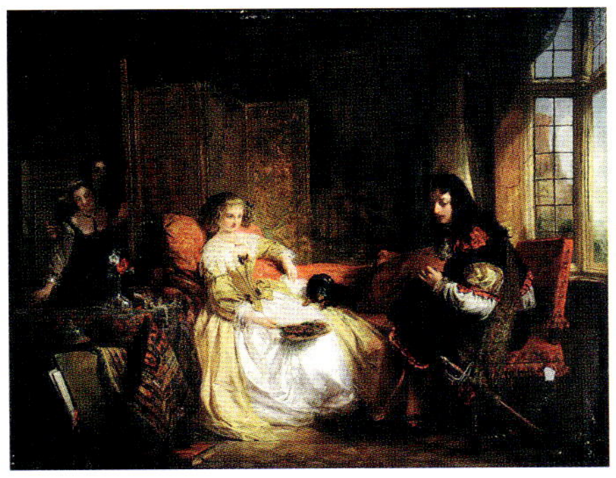

Solomon, Abraham 1824–1862
The Timid Suitor 1856
oil on canvas 102 x 127.2
VIS.1527

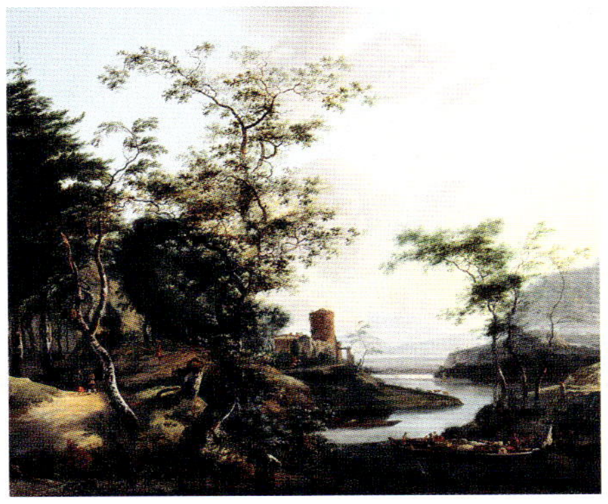

Sonje, Jan Gabrielsz. (attributed to)
c.1625–1707
Landscape with a Ruined Castle c.1667
oil on canvas 91 x 108
VIS.3118

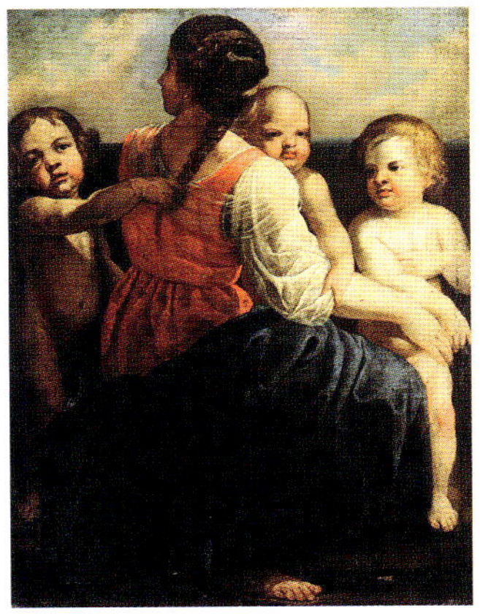

Spanish School 19th C
Mother and Three Children
oil on canvas 69.4 x 52.7
VIS.131

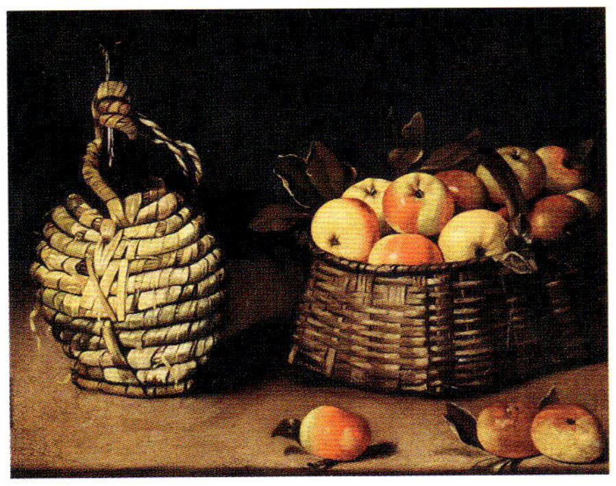

Spanish School (attributed to) 18th C
Wine Flask and Apples
oil on canvas 49.9 x 60.4
VIS.268

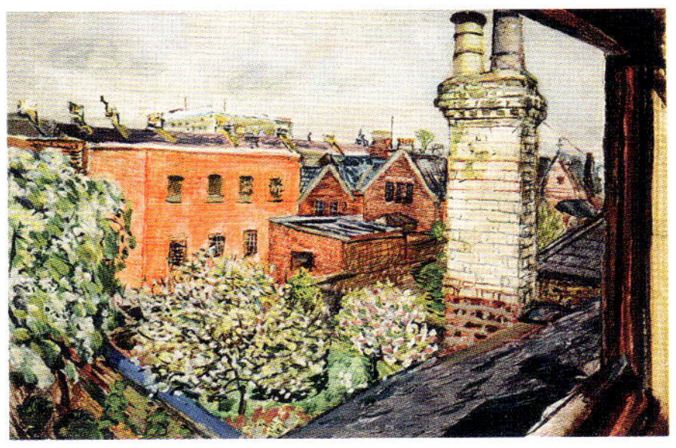

Spear, Ruskin 1911–1990
Rooftops
oil on panel 227 x 340
VIS.4553

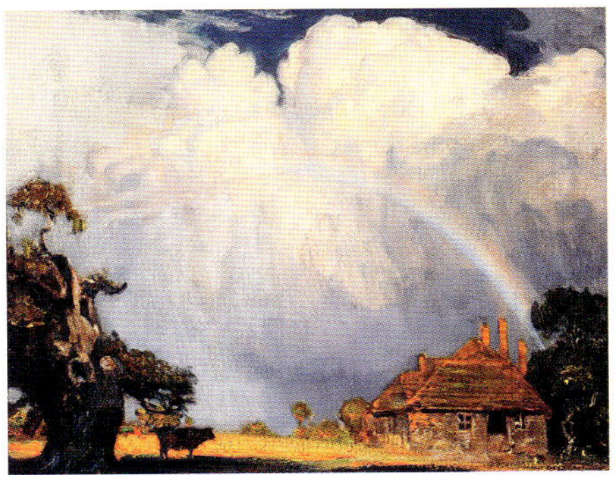

Speed, Harold 1872–1957
The Rainbow 1908
oil on canvas 53.1 x 65.5
VIS.595

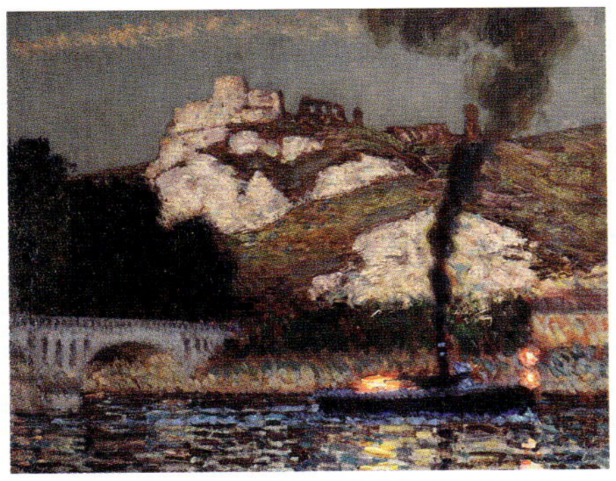

Speed, Harold 1872–1957
Château-Gaillard, Normandy, France, after Sunset
oil on canvas 49.5 x 62.1
VIS.2176

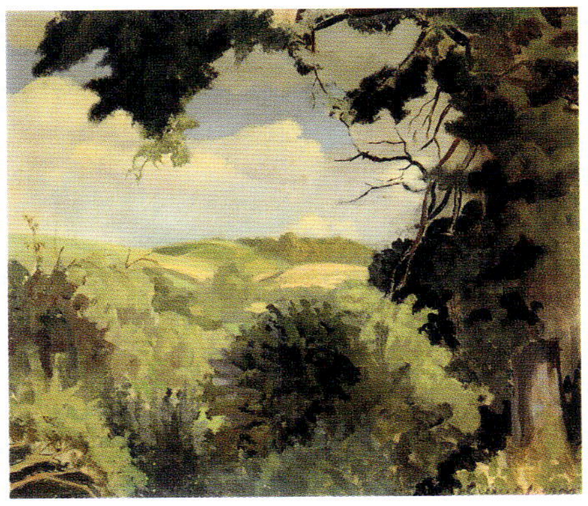

Spencer, Gilbert 1892–1979
Dorset Landscape No.1
oil on panel 34.2 x 39.3
VIS.5312

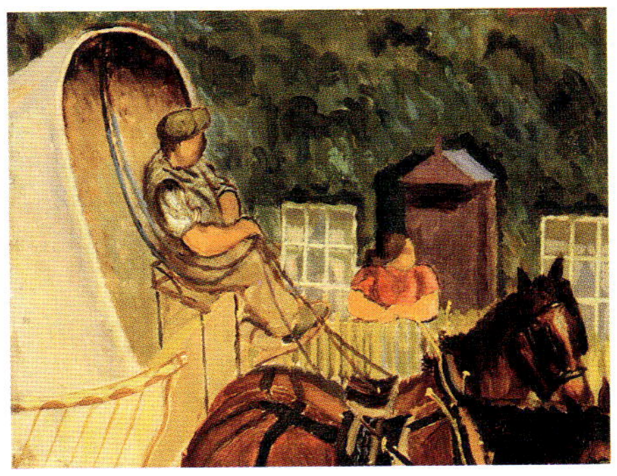

Spencer, Gilbert 1892–1979
The Drayman
oil on panel 30.6 x 39.3
VIS.2130

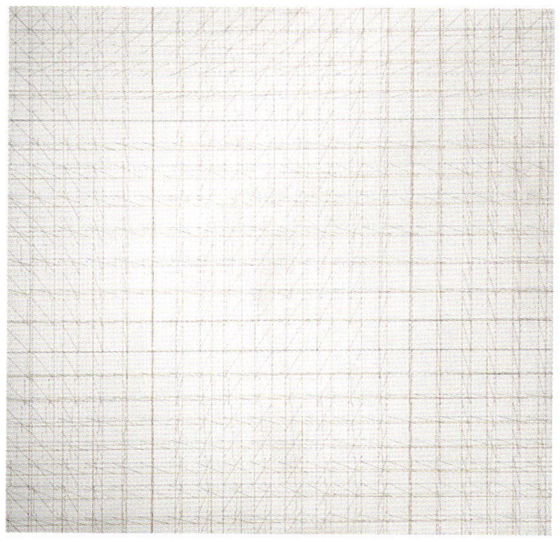

Spencer, Jean 1942–1998
Painting 1960–1972
oil on canvas 76.7 x 76.7
VIS.3910

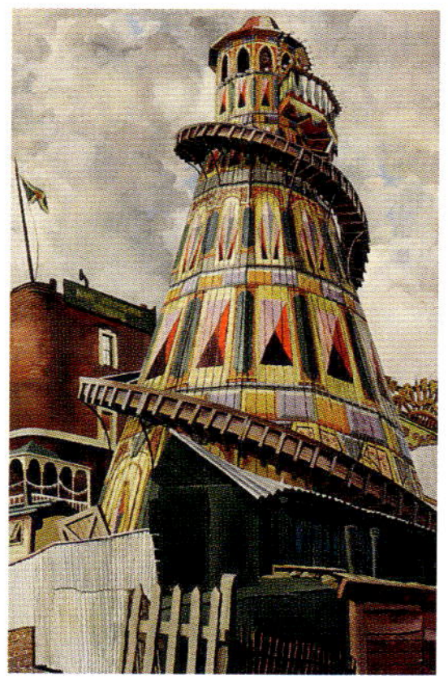

Spencer, Stanley 1891–1959
Helter Skelter 1937
oil on canvas 107.5 x 74.8
VIS.1849

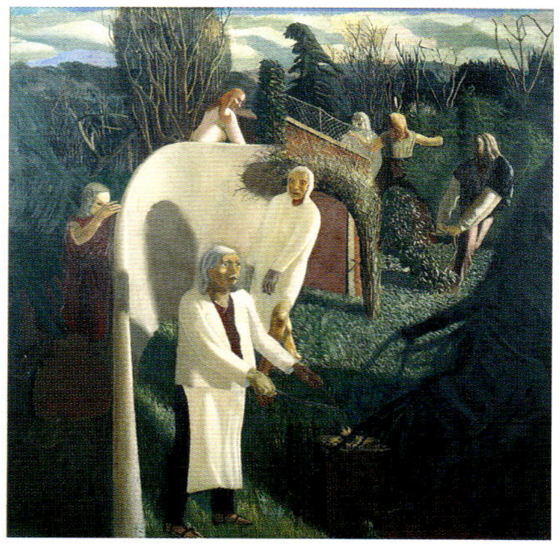

Spencer, Stanley 1891–1959
Zacharias and Elizabeth
oil on canvas 140 x 140
VIS.5307

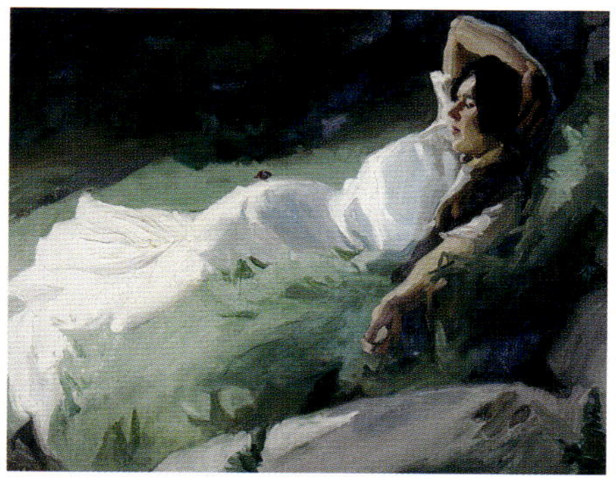

Spencer Pryse, Gerald 1882–1957
The Butterfly
oil on canvas 59.8 x 74.9
VIS.603

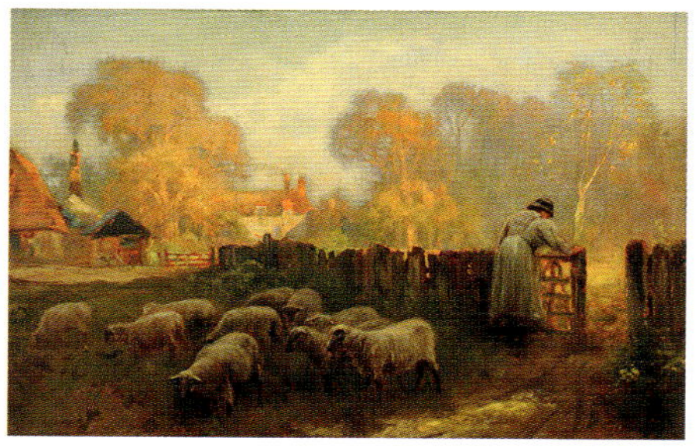

Spenlove-Spenlove, Frank 1866–1933
Evening Glow
oil on millboard 30 x 45
VIS.684

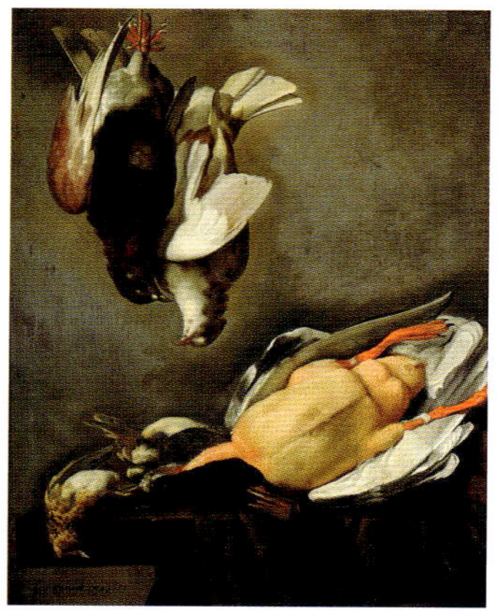

Spruyt, Johannes 1627/1628–1671
Dead Game 1659
oil on panel 63.5 x 49.5
VIS.2411

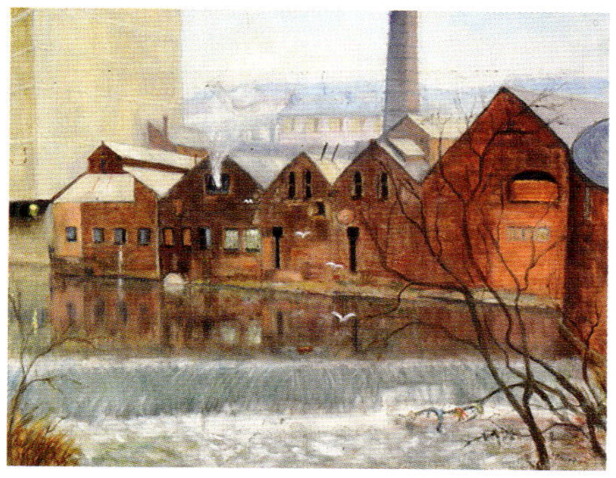

Spurr, Joyce b.1921
Steel Forging Works and the River Don from Effingham Street, South Yorkshire
oil on panel 48.5 x 62
1995.289

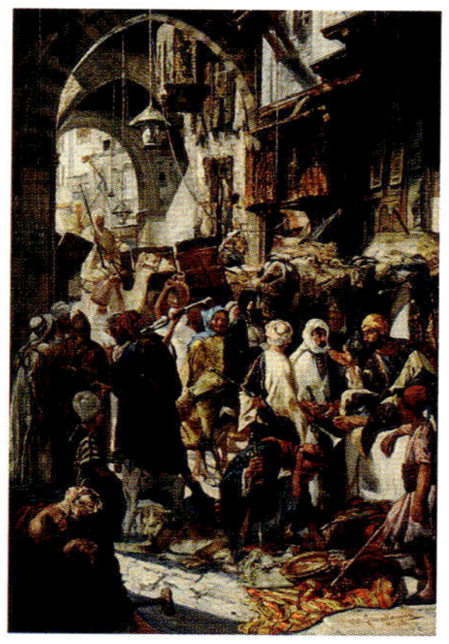

Staackmann, Heinrich Maria 1852–1940
Street in Cairo 1887
oil on panel 49.5 x 33.4
VIS.265

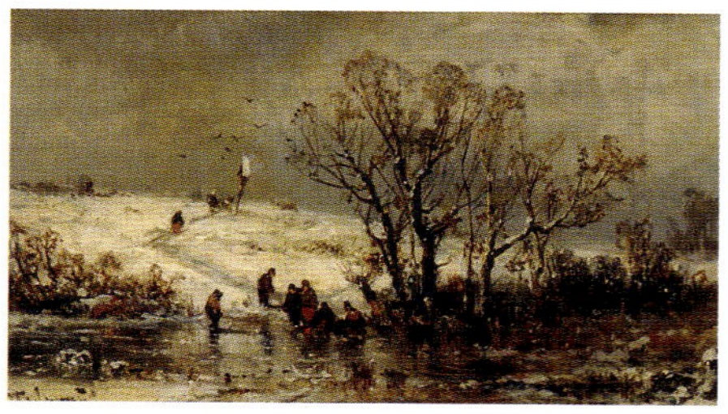

Stademann, Adolf 1824–1895
Winter Landscape
oil on panel 18.6 x 33.6
VIS.708

Facing page: Boyle, George A., 1842–1930, *Moonrise at Sea* (detail), 1914, Museums Sheffield, (p. 24)

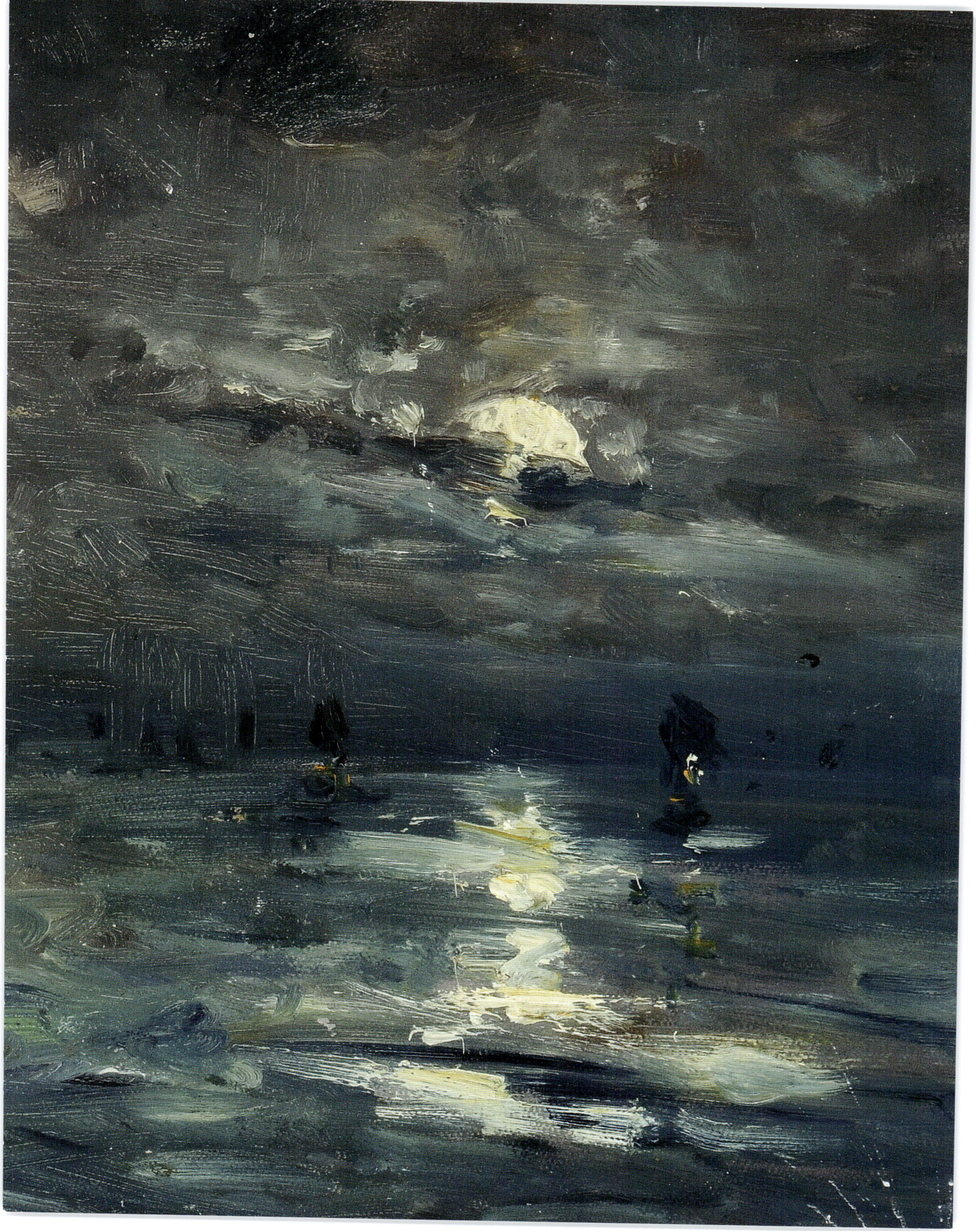

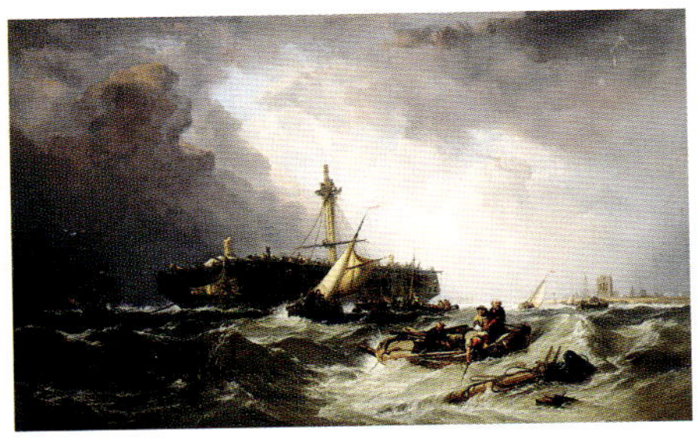

Stanfield, Clarkson 1793–1867
The Morning after the Wreck 1844
oil on canvas 153 x 232.4
VIS.1679

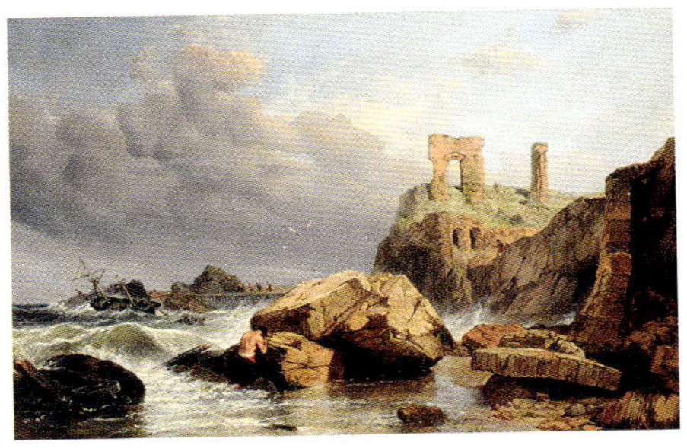

Stanfield, Clarkson 1793–1867
The Last of the Crew 1852
oil on canvas 59.6 x 90
VIS.1605

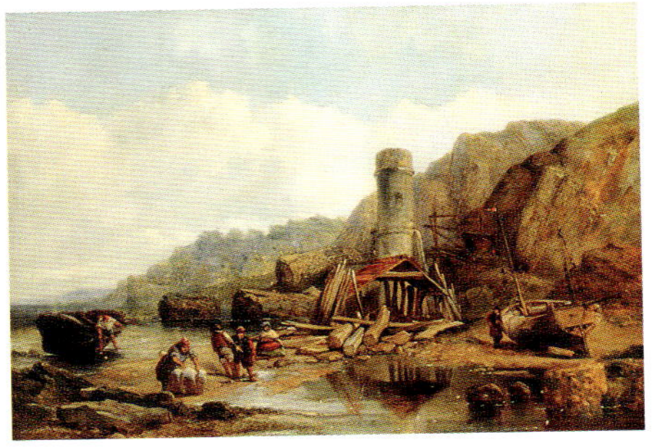

Stanfield, Clarkson 1793–1867
Coast Scene
oil on canvas 36.8 x 52.2
VIS.1567

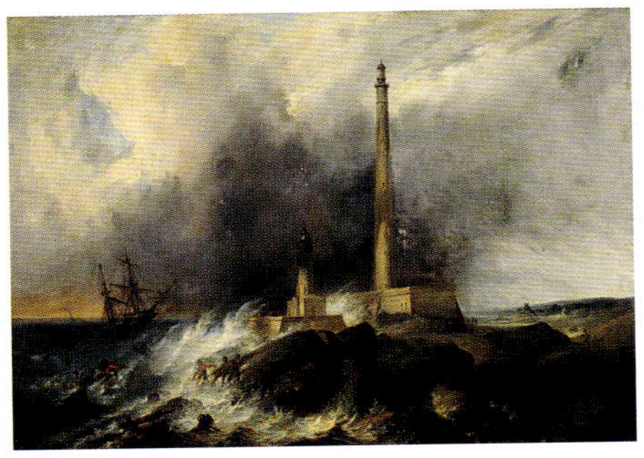

Stanfield, Clarkson 1793–1867
Eddystone Lighthouse
oil on canvas 101.4 x 140.5
VIS.3031

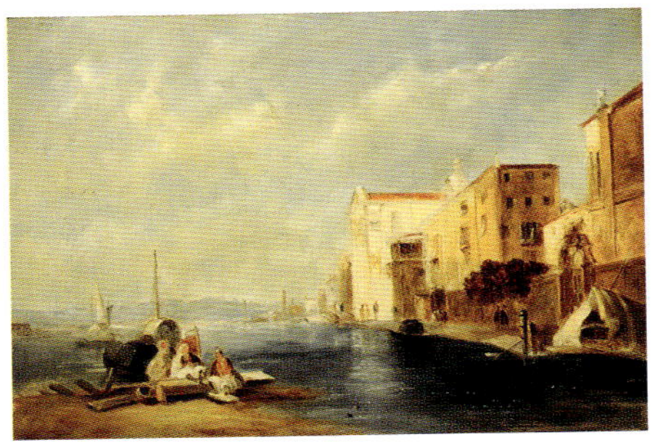

Stanfield, Clarkson 1793–1867
Italian Lake Scene
oil on canvas 35.3 x 50.5
VIS.285

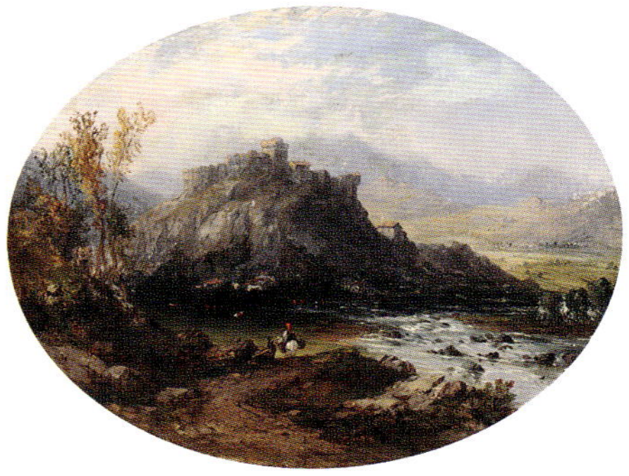

Stanfield, Clarkson 1793–1867
Landscape
oil on canvas 27.2 x 35.4
VIS.545

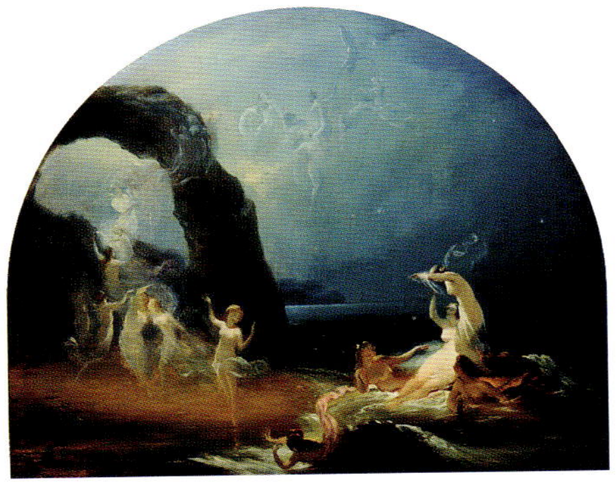

Stanier, Henry c.1832–1892
'Come unto these yellow sands' (from 'The Tempest' by William Shakespeare)
oil on panel 25.5 x 31
VIS.4200

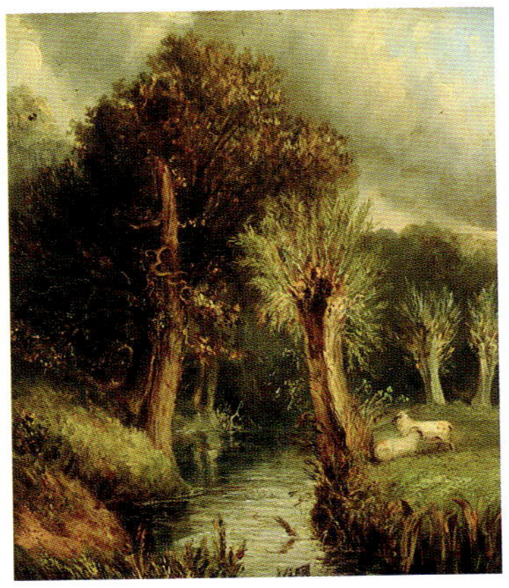

Stapleton, M. active from 1850
On the Frome
oil on panel 21.3 x 17.8
VIS.1243

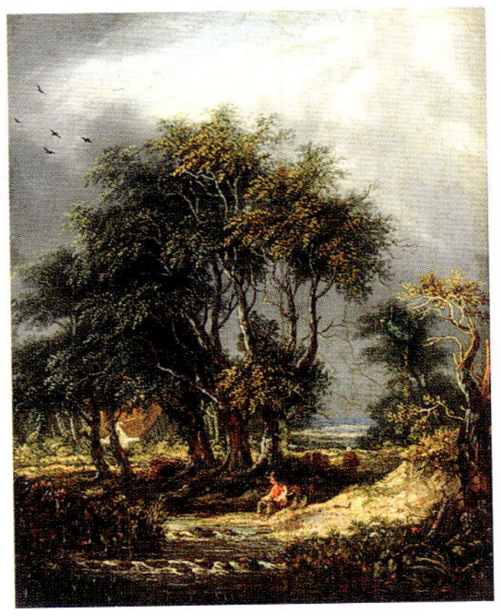

Stark, James 1794–1859
A Woody Landscape
oil on panel 25.5 x 20.8
VIS.349

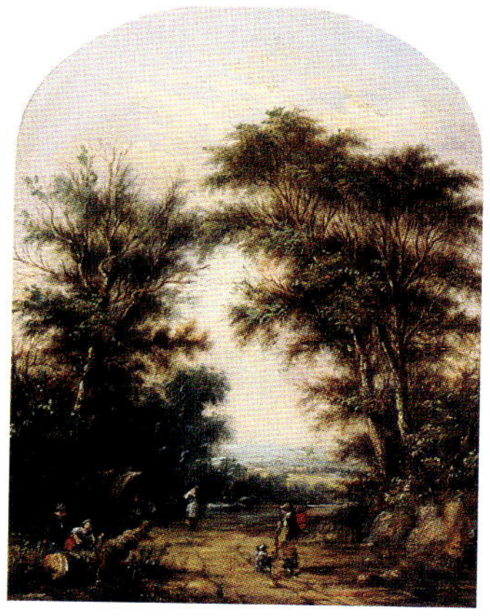

Stark, James 1794–1859
Landscape
oil on panel 18.5 x 14.5
VIS.1079

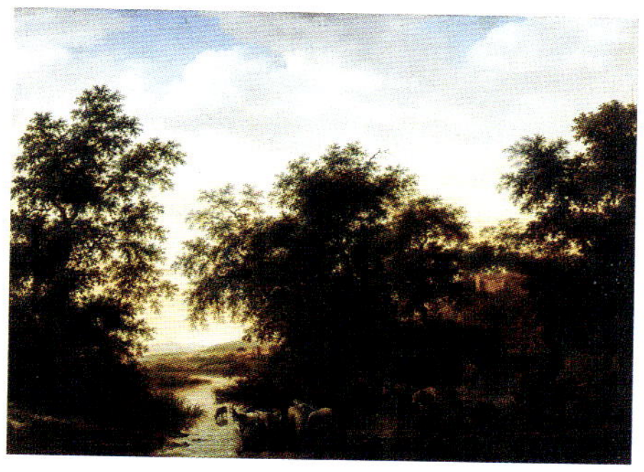

Stark, James 1794–1859
Landscape
oil on panel 45.4 x 60.9
VIS.1531

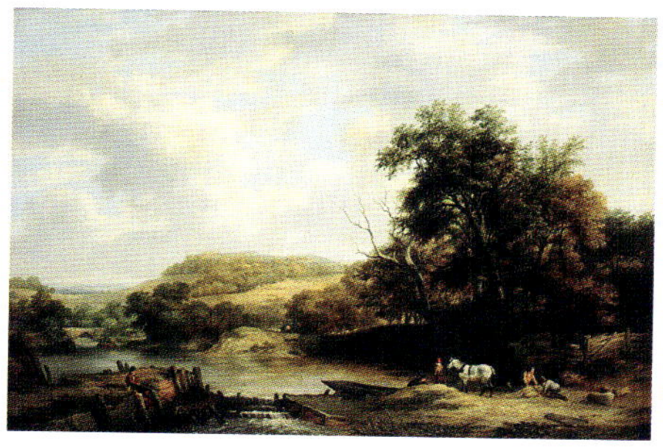

Stark, James 1794–1859
Landscape
oil on canvas 89 x 129.5
VIS.3147

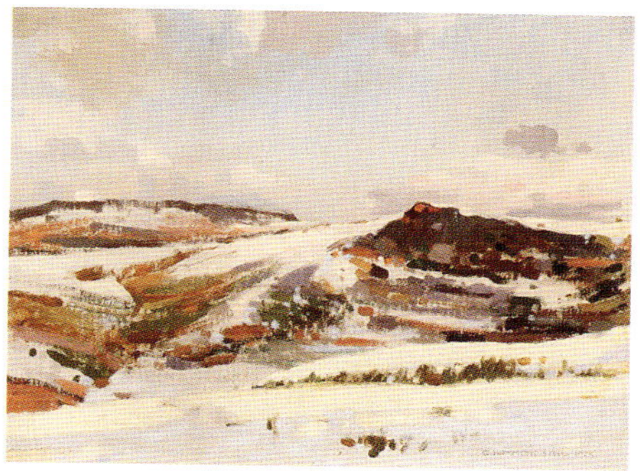

Steel, George Hammond 1900–1960
A Slight Fall 1925
oil on board 29.5 x 39.3
VIS.1242

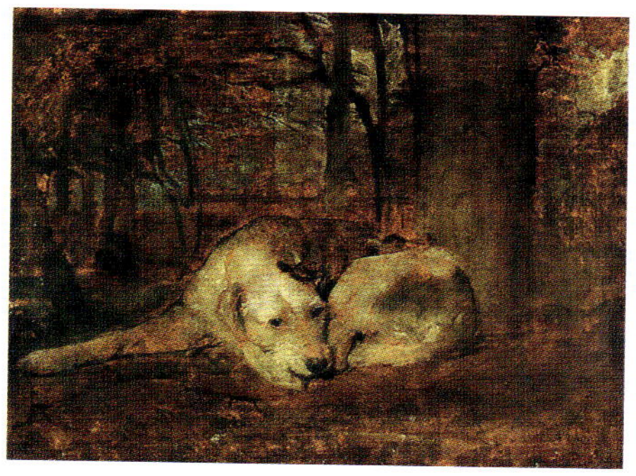

Stevens, Alfred George 1817–1875
Study of a Dog c.1851
oil on canvas 34.8 x 45.4
VIS.2312

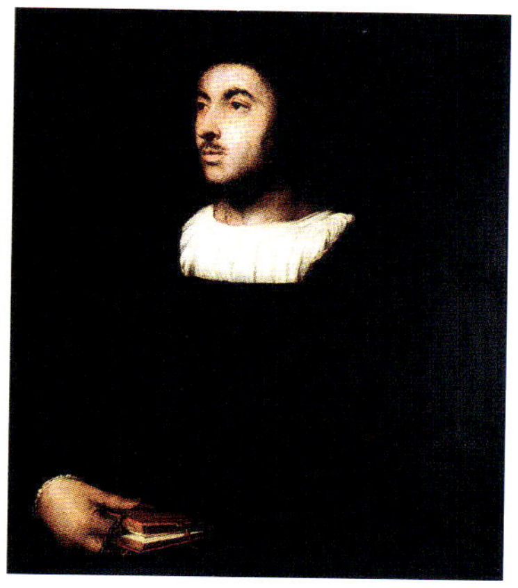

Stevens, Alfred George 1817–1875
A Venetian Gentleman at Hampton Court
(copy of Titian)
oil on canvas 81.8 x 69.9
VIS.2313

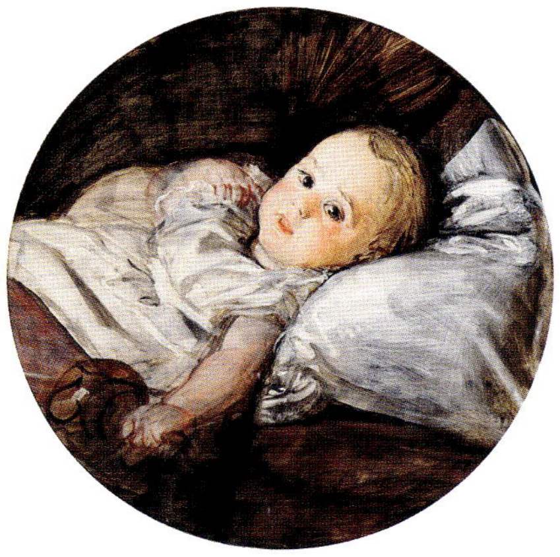

Stevens, Alfred George 1817–1875
Head of a Baby
oil on canvas 44.7
VIS.2314

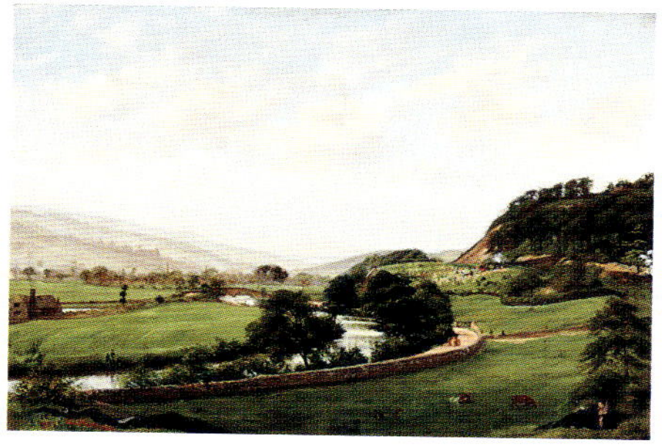

Stevenson, W. J. 1835–1905
River Don at Wardsend, Sheffield 1875
oil on canvas 44.2 x 64
1981.717

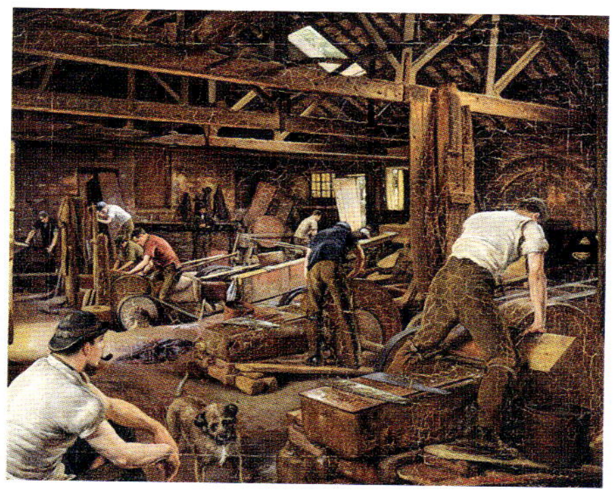

Stevenson, W. J. 1835–1905
Birley Meadow Grinding Wheel, Sheffield (August to September, 1870) 1876
oil on canvas 47.8 x 58
SH439

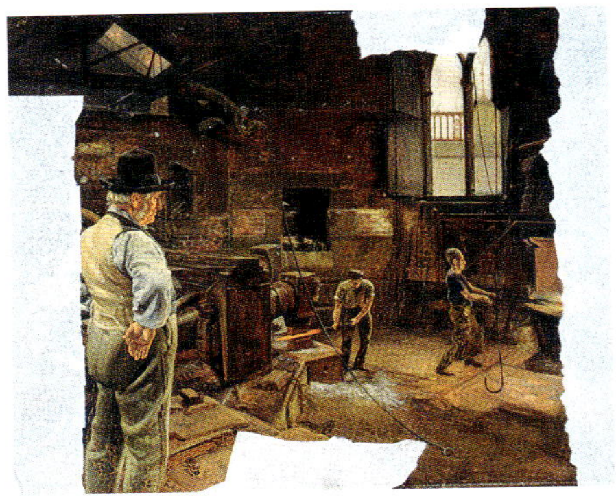

Stevenson, W. J. 1835–1905
Interior of a Tilt Forge, Lady's Bridge, Sheffield 1876
oil on canvas 50.1 x 60.1
K1956.7

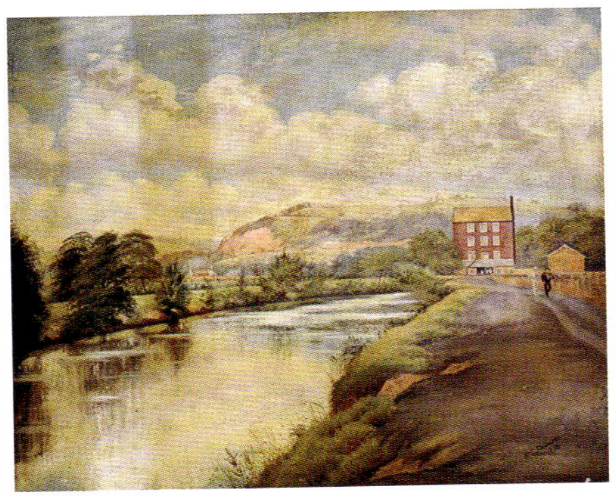

Stevenson, W. J. 1835–1905
Oughtibridge, Sheffield 1876
oil on canvas 63.5 x 76.4
VIS.2736

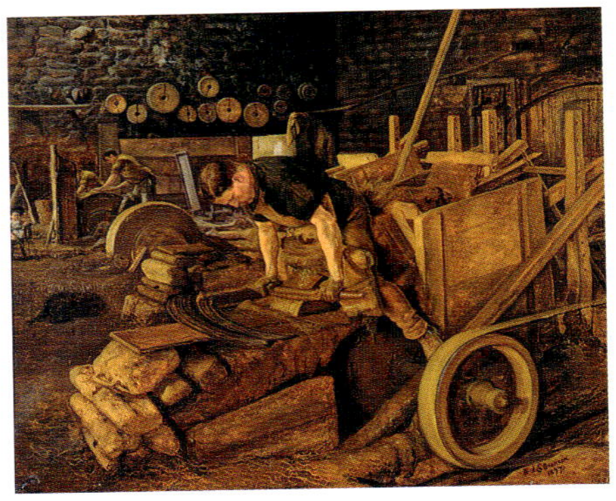

Stevenson, W. J. 1835–1905
Spooner's Wheel, Rivelin, Sheffield 1877
oil on canvas 49 x 58.5
K1956.8

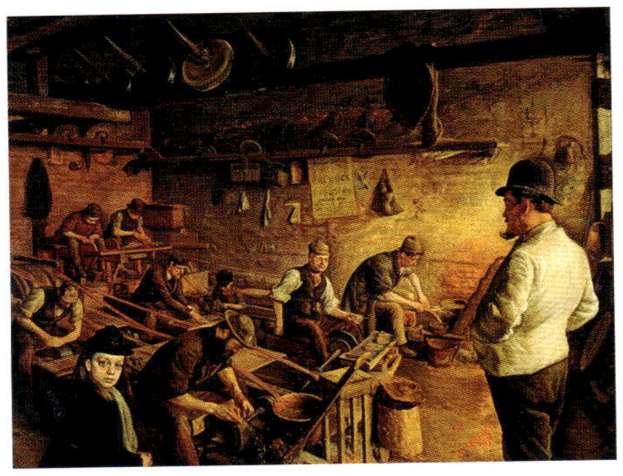

Stevenson, W. J. 1835–1905
Union Wheel, Sheffield 1877
oil on panel 47.2 x 59.5
K1956.9

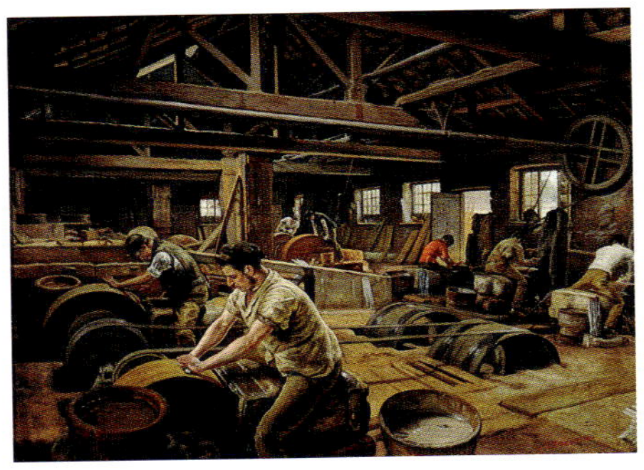

Stevenson, W. J. 1835–1905
Grinders' Workshop
oil on board 53.3 x 67.3
SH437

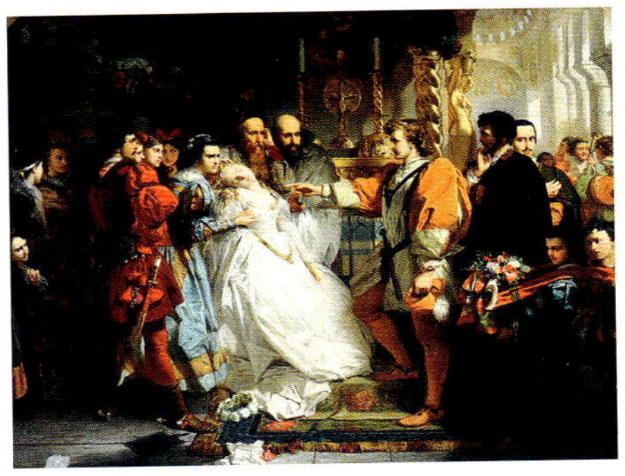

Stone, Marcus C. 1840–1921
Claudio, Deceived by Don Juan, Accuses Hero (from 'Measure for Measure' by William Shakespeare)
oil on canvas 85.1 x 109.1
VIS.1631

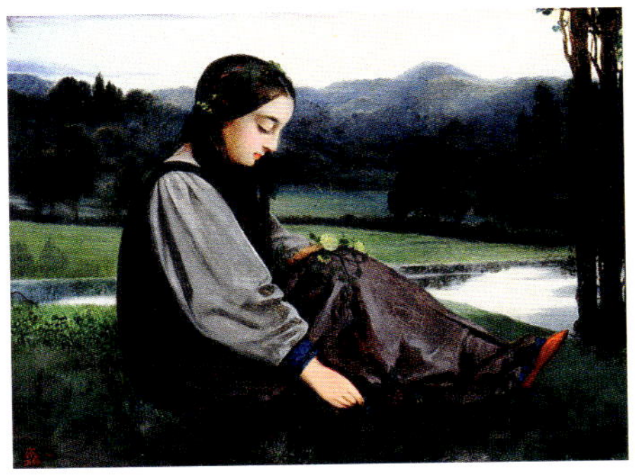

Storey, George Adolphus 1834–1919
Contemplation 1859
oil on canvas 31.9 x 41.9
VIS.844

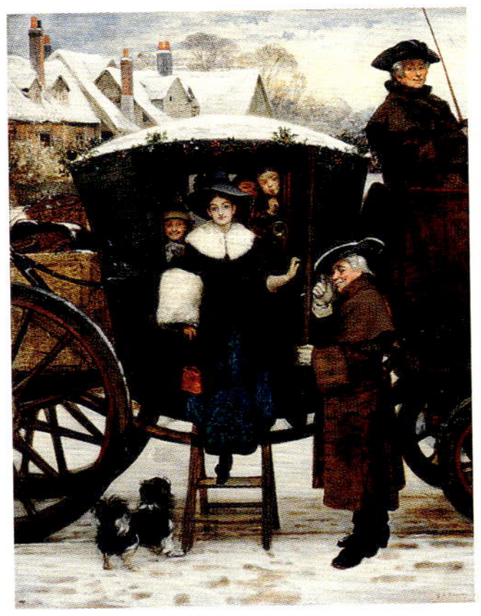

Storey, George Adolphus 1834–1919
Grandmamma's Christmas Visitors 1873
oil on canvas 117 x 97.5
VIS.1432

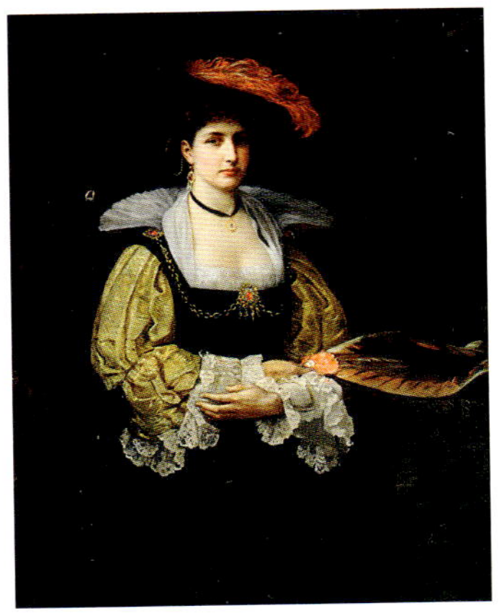

Storey, George Adolphus 1834–1919
Portrait of a Lady 1878
oil on canvas 127.7 x 102.6
VIS.1448

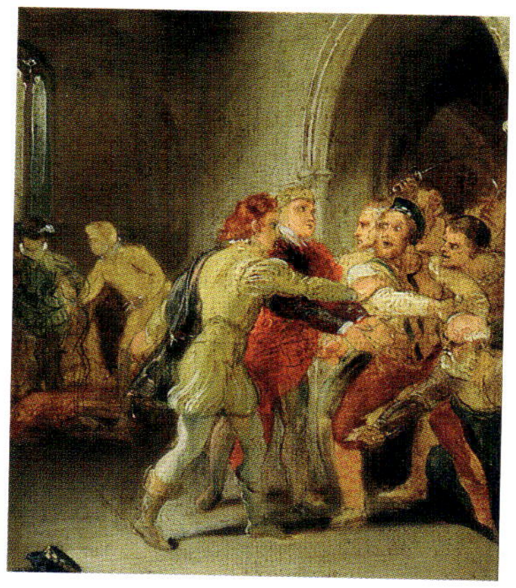

Stothard, Thomas 1755–1834
The Assassins
oil on panel 15.7 x 13.5
VIS.85

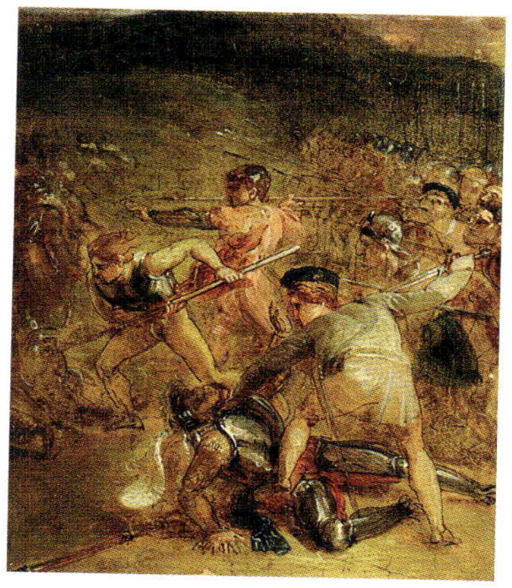

Stothard, Thomas 1755–1834
The Attack
oil on panel 15.9 x 13.6
VIS.66

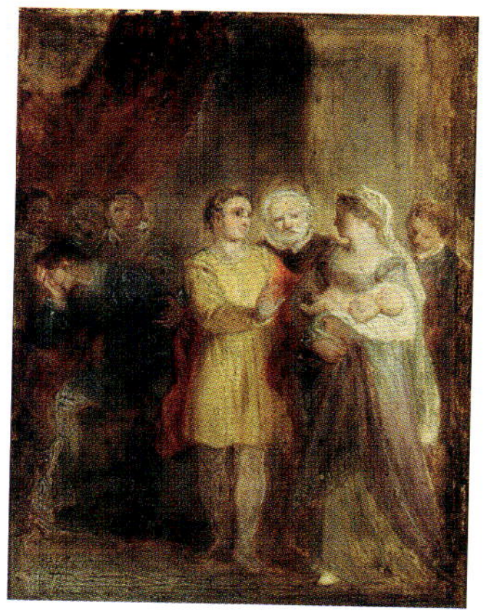

Stothard, Thomas 1755–1834
The Heir
oil on panel 17.6 x 13.2
VIS.86

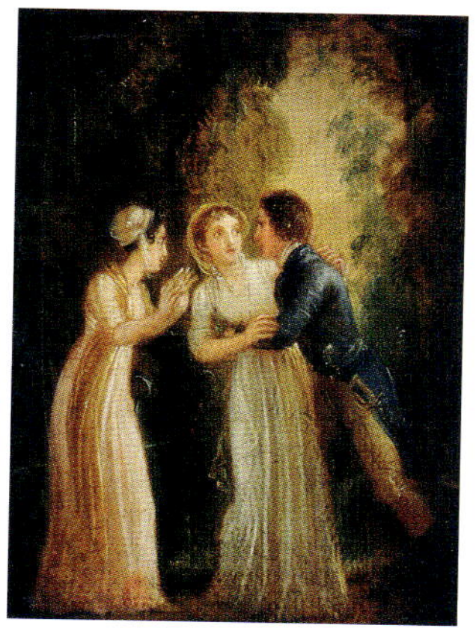

Stothard, Thomas 1755–1834
The Lovers' Meeting
oil on panel 19 x 13.8
VIS.79

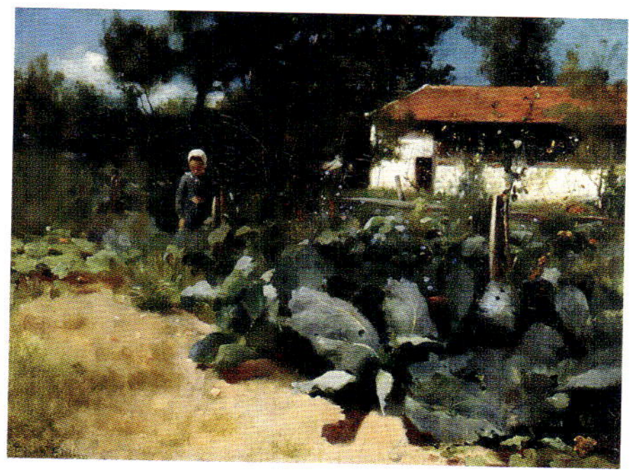

Stott, Edward William 1859–1918
A French Kitchen Garden 1883
oil on canvas 45.1 x 59.6
VIS.126

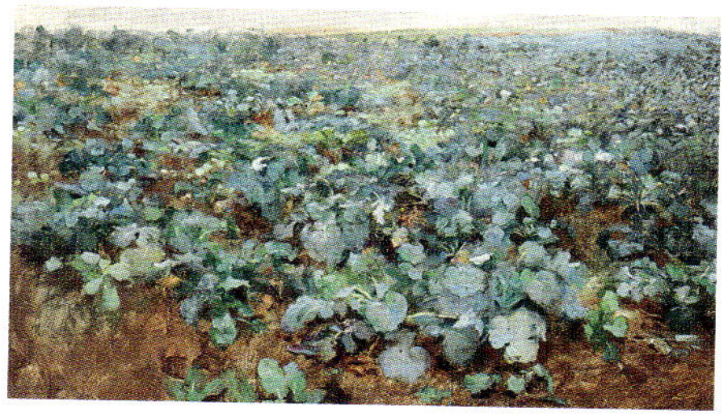

Stott, Edward William 1859–1918
The Turnip Field
oil on canvas 27.3 x 46.6
VIS.553

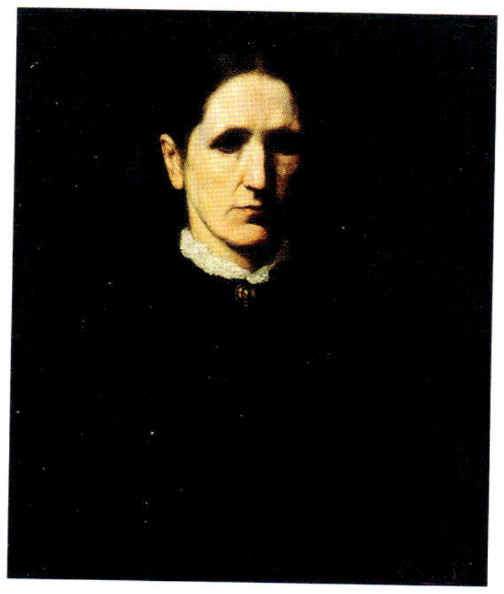

Strang, William 1859–1921
Miss Elizabeth Martin 1880
oil on canvas 60 x 49.5
VIS.216

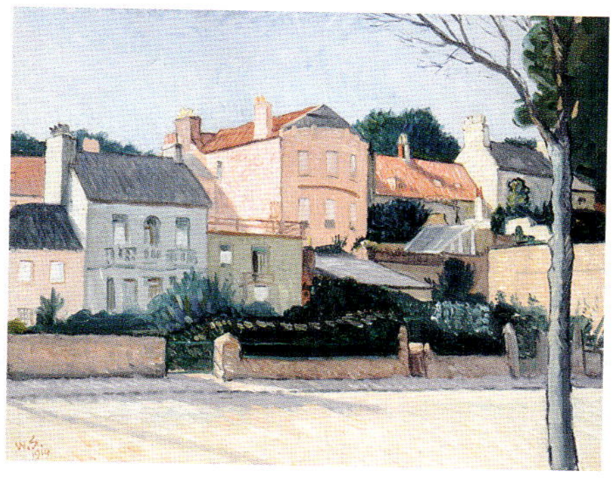

Strang, William 1859–1921
Houses 1914
oil on canvas 34.4 x 44.7
VIS.154

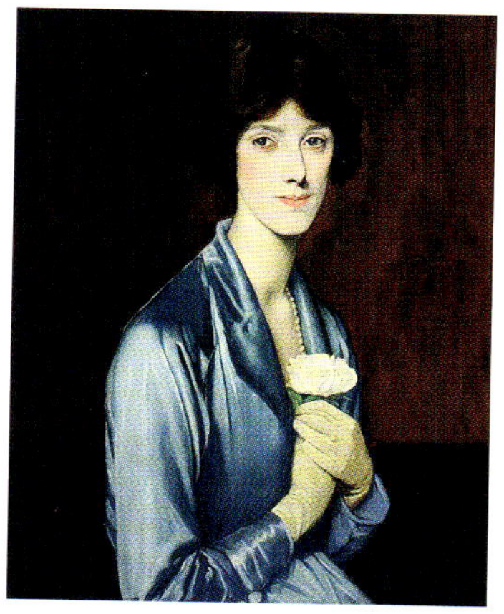

Strang, William 1859–1921
The White Rose 1919
oil on canvas 73 x 58.1
VIS.119

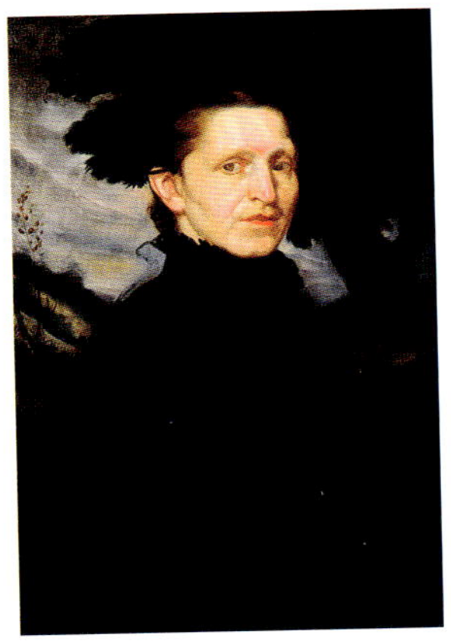

Strang, William 1859–1921
Miss Ann Martin
oil on canvas 75 x 49.8
VIS.130

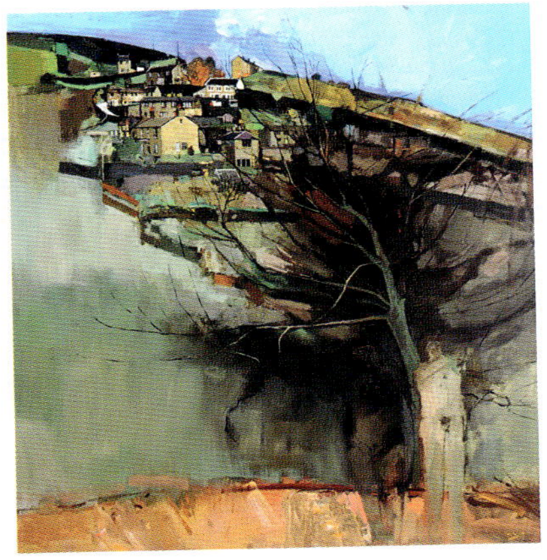

Stubley, Trevor 1932–2010
Holmfirth, West Yorkshire, Adam and Eve
oil on panel 126.4 x 118.8
VIS.5103

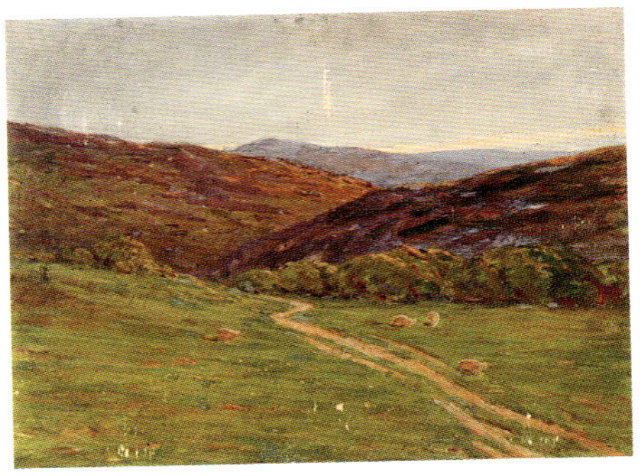

Styring, Elizabeth 1854–1940
Evening Stillness
oil on millboard 45 x 60
VIS.2363

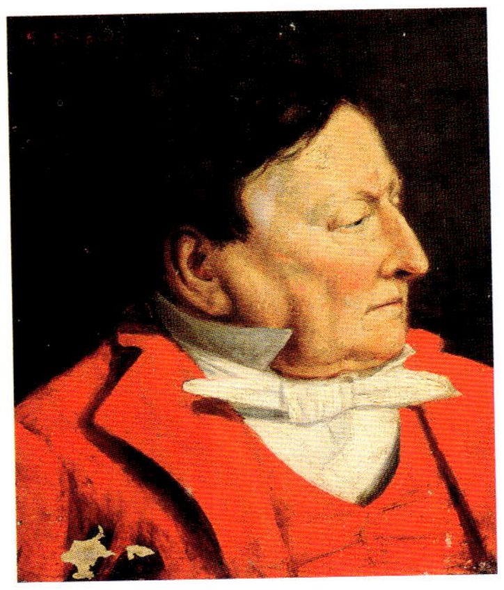

Styring, Elizabeth 1854–1940
The Pink Coat
oil on canvas 30.8 x 25.4
VIS.2356

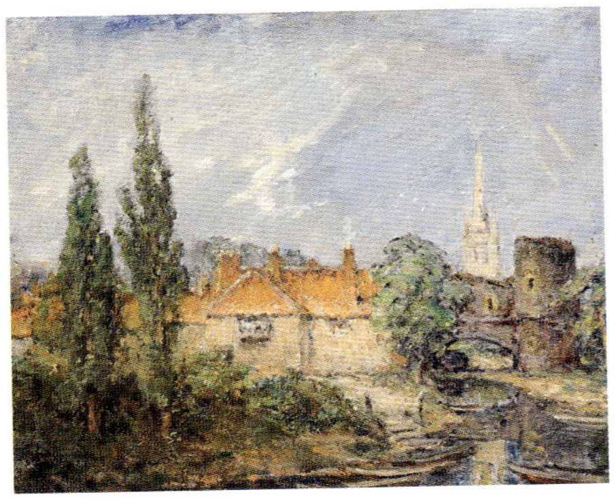

Styring, Elizabeth 1854–1940
The Poplars (recto)
oil on panel 49.4 x 59.5
VIS.2365

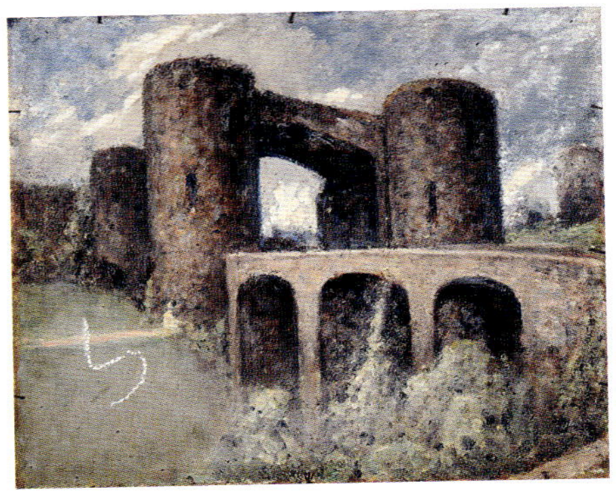

Styring, Elizabeth 1854–1940
Castle and Viaduct (verso)*
oil on panel 49.4 x 59.5
VIS.2365 VERSO

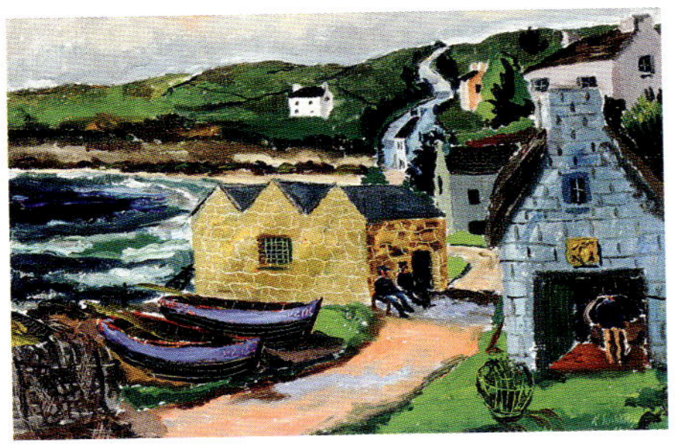

Suddaby, Rowland 1912–1972
Cape Cornwall 1956
oil on canvas 49.3 x 74.7
VIS.4026

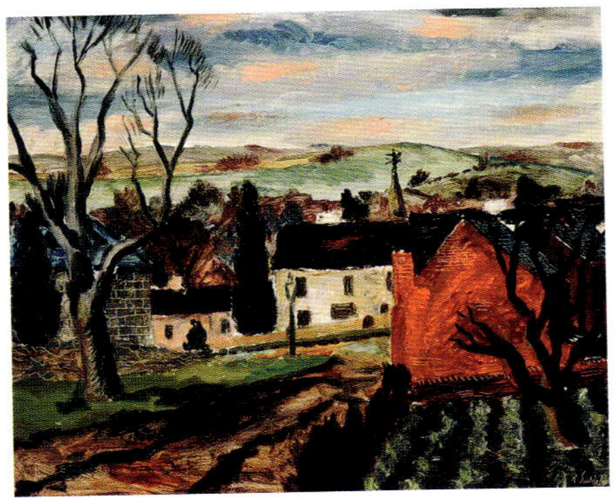

Suddaby, Rowland 1912–1972
Scholes, Yorkshire 1967
oil on millboard 50.1 x 60.5
VIS.1938

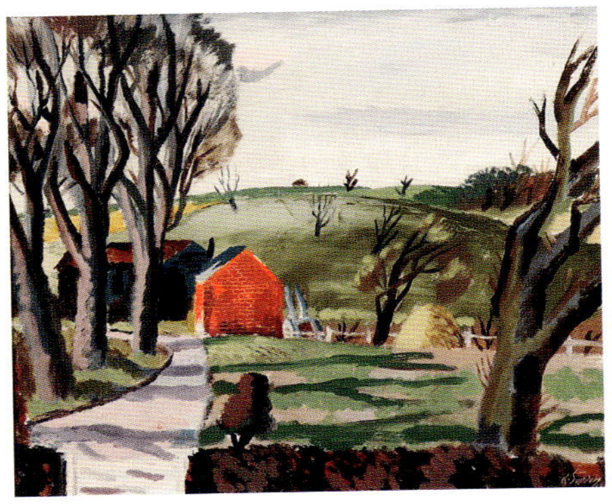

Suddaby, Rowland 1912–1972
Paddock at Stoke-by-Nayland, Essex
oil on canvas 48.9 x 59.2
VIS.5436

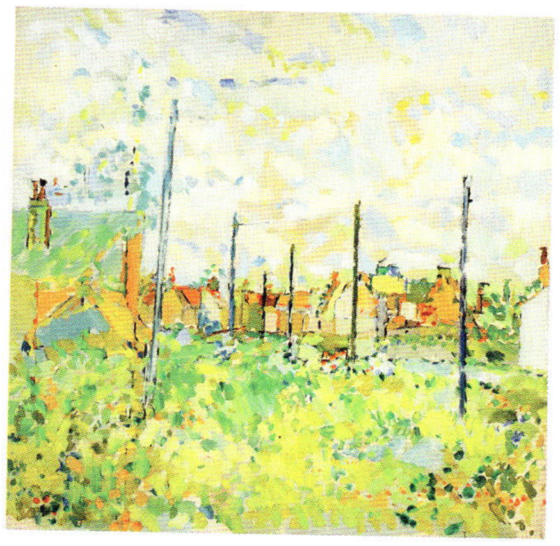

Sutton, Philip b.1928
Snape Village, Suffolk 1956
oil on canvas 70.5 x 70.8
VIS.3755

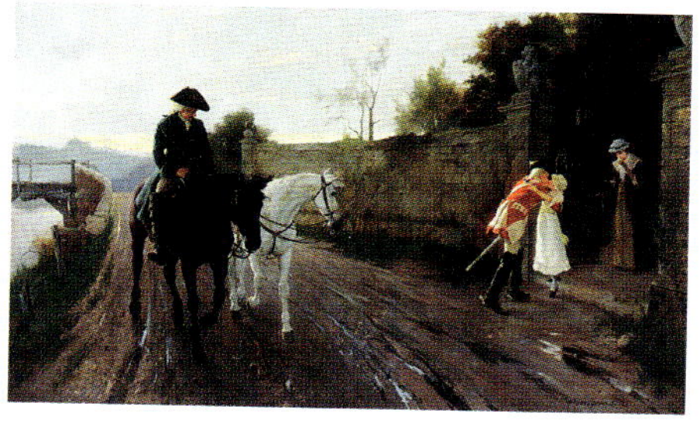

Swinstead, George Hillyard 1860–1926
When Trumpets Call, Then Homes Are Broken
oil on canvas 93.6 x 156
VIS.1589

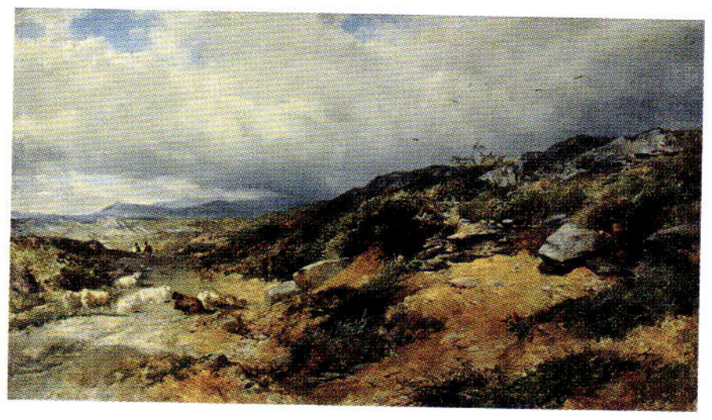

Syer, John 1815–1885
Landscape, North Wales 1864
oil on canvas 48.6 x 80
VIS.1566

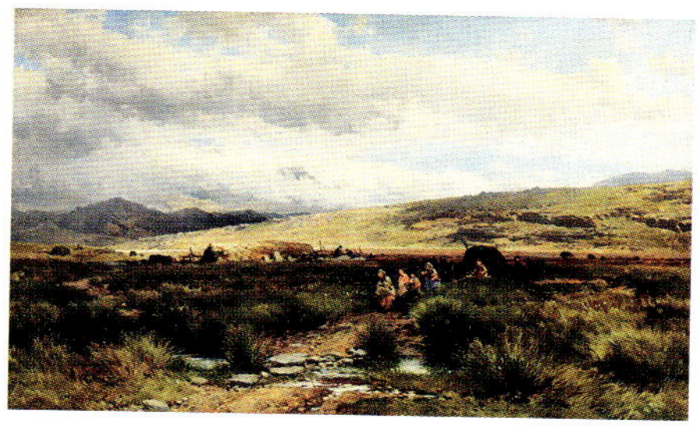

Syer, John 1815–1885
Among the Rushes 1868
oil on board 55.7 x 89.9
VIS.1626

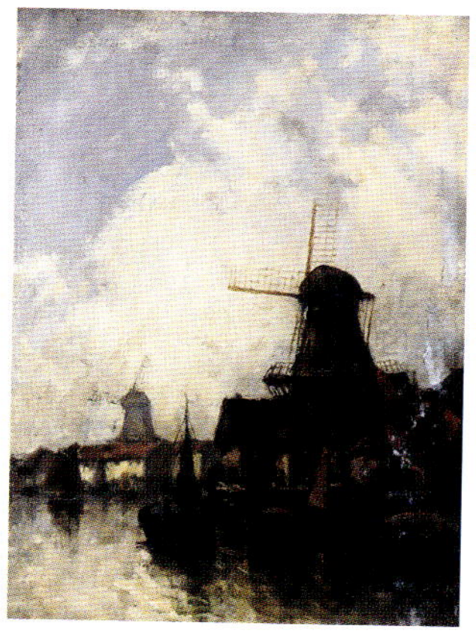

Syers, Rose Aspinall 1850–after 1926
A Dutch Town, Windmills
oil on canvas 49.6 x 36.7
VIS.636

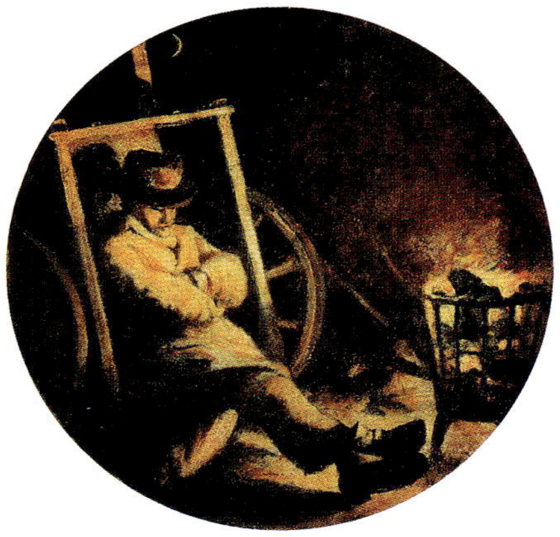

Sykes, Godfrey 1824–1866
The Watchman 1840–1842
oil on canvas 29.1
VIS.2939

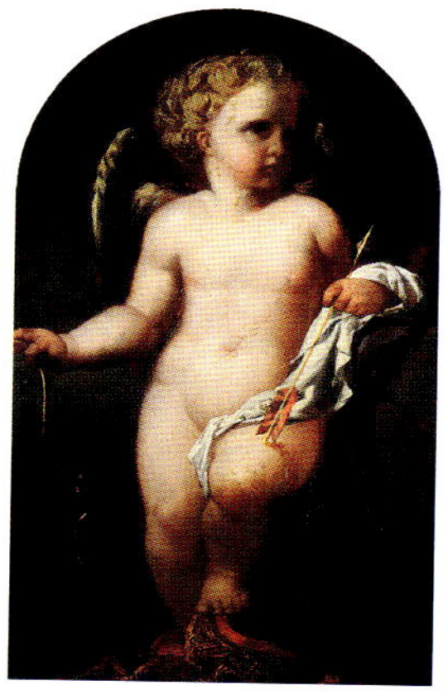

Sykes, Godfrey 1824–1866
Study of a Cherub 1855
oil on canvas 46.9 x 29
VIS.3023

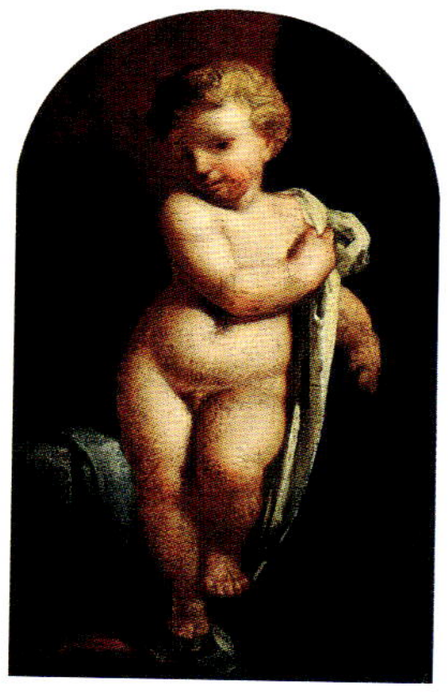

Sykes, Godfrey 1824–1866
Study of a Cherub 1855
oil on canvas 46.8 x 29.1
VIS.3024

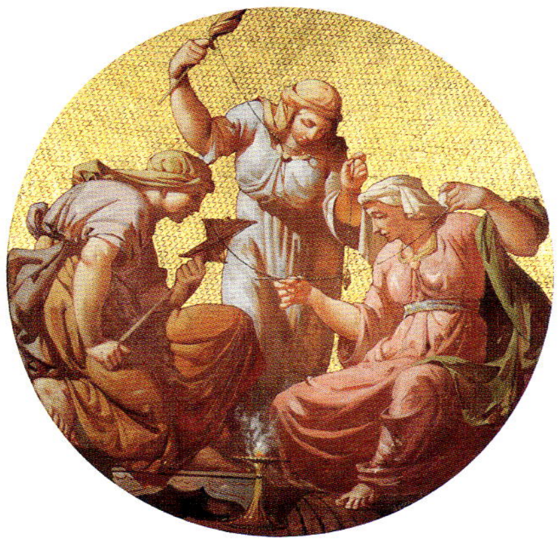

Sykes, Godfrey 1824–1866
The Three Fates 1855
tempera on paper on panel 82.3
VIS.1672

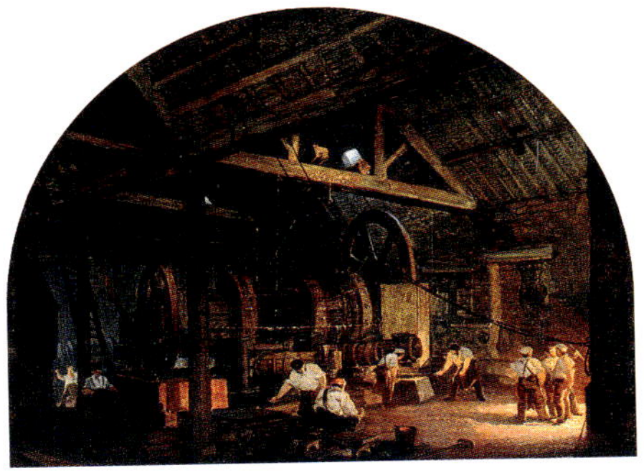

Sykes, Godfrey 1824–1866
The Tilt Forge c.1855
oil on canvas 36.2 x 48.8
K1923.5

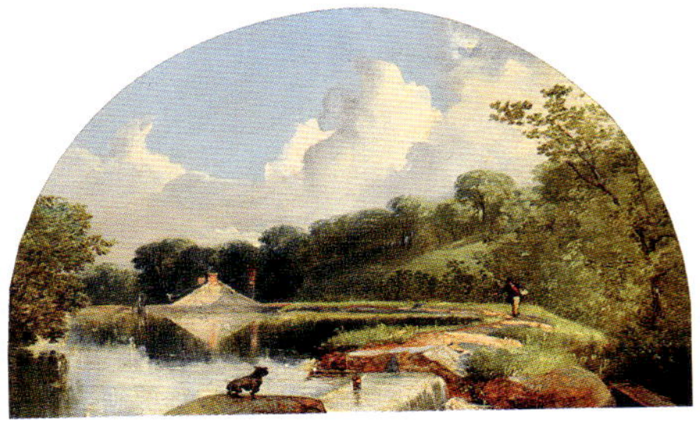

Sykes, Godfrey 1824–1866
Up the Porter 1856
oil on canvas 29 x 46.8
VIS.3243

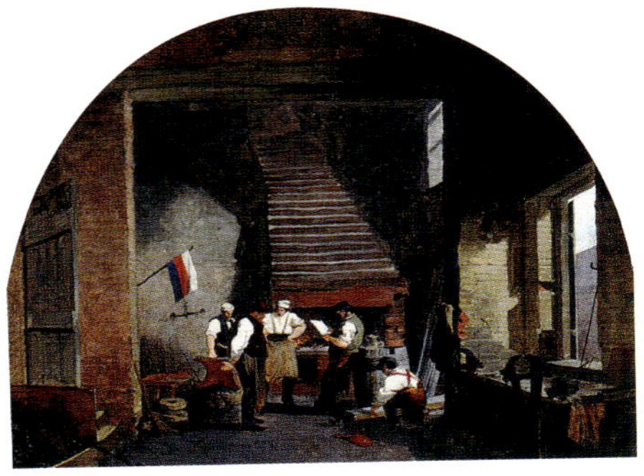

Sykes, Godfrey 1824–1866
A Smith's Shop c.1856
oil on canvas 36.2 x 48.8
K1923.4

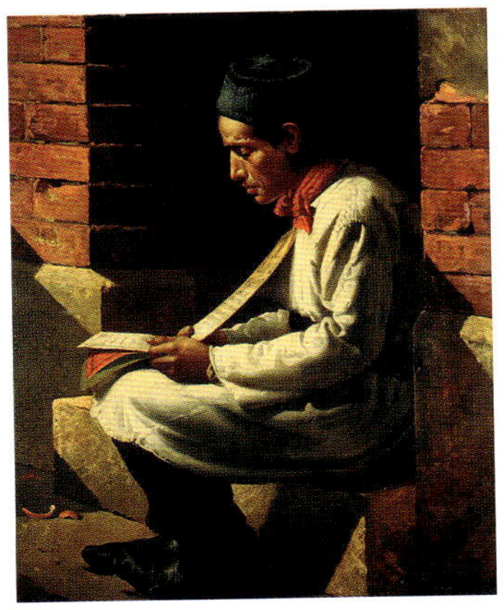

Sykes, Godfrey 1824–1866
Lascar 1857
oil on canvas 99.5 x 78.5
VIS.4209

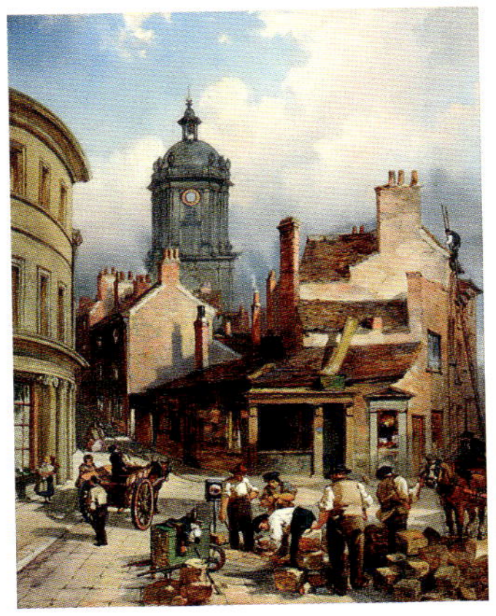

Sykes, Godfrey 1824–1866
Cheney Square with St Paul's, Sheffield 1858
oil on canvas 44.5 x 35.1
K1906.2

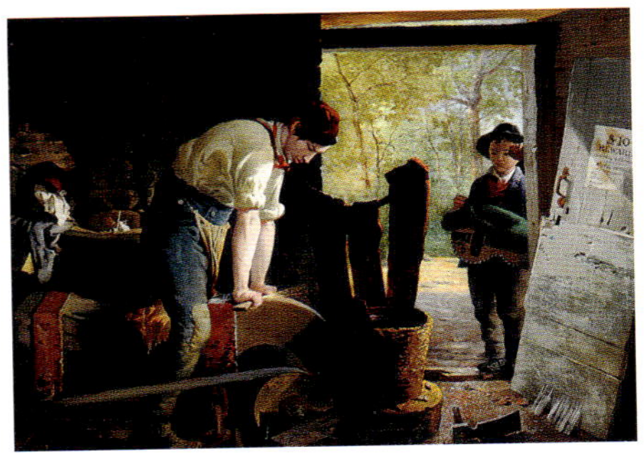

Sykes, Godfrey 1824–1866
The Two Grinders c.1858
oil on canvas 45.3 x 61.5
K1921.28

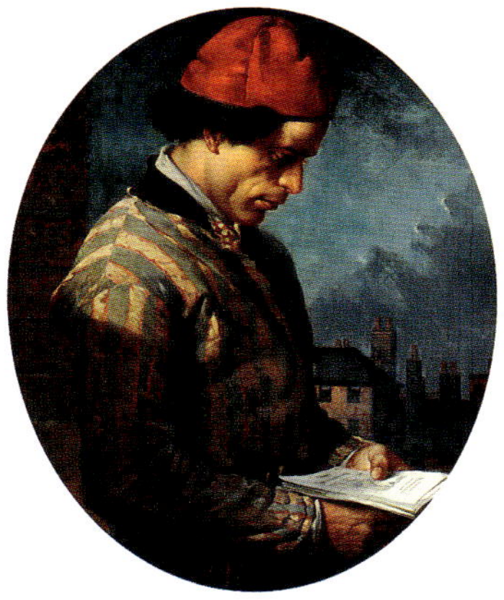

Sykes, Godfrey 1824–1866
Portrait of an Oriental 1859
oil on canvas 74.6 x 61.2
VIS.2715

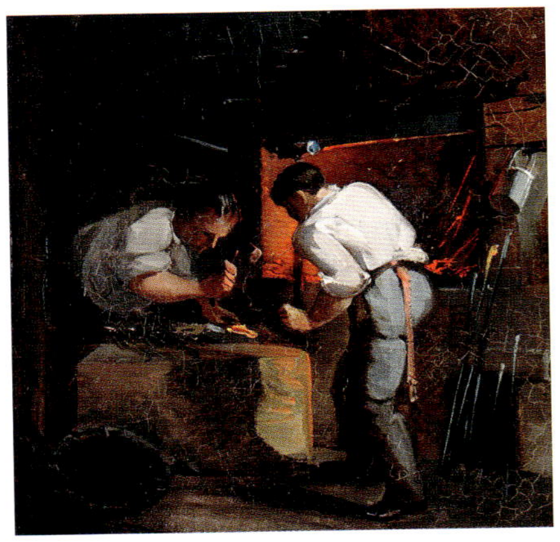

Sykes, Godfrey 1824–1866
A Blacksmith's Shop
oil on canvas 27.1 x 27
VIS.3092

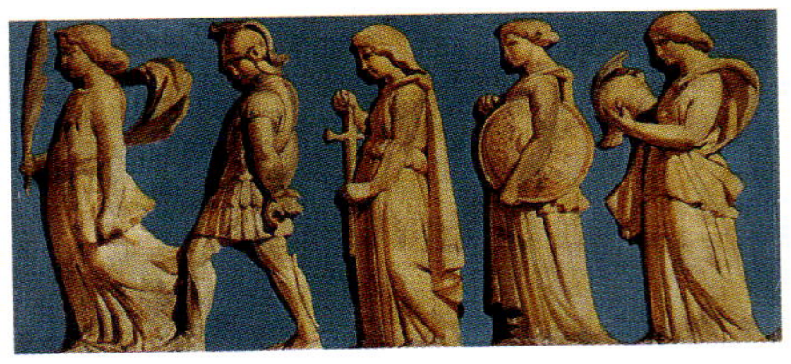

Sykes, Godfrey 1824–1866
Frieze with Figures (polyptych)
oil on paper on board 60 x 130.9
VIS.2385

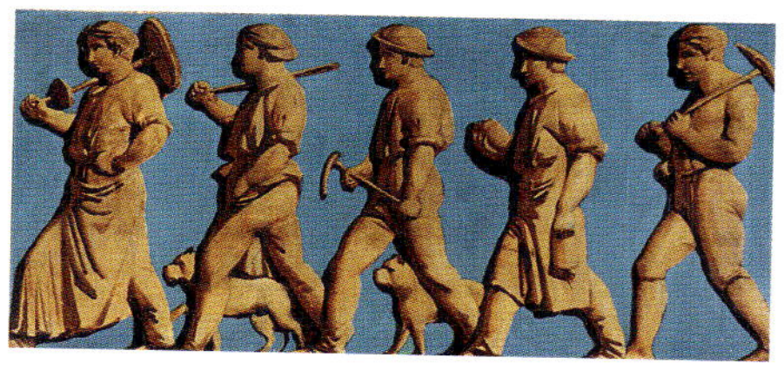

Sykes, Godfrey 1824–1866
Frieze with Figures (polyptych)
oil on paper on board 58.8 x 127
VIS.2386

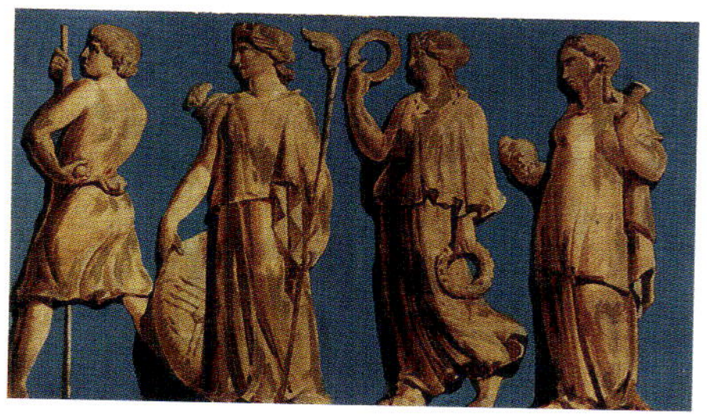

Sykes, Godfrey 1824–1866
Frieze with Figures (polyptych)
oil on paper on board 59.8 x 100.5
VIS.2387

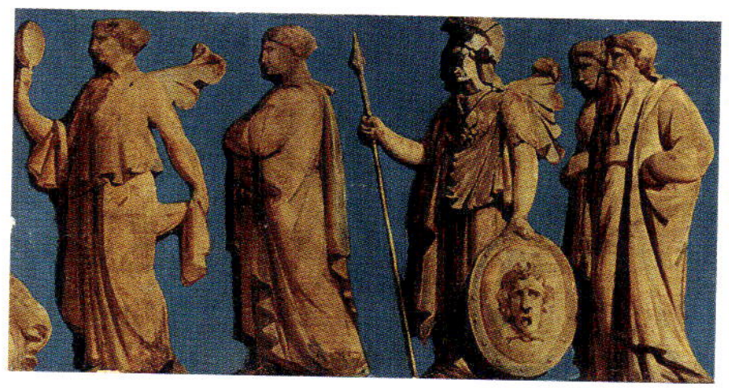

Sykes, Godfrey 1824–1866
Frieze with Figures (polyptych)
oil on paper on board 58.5 x 109.1
VIS.2388

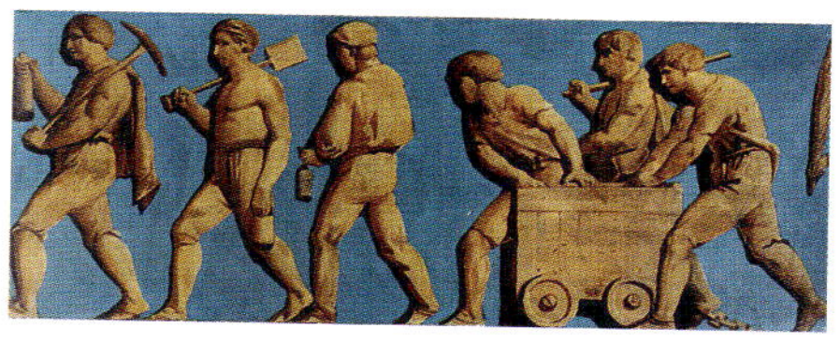

Sykes, Godfrey 1824–1866
Frieze with Figures (polyptych)
oil on paper on board 59.3 x 149.5
VIS.2390

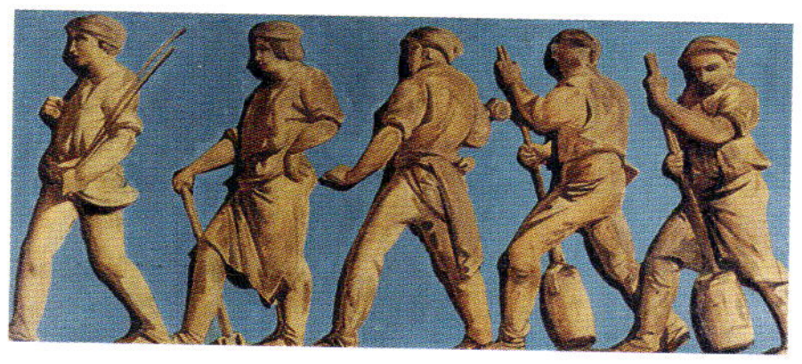

Sykes, Godfrey 1824–1866
Frieze with Figures (polyptych)
oil on paper on board 59 x 131.7
VIS.2391

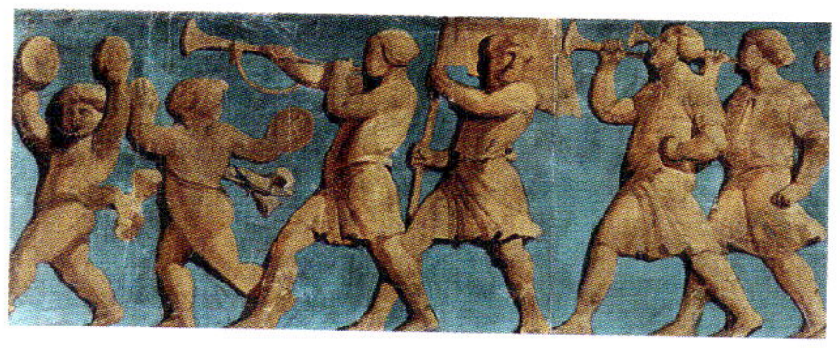

Sykes, Godfrey 1824–1866
Frieze with Figures (polyptych)
oil on paper on board 59 x 145.2
VIS.2392

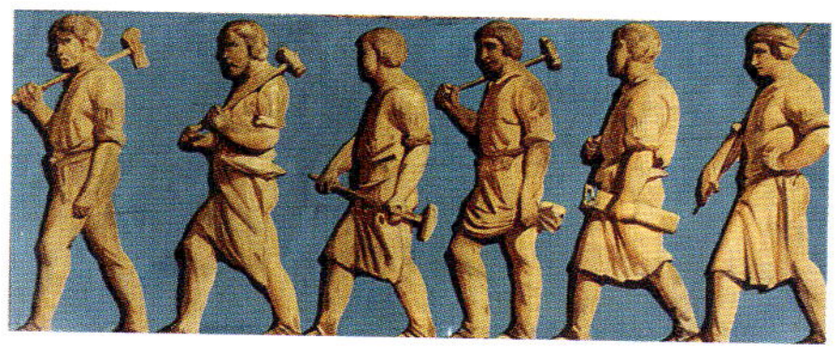

Sykes, Godfrey 1824–1866
Frieze with Figures (polyptych)
oil on paper on board 59.1 x 145.1
VIS.2393

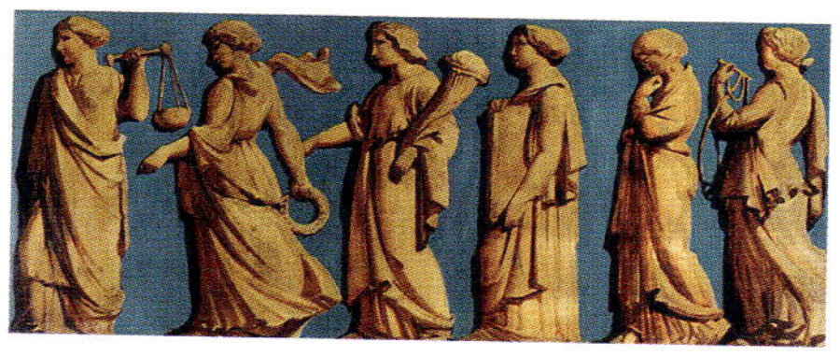

Sykes, Godfrey 1824–1866
Frieze with Figures (polyptych)
oil on paper on board 59.8 x 145.1
VIS.2394

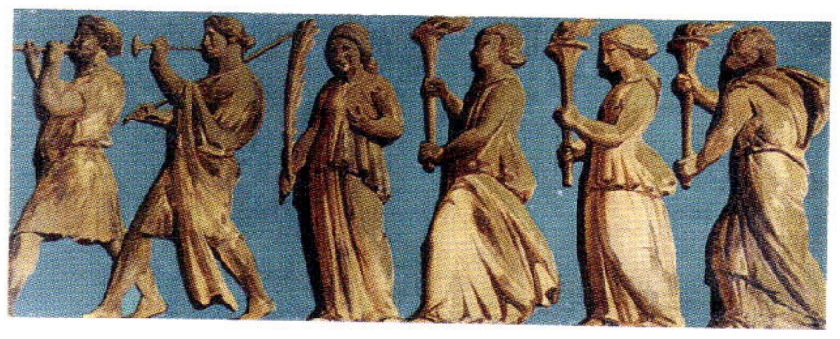

Sykes, Godfrey 1824–1866
Frieze with Figures (polyptych)
oil on paper on board 58.9 x 144.9
VIS.2395

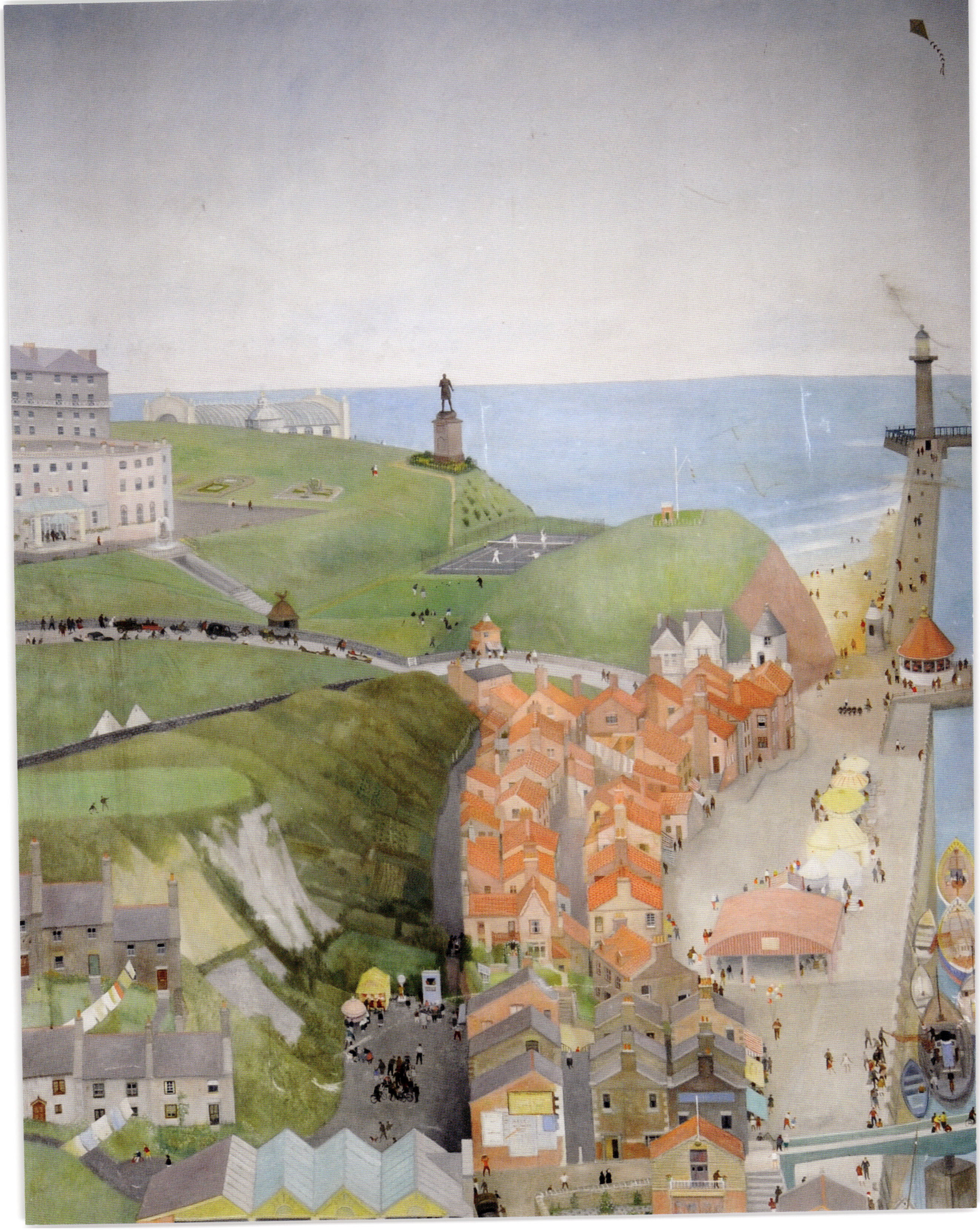

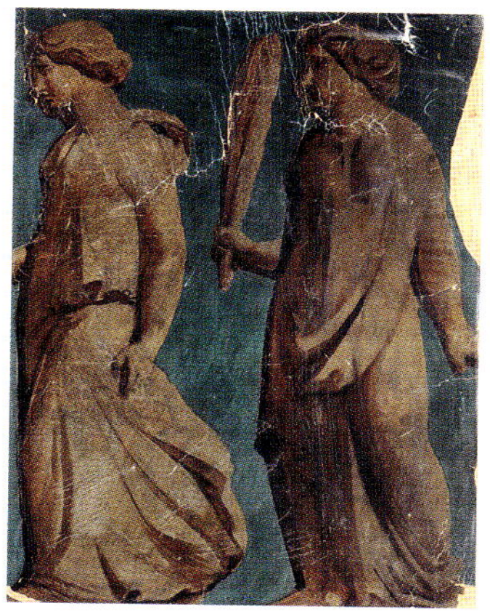

Sykes, Godfrey 1824–1866
Frieze with Figures (polyptych)
oil on paper on board 59 x 46
VIS.2397

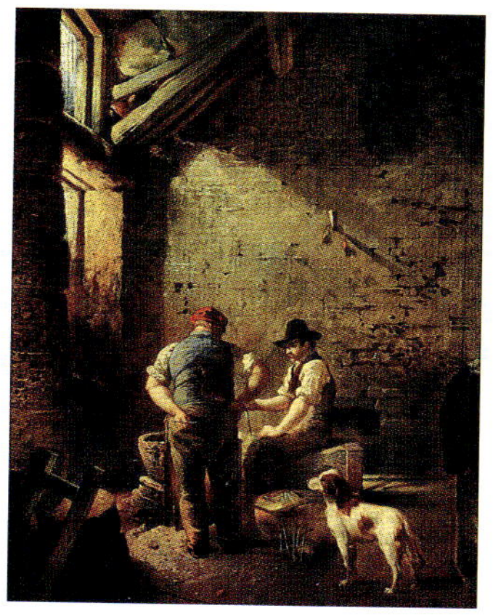

Sykes, Godfrey 1824–1866
Grinder's Hull
oil on canvas 44.5 x 34
K1923.3

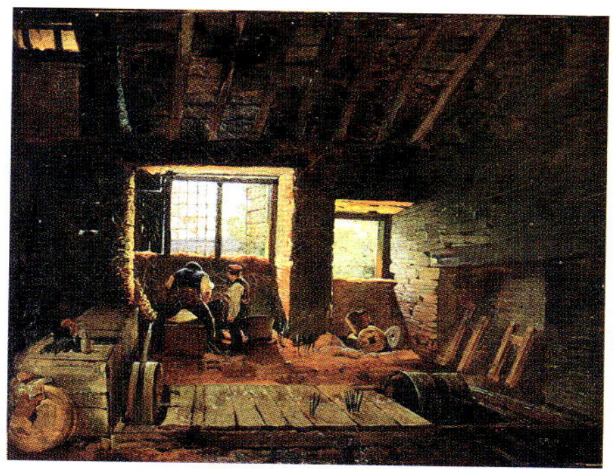

Sykes, Godfrey 1824–1866
Interior of a Sheffield Grinder's Hull
oil on canvas 34.9 x 44.8
VIS.2306

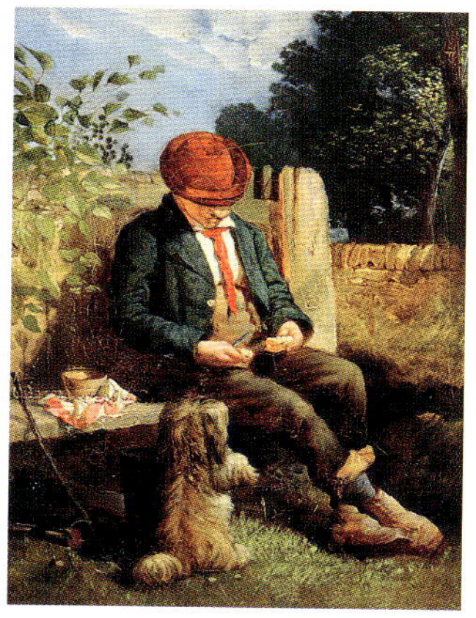

Sykes, Godfrey 1824–1866
Lunch Time
oil on canvas 39.7 x 29.7
VIS.2308

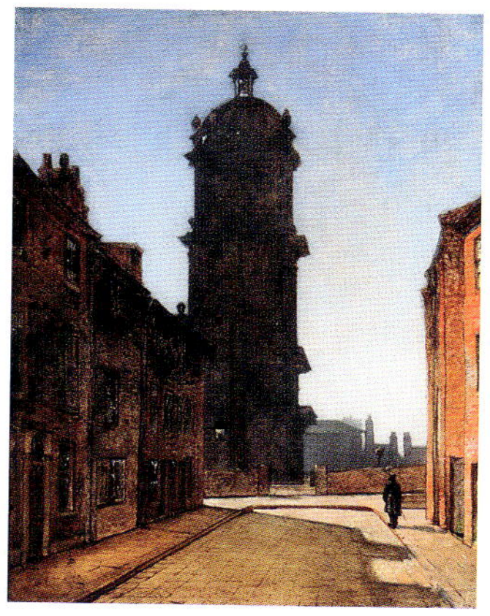

Sykes, Godfrey 1824–1866
St Paul's Church, Sheffield
oil on canvas 44.5 x 34.8
K1906.1

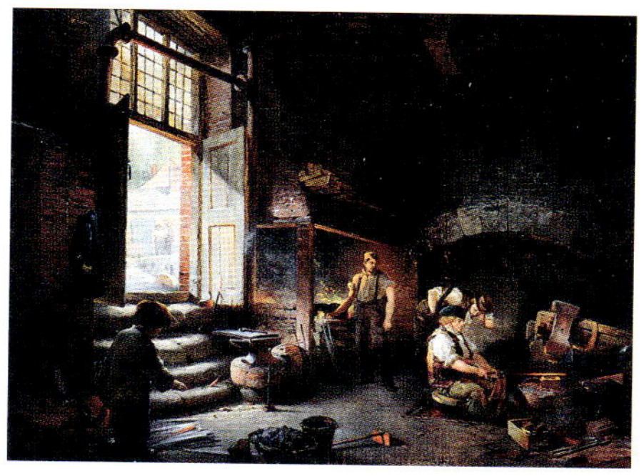

Sykes, Godfrey 1824–1866
Sheffield Scythe Tilters
oil on canvas 47.6 x 62.9
VIS.3244

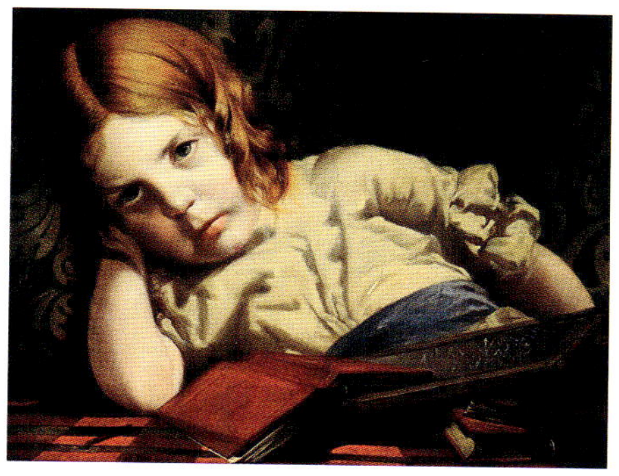

Sykes, Godfrey 1824–1866
The Pet in a Pet
oil on canvas 34.5 x 44.9
VIS.2307

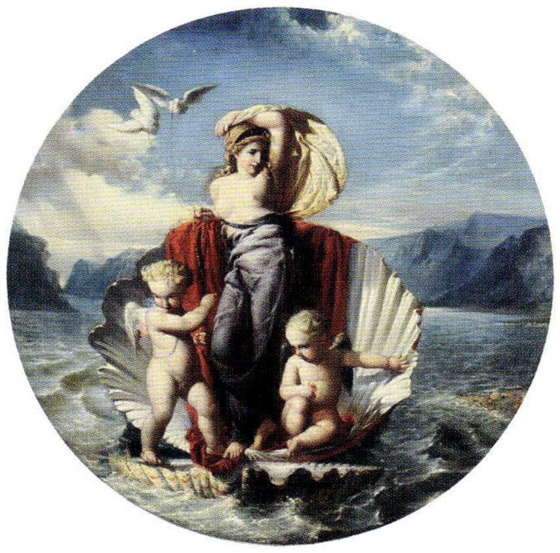

Sykes, Godfrey 1824–1866
Venus Arising from the Sea
oil on canvas 64.5
VIS.2020

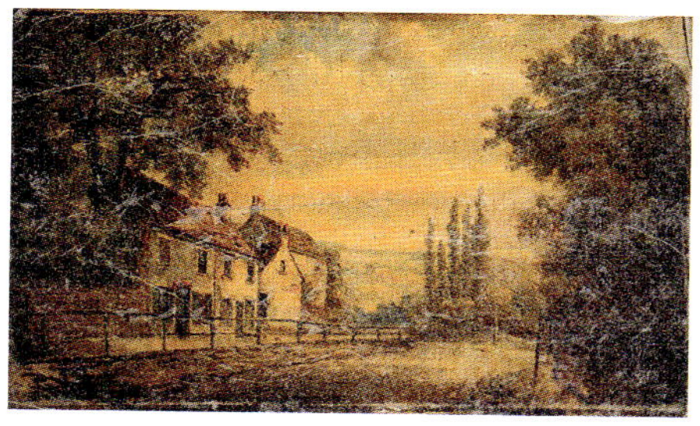

Sykes, Godfrey (attributed to) 1824–1866
Cottages in London Road, Highfields, Sheffield
oil on canvas 24.9 x 40
K1938.31

Facing page: Eurich, Richard Ernst, 1903–1992, *Whitby, to Represent Sheffield on Holiday* (one of a pair of murals to face east) (detail), 1960–1961, Sheffield Teaching Hospitals NHS Foundation Trust, (p. 270)

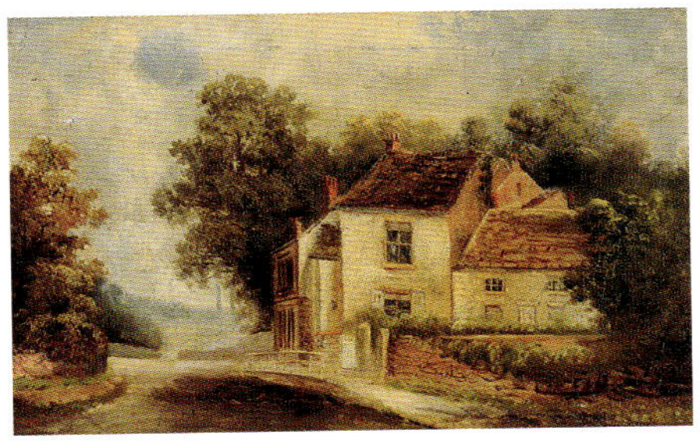

Sykes, Godfrey (attributed to) 1824–1866
Cottages in London Road, Highfields, Sheffield
oil on canvas 23.8 x 38.2
K1938.32

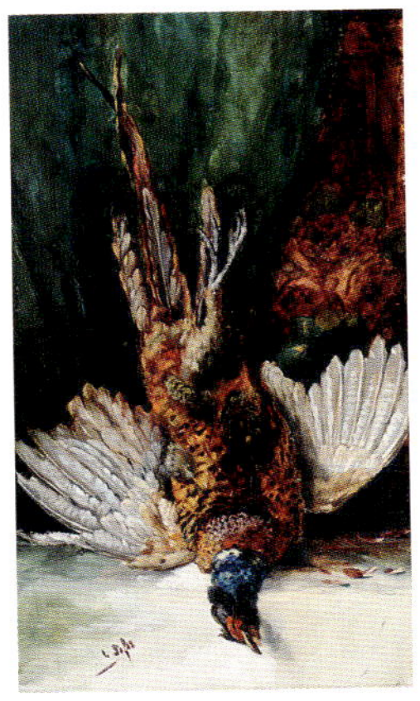

Sykes, Lilian active 1887–1890
Dead Pheasant
oil on canvas 99.3 x 57.4
VIS.1276

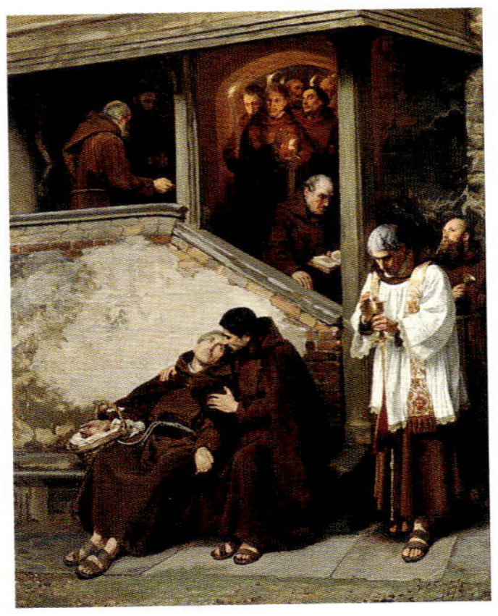

Symons, William Christian 1845–1911
In hora mortis 1875
oil on canvas 140.7 x 110.5
VIS.1587

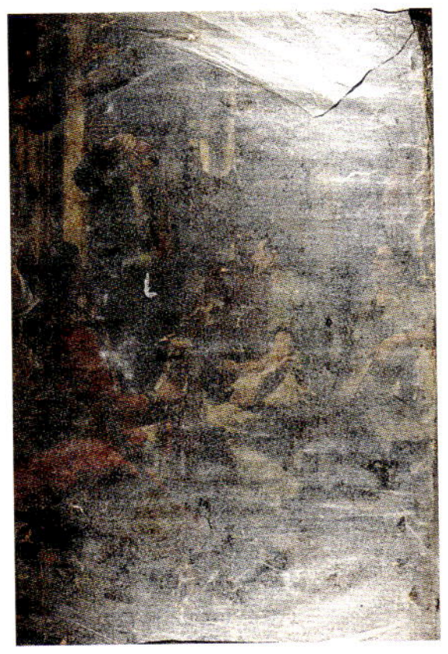

Symons, William Christian 1845–1911
Returned from the Wars
oil on canvas 188.5 x 137.8
VIS.2537

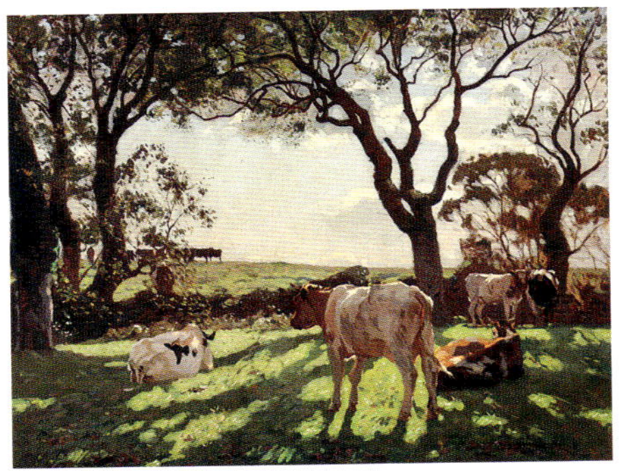

Talmage, Algernon Mayow 1871–1939
October Morning 1920
oil on canvas 110.2 x 140.8
VIS.969

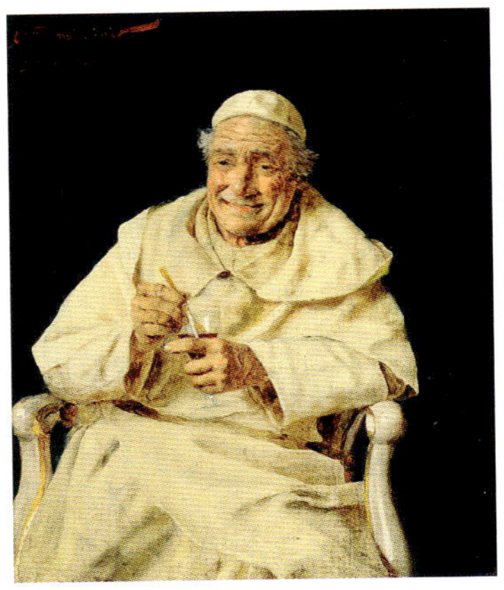

Tamburini, Arnaldo 1843–1908
The Monk 1870–1900
oil on canvas 27.5 x 23.3
VIS.2551

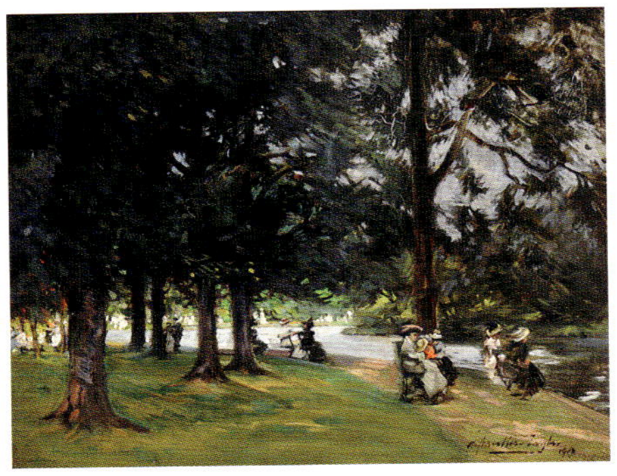

Tayler, Albert Chevallier 1862–1925
The Upper Thames 1913
oil on canvas 40.4 x 50.8
VIS.705

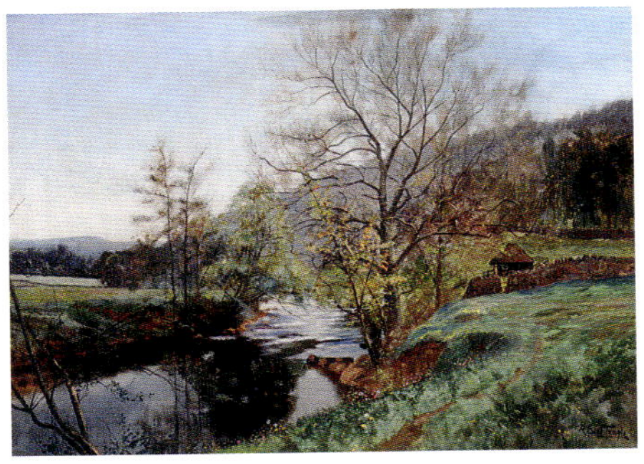

Temple, Robert Scott b.c.1853
Landscape with a River 1894–1905
oil on canvas 53.8 x 73.9
VIS.1460

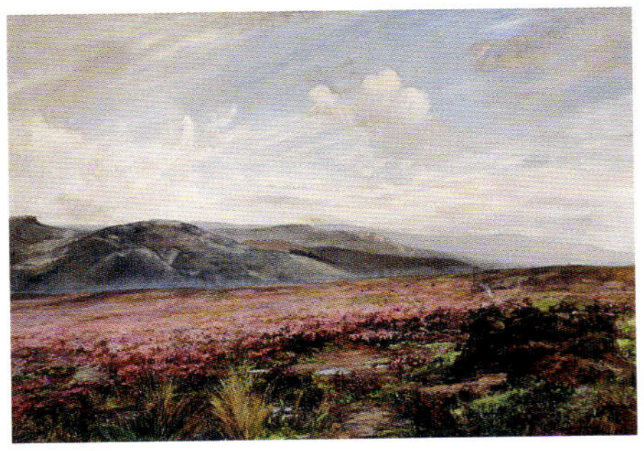

Temple, Robert Scott b.c.1853
The Old Woman of Moscar Moor, Derbyshire
1895
oil on canvas 74.3 x 105.4
VIS.1465

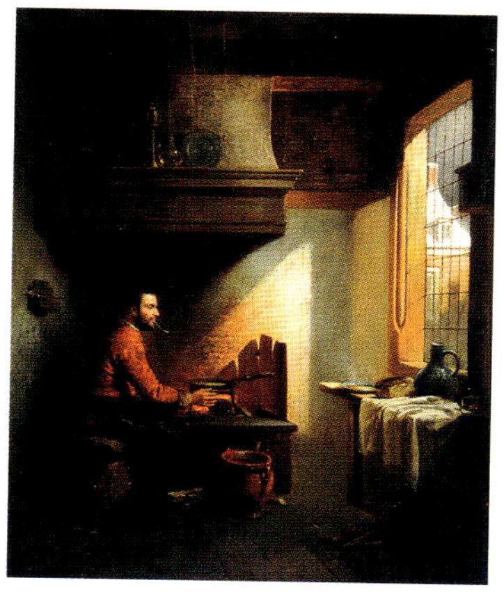

Ten Kate, Herman Frederik Carel
1822–1891
Interior 1855–1865
oil on panel 47 x 38.4
VIS.681

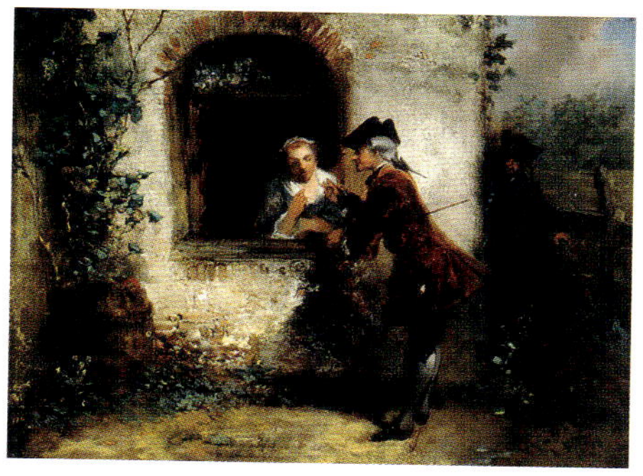

Ten Kate, Herman Frederik Carel
1822–1891
A Back Door Visitor 1856
oil on panel 15.2 x 20.8
VIS.1003

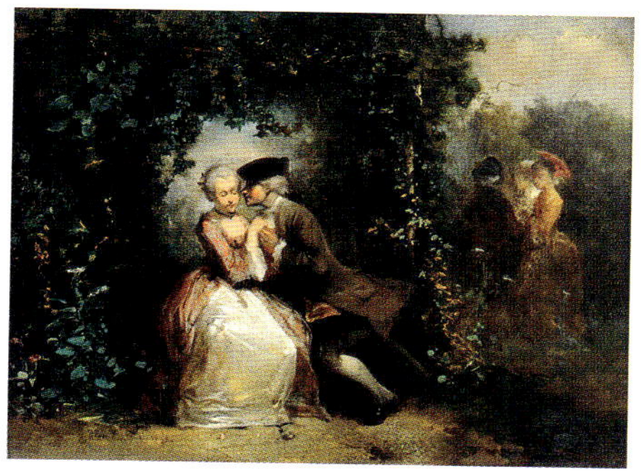

Ten Kate, Herman Frederik Carel
1822–1891
Lovers 1856
oil on panel 15.4 x 20.8
VIS.1055

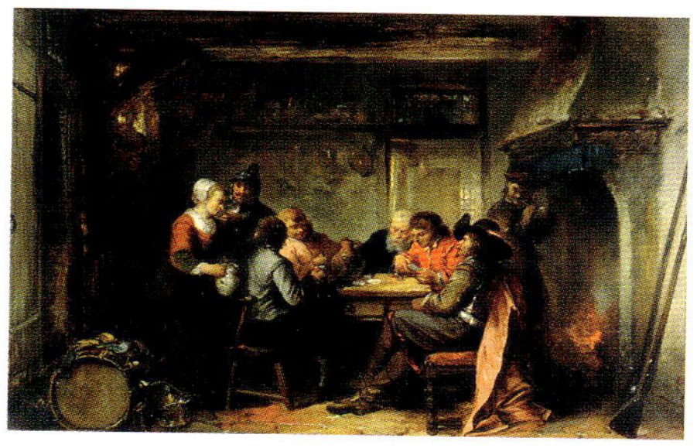

Ten Kate, Herman Frederik Carel
1822–1891
Card Players 1878
oil on panel 28 x 43.5
VIS.1409

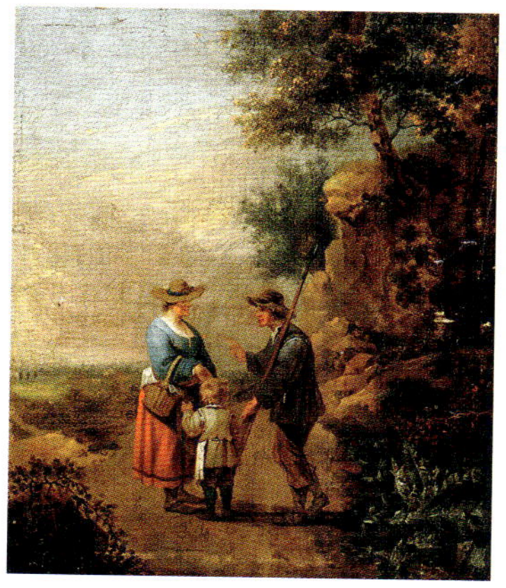

Teniers, David I 1582–1649
Landscape with Figures
oil on canvas 36.9 x 31.2
VIS.2382

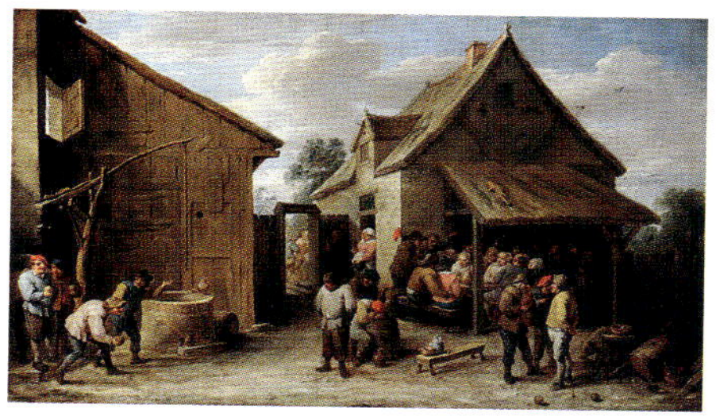

Teniers, David II 1610–1690
The Yard of an Inn 1650–1660
oil on canvas 52.8 x 85
VIS.5129

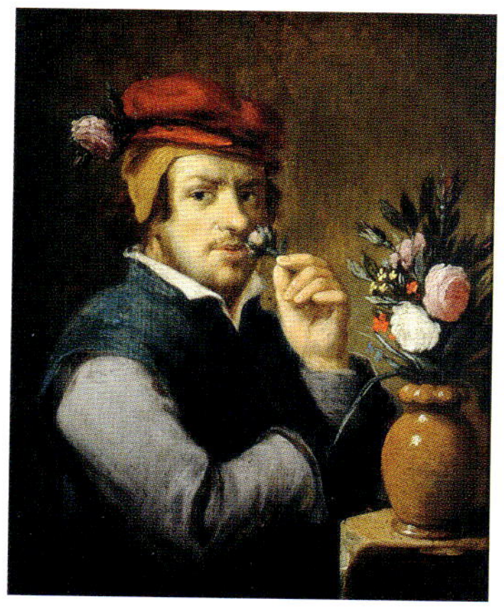

Teniers, David II (attributed to) 1610–1690
The Sense of Smell 1630–1640
oil on panel 30 x 24.1
VIS.1313

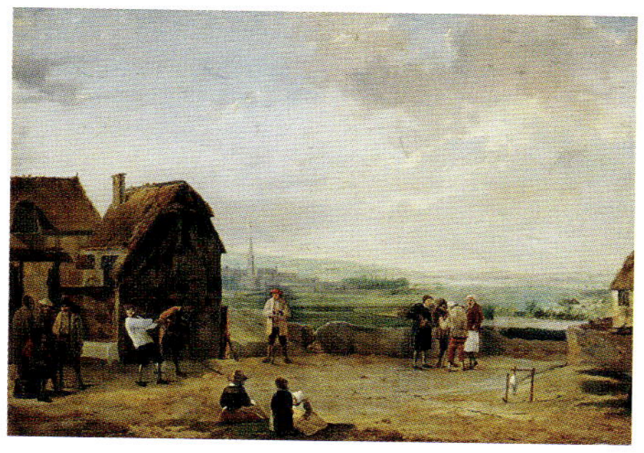

Teniers, David II (school of) 1610–1690
Shuttlecock
oil on panel 35.8 x 47.5
VIS.261

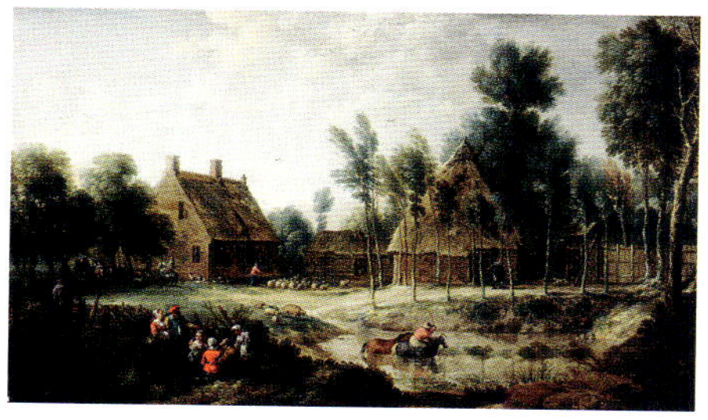

Teniers, David II 1610–1690 & **Peeters, Gillis**
1612–1653
A Scene in a Flemish Village 1645–1653
oil on copper 44.9 x 74
VIS.5131

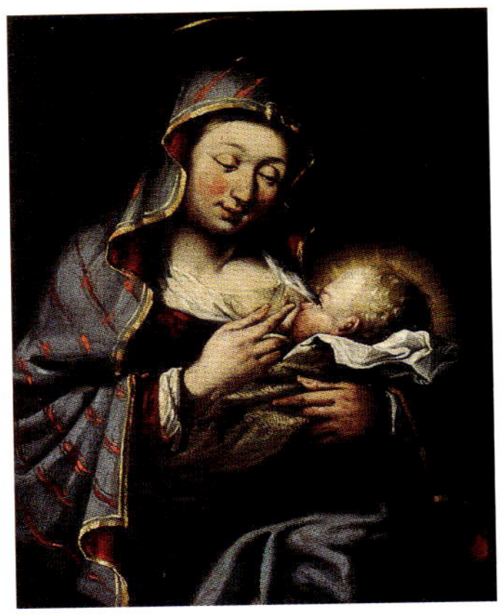

Teurdyghe, Carolus Ignatius (attributed to)
active c.1700
Madonna and Child 1702
oil on canvas 43.8 x 35.4
VIS.1878

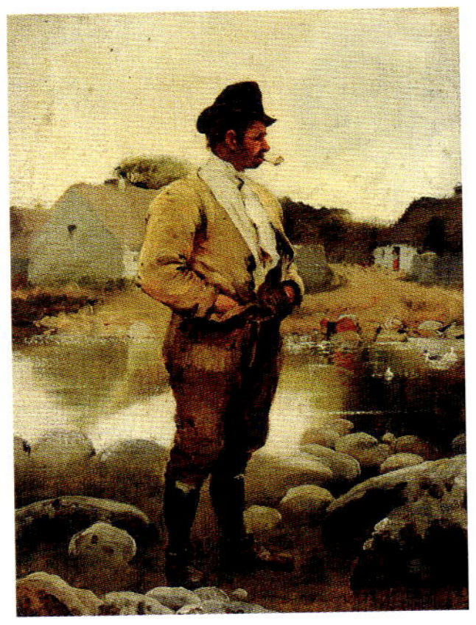

Thaddeus, Henry Jones 1860–1929
An Irish Peasant 1888
oil on canvas 29.3 x 21.2
VIS.156

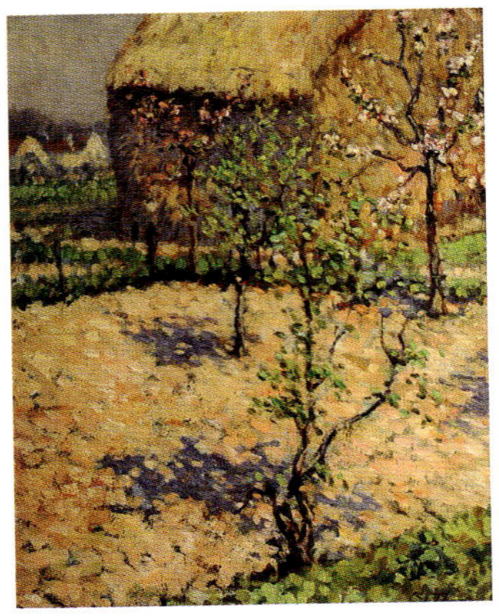

Tharp, Charles Julian 1878–1951
Blossom Time 1943
oil on canvas 48.7 x 37.5
VIS.1029

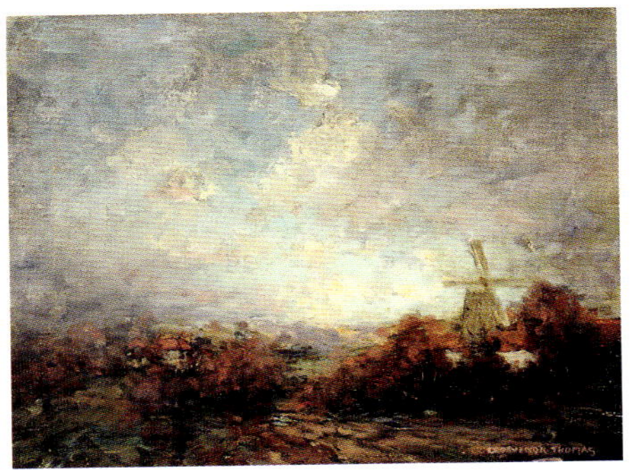

Thomas, Grosvenor 1856–1923
Landscape with a Windmill
oil on canvas 34.4 x 44.3
VIS.696

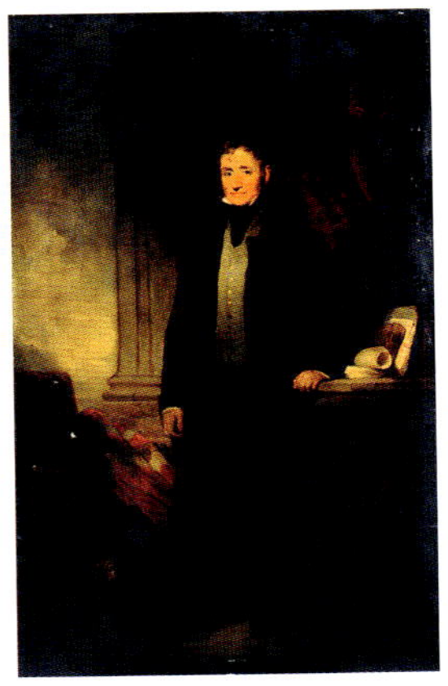

Thompson, Hugh 1810–1866
James Archibald Stuart-Wortley-Mackenzie (1776–1845), 1st Lord Wharncliffe
oil on canvas 246.9 x 152.4
VIS.LI.833 (P)

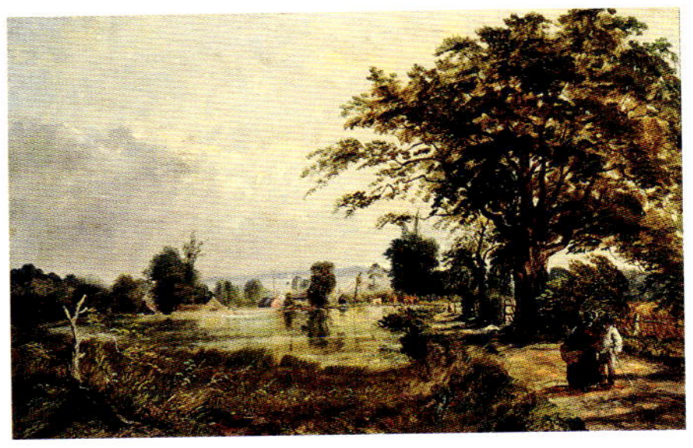

Thomson, Christopher 1799–1871
Little London Dam, Heeley, Sheffield 1857
oil on canvas 33.8 x 51.8
K1908.64

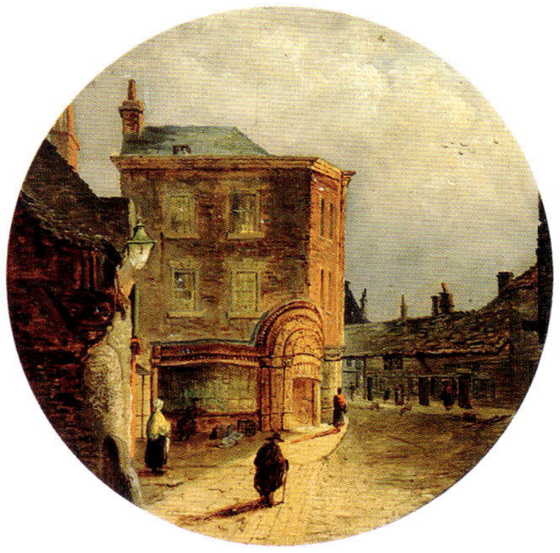

Thomson, Christopher 1799–1871
Sheffield Iris Office, Hartshead 1859
oil on canvas 18.8
K1934.28

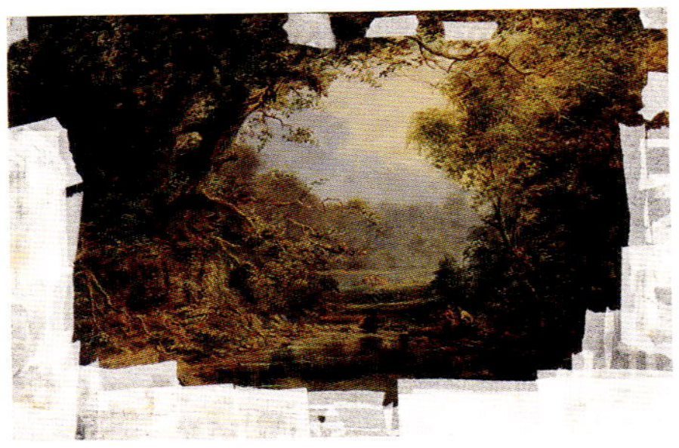

Thomson, Christopher 1799–1871
Rivelin Valley, near Black Brook, Sheffield
c.1860
oil on canvas 50.6 x 76.6
K1912.1

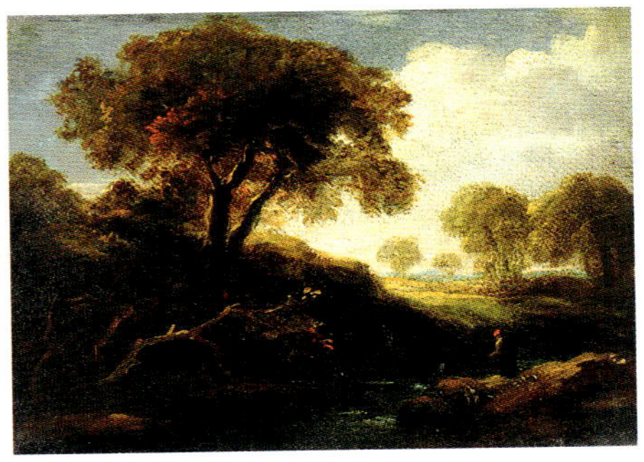

Thomson, John 1778–1840
Landscape
oil on panel 24 x 34.2
VIS.686

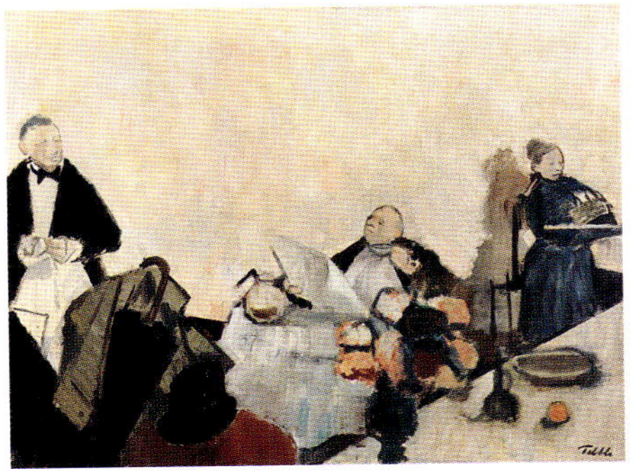

Tibble, Geoffrey Arthur 1909–1952
Chez Martin 1948
oil on canvas 85.3 x 110.8
VIS.3746

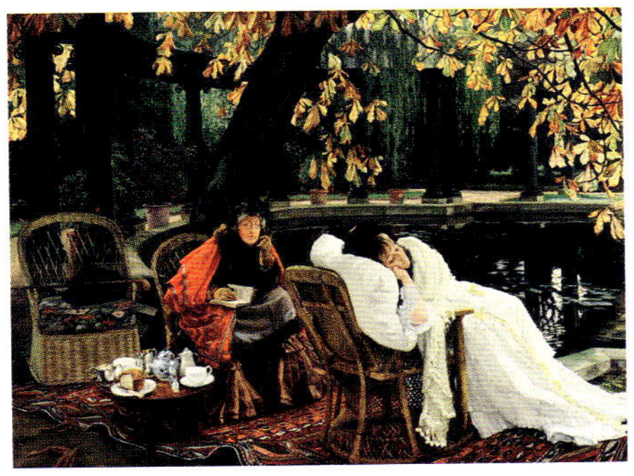

Tissot, James 1836–1902
The Convalescent c.1876
oil on canvas 75.4 x 98.4
VIS.2213

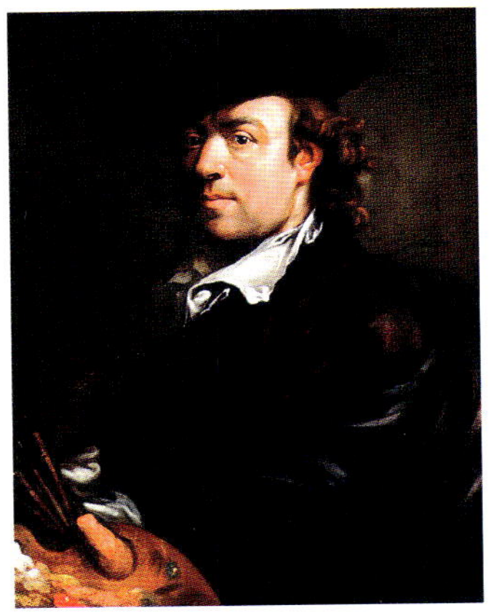

Tol, Dominicus van (attributed to)
c.1635–1676
Self Portrait 1660–1670
oil on canvas 72.4 x 55
VIS.287

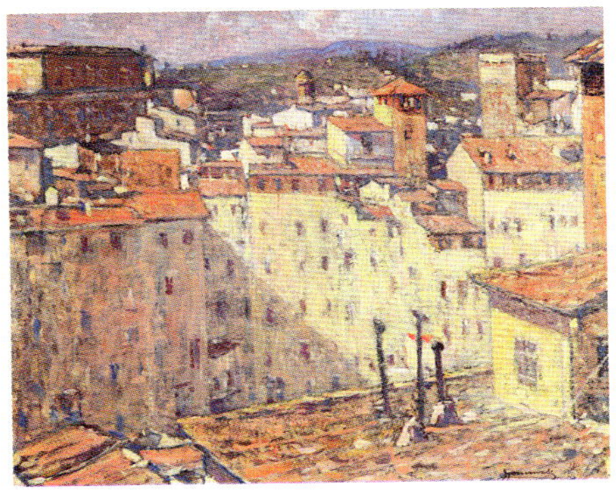

Tommasi, Adolfo 1851–1933
View of an Italian Town
oil on millboard 35.8 x 43.1
VIS.2895

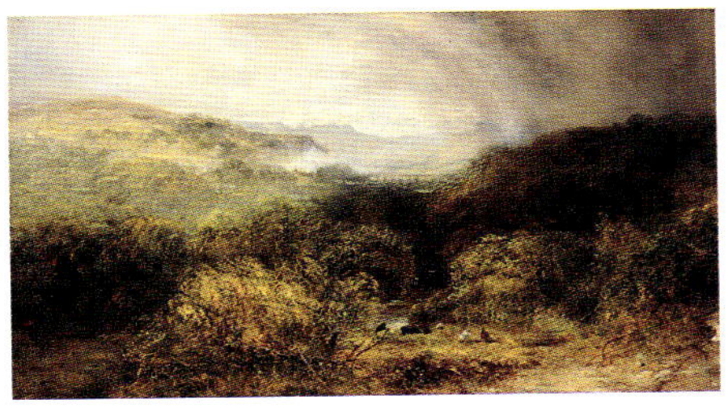

Tonge, Robert 1823–1856
Vale of Llangollen, Wales 1851
oil on canvas 34.6 x 59.5
VIS.1622

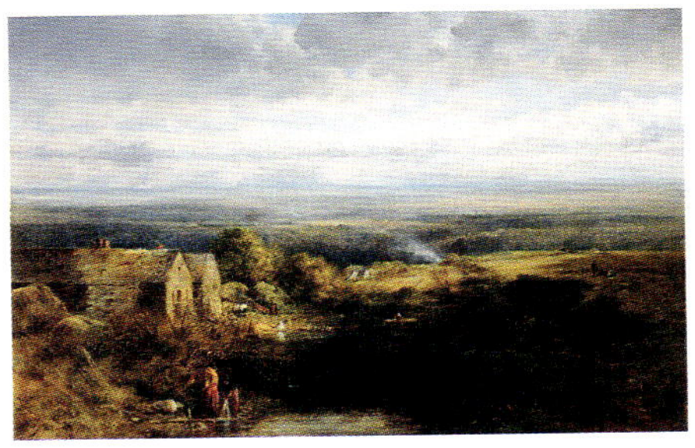

Tonge, Robert 1823–1856
The Valley of the Dee, Wales 1852
oil on canvas 39.9 x 60.9
VIS.1512

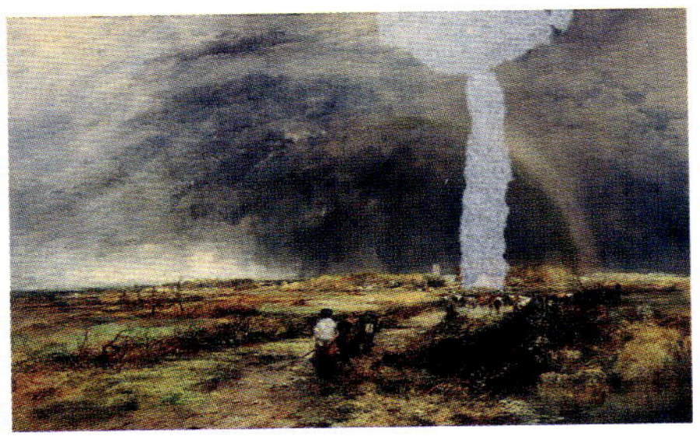

Tonge, Robert 1823–1856
The Rainbow 1854
oil on board 38.2 x 61.8
VIS.1401

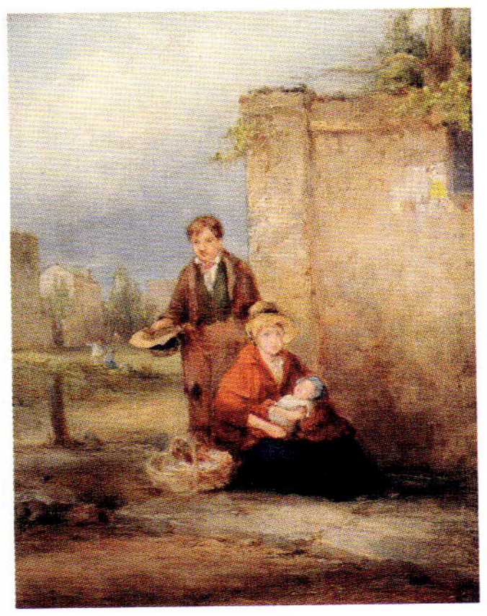

Topham, Francis Williams 1808–1877
The Mendicants 1833
oil on canvas 24 x 19
VIS.1057

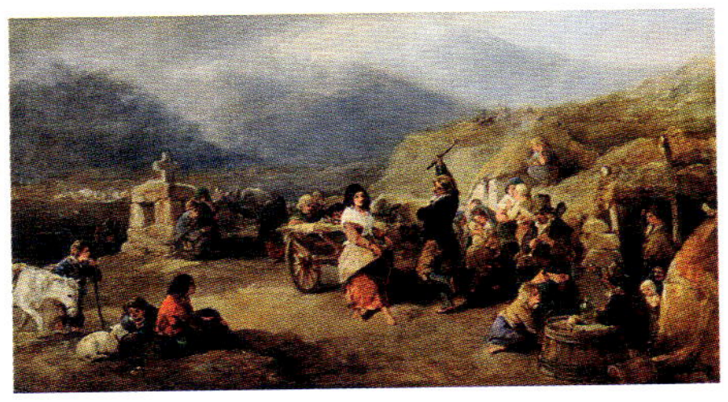

Topham, Francis Williams 1808–1877
Saturday Evening in Connemara, Ireland
oil on canvas 47.6 x 87.1
VIS.1556

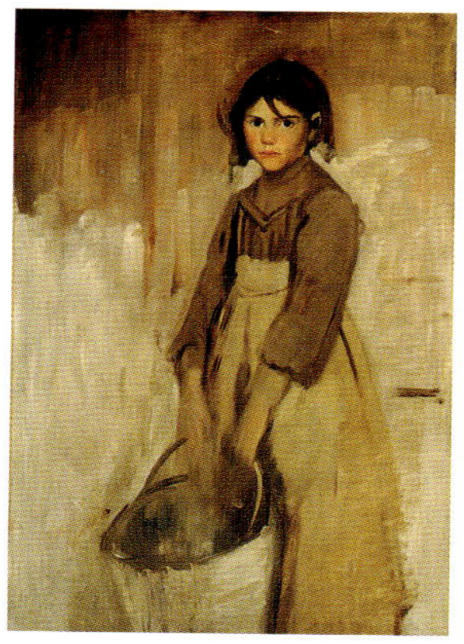

Torrance, James 1859–1916
The Pig Feeder's Daughter
oil on canvas 99 x 68.9
VIS.1914

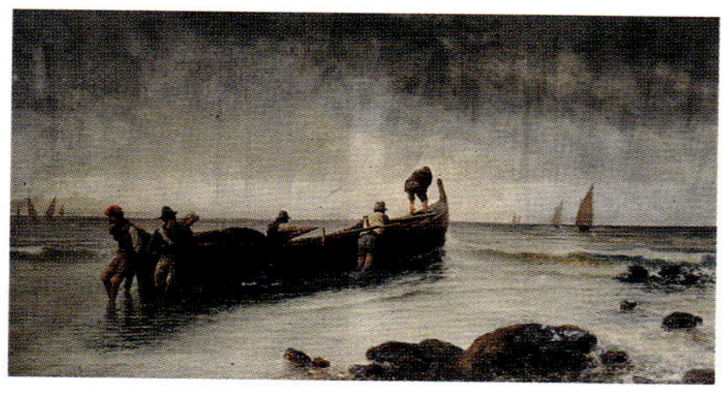

Torre, Raffaelo 1844–1927
A Gentle Breeze
oil on canvas 121.9 x 223.9
VIS.1455

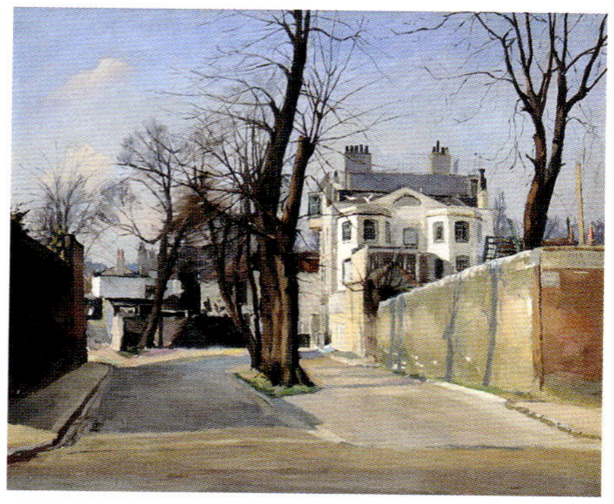

Towner, Donald Chisholm 1903–1985
Admiral's House, Hampstead, London 1932
oil on canvas 63 x 75.2
VIS.178

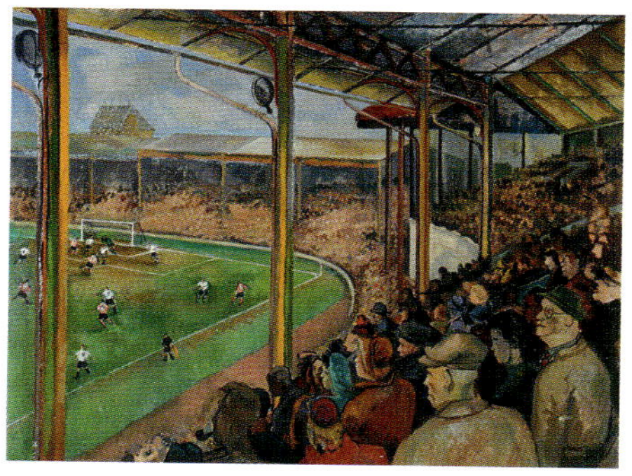

Townley, James Morrison 1917–1995
Bramall Lane, Sheffield 1953
acrylic on canvas 71 x 91.5
2008.389

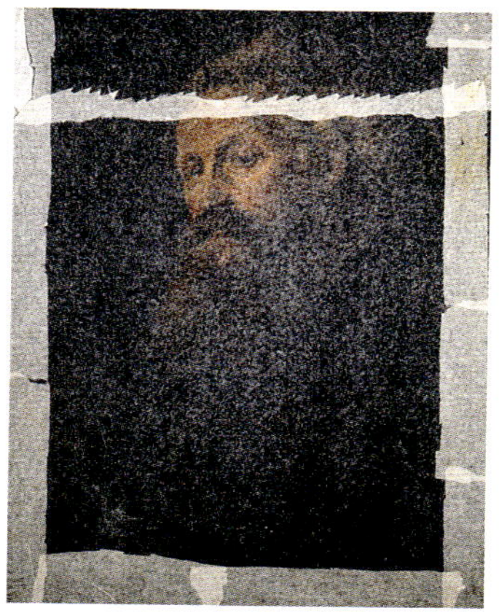

Townroe, Reuben 1835–1911
Robert Glassby
oil on canvas 62.5 x 48.5
K1929.19

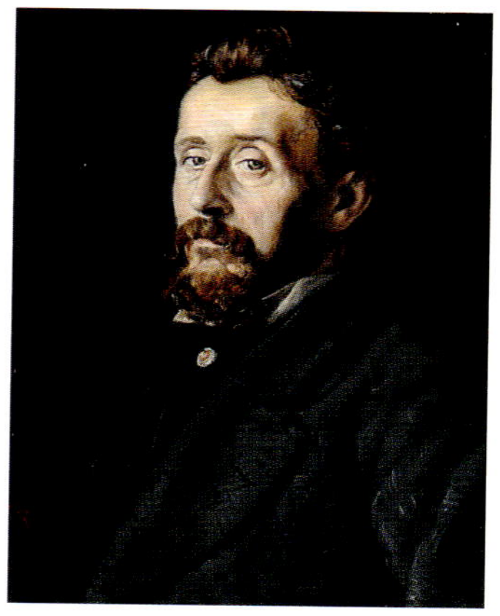

Townroe, Reuben 1835–1911
Self Portrait
oil on canvas 51.2 x 39.7
VIS.2310

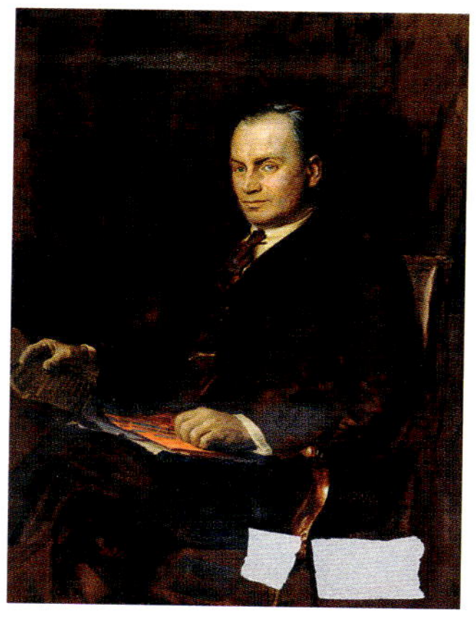

Townsend, Ernest 1885–1944
Ashley Ward 1928
oil on canvas 122.5 x 92
SH412

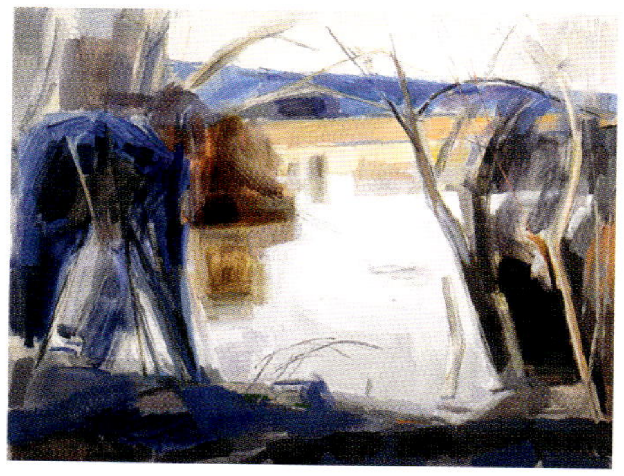

Townsend, William 1909–1973
Landscape with a Pond
oil on canvas 70.3 x 90.7
VIS.4516

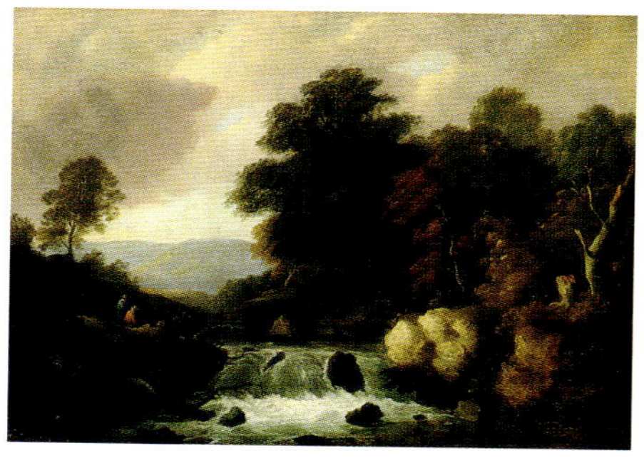

Traies, William 1789–1872
The Waterfall
oil on canvas 39.4 x 55.5
VIS.563

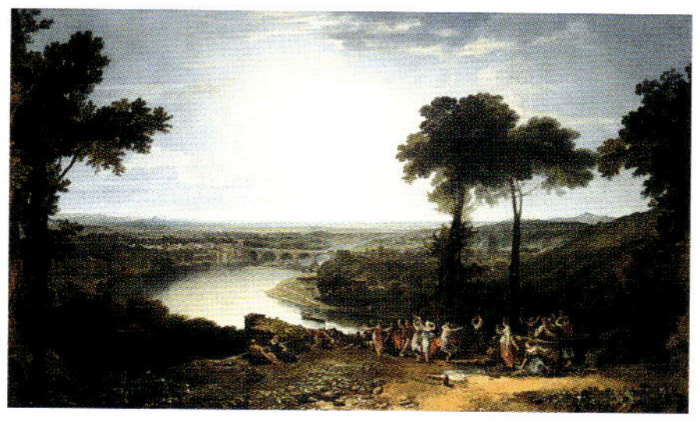

Turner, Joseph Mallord William 1775–1851
The Festival of the Opening of the Vintage at Mâcon, France c.1803
oil on canvas 182.5 x 274.4
VIS.3129

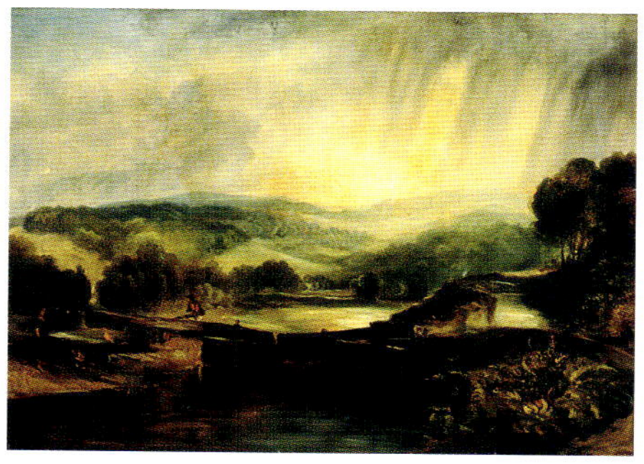

Turner, Joseph Mallord William (after) 1775–1851
A View on the Colne, Moor Park, Hertfordshire
oil on canvas 66 x 91.5
VIS.1630

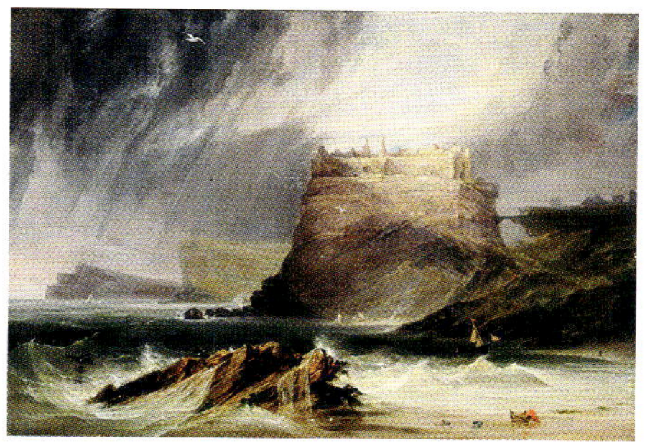

Turner, Joseph Mallord William (after) 1775–1851
Dunbar Castle, Scotland
oil on canvas 59.7 x 84.2
VIS.1417

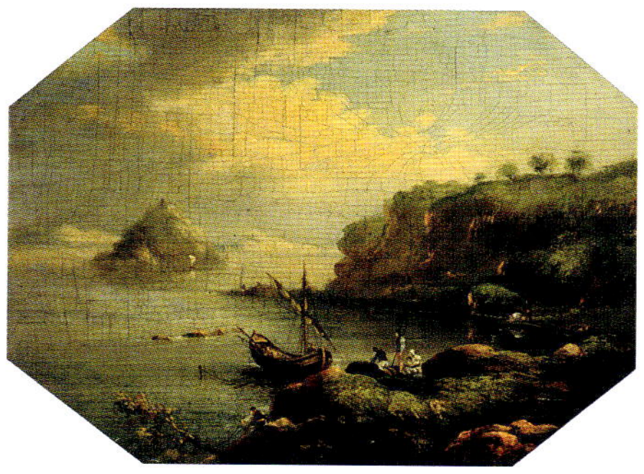

Turner, Joseph Mallord William (attributed to) 1775–1851
Seascape
oil on panel 21.6 x 28.4
VIS.1050

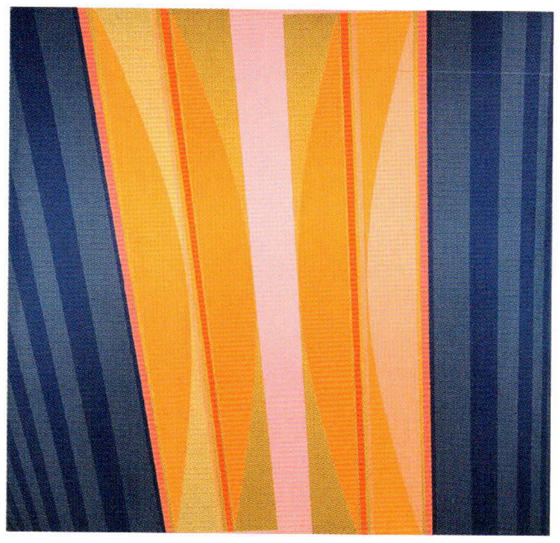

Tyzack, Michael 1933–2007
Wedge 1963
acrylic on board 160 x 159.5
VIS.3285

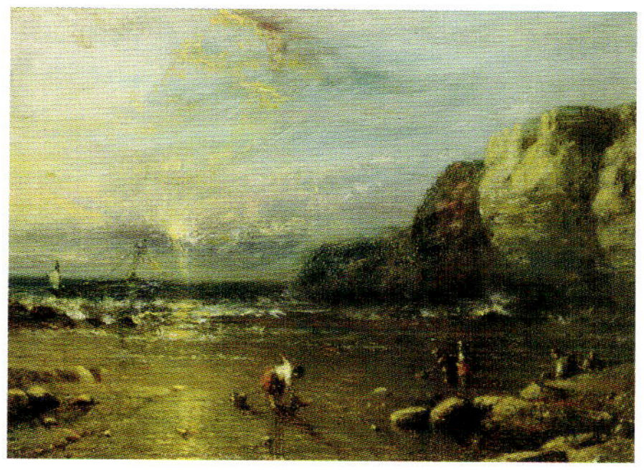

Underhill, Frederick Charles c.1832–1896
A Cornish Coast View
oil on board 22 x 29.8
VIS.1023

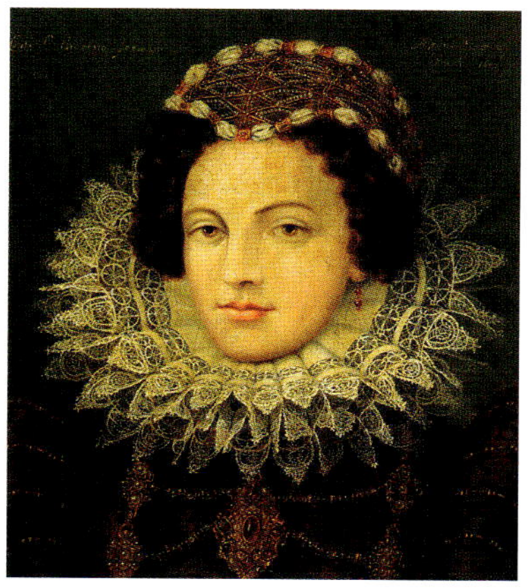

unknown artist
Lady Catherine Jermyn (b.1579) 1601
oil on panel 31.3 x 28
VIS.51

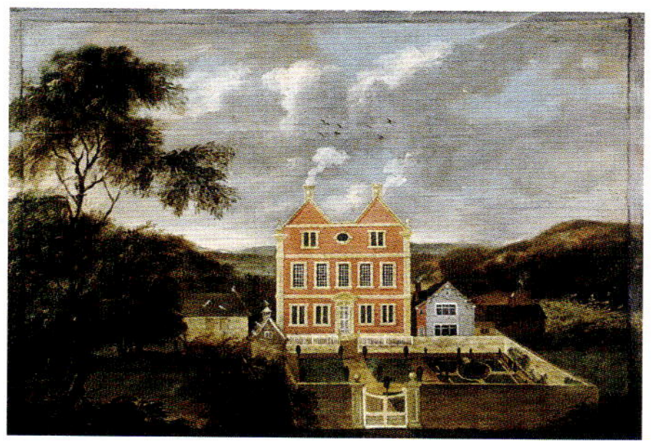

unknown artist
Norwood Hall, Sheffield 1775–1900
oil on panel 87.9 x 126.8
VIS.2129

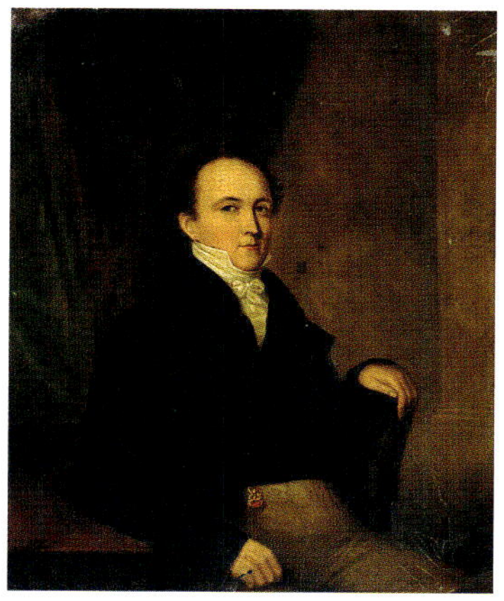

unknown artist
Frederick Woolhouse c.1820
oil on metal 29.5 x 24.5
1969.6

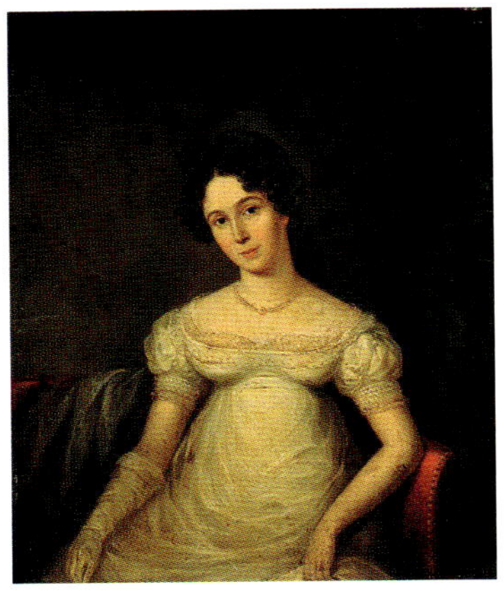

unknown artist
Anne Woolhouse c.1820
oil on metal 29.5 x 24.3
1969.7

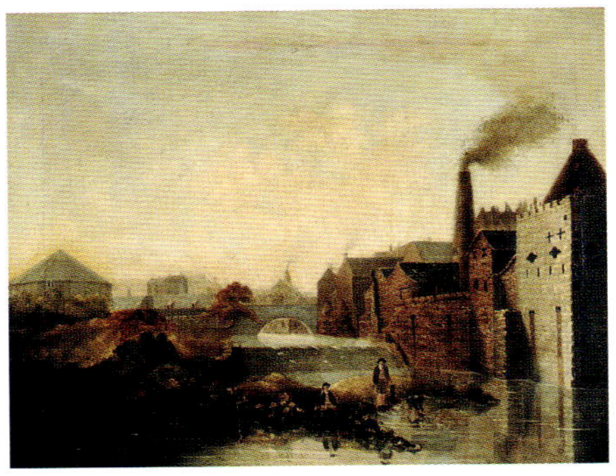

unknown artist
River Sheaf and Shrewsbury Hospital, Sheffield c.1825
oil on canvas 50.5 x 64
K1930.30

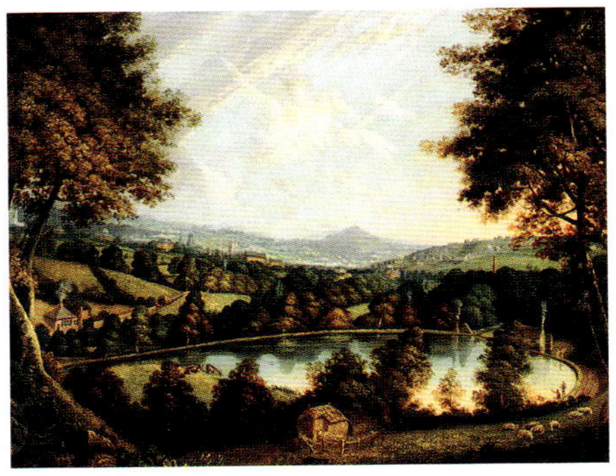

unknown artist
Sheffield from Heeley c.1830
oil on panel 48.3 x 62.2
K1938.42

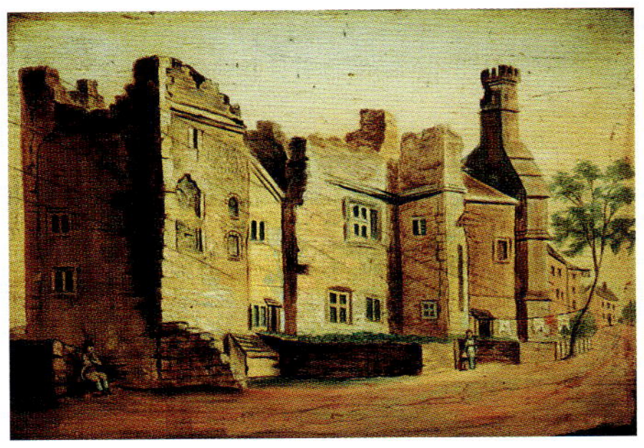

unknown artist
Sheffield Manor c.1830
oil on board 16.8 x 24.5
K1934.21

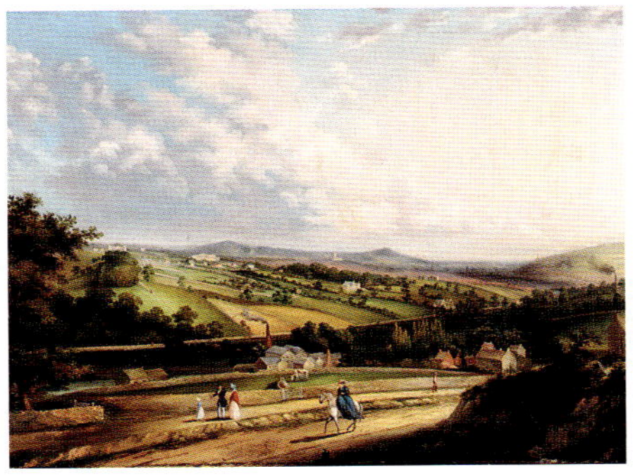

unknown artist
View of Sheffield from Sharrow Moor c.1838
oil on canvas 67.5 x 87.5
1981.707

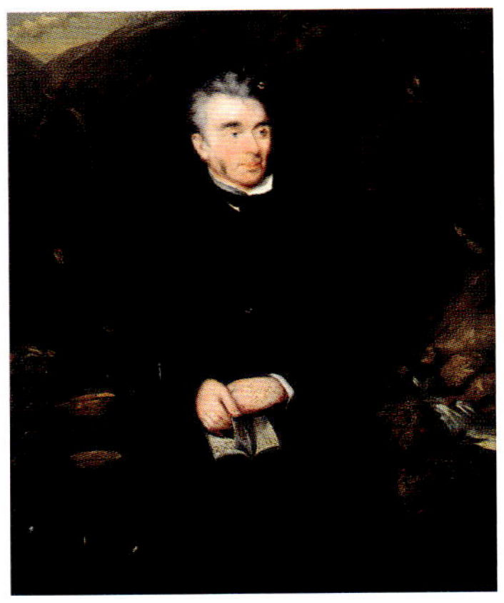

unknown artist
Ebenezer Elliott (1781–1849) 1839
oil on canvas 127.2 x 102.8
VIS.LI.815 (P)

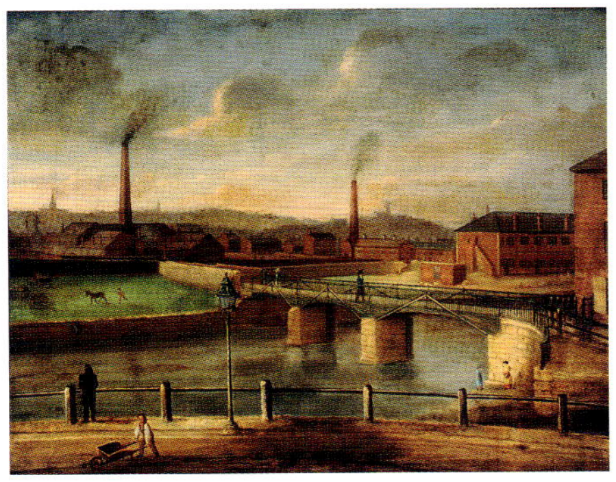

unknown artist
Bridge and White Rails at Bridgehouses, Sheffield c.1840
oil on canvas 71 x 88.3
K1909.56

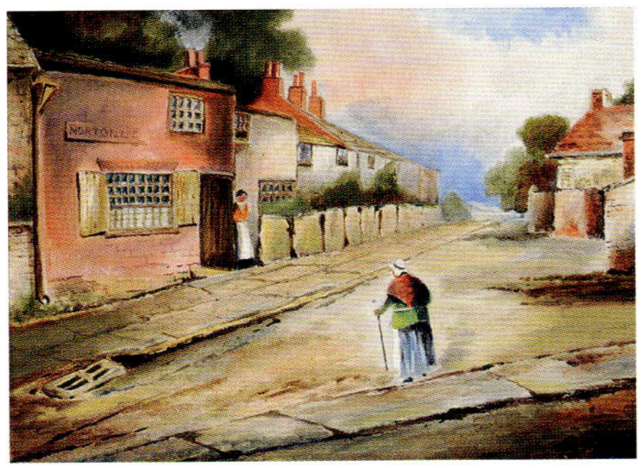

unknown artist
Cottage at Norton Lees, Sheffield 1850–1890
oil on panel 20.9 x 28.5
1981.705

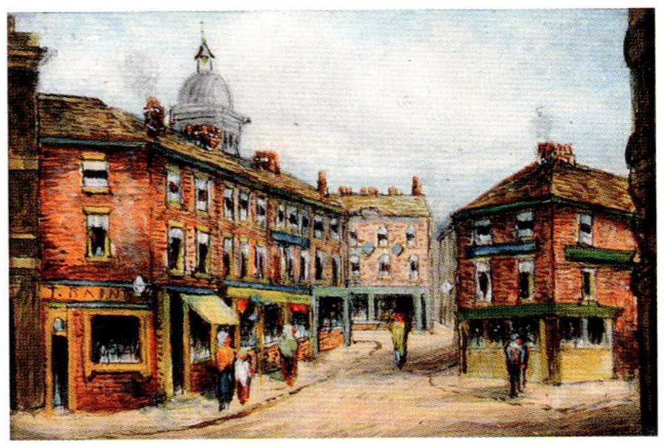

unknown artist
Corner of Fargate and Pinstone Street, Sheffield c.1850
oil on board 12.2 x 17.5
1974.542

Facing page: Cole, Leslie, 1910–1976, *Air Transport Auxiliary* (detail), 1943, Museums Sheffield, (p. 43)

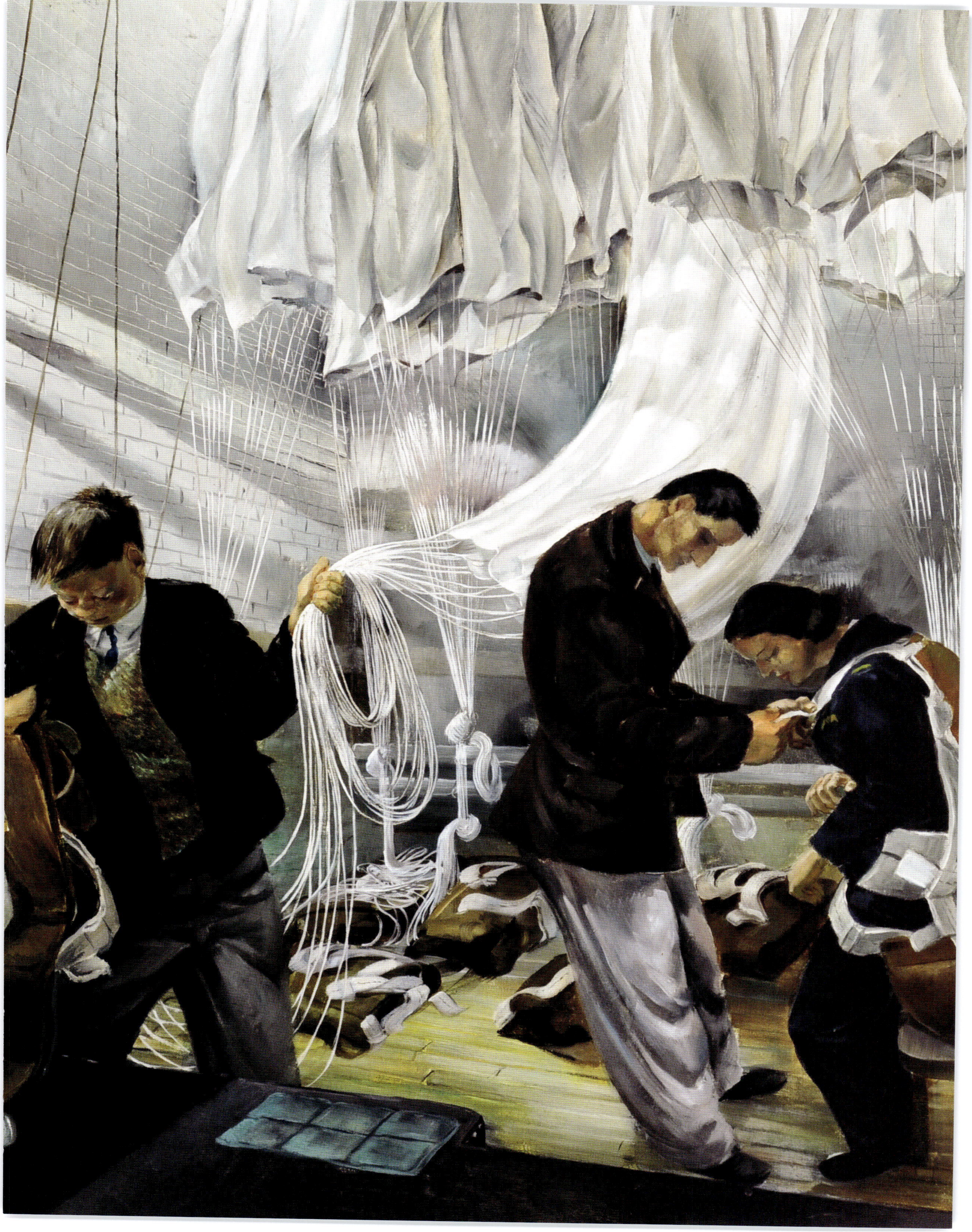

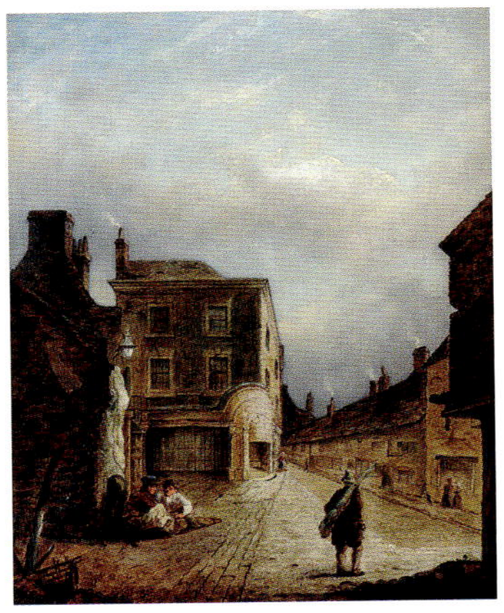

unknown artist
Montgomery Tavern, Sheffield 1856
oil on canvas 42.8 x 34.4
VIS.1899

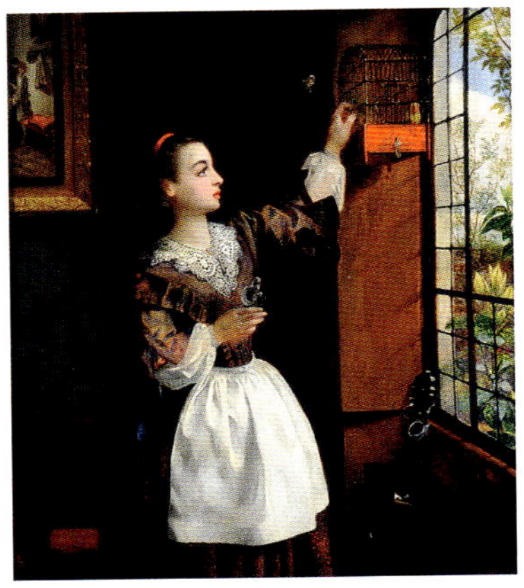

unknown artist
Feeding the Canary 1858
oil on canvas 39.8 x 34.7
VIS.161

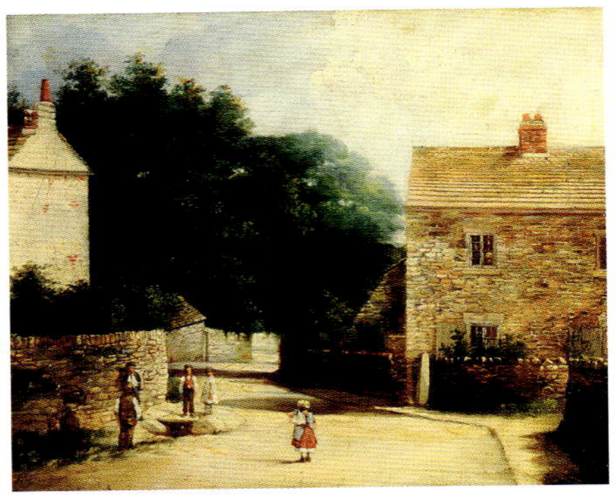

unknown artist
Cottages on Greystones Road, Sheffield c.1870
oil on canvas 29.6 x 37.6
K1930.36

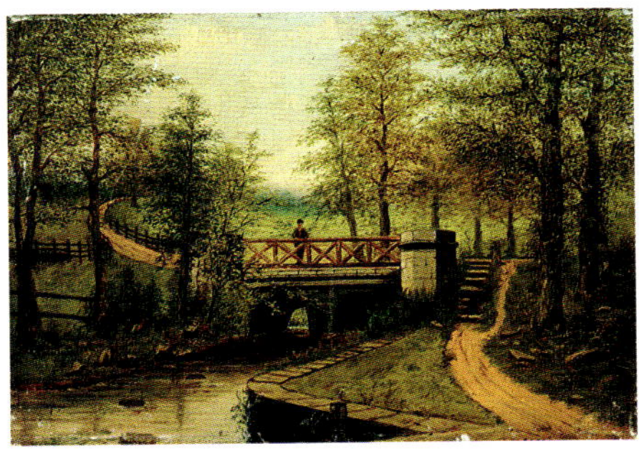

unknown artist
Whiteley Woods Bridge, Sheffield c.1870
oil on canvas 25.5 x 35.5
K1952.2

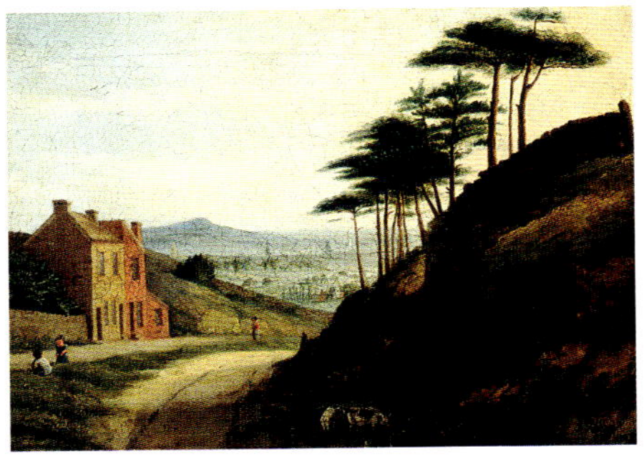

unknown artist
Sheffield from Psalter Lane 1921
oil on canvas 49.5 x 59
1985.65

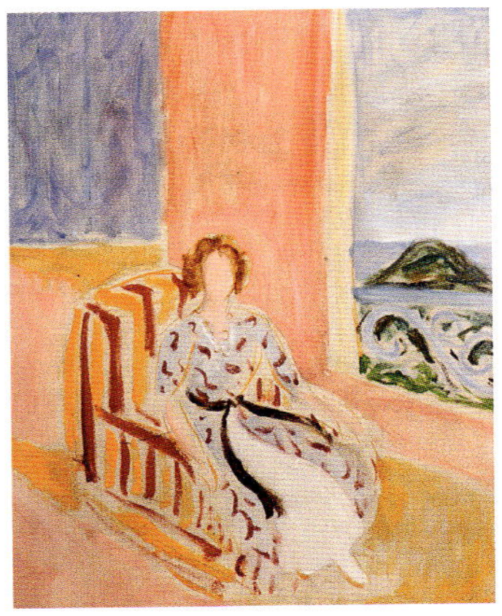

unknown artist (in the manner of Henri Matisse) 1869–1954
La femme au peignoir 1942
oil on canvas 39.1 x 31.3
VIS.3857

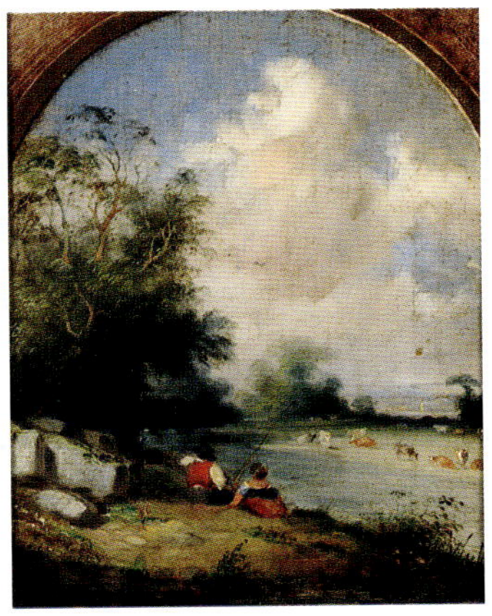

unknown artist
A Bavarian Landscape
oil on canvas 20.5 x 15.6
VIS.961

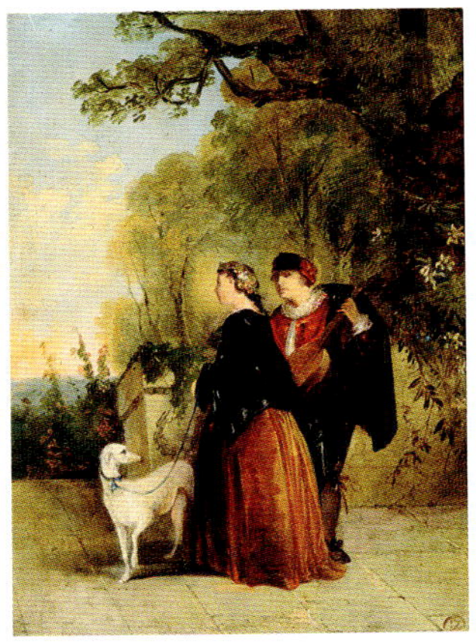

unknown artist
A Musician, and a Lady with a Dog in a Landscape
oil on millboard 27.8 x 20.2
VIS.960

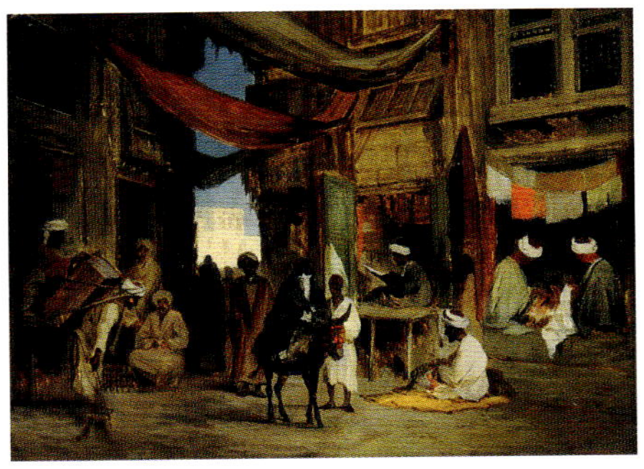

unknown artist
An Eastern Bazaar Scene
oil on panel 18.9 x 26.1
VIS.1039

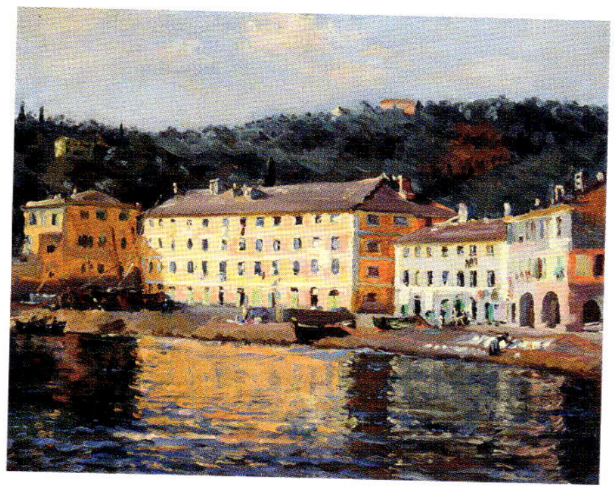

unknown artist
An Italian Bay
oil on canvas 39.3 x 49.4
VIS.2899

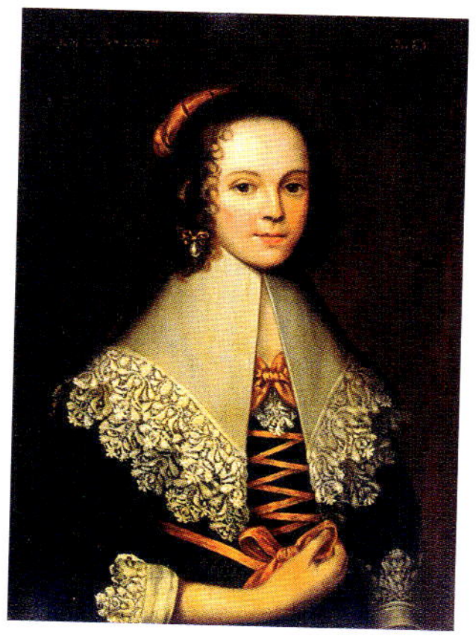

unknown artist
Ann Astley
oil on panel 29.5 x 20.9
VIS.54

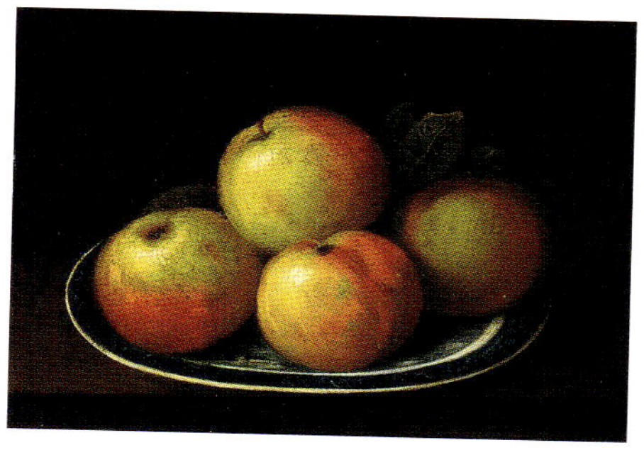

unknown artist
Apples on a Dish
oil on panel 19.3 x 27.8
VIS.1070

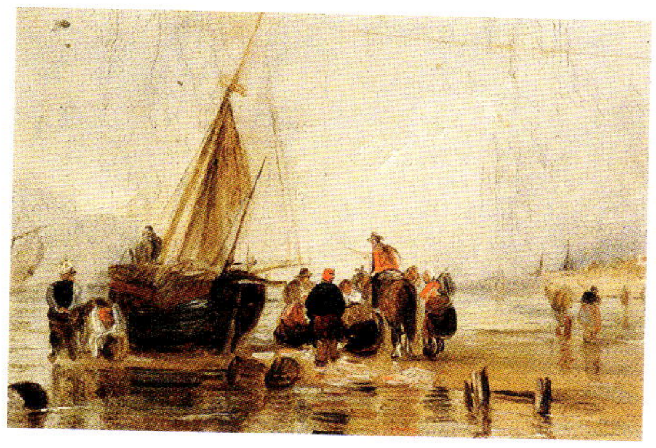

unknown artist
Beach Scene
oil on panel 16.5 x 24.1
VIS.1086

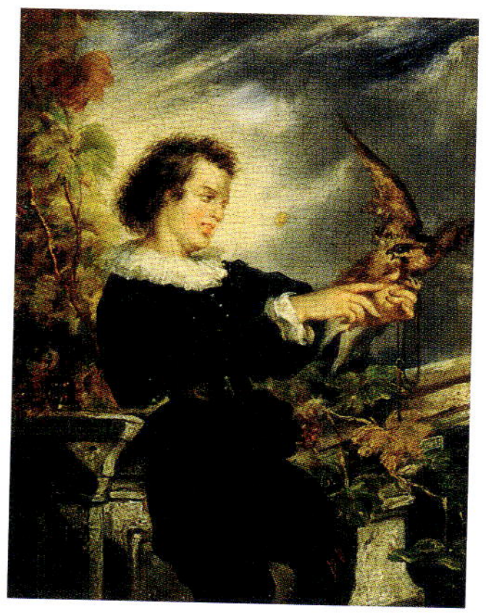

unknown artist
Boy with a Falcon
oil on panel 23 x 17.6
VIS.286

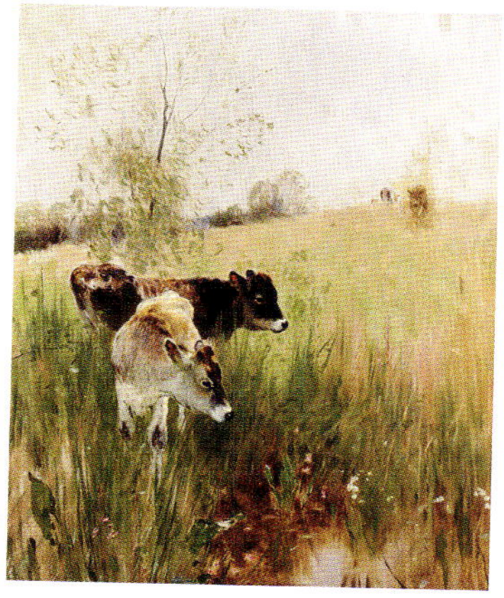

unknown artist
Calves
oil on canvas 59.7 x 49.6
VIS.1353

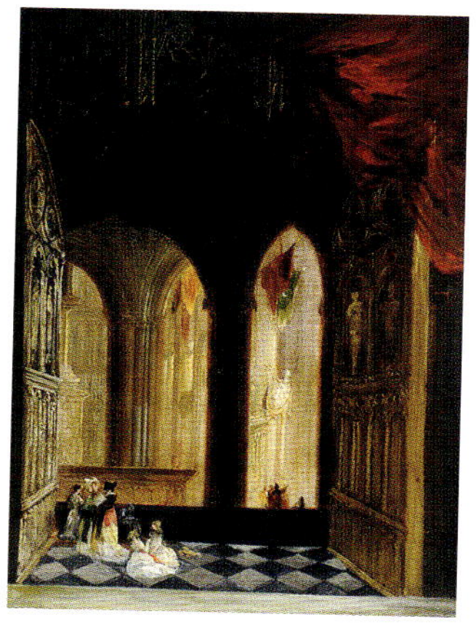

unknown artist
Cathedral with Figures
oil on canvas 39.1 x 29.1
VIS.1494

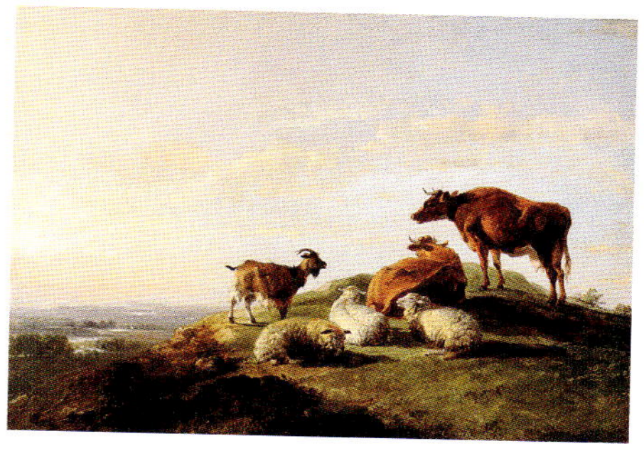

unknown artist
Cattle, Goats and Sheep
oil on canvas 43.4 x 62.5
VIS.1502

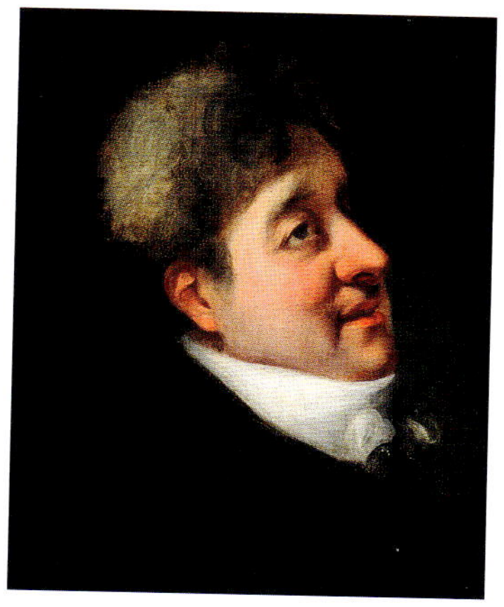

unknown artist
Charles Dibdin (1745?–1814)
oil on canvas 41.8 x 34.4
VIS.2592

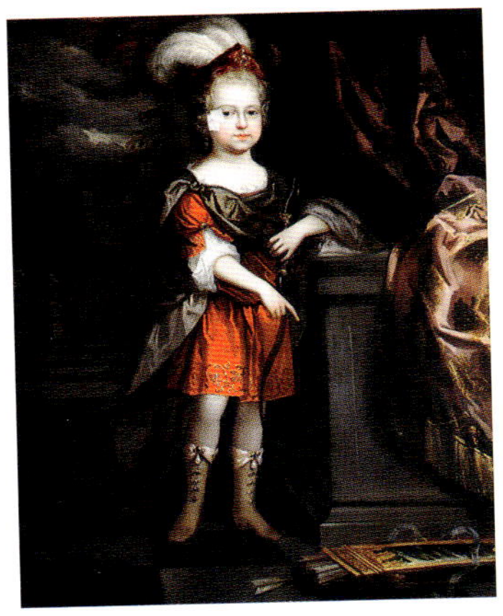

unknown artist
Charles Pye as a Child
oil on canvas 124.4 x 98.3
VIS.3233

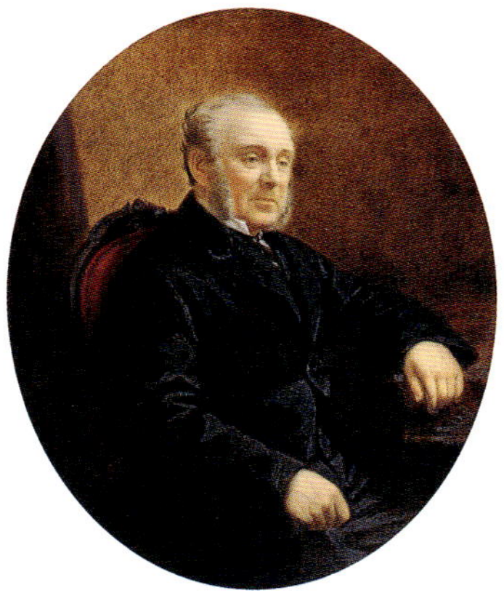

unknown artist
Christopher Johnson
oil on canvas 31 x 25.5
K1955.5

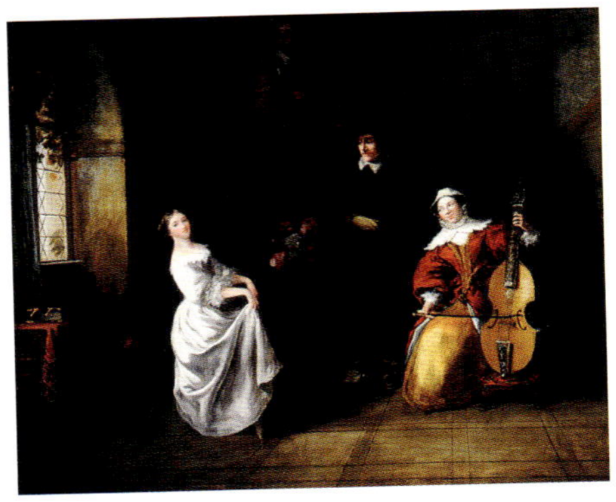

unknown artist
Conversation Piece with Three Figures
oil on canvas 62 x 74.6
VIS.2084

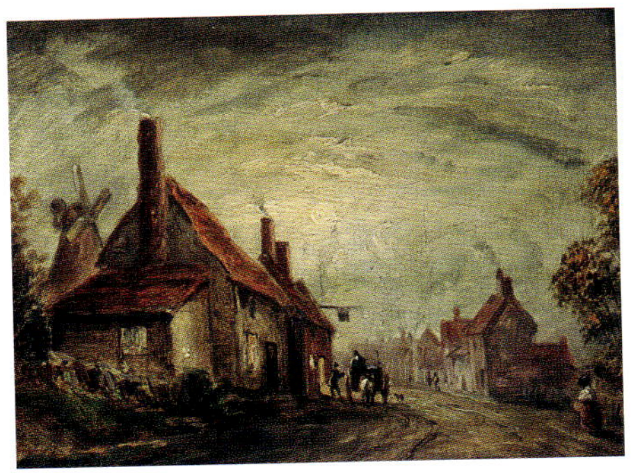

unknown artist
Country Inn
oil on panel 14.5 x 19.5
VIS.1020

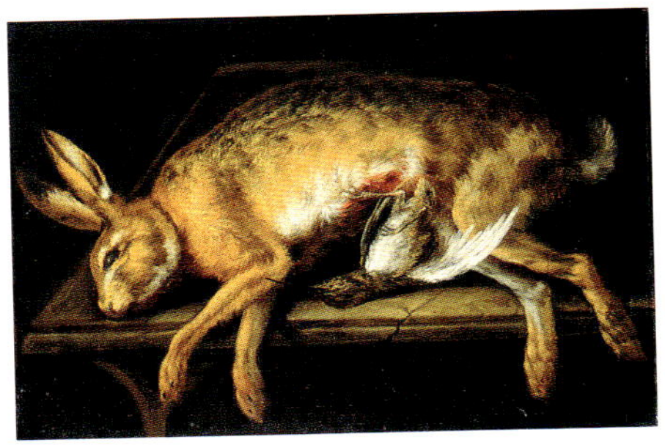

unknown artist
Dead Hare
oil on canvas 47.3 x 68.2
VIS.2600

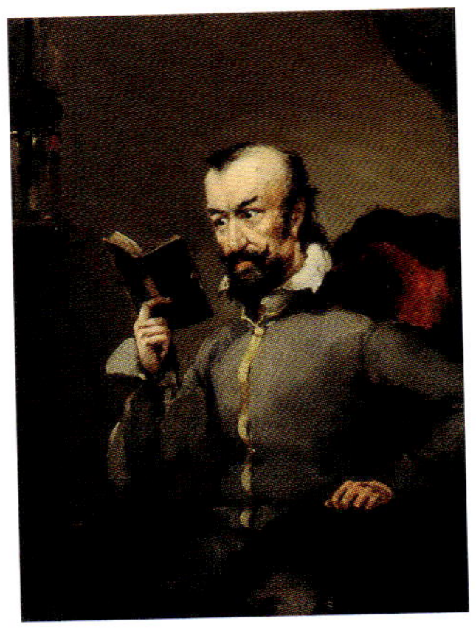

unknown artist
Don Quixote
oil on panel 28.1 x 20.6
VIS.1096

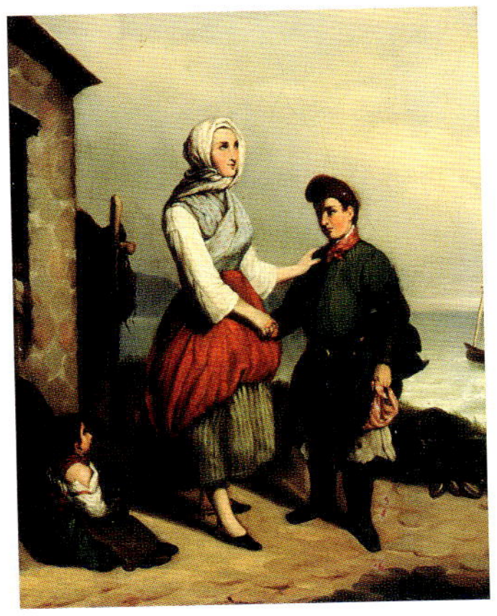

unknown artist
Farewell
oil on panel 23 x 18.4
VIS.954

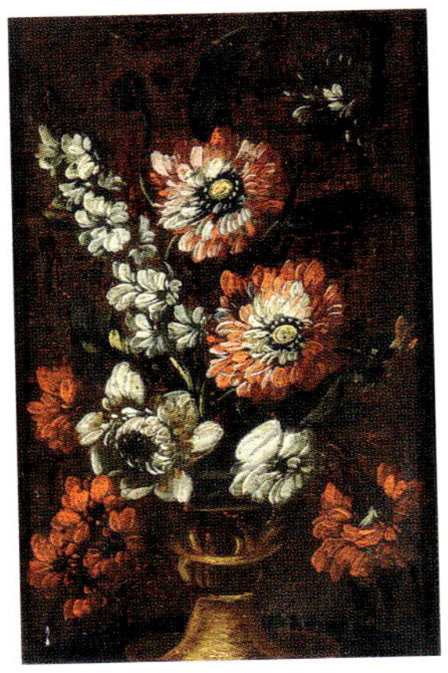

unknown artist
Flower Piece
oil on panel 32.8 x 20.4
VIS.122

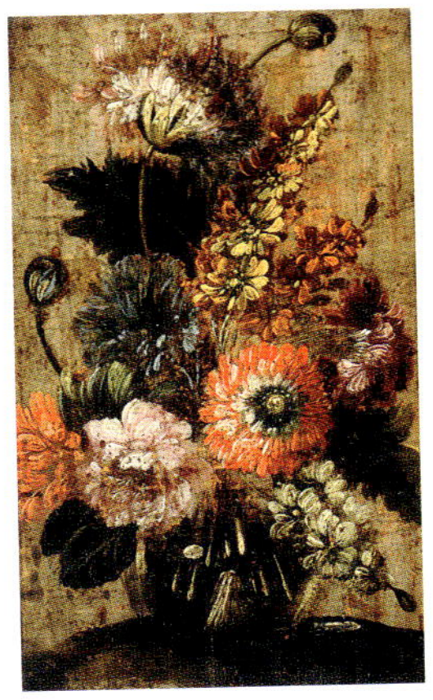

unknown artist
Flower Piece
oil on panel 33.2 x 20.5
VIS.123

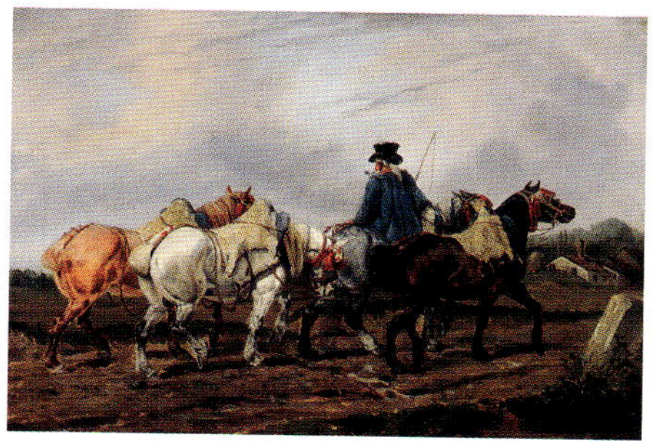

unknown artist
French Percheron Horses
oil on canvas 37.3 x 52.9
VIS.2727

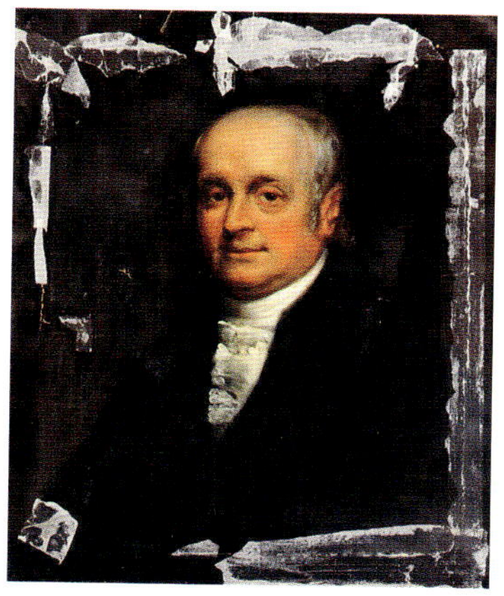

unknown artist
George Woolhouse
oil on canvas 73 x 61.6
1969.9

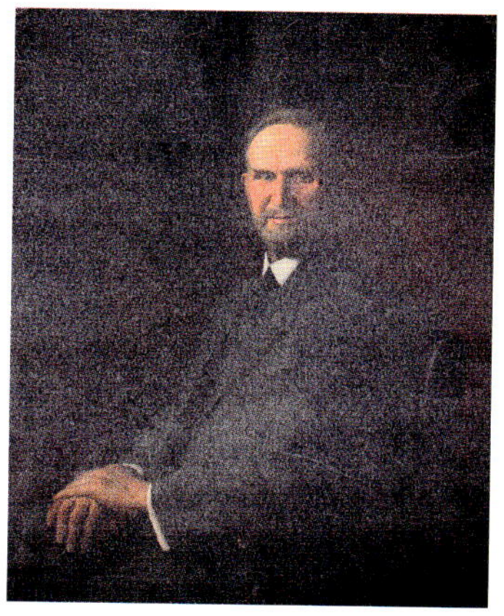

unknown artist
H. W. Lash
oil on canvas 112 x 86.5
SH416

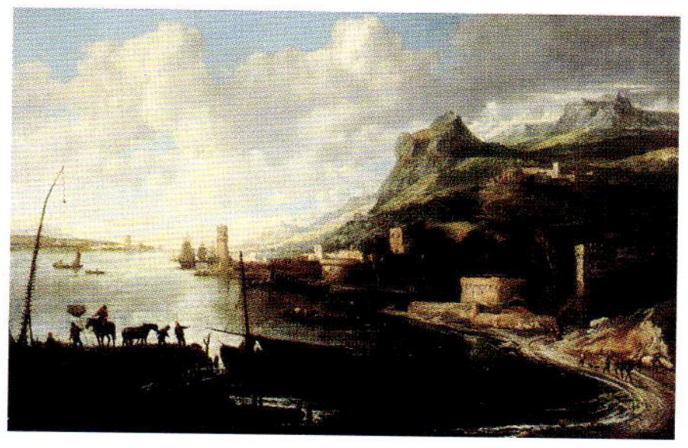

unknown artist
Harbour Scene
oil on canvas 94 x 140.1
VIS.3150

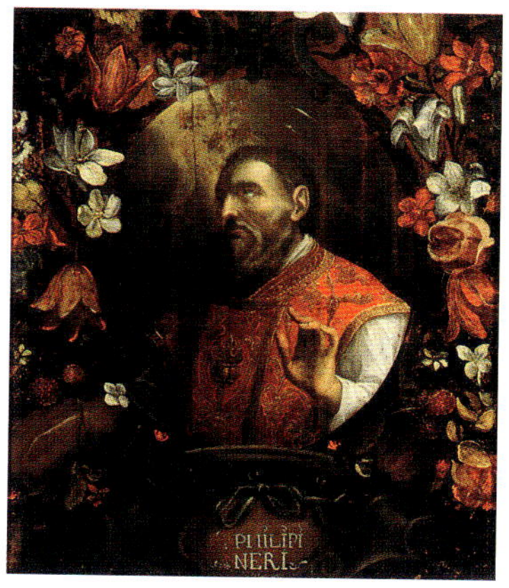

unknown artist
Head of Philip Neri (1515–1595)
oil on panel 37.8 x 31.7
VIS.1213

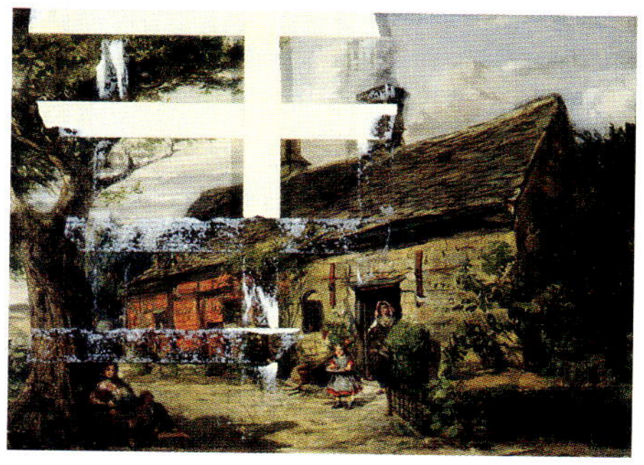

unknown artist
Helping the Poor
oil on panel 32.4 x 44.2
VIS.1372

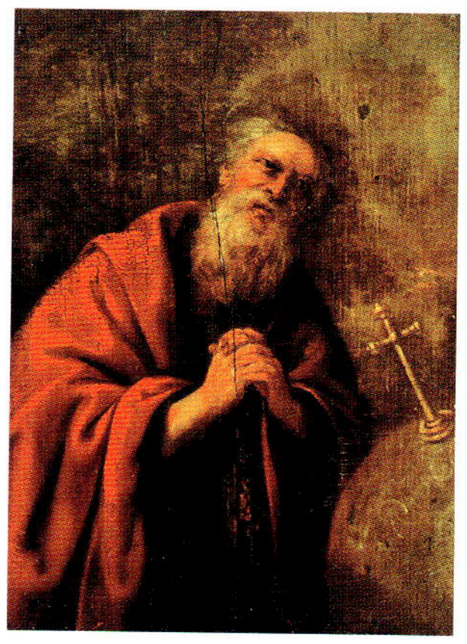

unknown artist
Heraclitus, Ancient Greek Scientist
oil on panel 17.6 x 12.9
VIS.965

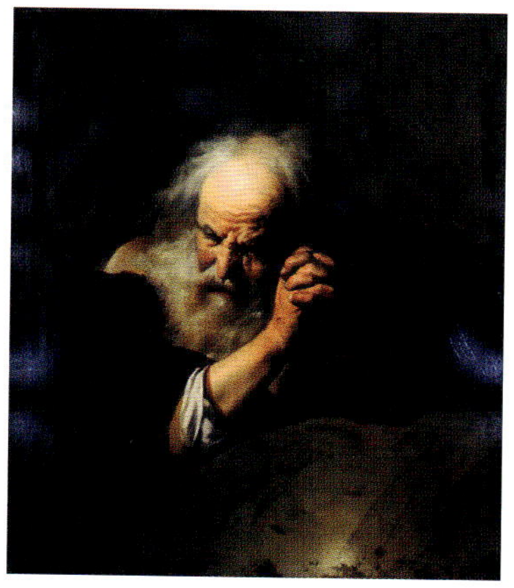

unknown artist
Heraclitus, Ancient Greek Scientist
oil on canvas 84.8 x 72
VIS.1671

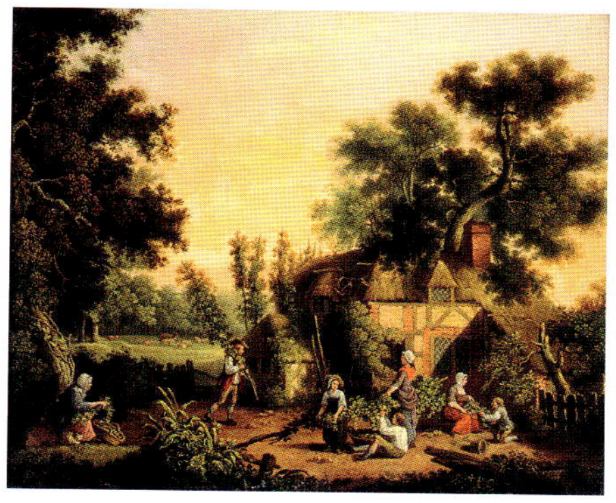

unknown artist
Hop Harvest, Bavaria
oil on panel 43.4 x 53
VIS.160

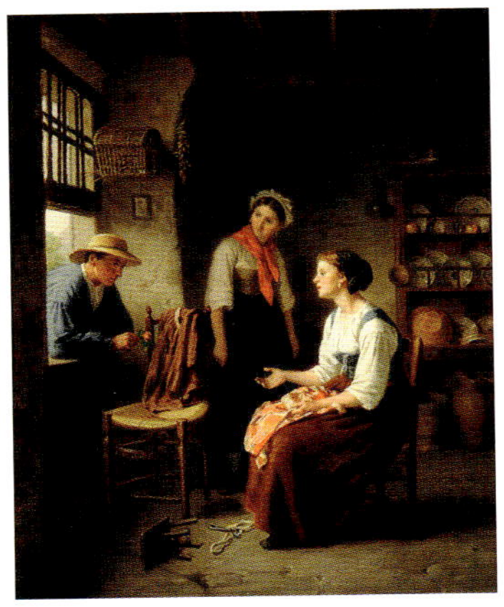

unknown artist
Interior of a Cottage with Figures
oil on panel 39.6 x 31.5
VIS.1405

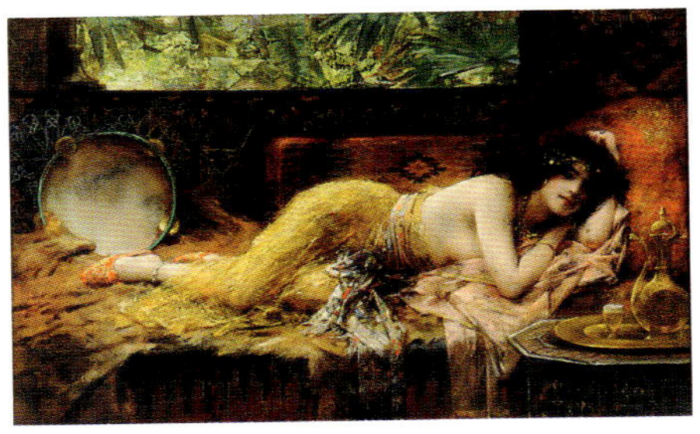

unknown artist
Interior with a Lady
oil on canvas 50.8 x 81.4
VIS.2361

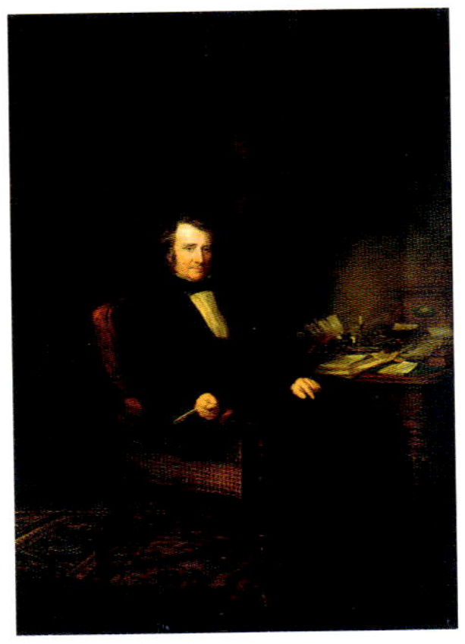

unknown artist
John Arthur Roebuck (1802–1879)
oil on canvas 216.5 x 153
VIS.LI.836 (P)

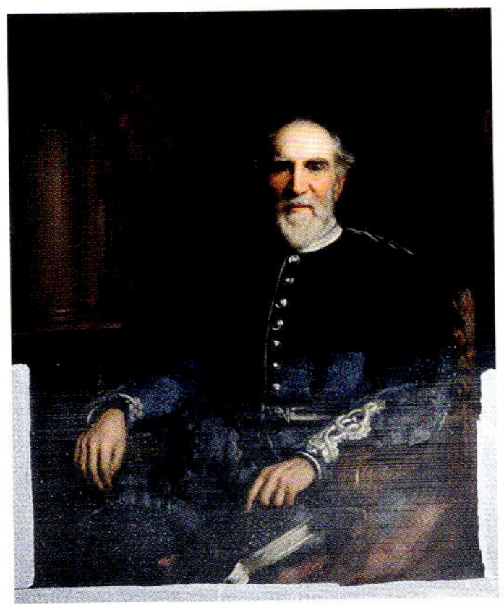

unknown artist
John Jackson (d.1895), Mayor of Sheffield (1889–1890)
oil on canvas 127 x 101.5
1992.1222

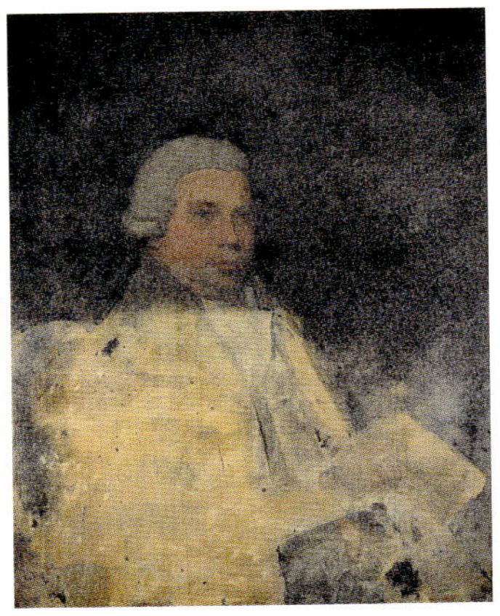

unknown artist
John Read (1744–1803), of Norton House
oil on canvas 91.5 x 71.2
SH419

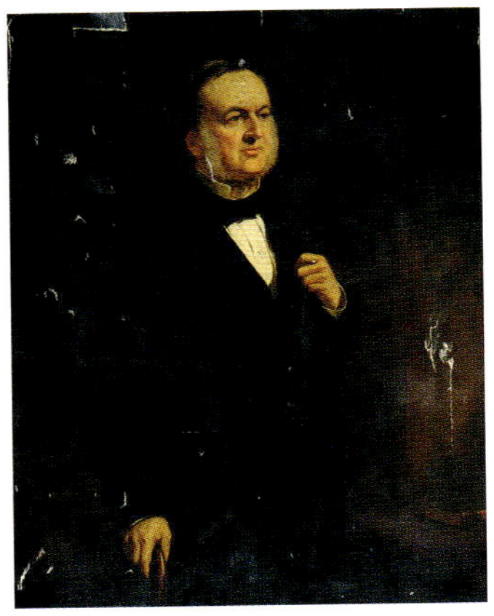

unknown artist
John Webster (d.1878), Mayor of Sheffield (1866–1868)
oil on canvas 118.1 x 93.1
VIS.LI.828 (P)

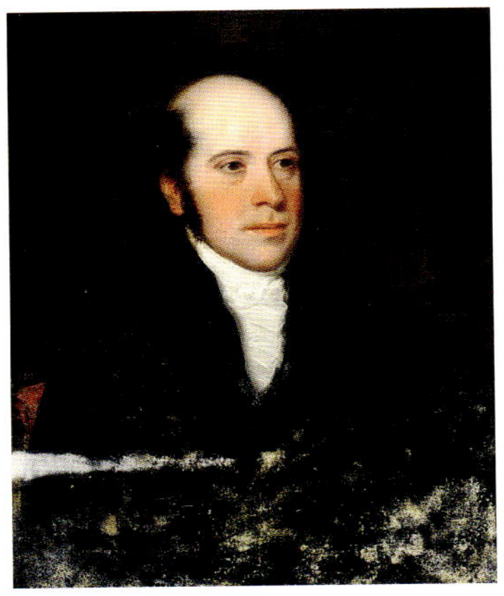

unknown artist
Joseph Read
oil on canvas 76 x 63
SH421

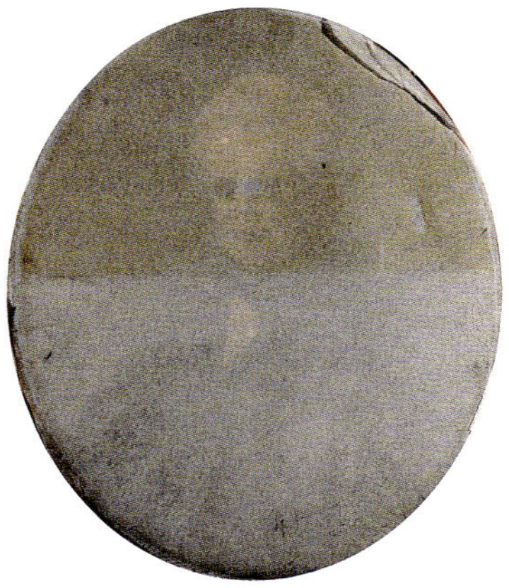

unknown artist
Joseph Rodgers (1785–1867)
oil on canvas 76.5 x 64
SH418

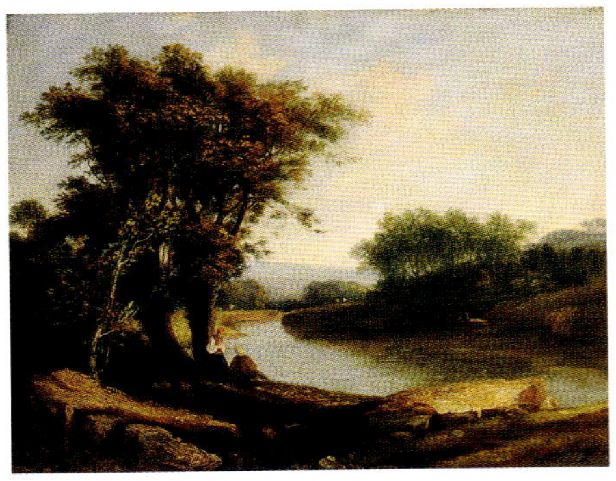

unknown artist
Landscape
oil on panel 26.5 x 34.1
VIS.18

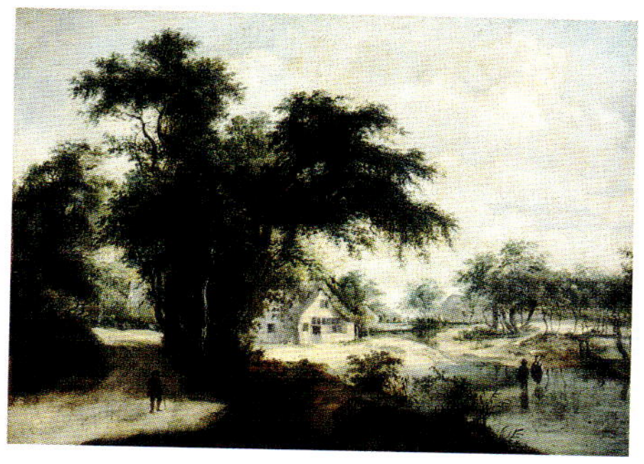

unknown artist
Landscape
oil on canvas 64.5 x 88.6
VIS.146

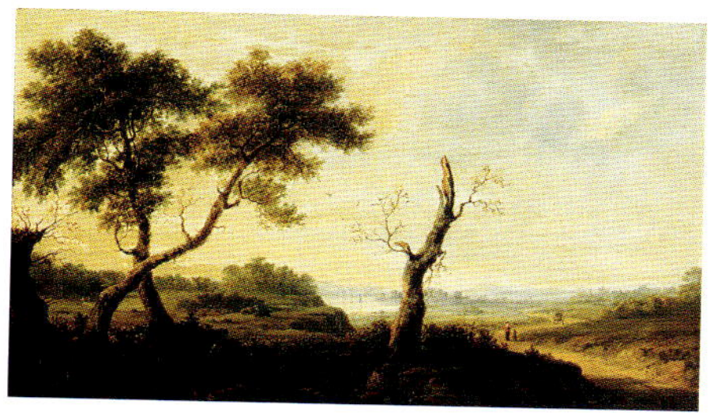

unknown artist
Landscape
oil on panel 31.6 x 54.1
VIS.159

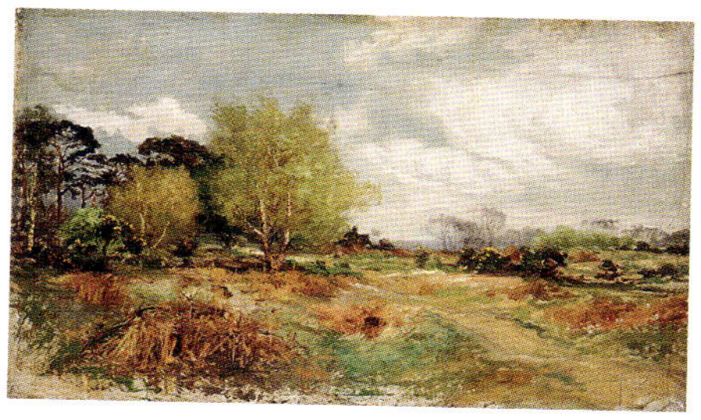

unknown artist
Landscape
oil on canvas 30.5 x 50.8
VIS.1000

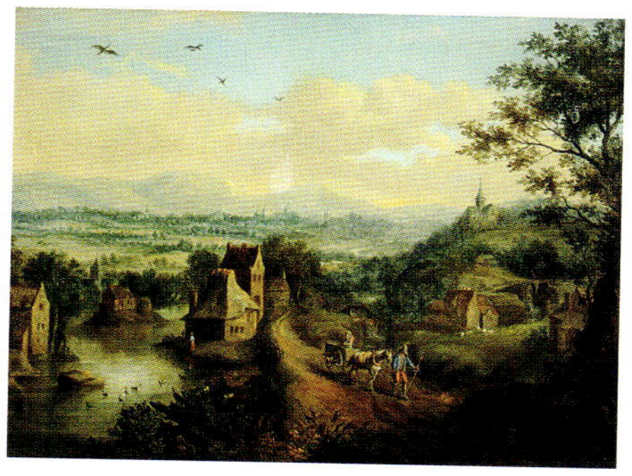

unknown artist
Landscape
oil on panel 31 x 41
VIS.1030

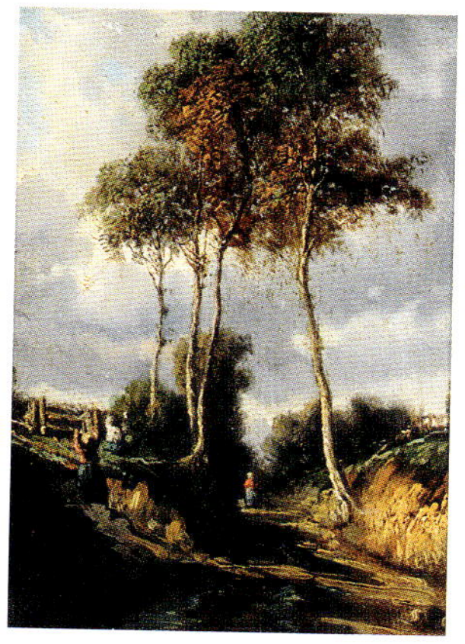

unknown artist
Landscape
oil on millboard 24 x 17
VIS.1084

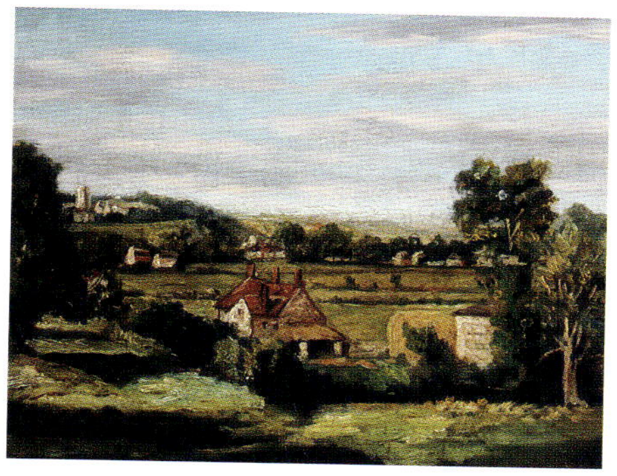

unknown artist
Landscape
oil on panel 22.5 x 28.5
VIS.1097

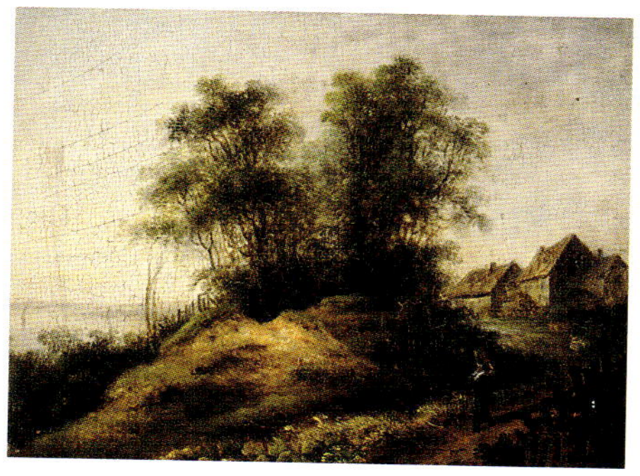

unknown artist
Landscape
oil on panel 16.4 x 22
VIS.1103

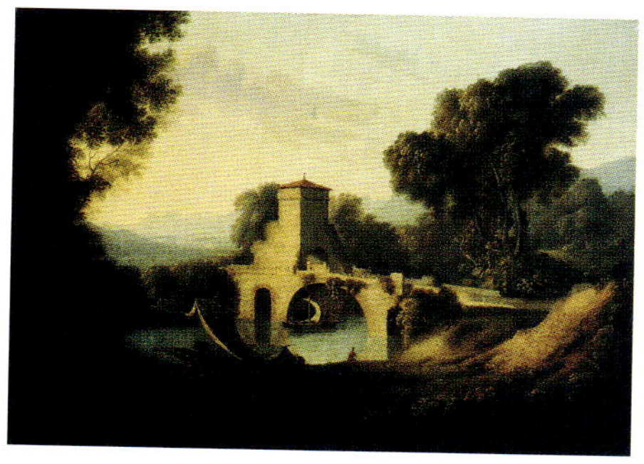

unknown artist
Landscape
oil on canvas 47.4 x 65.6
VIS.1308

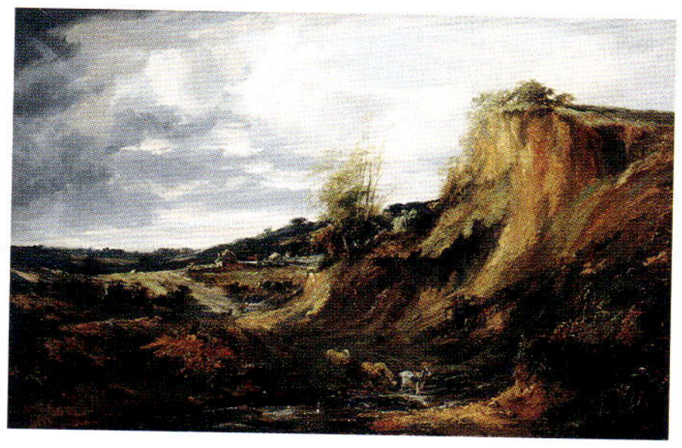

unknown artist
Landscape
oil on canvas 58.8 x 90
VIS.2615

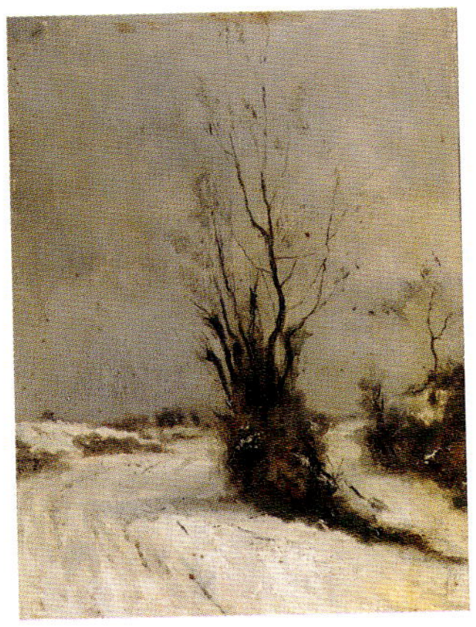

unknown artist
Landscape in Snow
oil on canvas 33.2 x 24.2
VIS.697

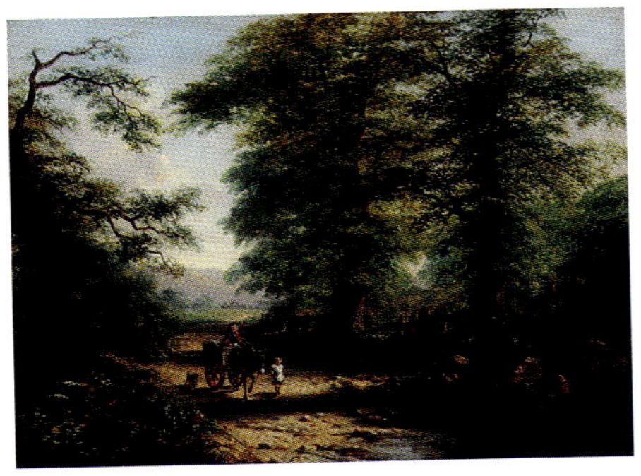

unknown artist
Landscape with a Cart
oil on canvas 44.6 x 59.7
VIS.1352

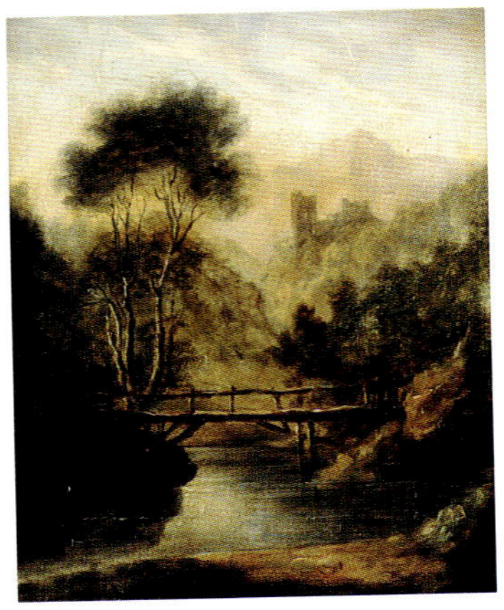

unknown artist
Landscape with a River
oil on panel 23.5 x 19
VIS.221

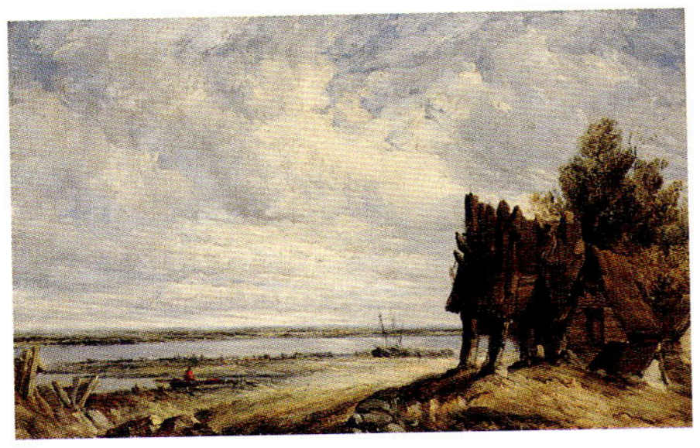

unknown artist
Landscape with a River
oil on canvas 35.2 x 46.1
VIS.1214

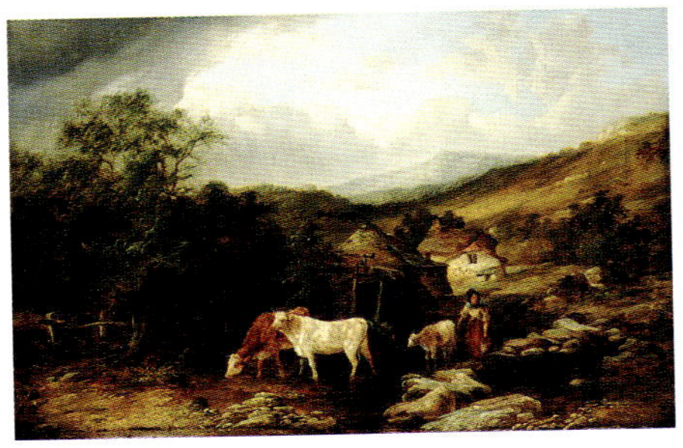

unknown artist
Landscape with a River and Cattle
oil on canvas 34.3 x 51
VIS.2731

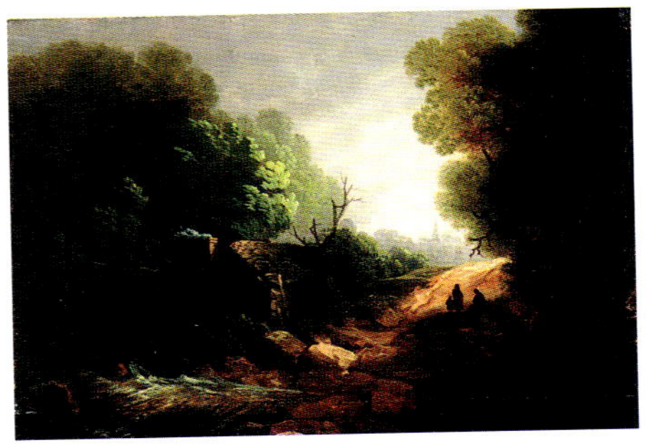

unknown artist
Landscape with a Small Cottage
oil on canvas 25.7 x 35.3
VIS.184

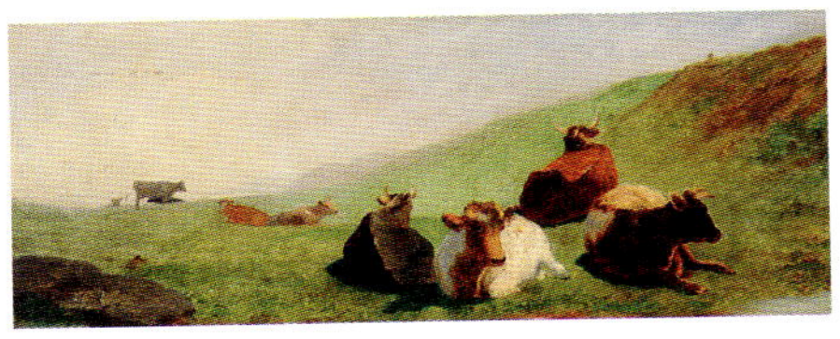

unknown artist
Landscape with Cattle
oil on plywood 22.4 x 59.1
VIS.1005

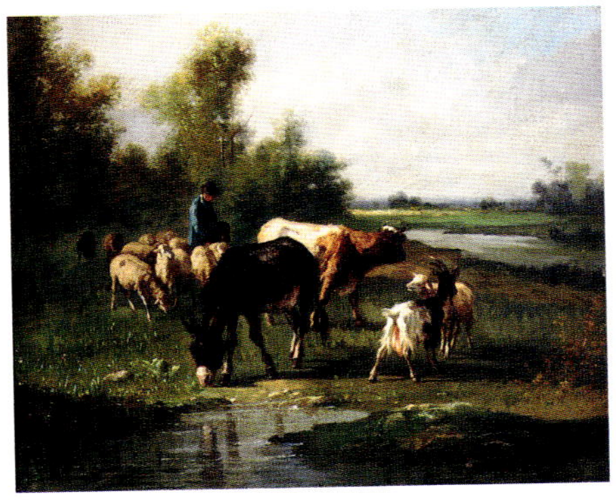

unknown artist
Landscape with Cattle, Goats and a Donkey
oil on canvas 36.8 x 44.7
VIS.364

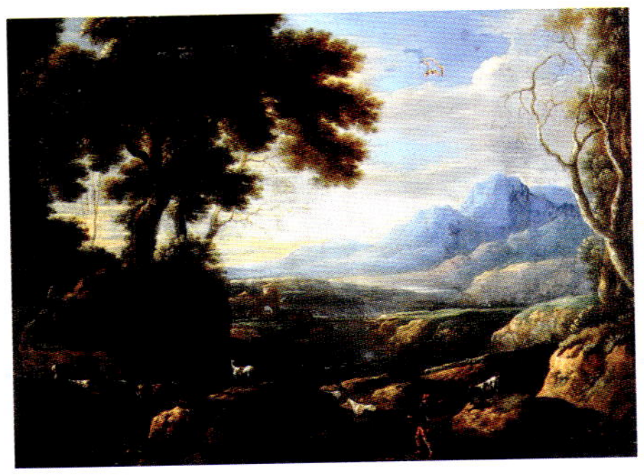

unknown artist
Landscape with Drovers
oil on canvas 51.1 x 68.1
VIS.2616

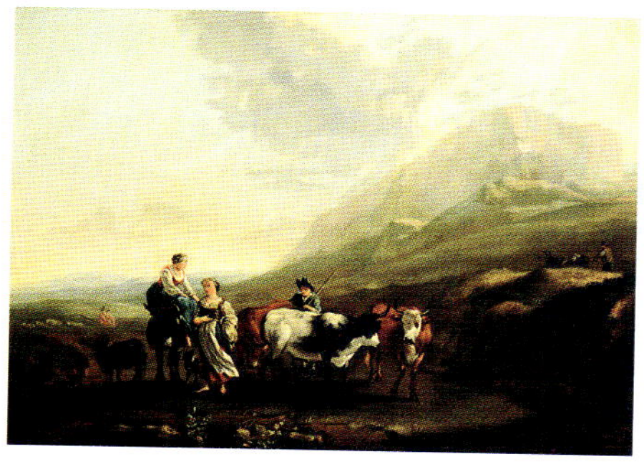

unknown artist
Landscape with Figures and Cattle
oil on panel 24.8 x 34.3
VIS.1245

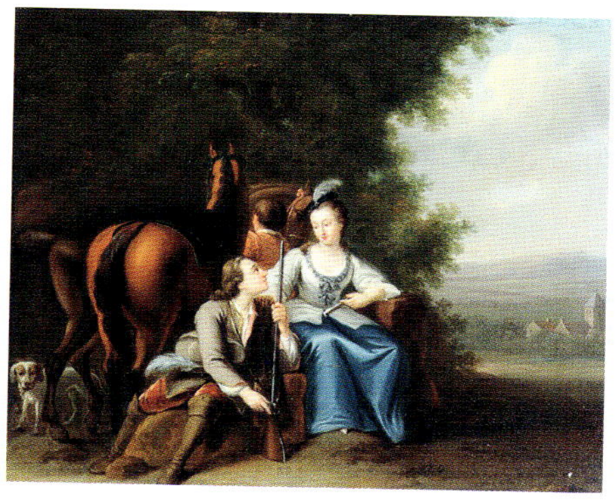

unknown artist
Landscape with Figures and Horses
oil on canvas 19.8 x 24.2
VIS.1068

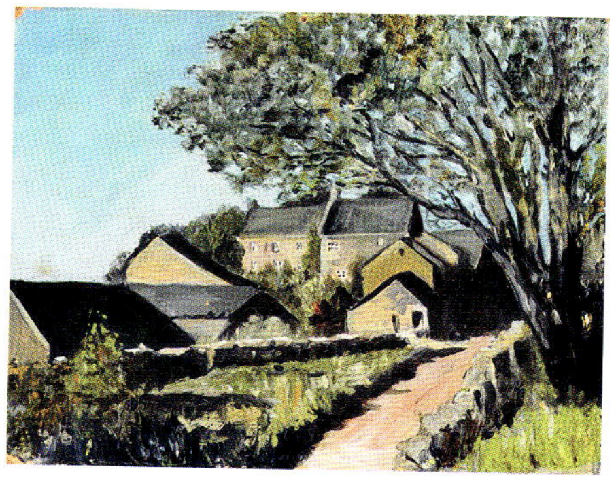

unknown artist
Lees Hall, Norton, Sheffield
oil on board 40.5 x 50.5
X1985.564

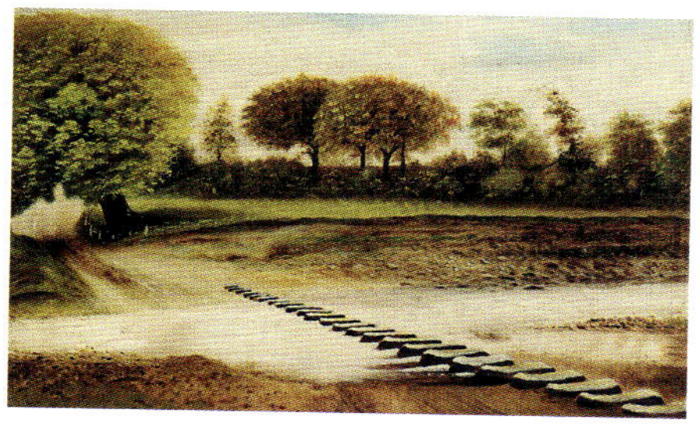

unknown artist
Lepping Stones, Wadsley Bridge, Sheffield
oil on canvas 24.2 x 39.5
K1959.9

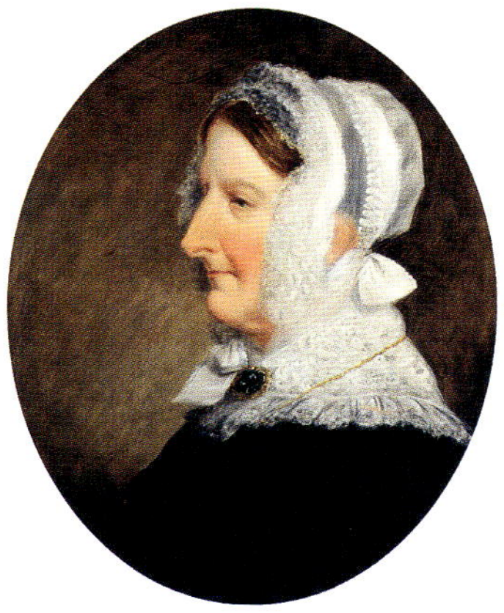

unknown artist
Miss Elizabeth Croft (1769–1859)
oil on canvas 52.1 x 41.6
VIS.2016

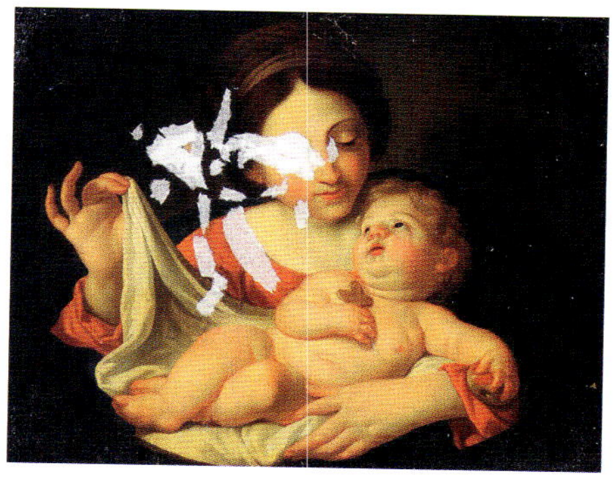

unknown artist
Mother and Child
oil on canvas 42.9 x 53.1
VIS.1295

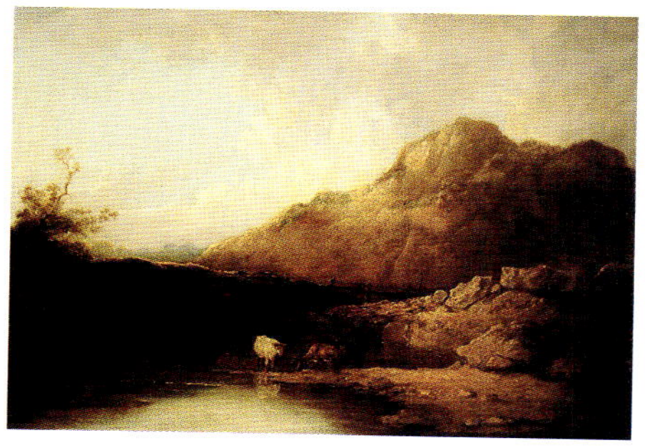

unknown artist
Mountain Landscape with Cattle
oil on panel 30.5 x 44
VIS.108

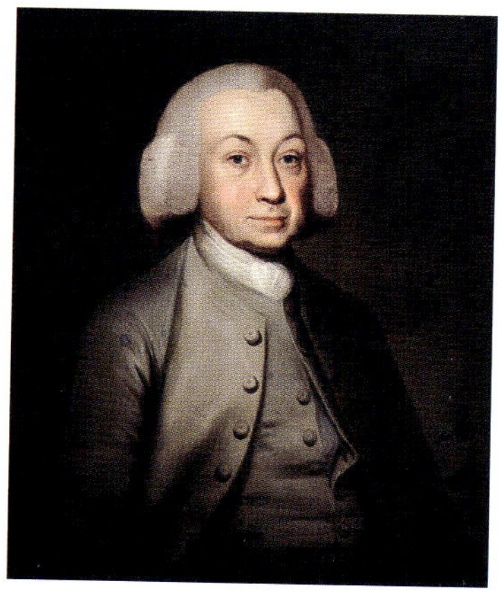

unknown artist
Mr Batty
oil on canvas 74.8 x 62.1
VIS.1912

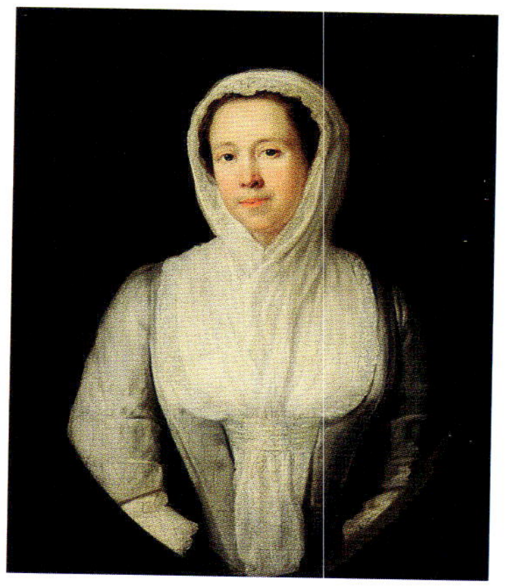

unknown artist
Mrs Batty
oil on canvas 73.6 x 61.6
VIS.2018

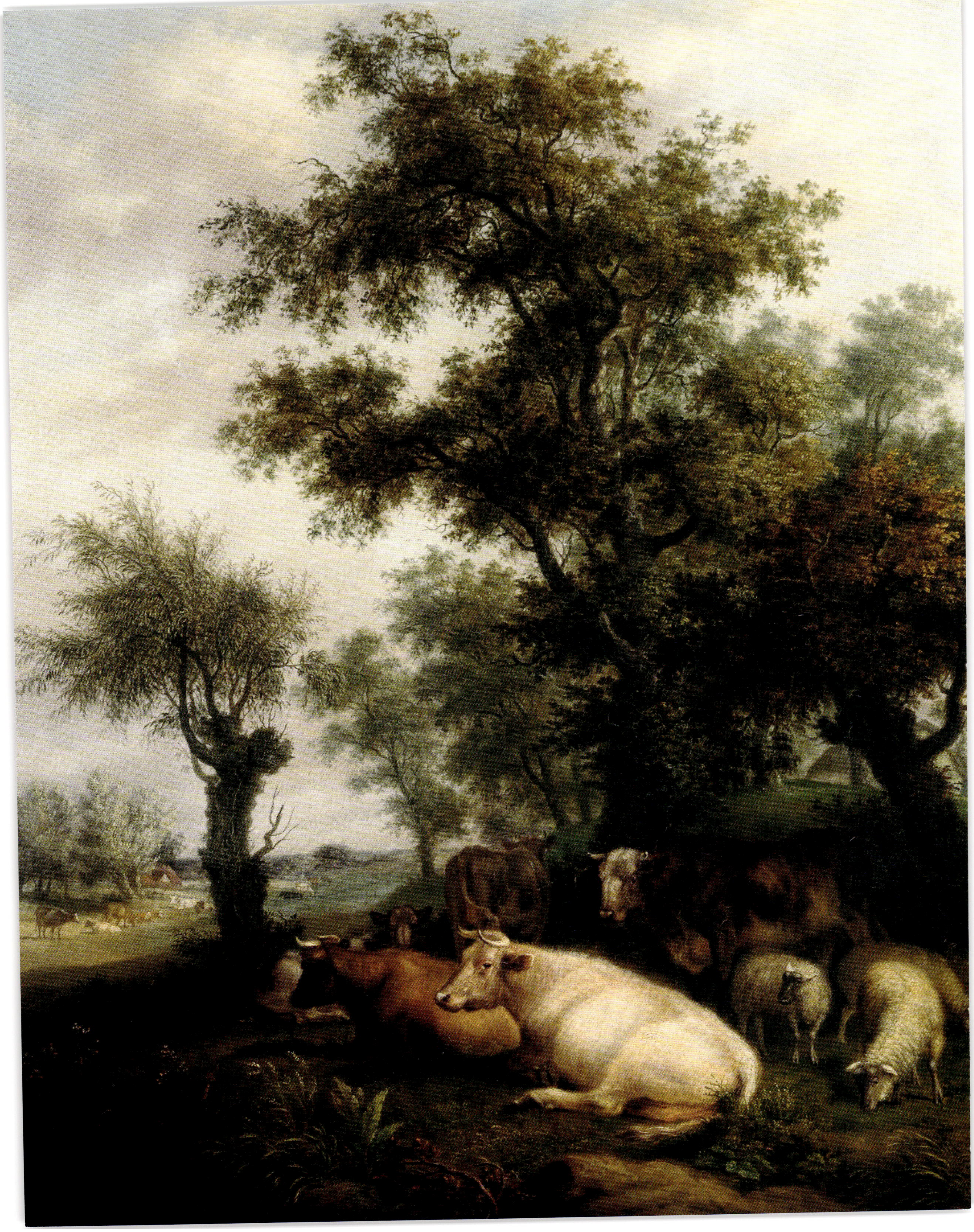

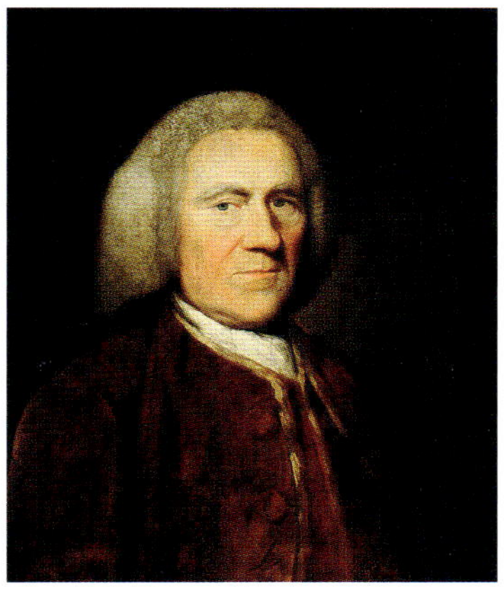

unknown artist
Portrait of a Gentleman
oil on canvas 59.5 x 49.5
VIS.489

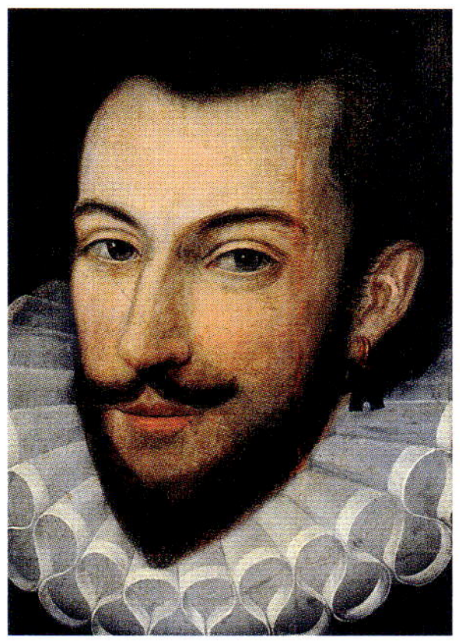

unknown artist
Portrait of a Gentleman
oil on panel 28.3 x 19.6
VIS.1087

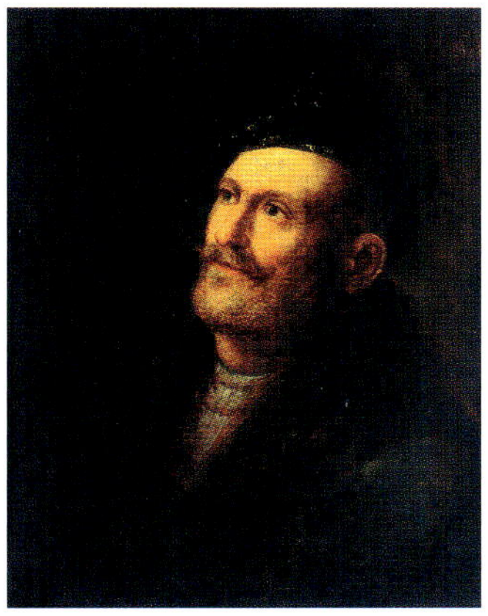

unknown artist
Portrait of a Gentleman
oil on canvas 56.5 x 43.5
VIS.1258

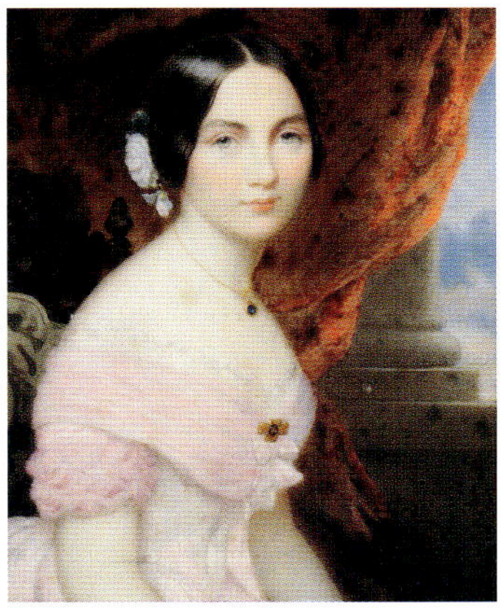

unknown artist
Portrait of a Lady
oil on millboard 11.5 x 9.5
VIS.1304

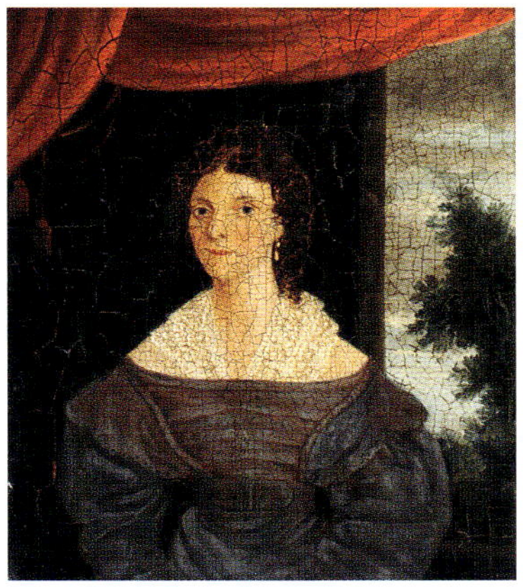

unknown artist
Portrait of a Lady
oil on panel 19.4 x 17
VIS.1955

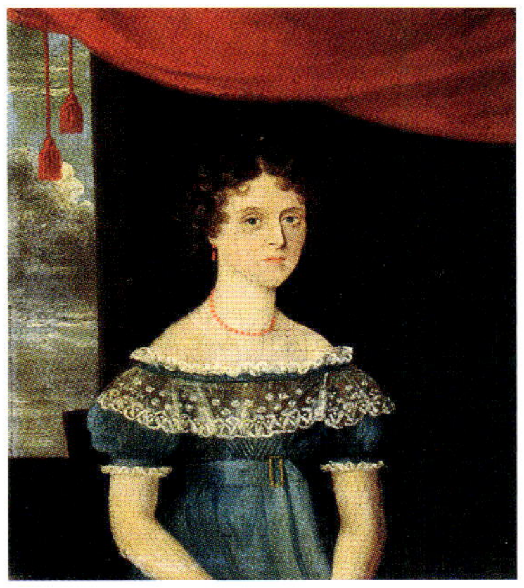

unknown artist
Portrait of a Lady
oil on panel 19.4 x 16.8
VIS.1956

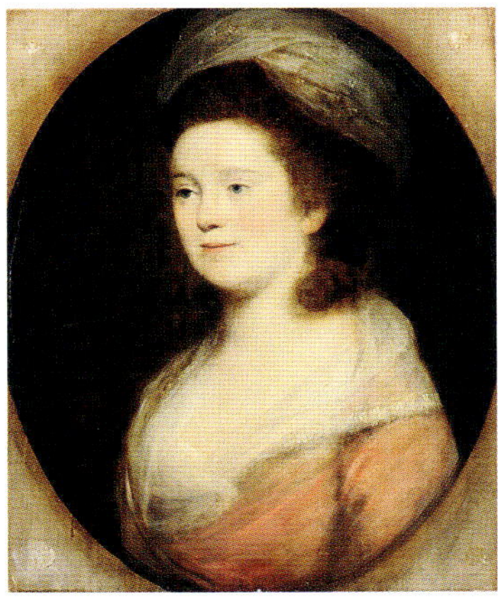

unknown artist
Portrait of a Lady
oil on canvas 60.9 x 50.8
VIS.3001

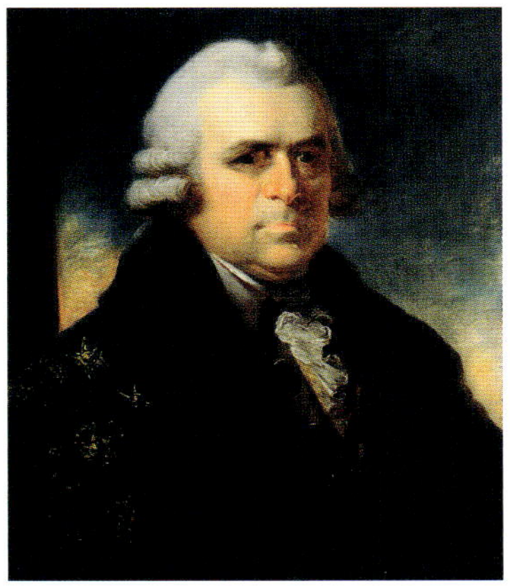

unknown artist
Portrait of a Lawyer
oil on canvas 55.4 x 47.4
VIS.279

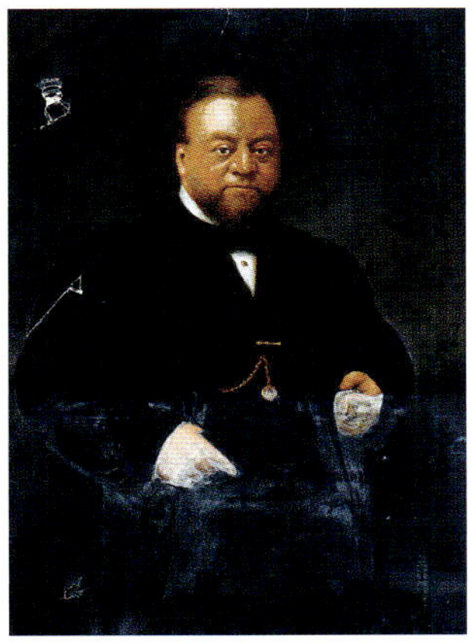

unknown artist
Portrait of a Man
oil on canvas 119.8 x 85.8
SH413

Facing page: Barker, Thomas, 1809–1869, *Cattle Group* (detail), Museums Sheffield, (p. 12)

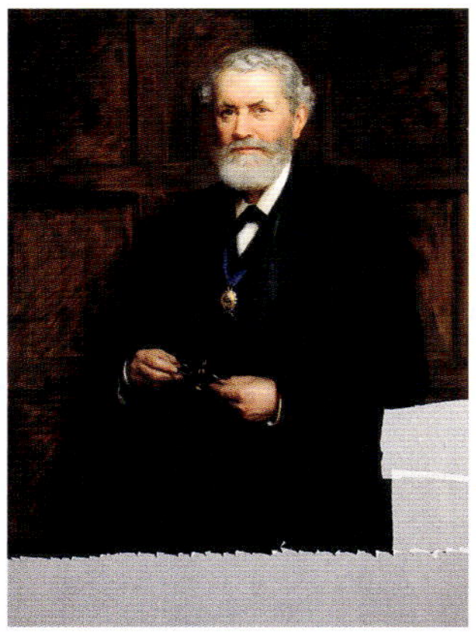

unknown artist
Portrait of a Man
oil on canvas 127.5 x 89
SH415

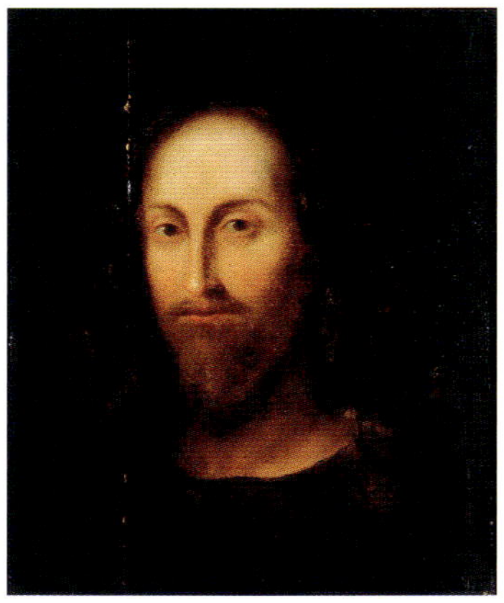

unknown artist
Portrait of a Man
oil on canvas 50.6 x 39.7
VIS.167

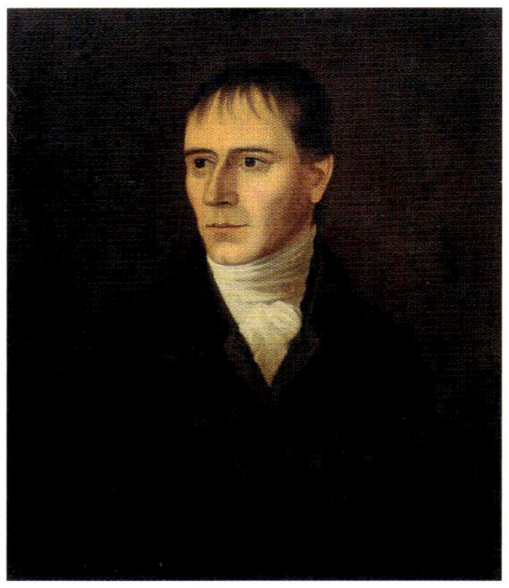

unknown artist
Portrait of a Man
oil on canvas 64.5 x 54.5
VIS.1953

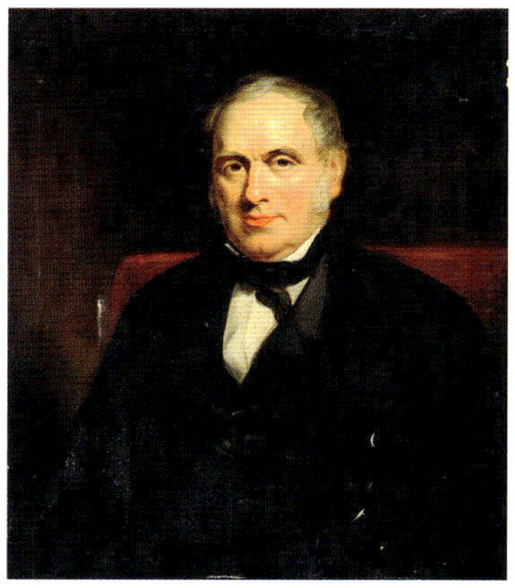

unknown artist
Portrait of a Man
oil on canvas 76 x 63.2
VIS.2126

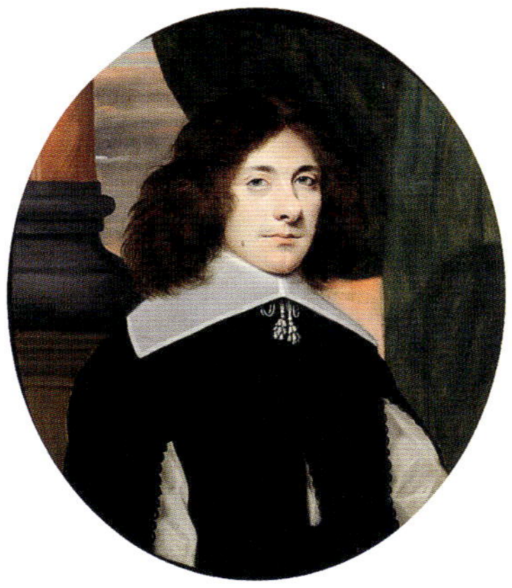

unknown artist
Portrait of a Man
oil on canvas 75.5 x 63.3
VIS.2244

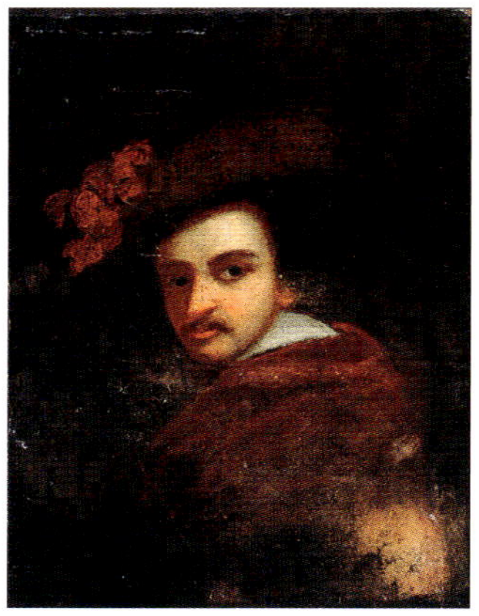

unknown artist
Portrait of a Man
oil on canvas 34 x 25.5
VIS.4962

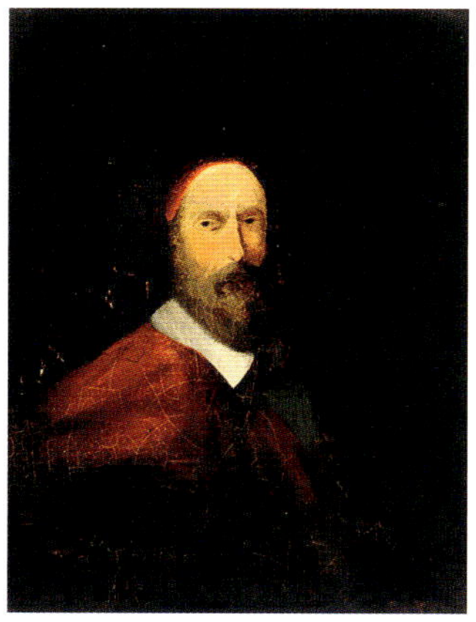

unknown artist
Portrait of a Man in a Red Cap
oil on panel 16.7 x 12.6
VIS.252

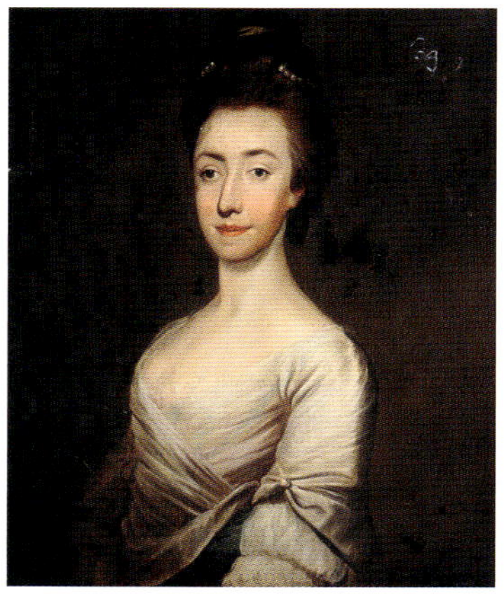

unknown artist
Portrait of a Member of the Batty Family
oil on canvas 74.9 x 62.1
VIS.1913

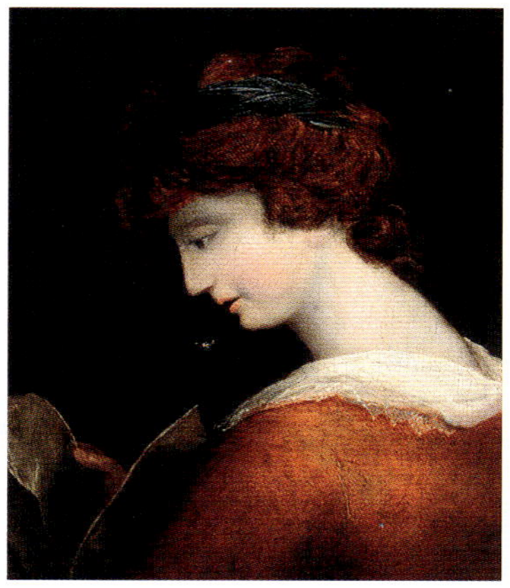

unknown artist
Portrait of a Woman
oil on canvas 21.3 x 17.8
VIS.1053

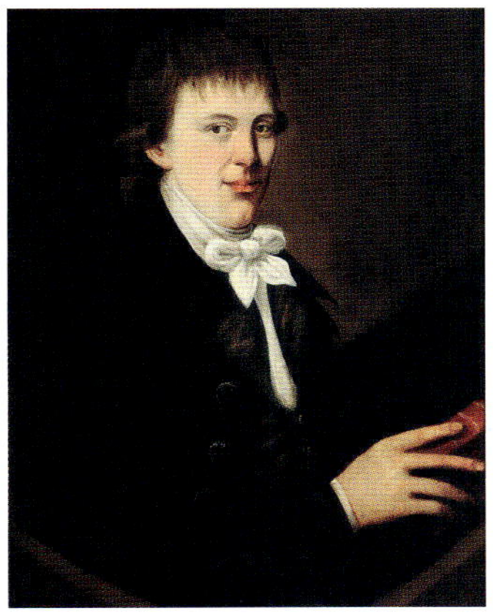

unknown artist
Portrait of a Young Man
oil on canvas 63.5 x 48.5
SH435

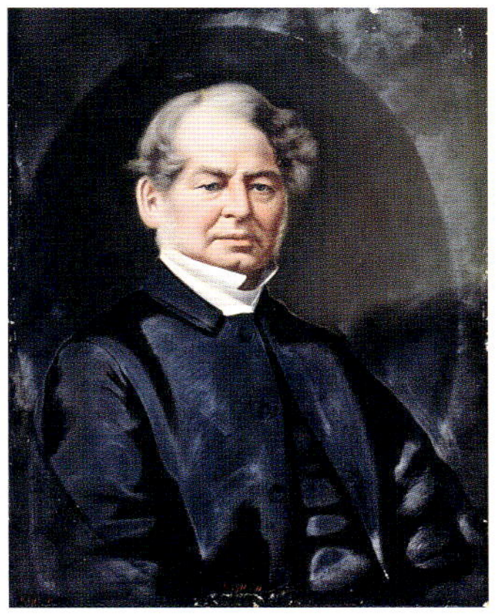

unknown artist
Reverend Thomas Sale (d.1873), Vicar of Sheffield
oil on board 61 x 48.2
K1916.13

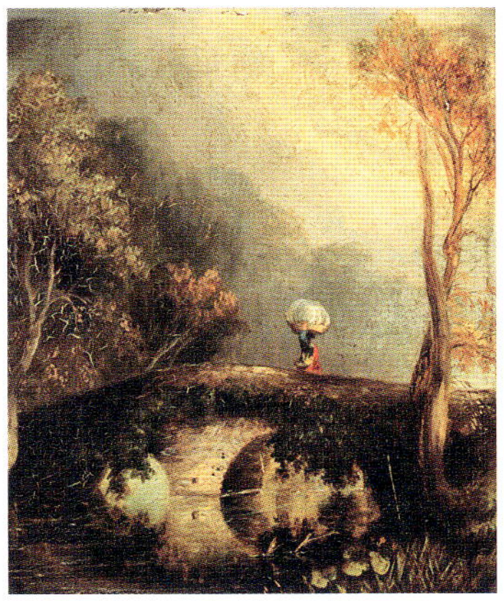

unknown artist
River Scene
oil on panel 21.8 x 17.7
VIS.1035

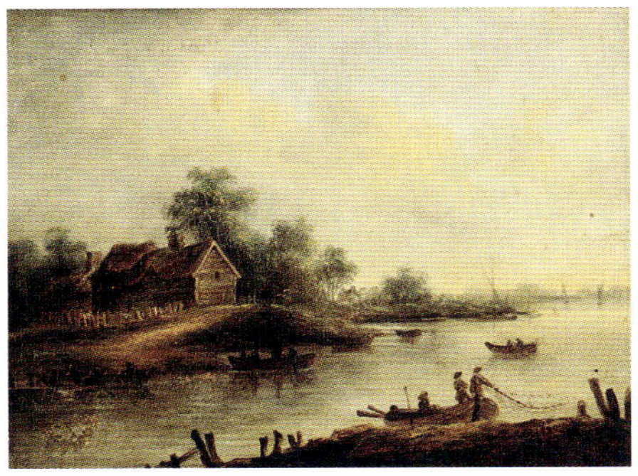

unknown artist
River Scene
oil on panel 16.7 x 21.9
VIS.1106

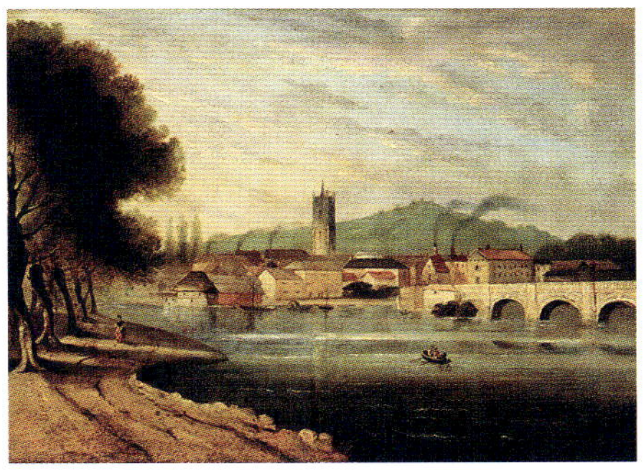

unknown artist
River Scene with a Bridge
oil on canvas 33.1 x 44.3
VIS.1251

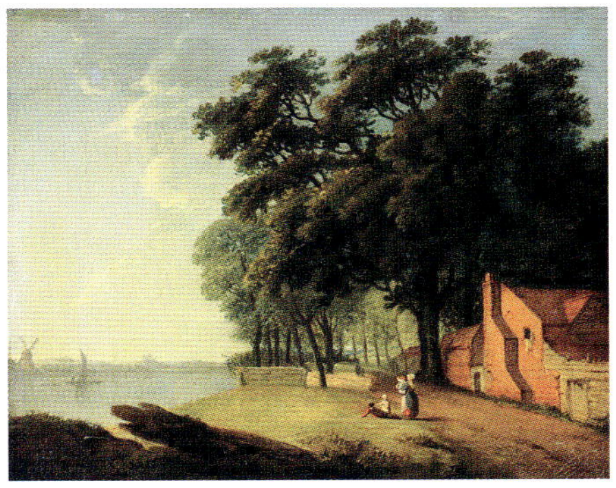

unknown artist
River Scene with a Cottage
oil on canvas 39.5 x 47.5
VIS.319

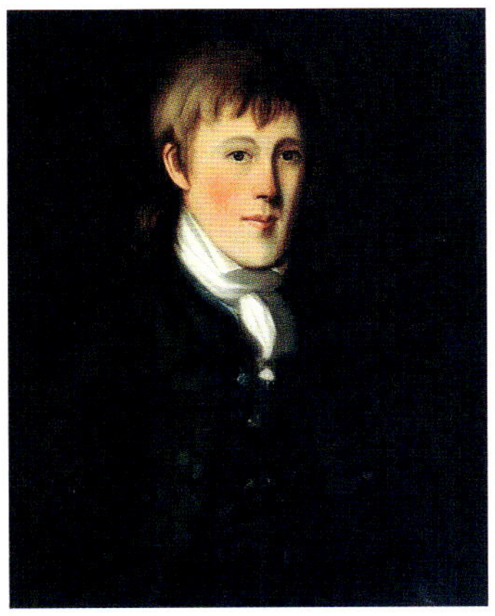

unknown artist
Samuel Osbourne
oil on canvas 65.5 x 53.8
SH436

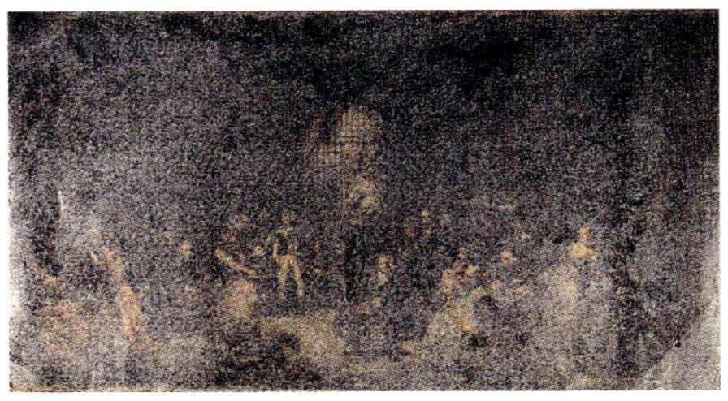

unknown artist
Scene from the French Revolution
oil on canvas 75.5 x 125.5
VIS.2710

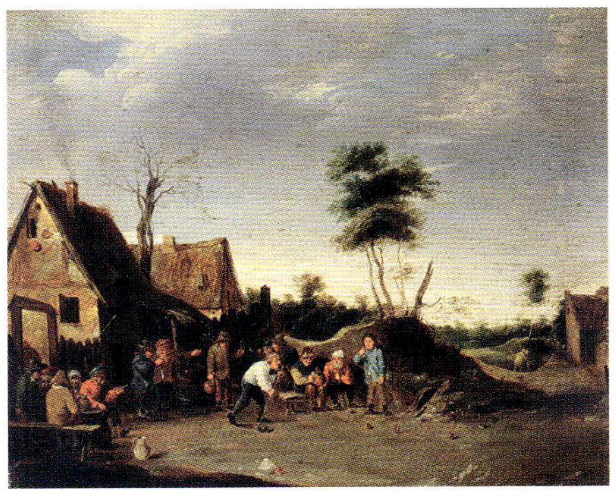

unknown artist
Scene Outside a Village Inn
oil on panel 16.4 x 21.8
VIS.1013

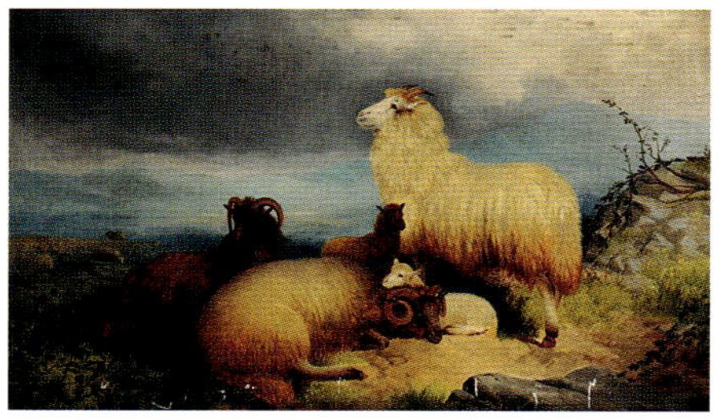

unknown artist
Sheep
oil on canvas 72.2 x 117.5
VIS.1280

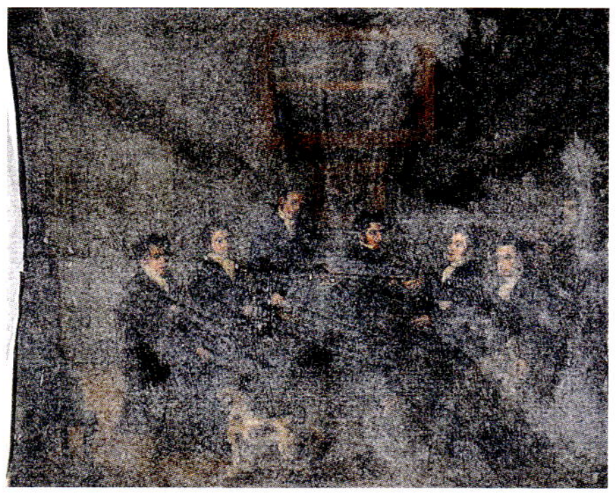

unknown artist
Six Sheffield Gentlemen at a Table
oil on canvas 64.3 x 77.2
K19.2.78.1

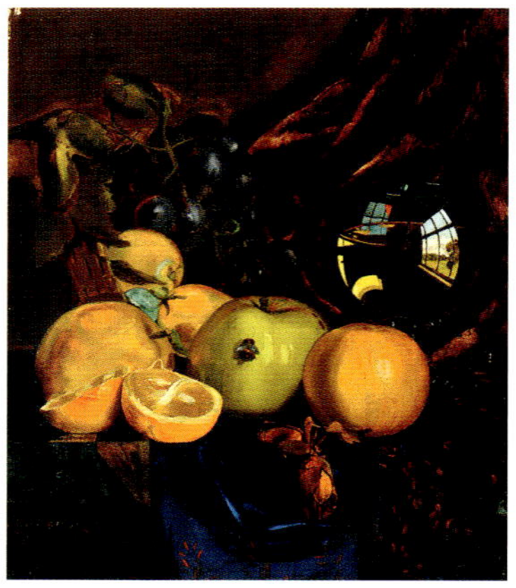

unknown artist
Still Life
oil on canvas 34 x 29
VIS.1235

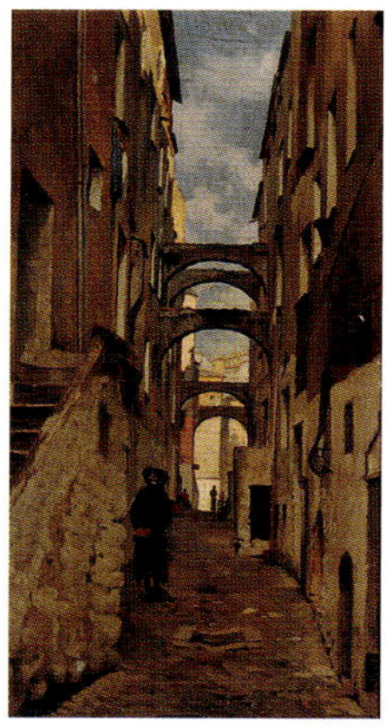

unknown artist
Street Scene
oil on canvas 37.9 x 19.9
VIS.1021

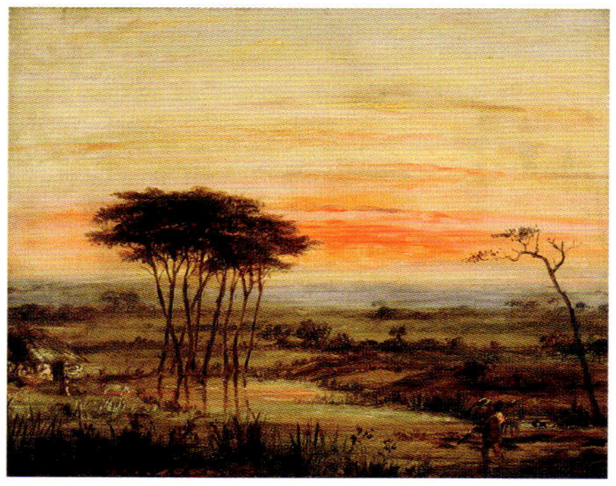

unknown artist
Sunset
oil on board 28.5 x 36
VIS.1095

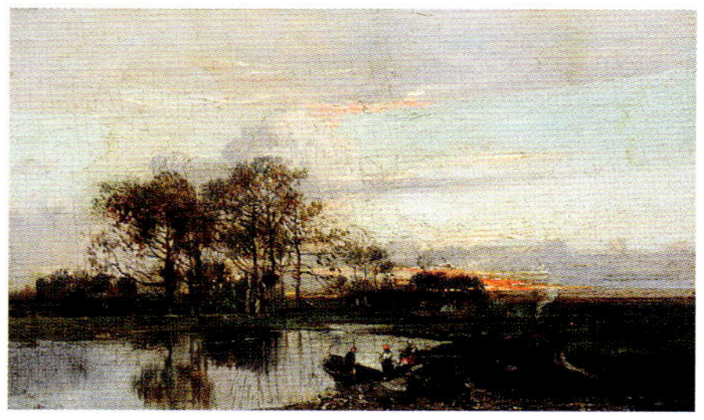

unknown artist
Sunset View
oil on panel 13.4 x 22.2
VIS.1002

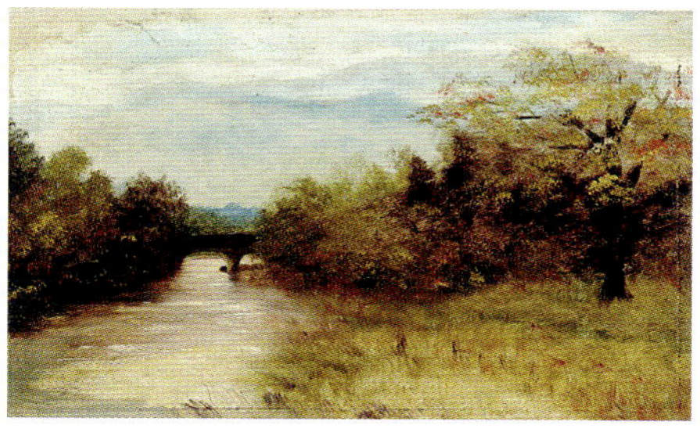

unknown artist
The Don Valley, Sheffield
oil on canvas 24.5 x 39.5
K1959.10

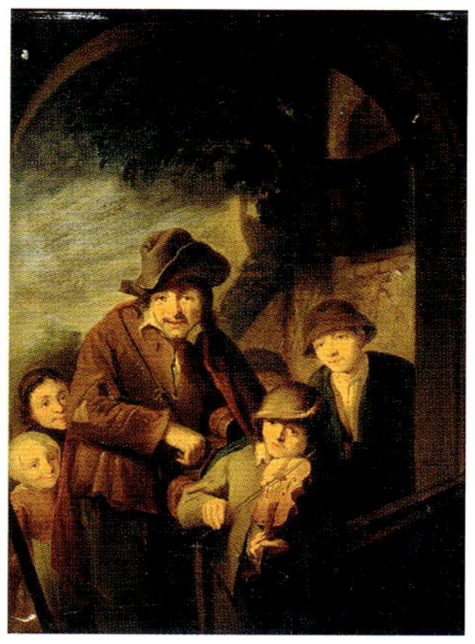

unknown artist
The Musician
oil on panel 40.2 x 29.6
VIS.1217

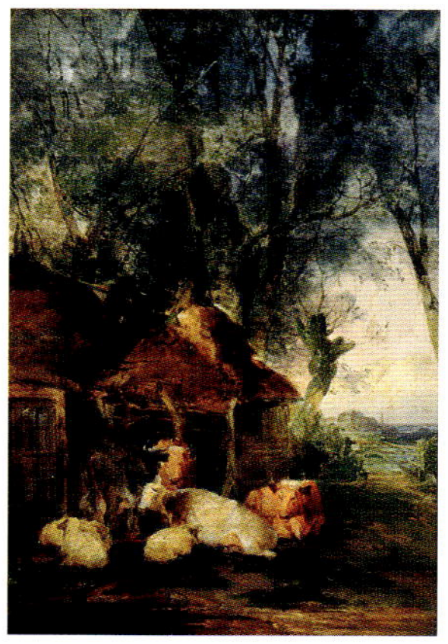

unknown artist
The Old Barn
oil on millboard 38.5 x 27
VIS.380

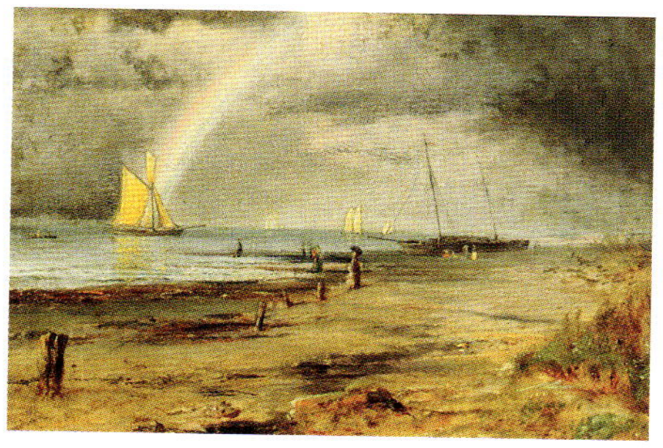

unknown artist
The Rainbow
oil on canvas 26.5 x 40
VIS.897

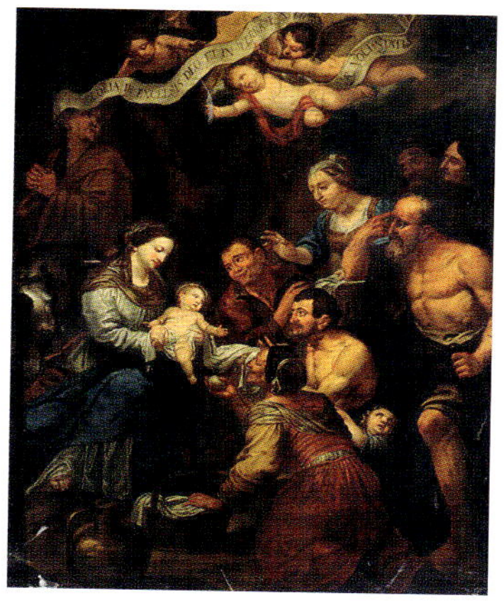

unknown artist
The Virgin Mary with the Infant Christ
oil on canvas 167.1 x 131.9
VIS.1690

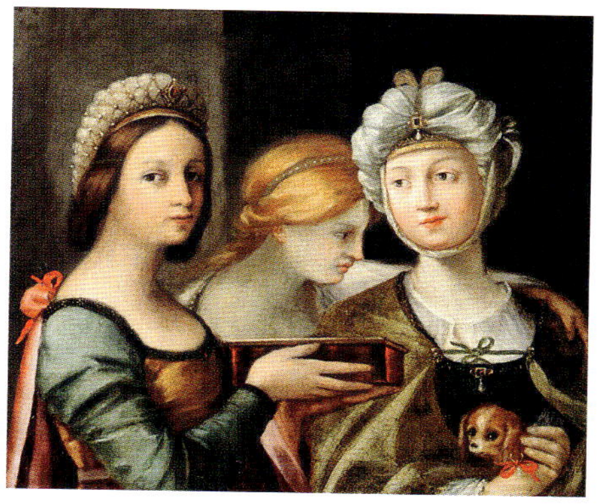

unknown artist
Three Female Figures
oil on canvas 43.9 x 50.8
VIS.2726

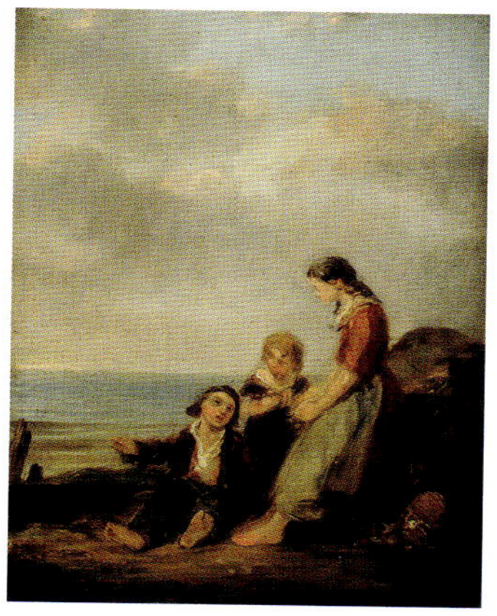

unknown artist
Three Figures on the Shore
oil on board 25.4 x 19.9
VIS.2359

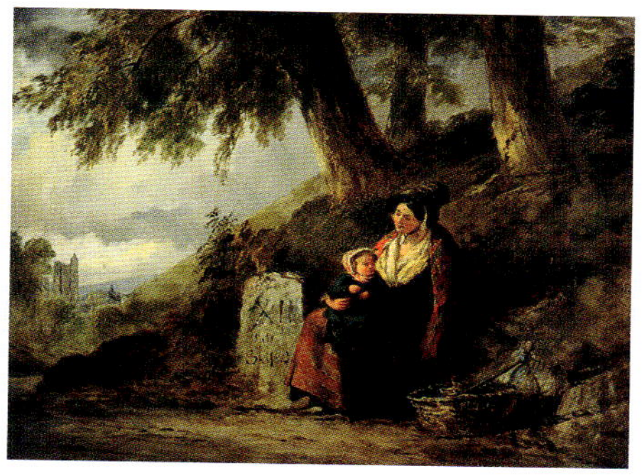

unknown artist
Wayfarers
oil on panel 45 x 59.3
VIS.547

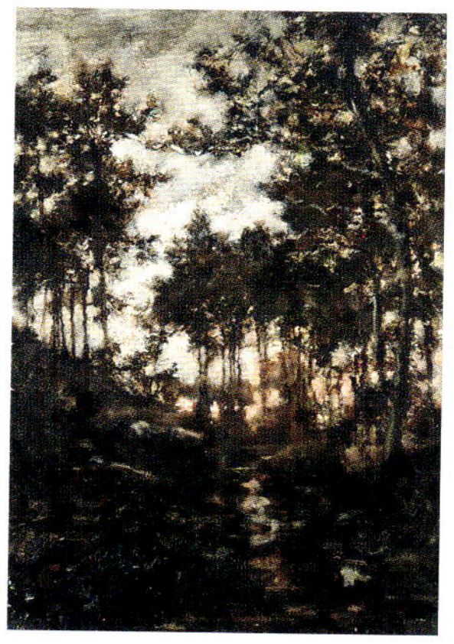

unknown artist
Woodland
oil on canvas 61.2 x 45.8
VIS.1221

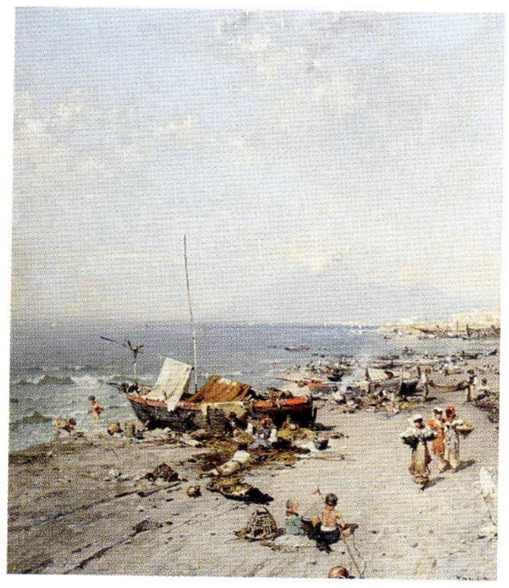

Unterberger, Franz Richard 1838–1902
Rivera de Castellammare, Italy 1870–1875
oil on canvas 79.1 x 66.4
VIS.695

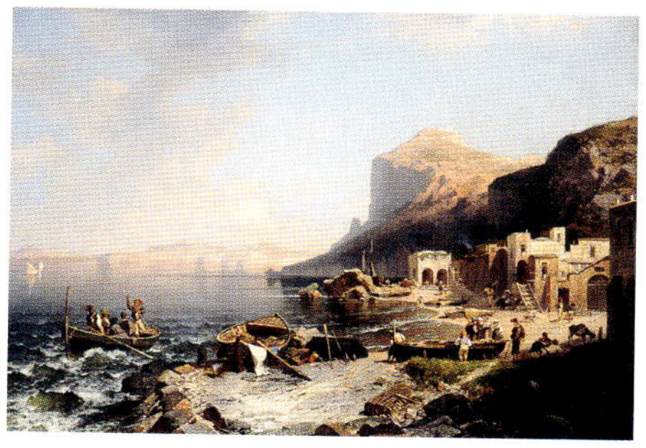

Unterberger, Franz Richard 1838–1902
Port of Capri, Italy
oil on canvas 66 x 94
VIS.116

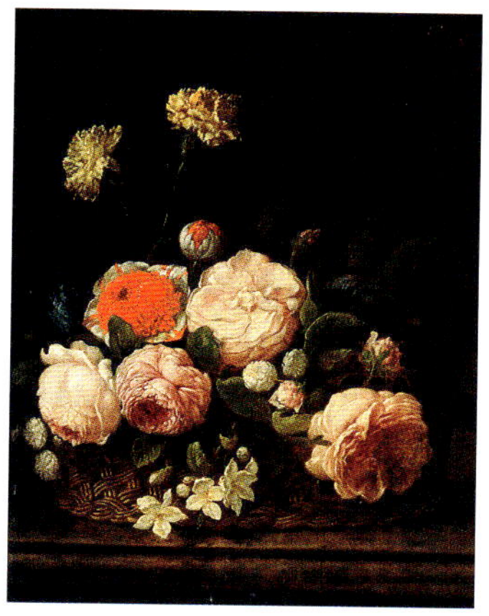

Van Assen, Benedictus Antonio 1788–1817
Flowers
oil on panel 39.4 x 30.4
VIS.27

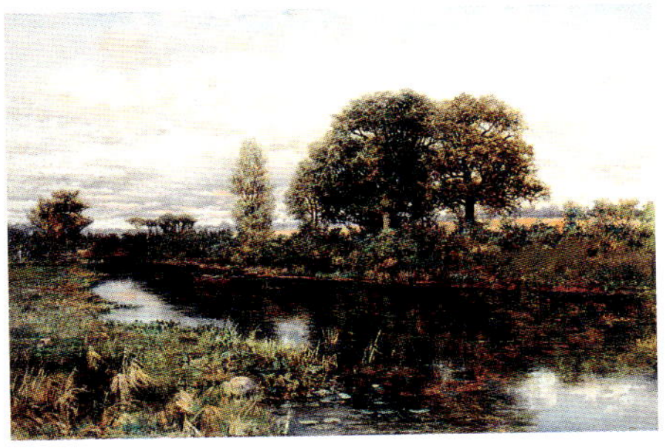

Van Boskerck, Robert Ward 1855–1932
A Rhode Island River, America
oil on canvas 112.4 x 163.4
VIS.1691

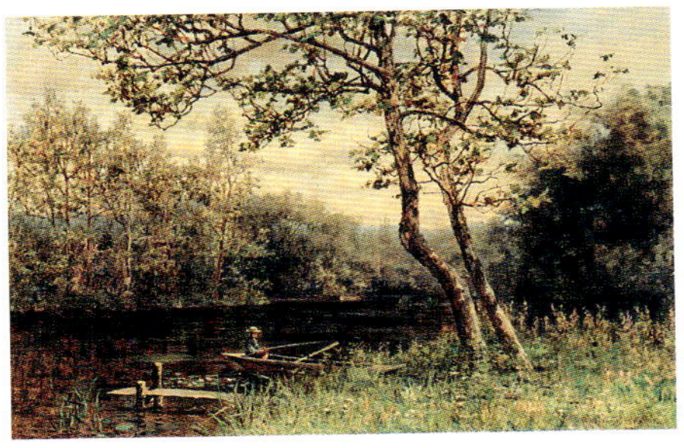

Van Boskerck, Robert Ward 1855–1932
American River Scene
oil on canvas 49.7 x 75.2
VIS.2856

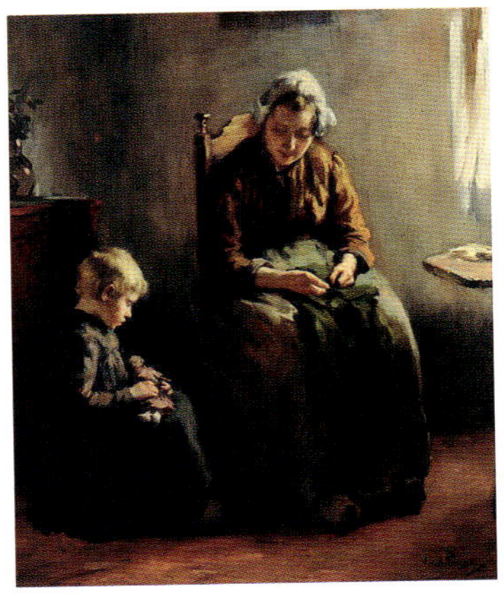

Van de Tonge, Louis 1871–1937
The New Doll
oil on canvas 52.9 x 43.7
VIS.632

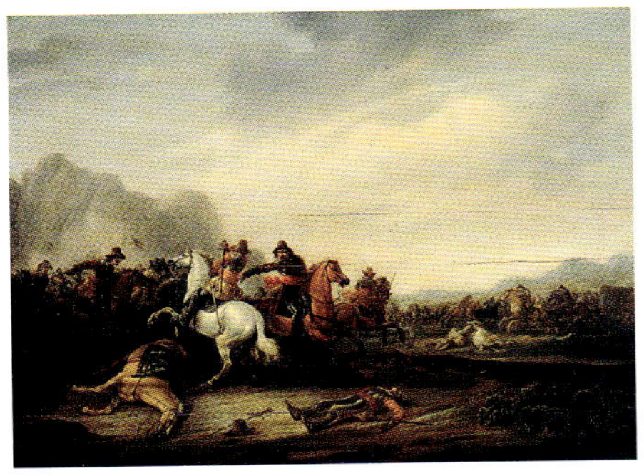

Van der Hoef, Abraham (attributed to)
1611/1612–1649
A Cavalry Skirmish 1630–1640
oil on panel 46.8 x 62.8
VIS.70

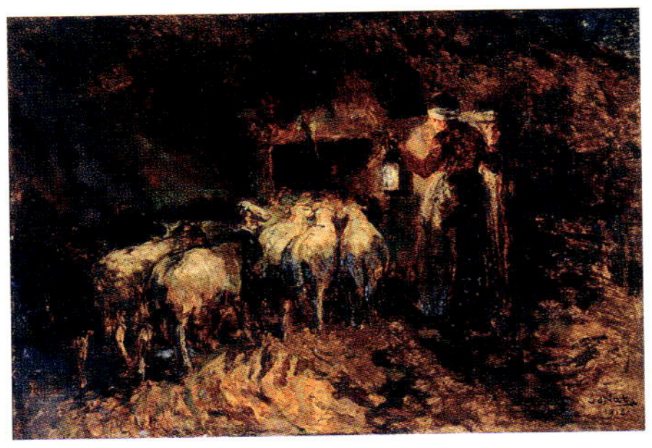

Van der Nat, Willem Hendrik 1865–1929
Sheep in a Barn 1918
oil on canvas 72.2 x 102
VIS.791

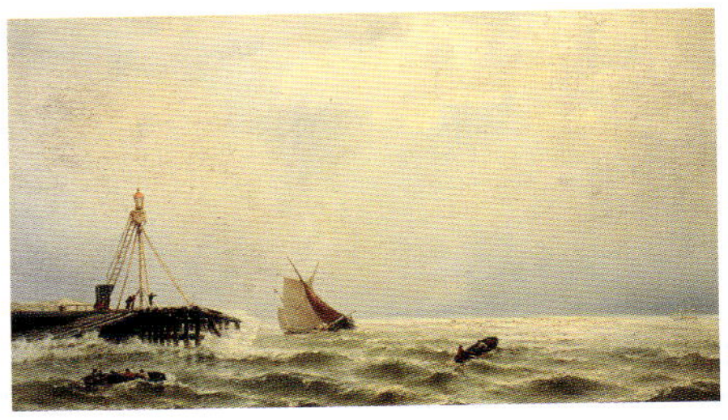

Van Heemskerck van Beest, Jacob Eduard
1828–1894
Sea View
oil on canvas 80.5 x 134.5
VIS.1470

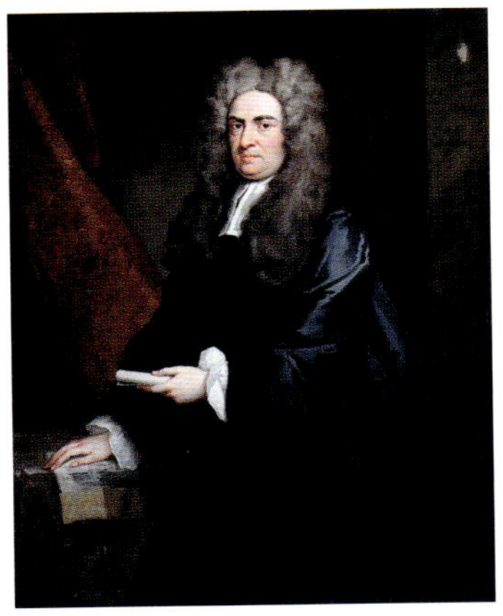

Vanderbank, John c.1694–1739
William Rogers of Dowdeswell, Master in the High Court of Chancery 1721
oil on canvas 127.4 x 102.2
VIS.3945

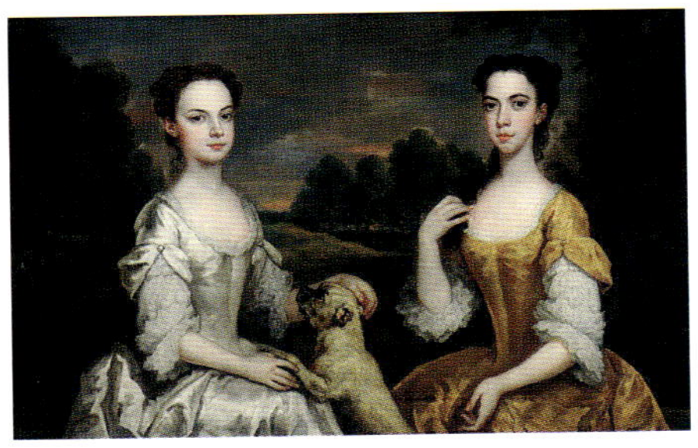

Vanderbank, John c.1694–1739
Anne and Mary Tonson 1734
oil on canvas 85.4 x 130.6
VIS.379

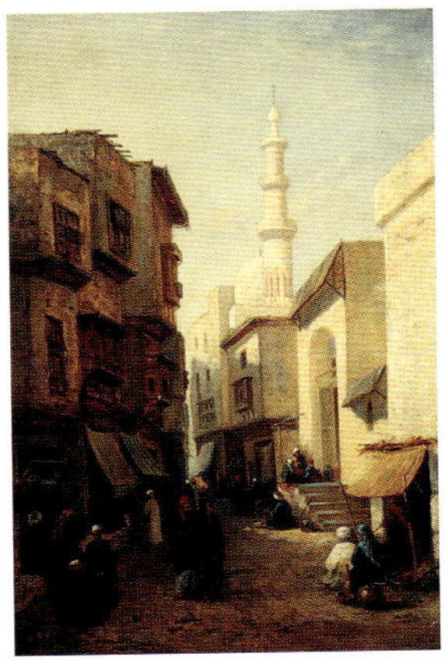

Varley, John II 1850–1933
Mosque near the Bab al-Nasr, Cairo 1878
oil on canvas 75 x 49.7
VIS.1275

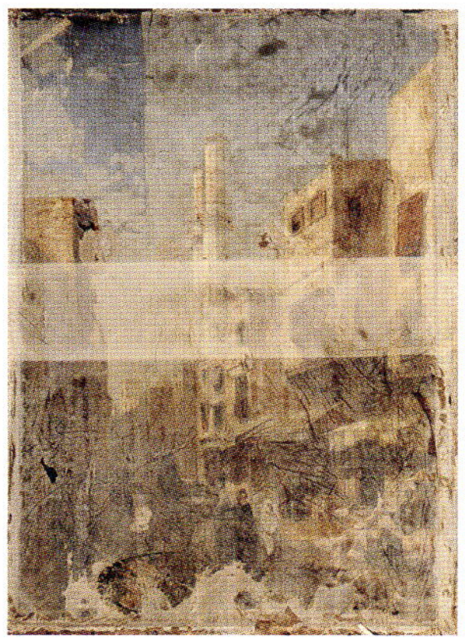

Varley, John II 1850–1933
Near the Gate of the Zueylah, Cairo 1878
oil on canvas 76 x 53.8
VIS.4744

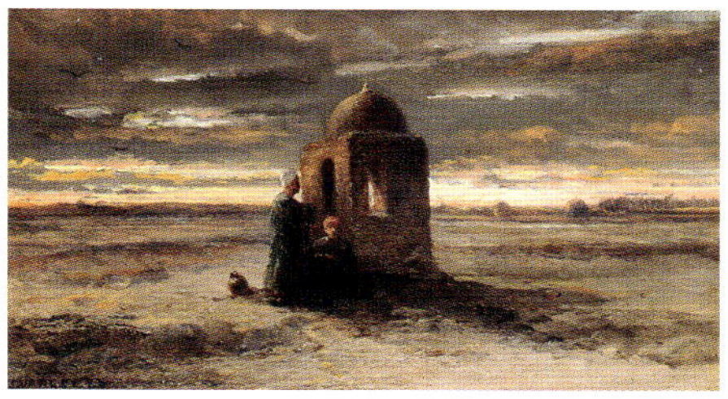

Varley, John II 1850–1933
A Well at Abbassieh, Near Cairo 1883
oil on panel 13.7 x 24.7
VIS.1054

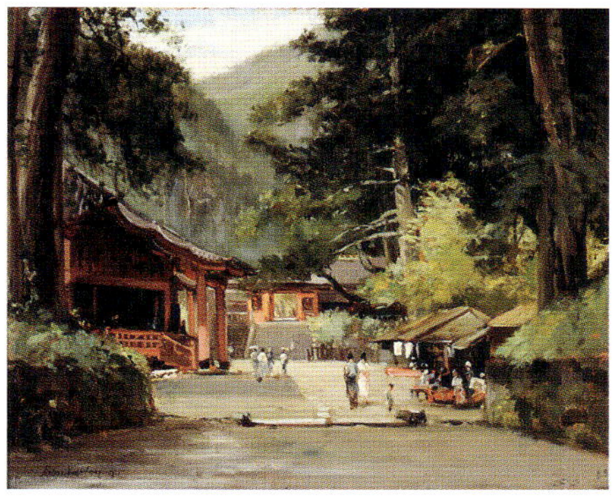

Varley, John II 1850–1933
Entrance to the Mausoleum of Jyemiten, Nikko, Japan 1890
oil on panel 27.6 x 33.6
VIS.640

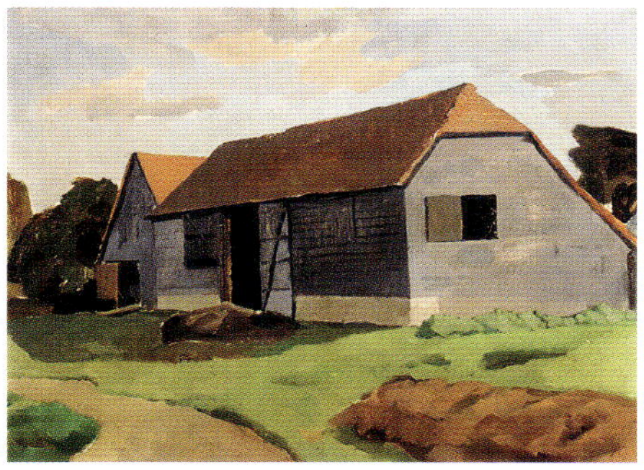

Vaughan, John Keith 1912–1977
The Barn 1935
oil on panel 43.3 x 58.7
VIS.4225

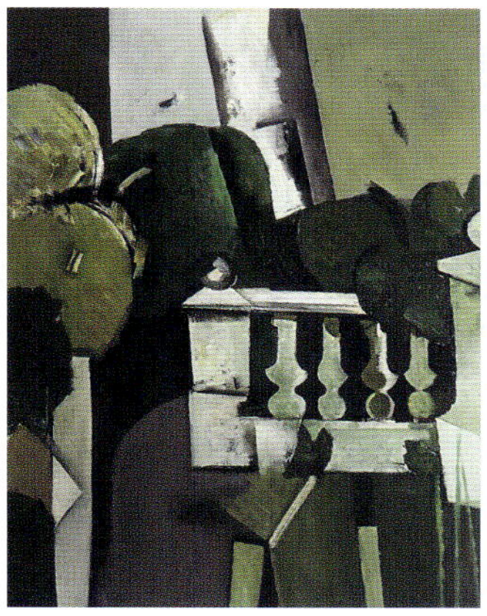

Vaughan, John Keith 1912–1977
Landscape in Belsize Park, London 1954
oil on canvas 89.4 x 68.9
VIS.4010

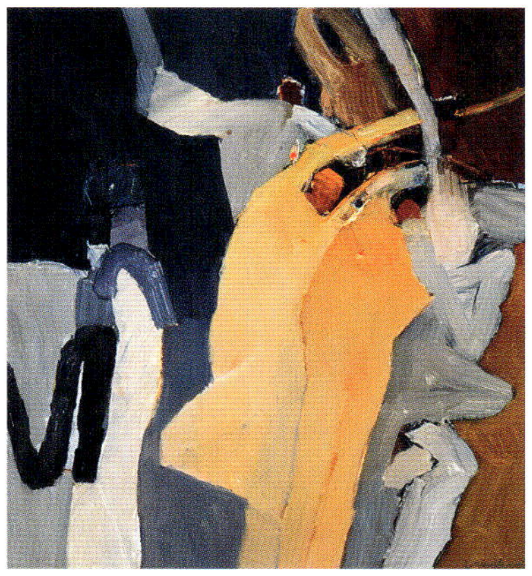

Vaughan, John Keith 1912–1977
Study for a Laocoon, VII 1964
oil on board 43.5 x 38.8
VIS.4070

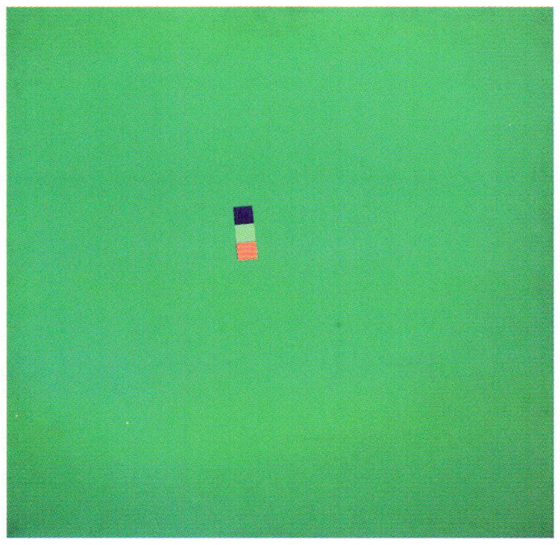

Vaux, Marc b.1932
L. S. Green 3 1969
acrylic on canvas 79.1 x 78.7
VIS.3712

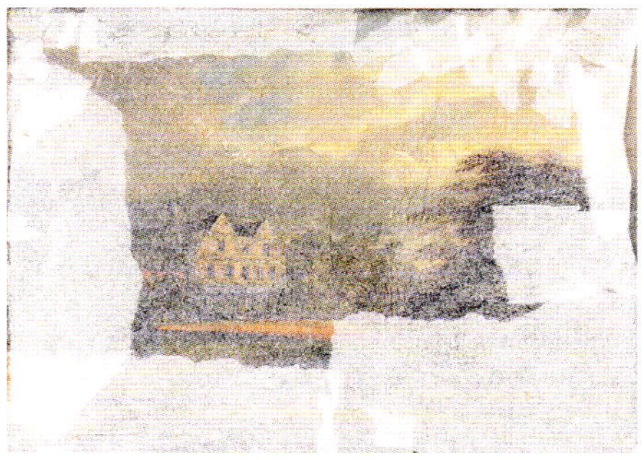

Vawser, George Robert 1815–1893
Norwood Hall, Pitsmoor, Sheffield 1854
oil on canvas 40.7 x 56.6
K1919.69

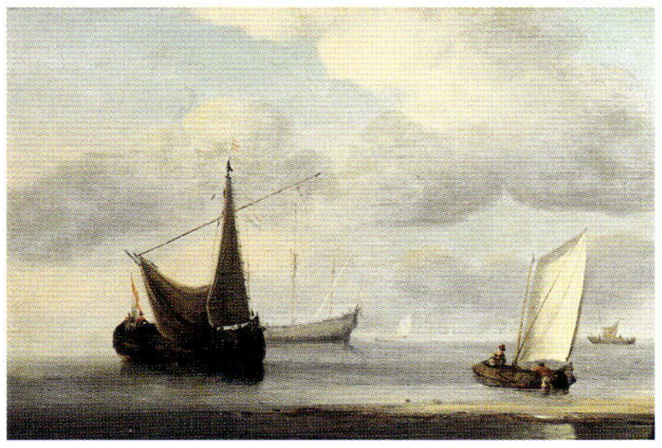

Velde, Willem van de II (school of) 1633–1707
Seascape 1660–1680
oil on panel 31 x 44.5
VIS.1312

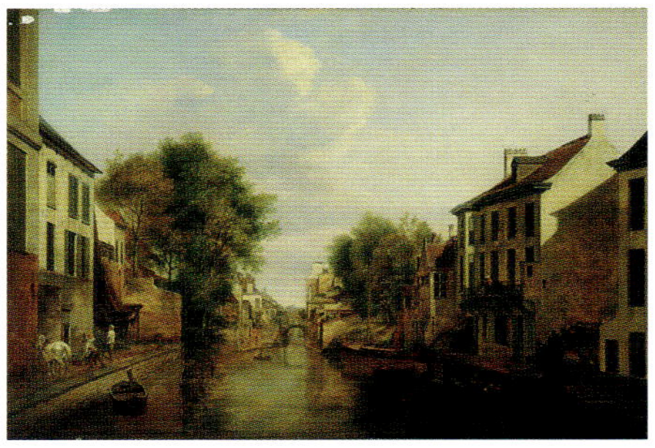

Verheyden, François (attributed to)
1806–1889/1890
The Canal, Bruges, Belgium 1850–1860
oil on panel 37.7 x 53.5
VIS.368

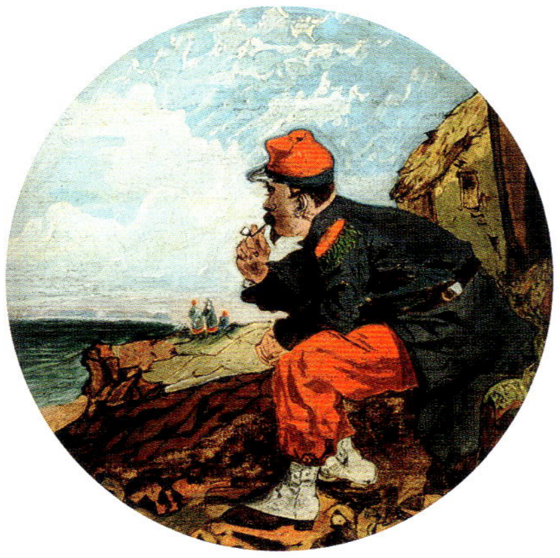

Vernet, Claude-Joseph 1714–1789
A French Soldier
oil on canvas 23.4
VIS.1025

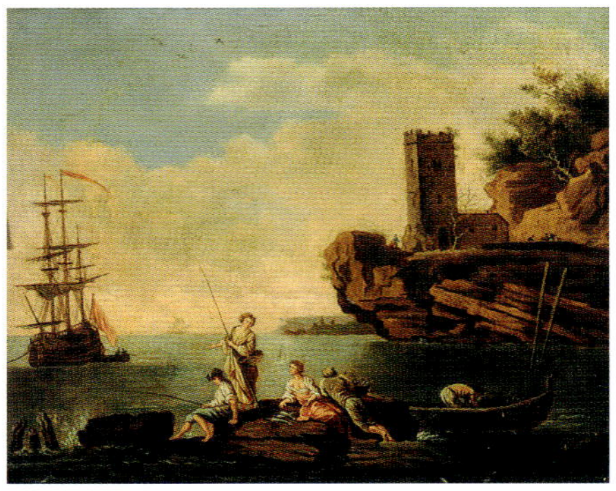

Vernet, Claude-Joseph 1714–1789
Sea Piece
oil on canvas 41.6 x 51.4
VIS.1237

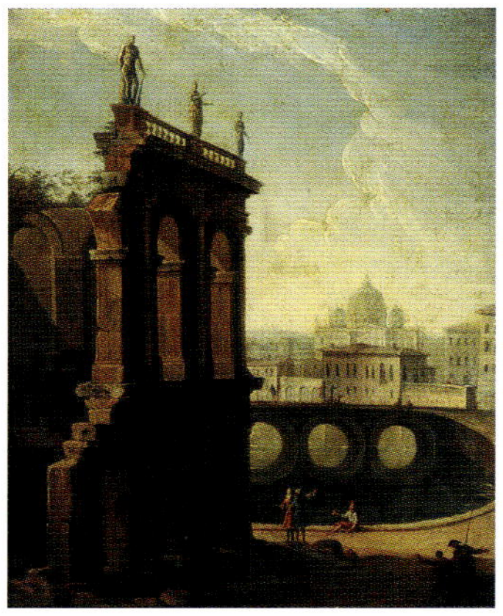

Vernet, Claude-Joseph (attributed to)
1714–1789
Castel Sant'Angelo, Rome 1750–1770
oil on canvas 44.2 x 35.4
VIS.139

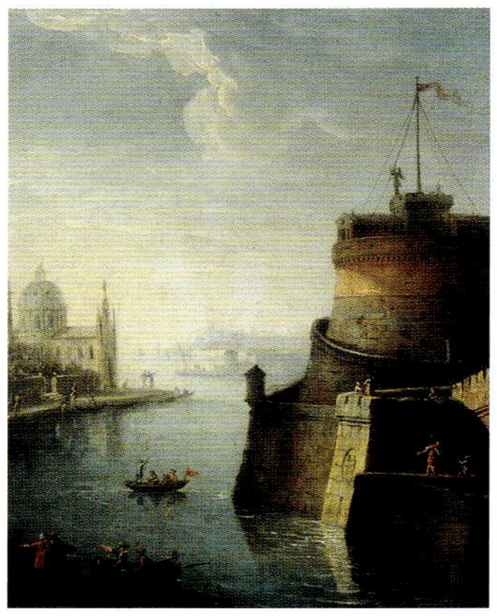

Vernet, Claude-Joseph (attributed to)
1714–1789
Scene on the Tiber 1750–1770
oil on canvas 44.2 x 35.4
VIS.138

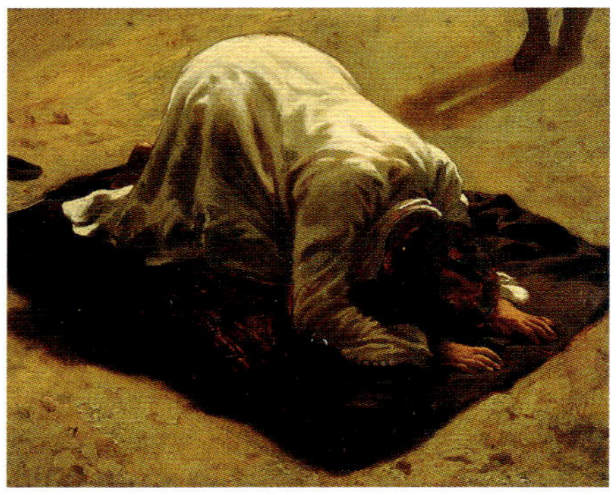

Vernet, Horace 1789–1863
An Arab at Prayer
oil on canvas on panel 24.5 x 29.2
VIS.950

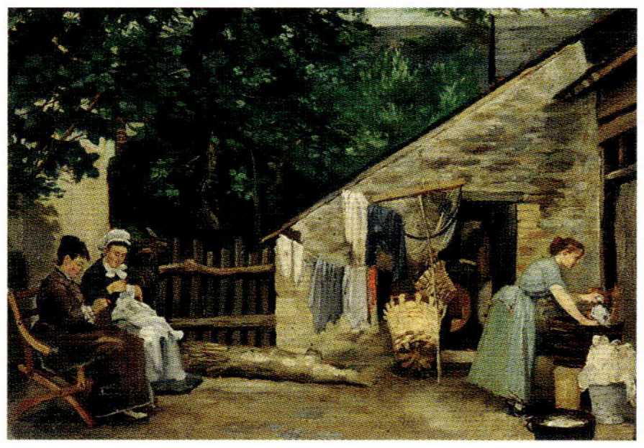

Vernier, Émile Louis (attributed to)
1829–1887
A Cottage at Amiens, France 1855–1860
oil on panel 23.8 x 33.9
VIS.530

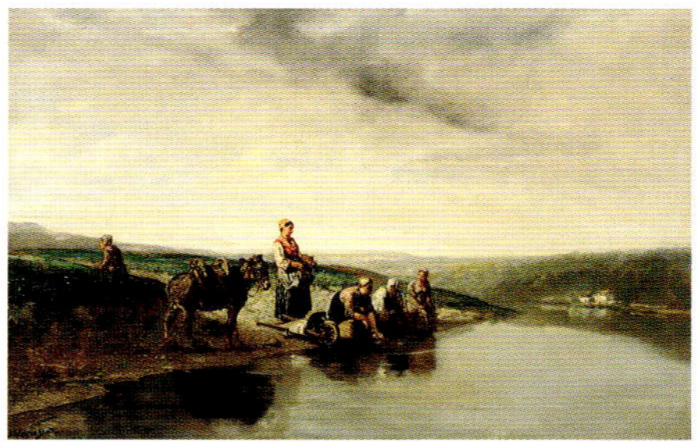

Veyrassat, Jules Jacques 1828–1893
Landscape with a River 1850–1855
oil on canvas 64 x 99.1
VIS.2845

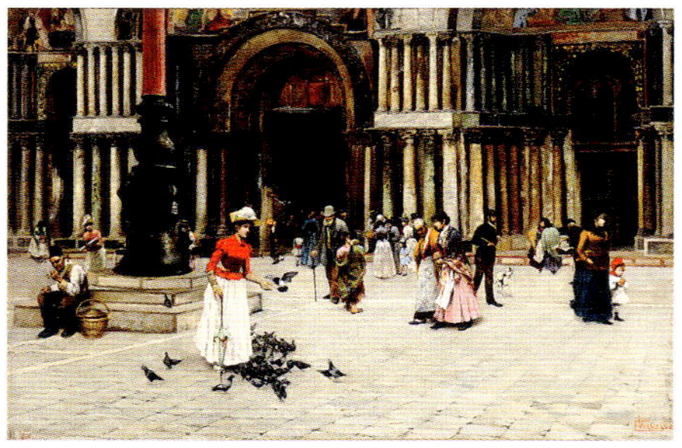

Vianello, Giovanni 1873–1926
Venezia
oil on canvas 59.5 x 89.9
VIS.2529

Facing page: Sickert, Walter Richard, 1860–1842, *Fred Winter* (detail), Museums Sheffield, (p. 194)

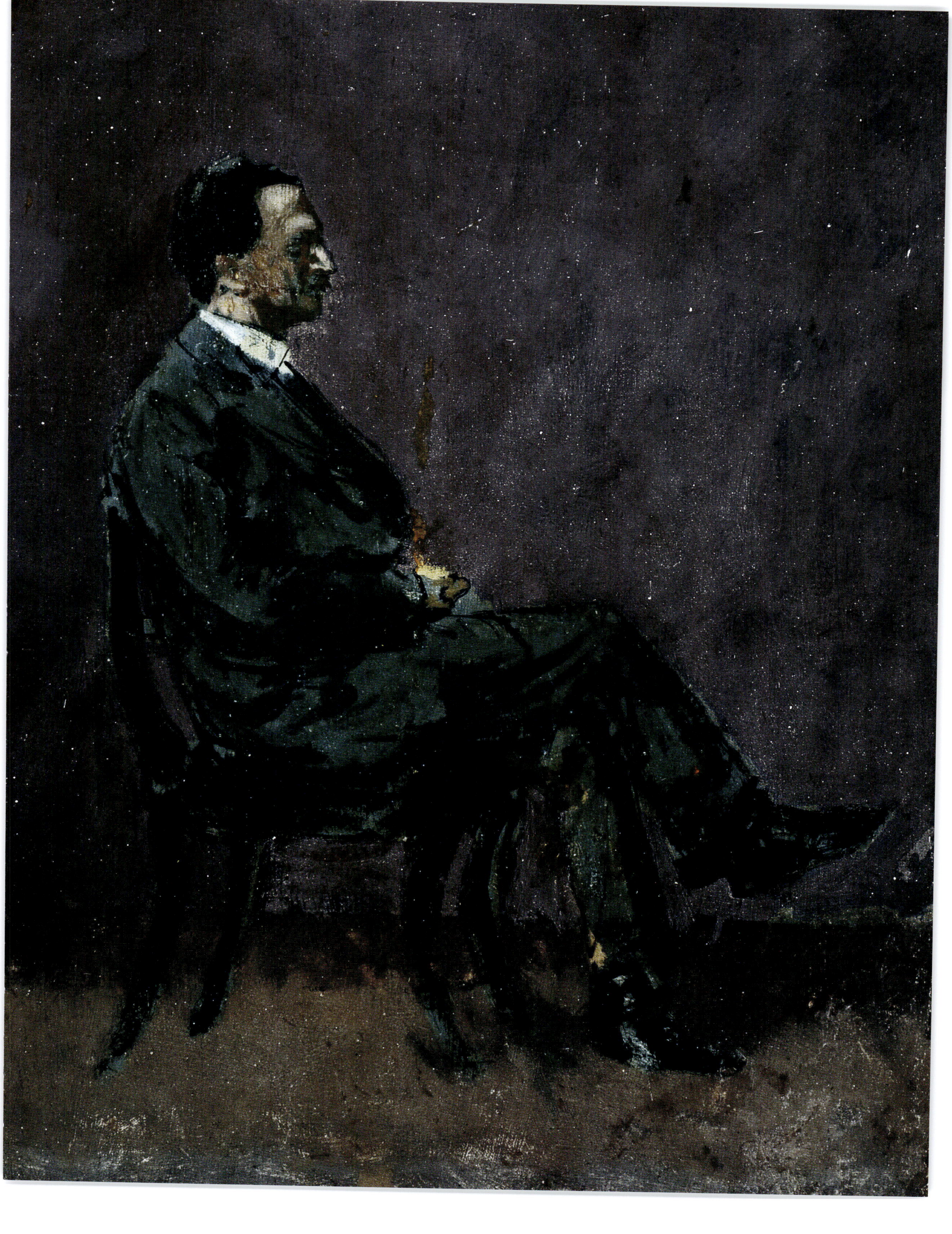

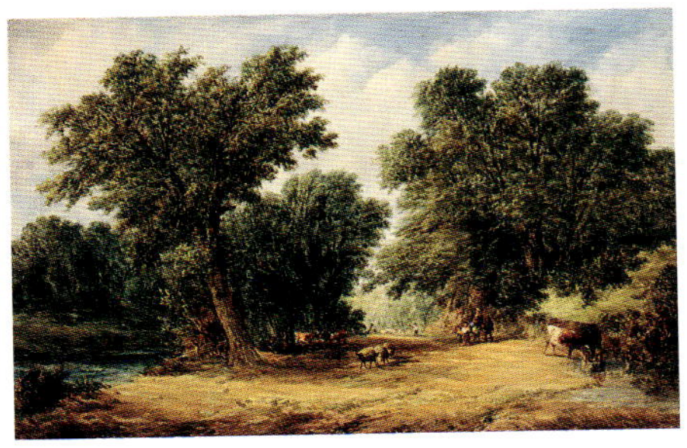

Vickers, Alfred 1786–1868
At Bolton Abbey, North Yorkshire 1858
oil on canvas 40.4 x 60.3
VIS.528

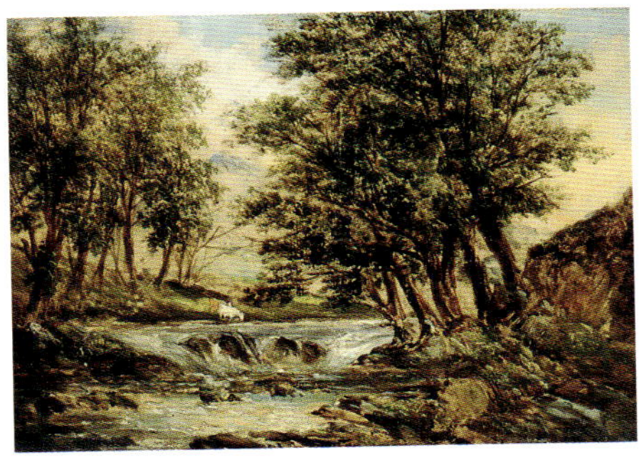

Vickers, Alfred 1786–1868
Near Beddgelert, North Wales 1859
oil on canvas 24.3 x 34.6
VIS.1047

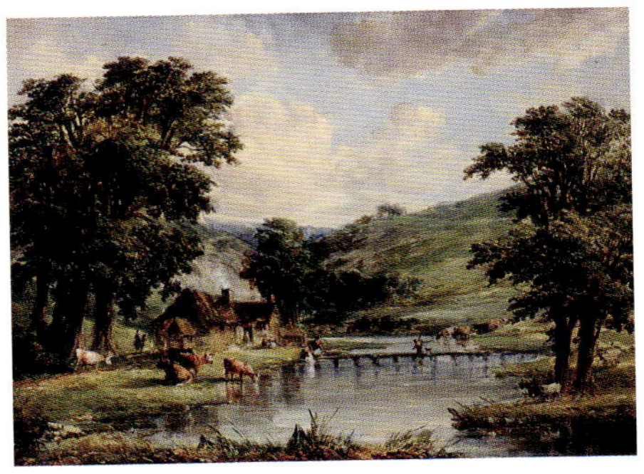

Vickers, Alfred 1786–1868
In Monsal Dale, Derbyshire 1862
oil on panel 32.3 x 43.1
VIS.1374

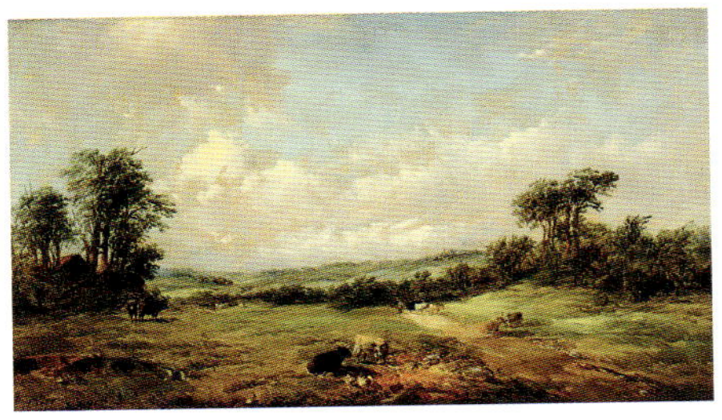

Vickers, Alfred 1786–1868
Landscape with Cattle 1864
oil on canvas 29.5 x 50
VIS.675

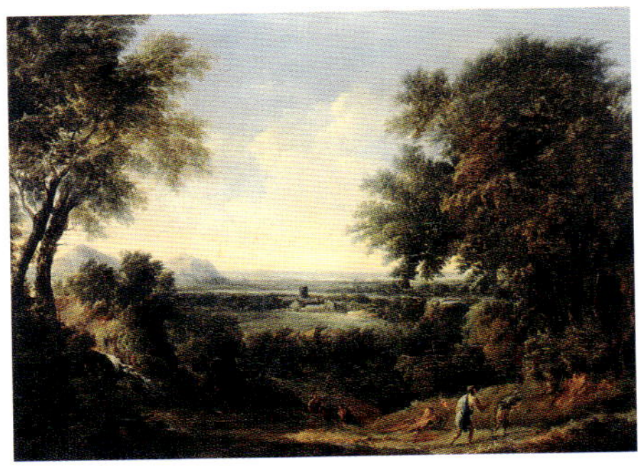

Vickers, Alfred 1786–1868
Abraham on His Way to the Sacrifice
oil on canvas 44.1 x 59.5
VIS.2370

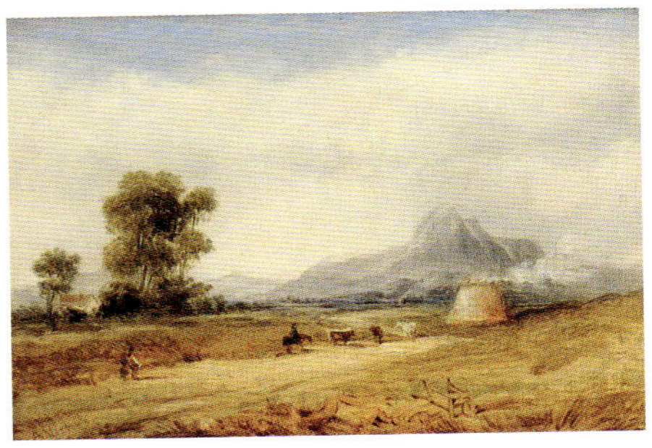

Vickers, Alfred 1786–1868
Landscape
oil on canvas 16.5 x 24.5
VIS.1022

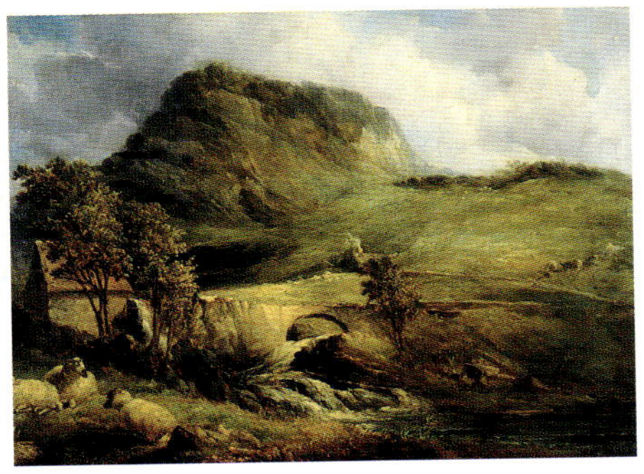

Vickers, Alfred 1786–1868
Landscape with a River
oil on canvas 43.8 x 59
VIS.1230

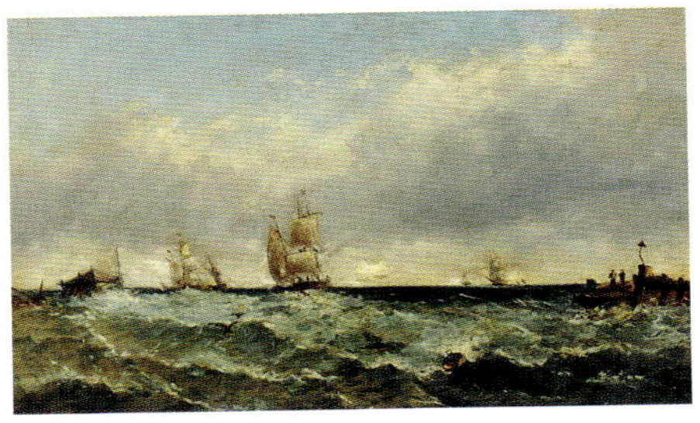

Vickers, Alfred 1786–1868
Off Calais, France
oil on canvas 42.6 x 67.9
VIS.634

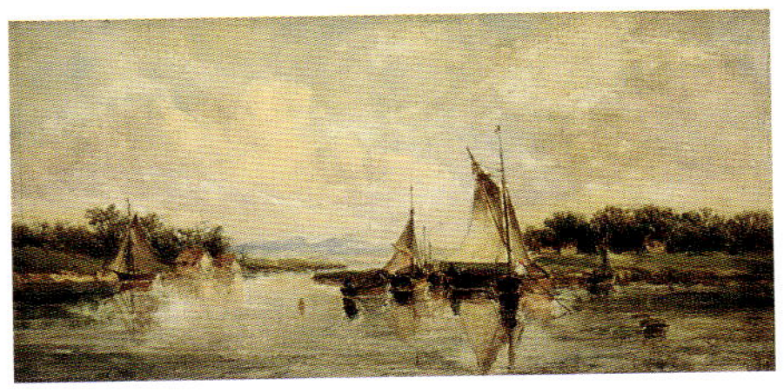

Vickers, Alfred 1786–1868
River Scene
oil on panel 17 x 34.6
VIS.774

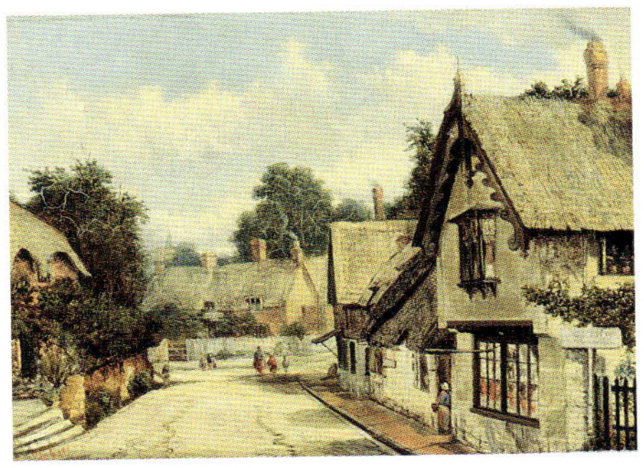

Vickers, Alfred 1786–1868
Village Street
oil on canvas 21.2 x 29.1
VIS.552

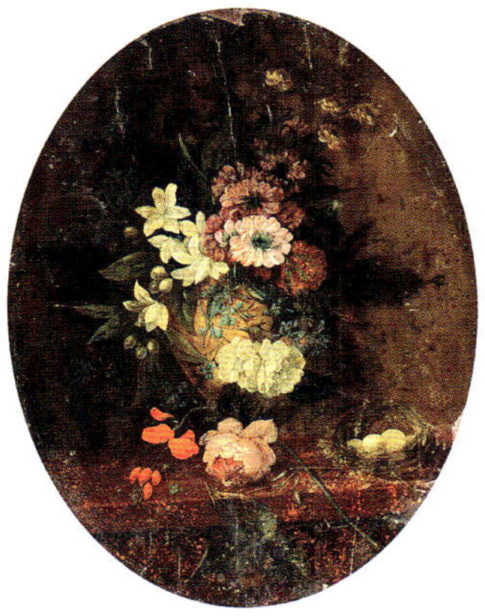

Vidal, Louis c.1754–1804
Vase of Flowers 1775–1785
oil on panel 43 x 33.1
VIS.29

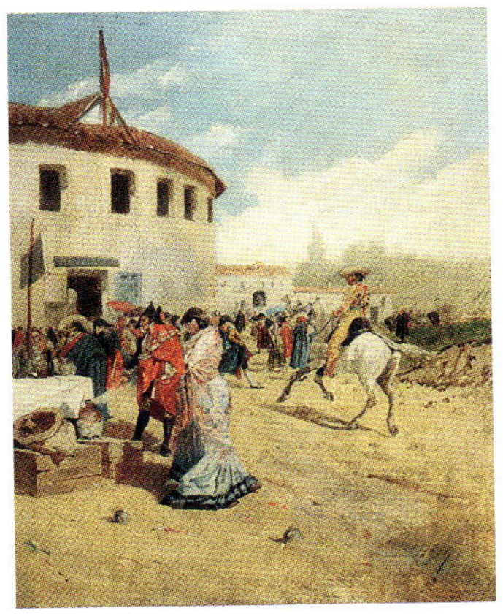

Villamil, Eugenio Lucas 1858–1918
To the Bull Ring
oil on canvas 56 x 44.5
VIS.621

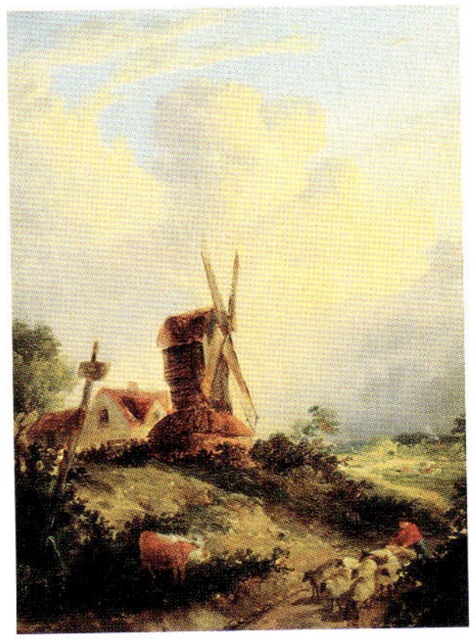

Vincent, George 1796–1831
A Norfolk Mill
oil on panel 32.8 x 24.2
VIS.348

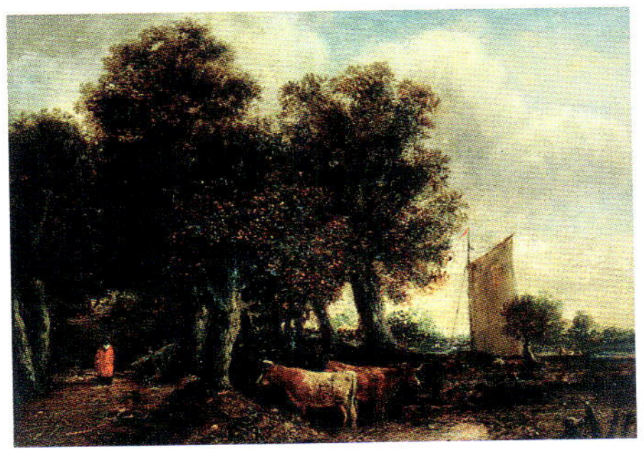

Vincent, George 1796–1831
A View near Thorpe, Norwich, Norfolk
oil on panel 23.8 x 33.8
VIS.315

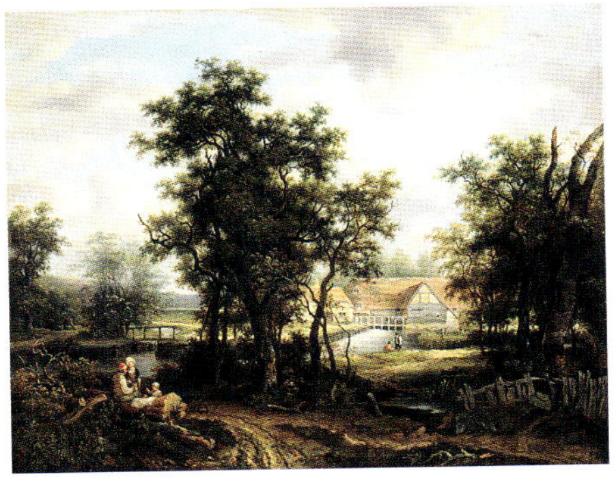

Vincent, George 1796–1831
A View of Suffolk
oil on canvas 90.6 x 113.4
VIS.1434

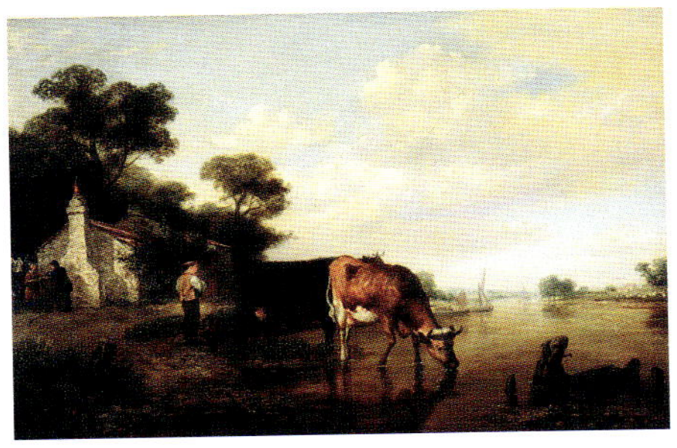

Vincent, George 1796–1831
Cattle Drinking
oil on canvas 49.8 x 75.1
VIS.373

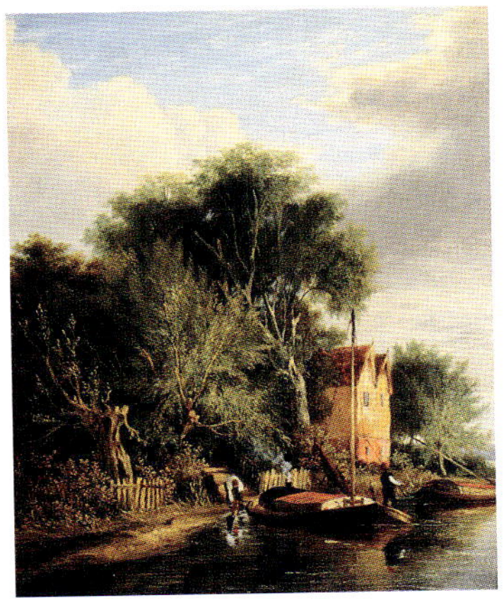

Vincent, George 1796–1831
On the Yare, Norfolk
oil on panel 28 x 22.3
VIS.2269

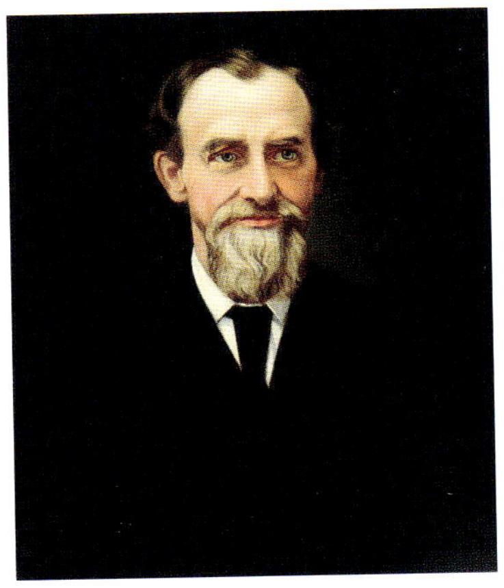

Vizard, W. active 1884–1903
Portrait of a Man 1884
oil on canvas 59.7 x 49.2
SH438

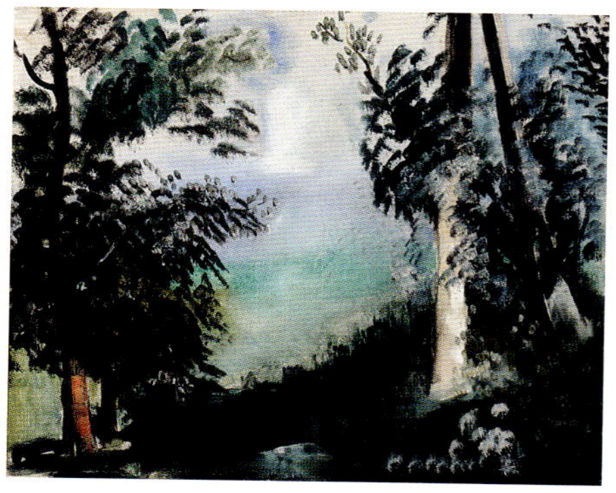

Vlaminck, Maurice de 1876–1958
The Edge of the Wood
oil on canvas 57.9 x 70.6
VIS.LI.894 (P)

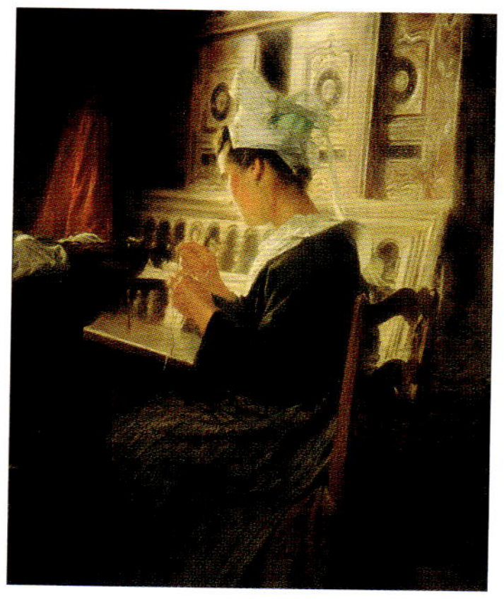

Vollon, Alexis 1865–1945
The Sewing Maid
oil on canvas 98.2 x 78.6
VIS.936

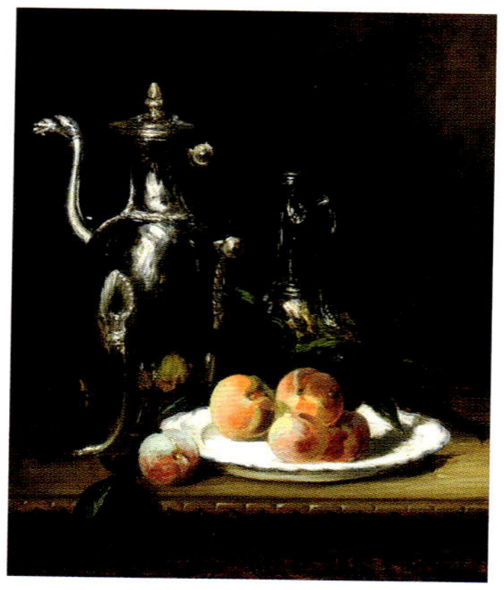

Vollon, Antoine 1833–1900
Peaches 1870–1875
oil on panel 44.7 x 37
VIS.271

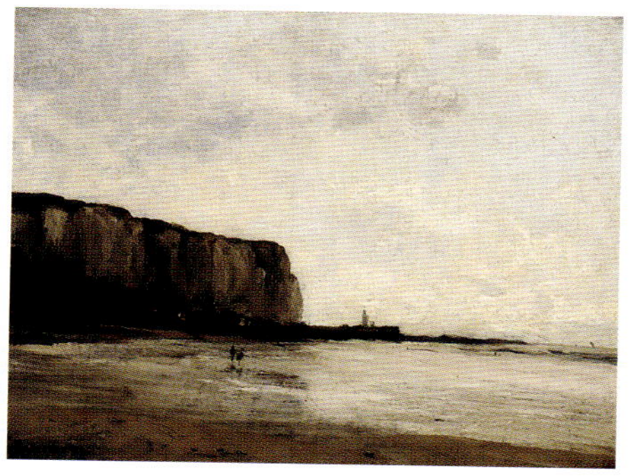

Vollon, Antoine 1833–1900
Coast near Étretat, France
oil on canvas 41.2 x 53.8
VIS.353

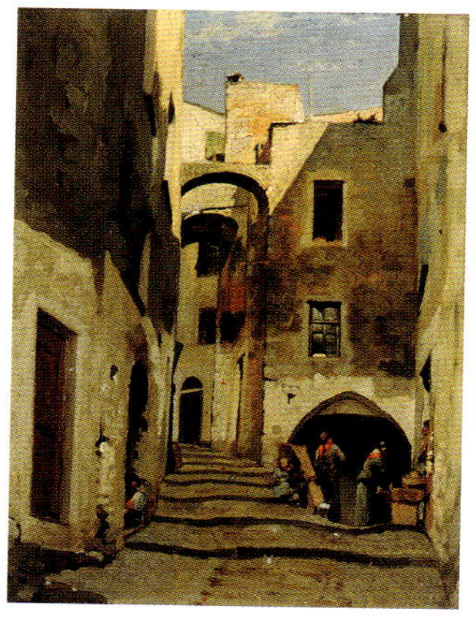

Von Gegerfeldt, Wilhelm 1844–1920
Eastern Scene
oil on panel 26.3 x 20
VIS.771

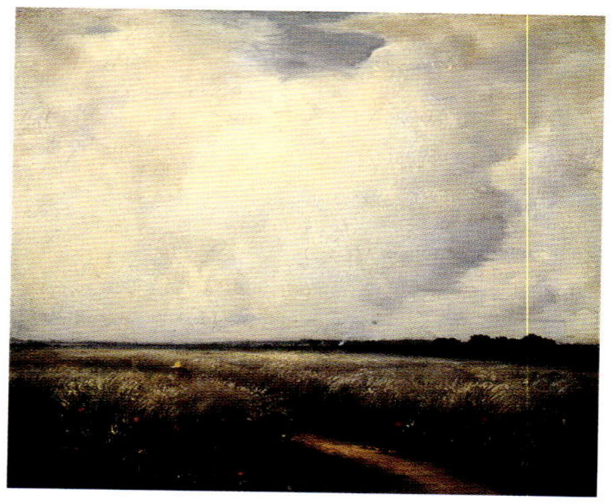

Von Löfftz, Ludwig 1845–1910
Cornfield 1907
oil on canvas 46 x 55.5
VIS.934

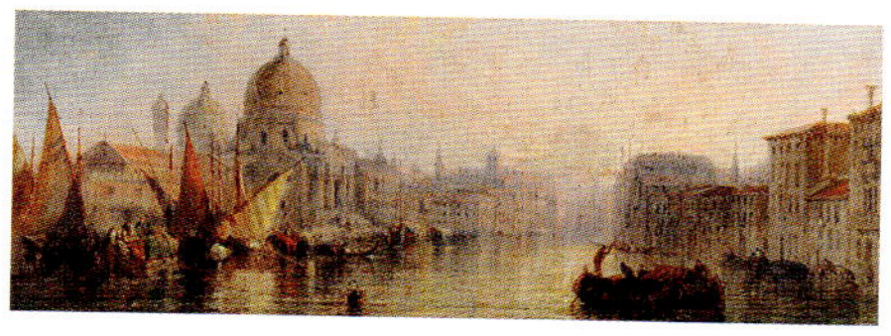

Vuram, J.
Entrance to the Grand Canal, Venice, Sunset
oil on canvas 26.4 x 72.2
VIS.1410

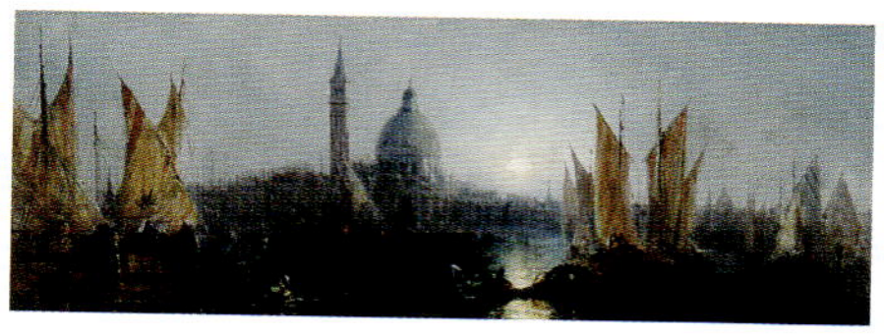

Vuram, J. (attributed to)
Santa Maria Maggiore, Venice, Moonlight
1840–1850
oil on canvas 26.4 x 72.2
VIS.1411

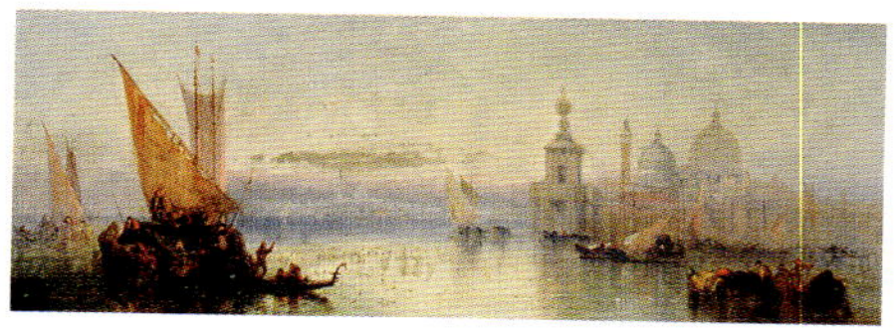

Vuram, J. (attributed to)
The Dogana, Venice, Early Morning
oil on canvas 26 x 71.5
VIS.1412

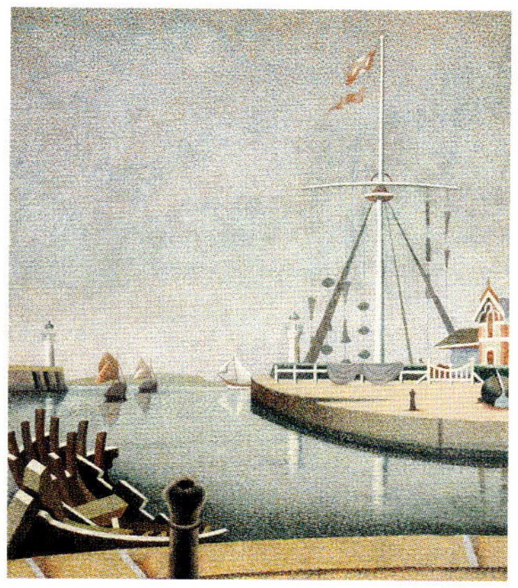

Wadsworth, Edward Alexander 1889–1949
Honfleur, France, Entrance to the Harbour
1939
tempera on cardboard 71 x 62
VIS.4284

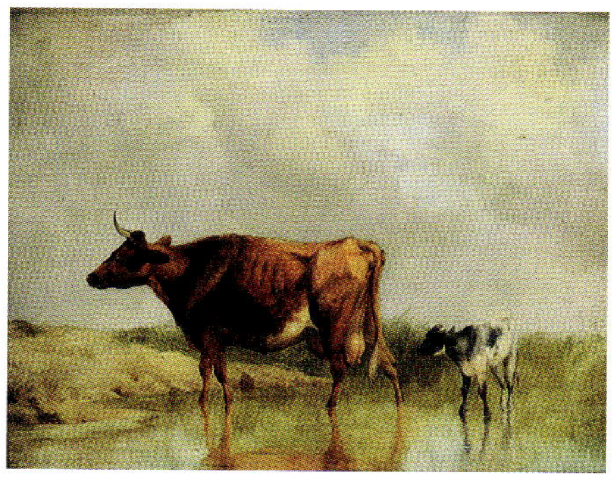

Wainewright, Thomas Francis 1794–1883
Landscape with Cattle
oil on panel 19 x 24.2
VIS.1066

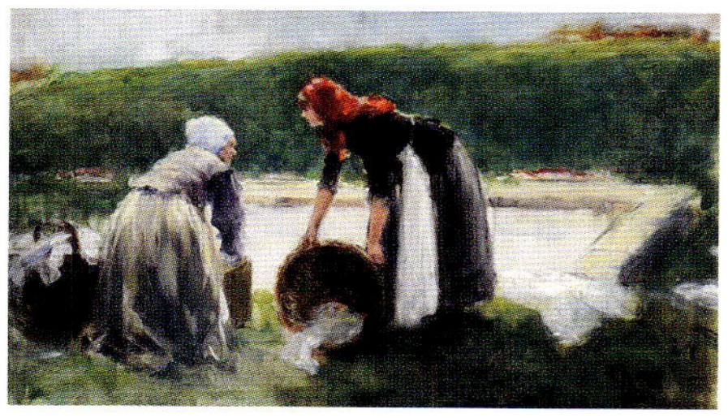

Wakle, J. F.
Washing Day
oil on canvas 34.7 x 60
VIS.1257

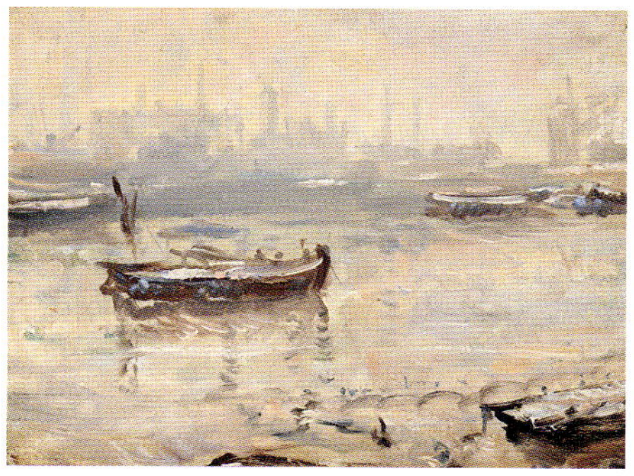

Walker, Ethel 1861–1951
Midday Shore
oil on panel 26.3 x 34.6
VIS.4343

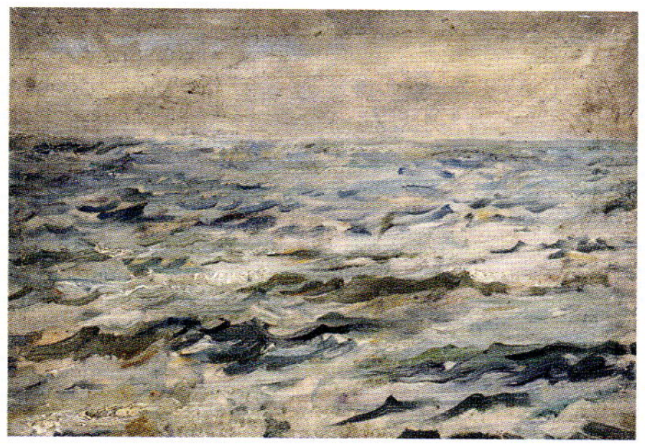

Walker, Ethel 1861–1951
Seascape
oil on panel 23.5 x 33.2
VIS.4344

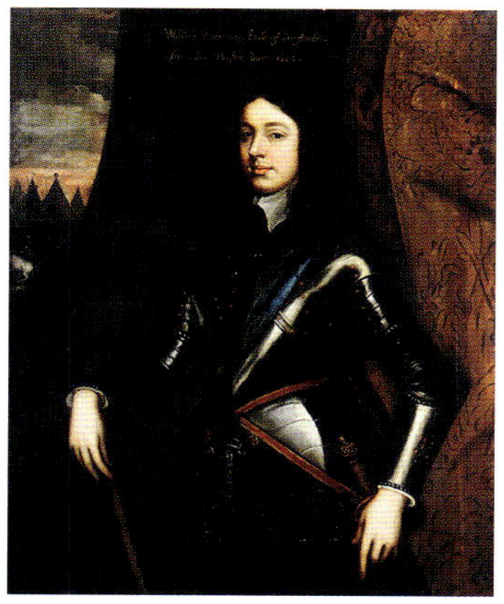

Walker, Robert 1599–1658
The Earl of Strafford (possibly Wiliam Wentworth, 1626–1695) 1654
oil on canvas 121.5 x 97.5
VIS.546

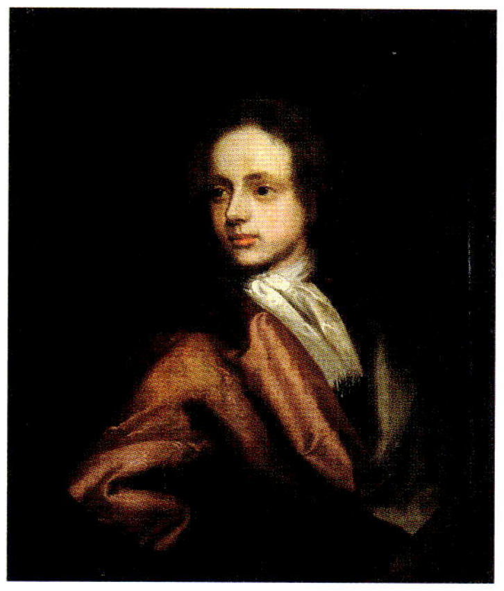

Walker, Robert (after) 1599–1658
Portrait of a Young Man
oil on canvas 76.7 x 63.5
VIS.2614

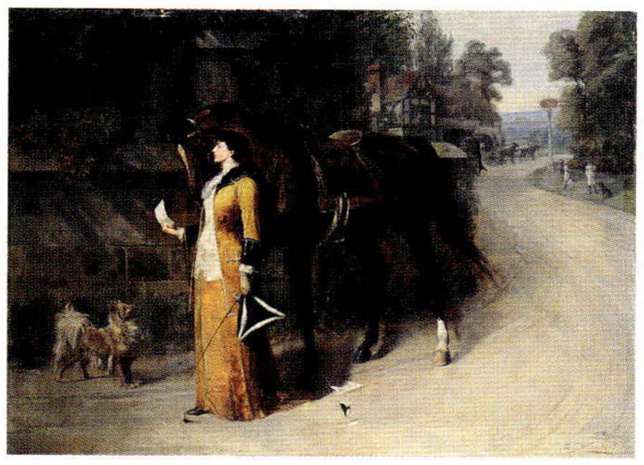

Waller, Samuel Edmund 1850–1903
Keep My Secret 1897
oil on canvas 124 x 168.6
VIS.1677

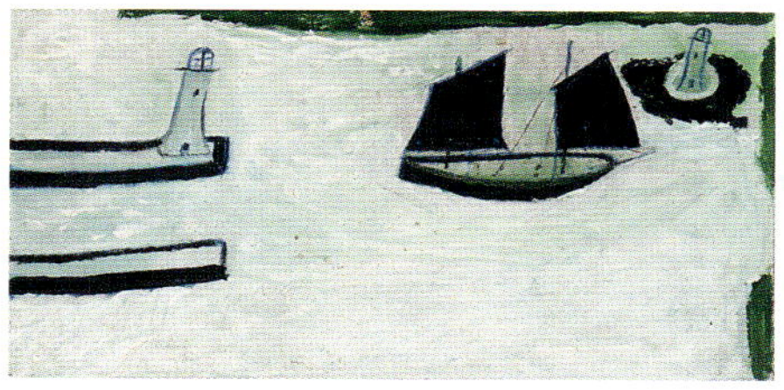

Wallis, Alfred 1855–1942
Fishing Boat Between Two Lighthouses
oil on board 34.5 x 52.4
VIS.3831

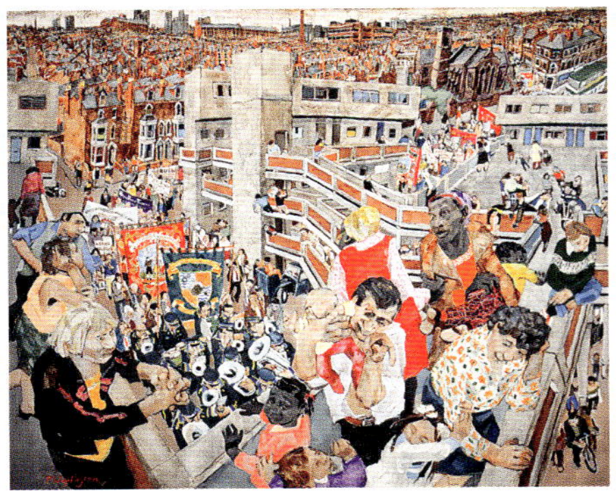

Waplington, Paul Anthony b.1938
May Day, Hyson Green, Nottinghamshire 1978
acrylic on canvas 150.5 x 181.5
VIS.4945

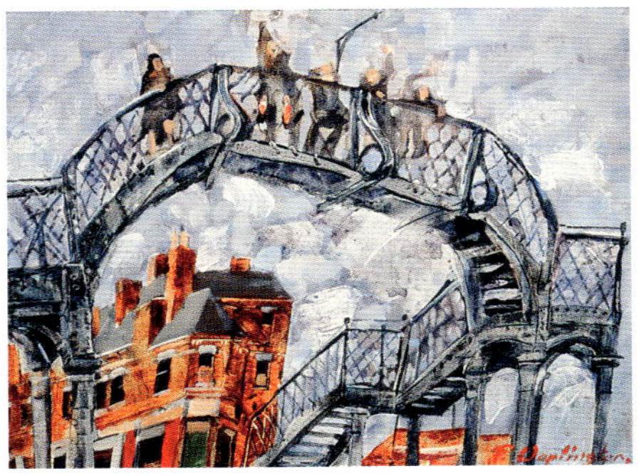

Waplington, Paul Anthony b.1938
Footbridge
acrylic on canvas 29.8 x 39.9
VIS.5437

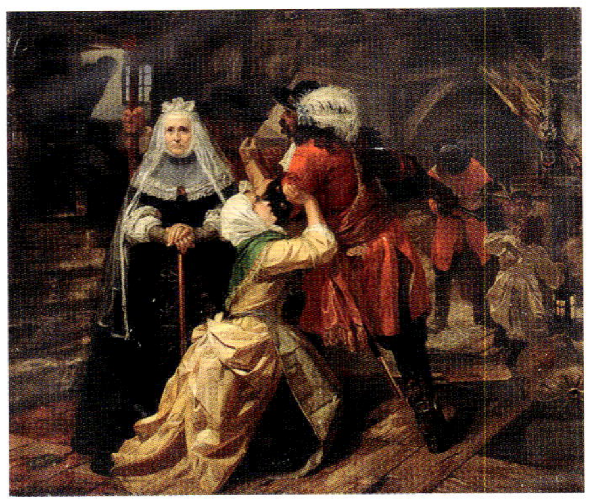

Ward, Edward Matthew 1816–1879
The Concealment of the Fugitive by Alice Lisle (after the Battle of Sedgemoor in the reign of James II) 1858
oil on canvas 205.8 x 235.8
VIS.1484

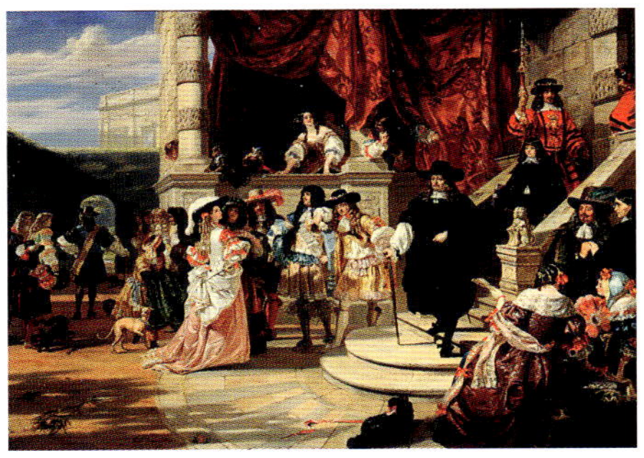

Ward, Edward Matthew 1816–1879
The Fall of Clarendon 1861
oil on canvas 65 x 89.4
VIS.1424

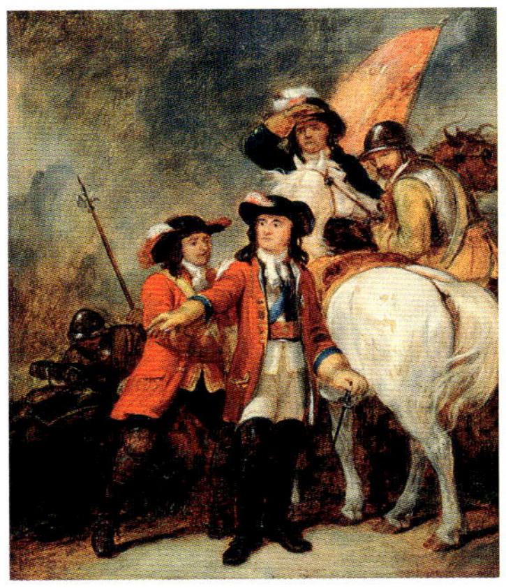

Ward, Edward Matthew 1816–1879
Cavalry Man
oil on canvas 22.7 x 19.2
VIS.1012

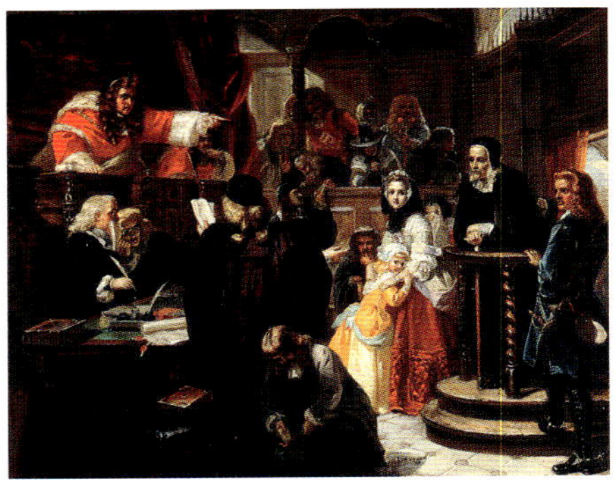

Ward, Edward Matthew 1816–1879
Judge Jeffreys Bullying Richard Baxter
oil on canvas 42.2 x 52.2
VIS.1578

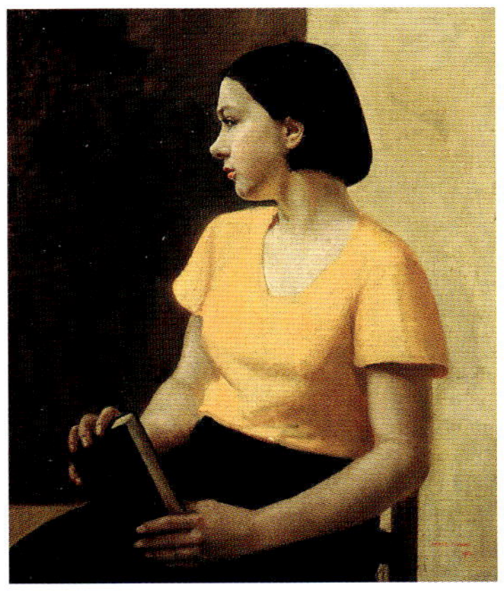

Ward, Grace active 1930–1940s
Juanita 1932
oil on canvas 59.2 x 49
VIS.674

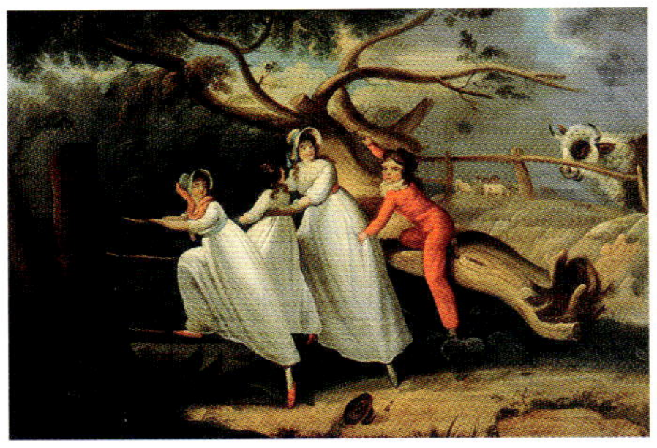

Ward, James 1769–1859
Disobedience in Danger
oil on iron 43.8 x 63.1
VIS.1685

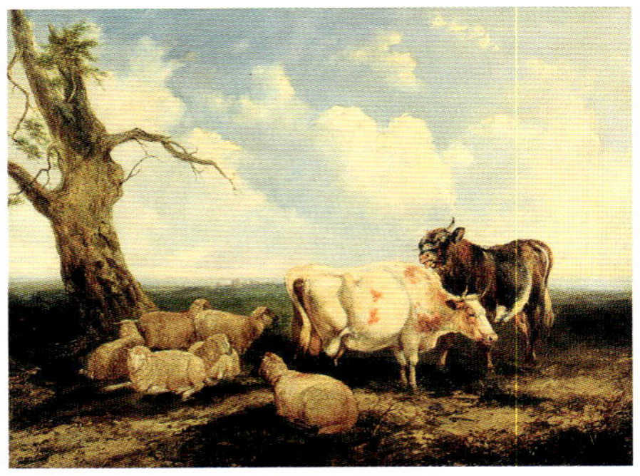

Ward, James 1769–1859
Landscape with Cattle
oil on canvas 67.5 x 89.2
VIS.2304

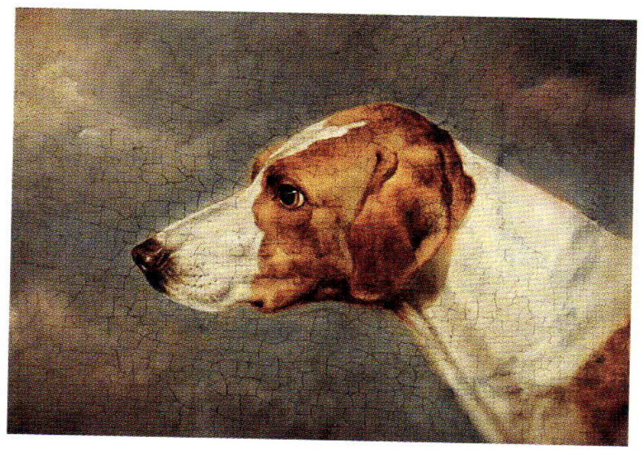

Ward, Martin Theodore 1799–1874
Dog's Head
oil on panel 30.6 x 42.9
VIS.616

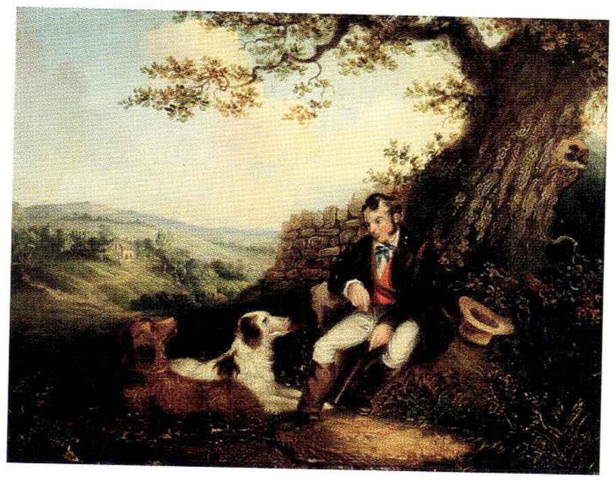

Ward, Martin Theodore 1799–1874
The Sportsman
oil on board 19.1 x 24.3
VIS.303

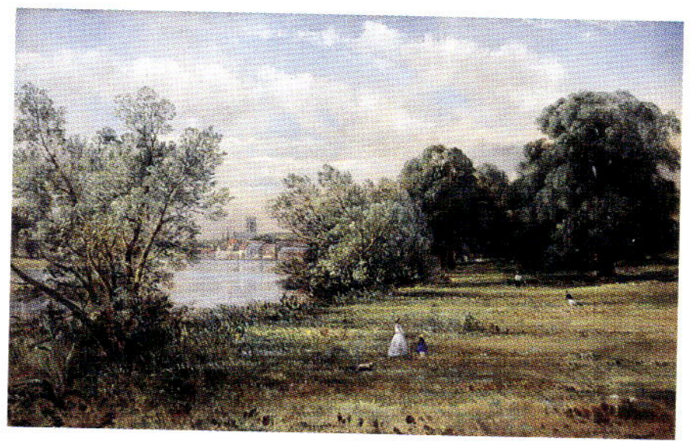

Ward, T. active 1819–1865
Henley-on-Thames, Oxfordshire 1865
oil on canvas 43.3 x 66.2
VIS.895

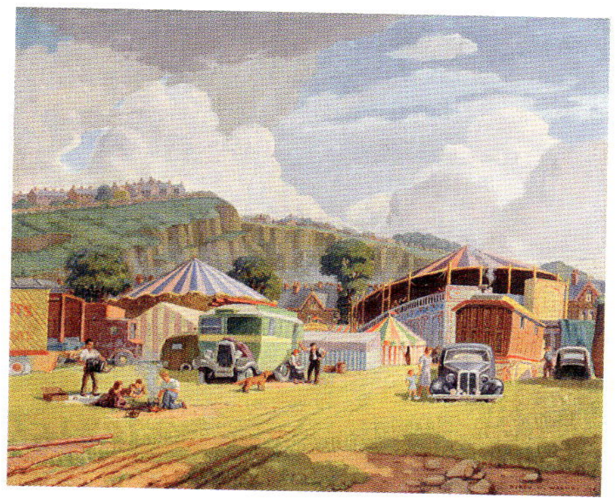

Warmby, Byron Winston 1902–1978
A Fair in Endcliffe Park, Sheffield 1944
oil on board 49.1 x 59
2008.361

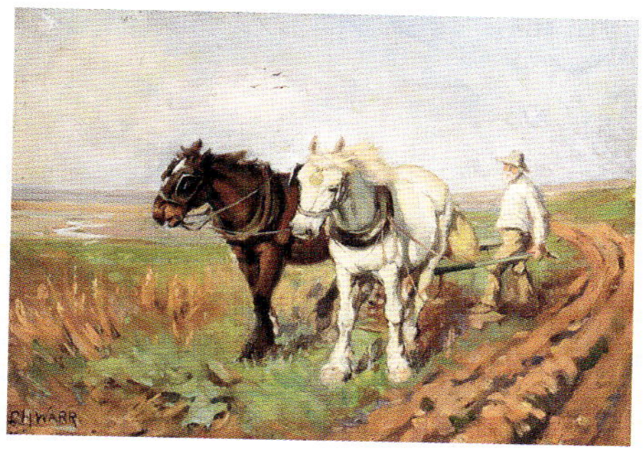

Warr, George H. 1907–1933
Ploughing Scene
oil on canvas 24 x 34.2
VIS.1959

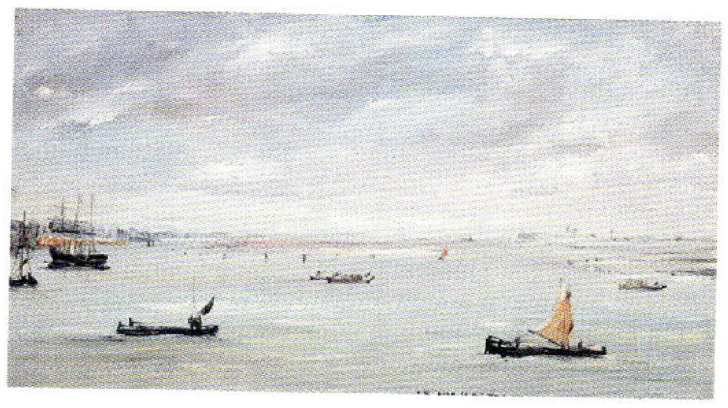

Warren, William White 1832–1915
Venice 1887
oil on paper 17.6 x 31.8
VIS.1356

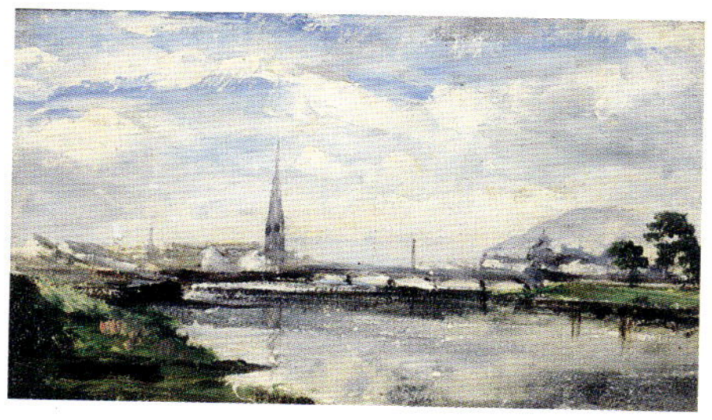

Warren, William White 1832–1915
River Scene with a Church
oil on plywood 17.6 x 30.7
VIS.752

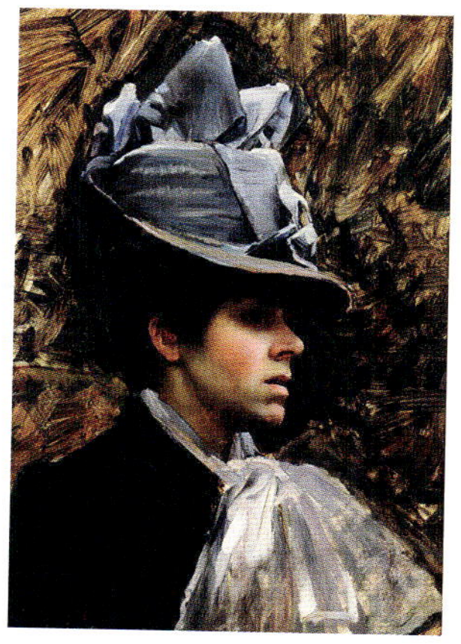

Waterhouse, John William 1849–1917
Portrait of the Artist's Wife
oil on board 56.1 x 39
VIS.4431

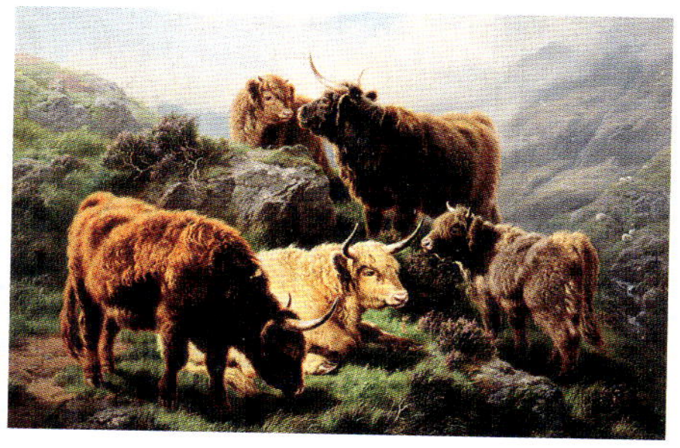

Watson, William II active 1866–1921
A Breezy Morn, Glen Massan, Argyllshire, Scotland 1894
oil on canvas 59.3 x 90
VIS.2423

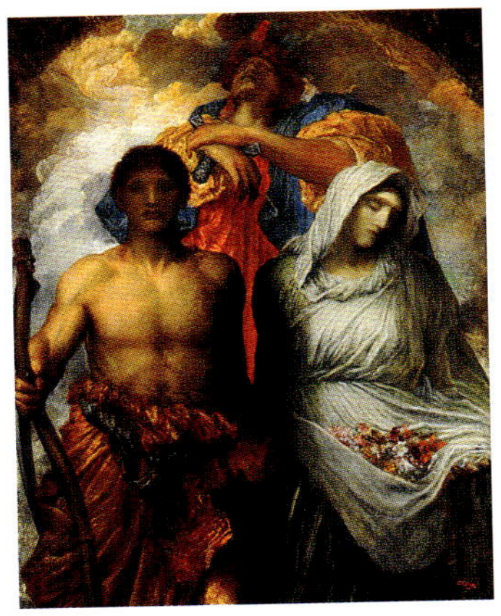

Watts, George Frederick 1817–1904
Time, Death and Judgement c.1895
oil on canvas 138.2 x 114.2
VIS.3375

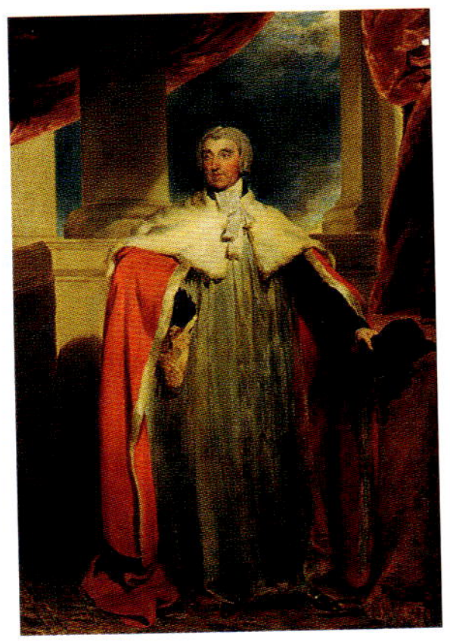

Watts, George Frederick 1817–1904
Dr Edward Venables-Vernon-Harcourt (1757–1847), Archbishop of York
oil on canvas 53 x 35.4
VIS.272

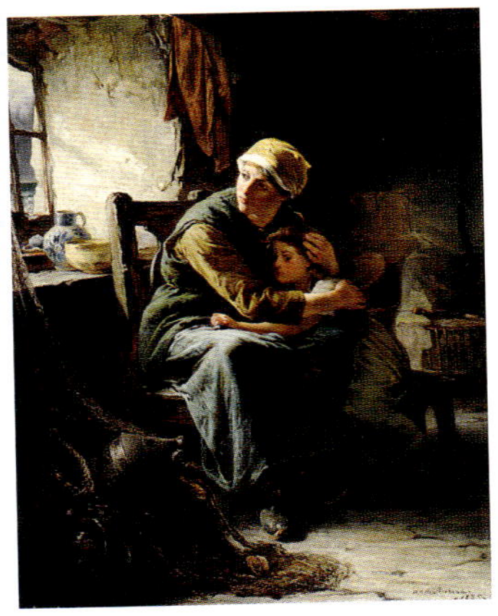

Weatherhead, William Harris 1843–1903
'For those in peril' 1885
oil on canvas 91.5 x 71.4
VIS.799

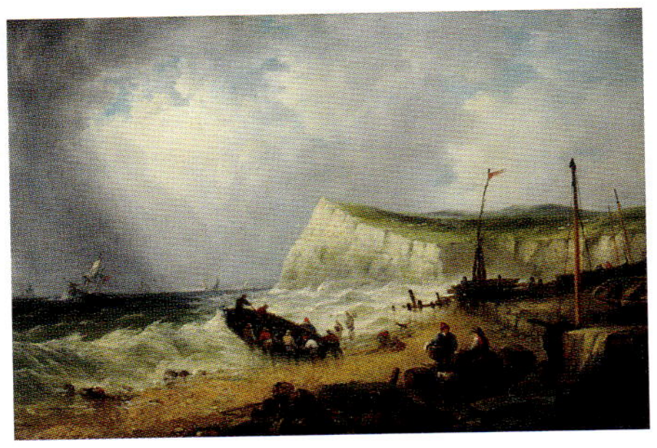

Webb, James 1825–1895
Coast Scene 1871
oil on canvas 30.5 x 42.9
VIS.611

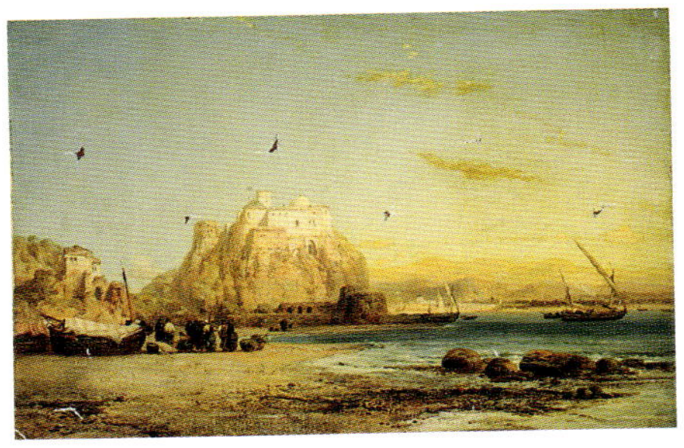

Webb, James 1825–1895
Mont Saint-Michel, Normandy, France 1873
oil on canvas 51.4 x 76.6
VIS.1608

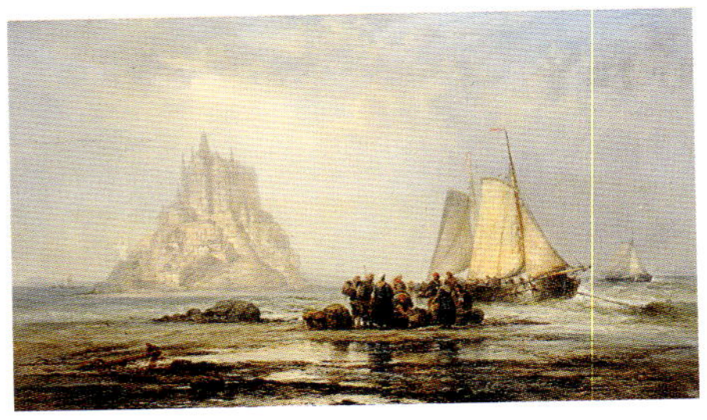

Webb, James 1825–1895
Mont Saint-Michel, Normandy, France 1873–1874
oil on canvas 59.8 x 100.4
VIS.1421

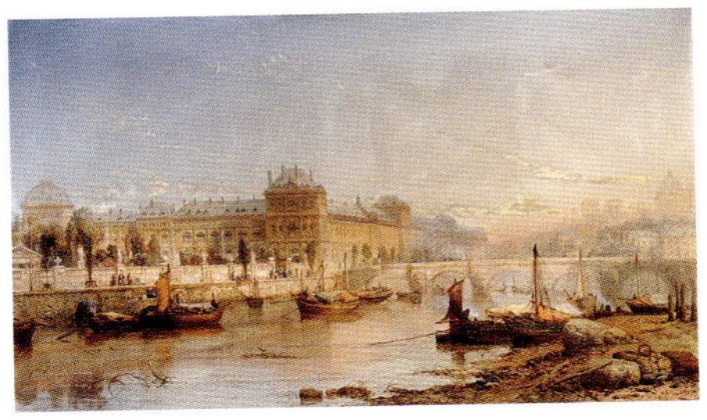

Webb, James 1825–1895
Paris 1874–1875
oil on canvas 75.3 x 126.6
VIS.1469

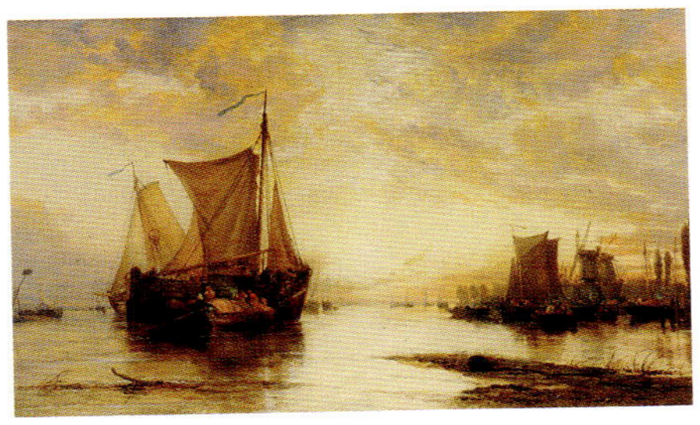

Webb, James 1825–1895
At Dordrecht, Holland 1875–1876
oil on canvas 61.5 x 101.5
VIS.1464

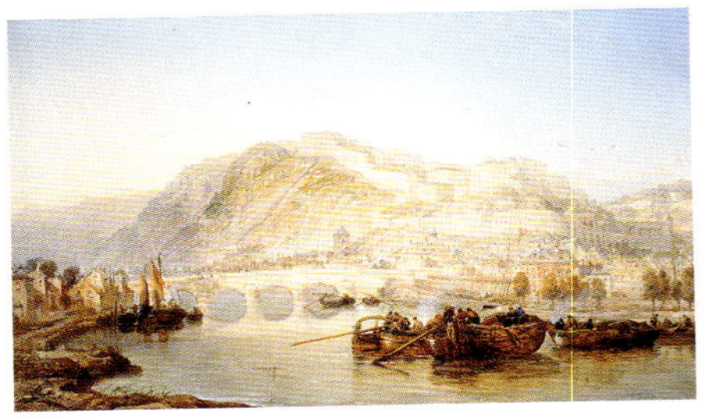

Webb, James 1825–1895
Namur, Belgium 1876–1878
oil on canvas 77.1 x 127.3
VIS.1585

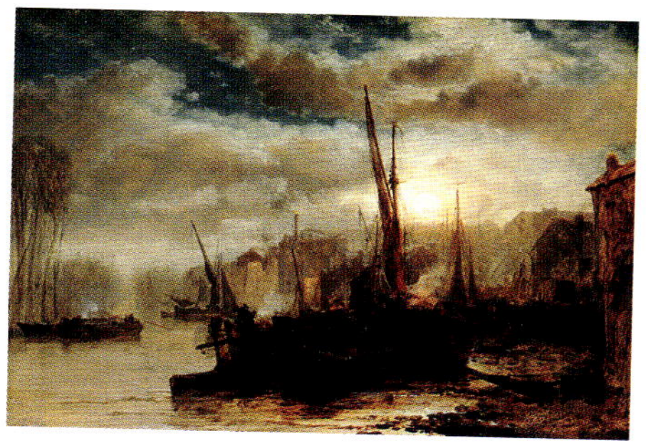

Webb, James 1825–1895
On the Thames, near Kew 1878
oil on panel 34.7 x 50.2
VIS.1288

Webb, James 1825–1895
The Sussex Weald 1880
oil on panel 17.3 x 24.7
VIS.562

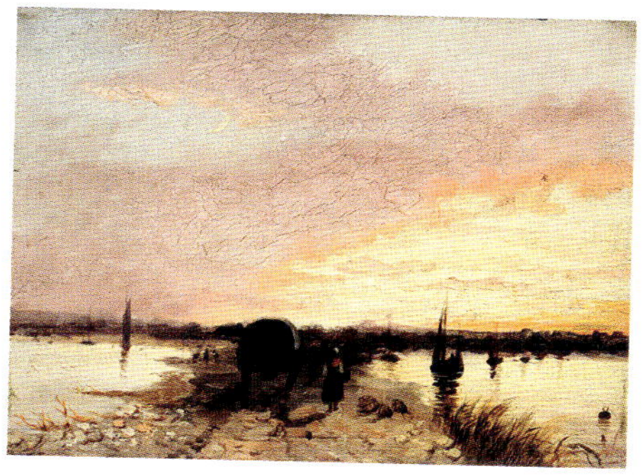

Webb, James 1825–1895
French Coast, near Calais, France
oil on panel 18.7 x 25.4
VIS.1088

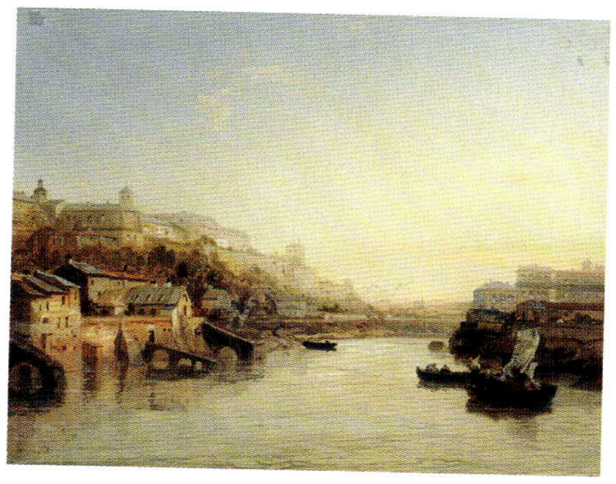

Webb, James 1825–1895
On the Meuse
oil on canvas 29 x 36.5
VIS.1344

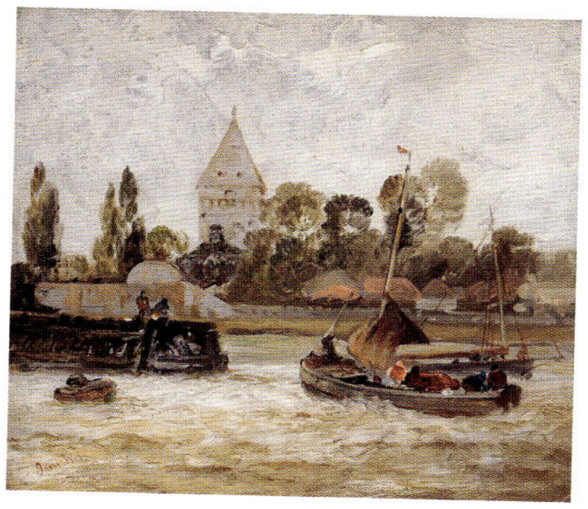

Webb, James 1825–1895
Seascape
oil on millboard 73.9 x 104
VIS.1004

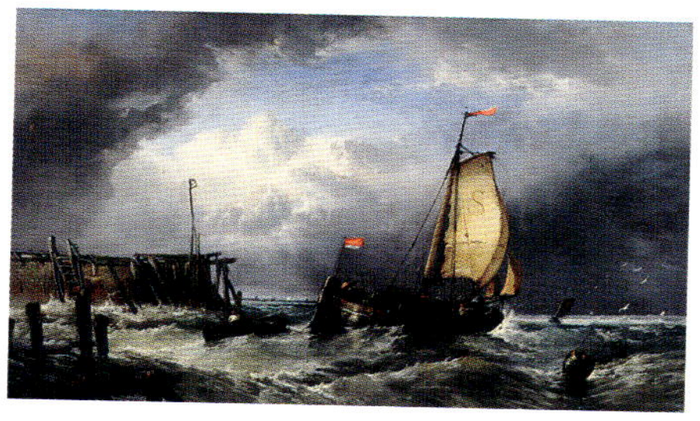

Webb, James 1825–1895
Seascape
oil on canvas 65 x 105.5
VIS.2322

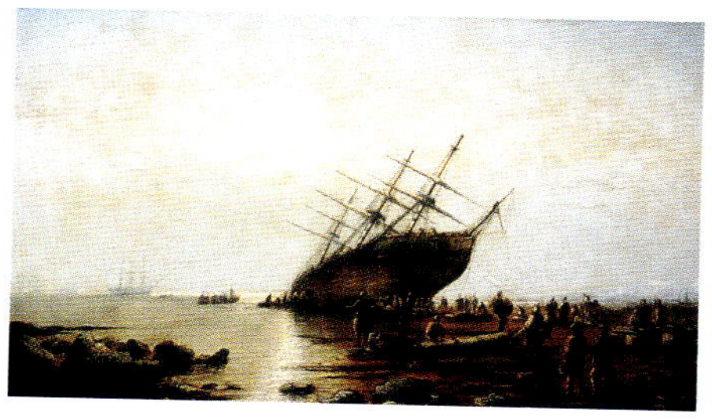

Webb, James 1825–1895
Ship Aground
oil on canvas 76.9 x 127.5
VIS.339

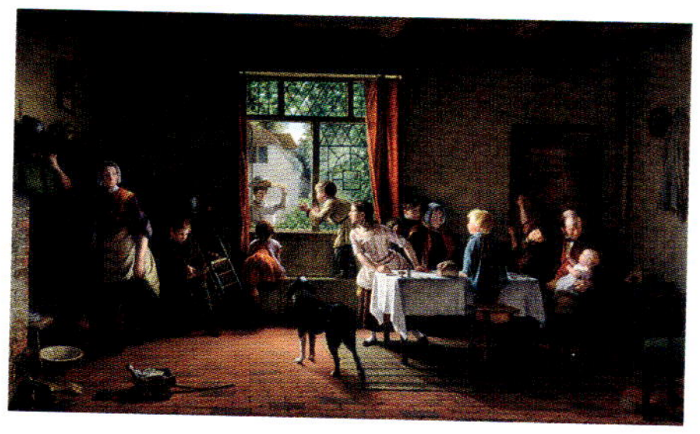

Webster, Thomas George 1800–1886
Roast Pig 1862
oil on canvas 73.2 x 118.6
VIS.1514

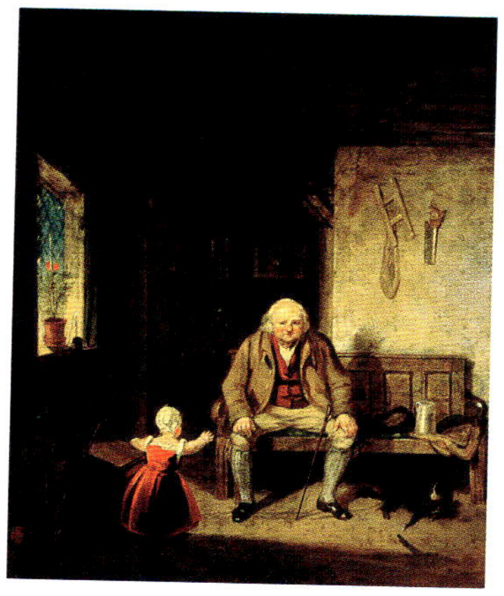

Webster, Thomas George 1800–1886
First Steps
oil on canvas 28.8 x 24
VIS.584

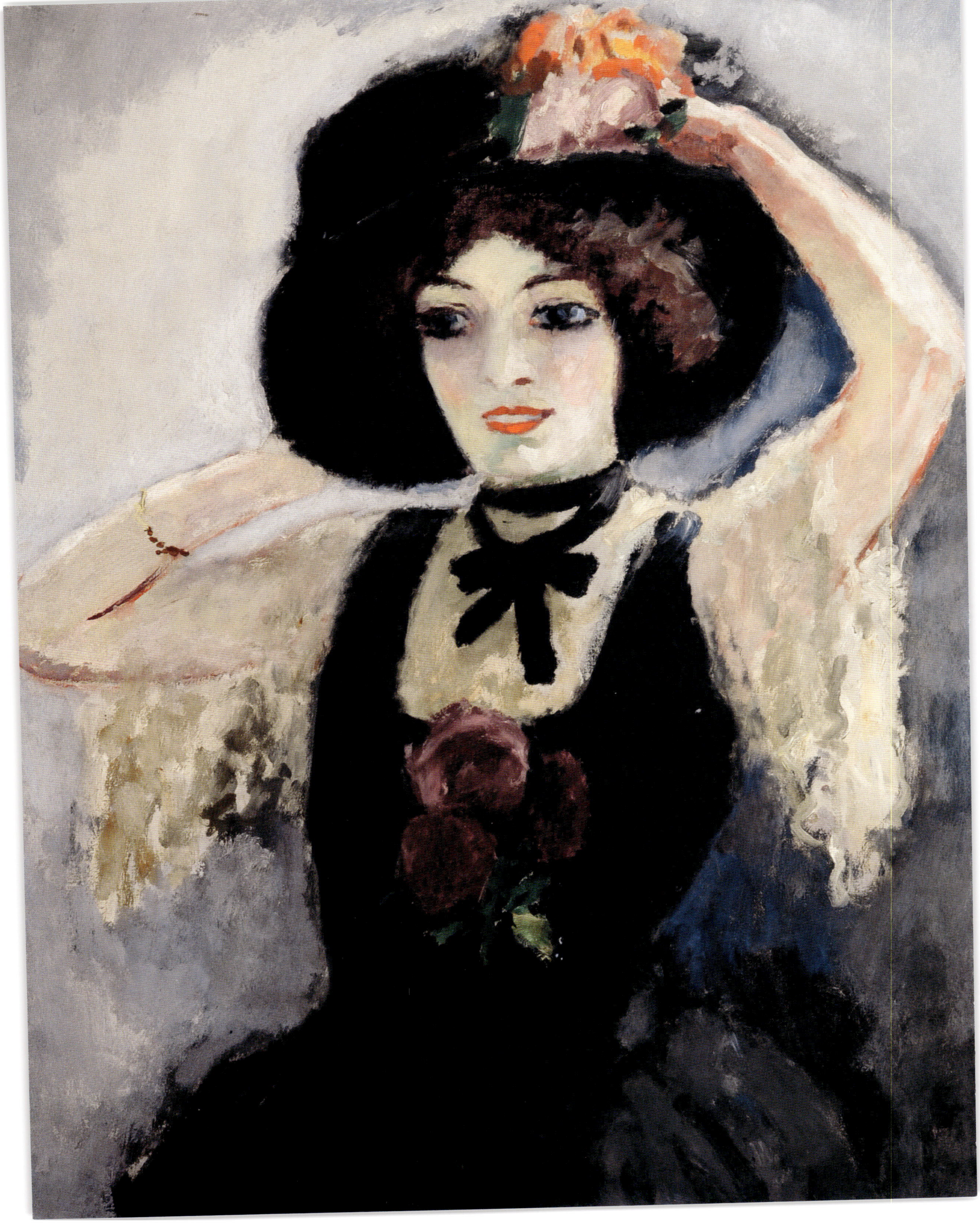

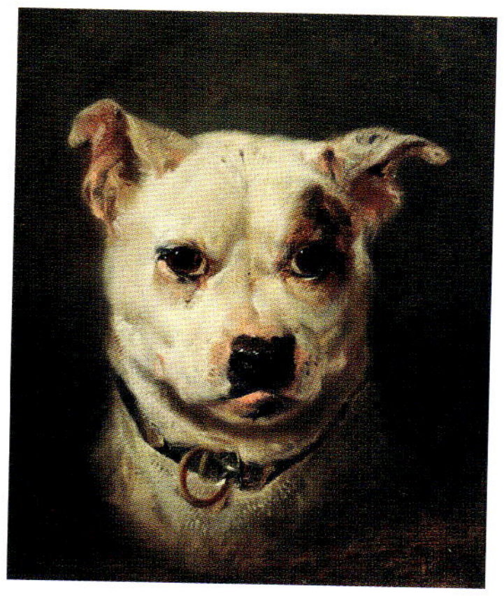

Weekes, Henry I 1807–1877
'Dan Leno' 1871
oil on canvas 29.5 x 24.1
VIS.417

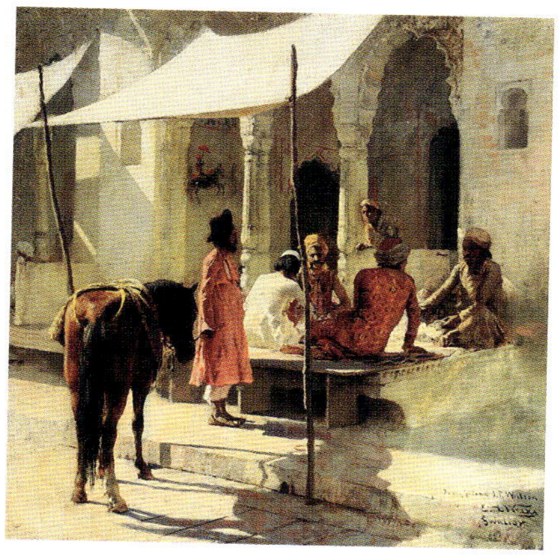

Weeks, Edwin Lord 1849–1903
An Indian Messenger
oil on canvas 42 x 41.3
VIS.599

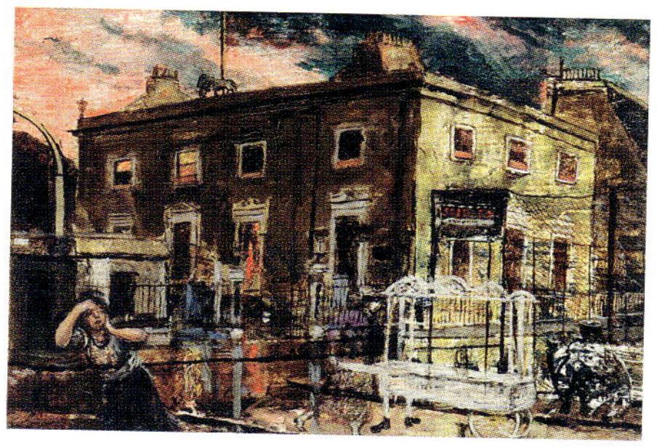

Weight, Carel Victor Morlais 1908–1997
'Cockles and mussels, alive, alive oh!'
oil on canvas 22 x 30.4
VIS.5442

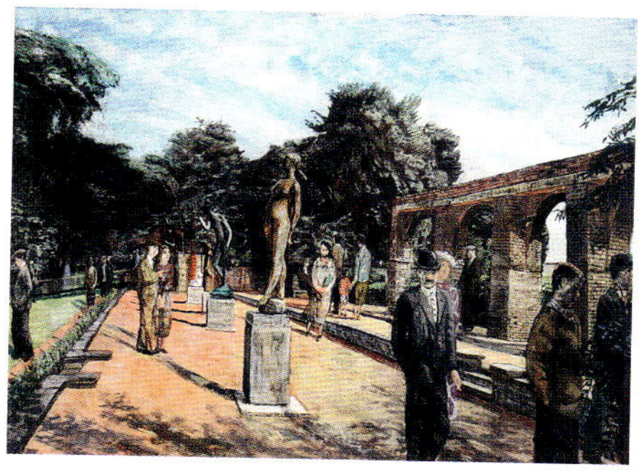

Weight, Carel Victor Morlais 1908–1997
Visitors to a Sculpture Park
oil on canvas 97.4 x 130.8
VIS.LI.1046 (P)

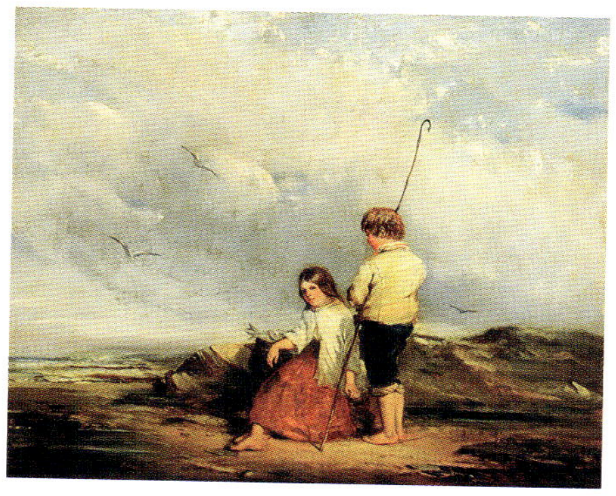

Weir, William d.1865
Fisher Girl and Boy 1855
oil on canvas 48 x 58.1
VIS.1501

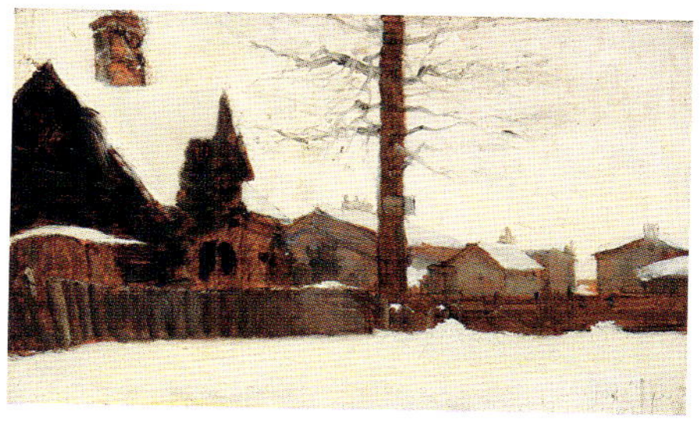

Weiss, José 1859–1919
A Winter Scene 1890
oil on panel 12.5 x 20.9
VIS.1001

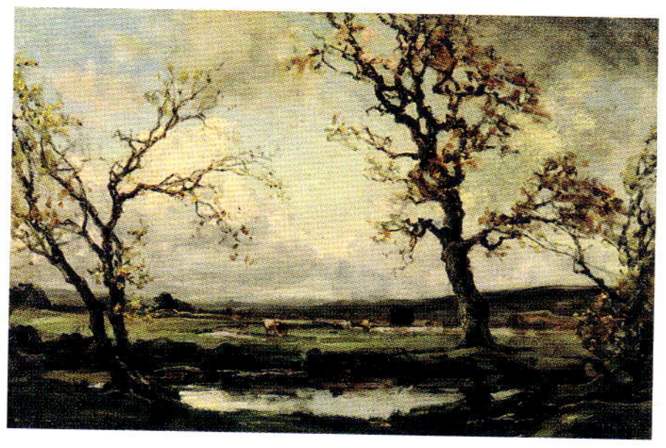

Weiss, José 1859–1919
A Sunlit Cloud
oil on canvas 50.8 x 76.1
VIS.700

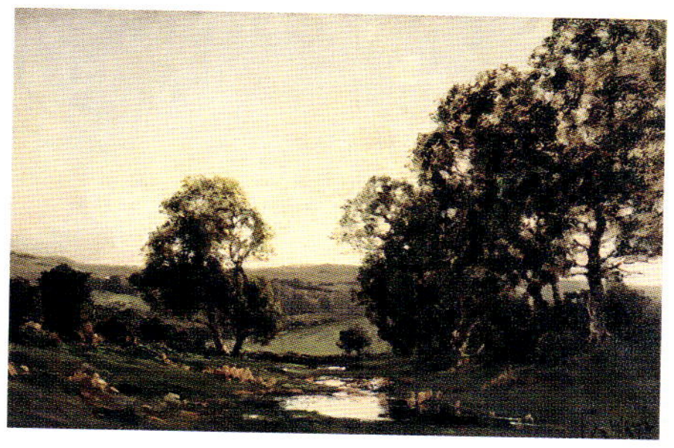

Weiss, José 1859–1919
Evening in South Devon
oil on canvas 40 x 60.4
VIS.767

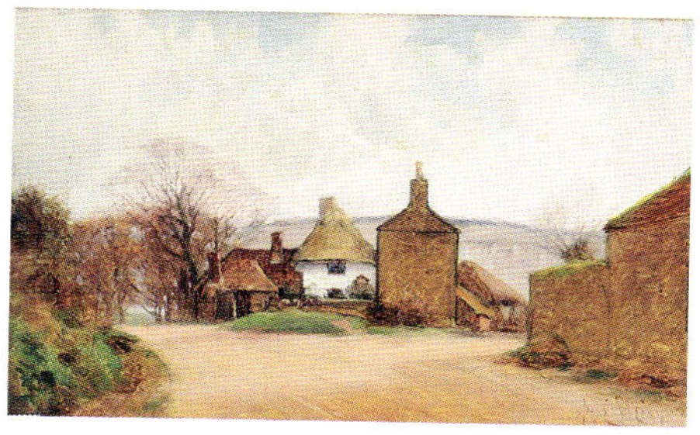

Weiss, José 1859–1919
Landscape
oil on panel 16 x 26
VIS.962

Facing page: Dongen, Kees van, 1877–1968, *Kiki de Montparnasse (1901–1953)* (detail), c.1909, Museums Sheffield, (p. 61)

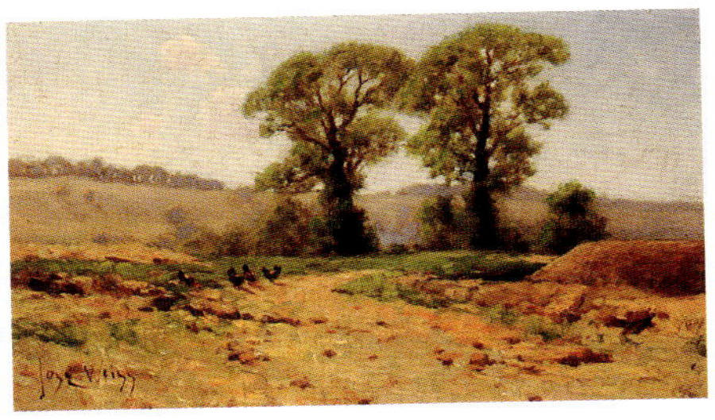

Weiss, José 1859–1919
Landscape
oil on panel 14.9 x 25.7
VIS.1052

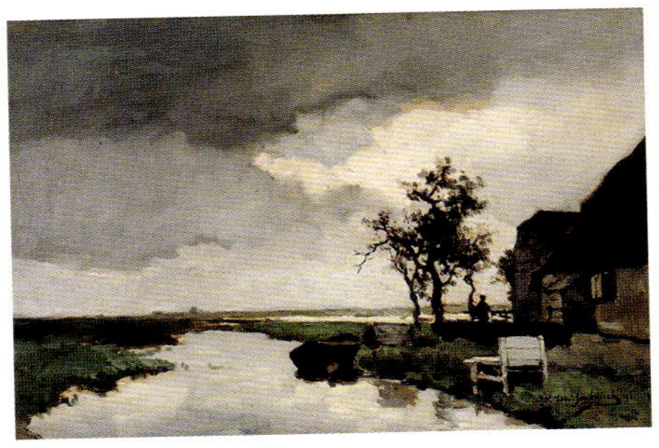

Weissenbruch, Jan Hendrik 1824–1903
A Dutch Canal 1891
oil on panel 34.5 x 49.5
VIS.570

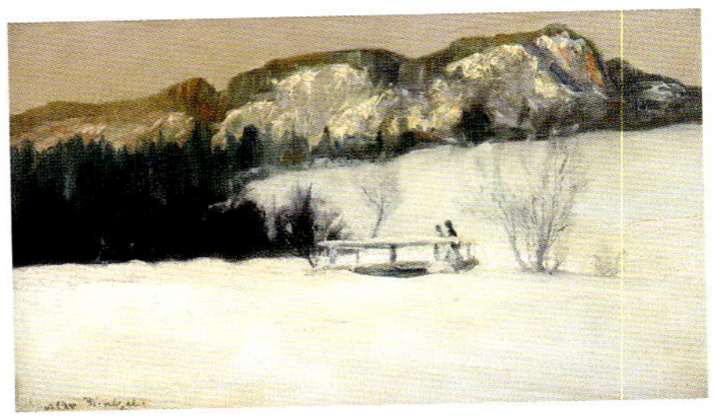

Wentzel, Niels Gustav 1859–1927
Snow Scene
oil on canvas 33.1 x 58.3
VIS.787

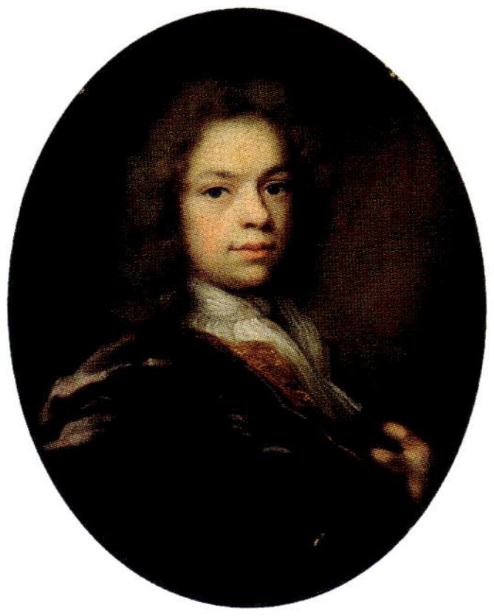

Werff, Adriaen van der (attributed to)
1659–1722
Portrait of a Young Man
oil on panel 33.1 x 25.4
VIS.49

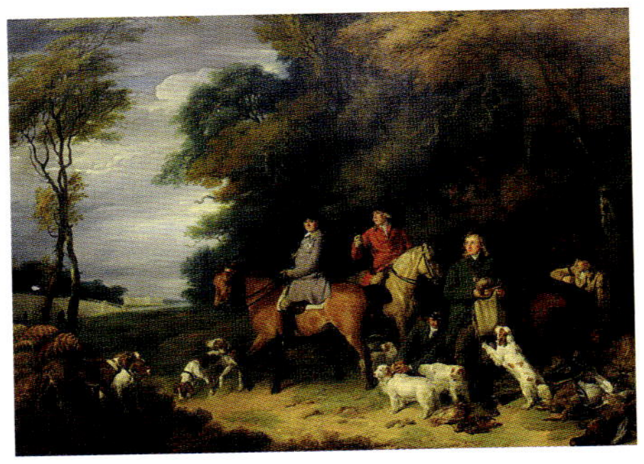

Wheatley, Francis 1747–1801
Return from the Shoot 1788
oil on canvas 156.1 x 210
VIS.5305

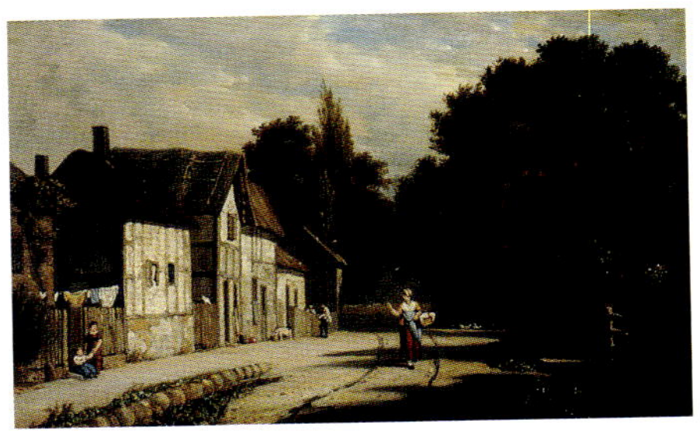

Wheatley, Francis 1747–1801
The Village Street
oil on canvas 30.8 x 48.9
VIS.76

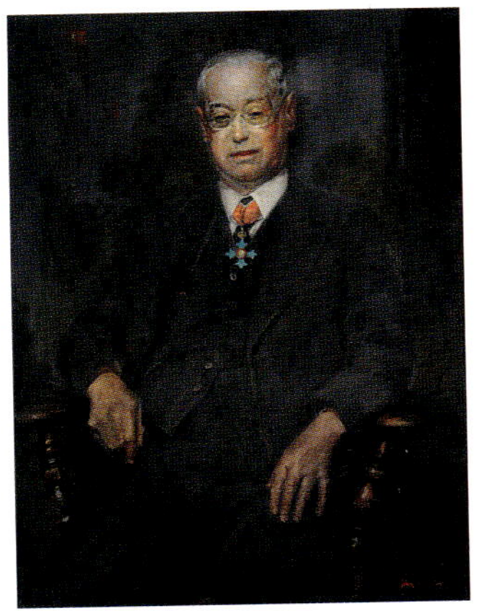

Wheatley, John 1892–1955
Sir Basil Gibson
oil on canvas 100.5 x 75.4
VIS.4133

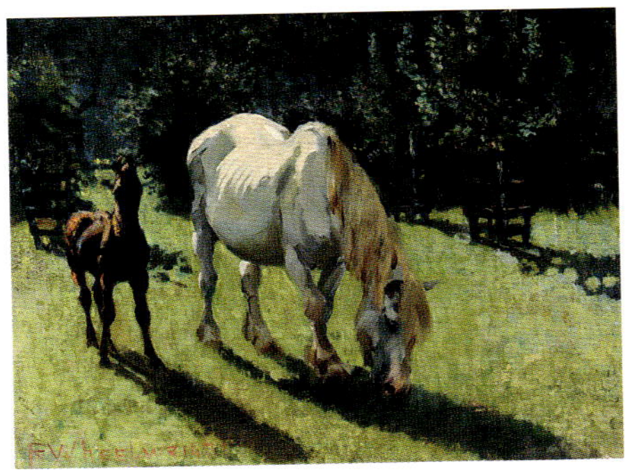

Wheelwright, Rowland 1870–1955
A Summer Afternoon
oil on canvas 32.8 x 43
VIS.620

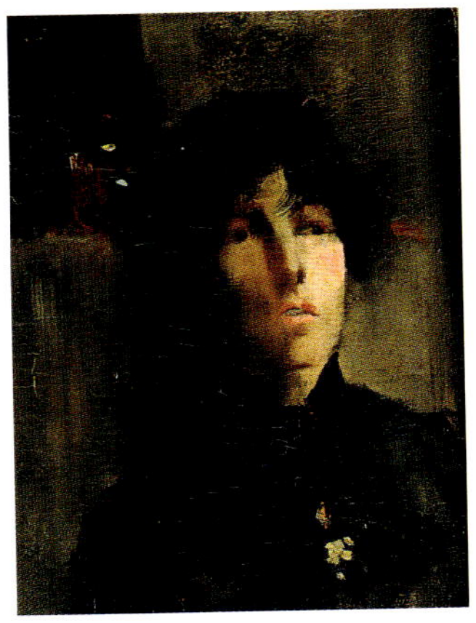

Whistler, James Abbott McNeill 1834–1903
Portrait
oil on canvas on board 18.9 x 14.2
VIS.510

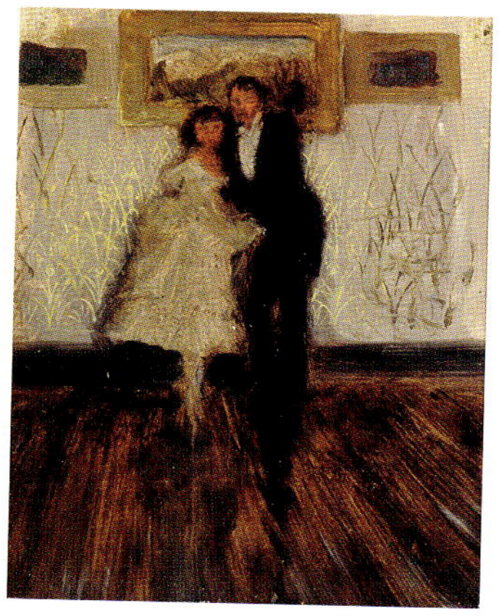

Whistler, James Abbott McNeill 1834–1903
The Dancing Lesson
oil on canvas 18.2 x 14
VIS.1051

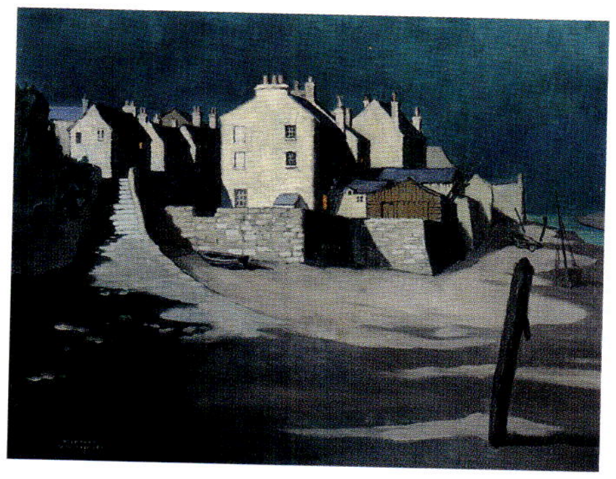

Whittington, Marjory active 20th C
At Appledore, Devon
oil on canvas 39.5 x 49.8
VIS.607

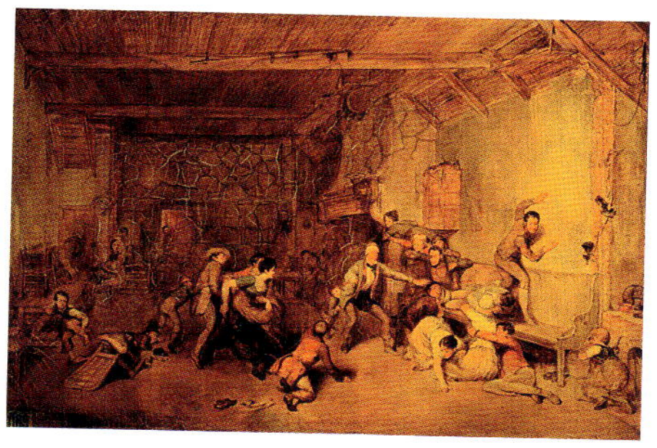

Wilkie, David 1785–1841
Blind Man's Bluff 1830
oil on canvas 59.8 x 88
VIS.1461

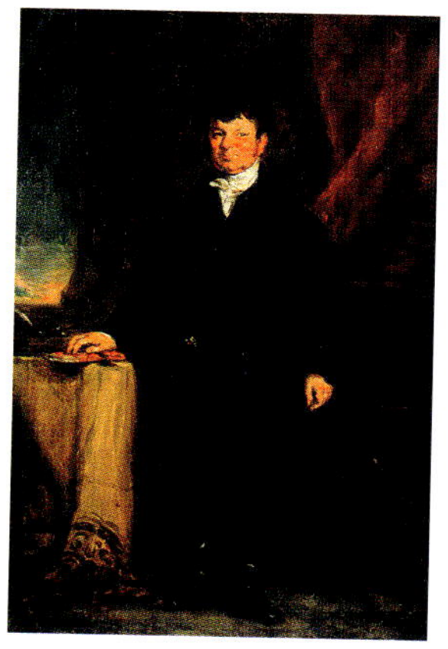

Wilkie, David 1785–1841
A Scottish Professor
oil on panel 29.1 x 19.1
VIS.28

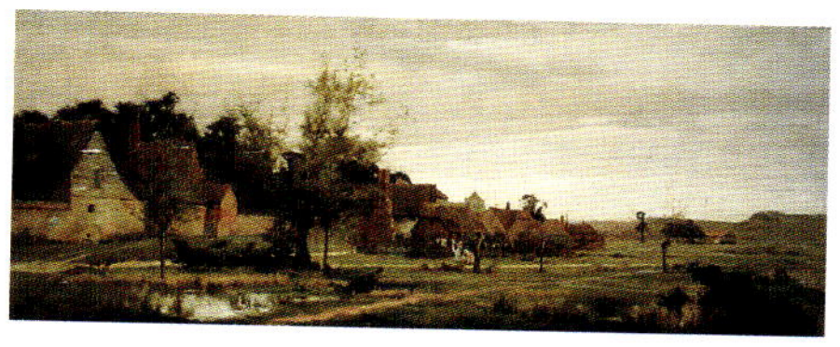

Wilkinson, Charles A. b.1830
Landscape 1884
oil on canvas 56.6 x 137.7
VIS.1296

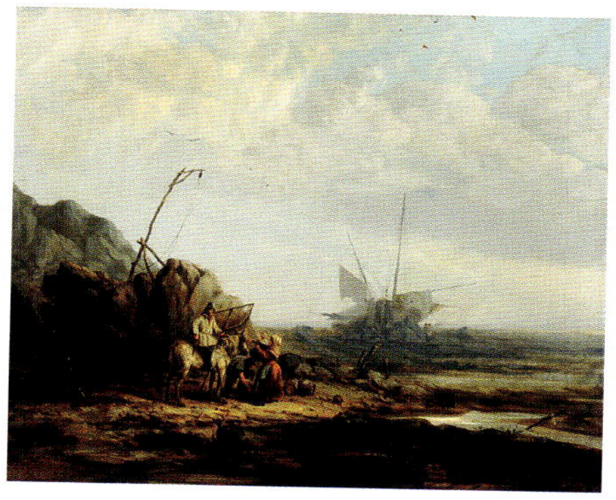

Willcock, George Burrell 1811–1852
Coast Scene
oil on canvas 63.5 x 76.2
VIS.533

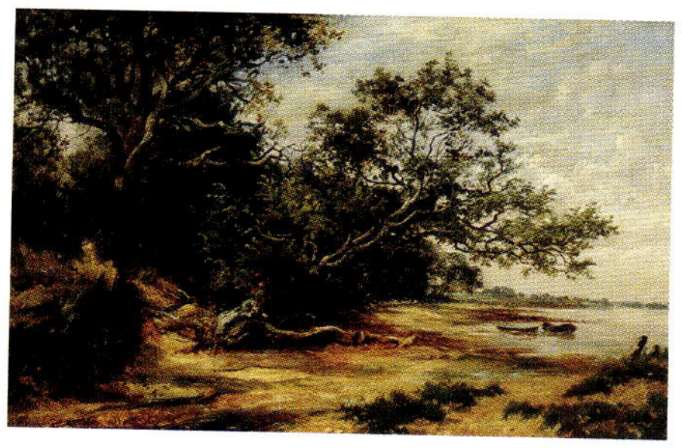

Willcock, George Burrell 1811–1852
View near Harwich, Essex
oil on canvas 28.9 x 44.5
VIS.369

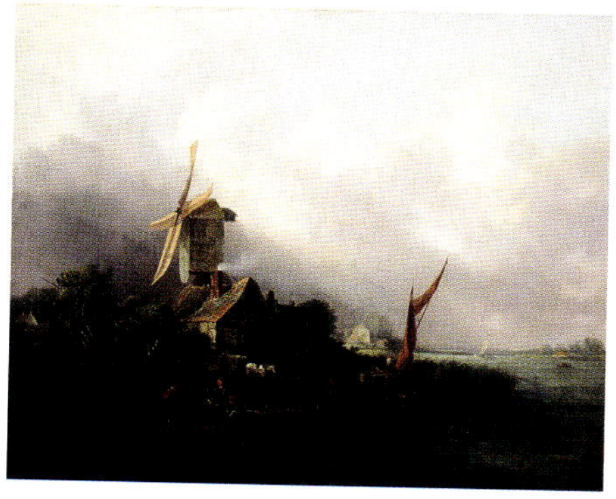

Williams, Edward 1782–1855
A Squally Day on the Yare, Norfolk
oil on canvas 70 x 84
VIS.2735

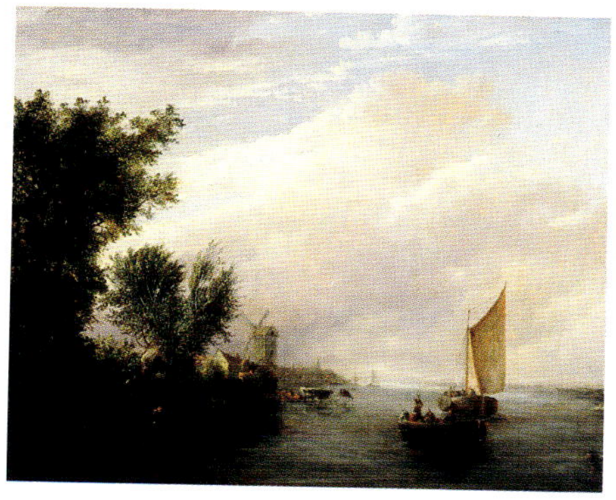

Williams, Edward 1782–1855
Barges on a River
oil on canvas 56.1 x 69.2
VIS.310

Williams, Edward 1782–1855
Castleman Villas, Moonlight
oil on canvas 27.5 x 51
VIS.309

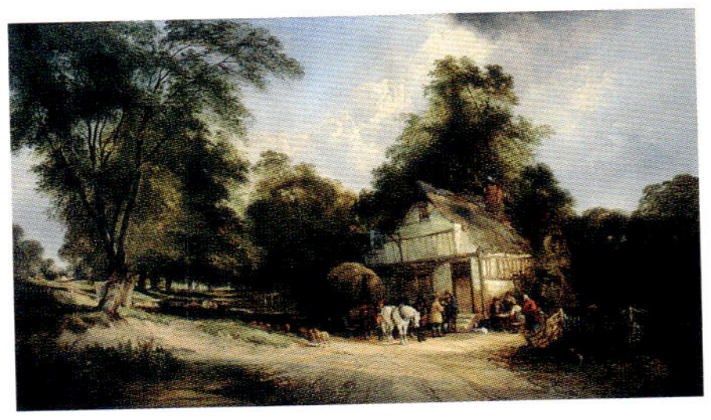

Williams, Edward Charles 1807–1881
A Roadside Inn at Rushington, Sussex 1851
oil on canvas 74.5 x 124.5
VIS.1949

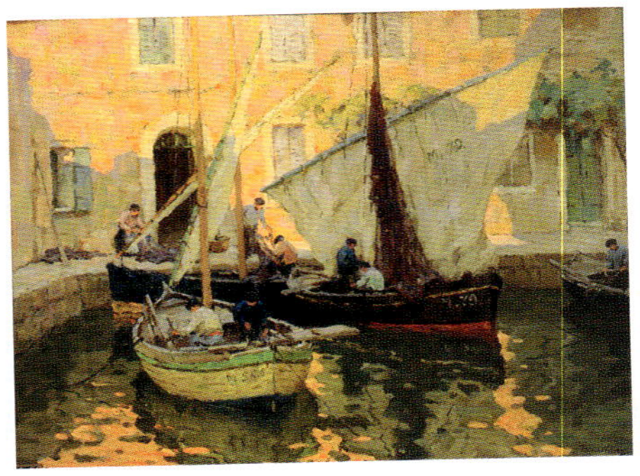

Williams, Terrick John 1860–1936
Golden Evening, Martigues, France
oil on canvas 59.8 x 80.5
VIS.2859

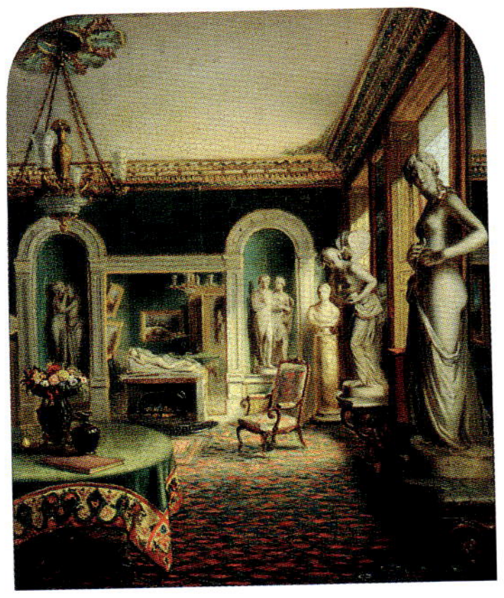

Wilson, Arthur 1838–1914
Interior of Doctor Cordell Thompson's House c.1870
oil on canvas 34.5 x 29.5
K1934.33

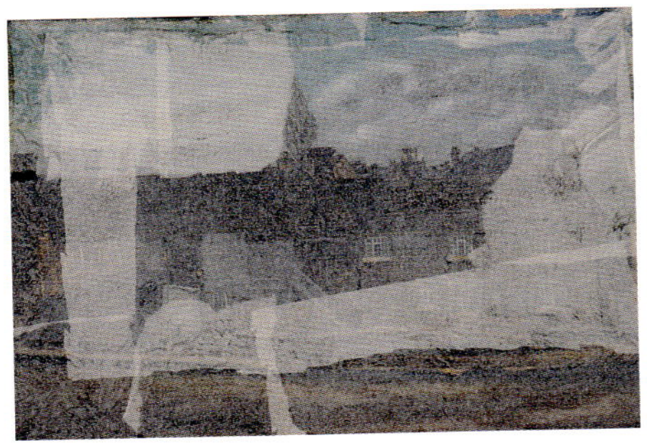

Wilson, Arthur 1838–1914
View of Cottages, Woodseats, Sheffield c.1900
oil on canvas 41.2 x 58.5
1963.96

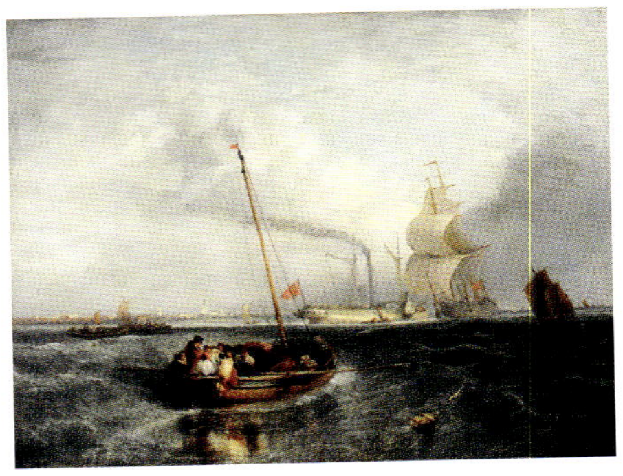

Wilson, John H. 'Jock' 1774–1855
Sea Piece
oil on canvas 71.5 x 91.7
VIS.1518

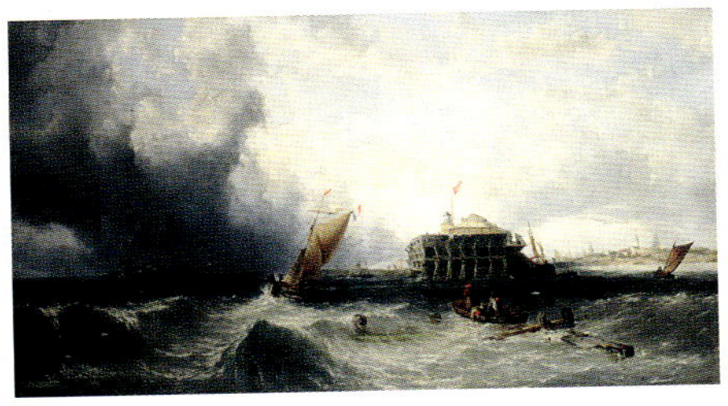

Wilson, John James II 1818–1875
Calais, Old Pier, France 1850
oil on canvas 61.5 x 110
VIS.1994

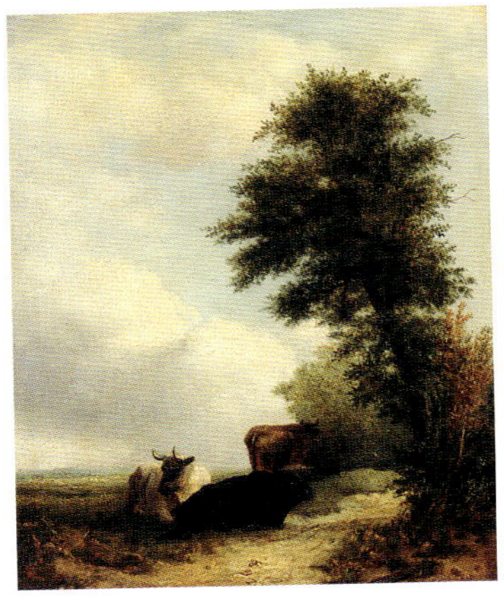

Wilson, John James II 1818–1875
Landscape with Cattle 1859
oil on canvas 29.3 x 24.2
VIS.1026

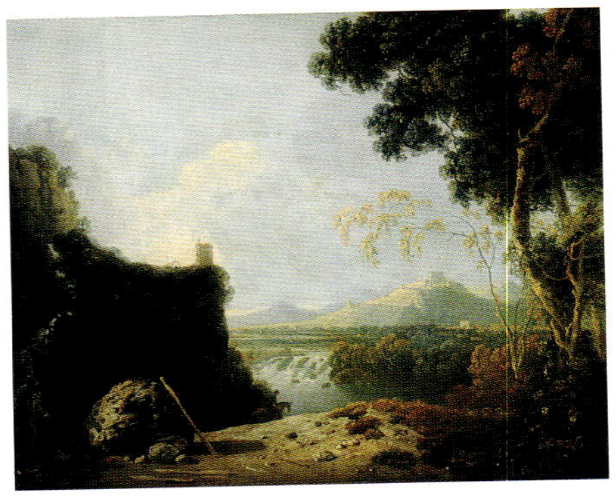

Wilson, Richard (after) 1712/1713–1782
Italian Landscape
oil on canvas 66.8 x 82.3
VIS.358

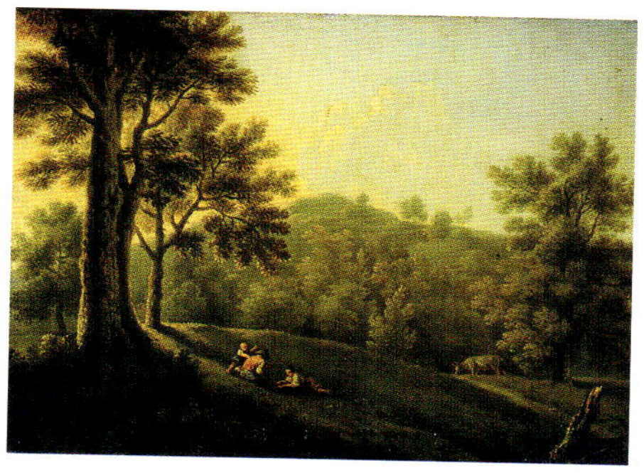

Wilson, Richard (attributed to) 1712/1713–1782
A View near Bologna, Italy
oil on canvas 24.1 x 33.4
VIS.326

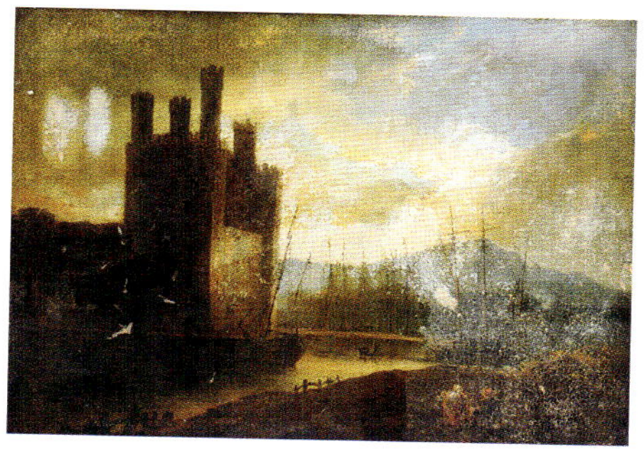

Wilson, Richard (attributed to) 1712/1713–1782
Caernarvon Castle, Wales
oil on panel 55.7 x 76
VIS.2719

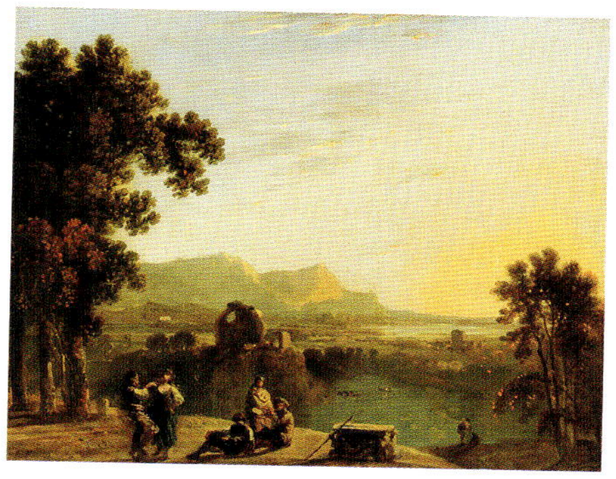

Wilson, Richard (attributed to) 1712/1713–1782
Italian Landscape with Figures
oil on canvas 40.9 x 51.2
VIS.75

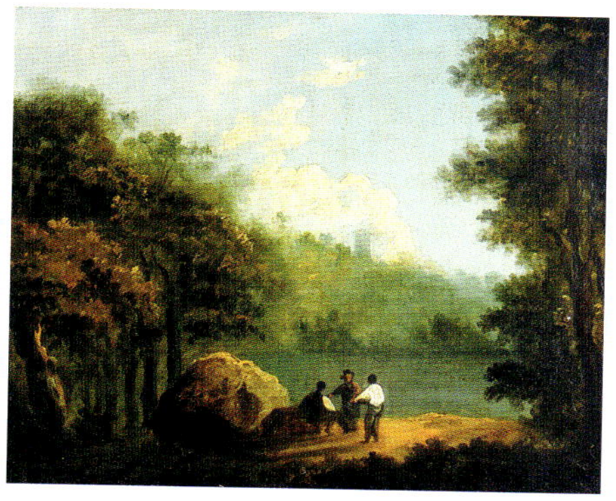

Wilson, Richard (attributed to) 1712/1713–1782
Lake Nemi, Rome
oil on canvas 29.3 x 34.5
VIS.137

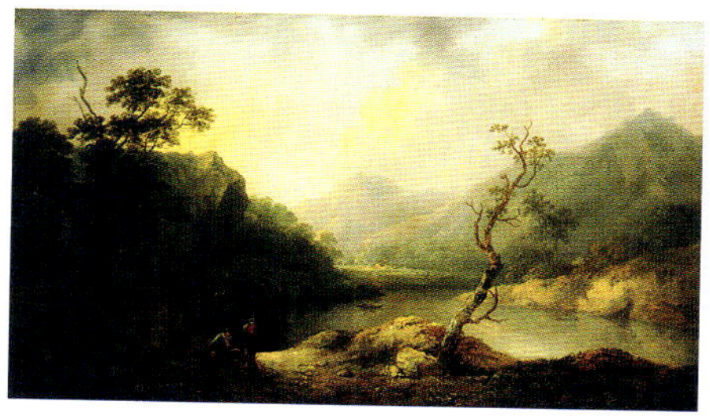

Wilson, Richard (attributed to) 1712/1713–1782
Lake Scene
oil on canvas 36.6 x 62
VIS.330

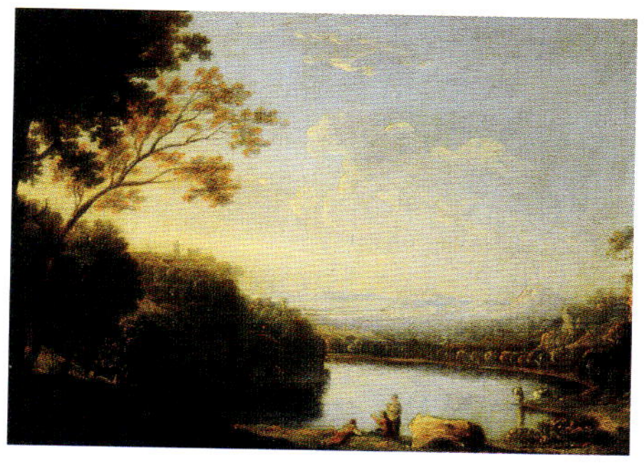

Wilson, Richard (attributed to) 1712/1713–1782
Landscape
oil on canvas 29.5 x 39
VIS.191

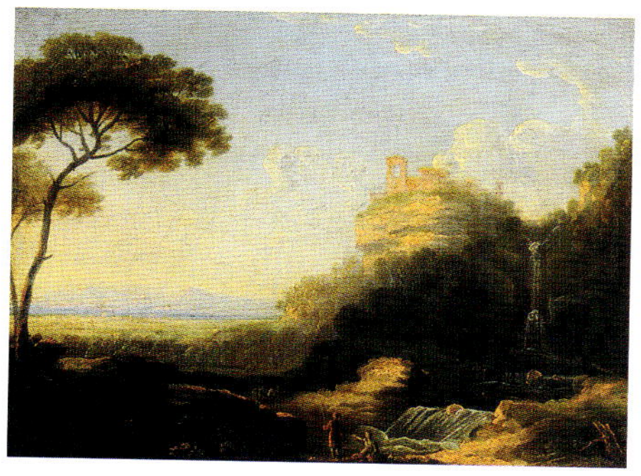

Wilson, Richard (attributed to) 1712/1713–1782
Landscape
oil on canvas 27.8 x 37.5
VIS.193

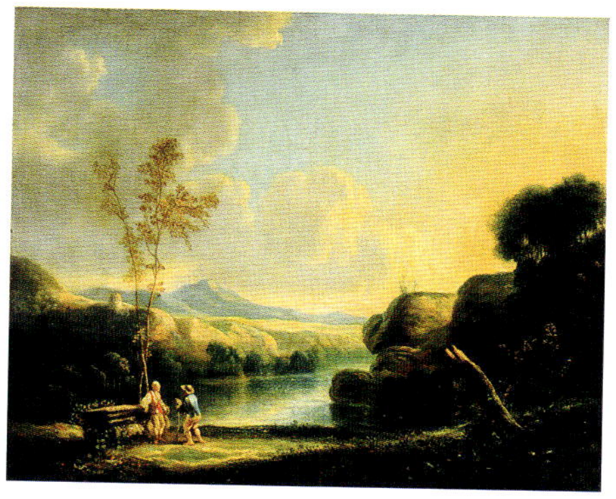

Wilson, Richard (attributed to) 1712/1713–1782
Landscape
oil on canvas 63.8 x 77.2
VIS.846

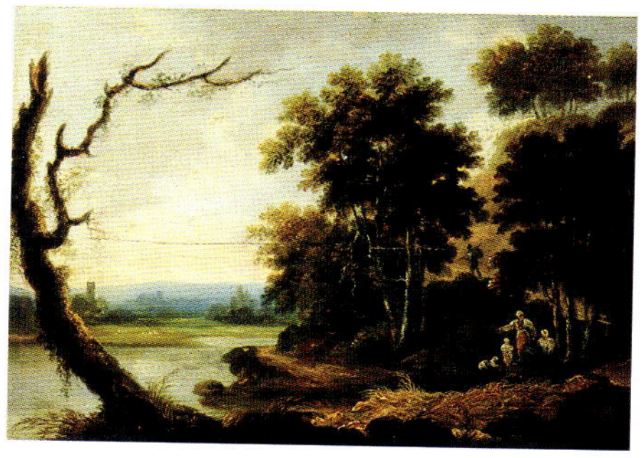

Wilson, Richard (attributed to) 1712/1713–1782
Landscape with a Church
oil on canvas 21.3 x 30.3
VIS.560

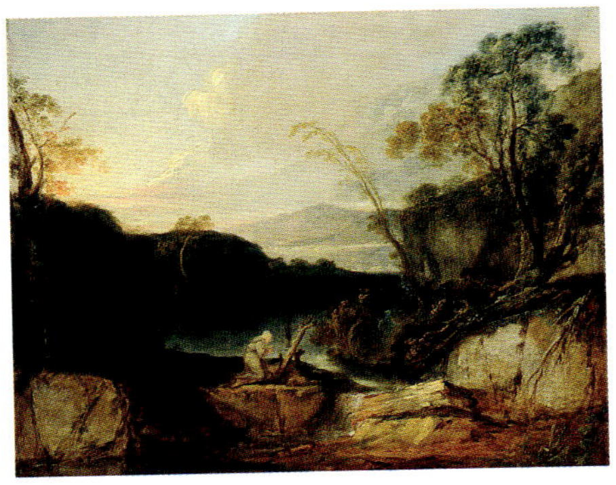

Wilson, Richard (attributed to) 1712/1713–1782
Landscape with a Monk at Devotion
oil on canvas 47.9 x 60.3
VIS.60

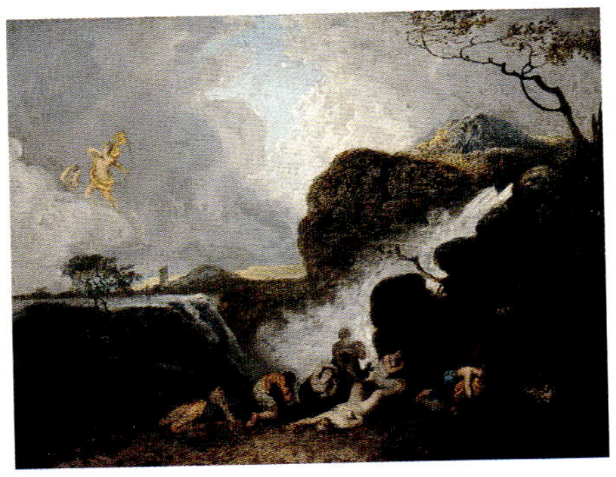

Wilson, Richard (attributed to) 1712/1713–1782
Niobe and Her Children
oil on canvas 78.7 x 100.2
VIS.LI.148 (P)

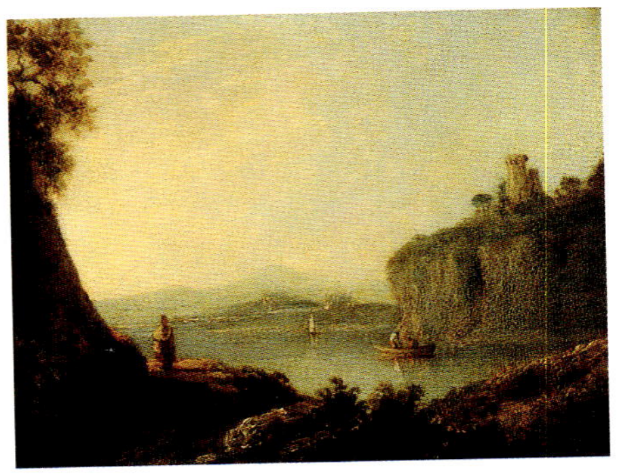

Wilson, Richard (attributed to) 1712/1713–1782
The Boat Man
oil on canvas 20.9 x 26.4
VIS.334

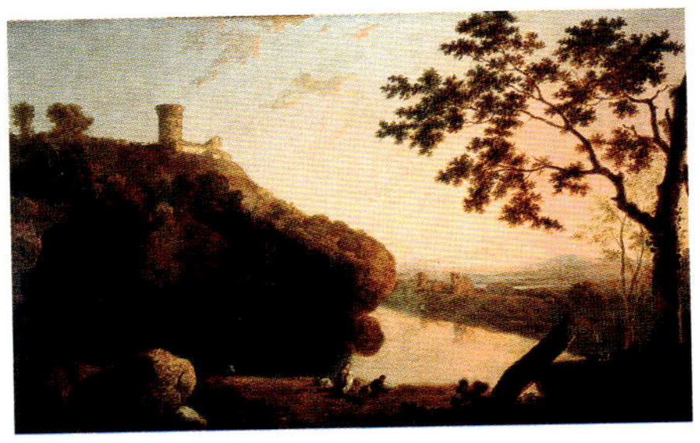

Wilson, Richard (attributed to) 1712/1713–1782
View on the Arno, Italy
oil on canvas 78.1 x 122.1
VIS.355

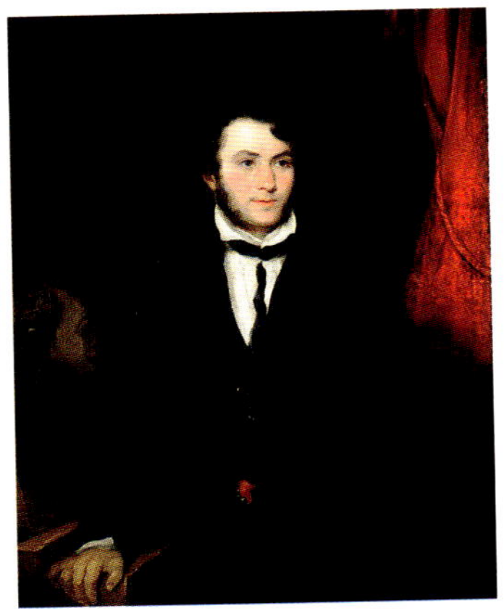

Wilson, W.
Edward Law (1790–1871), 1st Earl of Ellenborough, GCB, PC
oil on canvas 110.5 x 86.8
VIS.1843

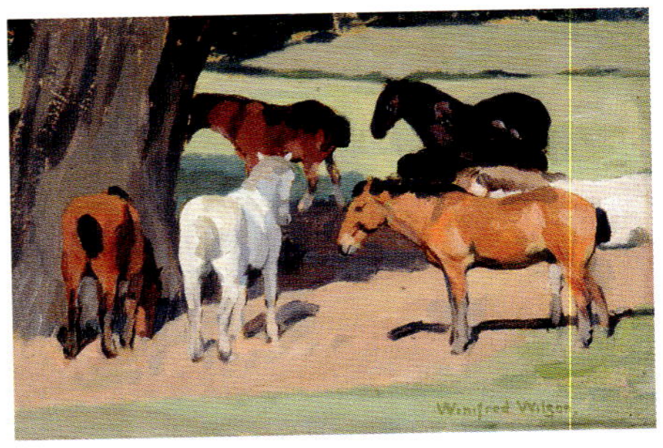

Wilson, Winifred 1882–1973
Pit Ponies
oil on panel 19.9 x 28.6
VIS.225

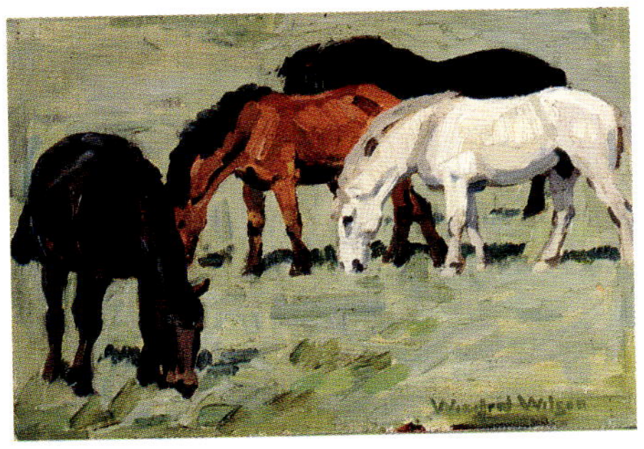

Wilson, Winifred 1882–1973
Ponies
oil on canvas on board 19 x 27.3
VIS.229

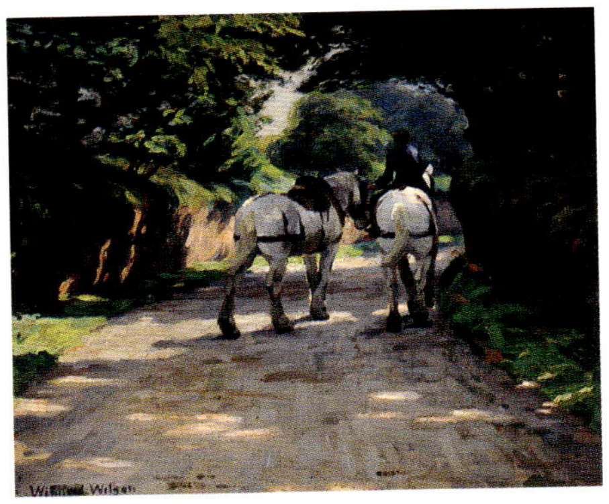

Wilson, Winifred 1882–1973
Up the Lane, Beauchief, Sheffield
oil on canvas 61.6 x 73.2
VIS.712

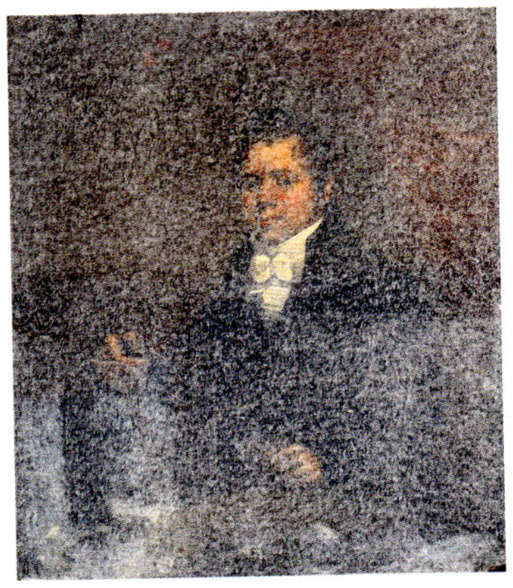

Wilson of Sheffield
Portrait of a Man c.1830
oil on canvas 40.5 x 34.4
X1974.183

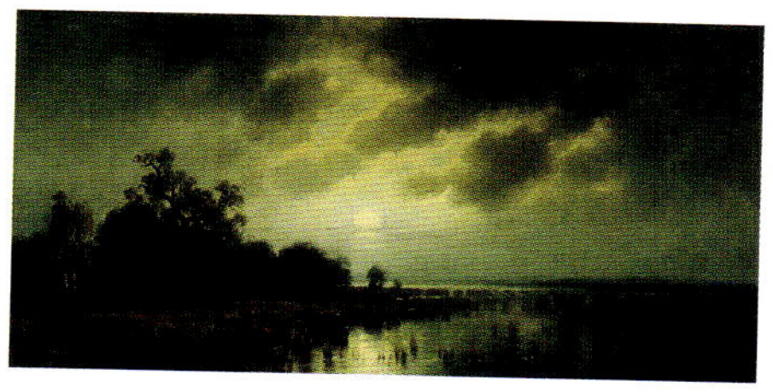

Wimmer, L.
Lake Scene 1877
oil on canvas 21.5 x 41.7
VIS.1031

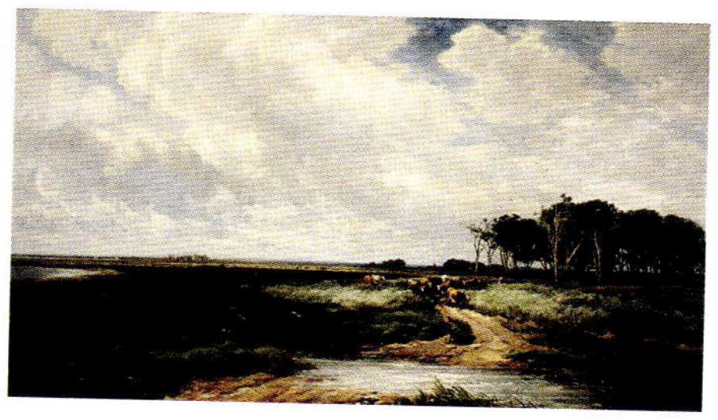

Wimperis, Edmund Morison 1835–1900
Moorland with Peat Gatherers 1886
oil on canvas 76.7 x 127.6
VIS.694

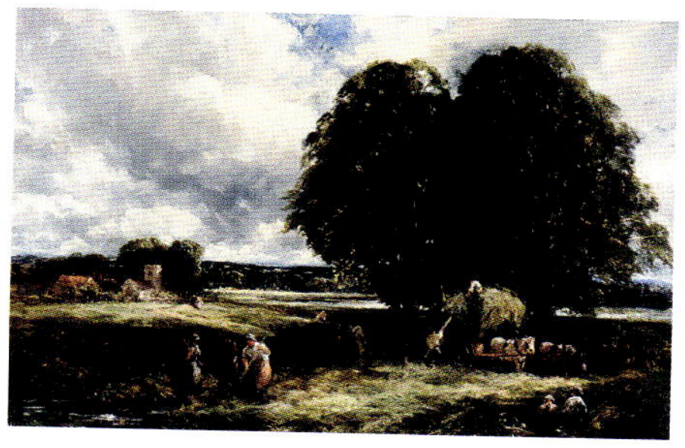

Wimperis, Edmund Morison 1835–1900
Haymaking 1898
oil on canvas 48.9 x 74.8
VIS.3287

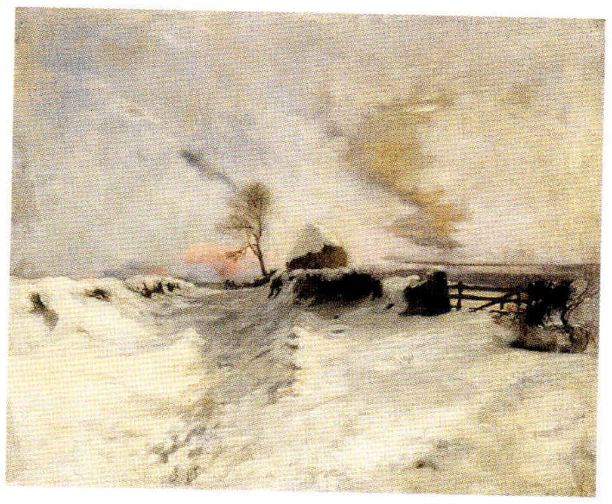

Winterbottom, Austin 1860–1919
Drifted Snow 1894
oil on canvas 50 x 60
VIS.2869

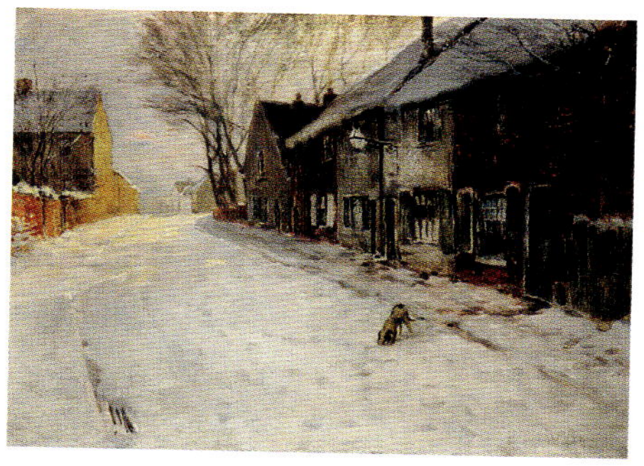

Winterbottom, Austin 1860–1919
The Village Street, Crookes, Sheffield 1901
oil on canvas 39 x 54
K1903.1

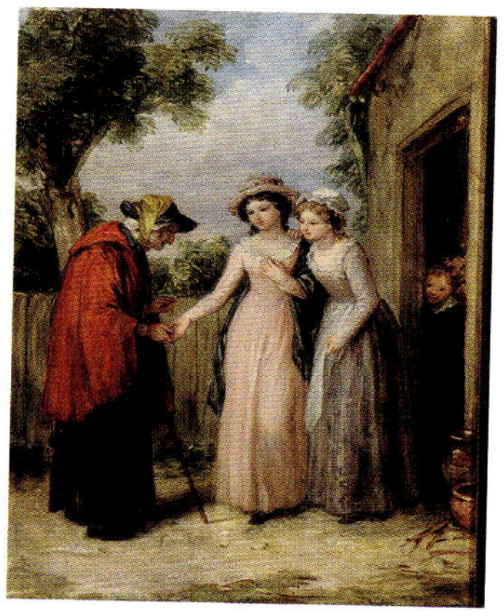

Witherington, William Frederick
1785–1865
The Fortune Teller
oil on board 29.5 x 22.7
VIS.80

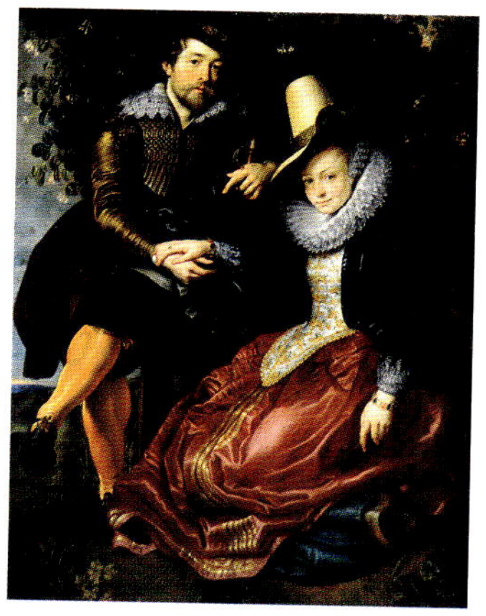

Wohlgarten, Joseph van
Peter Paul Rubens (1577–1640), and Isabella Brant (1591–1626), in the Honeysuckle Bower (after Peter Paul Rubens) 1883
oil on canvas 136.5 x 104.2
VIS.1582

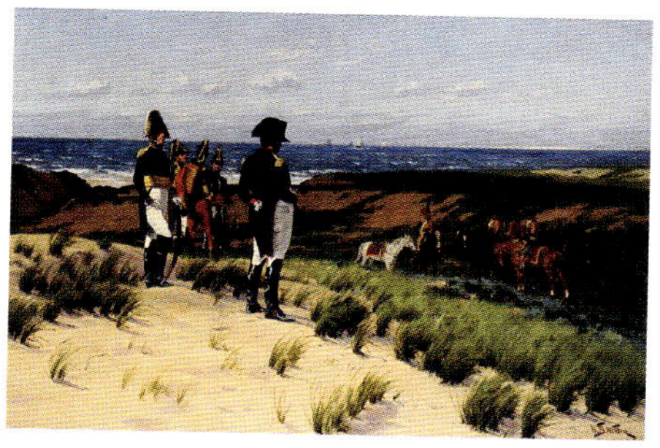

Wollen, William Barnes 1857–1936
Britain's Watch-Dogs
oil on canvas 43.5 x 64
VIS.1966

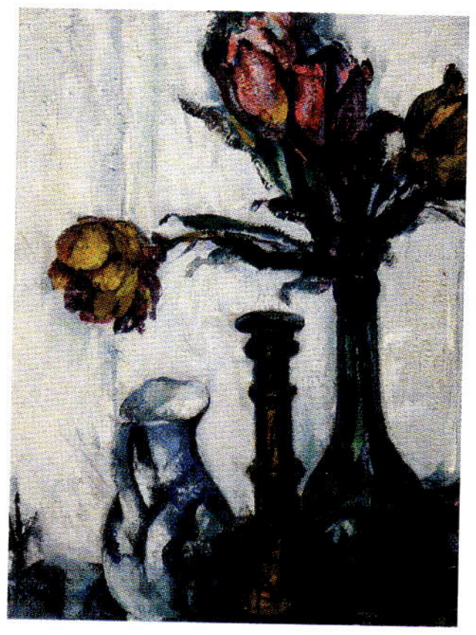

Wolmark, Alfred Aaron 1877–1961
Still Life with Tulips, a Jug and a Candlestick
1934
oil on board 44.5 x 33.8
VIS.4514

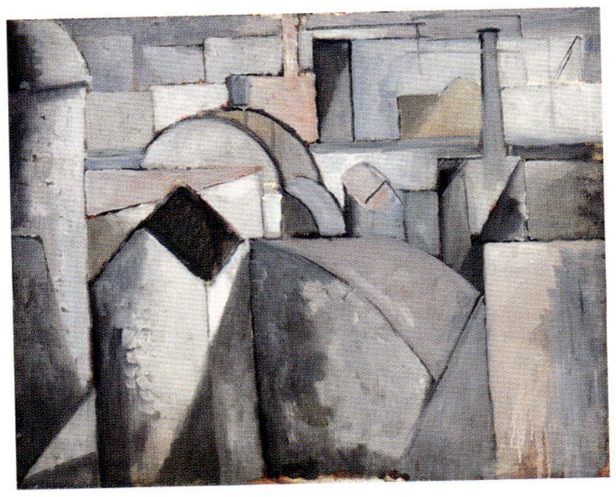

Wood, Christopher 1901–1930
Buildings at Passy, Paris 1927
oil on canvas 61.3 x 74.5
VIS.4340

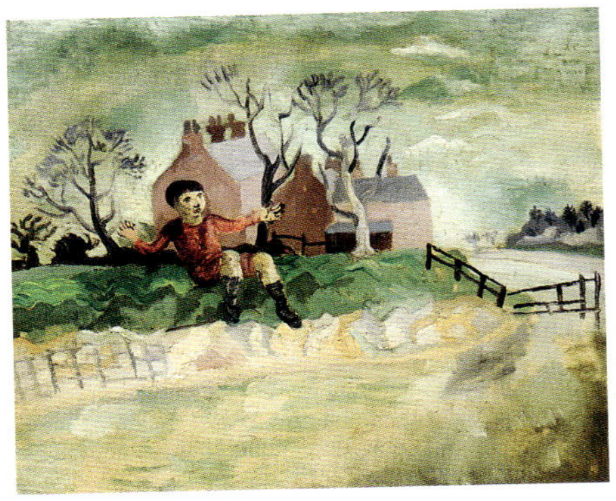

Wood, Christopher 1901–1930
The Jumping Boy, Arundel, West Sussex (recto) 1929
oil on canvas 63.4 x 72.8
VIS.3739

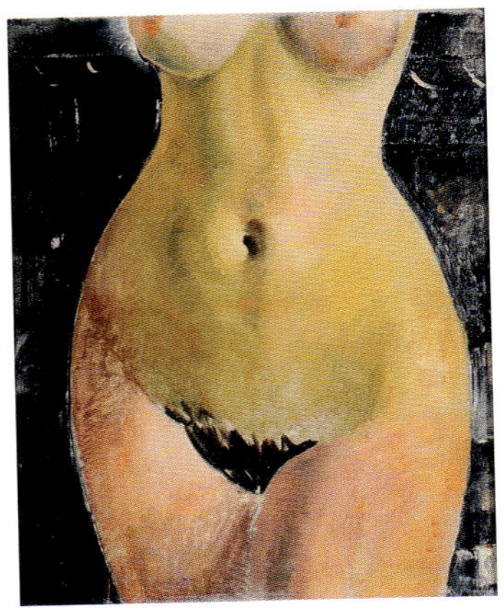

Wood, Christopher 1901–1930
*Female Nude** (verso) c.1929
oil on canvas 72.8 x 63.4
VIS.3739

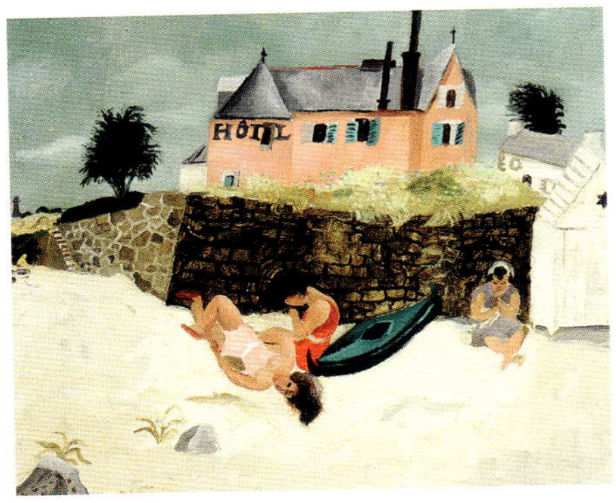

Wood, Christopher 1901–1930
La plage, Hotel Ty-Mad, Tréboul, France 1930
oil on board 43.4 x 52.5
VIS.4325

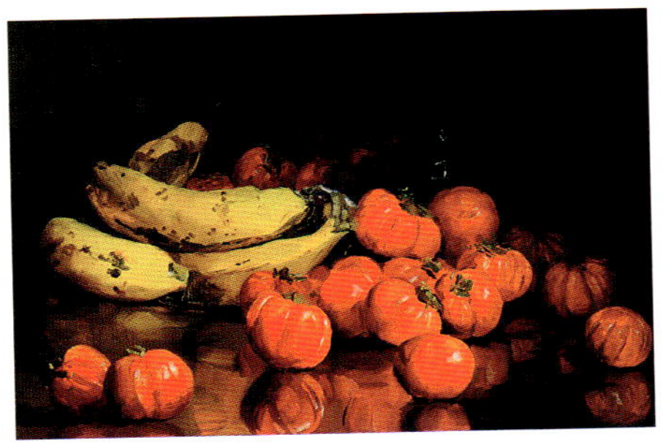

Woods, Grace Mary b.1909
Tomatoes and Bananas 1934–1937
oil on canvas 26.5 x 36.9
VIS.638

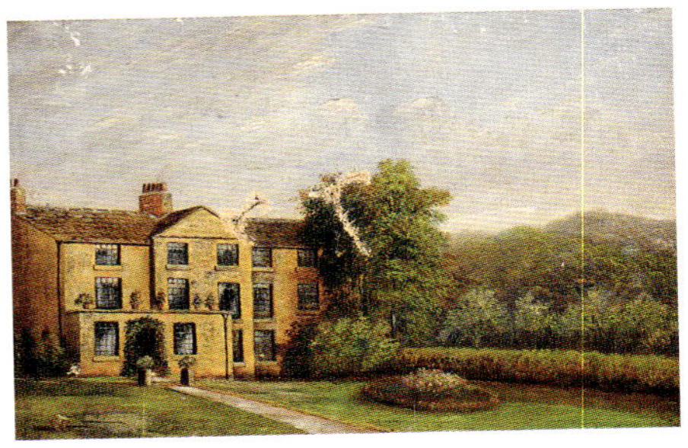

Woolhouse, George 1751–1835
Old House, Norfolk Street, Sheffield
oil on canvas 20.5 x 30.5
X1974.629

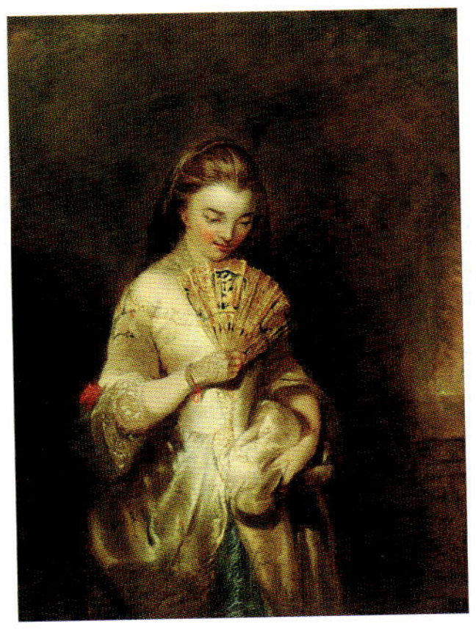

Woolmer, Alfred Joseph 1805–1892
Sweet Seventeen
oil on canvas 38.8 x 29
VIS.709

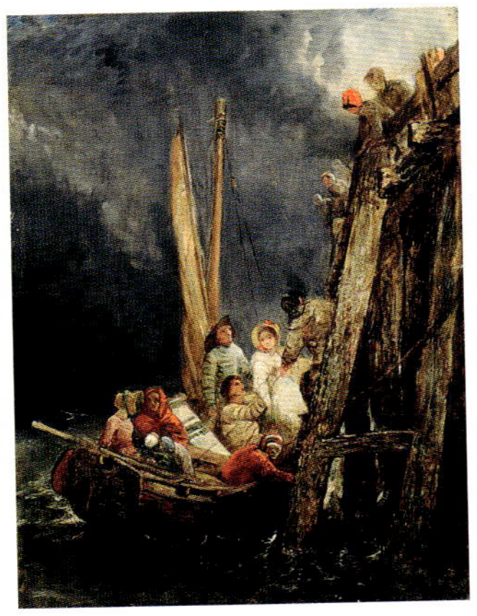

Woolner, Thomas (attributed to) 1825–1892
The Farewell
oil on canvas 39 x 29.1
VIS.532

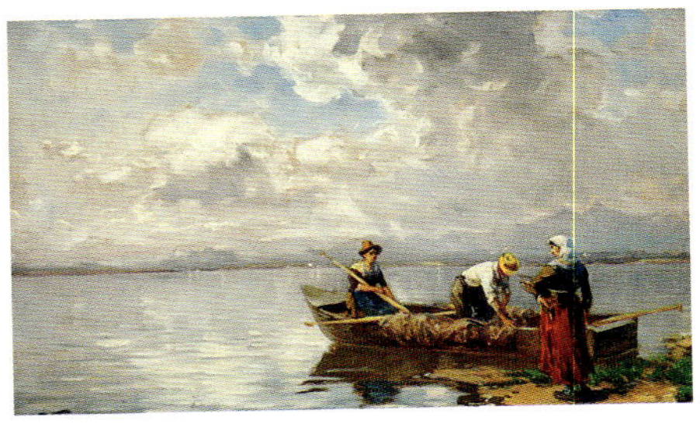

Wopfner, Josef 1843–1927
The Ferry
oil on canvas 31.8 x 54
VIS.1360

Facing page: Auerbach, Frank Helmuth, b.1931, *Head of J. Y. M.* (detail), 1973, Museums Sheffield, (p. 9)

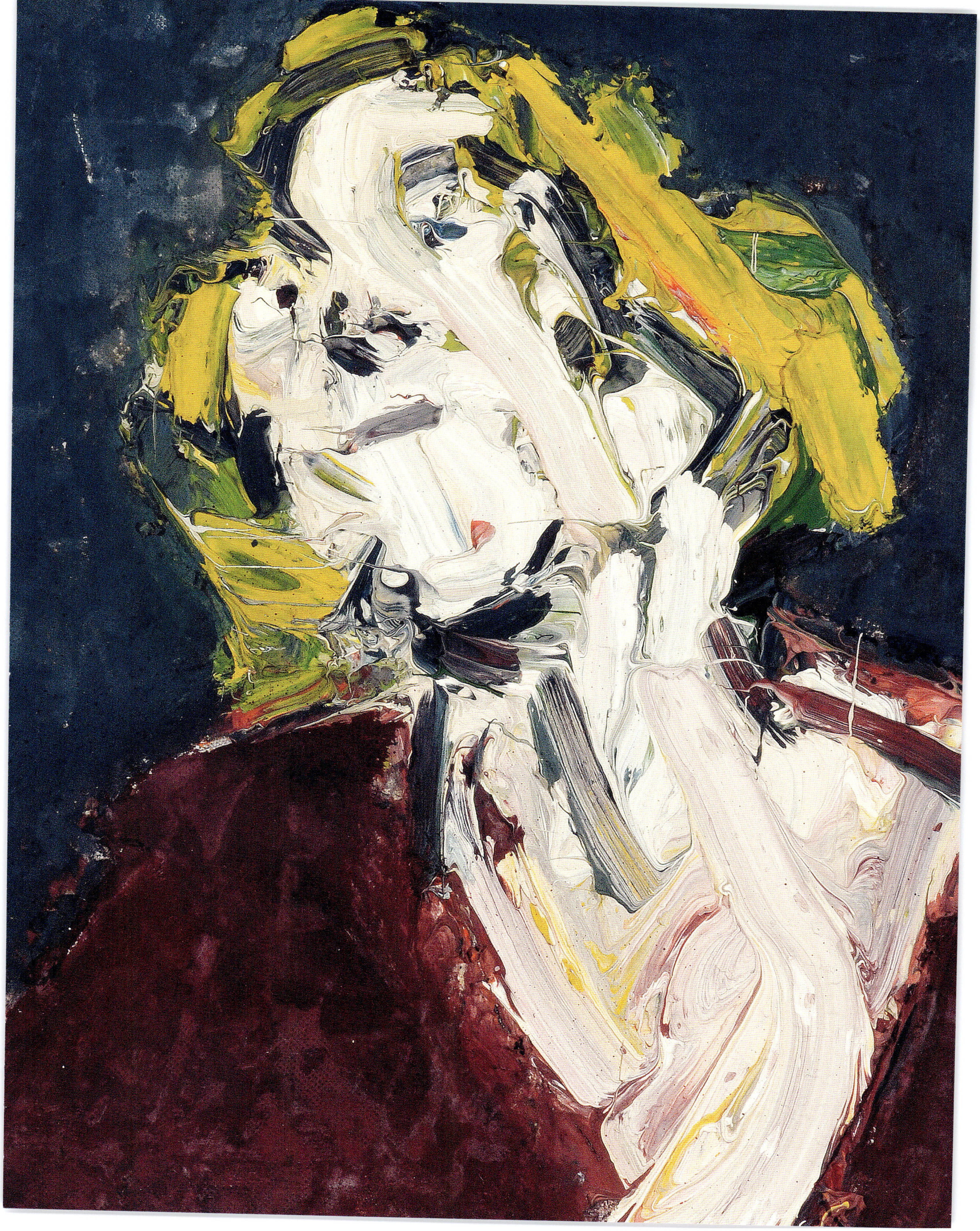

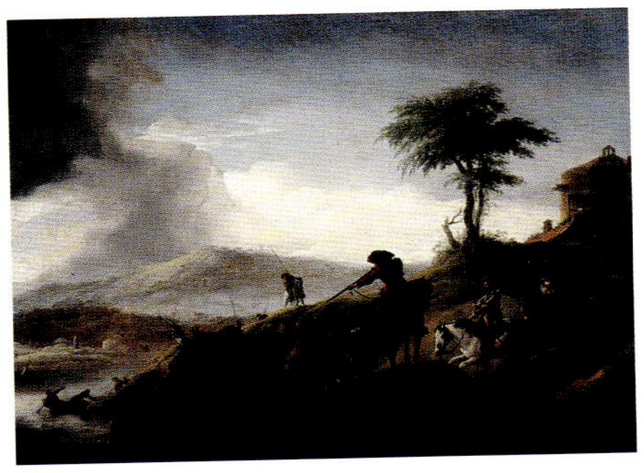

Wouwerman, Philips 1619–1668
A Stag Hunt 1639–1668
oil on panel 41.5 x 55.4
VIS.5130

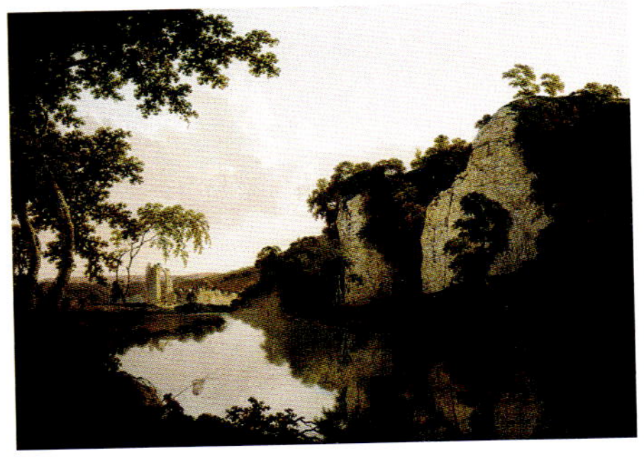

Wright, Joseph of Derby 1734–1797
Landscape with Dale Abbey, Derbyshire c.1785
oil on canvas 72.4 x 98.8
VIS.367

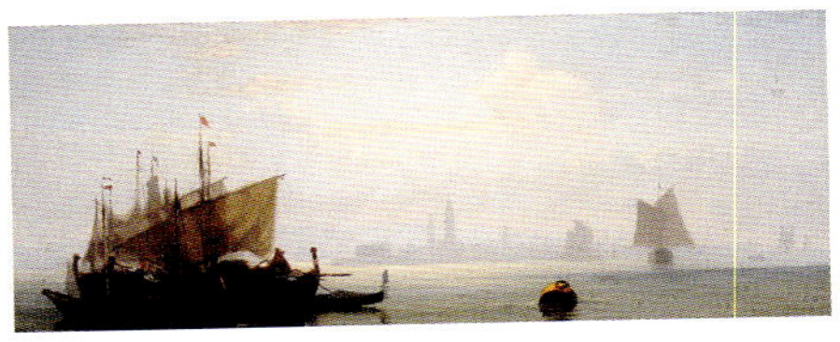

Wyld, William 1806–1889
Venice, Morning
oil on panel 13.5 x 34.4
VIS.1491

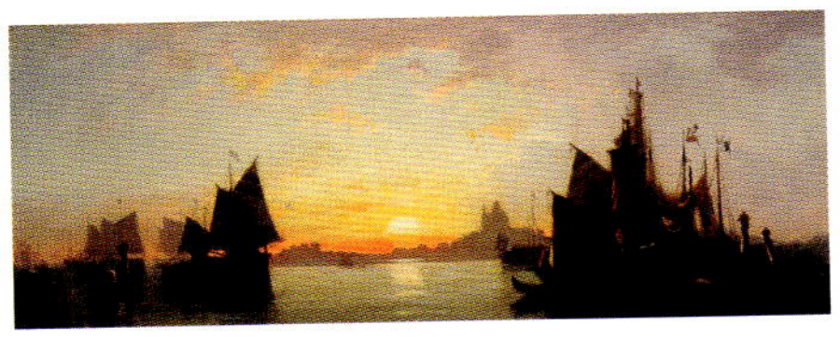

Wyld, William 1806–1889
Venice, Evening
oil on panel 13.5 x 34.4
VIS.1492

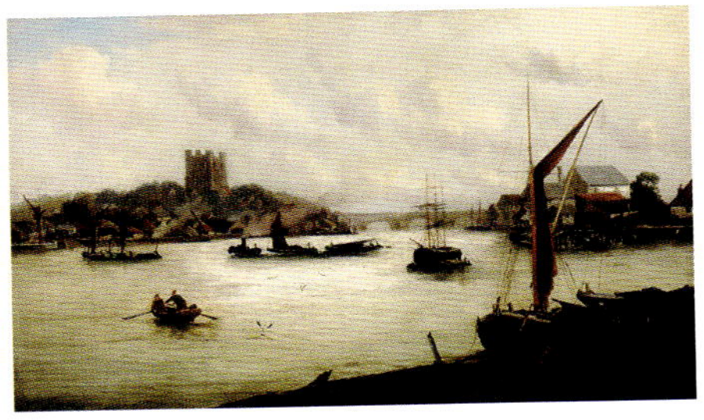

Wyllie, William Lionel 1851–1931
Rochester Castle, Kent 1891
oil on canvas 54.1 x 89.8
VIS.704

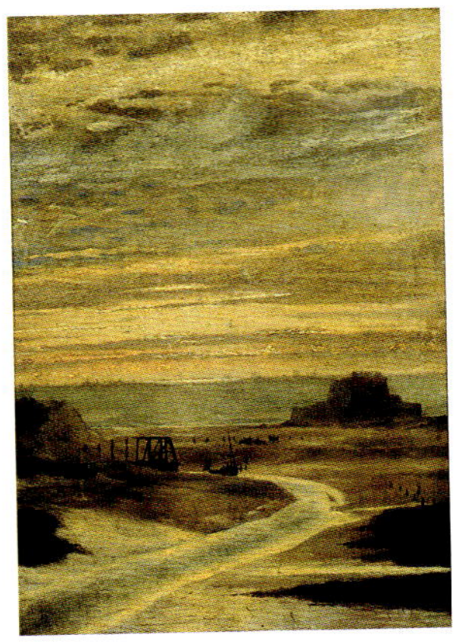

Wyllie, William Lionel 1851–1931
A Coast View
oil on millboard 28.8 x 19.6
VIS.1036

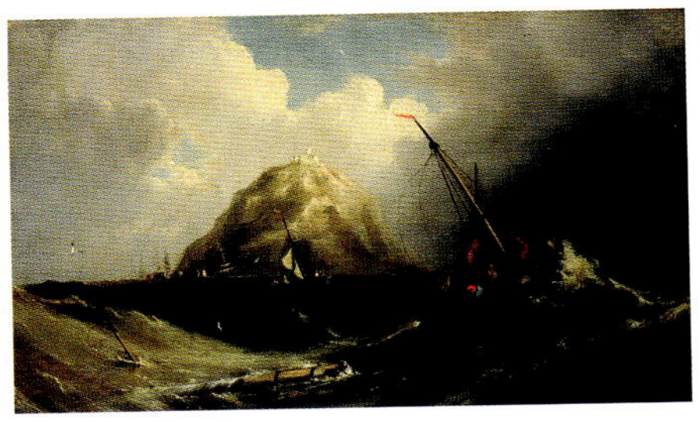

Yarnold, Joseph c.1817–1852
Seascape
oil on panel 23 x 38.4
VIS.124

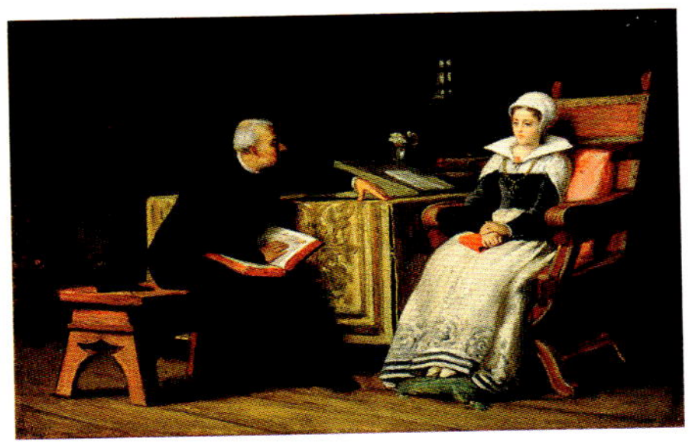

Yeames, William Frederick 1835–1918
Lady Jane Grey in the Tower 1867
oil on canvas 27 x 41.1
VIS.1386

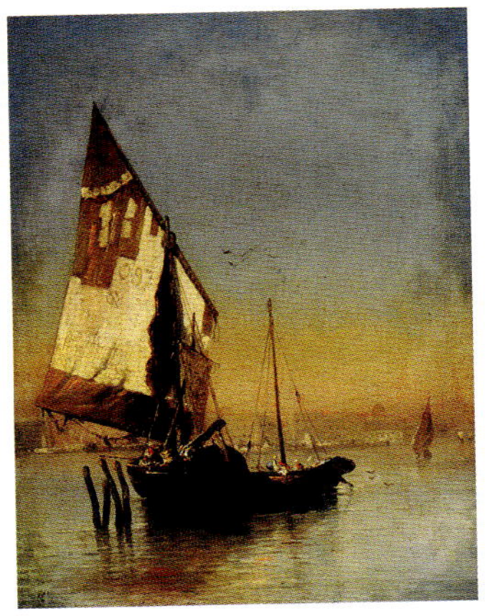

Ziem, Félix François Georges Philibert
1821–1911
Venetian Barges
oil on canvas 46.1 x 36
VIS.608

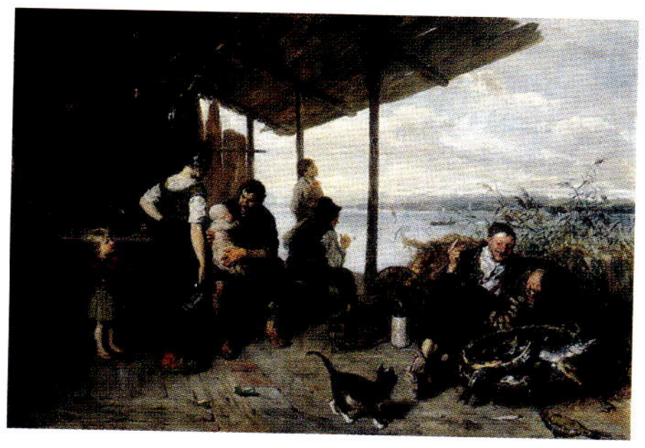

Zimmermann, Ernst Karl Georg 1852–1901
The Fisherman's Cottage c.1887
oil on panel 51 x 73
VIS.1558

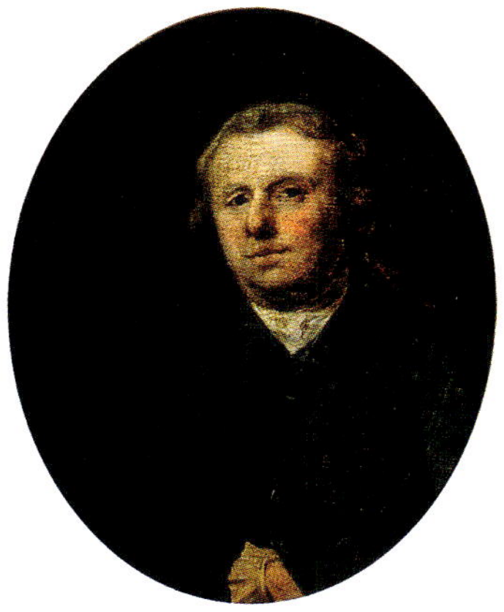

Zoffany, Johann 1733–1810
Peter Garrick
oil on canvas 24.1 x 19.4
VIS.773

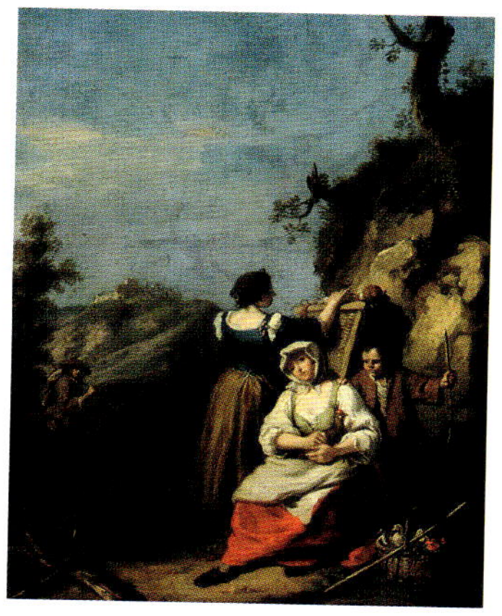

Zuccarelli, Franco (attributed to)
1702–1788
Italian Peasants 1760–1765
oil on canvas 56.5 x 44.3
VIS.247

Sheffield Central Library

Sheffield Central Library's mission statement is 'to provide opportunities and access to resources for everyone to learn, enjoy and discover'. This aim is met in many ways across the services which comprise the Central Library; over 30 local libraries and special services including libraries in hospitals and services for the housebound.

Amongst other intentions, the Libraries' Charter promises space to sit and read or study, opportunities to develop a love of reading in a group or individually, requested books delivered to a local library, and access to resources for learning. Many other services are also provided, including free internet access.

Library spaces are also ideal locations to promote art, both with long-term hangings and short exhibition runs. The 75-year-old Art Deco Central Library (which shares the same building as the Graves Gallery, whose collection is in Museums Sheffield) especially lends itself to long-term displays of work.

Our Collection of paintings by British artist Bob Brighton can be found in the newly-refurbished IT suite. His language is colour and his vocabulary a palette of over 90 hues. The artist's work has been described by one critic as 'brilliant abstractions that utilise colour in the most lyrical way'. Brighton's paintings are typically unstretched canvases of raw hessian, cotton and flax, sandwiched together, soaked in colour and pinned directly to the gallery wall. Most of the works are large and dramatic.

Since becoming a professional artist in 1983 Brighton has given most of his work away and lived a frugal existence. All these paintings were donated by the artist.

Martin Dutch, Head of Libraries, Archives and Information

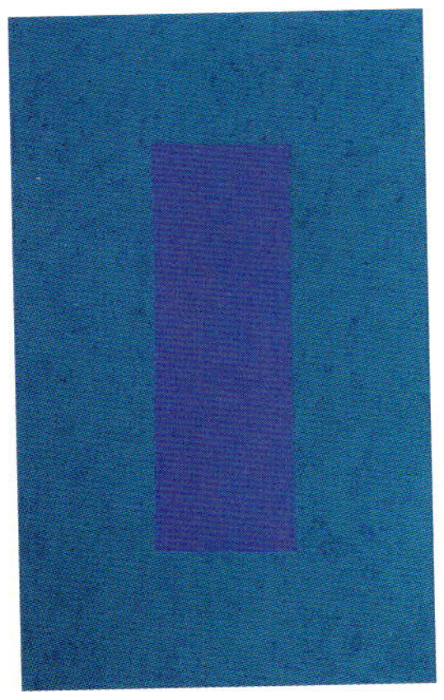

Brighton, Bob b.1936
579 2005
oil on canvas 77 x 46
PCF18

Brighton, Bob b.1936
580 2005
oil on canvas 77 x 46
PCF19

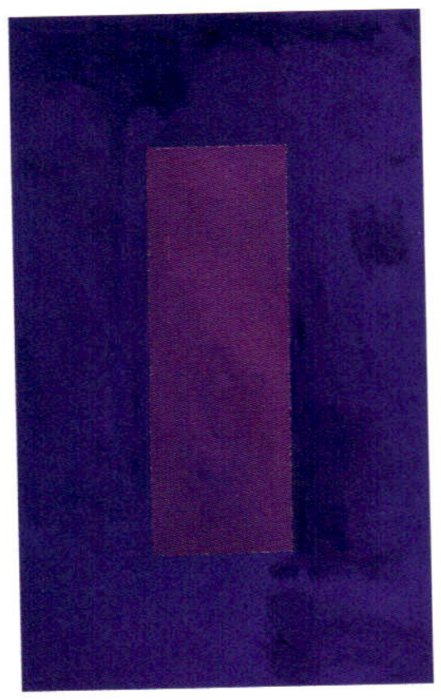

Brighton, Bob b.1936
581 2005
oil on canvas 77 x 46
PCF20

Brighton, Bob b.1936
582 2005
oil on canvas 77 x 46
PCF21

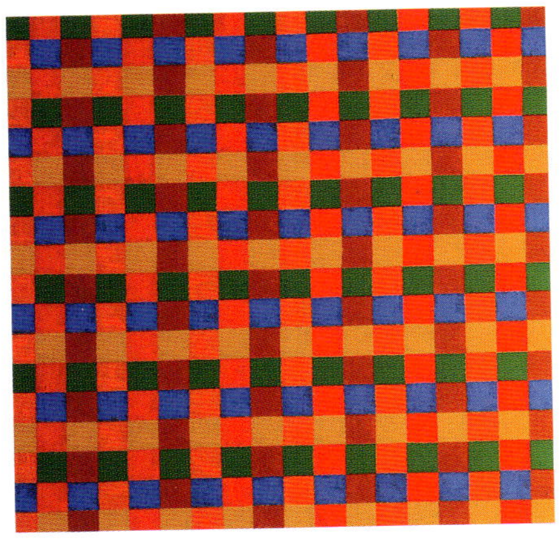

Brighton, Bob b.1936
Orange Blocks c.2009
oil on canvas 46 x 46
PCF3

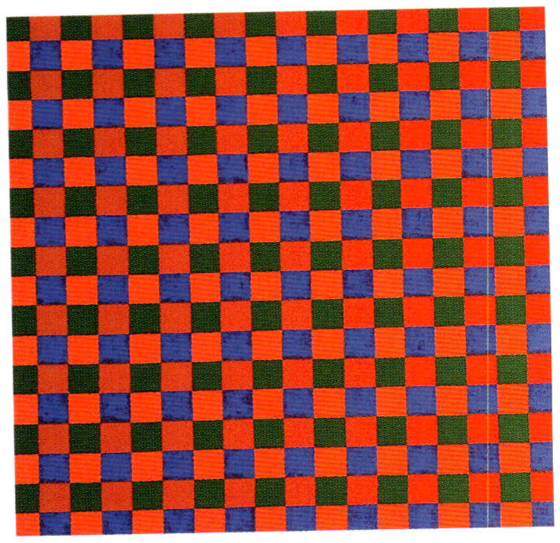

Brighton, Bob b.1936
Orange Multi-Coloured Squares c.2009
oil on canvas 46 x 46
PCF2

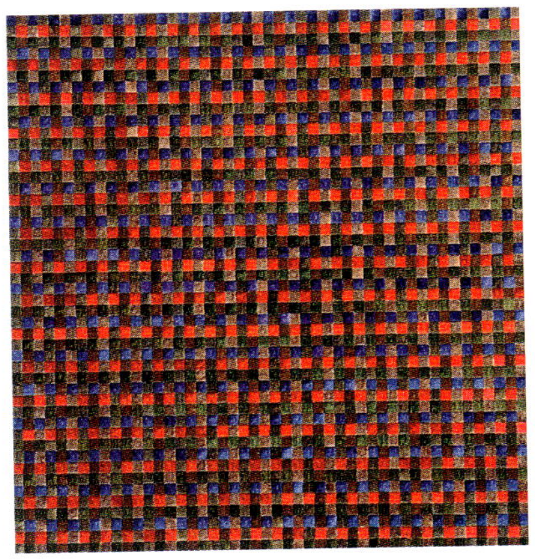

Brighton, Bob b.1936
Small Squares 1 c.2009
oil on canvas 66 x 62
PCF13

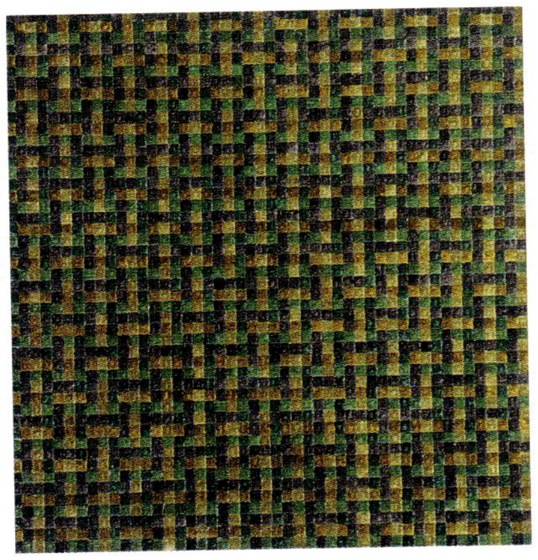

Brighton, Bob b.1936
Small Squares 2 c.2009
oil on canvas 66 x 62
PCF14

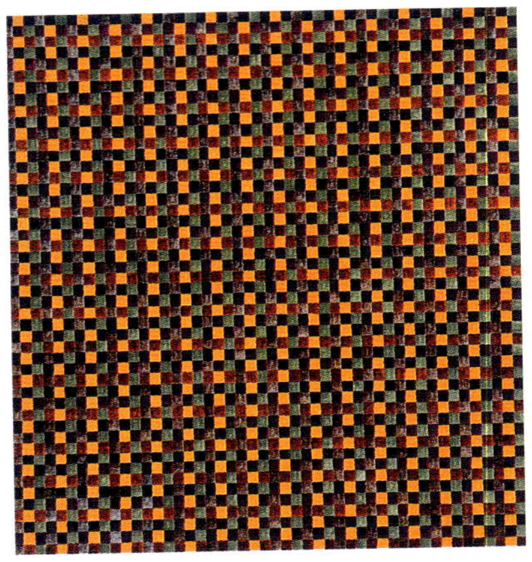

Brighton, Bob b.1936
Small Squares 3 c.2009
oil on canvas 66 x 62
PCF15

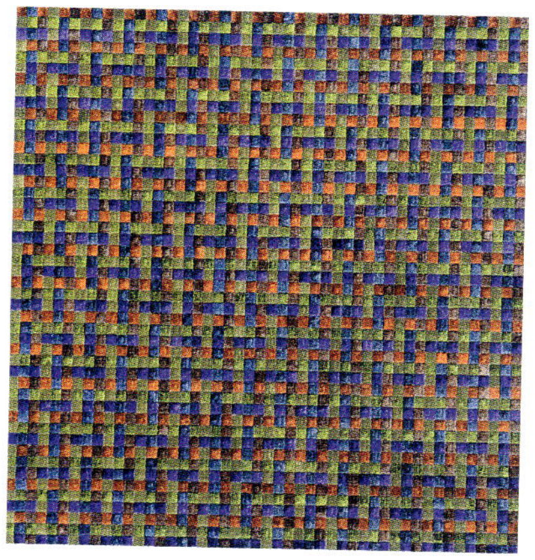

Brighton, Bob b.1936
Small Squares 4 c.2009
oil on canvas 66 x 62
PCF16

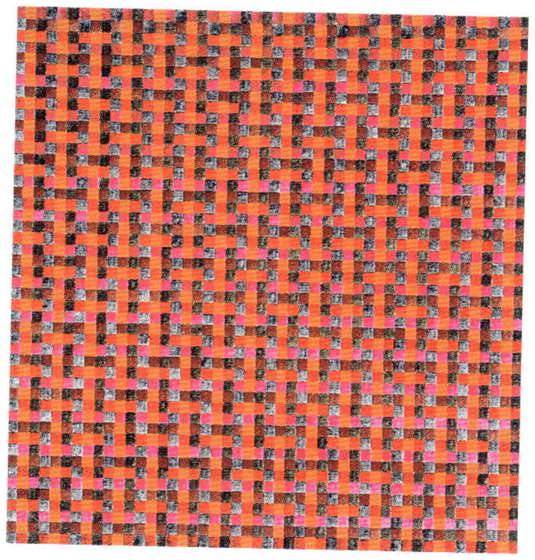

Brighton, Bob b.1936
Small Squares 5 c.2009
oil on canvas 66 x 62
PCF17

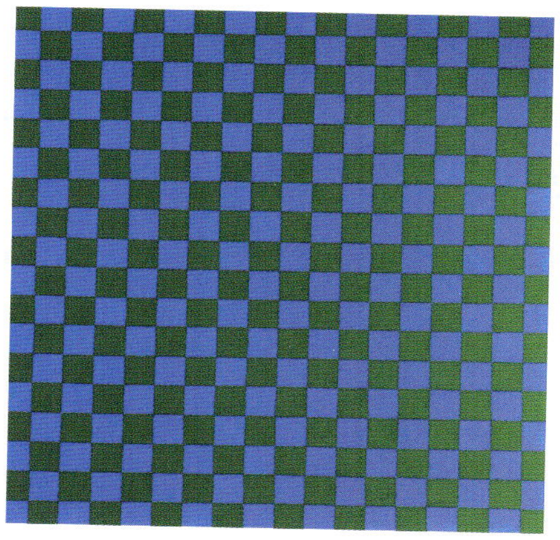

Brighton, Bob b.1936
Turquoise Squares c.2009
oil on canvas 46 x 46
PCF1

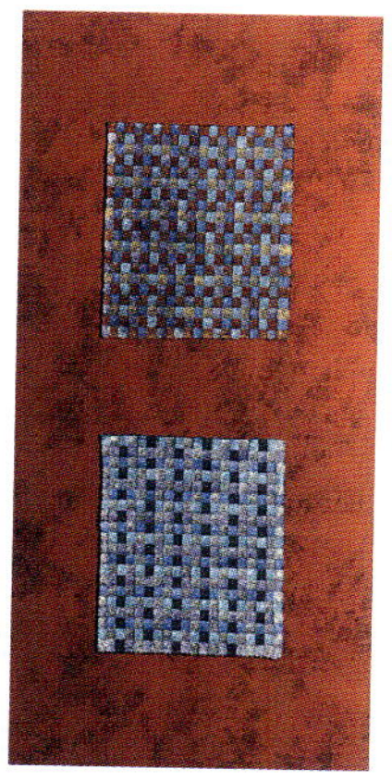

Brighton, Bob b.1936
Purple Squares on Brown c.2009
oil on canvas mounted on painted canvas 107 x 51
PCF11

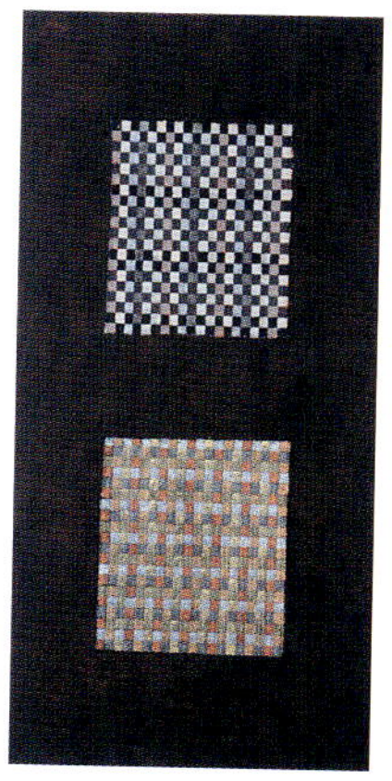

Brighton, Bob b.1936
Squares on Black c.2009
oil on canvas mounted on painted canvas 107 x 51
PCF12

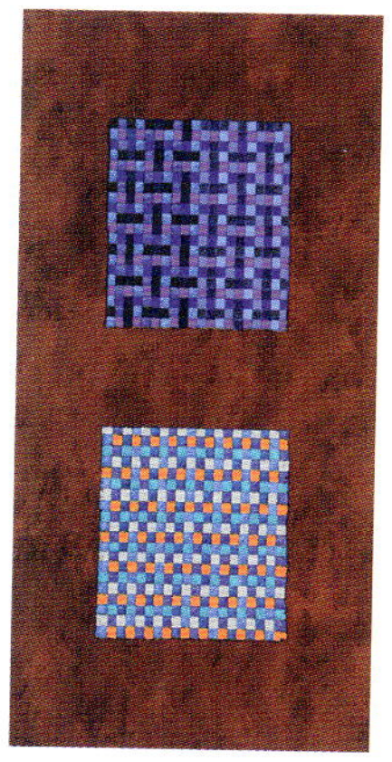

Brighton, Bob b.1936
Squares on Brown c.2009
oil on canvas mounted on painted canvas 107 x 51
PCF9

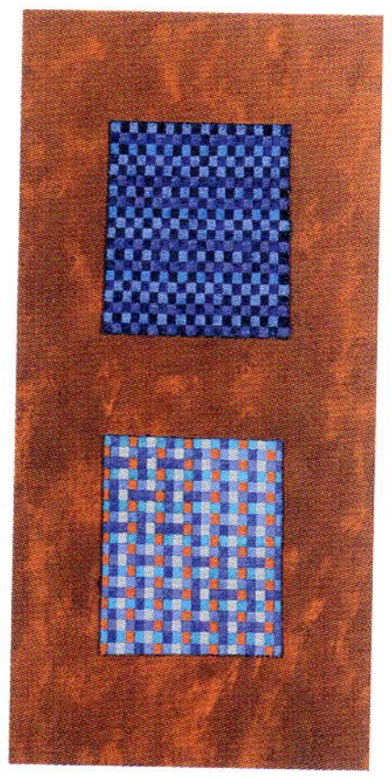

Brighton, Bob b.1936
Squares on Copper c.2009
oil on canvas mounted on painted canvas 107 x 51
PCF10

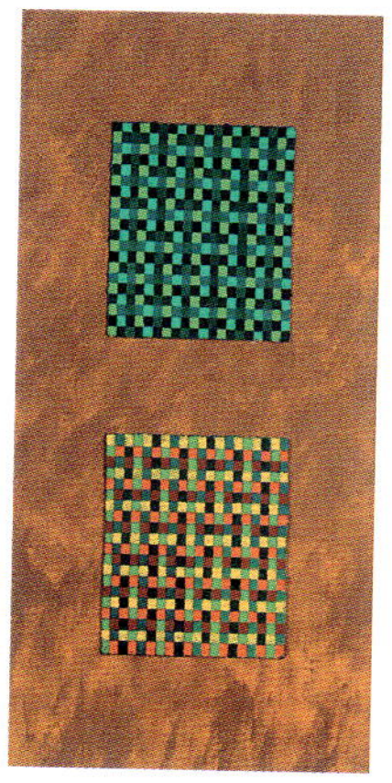

Brighton, Bob b.1936
Squares on Gold c.2009
oil on canvas mounted on painted canvas 107 x 51
PCF8

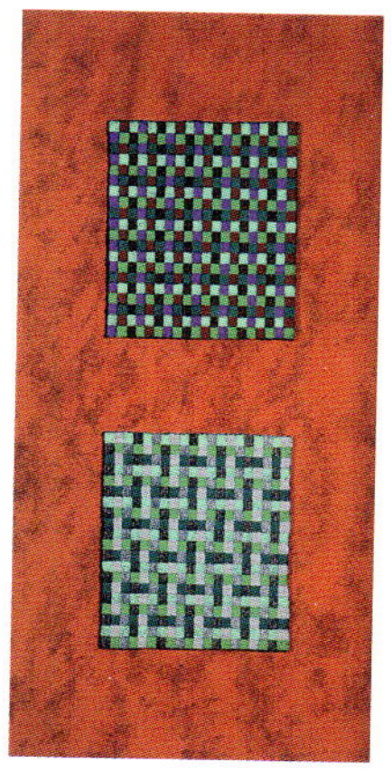

Brighton, Bob b.1936
Squares on Terracotta c.2009
oil on canvas mounted on painted canvas 107 x 51
PCF7

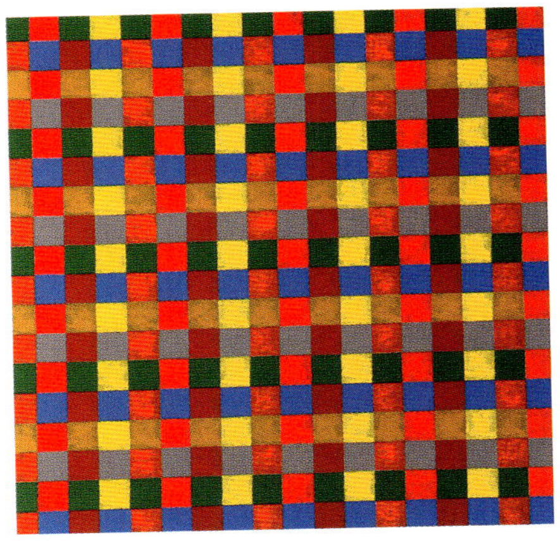

Brighton, Bob b.1936
Yellow Blue 1 c.2009
oil on canvas 46 x 46
PCF4

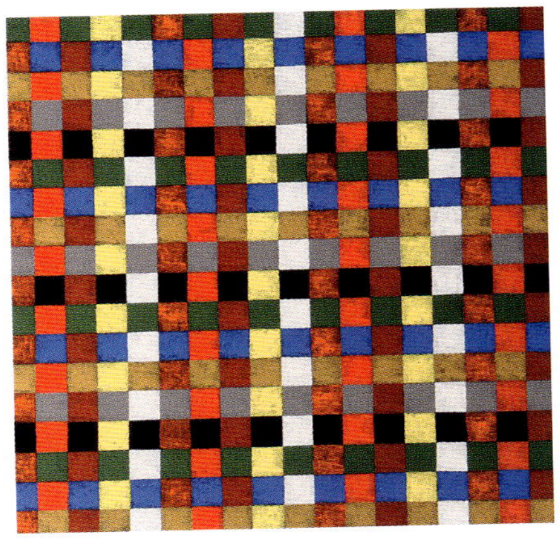

Brighton, Bob b.1936
Yellow Blue 2 c.2009
oil on canvas 46 x 46
PCF5

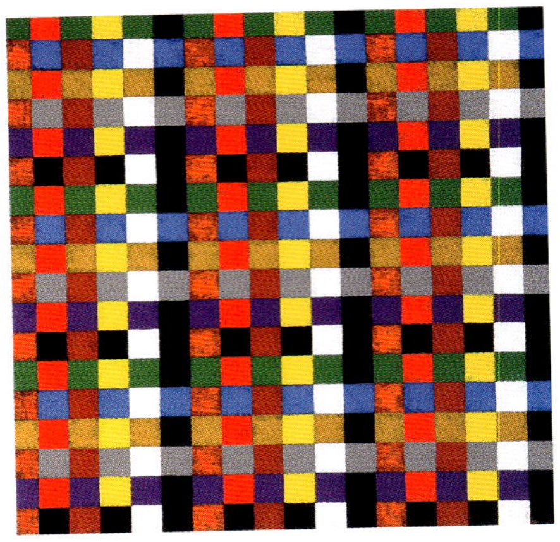

Brighton, Bob b.1936
Yellow Blue 3 c.2009
oil on canvas 46 x 46
PCF6

Sheffield Hallam University

Sheffield Hallam University is one of the country's most progressive and innovative universities. We pride ourselves on making a positive difference – to our students, to our staff, to the businesses we work with and to the local community. Our sought-after graduates contribute to the economic and social development of both our region and to the UK as a whole.

Our facilities are state-of-the-art and we have invested heavily in new technology to ensure that our capability matches the cutting-edge approach of our teaching. We are recognised as a Centre of Excellence for Teaching and Learning, e-learning and employability.

Sheffield Hallam plays a key role in the city and region in which it operates. We are located both in the heart of Sheffield and its leafy suburbs, and our students add to the vibrancy and diversity of the city.

The art Collection at the University is varied, featuring large canvasses by former students and also a series of formal portraits of governors, chancellors and vice-chancellors.

There are three portraits by Yorkshire-born Tom Wood, a former student and now renowned portrait painter and artist. The University commissioned a triptych of portraits of *Richard Gregory, Chairman of the Board of Governors of Sheffield Hallam University*, *Lord Robert Winston, Chancellor of Sheffield Hallam University*, and *Professor Diana Green, CBE, Vice-Chancellor of Sheffield Hallam University*.

Works by Sheffield-born artist, Joe Scarborough are well-represented in the Collection reflecting the University's support during the artist's early career.

In the University's Special Collections Department are *Life Study* by York-born artist William Etty, and *Self Portrait* by William Henry Sounes, a former Head of the School of Art; once more emphasising the richness of local connections within the University's art Collection.

Alex Pettifer, Director of Estates and Facilities

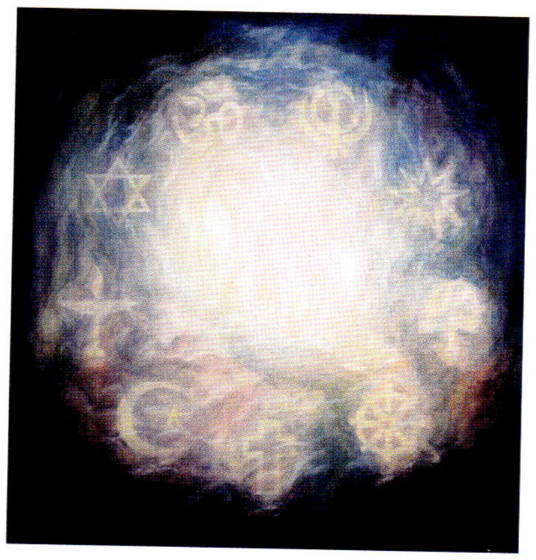

Brown, Colin b.1957
Cloud of Faith 2007
oil on canvas 80 x 75
PCF8

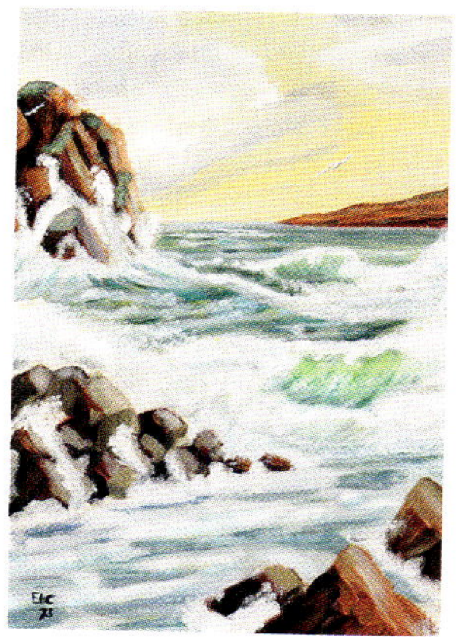

E. H. C.
The Sea and the Rocks 1973
oil on canvas 40.5 x 30
107

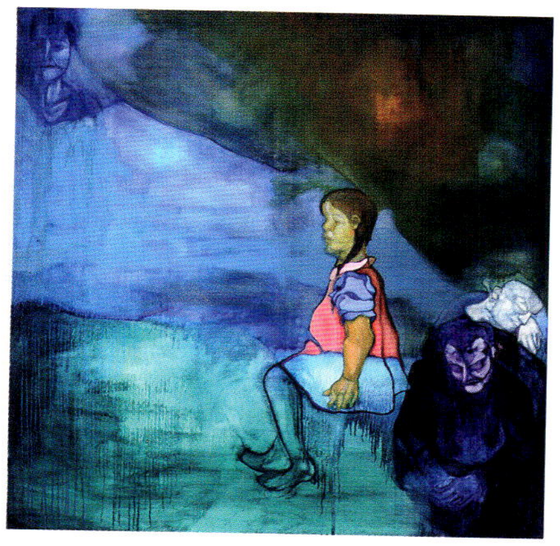

Dickens, Michelle Louise b.1970
Blue 1994–1995
oil on canvas 183 x 183
2

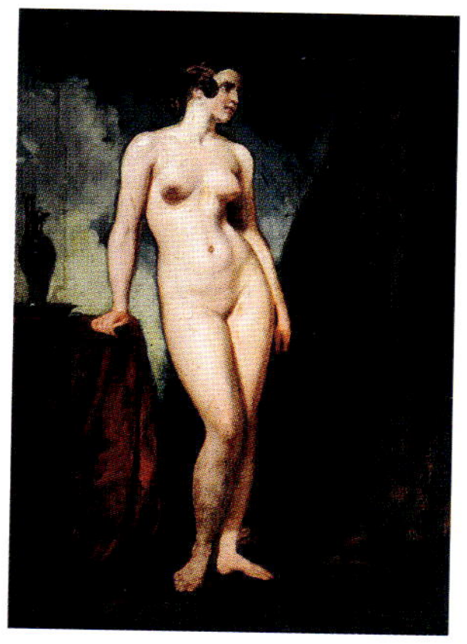

Etty, William 1787–1849
Life Study
oil on canvas 72 x 50
709.2 ETTY

Greene, Mary b.1953
Depths
oil on canvas 176 x 100
PCF20

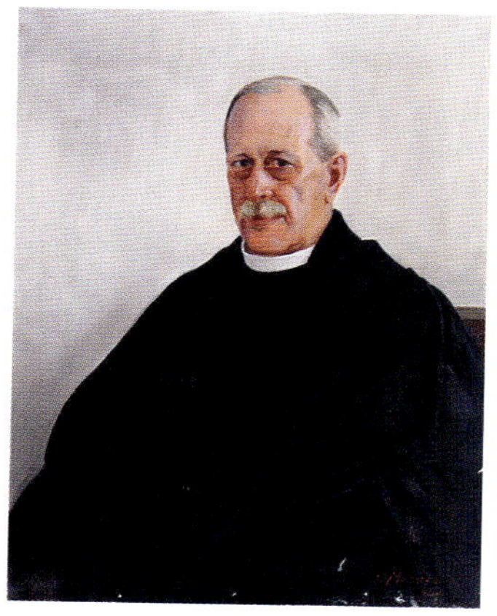

Morgan, E.
Reverend Valentine Ward Pearson, First Principal of Sheffield Training College for Teachers (1905–1921) 1926
oil on canvas 104 x 83
75

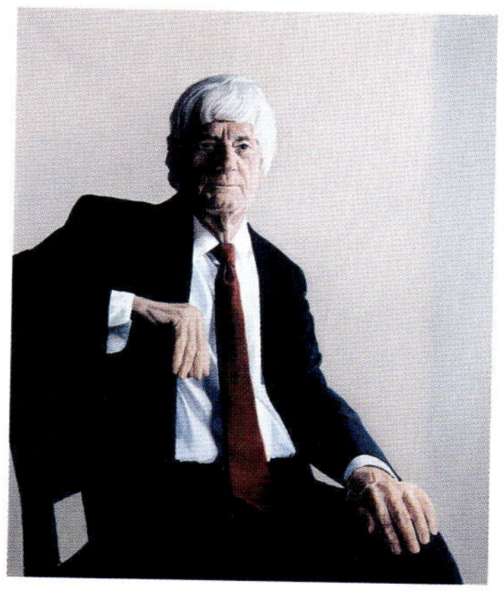

Priseman, Robert b.1965
Councillor William Owen (d.1922), JP, Chair of the Board of Governors (1975-1989), Deputy Chair of the Board of Governors (…) 1992
oil on canvas 89 x 75
PCF17

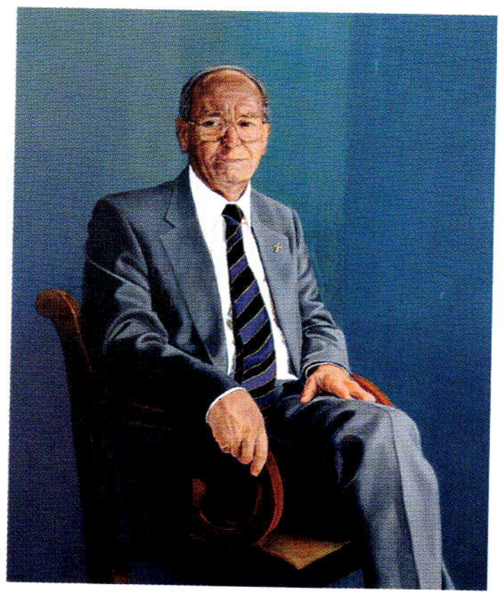

Priseman, Robert b.1965
Canon George Tolley, Principal of Sheffield City Polytechnic (1969–1982) 1993
oil on canvas 89 x 74
PCF13

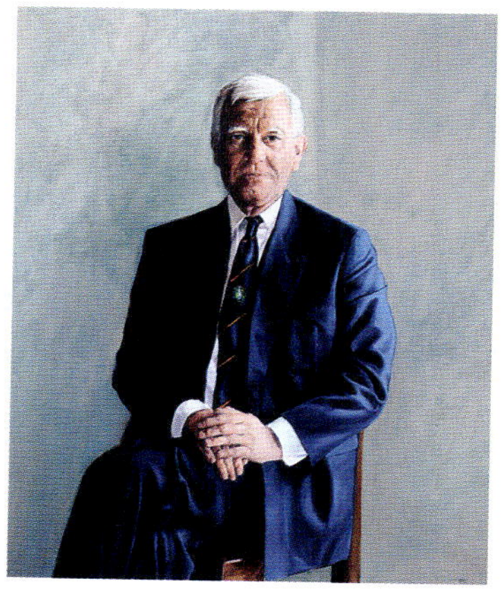

Priseman, Robert b.1965
Peter Newman, Chairman of Sheffield City Polytechnic Board of Governors (1988–1992) 1993
oil on canvas 89 x 75
PCF18

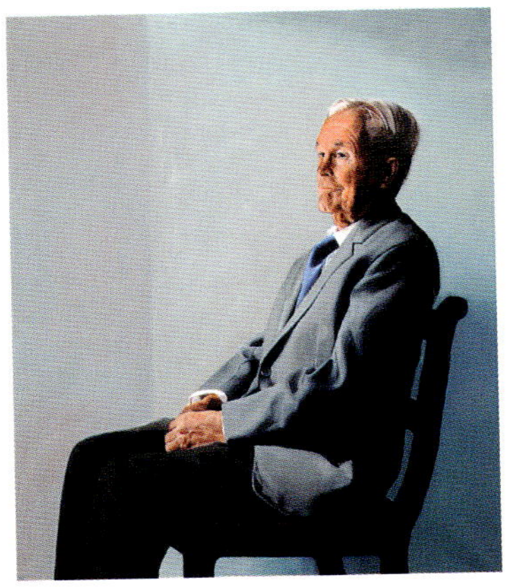

Priseman, Robert b.1965
Sir Eric Mensforth (1906–2000), CBE, First Chairman of the Governing Body of Sheffield City Polytechnic (1969–1975) 1993
oil on canvas 89 x 73
PCF16

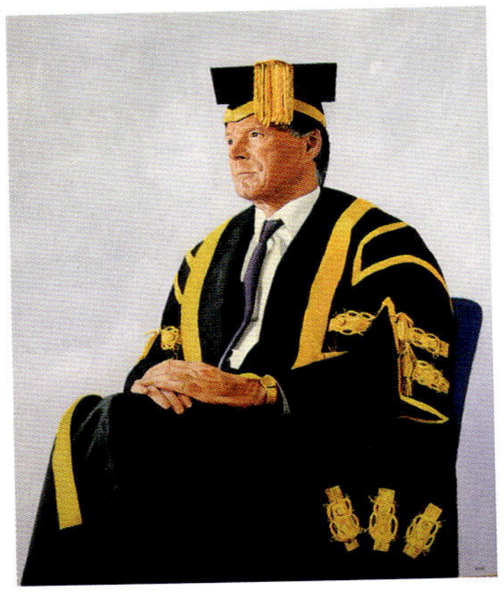

Priseman, Robert b.1965
John Stoddart, Principal, Sheffield Hallam University (c.1983–1998) 1994
oil on canvas 87 x 75
PCF14

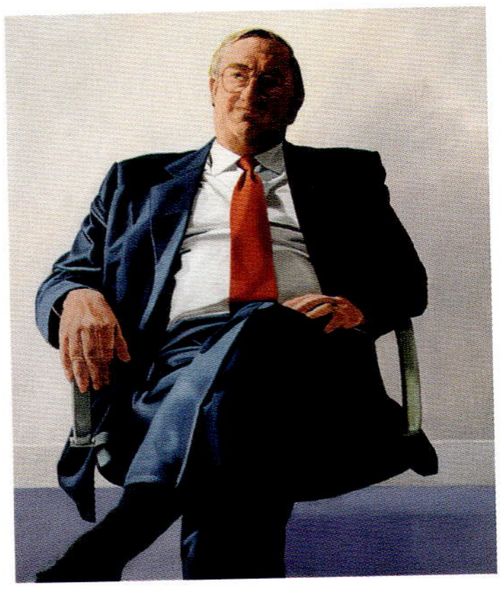

Priseman, Robert b.1965
Norman Adsetts (b.1931), OBE, Chairman of Sheffield Hallam University Board of Governors (1993–1999) 1994
oil on canvas 89 x 75
PCF19

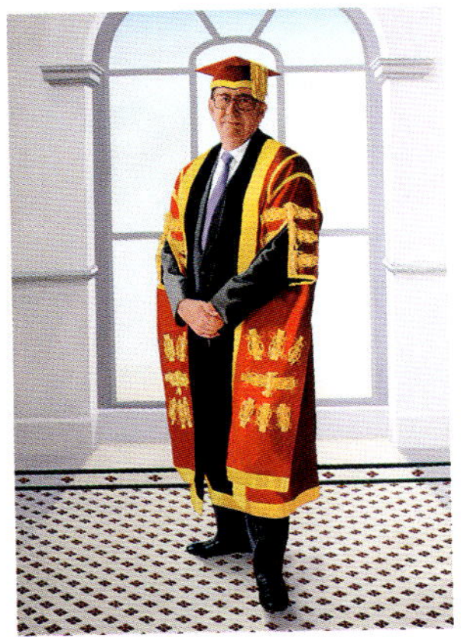

Priseman, Robert b.1965
Sir Bryan Nicholson, Chancellor of Sheffield Hallam University (c.1994–2001) 1995
oil on canvas 135 x 90
PCF15

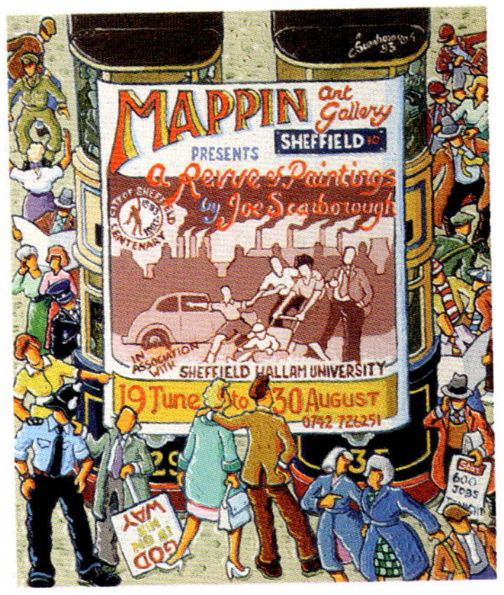

Scarborough, Joe b.1938
'A Review of Paintings by Joe Scarborough', Mappin Art Gallery, Sheffield, Advertisement 1993
oil on canvas 50 x 40
39

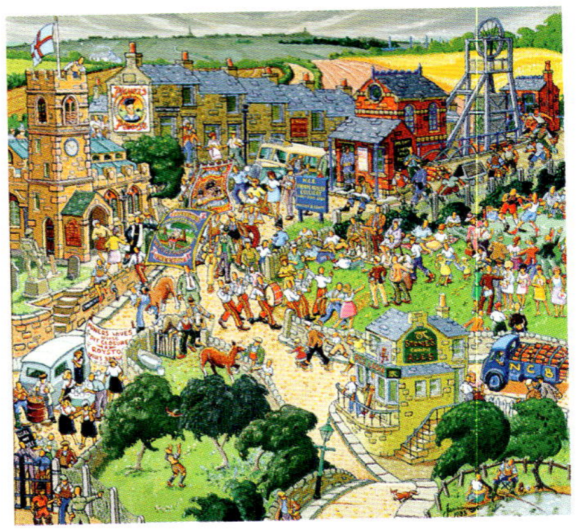

Scarborough, Joe b.1938
'Coal', A Celebration 1993
oil on canvas 98 x 100
PCF10

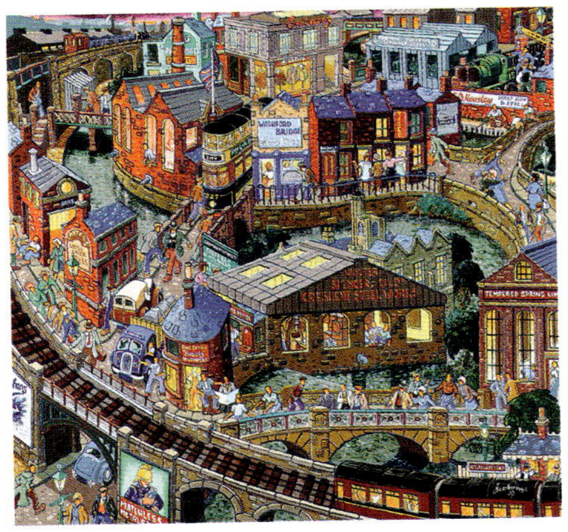

Scarborough, Joe b.1938
Steel and Steelworkers 1993
oil on canvas 100 x 110
PCF9

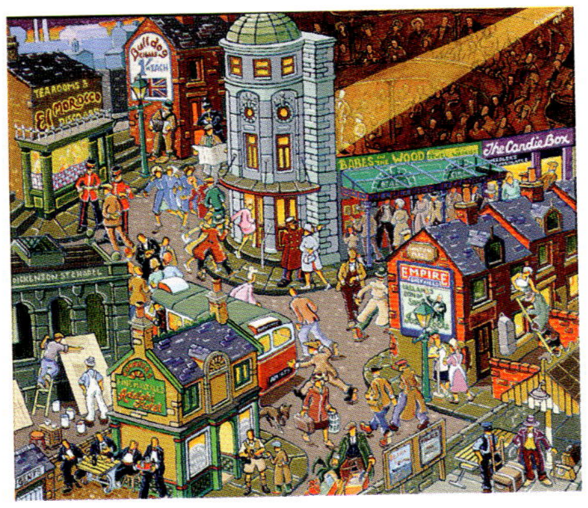

Scarborough, Joe b.1938
The Streets of Sheffield 1994
oil on canvas 80 x 90
68

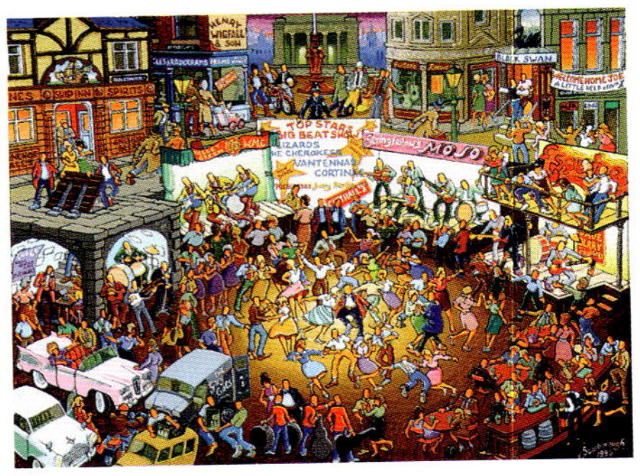

Scarborough, Joe b.1938
People Dancing to Bands, Sheffield 1996
oil on canvas 88 x 113
86

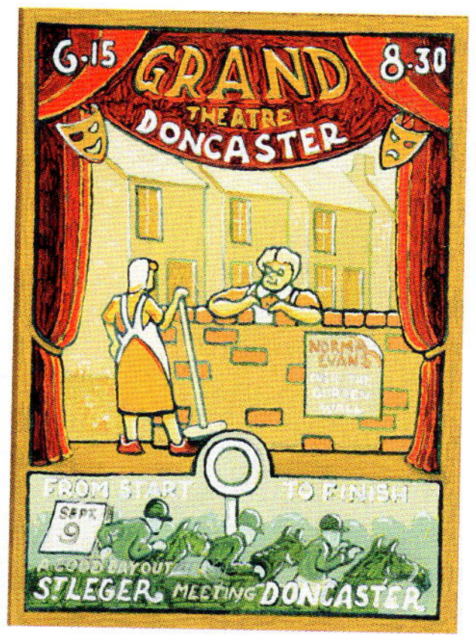

Scarborough, Joe b.1938
Grand Theatre, Doncaster, Advertisement mid-1990s
oil on canvas 45 x 35.5
70

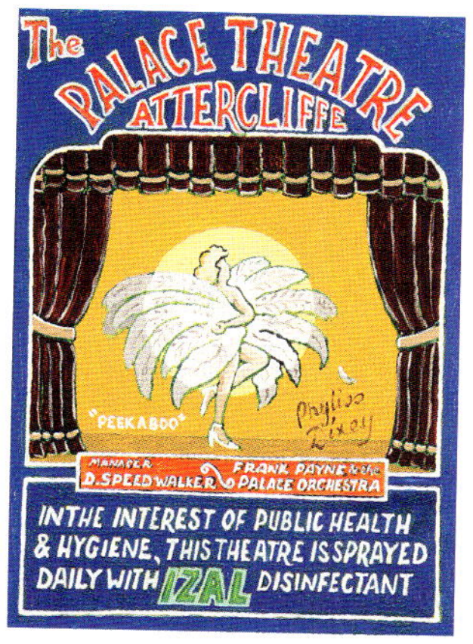

Scarborough, Joe b.1938
Palace Theatre, Attercliffe, Advertisement mid-1990s
oil on canvas 45 x 35.5
72

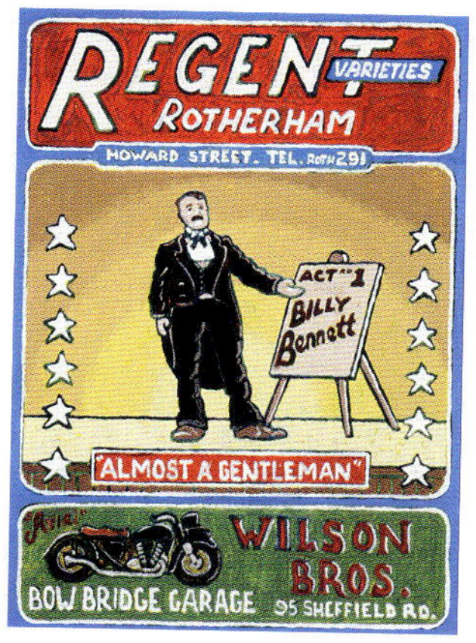

Scarborough, Joe b.1938
The Regent, Rotherham, Advertisement mid-1990s
oil on canvas 45 x 35.5
69

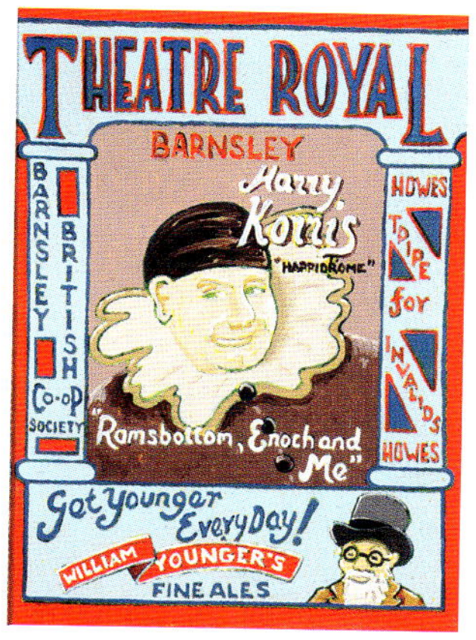

Scarborough, Joe b.1938
Theatre Royal, Barnsley, Advertisement mid-1990s
oil on canvas 45 x 35.5
71

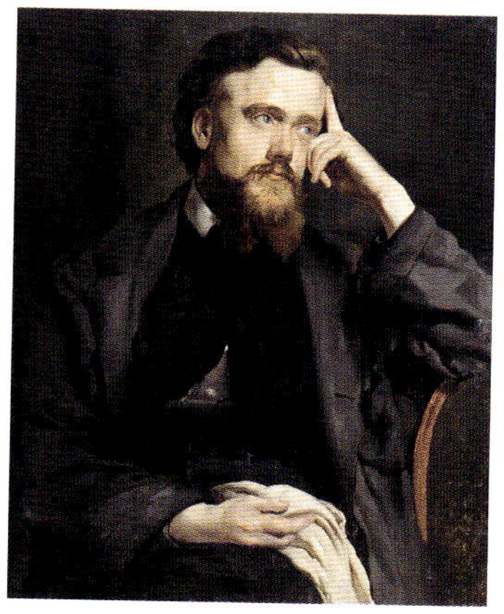

Sounes, William Henry 1830–1873
Self Portrait c.1865
oil on canvas 82 x 64
709.2 SOUNES

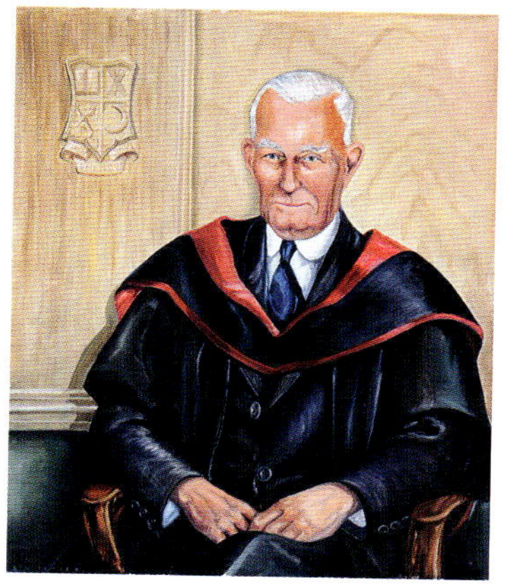

Tucker, R. A.
Ralf R. Kimbell
oil on canvas 104 x 88.5
81

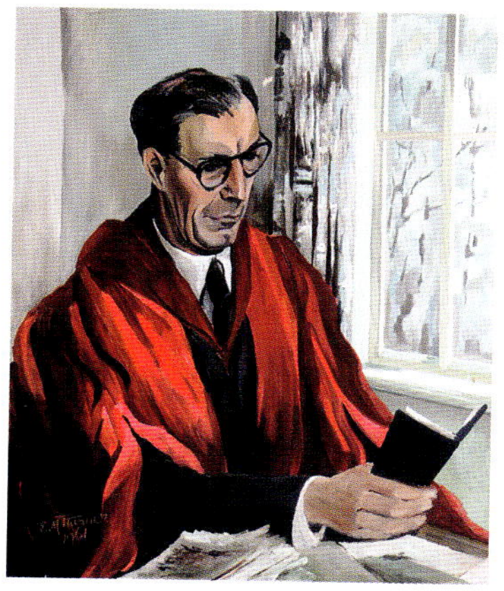

Turner, E. M. T.
Dr Herbert Wing 1961
oil on canvas 104 x 89
73

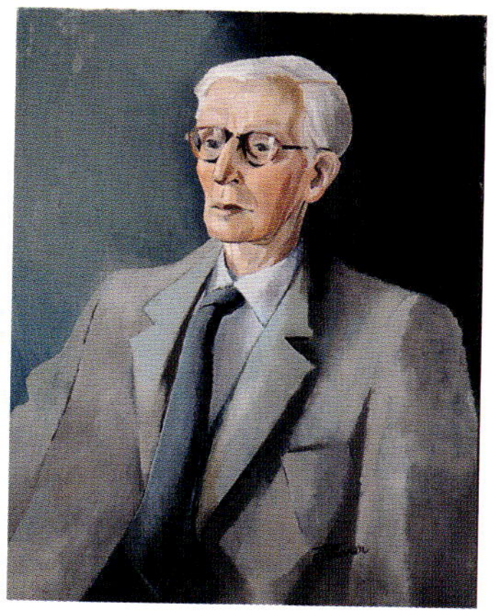

Turner, E. M. T.
Samuel Hoole
oil on canvas 93.5 x 75.5
82

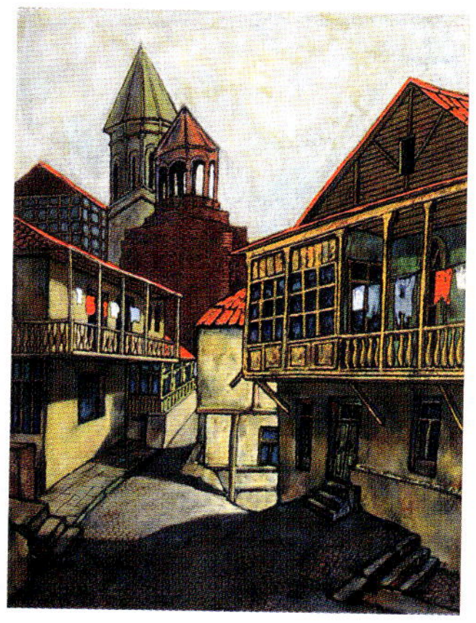

unknown artist
Street Scene, Old Quarter, Tbilisi, Georgia c.2001
oil on card 35 x 25
43

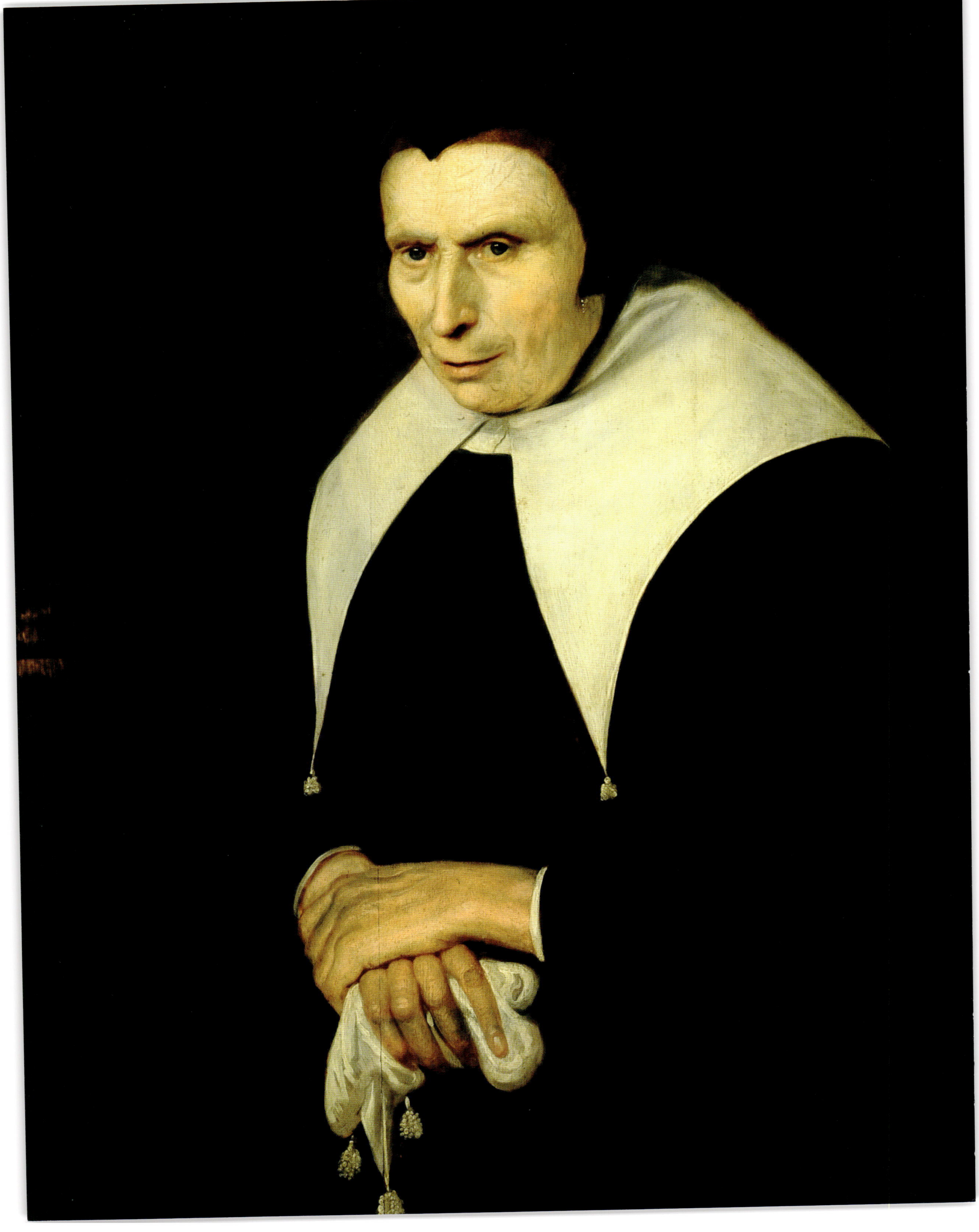

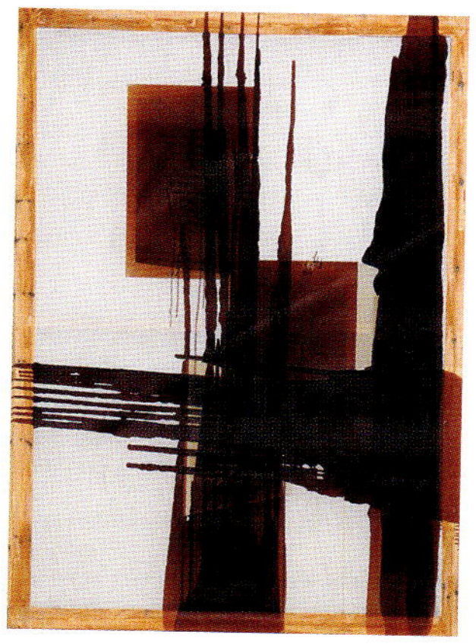

unknown artist
*Abstract** (triptych, left wing)
acrylic on board 250 x 170
PCF4

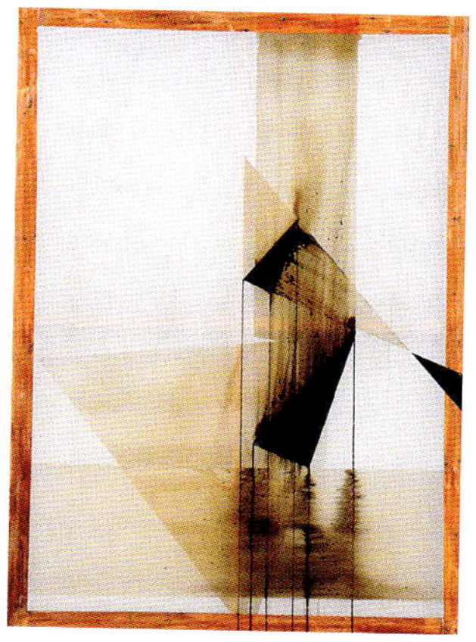

unknown artist
*Abstract** (triptych, centre panel)
acrylic on board 250 x 170
PCF5

unknown artist
*Abstract** (triptych, right wing)
acrylic on board 250 x 170
PCF6

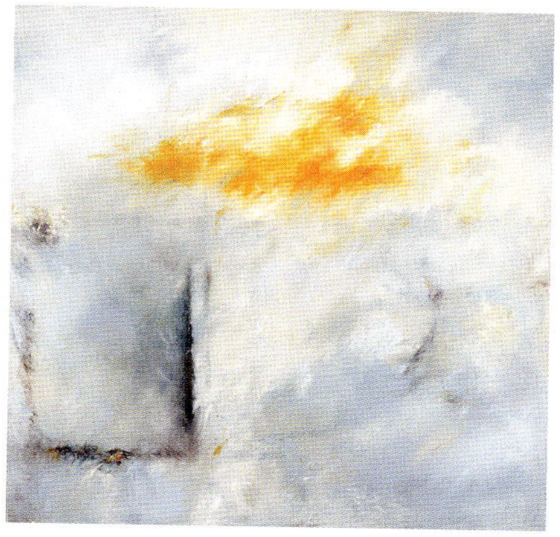

unknown artist
*Abstract in Blue and Orange**
oil on canvas 160 x 150
PCF12

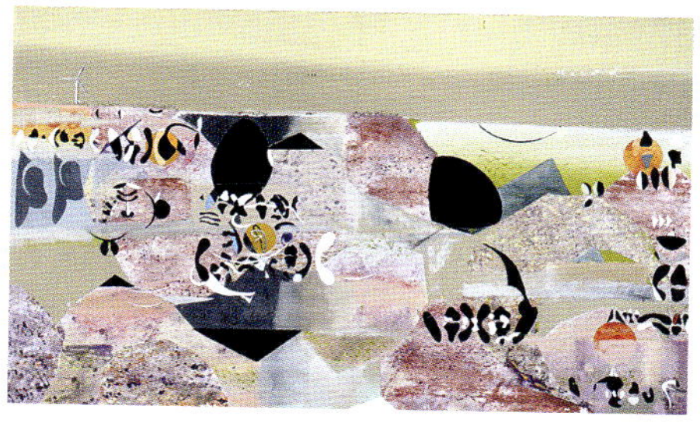

unknown artist
Abstract Landscape in Pale Pink and Green
oil on canvas 93 x 154
1

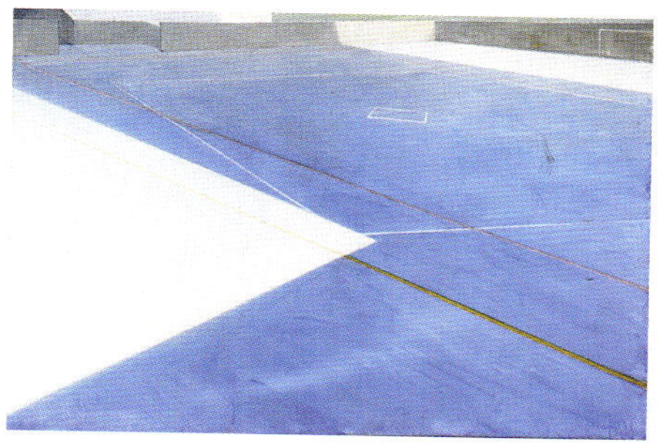

unknown artist
Courtyard in Light and Shadow with Geometric Shapes
oil on canvas 93 x 134
3

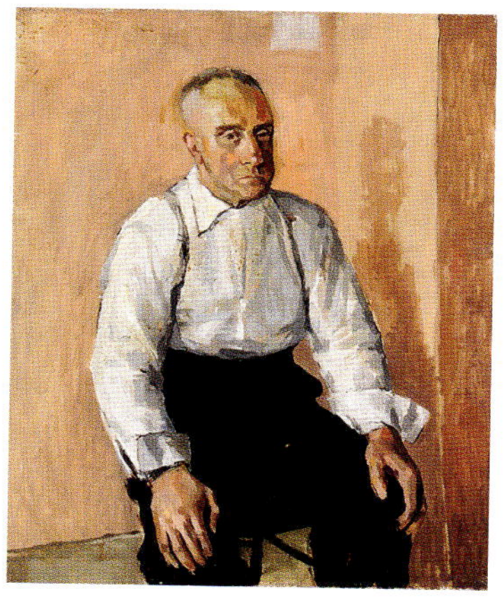

unknown artist
Old Man
oil on canvas 76 x 63
29

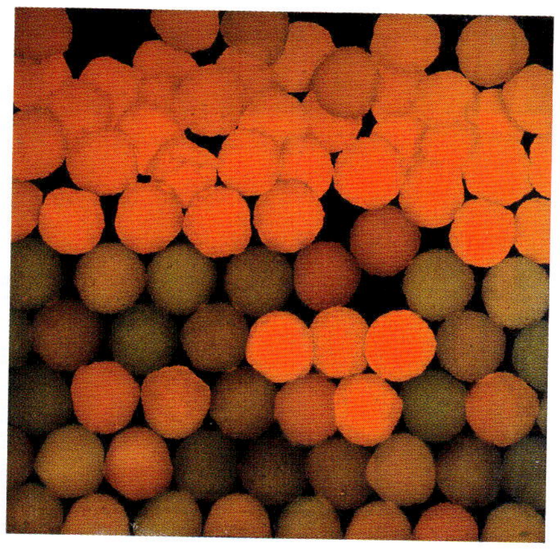

unknown artist
Orange and Green Circles
oil on canvas 92 x 92
10

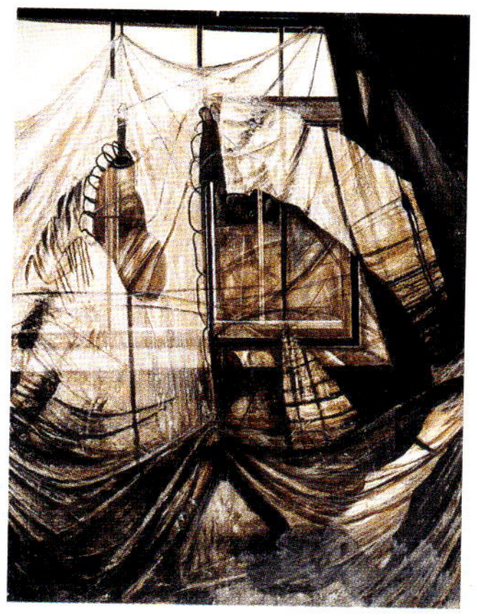

unknown artist
Window and Fabric
oil on board 122 x 92
9

Facing page: Beeldemaker, Adriaen Cornelisz., 1618–1709, *Portrait of an Old Woman* (detail), 1676, Museums Sheffield, (p. 16)

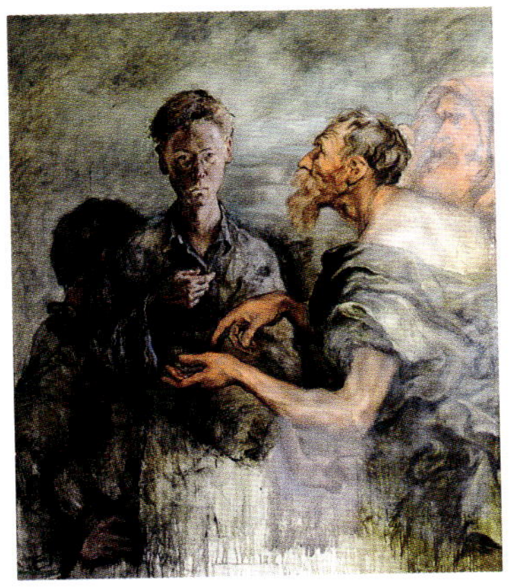

unknown artist
Youth and Age
oil on canvas 180 x 147
PCF7

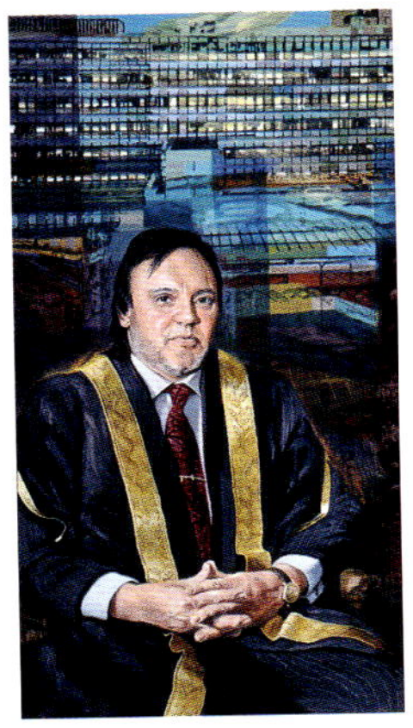

Wood, Tom b.1955
Richard Gregory, Chairman of the Board of Governors of Sheffield Hallam University
(triptych, left wing) c.2006
oil on canvas 165 x 80
PCF1

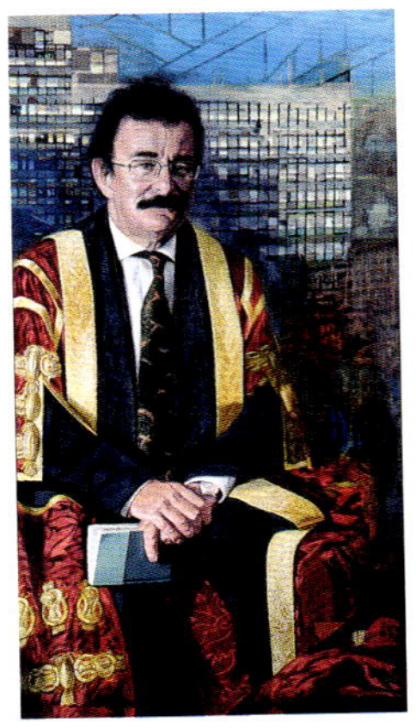

Wood, Tom b.1955
Lord Robert Winston (b.1940), Chancellor of Sheffield Hallam University from 2001
(triptych, centre panel) c.2006
oil on canvas 165 x 80
PCF2

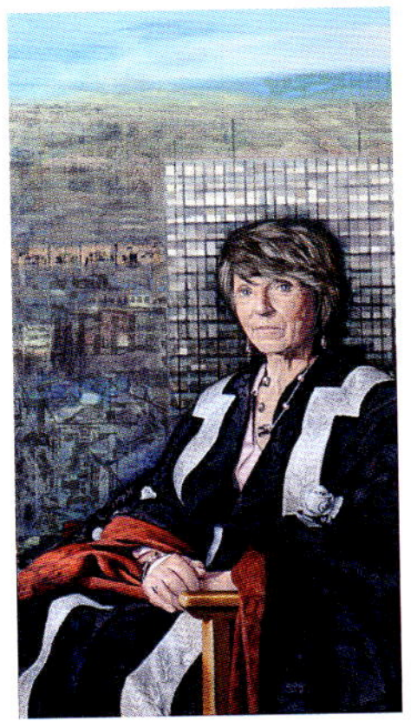

Wood, Tom b.1955
Professor Diana Green, CBE, Vice-Chancellor of Sheffield Hallam University (1998–2007)
(triptych, right wing) c.2006
oil on canvas 165 x 80
PCF3

Sheffield Industrial Museums Trust

The art collection managed by Sheffield Industrial Museums Trust is small but significant, as it provides an important insight into the places, people and processes relevant to the industrial heritage of Sheffield.

Each painting has a story to tell about the nature of working life for the people of the city of Sheffield. The diverse Collection consists of famous works, such as *The Wealth of England, the Bessemer Process of Making Steel* by William Holt Yates Titcomb, which captures the movement and drama of large-scale steel production, and more personal pieces such as *Detail of a Steel Ladle* by Mel G. Booth.

The portraits of the key players in Sheffield's industrial life provide not only a personal connection, but also allow access to a social-historical understanding of the period. The views of buildings and places are instrumental in setting the contextual background for the stories of the technological changes that are part of the history of the city.

Sheffield Industrial Museums Trust manages the industrial collections on behalf of Sheffield City Council and operates Kelham Island Museum and Abbeydale Industrial Hamlet. The collections cover the major manufacturing industries of Sheffield: the metallurgical industries, iron and steel-making, cutlery-making, tool-making, silver and hollow-ware manufacture, mechanical and electrical engineering, scientific and technological research, and other manufacturing industries around Sheffield, including the extraction of the raw materials which support these industries.

Alison Duce, Head of Curatorial Services

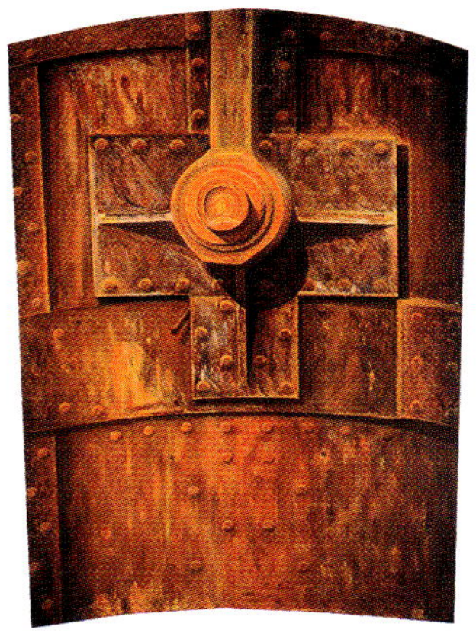

Booth, Mel G. active 1975–1990s
Detail of a Steel Ladle (from the ladle in Kelham Island Museum) 1984
oil on canvas 150 x 112 (E)
PN2029

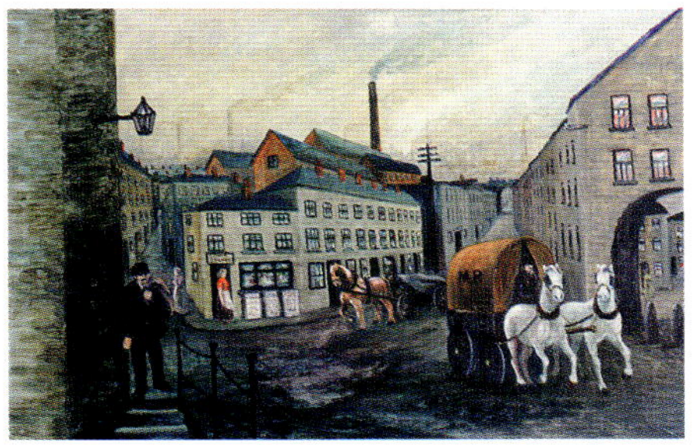

Brown, W.
Street Scene, East End, Sheffield 1930s
oil on board 39 x 57
PN0271

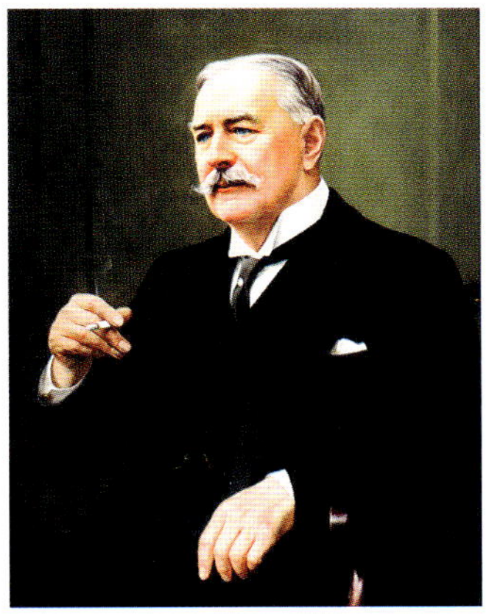

Corfield, Colin 1910–1991
Albert Vickers (1838–1919), Chairman of Vickers Ltd (1908–1918) 1957
oil on canvas 110 x 90
PN3711

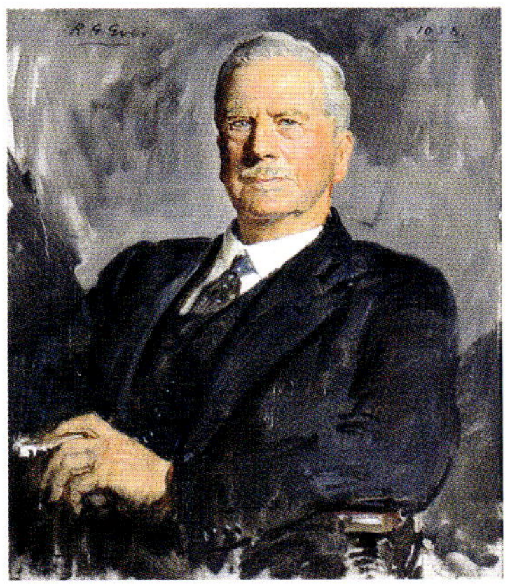

Eves, Reginald Grenville 1876–1941
P. B. Brown 1938
oil on canvas 88 x 77
PN2112

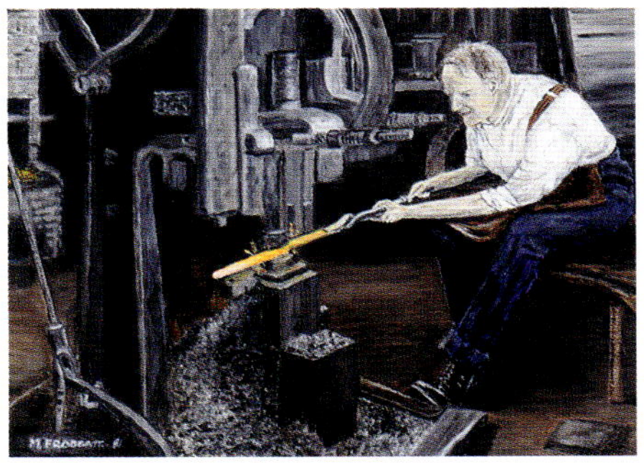

Froggatt, Muriel Alice 1909–1992
Memories of Unstone Mills, Ben the Smithy 1981
oil on board 29 x 39
PN2023

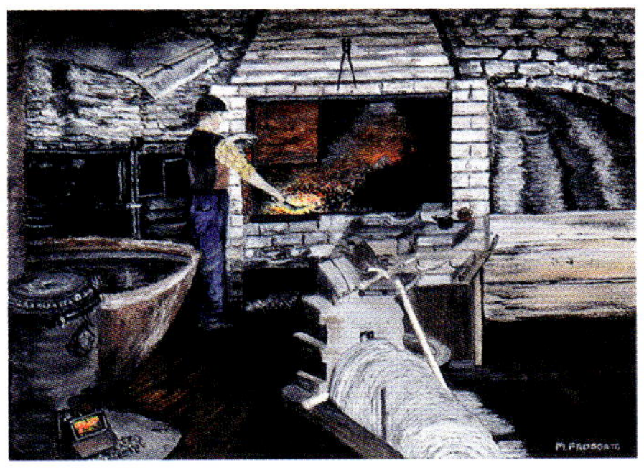

Froggatt, Muriel Alice 1909–1992
Sickle and Hook Maker, Unstone Mills
oil on board 29 x 39
PN2024

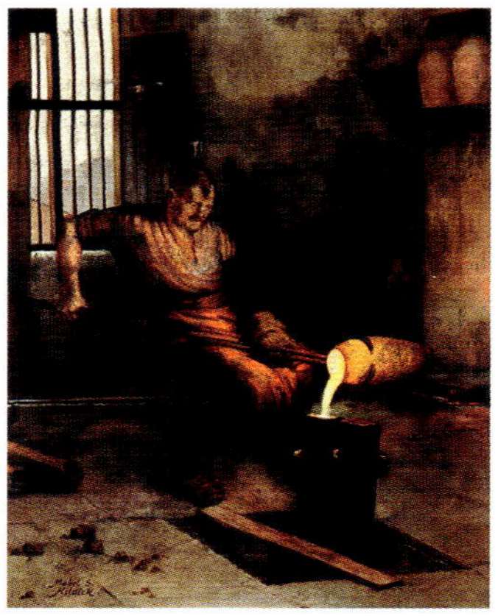

Hildick, Mabel Sarah 1884–1979
Crucible
oil on canvas 43 x 33
PN2020

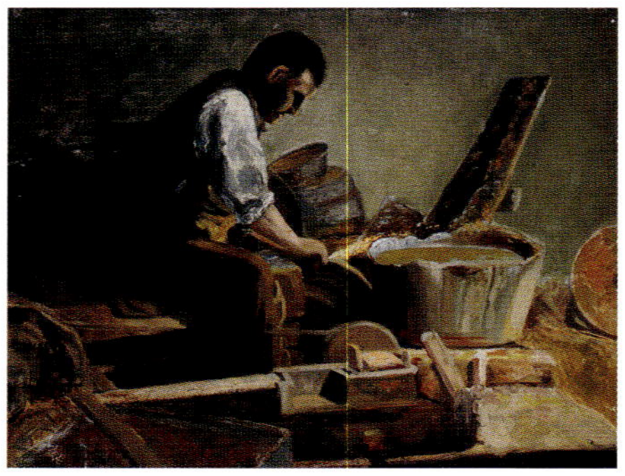

Laver, John Holmes 1880–1950
Jobbing Grinder, Rockingham Lane, Sheffield
1930s
oil on canvas 56 x 74 (E)
1980.966

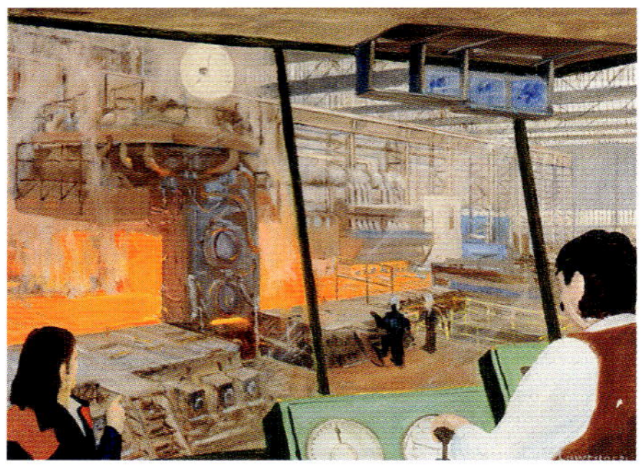

Lawrance, M.
Rolling Mill, Avesta, Sheffield 1990
oil on board 30 x 40
PN2295

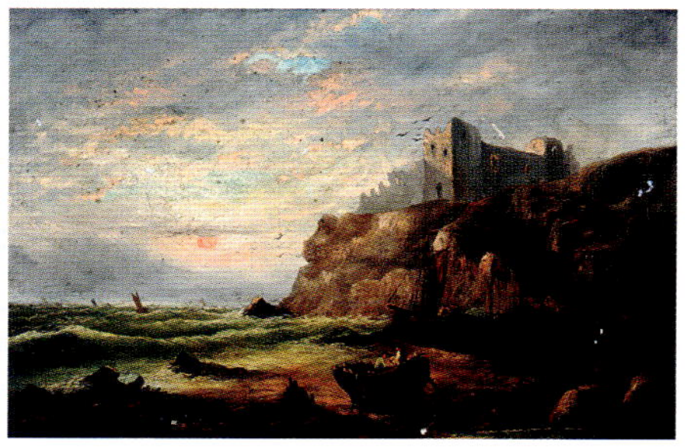

Martin, F.
Coastal View with a Castle
oil on canvas 40 x 58
AB3397

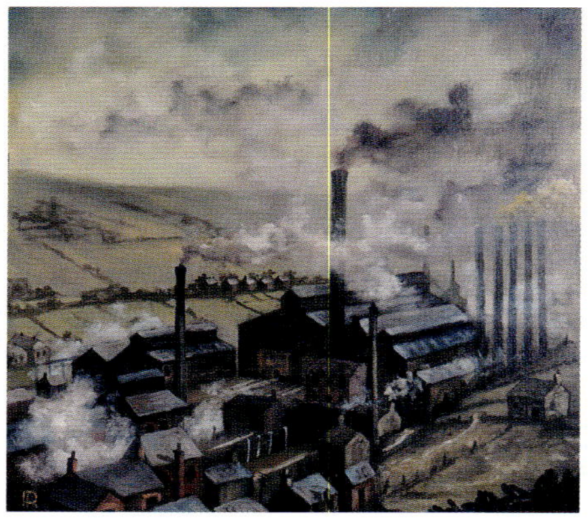

Penistone, Robert b.1946
Industrial Buildings with Chimneys and Smoke, Surrounded by Houses and Fields
1990s
oil on board 30.5 x 33
PN3627

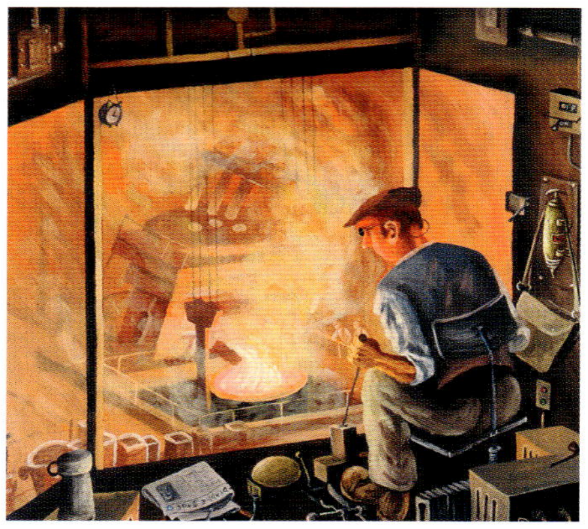

Penistone, Robert b.1946
Crane Driver, 1930 1997–1998
oil on board 46 x 48
PN3191

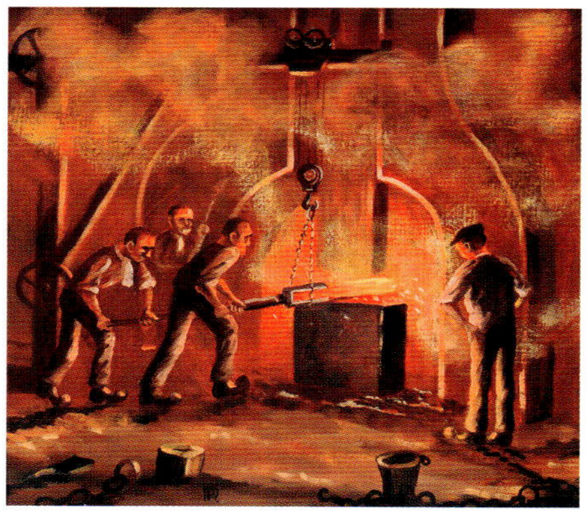

Penistone, Robert b.1946
Forging Steel under a Steam Hammer, 1930
c.1999
oil on canvas 37 x 40
PN3190

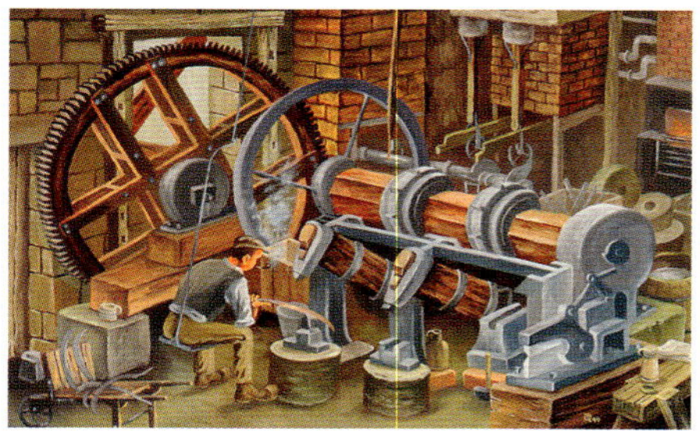

Penistone, Robert b.1946
Tilt Hammer, 1930 2000
oil on board 43 x 63
PN3192

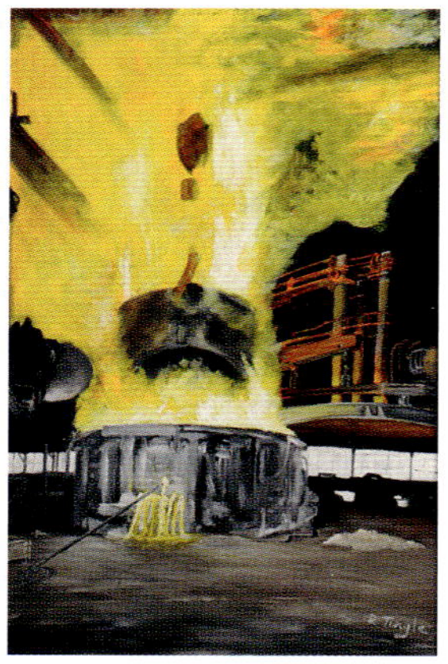

Tingle, Roy
Tinsley Park, Sheffield, Electric Arc Furnace Receiving a Charge of Scrap
oil on board 92 x 62
PN3662

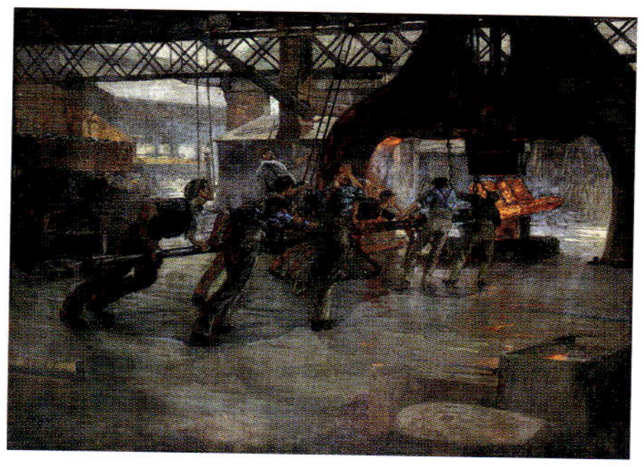

Titcomb, William Holt Yates 1858–1930
The Steam Hammer 1895
oil on canvas 110 x 148 (E)
PN0343 (P)

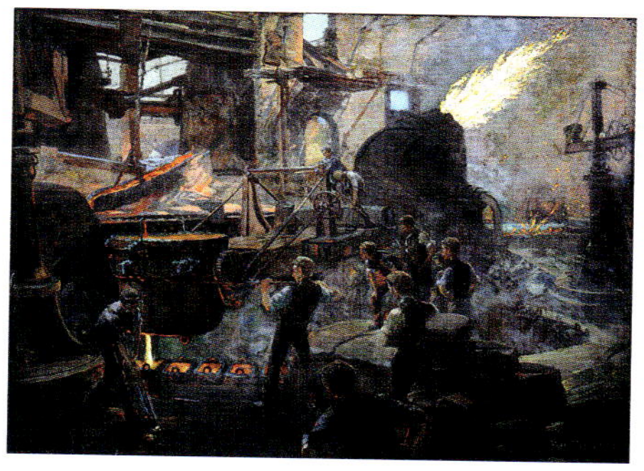

Titcomb, William Holt Yates 1858–1930
The Wealth of England, the Bessemer Process of Making Steel 1895
oil on canvas 114.5 x 152.7
PN0344 (P)

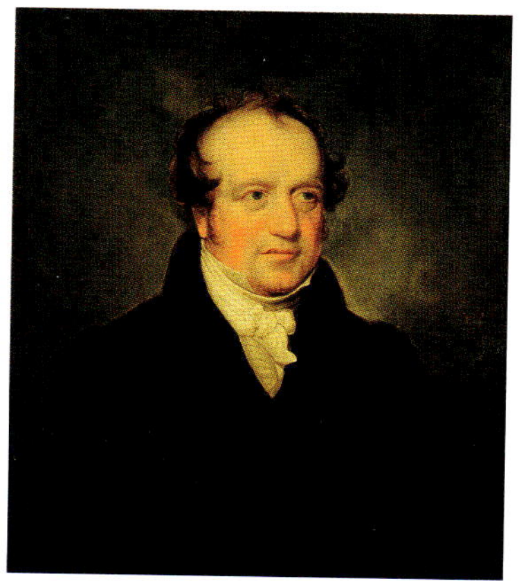

unknown artist early 19th C
Mr James Sanderson
oil on canvas 102 x 89
PN2110 (P)

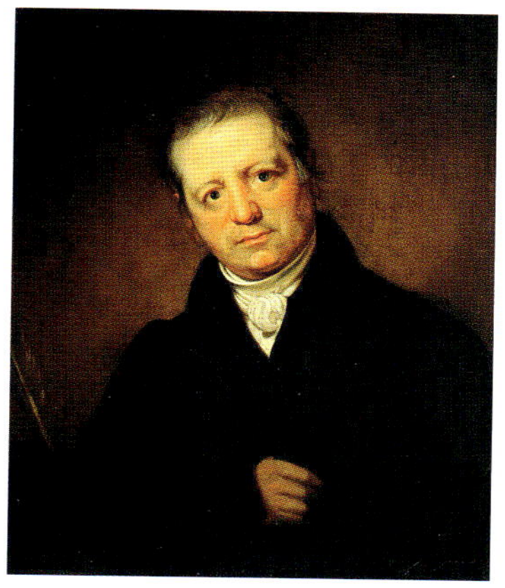

unknown artist early 19th C
Mr Thomas Sanderson
oil on canvas 102 x 89
PN2109 (P)

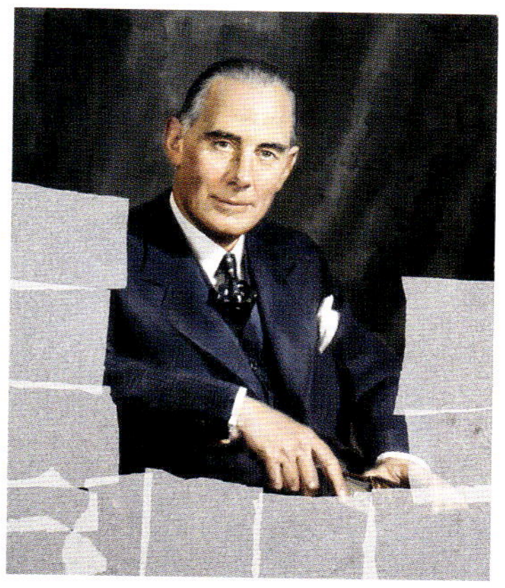

unknown artist
Robert Jardine of the Sheffield Smelting Company c.1960
oil on canvas 76 x 63.5
PN2252

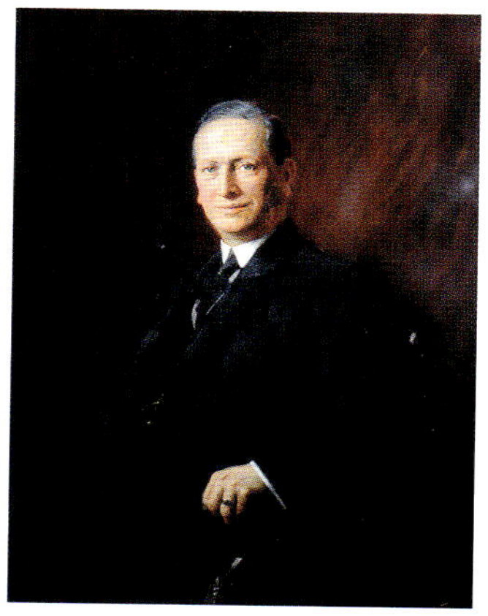

unknown artist
Arthur J. Ward, JP
oil on canvas 111 x 85
PN2113

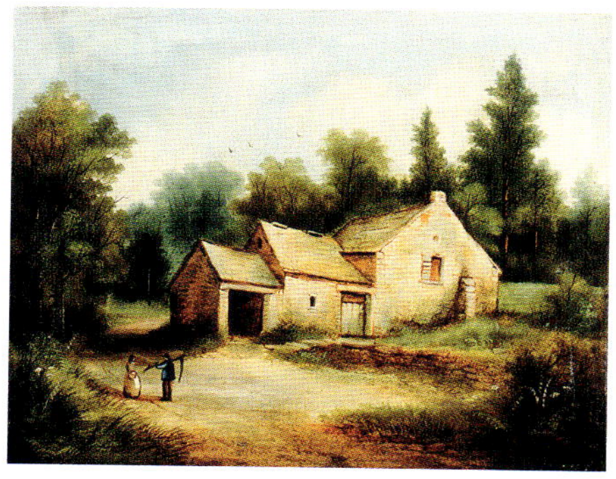

unknown artist
Ryecroft Mill, Dore, Sheffield
oil on canvas 51 x 66
AB3267

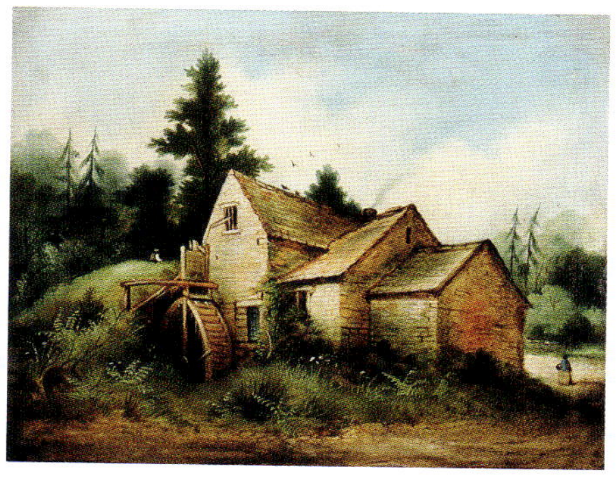

unknown artist
Ryecroft Mill Waterwheel, Dore, Sheffield
oil on canvas 51 x 66
AB3268

Sheffield Libraries Archives and Information: Sheffield Archives

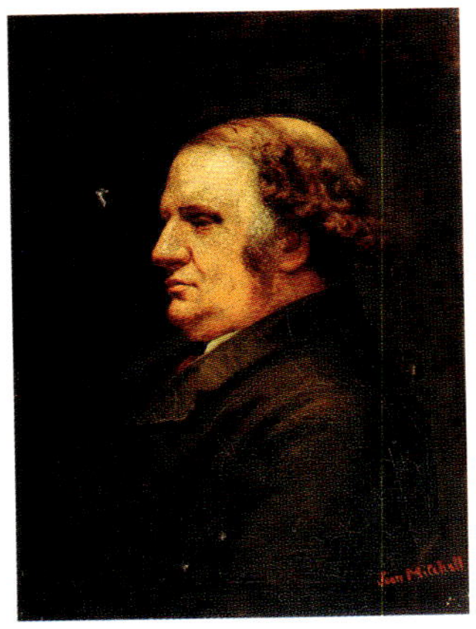

Mitchell, Jean 1861–1941
Dr Arthur Jackson c.1890
oil on canvas 55 x 40
2009/97

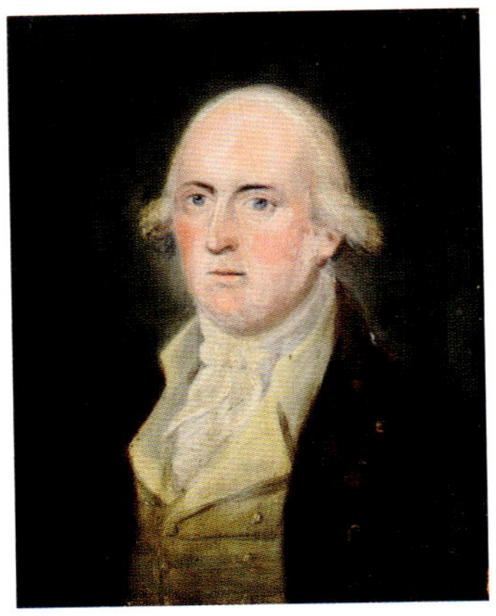

unknown artist
Captain John Peirson c.1810
oil on board 30.5 x 24.1
BUS8/6/5/1 (P)

Sheffield Magistrates' Court

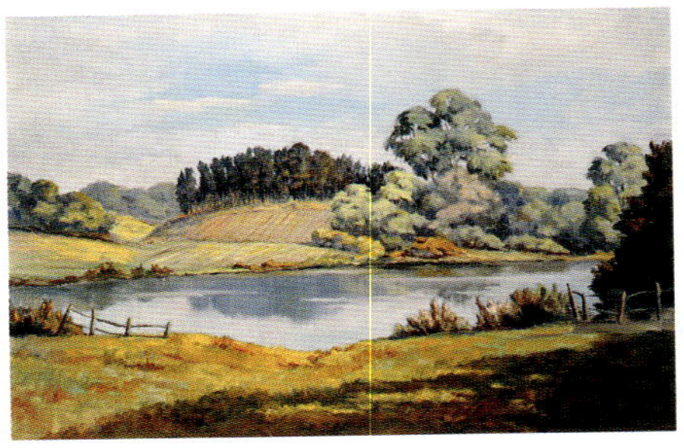

Bradbury, Mary 1909–2006
*Landscape with a River**
oil on canvas 58 x 88
PCF3

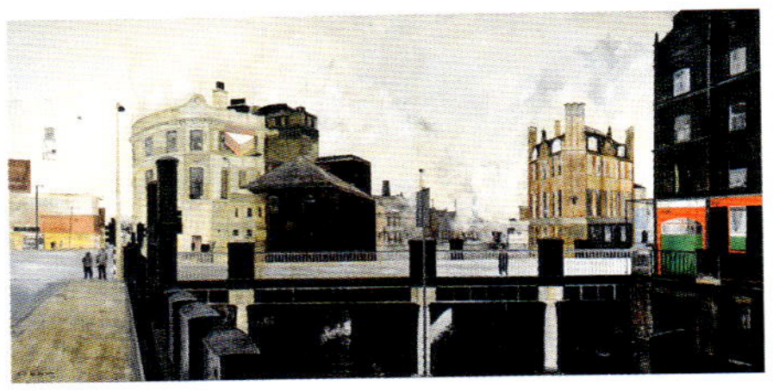

Lawton, Nigel Philip
Lady's Bridge, Sheffield 1974
oil on canvas 125 x 245
PCF2

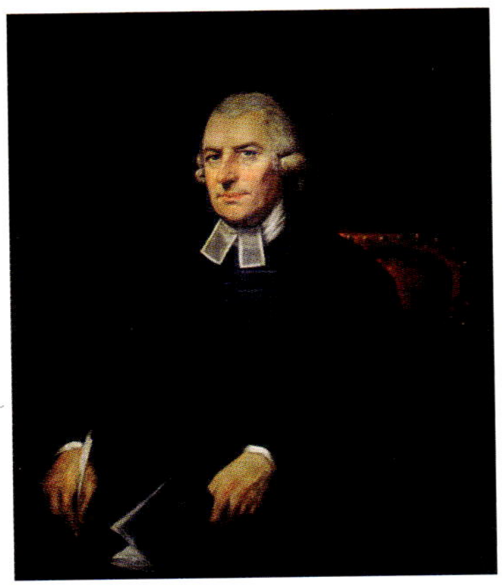

unknown artist
Reverend James Wilkinson (1730–1805), MA
1790s
oil on canvas 142 x 90
PCF1

Sheffield Teaching Hospitals NHS Foundation Trust

The oil paintings in this Collection largely come from the collections of the Sheffield Royal Infirmary (1797–1979) and the Sheffield Royal Hospital (1832–1979), two hospitals which were closed when the Royal Hallamshire Hospital opened in 1979. The two earlier hospitals were founded as charitable institutions, so-called 'voluntary hospitals', and were run by separate boards of governors until these merged in 1939. These were then known as The United Sheffield Hospitals until the start of the National Health Service in 1948.

The contents of the Collection reflects this history. The emphasis is on portraits of individuals who made significant contributions to the founding, and subsequent running, of the hospitals and the Medical School.

The Medical School, which was founded in 1828, became one of the founding institutions of the University of Sheffield in 1905. Some of the paintings are on display in the Hospital, or in the adjacent Medical School, with many held in storage as part of the Sheffield Teaching Hospitals Historic Collections. This collection also includes paintings in media other than oil (some of which are available online at www.picturesheffield.com), sculptures including early works by the locally born Francis Chantrey, and objects reflecting the history of medicine in Sheffield.

Dr C. Derek Holdsworth, Volunteer Curator to the Collection

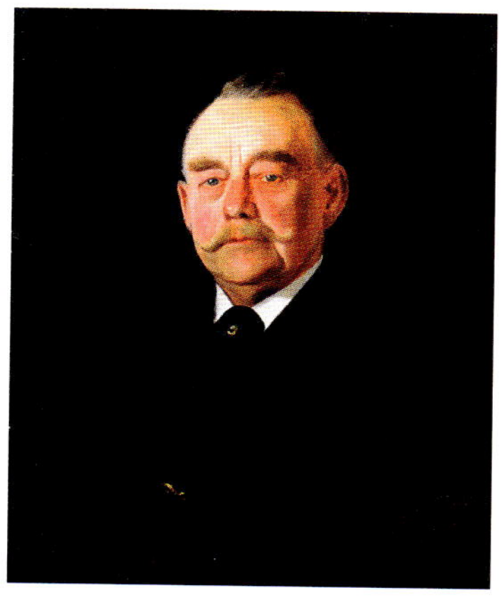

Assus, Maurice 1880–1955
William Edgar Allen (1837–1915), Founder of the Edgar Allen Institute 1907
oil on canvas 63.5 x 50.8
PCF5

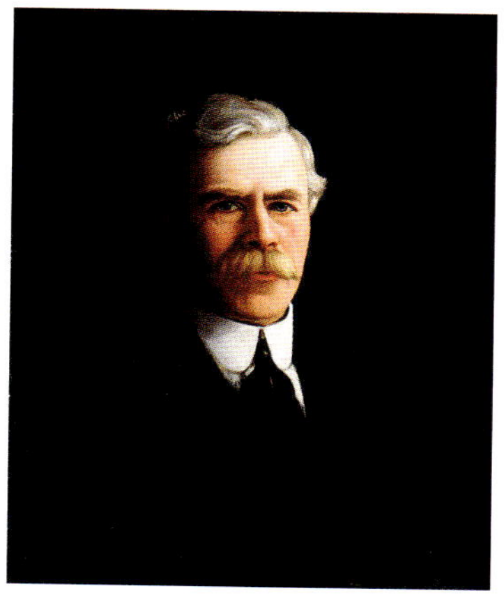

Bentley, Joseph Herbert 1866–1934
Sinclair White, MD, FRCS, Surgeon to the Royal Infirmary (1898–1920) 1921
oil on canvas 73.6 x 61
PCF28

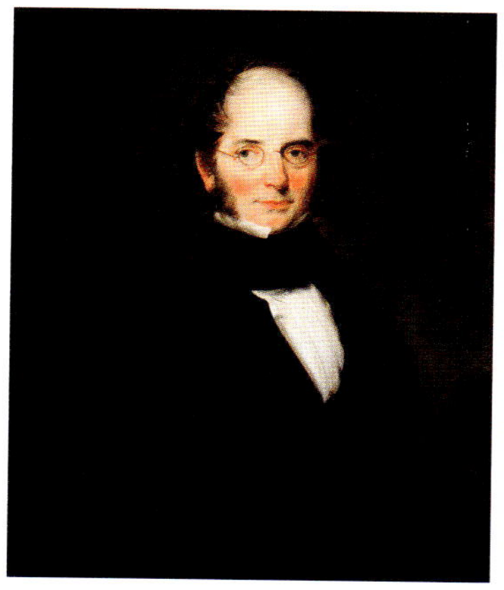

Birch, John (attributed to) 1807–1857
Sir Arnold Knight (1789–1871), Founder of the Sheffield Medical Institution (1829)
oil on canvas 76.2 x 63.5
PCF20

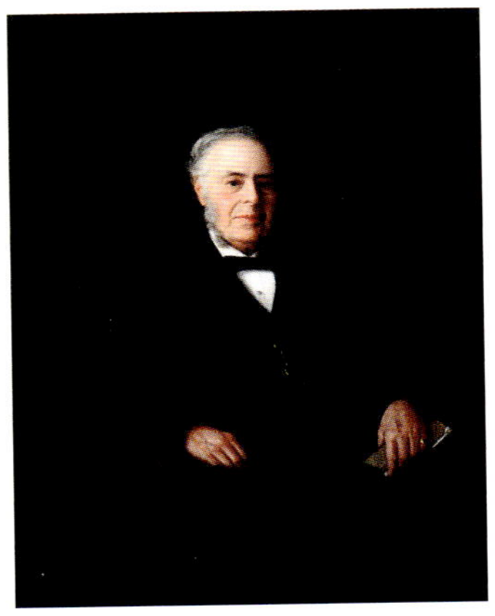

Cammell, Bernard Edward 1850–1932
Mariano Martin de Bartolomé (c.1810–1890), Physician at Sheffield Infirmary (1846–1889), First President of the Sheffield (...) 1888
oil on canvas 127 x 101.6
PCF7

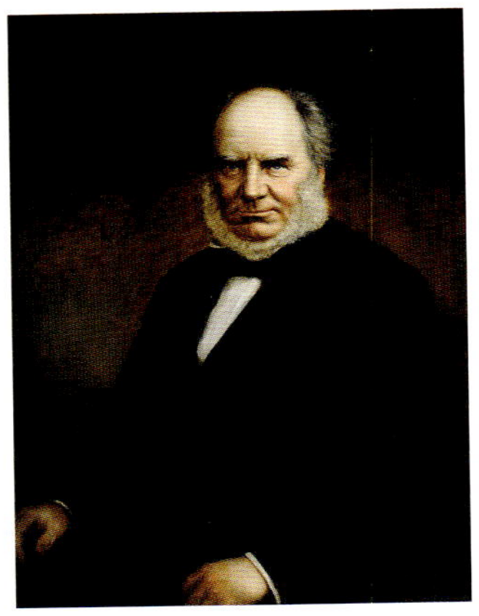

Crighton, Hugh Ford 1824–1886
Thomas Jessop (1804–1887), Founder of the Hospital (1846), Builder of the Jessop Hospital for Women, Leavygreave Road (1878)
oil on canvas 127 x 101.6
PCF19

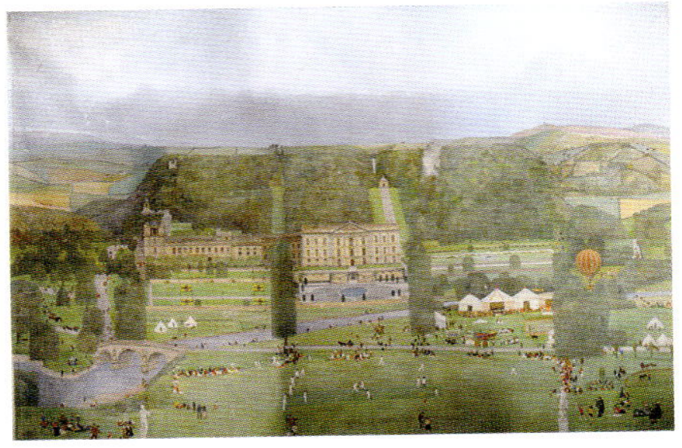

Eurich, Richard Ernst 1903–1992
Chatsworth, to Represent Sheffield at Play (one of a pair of murals to face west) 1960–1961
oil on canvas 304.8 x 426.7
PCF3

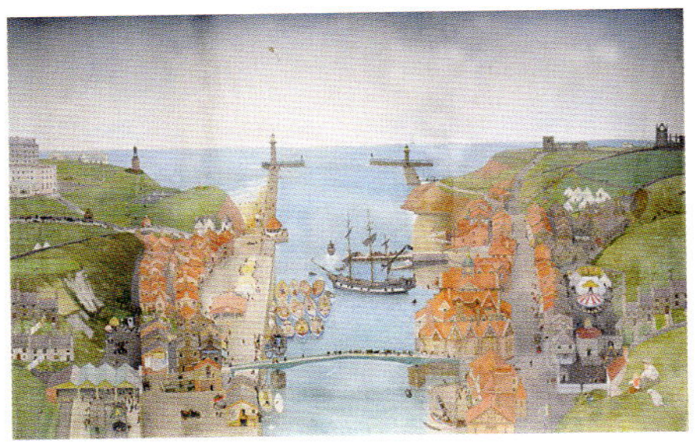

Eurich, Richard Ernst 1903–1992
Whitby, to Represent Sheffield on Holiday (one of a pair of murals to face east) 1960–1961
oil on canvas 304.8 x 426.7
PCF4

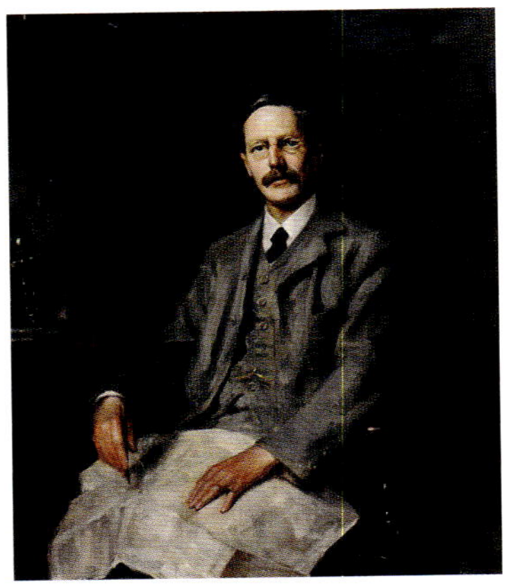

Fower, Robert 1866–1947
Sir William Henry Ellis (1860–1945), GBE, JP, Member of the Board of Management (1898–1945), Vice-Chairman (...) c.1918
oil on canvas 128 x 98
PCF11

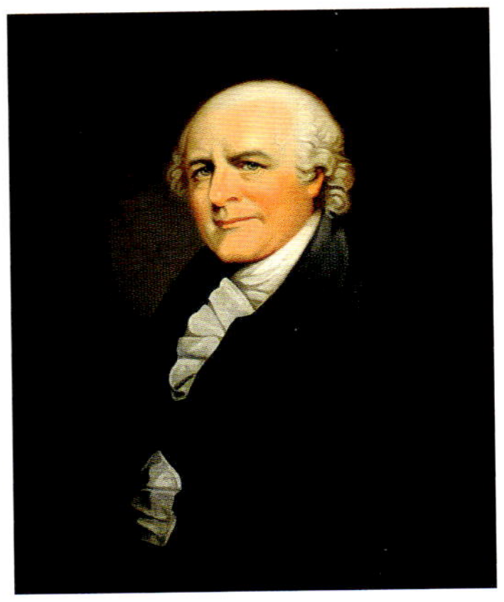

Gainsford, F. G. active 1805–1828
John Browne (c.1740–1810), MD, 'of the Lead Works', First Chairman of the Board
oil on canvas 76.2 x 61
PCF9

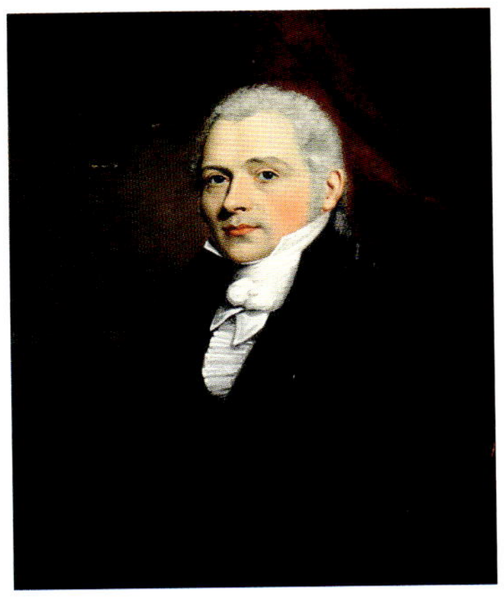

Gainsford, F. G. active 1805–1828
Robert Ernest (1771–1841), MD, House Surgeon to Sheffield Infirmary (1797–1841)
oil on canvas 73.7 x 61
PCF12

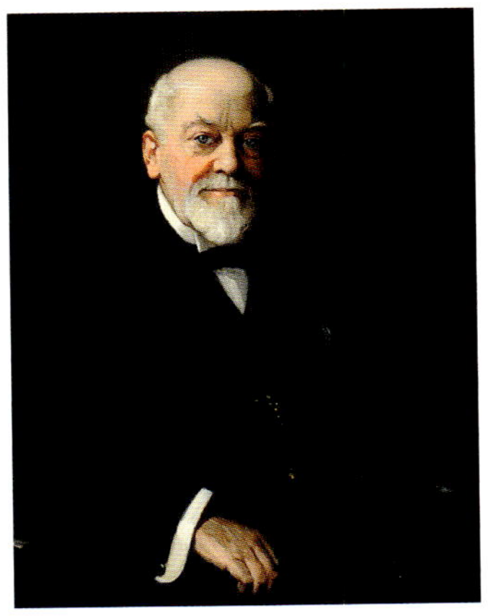

Garnett, Ruth 1836–1915
John Marshall, JP 1913
oil on canvas 91.4 x 71.1
PCF22

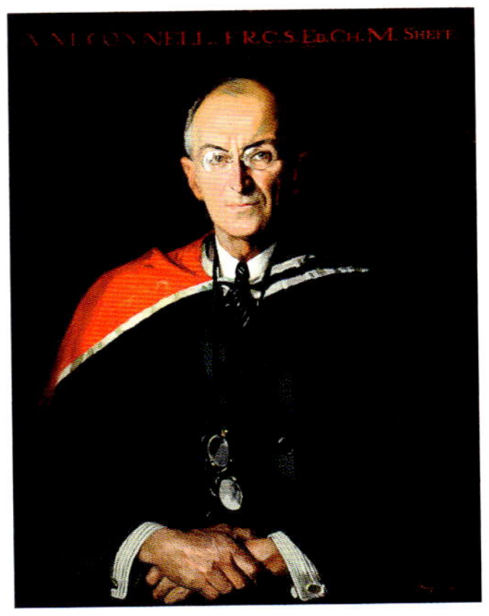

Hoyland, Henry George 1895–1948
A. M. Connell (1872–1945), FRCS, ED, CH, M SHEFF, Honorary Surgeon, Sheffield Infirmary (1901–1931), Professor of Surgery (1913–1930)
oil on canvas 91.4 x 71.1
PCF10

Facing page: Titcomb, William Holt Yates, 1858–1930, *The Steam Hammer* (detail), 1895, Sheffield Industrial Museums Trust, (p. 267)

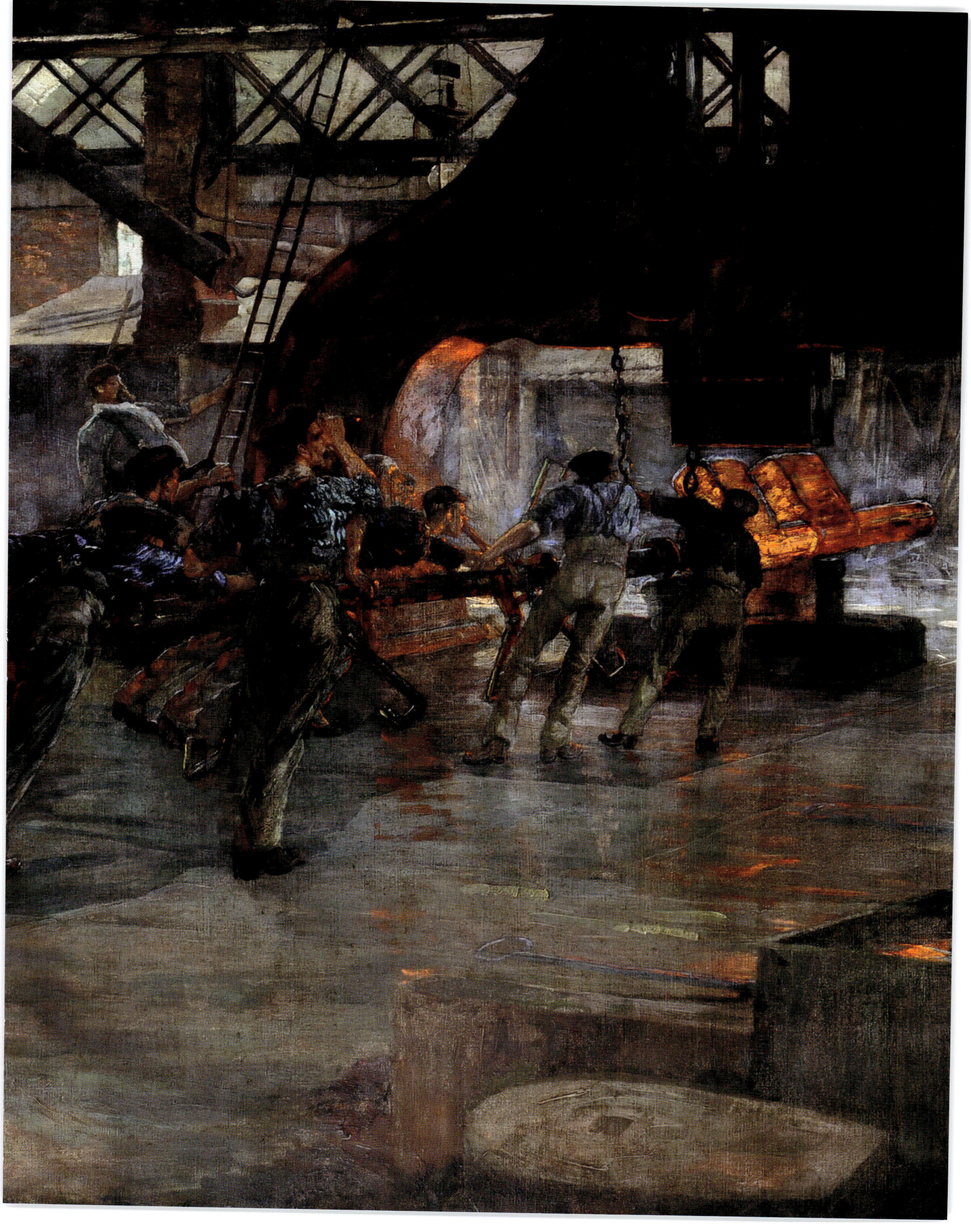

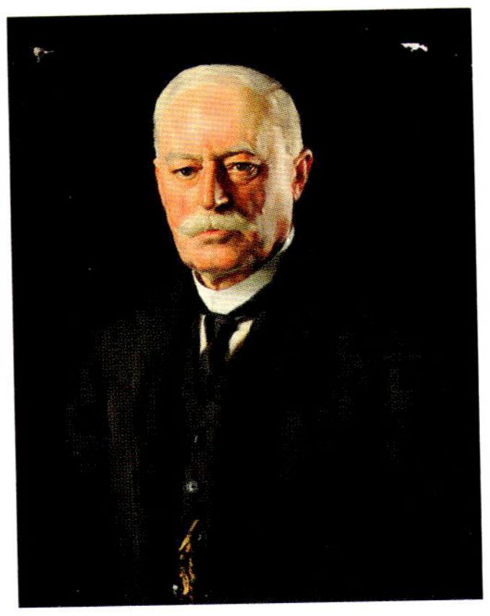

Jagger, David 1891–1958
Henry Hall Bedford, JP, Chairman of the Board (1913–1924) c.1924
oil on canvas 71.1 x 53.3
PCF8

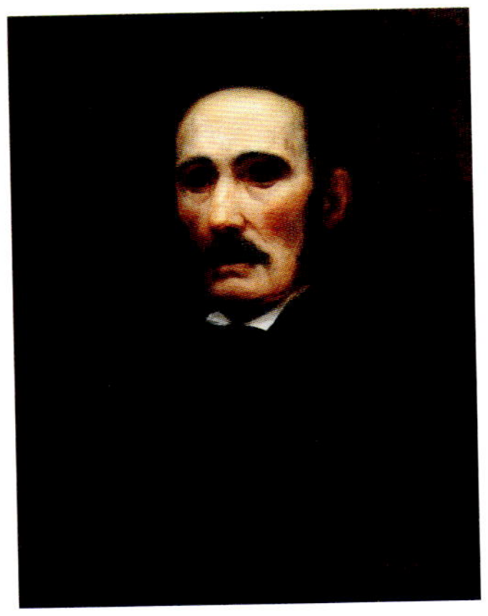

Mitchell, Jean 1861–1941
Joseph Law (d.1897), MD, Honorary Secretary to Sheffield Medical Society (1842–1852) 1892
oil on canvas 63.5 x 50.8
PCF21

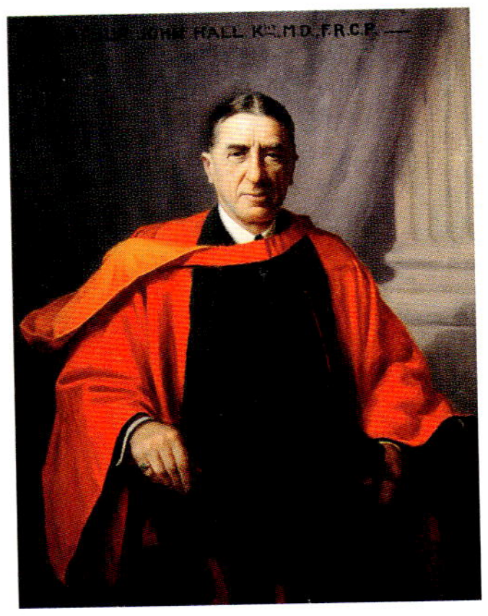

Moore, Ernest 1865–1940
Sir Arthur John Hall (1866–1951), KT, MD, DSc, FRCP, Professor of Physiology, Pathology and Medicine and Physician (...) 1937
oil on canvas 110 x 85
PCF15

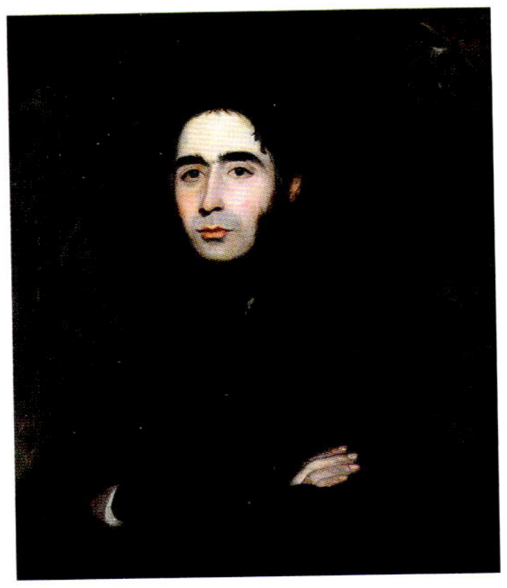

Moore, John 1801–1865
George Calvert Holland (1801–1865), MD, Physician, Sheffield General Infirmary (1832–1843), Physician, Sheffield (...)–1843
oil on canvas 76.2 x 63.5
PCF16

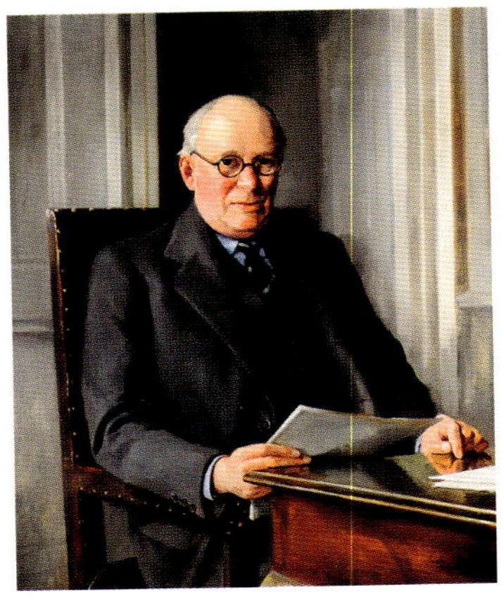

Platt, Joyce b.1920
Ronald Wilfred Matthews, KT, K St J, JP, Chairman of the Royal Infirmary, Sheffield (1924–1948), Member of the Board (...) 1949
oil on canvas 96.5 x 81.2
PCF24

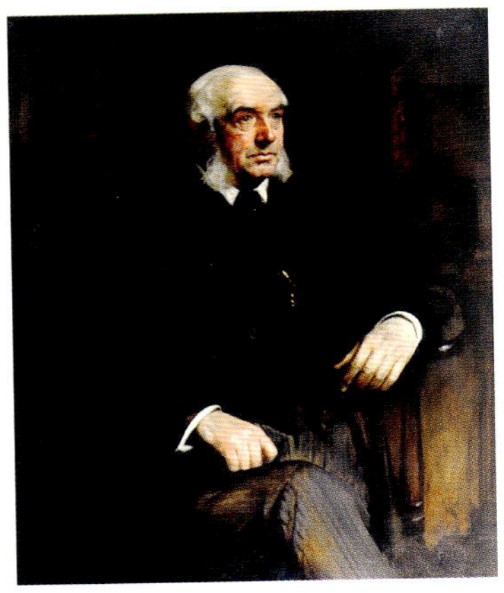

Shannon, James Jebusa 1862–1923
William Fisher Favell (1832–1896), Surgeon of Sheffield Infirmary (c.1857–1893) 1893
oil on canvas 137.1 x 111.8
PCF13

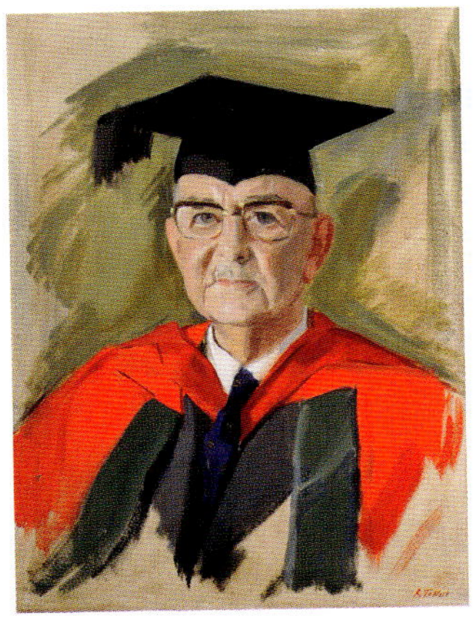

Tollast, Robert 1918–1996
John G. McCrie (1902–1977), OBE, TD, MD, FRCP (Ed), Dean of the Faculty of Medicine, Sheffield (1947–1968)
oil on canvas 60 x 46
PCF30

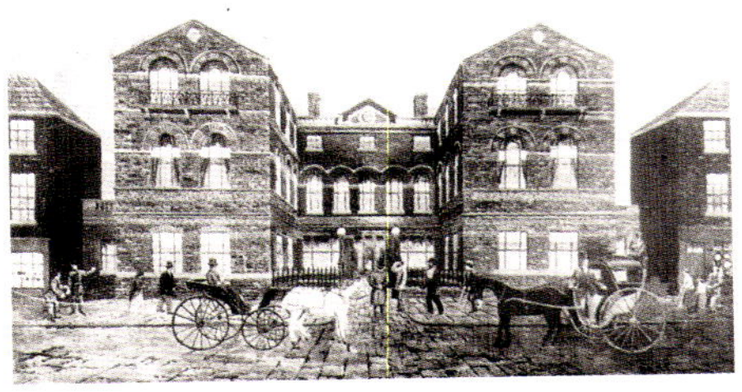

unknown artist
Sheffield Public Hospital and Dispensary of 1860 (showing physician Dr J. C. Hall and surgeon Mr Arthur Jackson) early 1870s
oil on canvas 50.8 x 77.3 (E)
PCF2

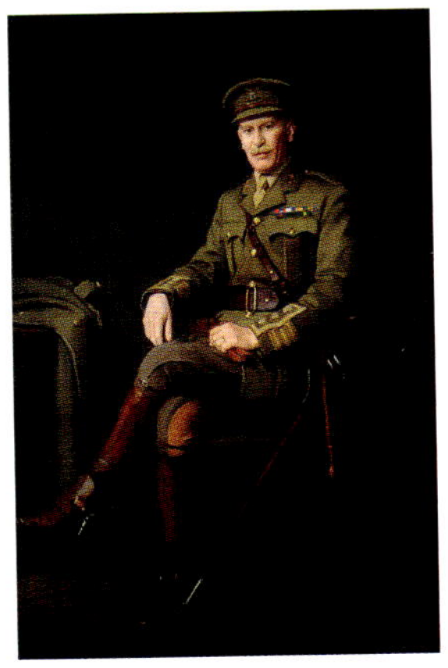

unknown artist
Colonel Charles Clifford (1860–1936), CMG, VD (donor of the land for the Sheffield Dental Hospital)* 1924
oil on canvas 190 x 129 (E)
PCF31

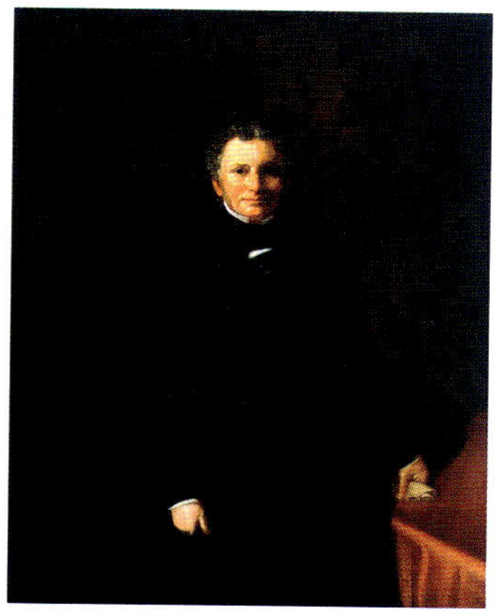

unknown artist
Corden Thompson (1793–1876), MD Edinburgh, Physician to Sheffield Infirmary (1831–1866)
oil on canvas 142.2 x 111.8
PCF27

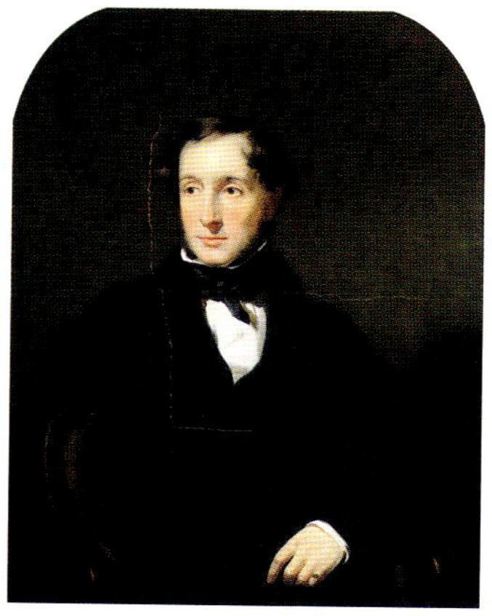

unknown artist
George Hounsfield, Esq., of the 'Clough', Sheffield (formerly a member of the Weekly Board and Treasurer of Sheffield) *(...)*
oil on canvas 91.4 x 71.1
PCF17

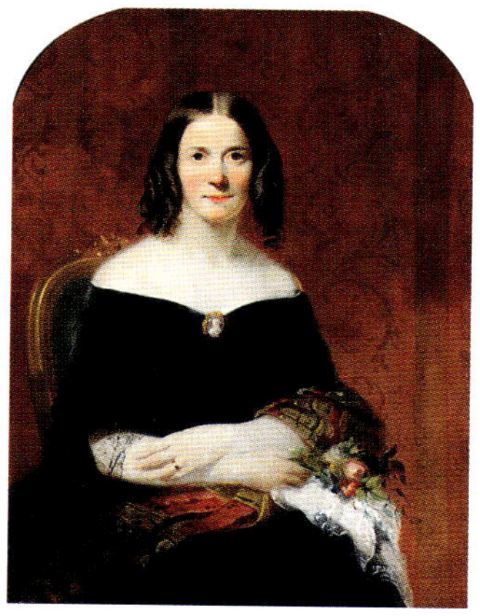

unknown artist
Maria Overend of West Retford House (d.1896), Nottinghamshire, Donor of the Overend Convalescent Fund (...)
oil on canvas 91.4 x 71.1
PCF26

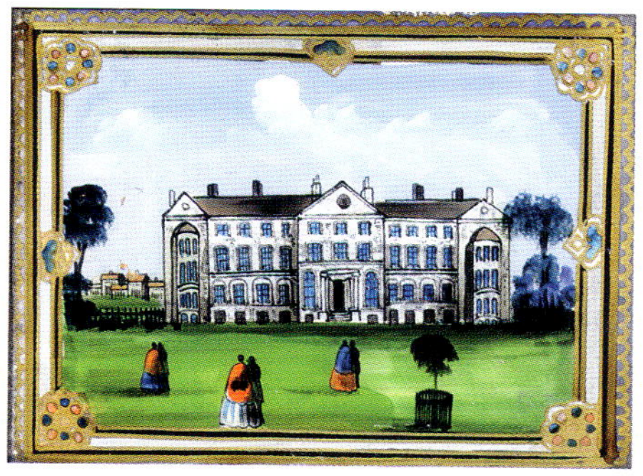

unknown artist
Sheffield General Infirmary
oil, foil & mother of pearl on glass 23 x 31 (E)
PCF1

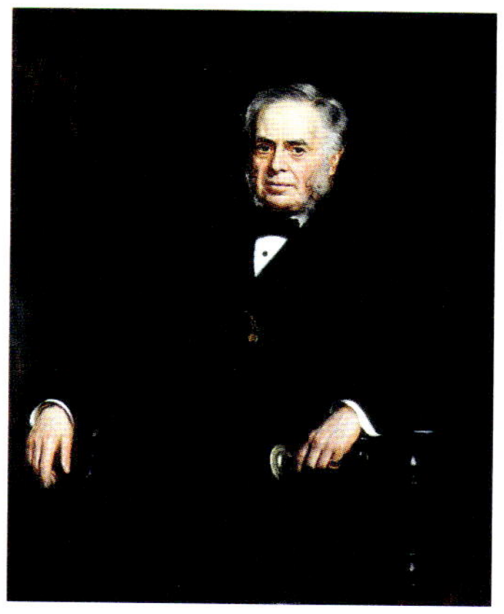

Waller, Mary Lemon 1852–c.1931
Mariano Martin de Bartolomé (c.1810–1890), Physician at Sheffield Infirmary (1846–1889), First President of the Sheffield (...) 1890
oil on canvas 127 x 101.6
PCF6

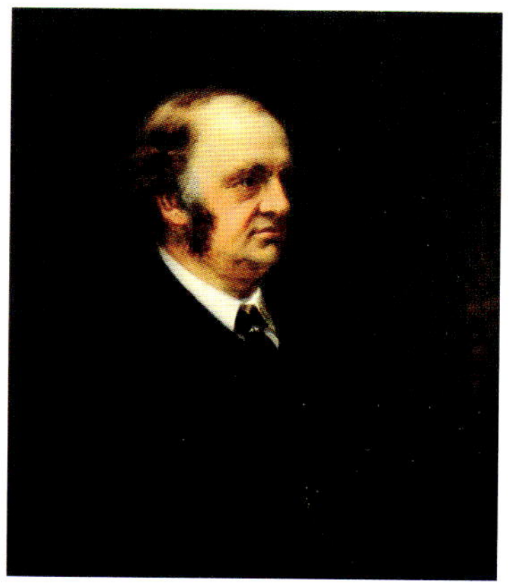

Waller, Mary Lemon 1852–c.1931
Arthur Jackson (c.1844–1895), Honorary Surgeon, Sheffield Public Hospital and Dispensary (1866–1877), Sheffield (...)
oil on canvas 76.2 x 66
PCF18

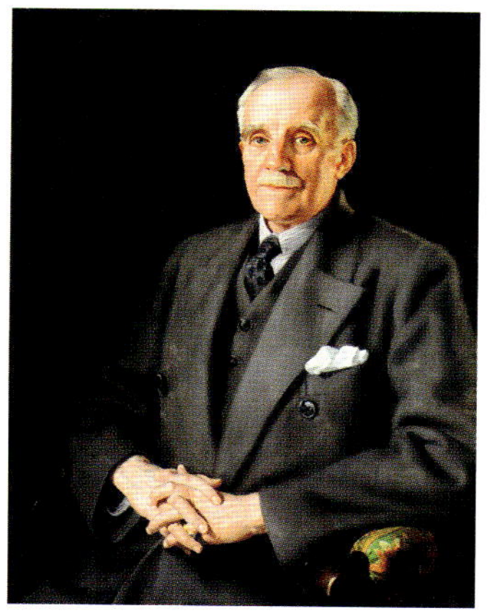

Williams, Margaret Lindsay 1887–1960
Frederick Marmaduke Osborn, Esq. (1874–1950), Chairman of the Sheffield Royal Hospital (1905–1948) (...) 1949
oil on canvas 76.2 x 66
PCF25

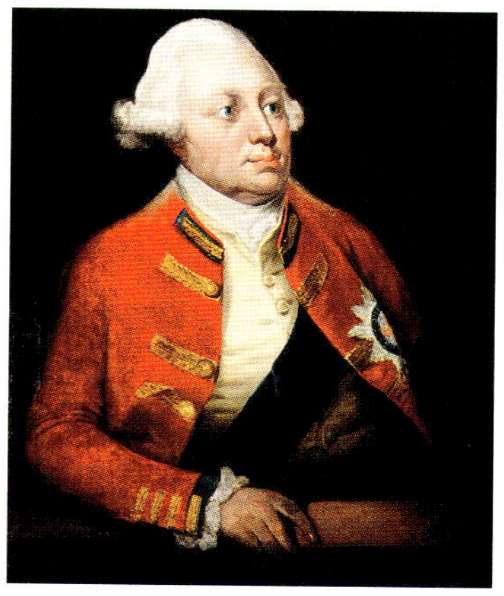

Zoffany, Johann (after) 1733–1810
George III (1738–1820)
oil on canvas 89 x 74
PCF14

Sheffield Town Hall

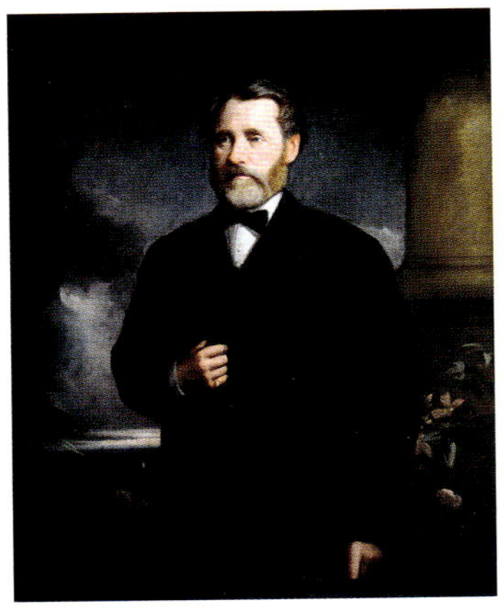

Barker, Thomas Jones 1815–1882
Mark Firth (1819–1880), Mayor of Sheffield (1874)
oil on canvas 120 x 100 (E)
PCF7

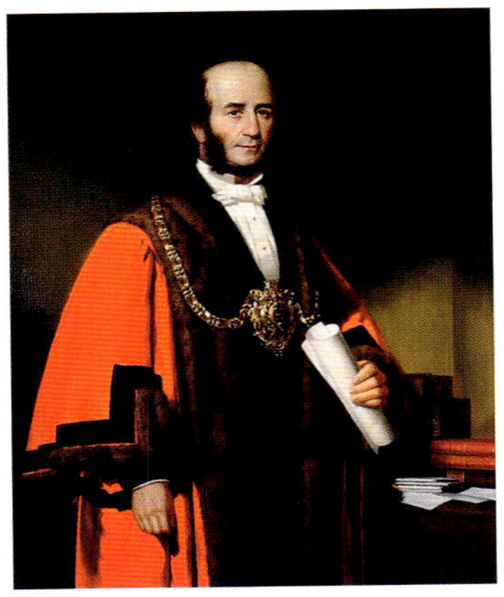

Crighton, Hugh Ford 1824–1886
Thomas Moore (1809–1880), Mayor of Sheffield (1868–1871) 1872
oil on canvas 122 x 100
PCF3

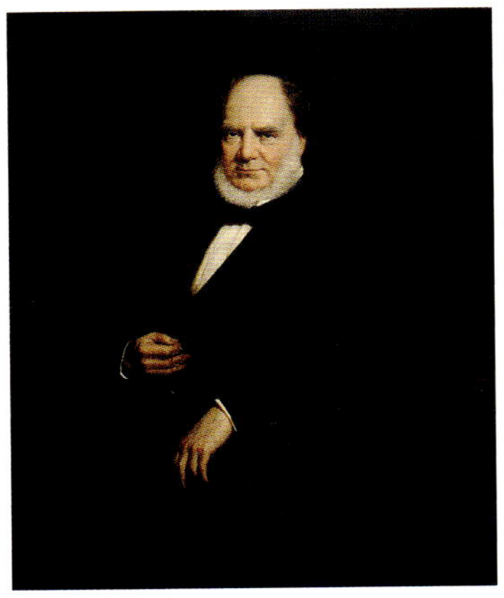

Crighton, Hugh Ford 1824–1886
Thomas Jessop (1804–1887), JP, Mayor of Sheffield (1865–1868)
oil on canvas 170 x 102 (E)
PCF2

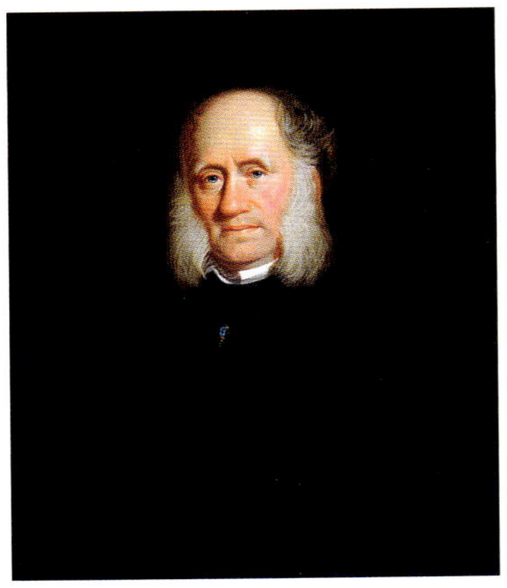

Crighton, Hugh Ford 1824–1886
William Jeffcock (1800–1877), First Mayor of Sheffield (1843–1844)
oil on canvas 90 x 70 (E)
PCF8

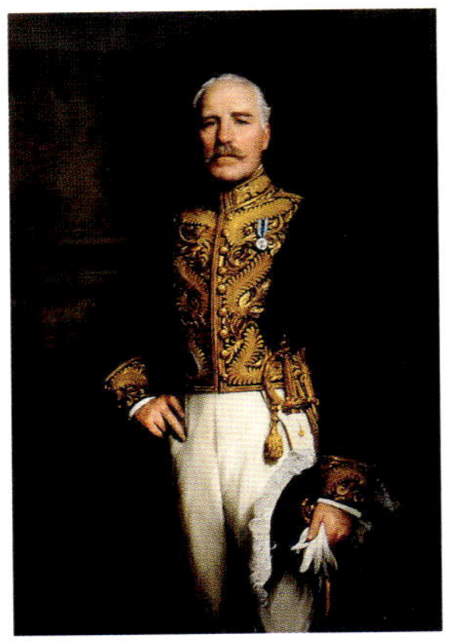

Fildes, Luke 1843–1927
The Right Honourable Charles B. Stuart-Wortley (1851–1926), MP for Sheffield (1880–1913) 1912
oil on canvas 170 x 102 (E)
PCF1

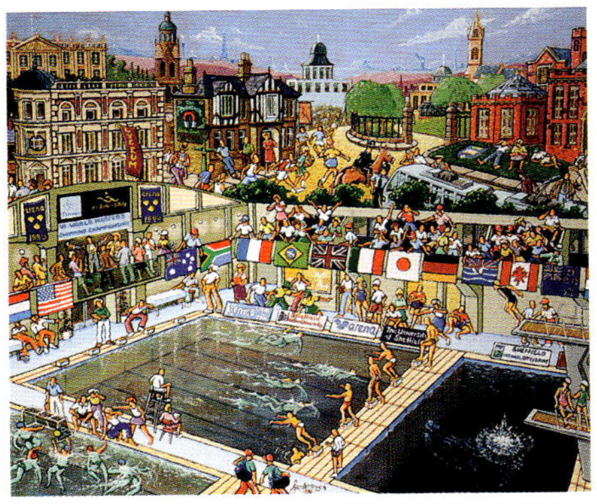

Scarborough, Joe b.1938
VI World Masters Swimming Championships, Sheffield 1996
oil on canvas 84 x 100
PCF4

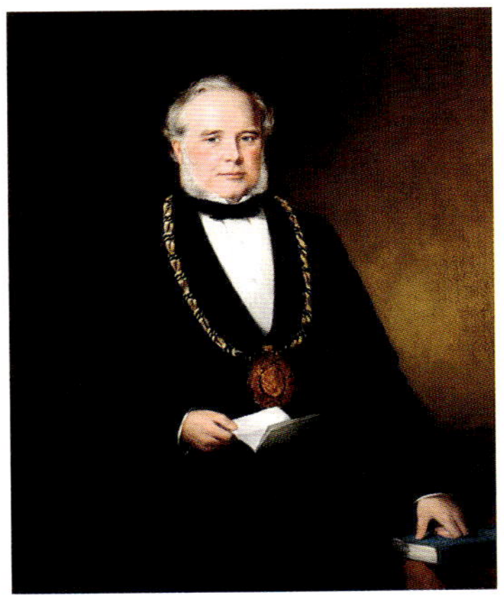

Smith, Richard 1818–1890
Sir John Brown (1816–1896), KT, DL, Mayor of Sheffield (1861–1862)
oil on canvas 120 x 100 (E)
PCF5

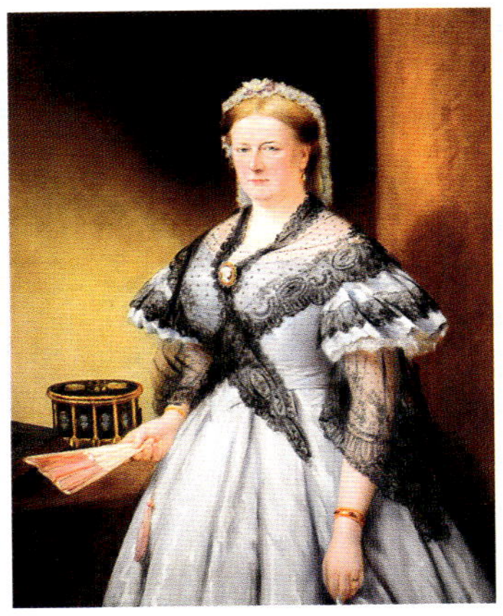

Smith, Richard 1818–1890
Lady Brown (1813–1881), Wife of Sir John Brown
oil on canvas 120 x 100 (E)
PCF6

South Yorkshire Fire and Rescue Training Centre

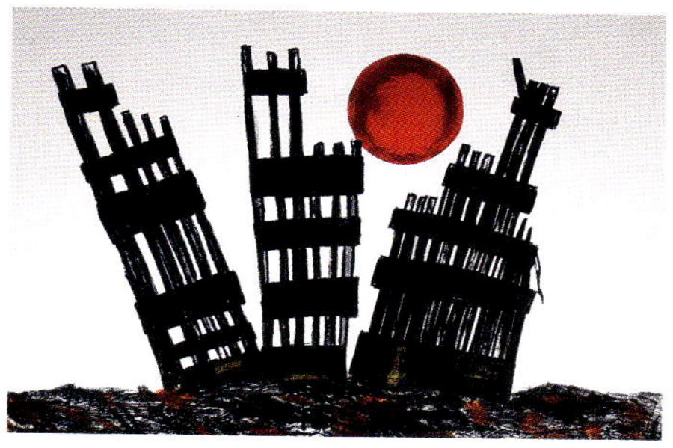

Jones, Donna active 2002–2003
*Ground Zero, 9/11 No.1** c.2002
oil (?) on board 66 x 97
PCF1

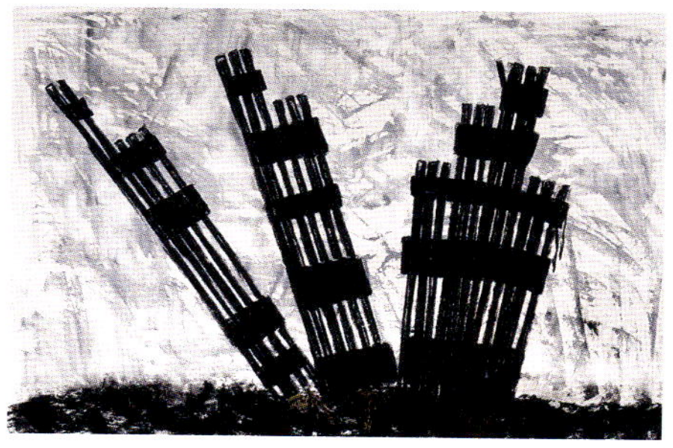

Jones, Donna active 2002–2003
*Ground Zero, 9/11 No.2** c.2002
oil (?) on board 66 x 97
PCF2

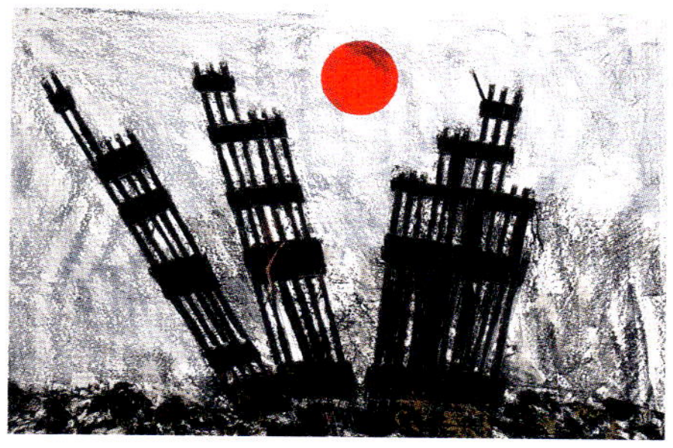

Jones, Donna active 2002–2003
*Ground Zero, 9/11 No.3** 2002
oil (?) on board 66 x 97
PCF3

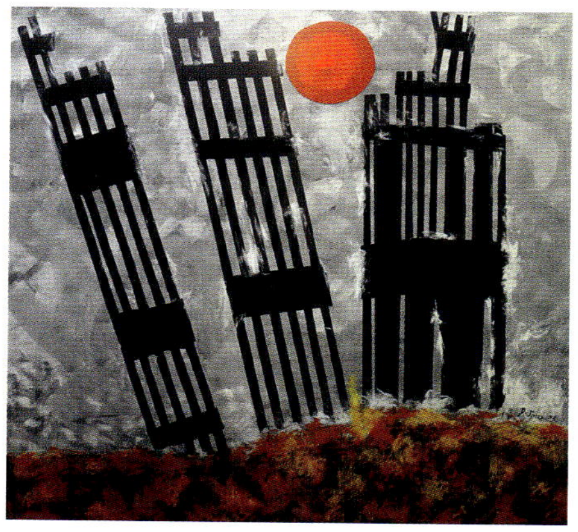

Jones, Donna active 2002–2003
*Ground Zero, 9/11 No.4** 2003
oil (?) on board 182 x 182 (E)
PCF4

Stocksbridge Town Council

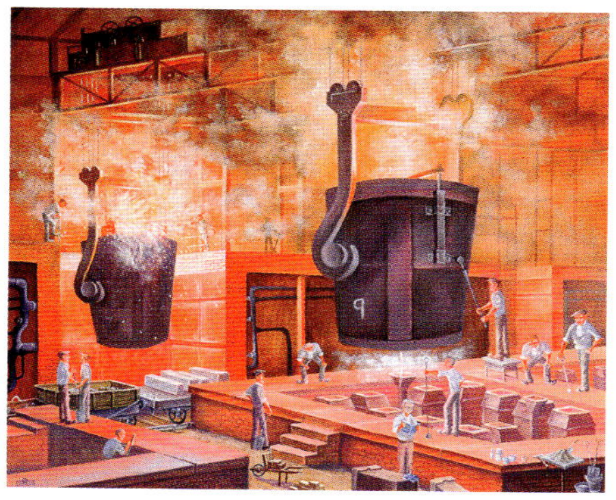

Penistone, Robert b.1946
Siemens Open Hearth, Sheffield, No.1 Melting Shop (1917–1968) 2008
oil on board 63 x 68
PCF3

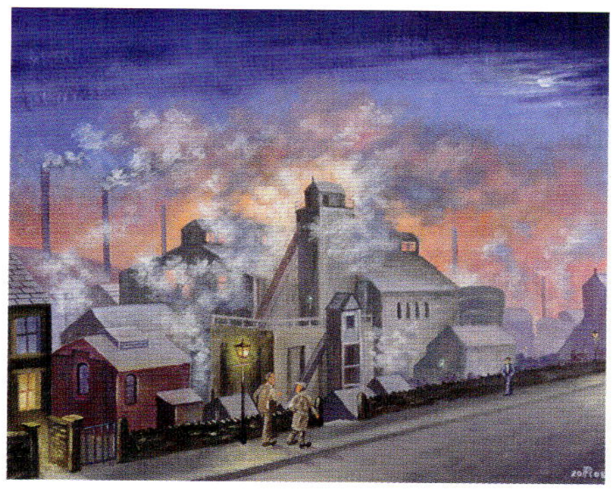

Penistone, Robert b.1946
Stocksbridge Coke Ovens, 1940s, Manchester Road, Sheffield 2008
oil on board 39 x 49
PCF1

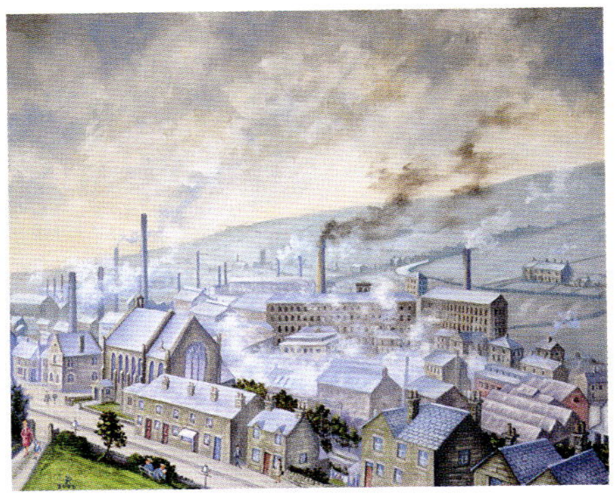

Penistone, Robert b.1946
View of Stocksbridge, Sheffield, from the Clock Tower Gardens, Late 1940s 2008
oil on canvas 49 x 59
PCF2

The Children's Hospital

The hospital environment can be a powerful contributory factor to patient wellbeing, improving staff morale, and reducing stress levels and the length of hospital stay. People using a dedicated children's facility expect high-quality medical care and the hospital environment is, even unconsciously, symbolic of that care. Visitors should feel welcomed as they enter the hospital and have the benefit of surroundings which are different, distracting, supportive and even uplifting as they care for the children. A relaxed, interesting and secure place, reduces fear and tension for both the child and their family.

The Arts for Health Programme at The Children's Hospital, Sheffield has been running for almost 10 years, and since summer 2008 has been entirely funded by The Children's Hospital Charity. Every year it strives to raise £65,000 towards enhancing the hospital environment and employs a full-time Arts for Health Coordinator.

Arts for Health is becoming increasingly involved in Trust redevelopment projects – advising on design, colour and equipment – as well as being committed to providing art activities on the wards to alleviate stress, pass the time, and encourage fun.

Our art collection at The Children's Hospital primarily comprises work purchased by Arts for Health or donated to the Charity, and predominantly dates from the past decade. We display a large variety of pieces, ranging from mosaics and ceramics to textiles and weavings. In the past year there has been a strong move away from traditional murals painted directly onto walls or ceilings, towards vinyl characters that provide a contemporary and more durable alternative, but the majority of our work consists of acrylic on board.

Our *Theo's Amazing Journey* series features the Charity mascot on a journey around the world, sending postcards back to the hospital en route, and patients using other stairwells can walk from sea to space, or learn the alphabet.

It is common for our art to be created in conjunction with our patients. Artists such as Andy Heath or Seiko Kinoshita have facilitated workshops in communal ward spaces or at the bedside. Patients can identify with the work of other children and be reassured by its presence, whilst its naivety makes the adults smile.

Seiko Kinoshita's work also heavily features in our newly completed Critical Care Unit, where the patients can be less aware of their surroundings. The brief was therefore to create an environment which was calming and tranquil for the patient's relatives. Kinoshita's painted wooden slats sit alongside textile weavings made from natural materials that captivate and distract the older audience who appreciate its intricate execution. Works like these, and Richard Firth's abstracts in the Child Assessment Unit, are used to encourage the mind to wander, creating its own interpretations, and feature in departments of the hospital where the reason for attendance can be distressing.

We are fortunate to have two large oil paintings, donated by locally famous artists Joe Scarborough and Kristan Paul Baggaley, which are displayed in prominent positions. Joe Scarborough's *Open Day at Sheffield Children's Hospital* hangs proudly behind our A&E Reception desk and provides a colourful welcome to the building. Painted in 1994, the piece is still popular today and a recent limited edition print run continues to raise profits for the Charity. Baggaley's beautiful depiction of the view towards *Sheffield from Dore Moor* was acquired in late 2009 and, hung at the junction of our main corridor, is attracting plenty of admiration. Part of Arts for Health's policy is to commission and support local artists above others and it is always wonderful when they decide to return the favour or are inspired by a visit to the Hospital.

Cat Powell, Arts for Health Coordinator

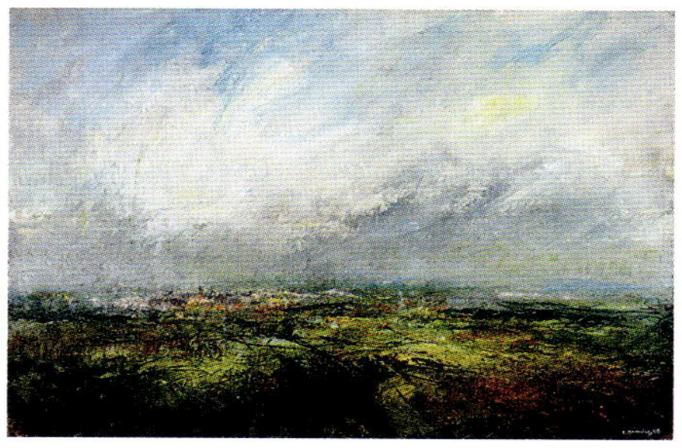

Baggaley, Kristan Paul b.1958
Sheffield from Dore Moor 2008
oil on canvas 100 x 150
PCF64

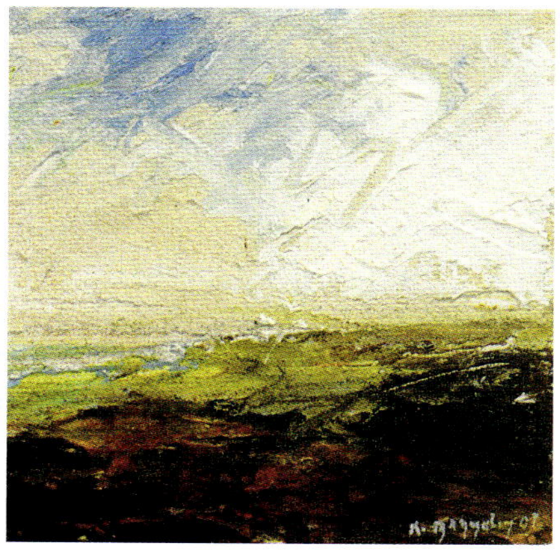

Baggaley, Kristan Paul b.1958
Peak District View 2009
oil on canvas 12.5 x 12.5
PCF65

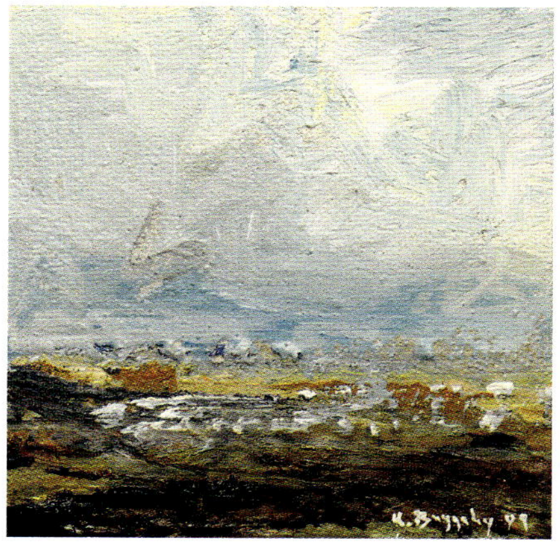

Baggaley, Kristan Paul b.1958
Peak District View 2009
oil on canvas 12.5 x 12.5
PCF66

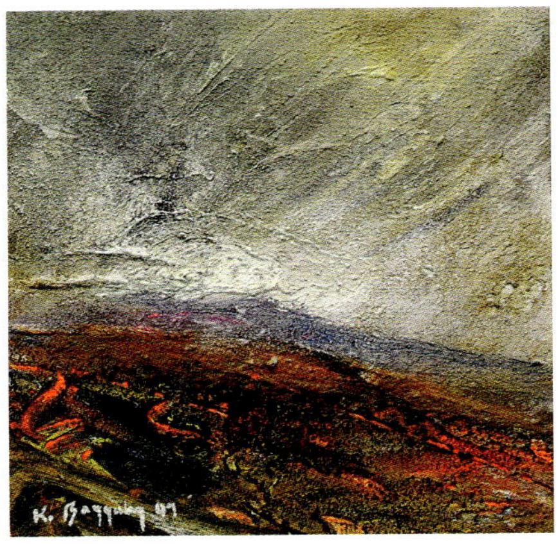

Baggaley, Kristan Paul b.1958
Peak District View 2009
oil on canvas 12.5 x 12.5
PCF67

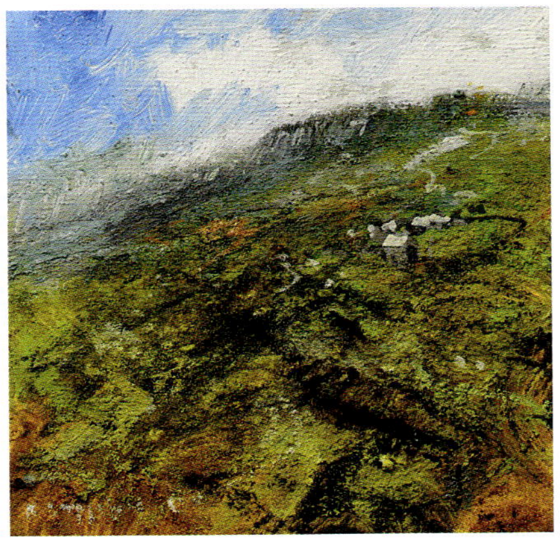

Baggaley, Kristan Paul b.1958
Peak District View 2009
oil on canvas 12.5 x 12.5
PCF68

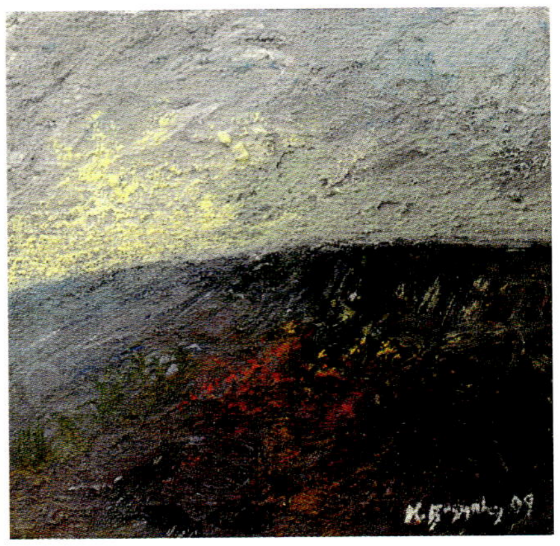

Baggaley, Kristan Paul b.1958
Peak District View 2009
oil on canvas 12.5 x 12.5
PCF69

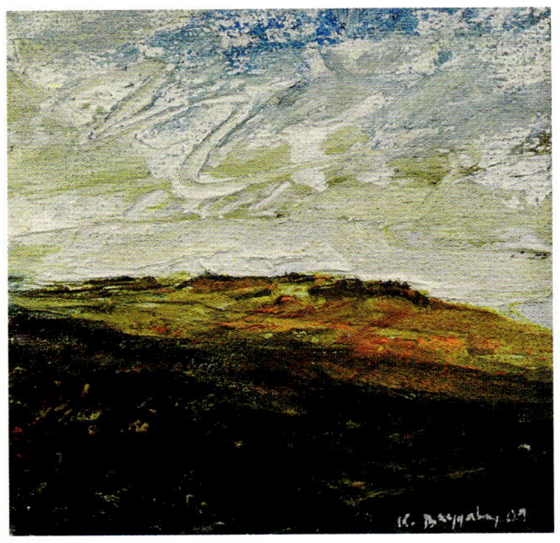

Baggaley, Kristan Paul b.1958
Peak District View 2009
oil on canvas 12.5 x 12.5
PCF70

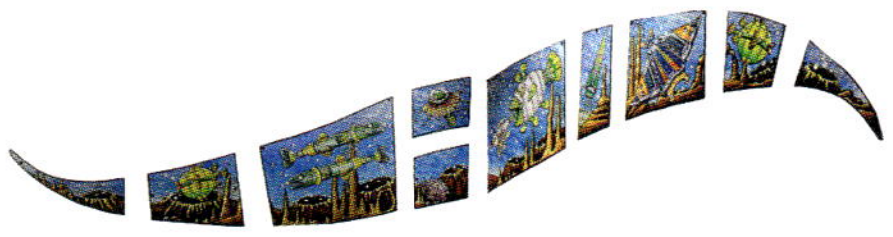

Field, Sandra b.1966
Robot Fish 1 (polyptych) 2001
acrylic on board 72 x 510 (E)
PCF18.1

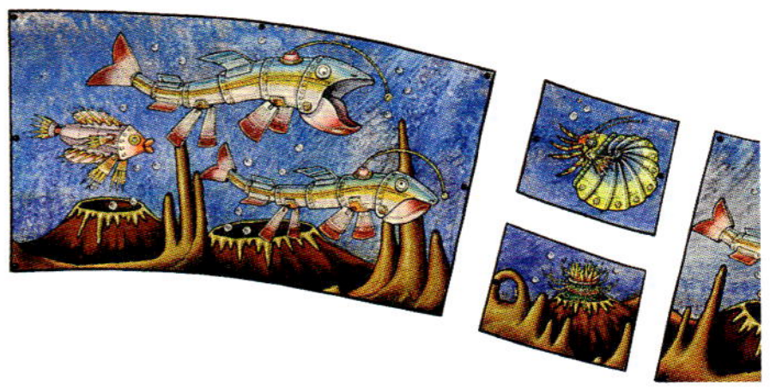

Field, Sandra b.1966
Robot Fish 2 (polyptych) (detail) 2001
acrylic on board 70 x 710 (E)
PCF18.2

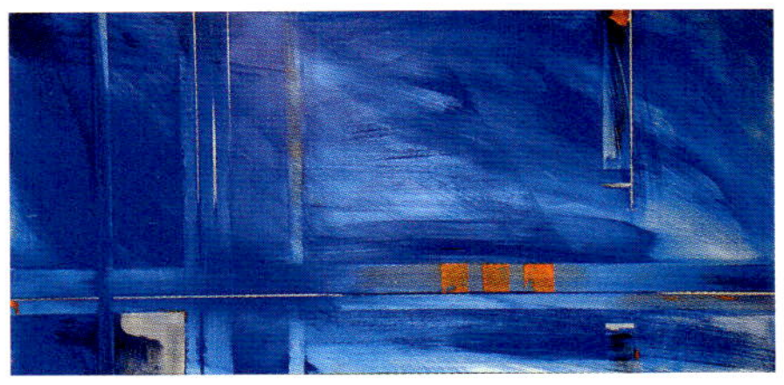

Firth, Richard b.1969
Blue Abstract 2004
acrylic on board 61 x 122
PCF3

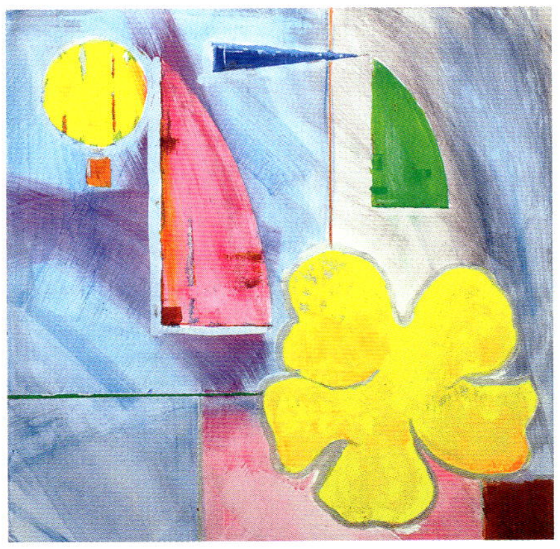

Firth, Richard b.1969
Boats and Flowers 2004
acrylic on board 71 x 71
PCF6

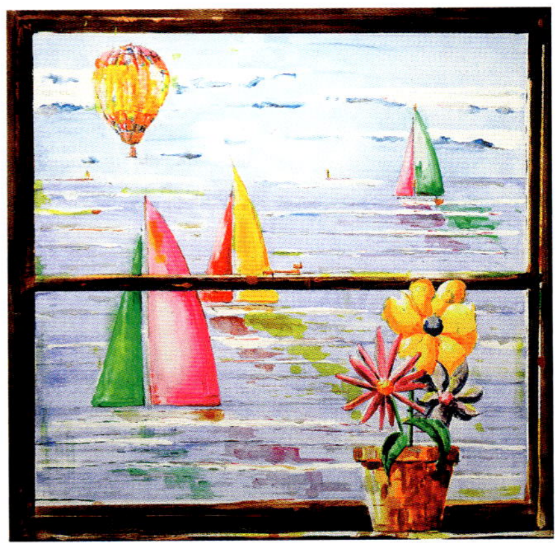

Firth, Richard b.1969
Boats through a Window 2004
acrylic on board 91.5 x 91.5
PCF5

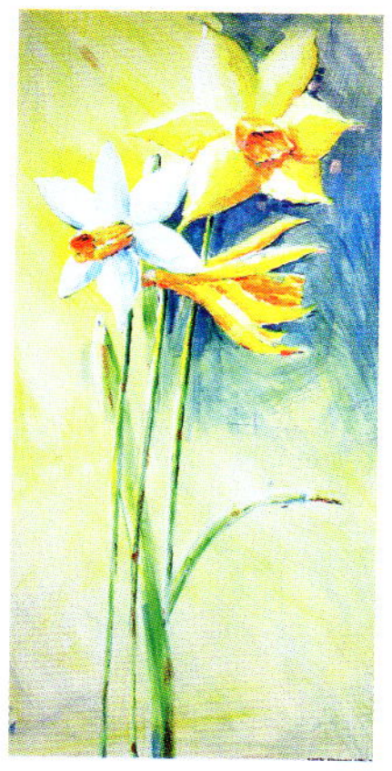

Firth, Richard b.1969
Daffodil 2004
acrylic on board 122 x 61
PCF7

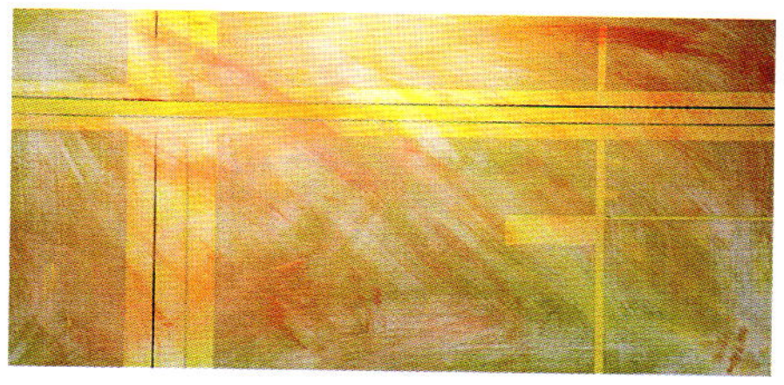

Firth, Richard b.1969
Yellow Abstract 2004
acrylic on board 61 x 122
PCF4

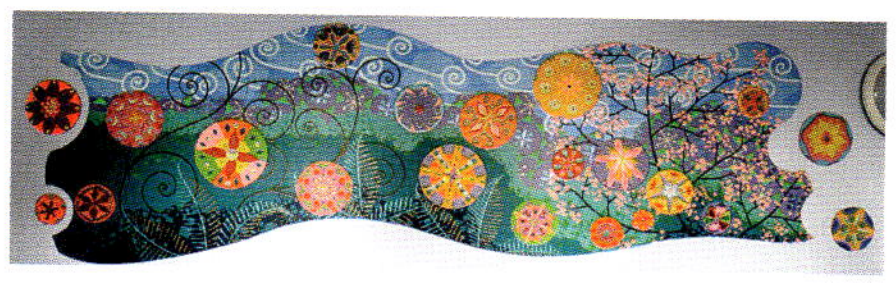

Heath, Andrew b.1962 & **Patients of The Children's Hospital, Sheffield**
Circles and Swirls (polyptych) 2005
acrylic on board 99 x 365.7
PCF23

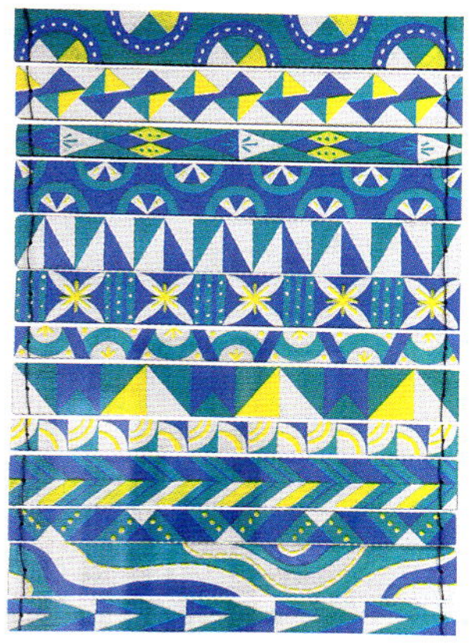

Kinoshita, Seiko b.1971
Large Blue Woven Slats 2009
acrylic on wood with weaving 42 x 30
PCF110

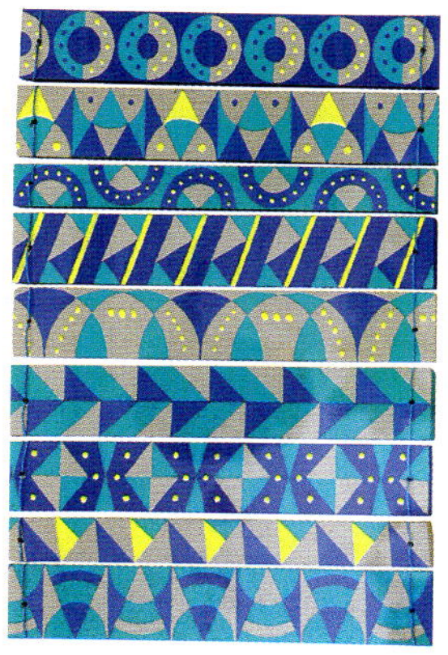

Kinoshita, Seiko b.1971
Large Purple Woven Slats 2009
acrylic on wood with weaving 30 x 23
PCF112

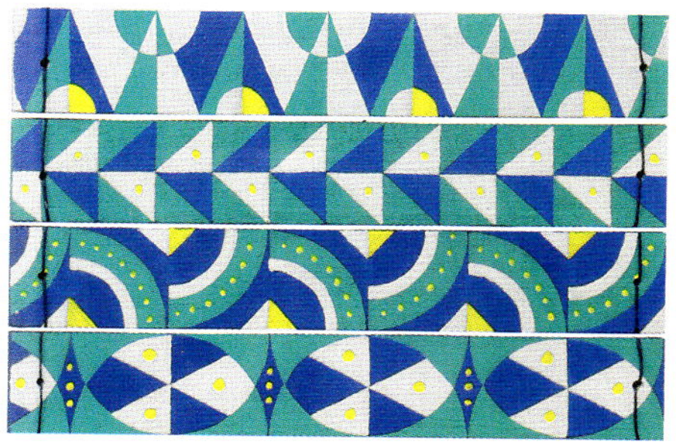

Kinoshita, Seiko b.1971
Small Blue Woven Slats 2009
acrylic on wood with weaving 15 x 23
PCF109

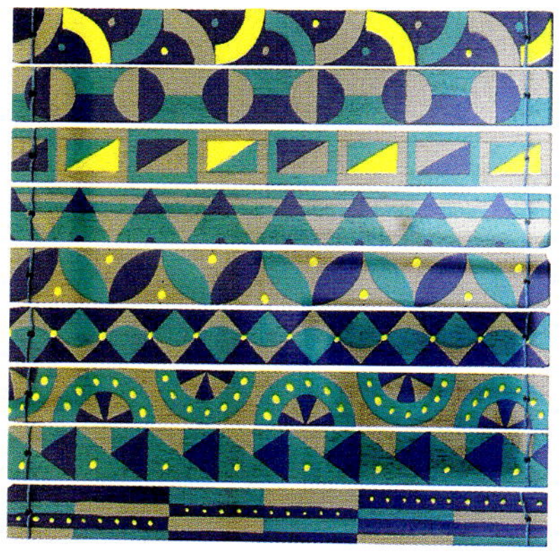

Kinoshita, Seiko b.1971
Small Purple Woven Slats 2009
acrylic on wood with weaving 21 x 23
PCF111

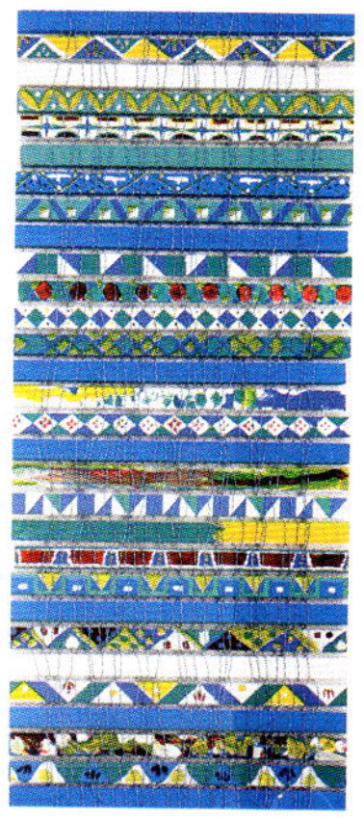

Kinoshita, Seiko b.1971 & **Patients of The Children's Hospital, Sheffield**
Blue Weaving 2007
acrylic on wood with weaving 85 x 45
PCF108

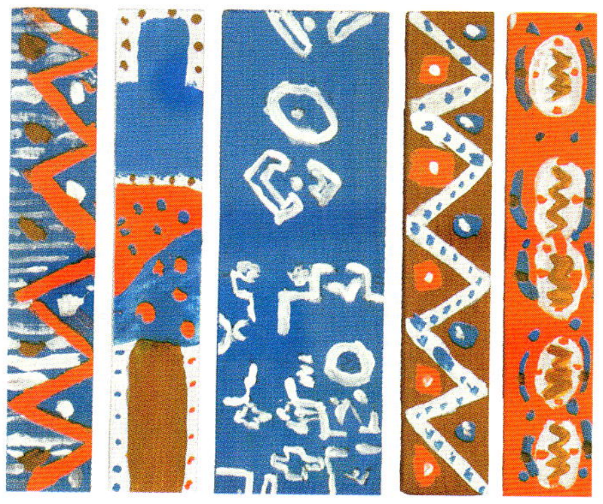

Kinoshita, Seiko b.1971 & **Patients of The Children's Hospital, Sheffield**
Blue Pink Woven Slats 2008
acrylic on wood with weaving 20 x 30
PCF113

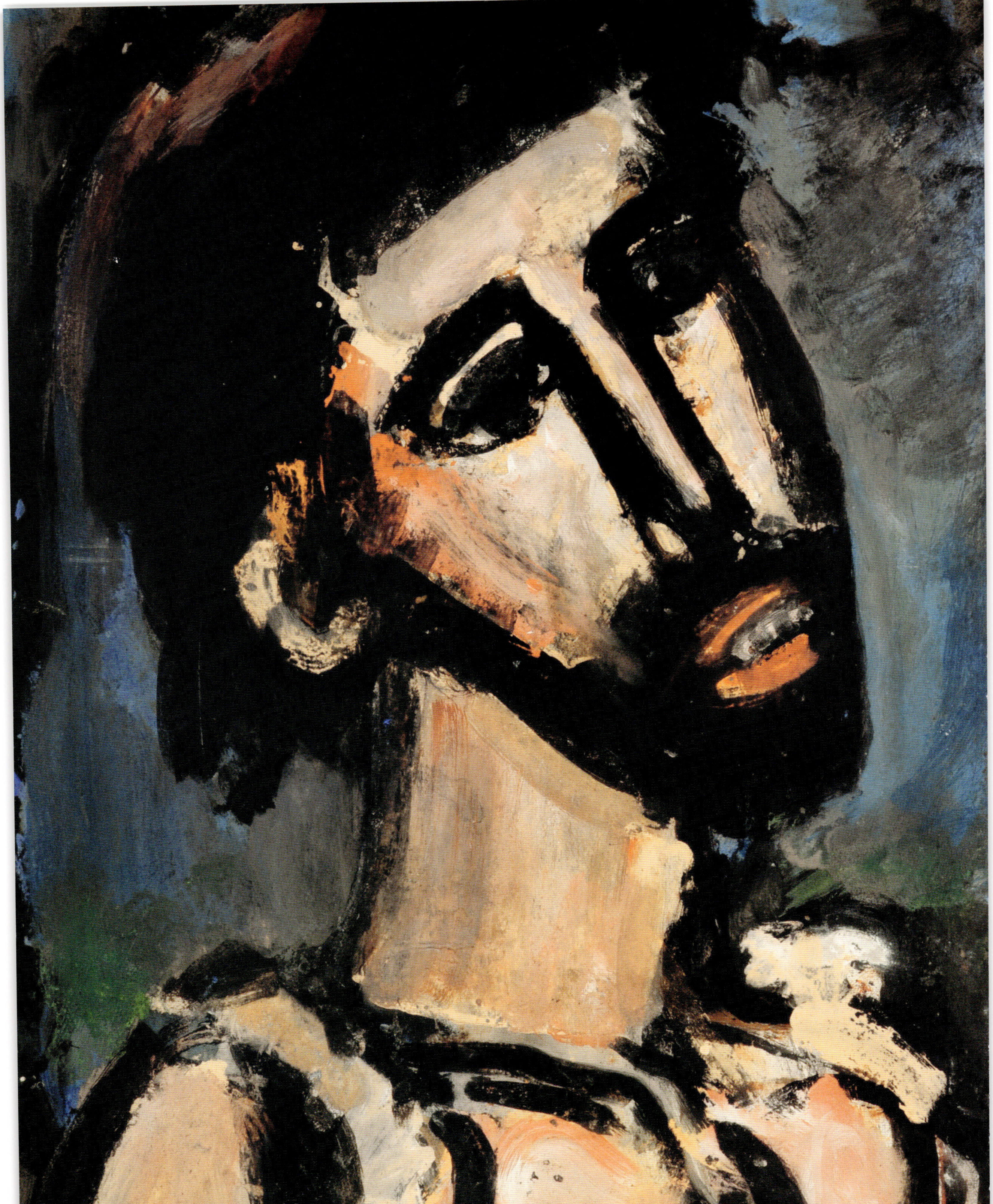

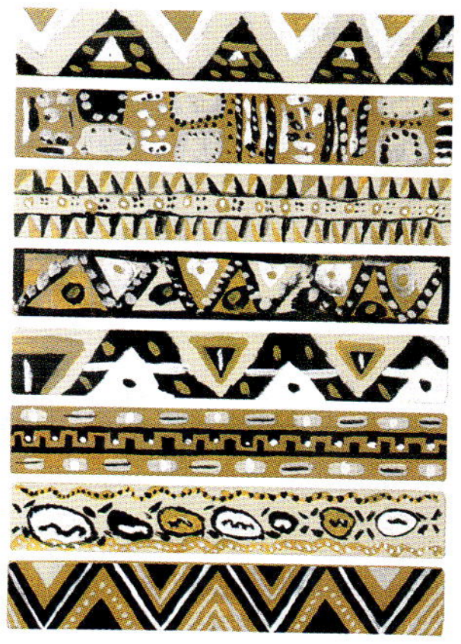

Kinoshita, Seiko b.1971 & **Patients of The Children's Hospital, Sheffield**
Brown Cream Woven Slats 2008
acrylic on wood with weaving 43 x 30
PCF115

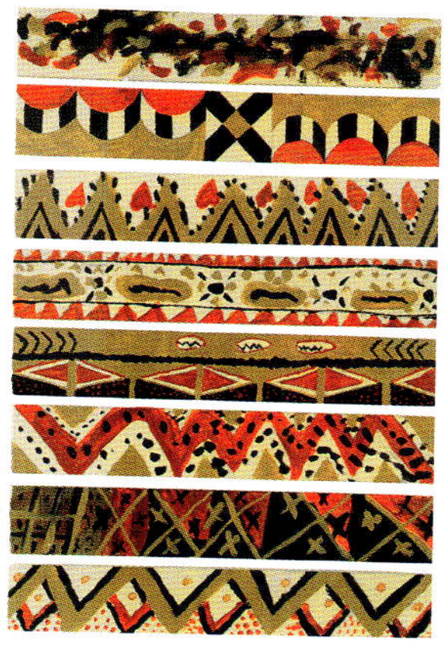

Kinoshita, Seiko b.1971 & **Patients of The Children's Hospital, Sheffield**
Brown Terracotta Woven Slats 2008
acrylic on wood with weaving 43 x 30
PCF116

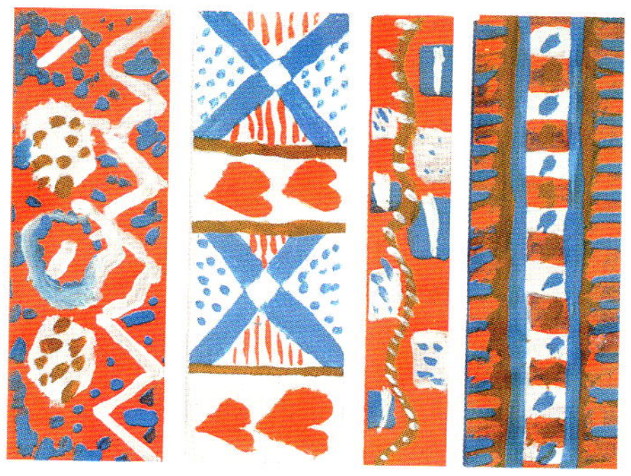

Kinoshita, Seiko b.1971 & **Patients of The Children's Hospital, Sheffield**
Pink Blue Woven Slats 2008
acrylic on wood with weaving 20 x 33
PCF114

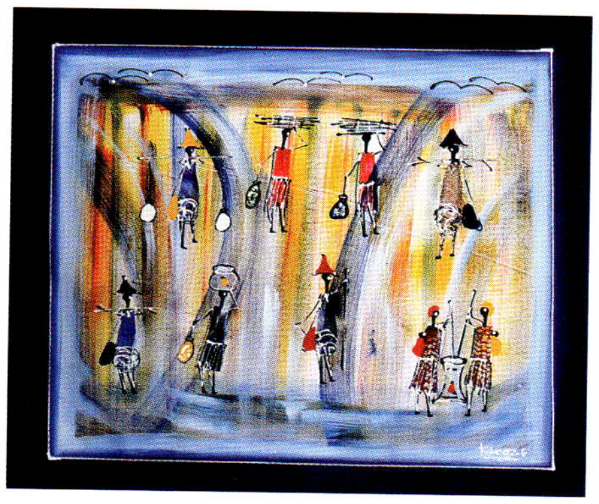

Klooze
Senegalese Figures
acrylic on canvas 84 x 95
PCF59

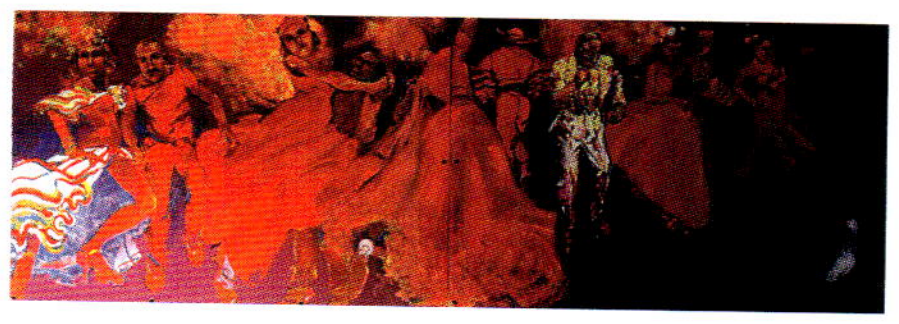

Lale, Hazel
Dancing 2001
oil on board 123 x 362
PCF55

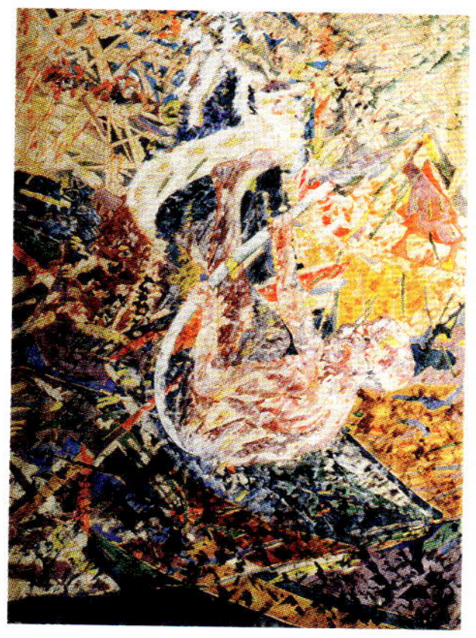

Parmakio, Rose active 1970s
All Fall Out No.1 1976
acrylic on paper 79 x 56
PCF56a

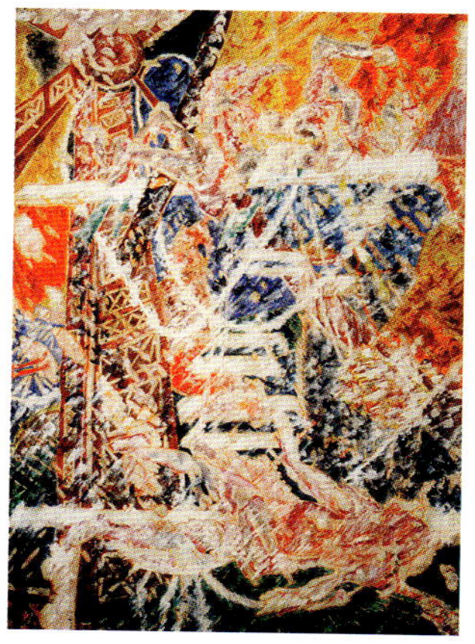

Parmakio, Rose active 1970s
All Fall Out No.2 1976
acrylic on paper 79 x 56
PCF56b

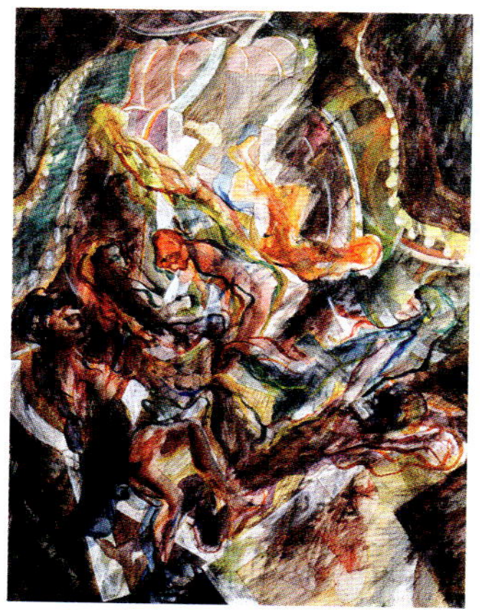

Parmakio, Rose active 1970s
All Fall Out No.3 1976
acrylic on paper 57 x 43
PCF56c

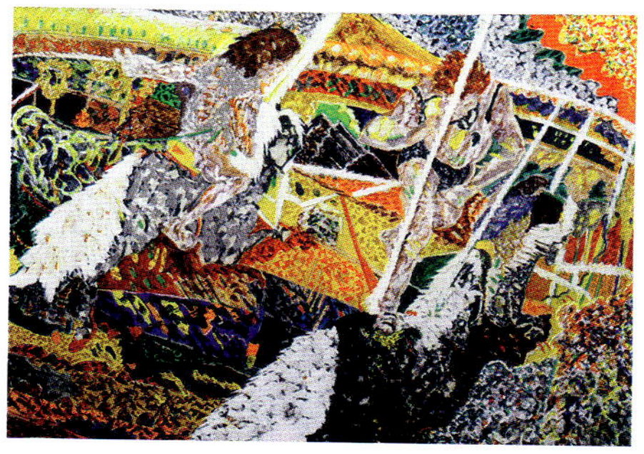

Parmakio, Rose active 1970s
All Fall Out No.4 1976
acrylic on paper 57 x 79
PCF56d

Facing page: Rouault, Georges, 1871–1959, *Head of Christ* (detail), Museums Sheffield, (p. 185)

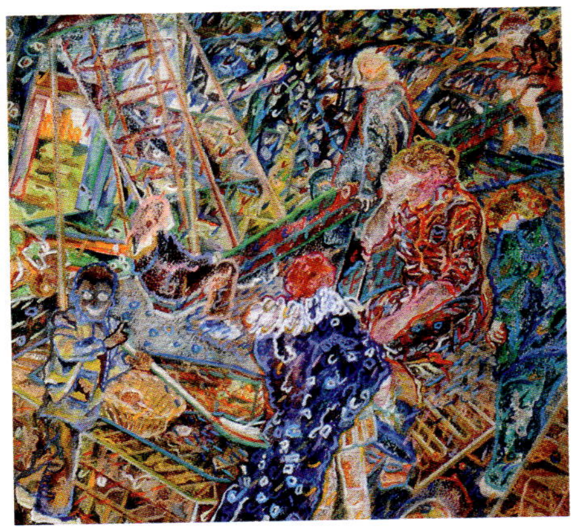

Parmakio, Rose active 1970s
Adventure Playground 1977
acrylic on paper 48 x 51
PCF57b

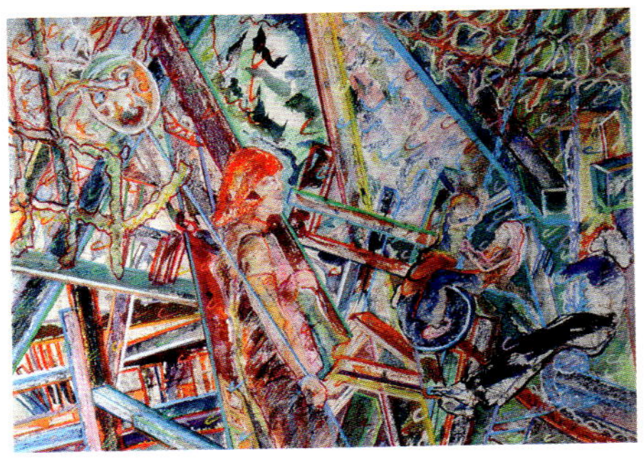

Parmakio, Rose active 1970s
Adventure Playground 1978
acrylic on paper 57 x 79
PCF57a

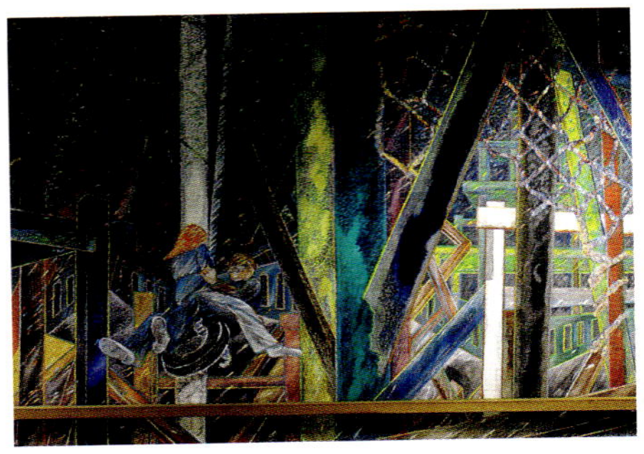

Parmakio, Rose active 1970s
Adventure Playground
oil on canvas 150 x 210
PCF61

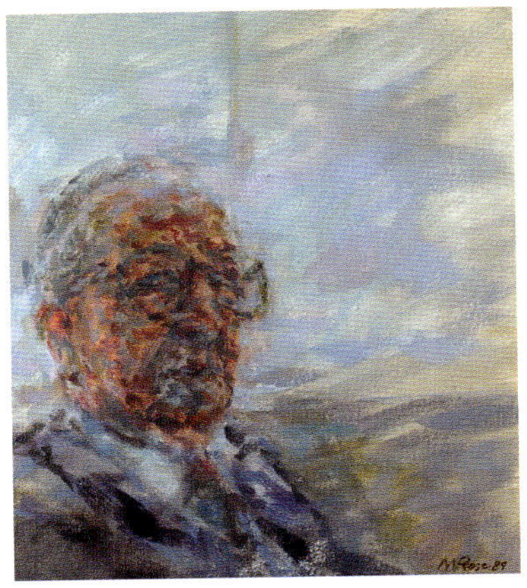

Rose, Martin H. b.1946
Professor Ronald Illingworth (1909–1990) 1989
oil on canvas 41 x 38
PCF60

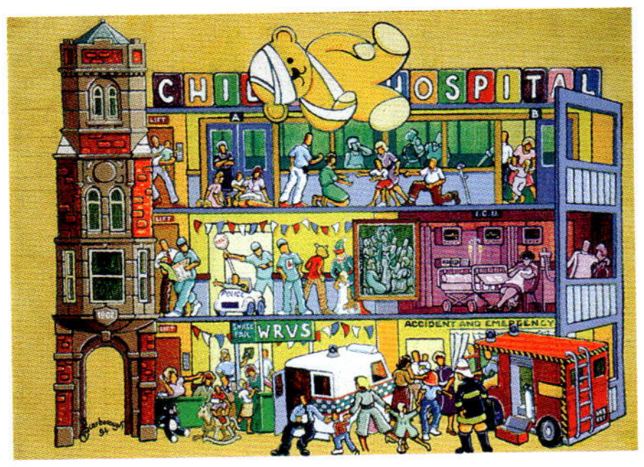

Scarborough, Joe b.1938
Open Day at Sheffield Children's Hospital 1994
oil on canvas 54 x 74
PCF12

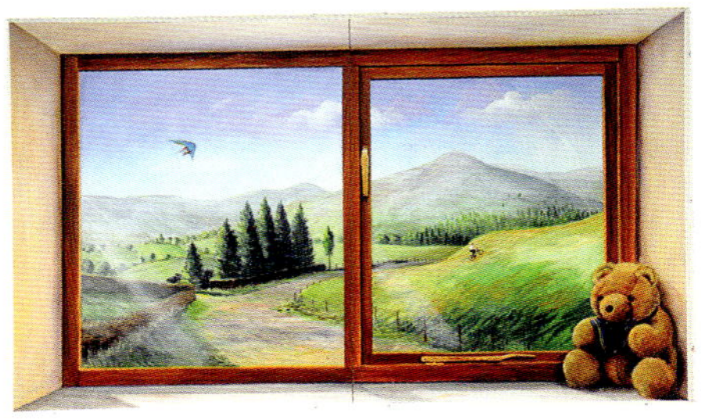

Taylor, Alan b.1958
Peak District Landscape 1
acrylic on board 114.3 x 243.8 (E)
PCF13

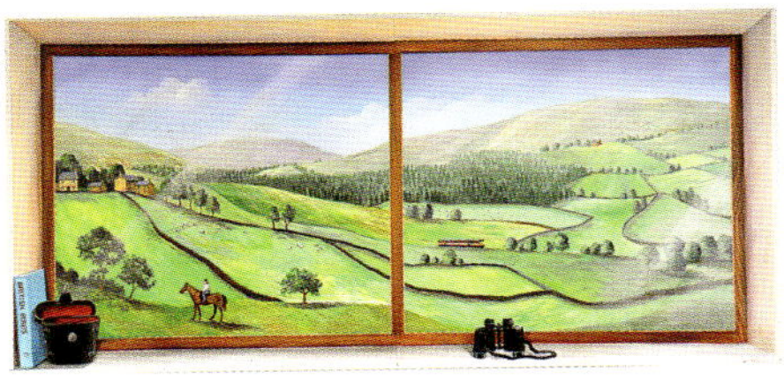

Taylor, Alan b.1958
Peak District Landscape 2
acrylic on board 114.3 x 182.8 (E)
PCF14

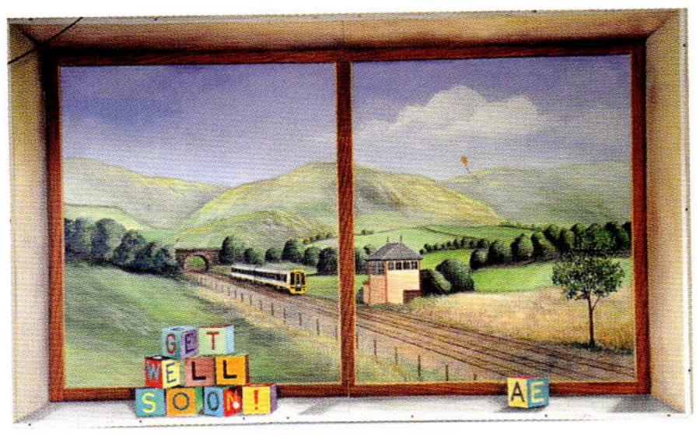

Taylor, Alan b.1958
Peak District Landscape 3
acrylic on board 162.5 x 170.2 (E)
PCF15

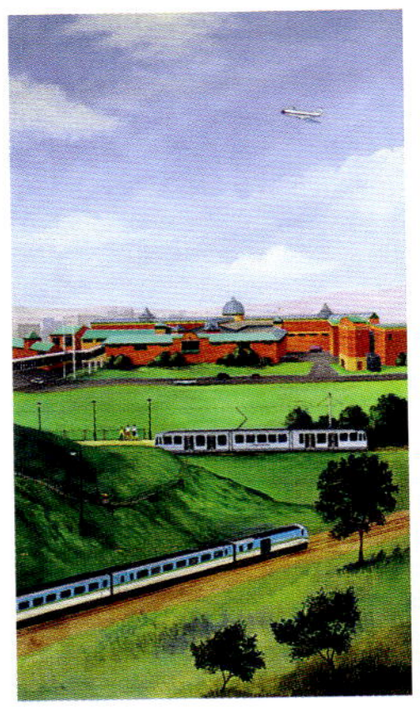

Taylor, Alan b.1958
Super Tram
acrylic on board 116.8 x 106.6
PCF17

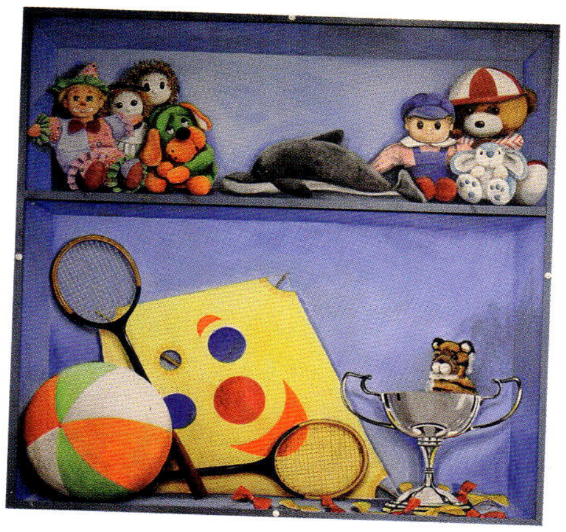

Taylor, Alan b.1958
Toy Cupboard
acrylic on board 121.9 x 121.9
PCF16

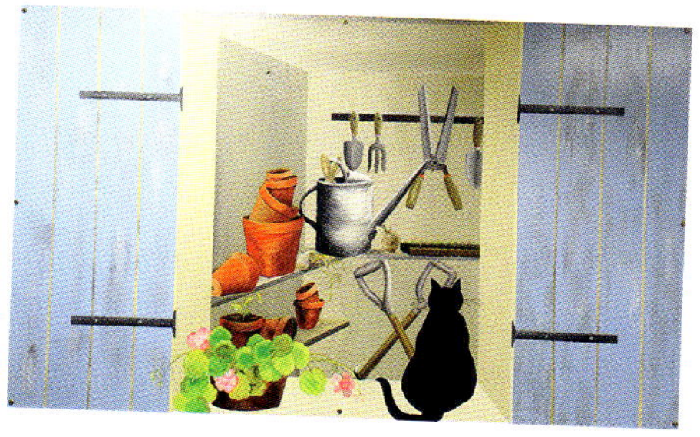

Taylor, Micheline & **Waite, Philippa**
Cat at a Window c.2003
acrylic on board 101.6 x 162.5
PCF2

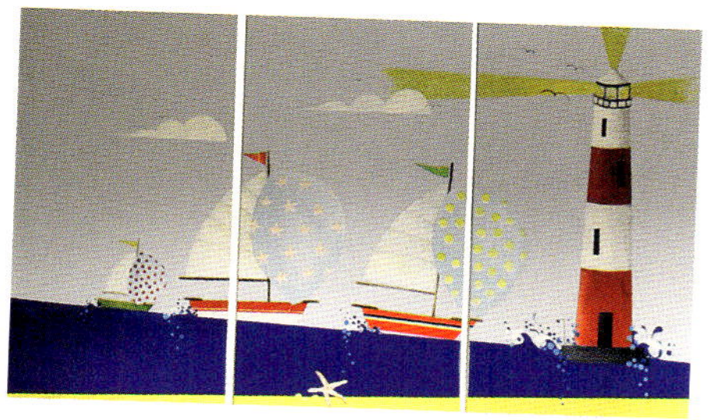

Taylor, Micheline & **Waite, Philippa**
Lighthouse and Ships (triptych)
acrylic on board 91 x 183
PCF19a

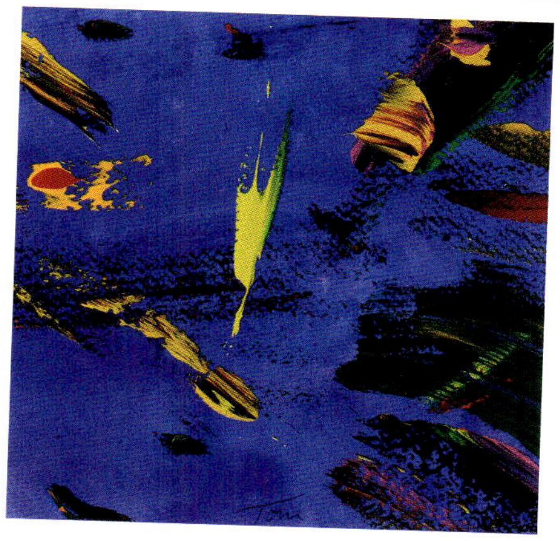

Tom
Dark Blue Abstract 2008
acrylic on paper 17 x 17
PCF58a

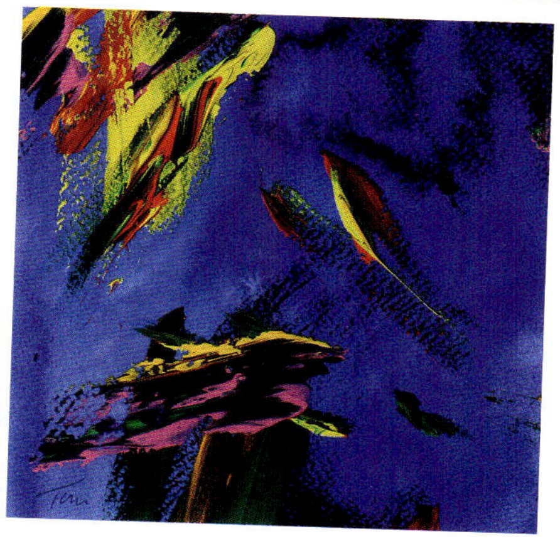

Tom
Dark Blue Abstract 2008
acrylic on paper 17 x 17
PCF58b

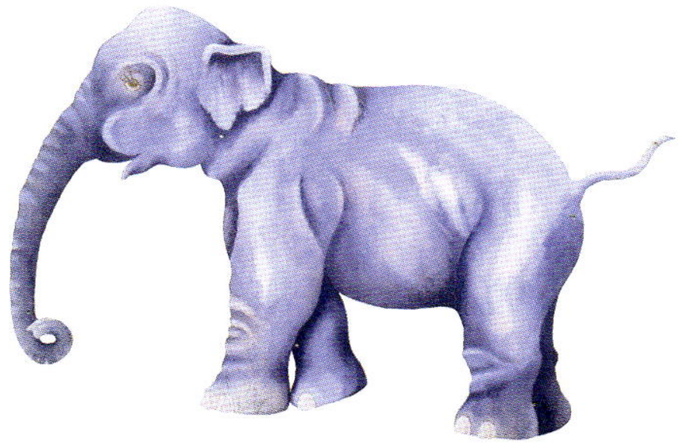

unknown artist
Elephants 1 c.2000
acrylic on board 99 x 163 (E)
PCF29.1

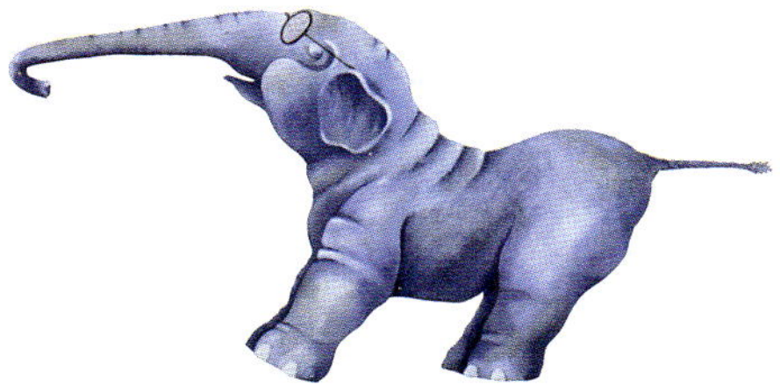

unknown artist
Elephants 2 c.2000
acrylic on board 100 x 200 (E)
PCF29.2

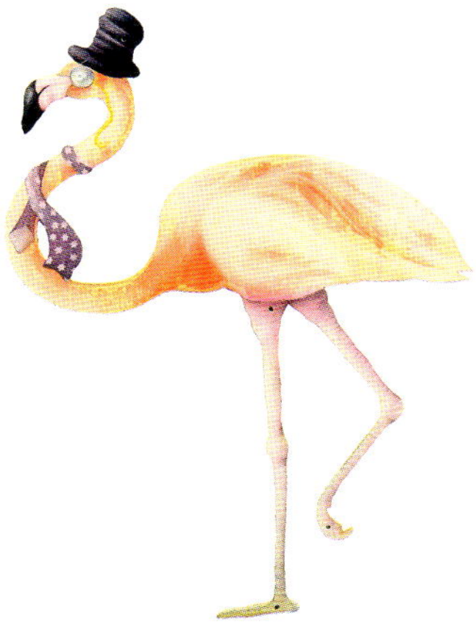

unknown artist
Flamingo 1 c.2000
acrylic on board 112 x 78 (E)
PCF102

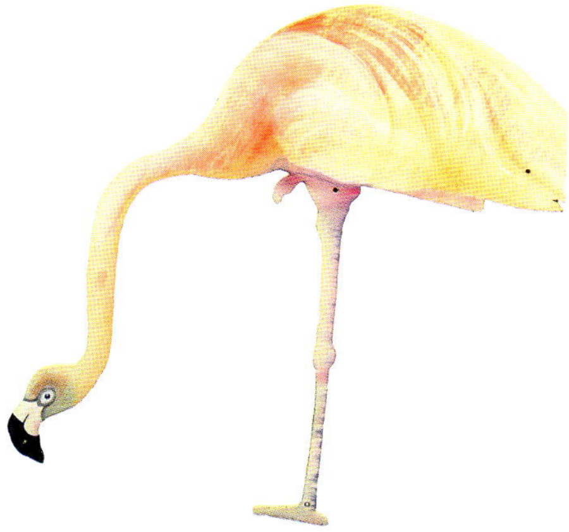

unknown artist
Flamingo 2 c.2000
acrylic on board 80 x 80 (E)
PCF104

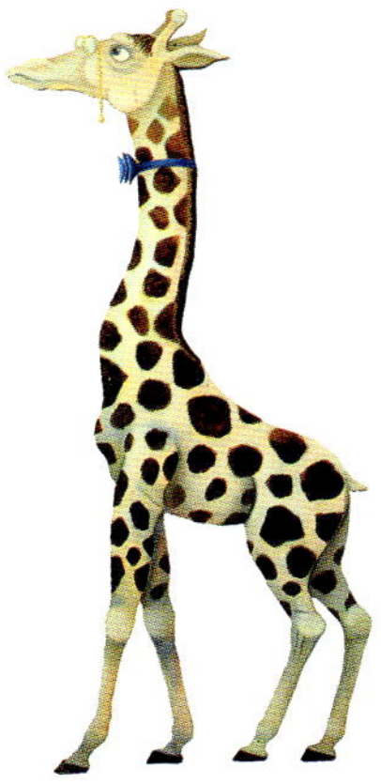

unknown artist
Giraffe c.2000
acrylic on board 190 x 70 (E)
PCF101

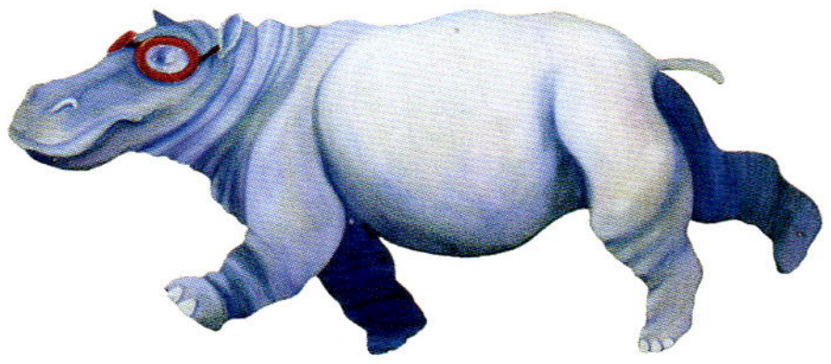

unknown artist
Hippopotamus c.2000
acrylic on board 60 x 140 (E)
PCF29.3

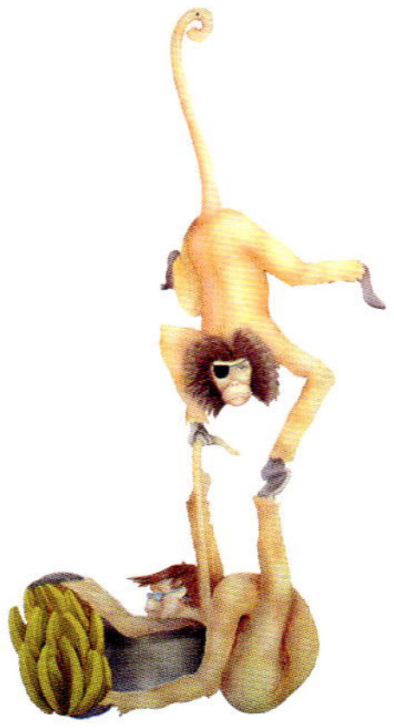

unknown artist
Monkeys c.2000
acrylic on board 193 x 111 (E)
PCF103

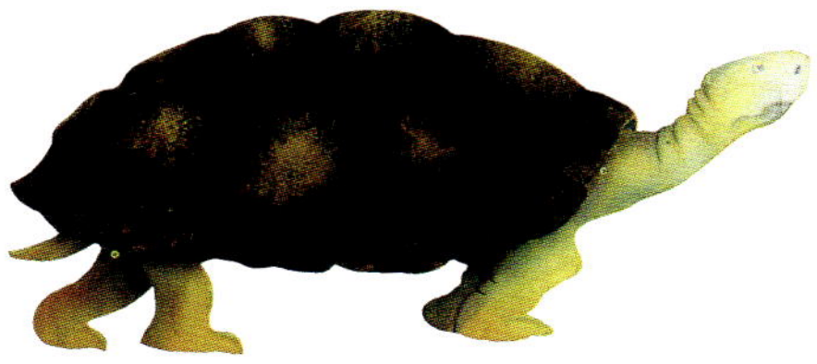

unknown artist
Tortoise 1 c.2000
acrylic on board 34 x 78 (E)
PCF105

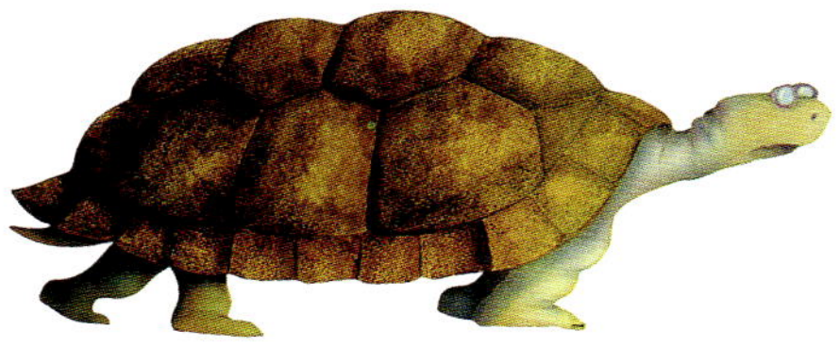

unknown artist
Tortoise 2 c.2000
acrylic on board 33 x 80 (E)
PCF106

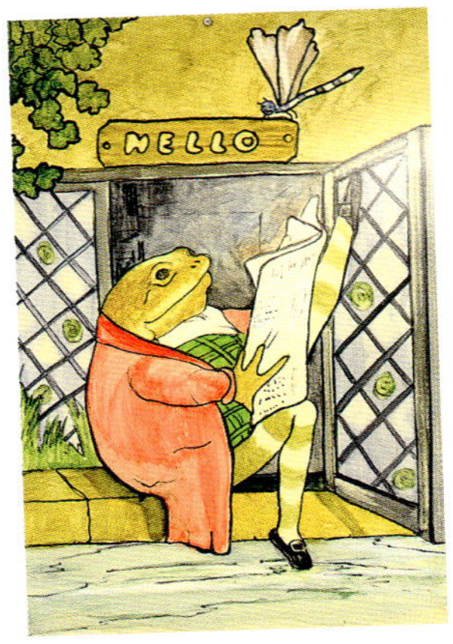

unknown artist
Beatrix Potter, Toad
acrylic on board 91 x 61
PCF24

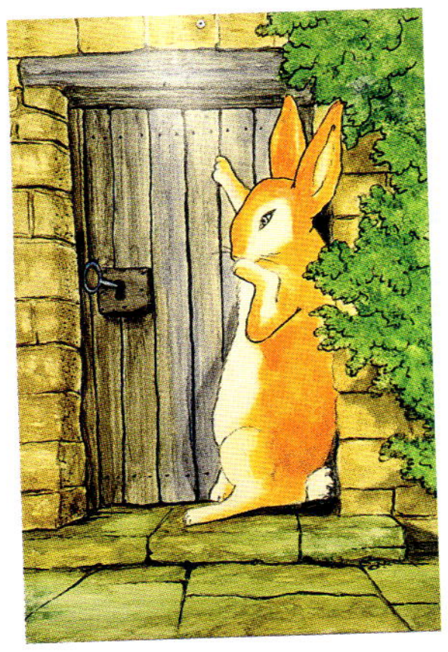

unknown artist
Beatrix Potter, Rabbit
acrylic on board 91 x 61
PCF25

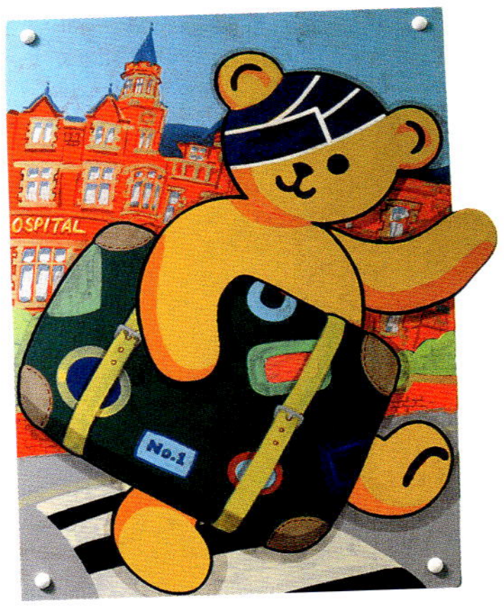

Wyatt, Houghton b.1953/1954
Theo's Amazing Journey, Theo Sets Off c.2001
acrylic & mixed media on board 61 x 44
PCF27.1

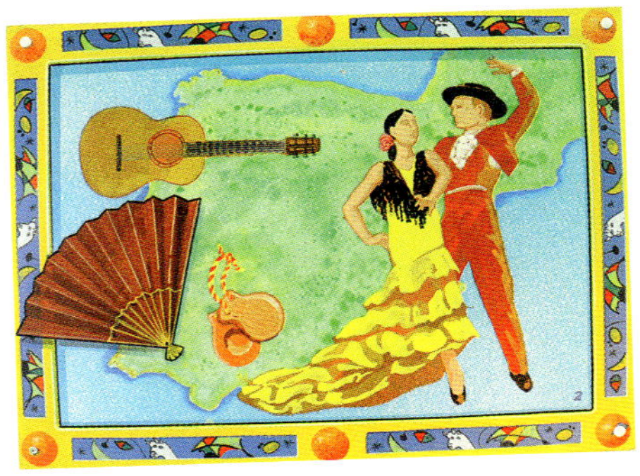

Wyatt, Houghton b.1953/1954
Theo's Amazing Journey, Spain c.2001
acrylic & mixed media on board 61 x 80
PCF27.2

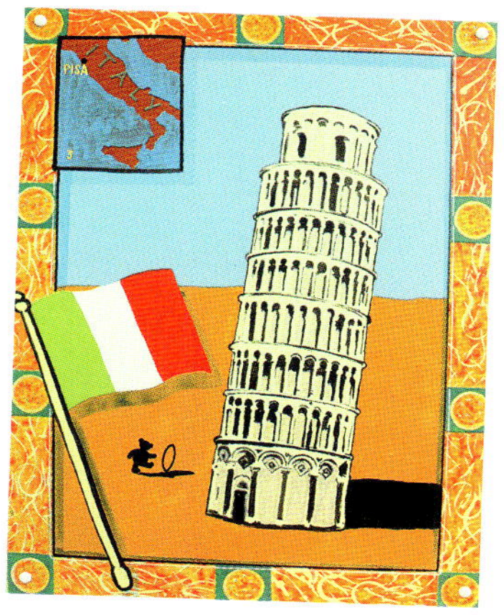

Wyatt, Houghton b.1953/1954
Theo's Amazing Journey, Italy c.2001
acrylic & mixed media on board 61 x 61 (E)
PCF27.3

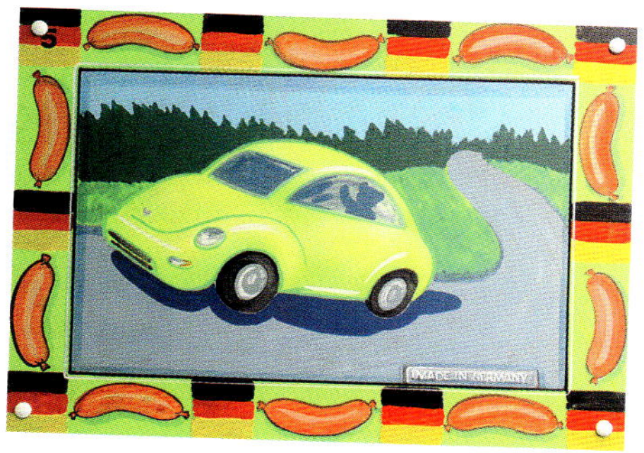

Wyatt, Houghton b.1953/1954
Theo's Amazing Journey, Germany c.2001
acrylic & mixed media on board 44 x 61
PCF27.4

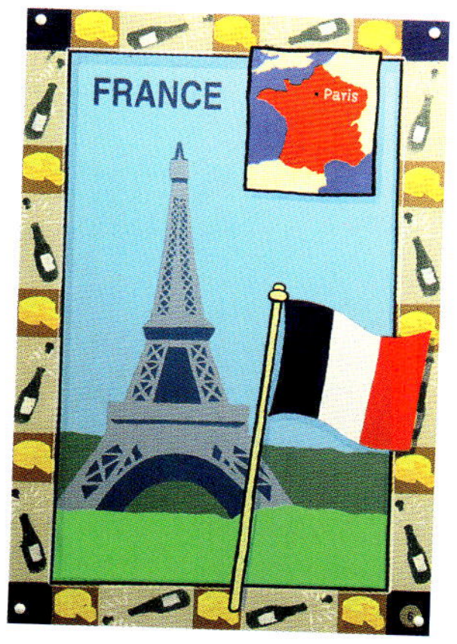

Wyatt, Houghton b.1953/1954
Theo's Amazing Journey, France c.2001
acrylic & mixed media on board 62 x 61
PCF27.5

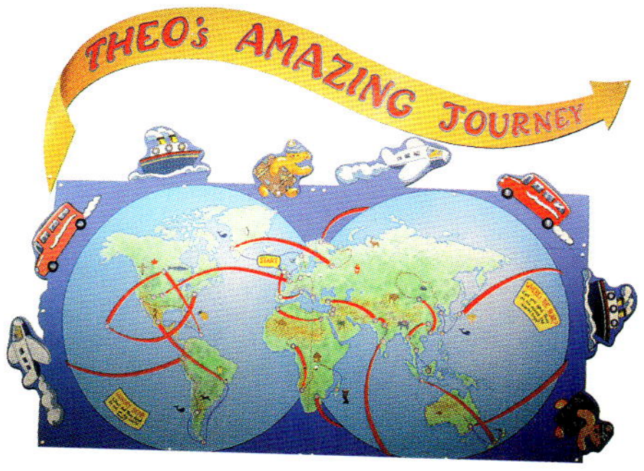

Wyatt, Houghton b.1953/1954
Theo's Amazing Journey, the World
(polyptych) c.2001
acrylic & mixed media on board 125 x 140
(E)
PCF27.6

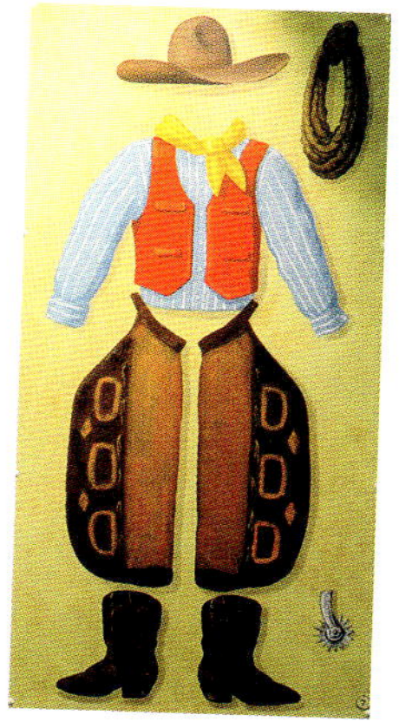

Wyatt, Houghton b.1953/1954
Theo's Amazing Journey, Cowboy c.2001
acrylic & mixed media on board 180 x 92
PCF27.7

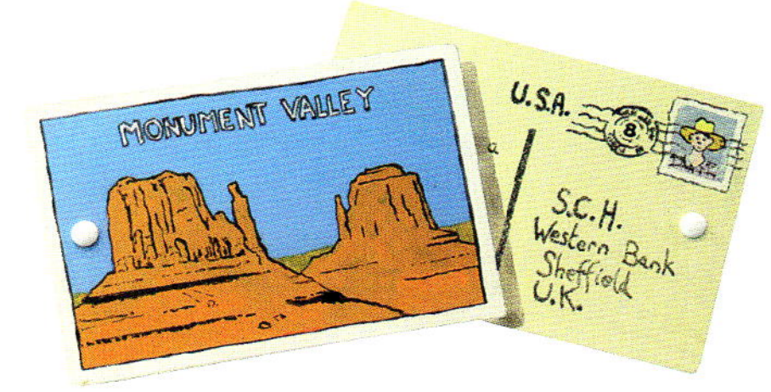

Wyatt, Houghton b.1953/1954
Theo's Amazing Journey, Postcard from Monument Valley, USA c.2001
acrylic & mixed media on board 20 x 40
PCF27.8

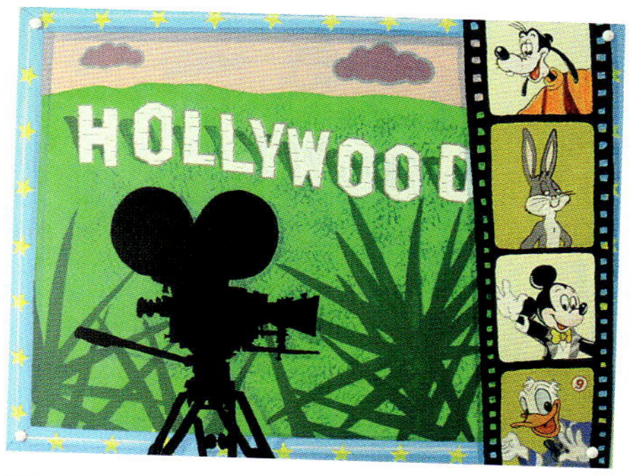

Wyatt, Houghton b.1953/1954
Theo's Amazing Journey, Hollywood c.2001
acrylic & mixed media on board 61 x 81
PCF27.9

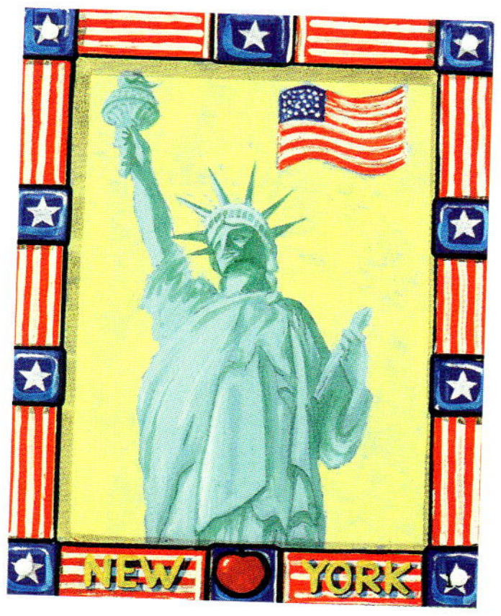

Wyatt, Houghton b.1953/1954
Theo's Amazing Journey, New York c.2001
acrylic & mixed media on board 56 x 44
PCF27.10

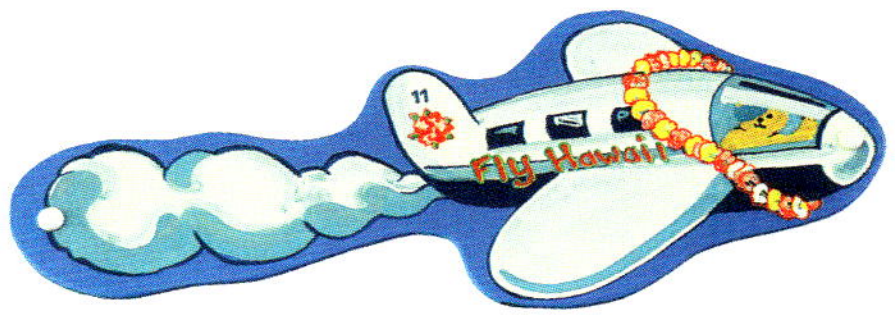

Wyatt, Houghton b.1953/1954
Theo's Amazing Journey, Hawaii c.2001
acrylic & mixed media on board 21 x 51 (E)
PCF27.11

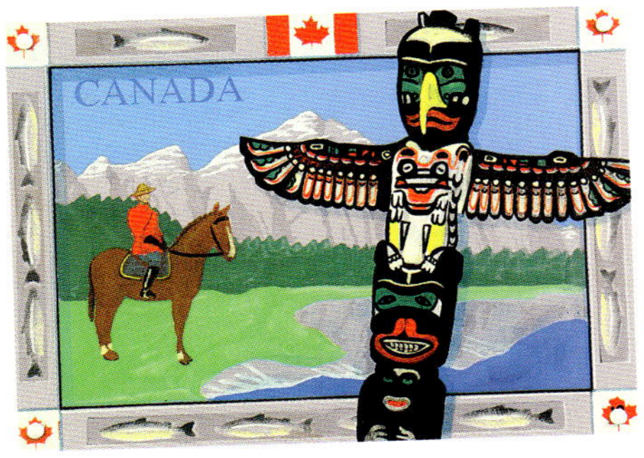

Wyatt, Houghton b.1953/1954
Theo's Amazing Journey, Canada c.2001
acrylic & mixed media on board 44 x 61
PCF27.12

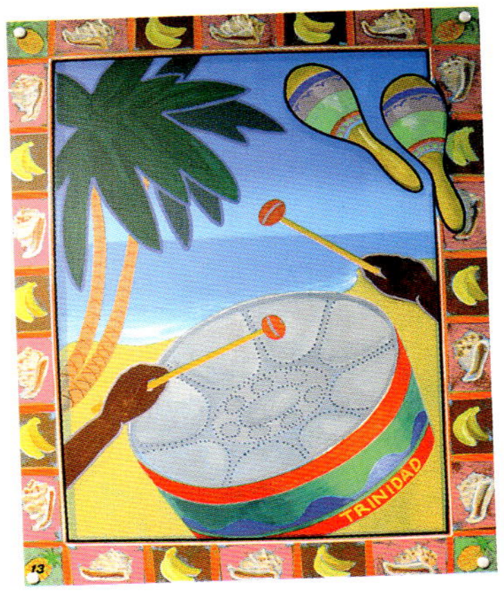

Wyatt, Houghton b.1953/1954
Theo's Amazing Journey, Trinidad c.2001
acrylic & mixed media on board 81 x 61
PCF27.13

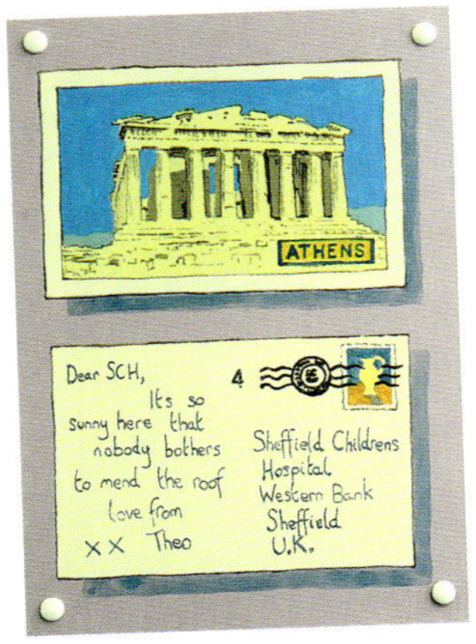

Wyatt, Houghton b.1953/1954
Theo's Amazing Journey, Postcard from Athens c.2001
acrylic & mixed media on board 44 x 30
PCF27.14

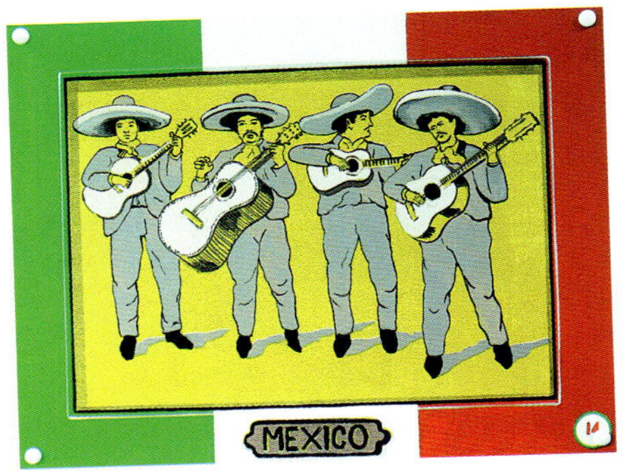

Wyatt, Houghton b.1953/1954
Theo's Amazing Journey, Mexico c.2001
acrylic & mixed media on board 44 x 56
PCF27.15

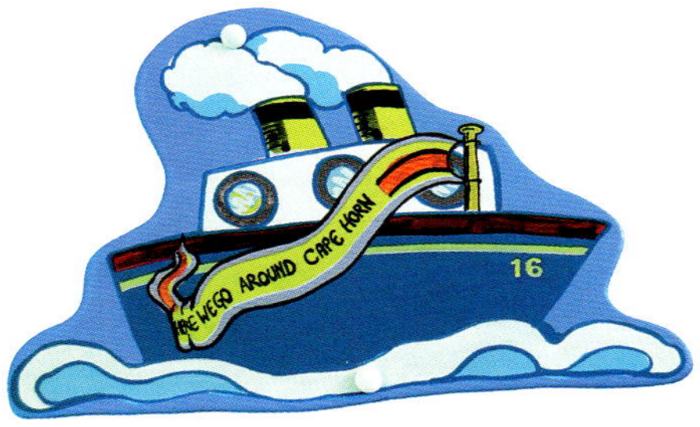

Wyatt, Houghton b.1953/1954
Theo's Amazing Journey, Cape Horn c.2001
acrylic & mixed media on board 25 x 39 (E)
PCF27.16

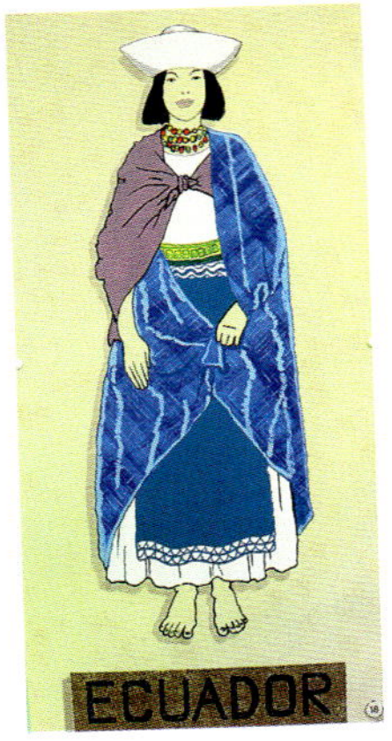

Wyatt, Houghton b.1953/1954
Theo's Amazing Journey, Ecuador c.2001
acrylic & mixed media on board 150 x 71
PCF27.17

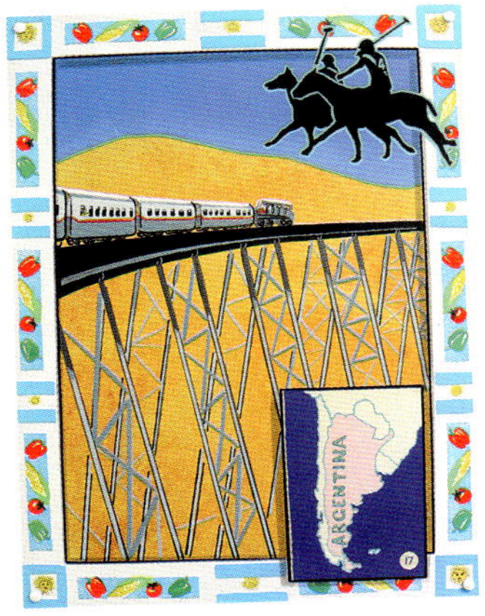

Wyatt, Houghton b.1953/1954
Theo's Amazing Journey, Argentina c.2001
acrylic & mixed media on board 81 x 61
PCF27.18

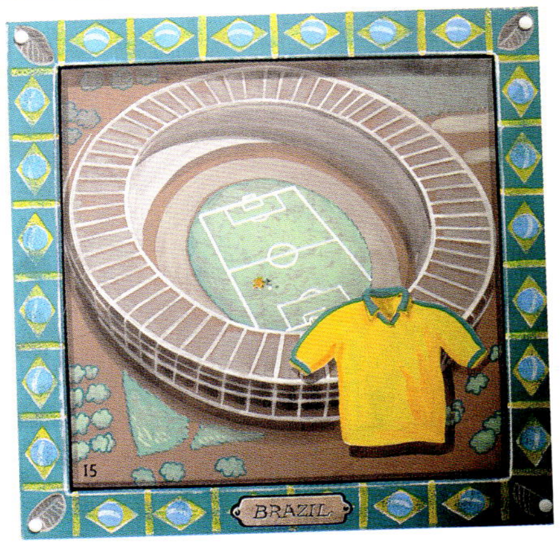

Wyatt, Houghton b.1953/1954
Theo's Amazing Journey, Brazil c.2001
acrylic & mixed media on board 60 x 61
PCF27.19

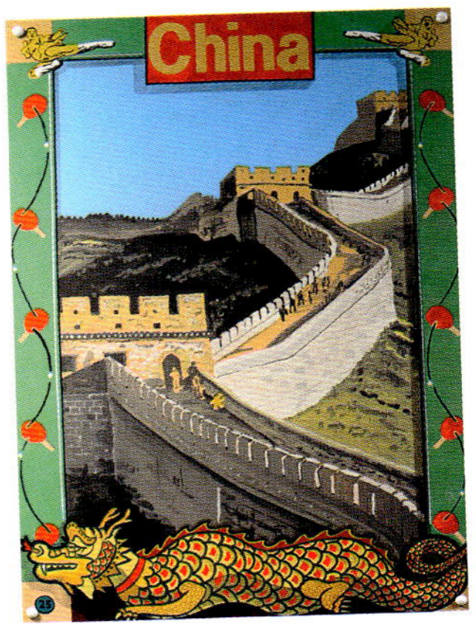

Wyatt, Houghton b.1953/1954
Theo's Amazing Journey, China c.2001
acrylic & mixed media on board 92 x 61
PCF27.20

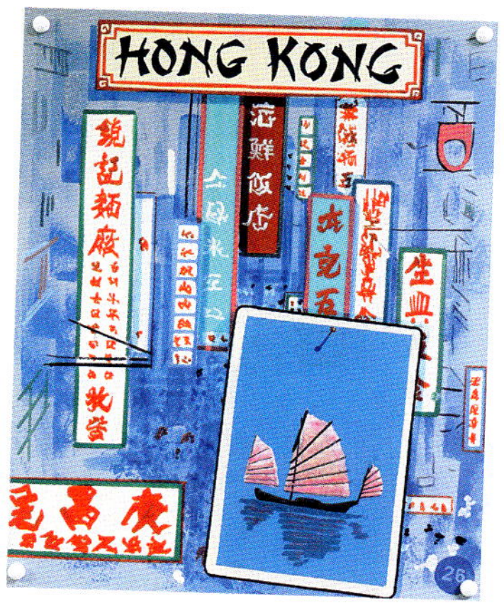

Wyatt, Houghton b.1953/1954
Theo's Amazing Journey, Hong Kong c.2001
acrylic & mixed media on board 56 x 43.5
PCF27.21

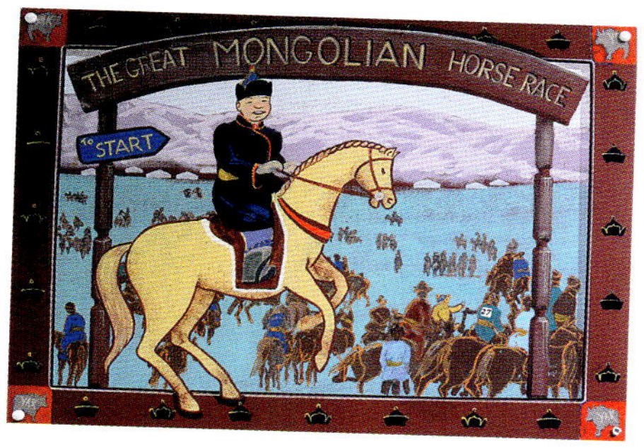

Wyatt, Houghton b.1953/1954
Theo's Amazing Journey, Mongolia c.2001
acrylic & mixed media on board 61 x 81
PCF27.22

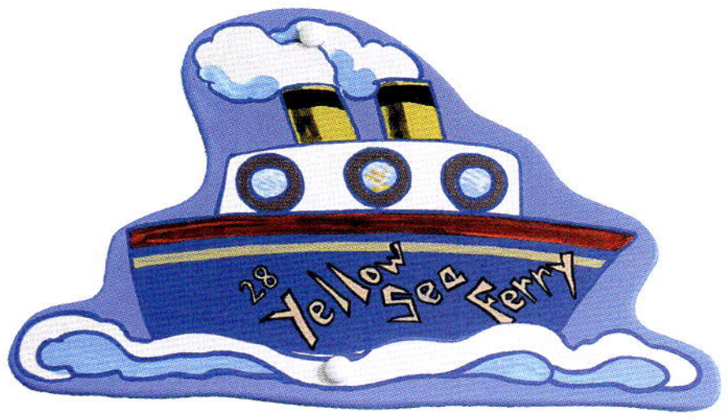

Wyatt, Houghton b.1953/1954
Theo's Amazing Journey, Yellow Sea Ferry c.2001
acrylic & mixed media on board 25 x 38
PCF27.23

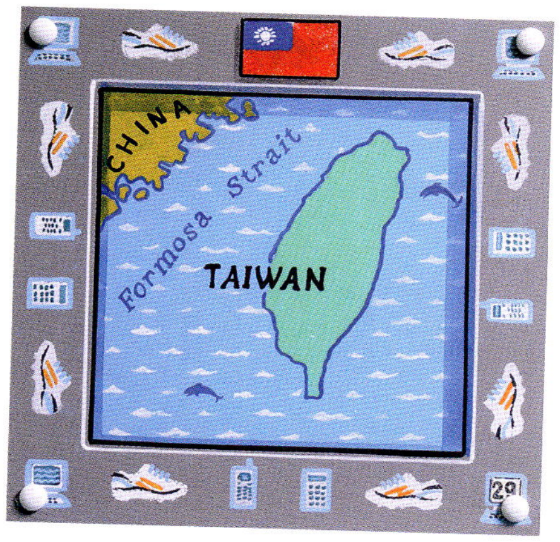

Wyatt, Houghton b.1953/1954
Theo's Amazing Journey, Taiwan c.2001
acrylic & mixed media on board 30 x 30
PCF27.24

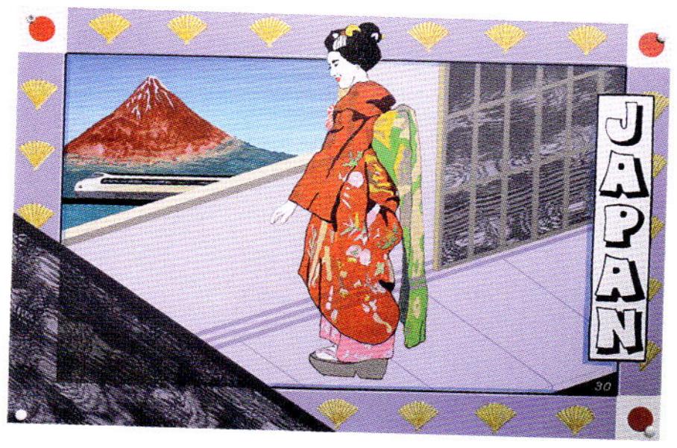

Wyatt, Houghton b.1953/1954
Theo's Amazing Journey, Japan c.2001
acrylic & mixed media on board 61 x 91.5
PCF27.25

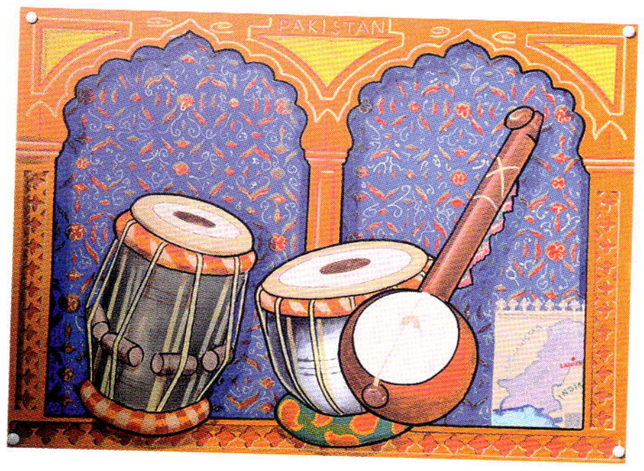

Wyatt, Houghton b.1953/1954
Theo's Amazing Journey, Pakistan c.2001
acrylic & mixed media on board 61 x 82.5
PCF27.26

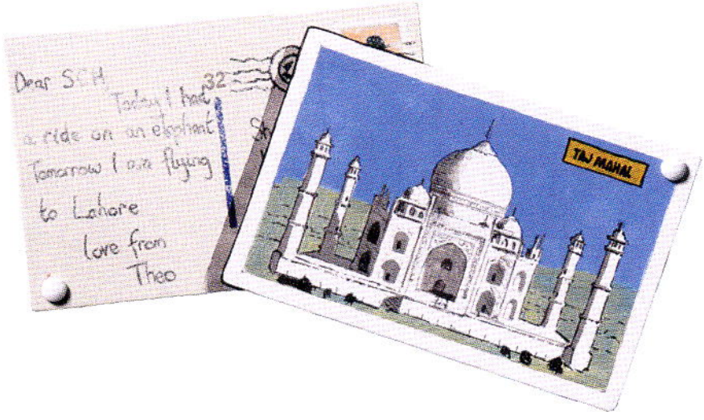

Wyatt, Houghton b.1953/1954
Theo's Amazing Journey, Postcard from the Taj Mahal, India c.2001
acrylic & mixed media on board 19 x 40
PCF27.27

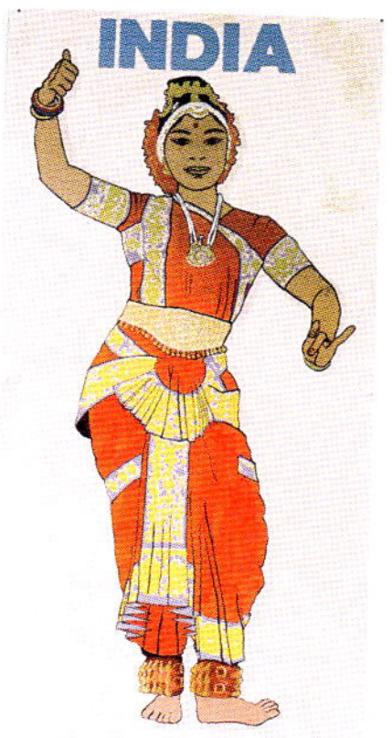

Wyatt, Houghton b.1953/1954
Theo's Amazing Journey, India c.2001
acrylic & mixed media on board 153 x 76
PCF27.28

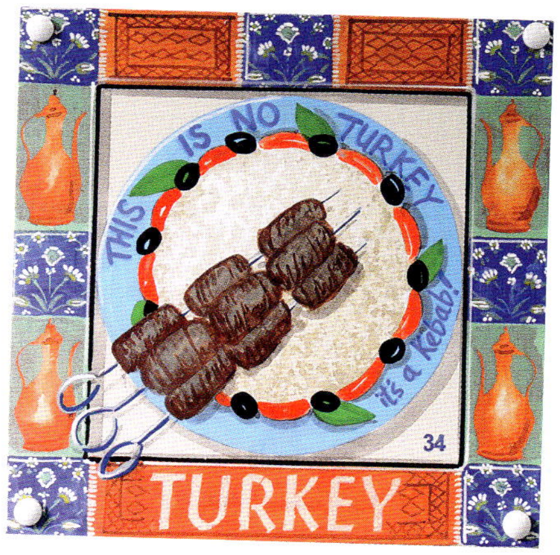

Wyatt, Houghton b.1953/1954
Theo's Amazing Journey, Turkey c.2001
acrylic & mixed media on board 30 x 30
PCF27.29

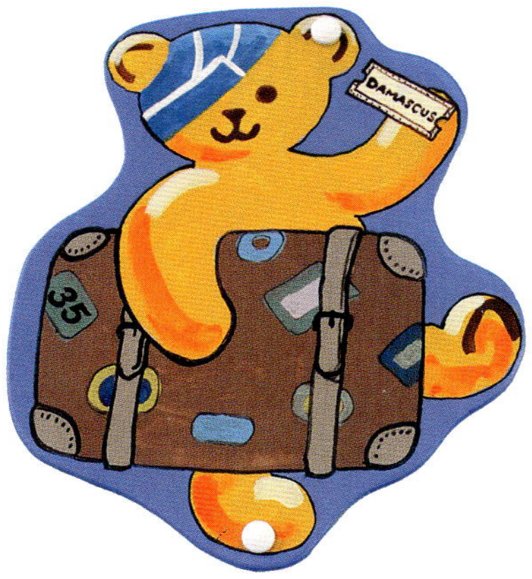

Wyatt, Houghton b.1953/1954
Theo's Amazing Journey, Theo in Damascus c.2001
acrylic & mixed media on board 28 x 23
PCF27.30

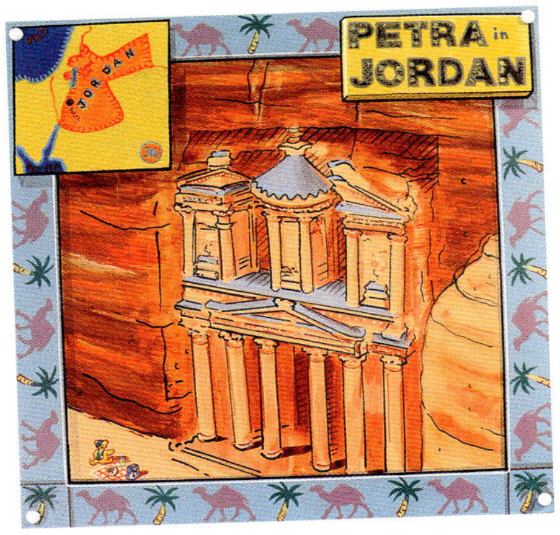

Wyatt, Houghton b.1953/1954
Theo's Amazing Journey, Jordan c.2001
acrylic & mixed media on board 61 x 61
PCF27.31

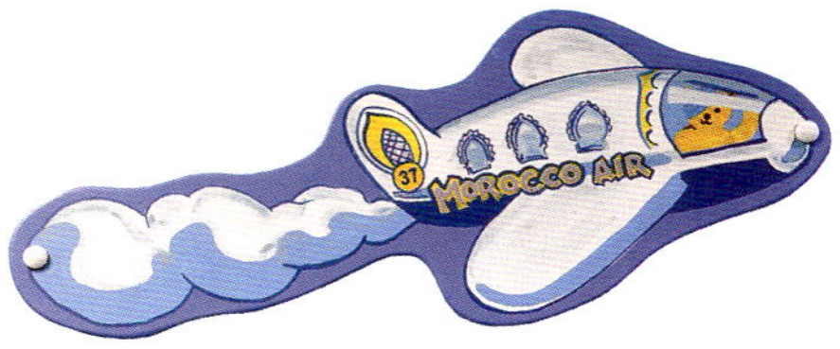

Wyatt, Houghton b.1953/1954
Theo's Amazing Journey, Morocco c.2001
acrylic & mixed media on board 22 x 56 (E)
PCF27.32

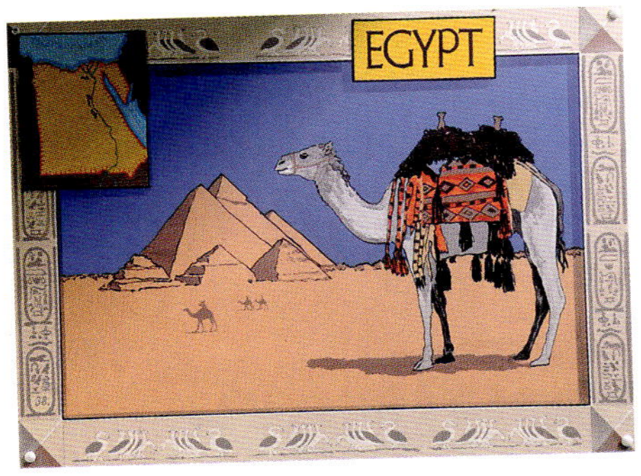

Wyatt, Houghton b.1953/1954
Theo's Amazing Journey, Egypt c.2001
acrylic & mixed media on board 61 x 92
PCF27.33

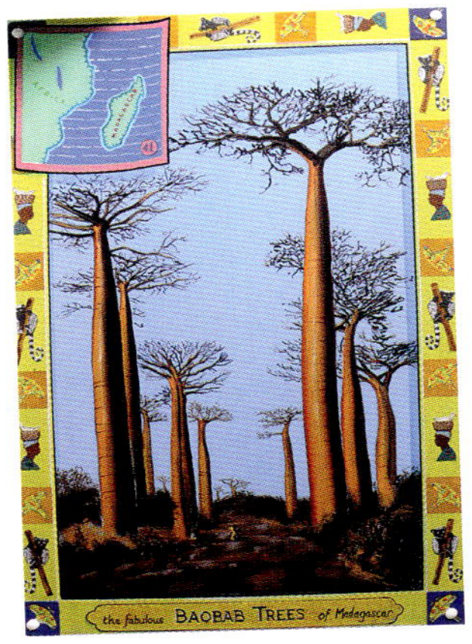

Wyatt, Houghton b.1953/1954
Theo's Amazing Journey, Madagascar c.2001
acrylic & mixed media on board 91 x 61
PCF27.34

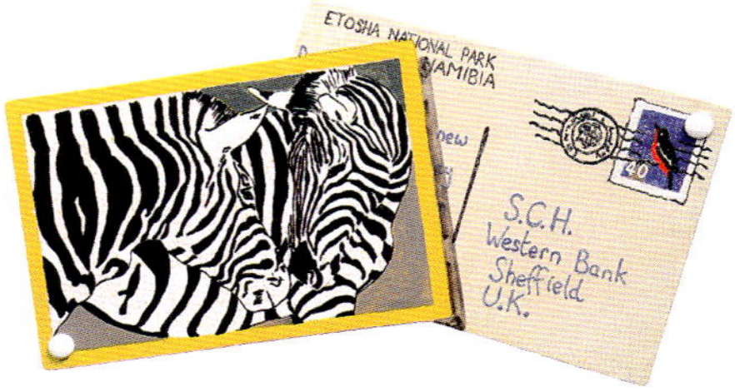

Wyatt, Houghton b.1953/1954
Theo's Amazing Journey, Postcard from Namibia c.2001
acrylic & mixed media on board 20 x 40
PCF27.35

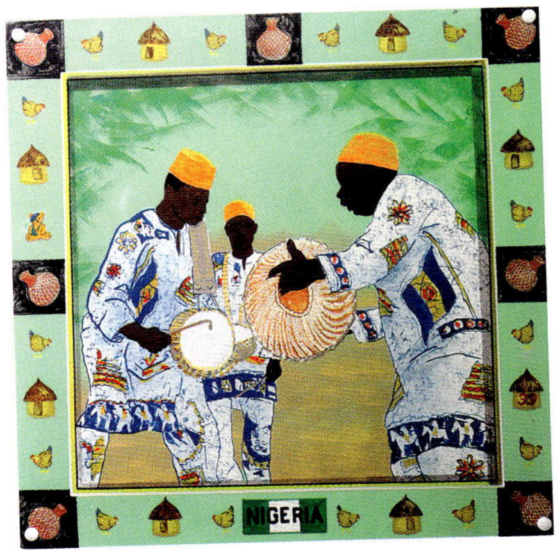

Wyatt, Houghton b.1953/1954
Theo's Amazing Journey, Nigeria c.2001
acrylic & mixed media on board 61 x 61
PCF27.36

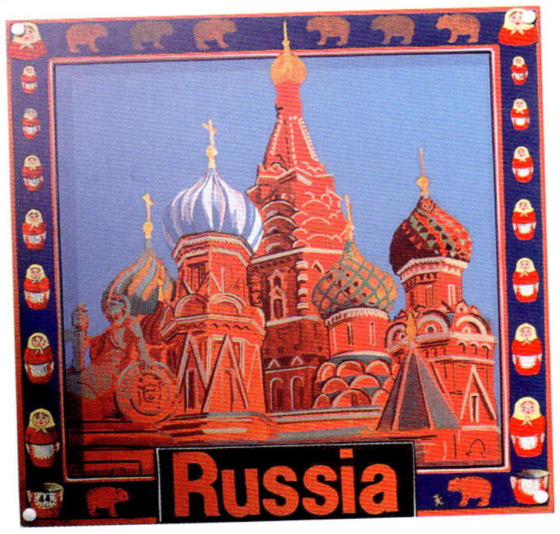

Wyatt, Houghton b.1953/1954
Theo's Amazing Journey, Russia c.2001
acrylic & mixed media on board 61 x 61
PCF27.37

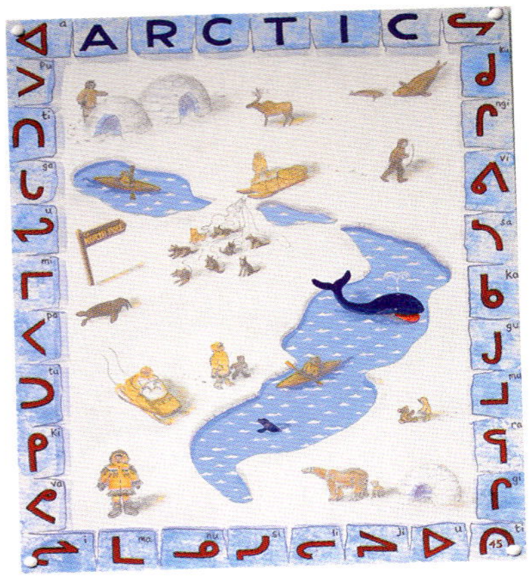

Wyatt, Houghton b.1953/1954
Theo's Amazing Journey, Arctic c.2001
acrylic & mixed media on board 81 x 61
PCF27.38

Facing page: Carline, Richard, 1896–1980, *Kate (Katherine Foster)* (detail), 1925, Museums Sheffield, (p. 35)

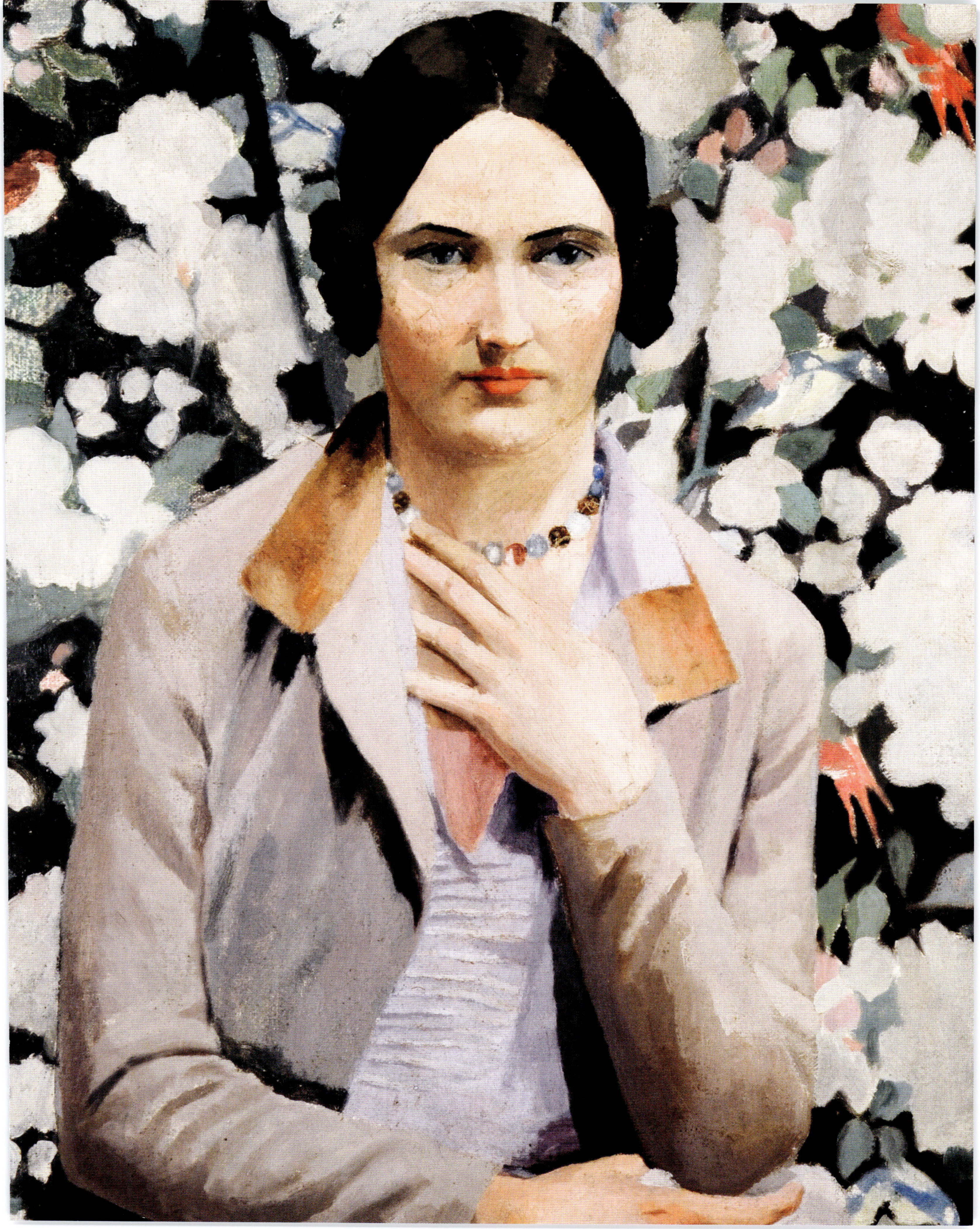

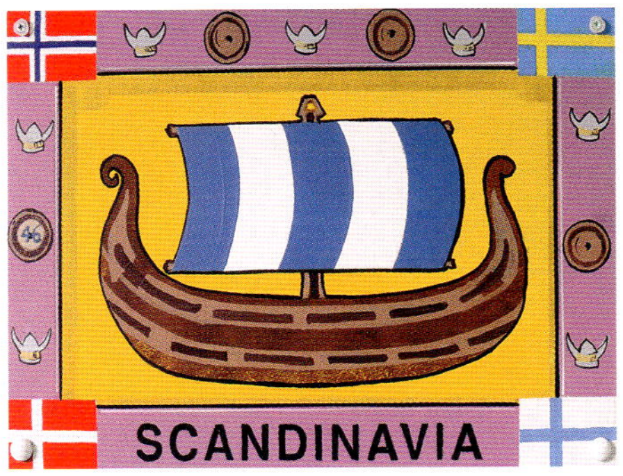

Wyatt, Houghton b.1953/1954
Theo's Amazing Journey, Scandinavia c.2001
acrylic & mixed media on board 31 x 45
PCF27.39

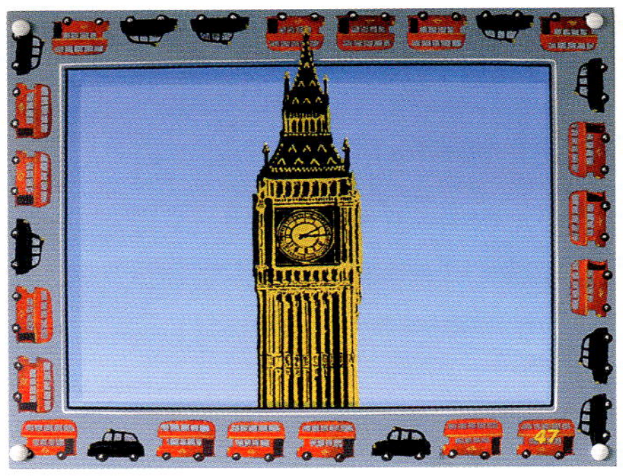

Wyatt, Houghton b.1953/1954
Theo's Amazing Journey, London c.2001
acrylic & mixed media on board 44 x 56
PCF27.40

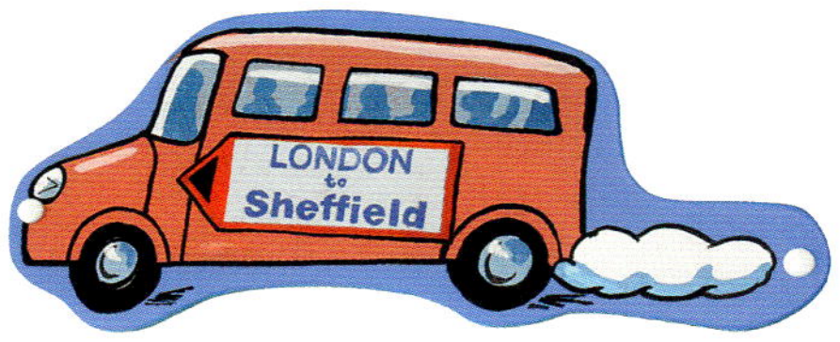

Wyatt, Houghton b.1953/1954
Theo's Amazing Journey, Theo Comes Home c.2001
acrylic & mixed media on board 18 x 48
PCF27.41

The Ken Hawley Collection Trust

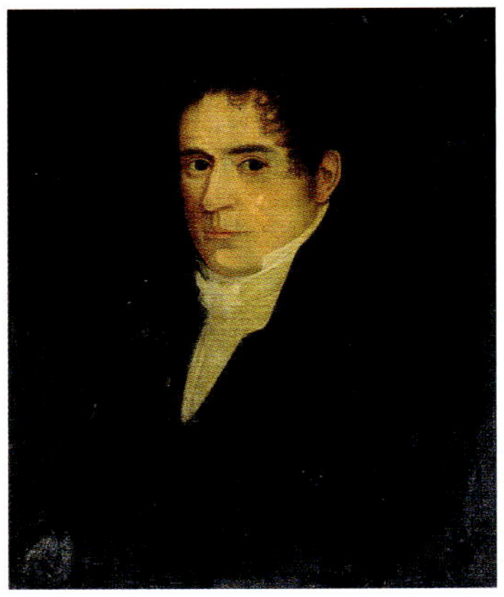

Kennedy, J.
Mr Turton c.1869
oil on canvas 59 x 49
PCF1

Traditional Heritage Museum, University of Sheffield

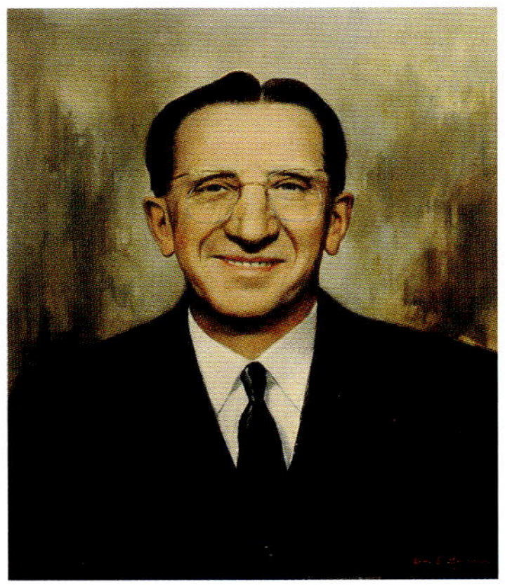

Brandon, Louis E.
Ernest Horton Senior (1895–1971), Proprietor of Horton Brothers and Austin and Dodson Ltd, Filemakers, Sheffield 1958
oil on board 72.5 x 63
PCF2

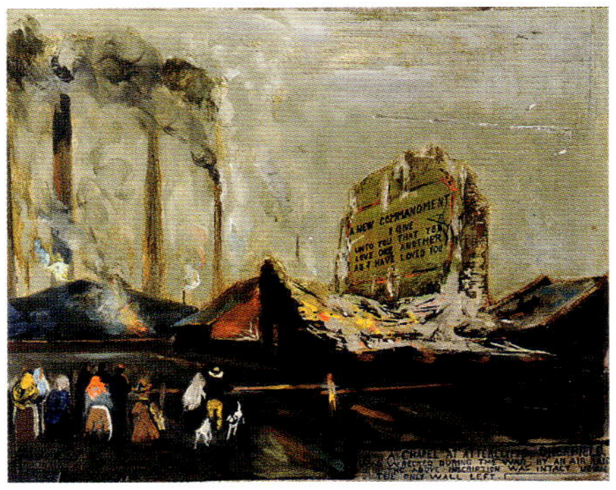

Keeling, William 1860–1930
A Memory Sketch: The Morning after the Zeppelin Raid on Attercliffe, Sheffield, 25 September 1916 1918
oil on board 39 x 46
PCF1

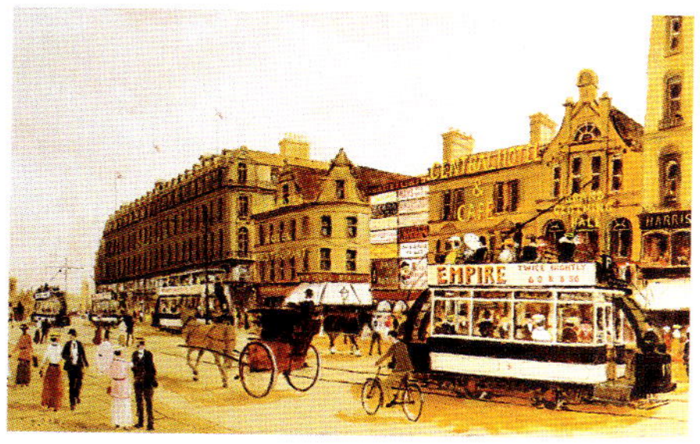

Little, Douglas Patrick active 1981–2007
High Street, Sheffield, 1904 1984
acrylic on board 46 x 63
PCF3

University of Sheffield

As with many university collections, the pictures owned by the University of Sheffield represent not so much a collection as an accumulation which has occurred over the 104 years of its existence; works have come into the University's possession either through donations, commissions or by purchases.

Around a third of the pictures are portraits of people significant in the University's history; usually distinguished academics, benefactors and lay officers, these paintings tend to be the result of commissions. This part of the Collection really proved its worth in 2005 when the University published a substantial and richly illustrated history to mark its centenary. Rows of portraits of dead white males in academic robes might not sound very exciting, but an investigation of their particular histories reveals some interesting stories. The portrait of Sir Joseph Jonas by an unknown artist is a case in point.

A millionaire steel manufacturer, Jonas was a Lord Mayor, and a generous donor of time and money to the University. However, German by birth, he was stripped of his title in 1918 because of allegations of passing beneficial business information to the Germans. In the same hall hangs a portrait by Mary Lemon Waller of *Henry Clifton Sorby (1826–1908)*, one of the last of the Victorian 'gentleman scientists'. Nationally distinguished as a geologist, metallurgist and zoologist, Sorby was the owner of a large yacht with a fitted laboratory, and was an enthusiastic watercolourist in his spare time.

The Collection has benefited greatly from donations by former students and other benefactors with connections to the University. The Department of Music houses *The Violinist* by Sir William Rothenstein, given by Rachel Ward, Rothenstein's daughter, who married a well-known bookshop owner in the city. More recently, a descendant of Sir Frederick Thorpe Mappin, an important supporter of the University's early Technical School, dispatched an impressive portrait by an unknown artist of his ancestor to us from New Zealand. A former professor of Law and Pro-Chancellor gave an 1840s oil painting attributed to Edward Matthew Ward, *Dr Johnson and Sir Joshua Reynolds Taking Tea with Mrs Thrale*, accompanied by a rather beautiful cat. A notable on-going source of pictures is the University's Fine Art Society, whose members not only organise exhibitions but also purchase pictures from them, which are then donated to the University for display.

The essential recording of people significant in the University's history and development still goes on but in recent years there has been an increased emphasis on the acquisition of art to enhance the work and leisure areas of students, staff and visitors. In other words, there has been a distinct decision to collect as well as merely to accumulate. This has been significantly stimulated by the striking new buildings which have appeared recently on campus, and demand strong contemporary works to complement their design.

Anthea Stephenson, Heritage Officer

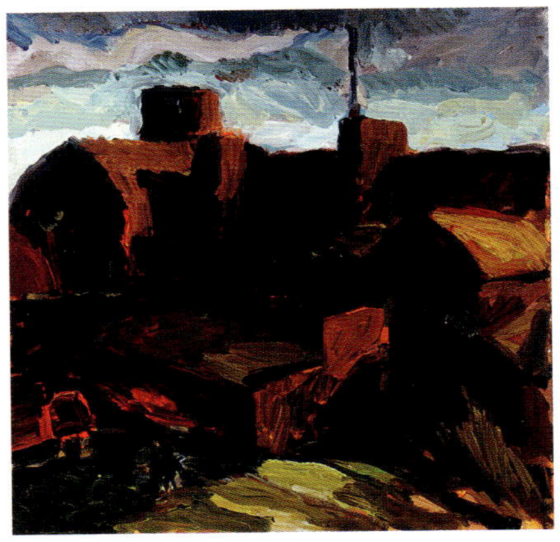

Attree, Jake b.1950
Robert Mart Mill 1 1990
oil on canvas 58 x 58
1083

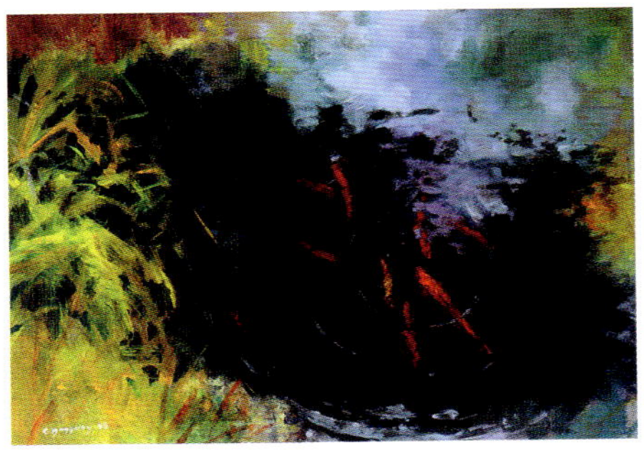

Baggaley, Kristan Paul b.1958
Deep Water 1998
acrylic on canvas 50 x 69
1069

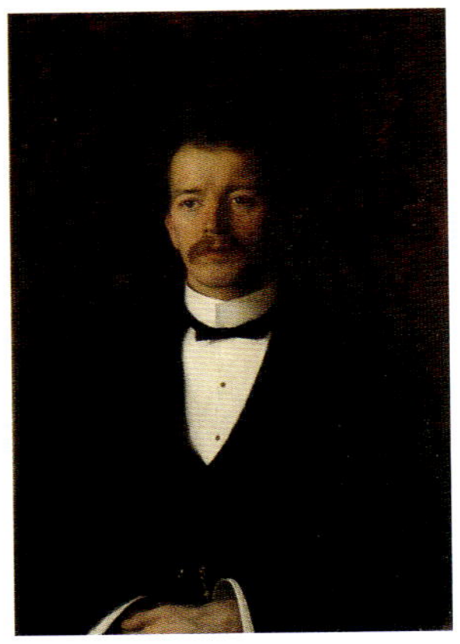

Barber, Reginald 1851–1928
Walter Butterworth (1862–1935) 1891
oil on canvas 75 x 50
380

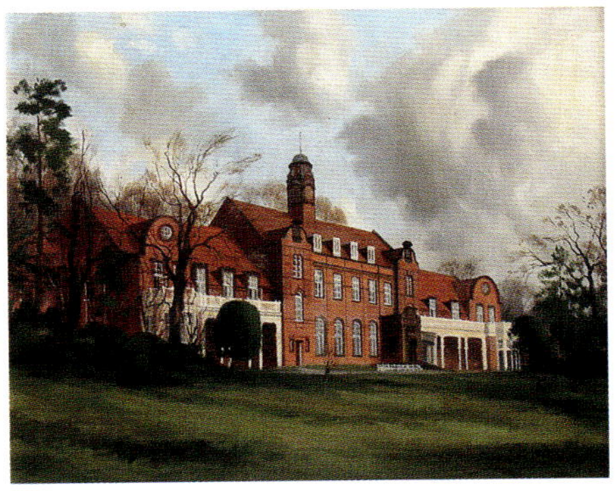

Billin, Edward Stanley 1911–1994
Whiteley Wood Clinic, Sheffield
oil on canvas 40 x 50 (E)
780

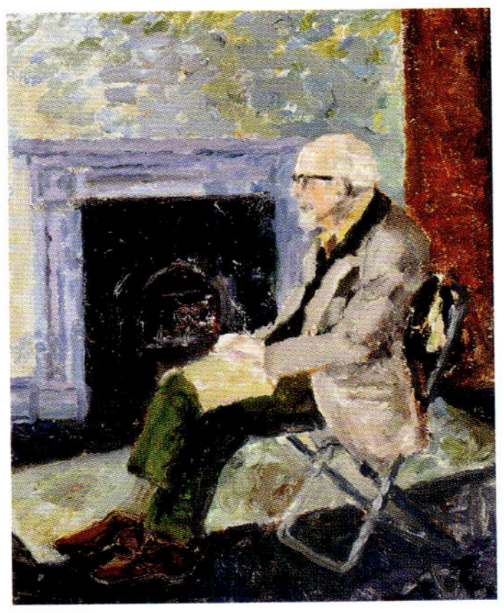

Blake, Valerie
Professor W. F. Mainland 1980
oil on board 31.5 x 26
1165

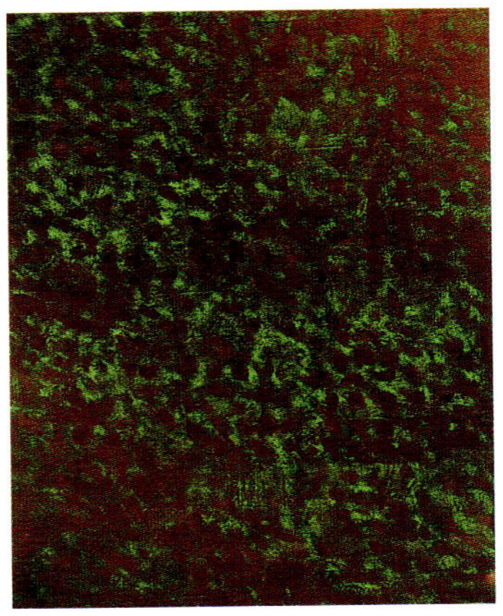

Brighton, Bob b.1936
13.9.94 1994
acrylic on canvas 152 x 122
1435

Brighton, Bob b.1936
15.9.94 1994
acrylic on canvas 152 x 122
1437

Brighton, Bob b.1936
21.9.94 1994
acrylic on canvas 152 x 122
1436

Brighton, Bob b.1936
12.10.94 1994
acrylic on canvas 152 x 122
1434

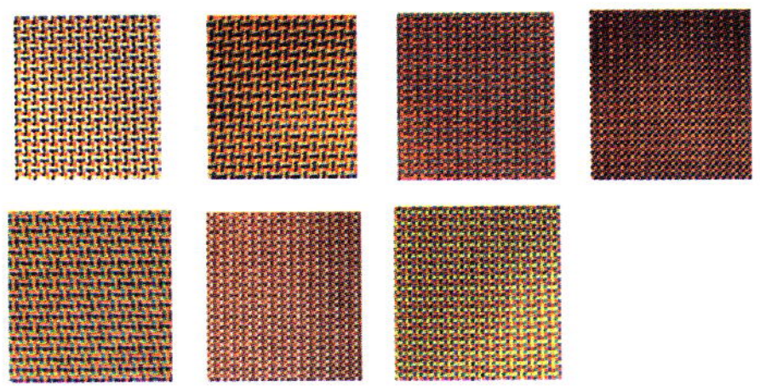

Brighton, Bob b.1936
Chequerboards (polyptych)
acrylic on canvas 134 x 244 (E)
1229

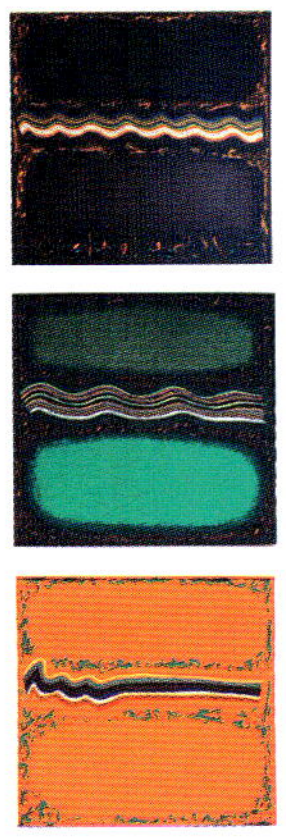

Brighton, Bob b.1936
Large Squares One (polyptych)
acrylic on canvas 555 x 185
1227

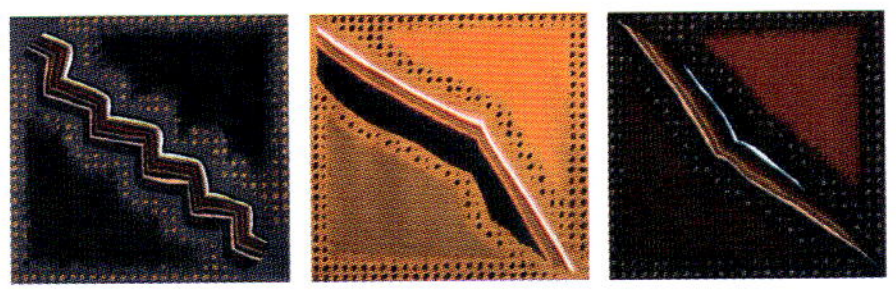

Brighton, Bob b.1936
Large Squares Two (polyptych)
acrylic on canvas 185 x 555 (E)
1228

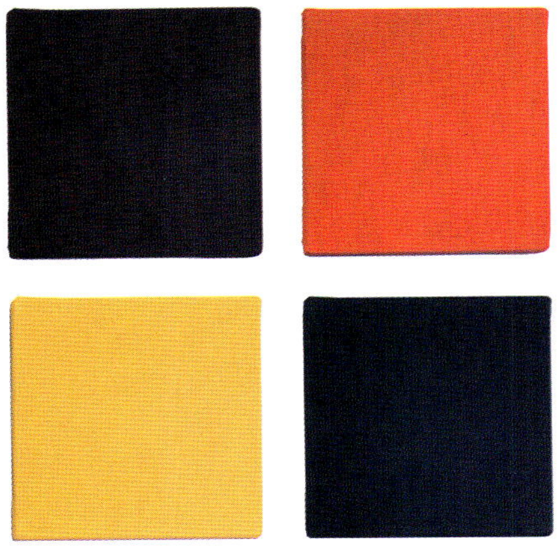

Brighton, Bob b.1936
Squares (polyptych)
acrylic on canvas 60 x 60 (E)
1225

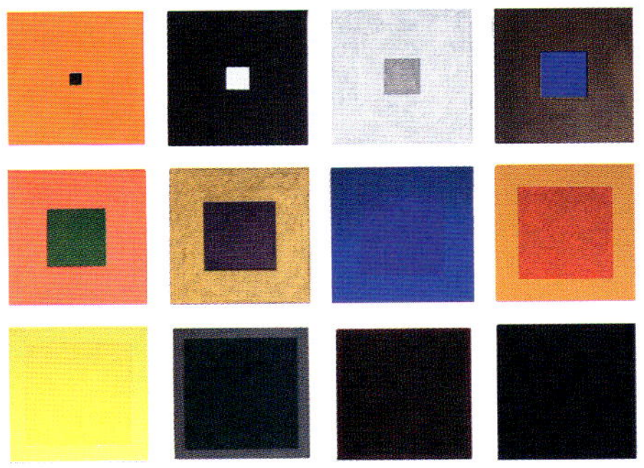

Brighton, Bob b.1936
Squares in Squares (polyptych)
acrylic on canvas 90 x 120 (E)
1226

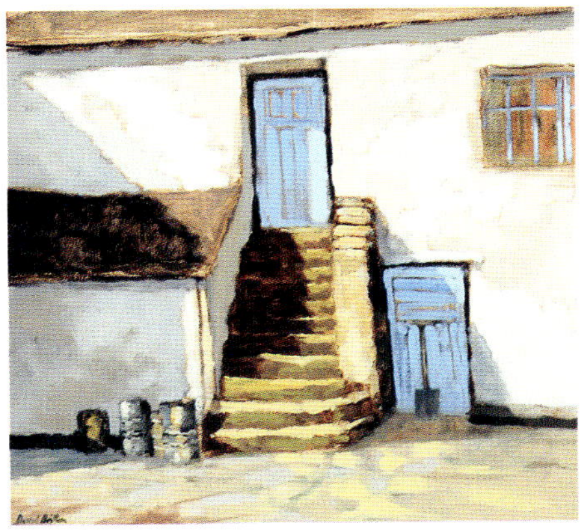

Britton, David Swinstead b.1937
Burnmoor Inn, Cumbria 1980
oil on canvas 46 x 49
1113

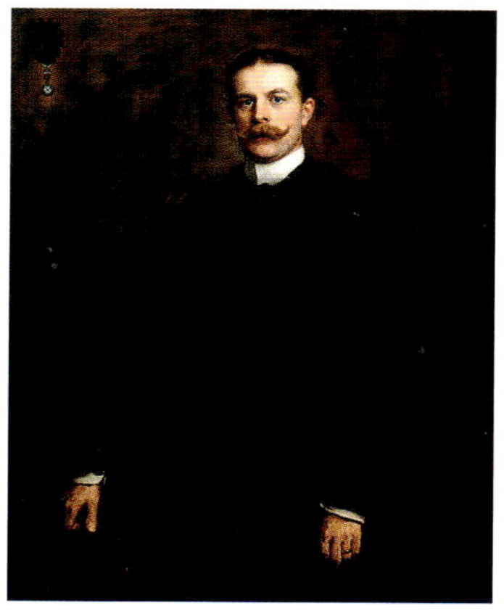

Carter, William 1863–1939
Robert Offley Ashburton Crewe-Milnes (1858–1945), 2nd Lord Haughton, Marquess of Crewe 1893
oil on canvas 125 x 100
389

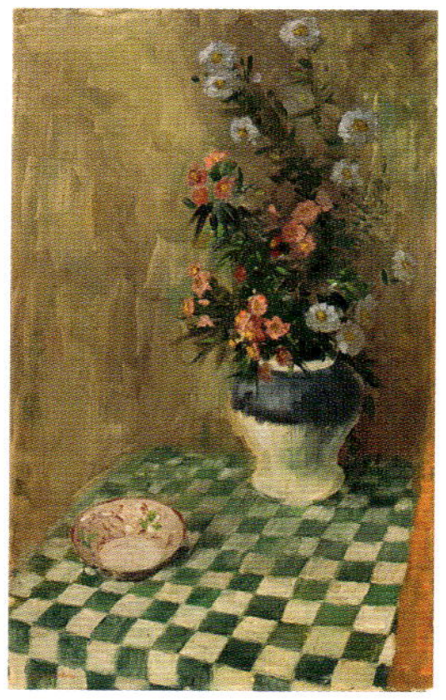

Constantine, Harry Francis b.1919
The Check Cloth
oil on canvas 55 x 33
1219

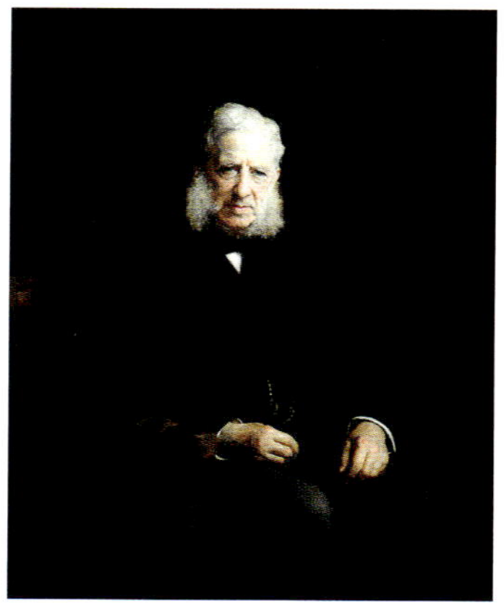

Cope, Arthur Stockdale 1857–1940
Sir Henry Stephenson (1826–1904) c.1899
oil on canvas 120 x 100
436

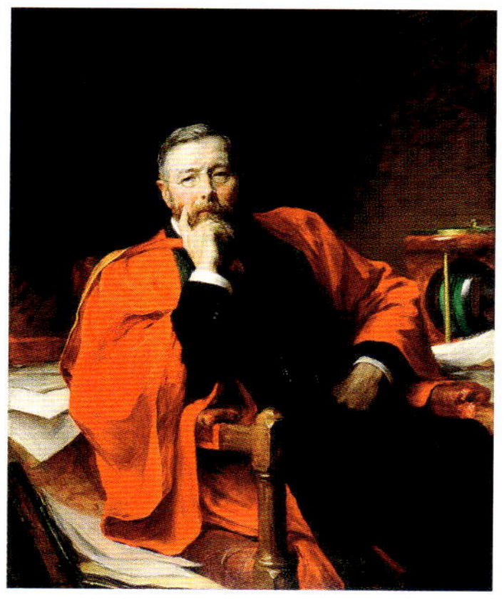

Cope, Arthur Stockdale 1857–1940
Professor William M. Hicks (1850–1934) 1909
oil on canvas 134 x 100 (E)
405

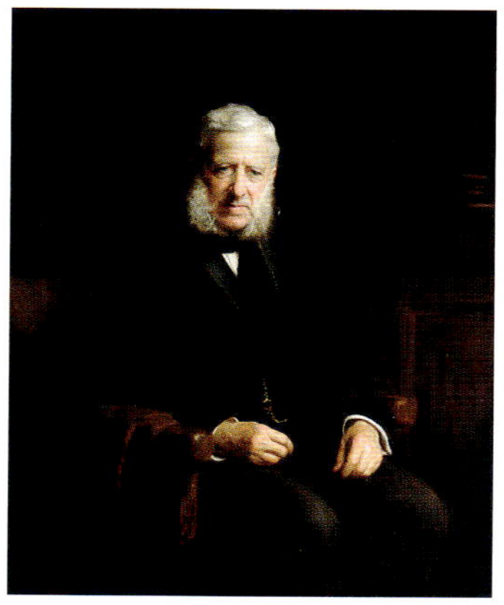

Cope, Arthur Stockdale 1857–1940
Sir Henry Stephenson (1826–1904)
oil on canvas 120 x 100
438

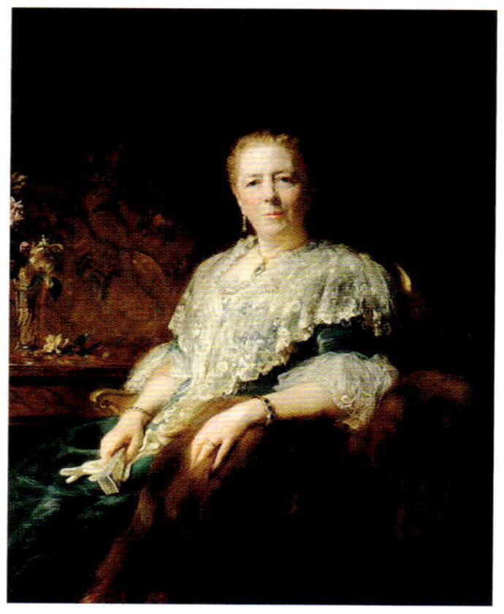

Cope, Arthur Stockdale 1857–1940
Lady Emma Stephenson
oil on canvas 120 x 100
439

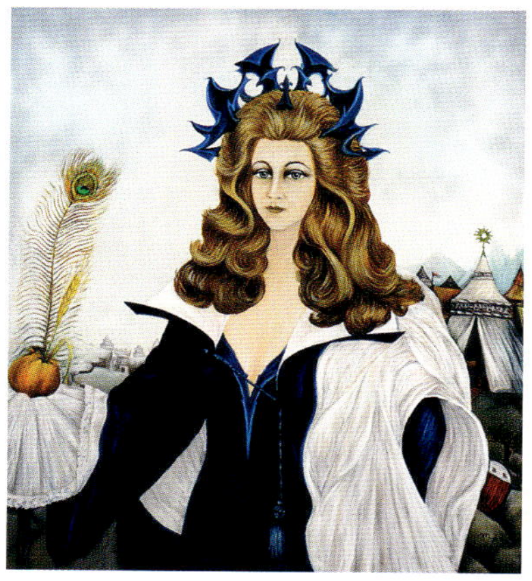

d'Aquavila, Walt
Nobel 1984
oil on canvas 100 x 90
459

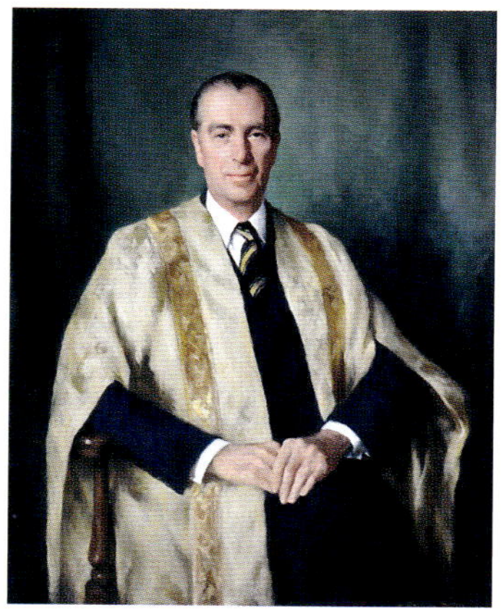

Dobson, Henry Raeburn 1901–1985
Sir Hugh Robson (1917–1977), Vice-Chancellor of the University of Sheffield (1966–1974) 1975
oil on canvas 129 x 102 (E)
432

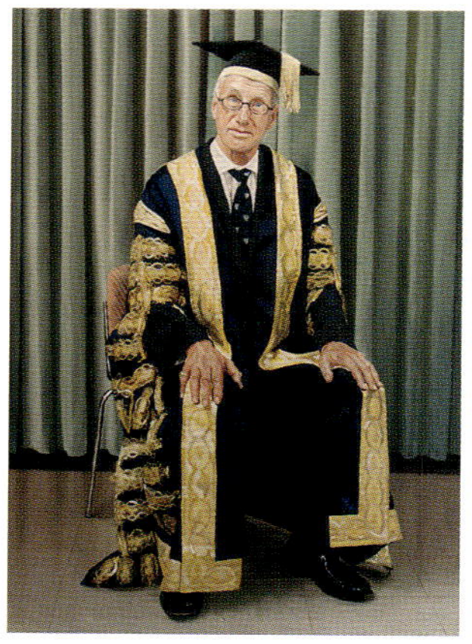

Edwards, Peter Douglas b.1955
Sir Peter Middleton (b.1934), Chancellor of the University of Sheffield (since 1999) 2009
oil on canvas 122 x 86
1424

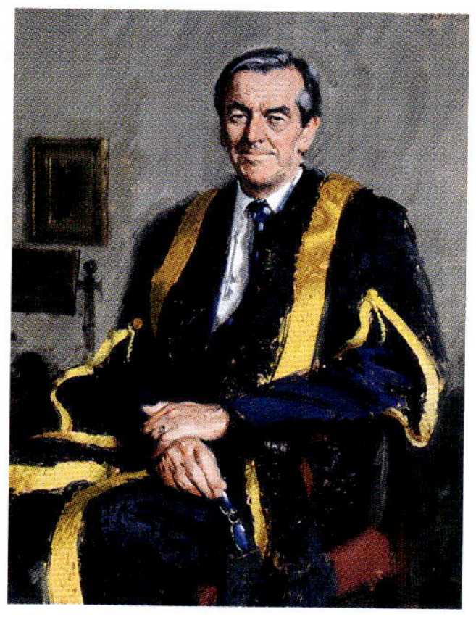

Festing, Andrew b.1941
Professor Robert Boucher (1940–2009), Vice-Chancellor of the University of Sheffield (2001–2007) 2007
oil on canvas 109 x 75 (E)
1184

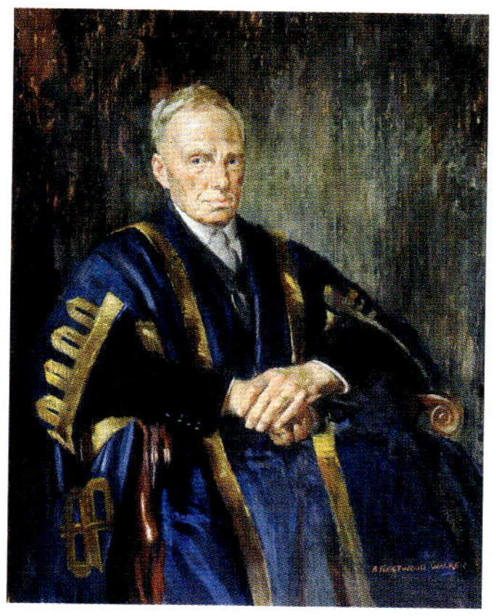

Fleetwood-Walker, Bernard 1893–1965
Dr Edward Bramley (1868–1969) 1950
oil on canvas 110 x 85
376

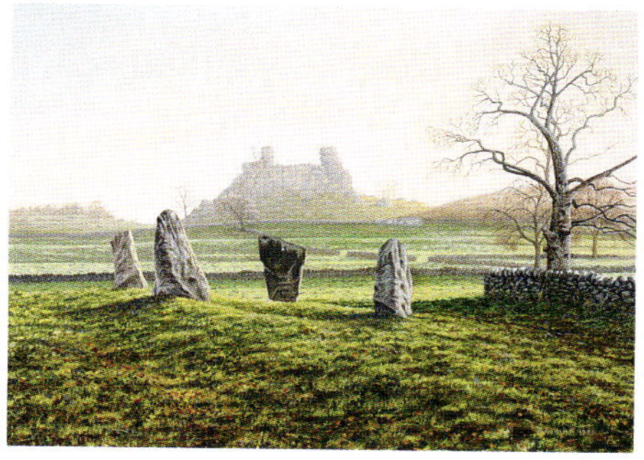

Gittins, John Steven b.1955
Robin Hood's Stride, Harthill Moor, Derbyshire 1981
oil on canvas 50 x 68
1217

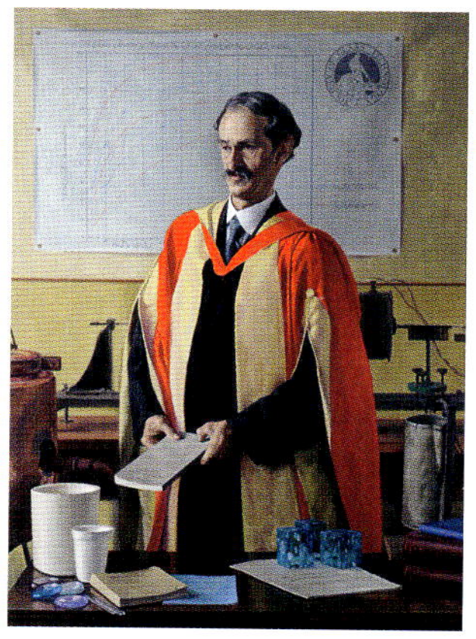

Halliday, Edward Irvine 1902–1984
Professor William Ernest Stephen Turner (1881–1963) 1938
oil on canvas 141 x 102
443

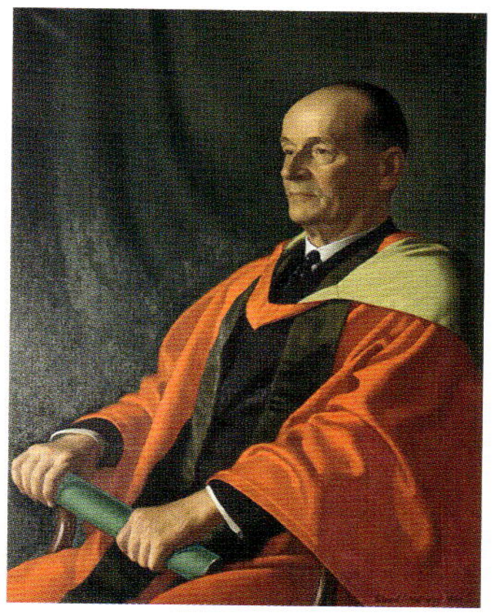

Halliday, Edward Irvine 1902–1984
Dr Stanley B. Bagley (1874–1957) 1939
oil on canvas 100 x 75
370

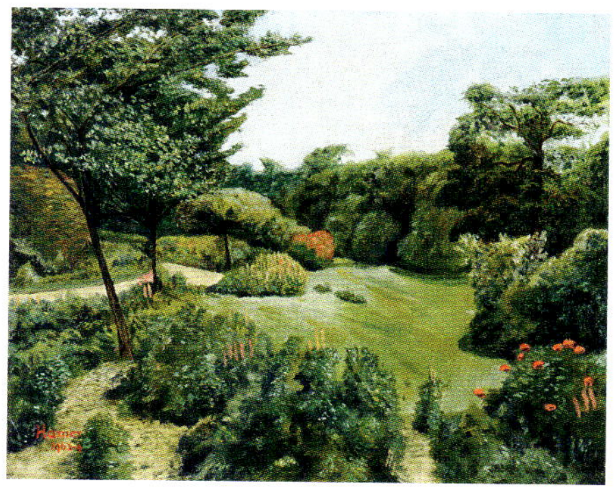

Hamer, Douglas 1897–1981
The Vice-Chancellor's Garden 1963–1964
oil on board 49 x 60
1163

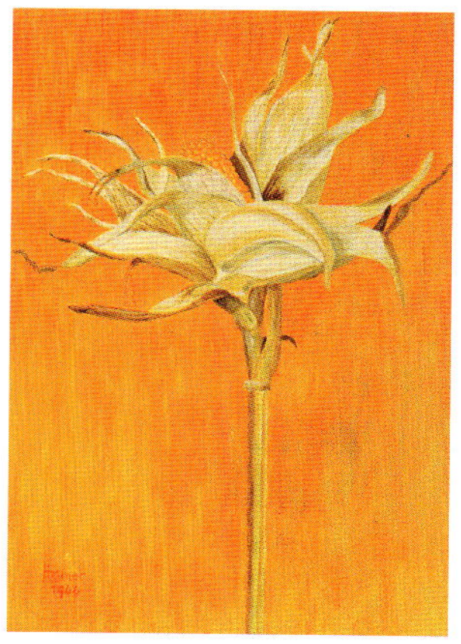

Hamer, Douglas 1897–1981
Corn 1966
oil on canvas 64 x 44
1127

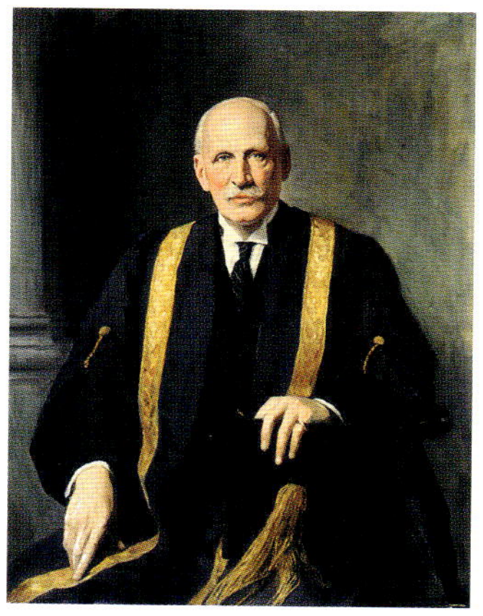

Harcourt, George 1868–1947
Sir Arthur Wallace Pickard-Cambridge (1873–1952), Vice-Chancellor of the University of Sheffield (1930–1938) 1938
oil on canvas 120 x 85 (E)
427

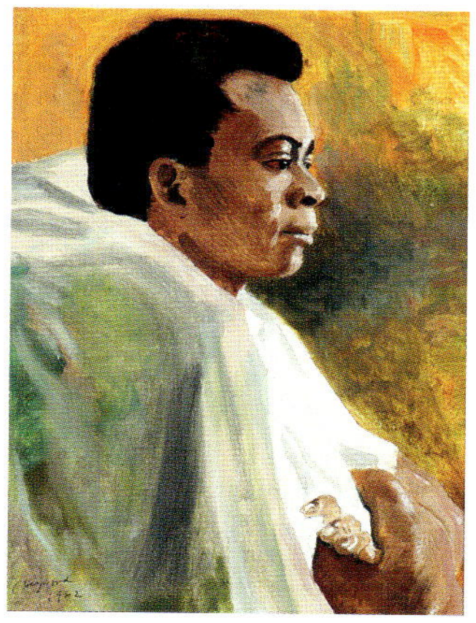

Heywood, Christopher b.1928
Portrait 1982
oil on canvas 45 x 34
1093

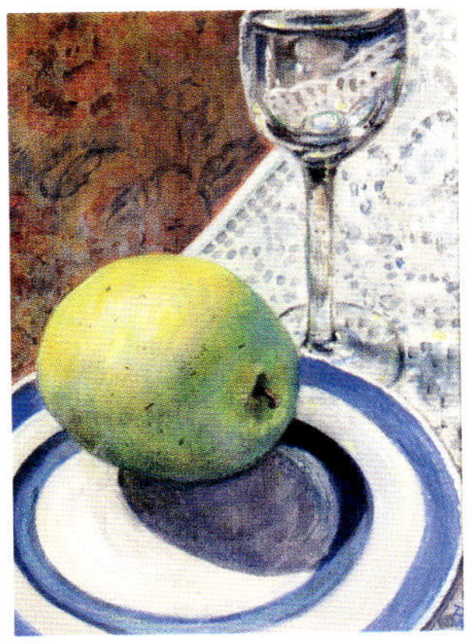

Holland, Diana
Still Life with a Golden Delicious 1996
oil on canvas 19 x 14
1224

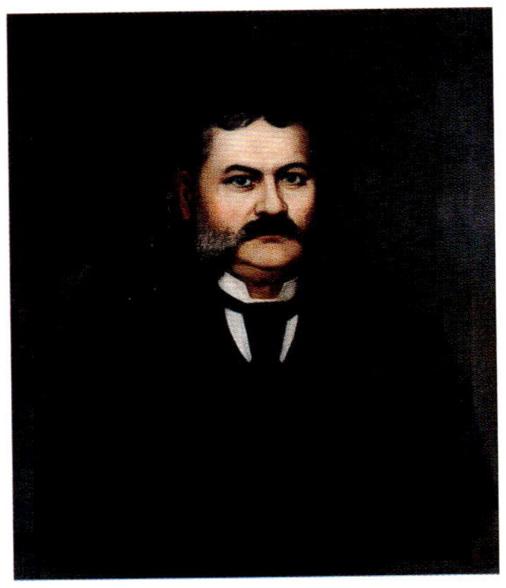

Hulett
Ezra Hounsfield Linley 1892
oil on canvas 75 x 62
415

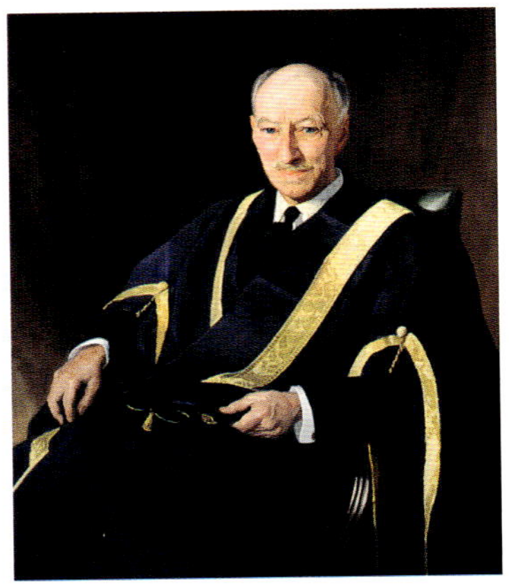

Hutchison, William Oliphant 1889–1970
Sir Irvine Masson (1887–1962), Vice-Chancellor of the University of Sheffield (1938–1953) 1952
oil on canvas 120 x 95 (E)
421

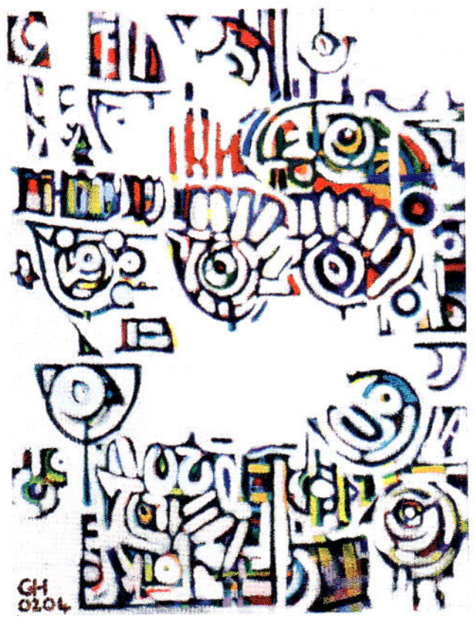

Hyde, Graham b.c.1979
Chicken Run 2004
acrylic on canvas 86 x 61
1086

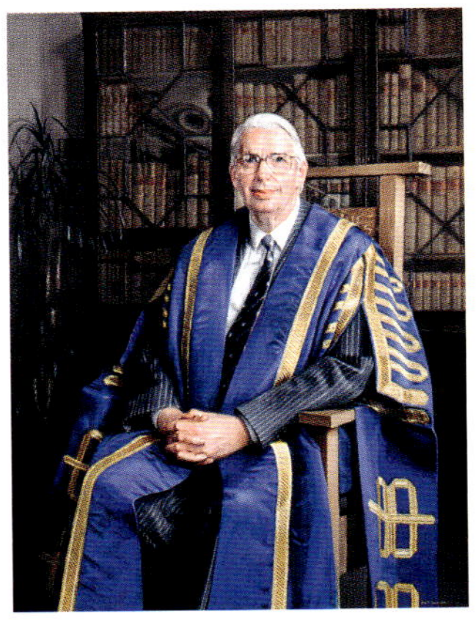

Jackson, Peter Kenneth Cowley 1930–2006
James E. Eardley 1994
oil on canvas 120 x 90
393

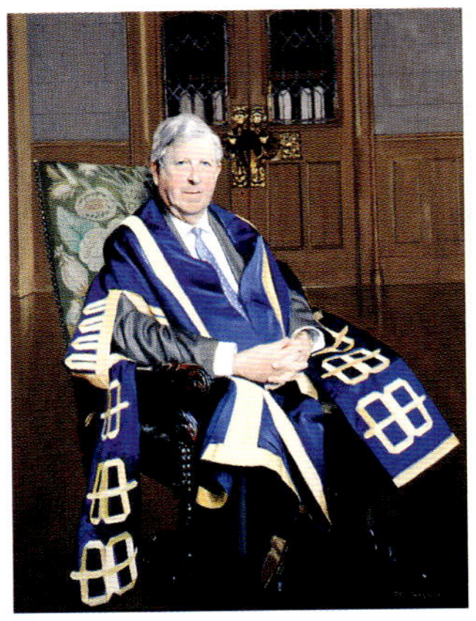

Jackson, Peter Kenneth Cowley 1930–2006
Peter Lee 2006
oil on canvas 125 x 94
1167

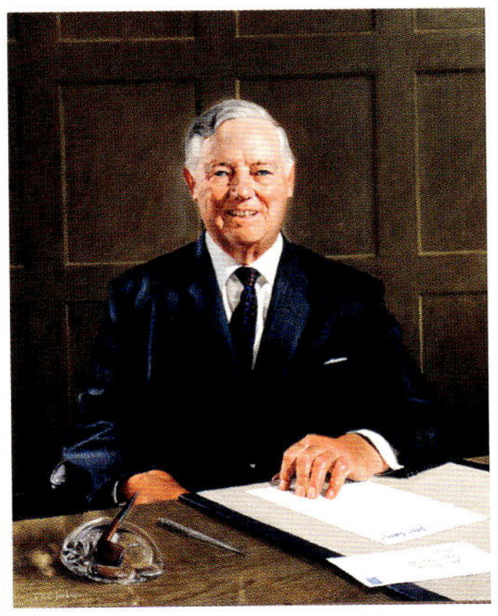

Jackson, Peter Kenneth Cowley 1930–2006
John Carr (1909–1992), MBE
acrylic on canvas 75 x 61
1286

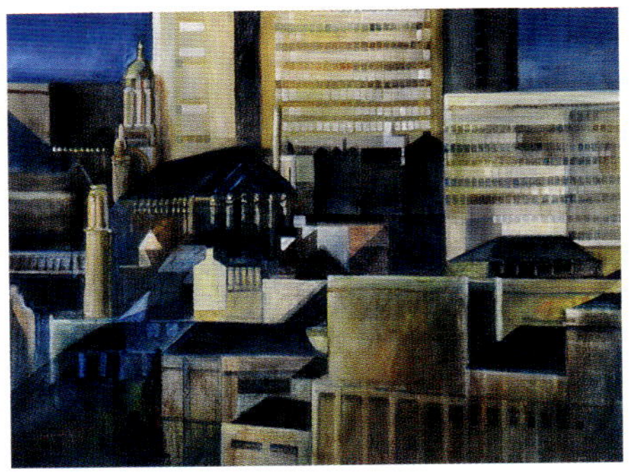

Kemp, Fiona Margaret b.1949
City View 1
acrylic on paper 34 x 45
1210

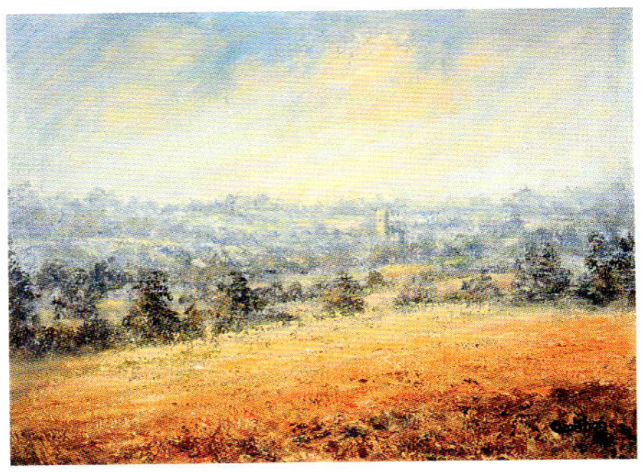

Kiddy, Gretchen 1910–2005
Dedham Vale, Essex 1981
oil on canvas 28 x 38
1087

Facing page: Rothenstein, Michael, 1908–1993, *Journey to the Promised Land* (detail), 1938, Museums Sheffield, (p. 184)

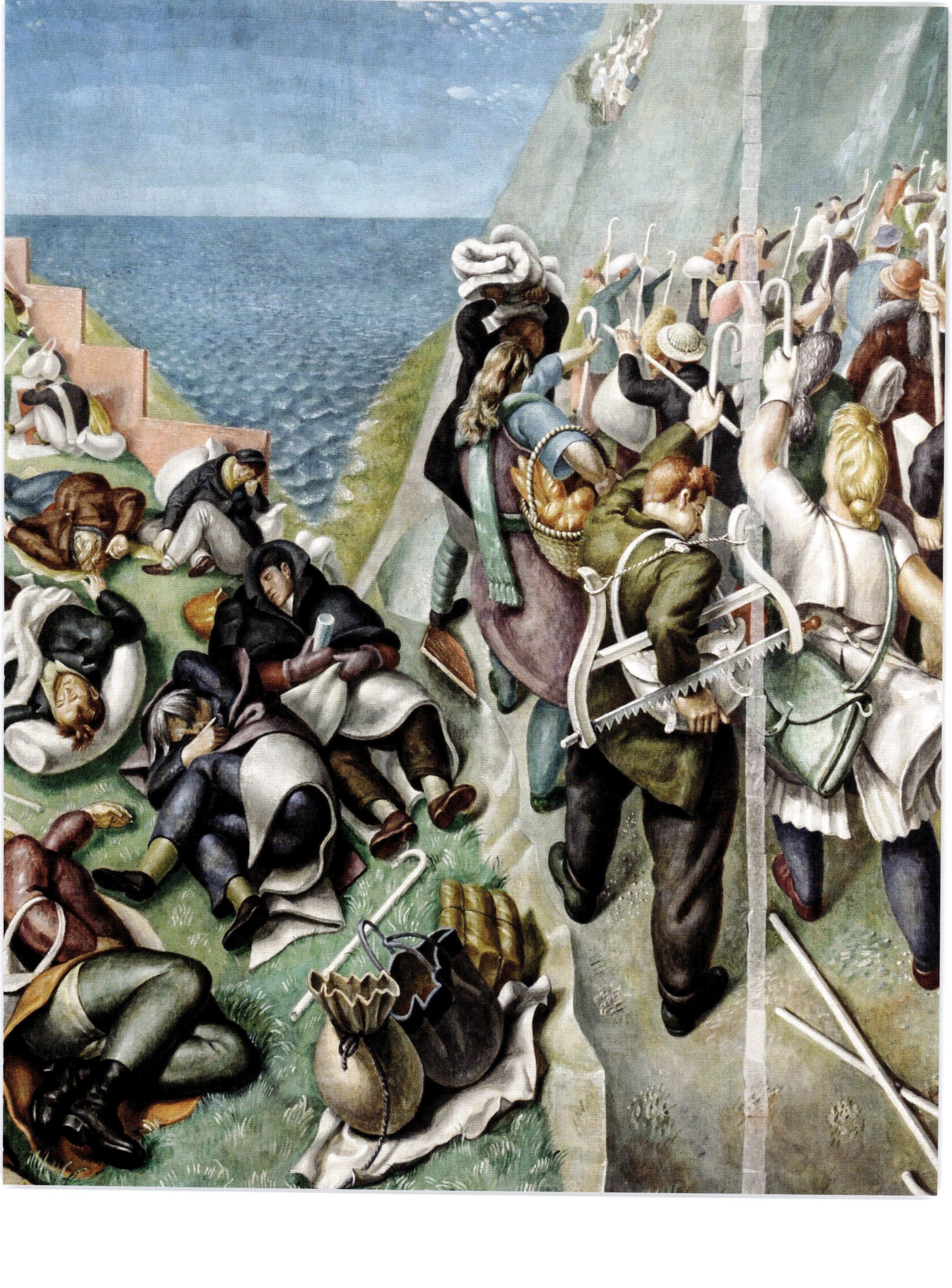

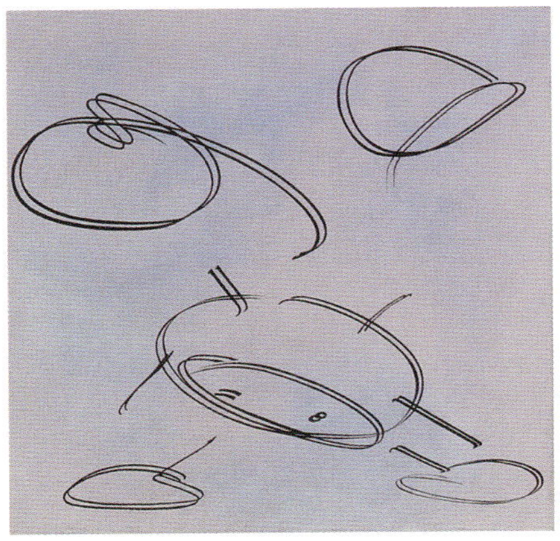

Lewis, Bethan Rhiannon b.1975
Doo-V 2003
oil on canvas 56 x 56
870

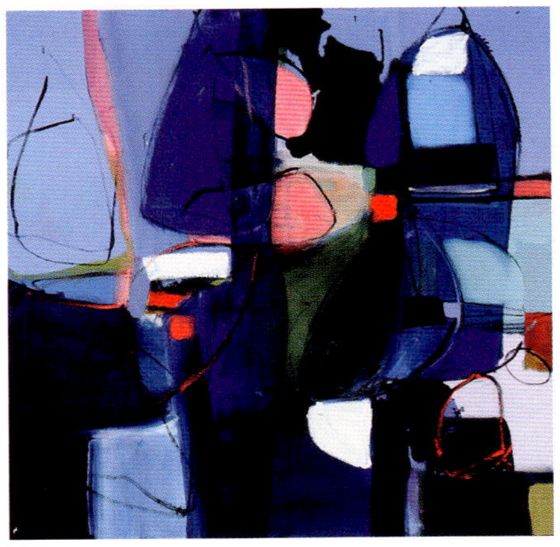

Little, Pauline b.1961
A New Beginning 2004
oil on canvas 77 x 77
1047

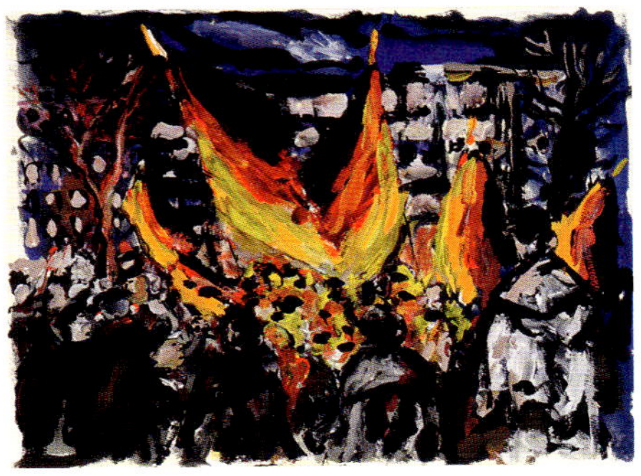

Lowe, Anthony b.1957
The German Choir 1991
acrylic on paper 38 x 50
1094

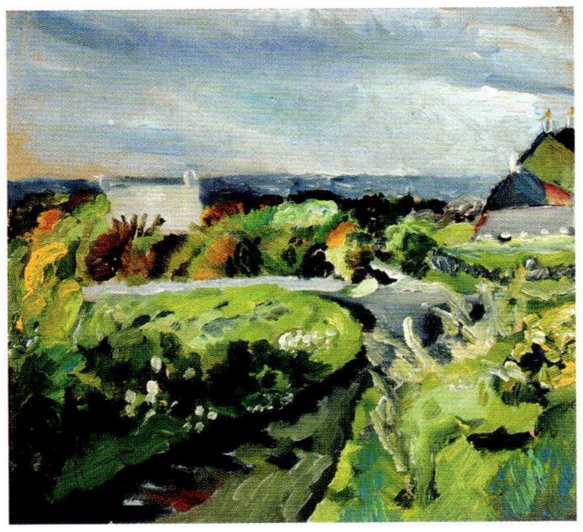

Lowe, Anthony b.1957
Brittany, France
oil on canvas 21 x 22
1088

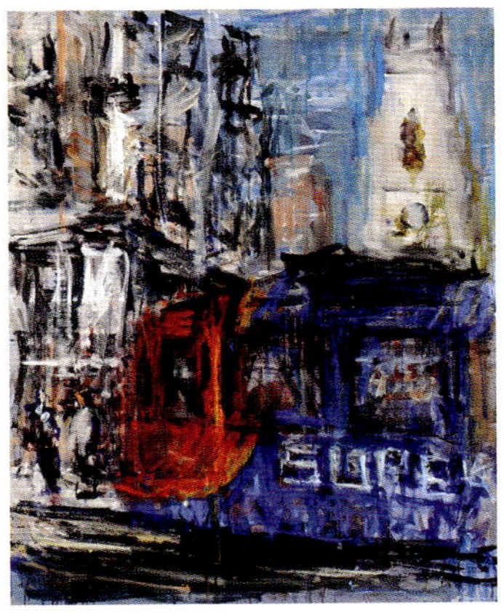

Machan, Robert b.1948
The Church, Regent Street, Sheffield 2008
oil on canvas 102 x 81
1255

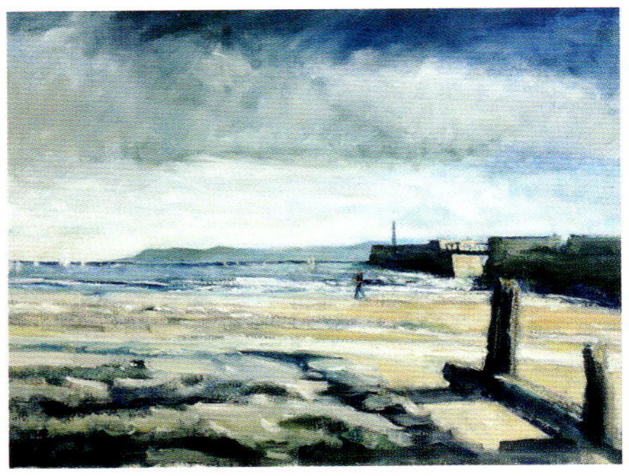

Mayne, Peter
Hartlepool, County Durham 1996
oil on board 29 x 39
1090

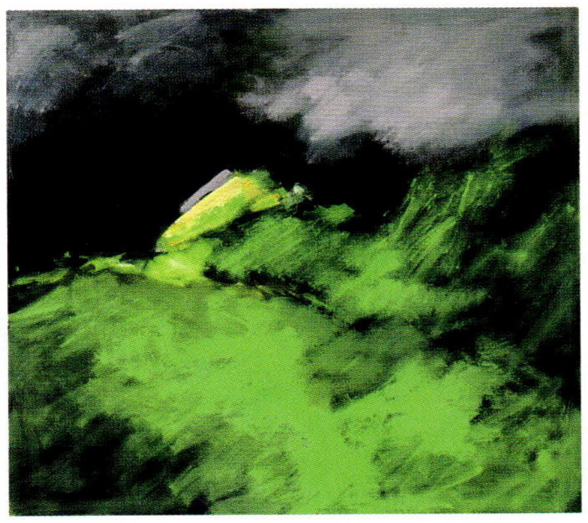

McCall, Susan b.1946
Gathering Storm 2004
oil on canvas 90 x 100
911

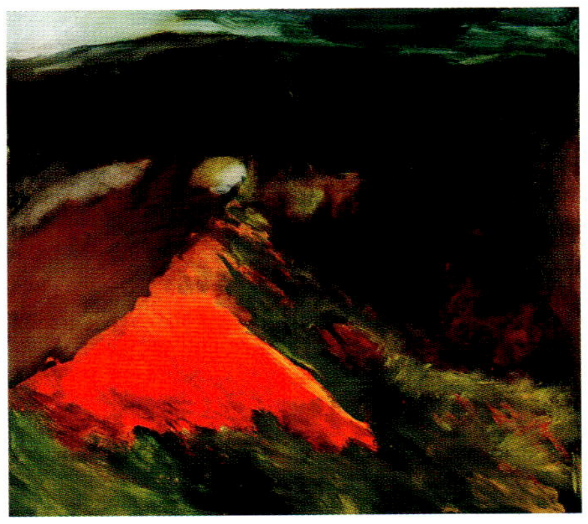

McCall, Susan b.1946
Red Grass 2004
oil on canvas 90 x 100
912

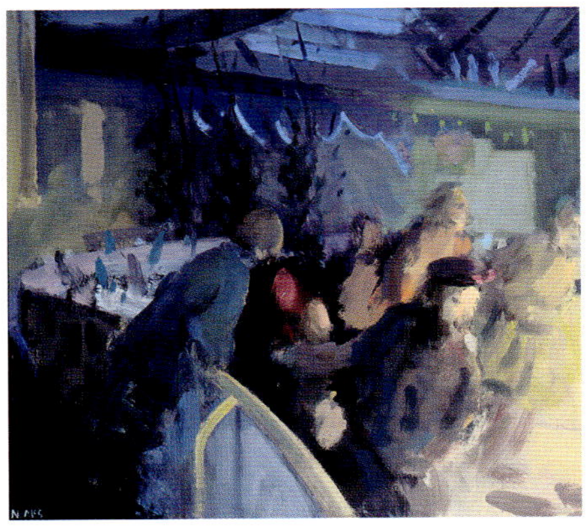

McGregor, Neil b.1963
Study for 'Skating Rink' 1994
oil on canvas 44 x 50
1068

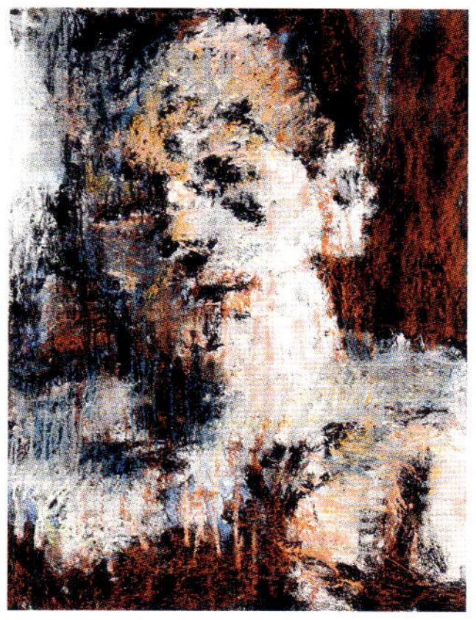

McPartland, Ian b.1963
Untitled 1993
oil/acrylic on paper 68 x 50
1135

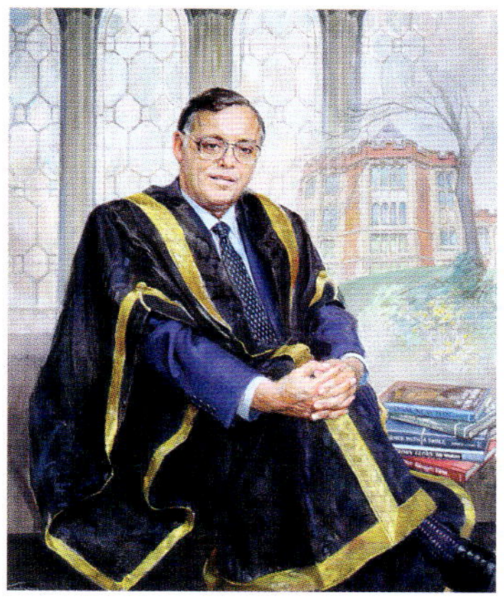

Mendoza, June b.1945
Sir Gareth Roberts (1940–2007) 1996
oil on canvas 133 x 100 (E)
431

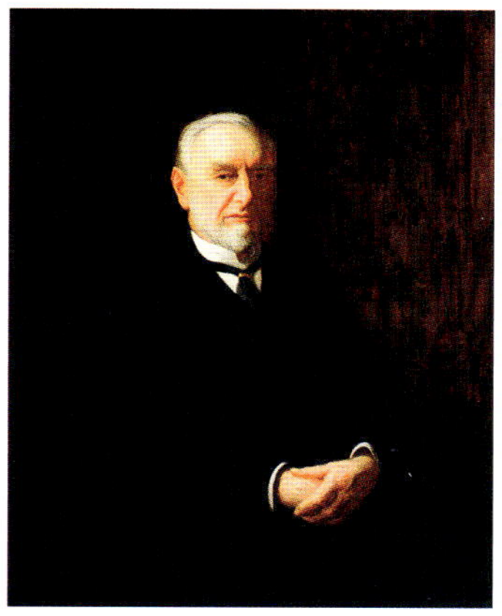

Moore, Ernest 1865–1940
Sir Frederick Thorpe Mappin (1821–1910)
1906
oil on canvas 115 x 87
418

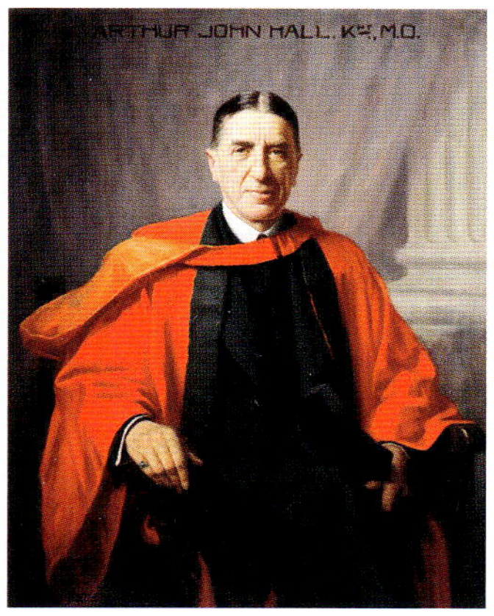

Moore, Ernest 1865–1940
Sir Arthur Hall (1866–1951), KT, MD 1936
oil on canvas 124 x 85 (E)
403

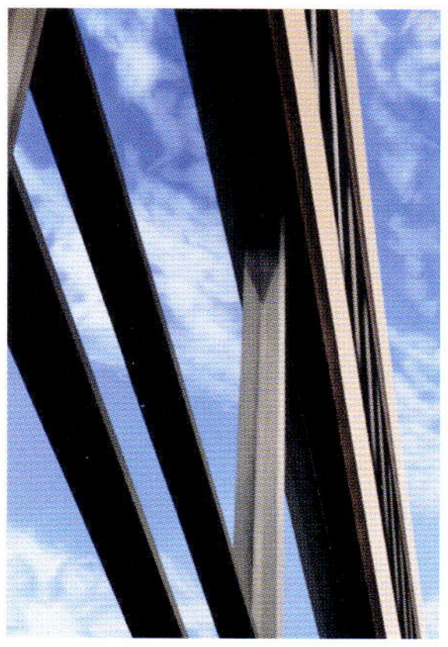

Neiland, Brendan b.1941
Rerum cognoscere causas 2002
acrylic on canvas 180 x 120 (E)
785

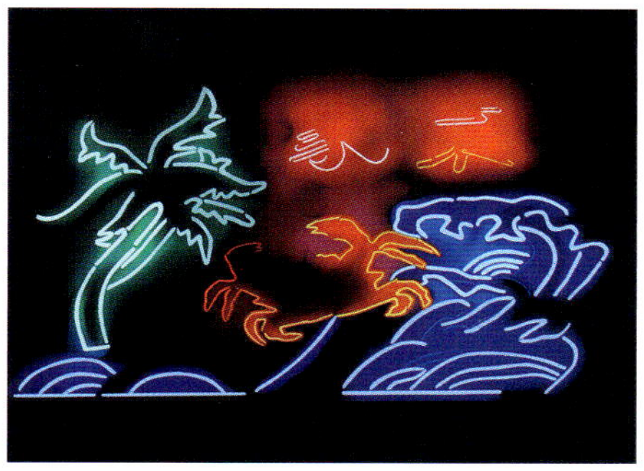

Neiland, Brendan b.1941
Crab 2007
acrylic on canvas 91.5 x 122
1282

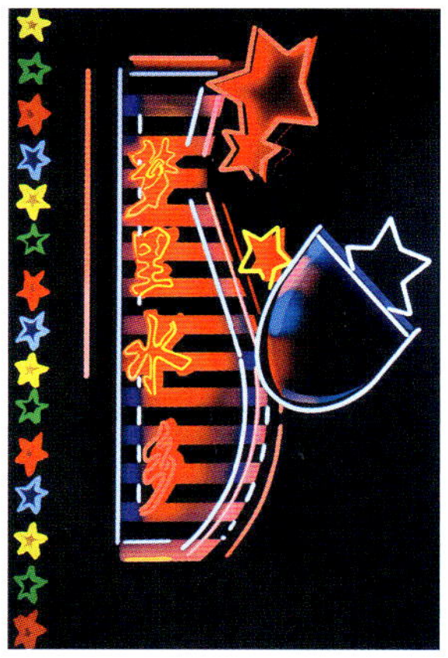

Neiland, Brendan b.1941
Effervescence 2007
acrylic on canvas 183 x 122
1438

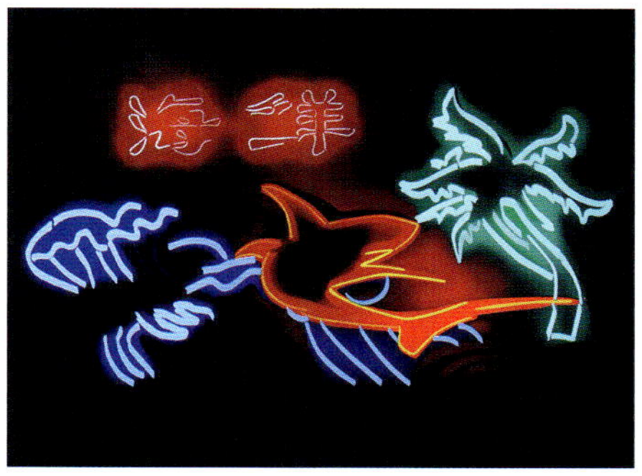

Neiland, Brendan b.1941
Shark 2007
acrylic on canvas 91.5 x 122
1283

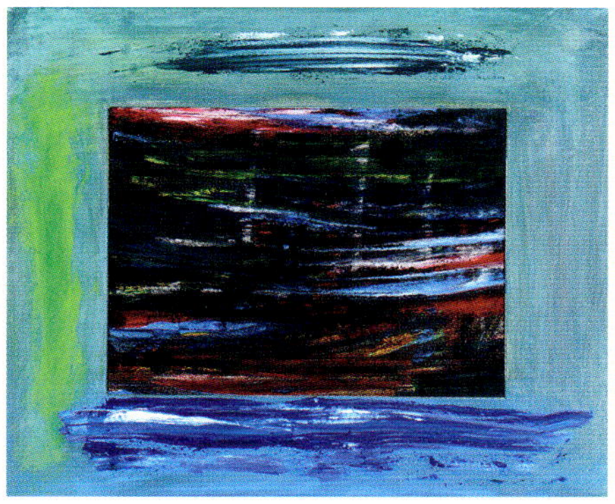

Ociepko, Mark b.1945
Tranquillo 2003
acrylic on board 47.5 x 50.8
1130

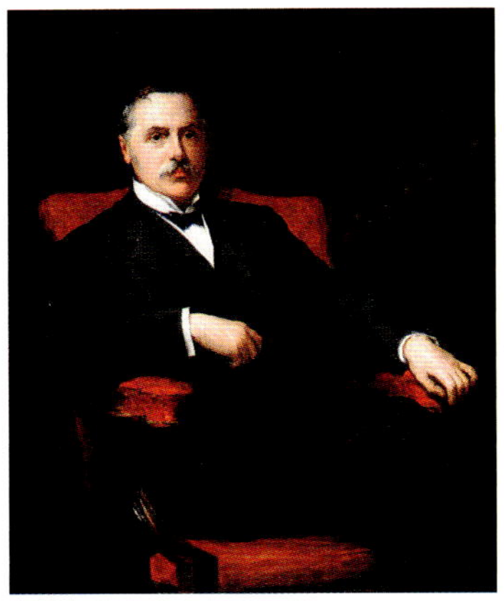

Ouless, Walter William 1848–1933
Sir George Franklin (d.1916) 1909
oil on canvas 138 x 101 (E)
397

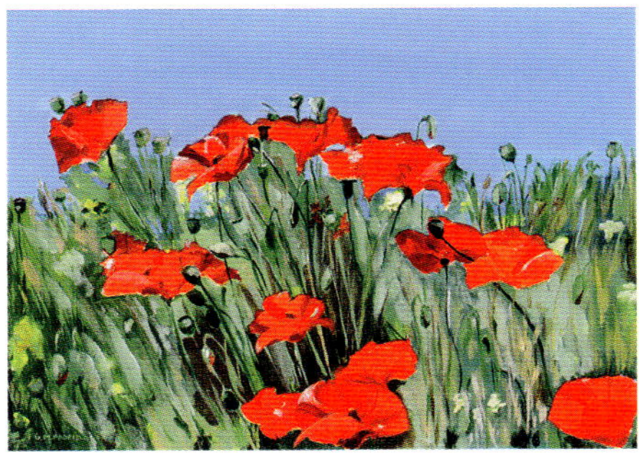

Padfield, Gillian Margaret 1939–2009
Poppy Field
acrylic on board 29 x 39
1308

Peacock, Brian 1935–2004
Beach Hut
oil on canvas 39 x 37
1098

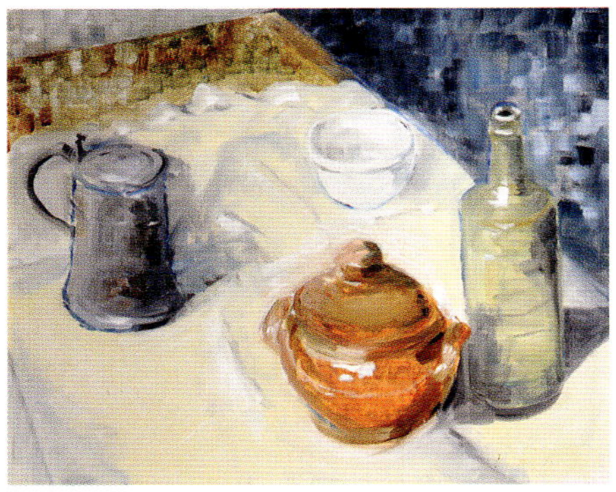

Pemberton, John active 1948
Still Life
oil on canvas 44 x 54
1112

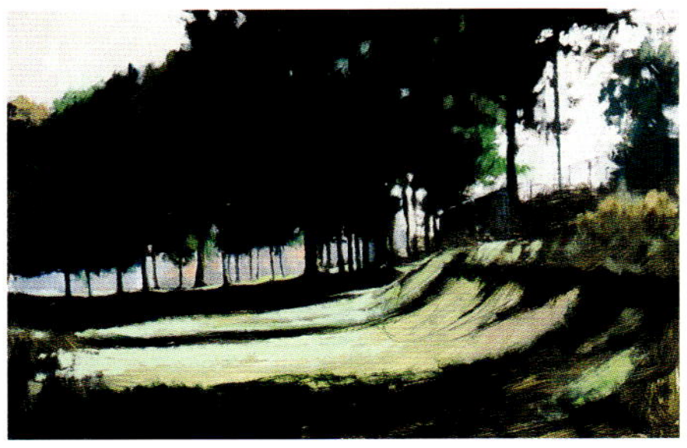

Reah, Ken
Parkscape with Railings 1989
oil on board 50 x 76
1221

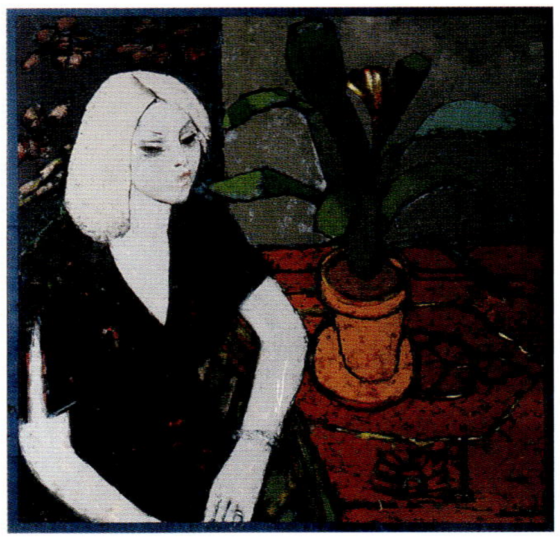

Röder, Endre Zoltan Eugene b.1933
Carole and Yucca 1989
oil on canvas 86 x 86
1058

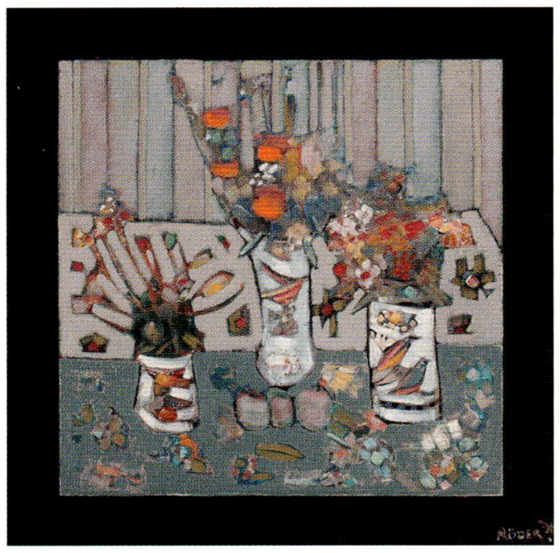

Röder, Endre Zoltan Eugene b.1933
Three Bouquets 1997
oil on canvas 90 x 90
1151

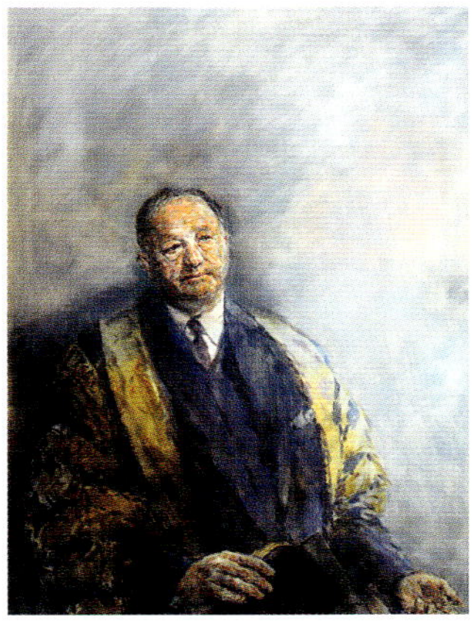

Rose, Martin H. b.1946
The Right Honourable Richard Austin Butler (1902–1982), Baron Butler of Saffron Walden, Chancellor of the University (…) 1977
oil on canvas 121 x 90
379

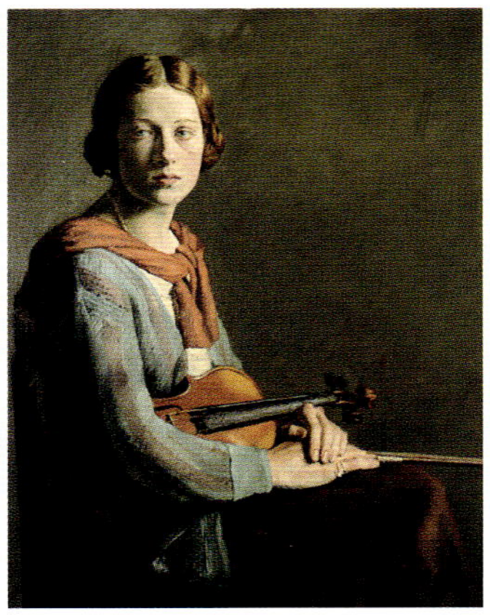

Rothenstein, William 1872–1945
The Violinist
oil on canvas 83 x 65
447

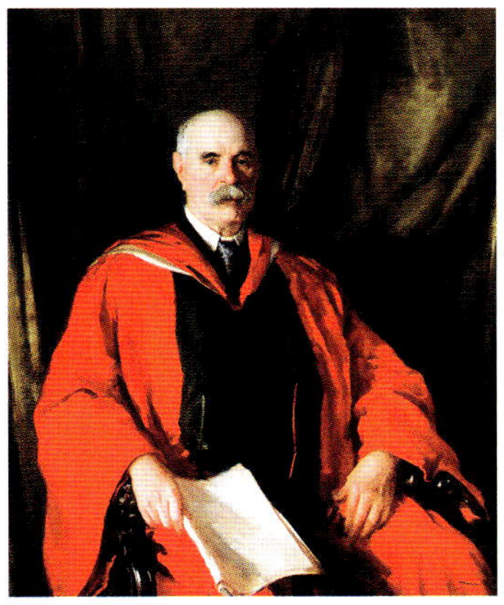

Russell, Walter Westley 1867–1949
Alderman Robert Styring, Lord Mayor of Sheffield (1906) 1926
oil on canvas 130 x 100 (E)
440

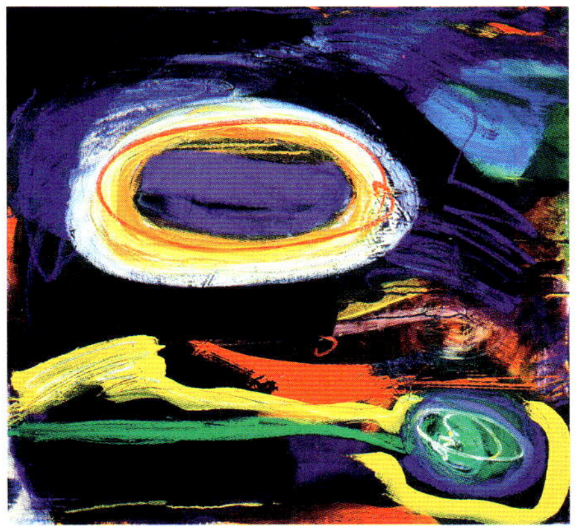

Sanderson, Helen
Untitled 1995
oil on canvas 88 x 92
1117

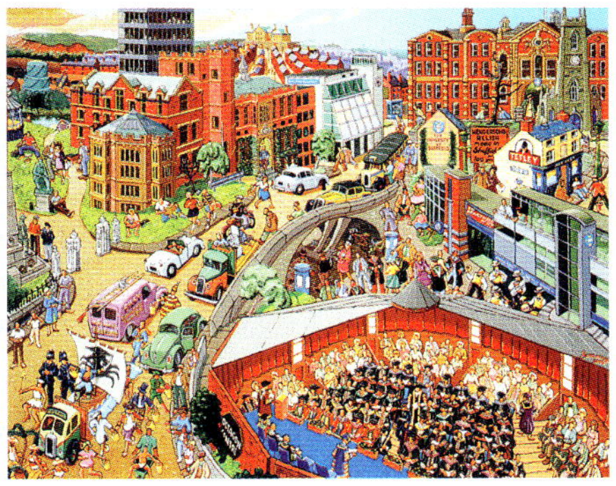

Scarborough, Joe b.1938
Our University 2004
oil on canvas 102 x 127
894

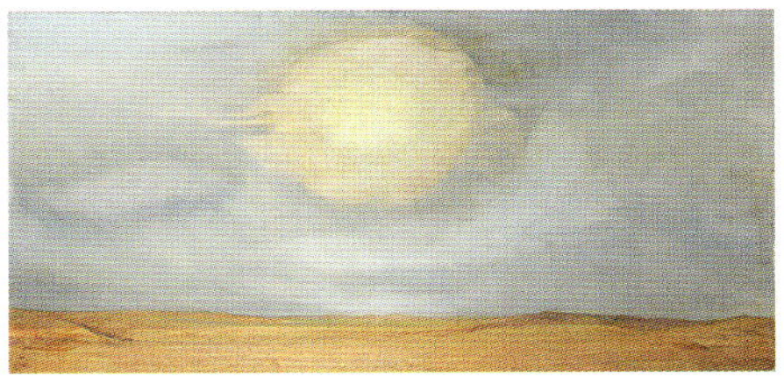

Shackleton, Judith
Desert Sun
oil on canvas 46 x 91
1119

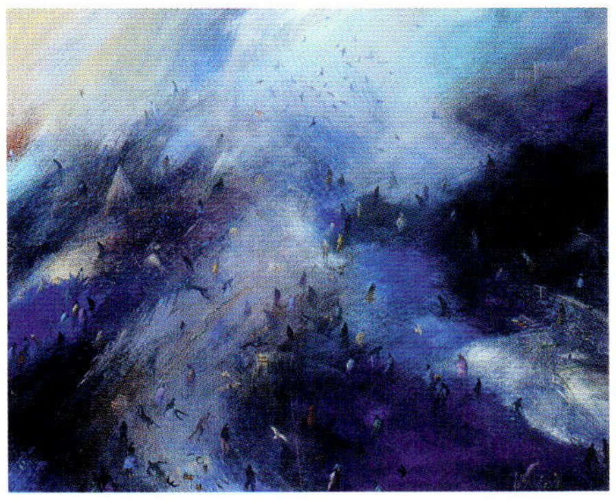

Shaw, David Carson b.1942
Perduta 1995
oil on canvas 24 x 29
1097

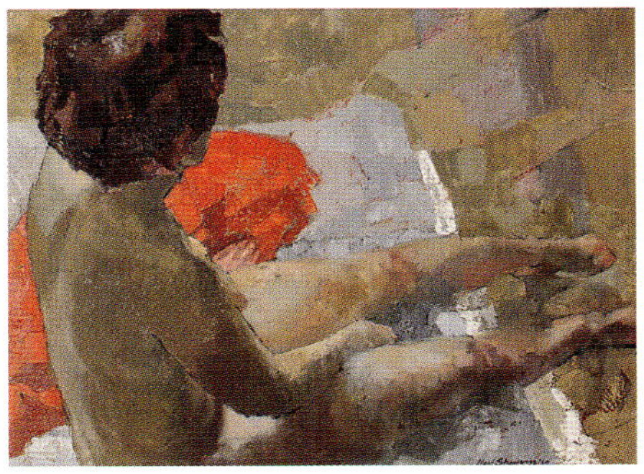

Shawcross, Neil b.1940
Nude 1960
oil on board 60 x 79
1158

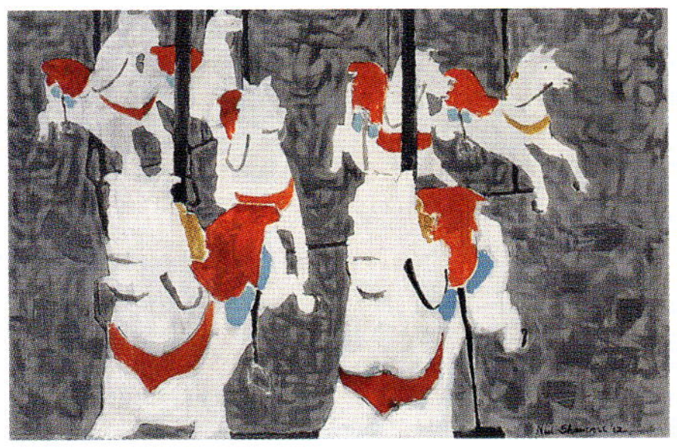

Shawcross, Neil b.1940
Fairground Horses 1962
acrylic on canvas 60 x 91
1161

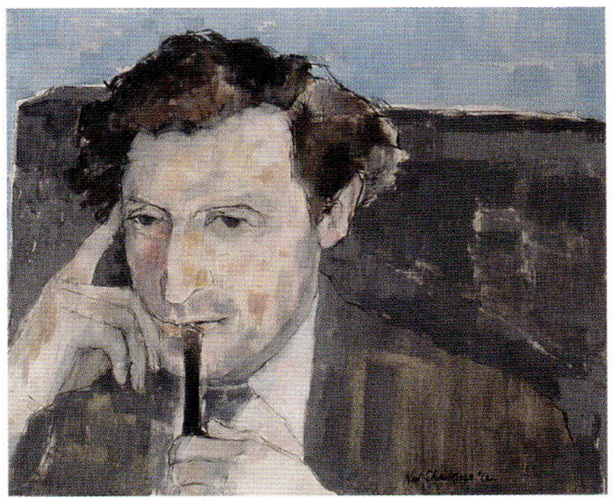

Shawcross, Neil b.1940
Howard Warrender (d.1985) 1962
acrylic on canvas 49 x 60
1160

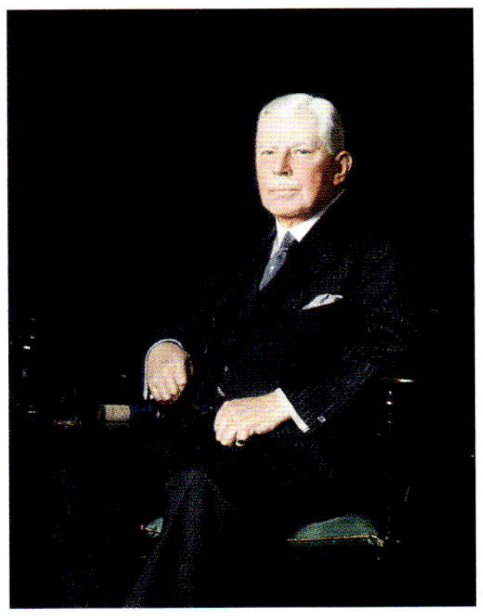

Somerville, Howard 1873–1952
Sir Henry Kenyon Stephenson (1865–1947), Treasurer of the University of Sheffield
oil on canvas 120 x 86 (E)
859

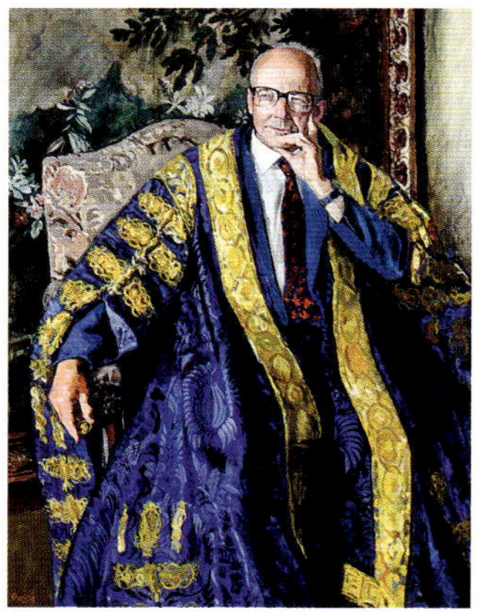

Stubley, Trevor 1932–2010
Lord Dainton of Hallam Moors (1914–1997) 1984
oil on canvas 120 x 90
391

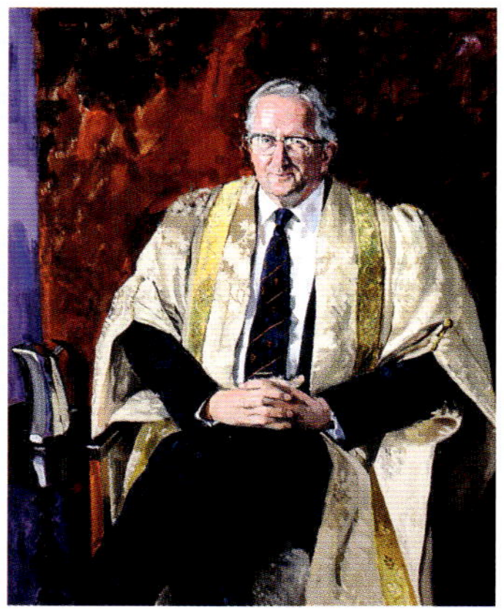

Stubley, Trevor 1932–2010
Professor Geoffrey Sims (b.1926), Vice-Chancellor of the University of Sheffield (1974–1991) 1985
oil on canvas 132 x 103 (E)
433

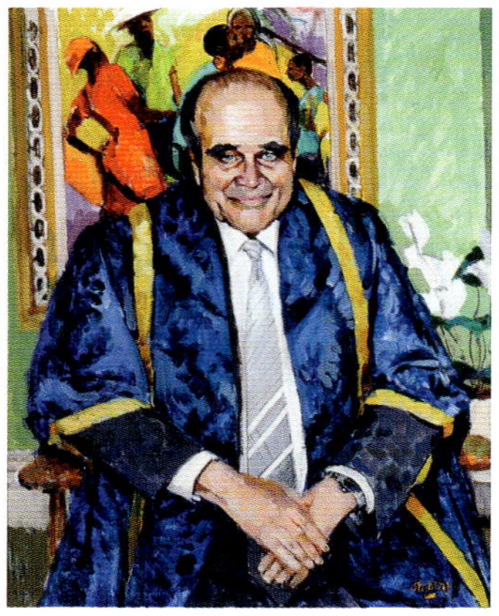

Stubley, Trevor 1932–2010
Sir Roy Marshall
oil on canvas 50 x 40
1230

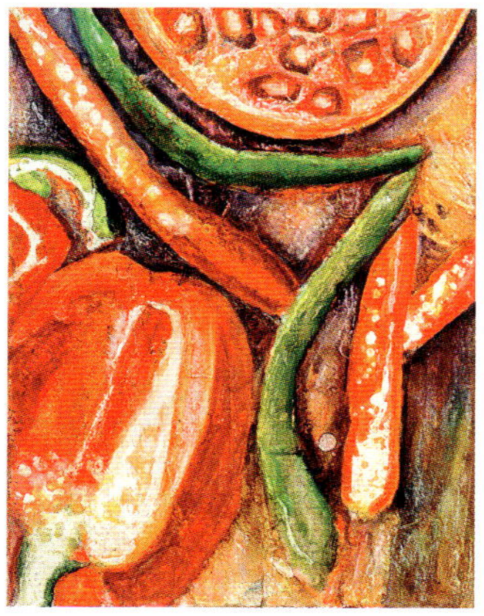

Suberu, Ade b.1968
Chillies 2 1999
acrylic on canvas 40 x 30
1439

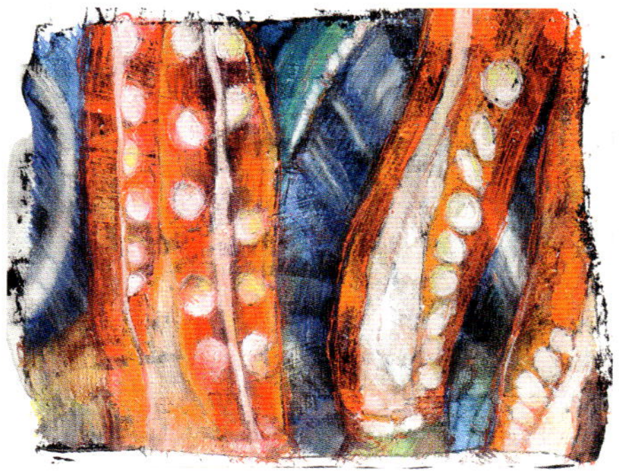

Suberu, Ade b.1968
Chillies 3 1999
acrylic on canvas 38 x 49
1073

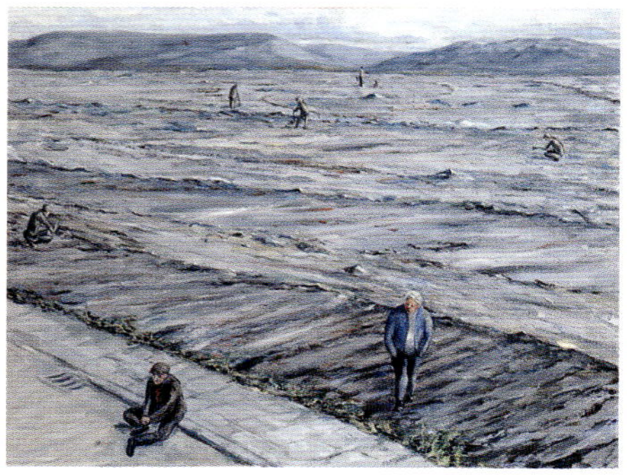

Teale, Dick b.1930
Scratin for Coal 1989
oil on canvas 61 x 79
1131

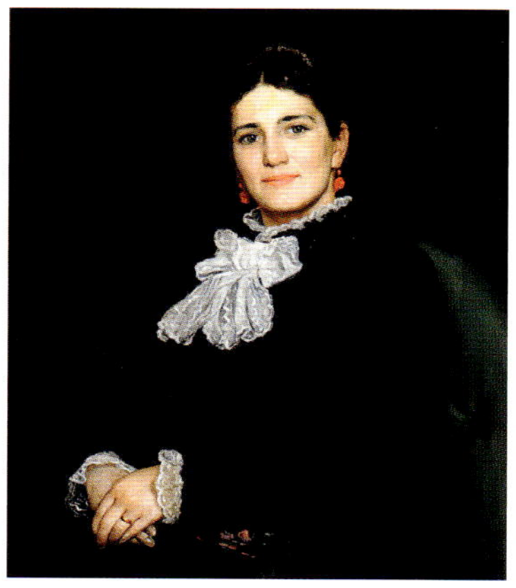

Tracy, John Martin 1843–1893
Mrs Ezra Hounsfield Linley 1877
oil on canvas 75 x 62
416

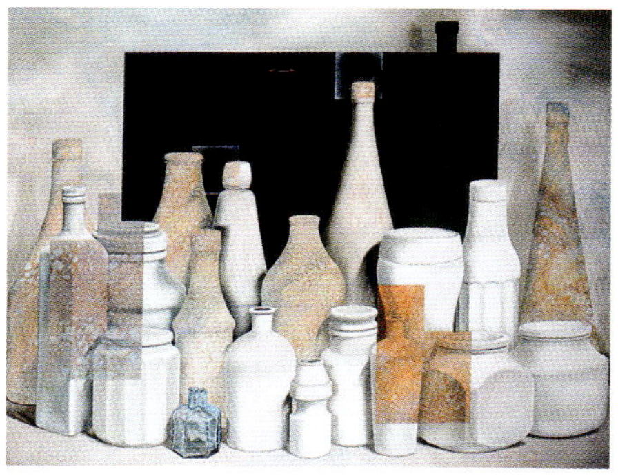

Underhill, Graham b.1946
Arrangement before a Void 2008
oil on canvas 99 x 130
1280

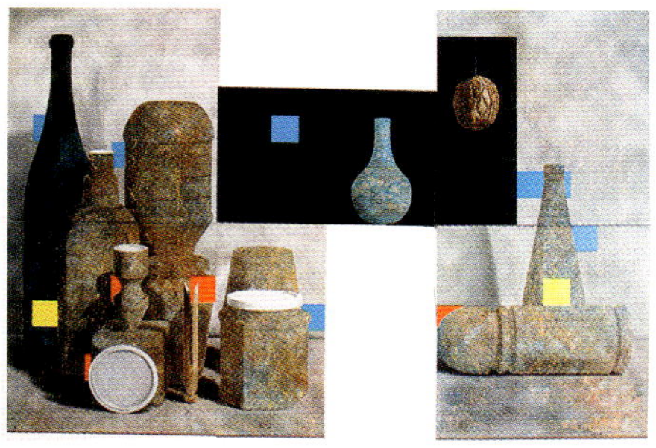

Underhill, Graham b.1946
Heroic Still Life with Hanging Nut (polyptych) 2008
oil on canvas 160 x 240
1279

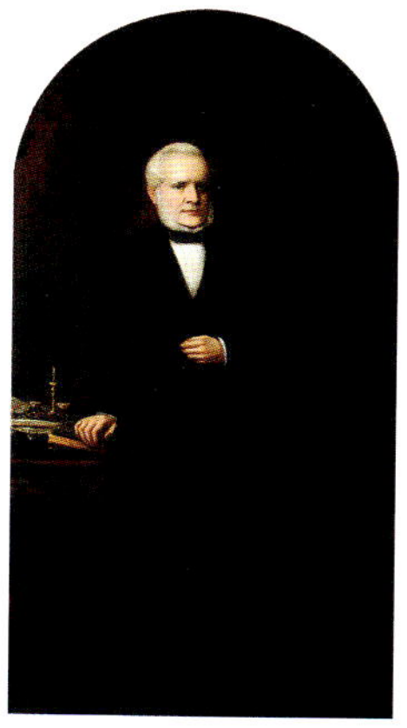

unknown artist
Sir John Brown (1816–1896), DL, Founder John Brown & Company (1838) 1870
oil on canvas 212 x 110
377

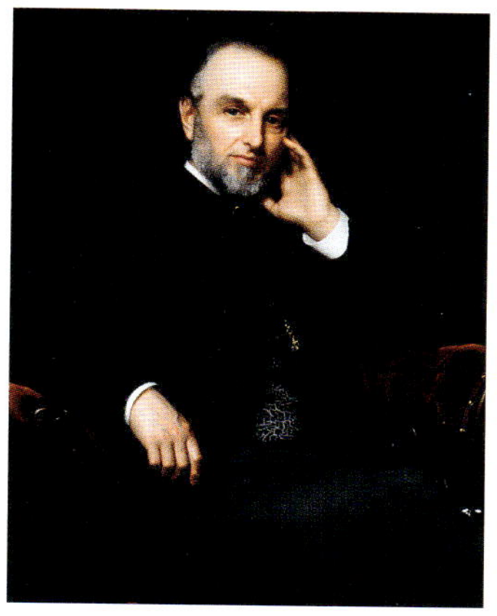

unknown artist
Sir Frederick Thorpe Mappin (1821–1910) 1884
oil on canvas 94 x 69 (E)
1029

unknown artist
Sir Albert John Hobson (1861–1923), Lord Mayor of Sheffield (1911) 1902
oil on canvas 125 x 100
406

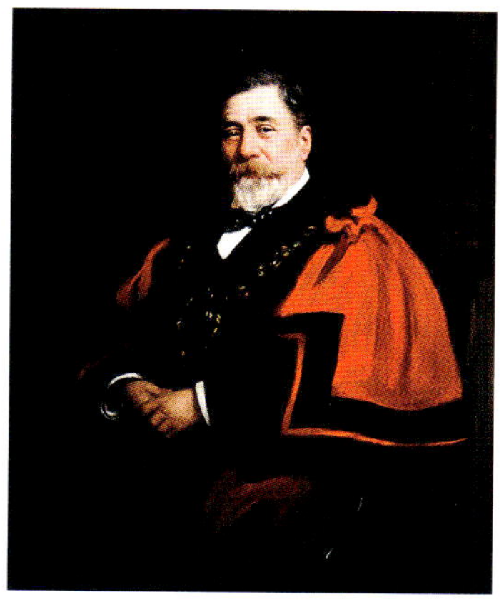

unknown artist
Sir Joseph Jonas (1845–1921), Lord Mayor of Sheffield (1904–1905) 1916
oil on canvas 125 x 99
410

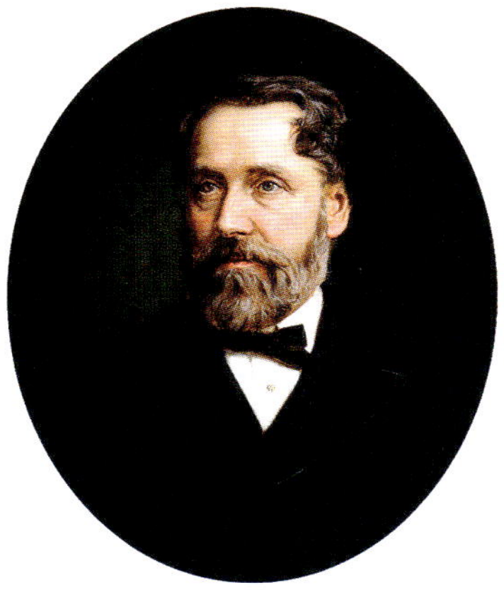

unknown artist
Mark Firth (1819–1880)
oil on canvas 60 x 50
1287

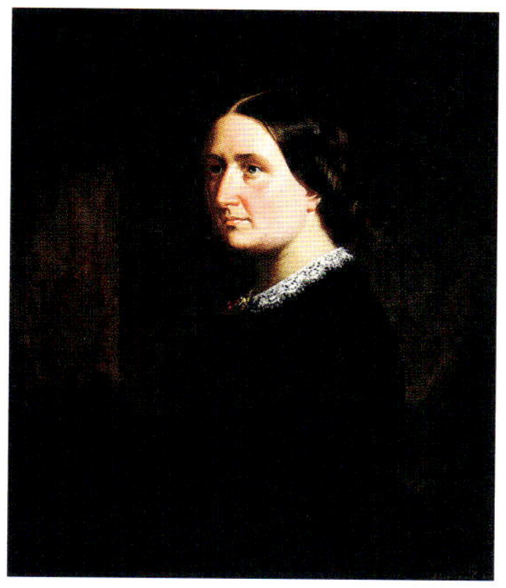

unknown artist
Mrs Firth
oil on canvas 75 x 61
1288

unknown artist
Misty Sunrise
acrylic on canvas 63 x 75
1162

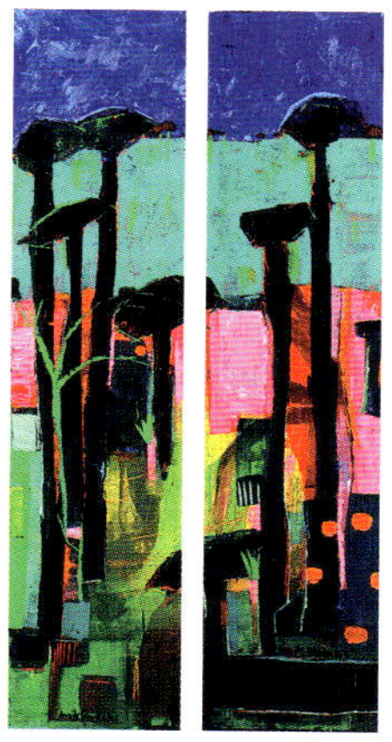

Varkalis, Amrik b.1949
Black Trees 1 and 2 (diptych) 2008
oil on board 122 x 30; 122 x 30
1237

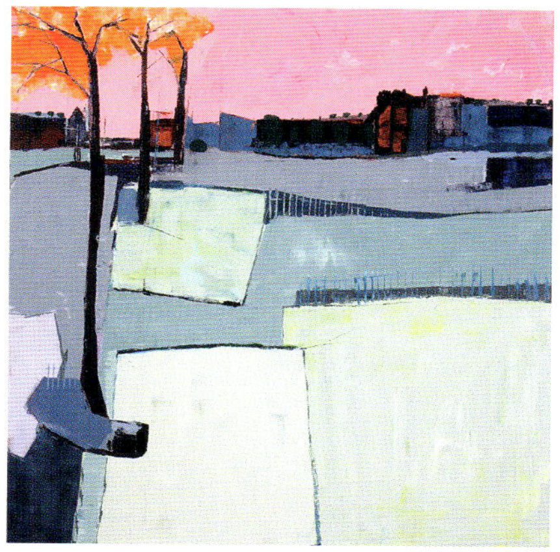

Varkalis, Amrik b.1949
Pink Sky
oil on canvas 91 x 91
1236

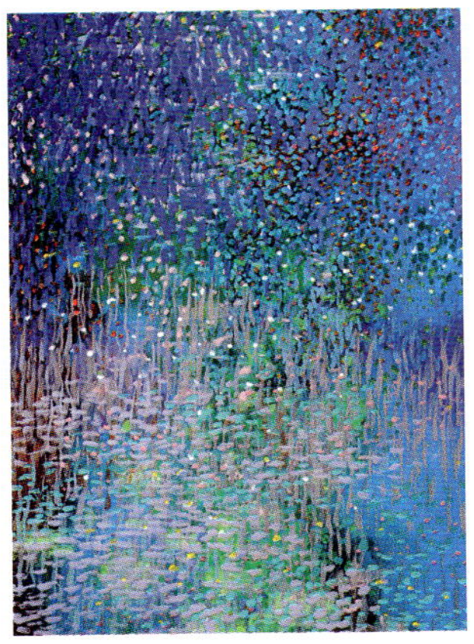

Wall, Tom 1941–1992
Stream 1975
acrylic on canvas 68 x 47
1121

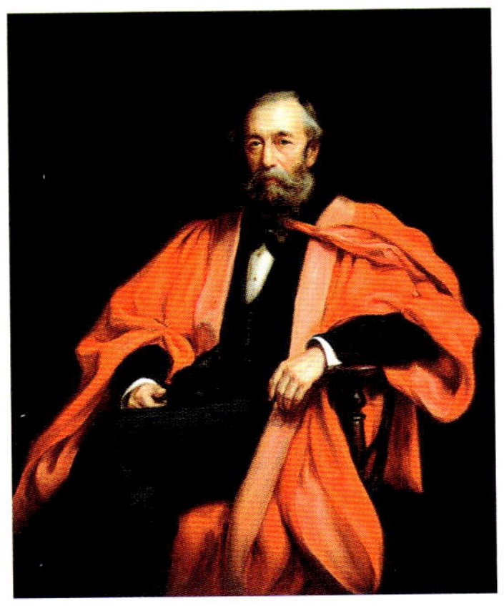

Waller, Mary Lemon 1852–c.1931
Henry Clifton Sorby (1826–1908), LLD, FRS
1906
oil on canvas 145 x 115
434

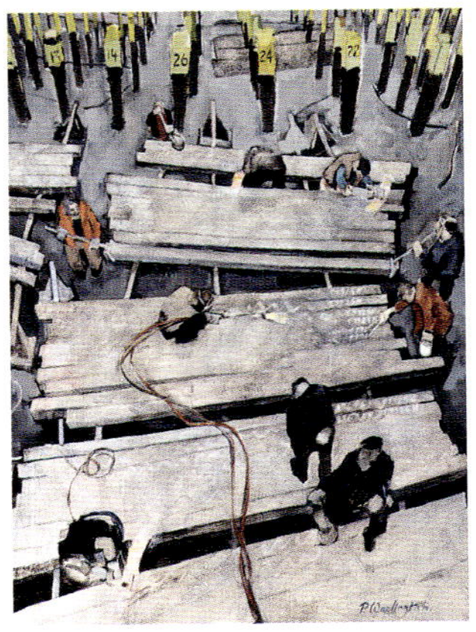

Waplington, Paul Anthony b.1938
Dressing Billets 1983
acrylic on canvas 127 x 98
454

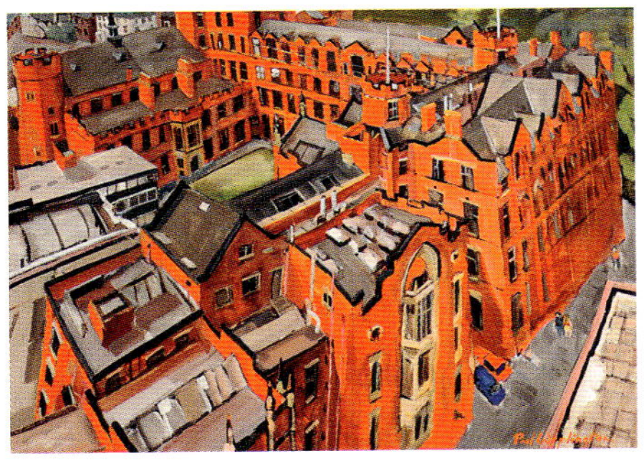

Waplington, Paul Anthony b.1938
The Quadrangle 1985
oil on canvas 107 x 130
455

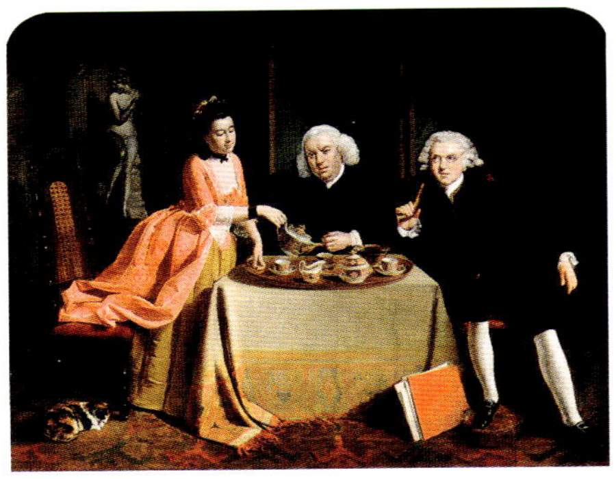

Ward, Edward Matthew (attributed to)
1816–1879
Dr Johnson and Sir Joshua Reynolds Taking Tea with Mrs Thrale 1848
oil on canvas 95 x 119
453

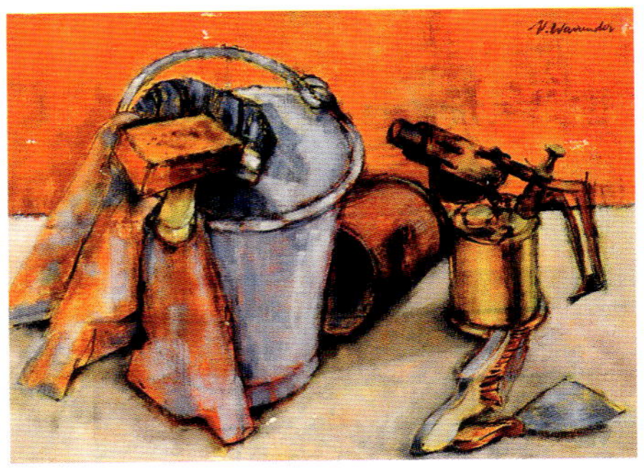

Warrender, Vera
Still Life with a Blowlamp
oil on canvas 44 x 59
1133

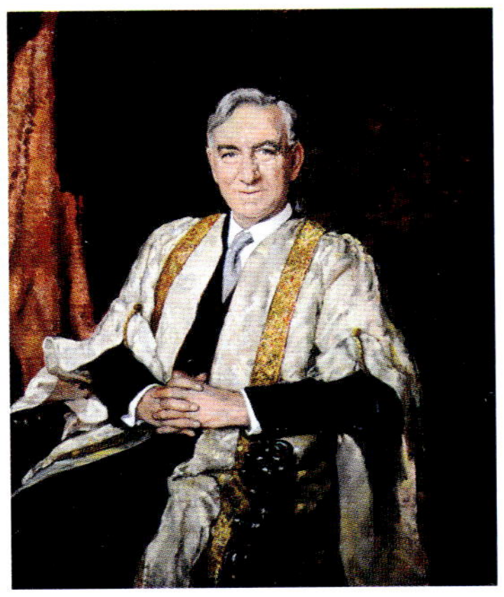

Wheatley, Grace 1888–1970
Dr John Macnaghten Whittaker (1905–1984), Vice-Chancellor of the University of Sheffield (1953–1965) 1965
oil on canvas 117 x 91 (E)
444

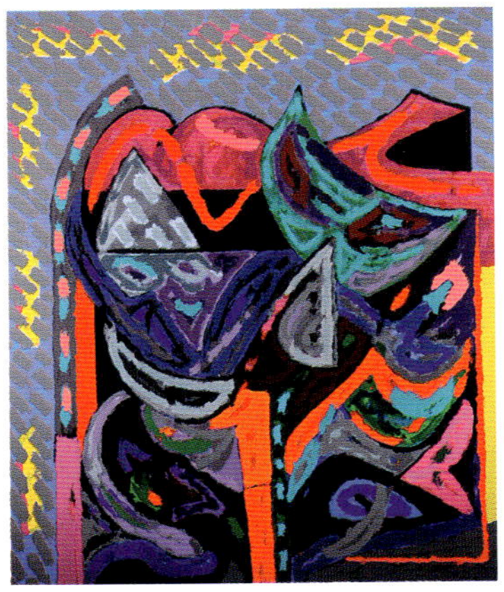

Widdop, John
Cycle XII 1994
acrylic on canvas 211 x 176
506

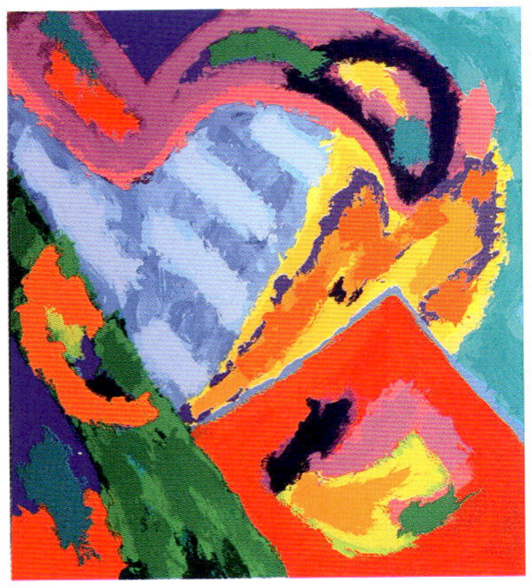

Widdop, John
Tantric Model VIII 1994
oil on canvas 57 x 50
1116

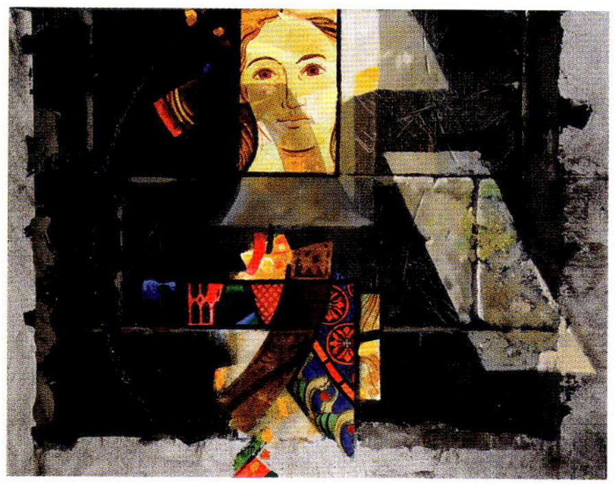

Wilson, Graeme b.1951
Annunciation 1990
oil on canvas 40 x 50
1064

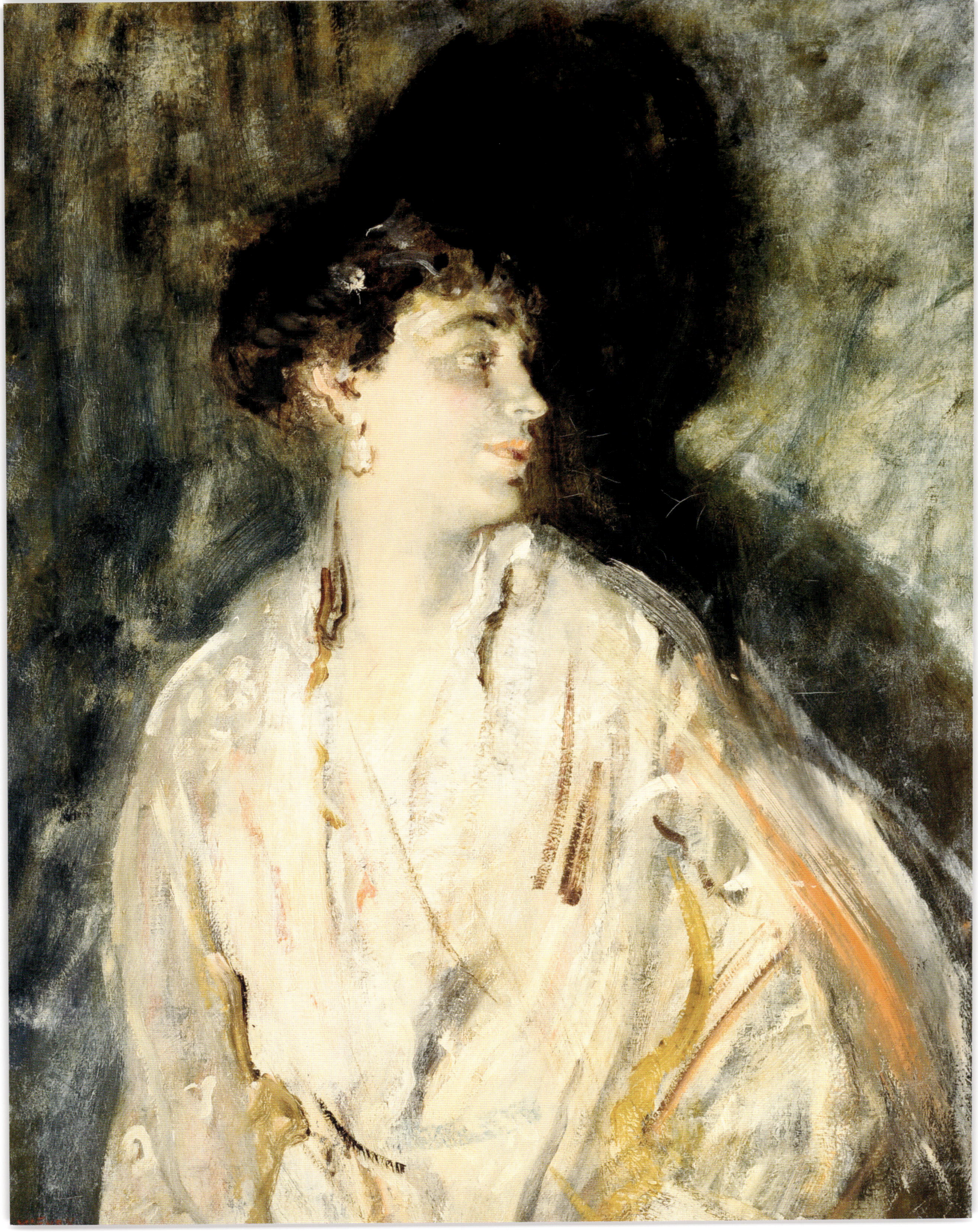

Paintings Without Reproductions

This section lists all the paintings that have not been included in the main pages of the catalogue. They were excluded as it was not possible to photograph them for this project. Additional information relating to acquisition credit lines or loan details is also included. For this reason the information below is not repeated in the Further Information section.

Museums Sheffield

Bartlett, Charles William 1860–1940, *A Festival in Brittany, France*, 1906, 119.7 x 144.2, oil on canvas, VIS.590, gift from Mr Graves, 1935, not available at the time of photography

Moes, Wally 1856–1918, *The First Prayer*, 1892, 98 x 123.5, oil on canvas, VIS.521, gift from Mr Graves, 1929, not available at the time of photography

Muller, William James 1812–1845, *Landscape*, 1836, 99.8 x 166.1, oil on canvas, VIS.1613, presented by F. T. Mappin, 1887, not available at the time of photography

Nash, John Northcote 1893–1977, *Landscape with Buildings*, c.1937, 67.9 x 85, oil on canvas, VIS.2947, purchased, 1937, not available at the time of photography

Rose, Rose b.1946, *Interior, Rock 'n' Roll*, oil & enamel on paper, VIS.5441, purchased, 1986, not available at the time of photography

Sheffield Industrial Museums Trust

Dean, K. *Cogging Down*, 1955, 39 x 48, oil on canvas, 1980.938, gift from Mr Hatcher, c.1980, not available at the time of photography

Penistone, Robert b.1946, *Men Pouring Crucible Steel into an Ingot*, 1920s, 58 x 68, oil on board, PN3193, not available at the time of photography

Penistone, Robert b.1946, *View Looking over Stocksbridge Steelworks, Sheffield*, 1920s, 35 x 38, oil & beeswax on board, PN3189, not available at the time of photography

Sheffield Town Hall

P. D. or **R. D.** *Farmhouse**, 1985, 24 x 35, oil on board, PCF9, gift, not available at the time of photography

The Children's Hospital, Sheffield

Artistic Licence *Entertainment Alphabet, Title Board*, 1992, 105 x 50 , acrylic & paper on board, PCF100, acquired through the fundraising efforts of PC Steve Hague of the Road Safety Department and the Motorcycle Wing of the South Yorkshire Police, 1992, copyright permission denied

Artistic Licence *Entertainment Alphabet A, Acrobat (detail)*, 1992, 122 x 122 , acrylic on board, PCF1a, acquired through the fundraising efforts of PC Steve Hague of the Road Safety Department and the Motorcycle Wing of the South Yorkshire Police, 1992, copyright permission denied

Artistic Licence *Entertainment Alphabet B, Ballooning (detail)*, 1992, 122 x 122 , acrylic on board, PCF1b, acquired through the fundraising efforts of PC Steve Hague of the Road Safety Department and the Motorcycle Wing of the South Yorkshire Police, 1992, copyright permission denied

Artistic Licence *Entertainment Alphabet C, Clowning (detail)*, 1992, 122 x 122 , acrylic on board, PCF1c, acquired through the fundraising efforts of PC Steve Hague of the Road Safety Department and the Motorcycle Wing of the South Yorkshire Police, 1992, copyright permission denied

Artistic Licence *Entertainment Alphabet D, Drawing (detail)*, 1992, 122 x 122 , acrylic on board, PCF1d, acquired through the fundraising efforts of PC Steve Hague of the Road Safety Department and the Motorcycle Wing of the South Yorkshire Police, 1992, copyright permission denied

Artistic Licence *Entertainment Alphabet E, Entertainment (detail)*, 1992, 122 x 122 , acrylic on board, PCF1e, acquired through the fundraising efforts of PC Steve Hague of the Road Safety Department and the Motorcycle Wing of the South Yorkshire Police, 1992, copyright permission denied

Artistic Licence *Entertainment Alphabet F, Fishing (detail)*, 1992, 122 x 122 , acrylic on board, PCF1f, acquired through the fundraising efforts of PC Steve Hague of the Road Safety Department and the Motorcycle Wing of the South Yorkshire Police, 1992, copyright permission denied

Artistic Licence *Entertainment Alphabet G, Golf (detail)*, 1992, 122 x 122 , acrylic on board, PCF1g, acquired through the fundraising efforts of PC Steve Hague of the Road Safety Department and the Motorcycle Wing of the South Yorkshire Police, 1992, copyright permission denied

Artistic Licence *Entertainment Alphabet H, Holidays (detail)*, 1992, 122 x 122 , acrylic on board, PCF1h, acquired through the fundraising efforts of PC Steve Hague of the Road Safety Department and the Motorcycle Wing of the South Yorkshire Police, 1992, copyright permission denied

Artistic Licence *Entertainment Alphabet I, Ice-Skating (detail)*, 1992, 122 x 122 , acrylic on board, PCF1i, acquired through the fundraising efforts of PC Steve Hague of the Road Safety Department and the Motorcycle Wing of the South Yorkshire Police, 1992, copyright permission denied

Artistic Licence *Entertainment Alphabet J, Juggling (detail)*, 1992, 122 x 122 , acrylic on board, PCF1j, acquired through the fundraising efforts of PC Steve Hague of the Road Safety Department and the Motorcycle Wing of the South Yorkshire Police, 1992, copyright permission denied

Artistic Licence *Entertainment Alphabet K, Kites (detail)*, 1992, 122 x 122 , acrylic on board, PCF1k, acquired through the fundraising efforts of PC Steve Hague of the Road Safety Department and the Motorcycle Wing of the South Yorkshire Police, 1992, copyright permission denied

Artistic Licence *Entertainment Alphabet L, Leap-Frog (detail)*, 1992, 122 x 122 , acrylic on board, PCF1l, acquired through the fundraising efforts of PC Steve Hague of the Road Safety Department and the Motorcycle Wing of the South Yorkshire Police, 1992, copyright permission denied

Artistic Licence *Entertainment Alphabet M, Magic (detail)*, 1992, 122 x 122 , acrylic on board, PCF1m, acquired through the fundraising efforts of PC Steve Hague of the Road Safety Department and the Motorcycle Wing of the South Yorkshire Police, 1992, copyright permission denied

Artistic Licence *Entertainment Alphabet N, Netball (detail)*, 1992, 122 x 122 , acrylic on board, PCF1n, acquired through the fundraising efforts of PC Steve Hague of the Road Safety Department and the Motorcycle Wing of the South Yorkshire Police, 1992, copyright permission denied

Artistic Licence *Entertainment Alphabet O, Opera (detail)*, 1992, 122 x 122 , acrylic on board, PCF1o, acquired through the fundraising efforts of PC Steve Hague of the Road Safety Department and the Motorcycle Wing of the South Yorkshire Police, 1992, copyright permission denied

Artistic Licence *Entertainment Alphabet P, Painting (detail)*, 1992, 122 x 122 , acrylic on board, PCF1p, acquired through the fundraising efforts of PC Steve Hague of the Road Safety Department and the Motorcycle Wing of the South Yorkshire Police, 1992, copyright permission denied

Artistic Licence *Entertainment Alphabet Q, Quiz (detail)*, 1992, 122 x 122 , acrylic on board, PCF1q, acquired through the fundraising efforts of PC Steve Hague of the Road Safety Department and the Motorcycle Wing of the South Yorkshire Police, 1992, copyright permission denied

Artistic Licence *Entertainment Alphabet R, Reading (detail)*, 1992, 122 x 122 , acrylic on board, PCF1r, acquired through the fundraising efforts of PC Steve Hague of the Road Safety Department and the Motorcycle Wing of the South Yorkshire Police, 1992, copyright permission denied

Artistic Licence *Entertainment Alphabet S, Skateboarding (detail)*, 1992, 122 x 122 , acrylic on board, PCF1s, acquired through the fundraising efforts of PC Steve Hague of the Road Safety Department and the Motorcycle Wing of the South Yorkshire Police, 1992, copyright permission denied

Artistic Licence *Entertainment Alphabet T, Television (detail)*, 1992, 122 x 122 , acrylic on board, PCF1t, acquired through the fundraising efforts of PC Steve Hague of the Road Safety Department and the Motorcycle Wing of the South Yorkshire Police, 1992, copyright permission denied

Artistic Licence *Entertainment Alphabet U, United (detail)*, 1992, 122 x 122 , acrylic on board, PCF1u, acquired through the fundraising efforts of PC Steve Hague of the Road Safety Department and the Motorcycle Wing of the South Yorkshire Police, 1992, copyright permission denied

Artistic Licence *Entertainment Alphabet V, Ventriloquism (detail)*, 1992, 122 x 122 , acrylic on board, PCF1v, acquired through the fundraising efforts of PC Steve Hague of the Road Safety Department and the Motorcycle Wing of the South Yorkshire

Facing page: McEvoy, Ambrose, 1878–1927, *The Honourable Mrs Akers-Douglas* (detail), Museums Sheffield, (p. 135)

Police, 1992, copyright permission denied

Artistic Licence *Entertainment Alphabet W, Weight-Lifting (detail)*, 1992, 122 x 122 , acrylic on board, PCF1w, acquired through the fundraising efforts of PC Steve Hague of the Road Safety Department and the Motorcycle Wing of the South Yorkshire Police, 1992, copyright permission denied

Artistic Licence *Entertainment Alphabet X, Xylophone (detail)*, 1992, 122 x 122 , acrylic on board, PCF1x, acquired through the fundraising efforts of PC Steve Hague of the Road Safety Department and the Motorcycle Wing of the South Yorkshire Police, 1992, copyright permission denied

Artistic Licence *Entertainment Alphabet Y, Yo-Yoing (detail)*, 1992, 122 x 122 , acrylic on board, PCF1y, acquired through the fundraising efforts of PC Steve Hague of the Road Safety Department and the Motorcycle Wing of the South Yorkshire Police, 1992, copyright permission denied

Artistic Licence *Entertainment Alphabet Z, Zoo (detail)*, 1992, 122 x 122 , acrylic on board, PCF1z, acquired through the fundraising efforts of PC Steve Hague of the Road Safety Department and the Motorcycle Wing of the South Yorkshire Police, 1992, copyright permission denied

Field, Sandra b.1966, *Road Signs* (a series of around 60 paintings), 2002, acrylic on board, PCF20.1, donated by the League of Friends, 2002, not available at the time of photography

Heath, Andrew b.1962, *Landscape*, acrylic on board, PCF53, not available at the time of photography

unknown artist *Ostrich 1*, c.2000, 122 x 61, acrylic on board, PCF107, purchased, c.2000, not available at the time of photography

unknown artist *Ostrich 2*, c.2000, 91 x 76, acrylic on board, PCF108b, purchased, c.2000, not available at the time of photography

unknown artist *Jungle*, acrylic on board, PCF54, not available at the time of photography

STOLEN

Sheffield Teaching Hospitals NHS Foundation Trust

C. K. *Sheffield General Infirmary from Port Mahon*, 1798, 25.4, oil on copper, PCF30, transferred from the Board Room, Royal Infirmary, stolen, 2003

unknown artist *Thomas Parr, known as 'Old Parr', Died Aged 152 (1483–1635)*, 19 x 11.43, oil on canvas (?), PCF29, gift from Mr Samuel Marshall, 1797, stolen, 2003

Further Information

The paintings listed in this section have additional information relating to one or more of the five categories outlined below. This extra information is only provided where it is applicable and where it exists. Paintings listed in this section follow the same order as in the illustrated pages of the catalogue.

I The full name of the artist if this was too long to display in the illustrated pages of the catalogue. Such cases are marked in the catalogue with a (…).

II The full title of the painting if this was too long to display in the illustrated pages of the catalogue. Such cases are marked in the catalogue with a (…).

III Acquisition information or acquisition credit lines as well as information about loans, copied from the records of the owner collection.

IV Artist copyright credit lines where the copyright owner has been traced. Exhaustive efforts have been made to locate the copyright owners of all the images included within this catalogue and to meet their requirements. Any omissions or mistakes brought to our attention will be duly attended to and corrected in future publications.

V The credit line of the lender of the transparency if the transparency has been borrowed. Bridgeman images are available subject to any relevant copyright approvals from the Bridgeman Art Library at www.bridgemanart.com

Bradfield Parish Council

Members of the Rural Youth Project *Under the Sea* (polyptych), acquired with the assistance of a Rural Youth Project grant, aided by Bradfield Parish Council, 2008
Rodgers, D. K. *Lower Bradfield, Sheffield*, gift, 2009

Fire and Police Museum at Sheffield

Brown, Chris active since c.1989, *The Story of a Day at Ringinglow Fire Station*, transferred from Ringinglow Fire Station, c.2007, © Fire and Police Museum
Brown, Chris active since c.1989, *Firefighters Entering a Burning Building*, presented by the artist, © Fire and Police Museum
Brown, Chris active since c.1989, *The Timeline of Firefighting* (a work in progress, polyptych), presented and regularly updated by the artist, since 1993, © Fire and Police Museum
Howard, Reg *Street Fire Rescue*, transferred from South Yorkshire Fire & Rescue Service Headquarters, Sheffield, 2009, © Fire and Police Museum
Muller, Axel *Division Street Fire Station Pole Drop*, presented by the artist, © Fire and Police Museum
Scarborough, Joe b.1938, *Fire*, commissioned by the South Yorkshire Fire Service Historical Society, 1985, © Fire and Police Museum

Museums Sheffield

Abbott, Lemuel Francis 1760–1803, *William Traies of Crediton* (father of the artist), gift from J. G. Graves, 1929
Abrahams, Philippa b.1947, *The Virgin Adoring the Infant Christ* (after Andrea del Verrocchio), on long-term loan from the Guild of St George, © the artist
Adams, Beatrice b.1877, *View of the Science Gallery at Weston Park Museum, Sheffield*, presented by the artist, 1921
Adams, John Clayton 1840–1906, *Harvest Time*, bequeathed by Sir Wilson Mappin, 1925
Adams, John Clayton 1840–1906, *Harvest Time*, presented by F. T. Mappin, 1887
Adams, John Clayton 1840–1906, *In the Surrey Woods*, gift from J. G. Graves, 1943
Adams, Norman 1927–2005, *St Peter*, purchased from the artist, 1972, © the artist's estate
Adamson, Dorothy 1894–1934, *Sunday*, gift from J. G. Graves, 1942
Adshead, Mary 1904–1995, *Self Portrait*, purchased from Sally Hunter Fine Art, 1986, © the artist's estate
Aldam, Thomas *Balm Green, Sheffield*, purchased, 1972
Alessandri, Angelo 1854–1931, *St Jerome Leading the Tame Lion into the Monastery* (detail) (after Vittore Carpaccio), on long-term loan from the Guild of St George
Alessandri, Angelo 1854–1931, *The Obsequies of St Jerome* (detail) (after Vittore Carpaccio), on long-term loan from the Guild of St George
Allan, Robert Weir 1852–1942, *The Old Harbour, Portsoy, Scotland*, gift from J. G. Graves, 1929
Allan, Robert Weir 1852–1942, *Venice*, gift from J. G. Graves, 1929
Allen, Harry Epworth 1894–1958, *Derbyshire Walls*, purchased from the artist, 1956, © Geraldine Lattey/Harry Epworth Allen Foundation
Allinson, Adrian Paul 1890–1959, *Moel Hebog, North Wales*, purchased at Sotheby's, 1978 © the artist's estate
Amigoni, Jacopo c.1682–1752, *Sir Thomas Reeve (1673–1737)*, purchased, 1953
Amigoni, Jacopo (attributed to) c.1682–1752, *Cupids at Play*, gift from J. G. Graves, 1929
Anderson, William 1757–1837, *Sea Piece*, gift from J. G. Graves, 1935
André, Edmond 1837–1877, *The Introduction*, presented by F. T. Mappin, 1891
Anker, Albert 1831–1910, *The Public Notary*, bequeathed by J. N. Mappin, 1887
Ansdell, Richard 1815–1885, *The Lost Shepherd*, presented by Miss Davy, 1929
Ansdell, Richard 1815–1885, *Dead Stag*, presented by F. T. Mappin, 1887
Armandi, Polermo b.1842, *Stormy Weather*, gift from J. G. Graves, 1943
Armitage, Edward 1817–1896, *Christ Calling the Apostles James and John*, bequeathed by J. N. Mappin, 1887
Armstrong, John 1893–1973, *Nocturne*, purchased at Sotheby's, 1967, © the artist's estate/Bridgeman Art Library
Arrowsmith, Thomas 1772–1830, *Portrait of a Boy* (probably George Woolhouse), presented by R. C. D. Fell, 1969
Atkinson, Conrad b.1940, *Goldfish*, purchased from the artist, 1986, © the artist
Atkinson, Conrad b.1940, *Measures*, purchased from the artist, © the artist
Auerbach, Frank Helmuth b.1931, *Head of J. Y. M.*, purchased from Marlborough Fine Art with the assistance of the Victoria and Albert Museum Purchase Grant Fund, 1974, © the artist
Auerbach, Frank Helmuth b.1931, *Looking towards Mornington Crescent Station, Night*, purchased from Marlborough Fine Art with the assistance of the Victoria and Albert Museum Purchase Grant Fund, 1974, © the artist
Aumonier, James 1832–1911, *A Bypath*, gift from J. G. Graves, 1937
Aumonier, James 1832–1911, *A Cambridgeshire Farm*, gift from J. G. Graves, 1929
Aumonier, James 1832–1911, *An English Cottage Home*, bequeathed by J. N. Mappin, 1887
Aumonier, James 1832–1911, *An Oxfordshire Sheep Farm*, gift from J. G. Graves, 1935
Aumonier, James 1832–1911, *Lancing Mill, Sussex*, gift from J. G. Graves, 1937
Aumonier, James 1832–1911, *Sussex Hayfields*, gift from J. G. Graves
Aumonier, James 1832–1911, *Village Street, Wendens Ambo, Essex*, gift from J. G. Graves, 1929
Ayres, Gillian b.1930, *Untitled 1980*, purchased from the Knoedler Gallery, 1981, © the artist
Ayres, Gillian b.1930, *Belt of Straw and Ivy Leaves*, on loan from a private collection, © the artist
Ayrton, Michael 1921–1975, *Norman Douglas (1868–1952)*, purchased from the Stone Gallery, 1975, © the artist's estate
Backhuysen, Ludolf I 1630–1708, *Self Portrait*, accepted by HM Government in lieu of inheritance tax and allocated to Museums Sheffield, 1970
Baker, Thomas 1809–1869, *Cattle Group*, gift from J. G. Graves, 1929
Balestra, Antonio 1666–1740, *Cain and Abel*, purchased at Sotheby's, 1951
Banks, James *John Skinner*, presented by Mr O. Skinner, 1962
Banks, Thomas Joseph 1828–1896, *Mrs Sarah Bateman with Her Three Daughters*, presented by Mrs R. T. Betts, 1961
Banks, Thomas Joseph 1828–1896, *Thomas Bateman (1821–1861), and His Son*, presented by Mrs R. T. Betts, 1961
Barber, Thomas 1771–1843, *James Montgomery (1771–1854)*, presented by Sheffield Literary &

Philosophical Society
Bargue, Charles (attributed to) 1826–1883, *Arabs at Prayer*, gift from J. G. Graves
Barker, Allen b.1937, *Painting*, purchased from the Lucy Milton Gallery, 1972
Barker, Benjamin II 1776–1838, *Coast Scene*, gift from J. G. Graves, 1935
Barker, David Walker b.1947, *Seascape*, purchased from the artist, 1974, © the artist
Barker, Kit 1916–1988, *Tan Hill*, on loan from a private collection, © the artist's estate
Barker, Thomas 1769–1847, *The Falls of Tivoli, Italy*, purchased, 1950
Barker, Thomas 1769–1847, *Landscape with a River*, gift from J. G. Graves, 1943
Barker, Thomas 1769–1847, *Landscape with Cattle*, gift from J. G. Graves, 1935
Barker, Thomas 1769–1847, *The Pool*, gift from J. G. Graves, 1935
Barker, Thomas 1769–1847, *The Shepherd*, gift from J. G. Graves, 1929
Barker, Thomas 1769–1847, *The Woodman*, gift from J. G. Graves, 1929
Barker, Thomas Jones 1815–1882, *John Newton Mappin (1800–1883)*, presented by J. Y. Cowlishaw, 1891
Barker, Thomas Jones 1815–1882, *The Faithful Knight*, gift from J. G. Graves, 1935
Barnes, Edward Charles 1830–1890, *Savoyard with a Clarionet*, bequeathed by J. N. Mappin, 1887
Barns-Graham, Wilhelmina 1912–2004, *Glacier Painting, Green and Brown*, purchased from the New Art Centre, 1978, © by courtesy of the Barns-Graham Charitable Trust
Barret, George the elder 1728/1732–1784, *Scene from 'The Tempest'* (from the play by William Shakespeare), gift from J. G. Graves, 1929
Barret, George the elder (attributed to) 1728/1732–1784, *Landscape with a Lake*, gift from J. G. Graves
Barry, James 1741–1806, *Jupiter Beguiled by Juno on Mount Ida*, presented by the Sheffield Art Collections Fund, 1937
Bassano, Leandro (school of) 1557–1622, *The Road to Calvary*, presented by Captain Penrose, 1955
Bastien-Lepage, Émile 1854–1938, *The Young Craftsman*, gift from J. G. Graves, 1935
Bayes, Walter 1869–1956, *The Lemon*, purchased from the D'Offay Cauper Gallery, 1972, © the artist's estate
Bayes, Walter 1869–1956, *On the Beach*, purchased from the Piccadilly Gallery, 1965, © the artist's estate
Baynes, John active 1935–1943, *Trees on an Island*, presented anonymously, 1936
Baynes, Keith 1887–1977, *In the Baltic*, presented by the Contemporary Art Society, 1931
Bazler, Fred b.1934, *Four on Four*, purchased from the artist, 1981
Bazler, Fred b.1934, *Two on Six*, purchased from the artist, 1981
Beaune, M. *The Chocolate Maiden* (after Jean-Etienne Liotard), gift from J. G. Graves, 1929
Beavis, Richard 1824–1896, *Scene from 'The Lay of the Last Minstrel'* (from the poem by Walter Scott), bequeathed by H. H. Andrews, 1903
Beavis, Richard 1824–1896, *Cattle Raid*, presented by F. T. Mappin, 1891
Beavis, Richard 1824–1896, *The Charcoal Burners*, bequeathed by Sir Wilson Mappin, 1925
Beavis, Richard 1824–1896, *Carting Bracken*, gift from J. G. Graves, 1937
Beavis, Richard 1824–1896, *Coast Scene near Sidmouth, Devon*, gift from J. G. Graves, 1943
Beavis, Richard 1824–1896, *Near Sidmouth, Devon*, gift from J. G. Graves, 1943
Beechey, William 1753–1839, *Colonel Milner of Totley Hall*, presented by W. A. Milner, 1944
Beechey, William 1753–1839, *George III (1738–1820), Reviewing His Troops*, presented by the Sheffield Society for the Encouragement of Art, 1938
Beechey, William 1753–1839, *Mrs Goldsmith*, presented by Mr Bingham, 1954
Beechey, William 1753–1839, *Portrait of an Officer*, gift from J. G. Graves, 1929
Beeldemaker, Adriaen Cornelisz. 1618–1709, *Portrait of an Old Woman*, gift from J. G. Graves, 1935
Beelt, Cornelis 1640–1702, *The Tinker's Shop*, presented by Father Cook, 1948
Beeton, J. *Landscape*, bequeathed by J. N. Mappin, 1887
Bell, Vanessa 1879–1961, *View of the Pond at Charleston, East Sussex*, purchased at Christie's, 1975, © 1961 estate of Vanessa Bell, courtesy Henrietta Garnett
Bell, Vanessa 1879–1961, *Still Life*, © 1961 estate of Vanessa Bell, courtesy Henrietta Garnett
Bell, Walter b.1904, *Derbyshire Quarry*, presented by the Sheffield Society for the Encouragement of Art, 1937
Bellany, John b.1942, *Celtic Feast* (triptych), purchased from Monika Kinley with the assistance of the Victoria and Albert Museum Purchase Grant Fund, 1981, © the artist/Bridgeman Art Library
Bellingham-Smith, Elinor 1906–1988, *Bullrushes*, purchased at Christie's, 1965, © the artist's estate
Bellingham-Smith, Hugh 1866–1922, *Children in an Orchard*, gift from J. G. Graves, 1943
Bembridge, John Conrad c.1822–1857, *Colonel Athorpe (d.1806)*, presented by the Cutlers Company, 1960
Bentley, Charles 1808–1854, *Seascape*, gift from J. G. Graves, 1935
Bentley, Joseph Clayton 1809–1851, *River Aire, near Appleby, Yorkshire*, bequeathed by Sir Wilson Mappin, 1925
Bentley, Joseph Herbert 1866–1934, *Miss Atkin*, bequeathed by E. W. Atkin, 1957
Berg, Gunnar 1864–1894, *Cattle in a Landscape*, gift from J. G. Graves, 1935
Bergen, Hans *Cattle in a Stall*, gift from J. G. Graves, 1937
Bevan, Norman b.1900, *Seahouses Harbour, Northumberland*, purchased from the artist, 1979
Bevan, Robert Polhill 1865–1925, *Farm Landscape*, purchased at Christie's, 1968
Birch, John 1807–1857, *Sir Arnold Knight (1789–1871), MD*, transferred from Sheffield Central Library, 1936
Birch, Samuel John Lamorna 1869–1955, *Trewoofe from the Cairn, Cornwall*, gift from J. G. Graves, 1943, © the artist's estate
Bird, Edward 1772–1819, *The Discovered Correspondence*, gift from J. G. Graves, 1935
Birley, Oswald Hornby Joseph 1880–1952, *The Spanish Plume*, presented by Miss Ezme Vickers, 1953, © the artist's estate
Bishop, Henry 1868–1939, *Houses in Provence, France*, gift from J. G. Graves, 1943
Bishop, Henry 1868–1939, *Market Place, Concarneau, France*, gift from J. G. Graves, 1937
Bisson, Edouard 1856–1939, *A Springtime Idyll*, gift from J. G. Graves, 1929
Blaas, Eugen von 1843–1931, *Dressing for the Masquerade*, presented by F. T. Mappin, 1887
Blaas, Eugen von 1843–1931, *Portrait of a Boy*, gift from J. G. Graves, 1929
Blake, Peter b.1932, *Footsteps*, purchased from the Waddington Gallery with the assistance of the Victoria and Albert Museum Purchase Grant Fund, 1980, © Peter Blake. All rights reserved, DACS 2012
Blanche, Jacques-Emile 1861–1942, *Mabel Beardsley (1871–1916)*, presented by the Contemporary Art Society, 1952, © ADAGP, Paris and DACS, London 2012
Boden, William 1840–1920, *Long Steps, Bernard Street, Sheffield*, purchased, 1905
Boden, William 1840–1920, *Wagwood Stone Quarries, Dore, Derbyshire*, bequeathed by Major W. Boden, 1922
Boler, Albert Edward 1864–1939, *Banner Cross*, presented by Mr T. Roper, 1963
Bomberg, David 1890–1957, *Valley of La Hermida: Picos de Europa, Asturias, Spain*, purchased with the assistance of the Victoria and Albert Museum Purchase Grant Fund, 1965, © the estate of David Bomberg. All rights reserved, DACS 2012
Bond, William Joseph Julius Caesar 1833–1926, *The Duck Pond*, gift from J. G. Graves, 1935
Bone, Stephen 1904–1958, *Christchurch Bay, Dorset*, purchased, 1947, © estate of Stephen Bone. All rights reserved, DACS 2012
Bone, Stephen 1904–1958, *Sheffield Cathedral*, purchased from the artist's wife, 1976, © estate of Stephen Bone. All rights reserved, DACS 2012
Bonheur, Auguste-François 1824–1884, *Cattle*, presented by F. T. Mappin, 1891
Bonheur, Auguste-François 1824–1884, *Landscape with Cattle*, bequeathed by Sir Wilson Mappin, 1925
Bonheur, Rosa 1822–1899, *Sheep in a Landscape*, gift from J. G. Graves, 1929
Bonington, Richard Parkes 1802–1828, *Old Cherbourg, France*, gift from J. G. Graves, 1935
Bonington, Richard Parkes 1802–1828, *The Piazzetta, Venice*, gift from J. G. Graves, 1929
Bonington, Richard Parkes 1802–1828, *View of the City of Lyons, France*, gift from J. G. Graves, 1943
Bonnard, Pierre 1867–1947, *Nu aux bas noires*, on loan from a private collection, © ADAGP, Paris and DACS, London 2012
Bortoluzzi, Camillo 1868–1933, *Venetian Houses*, gift from J. G. Graves, 1937
Boshier, Derek b.1937, *First Toothpaste Painting*, purchased from the Waddington Gallery with the assistance of the Victoria and Albert Museum Purchase Grant Fund, 1979, © the artist/ courtesy Flowers Gallery, London
Bossuet, François Antoine 1798–1889, *Place de la Constitution à Jaen, Espagne*, bequeathed by H. H. Andrews, 1903
Bottomley, Albert Ernest 1873–1950, *March Morning*, gift from J. G. Graves, 1943
Boudin, Eugène Louis 1824–1898, *The Quay at Antwerp, Belgium*, gift from J. G. Graves, 1935
Boudin, Eugène Louis 1824–1898, *Plage en Normandie, France*, on loan from a private collection
Boudin, Eugène Louis 1824–1898, *The Water Meadows at Deauville, France*, gift from J. G. Graves, 1935
Bough, Samuel 1822–1878, *Coast Scene*, gift from J. G. Graves, 1937
Boughton, George Henry 1833–1905, *The Landing of the Pilgrim Fathers*, bequeathed by J. N. Mappin, 1887
Boughton, George Henry 1833–1905, *The Ferry, a Dainty Fare*, gift from J. G. Graves, 1935
Bource, Henri Jacques 1826–1899, *On the Beach, Scheveningen, Holland*, bequeathed by J. N. Mappin, 1887
Bouvet, Henri Marius Camille 1859–1945, *River Scene, Evening*, gift from J. G. Graves, 1937
Bower, Reuben 1828–1912, *St James's Church, Norton, Sheffield*, gift from the Norton History Group and Mrs E. Purnell, 2009
Bower, Reuben 1828–1912, *Beauchief Abbey, Derbyshire*, presented by Mrs Johnson, 1955
Bower, Reuben 1828–1912, *Cottage at Backmoor, Norton, Sheffield*, gift from the Norton History Group and Mrs E. Purnell, 2009
Boyd, Fionnuala b.1944 & **Evans, Leslie** b.1945, *Evidence Wind*, purchased from the Angela Flowers Gallery, 1975, © Boyd & Evans
Boyle, George A. 1826–1899, *Moonrise at Sea*, gift from J. G. Graves, 1943
Bradley, Andrea 1970–2009, *The River Rother*, presented by the artist, 1996 © the artist's estate
Bradley, Andrea 1970–2009, *Clumber Park and Church, Nottinghamshire*, presented by the artist, 1996 © the artist's estate
Brammall, J. H. active c.1860–1880, *Endcliffe Hall, Sheffield*, presented by E. C. Shrewsbury
Brammall, J. H. active c.1860–1880, *Manor Lodge, Sheffield*, presented by E. C. Shrewsbury
Brangwyn, Frank 1867–1956, *Fishermen at Funchal, Madeira, Portugal*, on loan from a private collection, © the artist's estate/ Bridgeman Art Library
Brangwyn, Frank 1867–1956, *Loading the Boat*, purchased from the Belgrave Gallery, 1977, © the artist's estate/Bridgeman Art Library
Branwhite, Charles 1817–1880, *Winter Scene*, bequeathed by J. N. Mappin, 1887
Bratby, John Randall 1928–1992, *Jean and Table Top (Girl in a Yellow Jumper)*, purchased from the Sandford Gallery with the assistance of the Victoria and Albert Museum Purchase Grant Fund, 1980, © the artist's estate/ Bridgeman Art Library
Bratby, John Randall 1928–1992, *Hardy Road in November, II*, purchased at Sotheby's, 1978, © the artist's estate/Bridgeman Art Library
Bratby, John Randall 1928–1992, *Antonia Fraser (b.1932)*, purchased from the artist with the assistance of the Victoria and Albert Museum Purchase Grant Fund, 1984, © the artist's estate/Bridgeman Art Library
Bratby, John Randall 1928–1992, *The Artist Painting a Picture*,

purchased from the artist with the assistance of the Victoria and Albert Museum Purchase Grant Fund, 1984, © the artist's estate/ Bridgeman Art Library
Brealey, William Ramsden 1889–1949, *Frederick Bradbury*, © the artist's estate
Brealey, William Ramsden 1889–1949, *The Waiter, Dieppe*, presented by Mr R. H. Parks, 1950, © the artist's estate
Brealey, William Ramsden 1889–1949, *Self Portrait*, presented by the artist, 1933, © the artist's estate
Brealey, William Ramsden 1889–1949, *Portrait of a Baby*, presented by Mr R. H. Parks, 1950, © the artist's estate
Brealey, William Ramsden 1889–1949, *The Huntsman*, presented by Mr R. H. Parks, 1950, © the artist's estate
Breanski, Alfred de 1852–1928, *A Glint of Sunshine, Glen Ogle, Scotland*, bequeathed by J. Slagg, 1979
Breanski, Alfred de 1852–1928, *Moorland*, gift from J. G. Graves, 1937
Brekelenkam, Quiringh van (attributed to) after 1622–1669 or after, *Old Woman*, gift from J. G. Graves, 1935
Brest, Germain Fabius 1823–1900, *A Town on a French River*, gift from J. G. Graves, 1943
Breton, Jules Adolphe Aimé Louis 1827–1906, *Landscape, Courrières, France*, gift from J. G. Graves, 1937
Brett, John 1830–1902, *Mount Etna from Taormina, Sicily*, gift from J. G. Graves, 1935
Brewtnall, Edward Frederick 1846–1902, *The Model's Luncheon*, presented by F. T. Mappin, 1891
Bright, Henry 1814–1873, *A Moorland View*, gift from J. G. Graves, 1935
Bright, Henry 1814–1873, *Mountainous Landscape with a Ruin*, bequeathed by Sir Wilson Mappin, 1925
Bright, Henry 1814–1873, *The Mill*, gift from J. G. Graves, 1935
Bright, Henry 1814–1873, *The Old Hall, Lincolnshire*, bequeathed by J. N. Mappin, 1887
Bright, Henry 1814–1873, *Woody Landscape*, gift from J. G. Graves, 1929
Bright, Henry 1814–1873 & **Hill** *Landscape with Figures*, bequeathed by Sir Wilson Mappin, 1925
Bristow, Edmund 1787–1876, *Landscape with Cattle*, gift from J. G. Graves, 1935
British (English) School 17th C, *An Unknown Lady* (possibly Lady Jane Grey, 1537–1554), gift from J. G. Graves, 1935
British (Norwich) School *At Norwich, Norfolk*, gift from J. G. Graves, 1935
British School 17th C, *Portrait of a Lady*, gift from J. G. Graves, 1942
British School 17th C, *William Mompesson (1639–1709), Rector of Eyam*, presented by D. Sutton, 1961
British School 18th C, *Mr Batty, a Sheffield Solicitor*, presented by Colonel McKenzie-Smith, 1949
British School 18th C, *Portrait of a Lady*, purchased, 1948
British School (attributed to) *Portrait of a Man, Aged 29*, gift from J. G. Graves, 1942
British School (attributed to) 19th C, *Persian Sibyl*, gift from J. G. Graves, 1929
Brockhurst, Gerald Leslie 1890–1978, *Ranunculus*, gift from J. G. Graves, 1935 © the artist's estate
Brocky, Charles (attributed to) 1807–1855, *Head of a Girl with Roses*, bequeathed by J. N. Mappin, 1887
Bromley, Valentine Walter 1848–1877, *Girl Resting*, gift from J. G. Graves, 1943
Brooker, William 1918–1983, *Interior by Lamplight*, purchased at Christie's, 1980, © the artist's estate
Brown, Thomas Austen 1859–1924, *Fisherfolk*, gift from J. G. Graves, 1929
Brown, Thomas Austen 1859–1924, *Sunshine and Shadow*, gift from J. G. Graves, 1935
Brown, Thomas Austen 1859–1924, *Turnip Hoeing*, gift from J. G. Graves, 1929
Brueghel, Jan the elder (attributed to) 1568–1625, *A Village*, gift from J. G. Graves
Brundrit, Reginald Grange 1883–1960, *Clouds from the West*, purchased from the artist, 1948
Bryant, Henry Charles 1836–1915, *Market Scene*, bequeathed by Sir Wilson Mappin, 1925
Bryant, Henry Charles 1836–1915, *Portsmouth Market*, bequeathed by Sir Wilson Mappin, 1925
Buhler, Robert A. 1916–1989, *The Orchard*, purchased from the New Grafton Gallery, 1970, © the artist's estate/Bridgeman Art Library
Bunce, William Gedney 1840–1916, *A Hot Day on the Lagoons, Venice*, gift from J. G. Graves, 1929
Bundy, Edgar 1862–1922, *Man Eating Lunch*, presented by Thomas Cocking & Sons, 1949
Bunney, John Wharlton 1828–1882, *Exterior of a Church, Ravenna, Italy*, accepted by HM Government in lieu of inheritance tax and allocated to the Guild of St George, 2002
Bunney, John Wharlton 1828–1882, *Lake with Islands and a Mountain Backdrop*, accepted by HM Government in lieu of inheritance tax and allocated to the Guild of St George, 2002
Bunney, John Wharlton 1828–1882, *Study of Tree Branches*, accepted by HM Government in lieu of inheritance tax and allocated to the Guild of St George, 2002
Bunney, John Wharlton 1828–1882, *The Piazzetta of San Marco* (unfinished), *Venice*, accepted by HM Government in lieu of inheritance tax and allocated to the Guild of St George, 2002
Bunney, John Wharlton 1828–1882, *Colonnaded Street Scene, Serravalle, Italy*, accepted by HM Government in lieu of inheritance tax and allocated to the Guild of St George, 2002
Bunney, John Wharlton 1828–1882, *St Ursula's Banners, St Ursula Receiving the Pope's Benediction* (detail) (after Vittore Carpaccio), on long-term loan from the Guild of St George, 1877
Bunney, John Wharlton 1828–1882, *Interior of the Sala del Senato, Doge's Palace, Venice*, accepted by HM Government in lieu of inheritance tax and allocated to the Guild of St George, 2002
Bunney, John Wharlton 1828–1882, *Outside the Public Gardens, Sant'Elena, Venice*, accepted by HM Government in lieu of inheritance tax and allocated to the Guild of St George, 2002
Bunney, John Wharlton 1828–1882, *Sailing Ship by the Ponte Veneta Marina, Venice*, accepted by HM Government in lieu of inheritance tax and allocated to the Guild of St George, 2002
Bunney, John Wharlton 1828–1882, *View of the Piazzetta di San Marco from San Giorgio, Venice*, accepted by HM Government in lieu of inheritance tax and allocated to the Guild of St George, 2002
Bunney, John Wharlton 1828–1882, *Lake Geneva and the Castle of Chillon, Switzerland*, accepted by HM Government in lieu of inheritance tax and allocated to the Guild of St George, 2002
Bunney, John Wharlton 1828–1882, *Venus, Vulcan and Cupid* (after Jacopo Tintoretto), accepted by HM Government in lieu of inheritance tax and allocated to the Guild of St George, 2002
Bunney, John Wharlton 1828–1882, *Interior of San Marco, with the Baptistery, Venice*, accepted by HM Government in lieu of inheritance tax and allocated to the Guild of St George, 2002
Bunney, John Wharlton 1828–1882, *The Vision of St Ursula* (detail) (after Vittore Carpaccio), accepted by HM Government in lieu of inheritance tax and allocated to the Guild of St George, 1877
Bunney, John Wharlton 1828–1882, *Western Facade of the Basilica of San Marco, Venice*, on long-term loan from the Guild of St George, 1882
Burgers, Hendricus-Jacobus 1834–1899, *Dutch Courtship*, bequeathed by Thomas Heiffor, 1886
Burgess, Arthur James Wetherall 1879–1957, *Destroyers on Scapa Flow*, gift from J. G. Graves, 1929, © the artist's estate
Burgin, Victor b.1941, *Escalator*, presented, 1966, © the artist
Burne-Jones, Edward 1833–1898, *Cupid Delivering Psyche*, purchased from Hartnoll & Eyre, 1971
Burne-Jones, Edward 1833–1898, *The Hours*, gift from J. G. Graves, 1935
Burr, Alexander Hohenlohe 1835–1898, *Grace before Meat*, presented by Mr R. W. Moore
Burr, Alexander Hohenlohe 1835–1898, *The Musical Party*, bequeathed by J. N. Mappin, 1887
Burr, Alexander Hohenlohe 1835–1898, *Blind Man's Buff*, gift from J. G. Graves, 1929
Burr, Alexander Hohenlohe 1835–1898, *The Rustic Crop*, bequeathed by J. N. Mappin, 1887
Burr, John P. 1831–1893, *The Travelling Tinker*, bequeathed by J. N. Mappin, 1887
Burr, John P. 1831–1893, *A Flock of Sheep*, bequeathed by E. G. Wragg, 1928
Burr, John P. 1831–1893, *The New Dress*, bequeathed by H. H. Andrews, 1903
Burrows, Robert 1810–1893, *A Wooded Glade*, gift from J. G. Graves, 1935
Bussy, Simon 1870–1954, *Mixed Flowers in a White Jug*, presented by Dick Rainer, 1970
Butler, J. active 19th C, *Cromwellian Soldier*, bequeathed by Sir Wilson Mappin, 1925
Buttersworth, Thomas 1768–1842, *The Squall*, gift from J. G. Graves, 1935
Cadell, Francis Campbell Boileau 1883–1937, *Iona, Scotland*, purchased from the Scottish Gallery with the assistance of the Victoria and Albert Museum Purchase Grant Fund, 1976 © Cadell Estate, courtesy Portland Gallery, London
Cairns, Joyce W. b.1947, *Martini Rose with the Captain of the 'Stirling Teal'*, purchased, 1986, © the artist
Caldecott, Randolph 1846–1886, *Monaco*, gift from J. G. Graves, 1935
Callow, William (attributed to) 1812–1908, *A Street in Bruges, Belgium*, bequeathed by J. N. Mappin, 1887
Cameron, David Young 1865–1945, *La Roche, Belgium*, gift from J. G. Graves, 1935
Cameron, David Young 1865–1945, *Sunset on the Firth*, purchased from the Fine Art Society, 1981
Cameron, Duncan 1837–1916, *Harvest Time near St Fillans, Perthshire, Scotland*, bequeathed by Sir Wilson Mappin, 1925
Cameron, Duncan 1837–1916, *Largo Bay, Scotland*, bequeathed by Sir Wilson Mappin, 1925
Campo, Federico del 1837–1923, *Canal with a Bridge*, gift from J. G. Graves, 1929
Canaletto (school of) 1697–1768, *Santa Maria della Salute, Venice*, gift from J. G. Graves, 1942
Carline, Richard 1896–1980, *Kate (Katherine Foster)*, purchased from Mary Carline, 1984, © the artist's estate
Carr, Henry Marvell 1894–1970, *Henry Rushbury's Daughter*, purchased from the artist, 1953
Carr, Henry Marvell 1894–1970, *Portrait of a Girl*, purchased from the artist, 1953
Carracci, Annibale (after) 1560–1609, *The Death of St Francis (The Ecstasy of St Francis)*, presented by Mrs Carter, 1956
Carrington, Donald P. b.1907, *Still Life*, presented by J. Rothenstein, 1936
Carter, William 1863–1939, *Still Life*, bequeathed by the artist, 1939
Castro, Manuel active before 1795–1805, *A Spanish Music Girl*, gift from J. G. Graves, 1943
Cattermole, George 1800–1868, *A Conference at the Monastery*, gift from J. G. Graves, 1929
Cattermole, George 1800–1868, *Rosslyn Chapel, Scotland*, gift from J. G. Graves, 1937
Caulfield, Patrick 1936–2005, *The Hermit*, purchased from David Philips with the assistance of the Victoria and Albert Museum Purchase Grant Fund, 1979, © the estate of Patrick Caulfield. All rights reserved, DACS 2012
Cazin, Jean-Charles 1841–1901, *Harvest Time*, gift from J. G. Graves, 1937
Cazin, Marie 1844–1924, *The Harbour Lights*, gift from J. G. Graves, 1937
Cazin, Marie (attributed to) 1844–1924, *Outskirts of Abbeville, France*, gift from J. G. Graves, 1935
Ceriez, Theodore 1832–1904, *A Savoyard in the Time of Louis XV*, bequeathed by J. N. Mappin, 1887
Cézanne, Paul 1839–1906, *Bassin du Jas de Bouffan*, bequeathed by R. A. Peto, 1964
Chaillou, Narcisse 1837–1896, *A Rat Seller during the Siege of Paris*, bequeathed by J. N. Mappin, 1887
Chaillou, Narcisse (attributed to) 1837–1896, *The Knife Grinder*, bequeathed by J. N. Mappin, 1887
Chambers, George 1803–1840, *Sailing Ships*, gift from J. G. Graves, 1935
Chambers, George 1803–1840, *Sea Piece*, bequeathed by J. N. Mappin, 1887
Chambers, George 1803–1840, *Coast Scene*, gift from J. G. Graves, 1935
Chantrey, Francis Leggatt 1781–1842, *Captain Thomas Asline Ward (1781–1871)*, presented by Lieutenant Colonel E. R. Bradley, 1950
Chantrey, Francis Leggatt 1781–1842, *Ebenezer Rhodes (1762–1839)*, presented by W. Mitchell Eadon, 1887

Chantrey, Francis Leggatt 1781–1842, *John B. Morton, Esq.*, purchased from Denis Schofield, 1951
Chantrey, Francis Leggatt 1781–1842, *John Fox of Dore*, presented by Mrs S. Sellars
Chantrey, Francis Leggatt 1781–1842, *John Porter (1736–1812)*, presented by Miss Mary Porter, 1940
Chantrey, Francis Leggatt 1781–1842, *Miss Bramall (b.1784)*, bequeathed by A. J. Milner, 1913
Chantrey, Francis Leggatt 1781–1842, *Portrait of a Lady (Miss Bramall)*, presented by T. S. Bramall, 1959
Chantrey, Francis Leggatt 1781–1842, *Self Portrait*, bequeathed by A. J. Milner, 1913
Chapman, Carlton Theodore 1860–1925, *Coast Scene*, bequeathed by H. H. Andrews, 1903
Charvot, Eugène (attributed to) 1847–1924, *Landscape with Cattle*, gift from J. G. Graves, 1929
Chialiva, Luigi 1842–1914, *Landscape with Cattle*, presented by F. T. Mappin, 1887
Churchyard, Thomas 1798–1865, *Seascape*, presented by the Sheffield Society for the Encouragement of Art, 1938
Clark, Joseph 1834–1926, *The Labourer's Welcome*, gift from J. G. Graves, 1929
Clarke, Brian b.1953, *Site Plan*, purchased from the artist, 1979, © Brian Clarke. All rights reserved, DACS 2012
Clarke, Pete b.1951, *Ways of Living: Inside Looking Out, a Monument*, purchased from the artist, 1984, © the artist
Clays, Paul Jean 1819–1900, *The Calm*, bequeathed by J. N. Mappin, 1887
Clays, Paul Jean 1819–1900, *The Storm*, bequeathed by J. N. Mappin, 1887
Clays, Paul Jean 1819–1900, *Dutch Fishing Boats*, presented by F. T. Mappin, 1887
Cleveley, John c.1712–1777, *Deptford Dockyard*, purchased from Wharncliffe Estates Co., 1956
Clouet, François (school of) c.1515–1572, *Diane de Poitiers (1499–1566), Duchess of Valentinois*, gift from J. G. Graves, 1935
Clough, Prunella 1919–1999, *Telephone Engineer II*, purchased from Ball & Hargreaves, 1979, © estate of Prunella Clough 2012. All rights reserved, DACS
Clough, Prunella 1919–1999, *Building Site*, purchased at Sotheby's, 1968, © estate of Prunella Clough 2012. All rights reserved, DACS
Clough, Prunella 1919–1999, *Landscape in a Mining Area*, purchased from Monika Kinley, 1972, © estate of Prunella Clough 2012. All rights reserved, DACS
Clough, Prunella 1919–1999, *Discovered Check*, purchased from the artist, 1973, © estate of Prunella Clough 2012. All rights reserved, DACS
Cluysenaar, André 1872–1939, *Arthur Balfour (1848–1930)*, presented by Balfour Darwins, 1975, © Anne Cluysenaar
Coates, Colin 1908–1991, *Jansen Street, Sheffield*, purchased, 1974, © the artist's estate
Coccorante, Leonardo (school of) 1680–1750, *The Pool of Bethesda*, presented by the National Union of Mineworkers, Barnsley, 1963
Cohen, Harold b.1928, *As If*, purchased from the artist, 1976, © the artist
Coker, Peter 1926–2004, *Butcher's Shop No.1*, purchased at Sotheby's with the assistance of the Victoria and Albert Museum Purchase Grant Fund, 1973, © the estate of Peter Coker, RA
Coker, Peter 1926–2004, *Cliff at Étretat, France*, purchased from the artist with the assistance of the Victoria and Albert Museum Purchase Grant Fund, 1984, © the estate of Peter Coker, RA
Coker, Peter 1926–2004, *Seascape*, purchased from Abbott and Holder, 1983, © the estate of Peter Coker, RA
Coldstream, William Menzies 1908–1987, *Rimini, Italy*, presented by the Women's Auxiliary Air Corps, 1947, © the artist's estate/Bridgeman Art Library
Cole, George 1810–1883, *Landscape*, presented by F. T. Mappin, 1891
Cole, George Vicat 1833–1893, *Landscape with Sheep and Figures*, bequeathed by E. G. Wragg, 1928
Cole, George Vicat 1833–1893, *Landscape with Sheep*, gift from J. G. Graves, 1943
Cole, George Vicat 1833–1893, *Near Petersfield, Hampshire*, gift from J. G. Graves, 1937
Cole, George Vicat 1833–1893, *On the Thames*, presented by J. A. Crammond, 1949
Cole, George Vicat 1833–1893, *Dorchester Abbey, Oxfordshire*, gift from J. G. Graves, 1929
Cole, George Vicat 1833–1893, *Churchyard, Dorchester Abbey, Oxfordshire*, gift from J. G. Graves, 1929
Cole, Leslie 1910–1976, *Air Transport Auxiliary*, presented by the Women's Auxiliary Air Corps, 1947, © the artist's estate
Collins, Cecil 1908–1989, *The Artist's House*, presented by the National Art Collections Fund, 2002, © Tate, London 2012
Collins, Cecil 1908–1989, *Still Life*, presented by the National Art Collections Fund, 2002, © Tate, London 2012
Collins, William 1788–1847, *Cromer Sands, Norfolk*, gift from J. G. Graves, 1929
Collins, William 1788–1847, *English Cottage Scene*, gift from J. G. Graves, 1929
Collinson, James 1825–1881, *The Landlady*, gift from J. G. Graves, 1929
Collinson, James 1825–1881, *At the Bazaar*, gift from J. G. Graves, 1929
Compton, Edward Theodore 1849–1921, *Snow Scene on the Col d'Orny, Valais, Switzerland*, bequeathed by A. Davy, 1946
Compton, Edward Theodore 1849–1921, *Loch Ness, Scotland*, gift from J. G. Graves, 1929
Conder, Charles 1868–1909, *French Beach Scene, Dieppe*, gift from J. G. Graves, 1942
Conder, Charles 1868–1909, *On the Seashore*, purchased, 1938
Conder, Charles 1868–1909, *Watching the Fireworks at Saint-Cloud, France*, gift from J. G. Graves, 1935
Constable, John (after) 1776–1837, *Cornfield (Country Lane)*, bequeathed by J. N. Mappin, 1887
Constable, John (attributed to) 1776–1837, *Salisbury Cathedral, Wiltshire*, gift from J. G. Graves, 1929
Constable, John (attributed to) 1776–1837, *Landscape*, bequeathed by J. N. Mappin, 1887
Constable, John (attributed to) 1776–1837, *Arundel Castle, West Sussex*, gift from J. G. Graves, 1943
Constable, John (attributed to) 1776–1837, *Hampstead, London*, gift from J. G. Graves, 1937
Constable, John (attributed to) 1776–1837, *The Water Meadows, Salisbury, Wiltshire*, gift from J. G. Graves, 1935
Constant, Jean Joseph Benjamin 1845–1902, *Portrait of the Artist*, gift from J. G. Graves, 1935
Constant, Jean Joseph Benjamin 1845–1902, *Venetian Scene*, presented by Madame De Runkel, 1938
Constant, Jean Joseph Benjamin 1845–1902, *Portrait*, presented by Madame De Runkel, 1938
Constantine, George Hamilton 1875–1968, *March Afternoon*, presented by A. L. Gibson, 1937, © the artist's estate
Constantine, Harry Francis b.1919, *A Winter Garden (Brocco Bank, Sheffield)*, purchased from the artist, 1982, © the artist
Constantine, Harry Francis b.1919, *Cemaes Bay, Anglesey, Wales*, purchased from the artist, 1982, © the artist
Constantine, Harry Francis b.1919, *Sun, Sea and Cloud, Irish Sea from Anglesey, Wales*, purchased from the artist, 1982, © the artist
Cooke, Edward William 1811–1880, *Venetian Fishing Craft off the Adriatic Shore of the Lido*, bequeathed by J. N. Mappin, 1887
Cooke, Edward William 1811–1880, *A Village Scene*, gift from J. G. Graves, 1937
Cooke, Edward William 1811–1880, *Venice*, gift from J. G. Graves, 1929
Cookesley, Margaret Deborah 1844–1927, *The Egg Seller*, gift from J. G. Graves, 1937
Cooper, Thomas Sidney 1803–1902, *Cattle and Sheep*, gift from J. G. Graves, 1935
Cooper, Thomas Sidney 1803–1902, *The Halt on the Hills*, presented by F. T. Mappin
Cooper, Thomas Sidney 1803–1902, *In the Whitehall Meadows, Canterbury, Kent*, bequeathed by J. N. Mappin, 1887
Cooper, Thomas Sidney 1803–1902, *Morning, Canterbury Meadows, Kent*, bequeathed by H. H. Andrews, 1903
Cooper, Thomas Sidney 1803–1902, *Amongst the Fells, East Cumberland*, bequeathed by Sir Wilson Mappin, 1925
Cooper, Thomas Sidney 1803–1902 & **Lee, Frederick Richard** 1798–1879, *Landscape, Sheep Crossing a Bridge*, presented by F. T. Mappin, 1887
Cooper, Thomas Sidney 1803–1902, **Creswick, Thomas** 1811–1869 & **Frith, William Powell** 1819–1909, *Landscape with Cattle*, presented by F. T. Mappin, 1891
Cope, Arthur Stockdale 1857–1940, *The Right Honourable Anthony John Mundella (1825–1897), MP*, on loan from a private collection
Cope, Charles West 1811–1890, *Edward III Conferring the Order of the Garter on Edward the Black Prince*, purchased from J. S. Maas, 1971
Corbet, Matthew Ridley 1850–1902, *Landscape Study for 'Val d'Arno, Italy, Evening'*, purchased from the Fine Art Society, 1976
Corot, Jean-Baptiste-Camille 1796–1875, *Au Petit Chaville*, purchased from Alex Reid & Lefevre with the assistance of the Victoria and Albert Museum Purchase Grant Fund, 1964
Corot, Jean-Baptiste-Camille (attributed to) 1796–1875, *Landscape and Farm Buildings*, gift from J. G. Graves, 1942
Corot, Jean-Baptiste-Camille (attributed to) 1796–1875, *Landscape*, gift from J. G. Graves, 1943
Cossaar, Jacobus Cornelis Wyand 1874–1966, *Rotterdam Boats*, gift from J. G. Graves, 1937
Coster, Jan Herman 1846–1920, *River Scene*, gift from J. G. Graves, 1929
Cotman, Frederick George 1850–1920, *Sunday Morning*, gift from J. G. Graves, 1929
Cotman, John Sell 1782–1842, *Village in Normandy, France, Noon*, gift from J. G. Graves, 1935
Cotman, John Sell (attributed to) 1782–1842, *Consett Iron Works, Durham*, gift from J. G. Graves, 1935
Coulaud, Martin d.1906, *Returning to the Fold*, gift from J. G. Graves, 1943
Courbet, Gustave 1819–1877, *Boy with a Parrot*, gift from J. G. Graves, 1935
Cousin, Charles-Louis-Auguste 1807–1887, *A Venetian Byway*, gift from J. G. Graves, 1943
Couture, Thomas (attributed to) 1815–1879, *A Portrait Study*, gift from J. G. Graves, 1943
Cowen, William 1791–1864, *View of Sheffield from Meersbrook*, presented by J. E. Cutler, 1886
Cowen, William 1791–1864, *View of Sheffield from Shrewsbury Road*, purchased, 1952
Cox, David the elder 1783–1859, *On the Lledr, North Wales*, presented by the Nettlefold Collection, 1948
Cox, David the elder 1783–1859, *Darley Churchyard, Derbyshire*, gift from J. G. Graves, 1935
Cox, David the elder 1783–1859, *Crossing the Heath*, gift from J. G. Graves, 1929
Cox, David the elder 1783–1859, *Landscape*, bequeathed by J. N. Mappin, 1887
Cox, David the elder 1783–1859, *Riverside Path*, gift from J. G. Graves, 1942
Cox, David the elder 1783–1859, *The Wayfarers*, gift from J. G. Graves, 1929
Coxon, Raymond James 1896–1997, *Near Portmadoc, Wales*, presented by the Sheffield Society for the Encouragement of Art, 1937, © the artist's estate
Cradock, Marmaduke (after) c.1660–1717, *Peacocks and Poultry*, bequeathed by Mr J. Wigfull, 1936
Craxton, John 1922–2009, *Cat and Snail*, purchased from Ball & Hargreaves, 1977, © John Craxton 2012. All rights reserved, DACS
Creswick, Thomas 1811–1869, *Glengarriff, County Cork, Ireland*, bequeathed by J. N. Mappin, 1887
Creswick, Thomas 1811–1869, *High Tor, Matlock, Derbyshire*, gift from J. G. Graves, 1935
Creswick, Thomas 1811–1869, *Landscape, River Scene*, bequeathed by Bertha Annie Sykes, 1949
Creswick, Thomas 1811–1869, *A Mill Stream in Eskdale, Cumbria*, bequeathed by J. N. Mappin, 1887
Creswick, Thomas 1811–1869, *A Road near Sheffield*, gift from J. G. Graves, 1929
Creswick, Thomas 1811–1869, *A Welsh Landscape*, gift from J. G. Graves, 1935
Creswick, Thomas 1811–1869, *Across the Common*, gift from J. G. Graves, 1935
Creswick, Thomas 1811–1869, *Brighton Pier, East Sussex*, bequeathed by J. N. Mappin, 1887

Creswick, Thomas 1811–1869, *Cumberland*, gift from J. G. Graves, 1929

Creswick, Thomas 1811–1869, *Hillsborough, Sheffield*, gift from J. G. Graves, 1929

Creswick, Thomas 1811–1869, *Italian Landscape*, gift from J. G. Graves, 1935

Creswick, Thomas 1811–1869, *Landscape*, bequeathed by J. N. Mappin, 1887

Creswick, Thomas 1811–1869, *Landscape with Cattle*, gift from J. G. Graves

Creswick, Thomas 1811–1869, *Landscape with Trees*, gift from J. G. Graves, 1935

Creswick, Thomas 1811–1869, *Near Ashover, Derbyshire*, gift from J. G. Graves, 1935

Creswick, Thomas 1811–1869, *Near Barmouth, Wales*, gift from J. G. Graves, 1935

Creswick, Thomas 1811–1869, *Smoo Cave, Sutherland, Scotland*, gift from J. G. Graves, 1935

Creswick, Thomas 1811–1869, *South Stack Lighthouse, Holyhead, Wales*, bequeathed by J. N. Mappin, 1887

Creswick, Thomas 1811–1869, *Stepping Stones*, bequeathed by H. H. Andrews, 1903

Creswick, Thomas 1811–1869, *Surrey Sandhills*, presented by the family of the late H. Bramley, 1922

Creswick, Thomas 1811–1869, *The Fairy Glen, Betws-y-Coed, Wales*, gift from J. G. Graves, 1935

Creswick, Thomas 1811–1869, *The Ferry*, gift from J. G. Graves, 1935

Creswick, Thomas 1811–1869, *The Ford*, bequeathed by H. C. Brunning, 1908

Creswick, Thomas 1811–1869, *The Millstream*, gift from J. G. Graves, 1935

Creswick, Thomas 1811–1869, *The Priory*, gift from J. G. Graves, 1935

Creswick, Thomas 1811–1869, *The River Road*, gift from J. G. Graves

Creswick, Thomas 1811–1869, *The Trout Stream*, gift from J. G. Graves, 1935

Crighton, Hugh Ford 1824–1886, *Thomas Moore (1809–1880), Mayor of Sheffield (1868–1871)*, on loan from a private collection

Crighton, Hugh Ford 1824–1886, *Henry Seebohm (1832–1895)*, presented by George W. Staniforth, 1945

Crighton, Hugh Ford 1824–1886, *Thomas Jessop (1804–1887), JP, Mayor of Sheffield (1863–1864)*, on loan from a private collection

Crighton, Hugh Ford 1824–1886, *Self Portrait*, presented by Thomas Winder, 1910

Crighton, Hugh Ford 1824–1886, *Thomas Moore (1809–1880), Mayor of Sheffield (1868–1871)*, on loan from a private collection

Crofts, Ernest 1847–1911, *The Morning of the Battle of Waterloo*, bequeathed by J. N. Mappin, 1887

Crofts, Ernest 1847–1911, *The Empty Saddle*, bequeathed by J. N. Mappin, 1887

Crofts, Ernest 1847–1911, *Cromwell Questioning a Prisoner*, presented by J. S. Watson, 1945

Crofts, Ernest 1847–1911, *Wellington's March from Quatre Bras to Waterloo*, bequeathed by J. N. Mappin, 1887

Crome, John 1768–1821, *A Harvest*, gift from J. G. Graves, 1935

Crome, John 1768–1821, *Landscape with a River*, gift from J. G. Graves, 1943

Crome, John 1768–1821, *Near St Martin, Norfolk*, bequeathed by W. Adlington, 1946

Crome, John 1768–1821, *The Windmill*, bequeathed by J. N. Mappin, 1887

Crome, John Berney 1794–1842, *Barges by a Jetty*, gift from J. G. Graves

Crome, John Berney 1794–1842, *On the Yare, Norfolk*, gift from J. G. Graves, 1935

Crozier, William 1930–2011, *Putney Heath, London*, purchased at Sotheby's, 1965, © the estate of William Crozier/ courtesy Flowers Gallery, London

Danby, Francis 1793–1861, *A Misty Spring Morning*, gift from J. G. Graves, 1943

Danby, Francis 1793–1861, *Sunset*, purchased from Agnew's, 1966

Dansaert, Léon Marie Constant 1830–1909, *The Promenade of Versailles in the Time of Louis XV*, bequeathed by J. N. Mappin, 1887

Daubigny, Charles-François 1817–1878, *Fishing Boats by a Stream*, gift from J. G. Graves, 1935

Davie, Alan b.1920, *Tree into Animal No.1*, purchased from Gimpel Fils with the assistance of the Victoria and Albert Museum Purchase Grant Fund, 1980, © the artist

Davie, Alan b.1920, *Prize for a Serpent*, purchased from Gimpel Fils, © the artist

Davis, Henry William Banks 1833–1914, *Landscape with Cattle*, presented by Mr Cramond, 1949

Davis, Henry William Banks 1833–1914, *A Summer Afternoon*, presented by F. T. Mappin

Davis, Henry William Banks 1833–1914, *Landscape in Wiltshire*, bequeathed by J. N. Mappin, 1887

Davis, Henry William Banks 1833–1914, *Landscape with Cattle and Sheep*, bequeathed by Sir Wilson Mappin, 1925

Davis, Richard Barrett 1782–1854, *Cattle*, gift from J. G. Graves, 1935

Dawson, Henry 1811–1878, *View on the Thames Looking towards St Paul's, London*, presented by F. T. Mappin, 1887

Dawson, Henry 1811–1878, *Cattle Sheltering*, gift from J. G. Graves, 1929

Dawson, Henry 1811–1878, *The Last Load*, gift from J. G. Graves, 1935

De Cock, Xavier 1818–1896, *Evening*, gift from J. G. Graves, 1937

de Francia, Peter 1921–2012, *Portrait of an African Girl*, purchased from the artist, 1984, © estate of Peter de Francia, courtesy James Hyman Fine Art, London

de Francia, Peter 1921–2012, *Figure Study for 'The Bombing of Sakiet'*, purchased, 1986, © estate of Peter de Francia, courtesy James Hyman Fine Art, London

de Francia, Peter 1921–2012, *Oil Sketch for 'The Bombing of Sakiet'*, purchased, 1986, © estate of Peter de Francia, courtesy James Hyman Fine Art, London

de Francia, Peter 1921–2012, *African Prison*, purchased from the artist with the assistance of the Victoria and Albert Museum Purchase Grant Fund, 1984, © estate of Peter de Francia, courtesy James Hyman Fine Art, London

de Francia, Peter 1921–2012, *Old Man and a Boy*, purchased from the artist, 1984, © estate of Peter de Francia, courtesy James Hyman Fine Art, London

de Groot, Adelaide Milton 1876–1967, *The Dutch Canal*, gift from J. G. Graves, 1943

De Sausmarez, Lionel Maurice 1915–1969, *Lodge Moor, Sheffield, in the Evening*, presented by C. A. Humphrey, 1981, © the artist's estate

De Sausmarez, Lionel Maurice 1915–1969, *Apples, Apple Peel and a Knife on a Table* (recto), purchased at Christie's, 1980, © the artist's estate

De Sausmarez, Lionel Maurice 1915–1969, *Portrait of an Unknown Woman* (verso)*, purchased at Christie's, 1980, © the artist's estate

De Wint, Peter 1784–1849, *The Wayside Pool*, gift from J. G. Graves, 1935

De Wint, Peter 1784–1849, *William Hilton Senior*, gift from J. G. Graves, 1935

Dearle, John Henry 1860–1932, *A Straw Barge*, gift from J. G. Graves, 1935

Dearman, John active 1824–1857, *Landscape with Cattle*, gift from J. G. Graves, 1929

Debuche, Georges L. active 1925–1928, *The Silver Coffee Service*, gift from J. G. Graves, 1943

Decamps, Alexandre-Gabriel 1803–1860, *The Blind Beggar*, gift from J. G. Graves, 1935

Decamps, Alexandre-Gabriel (attributed to) 1803–1860, *An Arab and His Steed*, gift from J. G. Graves, 1929

Delamotte, A. *Oriental Poppies*, gift from J. G. Graves

Denny, Robyn b.1930, *Rising I*, purchased from the Kasmin Gallery, 1972, © the artist

Deutsch, Ludwig 1855–1935, *The Sultan's Daughter*, gift from J. G. Graves, 1937

Devas, Anthony 1911–1958, *St Margaret's Bay, Kent*, presented by the family of the artist, 1991, © the artist's estate/Bridgeman Art Library

Devis, Arthur William 1762–1822, *The Swing*, gift from J. G. Graves, 1935

Diaz de la Peña, Narcisse Virgile (attributed to) 1808–1876, *A Wood Scene*, gift from J. G. Graves, 1942

Dibdin, Thomas Colman 1810–1893, *Landscape*, presented by A. Wood, 1969

Dicksee, Frank 1853–1928, *Interior with a Lady*, gift from J. G. Graves, 1943

Dismorr, Jessica 1885–1939, *Landscape with Figures*, purchased at Phillips, 1991

Dobson, Frank 1888–1963, *Portrait of the Artist's Wife*, purchased at Christie's, 1974

Dobson, William Charles Thomas 1817–1898, *The Good Shepherd*, bequeathed by J. N. Mappin, 1887

Dongen, Kees van 1877–1968, *Kiki de Montparnasse (1901–1953)*, on loan from a private collection, © ADAGP, Paris and DACS, London 2012

Doré, Gustave 1832–1883, *Three Figures*, presented by F. T. Mappin

Downman, John 1750–1824, *Lady in a Grey Dress*, gift from J. G. Graves, 1935

Downman, John 1750–1824, *Portrait of a Gentleman*, gift from J. G. Graves, 1929

Downton, John 1906–1991, *Joan Harris*, © Museums Sheffield

Drummond, Malcolm 1880–1945, *The Artist's Desk*, purchased from Anthony D'Offay with the assistance of the Victoria and Albert Museum Purchase Grant Fund, 1975, © the artist's estate

Drummond, Malcolm 1880–1945, *Near Beaconsfield, Buckinghamshire*, presented by Mrs V. M. Carr, 1972, © the artist's estate

Dubufe, Guillaume 1853–1909, *Spring Time in Italy*, presented by the Right Honourable A. J. Mundella, MP

Dugdale, Thomas Cantrell 1880–1952, *Un quai à Paris*, purchased at Sotheby's, 1976, © Joanna Dunham

Dunbar, Evelyn Mary 1906–1960, *The Garden*, presented by the Sheffield Society for the Encouragement of Art, 1937, © the artist's estate

Duncan, Edward 1803–1882, *The Wreck*, presented by F. T. Mappin, 1891

Dunlop, Ronald Ossory 1894–1973, *Portrait*, purchased from the artist, 1952

Dunlop, Ronald Ossory 1894–1973, *The Untidy Farmyard*, purchased from the artist, 1952

Dupré, Jules 1811–1889, *A Stiff Breeze*, gift from J. G. Graves, 1935

Dupré, Jules 1811–1889, *Coucher du soleil*, presented by the Nettlefold Collection, 1948

Dusart, Cornelis 1660–1704, *A Merrymaking*, gift from J. G. Graves, 1935

Dutch School *Soldiers Attacking Villagers*, gift from J. G. Graves, 1943

Dutch School 17th C, *Portrait*, gift from J. G. Graves, 1942

Dutch School 17th C, *Portrait of a Gentleman*, gift from J. G. Graves, 1935

Dutch School 17th C, *River Scene*, gift from J. G. Graves, 1942

Dutch School 17th C, *The Denial of Christ*, presented by Captain Penrose, 1955

Dutch School 17th C, *View of a Waterway*, gift from J. G. Graves, 1937

Dutch School 18th C, *Skating in Holland*, bequeathed by J. N. Mappin, 1887

Dutch School 18th C, *The Artist's Studio*, gift from J. G. Graves, 1942

Dutch School *Flower Piece*, gift from J. G. Graves, 1942

Dutch School *River Scene*, gift from J. G. Graves, 1942

Dutch School (attributed to) *Lady in a Ruff*, gift from J. G. Graves, 1935

Dutch School (attributed to) 18th C, *Flowers in a Vase*, gift from J. G. Graves, 1935

Dutch School (attributed to) 18th C, *Harbour Scene*, gift from J. G. Graves, 1935

Duval, John 1816–1892, *John Bunyan in Bedford Gaol*, gift from J. G. Graves, 1942

Duverger, Théophile Emmanuel 1821–1901, *When the Cat's Away the Mice Will Play*, bequeathed by J. N. Mappin, 1887

Eadon, Willis 1870–1945, *Shore Scene*, presented by Mrs Tyzack, 1996

Earl, Thomas 1810–1876, *Dog and Rabbit*, bequeathed by J. N. Mappin, 1887

Eatwell, W. active 1862, *Sir Walter Scott (1771–1832), Bt*, gift from J. G. Graves, 1942

Egg, Augustus Leopold 1816–1863, *Lady in a Green Dress*, gift from J. G. Graves, 1935

Egg, Augustus Leopold 1816–1863, *Le diable boiteux*, presented by F. T. Mappin, 1887

Egley, William Maw 1826–1916, *The Lady of Shalott*, gift from J. G. Graves, 1937

Elliott, John b.1953, *Not Quite Social*, purchased from the Anne Berthoud Gallery, 1981

Ellis, Edwin 1841–1895, *Cliffs and Sea*, gift from J. G. Graves, 1937

Ellis, Edwin 1841–1895, *Coast View*, gift from J. G. Graves, 1929

Ellis, Edwin 1841–1895, *Landing the Catch*, gift from J. G. Graves

Ellis, Edwin 1841–1895, *Landscape and a River*, gift from J. G. Graves, 1929

Ellis, Edwin 1841–1895, *Over the Harbour Bar*, presented by F. T. Mappin, 1887

Elsheimer, Adam (attributed to) 1578–1610, *The Betrayal of Christ*, gift from J. G. Graves, 1929
Eluke, Julius active 20th C, *The Lion of St Mark, Venice*, gift from J. G. Graves, 1937
Elwell, Frederick William 1870–1958, *The New Frock*, gift from J. G. Graves, 1935
Emms, John 1843–1912, *Hunting Scene*, bequeathed by H. H. Andrews, 1903
Emms, John 1843–1912, *Run to Earth*, bequeathed by H. H. Andrews, 1903
Engel, Fritz Franz c.1878–1956, *Summer Day*, presented by Mrs Tozer, 1967
Etty, William 1787–1849, *Classical Subject*, presented by Mrs Roddis, 1952
Etty, William 1787–1849, *Head of a Girl*, gift from J. G. Graves, 1935
Etty, William 1787–1849, *Judas Iscariot*, gift from J. G. Graves, 1929
Etty, William 1787–1849, *Nude*, gift from J. G. Graves, 1937
Etty, William 1787–1849, *Nude*, presented by the Sheffield Society for the Encouragement of Art, 1938
Etty, William 1787–1849, *Titania and the Fairies*, gift from J. G. Graves
Eurich, Richard Ernst 1903–1992, *Crab Boat*, purchased from Arthur Tooth, 1973, © the artist's estate/Bridgeman Art Library
Eyre, James 1802–1838, *A Windmill in Derbyshire*, gift from J. G. Graves, 1937
Faed, John 1820–1902, *Highland Interior with Figures*, bequeathed by Sir Wilson Mappin, 1925
Faed, Thomas 1826–1900, *Auld Robin Gray*, bequeathed by J. N. Mappin, 1887
Faed, Thomas 1826–1900, *Robert Burns and Highland Mary*, bequeathed by J. N. Mappin, 1887
Faed, Thomas 1826–1900, *A Game of Draughts*, presented by F. T. Mappin
Faed, Thomas 1826–1900, *Cottage Interior*, gift from J. G. Graves, 1935
Fahey, Edward Henry 1844–1907, *The Via Massala, Rapallo, Italy*, gift from J. G. Graves, 1929
Fantin-Latour, Henri 1836–1904, *The Crucifixion*, gift from J. G. Graves, 1935
Fantin-Latour, Henri (attributed to) 1836–1904, *The Trysting Place*, gift from J. G. Graves, 1935
Farquharson, David 1839–1907, *Eventide*, bequeathed by Sir Wilson Mappin, 1925
Farren, Robert Dennis 1832–1912, *Potato Picking in Cambridgeshire*, gift from J. G. Graves, 1929
Farthing, Stephen b.1950, *Room in Samur*, presented by the Contemporary Art Society, 1992, © the artist
Fawley, J. F. *Rural Cottage**, bequeathed by Miss Ada Fawley, 1978
Fedden, Mary b.1915, *Red Still Life*, purchased from the Sandford Gallery, 1980, © the artist
Fedden, Mary b.1915, *Shetland Still Life*, purchased from the Sandford Gallery, 1980, © the artist
Fedden, Mary b.1915, *Three Mauve Flowers*, presented by the artist, 1997, © the artist
Feiler, Paul b.1918, *Strata Brown and Grey*, on loan from a private collection, © the artist/Bridgeman Art Library
Fell, Sheila Mary 1931–1979, *Snowscape, Cumbria*, purchased from the artist, 1977
Ferg, Franz de Paula 1689–1740, *A Street Scene*, presented by the Nettlefold Collection, 1948
Ferg, Franz de Paula 1689–1740, *The Fountain*, gift from J. G. Graves, 1935
Ferg, Franz de Paula (attributed to) 1689–1740, *The Ferryboat*, gift from J. G. Graves, 1935
Fieldhouse, Florence 1898–1974, *Alderman Mrs A. E. Longden (d.1952), First Lady Lord Mayor of Sheffield*, presented by J. D. W. Longden, 1976
Fielding, Anthony V. C. 1787–1855, *A Rough Sea off Dover, Kent*, bequeathed by J. N. Mappin, 1887
Fielding, Anthony V. C. 1787–1855, *Ben Venue, Scotland*, gift from J. G. Graves, 1935
Fielding, Anthony V. C. 1787–1855, *Landscape*, gift from J. G. Graves, 1935
Fielding, Anthony V. C. 1787–1855, *Landscape with Cattle*, gift from J. G. Graves, 1937
Fielding, Brian 1933–1987, *Baltic Angel*, purchased from the artist, 1987, © the artist's estate
Fielding, Brian 1933–1987, *Ink City*, purchased, 1986, © the artist's estate
Fisher, Mark 1841–1923, *A Grey Day*, gift from J. G. Graves, 1929
Fleetwood-Walker, Bernard 1893–1965, *Head of a Girl*, purchased, 1948, © the estate of Mrs P. Fleetwood-Walker
Fleetwood-Walker, Bernard 1893–1965, *Miss Bryan*, © the estate of Mrs P. Fleetwood-Walker
Flemish School 15th C, *Man with a Red Cap*, gift from J. G. Graves, 1935
Flemish School 16th C, *Mary Tudor (1516–1558)*, gift from J. G. Graves, 1935
Flemish School 19th C, *Peasants (Skittle Alley)*, gift from J. G. Graves, 1935
Flemish School (attributed to) 16th C, *Fortress*, gift from J. G. Graves, 1935
Focardi, Ruggero 1864–1934, *A Spanish Street Scene*, gift from J. G. Graves, 1942
Focardi, Ruggero 1864–1934, *The Olive Grove*, gift from J. G. Graves, 1943
Forbes, Stanhope Alexander 1857–1947, *Sheffield, River and Smoking Chimneys*, purchased from the Fine Art Society, 1980, © the artist's estate/Bridgeman Art Library
Formois, Théodore 1814–1871, *In the Belgian Ardennes*, gift from J. G. Graves, 1929
Foster, Myles Birket 1825–1899, *The Ruined Mill*, gift from J. G. Graves, 1935
Fowler, Robert 1853–1926, *Halcyon Weather*, presented by R. Fowler Junior, 1932
Fragonard, Jean-Honoré (attributed to) 1732–1806, *The Sketching Lesson*, gift from J. G. Graves, 1943
Franco-Flemish School *The Triumph of Bacchus*, purchased from the Castle Hill Club, 1950
Fraser, Alexander b.1940, *Pink Beach*, purchased from the artist, 1970, © the artist
Fraser, Alexander George 1786–1865, *The Goose Girl*, gift from J. G. Graves, 1943
Freedman, Barnett 1901–1958, *The Farmyard*, purchased, 1934, © V. C. Freedman and descendants
French School 18th C, *Classical Landscape*, bequeathed by Mrs Handley, 1951
French School 18th C, *The Arts*, purchased from Hallsborough, 1951
French School *Self Portrait*, gift from J. G. Graves, 1942
French School *The Holy Well*, gift from J. G. Graves, 1942
French School (attributed to) 18th C, *Maximilien François Marie Isidore de Robespierre (1758–1794)*, gift from J. G. Graves, 1935
French School (attributed to) 19th C, *A Musical Party*, gift from J. G. Graves, 1935
French School (attributed to) 19th C, *Peasants in a Field at Rest*, gift from J. G. Graves, 1943
French School (attributed to) 19th C, *Still Life, Peaches on a Dish*, gift from J. G. Graves, 1935
Frère, Charles Édouard 1837–1894, *Shoeing Forge*, presented by F. T. Mappin, 1887
Frère, Pierre Edouard 1819–1886, *Waiting for Visitors*, gift from J. G. Graves, 1929
Frère, Pierre Edouard 1819–1886, *In Front of the School*, bequeathed by J. N. Mappin, 1887
Frère, Pierre Edouard 1819–1886, *Sewing on a Button*, presented by F. T. Mappin, 1887
Frith, William Powell 1819–1909, *John Knox Reproving Mary Queen of Scots*, bequeathed by J. N. Mappin, 1887
Frith, William Powell 1819–1909, *The Toilet*, bequeathed by Sir Wilson Mappin, 1925
Frith, William Powell 1819–1909, *The Bride of Lammermoor* (from the novel by Walker Scott), bequeathed by H. H. Andrews, 1903
Frost, Terry 1915–2003, *Green and Maroon Movement*, purchased, 1984, © estate of Terry Frost. All rights reserved, DACS 2012
Frost, Terry 1915–2003, *Abstract Painting*, on loan from a private collection, © estate of Terry Frost. All rights reserved. DACS 2012
Fry, Anthony b.1927, *Dancing Figures No.9*, purchased from the New Art Centre, 1969, © the artist
Fry, Roger Eliot 1866–1934, *Edith Sitwell (1887–1964)*, gift from J. G. Graves, 1935
Fry, Roger Eliot 1866–1934, *Quarry, Bo Peep Farm, Sussex*, gift from J. G. Graves, 1937
Fry, Roger Eliot 1866–1934, *Rabat, Morocco*, presented by Lord Lee of Fareham, 1935
Fumi, Tebaldo active 1870–1880, *Madonna del Cardelino* (after Raphael), on long-term loan from the Guild of St George, 1923
Fuseli, Henry 1741–1825, *The Tempest*, purchased from Colonel Hollingworth, 1950
Fuseli, Henry (attributed to) 1741–1825, *Albermarle Street, London*, gift from J. G. Graves, 1935
Fyfe, William Baxter Collier 1836–1882, *Landscape in West Ireland*, gift from J. G. Graves, 1943
Gainsborough, Thomas (attributed to) 1727–1788, *Landscape*, gift from J. G. Graves, 1942
Garay Arévalo, Manuel 1844–1911, *The Mouse*, bequeathed by Thomas Heiffor, 1886
Garstin, Norman 1847–1926, *Wren's Monument (St Paul's Cathedral, London)*, purchased from the artist, 1921
Garstin, Norman 1847–1926, *Béguinage Church*, presented by the Contemporary Art Society, 1980
Gaubault, Alfred Émile d.1895, *A French Guardsman*, gift from J. G. Graves, 1943
Gaubault, Alfred Émile d.1895, *A French Guardsman*, gift from J. G. Graves, 1943
Gauguin, Paul 1848–1903, *Interieur avec Aline Gauguin*, on loan from a private collection
Geefs, Fanny 1807–1883, *Meditation*, gift from J. G. Graves, 1943
Geoffroy, Jean Jules Henry 1853–1924, *Visiting Day*, gift from J. G. Graves, 1929
Gérome, Jean-Léon 1824–1904, *The Execution of Marshal Ney*, presented by Lord Faringdon, 1931
Gheeraerts, Marcus the elder (attributed to) c.1520–before 1604, *Lord Hunsdon (1526–1596)*, gift from J. G. Graves, 1935
Gibbs, Lewis T. *Evening Stillness*, gift from J. G. Graves, 1942
Gibbs, Percy William 1894–1937, *Landing the Catch*, gift from J. G. Graves, 1937
Gibbs, Thomas Binney 1870–1947, *Edward Carpenter (1844–1929)*, presented by Gilbert Beith, 1949
Gilbert, John 1817–1897, *Charles I Leaving Westminster after His Death Sentence Had Been Passed*, presented by F. T. Mappin
Giles, Frank Lynton 1910–2003, *The Elements*, presented by the artist, 1981, © the artist's estate
Gill, Edmund Marriner 1820–1894, *A Welsh Mountain Torrent*, gift from J. G. Graves, 1943
Gillet, Numa François 1868–1940, *Summer Sunshine*, gift from J. G. Graves, 1943
Gillies, William George 1898–1973, *Flowers in a Vase*, purchased from the collection of the late J. W. Blyth, 1965, © Royal Scottish Academy
Gillies, William George 1898–1973, *Temple, Midlothian, Scotland*, purchased, 1966, © Royal Scottish Academy
Gillray, James 1757–1815, *A Country Fair*, gift from J. G. Graves, 1935
Gilman, Harold 1876–1919, *Eating House*, purchased from the Piccadilly Gallery, 1965
Ginner, Charles 1878–1952, *Le quai Duquesne, Dieppe, France*, purchased from the Fine Art Society, 1976
Ginner, Charles 1878–1952, *St John's Church, Chester*, purchased from H. Booth, 1952
Girardet, Léopold-Henri 1848–1904, *The Sick Child*, bequeathed by Sir Wilson Mappin, 1925
Girardot, Ernest Gustave 1840–1904, *Scene from 'The Vicar of Wakefield'* (from the novel by Oliver Goldsmith), presented by Mrs J. D. Dickinson Eaton, 1913
Gogin, Charles 1844–1931, *Ivy Leaves*, presented by F. T. Mappin, 1887
Gogin, Charles 1844–1931, *A Profile*, presented by Mrs Alma Gogin, 1931
Gomez *Portrait*, gift from J. G. Graves, 1943
Goodall, Frederick 1822–1904, *The Village Holiday* (after David Wilkie), bequeathed by J. N. Mappin, 1887
Goodall, Frederick 1822–1904, *The Sick Child*, bequeathed by J. N. Mappin, 1887
Goodall, Frederick 1822–1904, *Felice Ballarin Reciting Tasso to the People of Chioggia*, bequeathed by Sir Wilson Mappin, 1925
Goodall, Frederick 1822–1904, *The Relief of Lucknow (Jessie's Dream)*, bequeathed by J. N. Mappin, 1887
Goodall, Frederick 1822–1904, *Winnowing Corn in Brittany, France*, bequeathed by J. N. Mappin, 1887
Goodall, Frederick 1822–1904, *Hunt the Slipper*, bequeathed by J. N. Mappin, 1887
Goodall, Frederick 1822–1904, *The First Born*, presented by F. T. Mappin, 1887
Goodall, Frederick 1822–1904, *Agriculture in the Valley of the Nile*,

bequeathed by J. N. Mappin, 1887
Goodall, Howard 1850–1874, *Capri Girls Winnowing Corn*, presented by F. T. Mappin, 1887
Goodwin, Albert 1845–1932, *London Flower Girl*, gift from J. G. Graves, 1929
Goodwin, Albert 1845–1932, *Lincoln*, gift from J. G. Graves, 1935
Goodwin, Albert 1845–1932, *Pevensey Castle, East Sussex*, presented, 1941
Goodwin, Albert 1845–1932, *Scene from 'The Tempest'* (from the play by William Shakespeare), gift from J. G. Graves, 1935
Gore, Spencer 1878–1914, *Harold Gilman's House at Letchworth, Hertfordshire*, purchased at Christie's with the assistance of the Victoria and Albert Museum Purchase Grant Fund, 1978
Gore, Spencer 1878–1914, *Reclining Nude*, presented by M. R. Wilfred Jonson, 1935
Gosse, Laura Sylvia 1881–1968, *Dancing Negro*, gift from J. G. Graves, 1935, © the artist's estate/ Bridgeman Art Library
Gosse, Laura Sylvia 1881–1968, *Homeward Bound, la rue St Remi, Dieppe, France*, gift from J. G. Graves, 1935, © the artist's estate/ Bridgeman Art Library
Gosse, Laura Sylvia 1881–1968, *Les rentiers*, gift from J. G. Graves, 1935, © the artist's estate/ Bridgeman Art Library
Gotch, Thomas Cooper 1854–1931, *The Mother Enthroned*, presented by C. Boot, 1925
Gotch, Thomas Cooper 1854–1931, *Winter Sketch, Provence, France*, presented by the Fine Art Society, 1978
Goupil, Jules Adolphe 1839–1883, *Landscape with a Church*, gift from J. G. Graves, 1943
Gowing, Lawrence 1918–1991, *Apples*, purchased at Sotheby's, 1967, © estate of Sir Lawrence Gowing
Gowing, Lawrence 1918–1991, *Barbara Saxon*, © estate of Sir Lawrence Gowing
Goyen, Jan van 1596–1656, *Landscape with Cottages on the Dunes*, purchased from P. & D. Colnaghi Co. Ltd, 1954
Goyen, Jan van (school of) 1596–1656, *River Scene with Boats*, gift from J. G. Graves, 1943
Goyen, Jan van (style of) 1596–1656, *Landscape*, gift from J. G. Graves
Graham, George 1881–1949, *The Look Out, Winchelsea, East Sussex*, gift from J. G. Graves, 1935
Graham Bell, Frank 1910–1943, *Brunswick Square, London*, purchased at Sotheby's, 1984, © the artist's estate
Gran, Daniel 1694–1757, *The Charity of St Elizabeth of Hungary*, purchased with the assistance of the Victoria and Albert Museum Purchase Grant Fund, 1966
Graner, Luis 1863–1929, *The Losing Candidates*, gift from J. G. Graves, 1929
Graner, Luis 1863–1929, *The Winning Candidates*, gift from J. G. Graves, 1929
Grant, Duncan 1885–1978, *Bea Howe*, purchased from the Mayor Gallery, 1977, © estate of Duncan Grant. All rights reserved, DACS 2012
Greaves, Derrick b.1927, *Sheffield*, purchased from the Balliol College Junior Common Room, 1979, © the artist
Greaves, Derrick b.1927, *Venice in the Rain*, presented by the Contemporary Art Society, 1956, © the artist
Greaves, Derrick b.1927, *Flower and Collage*, purchased from Monika Kinley, 1972, © the artist
Greaves, Derrick b.1927, *In the Studio 2, Flowers in the Studio*, purchased at Christie's, 1980, © the artist
Greaves, Walter 1846–1930, *Nocturne, Battersea Reach, London*, purchased at Christie's, 1974
Greaves, Walter 1846–1930, *The Thames at Chelsea, London*, purchased from P. H. Spurr, 1937
Greenham, Robert Duckworth 1906–1976, *Mary*, purchased from the Piccadilly Gallery with the assistance of the Victoria and Albert Museum Purchase Grant Fund, 1981
Greiffenhagen, Maurice 1862–1931, *Portrait of a Boy*, presented by the artist's son, 1949
Greiffenhagen, Maurice 1862–1931, *Portrait of a Lady*, presented by Mrs E. Greiffenhagen, 1949
Greuze, Jean-Baptiste 1725–1805, *Portrait of a Girl*, gift from J. G. Graves, 1943
Griffin, Paul b.1955, *Strange Time*, purchased from the artist, 1981
Grimm, Stanley 1891–1966, *Flower Piece*, gift from J. G. Graves, 1937
Grönland, Theude 1817–1876, *Fruit*, gift from J. G. Graves, 1929
Guise, A. *A Japanese Girl*, gift from J. G. Graves, 1943
Gunn, Herbert James 1893–1964, *Le pont de Napoléon, Paris*, purchased from N. Coker, 1973, © estate of the artist
Gussoni, Vittorio 1893–1968, *Lady's Head*, gift from J. G. Graves, 1935
Gussow, Carl 1843–1907, *Autumn Flowers*, bequeathed by J. N. Mappin, 1887
Guttman, J. b.1869, *Self Portrait* (after Rembrandt van Rijn), presented by F. T. Mappin, 1891
Guttman, J. b.1869, *Rembrandt's Mother* (after Rembrandt van Rijn), presented by F. T. Mappin, 1891
Haanen, Adriana Johanna 1814–1895, *Flowers*, bequeathed by J. N. Mappin, 1887
Haghe, Louis 1806–1885, *The Church of St Jacques, Antwerp, Belgium*, presented by F. T. Mappin, 1891
Hallé, Charles Edward 1846–1919, *The Fortune Teller*, bequeathed by Sir Wilson Mappin, 1925
Hallé, Charles Edward 1846–1919, *The Rivals*, presented by F. T. Mappin
Halswelle, Keeley 1832–1891, *A Rainy Night*, gift from J. G. Graves, 1929
Hanneman, Adriaen c.1601–1671, *Portrait of a Lady*, purchased from F. Slater, 1952
Hardy, Dudley 1866–1922, *Madame Sarah Bernhardt (1844–1923)*, gift from J. G. Graves, 1935
Hardy, Dudley 1866–1922, *Madame Sarah Bernhardt (1844–1923)*, presented by Miss Rudge
Hardy, Heywood 1842–1933, *Country Scene*, bequeathed by Mrs A. G. Yeomans, 1972
Hardy, Thomas Bush 1842–1897, *Sea Piece*, gift from J. G. Graves, 1943
Hardy, Thomas Bush 1842–1897, *Seascape*, gift from J. G. Graves, 1942
Hardy, Thomas Bush 1842–1897, *Sea Piece*, gift from J. G. Graves, 1929
Hargitt, Edward 1835–1895, *The Goose Girl*
Harnett, William Michael 1848–1892, *The Old Cupboard Door*, bequeathed by H. H. Andrews, 1903
Harpignies, Henri-Joseph 1819–1916, *Farmhouses, St Aubin, Jersey*, gift from J. G. Graves, 1935
Harpignies, Henri-Joseph 1819–1916, *Sunset*, gift from J. G. Graves, 1935
Harris, Thomas 1787–1817, *St Paul's Parish Church of Sheffield*, gift from J. G. Graves, 1937
Hattersley, George Pearson 1858–1937, *Site of Crookes Valley Road (Great Dam Road from Mushroom Lane, Western Park, Sheffield)*, presented by H. E. Robinson, 1929
Hauve, A. van *The Soldier's Return*, gift from J. G. Graves, 1942
Havell, William 1782–1857, *Mountain Pass near Subiaco, Roman States*, presented by F. T. Mappin, 1887
Havers, Alice 1850–1890, *Roses in a Vase*, gift from J. G. Graves, 1943
Havers, Alice 1850–1890, *Rush Cutters*, presented by F. T. Mappin, 1887
Havers, Val 1873–1912, *A Turkish Lady*, gift from J. G. Graves, 1929
Hawkesworth, Joseph Hallam 1827–1908, *Landscape*, presented by Mr and Mrs Walker, 1938
Hawkesworth, Joseph Hallam 1827–1908, *Old Endcliffe Woods, Sheffield*, gift from J. G. Graves, 1935
Hawkesworth, Joseph Hallam 1827–1908, *Rivelin Valley, Sheffield*, presented by Mr F. S. Pulland, 1939
Hawkesworth, Joseph Hallam 1827–1908, *Winter Scene*, purchased from Mr H. Booth, 1954
Hawkesworth, Joseph Hallam 1827–1908 or **Pickford, Ralph Randolphus (attributed to)** 1834–1911, *High Street, Sheffield*
Hawksley, Arthur 1842–1915, *Robin Hood's Bay, North Yorkshire*, presented by Mrs Hawksley
Hayes, Edwin 1819–1904, *Port Rush*, gift from J. G. Graves, 1937
Hayes, Edwin 1819–1904, *Sea Piece*, presented by F. T. Mappin
Hayes, Edwin 1819–1904, *Seascape*, gift from J. G. Graves, 1937
Hayes, Edwin 1819–1904, *Broadstairs Harbour, Kent*, gift from J. G. Graves, 1943
Hayes, Edwin 1819–1904, *Shipping Making for a Harbour in a Rough Sea*, gift from J. G. Graves, 1929
Head, B. G. active 1867–1890, *William Gladstone (1809–1898)*, gift from J. G. Graves, 1942
Heath, Adrian 1920–1992, *Divided*, purchased from the artist, 1972, © the estate of Adrian Heath
Heath, Adrian 1920–1992, *Divided Form*, purchased from the artist, 1972, © the estate of Adrian Heath
Heeremans, Thomas c.1640–1697, *Winter Landscape*, purchased from W. M. Saline & Sons, 1954
Heinish, Karl Adam 1847–1923, *Cottages*, gift from J. G. Graves, 1929
Hellewell, Jack 1920–2000, *Libya in January*, on loan from a private collection, presented by the Sheffield Society for the Encouragement of Art
Helmick, Howard 1845–1907, *A Frugal Meal*, bequeathed by Bertha Annie Sykes, 1949
Helmick, Howard 1845–1907, *The Gossips*, bequeathed by H. H. Andrews, 1903
Helmick, Howard 1845–1907, *A Stitch in Time Saves Nine*, bequeathed by H. H. Andrews, 1903
Helmick, Howard 1845–1907, *The Alchemist*, bequeathed by H. H. Andrews, 1903
Helmick, Howard 1845–1907, *The Connoisseurs*, bequeathed by H. H. Andrews, 1903
Hemy, Charles Napier 1841–1917, *Whitby, North Yorkshire*, gift from J. G. Graves, 1943
Hemy, Charles Napier 1841–1917, *How the Boat Came Home*, presented by F. T. Mappin, 1887
Hemy, Charles Napier 1841–1917, *A Pull to Windward, Falmouth, Cornwall*, presented by Mr Gaymond, 1949
Henry, Émile (attributed to) 1844–1920, *Travellers on a Showery Day*, gift from J. G. Graves, 1935
Henry, George 1858–1943, *Hikers at Goodwood Downs, West Sussex*, presented by the Trustees of the estate of the artist, 1945
Henry, Paul 1876–1958, *The Village by the Lake*, purchased from the Imperial Gallery, 1929
Henshaw, Frederick Henry 1807–1891, *In the Forest of Arden, Warwickshire*, gift from J. G. Graves, 1935
Henzell, Isaac 1815–1876, *The Crab Catcher*, presented by F. T. Mappin, 1891
Hepher, David b.1935, *Still Life*, purchased from the artist, 1972, © the artist/ courtesy Flowers Gallery, London
Hepher, David b.1935, *No.21* (diptych), purchased from the Angela Flowers Gallery, 1972, © the artist/ courtesy Flowers Gallery, London
Hepher, David b.1935, *Upperthorpe, Sheffield*, purchased from the artist, 1974, © the artist/ courtesy Flowers Gallery, London
Her, Theodor 1838–1892, *Landscape with Figures*, gift from J. G. Graves, 1943
Herdman, Robert Duddingstone 1863–1922, *Head of a Man*, gift from J. G. Graves, 1929
Hering, George Edwards 1805–1879, *On Lake Como, Italy*, gift from J. G. Graves,1929
Hering, George Edwards 1805–1879, *William Tell's Chapel on the Lake of Lucerne, Switzerland*, gift from J. G. Graves, 1943
Herring, John Frederick I 1795–1865, *Horses in a Landscape*, bequeathed by E. Buxton, 1946
Herring, John Frederick I 1795–1865, *The Good Templars*, gift from J. G. Graves, 1943
Herring, John Frederick I 1795–1865, *The White Horse*, gift from J. G. Graves, 1942
Highfield, William 1870–1957, *Broadfield Toll-Bar, Sheffield*, presented by Mrs E. Wilson, 1956
Highfield, William 1870–1957, *Heeley Toll-Bar, Sheffield*, presented by Mrs E. Wilson, 1956
Highfield, William 1870–1957, *Pitsmoor Toll-Bar, Sheffield*, purchased, 1981
Highfield, William 1870–1957, *Norton Church, Sheffield*, presented by D. L. Johnson, 1957
Highfield, William 1870–1957, *Beauchief Abbey, Sheffield*, presented by R. Covill, 1972
Highfield, William 1870–1957, *Broadfield Road Toll-Bar, Sheffield*, presented by R. Covill, 1972
Highfield, William 1870–1957, *Heeley Toll-Bar, Sheffield*, presented by R. Covill, 1972
Highmore, Joseph 1692–1780, *Portrait of a Lady with a Pug Dog*, on loan from the Maleham Bequest, 1955
Highmore, Joseph 1692–1780, *Portrait of a Divine, Laurence Degge*, presented by Mr Bingham, 1954
Hill, Arthur c.1829–1894, *A Study of Beeches*, gift from J. G. Graves with the assistance of the Victoria and Albert Museum Purchase Grant Fund, 1943
Hill, James Stevens 1854–1921, *Landscape with a Church*, gift from J. G. Graves, 1943

Hill, James Stevens 1854–1921, *Marguerites in a Vase*, gift from J. G. Graves, 1943

Hillingford, Robert Alexander 1825–1904, *The Dunmow Flitch*, bequeathed by H. H. Andrews, 1903

Hilton, Roger 1911–1975, *Composition*, purchased from Ganymede Press, 1968, © estate of Roger Hilton. All rights reserved, DACS 2012

Hilton, Roger 1911–1975, *Fish and Two Lemons*, © estate of Roger Hilton. All rights reserved, DACS 2012

Hitchens, Ivon 1893–1979, *Flower Piece*, purchased from the Waddington Galleries, 1975, © Ivon Hitchens' estate/Jonathan Clark & Co.

Hobbema, Meindert (after) 1638–1709, *The Watermill*, gift from J. G. Graves, 1937

Hofland, Thomas Christopher 1777–1843, *Sheffield from Crookes*, purchased, 1972

Hofland, Thomas Christopher 1777–1843, *Sheffield General Cemetery*, purchased, 1903

Holl, Frank 1845–1888, *Her First Born*, purchased at Sotheby's, 1983

Holland, James 1799–1870, *Head of Lake Geneva, Switzerland*, gift from J. G. Graves, 1942

Holland, James 1799–1870, *A Highland River Scene with a Salmon Trap*, presented by F. T. Mappin, 1887

Holland, James 1799–1870, *Italian Village*, gift from J. G. Graves

Holland, James 1799–1870, *The Rialto, Venice*, bequeathed by J. N. Mappin, 1887

Holland, James 1799–1870, *Venice*, gift from J. G. Graves

Hollingsworth, Ruth b. 1880, *Daydreams*, gift from J. G. Graves, 1929

Hollingsworth, Ruth b. 1880, *Landscape*, gift from J. G. Graves, 1942

Hone, Nathaniel I 1718–1784, *The Honourable David Murray (1748–1794), MP for Peebleshire*, purchased at Christie's, 1972

Hook, James Clarke 1819–1907, *A Dream of Venice*, bequeathed by Sir Wilson Mappin, 1925

Hope, Robert 1869–1936, *Stream in Galloway, Scotland*, purchased at Christie's, 1978

Hoppner, John 1758–1810, *Mary Anne Sykes*, purchased, 1953

Hornel, Edward Atkinson 1864–1933, *Children by the Sea*, gift from J. G. Graves, 1935

Horsley, Walter Charles 1855–1934, *The French in Cairo*, presented by F. T. Mappin, 1887

Horton, Percy Frederick 1897–1970, *House on the Seine*, © the artist's estate

Horton, Percy Frederick 1897–1970, *Unemployed Man*, presented, 1937, © the artist's estate

Houston, George 1869–1947, *Port Askaig, Islay, Scotland*, purchased, 1929, © the artist's estate

Houthuesen, Albert Anthony 1903–1979, *Grain Barrels*, purchased, 1938, © reproduced by permission of the Trustees of the Albert Houthuesen Trust

Houthuesen, Albert Anthony 1903–1979, *The Collier*, purchased from the artist, 1934, © reproduced by permission of the Trustees of the Albert Houthuesen Trust

Hoyland, Henry George 1895–1948, *'Saint Thomas, 1914–1918'*, gift from J. G. Graves, 1937, © the artist's estate

Hoyland, John 1934–2011, *12.1.1969*, presented by the Contemporary Art Society, 1972, © the estate of John Hoyland. All rights reserved, DACS 2012

Hoyland, John 1934–2011, *Composition XVIII*, purchased from the Anti-Apartheid Auction arranged by the British Defence & Aid Fund for Southern Africa, 1983, © the estate of John Hoyland. All rights reserved, DACS 2012

Hubbard, Eric Hesketh 1892–1957, *A London Winter View*, gift from J. G. Graves, 1937

Hudson, Robert 1852–1884, *After Rain of the Tummell, Perthshire, Scotland*, bequeathed by Mrs Linley, 1920

Hudson, Robert 1852–1884, *Mountain Scene*

Hudson, Robert 1852–1884, *Brook Scene, Endcliffe Woods, Sheffield*, bequeathed by H. H. Andrews, 1903

Hudson, Thomas 1701–1779, *Dormer Fynes*, presented by the J. G. Graves Charitable Trust, 1950

Hughes, Arthur 1832–1915, *In the Grass*, gift from J. G. Graves, 1935

Hughes, Malcolm Edward 1920–1997, *Street Gossip*, © the artist's estate

Hughes-Stanton, Herbert Edwin Pelham 1870–1937, *Peat Gatherers*, gift from J. G. Graves, 1929

Hughes-Stanton, Herbert Edwin Pelham 1870–1937, *Moonrise*, gift from J. G. Graves, 1937

Hulme, Frederick William 1816–1884, *Ventnor from St Lawrence, Isle of Wight*, gift from J. G. Graves, 1929

Hulsdonck, Jacob van (attributed to) 1582–1647, *Still Life*, gift from J. G. Graves, 1935

Hume, Edith 1843–1906, *Packing Fish*, bequeathed by J. N. Mappin, 1887

Humphrey, Edward J. active 1872–1890, *Resting*, bequeathed by J. N. Mappin, 1887

Humphry, Ozias 1742–1810, *Francis Austen, Esq., of Sevenoaks*, gift from J. G. Graves, 1935

Hunt, Edgar 1876–1953, *Dog and Pigeons*, gift from J. G. Graves, 1942

Hunt, Thomas 1854–1929, *Home Sunshine*, gift from J. G. Graves, 1943

Hunt, William Holman 1827–1910, *Little Nell and Her Grandfather*, gift from J. G. Graves, 1935

Hunter, George Leslie 1877–1931, *Still Life with Fruit and a Black Fan*, purchased from the Fine Art Society with the assistance of the Victoria and Albert Museum Purchase Grant Fund, 1975

Hurt, Louis Bosworth 1856–1929, *At the Head of Glen Etive, Scotland*, bequeathed by Mrs Fisher,1930

Hutchison, William Oliphant 1889–1970, *The Hills of Fife, Scotland*, purchased at Christie's, 1978, © the artist's estate

Huysum, Jacob van 1686–1740, *Flowers in a Sculptured Vase*, gift from J. G. Graves, 1935

Hyatt, Derek James b.1931, *Woodpecker Woods, Autumn*, purchased from the artist, © the artist

Hyneman, Herman N. 1859–1907, *River Scene*, gift from J. G. Graves, 1937

Ibbetson, Julius Caesar 1759–1817, *Mountain Landscape*, purchased, 1950

Ibbetson, Julius Caesar 1759–1817, *A View in North Wales*, gift from J. G. Graves, 1937

Ibbetson, Julius Caesar 1759–1817, *The Harrow*, gift from J. G. Graves, 1935

Ibbetson, Julius Caesar 1759–1817, *Welsh Landscape*, gift from J. G. Graves, 1942

Ibbitt, William 1804–1869, *Wardsend Arches, Sheffield*, purchased, 1911

Ibbitt, William 1804–1869, *Sheffield from Crookesmoor*, presented by Herbert Barnes, 1931

Ibbitt, William 1804–1869, *Dam House, Crookesmoor, Sheffield*, purchased, 1903

Ifold, Frederick 1821–1904, *In Northern France*, gift from J. G. Graves

Inlander, Henry 1925–1983, *Mountains in Tuscany, Italy*, purchased at Sotheby's, 1973, © the artist's estate

Innes, James Dickson 1887–1914, *Mediterranean Coast Scene (Landscape Pyrenees)*, purchased from Dorelia John, 1964

Innes, James Dickson 1887–1914, *Landscape with a Figure, Arenig, Wales*, purchased from Dorelia John, 1964

Irvin, Albert b.1922, *Cathay*, purchased with the assistance of the Victoria and Albert Museum Purchase Grant Fund, 1986, © Albert Irvin. All rights reserved, DACS 2012

Irving, J. Thwaite active 1888–1909, *Lambing Time*, gift from J. G. Graves, 1929

Irwin, Gwyther 1931–2008, *Daymer, 1961*, purchased from New Art Centre with the assistance of the Victoria and Albert Museum Purchase Grant Fund, 1981, © the artist's estate

Israëls, Jozef (attributed to) 1824–1911, *Peasant Children*, gift from J. G. Graves, 1929

Italian School *Portrait of a Gentleman*, gift from J. G. Graves, 1935

Italian School 16th C, *San Rocco*, gift from J. G. Graves, 1943

Italian School 17th C, *Cupid and Monk*, gift from J. G. Graves

Italian School 18th C, *Cattle Drovers*, gift from J. G. Graves, 1935

Italian School 18th C, *Madonna and Child*, gift from J. G. Graves, 1943

Italian School 18th C, *The Grand Canal* (diptych), purchased, 1950

Italian School 18th C, *Venetian Canal*, gift from J. G. Graves

Italian School 19th C, *The Grand Canal, Venice*, gift from J. G. Graves, 1929

Italian School (attributed to) 15th C, *St Barbara*, presented by G. J. Chester to Sheffield Public Museum, 1886; transferred to Sheffield City Art Galleries, 1934

Italian School (attributed to) 18th C, *Portrait of a Cardinal*, gift from J. G. Graves, 1935

Jack, Richard 1866–1952, *Richmond Castle, North Yorkshire*, presented by B. A. Jones, 1927, © the artist's estate

Jacque, Charles Émile 1813–1894, *Forest Scene*, presented by F. T. Mappin, 1891

Jacque, Charles Émile 1813–1894, *The Flock*, presented by F. T. Mappin, 1887

Jacques, Marie b.1868, *Moonlight*, gift from J. G. Graves, 1937

Jacquet, Gustave Jean 1846–1909, *Good News*, bequeathed by H. H. Andrews, 1903

Jacquet, Gustave Jean 1846–1909, *Sport*, bequeathed by H. H. Andrews, 1903

Jacquet, Gustave Jean 1846–1909, *Music*, bequeathed by H. H. Andrews, 1903

Jagger, David 1891–1958, *Charles Jagger (1885–1934)*, bequeathed by J. S. Austin, 1942, © the artist's estate

Jagger, David 1891–1958, *Dr John George Graves (1866–1945)*, gift from the sitter, 1943, © the artist's estate

Jagger, David 1891–1958, *Portrait of a Lady*, purchased from Phillip's with the assistance of the Victoria and Albert Museum Purchase Grant Fund and the J. G. Graves Trust, 1996, © the artist's estate

Jagger, David 1891–1958, *Portrait of a Man*, presented by Willis Eadon, 1940, © the artist's estate

Jagger, David 1891–1958, *The Late Cyrus Jones*, presented by Mrs J. M. Jones, 1976, © the artist's estate

James, David 1834–1897, *A Cornish Breaker*, presented by Mrs Scott Walker, 1929

Jamieson, Alexander 1873–1937, *Fontainebleau, France*, purchased from the artist, 1921

Janssens van Ceulen, Cornelis 1593–1661, *Lady Coventry*, purchased from Leggatt Bros, 1970

Janssens van Ceulen, Cornelis (attributed to) 1593–1661, *Portrait of a Gentleman*, gift from J. G. Graves, 1935

Jaray, Tess b.1937, *Minuet*, presented by the artist, 1972, © the artist

Jennings, Roberta Louise b.1919, *Christmas Eve, 1932 (First Night of the Pantomime at the Lyceum Theatre, Sheffield)*, presented by Mr Hedley Oldfield and the Sheffield Society for the Encouragement of Art, 2004, © the artist

John, Augustus Edwin 1878–1961, *Señora Gandarillas*, on loan from the Maleham Bequest, 1972, © the artist's estate/Bridgeman Art Library

John, Augustus Edwin 1878–1961, *Robin John*, purchased from Admiral Sir Caspar John with the assistance of the Victoria and Albert Museum Purchase Grant Fund, 1970, © the artist's estate/ Bridgeman Art Library

John, Gwen 1876–1939, *A Corner of the Artist's Room in Paris*, presented by Dorelia John, 1984

Johnson, Charles Edward 1832–1913, *The Last of the Spanish Armada*, bequeathed by J. N. Mappin, 1887

Johnson, Harry John 1826–1884, *The Salmon Trap*, bequeathed by J. N. Mappin, 1887

Johnson, Valentine active 1777–1799, *Reverend Alexander McKenzie (1755–1816), Curate of St Paul's, Sheffield*, presented by Colonel McKenzie Smith, 1956

Johnston, Alexander 1815–1891, *Flora MacDonald's Introduction to Bonnie Prince Charlie*, bequeathed by J. N. Mappin, 1887

Johnston, Alexander 1815–1891, *Robin Adair*, presented by F. T. Mappin, 1887

Johnston, Alexander 1815–1891, *The Peaceful Cottagers*, gift from J. G. Graves, 1937

Jones, Allen b.1937, *Black Hat*, purchased from the Waddington Galleries with the assistance of the Victoria and Albert Museum Purchase Grant Fund, 1977, © Allen Jones

Jones, Stanley Robert b.1927, *Hopeless Dawn, Sheffield*, purchased at the Open Air Exhibition, 1963, © the artist

Jones, Stanley Robert b.1927, *St Nicholas Cole Abbey, London*, purchased from the artist, 1966, © the artist

Jongkind, Johan Barthold 1819–1891, *River Scene with Barges and Figures*, bequeathed by Sir Wilson Mappin, 1925

Jordaens, Jacob 1593–1678, *Tasting*, on loan from a private collection

Joseph, Tam b.1947, *School Report*, purchased from the artist, 1984, © the artist
Jungman, Nico 1872–1935, *Les Avants, Switzerland*, presented by Lord Lee of Fareham, 1935
Kay, Ernest active 1907, *Landscape*, presented by Mrs Banks, 1965
Kay, Ernest active 1907, *Landscape*, presented by Mrs Banks, 1952
Keeling, William 1860–1930, *A Derbyshire Road*, presented by Miss E. Keeling, 1931
Kelly, Felix Runcie 1914–1994, *Pink House on a Hill*, purchased at Sotheby's,1978, © the artist's estate
Kelly, Gerald Festus 1879–1972, *Les Halles Centrales, Paris*, purchased from the Belgrave Gallery, 1977
Kemm, Robert 1830–1895, *A Spanish Lady*, gift from J. G. Graves, 1943
Kemp-Welch, Lucy 1869–1958, *The Riders*, presented by Miss M. Frobisher, 1965, © David Messum
Kennedy, William Denholm 1813–1865, *River Scene*, gift from J. G. Graves, 1929
Kessell, Mary 1914–1977, *Portrait of a Woman*, presented by the Contemporary Art Society, 1948
Kettell, Jack *Rebuilding a Blast Furnace*, purchased, 1988
Kidd, William 1790–1863, *A Scene from a Work by Walter Scott*, gift from J. G. Graves, 1935
Kilgore, Constance b.1951, *Haptic*, purchased from the artist, 1981, © the artist
King, Gunning 1859–1940, *The Letter*, gift from J. G. Graves, 1935
King, Henry John Yeend 1855–1924, *Lathkill Dale, Derbyshire*, bequeathed by H. H. Andrews, 1903
Kitaj, R. B. 1932–2007, *The Rival Poet*, purchased from Marlborough Fine Art with the assistance of the Victoria and Albert Museum Purchase Grant Fund, 1970, © estate of R. B. Kitaj
Knapton, George 1698–1778, *Portrait of a Scholar*, bequeathed by J. R. Wigfull, 1936
Kneller, Godfrey 1646–1723, *Hortense Mancini (1646–1699), Duchess of Mazarin*, purchased at Christie's, 1973
Kneller, Godfrey 1646–1723, *Governor Harrison*, purchased, 1955
Kneller, Godfrey 1646–1723, *Portrait*, gift from J. G. Graves, 1942
Knight, John William Buxton 1842/1843–1908, *River Scene*, presented by the Sheffield Society for the Encouragement of Art, 1938
Koekkoek, Barend Cornelis 1803–1862, *Landscape*, bequeathed by J. N. Mappin, 1887
Koekkoek, Barend Cornelis 1803–1862, *A Coming Storm*, bequeathed by J. N. Mappin, 1887
Koekkoek, Hermanus the elder 1815–1882, *Ships at Sea*, presented by F. T. Mappin, 1887
Koekkoek, Hermanus the younger 1836–1909, *Flushing, Holland*, gift from J. G. Graves, 1937
Koekkoek, Johannes Hermanus 1778–1851, *Sea Piece*, presented by F. T. Mappin, 1887
Koekkoek, Johannes Hermanus 1778–1851, *Seascape*, bequeathed by Sir Wilson Mappin, 1925
Koekkoek, Marinus Adrianus (attributed to) 1807–1870, *Landscape*, bequeathed by J. N. Mappin, 1887
Koerner, Ernest Carl 1846–1927, *Temple of the Medinet Habu, Upper Egypt*, gift from J. G. Graves, 1937
Kotasz, Károly 1872–1941, *A Figure Group*, gift from J. G. Graves, 1937
Ladell, Edward 1821–1886, *Birds from Nature*, presented by W. Turner, 1875
Laidlay, William James 1846–1912, *On the Nile at Luxor, Egypt*, gift from J. G. Graves, 1939
Lamb, Henry 1883–1960, *Edward Hector Bent, GM*, presented by the Women's Auxiliary Air Corps, 1947, © estate of Henry Lamb
Lamb, Henry 1883–1960, *The Night Watch, Canadian Heavy Gunners, 2nd A. A. Battery*, presented by the Women's Auxiliary Air Corps, 1947, © estate of Henry Lamb
Lamb, Henry 1883–1960, *Donegal Potato Pickers*, purchased from the Angela Flowers Gallery, 1973, © estate of Henry Lamb
Lambeaux, Jules (attributed to) 1858–1890, *Infant and Nurse*, gift from J. G. Graves, 1935
Lambert, Clement 1855–1925, *A Marshland*, gift from J. G. Graves, 1942
Lambert, Clement 1855–1925, *Romantic Landscape*, purchased, 1952
Lambinet, Emile Charles 1815–1877, *Landscape*, presented by F. T. Mappin, 1887
Lambinet, Emile Charles 1815–1877, *River Scene with Barges*, gift from J. G. Graves, 1935
Lancret, Nicolas (attributed to) 1690–1743, *Conversation Piece*, presented by the National Union of Mineworkers, Barnsley, 1963
Landseer, Edwin Henry 1802–1873, *Count d'Orsay's Charger*, bequeathed by J. N. Mappin, 1887
Landseer, Edwin Henry 1802–1873, *A Stray Shot*, bequeathed by J. N. Mappin, 1887
Landseer, Edwin Henry 1802–1873, *Chevy Chase*, bequeathed by J. N. Mappin, 1887
Landseer, Edwin Henry 1802–1873, *The Young Laird*, gift from J. G. Graves, 1929
Lascaux, Elie 1888–1969, *Avignon, France*, gift from J. G. Graves, 1935, © ADAGP, Paris and DACS, London 2012
Lavery, John 1856–1941, *Dar el Cadi, Interior of a Mosque*, gift from J. G. Graves, 1929, © the estate of Sir John Lavery by courtesy of Felix Rosenstiel's Widow & Son Ltd
Lavery, John 1856–1941, *The Harbour at St Jean de Luz, France: Early Morning*, purchased from Arthur Tooth, 1969, © the estate of Sir John Lavery by courtesy of Felix Rosenstiel's Widow & Son Ltd
Lavery, John 1856–1941, *Portrait of a Lady*, gift from J. G. Graves, 1943, © the estate of Sir John Lavery by courtesy of Felix Rosenstiel's Widow & Son Ltd
Lavoine, Louis Victor (attributed to) 1808–1861, *Young Mitchell (1811–1865)*, purchased, 1952
Lawrence, Thomas 1769–1830, *Head of a Girl*, gift from J. G. Graves, 1935
Lawrence, Thomas 1769–1830, *Master Charles Hope*, on loan from a private collection
Lawrence, Thomas 1769–1830, *Sir William Grant (1752–1832)*, presented by Colonel McKenzie Smith, 1955
Lawson, Cecil Gordon 1851–1882, *River Scene with Shipping*, bequeathed by Sir Wilson Mappin, 1925
Lawson, Cecil Gordon 1851–1882, *The Hayfield*, gift from J. G. Graves, 1929
Lawson, Sonia b.1934, *Frail Peace*, purchased from the artist, 1983, © the artist
Le Bas, Edward 1904–1966, *The Bandstand at Hyde Park, London*, purchased from Spink & Son with the assistance of the Victoria and Albert Museum Purchase Grant Fund, 1980
Le Sidaner, Henri Eugène 1862–1939, *The Belfry at Bruges, Belgium*, gift from J. G. Graves, 1935
Le Sidaner, Henri Eugène 1862–1939, *Nemours, Seine-et-Marne, France*, gift from J. G. Graves, 1935
Leader, Benjamin Williams 1831–1923, *The River Llugwy, Betws-y-Coed, Wales*, gift from J. G. Graves, 1943
Leader, Benjamin Williams 1831–1923, *The Lledr Bridge, near Betws-y-Coed, Wales*, purchased at Christie's, 1910
Leader, Benjamin Williams 1831–1923, *The Close of Summer*, bequeathed by Sir Wilson Mappin, 1925
Leader, Benjamin Williams 1831–1923, *The Last Gleam*, bequeathed by H. H. Andrews, 1903
Leader, Benjamin Williams 1831–1923, *Betws-y-Coed, Wales*, bequeathed by J. N. Mappin, 1887
Leader, Benjamin Williams 1831–1923, *On the Severn*, gift from J. G. Graves, 1929
Leader, Benjamin Williams 1831–1923, *A Country Churchyard*, gift from J. G. Graves, 1937
Leader, Benjamin Williams 1831–1923, *Seascape, North Welsh Coast*, bequeathed by Mrs Wing through the Sheffield Society for the Encouragement of Art, 1938
Leader, Benjamin Williams 1831–1923, *On the Severn*, bequeathed by H. H. Andrews, 1903
Leader, Benjamin Williams 1831–1923, *Near Moel Siabod, Wales*, gift from J. G. Graves, 1937
Leader, Benjamin Williams 1831–1923, *Across the Common*, gift from J. G. Graves, 1937
Leader, Benjamin Williams 1831–1923, *Morning*, presented by Mrs S. Stanley Watson, 1945
Leadley, W. E. 1903–1973, *Driftwood*, purchased from the artist, 1966
Lear, Edward 1812–1888, *Buon Ricovero, in the Roman Campagna*, purchased at Sotheby's, 1970
Lee, Frederick Richard 1798–1879, *Birds and Fruit*, gift from J. G. Graves, 1929
Lee, Frederick Richard 1798–1879, *Landscape with a River*, gift from J. G. Graves, 1943
Lee, Terry b.1932, *Self Portrait*, presented by the artist, 1964, © the artist
Lee, Terry b.1932, *Ask for Whom*, purchased from the artist, 1966, © the artist
Lee, Terry b.1932, *Adam's Tree*, on loan from a private collection, © the artist
Lee, Terry b.1932, *The Swinger*, purchased from the artist, 1968, © the artist
Lee, Terry b.1932, *Sheffield River*, purchased from the artist, 1980, © the artist
Lee-Hankey, William 1869–1952, *A French Market Place*, gift from J. G. Graves, 1942
Lee-Hankey, William 1869–1952, *Anxious Thoughts*, gift from J. G. Graves, 1943
Lee-Hankey, William 1869–1952, *'In the silent woody places by the home that gave me birth'*, gift from J. G. Graves, 1935
Leemputten, Cornelis van 1841–1902, *Sheep and Poultry*, bequeathed by J. N. Mappin, 1887
Lees, Derwent 1885–1931, *A Girl Standing by a Hay Cart*, purchased from Arthur Tooth, 1969
Legros, Alphonse 1837–1911, *Blessing the Sea*, gift from J. G. Graves, 1935
Lehmann, Rudolph 1819–1905, *Portrait of a Lady*, gift from J. G. Graves, 1929
Leist, Frederick William 1878–1945, *A Carnival Souvenir*, purchased from the artist, 1921
Leitch, William Leighton 1804–1883, *View above the Capua, Southern Italy*, presented by F. T. Mappin, 1891
Lely, Peter 1618–1680, *Margaret Brooke (c.1647–1667), Lady Denham*, on loan from the Maleham Bequest, since 1955
Lely, Peter (after) 1618–1680, *Oliver Cromwell (1599–1658)*, bequeathed by J. N. Mappin, 1887
Lemon, Arthur 1850–1912, *Harvest in Tuscany*, presented by V. Machall, 1947
Lemon, Arthur 1850–1912, *Landscape*, presented by V. Machall, 1947
Leslie, Charles Robert 1794–1859, *Scene from William Shakespeare's 'The Merry Wives of Windsor'*, bequeathed by Sir Wilson Mappin, 1925
Lessore, Thérèse 1884–1945, *Saturday Evening*, presented by the Contemporary Art Society, 1927, © Henry & John Lessore
Levis, Maurice 1860–1940, *On the River Yonne, France*, gift from J. G. Graves, 1935
Levis, Maurice 1860–1940, *At Boutigny, France*, gift from J. G. Graves, 1937
Levis, Maurice 1860–1940, *Les vieux ramparts*, gift from J. G. Graves, 1943
Levis, Maurice 1860–1940, *The Old Ramparts, Mailly-le-Château, France*, gift from J. G. Graves, 1943
Levy, Émile 1826–1890, *The First Lilac*, gift from J. G. Graves, 1943
Lewin, Stephen Samuel 1848–1909, *End of the Game*, bequeathed by H. H. Andrews, 1903
Lewin, Stephen Samuel 1848–1909, *Forty Winks*, bequeathed by H. H. Andrews, 1903
Lewin, Stephen Samuel 1848–1909, *The Toilet*, bequeathed by H. H. Andrews, 1903
Lewis, John Frederick 1805–1876, *Persian Interior*, purchased from the Fine Art Society, 1973
Lhermitte, Léon-Augustin (attributed to) 1844–1925, *Landscape*, gift from J. G. Graves, 1937
Lidderdale, Charles Sillem 1831–1895, *Portrait with Bullrushes*, unknown acquisition method
Lidderdale, Charles Sillem 1831–1895, *Portrait of a Lady*, gift from J. G. Graves, 1943
Linderum, Richard 1851–1926, *The Scientist*, gift from J. G. Graves, 1942
Lindley, W. *Reuben Hallam (1818–1908)*, purchased, 1913
Linnell, James Thomas 1826–1905, *The Haymakers*, bequeathed by J. N. Mappin, 1887
Linnell, James Thomas 1826–1905, *Knole Park, Kent*, gift from J. G. Graves, 1935
Linnell, John 1792–1882, *Portrait of a Man* (possibly W. J. White, the Engraver), gift from J. G. Graves, 1929
Linnell, John 1792–1882, *Landscape with Sheep*, bequeathed by J. N. Mappin, 1887
Linnell, John 1792–1882, *The Timber Wagon*, bequeathed by J. N. Mappin, 1887
Linnell, John 1792–1882, *A View of Hampstead Heath, London*, gift from J. G. Graves, 1935
Linnell, John 1792–1882, *In Windsor Forest, Berkshire*, purchased from David Walker-Barker, 1974
Linnell, John 1792–1882, *Rest Time*, gift from J. G. Graves, 1935

Linnell, William 1826–1906, *'Where the nibbling flocks do stray'*, bequeathed by J. N. Mappin, 1887
Linnell, William 1826–1906, *The Distaff*, bequeathed by J. N. Mappin, 1887
Linnell, William 1826–1906, *In viaggio*, bequeathed by J. N. Mappin, 1887
Linton, James Dromgole 1840–1916, *Queen Elizabeth of Hungary and the Court Painter*, gift from J. G. Graves, 1929
Linton, William 1791–1876, *Italian Landscape*, gift from J. G. Graves, 1943
Lisle, Frank 1916–1986, *Flat Iron*, purchased from the artist, 1981, © the artist's estate
Lismer, Arthur 1885–1969, *Little Seaboat*, presented by Mrs W. Hague, 1962
Little, Douglas Patrick active 1981–1985, *The Philadelphian (Interior of a Strip Mill at Shalesmoor, Sheffield)*, gift from the artist, 1985
Lloyd, Stuart active 1875–1929, *Sheep in Pasture*, gift from J. G. Graves, 1929
Lloyd, Stuart active 1875–1929, *On the Stour*, gift from J. G. Graves, 1929
Lloyd-Jones, Peter 1940–2001, *Early Theme*, purchased from the artist, 1970, © the artist's estate
Lomax, John Arthur 1857–1923, *Aren't You Ready?*
Long, Edwin 1829–1891, *Princess Helen Randis Singh*, gift from J. G. Graves, 1943
Lorein, Victor 1894–1954, *Portrait of the Artist*, gift from J. G. Graves, 1937
Los, Waldermar 1849–1888, *The Outpost*, gift from J. G. Graves, 1937
Lotz, H. J. *Battersea Reach, London*, gift from J. G. Graves, 1937
Loudin, H. D. *An Evening View*, gift from J. G. Graves
Loudin, H. D. *The Storm Cloud*, gift from J. G. Graves, 1937
Loutherbourg, Philip James de 1740–1812, *Landscape with Shepherds*, gift from J. G. Graves, 1942
Loutherbourg, Philip James de 1740–1812, *Landscape*, gift from J. G. Graves, 1935
Lowe, Anthony b.1957, *Hole in the Road, Sheffield*
Lowe, Anthony b.1957, *Pond Street Bus Station, Sheffield*, acquired via the Bassetts Purchase Commission, 1986
Lowe, Arthur 1866–1940, *The Canal Bend*, presented by Mrs Lowe, 1944
Lowe, David active 19th C, *Portrait of a Man*
Lowinsky, Thomas Esmond 1892–1947, *Miss Cicely Hamilton (1872–1952)*, presented by Mr W. Jansen, 1936
Lowinsky, Thomas Esmond 1892–1947, *The Offering of Cain and Offering of Abel*, purchased from the artist, 1936
Lowndes, Alan 1921–1978, *Halifax, West Yorkshire*, purchased from the Crane Kalman Gallery, 1984, © the artist's estate
Lowry, Laurence Stephen 1887–1976, *Fire Watcher* (recto), purchased from Reid & Lefevre with the assistance of the Victoria and Albert Museum Purchase Grant Fund, 1965, © the estate of L. S. Lowry. All rights reserved, DACS 2012
Lowry, Laurence Stephen 1887–1976, *Street Scene* (verso), purchased from Reid & Lefevre with the assistance of the Victoria and Albert Museum Purchase Grant Fund, 1965, © the estate of L. S. Lowry. All rights reserved, DACS 2012
Lowry, Laurence Stephen 1887–1976, *Northern Race Meeting*, on loan from a private collection, © the estate of L. S. Lowry. All rights reserved, DACS 2012
Lowry, Laurence Stephen 1887–1976, *Meeting Point*, on loan from a private collection, © the estate of L. S. Lowry. All rights reserved, DACS 2012
Ludovici, Albert 1852–1932, *London Street Arabs Struggling for a Coin*, gift from J. G. Graves, 1942
Ludovici, Albert 1852–1932, *The Picnic Party*, gift from J. G. Graves, 1937
Ludovici, Albert 1852–1932, *The Dancing Lesson*, bequeathed by H. H. Andrews, 1903
Luker, William 1828–1892, *Aberfoyle, Highland Cattle*, gift from J. G. Graves, 1943
Luker, William 1828–1892, *Highland Cattle*, gift from J. G. Graves, 1937
Luny, Thomas 1759–1837, *Sea Piece*, gift from J. G. Graves
Lutzens *Cupid and Birds*, bequeathed by J. N. Mappin, 1887
Lutzens *Cupids and Flowers*, bequeathed by J. N. Mappin, 1887
Lyons, L. *The Wood Gatherer*, bequeathed by Bertha Annie Sykes, 1949
Macbeth, Robert Walker 1848–1910, *Late for the Ferry, King's Lynn, Norfolk*, gift from J. G. Graves, 1937
MacGeorge, William Stewart 1861–1931, *A Children's Picnic*, gift from J. G. Graves, 1937
MacGregor, William York 1855–1923, *Chepstow Castle, Wales*, gift from J. G. Graves, 1942
MacIntyre, James Crichton active 1867–c.1911, *A View of Sheffield from Psalter Lane*, presented, 1938
McIntyre, James active 1867–1909, *A Gleam of Hope*, presented by Mr J. Beal, 1976
MacIntyre, Joseph Wrightson 1842–1897, *Interior of Holme Head Wheel, Rivelin Valley, Sheffield*, presented by T. Crossland, 1955
MacIntyre, Joseph Wrightson 1842–1897, *Mary (Anne) Beal*, presented by Mr J. Beal, 1961
MacIntyre, Joseph Wrightson 1842–1897, *Michael Beal*, presented by Mr J. Beal, 1961
MacIntyre, Joseph Wrightson 1842–1897, *Men Seated around a Fire in a Grinding Shop*, purchased, 1960
Maclise, Daniel 1806–1870, *The Spirit of Chivalry*, presented by F. T. Mappin, 1887
Maclise, Daniel 1806–1870, *Yes or No?*, gift from J. G. Graves, 1935
Madliner, W. J. *The Windmill*, bequeathed by J. N. Mappin, 1887
Mahoney, Charles 1903–1968, *Hampstead Backs, London*, purchased from the artist, 1927, © the artist's estate
Mahoney, Charles 1903–1968, *The Plant Table*, presented by the Sheffield Society for the Encouragement of Art, 1937, © the artist's estate
Maitland, Paul Fordyce 1863–1909, *Battersea Reach, London*, gift from J. G. Graves, 1937
Maitland, Paul Fordyce 1863–1909, *Cheyne Walk, Chelsea, London*, gift from J. G. Graves, 1929
Malbon, William 1805–1877, *'Samson', Sire of 'Sally'*, bequeathed by Miss A. J. Watson, 1953
Malbon, William 1805–1877, *Dog and Hare*, presented, 1953
Malbon, William 1805–1877, *Horse in a Stable Yard*, purchased, 1953
Malbon, William 1805–1877, *Mare and Foal*, purchased, 1953
Malbon, William 1805–1877, *The Sherwood Rangers*, purchased, 1949
Malbon, William 1805–1877, *'Sally'*, bequeathed by Miss A. J. Watson, 1953
Malbon, William 1805–1877, *Winter Scene*, presented by Mr Booth, 1953
Mancini, Antonio 1852–1930, *Portrait of a Man*, gift from J. G. Graves, 1929
Mann, Cathleen 1896–1959, *Portrait of a Lady*, gift from J. G. Graves, 1943, © the artist's estate
Marchetti, Ludovico 1853–1909, *Ducal Wedding*, presented by Mrs Jones, 1940
Maris, Jacob Henricus 1837–1899, *Shore Scene*, gift from J. G. Graves, 1943
Maris, Willem 1844–1910, *Cattle*, gift from J. G. Graves, 1929
Marks, Henry Stacey 1829–1898, *At the Piano*, gift from J. G. Graves, 1935
Marlow, William 1740–1813, *Le pont du gard, Nimes, France*, purchased, 1951
Marten, J. active 19th C, *A Visit to the Lawyer*, gift from J. G. Graves, 1929
Martin, Florence b.c.1845, *The Art Student*, bequeathed by Sir Wilson Mappin, 1925
Martin, Kenneth 1905–1984, *Chance, Order, Change, 24 History Painting A*, purchased from the Waddington Galleries with the assistance of the Victoria and Albert Museum Purchase Grant Fund, 1984, © the artist's estate
Masaccio (after) 1401–1428, *Girolamo Savonarola (1452–1498)*, gift from J. G. Graves, 1943
Masoero, Jeanne b.1937, *Kenneth Martin (1905–1984)*, presented by the artist, 2009, © the artist
Mason, William Henry active 1858–1917, *Coast Scene with Shipping*, bequeathed by Sir Wilson Mappin, 1925
Masquerier, John James 1778–1855, *Portrait of a Lady*, gift from J. G. Graves, 1937
Mastin, John 1865–1932, *Alderman George Senior (d.1915), JP, Lord Mayor of Sheffield (1901)*, on loan from a private collection
Matesdorf, Théodore (attributed to) 1849–1909, *Interior*, gift from J. G. Graves, 1937
Mauve, Anton 1838–1888, *On the Sea Shore*, bequeathed by J. N. Mappin, 1887
McBey, James 1883–1959, *Lady in a Red Dress*, gift from J. G. Graves, 1937, © the artist's estate
McCulloch, Horatio 1805–1867, *Newark Castle Overlooking the Yarrow, Scotland*, bequeathed by E. G. Wragg, 1928
McCulloch, Horatio 1805–1867, *Old Mortality Recutting the Tomb Stones of the Covenanters*, gift from J. G. Graves, 1929
McEvoy, Ambrose 1878–1927, *Miss Joan Claudia Johnson, in Green*, purchased from H. Riddle, 1969
McEvoy, Ambrose 1878–1927, *View from the Adelphi, London*, purchased from Mrs Alan Bazell, 1969
McEvoy, Ambrose 1878–1927, *The Honourable Mrs Akers-Douglas*, on loan from a private collection
McEvoy, Ambrose 1878–1927, *Viscountess Cranborne*, purchased, 1943
McFadyen, Jock b.1950, *When Not Driving Fast Cars Queenie Loved to Dance*, purchased from Blond Fine Art, 1981, © the artist
McLaughlin, John 1885–1957, *Obelisque de Luxor, Paris*, gift from J. G. Graves, 1937
Meadows, Arthur Joseph 1843–1907, *Venice*, gift from J. G. Graves, 1943
Meadows, Arthur Joseph 1843–1907, *Seascape*, gift from J. G. Graves, 1943
Meffsner, Ernst (attributed to) active mid-19th C, *Feeding Sheep*, bequeathed by H. H. Andrews, 1903
Meissonier, Jean Louis Ernest 1815–1891, *Strolling Players*, gift from J. G. Graves, 1935
Melby, William 1824–1882, *Seascape*, bequeathed by Sir Wilson Mappin, 1925
Mellis, Margaret 1914–2009, *Red Flower*, purchased from the artist, 1981, © the estate of Margaret Mellis
Mellon, Campbell Archibald 1876–1955, *Foreshore at Gorleston, Norfolk*, gift from J. G. Graves, 1943
Mellon, Campbell Archibald 1876–1955, *The Gap, Kessingland, Suffolk*, gift from J. G. Graves
Mengs, Anton Raphael 1728–1779, *Portrait of the Artist's Father*, gift from J. G. Graves, 1935
Meninsky, Bernard 1891–1950, *Portrait of a Girl*, gift from J. G. Graves, 1935, © the artist's estate/ Bridgeman Art Library
Menpes, Mortimer L. 1855–1938, *A Courtyard*, gift from J. G. Graves, 1943
Menpes, Mortimer L. 1855–1938, *All the Day's Work (Lahore)*, gift from J. G. Graves, 1929
Menpes, Mortimer L. 1855–1938, *Entrance to a Japanese Garden*, gift from J. G. Graves, 1937
Menpes, Mortimer L. 1855–1938, *On the Balcony*, gift from J. G. Graves, 1937
Menpes, Mortimer L. 1855–1938, *Spinning (Ajmere)*, gift from J. G. Graves, 1929
Menpes, Mortimer L. 1855–1938, *Venice*, gift from J. G. Graves
Mesdag, Hendrik Willem 1831–1915, *A Fisher Girl*, gift from J. G. Graves, 1935
Mettling, Louis 1847–1904, *The Washing*, gift from J. G. Graves, 1937
Meulen, Steven van der 1493–1563, *Portrait of a Member of the Tichborne Family*, gift from J. G. Graves
Meyerheim, Robert Gustav 1847–1920, *A Pastoral*, gift from J. G. Graves, 1937
Meyerheim, Robert Gustav (attributed to) 1847–1920, *The Goose Girl*, gift from J. G. Graves, 1935
Michel, Georges 1763–1843, *Landscape with Windmills*, gift from J. G. Graves, 1935
Michel, Georges 1763–1843, *Stormy Landscape*, gift from J. G. Graves, 1935
Middleditch, Edward 1923–1987, *Cat on a Chair*, purchased at Sotheby's, 1966, © the estate of Edward Middleditch, courtesy James Hyman Gallery, London
Middleton, James Godsell 1805–1874, *George Hadfield (1787–1879)*, on loan from a private collection
Miereveld, Michiel Jansz. van 1567–1641, *Johanna de Witt*, gift from J. G. Graves, 1942
Millais, John Everett 1829–1896, *Portrait of a Girl*, presented by the Graves Trust, 1957
Millais, John Everett 1829–1896, *The Proposal*, bequeathed by J. N. Mappin, 1887
Milne, John Maclauchlan 1886–1957, *La fontain*, gift from J. G. Graves, 1943 © John Maclauchlan Milne, care of Portland Gallery, London
Milne, John Maclauchlan 1886–1957, *Concert au Jardin du Luxembourg, Paris*, gift from J. G.

Graves, 1937 © John Maclauchlan Milne, care of Portland Gallery, London
Milne, John Maclauchlan 1886–1957, *La fontain*, gift from J. G. Graves, 1943 © John Maclauchlan Milne, care of Portland Gallery, London
Mion, Luigi 1843–c.1920, *Study of a Girl*, gift from J. G. Graves, 1942
Mitchell, J. Young 1811–1865, *Self Portrait*, presented by Mrs Jean Mitchell Saltfleet, 1934
Mitchell, Jean 1861–1941, *Portrait of a Man*, bequeathed by A. Howe, 1957
Mitchell, Jean 1861–1941, *An Old Italian*, purchased from J. M. Saltfleet, 1926
Mitchell, Jean 1861–1941, *The Deaconess*, gift from J. G. Graves, 1937
Moermans, Frans (attributed to) active 1871–1878, *Gypsies in a Spanish Château*, bequeathed by J. Heiffor, 1886
Momper, Joos de the younger (attributed to) 1564–1635, *Winter Landscape with Buildings and Figures*, purchased from W. M. Saline & Sons, 1954
Monamy, Peter 1681–1749, *Men o' War in a Choppy Sea*, purchased at Sotheby's, 1970
Monnoyer, Jean-Baptiste 1636–1699, *Leaves and Flowers with a Butterfly*, gift from J. G. Graves, 1943
Monnoyer, Jean-Baptiste (attributed to) 1636–1699, *Flower Piece*, gift from J. G. Graves, 1935
Monnoyer, Jean-Baptiste (attributed to) 1636–1699, *Still Life*, gift from J. G. Graves, 1935
Montalba, Hilda 1946–1919, *Boy Unloading a Venetian Market Boat*, presented by F. T. Mappin, 1891
Montalba, Hilda 1946–1919, *Venetian Boatman*, gift from J. G. Graves, 1942
Monticelli, Adolphe Joseph Thomas 1824–1886, *The Piazzetta, Venice*, gift from J. G. Graves, 1929
Monticelli, Adolphe Joseph Thomas 1824–1886, *Figure Composition*, gift from J. G. Graves, 1935
Monticelli, Adolphe Joseph Thomas 1824–1886, *Echo in the Wood*, gift from J. G. Graves, 1935
Monticelli, Adolphe Joseph Thomas (attributed to) 1824–1886, *The Bouquet*, gift from J. G. Graves, 1935
Mooney, Edward Hartley c.1878–1938, *Marigolds*, gift from J. G. Graves, 1937
Moore, Albert Joseph 1841–1893, *Battledore and Shuttlecock*, gift from J. G. Graves, 1935
Moore, Albert Joseph 1841–1893, *Battledore and Shuttlecock*, gift from J. G. Graves, 1935
Moore, Ernest 1865–1940, *Henry Fitzalan-Howard (1847–1917), 15th Duke of Norfolk, First Lord Mayor of Sheffield*, on loan from a private collection
Moore, Ernest 1865–1940, *Alderman William Johnson Clegg (1827–1895), JP, Mayor of Sheffield (1887–1888)*, on loan from a private collection
Moore, Ernest 1865–1940, *Rejected*, purchased from Mr Wilkinson, 1954
Moore, Ernest 1865–1940, *Alderman Edward Saville Foster (d.1894), Mayor of Sheffield (1893–1894)*, on loan from a private collection
Moore, Ernest 1865–1940, *Charles William Styring*
Moore, Ernest 1865–1940, *Robert J. Wales*
Moore, Ernest 1865–1940, *William Ward*
Moore, Henry 1831–1895, *Sea Shore*, bequeathed by Lady Osbourne, 1955
Moore, Henry 1831–1895, *Sea Piece*, gift from J. G. Graves, 1929
Moore, Henry 1831–1895, *Shipping off the Coast*, gift from J. G. Graves, 1937
Mor, Antonis (attributed to) 1512–1516–c.1576, *St Sebastian*, purchased jointly with the Sheffield Society for the Encouragement of Art, 1937
Morales, Luis de (school of) c.1509–c.1586, *Christ Carrying the Cross*, purchased, 1949
Morgan, Frederick 1856–1927, *Gleaners*, presented by F. T. Mappin, 1891
Morgan, John 1823–1886, *Interior of a Village School*, bequeathed by Sir Wilson Mappin, 1925
Morland, George 1763–1804, *Breaking the Ice*, purchased from the Fine Art Society, 1949
Morland, George 1763–1804, *In the Hayfield*, gift from J. G. Graves, 1942
Morland, George 1763–1804, *Donkeys*, purchased, 1938
Morland, George 1763–1804, *Landscape*, gift from J. G. Graves, 1935
Morland, George 1763–1804, *Pigs*, gift from J. G. Graves, 1935
Morland, George 1763–1804, *Pigs in a Sty*, gift from J. G. Graves, 1935
Morland, George 1763–1804, *The Approaching Storm*, gift from J. G. Graves, 1935
Morland, George 1763–1804, *The Village Inn*, bequeathed by J. N. Mappin, 1887
Morland, George 1763–1804, *Travelling Gypsies*, gift from J. G. Graves, 1935
Morris, Philip Richard 1834–1902, *March Winds*, gift from J. G. Graves, 1937
Morris, Stephen b.1935, *Untitled*, on long-term loan from the Guild of St George, © the artist
Mostyn, Thomas Edwin 1864–1930, *The Enchanted Garden*, bequeathed by J. N. Mappin, 1887
Mostyn, Thomas Edwin 1864–1930, *The Garden of Memory*, gift from J. G. Graves, 1937
Mouillot, Marcel 1889–1972, *Shipping in a Port*, gift from J. G. Graves, 1937
Mücke, Karl Anton Heinrich 1806–1891, *Still Life*, gift from J. G. Graves, 1935
Muckley, William Jabez 1829–1905, *Grapes*, bequeathed by J. N. Mappin, 1887
Muirhead, David 1867–1930, *Farmyard*, purchased at Christie's, 1970
Müller, Alfredo 1869–1940, *Landscape*, gift from J. G. Graves, 1942
Müller, Alfredo 1869–1940, *Landscape*, gift from J. G. Graves, 1942
Müller, Alfredo 1869–1940, *Ruins*, gift from J. G. Graves, 1942
Müller, Alfredo 1869–1940, *Sicily*, gift from J. G. Graves, 1942
Müller, Alfredo 1869–1940, *A Rocky Landscape*, gift from J. G. Graves, 1942
Müller, Alfredo 1869–1940, *Landscape*, gift from J. G. Graves, 1942
Müller, Alfredo 1869–1940, *Old Bridge, Sicily*, gift from J. G. Graves, 1942
Müller, Alfredo 1869–1940, *Study*, gift from J. G. Graves, 1942
Muller, William James 1812–1845, *Landscape with a Little Boy and a Basket*, bequeathed by J. N. Mappin, 1887
Muller, William James 1812–1845, *Grand Canal, Venice*, bequeathed by Sir Wilson Mappin, 1925
Muller, William James 1812–1845, *A Peasant Girl*, gift from J. G. Graves, 1942
Muller, William James 1812–1845, *Landscape*, bequeathed by J. N. Mappin, 1887
Muller, William James 1812–1845, *A Moorish Nobleman and His Attendants*, purchased from the Brighouse Art Gallery, 1971
Muller, William James 1812–1845, *A Mountain Waterfall in Snowdonia, Wales*, presented by F. T. Mappin, 1887
Muller, William James 1812–1845, *A Persian Group*, gift from J. G. Graves, 1929
Muller, William James 1812–1845, *A Sketch in Wales*, gift from J. G. Graves, 1935
Muller, William James 1812–1845, *Evening Sketch*, gift from J. G. Graves, 1943
Muller, William James 1812–1845, *Landscape*, gift from J. G. Graves, 1929
Muller, William James 1812–1845, *Landscape*, bequeathed by J. N. Mappin, 1887
Muller, William James 1812–1845, *Oriental and Girl*, bequeathed by J. N. Mappin, 1887
Muller, William James 1812–1845, *Scene in Algiers*, bequeathed by J. N. Mappin, 1887
Muller, William James 1812–1845, *Scene in Morocco*, bequeathed by J. N. Mappin, 1887
Muller, William James 1812–1845, *The Village Smithy*, gift from J. G. Graves, 1935
Mulready, Augustus Edwin 1844–1905, *A Share of a Crust*, bequeathed by Sir Wilson Mappin, 1925
Mulready, William 1786–1863, *Farmhouse with a White Horse*, gift from J. G. Graves, 1937
Mulready, William 1786–1863, *The Cottage*, gift from J. G. Graves, 1937
Mulready, William 1786–1863, *The Dead Canary*, gift from J. G. Graves, 1937
Muncaster, Claude 1903–1974, *Winter's Morning, Cartmel Priory, Cumbria*, on loan from the Maleham Bequest, © the artist's estate
Munnings, Alfred James 1878–1959, *Goats on a Common*, gift from J. G. Graves, 1929, © the artist's estate courtesy of Felix Rosenstiel's Widow & Son Ltd
Munnings, Alfred James 1878–1959, *Hop-Picking*, gift from J. G. Graves, 1935, © the artist's estate courtesy of Felix Rosenstiel's Widow & Son Ltd
Munnings, Alfred James 1878–1959, *The Grey Mare*, purchased from the artist, 1921, © the artist's estate courtesy of Felix Rosenstiel's Widow & Son Ltd
Munthe, Ludwig 1841–1896, *Winter Scene*, bequeathed by J. N. Mappin, 1887
Murillo, Bartolomé Esteban 1618–1682, *The Infant Christ Asleep on the Cross*, gift from J. G. Graves, 1935
Murray, Charles 1894–1954, *Russian Village, Winter*, purchased, 1934
Murray, Charles 1894–1954, *Scottish Fisherwomen*, purchased from the Leicester Galleries, 1966
Murray, Charles Fairfax 1849–1919, *Mandolin Player*, gift from J. G. Graves, 1935
Murray, Charles Fairfax (attributed to) 1849–1919, *Guitar Player*, gift from J. G. Graves, 1935
Murray, David 1849–1933, *Homeward, Sunset*, purchased by the Fine Art Society, 1978
Murray, David 1849–1933, *The Stream*, gift from J. G. Graves, 1935
Musin, François Etienne 1820–1888, *Sea Fight*, bequeathed by J. N. Mappin, 1887
Mytens, Daniel I c.1590–1647, *James Hamilton (1589–1625), 2nd Marquess of Hamilton and 4th Earl of Arran, KG, PC*, purchased from Thomas Agnews, 1970
Mytens, Jan (attributed to) c.1614–1670, *Admiral Cornelius Tromp (1629–1691)*, gift from J. G. Graves, 1935
Nash, John Northcote 1893–1977, *Ashby's Pond*, purchased, 1937, © the artist's estate/Bridgeman Art Library
Nash, Paul 1889–1946, *Iver Heath, Buckinghamshire, Snow*, purchased at Sotheby's with the assistance of the Victoria and Albert Museum Purchase Grant Fund, 1976, © Tate, London 2012
Nash, Paul 1889–1946, *March Landscape*, purchased from the New Art Centre with the assistance of the Victoria and Albert Museum Purchase Grant Fund, 1984, © Tate, London 2012
Nasmyth, Patrick 1787–1831, *Landscape*, bequeathed by J. N. Mappin, 1887
Nasmyth, Patrick 1787–1831, *Landscape*, gift from J. G. Graves, 1935
Nasmyth, Patrick 1787–1831, *Landscape*, bequeathed by J. N. Mappin, 1887
Nasmyth, Patrick 1787–1831, *Landscape*, gift from J. G. Graves, 1943
Neer, Aert van der 1603–1677, *Frozen River Scene*, accepted by HM Government in lieu of inheritance tax and allocated to Museums Sheffield, 1980
Neiland, Brendan b.1941, *Corner*, purchased from the Angela Flowers Gallery with the assistance of the Victoria and Albert Museum Purchase Grant Fund, 1976, © the artist
Netscher, Wilhelm Adrian 1791–1851, *Landscape with Figures*, gift from J. G. Graves, 1943
Nevinson, Christopher 1889–1946, *Ypres after the First Bombardment*, purchased via the Redfern Gallery from the Rex Nan Kivell Collection with the assistance of the Victoria and Albert Museum Purchase Grant Fund, 1977, © the artist's estate/Bridgeman Art Library
Nevinson, Christopher 1889–1946, *Rain and Mud after the Battle*, purchased from the Leicester Galleries with the assistance of the Victoria and Albert Museum Purchase Grant Fund, 1970, © the artist's estate/Bridgeman Art Library
Nicholls, Bertram 1883–1974, *View in Provence, France*, gift from J. G. Graves, 1942
Nicholls, Bertram 1883–1974, *The Windmill at Rye, East Sussex*, gift from J. G. Graves, 1935
Nicholson, Ben 1894–1982, *1917 (portrait of Edie)*, gift from J. G. Graves, 1935, © Angela Verren Taunt 2012. All rights reserved, DACS
Nicholson, Walter 1830–1907, *Old Chapel Steps, Haddon Hall, Derbyshire*, bequeathed by Sir Wilson Mappin, 1925
Nicholson, William 1872–1949, *The Devil's Flight, Gloucestershire*, gift from J. G. Graves, 1929, © Elizabeth Banks
Nicholson, William 1872–1949, *The Road to Zamarramala, Spain*, purchased at Christie's with the assistance of the Victoria and Albert Museum Purchase Grant Fund, 1974, © Elizabeth Banks

Nicholson, Winifred 1893–1981, *Cockley Moor, Cumbria*, purchased from Martin & Sewell, 1971, © Trustees of Winifred Nicholson

Nicholson, Winifred 1893–1981, *Kathleen's Bunch II*, purchased at Sotheby's, 1973, © Trustees of Winifred Nicholson

Nicol, Erskine 1825–1904, *The Errand Boy*, gift from J. G. Graves, 1943

Nicol, Erskine 1825–1904, *Scene in an Irish Cabin*, bequeathed by J. N. Mappin, 1887

Nicol, Erskine 1825–1904, *The Perch Fishers*, bequeathed by J. N. Mappin, 1887

Nicol, Erskine 1825–1904, *Notice to Quit*, gift from J. G. Graves, 1935

Nicol, Erskine 1825–1904, *Irish Emigrants Waiting for the Train*, bequeathed by J. N. Mappin, 1887

Nicol, Erskine 1825–1904, *Collecting His Thoughts*, presented by F. T. Mappin, 1891

Nicol, Erskine 1825–1904, *An Irish Peasant*, gift from J. G. Graves, 1937

Nicol, John Watson 1856–1926, *For Better, for Worse: Rob Roy and the Baillie*, presented by F. T. Mappin, 1887

Niemann, Edmund John 1813–1876, *Salisbury, Wiltshire*, gift from J. G. Graves, 1935

Niemann, Edmund John 1813–1876, *View at Hertford*, bequeathed by J. N. Mappin, 1887

Niemann, Edmund John 1813–1876, *A Wooded Glade*, bequeathed by J. N. Mappin, 1887

Niemann, Edmund John 1813–1876, *Mountain Scene near Barmouth, Wales*, gift from J. G. Graves, 1929

Niemann, Edmund John 1813–1876, *The River Don after the Flood*, gift from Mr E. Pepper, 1955

Niemann, Edmund John 1813–1876, *Cookham on Thames, Berkshire*, gift from J. G. Graves, 1943

Niemann, Edmund John 1813–1876, *Flock of Sheep*, gift from J. G. Graves

Niemann, Edmund John 1813–1876, *A Storm on the Moors*, presented by H. Bramley

Niemann, Edmund John 1813–1876, *In the Valley of the Nidd, Yorkshire*, gift from J. G. Graves, 1929

Niemann, Edmund John 1813–1876, *Moonrise*, gift from J. G. Graves, 1942

Niemann, Edmund John 1813–1876, *Near Richmond, Yorkshire*, bequeathed by J. N. Mappin, 1887

Niemann, Edmund John 1813–1876, *The Guardship of the Nore*, presented by F. T. Mappin, 1887

Niemann, Edmund John 1813–1876 & **Prades, Alfred F. de** active 1844–1883, *Pateley Moor, North Yorkshire*, gift from J. G. Graves, 1937

Niemann, Edmund John (school of) 1813–1876, *Sailing Ship in a Storm*, bequeathed by Bertha Annie Sykes, 1949

Nieuwal, Jan Rutgers active 1620–1661, *Portrait of a Lady, Aged 58*, gift from J. G. Graves, 1943

Noble, James Campbell 1846–1913, *Tarbert, Scotland*, gift from J. G. Graves, 1935

Normann, Adelsteen 1848–1918, *Lake Scene*, gift from J. G. Graves, 1942

O'Briton (attributed to) *Landscape*, gift from J. G. Graves, 1943

O'Connor, Aloysius Patrick *Overgang, Brixham, Devon*, gift from J. G. Graves, 1937

O'Connor, James Arthur 1792–1841, *In the Dargle Country, Ireland*, presented by F. T. Mappin, 1887

O'Connor, James Arthur 1792–1841, *Landscape*, bequeathed by J. N. Mappin, 1887

O'Connor, James Arthur 1792–1841, *Evening*, gift from J. G. Graves, 1935

O'Conor, Roderic 1860–1940, *Jeune paysanne Bretonne*, on loan from a private collection, © the artist's estate

Oliver, Ken b.1948, *The Visit*, purchased from Moira Kelly Ltd with grant aid from the Contemporary Art Society, 1982

Oliver, William 1823–1901, *Gathering ye Roses*, bequeathed by M. J. Linley, 1920

Oliver, William 1823–1901, *Hark*, bequeathed by M. J. Linley, 1920

Oliver, William 1823–1901, *Sketching from Nature*, bequeathed by M. J. Linley, 1920

Oliver, William 1823–1901, *Industry*, bequeathed by M. J. Linley, 1920

Oliver, William 1823–1901, *Pity, Oh the Pity*, bequeathed by J. Waterhouse, 1902

Oliver, William 1823–1901, *At the Well*, bequeathed by Thomas Waterhouse, 1902

Oliver, William 1823–1901, *Red Riding Hood* (a portrait of the artist's granddaughter), bequeathed by Thomas Waterhouse, 1902

Oliver, William 1823–1901, *A Lady*, bequeathed by H. H. Andrews, 1903

Oliver, William 1823–1901, *A Spanish Lady*, bequeathed by J. Waterhouse, 1902

Oliver, William 1823–1901, *The Gipsy*, bequeathed by H. H. Andrews, 1903

Oliver, William 1823–1901, *The Lesson*, bequeathed by H. H. Andrews, 1903

Oliver, William 1823–1901, *The Letter*, bequeathed by H. H. Andrews, 1903

Olsson, Albert Julius 1864–1942, *Off the Isle of Wight*, gift from J. G. Graves, 1942

Ommeganck, Balthazar Paul 1755–1826, *Canal Scene*, gift from J. G. Graves, 1935

O'Neill, George Bernard 1828–1917, *Grandfather's Advice*, bequeathed by J. N. Mappin, 1887

O'Neill, George Bernard 1828–1917, *The Letter*, gift from J. G. Graves, 1935

O'Neill, George Bernard 1828–1917, *The Travelling Artist*, gift from J. G. Graves, 1929

Oram, Edward d.1810, *Landscape*, gift from J. G. Graves, 1935

Orchardson, William Quiller 1832–1910, *Little Nell and Her Grandfather in the Wood*, bequeathed by J. N. Mappin, 1887

Orchardson, William Quiller 1832–1910, *A Girl in a Muslin Dress*, gift from J. G. Graves, 1935

Orchardson, William Quiller 1832–1910, *Cottages, Stanstead, Essex*, gift from J. G. Graves, 1935

Orpen, William 1878–1931, *Portrait of a Youth*, gift from J. G. Graves, 1935

Ouless, Walter William 1848–1933, *Sir Frederick Thorpe Mappin (1821–1910), Bt*, presented by a fellow townsman

Ouless, Walter William 1848–1933, *Alderman George Franklin (d.1916), JP, Lord Mayor of Sheffield (1897–1898)*, on loan from a private collection

Ouless, Walter William 1848–1933, *Scene from the French Revolution*, bequeathed by J. N. Mappin, 1887

Owen, William 1769–1825, *John Kemble in 'The Stranger'* (an adaptation of August von Kotzebue's 'Menschenhaß und Reue'), bequeathed by A. Daubney, 1905

Pace del Campidoglio, Michele (attributed to) 1610–probably 1670, *Flowers and Fruit*, bequeathed by Mrs Handley, 1951

Padgett, William 1851–1904, *The Old Wife's Work*, gift from J. G. Graves, 1937

Palizzi, Filippo 1818–1899, *Mother and Child*, bequeathed by J. N. Mappin, 1887

Paoletti, Antonio Ermolao 1834–1912, *The Girl at the Well*, bequeathed by H. H. Andrews, 1903

Paoletti, Antonio Ermolao 1834–1912, *The Match Seller*, bequeathed by H. H. Andrews, 1903

Papperitz, Friedrich Georg 1846–1918, *The Procession to Calvary, Christ Falling under the Weight of the Cross*, presented by F. T. Mappin, 1887

Park, Henry 1816–1871, *Gipsy Encampment*, presented by W. E. Prest, 1951

Park, Stuart 1862–1933, *Roses*, gift from J. G. Graves, 1935

Parker, Henry Perlee 1795–1873, *The Burial of Sir Francis Chantrey in Norton Churchyard, Sheffield*, purchased, 1905

Parker, Henry Perlee 1795–1873, *The Milk Boys*, purchased, 1929

Parrott, William 1813–after 1891, *Turner on Varnishing Day*, on long-term loan from the Guild of St George

Parsons, Alfred William 1847–1920, *Ash Trees at Cropthorne, Worcestershire*, gift from J. G. Graves, 1943

Pasmore, Daniel I c.1815–1893, *Interior with Figures*, bequeathed by Sir Wilson Mappin, 1925

Pasmore, Victor 1908–1998, *Vase of Flowers*, purchased at Christie's, 1966, © Victor Pasmore estate

Patel, Pierre I c.1605–1676, *The Flight into Egypt*, purchased, 1949

Paton, Joseph Noel 1821–1901, *The Fairy Queen*, purchased at Sotheby's, 1976

Paul, Paul 1865–1937, *Landscape with a River*, gift from J. G. Graves, 1943

Pavy, Philippe b.1860, *The Sacred Lion*, gift from J. G. Graves, 1937

Pavy, Philippe b.1860, *Farmyard Scene*, presented, 1906

Peel, James 1811–1906, *Landscape with a River*, gift from J. G. Graves, 1943

Peele, John Thomas 1822–1897, *Landscape*, bequeathed by Bertha Annie Sykes, 1949

Peeters, Bonaventura I 1614–1652, *Coast Scene with Shipping*, on loan from a private collection

Peppercorn, Arthur Douglas 1847–1926, *A Fishing Village*, gift from J. G. Graves, 1935

Peppercorn, Arthur Douglas 1847–1926, *Landscape*, gift from J. G. Graves

Peppercorn, Arthur Douglas 1847–1926, *Moonlight*, gift from J. G. Graves, 1929

Peppercorn, Arthur Douglas 1847–1926, *River Scene*, gift from J. G. Graves

Peppercorn, Arthur Douglas 1847–1926, *Two Pollards*, gift from J. G. Graves, 1935

Peppercorn, Arthur Douglas 1847–1926, *View near Portsmouth, Hampshire*, gift from J. G. Graves, 1935

Percy, Sidney Richard 1821–1886, *Coniston Lake, Cumbria*, presented by F. T. Mappin, 1887

Perkins, J. M. *An Old Courtyard, Greenwich, London*, gift from J. G. Graves, 1943

Perronneau, Jean-Baptiste (attributed to) 1715–1783, *Portrait of an Actor*, gift from J. G. Graves, 1935

Pether, Henry c.1801–1880, *A View of the Thames*, gift from J. G. Graves, 1935

Pettie, John 1839–1893, *The Drumhead Court Martial*, bequeathed by J. N. Mappin, 1887

Pettie, John 1839–1893, *Hudibras and Ralpho in the Stocks* (from the poem by Samuel Butler), bequeathed by J. N. Mappin, 1887

Pettie, John 1839–1893, *Treason*, bequeathed by J. N. Mappin, 1887

Pettie, John 1839–1893, *The Disgrace of Cardinal Wolsey*, presented by T. Firth, 1919

Pettie, John 1839–1893, *The Puritan*, bequeathed by J. N. Mappin, 1887

Pettie, John 1839–1893, *A Lady of the Seventeenth Century*, bequeathed by J. N. Mappin, 1887

Pettie, John 1839–1893, *To the Death*, bequeathed by J. N. Mappin, 1887

Pettie, John 1839–1893, *The Edge of the Wood*, purchased from the Fine Art Society with the assistance of the Victoria and Albert Museum Purchase Grant Fund, 1981

Pettie, John 1839–1893, *The Flag of Truce*, bequeathed by J. N. Mappin, 1887

Pettie, John 1839–1893, *The Royalist*, bequeathed by J. N. Mappin, 1887

Pettie, John 1839–1893, *The Sally*, bequeathed by J. N. Mappin, 1887

Pettit, Joseph Paul 1812–1882, *Mont St Michel, France*, gift from J. G. Graves, 1937

Pezzoia *Portrait of an Italian Girl*, gift from J. G. Graves, 1943

Philips, Hermann August 1844–1927, *Reverie*, gift from J. G. Graves, 1937

Philipson, Robin 1916–1992, *Dancing Odalisque*, purchased from the artist, 1965, © the artist's estate

Phillip, John 1817–1867, *Carnival Time, Seville, Spain*, bequeathed by J. N. Mappin, 1887

Phillip, John 1817–1867, *The Fair Maid of Perth*, bequeathed by J. N. Mappin, 1887

Phillip, John 1817–1867, *The Highland Gillie*, bequeathed by J. N. Mappin, 1887

Phillip, John 1817–1867, *The Water Drinkers*, bequeathed by J. N. Mappin, 1887

Phillip, John 1817–1867, *Vintage of Seville*, bequeathed by J. N. Mappin, 1887

Phillips, Thomas 1770–1845, *Master Millward*, on loan from the Maleham Bequest, 1950

Phillips, Tom b.1937, *Synthetic English Landscape No.3*, purchased, 1973, © Tom Phillips. All rights reserved, DACS 2012

Phillips, Tom b.1937, *Fisherman's Walk Gardens*, purchased from Marlborough Fine Art with the assistance of the Victoria and Albert Museum Purchase Grant Fund, 1973, © Tom Phillips. All rights reserved, DACS 2012

Pickersgill, Henry William 1782–1875, *Reverend Joseph Hunter (1783–1861)*, presented by the Archaeological Society, 1961

Pigott, William Henry c.1810–1901, *Bakewell Meadows, Derbyshire*, gift from J. G. Graves, 1929

Pinwell, George John 1842–1875, *Portrait*, gift from J. G. Graves, 1943

Pinwell, George John 1842–1875, *The Garden Gate*, gift from J. G. Graves, 1935

Pisa, Alberto 1864–1931, *Hampstead Heath, London*, gift from J. G. Graves, 1929

Pissarro, Camille 1831–1903, *Paysannes plantant des rammes*, on loan from a private collection

Pissarro, Lucien 1863–1944, *A February Morning, East Knoyle, Wiltshire*, bequeathed by Lady Osbourne, 1955, © the artist's estate

Pittman, Osmund 1874–1968, *Loch Crocach, Scotland*, gift from J. G. Graves, 1942

Pittoni, Giovanni Battista the younger 1687–1767, *The Adulteress before Christ*, purchased from P. & D. Colnaghi Co. Ltd, 1951

Plummer, Robin b.1931, *Blackberry*, presented by the artist, 1968, © the artist

Plummer, Robin b.1931, *Squash*, presented by the artist, 1968, © the artist

Poole, James 1803–1886, *Donati's Comet*, presented by the Trustees of the estate of William Lavers, 1908

Poole, James 1803–1886, *Clogwyn Mawr, near Capel Curig, Wales*, bequeathed by William Lavers, 1908

Poole, James 1803–1886, *Clogwyn Mawr, near Capel Curig, Wales*, bequeathed by William Lavers

Poole, James 1803–1886, *Falls near Pont-y-Cefn, North Wales*, bequeathed by William Lavers, 1908

Poole, James 1803–1886, *Landscape*

Poole, James 1803–1886, *Landscape*

Poole, James 1803–1886, *Landscape with Gypsies*, presented by Mr and Mrs Percy Carlise,1927

Poole, James 1803–1886, *Mountain Landscape*, bequeathed by Dr H. C. Sorby

Poole, James 1803–1886, *Off Machon Bank, Sheffield*

Poole, James 1803–1886, *On the Conway, Betws-y-Coed, North Wales*, bequeathed by Dr H. C. Sorby

Poole, James 1803–1886, *The Head of Lake Lucerne, Switzerland*, bequeathed by E. G. Wragg, 1928

Poole, James 1803–1886, *View on the River Llugwy, North Wales*, bequeathed by Sir Wilson Mappin, 1925

Poole, Paul Falconer 1807–1879, *Solomon Eagle*, presented by F. T. Mappin, 1891

Poole, Paul Falconer 1807–1879, *A Capri Girl*, presented by F. T. Mappin

Poole, Paul Falconer 1807–1879, *Gypsy Children*, gift from J. G. Graves, 1935

Poole, William c.1798–1888, *'Let 'em Come'*, presented by Mrs E. Bastin

Poole, William c.1798–1888, *Samuel Bailey (1791–1870), Poet and Philosopher*, transferred from Sheffield Central Library, 1936

Poole, William c.1798–1888, *Samuel Bailey (1791–1870), Poet and Philosopher*, on loan from a private collection

Poole, William c.1798–1888, *William Wentworth-Fitzwilliam (1748–1833), 4th Earl Fitzwilliam*, on loan from a private collection

Pope, Alexander 1849–1924, *Still Life (Sporting Equipment)*, bequeathed by H. H. Andrews, 1903

Porter, Frederick James 1883–1944, *River Scene*, purchased at Christie's, 1972

Pott, Laslett John 1837–1898, *The Return of the Victors*, bequeathed by M. J. Linley, 1920

Pott, Laslett John 1837–1898, *Waiting for the King's Favourite*, bequeathed by H. H. Andrews, 1903

Pott, Laslett John 1837–1898, *The Sisters*, bequeathed by H. H. Andrews, 1903

Pott, Laslett John 1837–1898, *Sir Peter Teazle*, bequeathed by H. H. Andrews, 1903

Potten, Christopher Nerry 1849–1934, *Landscape*, gift from J. G. Graves, 1943

Potter, Mary 1900–1981, *End of Daylight*, purchased from the artist, 1965, © estate of Mary Potter. All rights reserved, DACS 2012

Potter, Mary 1900–1981, *Evening Light on the Trees*, purchased from the New Art Centre, 1984, © estate of Mary Potter. All rights reserved, DACS 2012

Potter, Mary 1900–1981, *Still Life with a Vase*, presented by C. Boot, 1925, © estate of Mary Potter. All rights reserved, DACS 2012

Poynter, Edward John 1836–1919, *Edward Montagu Stuart Granville Montagu-Stuart-Wortley-Mackenzie (1827–1899), 1st Earl of Wharncliffe*, accepted by HM Government in lieu of inheritance tax and allocated to Museums Sheffield, 2005

Poynter, Edward John 1836–1919, *Corner of the Market Place*, on loan from a private collection

Price, Edward 1800–1885, *Sheffield and the Valley of the Don*, presented by J. J. Greaves & Son, 1948

Priestman, Bertram 1868–1951, *Wareham Channel, Dorset*, gift from J. G. Graves, 1935

Prinsep, Valentine Cameron 1838–1904, *Girl Blowing Soap Bubbles*, bequeathed by J. N. Mappin, 1887

Prinsep, Valentine Cameron 1838–1904, *To Versailles, an Incident in the French Revolution*, presented by F. T. Mappin, 1895

Pritchett, Edward active c.1828–1879, *The Piazzetta, Venice*, gift from J. G. Graves, 1937

Procaccini, Giulio Cesare 1574–1625, *The Mocking of Christ*, presented by the National Union of Mineworkers, Barnsley, 1963

Procktor, Patrick 1936–2003, *Figures, Red and Blue*, on loan from a private collection, © the artist's estate

Procktor, Patrick 1936–2003, *Beneath the Surface*, purchased from David Schilling, 1974, © the artist's estate

Procter, Dod 1892–1972, *Nasturtiums*, purchased from the Leicester Galleries, 1966, © the artist's estate/Bridgeman Art Library

Prout, Samuel 1783–1852, *River Scene*, gift from J. G. Graves, 1929

Prout, Samuel 1783–1852, *The Fountain*, gift from J. G. Graves, 1943

Pyne, James Baker 1800–1870, *Marine Piece*, bequeathed by J. N. Mappin, 1887

Pyne, James Baker 1800–1870, *Marine Piece*, bequeathed by J. N. Mappin, 1887

Pyne, James Baker 1800–1870, *Rome from Tivoli, Italy*, gift from J. G. Graves, 1929

Pyne, James Baker 1800–1870, *Moel Hebog, North Wales*, gift from J. G. Graves, 1943

Pyne, James Baker 1800–1870, *Near Eastbourne, East Sussex, with a View of Pevensey Bay*, gift from J. G. Graves, 1929

Pyne, James Baker 1800–1870, *Scarborough, North Yorkshire*, gift from J. G. Graves, 1935

Quizet, Alphonse 1885–1955, *The Canal at La Villette, Paris*, gift from J. G. Graves, 1937, © ADAGP, Paris and DACS, London 2012

Raeburn, Henry 1756–1823, *Head of a Man*, gift from J. G. Graves, 1935

Raeburn, Henry 1756–1823, *Lady Mary Lyon, Daughter of the Earl of Strathmore*, gift from J. G. Graves, 1935

Ragon, Adolphe 1847–1924, *Coast Scene*, gift from J. G. Graves, 1942

Ragon, Adolphe 1847–1924, *Gravesend, Kent*, gift from J. G. Graves, 1942

Rainer, Richard b.1933, *Fecundity*, presented by the artist, 1970, © the artist

Rainer, Richard b.1933, *Fecundity II*, presented by the artist, 1970, © the artist

Ramsay, Allan 1713–1784, *The Honourable Mrs Clarges* (daughter of the 1st Viscount Barrington), purchased at Christie's, 1972

Ramsay, Allan 1852–1912, *The Old Green Tree and Gateway at Edzell Castle, Scotland*, gift from J. G. Graves

Ramsay, Patricia 1886–1974, *Banana Tree*, presented by the Contemporary Art Society, 1935, © the artist's estate

Raphael (after) 1483–1520, *Madonna and Child*, gift from J. G. Graves, 1943

Rathbone, John 1750–1807, *Evening*, gift from J. G. Graves, 1935

Rathbone, John 1750–1807, *Morning*, gift from J. G. Graves, 1935

Rathbone, John 1750–1807, *Sunset*, gift from J. G. Graves, 1935

Rattray, Alexander William Wellwood 1849–1902, *Black Water Bay, Isle of Arran, Scotland*, gift from J. G. Graves, 1929

Ravesteyn, Jan Anthonisz. van (attributed to) c.1570–1657, *Portrait of a Lady*, gift from J. G. Graves, 1935

Rea, Cecil William 1860–1935, *Nude*, presented by Mrs Rea, 1939

Rea, Constance 1891–1935, *Interior with Figures*, gift from J. G. Graves, 1943

Redpath, Anne 1895–1965, *Altar in Lisbon*, presented by Park Division Labour Party, 1964, © the artist's estate/Bridgeman Art Library

Redpath, Anne 1895–1965, *Still Life on a Table*, purchased from Aitken Dot, 1977, © the artist's estate/Bridgeman Art Library

Reinagle, George Philip c.1802–1835, *A Lake Scene*, gift from J. G. Graves, 1929

Reinagle, Philip 1749–1833, *The Heron Shoot*, gift from J. G. Graves, 1929

Reinagle, Ramsay Richard 1775–1862, *Forest, Gowbarrow Park, Ullswater, Cumbria*, gift from J. G. Graves, 1937

Reinagle, Ramsay Richard 1775–1862, *Gypsy Encampment*, gift from J. G. Graves, 1929

Renoir, Pierre-Auguste 1841–1919, *La rivière*, on loan from a private collection

Réol, Marie Marguerite 1880–1963, *Christmas Roses*, gift from J. G. Graves, 1943

Réol, Marie Marguerite 1880–1963, *Winter Roses*, gift from J. G. Graves, 1943

Reynolds, Joshua (attributed to) 1723–1792, *A Storm on the Coast near Plympton, Devon*, gift from J. G. Graves, 1929

Rhoades, Geoffrey 1898–1980, *Noon's Farm, Oxenwood, Wiltshire*, purchased, 1934

Rhodes, M. active 19th C, *Bothered*, bequeathed by J. N. Mappin, 1887

Ribera, Jusepe de 1591–1652, *Man with a Skull*, gift from J. G. Graves, 1935

Ribera, Jusepe de (attributed to) 1591–1652, *Head of an Apostle*, presented by the Sheffield Art Collections Fund, 1937

Ricci, Sebastiano 1659–1734, *Christ and the Woman of Samaria*, purchased, 1949

Richardson, Jonathan the elder 1664/1665–1745, *Lady Mary Wortley Montagu (1689–1762)*, purchased from Spinks with the assistance of the Victoria and Albert Museum Purchase Grant Fund, 1977

Richmond, William Blake 1842–1921, *Valley of the Eurotas, Pastoral, Greece*, purchased from the Fine Art Society, 1977

Riegen, Nicholaas 1827–1889, *French Shipping*, gift from J. G. Graves, 1935

Rigg, Ernest Higgins 1868–1947, *Quiet Hour*, gift from J. G. Graves, 1935

Riley, Bridget b.1931, *Rise I*, purchased from the Juda Rowan Gallery, 1983, © the artist

Riley, John 1646–1691, *James Scott (1649–1685), 1st Duke of Monmouth*, purchased, 1955

Rivers, Leopold 1852–1905, *Landscape with a Bridge*, gift from J. G. Graves, 1937

Rivers, Leopold 1852–1905, *Landscape with Cottages*, gift from J. G. Graves, 1929

Rivers, Leopold 1852–1905, *Littlehampton, Sussex*, gift from J. G. Graves, 1929

Rivers, Leopold 1852–1905, *Near Newbury, Berkshire*, gift from J. G. Graves, 1929

Robert, Hubert 1733–1808, *Landscape with Ruins*, gift from J. G. Graves, 1929

Robert, Hubert 1733–1808, *Pyramid of Cestius, Rome*, gift from J. G. Graves, 1943

Robert, Hubert (attributed to) 1733–1808, *Classical Landscape*, gift from J. G. Graves, 1935

Robert, Hubert (attributed to) 1733–1808, *Classical Landscape*, gift from J. G. Graves, 1935

Roberts, David 1796–1864, *The Piazza Navona at Rome*, bequeathed by J. N. Mappin, 1887

Roberts, David 1796–1864, *The Ruins of Tyre, Lebanon*, gift from J. G. Graves, 1935

Roberts, David 1796–1864, *Church of Santa Maria della Salute, Venice*, bequeathed by J. N. Mappin, 1887

Roberts, David 1796–1864, *Canal Scene, Venice*, gift from J. G. Graves, 1943

Roberts, David 1796–1864, *Cathedral, France*, gift from J. G. Graves, 1935

Roberts, David 1796–1864, *Cathedral Interior*, gift from J. G. Graves, 1929

Roberts, William Patrick 1895–1980, *The Red Turban*, presented by the Contemporary Art Society, 1928, © estate of John David Roberts. By courtesy of The William Roberts Society

Robertson, Henry Robert 1839–1921, *Winter*, bequeathed by J. N. Mappin, 1887

Roe, Colin Graeme 1857–1910, *Study of a Horse*, purchased, 1954

Roestraten, Pieter Gerritsz. van 1629/1630–1700, *Still Life with Tea Cups*, gift from J. G. Graves, 1935

Rogers, Claude 1907–1979, *Nude*, presented by the Contemporary Art Society, 1950, © Crispin Rogers

Rögge, Wilhelm 1829–1908, *The Frenchman Playing to His Bird*, bequeathed by J. N. Mappin, 1887

Romney, George 1734–1802, *Edward Wortley Montagu (1713–1776), MP*, accepted by HM Government in lieu of inheritance tax and allocated to Museums Sheffield, 2005

Romney, George 1734–1802, *Head of an Apostle*, purchased from W. Wheeler, 1938

Romney, George 1734–1802, *Head of an Apostle*, purchased, 1938

Roos, Philipp Peter 1657–1706, *Landscape with Goats and Cattle*, presented by Dr Maynski, 1954

Roos, Philipp Peter 1657–1706, *Landscape with Sheep*, presented by Dr Maynski, 1954

Rosa, Salvator (attributed to) 1615–1673, *Figures by a Mountain Stream*, purchased, 1950

Rose, Magnus 1859–1900, *Flowers and Fruit*, presented by F. T. Mappin, 1887

Rose, Martin H. b.1946, *Martin Harris, an Art Student*, purchased from the artist, 1982, © the artist

Rosselli, Cosimo 1439–1507, *Virgin and Child with Angels*, on long-term loan from the Guild of St George, 1935

Rossetti, Dante Gabriel 1828–1882, *Portrait of a Musician*, gift from J. G. Graves, 1929

Rothenstein, Anne b.1949, *Figure on a Bed*, presented by the artist, 1996, © the artist/Bridgeman Art Library

Rothenstein, Michael 1908–1993, *Journey to the Promised Land*, presented by Mrs Alan Ward, 1973, © the artist's estate

Rothenstein, William 1872–1945, *Interior (Lady with a Hat)*, bequeathed by Rachel Ward, 1989, © the artist's estate/Bridgeman Art Library

Rothenstein, William 1872–1945, *Coster Girls*, presented by the Sheffield Society for the Encouragement of Art, 1938, © the artist's estate/Bridgeman Art Library

Rothenstein, William 1872–1945, *Evening in Benares, India*, presented by Mrs A. B. Ward, 1958, © the artist's estate/Bridgeman Art Library

Rothenstein, William 1872–1945, *Buffer Girls*, presented by Sir Robert Hadfield through the Sheffield Art Collections Fund, 1937, © the artist's estate/ Bridgeman Art Library

Rothenstein, William 1872–1945, *Rachael and Betty*, presented by Mrs A. B. Ward, 1973, © the artist's estate/Bridgeman Art Library

Rothenstein, William 1872–1945, *Self Portrait*, presented by the Contemporary Art Society, 1938, © the artist's estate/Bridgeman Art Library

Rouault, Georges 1871–1958, *Head of Christ*, on loan from a private collection, © ADAGP, Paris and DACS, London 2012

Rousseau, Théodore (attributed to) 1812–1867, *Pastoral Scene*, gift from J. G. Graves, 1935

Rousseau, Théodore (attributed to) 1812–1867, *Landscape*, gift from J. G. Graves, 1935

Roussel, Théodore Casimir 1847–1926, *Flowers*, gift from J. G. Graves, 1935

Rowles, Marjorie Kathleen active 1923–1929, *The Coming Thunderstorm*, presented by the Contemporary Art Society, 1931

Royle, Stanley 1888–1961, *The Farmyard*, presented by Miss Royle, 1980, © the artist's estate/ Bridgeman Art Library

Royle, Stanley 1888–1961, *Ploughing*, presented by Willis Eadon through the Sheffield Society for the Encouragement of Art, 1937, © the artist's estate/ Bridgeman Art Library

Royle, Stanley 1888–1961, *Landscape*, presented by Mrs Tozer, 1966, © the artist's estate/ Bridgeman Art Library

Royle, Stanley 1888–1961, *Morning on the Derbyshire Moors*, presented by L. Spencer, 1924, © the artist's estate/Bridgeman Art Library

Royle, Stanley 1888–1961, *Bents Green, Sheffield*, bequeathed by P. Goodwin, 1964, © the artist's estate/Bridgeman Art Library

Royle, Stanley 1888–1961, *Sheffield from Crookes*, purchased by the Art Galleries Sub-Committee, 1953, © the artist's estate/Bridgeman Art Library

Royle, Stanley 1888–1961, *Sheffield from the Park*, purchased by the Art Galleries Sub-Committee, 1953, © the artist's estate/Bridgeman Art Library

Royle, Stanley 1888–1961, *Sheffield from Wincobank Wood*, purchased by the Art Galleries Sub-Committee, 1953, © the artist's estate/Bridgeman Art Library

Royle, Stanley 1888–1961, *View from the Cupola, Derbyshire*, gift from J. G. Graves, 1942, © the artist's estate/Bridgeman Art Library

Royle, Stanley 1888–1961, *Packhorse Bridge, Derwent, Derbyshire*, gift from J. G. Graves, 1929, © the artist's estate/ Bridgeman Art Library

Royle, Stanley 1888–1961, *Bluebell Wood*, presented by Mrs Tyzack, 1996, © the artist's estate/ Bridgeman Art Library

Royle, Stanley 1888–1961, *Mevagissey, Cornwall*, presented by Mr Packer, 1970, © the artist's estate/Bridgeman Art Library

Royle, Stanley 1888–1961, *Burbage Brook, Derbyshire*, purchased from Mrs F. A. Miller, 1962, © the artist's estate/Bridgeman Art Library

Royle, Stanley 1888–1961, *Burbage Brook, Derbyshire* (recto), purchased from Mrs Copleston, 1968, © the artist's estate/ Bridgeman Art Library

Royle, Stanley 1888–1961, *Landscape with a Church and Corn Stooks* (verso)*, purchased from Mrs Copleston, 1968, © the artist's estate/Bridgeman Art Library

Royle, Stanley 1888–1961, *Rock Formation, Nova Scotia, Canada*, purchased, 1987, © the artist's estate/Bridgeman Art Library

Rubens, Peter Paul (studio of) 1577–1640, *Virgin and Child*, gift from J. G. Graves, 1929

Russell, Walter Westley 1867–1949, *Girl in a Muslin Dress*, purchased, 1947

Russell, Walter Westley 1867–1949, *Marion*, purchased from the artist, 1947

Russian School *Russian Painted Icon*, presented by Mrs Loy-Smith, 1889

Ryder, J. T. active c.1933–c.1960, *St John's Church, Sheffield*, presented by Peter Barnes, 2008

Ryder, J. T. active c.1933–c.1960, *Mary Queen of Scots' Shoes*, gift from Mr H. Cowlishaw, c.1979

Sadée, Philip Lodewijk Jacob Frederik 1837–1904, *Figure Piece*, bequeathed by J. N. Mappin, 1887

Sadée, Philip Lodewijk Jacob Frederik (attributed to) 1837–1904, *The End of the Day*, presented by F. T. Mappin, 1891

Safonov, N. *Woodland Path*, gift from J. G. Graves

Sanderson-Wells, John 1872–1955, *Hunting Scene*, gift from J. G. Graves, 1943

Sandys, Frederick 1829–1904, *William H. Clabburn*, gift from J. G. Graves, 1935

Sant, James 1820–1916, *Meditation*, gift from J. G. Graves, 1929

Sant, James 1820–1916, *The Bride*, gift from J. G. Graves, 1937

Santoro, Rubens 1859–1942, *Capri, Italy*, bequeathed by H. H. Andrews, 1903

Saraceni, Carlo (after) 1579–1620, *Judith with the Head of Holofernes*, purchased at Christie's, 1970

Sargent, John Singer 1856–1925, *The Misses Vickers*, presented by D. Vickers, 1938

Sargent, Louis Augustus b.1881, *Atlantic Shore, Cornwall*, purchased via public subscription and a city grant, 1921

Sarto, Andrea del (after) 1486–1530, *Figure of Charity*, presented by Mrs Mitchell, 1949

Sartorius, John Nost 1759–1828, *Fox Hunting*, gift from J. G. Graves, 1935

Sassoferrato (attributed to) 1609–1685, *Madonna and Child*, gift from J. G. Graves, 1935

Scarborough, Joe b.1938, *Britannia Works on Love Street* (recto), purchased, 1971, © the artist

Scarborough, Joe b.1938, *Landscape with Fighter Planes** (verso), purchased, 1971, © the artist

Scarborough, Joe b.1938, *Pub Interior*, presented by the artist, 1975, © the artist

Schalch, Johann Jacob 1723–1789, *Schaffhausen Falls, Switzerland*, gift from J. G. Graves, 1935

Schampheleer, Edmond de 1824–1899, *River Scene with a Steam Boat*, bequeathed by Sir Wilson Mappin, 1925

Schenck, August Friedrich Albrecht 1828–1901, *Donkey Surprised by a Wolf*, presented by F. T. Mappin, 1887

Schieler, Robert *Village Church*, gift from J. G. Graves, 1942

Scholderer, Otto 1834–1902, *Man and Hares*, presented by F. T. Mappin, 1891

Schreyer, Christian Adolf 1828–1899, *The Approach to Cairo*, bequeathed by J. N. Mappin, 1887

Schröder, Albert Friedrich 1854–1939, *The Love Song*, bequeathed by E. G. Wragg, 1928

Seabrooke, Elliott 1886–1950, *The Coffee Pot*, presented by Mr Stephenson, 1935

Seabrooke, Elliott 1886–1950, *Landscape*, presented by C. D. Stephenson, 1935

Seddon, Richard 1915–2002, *Suffolk Village*, purchased from the artist, 1956

Selden, Roger b.1945, *Composition*, purchased from the Edward Torah Gallery, 1982, © the artist

Shackleton, William 1872–1933, *Shore Scene*, presented, 1938

Shannon, James Jebusa 1862–1923, *Portrait of a Lady*, presented by Mr Bingham, 1954

Shannon, James Jebusa 1862–1923, *The Children of Douglas Vickers*, bequeathed by D. Vickers, 1938

Shayer, William 1788–1879, *Coast Scene*, gift from J. G. Graves, 1937

Shayer, William 1788–1879, *The White Cow*, gift from J. G. Graves, 1935

Shayer, William 1788–1879, *Shore Scene*, gift from J. G. Graves

Shayer, William 1788–1879, *Coast Scene*, gift from J. G. Graves, 1935

Shayer, William 1788–1879, *Donkey and Sheep*, gift from J. G. Graves, 1937

Shayer, William 1788–1879, *Fisherman's Children near Blackgang, Isle of Wight*, gift from J. G. Graves, 1943

Shepherd, F. H. S. 1877–1948, *Drawing Room Interior*, presented by Mr J. M. Booth, 1950

Shepherd, Kate active 1888–1916, *Portrait of an Arab*, gift from J. G. Graves, 1929

Sherrin, Daniel 1869–1940, *Sunset near Canterbury, Kent*, bequeathed by H. H. Andrews, 1903

Sichel, Ernest Leopold 1862–1941, *Globe and Maps*, presented by the Sheffield Society for the Encouragement of Art, 1937

Sickert, Bernard 1863–1932, *The Lutheran Church, Amsterdam*, gift from J. G. Graves, 1935

Sickert, Walter Richard 1860–1942, *L'Hotel Royal, Dieppe, France*, purchased at Christie's, 1983, © estate of Walter R. Sickert. All rights reserved, DACS 2012

Sickert, Walter Richard 1860–1942, *Soldiers of King Albert at the Ready*, presented by A. Wood, 1969, © estate of Walter R. Sickert. All rights reserved, DACS 2012

Sickert, Walter Richard 1860–1942, *Chagford, Devon*, gift from J. G. Graves, 1935, © estate of Walter R. Sickert. All rights reserved, DACS 2012

Sickert, Walter Richard 1860–1942, *Portrait of a Woman*, gift from J. G. Graves, 1935, © estate of Walter R. Sickert. All rights reserved, DACS 2012

Sickert, Walter Richard 1860–1942, *A Dead Hare*, gift from J. G. Graves, 1935, © estate of Walter R. Sickert. All rights reserved, DACS 2012

Sickert, Walter Richard 1860–1942, *Fred Winter*, purchased at Sotheby's, 1968, © estate of Walter R. Sickert. All rights reserved, DACS 2012

Simcock, Jack b.1929, *Cottage and Woman (Biddulph, near Stoke-on-Trent, Staffordshire)*, purchased from the Piccadilly Gallery, 1968, © the artist

Simmons, John 1871–1944, *Sheffield Fair*, presented by Mrs Simmons, 1945

Simon, Lucien 1861–1945, *A Parisian Funeral*, gift from J. G. Graves, 1937, © ADAGP, Paris and DACS, London 2012

Simpson, Charles Walter 1885–1971, *Dartmoor Ponies*, purchased from the artist, 1932, © the artist's estate

Simpson, Charles Walter 1885–1971, *Mallard Drake*, purchased from the artist, 1932, © the artist's estate

Singleton, Henry 1766–1839, *The Tired Soldier*, gift from J. G. Graves, 1935

Sisley, Alfred 1839–1899, *Le barrage à Saint-Mammes, France*, on loan from a private collection

Sisley, Alfred 1839–1899, *The Banks of the River Seine around Louveciennes, France*, on loan from a private collection

Smart, Robert Borlase 1881–1947, *In the Bay of Biscay*, gift from J. G. Graves, 1929, © the artist's estate

Smith, Jack 1928–2011, *The Pink Shirt*, presented by the Contemporary Art Society, 1959, © the artist's estate/ courtesy Flowers Gallery, London

Smith, Jack 1928–2011, *Sounds on Grey*, presented by the Contemporary Art Society, 1975, © the artist's estate/ courtesy Flowers Gallery, London

Smith, Jack 1928–2011, *Spanish Still Life*, purchased from the Hanover Gallery, 1971, © the artist's estate/ courtesy Flowers Gallery, London

Smith, Matthew Arnold Bracey 1879–1959, *Tulips*, purchased from the Redfern Gallery with grant aid from the Contemporary Art

Society, 1953, © by permission of the copyright holder
Smith, Richard 1818–1890, *John Holland*, on loan from a private collection
Smith, Richard 1818–1890, *Arthur Thomas, Capital Church Burgess of Sheffield*, on loan from a private collection
Smith, Richard 1818–1890, *John Brown (1816–1896), Mayor of Sheffield (1861–1863)*, on loan from a private collection
Smith, Richard 1818–1890, *William Smith*, on loan from a private collection
Smith, W. E. *Rivelin Valley, Sheffield*, presented by Mr Smith, 1966
Solomon, Abraham 1824–1862, *The Timid Suitor*, bequeathed by J. N. Mappin, 1887
Sonje, Jan Gabrielsz. (attributed to) c.1625–1707, *Landscape with a Ruined Castle*, on loan from the Maleham Bequest, 1955
Spanish School 19th C, *Mother and Three Children*, gift from J. G. Graves, 1942
Spanish School (attributed to) 18th C, *Wine Flask and Apples*, gift from J. G. Graves, 1935
Spear, Ruskin 1911–1990, *Rooftops*, purchased at Sotheby's, 1979, © the artist's estate/Bridgeman Art Library
Speed, Harold 1872–1957, *The Rainbow*, gift from J. G. Graves, 1937
Speed, Harold 1872–1957, *Château-Gaillard, Normandy, France, after Sunset*, presented by J. Ward, 1940
Spencer, Gilbert 1892–1979, *Dorset Landscape No.1*, presented by the National Art Collections Fund, 2001, © the artist's estate/ Bridgeman Art Library
Spencer, Gilbert 1892–1979, *The Drayman*, purchased, 1934, © the artist's estate/Bridgeman Art Library
Spencer, Jean 1942–1998, *Painting*, purchased from the Lucy Milton Gallery, 1972, © the artist's estate
Spencer, Stanley 1891–1959, *Helter Skelter*, purchased, 1937, © the estate of Stanley Spencer. All rights reserved, DACS 2012
Spencer, Stanley 1891–1959, *Zacharias and Elizabeth*, purchased jointly with the Tate Gallery with assistance from the National Lottery through the Heritage Lottery Fund, the National Art Collections Fund, the Friends of the Tate Gallery, Howard and Roberta Ahmanson and private benefactors, 1999, © the estate of Stanley Spencer. All rights reserved, DACS 2012
Spencer Pryse, Gerald 1882–1957, *The Butterfly*, gift from J. G. Graves, 1937 © the artist's estate
Spenlove-Spenlove, Frank 1866–1933, *Evening Glow*, gift from J. G. Graves, 1929
Spruyt, Johannes 1627/1628–1671, *Dead Game*
Spurr, Joyce b.1921, *Steel Forging Works and the River Don from Effingham Street, South Yorkshire*, presented by the artist, 1995, © the artist
Staackmann, Heinrich Maria 1852–1940, *Street in Cairo*, gift from J. G. Graves, 1937
Stademann, Adolf 1824–1895, *Winter Landscape*, gift from J. G. Graves, 1929
Stanfield, Clarkson 1793–1867, *The Morning after the Wreck*, presented by Paul R. Kulhnrich, 1929
Stanfield, Clarkson 1793–1867, *The Last of the Crew*, bequeathed by J. N. Mappin, 1887
Stanfield, Clarkson 1793–1867, *Coast Scene*, bequeathed by J. N. Mappin, 1887
Stanfield, Clarkson 1793–1867, *Eddystone Lighthouse*
Stanfield, Clarkson 1793–1867, *Italian Lake Scene*, gift from J. G. Graves, 1935
Stanfield, Clarkson 1793–1867, *Landscape*, gift from J. G. Graves, 1935
Stanier, Henry c.1832–1892, *Come unto these yellow sands'* (from 'The Tempest' by William Shakespeare), purchased at Sotheby's, 1976
Stapleton, M. active from 1850, *On the Frome*, gift from J. G. Graves
Stark, James 1794–1859, *A Woody Landscape*, gift from J. G. Graves, 1935
Stark, James 1794–1859, *Landscape*, gift from J. G. Graves, 1943
Stark, James 1794–1859, *Landscape*, bequeathed by J. N. Mappin, 1887
Stark, James 1794–1859, *Landscape*, presented by Mrs Atkin, 1957
Steel, George Hammond 1900–1960, *A Slight Fall*, gift from J. G. Graves, 1943
Stevens, Alfred George 1817–1875, *Study of a Dog*, presented by Mrs Jean Mitchell Saltfleet, 1934
Stevens, Alfred George 1817–1875, *A Venetian Gentleman at Hampton Court* (copy of Titian), purchased, 1950
Stevens, Alfred George 1817–1875, *Head of a Baby*, presented by the National Art Collections Fund, 1937
Stevenson, W. J. 1835–1905, *River Don at Wardsend, Sheffield*, purchased, 1981
Stevenson, W. J. 1835–1905, *Birley Meadow Grinding Wheel, Sheffield (August to September, 1870)*
Stevenson, W. J. 1835–1905, *Interior of a Tilt Forge, Lady's Bridge, Sheffield*, presented by the Parks Department, Sheffield, 1956
Stevenson, W. J. 1835–1905, *Oughtibridge, Sheffield*, presented by F. Bradbury through the Sheffield Art Collections Fund
Stevenson, W. J. 1835–1905, *Spooner's Wheel, Rivelin, Sheffield*, presented by the Parks Department, Sheffield, 1956
Stevenson, W. J. 1835–1905, *Union Wheel, Sheffield*, presented by the Parks Department, Sheffield, 1956
Stevenson, W. J. 1835–1905, *Grinders' Workshop*
Stone, Marcus C. 1840–1921, *Claudio, Deceived by Don Juan, Accuses Hero* (from 'Measure for Measure' by William Shakespeare), bequeathed by J. N. Mappin, 1887
Storey, George Adolphus 1834–1919, *Contemplation*, gift from J. G. Graves, 1942
Storey, George Adolphus 1834–1919, *Grandmamma's Christmas Visitors*, bequeathed by J. N. Mappin, 1887
Storey, George Adolphus 1834–1919, *Portrait of a Lady*, presented by F. T. Mappin, 1891
Stothard, Thomas 1755–1834, *The Assassins*, gift from J. G. Graves, 1935
Stothard, Thomas 1755–1834, *The Attack*, gift from J. G. Graves, 1935
Stothard, Thomas 1755–1834, *The Heir*, gift from J. G. Graves, 1935
Stothard, Thomas 1755–1834, *The Lovers' Meeting*, gift from J. G. Graves, 1935
Stott, Edward William 1859–1918, *A French Kitchen Garden*, gift from J. G. Graves, 1937
Stott, Edward William 1859–1918, *The Turnip Field*, gift from J. G. Graves, 1935
Strang, William 1859–1921, *Miss Elizabeth Martin*, gift from J. G. Graves, 1935
Strang, William 1859–1921, *Houses*, gift from J. G. Graves, 1935
Strang, William 1859–1921, *The White Rose*, gift from J. G. Graves, 1935
Strang, William 1859–1921, *Miss Ann Martin*, gift from J. G. Graves, 1935
Stubley, Trevor 1932–2010, *Holmfirth, West Yorkshire, Adam and Eve*, presented by Yorkshire Television, 1982, © the artist's estate
Styring, Elizabeth 1854–1940, *Evening Stillness*, bequeathed by the artist, 1940
Styring, Elizabeth 1854–1940, *The Pink Coat*, bequeathed by the artist, 1940
Styring, Elizabeth 1854–1940, *The Poplars* (recto), bequeathed by the artist, 1940
Styring, Elizabeth 1854–1940, *Castle and Viaduct* (verso)*, bequeathed by the artist, 1940
Suddaby, Rowland 1912–1972, *Cape Cornwall*, purchased at Christie's, 1974, © the artist's estate
Suddaby, Rowland 1912–1972, *Scholes, Yorkshire*, © the artist's estate
Suddaby, Rowland 1912–1972, *Paddock at Stoke-by-Nayland, Essex*, purchased from Martin & Sewell, 1971, © the artist's estate
Sutton, Philip b.1928, *Snape Village, Suffolk*, purchased at Christie's, 1970, © Philip Sutton. All rights reserved, DACS 2012
Swinstead, George Hillyard 1860–1926, *When Trumpets Call, Then Homes Are Broken*, bequeathed by J. N. Mappin, 1887
Syer, John 1815–1885, *Landscape, North Wales*, presented by F. T. Mappin, 1887
Syer, John 1815–1885, *Among the Rushes*, bequeathed by J. N. Mappin, 1887
Syers, Rose Aspinall 1850–after 1926, *A Dutch Town, Windmills*, gift from J. G. Graves, 1937
Sykes, Godfrey 1824–1866, *The Watchman*
Sykes, Godfrey 1824–1866, *Study of a Cherub*, purchased, 1954
Sykes, Godfrey 1824–1866, *Study of a Cherub*, purchased, 1954
Sykes, Godfrey 1824–1866, *The Three Fates*, presented by Mrs Barbara H. Rodgers, 1930
Sykes, Godfrey 1824–1866, *The Tilt Forge*, presented by the sons of Robert Beckett, 1923
Sykes, Godfrey 1824–1866, *Up the Porter*, purchased from H. Baxter, 1923
Sykes, Godfrey 1824–1866, *A Smith's Shop*, presented by the sons of Robert Beckett, 1923
Sykes, Godfrey 1824–1866, *Lascar*, purchased from Mr Bajorak, 1976
Sykes, Godfrey 1824–1866, *Cheney Square with St Paul's, Sheffield*, bequeathed by Mrs Ann Beckett, 1906
Sykes, Godfrey 1824–1866, *The Two Grinders*, purchased, 1921
Sykes, Godfrey 1824–1866, *Portrait of an Oriental*, purchased from Mr H. Atkins, 1940
Sykes, Godfrey 1824–1866, *A Blacksmith's Shop*, purchased from Mr H. Booth, 1954
Sykes, Godfrey 1824–1866, *Frieze with Figures* (polyptych), presented, 1935
Sykes, Godfrey 1824–1866, *Frieze with Figures* (polyptych), presented, 1935
Sykes, Godfrey 1824–1866, *Frieze with Figures* (polyptych), presented, 1935
Sykes, Godfrey 1824–1866, *Frieze with Figures* (polyptych), presented, 1935
Sykes, Godfrey 1824–1866, *Frieze with Figures* (polyptych), presented, 1935
Sykes, Godfrey 1824–1866, *Frieze with Figures* (polyptych), presented, 1935
Sykes, Godfrey 1824–1866, *Frieze with Figures* (polyptych), presented, 1935
Sykes, Godfrey 1824–1866, *Frieze with Figures* (polyptych), presented, 1935
Sykes, Godfrey 1824–1866, *Frieze with Figures* (polyptych), presented, 1935
Sykes, Godfrey 1824–1866, *Frieze with Figures* (polyptych), presented, 1935
Sykes, Godfrey 1824–1866, *Frieze with Figures* (polyptych), presented, 1935
Sykes, Godfrey 1824–1866, *Grinder's Hull*, presented by the sons of Robert Beckett
Sykes, Godfrey 1824–1866, *Interior of a Sheffield Grinder's Hull*, presented by the Sheffield Society for the Encouragement of Art, 1937
Sykes, Godfrey 1824–1866, *Lunch Time*, presented by B. M. Rodgers, 1934
Sykes, Godfrey 1824–1866, *St Paul's Church, Sheffield*, bequeathed by Mrs Ann Beckett, 1906
Sykes, Godfrey 1824–1866, *Sheffield Scythe Tilters*, purchased from H. Baxter, 1923
Sykes, Godfrey 1824–1866, *The Pet in a Pet*, presented by Alderman W. H. Brittain, 1906
Sykes, Godfrey 1824–1866, *Venus Arising from the Sea*, purchased from Mr Harry Aitkin, 1940
Sykes, Godfrey (attributed to) 1824–1866, *Cottages in London Road, Highfields, Sheffield*, presented by Mrs H. Hemingway, 1838
Sykes, Godfrey (attributed to) 1824–1866, *Cottages in London Road, Highfields, Sheffield*, presented by Mrs H. Hemingway, 1838
Sykes, Lilian active 1887–1890, *Dead Pheasant*, gift from J. G. Graves
Symons, William Christian 1845–1911, *In hora mortis*, presented by F. T. Mappin, 1887
Symons, William Christian 1845–1911, *Returned from the Wars*, presented by John Eadon, 1894
Talmage, Algernon Mayow 1871–1939, *October Morning*, gift from J. G. Graves, 1929
Tamburini, Arnaldo 1843–1908, *The Monk*, bequeathed by H. H. Andrews, 1903
Tayler, Albert Chevallier 1862–1925, *The Upper Thames*, gift from J. G. Graves, 1929
Temple, Robert Scott b.c.1853, *Landscape with a River*, bequeathed by Sir Wilson Mappin, 1925
Temple, Robert Scott b.c.1853, *The Old Woman of Moscar Moor, Derbyshire*, bequeathed by Sir Wilson Mappin, 1925
Ten Kate, Herman Frederik Carel 1822–1891, *Interior*, gift from J. G. Graves, 1929
Ten Kate, Herman Frederik Carel 1822–1891, *A Back Door Visitor*, gift from J. G. Graves, 1943
Ten Kate, Herman Frederik Carel 1822–1891, *Lovers*, gift from J. G. Graves, 1943
Ten Kate, Herman Frederik Carel 1822–1891, *Card Players*, presented by F. T. Mappin, 1887

Teniers, David I 1582–1649, *Landscape with Figures*
Teniers, David II 1610–1690, *The Yard of an Inn*, accepted by HM Government in lieu of inheritance tax and allocated to Museums Sheffield, 1980
Teniers, David II (attributed to) 1610–1690, *The Sense of Smell*, gift from J. G. Graves, 1943
Teniers, David II (school of) 1610–1690, *Shuttlecock*, gift from J. G. Graves, 1935
Teniers, David II 1610–1690 & **Peeters, Gillis** 1612–1653, *A Scene in a Flemish Village*, accepted by HM Government in lieu of inheritance tax and allocated to Museums Sheffield, 1980
Teurdyghe, Carolus Ignatius (attributed to) active c.1700, *Madonna and Child*, presented by Lord Lee of Fareham, 1935
Thaddeus, Henry Jones 1860–1929, *An Irish Peasant*, gift from J. G. Graves, 1935
Tharp, Charles Julian 1878–1951, *Blossom Time*, gift from J. G. Graves, 1943, © the artist's estate
Thomas, Grosvenor 1856–1923, *Landscape with a Windmill*, gift from J. G. Graves, 1937
Thompson, Hugh 1810–1866, *James Archibald Stuart-Wortley-Mackenzie (1776–1845), 1st Lord Wharncliffe*, on loan from a private collection
Thomson, Christopher 1799–1871, *Little London Dam, Heeley, Sheffield*, presented by George H. Beal, 1908
Thomson, Christopher 1799–1871, *Sheffield Iris Office, Hartshead*, purchased, 1934
Thomson, Christopher 1799–1871, *Rivelin Valley, near Black Brook, Sheffield*, purchased, 1912
Thomson, John 1778–1840, *Landscape*, gift from J. G. Graves, 1937
Tibble, Geoffrey Arthur 1909–1952, *Chez Martin*, purchased at Christie's, 1970
Tissot, James 1836–1902, *The Convalescent*, purchased, 1949
Tol, Dominicus van (attributed to) c.1635–1676, *Self Portrait*, gift from J. G. Graves, 1935
Tommasi, Adolfo 1851–1933, *View of an Italian Town*, gift from J. G. Graves, 1943
Tonge, Robert 1823–1856, *Vale of Llangollen, Wales*, bequeathed by J. N. Mappin, 1887
Tonge, Robert 1823–1856, *The Valley of the Dee, Wales*, bequeathed by J. N. Mappin, 1887
Tonge, Robert 1823–1856, *The Rainbow*, bequeathed by J. N. Mappin, 1887
Topham, Francis Williams 1808–1877, *The Mendicants*, gift from J. G. Graves, 1943
Topham, Francis Williams 1808–1877, *Saturday Evening in Connemara, Ireland*, bequeathed by J. N. Mappin, 1887
Torrance, James 1859–1916, *The Pig Feeder's Daughter*, presented by the Trustees of Mrs Torrance, 1921
Torre, Raffaelo 1844–1927, *A Gentle Breeze*, bequeathed by Sir Wilson Mappin, 1925
Towner, Donald Chisholm 1903–1985, *Admiral's House, Hampstead, London*, gift from J. G. Graves, 1935, © the artist's estate
Townley, James Morrison 1917–1995, *Bramall Lane, Sheffield*, presented by B. Molnar, 2008
Townroe, Reuben 1835–1911, *Robert Glassby*, purchased, 1929
Townroe, Reuben 1835–1911, *Self Portrait*, presented by the Sheffield Society for the Encouragement of Art, 1943
Townsend, Ernest 1885–1944, *Ashley Ward*
Townsend, William 1909–1973, *Landscape with a Pond*, purchased at Christie's, 1978, © the artist's estate
Traies, William 1789–1872, *The Waterfall*, gift from J. G. Graves, 1935
Turner, Joseph Mallord William 1775–1851, *The Festival of the Opening of the Vintage at Mâcon, France*, bequeathed by Ernest Cook through the National Art Collections Fund, 1955
Turner, Joseph Mallord William (after) 1775–1851, *A View on the Colne, Moor Park, Hertfordshire*, bequeathed by J. N. Mappin, 1887
Turner, Joseph Mallord William (after) 1775–1851, *Dunbar Castle, Scotland*, bequeathed by J. N. Mappin, 1887
Turner, Joseph Mallord William (attributed to) 1775–1851, *Seascape*, gift from J. G. Graves, 1943
Tyzack, Michael 1933–2007, *Wedge*, purchased with the assistance of the Victoria and Albert Museum Purchase Grant Fund, 1966, © the artist's estate
Underhill, Frederick Charles c.1832–1896, *A Cornish Coast View*, gift from J. G. Graves, 1943
unknown artist *Lady Catherine Jermyn (b.1579)*, gift from J. G. Graves, 1935
unknown artist *Norwood Hall, Sheffield*, presented by Mrs J. Wheat, 1938
unknown artist *Frederick Woolhouse*, presented by R. C. D. Fell, 1969
unknown artist *Anne Woolhouse*, presented by R. C. D. Fell, 1969
unknown artist *River Sheaf and Shrewsbury Hospital, Sheffield*, presented by Mrs E. A. Roper, 1930
unknown artist *Sheffield from Heeley*, bequeathed by Dr John Stokes, 1938
unknown artist *Sheffield Manor*, purchased, 1934
unknown artist *View of Sheffield from Sharrow Moor*, presented by Mr A. H. Butler, 1980
unknown artist *Ebenezer Elliott (1781–1849)*, on loan from a private collection
unknown artist *Bridge and White Rails at Bridgehouses, Sheffield*, purchased, 1909
unknown artist *Cottage at Norton Lees, Sheffield*, presented by Miss O. Hallesworth, 1980
unknown artist *Corner of Fargate and Pinstone Street, Sheffield*, presented by Mrs Ferguson, 1974
unknown artist *Montgomery Tavern, Sheffield*, presented by A. Goodwin, 1936
unknown artist *Feeding the Canary*, gift from J. G. Graves, 1937
unknown artist *Cottages on Greystones Road, Sheffield*, presented by E. Jameson, 1930
unknown artist *Whiteley Woods Bridge, Sheffield*, presented by J. H. Beardshaw, 1952
unknown artist *Sheffield from Psalter Lane*, purchased, 1985
unknown artist (in the manner of Henri Matisse) *La femme au peignoir*, purchased from H. L. Good with the assistance of the Victoria and Albert Museum Purchase Grant Fund, 1972
unknown artist *A Bavarian Landscape*, gift from J. G. Graves, 1943
unknown artist *A Musician, and a Lady with a Dog in a Landscape*, gift from J. G. Graves, 1943
unknown artist *An Eastern Bazaar Scene*, gift from J. G. Graves, 1943
unknown artist *An Italian Bay*
unknown artist *Ann Astley*, gift from J. G. Graves, 1935
unknown artist *Apples on a Dish*, gift from J. G. Graves, 1943
unknown artist *Beach Scene*, gift from J. G. Graves
unknown artist *Boy with a Falcon*, gift from J. G. Graves, 1937
unknown artist *Calves*, gift from J. G. Graves
unknown artist *Cathedral with Figures*, bequeathed by Sir Wilson Mappin, 1925
unknown artist *Cattle, Goats and Sheep*, bequeathed by Sir Wilson Mappin, 1925
unknown artist *Charles Dibdin (1745?–1814)*, presented by Mr Willis Dixon, 1965
unknown artist *Charles Pye as a Child*, presented by the Elmhirst foundation, 1961
unknown artist *Christopher Johnson*, presented by Mr J. M. Denton, 1955
unknown artist *Conversation Piece with Three Figures*, bequeathed by Mrs Dawson, 1963
unknown artist *Country Inn*, gift from J. G. Graves
unknown artist *Dead Hare*
unknown artist *Don Quixote*, gift from J. G. Graves
unknown artist *Farewell*, gift from J. G. Graves
unknown artist *Flower Piece*, gift from J. G. Graves, 1943
unknown artist *Flower Piece*, gift from J. G. Graves, 1943
unknown artist *French Percheron Horses*, gift from J. G. Graves
unknown artist *George Woolhouse*, presented by R. C. D. Fell, 1969
unknown artist *H. W. Lash*
unknown artist *Harbour Scene*, presented by Mr Eberlyn, 1957
unknown artist *Head of Philip Neri (1515–1595)*, gift from J. G. Graves, 1943
unknown artist *Helping the Poor*, bequeathed by J. N. Mappin, 1887
unknown artist *Heraclitus, Ancient Greek Scientist*, gift from J. G. Graves, 1942
unknown artist *Heraclitus, Ancient Greek Scientist*, presented by Miss M. Deakin, 1980
unknown artist *Hop Harvest, Bavaria*, gift from J. G. Graves, 1942**unknown artist** *Interior of a Cottage with Figures*, bequeathed by J. N. Mappin, 1887
unknown artist *Interior with a Lady*
unknown artist *John Arthur Roebuck (1802–1879)*, on loan from a private collection
unknown artist *John Jackson (d.1895), Mayor of Sheffield (1889–1890)*, presented by R. P. Barlow, 1993
unknown artist *John Read (1744–1803), of Norton House*
unknown artist *John Webster (d.1878), Mayor of Sheffield (1866–1868)*, on loan from a private collection
unknown artist *Joseph Read*
unknown artist *Joseph Rodgers (1785–1867)*
unknown artist *Landscape*, gift from J. G. Graves
unknown artist *Landscape*, gift from J. G. Graves, 1937
unknown artist *Landscape*, gift from J. G. Graves
unknown artist *Landscape*, gift from J. G. Graves
unknown artist *Landscape*, gift from J. G. Graves
unknown artist *Landscape*, gift from J. G. Graves
unknown artist *Landscape*, gift from J. G. Graves
unknown artist *Landscape*, gift from J. G. Graves
unknown artist *Landscape*, gift from J. G. Graves
unknown artist *Landscape*, presented by Dr Naish, 1951
unknown artist *Landscape in Snow*, gift from J. G. Graves, 1943
unknown artist *Landscape with a Cart*, gift from J. G. Graves, 1942
unknown artist *Landscape with a River*, gift from J. G. Graves, 1943
unknown artist *Landscape with a River*, gift from J. G. Graves, 1942
unknown artist *Landscape with a River and Cattle*
unknown artist *Landscape with a Small Cottage*, gift from J. G. Graves
unknown artist *Landscape with Cattle*, gift from J. G. Graves
unknown artist *Landscape with Cattle, Goats and a Donkey*, gift from J. G. Graves, 1937
unknown artist *Landscape with Drovers*, bequeathed by Mrs Handley, 1951
unknown artist *Landscape with Figures and Cattle*, gift from J. G. Graves
unknown artist *Landscape with Figures and Horses*, gift from J. G. Graves, 1943
unknown artist *Lees Hall, Norton, Sheffield*
unknown artist *Lepping Stones, Wadsley Bridge, Sheffield*, presented by Mr and Mrs S. G. Newham, 1959
unknown artist *Miss Elizabeth Croft (1769–1859)*, presented by Colonel McKenzie-Smith, 1949
unknown artist *Mother and Child*, gift from J. G. Graves, 1942
unknown artist *Mountain Landscape with Cattle*, gift from J. G. Graves, 1943
unknown artist *Mr Batty*, presented by Colonel McKenzie-Smith, 1949
unknown artist *Mrs Batty*, presented by Colonel McKenzie-Smith, 1949
unknown artist *Portrait of a Gentleman*, gift from J. G. Graves
unknown artist *Portrait of a Gentleman*, gift from J. G. Graves
unknown artist *Portrait of a Gentleman*, gift from J. G. Graves
unknown artist *Portrait of a Lady*, presented
unknown artist *Portrait of a Lady*, presented
unknown artist *Portrait of a Lady*, bequeathed by Miss Watson, 1953
unknown artist *Portrait of a Lawyer*, gift from J. G. Graves
unknown artist *Portrait of a Man*
unknown artist *Portrait of a Man*
unknown artist *Portrait of a Man*, gift from J. G. Graves, 1942
unknown artist *Portrait of a Man*
unknown artist *Portrait of a Man*
unknown artist *Portrait of a Man*, purchased, 1949
unknown artist *Portrait of a Man*, presented by Mr Crofts, 1981
unknown artist *Portrait of a Man in a Red Cap*, gift from J. G. Graves
unknown artist *Portrait of a Member of the Batty Family*, presented by Colonel McKenzie-Smith, 1949
unknown artist *Portrait of a Woman*, gift from J. G. Graves
unknown artist *Portrait of a Young Man*
unknown artist *Reverend Thomas Sale (d.1873), Vicar of Sheffield*, purchased from William Challenger, 1916
unknown artist *River Scene*, gift from J. G. Graves
unknown artist *River Scene*, gift from J. G. Graves
unknown artist *River Scene with a Bridge*, gift from J. G. Graves, 1943
unknown artist *River Scene with a Cottage*, gift from J. G. Graves, 1935

unknown artist *Samuel Osbourne*
unknown artist *Scene from the French Revolution*
unknown artist *Scene Outside a Village Inn*, gift from J. G. Graves
unknown artist *Sheep*, gift from J. G. Graves
unknown artist *Six Sheffield Gentlemen at a Table*, presented by J. Skelton, 1878
unknown artist *Still Life*, gift from J. G. Graves, 1929
unknown artist *Street Scene*, gift from J. G. Graves
unknown artist *Sunset*, gift from J. G. Graves, 1943
unknown artist *Sunset View*, gift from J. G. Graves
unknown artist *The Don Valley, Sheffield*, presented by Mr and Mrs S. G. Newham, 1959
unknown artist *The Musician*, gift from J. G. Graves
unknown artist *The Old Barn*, gift from J. G. Graves, 1935
unknown artist *The Rainbow*, gift from J. G. Graves, 1943
unknown artist *The Virgin Mary with the Infant Christ*
unknown artist *Three Female Figures*
unknown artist *Three Figures on the Shore*, bequeathed by Bertha Annie Sykes, 1949
unknown artist *Wayfarers*, gift from J. G. Graves, 1935
unknown artist *Woodland*, gift from J. G. Graves, 1943
Unterberger, Franz Richard 1838–1902, *Rivera de Castellammare, Italy*, gift from J. G. Graves, 1937
Unterberger, Franz Richard 1838–1902, *Port of Capri, Italy*, gift from J. G. Graves, 1929
Van Assen, Benedictus Antonio 1788–1817, *Flowers*, gift from J. G. Graves, 1929
Van Boskerck, Robert Ward 1855–1932, *A Rhode Island River, America*, bequeathed by H. H. Andrews, 1903
Van Boskerck, Robert Ward 1855–1932, *American River Scene*, bequeathed by H. H. Andrews, 1903
Van de Tonge, Louis 1871–1937, *The New Doll*, gift from J. G. Graves, 1937
Van der Hoef, Abraham (attributed to) 1611/1612–1649, *A Cavalry Skirmish*, gift from J. G. Graves, 1935
Van der Nat, Willem Hendrik 1865–1929, *Sheep in a Barn*, gift from J. G. Graves, 1937
Van Heemskerck van Beest, Jacob Eduard 1828–1894, *Sea View*, bequeathed by Sir Wilson Mappin, 1925
Vanderbank, John c.1694–1739, *William Rogers of Dowdeswell, Master in the High Court of Chancery*, purchased at Christie's, 1972
Vanderbank, John c.1694–1739, *Anne and Mary Tonson*, presented by the J. G. Graves Charitable Trust, 1950
Varley, John II 1850–1933, *Mosque near the Bab al-Nasr, Cairo*, gift from J. G. Graves, 1943
Varley, John II 1850–1933, *Near the Gate of the Zueylah, Cairo*, presented by F. T. Mappin, 1887
Varley, John II 1850–1933, *A Well at Abbassieh, Near Cairo*, gift from J. G. Graves, 1929
Varley, John II 1850–1933, *Entrance to the Mausoleum of Jyemiten, Nikko, Japan*, gift from J. G. Graves, 1929
Vaughan, John Keith 1912–1977, *The Barn*, purchased at Sotheby's, 1976, © the estate of Keith Vaughan. All rights reserved, DACS 2012
Vaughan, John Keith 1912–1977, *Landscape in Belsize Park, London*, purchased from the Mercury Gallery with the assistance of the Victoria and Albert Museum Purchase Grant Fund, 1973, © the estate of Keith Vaughan. All rights reserved, DACS 2012
Vaughan, John Keith 1912–1977, *Study for a Laocoon, VII*, purchased from Marlborough Fine Art, 1974, © the estate of Keith Vaughan. All rights reserved, DACS 2012
Vaux, Marc b.1932, *L. S. Green 3*, purchased from the Axiom Gallery, 1970, © the artist
Vawser, George Robert 1815–1893, *Norwood Hall, Pitsmoor, Sheffield*, presented by Dr Henry Jackson, 1919
Velde, Willem van de II (school of) 1633–1707, *Seascape*, gift from J. G. Graves, 1935
Verheyden, François (attributed to) 1806–1889/1890, *The Canal, Bruges, Belgium*, gift from J. G. Graves, 1935
Vernet, Claude-Joseph 1714–1789, *A French Soldier*, gift from J. G. Graves
Vernet, Claude-Joseph 1714–1789, *Sea Piece*, gift from J. G. Graves, 1887
Vernet, Claude-Joseph (attributed to) 1714–1789, *Castel Sant'Angelo, Rome*, gift from J. G. Graves, 1942
Vernet, Claude-Joseph (attributed to) 1714–1789, *Scene on the Tiber*, gift from J. G. Graves, 1942
Vernet, Horace 1789–1863, *An Arab at Prayer*, gift from J. G. Graves
Vernier, Émile Louis (attributed to) 1829–1887, *A Cottage at Amiens, France*, gift from J. G. Graves, 1929
Veyrassat, Jules Jacques 1828–1893, *Landscape with a River*, gift from J. G. Graves, 1943
Vianello, Giovanni 1873–1926, *Venezia*, bequeathed by H. H. Andrews, 1903
Vickers, Alfred 1786–1868, *At Bolton Abbey, North Yorkshire*, gift from J. G. Graves, 1935
Vickers, Alfred 1786–1868, *Near Beddgelert, North Wales*, gift from J. G. Graves, 1943
Vickers, Alfred 1786–1868, *In Monsal Dale, Derbyshire*, bequeathed by J. N. Mappin, 1887
Vickers, Alfred 1786–1868, *Landscape with Cattle*, gift from J. G. Graves, 1943
Vickers, Alfred 1786–1868, *Abraham on His Way to the Sacrifice*, bequeathed by Thomas Heiffor
Vickers, Alfred 1786–1868, *Landscape*, gift from J. G. Graves, 1929
Vickers, Alfred 1786–1868, *Landscape with a River*, gift from J. G. Graves, 1943
Vickers, Alfred 1786–1868, *Off Calais, France*, gift from J. G. Graves, 1929
Vickers, Alfred 1786–1868, *River Scene*, gift from J. G. Graves, 1943
Vickers, Alfred 1786–1868, *Village Street*, gift from J. G. Graves, 1929
Vidal, Louis c.1754–1804, *Vase of Flowers*, gift from J. G. Graves, 1935
Villamil, Eugenio Lucas 1858–1918, *To the Bull Ring*, gift from J. G. Graves, 1929
Vincent, George 1796–1831, *A Norfolk Mill*, gift from J. G. Graves, 1935
Vincent, George 1796–1831, *A View near Thorpe, Norwich, Norfolk*, gift from J. G. Graves, 1929
Vincent, George 1796–1831, *A View of Suffolk*, bequeathed by J. N. Mappin, 1887
Vincent, George 1796–1831, *Cattle Drinking*, gift from J. G. Graves
Vincent, George 1796–1831, *On the Yare, Norfolk*, presented by the Nettlefold Collection, 1948
Vizard, W. active 1884–1903, *Portrait of a Man*
Vlaminck, Maurice de 1876–1958, *The Edge of the Wood*, on loan from a private collection, © ADAGP, Paris and DACS, London 2012
Vollon, Alexis 1865–1945, *The Sewing Maid*, gift from J. G. Graves, 1943, © ADAGP, Paris and DACS, London 2012
Vollon, Antoine 1833–1900, *Peaches*, gift from J. G. Graves, 1935
Vollon, Antoine 1833–1900, *Coast near Étretat, France*, gift from J. G. Graves, 1935
Von Gegerfeldt, Wilhelm 1844–1920, *Eastern Scene*, gift from J. G. Graves, 1929
Von Löfftz, Ludwig 1845–1910, *Cornfield*, gift from J. G. Graves, 1943
Vuram, J. *Entrance to the Grand Canal, Venice, Sunset*, bequeathed by J. N. Mappin, 1887
Vuram, J. (attributed to) *Santa Maria Maggiore, Venice, Moonlight*, bequeathed by J. N. Mappin, 1887
Vuram, J. (attributed to) *The Dogana, Venice, Early Morning*, bequeathed by J. N. Mappin, 1887
Wadsworth, Edward Alexander 1889–1949, *Honfleur, France, Entrance to the Harbour*, purchased with the assistance of the Victoria and Albert Museum Purchase Grant Fund, 1977, © estate of Edward Wadsworth. All rights reserved, DACS 2012
Wainewright, Thomas Francis 1794–1883, *Landscape with Cattle*, gift from J. G. Graves
Wakle, J. F. *Washing Day*, gift from J. G. Graves, 1943
Walker, Ethel 1861–1951, *Midday Shore*, purchased from the Redfern Gallery, 1977, © the artist's estate/ Bridgeman Art Library
Walker, Ethel 1861–1951, *Seascape*, purchased from the Redfern Gallery, 1977, © the artist's estate/ Bridgeman Art Library
Walker, Robert 1599–1658, *The Earl of Strafford* (possibly William Wentworth, 1626–1695), gift from J. G. Graves
Walker, Robert (after) 1599–1658, *Portrait of a Young Man*, presented by Dr Naish, 1951
Waller, Samuel Edmund 1850–1903, *Keep My Secret*, presented by Reginald Vaile, 1901
Wallis, Alfred 1855–1942, *Fishing Boat Between Two Lighthouses*, purchased at Christie's, 1972
Waplington, Paul Anthony b.1938, *May Day, Hyson Green, Nottinghamshire*, purchased from the artist with the assistance of the Victoria and Albert Museum Purchase Grant Fund, 1981, © the artist
Waplington, Paul Anthony b.1938, *Footbridge*, purchased from the artist, 1981, © the artist
Ward, Edward Matthew 1816–1879, *The Concealment of the Fugitive by Alice Lisle* (after the Battle of Sedgemoor in the Reign of James II), presented by F. T. Mappin
Ward, Edward Matthew 1816–1879, *The Fall of Clarendon*, bequeathed by J. N. Mappin, 1887
Ward, Edward Matthew 1816–1879, *Cavalry Man*, gift from J. G. Graves
Ward, Edward Matthew 1816–1879, *Judge Jeffreys Bullying Richard Baxter*, presented by F. T. Mappin, 1897
Ward, Grace active 1930–1940s, *Juanita*, gift from J. G. Graves, 1937
Ward, James 1769–1859, *Disobedience in Danger*, gift from J. G. Graves
Ward, James 1769–1859, *Landscape with Cattle*, presented by the Sheffield Society for the Encouragement of Art
Ward, Martin Theodore 1799–1874, *Landscape with Cattle*, gift from J. G. Graves, 1937
Ward, Martin Theodore 1799–1874, *The Sportsman*, gift from J. G. Graves, 1935
Ward, T. active 1819–1865, *Henley-on-Thames, Oxfordshire*, gift from J. G. Graves, 1935
Warmby, Byron Winston 1902–1978, *A Fair in Endcliffe Park, Sheffield*, purchased, 1982
Warr, George H. 1907–1933, *Ploughing Scene*, bequeathed by Bertha Annie Sykes, 1949
Warren, William White 1832–1915, *Venice*, gift from J. G. Graves, 1943
Warren, William White 1832–1915, *River Scene with a Church*, gift from J. G. Graves, 1937
Waterhouse, John William 1849–1917, *Portrait of the Artist's Wife*, purchased from Jeremy Maas & Co. with the assistance of the Victoria and Albert Museum Purchase Grant Fund, 1978
Watson, William II active 1866–1921, *A Breezy Morn, Glen Massan, Argyllshire, Scotland*, bequeathed by H. H. Andrews, 1903
Watts, George Frederick 1817–1904, *Time, Death and Judgement*, purchased from the Fine Art Society, 1969
Watts, George Frederick 1817–1904, *Dr Edward Venables-Vernon-Harcourt (1757–1847), Archbishop of York*, gift from J. G. Graves, 1932
Weatherhead, William Harris 1843–1903, *'For those in peril'*, gift from J. G. Graves, 1929
Webb, James 1825–1895, *Coast Scene*, gift from J. G. Graves, 1937
Webb, James 1825–1895, *Mont Saint-Michel, Normandy, France*, bequeathed by H. H. Andrews, 1903
Webb, James 1825–1895, *Mont Saint-Michel, Normandy, France*, bequeathed by J. N. Mappin, 1887
Webb, James 1825–1895, *Paris*, bequeathed by Sir Wilson Mappin, 1925
Webb, James 1825–1895, *At Dordrecht, Holland*, bequeathed by Sir Wilson Mappin, 1925
Webb, James 1825–1895, *Namur, Belgium*, presented by F. T. Mappin, 1887
Webb, James 1825–1895, *On the Thames, near Kew*, gift from J. G. Graves, 1943
Webb, James 1825–1895, *The Sussex Weald*, gift from J. G. Graves, 1935
Webb, James 1825–1895, *French Coast, near Calais, France*, gift from J. G. Graves, 1929
Webb, James 1825–1895, *On the Meuse*, gift from J. G. Graves, 1929
Webb, James 1825–1895, *Seascape*, gift from J. G. Graves, 1943
Webb, James 1825–1895, *Seascape*, bequeathed by H. H. Andrews, 1903
Webb, James 1825–1895, *Ship Aground*, gift from J. G. Graves, 1942
Webster, Thomas George 1800–1886, *Roast Pig*, bequeathed by Sir Wilson Mappin, 1925
Webster, Thomas George 1800–1886, *First Steps*, gift from J. G. Graves, 1935
Weekes, Henry I 1807–1877, *'Dan Leno'*, gift from J. G. Graves, 1942
Weeks, Edwin Lord 1849–1903, *An Indian Messenger*, gift from J. G. Graves, 1937

Weight, Carel Victor Morlais 1908–1997, *'Cockles and mussels, alive, alive oh!'*, purchased from the Leicester Galleries, 1964, © the estate of the artist/Bridgeman Art Library
Weight, Carel Victor Morlais 1908–1997, *Visitors to a Sculpture Park*, on loan from a private collection, © the estate of the artist/Bridgeman Art Library
Weir, William d.1865, *Fisher Girl and Boy*, bequeathed by Sir Wilson Mappin, 1925
Weiss, José 1859–1919, *A Winter Scene*, gift from J. G. Graves, 1943
Weiss, José 1859–1919, *A Sunlit Cloud*, gift from J. G. Graves, 1937
Weiss, José 1859–1919, *Evening in South Devon*, gift from J. G. Graves, 1937
Weiss, José 1859–1919, *Landscape*, gift from J. G. Graves, 1943
Weiss, José 1859–1919, *Landscape*, gift from J. G. Graves, 1943
Weissenbruch, Jan Hendrik 1824–1903, *A Dutch Canal*, gift from J. G. Graves
Wentzel, Niels Gustav 1859–1927, *Snow Scene*, gift from J. G. Graves, 1937
Werff, Adriaen van der (attributed to) 1659–1722, *Portrait of a Young Man*, gift from J. G. Graves, 1935
Wheatley, Francis 1747–1801, *Return from the Shoot*, accepted by HM Government in lieu of inheritance tax and allocated to Museums Sheffield
Wheatley, Francis 1747–1801, *The Village Street*, gift from J. G. Graves, 1935
Wheatley, John 1892–1955, *Sir Basil Gibson*, presented by the Trent Regional Health Authority, 1975
Wheelwright, Rowland 1870–1955, *A Summer Afternoon*, gift from J. G. Graves, 1929
Whistler, James Abbott McNeill 1834–1903, *Portrait*, gift from J. G. Graves, 1935
Whistler, James Abbott McNeill 1834–1903, *The Dancing Lesson*, gift from J. G. Graves, 1943
Whittington, Marjory active 20th C, *At Appledore, Devon*, gift from J. G. Graves
Wilkie, David 1785–1841, *Blind Man's Bluff*, bequeathed by Sir Wilson Mappin, 1925
Wilkie, David 1785–1841, *A Scottish Professor*, gift from J. G. Graves, 1929
Wilkinson, Charles A. b.1830, *Landscape*, gift from J. G. Graves, 1942
Willcock, George Burrell 1811–1852, *Coast Scene*, gift from J. G. Graves, 1935
Willcock, George Burrell 1811–1852, *View near Harwich, Essex*, gift from J. G. Graves, 1935
Williams, Edward 1782–1855, *A Squally Day on the Yare, Norfolk*, bequeathed by J. B. Styring, 1941
Williams, Edward 1782–1855, *Barges on a River*, gift from J. G. Graves, 1935
Williams, Edward 1782–1855, *Castleman Villas, Moonlight*, gift from J. G. Graves
Williams, Edward Charles 1807–1881, *A Roadside Inn at Rushington, Sussex*, bequeathed by James Wing, 1941
Williams, Terrick John 1860–1936, *Golden Evening, Martigues, France*, presented by B. A. Jones, 1928
Wilson, Arthur 1838–1914, *Interior of Doctor Cordell Thompson's House*, presented by Sir Arthur J. Hall, 1934
Wilson, Arthur 1838–1914, *View of Cottages, Woodseats, Sheffield*, purchased, 1963
Wilson, John H. 'Jock' 1774–1855, *Sea Piece*, presented by F. T. Mappin, 1891
Wilson, John James II 1818–1875, *Calais, Old Pier, France*, bequeathed by Thomas Waterhouse, 1902
Wilson, John James II 1818–1875, *Landscape with Cattle*, gift from J. G. Graves, 1929
Wilson, Richard (after) 1712/1713–1782, *Italian Landscape*, gift from J. G. Graves, 1942
Wilson, Richard (attributed to) 1712/1713–1782, *A View near Bologna, Italy*, gift from J. G. Graves, 1929
Wilson, Richard (attributed to) 1712/1713–1782, *Caernarvon Castle, Wales*, presented by Reverend Grenville John Cherter, 1888
Wilson, Richard (attributed to) 1712/1713–1782, *Italian Landscape with Figures*, gift from J. G. Graves, 1935
Wilson, Richard (attributed to) 1712/1713–1782, *Lake Nemi, Rome*, gift from J. G. Graves, 1943
Wilson, Richard (attributed to) 1712/1713–1782, *Lake Scene*, gift from J. G. Graves, 1935
Wilson, Richard (attributed to) 1712/1713–1782, *Landscape*, gift from J. G. Graves, 1935
Wilson, Richard (attributed to) 1712/1713–1782, *Landscape*, gift from J. G. Graves, 1935
Wilson, Richard (attributed to) 1712/1713–1782, *Landscape*, gift from J. G. Graves, 1935
Wilson, Richard (attributed to) 1712/1713–1782, *Landscape with a Church*, gift from J. G. Graves, 1935
Wilson, Richard (attributed to) 1712/1713–1782, *Landscape with a Monk at Devotion*, gift from J. G. Graves, 1935
Wilson, Richard (attributed to) 1712/1713–1782, *Niobe and Her Children*, on loan from a private collection
Wilson, Richard (attributed to) 1712/1713–1782, *The Boat Man*, gift from J. G. Graves, 1935
Wilson, Richard (attributed to) 1712/1713–1782, *View on the Arno, Italy*, gift from J. G. Graves, 1935
Wilson, W. *Edward Law (1790–1871), 1st Earl of Ellenborough, GCB, PC*, presented by Mr Bernard Hoole, 1937
Wilson, Winifred 1882–1973, *Pit Ponies*, gift from J. G. Graves, 1942
Wilson, Winifred 1882–1973, *Ponies*, gift from J. G. Graves, 1942
Wilson, Winifred 1882–1973, *Up the Lane, Beauchief, Sheffield*, gift from J. G. Graves, 1937
Wilson of Sheffield *Portrait of a Man*, gift from E. Speed
Wimmer, L. *Lake Scene*, gift from J. G. Graves, 1942
Wimperis, Edmund Morison 1835–1900, *Moorland with Peat Gatherers*, gift from J. G. Graves, 1937
Wimperis, Edmund Morison 1835–1900, *Haymaking*, presented by Mrs Tozer, 1967
Winterbottom, Austin 1860–1919, *Drifted Snow*, presented by the artist's pupils, 1920
Winterbottom, Austin 1860–1919, *The Village Street, Crookes, Sheffield*, purchased, 1903
Witherington, William Frederick 1785–1865, *The Fortune Teller*, gift from J. G. Graves, 1935
Wohlgarten, Joseph van *Peter Paul Rubens (1577–1640), and Isabella Brant (1591–1626), in the Honeysuckle Bower* (after Peter Paul Rubens), presented by F. T. Mappin
Wollen, William Barnes 1857–1936, *Britain's Watch-Dogs*
Wolmark, Alfred Aaron 1877–1961, *Still Life with Tulips, a Jug and a Candlestick*, purchased from David Hepher, 1974, © permission of Mrs Diana S. Hall
Wood, Christopher 1901–1930, *Buildings at Passy, Paris*, purchased from the Redfern Gallery, 1977
Wood, Christopher 1901–1930, *The Jumping Boy, Arundel, West Sussex* (recto), purchased at Christie's, 1970
Wood, Christopher 1901–1930, *Female Nude** (verso), purchased at Christie's, 1970
Wood, Christopher 1901–1930, *La Plage, Hotel Ty-Mad, Tréboul, France*, purchased from the Redfern Gallery, 1978
Woods, Grace Mary b.1909, *Tomatoes and Bananas*, gift from J. G. Graves, 1937
Woolhouse, George 1751–1835, *Old House, Norfolk Street, Sheffield*
Woolmer, Alfred Joseph 1805–1892, *Sweet Seventeen*, gift from J. G. Graves, 1937
Woolner, Thomas (attributed to) 1825–1892, *The Farewell*, gift from J. G. Graves, 1929
Wopfner, Josef 1843–1927, *The Ferry*, gift from J. G. Graves, 1943
Wouwerman, Philips 1619–1668, *A Stag Hunt*, accepted by HM Government in lieu of inheritance tax and allocated to Museums Sheffield, 1980
Wright, Joseph of Derby 1734–1797, *Landscape with Dale Abbey, Derbyshire*, gift from J. G. Graves, 1935
Wyld, William 1806–1889, *Venice, Morning*, bequeathed by Sir Wilson Mappin, 1925
Wyld, William 1806–1889, *Venice, Evening*, bequeathed by Sir Wilson Mappin, 1925
Wyllie, William Lionel 1851–1931, *Rochester Castle, Kent*, gift from J. G. Graves, 1937
Wyllie, William Lionel 1851–1931, *A Coast View*, gift from J. G. Graves, 1943
Yarnold, Joseph c.1817–1852, *Seascape*, gift from J. G. Graves, 1943
Yeames, William Frederick 1835–1918, *Lady Jane Grey in the Tower*, bequeathed by J. N. Mappin, 1887
Ziem, Félix François Georges Philibert 1821–1911, *Venetian Barges*, gift from J. G. Graves, 1937
Zimmermann, Ernst Karl Georg 1852–1901, *The Fisherman's Cottage*, bequeathed by J. N. Mappin, 1887
Zoffany, Johann 1733–1810, *Peter Garrick*, gift from J. G. Graves, 1937
Zuccarelli, Franco (attributed to) 1702–1788, *Italian Peasants*, gift from J. G. Graves, 1929

Sheffield Central Library

Brighton, Bob b.1936, *579*, gift from the artist, 2009, © the artist
Brighton, Bob b.1936, *580*, gift from the artist, 2009, © the artist
Brighton, Bob b.1936, *581*, gift from the artist, 2009, © the artist
Brighton, Bob b.1936, *582*, gift from the artist, 2009, © the artist
Brighton, Bob b.1936, *Orange Blocks*, gift from the artist, 2009, © the artist
Brighton, Bob b.1936, *Orange Multi-Coloured Squares*, gift from the artist, 2009, © the artist
Brighton, Bob b.1936, *Small Squares 1*, gift from the artist, 2009, © the artist
Brighton, Bob b.1936, *Small Squares 2*, gift from the artist, 2009, © the artist
Brighton, Bob b.1936, *Small Squares 3*, gift from the artist, 2009, © the artist
Brighton, Bob b.1936, *Small Squares 4*, gift from the artist, 2009, © the artist
Brighton, Bob b.1936, *Small Squares 5*, gift from the artist, 2009, © the artist
Brighton, Bob b.1936, *Turquoise Squares*, gift from the artist, 2009, © the artist
Brighton, Bob b.1936, *Purple Squares on Brown*, gift from the artist, 2009, © the artist
Brighton, Bob b.1936, *Squares on Black*, gift from the artist, 2009, © the artist
Brighton, Bob b.1936, *Squares on Brown*, gift from the artist, 2009, © the artist
Brighton, Bob b.1936, *Squares on Copper*, gift from the artist, 2009, © Sheffield Central Library
Brighton, Bob b.1936, *Squares on Gold*, gift from the artist, 2009, © the artist
Brighton, Bob b.1936, *Squares on Terracotta*, gift from the artist, 2009, © the artist
Brighton, Bob b.1936, *Yellow Blue 1*, gift from the artist, 2009, © the artist
Brighton, Bob b.1936, *Yellow Blue 2*, gift from the artist, 2009, © the artist
Brighton, Bob b.1936, *Yellow Blue 3*, gift from the artist, 2009, © the artist

Sheffield Hallam University

Brown, Colin b.1957, *Cloud of Faith*, commissioned to commemorate the opening of the Multifaith Centre by the Chancellor, Lord Robert Winston, 2007, © the artist
E. H. C. *The Sea and the Rocks*
Dickens, Michelle Louise b.1970, *Blue*, © the artist
Etty, William 1787–1849, *Life Study*, purchased by the Sheffield School of Art, 1865
Greene, Mary b.1953, *Depths*, acquired from a former student, © the artist
Morgan, E. *Reverend Valentine Ward Pearson, First Principal of Sheffield Training College for Teachers (1905–1921)*
Priseman, Robert b.1965, *Councillor William Owen (d.1922), JP, Chair of the Board of Governors (1975-1989), Deputy Chair of the Board of Governors (1989–1991)*, commissioned, 1992, © the artist
Priseman, Robert b.1965, *Canon George Tolley, Principal of Sheffield City Polytechnic (1969–1982)*, commissioned, 1993, © the artist
Priseman, Robert b.1965, *Peter Newman, Chairman of Sheffield City Polytechnic Board of Governors (1988–1992)*, commissioned, 1993, © the artist
Priseman, Robert b.1965, *Sir Eric Mensforth (1906–2000), CBE, First Chairman of the Governing Body of Sheffield City Polytechnic (1969–1975)*, commissioned, 1993, © the artist
Priseman, Robert b.1965, *John Stoddart, Principal, Sheffield Hallam University (c.1983–1998)*, commissioned, 1994, © the artist
Priseman, Robert b.1965, *Norman Adsetts (b.1931), OBE, Chairman of Sheffield Hallam University Board of Governors (1993–1999)*, commissioned, 1994, © the artist
Priseman, Robert b.1965, *Sir Bryan Nicholson, Chancellor of Sheffield Hallam University (c.1994–2001)*, commissioned, 1995, © the artist
Scarborough, Joe b.1938, *'A Review of Paintings by Joe Scarborough', Mappin Art Gallery,*

Sheffield, Advertisement, gift from the artist, © the artist
Scarborough, Joe b.1938, *'Coal', A Celebration*, produced for an Art for the Community Project; gift from the artist, 1993, © the artist
Scarborough, Joe b.1938, *Steel and Steelworkers*, produced for an Art for the Community Project; gift from the artist, 1993, © the artist
Scarborough, Joe b.1938, *The Streets of Sheffield*, gift from the artist, © the artist
Scarborough, Joe b.1938, *People Dancing to Bands, Sheffield*, gift from the artist, © the artist
Scarborough, Joe b.1938, *Grand Theatre, Doncaster, Advertisement*, gift from the artist, © the artist
Scarborough, Joe b.1938, *Palace Theatre, Attercliffe, Advertisement*, gift from the artist, © the artist
Scarborough, Joe b.1938, *The Regent, Rotherham, Advertisement*, gift from the artist, © the artist
Scarborough, Joe b.1938, *Theatre Royal, Barnsley, Advertisement*, gift from the artist, © the artist
Sounes, William Henry 1830–1873, *Self Portrait*
Tucker, R. A. *Ralf R. Kimbell*
Turner, E. M. T. *Dr Herbert Wing*
Turner, E. M. T. *Samuel Hoole*
unknown artist *Street Scene, Old Quarter, Tbilisi, Georgia*, gift from the Georgian members of the Linguistic Politeness Research Group, 2001
unknown artist *Abstract** (triptych, left wing)
unknown artist *Abstract** (triptych, centre panel)
unknown artist *Abstract** (triptych, right wing)
unknown artist *Abstract in Blue and Orange**
unknown artist *Abstract Landscape in Pale Pink and Green*
unknown artist *Courtyard in Light and Shadow with Geometric Shapes*
unknown artist *Old Man*
unknown artist *Orange and Green Circles*
unknown artist *Window and Fabric*
unknown artist *Youth and Age*, acquired from a former student
Wood, Tom b.1955, *Richard Gregory, Chairman of the Board of Governors of Sheffield Hallam University* (triptych, left wing), commissioned, © the artist
Wood, Tom b.1955, *Lord Robert Winston (b.1940), Chancellor of Sheffield Hallam University from 2001* (triptych, centre panel), commissioned, © the artist
Wood, Tom b.1955, *Professor Diana Green, CBE, Vice-Chancellor of Sheffield Hallam University (1998–2007)* (triptych, right wing), commissioned, © the artist

Sheffield Industrial Museums Trust

Booth, Mel G. active 1975–1990s, *Detail of a Steel Ladle* (from the ladle in Kelham Island Museum), commissioned, 1984
Brown, W. *Street Scene, East End, Sheffield*, bequeathed
Corfield, Colin 1910–1991, *Albert Vickers (1838–1919), Chairman of Vickers Ltd (1908–1918)*, gift, 2006
Eves, Reginald Grenville 1876–1941, *P. B. Brown*
Froggatt, Muriel Alice 1909–1992, *Memories of Unstone Mills, Ben the Smithy*, gift
Froggatt, Muriel Alice 1909–1992, *Sickle and Hook Maker, Unstone Mills*, gift
Hildick, Mabel Sarah 1884–1979, *Crucible*, purchased with the assistance of the Preservation of Industrial and Scientific Materials Grant Fund, 1991
Laver, John Holmes 1880–1950, *Jobbing Grinder, Rockingham Lane, Sheffield*, purchased from Mrs Laver (daughter-in-law of the artist)
Lawrence, M. *Rolling Mill, Avesta, Sheffield*, gift from D. Kennedy, 1990
Martin, F. *Coastal View with a Castle*
Penistone, Robert b.1946, *Industrial Buildings with Chimneys and Smoke, Surrounded by Houses and Fields*, © the artist
Penistone, Robert b.1946, *Crane Driver, 1930*, © the artist
Penistone, Robert b.1946, *Forging Steel under a Steam Hammer, 1930*, © the artist
Penistone, Robert b.1946, *Tilt Hammer, 1930*, © the artist
Tingle, Roy *Tinsley Park, Sheffield, Electric Arc Furnace Receiving a Charge of Scrap*
Titcomb, William Holt Yates 1858–1930, *The Steam Hammer*, on loan from the British Steel Corporation
Titcomb, William Holt Yates 1858–1930, *The Wealth of England, the Bessemer Process of Making Steel*, on loan from the British Steel Corporation
unknown artist early 19th C, *Mr James Sanderson*, on loan from Sanderson Kayser
unknown artist early 19th C, *Mr Thomas Sanderson*, on loan from Sanderson Kayser
unknown artist *Robert Jardine of the Sheffield Smelting Company*
unknown artist *Arthur J. Ward, JP*
unknown artist *Ryecroft Mill, Dore, Sheffield*
unknown artist *Ryecroft Mill Waterwheel, Dore, Sheffield*

Sheffield Libraries Archives and Information: Sheffield Archives

Mitchell, Jean 1861–1941, *Dr Arthur Jackson*, gift from Dr Henry Jackson
unknown artist *Captain John Peirson*, on loan from the Imperial Tobacco Group Plc

Sheffield Magistrates' Court

Bradbury, Mary 1909–2006, *Landscape with a River**, donated, © the artist's estate
Lawton, Nigel Philip *Lady's Bridge, Sheffield*, donated
unknown artist *Reverend James Wilkinson (1730–1805), MA*, donated

Sheffield Teaching Hospitals NHS Foundation Trust

Assus, Maurice 1880–1955, *William Edgar Allen (1837–1915), Founder of the Edgar Allen Institute*, transferred from the Edgar Allen Physical Treatment Centre
Bentley, Joseph Herbert 1866–1934, *Sinclair White, MD, FRCS, Surgeon to the Royal Infirmary (1898–1920)*, transferred from the Royal Infirmary
Birch, John (attributed to) 1807–1857, *Sir Arnold Knight (1789–1871), Founder of the Sheffield Medical Institution (1829)*, presented by the Sheffield Mechanics Institution
Cammell, Bernard Edward 1850–1932, *Mariano Martin de Bartolomé (c.1810–1890), Physician at Sheffield Infirmary (1846–1889), First President of the Sheffield Medico-Chirurgical Society (1869)*
Crighton, Hugh Ford 1824–1886, *Thomas Jessop (1804–1887), Founder of the Hospital (1846), Builder of the Jessop Hospital for Women, Leavygreave Road (1878)*
Eurich, Richard Ernst 1903–1992, *Chatsworth, North Yorkshire, to Represent Sheffield at Play* (one of a pair of murals to face west), commissioned by the Board of Governors of the United Sheffield Hospitals with the asssitance of the Edwin Austin Abbey Memorial Trust, © the artist's estate/ Bridgeman Art Library
Eurich, Richard Ernst 1903–1992, *Whitby, North Yorkshire, to Represent Sheffield on Holiday* (one of a pair of murals to face east), commissioned by the Board of Governors of the United Sheffield Hospitals with the assistance of the Edwin Austin Abbey Memorial Trust, © the artist's estate/ Bridgeman Art Library
Fower, Robert 1866–1947, *Sir William Henry Ellis (1860–1945), GBE, JP, Member of the Board of Management (1898–1945), Vice-Chairman of the Board (1935–1945)* (after Arthur Hacker), transferred from the Royal Infirmary
Gainsford, F. G. active 1805–1828, *John Browne (c.1740–1810), MD, 'of the Lead Works', First Chairman of the Board*
Gainsford, F. G. active 1805–1828, *Robert Ernest (1771–1841), MD, House Surgeon to Sheffield Infirmary (1797–1841)*, presented to the Infirmary by Joseph Hadfield, 1844, transferred from the Royal Infirmary
Garnett, Ruth 1836–1915, *John Marshall, JP*, transferred from the Royal Infirmary
Hoyland, Henry George 1895–1948, *A. M. Connell (1872–1945), FRCS, ED, CH, M SHEFF, Honorary Surgeon, Sheffield Infirmary (1901–1931), Professor of Surgery (1913–1930)*, transferred from the Board Room at the Royal Infirmary, © the artist's estate
Jagger, David 1891–1958, *Henry Hall Bedford, JP, Chairman of the Board (1913–1924)*, presented by members of the Weekly Board and Honorary Medical Staff in recognition of the sitter's valuable services, 1925; transferred from the Royal Infirmary, © the artist's estate
Mitchell, Jean 1861–1941, *Joseph Law (d.1897), MD, Honorary Secretary to Sheffield Medical Society (1842–1852)*, presented to be hung in the library of the Medical School, transferred from the Medical Library, University of Sheffield, 1892
Moore, Ernest 1865–1940, *Sir Arthur John Hall (1866–1951), KT, MD, DSc, FRCP, Professor of Physiology, Pathology and Medicine and Physician at the Royal Hospital*, presented by Sir Arthur Hall, 1937
Moore, John 1801–1865, *George Calvert Holland (1801–1865), MD, Physician, Sheffield General Infirmary (1832–1843), Physician, Sheffield Public Dispensary (1838)*, transferred from the Royal Infirmary
Platt, Joyce b.1920, *Ronald Wilfred Matthews, KT, K St J, JP, Chairman of the Royal Infirmary, Sheffield (1924–1948), Member of the Board (1908–1948)*, transferred from the Royal Infirmary, © the artist
Shannon, James Jebusa 1862–1923, *William Fisher Favell (1832–1896), Surgeon of Sheffield Infirmary (c.1857–1893)*, paid for by public subscription, 1893, transferred from the Royal Infirmary
Tollast, Robert 1918–1996, *John G. McCrie (1902–1977), OBE, TD, MD, FRCP (Ed), Dean of the Faculty of Medicine, Sheffield (1947–1968)*, transferred from the Royal Infirmary
unknown artist *Sheffield Public Hospital and Dispensary of 1860* (showing physician Dr J. C. Hall and surgeon Mr Arthur Jackson), transferred from the Royal Hospital
unknown artist *Colonel Charles Clifford (1860–1936), CMG, VD* (donor of the land for the Sheffield Dental Hospital)*, presented to Colonel Charles Clifford, 1924; bequeathed to the Dental Hospital, c.1936
unknown artist *Corden Thompson (1793–1876), MD Edinburgh, Physician to Sheffield Infirmary (1831–1866)*
unknown artist *George Hounsfield, Esq., of the 'Clough', Sheffield* (formerly a member of the Weekly Board and Treasurer of Sheffield Infirmary, 1860), presented by Mrs Arthur Jackson in accordance with the wishes of Mrs Overend, transferred from the Royal Infirmary
unknown artist *Maria Overend of West Retford House (d.1896), Nottinghamshire, Donor of the Overend Convalescent Fund* (Mrs William Overend, previously Hounsfield), transferred from the Royal Infirmary
unknown artist *Sheffield General Infirmary*, presented to the Royal Infirmary by Professor A. M. Connell, FRCS, 1938
Waller, Mary Lemon 1852–c.1931, *Mariano Martin de Bartolomé (c.1810–1890), Physician at Sheffield Infirmary (1846–1889), First President of the Sheffield Medico-Chirurgical Society (1869)*, transferred from the Royal Infirmary
Waller, Mary Lemon 1852–c.1931, *Arthur Jackson (c.1844–1895), Honorary Surgeon, Sheffield Public Hospital and Dispensary (1866–1877), Sheffield General Infirmary (1877–1895)*, funded by public subscription; transferred from the Royal Infirmary
Williams, Margaret Lindsay 1887–1960, *Frederick Marmaduke Osborn, Esq. (1874–1950), Chairman of the Sheffield Royal Hospital (1905–1948), Member of the Board (1912–1948)*, transferred from the Royal Hospital
Zoffany, Johann (after) 1733–1810, *George III (1738–1820)*, gift from Mr Samuel Marshall, 1790s (?)

Sheffield Town Hall

Barker, Thomas Jones 1815–1882, *Mark Firth (1819–1880), Mayor of Sheffield (1874)*
Crighton, Hugh Ford 1824–1886, *Thomas Moore (1809–1880), Mayor of Sheffield (1868–1871)*, donated by Mrs Patricia Smith, great-great-granddaughter of the sitter, 2003
Crighton, Hugh Ford 1824–1886, *Thomas Jessop (1804–1887), JP, Mayor of Sheffield (1865–1868)*
Crighton, Hugh Ford 1824–1886, *William Jeffcock (1800–1877), First Mayor of*

Sheffield (1843–1844), donated by William Parkyn Jeffcock, 2008
Fildes, Luke 1843–1927, *The Right Honourable Charles B. Stuart-Wortley (1851–1926), MP for Sheffield (1880–1913)*
Scarborough, Joe b.1938, *VI World Masters Swimming Championships, Sheffield*, gift from the VI World Masters Swimming Championships, 1996, © the artist
Smith, Richard 1818–1890, *Sir John Brown (1816–1896), KT, DL, Mayor of Sheffield (1861–1862)*
Smith, Richard 1818–1890, *Lady Brown (1813–1881), Wife of Sir John Brown*

South Yorkshire Fire and Rescue Training Centre

Jones, Donna active 2002–2003, *Ground Zero, 9/11 No.1**, gift from the artist, c.2003
Jones, Donna active 2002–2003, *Ground Zero, 9/11 No.2**, gift from the artist, c.2003
Jones, Donna active 2002–2003, *Ground Zero, 9/11 No.3**, gift from the artist, c.2003
Jones, Donna active 2002–2003, *Ground Zero, 9/11 No.4**, gift from the artist, c.2003

Stocksbridge Town Council

Penistone, Robert b.1946, *Siemens Open Hearth, Sheffield, No.1 Melting Shop (1917–1968)*, commissioned, 2008, © the artist
Penistone, Robert b.1946, *Stocksbridge Coke Ovens, 1940s, Manchester Road, Sheffield*, commissioned, 2008, © the artist
Penistone, Robert b.1946, *View of Stocksbridge, Sheffield, from the Clock Tower Gardens, Late 1940s*, commissioned, 2008, © the artist

The Children's Hospital, Sheffield

Baggaley, Kristan Paul b.1958, *Sheffield from Dore Moor*, gift from the artist, 2009, © the artist
Baggaley, Kristan Paul b.1958, *Peak District View*, purchased from the artist, 2009, © the artist
Baggaley, Kristan Paul b.1958, *Peak District View*, purchased from the artist, 2009, © the artist
Baggaley, Kristan Paul b.1958, *Peak District View*, purchased from the artist, 2009, © the artist
Baggaley, Kristan Paul b.1958, *Peak District View*, purchased from the artist, 2009, © the artist
Baggaley, Kristan Paul b.1958, *Peak District View*, purchased from the artist, 2009, © the artist
Field, Sandra b.1966, *Robot Fish 1* (polyptych), commissioned, c.2001, © the artist
Field, Sandra b.1966, *Robot Fish 2* (polyptych) (detail), commissioned, c.2001, © the artist
Firth, Richard *Blue Abstract*, purchased, 2004, © the artist
Firth, Richard *Boats and Flowers*, purchased, 2004, © the artist
Firth, Richard *Boats through a Window*, purchased, 2004, © the artist
Firth, Richard *Daffodil*, purchased, 2004, © the artist
Firth, Richard *Yellow Abstract*, purchased, 2004, © the artist
Heath, Andrew b. 1962 & **Patients of The Children's Hospital, Sheffield** *Circles and Swirls* (polyptych) (detail), commissioned, 2005, © the artist
Kinoshita, Seiko b.1971, *Large Blue Woven Slats*, commissioned, 2009, © the artist
Kinoshita, Seiko b.1971, *Large Purple Woven Slats*, commissioned, 2009, © the artist
Kinoshita, Seiko b.1971, *Small Blue Woven Slats*, commissioned, 2009, © the artist
Kinoshita, Seiko b.1971, *Small Purple Woven Slats*, commissioned, 2009, © the artist
Kinoshita, Seiko b.1971 & **Patients of The Children's Hospital, Sheffield** *Blue Weaving*, commissioned, 2007, © the artist
Kinoshita, Seiko b.1971 & **Patients of The Children's Hospital, Sheffield** *Blue Pink Woven Slats*, commissioned, 2008, © the artist
Kinoshita, Seiko b.1971 & **Patients of The Children's Hospital, Sheffield** *Brown Cream Woven Slats*, commissioned, 2008, © the artist
Kinoshita, Seiko b.1971 & **Patients of The Children's Hospital, Sheffield** *Brown Terracotta Woven Slats*, commissioned, 2008, © the artist
Kinoshita, Seiko b.1971 & **Patients of The Children's Hospital, Sheffield** *Pink Blue Woven Slats*, commissioned, 2008, © the artist
Klooze *Senegalese Figures*, purchased
Lale, Hazel *Dancing*, donated, 2001
Parmakio, Rose active 1970s, *All Fall Out No.1*
Parmakio, Rose active 1970s, *All Fall Out No.2*
Parmakio, Rose active 1970s, *All Fall Out No.3*
Parmakio, Rose active 1970s, *All Fall Out No.4*
Parmakio, Rose active 1970s, *Adventure Playground*
Parmakio, Rose active 1970s, *Adventure Playground*
Parmakio, Rose active 1970s, *Adventure Playground*
Rose, Martin H. b.1946, *Professor Ronald Illingworth (1909–1990)*, donated © the artist
Scarborough, Joe b.1938, *Open Day at Sheffield Children's Hospital*, donated by the artist, 1994, © the artist
Taylor, Alan b.1958, *Peak District Landscape 1*, purchased, c.1997, © the artist
Taylor, Alan b.1958, *Peak District Landscape 2*, purchased, c.1997, © the artist
Taylor, Alan b.1958, *Peak District Landscape 3*, purchased, c.1997, © the artist
Taylor, Alan b.1958, *Super Tram*, purchased, c.1997, © the artist
Taylor, Alan b.1958, *Toy Cupboard*, purchased, c.1997, © the artist
Taylor, Micheline & **Waite, Philippa** *Cat at a Window*, purchased, c.2003
Taylor, Micheline & **Waite, Philippa** *Lighthouse and Ships* (triptych), purchased, c.2003
Tom *Dark Blue Abstract*, purchased, 2008
Tom *Dark Blue Abstract*, purchased, 2008
unknown artist *Elephants 1*, purchased, c.2000
unknown artist *Elephants 2*, purchased, c.2000
unknown artist *Flamingo 1*, purchased, c.2000
unknown artist *Flamingo 2*, purchased, c.2000
unknown artist *Giraffe*, purchased, c.2000
unknown artist *Hippopotamus*, purchased, c.2000
unknown artist *Monkeys*, purchased, c.2000
unknown artist *Tortoise 1*, purchased, c.2000
unknown artist *Tortoise 2*, purchased, c.2000
unknown artist *Beatrix Potter, Toad*, purchased
unknown artist *Beatrix Potter, Rabbit*, purchased
Wyatt, Houghton b.1953/1954, *Theo's Amazing Journey, Theo Sets Off*, purchased, c.2001, © Houghton Wyatt
Wyatt, Houghton b.1953/1954, *Theo's Amazing Journey, Spain*, purchased, c.2001, © Houghton Wyatt
Wyatt, Houghton b.1953/1954, *Theo's Amazing Journey, Italy*, purchased, c.2001, © Houghton Wyatt
Wyatt, Houghton b.1953/1954, *Theo's Amazing Journey, Germany*, purchased, c.2001, © Houghton Wyatt
Wyatt, Houghton b.1953/1954, *Theo's Amazing Journey, France*, purchased, c.2001, © Houghton Wyatt
Wyatt, Houghton b.1953/1954, *Theo's Amazing Journey, the World* (polyptych), purchased, c.2001, © Houghton Wyatt
Wyatt, Houghton b.1953/1954, *Theo's Amazing Journey, Cowboy*, purchased, c.2001, © Houghton Wyatt
Wyatt, Houghton b.1953/1954, *Theo's Amazing Journey, Postcard from Monument Valley, USA*, purchased, c.2001, © Houghton Wyatt
Wyatt, Houghton b.1953/1954, *Theo's Amazing Journey, Hollywood*, purchased, © Houghton Wyatt
Wyatt, Houghton b.1953/1954, *Theo's Amazing Journey, New York*, purchased, c.2001, © Houghton Wyatt
Wyatt, Houghton b.1953/1954, *Theo's Amazing Journey, Hawaii*, purchased, © Houghton Wyatt
Wyatt, Houghton b.1953/1954, *Theo's Amazing Journey, Canada*, purchased, © Houghton Wyatt
Wyatt, Houghton b.1953/1954, *Theo's Amazing Journey, Trinidad*, purchased, © Houghton Wyatt
Wyatt, Houghton b.1953/1954, *Theo's Amazing Journey, Postcard from Athens*, purchased, © Houghton Wyatt
Wyatt, Houghton b.1953/1954, *Theo's Amazing Journey, Mexico*, purchased, © Houghton Wyatt
Wyatt, Houghton b.1953/1954, *Theo's Amazing Journey, Cape Horn*, purchased, © Houghton Wyatt
Wyatt, Houghton b.1953/1954, *Theo's Amazing Journey, Ecuador*, purchased, © Houghton Wyatt
Wyatt, Houghton b.1953/1954, *Theo's Amazing Journey, Argentina*, purchased, © Houghton Wyatt
Wyatt, Houghton b.1953/1954, *Theo's Amazing Journey, Brazil*, purchased, © Houghton Wyatt
Wyatt, Houghton b.1953/1954, *Theo's Amazing Journey, China*, purchased, © Houghton Wyatt
Wyatt, Houghton b.1953/1954, *Theo's Amazing Journey, Hong Kong*, purchased, © Houghton Wyatt
Wyatt, Houghton b.1953/1954, *Theo's Amazing Journey, Mongolia*, purchased, © Houghton Wyatt
Wyatt, Houghton b.1953/1954, *Theo's Amazing Journey, Yellow Sea Ferry*, purchased, © Houghton Wyatt
Wyatt, Houghton b.1953/1954, *Theo's Amazing Journey, Taiwan*, purchased, © Houghton Wyatt
Wyatt, Houghton b.1953/1954, *Theo's Amazing Journey, Japan*, purchased, © Houghton Wyatt
Wyatt, Houghton b.1953/1954, *Theo's Amazing Journey, Pakistan*, purchased, © Houghton Wyatt
Wyatt, Houghton b.1953/1954, *Theo's Amazing Journey, Postcard from the Taj Mahal, India*, purchased, c.2001, © Houghton Wyatt
Wyatt, Houghton b.1953/1954, *Theo's Amazing Journey, India*, purchased, c.2001, © Houghton Wyatt
Wyatt, Houghton b.1953/1954, *Theo's Amazing Journey, Turkey*, purchased, © Houghton Wyatt
Wyatt, Houghton b.1953/1954, *Theo's Amazing Journey, Theo in Damascus*, purchased, c.2001, © Houghton Wyatt
Wyatt, Houghton b.1953/1954, *Theo's Amazing Journey, Jordan*, purchased, c.2001, © Houghton Wyatt
Wyatt, Houghton b.1953/1954, *Theo's Amazing Journey, Morocco*, purchased, c.2001, © Houghton Wyatt
Wyatt, Houghton b.1953/1954, *Theo's Amazing Journey, Egypt*, purchased, c.2001, © Houghton Wyatt
Wyatt, Houghton b.1953/1954, *Theo's Amazing Journey, Madagascar*, purchased, c.2001, © Houghton Wyatt
Wyatt, Houghton b.1953/1954, *Theo's Amazing Journey, Postcard from Namibia*, purchased, c.2001, © Houghton Wyatt
Wyatt, Houghton b.1953/1954, *Theo's Amazing Journey, Nigeria*, purchased, c.2001, © Houghton Wyatt
Wyatt, Houghton b.1953/1954, *Theo's Amazing Journey, Russia*, purchased, © Houghton Wyatt
Wyatt, Houghton b.1953/1954, *Theo's Amazing Journey, Arctic*, purchased, c.2001, © Houghton Wyatt
Wyatt, Houghton b.1953/1954, *Theo's Amazing Journey, Scandinavia*, purchased, c.2001, © Houghton Wyatt
Wyatt, Houghton b.1953/1954, *Theo's Amazing Journey, London*, purchased, c.2001, © Houghton Wyatt
Wyatt, Houghton b.1953/1954, *Theo's Amazing Journey, Theo Comes Home*, purchased, c.2001, © Houghton Wyatt

The Ken Hawley Collection Trust

Kennedy, J. *Mr Turton*

Traditional Heritage Museum, University of Sheffield

Brandon, Louis E. *Ernest Horton Senior (1895–1971), Proprietor of Horton Brothers and Austin and Dodson Ltd, Filemakers, Sheffield*, donated by Mrs Margaret Laycock (daughter of the sitter), 2008
Keeling, William 1860–1930, *A Memory Sketch: The Morning after the Zeppelin Raid on Attercliffe, Sheffield, 25 September 1916*, donated by Mrs E. Beet-Wagner, 2004
Little, Douglas Patrick active 1981–2007, *High Street, Sheffield, 1904*, donated by the artist, 2007

University of Sheffield

Attree, Jake b.1950, *Robert Mart Mill 1*, donated by Sheffield University Fine Art Society, © the artist
Baggaley, Kristan Paul b.1958, *Deep Water*, donated by Sheffield

University Fine Art Society, © the artist
Barber, Reginald 1851–1928, *Walter Butterworth (1862–1935)*, acquired, 1980
Billin, Edward Stanley 1911–1994, *Whiteley Wood Clinic, Sheffield*, donated by Professor Erwin Stengel
Blake, Valerie *Professor W. F. Mainland*
Brighton, Bob b.1936, *13.9.94*, donated by the artist, 2007, © University of Sheffield
Brighton, Bob b.1936, *15.9.94*, donated by the artist, 2007, © University of Sheffield
Brighton, Bob b.1936, *21.9.94*, donated by the artist, 2007, © University of Sheffield
Brighton, Bob b.1936, *12.10.94*, donated by the artist, 2007, © University of Sheffield
Brighton, Bob b.1936, *Chequerboards* (polyptych), donated by the artist, 2007, © University of Sheffield
Brighton, Bob b.1936, *Large Squares One* (polyptych), donated by the artist, 2007, © University of Sheffield
Brighton, Bob b.1936, *Large Squares Two* (polyptych), donated by the artist, 2007, © University of Sheffield
Brighton, Bob b.1936, *Squares* (polyptych), donated by the artist, 2007, © University of Sheffield
Brighton, Bob b.1936, *Squares in Squares* (polyptych), donated by the artist, 2007, © University of Sheffield
Britton, David Swinstead b.1937, *Burnmoor Inn, Cumbria*, donated by Sheffield University Fine Art Society, © the artist
Carter, William 1863–1939, *Robert Offley Ashburton Crewe-Milnes (1858–1945), 2nd Lord Haughton, Marquess of Crewe*
Constantine, Harry Francis b.1919, *The Check Cloth*, donated by Sheffield University Fine Art Society, © the artist
Cope, Arthur Stockdale 1857–1940, *Sir Henry Stephenson (1826–1904)*, presented to Sir Henry Stephenson by his fellow citizens, 1899
Cope, Arthur Stockdale 1857–1940, *Professor William M. Hicks (1850–1934)*, donated by public subscription
Cope, Arthur Stockdale 1857–1940, *Sir Henry Stephenson (1826–1904)*
Cope, Arthur Stockdale 1857–1940, *Lady Emma Stephenson*
d'Aquavila, Walt *Nobel*, donated by the artist
Dobson, Henry Raeburn 1901–1985, *Sir Hugh Robson (1917–1977), Vice-Chancellor of the University of Sheffield (1966–1974)*, commissioned
Edwards, Peter Douglas b.1955, *Sir Peter Middleton (b.1934), Chancellor of the University of Sheffield (since 1999)*, commissioned, © the artist
Festing, Andrew b.1941, *Professor Robert Boucher (1940–2009), Vice-Chancellor of the University of Sheffield (2001–2007)*, purchased, 2007, © the artist
Fleetwood-Walker, Bernard 1893–1965, *Dr Edward Bramley (1868–1969)*, donated by the sitter, © the estate of Mrs P. Fleetwood-Walker
Gittins, John Steven b.1955, *Robin Hood's Stride, Harthill Moor, Derbyshire*, donated by Sheffield University Fine Art Society, © the artist
Halliday, Edward Irvine 1902–1984, *Professor William Ernest Stephen Turner (1881–1963)*, donated by Fellows of the Society of Glass Technology, 1938, © the artist's estate
Halliday, Edward Irvine 1902–1984, *Dr Stanley B. Bagley (1874–1957)*, donated by the sitter, © the artist's estate
Hamer, Douglas 1897–1981, *The Vice-Chancellor's Garden*
Hamer, Douglas 1897–1981, *Corn*, donated by Sheffield University Fine Art Society
Harcourt, George 1868–1947, *Sir Arthur Wallace Pickard-Cambridge (1873–1952), Vice-Chancellor of the University of Sheffield (1930–1938)*, commissioned at the time of the sitter's retirement
Heywood, Christopher b.1928, *Portrait*, donated by Sheffield University Fine Art Society, © the artist
Holland, Diana *Still Life with a Golden Delicious*, donated by Sheffield University Fine Art Society
Hulett *Ezra Hounsfield Linley*, donated
Hutchison, William Oliphant 1889–1970, *Sir Irvine Masson (1887–1962), Vice-Chancellor of the University of Sheffield (1938–1953)*, commissioned at the time of the sitter's retirement, © the artist's estate
Hyde, Graham b.c.1979, *Chicken Run*, donated by Sheffield University Fine Art Society
Jackson, Peter Kenneth Cowley 1930–2006, *James E. Eardley*, purchased, 1994, © the artist's estate
Jackson, Peter Kenneth Cowley 1930–2006, *Peter Lee*, purchased, 2006, © the artist's estate
Jackson, Peter Kenneth Cowley 1930–2006, *John Carr (1909–1992), MBE*, donated by Mrs Carr, 1995, © the artist's estate
Kemp, Fiona Margaret b.1949, *City View 1*, donated by Sheffield University Fine Art Society, © the artist
Kiddy, Gretchen 1910–2005, *Dedham Vale, Essex*, donated by Sheffield University Fine Art Society
Lewis, Bethan Rhiannon b.1975, *Doo-V*, purchased from the Royal Academy Schools, © the artist
Little, Pauline b.1961, *A New Beginning*, donated by Sheffield University Fine Art Society
Lowe, Anthony b.1957, *The German Choir*, donated by Sheffield University Fine Art Society
Lowe, Anthony b.1957, *Brittany, France*, donated by Sheffield University Fine Art Society
Machan, Robert b.1948, *The Church, Regent Street, Sheffield*, donated by Sheffield University Fine Art Society, 2008, © the artist
Mayne, Peter *Hartlepool, County Durham*, donated by Sheffield University Fine Art Society
McCall, Susan b.1946, *Gathering Storm*, purchased from a Sheffield University Fine Art Society exhibition, 2005, © the artist
McCall, Susan b.1946, *Red Grass*, purchased, 2004, © the artist
McGregor, Neil b.1963, *Study for 'Skating Rink'*, donated by Sheffield University Fine Art Society, © the artist
McPartland, Ian b.1963, *Untitled*, donated by Sheffield University Fine Art Society, © the artist
Mendoza, June b.1945, *Sir Gareth Roberts (1940–2007)*, commissioned, 1996, © the artist
Moore, Ernest 1865–1940, *Sir Frederick Thorpe Mappin (1821–1910)*, donated by public subscription
Moore, Ernest 1865–1940, *Sir Arthur Hall (1866–1951), KT, MD*, acquired, 1936
Neiland, Brendan b.1941, *Rerum cognoscere causas*, purchased, 2002, © the artist
Neiland, Brendan b.1941, *Crab*, purchased, 2008, © the artist
Neiland, Brendan b.1941, *Effervescence*, purchased, 2008, © the artist
Neiland, Brendan b.1941, *Shark*, acquired, 2008, © the artist
Ociepko, Mark b.1945, *Tranquillo*, donated by Sheffield University Fine Art Society, © the artist
Ouless, Walter William 1848–1933, *Sir George Franklin (d.1916)*, donated by Miss Franklin, the daughter of the sitter
Padfield, Gillian Margaret 1939–2009, *Poppy Field*, donated by Dr Adrian Padfield, the husband of the artist, 2009, © the artist's estate
Peacock, Brian 1935–2004, *Beach Hut*, donated by Sheffield University Fine Art Society, © the artist's estate
Pemberton, John active 1948, *Still Life*, donated by Sheffield University Fine Art Society
Reah, Ken *Parkscape with Railings*, donated by Sheffield University Fine Art Society
Röder, Endre Zoltan Eugene b.1933, *Carole and Yucca*, donated by Sheffield University Fine Art Society, © the artist
Röder, Endre Zoltan Eugene b.1933, *Three Bouquets*, donated by Carole and Endre Röder, © the artist
Rose, Martin H. b.1946, *The Right Honourable Richard Austin Butler (1902–1982), Baron Butler of Saffron Walden, Chancellor of the University of Sheffield (1959–1977)*, purchased, 1977 © the artist
Rothenstein, William 1872–1945, *The Violinist*, donated by Mrs Rachel Ward, 1961, © the artist's estate/Bridgeman Art Library
Russell, Walter Westley 1867–1949, *Alderman Robert Styring, Lord Mayor of Sheffield (1906)*, donated by Constance Styring, daughter of the sitter
Sanderson, Helen *Untitled*, donated by Sheffield University Fine Art Society
Scarborough, Joe b.1938, *Our University*, purchased by the Sheffield University Association, © the artist
Shackleton, Judith *Desert Sun*, donated by Sheffield University Fine Art Society
Shaw, David Carson b.1942, *Perduta*, donated by Sheffield University Fine Art Society, © the artist
Shawcross, Neil b.1940, *Nude*, donated, © the artist
Shawcross, Neil b.1940, *Fairground Horses*, donated, © the artist
Shawcross, Neil b.1940, *Howard Warrender (d.1985)*, donated, © the artist
Somerville, Howard 1873–1952, *Sir Henry Kenyon Stephenson (1865–1947), Treasurer of the University of Sheffield*
Stubley, Trevor 1932–2010, *Lord Dainton of Hallam Moors (1914–1997)*, purchased, 1984, © the artist's estate
Stubley, Trevor 1932–2010, *Professor Geoffrey Sims (b.1926), Vice-Chancellor of the University of Sheffield (1974–1991)*, commissioned, © the artist's estate
Stubley, Trevor 1932–2010, *Sir Roy Marshall*, donated by Sir John Wood, Professor of Law, © the artist's estate
Suberu, Ade b.1968, *Chillies 2*, donated by Sheffield University Fine Art Society
Suberu, Ade b.1968, *Chillies 3*, donated by Sheffield University Fine Art Society
Teale, Dick b.1930, *Scratin for Coal*, donated by Sheffield University Fine Art Society, © the artist
Tracy, John Martin 1843–1893, *Mrs Ezra Hounsfield Linley*
Underhill, Graham b.1946, *Arrangement before a Void*, purchased from a Sheffield University Fine Art Society exhibition, 2008, © the artist
Underhill, Graham b.1946, *Heroic Still Life with Hanging Nut* (polyptych), purchased from a Sheffield University Fine Art Society exhibition, 2008, © the artist
unknown artist *Sir John Brown (1816–1896), DL, Founder John Brown & Company (1838)*, donated by John Brown Plc (now part of Trafalgar House Plc), 1993
unknown artist *Sir Frederick Thorpe Mappin (1821–1910)*, donated by Mr Robert Fenwick, 2007
unknown artist *Sir Albert John Hobson (1861–1923), Lord Mayor of Sheffield (1911)*, presented to the sitter by the staff of Suffolk Works in commemoration of his master cutlership, 1902
unknown artist *Sir Joseph Jonas (1845–1921), Lord Mayor of Sheffield (1904–1905)*
unknown artist *Mark Firth (1819–1880)*
unknown artist *Mrs Firth*
unknown artist *Misty Sunrise*
Varkalis, Amrik b.1949, *Black Trees 1 and 2* (diptych), purchased from a Sheffield University Fine Art Society exhibition, 2008, © the artist
Varkalis, Amrik b.1949, *Pink Sky*, purchased jointly by the University of Sheffield and Sheffield University Fine Art Society, © the artist
Wall, Tom 1941–1992, *Stream*, donated by Sheffield University Fine Art Society
Waller, Mary Lemon 1852–c.1931, *Henry Clifton Sorby (1826–1908), LLD, FRS*, presented by some of the sitter's friends as a mark of personal regard, 1906
Waplington, Paul Anthony b.1938, *Dressing Billets*, purchased, © the artist
Waplington, Paul Anthony b.1938, *The Quadrangle*, commissioned, 1983, © the artist
Ward, Edward Matthew (attributed to) 1816–1879, *Dr Johnson and Sir Joshua Reynolds Taking Tea with Mrs Thrale*, donated by Dr Edward Bramley
Warrender, Vera *Still Life with a Blowlamp*, donated by Sheffield University Fine Art Society
Wheatley, Grace 1888–1970, *Dr John Macnaghten Whittaker (1905–1984), Vice-Chancellor of the University of Sheffield (1953–1965)*, commissioned
Widdop, John *Cycle XII*, purchased from an exhibition of the artist's work organised by the Sheffield University Fine Art Society, 1994
Widdop, John *Tantric Model VIII*, donated by Sheffield University Fine Art Society
Wilson, Graeme b.1951, *Annunciation*, donated by Sheffield University Fine Art Society © the artist

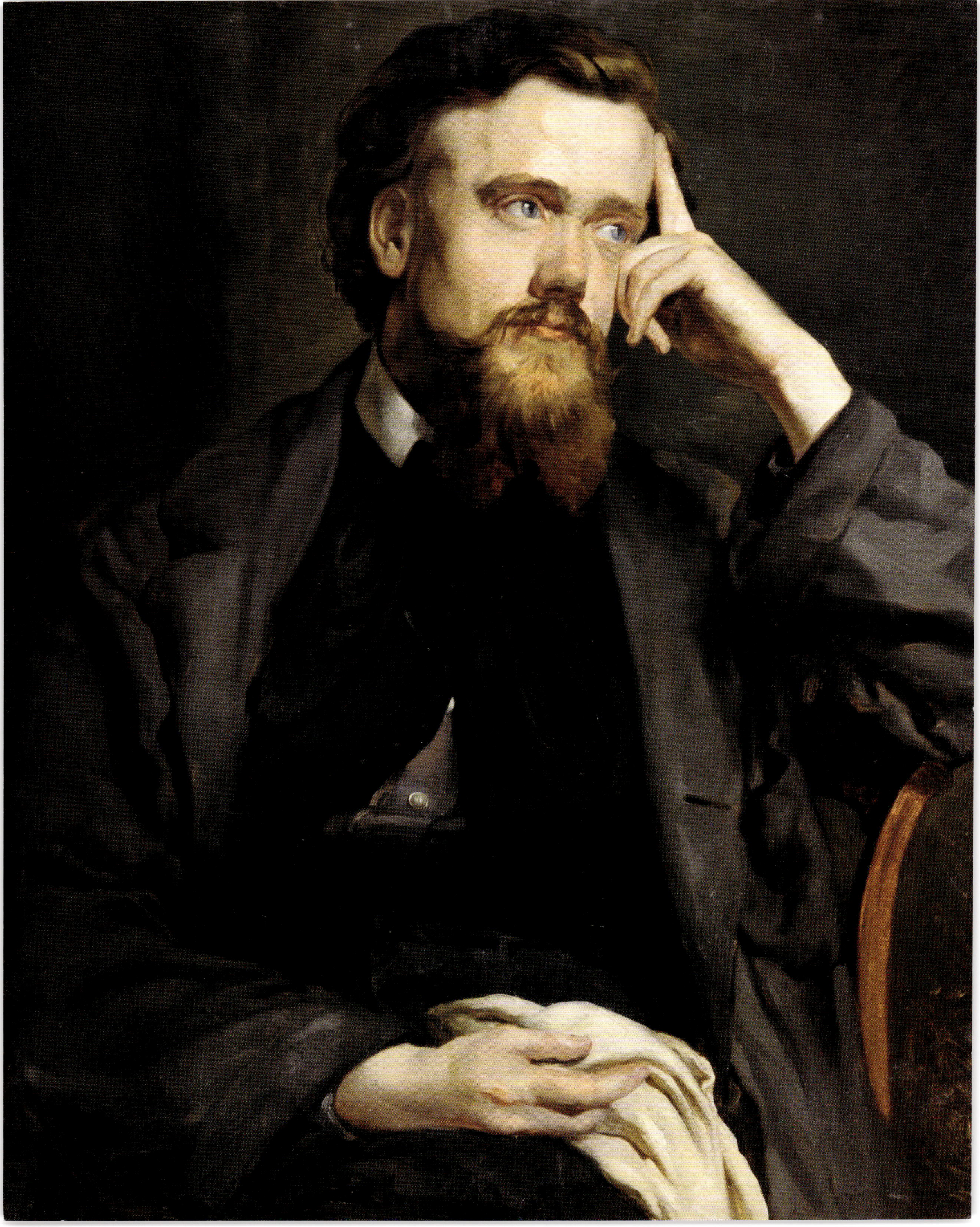

Collection Addresses

Bradfield Parish Council
Council Offices, Mill Lee Road, Low Bradfield
Sheffield S6 6LB
Telephone 01142 851375

Fire & Police Museum at Sheffield
Old Fire Station, West Bar, Sheffield S3 8PT
Telephone 01142 491999

Museums Sheffield:

Museums Sheffield
Leader House, Surrey Street, Sheffield S1 2LH
Telephone 01142 782600

Graves Gallery
Surrey Street, Sheffield S1 1XZ
Telephone 01142 782600

Millennium Gallery
Arundel Gate, Sheffield S1 2PP
Telephone 01142 782600

Weston Park
Western Bank, Sheffield S10 2TP
Telephone 01142 782600

Sheffield Central Library
Surrey Street, Sheffield S1 1XZ
Telephone 01142 734747

Sheffield Hallam University
Howard Street, Sheffield S1 1WB
Telephone 01142 255555

Sheffield Industrial Museums Trust:

Sheffield Industrial Museums Trust
Kelham Island Museum
Alma Street, Sheffield S3 8RY
Telephone 01142 722106

Abbeydale Industrial Hamlet
Abbeydale Road South, Sheffield S7 2QW
Telephone 01142 367731

Kelham Island Museum
Alma Street, Sheffield S3 8RY
Telephone 01142 7 2106

The Ken Hawley Collection Trust
c/o Kelham Island Museum
Alma Street, Sheffield S3 8RY
Telephone 01142 722106

Sheffield Libraries Archives and Information:
Sheffield Archives
52 Shoreham Street, Sheffield S1 4SP
Telephone 01142 039395

Sheffield Magistrates' Court
Castle Street, Sheffield S3 8LU
Telephone 01142 760760

Sheffield Teaching Hospitals NHS Foundation Trust
Royal Hallamshire Hospital, Glossop Road
Sheffield ST10 2JF
Telephone 01142 713071

Sheffield Town Hall
Town Hall, Sheffield S1 2HH
Telephone 01142 726444

South Yorkshire Fire and Rescue Training Centre
Training & Development Centre, Beaver Hill Road
Handsworth, Sheffield S13 9QA
Telephone 01142 692230

Stocksbridge Town Council
Town Hall, The ARC, Manchester Road, Stocksbridge
Sheffield S36 2DT
Telephone 01142 887895

The Children's Hospital
Western Bank, Sheffield S10 2TH
Telephone 01142 717000

The Ken Hawley Collection Trust
c/o Kelham Island Museum, Alma Street, Sheffield S3 8RY
Telephone 01142 722106

Traditional Heritage Museum, University of Sheffield
605 Ecclesall Road, Sheffield S11 8PR
Telephone 01142 681270

Facing page: Sounes, William Henry, 1830–1873, *Self Portrait* (detail), c.1865, Sheffield Hallam University, (p. 261)

University of Sheffield:

University of Sheffield
Heritage Office, University of Sheffield
2 Hounsfield Road, Sheffield S3 7FR
Telephone 01142 221369

University of Sheffield, Heritage Collection
Western Bank, Sheffield S10 2TN
Telephone 01142 222000

Turner Glass Museum
Department of Engineering Materials
University of Sheffield
Sir Robert Hadfield Building, Portobello Street
Sheffield S1 4DU
Telephone 01142 225500

Index of Artists

In this catalogue, artists' names and the spelling of their names follow the preferred presentation of the name in the Getty Union List of Artist Names (ULAN) as of February 2004, if the artist is listed in ULAN.

The page numbers next to each artist's name below direct readers to paintings that are by the artist; are attributed to the artist; or, in a few cases, are more loosely related to the artist being, for example, 'after', 'the circle of' or copies of a painting by the artist. The precise relationship between the artist and the painting is listed in the catalogue.

Abbott, Lemuel Francis (1760–1803) 6
Abrahams, Philippa (b.1947) 6
Adams, Beatrice (b.1877) 6
Adams, John Clayton (1840–1906) 6
Adams, Norman (1927–2005) 7
Adamson, Dorothy (1894–1934) 7
Adshead, Mary (1904–1995) 7
Aldam, Thomas 7
Alessandri, Angelo (1854–1931) 7
Allan, Robert Weir (1852–1942) 7
Allen, Harry Epworth (1894–1958) 7
Allinson, Adrian Paul (1890–1959) 8
Amigoni, Jacopo (c.1682–1752) 8
Anderson, William (1757–1837) 8
André, Edmond (1837–1877) 8
Anker, Albert (1831–1910) 8
Ansdell, Richard (1815–1885) 8
Armandi, Polermo (b.1842) 8
Armitage, Edward (1817–1896) 9
Armstrong, John (1893–1973) 9
Arrowsmith, Thomas (1772–1830) 9
Artistic Licence 309, 310
Assus, Maurice (1880–1955) 269
Atkinson, Conrad (b.1940) 9
Attree, Jake (b.1950) 292
Auerbach, Frank Helmuth (b.1931) 9, 253
Aumonier, James (1832–1911) 9, 11
Ayres, Gillian (b.1930) 11
Ayrton, Michael (1921–1975) 11
Backhuysen, Ludolf I (1630–1708) 11
Baggaley, Kristan Paul (b.1958) 277, 278, 292
Balestra, Antonio (1666–1740) 12
Banks, James 12
Banks, Thomas Joseph (1828–1896) 12
Barber, Reginald (1851–1928) 292
Barber, Thomas (1771–1843) 12
Bargue, Charles (1826–1883) 12
Barker, Allen (b.1937) 12
Barker, Benjamin II (1776–1838) 12
Barker, David Walker (b.1947) 13
Barker, Kit (1916–1988) 13
Barker, Thomas (1769–1847) 13
Barker, Thomas Jones (1815–1882) 13, 14, 274
Baker, Thomas (1809–1869) 12
Barnes, Edward Charles (1830–1890) 14
Barns-Graham, Wilhelmina (1912–2004) 14
Barret, George the elder (1728/1732–1784) 14
Barry, James (1741–1806) 14
Bartlett, Charles William (1860–1940) 309
Bassano, Leandro (1557–1622) 14
Bastien-Lepage, Émile (1854–1938) 14
Bayes, Walter (1869–1956) 14, 15
Baynes, John (active 1935–1943) 15
Baynes, Keith (1887–1977) 15
Bazler, Fred (b.1934) 15
Beaune, M. 15
Beavis, Richard (1824–1896) 15, 16
Beechey, William (1753–1839) 16
Beeldemaker, Adriaen Cornelisz. (1618–1709) 16, 262
Beelt, Cornelis (1640–1702) 16
Beeton, J. 17
Bell, Vanessa (1879–1961) 17
Bell, Walter (b.1904) 17
Bellany, John (b.1942) 17
Bellingham-Smith, Elinor (1906–1988) 17
Bellingham-Smith, Hugh (1866–1922) 17
Bembridge, John Conrad (c.1822–1857) 17
Bentley, Charles (1808–1854) 17
Bentley, Joseph Clayton (1809–1851) 18
Bentley, Joseph Herbert (1866–1934) 18, 269
Berg, Gunnar (1864–1894) 18
Bergen, Hans 18
Bevan, Norman (b.1900) 18
Bevan, Robert Polhill (1865–1925) 18
Billin, Edward Stanley (1911–1994) 292
Birch, John (1807–1857) 18, 269
Birch, Samuel John Lamorna (1869–1955) 18
Bird, Edward (1772–1819) 18
Birley, Oswald Hornby Joseph (1880–1952) 20
Bishop, Henry (1868–1939) 20
Bisson, Edouard (1856–1939) 20
Blaas, Eugen von (1843–1931) 20
Blake, Peter (b.1932) 20
Blake, Valerie 292
Blanche, Jacques-Emile (1861–1942) 20
Boden, William (1840–1920) 20, 21
Boler, Albert Edward (1864–1939) 21
Bomberg, David (1890–1957) 21

Bond, William Joseph Julius Caesar (1833–1926) 21
Bone, Stephen (1904–1958) 21
Bonheur, Auguste-François (1824–1884) 21
Bonheur, Rosa (1822–1899) 21
Bonington, Richard Parkes (1802–1828) 22
Bonnard, Pierre (1867–1947) 22, 64
Booth, Mel G. (active 1975–1990s) 265
Bortoluzzi, Camillo (1868–1933) 22
Boshier, Derek (b.1937) 22
Bossuet, François Antoine (1798–1889) 22
Bottomley, Albert Ernest (1873–1950) 22
Boudin, Eugène Louis (1824–1898) 22, 23
Bough, Samuel (1822–1878) 23
Boughton, George Henry (1833–1905) 23
Bource, Henri Jacques (1826–1899) 23
Bouvet, Henri Marius Camille (1859–1945) 23
Bower, Reuben (1828–1912) 23, 24
Boyd, Fionnuala (b.1944) 24
Boyle, George A. (1826–1899) 24, 199
Bradbury, Mary (1909–2006) 268
Bradley, Andrea (1970–2009) 24
Brammall, J. H. (active c.1860–1880) 24
Brandon, Louis E. 290
Brangwyn, Frank (1867–1956) 24
Branwhite, Charles (1817–1880) 25
Bratby, John Randall (1928–1992) 25
Brealey, William Ramsden (1889–1949) 25, 26
Breanski, Alfred de (1852–1928) 26
Brekelenkam, Quiringh van (after 1622–1669 or after) 26
Brest, Germain Fabius (1823–1900) 26
Breton, Jules Adolphe Aimé Louis (1827–1906) 26
Brett, John (1830–1902) 26
Brewtnall, Edward Frederick (1846–1902) 26
Bright, Henry (1814–1873) 26, 27
Brighton, Bob (b.1936) vi, 256–258, 292, 293
Bristow, Edmund (1787–1876) 27
British (English) School 27
British (Norwich) School 27
British School 27, 29
Britton, David Swinstead (b.1937) 293
Brockhurst, Gerald Leslie (1890–1978) 29
Brocky, Charles (1807–1855) 29
Bromley, Valentine Walter (1848–1877) 29
Brooker, William (1918–1983) 29
Brown, Chris (active since c.1989) 3
Brown, Colin (b.1957) 259
Brown, Thomas Austen (1859–1924) 30
Brown, W. 265
Brueghel, Jan the elder (1568–1625) 30
Brundrit, Reginald Grange (1883–1960) 30
Bryant, Henry Charles (1836–1915) 30
Buhler, Robert A. (1916–1989) 30
Bunce, William Gedney (1840–1916) 30
Bundy, Edgar (1862–1922) 31
Bunney, John Wharlton (1828–1882) 31, 32
Burgers, Hendricus-Jacobus (1834–1899) 32
Burgess, Arthur James Wetherall (1879–1957) 32
Burgin, Victor (b.1941) 33, 46
Burne-Jones, Edward (1833–1898) 33
Burr, Alexander Hohenlohe (1835–1898) 33
Burr, John P. (1831–1893) 33, 34
Burrows, Robert (1810–1893) 34
Bussy, Simon (1870–1954) 34
Butler, J. (active 19th C) 34
Buttersworth, Thomas (1768–1842) 34
E. H. C. 259
Cadell, Francis Campbell Boileau (1883–1937) 34
Cairns, Joyce W. (b.1947) 34
Caldecott, Randolph (1846–1886) 34
Callow, William (1812–1908) 34
Cameron, David Young (1865–1945) 35
Cameron, Duncan (1837–1916) 35
Cammell, Bernard Edward (1850–1932) 270
Campo, Federico del (1837–1923) 35
Canaletto (1697–1768) 35
Carline, Richard (1896–1980) 35, 289
Carpaccio, Vittore (c.1460–c.1526) 7, 31, 32
Carr, Henry Marvell (1894–1970) 35
Carracci, Annibale (1560–1609) 36
Carrington, Donald P. (b.1907) 36
Carter, William (1863–1939) 36, 294
Castro, Manuel (active before 1795–1805) 36
Cattermole, George (1800–1868) 36
Caulfield, Patrick (1936–2005) 36
Cazin, Jean-Charles (1841–1901) 36
Cazin, Marie (1844–1924) 36, 38
Ceriez, Theodore (1832–1904) 38
Cézanne, Paul (1839–1906) 38
Chaillou, Narcisse (1837–1896) 38
Chambers, George (1803–1840) 38
Chantrey, Francis Leggatt (1781–1842) 38, 39
Chapman, Carlton Theodore (1860–1925) 39
Charvot, Eugène (1847–1924) 39
Chialiva, Luigi (1842–1914) 40
Churchyard, Thomas (1798–1865) 40
Clark, Joseph (1834–1926) 40
Clarke, Brian (b.1953) 40
Clarke, Pete (b.1951) 40
Clays, Paul Jean (1819–1900) 40
Cleveley, John (c.1712–1777) 40
Clouet, François (c.1515–1572) 41
Clough, Prunella (1919–1999) 41
Cluysenaar, André (1872–1939) 41
Coates, Colin (1908–1991) 41
Coccorante, Leonardo (1680–1750) 41
Cohen, Harold (b.1928) 41
Coker, Peter (1926–2004) 42
Coldstream, William Menzies (1908–1987) 42
Cole, George (1810–1883) 42
Cole, George Vicat (1833–1893) 42, 43
Cole, Leslie (1910–1976) 43
Collins, Cecil (1908–1989) 43
Collins, William (1788–1847) 43
Collinson, James (1825–1881) 43
Compton, Edward Theodore (1849–1921) 44
Conder, Charles (1868–1909) 44
Constable, John (1776–1837) 44, 45
Constant, Jean Joseph Benjamin (1845–1902) 45

Constantine, George Hamilton (1875–1968) 45
Constantine, Harry Francis (b.1919) 45, 296, 294
Cooke, Edward William (1811–1880) 47
Cookesley, Margaret Deborah (1844–1927) 47
Cooper, Thomas Sidney (1803–1902) 47, 48
Cope, Arthur Stockdale (1857–1940) 48, 294
Cope, Charles West (1811–1890) 48
Corbet, Matthew Ridley (1850–1902) 48
Corfield, Colin (1910–1991) 265
Corot, Jean-Baptiste-Camille (1796–1875) 48
Cossaar, Jacobus Cornelis Wyand (1874–1966) 48
Coster, Jan Herman (1846–1920) 49
Cotman, Frederick George (1850–1920) 49
Cotman, John Sell (1782–1842) 49
Coulaud, Martin (d.1906) 49
Courbet, Gustave (1819–1877) 49
Cousin, Charles-Louis-Auguste (1807–1887) 49
Couture, Thomas (1815–1879) 49
Cowen, William (1791–1864) 49, 50
Cox, David the elder (1783–1859) 50
Coxon, Raymond James (1896–1997) 50
Cradock, Marmaduke (c.1660–1717) 50
Craxton, John (1922–2009) 51
Creswick, Thomas (1811–1869) 48, 51–54
Crighton, Hugh Ford (1824–1886) 54, 270, 274
Crofts, Ernest (1847–1911) 54, 57
Crome, John (1768–1821) 56
Crome, John Berney (1794–1842) 56
Crozier, William (1930–2011) 56
P. D. 309
R. D. 309
Danby, Francis (1793–1861) 56, 57
Dansaert, Léon Marie Constant (1830–1909) 57
d'Aquavila, Walt 294
Daubigny, Charles-François (1817–1878) 57
Davie, Alan (b.1920) 57
Davis, Henry William Banks (1833–1914) 57
Davis, Richard Barrett (1782–1854) 58
Dawson, Henry (1811–1878) 58
De Cock, Xavier (1818–1896) 58
de Francia, Peter (1921–2012) 58, 59, 91
de Groot, Adelaide Milton (1876–1967) 59
De Sausmarez, Lionel Maurice (1915–1969) 59
De Wint, Peter (1784–1849) 59
Dean, K. 309
Dearle, John Henry (1860–1932) 59
Dearman, John (active 1824–1857) 59
Debuche, Georges L. (active 1925–1928) 60
Decamps, Alexandre-Gabriel (1803–1860) 60
Delamotte, A. 60
Denny, Robyn (b.1930) 60
Deutsch, Ludwig (1855–1935) 60
Devas, Anthony (1911–1958) 60
Devis, Arthur William (1762–1822) 60
Diaz de la Peña, Narcisse Virgile (1808–1876) 60
Dibdin, Thomas Colman (1810–1893) 61
Dickens, Michelle Louise (b.1970) 259
Dicksee, Frank (1853–1928) 61
Dismorr, Jessica (1885–1939) 61
Dobson, Frank (1888–1963) 61
Dobson, Henry Raeburn (1901–1985) 294
Dobson, William Charles Thomas (1817–1898) 61
Dongen, Kees van (1877–1968) 61, 244
Doré, Gustave (1832–1883) 61
Downman, John (1750–1824) 61
Drummond, Malcolm (1880–1945) 62
Dubufe, Guillaume (1853–1909) 62
Dugdale, Thomas Cantrell (1880–1952) 62
Dunbar, Evelyn Mary (1906–1960) 62
Duncan, Edward (1803–1882) 62
Dunlop, Ronald Ossory (1894–1973) 62
Dupré, Jules (1811–1889) 63
Dusart, Cornelis (1660–1704) 63
Dutch School 63, 65, 109
Duval, John (1816–1892) 65
Duverger, Théophile Emmanuel (1821–1901) 65
Eadon, Willis (1870–1945) 66
Earl, Thomas (1810–1876) 66
Eatwell, W. (active 1862) 66
Edwards, Peter Douglas (b.1955) 294
Egg, Augustus Leopold (1816–1863) 66
Egley, William Maw (1826–1916) 66
Elliott, John (b.1953) 66
Ellis, Edwin (1841–1895) 66, 67
Elsheimer, Adam (1578–1610) 67
Eluke, Julius (active 20th C) 67
Elwell, Frederick William (1870–1958) 67
Emms, John (1843–1912) 67
Engel, Fritz Franz (c.1878–1956) 67
Etty, William (1787–1849) 68, 259
Eurich, Richard Ernst (1903–1992) 68, 208, 270
Evans, Leslie (b.1945) 24
Eves, Reginald Grenville (1876–1941) 265
Eyre, James (1802–1838) 68
Faed, John (1820–1902) 68
Faed, Thomas (1826–1900) 69
Fahey, Edward Henry (1844–1907) 69
Fantin-Latour, Henri (1836–1904) 69
Farquharson, David (1839–1907) 69
Farren, Robert Dennis (1832–1912) 69
Farthing, Stephen (b.1950) 70
Fawley, J. F. 70
Fedden, Mary (b.1915) 70
Feiler, Paul (b.1918) 70
Fell, Sheila Mary (1931–1979) 70
Ferg, Franz de Paula (1689–1740) 70, 71
Festing, Andrew (b.1941) 295
Field, Sandra (b.1966) 278
Fieldhouse, Florence (1898–1974) 71
Fielding, Anthony V. C. (1787–1855) 71
Fielding, Brian (1933–1987) 71
Fildes, Luke (1843–1927) 274
Firth, Richard (b.1969) 278, 279
Fisher, Mark (1841–1923) 71
Fleetwood-Walker, Bernard (1893–1965) 72, 295
Flemish School (15th C) 72
Focardi, Ruggero (1864–1934) 72
Forbes, Stanhope Alexander (1857–1947) 72

Formois, Théodore (1814–1871) 74
Foster, Myles Birket (1825–1899) 74
Fower, Robert (1866–1947) 270
Fowler, Robert (1853–1926) 74
Fragonard, Jean-Honoré (1732–1806) 74
Franco-Flemish School 74
Fraser, Alexander (b.1940) 74
Fraser, Alexander George (1786–1865) 74
Freedman, Barnett (1901–1958) 74
French School 74, 75
Frère, Charles Édouard (1837–1894) 75
Frère, Pierre Edouard (1819–1886) 76
Frith, William Powell (1819–1909) 48, 76
Froggatt, Muriel Alice (1909–1992) 265
Frost, Terry (1915–2003) 76
Fry, Anthony (b.1927) 76
Fry, Roger Eliot (1866–1934) 76, 77
Fumi, Tebaldo (active 1870–1880) 77
Fuseli, Henry (1741–1825) 77
Fyfe, William Baxter Collier (1836–1882) 77
Gainsborough, Thomas (1727–1788) 77
Gainsford, F. G. (active 1805–1828) 270
Garay Arévalo, Manuel (1844–1911) 77
Garnett, Ruth (1836–1915) 270
Garstin, Norman (1847–1926) 77, 78
Gaubault, Alfred Émile (d.1895) 78
Gauguin, Paul (1848–1903) 78
Geefs, Fanny (1807–1883) 78
Geoffroy, Jean Jules Henry (1853–1924) 78
Gérome, Jean-Léon (1824–1904) 78
Gheeraerts, Marcus the elder (c.1520–before 1604) 78
Gibbs, Lewis T. 78
Gibbs, Percy William (1894–1937) 79
Gibbs, Thomas Binney (1870–1947) 79
Gilbert, John (1817–1897) 79
Giles, Frank Lynton (1910–2003) 79
Gill, Edmund Marriner (1820–1894) 79
Gillet, Numa François (1868–1940) 79
Gillies, William George (1898–1973) 79
Gillray, James (1757–1815) 79
Gilman, Harold (1876–1919) 80
Ginner, Charles (1878–1952) 80
Girardet, Léopold-Henri (1848–1904) 80
Girardot, Ernest Gustave (1840–1904) 80
Gittins, John Steven (b.1955) 295
Gogin, Charles (1844–1931) 80
Gomez 80
Goodall, Frederick (1822–1904) 80, 81
Goodall, Howard (1850–1874) 81
Goodwin, Albert (1845–1932) 81, 83
Gore, Spencer (1878–1914) 83
Gosse, Laura Sylvia (1881–1968) 83
Gotch, Thomas Cooper (1854–1931) 83, 84
Goupil, Jules Adolphe (1839–1883) 84
Gowing, Lawrence (1918–1991) 84
Goyen, Jan van (1596–1656) 84
Graham, George (1881–1949) 84
Graham Bell, Frank (1910–1943) 84
Gran, Daniel (1694–1757) 85
Graner, Luis (1863–1929) 85
Grant, Duncan (1885–1978) 85
Greaves, Derrick (b.1927) 85
Greaves, Walter (1846–1930) 85, 86
Greene, Mary (b.1953) 259
Greenham, Robert Duckworth (1906–1976) 86
Greiffenhagen, Maurice (1862–1931) 86
Greuze, Jean-Baptiste (1725–1805) 86
Griffin, Paul (b.1955) 86
Grimm, Stanley (1891–1966) 86
Grönland, Theude (1817–1876) 86
Guise, A. 86
Gunn, Herbert James (1893–1964) 87
Gussoni, Vittorio (1893–1968) 87
Gussow, Carl (1843–1907) 87
Guttman, J. (b.1869) 87
Haanen, Adriana Johanna (1814–1895) 87
Hacker, Arthur (1858–1919) 270
Haghe, Louis (1806–1885) 87
Hallé, Charles Edward (1846–1919) 87
Halliday, Edward Irvine (1902–1984) 295
Halswelle, Keeley (1832–1891) 88
Hamer, Douglas (1897–1981) 295
Hanneman, Adriaen (c.1601–1671) 88
Harcourt, George (1868–1947) 295
Hardy, Dudley (1866–1922) 88
Hardy, Heywood (1842–1933) 88
Hardy, Thomas Bush (1842–1897) 88
Hargitt, Edward (1835–1895) 88
Harnett, William Michael (1848–1892) 89
Harpignies, Henri-Joseph (1819–1916) 89
Harris, Thomas (1787–1817) 89
Hattersley, George Pearson (1858–1937) 89
Hauve, A. van 89
Havell, William (1782–1857) 89
Havers, Alice (1850–1890) 89
Havers, Val (1873–1912) 90
Hawkesworth, Joseph Hallam (1827–1908) 90
Hawksley, Arthur (1842–1915) 90
Hayes, Edwin (1819–1904) 90, 92
Head, B. G. (active 1867–1890) 92
Heath, Adrian (1920–1992) 92
Heath, Andrew (b.1962) 279
Heeremans, Thomas (c.1640–1697) 92
Heinish, Karl Adam (1847–1923) 92
Hellewell, Jack (1920–2000) 92
Helmick, Howard (1845–1907) 93
Hemy, Charles Napier (1841–1917) 93
Henry, Émile (1844–1920) 93
Henry, George (1858–1943) 94
Henry, Paul (1876–1958) 94
Henshaw, Frederick Henry (1807–1891) 94
Henzell, Isaac (1815–1876) 94
Hepher, David (b.1935) 94
Her, Theodor (1838–1892) 94
Herdman, Robert Duddingstone (1863–1922) 94
Hering, George Edwards (1805–1879) 95
Herring, John Frederick I (1795–1865) 95
Heywood, Christopher (b.1928) 295

Highfield, William (1870–1957) 95, 96
Highmore, Joseph (1692–1780) 96
Hildick, Mabel Sarah (1884–1979) 266
Hill 27
Hill, Arthur (c.1829–1894) 96
Hill, James Stevens (1854–1921) 96
Hillingford, Robert Alexander (1825–1904) 96
Hilton, Roger (1911–1975) 97
Hitchens, Ivon (1893–1979) 97
Hobbema, Meindert (1638–1709) 97
Hofland, Thomas Christopher (1777–1843) 97
Holl, Frank (1845–1888) 97
Holland, Diana 296
Holland, James (1799–1870) 97, 98
Hollingsworth, Ruth (b.1880) 98
Hone, Nathaniel I (1718–1784) 98
Hook, James Clarke (1819–1907) 98
Hope, Robert (1869–1936) 98
Hoppner, John (1758–1810) 98
Hornel, Edward Atkinson (1864–1933) 99
Horsley, Walter Charles (1855–1934) 99
Horton, Percy Frederick (1897–1970) 99
Houston, George (1869–1947) 99
Houthuesen, Albert Anthony (1903–1979) 99
Howard, Reg 3
Hoyland, Henry George (1895–1948) 99, 270
Hoyland, John (1934–2011) 99, 101
Hubbard, Eric Hesketh (1892–1957) 101
Hudson, Robert (1852–1884) 101
Hudson, Thomas (1701–1779) 101
Hughes, Arthur (1832–1915) 101
Hughes, Malcolm Edward (1920–1997) 101
Hughes-Stanton, Herbert Edwin Pelham (1870–1937) 101, 102
Hulett 296
Hulme, Frederick William (1816–1884) 102
Hulsdonck, Jacob van (1582–1647) 102
Hume, Edith (1843–1906) 102
Humphrey, Edward J. (active 1872–1890) 102
Humphry, Ozias (1742–1810) 102
Hunt, Edgar (1876–1953) 102
Hunt, Thomas (1854–1929) 102
Hunt, William Holman (1827–1910) 102
Hunter, George Leslie (1877–1931) 103
Hurt, Louis Bosworth (1856–1929) 103
Hutchison, William Oliphant (1889–1970) 296, 303
Huysum, Jacob van (1686–1740) 103
Hyatt, Derek James (b.1931) 103
Hyde, Graham (b.c.1979) 296
Hyneman, Herman N. (1859–1907) 103
Ibbetson, Julius Caesar (1759–1817) 103, 104
Ibbitt, William (1804–1869) 104
Ifold, Frederick (1821–1904) 104
Inlander, Henry (1925–1983) 104
Innes, James Dickson (1887–1914) 104
Irvin, Albert (b.1922) 104
Irving, J. Thwaite (active 1888–1909) 105
Irwin, Gwyther (1931–2008) 105
Israëls, Jozef (1824–1911) 105
Italian School 105, 106
Jack, Richard (1866–1952) 106
Jackson, Peter Kenneth Cowley (1930–2006) 296
Jacque, Charles Émile (1813–1894) 106
Jacques, Marie (b.1868) 106
Jacquet, Gustave Jean (1846–1909) 106, 107
Jagger, David (1891–1958) 272
James, David (1834–1897) 107
Jamieson, Alexander (1873–1937) 107
Janssens van Ceulen, Cornelis (1593–1661) 108
Jaray, Tess (b.1937) 108
Jennings, Roberta Louise (b.1919) 108
John, Augustus Edwin (1878–1961) 108
John, Gwen (1876–1939) 108
Johnson, Charles Edward (1832–1913) 108
Johnson, Harry John (1826–1884) 108
Johnson, Valentine (active 1777–1799) 110
Johnston, Alexander (1815–1891) 110
Jones, Allen (b.1937) 110
Jones, Donna (active 2002–2003) 275
Jones, Stanley Robert (b.1927) 110
Jongkind, Johan Barthold (1819–1891) 110
Jordaens, Jacob (1593–1678) 110
Joseph, Tam (b.1947) 111
Jungman, Nico (1872–1935) 111
C. K. 310
Kay, Ernest (active 1907) 111
Keeling, William (1860–1930) 111, 290
Kelly, Felix Runcie (1914–1994) 111
Kelly, Gerald Festus (1879–1972) 111
Kemm, Robert (1830–1895) 111
Kemp, Fiona Margaret (b.1949) 296
Kemp-Welch, Lucy (1869–1958) 111, 190
Kennedy, J. 290
Kennedy, William Denholm (1813–1865) 112
Kessell, Mary (1914–1977) 112
Kettell, Jack 112
Kidd, William (1790–1863) 112
Kiddy, Gretchen (1910–2005) 296
Kilgore, Constance (b.1951) 112
King, Gunning (1859–1940) 112
King, Henry John Yeend (1855–1924) 112
Kinoshita, Seiko (b.1971) 279, 281
Kitaj, R. B. (1932–2007) iv, 112
Klooze 281
Knapton, George (1698–1778) 112
Kneller, Godfrey (1646–1723) 113
Knight, John William Buxton (1842/1843–1908) 113
Koekkoek, Barend Cornelis (1803–1862) 113
Koekkoek, Hermanus the elder (1815–1882) 113
Koekkoek, Hermanus the younger (1836–1909) 113
Koekkoek, Johannes Hermanus (1778–1851) 113, 114
Koekkoek, Marinus Adrianus (1807–1870) 114
Koerner, Ernest Carl (1846–1927) 114
Kotasz, Károly (1872–1941) 114
Ladell, Edward (1821–1886) 114
Laidlay, William James (1846–1912) 114
Lale, Hazel 281
Lamb, Henry (1883–1960) 114
Lambeaux, Jules (1858–1890) 115

Lambert, Clement (1855–1925) 115
Lambinet, Emile Charles (1815–1877) 115
Lancret, Nicolas (1690–1743) 115
Landseer, Edwin Henry (1802–1873) 115, 116
Lascaux, Elie (1888–1969) 116
Laver, John Holmes (1880–1950) 266
Lavery, John (1856–1941) 116
Lavoine, Louis Victor (1808–1861) 116
Lawrance, M. 266
Lawrence, Thomas (1769–1830) 116
Lawson, Cecil Gordon (1851–1882) 117
Lawson, Sonia (b.1934) 117
Lawton, Nigel Philip 268
Le Bas, Edward (1904–1966) 117
Le Sidaner, Henri Eugène (1862–1939) 117
Leader, Benjamin Williams (1831–1923) 117, 119
Leadley, W. E. (1903–1973) 120
Lear, Edward (1812–1888) 120
Lee, Frederick Richard (1798–1879) 48, 120
Lee, Terry (b.1932) 120
Lee-Hankey, William (1869–1952) 121
Leemputten, Cornelis van (1841–1902) 121
Lees, Derwent (1885–1931) 121
Legros, Alphonse (1837–1911) 121
Lehmann, Rudolph (1819–1905) 121
Leist, Frederick William (1878–1945) 121
Leitch, William Leighton (1804–1883) 121
Lely, Peter (1618–1680) 122
Lemon, Arthur (1850–1912) 122
Leslie, Charles Robert (1794–1859) 122
Lessore, Thérèse (1884–1945) 122
Levis, Maurice (1860–1940) 122, 123
Levy, Émile (1826–1890) 123
Lewin, Stephen Samuel (1848–1909) 123
Lewis, Bethan Rhiannon (b.1975) 298
Lewis, John Frederick (1805–1876) 123
Lhermitte, Léon-Augustin (1844–1925) 123
Lidderdale, Charles Sillem (1831–1895) 123
Linderum, Richard (1851–1926) 124
Lindley, W. 124
Linnell, James Thomas (1826–1905) 124
Linnell, John (1792–1882) 124, 125
Linnell, William (1826–1906) 125
Linton, James Dromgole (1840–1916) 125
Linton, William (1791–1876) 125
Liotard, Jean-Étienne (1702–1789) 15
Lisle, Frank (1916–1986) 125
Lismer, Arthur (1885–1969) 125
Little, Douglas Patrick (active 1981–1985) 125, 291
Little, Pauline (b.1961) 298
Lloyd, Stuart (active 1875–1929) 126
Lloyd-Jones, Peter (1940–2001) 126
Lomax, John Arthur (1857–1923) 126
Long, Edwin (1829–1891) 126
Lorein, Victor (1894–1954) 126
Los, Waldermar (1849–1888) 126
Lotz, H. J. 126
Loudin, H. D. 128
Loutherbourg, Philip James de (1740–1812) 128
Lowe, Anthony (b.1957) 128, 298
Lowe, Arthur (1866–1940) 128
Lowe, David (active 19th C) 128
Lowinsky, Thomas Esmond (1892–1947) 128, 129
Lowndes, Alan (1921–1978) 129
Lowry, Laurence Stephen (1887–1976) 129, 145
Ludovici, Albert (1852–1932) 129
Luker, William (1828–1892) 129, 130
Luny, Thomas (1759–1837) 130
Lutzens 130
Lyons, L. 130
Macbeth, Robert Walker (1848–1910) 130
MacGeorge, William Stewart (1861–1931) 130
MacGregor, William York (1855–1923) 130
Machan, Robert (b.1948) 298
MacIntyre, James Crichton (active 1867–c.1911) 130
MacIntyre, Joseph Wrightson (1842–1897) 131
Maclise, Daniel (1806–1870) 131
Madliner, W. J. 131
Mahoney, Charles (1903–1968) 131, 132
Maitland, Paul Fordyce (1863–1909) 132
Malbon, William (1805–1877) 132, 133
Mancini, Antonio (1852–1930) 133
Mann, Cathleen (1896–1959) 133
Marchetti, Ludovico (1853–1909) 133
Maris, Jacob Henricus (1837–1899) 133
Maris, Willem (1844–1910) 133
Marks, Henry Stacey (1829–1898) 133
Marlow, William (1740–1813) 133
Marten, J. (active 19th C) 133
Martin, F. 266
Martin, Florence (b.c.1845) 134
Martin, Kenneth (1905–1984) 134
Masaccio (1401–1428) 134
Masoero, Jeanne (b.1937) 134
Mason, William Henry (active 1858–1917) 134
Masquerier, John James (1778–1855) 134
Mastin, John (1865–1932) 134
Matesdorf, Théodore (1849–1909) 134
Matisse, Henri (1869–1954) 218
Mauve, Anton (1838–1888) 134
Mayne, Peter 298
McBey, James (1883–1959) 135
McCall, Susan (b.1946) 298
McCulloch, Horatio (1805–1867) 135
McEvoy, Ambrose (1878–1927) 135, 306
McFadyen, Jock (b.1950) 135
McGregor, Neil (b.1963) 298
McLaughlin, John (1885–1957) 135
McPartland, Ian (b.1963) 299
Meadows, Arthur Joseph (1843–1907) 137
Meffsner, Ernst (active mid-19th C) 137
Meissonier, Jean Louis Ernest (1815–1891) 137
Melby, William (1824–1882) 137
Mellis, Margaret (1914–2009) 137
Mellon, Campbell Archibald (1876–1955) 137
Members of the Rural Youth Project 3
Mendoza, June (b.1945) 299
Mengs, Anton Raphael (1728–1779) 137

Meninsky, Bernard (1891–1950) 138
Menpes, Mortimer L. (1855–1938) 138
Mesdag, Hendrik Willem (1831–1915) 138
Mettling, Louis (1847–1904) 138
Meulen, Steven van der (1493–1563) 139
Meyerheim, Robert Gustav (1847–1920) 139
Michel, Georges (1763–1843) 139
Middleditch, Edward (1923–1987) 139
Middleton, James Godsell (1805–1874) 139
Miereveld, Michiel Jansz. van (1567–1641) 139
Millais, John Everett (1829–1896) 139, 140
Milne, John Maclauchlan (1886–1957) 140
Mion, Luigi (1843–c.1920) 140
Mitchell, J. Young (1811–1865) 140
Mitchell, Jean (1861–1941) 140, 268, 272
Moermans, Frans (active 1871–1878) 141
Moes, Wally (1856–1918) 309
Momper, Joos de the younger (1564–1635) 141
Monamy, Peter (1681–1749) 141
Monnoyer, Jean-Baptiste (1636–1699) 141
Montalba, Hilda (1846–1919) 141
Monticelli, Adolphe Joseph Thomas (1824–1886) 141, 142
Mooney, Edward Hartley (c.1878–1938) 142
Moore, Albert Joseph (1841–1893) 142
Moore, Ernest (1865–1940) 142, 143, 272, 299
Moore, Henry (1831–1895) 143
Moore, John (1801–1865) 272
Mor, Antonis (1512–1516–c.1576) 143
Morales, Luis de (c.1509–c.1586) 82, 143
Morgan, E. 259
Morgan, Frederick (1856–1927) 144
Morgan, John (1823–1886) 144
Morland, George (1763–1804) 144, 146
Morris, Philip Richard (1834–1902) 146
Morris, Stephen (b.1935) 146
Mostyn, Thomas Edwin (1864–1930) 146
Mouillot, Marcel (1889–1972) 146
Mücke, Karl Anton Heinrich (1806–1891) 146
Muckley, William Jabez (1829–1905) 146
Muirhead, David (1867–1930) 147
Muller, Axel 3
Muller, William James (1812–1845) 148, 149, 309
Müller, Alfredo (1869–1940) 55, 147
Mulready, Augustus Edwin (1844–1905) 149
Mulready, William (1786–1863) 149, 150
Muncaster, Claude (1903–1974) 150
Munnings, Alfred James (1878–1959) 150
Munthe, Ludwig (1841–1896) 150
Murillo, Bartolomé Esteban (1618–1682) ii, 150
Murray, Charles (1894–1954) 150
Murray, Charles Fairfax (1849–1919) 151
Murray, David (1849–1933) 151
Musin, François Etienne (1820–1888) 151
Mytens, Daniel I (c.1590–1647) 151
Mytens, Jan (c.1614–1670) 151
Nash, John Northcote (1893–1977) 151, 309
Nash, Paul (1889–1946) 151, 152
Nasmyth, Patrick (1787–1831) 152
Neer, Aert van der (1603–1677) 152
Neiland, Brendan (b.1941) 1, 152, 299
Netscher, Wilhelm Adrian (1791–1851) 152
Nevinson, Christopher (1889–1946) 152, 153
Nicholls, Bertram (1883–1974) 153
Nicholson, Ben (1894–1982) 153
Nicholson, Walter (1830–1907) 153
Nicholson, William (1872–1949) 153
Nicholson, Winifred (1893–1981) 154
Nicol, Erskine (1825–1904) 155
Nicol, John Watson (1856–1926) 155
Niemann, Edmund John (1813–1876) 155, 156, 157, 174
Nieuwal, Jan Rutgers (active 1620–1661) 157
Noble, James Campbell (1846–1913) 157
Normann, Adelsteen (1848–1918) 157
O'Briton 157
Ociepko, Mark (b.1945) 299
O'Connor, Aloysius Patrick 157
O'Connor, James Arthur (1792–1841) 158
O'Conor, Roderic (1860–1940) 158
Oliver, Ken (b.1948) 158
Oliver, William (1823–1901) 158, 159
Olsson, Albert Julius (1864–1942) 159
Ommeganck, Balthazar Paul (1755–1826) 160
O'Neill, George Bernard (1828–1917) 160
Oram, Edward (d.1810) 160
Orchardson, William Quiller (1832–1910) 160
Orpen, William (1878–1931) 160
Ouless, Walter William (1848–1933) 161, 300
Owen, William (1769–1825) 161
Pace del Campidoglio, Michele (1610–probably 1670) 161
Padfield, Gillian Margaret (1939–2009) 300
Padgett, William (1851–1904) 161
Palizzi, Filippo (1818–1899) 161
Paoletti, Antonio Ermolao (1834–1912) 161
Papperitz, Friedrich Georg (1846–1918) 162
Park, Henry (1816–1871) 162
Park, Stuart (1862–1933) 162
Parker, Henry Perlee (1795–1873) 162
Parmakio, Rose (active 1970s) 281, 282
Parrott, William (1813–after 1891) 162
Parsons, Alfred William (1847–1920) 162
Pasmore, Daniel I (c.1815–1893) 162
Pasmore, Victor (1908–1998) 162
Patel, Pierre I (c.1605–1676) 164
Patients of The Children's Hospital, Sheffield 179, 281
Paton, Joseph Noel (1821–1901) 164
Paul, Paul (1865–1937) 164
Pavy, Philippe (b.1860) 164
Peacock, Brian (1935–2004) 300
Peel, James (1811–1906) 164
Peele, John Thomas (1822–1897) 164
Peeters, Bonaventura I (1614–1652) 164
Peeters, Gillis (1612–1653) 211
Pemberton, John (active 1948) 300
Penistone, Robert (b.1946) 266, 275, 276, 309
Peppercorn, Arthur Douglas (1847–1926) 164, 165
Percy, Sidney Richard (1821–1886) 165
Perkins, J. M. 165
Perronneau, Jean-Baptiste (1715–1783) 165

Pether, Henry (c.1801–1880) 165
Pettie, John (1839–1893) 166, 167
Pettit, Joseph Paul (1812–1882) 167
Pezzoia 167
Philips, Hermann August (1844–1927) 167
Philipson, Robin (1916–1992) 167
Phillip, John (1817–1867) 167, 168
Phillips, Thomas (1770–1845) 168
Phillips, Tom (b.1937) 168
Pickersgill, Henry William (1782–1875) 168
Pickford, Ralph Randolphus (1834–1911) 90
Pigott, William Henry (c.1810–1901) 168
Pinwell, George John (1842–1875) 168
Pisa, Alberto (1864–1931) 169
Pissarro, Camille (1831–1903) 100, 169
Pissarro, Lucien (1863–1944) 169
Pittman, Osmund (1874–1968) 169
Pittoni, Giovanni Battista the younger (1687–1767) 169
Platt, Joyce (b.1920) 272
Plummer, Robin (b.1931) 169
Poole, James (1803–1886) 169–170, 171
Poole, Paul Falconer (1807–1879) 171
Poole, William (c.1798–1888) 171
Pope, Alexander (1849–1924) 127, 171
Porter, Frederick James (1883–1944) 173
Pott, Laslett John (1837–1898) 173
Potten, Christopher Nerry (1849–1934) 173
Potter, Mary (1900–1981) 173
Poynter, Edward John (1836–1919) 174
Prades, Alfred F. De (active 1844–1883) 157
Price, Edward (1800–1885) 174
Priestman, Bertram (1868–1951) 174
Prinsep, Valentine Cameron (1838–1904) 174
Priseman, Robert (b.1965) 259, 260
Pritchett, Edward (active c.1828–1879) 174
Procaccini, Giulio Cesare (1574–1625) 174
Procktor, Patrick (1936–2003) 174, 175
Procter, Dod (1892–1972) 175
Prout, Samuel (1783–1852) 175
Pyne, James Baker (1800–1870) 175, 176
Quizet, Alphonse (1885–1955) 176
Raeburn, Henry (1756–1823) 176
Ragon, Adolphe (1847–1924) 176
Rainer, Richard (b.1933) 176
Ramsay, Allan (1852–1912) 176, 177
Ramsay, Patricia (1886–1974) 177
Raphael (1483–1520) 77, 177
Rathbone, John (1750–1807) 177
Rattray, Alexander William Wellwood (1849–1902) 177
Ravesteyn, Jan Anthonisz. van (c.1570–1657) 177
Rea, Cecil William (1860–1935) 177
Rea, Constance (1891–1935) 178
Reah, Ken 300
Redpath, Anne (1895–1965) 19, 178
Reinagle, George Philip (c.1802–1835) 178
Reinagle, Philip (1749–1833) 178
Reinagle, Ramsay Richard (1775–1862) 178
Rembrandt van Rijn (1606–1669) 87
Renoir, Pierre-Auguste (1841–1919) 178
Réol, Marie Marguerite (1880–1963) 178, 179
Reynolds, Joshua (1723–1792) 179
Rhoades, Geoffrey (1898–1980) 179
Rhodes, M. (active 19th C) 179
Ribera, Jusepe de (1591–1652) 179
Ricci, Sebastiano (1659–1734) 179, 181
Richardson, Jonathan the elder (1664/1665–1745) 179
Richmond, William Blake (1842–1921) 179
Riegen, Nicholaas (1827–1889) 180
Rigg, Ernest Higgins (1868–1947) 180
Riley, Bridget (b.1931) 180
Riley, John (1646–1691) 180
Rivers, Leopold (1852–1905) 180
Robert, Hubert (1733–1808) 180, 182
Roberts, David (1796–1864) 163, 182
Roberts, William Patrick (1895–1980) 118, 183
Robertson, Henry Robert (1839–1921) 183
Röder, Endre Zoltan Eugene (b.1933) 300
Rodgers, D. K. 3
Roe, Colin Graeme (1857–1910) 183
Roestraten, Pieter Gerritsz. van (1629/1630–1700) 183
Rogers, Claude (1907–1979) 183
Rögge, Wilhelm (1829–1908) 183
Romney, George (1734–1802) 183
Roos, Philipp Peter (1657–1706) 184
Rosa, Salvator (1615–1673) 184
Rose, Magnus (1859–1900) 184
Rose, Martin H. (b.1946) 184, 282, 300
Rose, Rose (b.1946) 309
Rosselli, Cosimo (1439–1507) 184
Rossetti, Dante Gabriel (1828–1882) 184
Rothenstein, Anne (b.1949) 184
Rothenstein, Michael (1908–1993) 184, 297
Rothenstein, William (1872–1945) 172, 185, 300
Rouault, Georges (1871–1958) 185, 280
Rousseau, Théodore (1812–1867) 185
Roussel, Théodore Casimir (1847–1926) 186
Rowles, Marjorie Kathleen (active 1923–1929) 186
Royle, Stanley (1888–1961) 186, 187
Rubens, Peter Paul (1577–1640) 188, 251
Russell, Walter Westley (1867–1949) 188, 301
Russian School 188
Ryder, J. T. (active c.1933–c.1960) 188
Sadée, Philip Lodewijk Jacob Frederik (1837–1904) 188
Safonov, N. 188
Sanderson, Helen 301
Sanderson-Wells, John (1872–1955) 189
Sandys, Frederick (1829–1904) 189
Sant, James (1820–1916) 189
Santoro, Rubens (1859–1942) 189
Saraceni, Carlo (1579–1620) 189
Sargent, John Singer (1856–1925) 189
Sargent, Louis Augustus (b.1881) 189
Sarto, Andrea del (1486–1530) 189
Sartorius, John Nost (1759–1828) 191
Sassoferrato (1609–1685) 191
Scarborough, Joe (b.1938) 4, 73, 191, 260, 261, 274, 282, 301
Schalch, Johann Jacob (1723–1789) 191
Schampheleer, Edmond de (1824–1899) 191

Schenck, August Friedrich Albrecht (1828–1901) 191
Schieler, Robert 191
Scholderer, Otto (1834–1902) viii, 192
Schreyer, Christian Adolf (1828–1899) 192
Schröder, Albert Friedrich (1854–1939) 192
Seabrooke, Elliott (1886–1950) 192
Seddon, Richard (1915–2002) 192
Selden, Roger (b.1945) 192
Shackleton, Judith 301
Shackleton, William (1872–1933) 192
Shannon, James Jebusa (1862–1923) 192, 193, 272
Shaw, David Carson (b.1942) 301
Shawcross, Neil (b.1940) 301
Shayer, William (1788–1879) 193
Shepherd, F. H. S. (1877–1948) 193
Shepherd, Kate (active 1888–1916) 193
Sherrin, Daniel (1869–1940) 194
Sichel, Ernest Leopold (1862–1941) 194
Sickert, Bernard (1863–1932) 194
Sickert, Walter Richard (1860–1942) 194, 235
Simcock, Jack (b.1929) 195
Simmons, John (1871–1944) 195
Simon, Lucien (1861–1945) 195
Simpson, Charles Walter (1885–1971) 195
Singleton, Henry (1766–1839) 195
Sisley, Alfred (1839–1899) 195
Smart, Robert Borlase (1881–1947) 195
Smith, Jack (1928–2011) 196
Smith, Matthew Arnold Bracey (1879–1959) 196
Smith, Richard (1818–1890) 196, 274
Smith, W. E. 196
Solomon, Abraham (1824–1862) 197
Somerville, Howard (1873–1952) 301
Sonje, Jan Gabrielsz. (c.1625–1707) 197
Sounes, William Henry (1830–1873) 261, 331
Spanish School (19th C) 197
Spear, Ruskin (1911–1990) 197
Speed, Harold (1872–1957) 197
Spencer, Gilbert (1892–1979) 197
Spencer, Jean (1942–1998) 198
Spencer, Stanley (1891–1959) 198
Spencer Pryse, Gerald (1882–1957) 198
Spenlove-Spenlove, Frank (1866–1933) 198
Spruyt, Johannes (1627/1628–1671) 198
Spurr, Joyce (b.1921) 198
Staackmann, Heinrich Maria (1852–1940) 198
Stademann, Adolf (1824–1895) 198
Stanfield, Clarkson (1793–1867) 200
Stanier, Henry (c.1832–1892) 200
Stapleton, M. (active from 1850) 200
Stark, James (1794–1859) 200, 201
Steel, George Hammond (1900–1960) 201
Stevens, Alfred George (1817–1875) 201
Stevenson, W. J. (1835–1905) 201, 202
Stone, Marcus C. (1840–1921) 202
Storey, George Adolphus (1834–1919) 202
Stothard, Thomas (1755–1834) 203
Stott, Edward William (1859–1918) 203
Strang, William (1859–1921) 203, 204
Stubley, Trevor (1932–2010) 204, 302
Styring, Elizabeth (1854–1940) 204
Suberu, Ade (b.1968) 302
Suddaby, Rowland (1912–1972) 204
Sutton, Philip (b.1928) 205
Swinstead, George Hillyard (1860–1926) 205
Syer, John (1815–1885) 205
Syers, Rose Aspinall (1850–after 1926) 205
Sykes, Godfrey (1824–1866) 205–207, 209, 210
Sykes, Lilian (active 1887–1890) 210
Symons, William Christian (1845–1911) 210
Talmage, Algernon Mayow (1871–1939) 210
Tamburini, Arnaldo (1843–1908) 210
Tayler, Albert Chevallier (1862–1925) 210
Taylor, Alan (b.1958) 282, 283
Taylor, Micheline 283
Teale, Dick (b.1930) 302
Temple, Robert Scott (b.c.1853) 210
Ten Kate, Herman Frederik Carel (1822–1891) 211
Teniers, David I (1582–1649) 211
Teniers, David II (1610–1690) 211
Teurdyghe, Carolus Ignatius (active c.1700) 212
Thaddeus, Henry Jones (1860–1929) 212
Tharp, Charles Julian (1878–1951) 212
Thomas, Grosvenor (1856–1923) 212
Thompson, Hugh (1810–1866) 212
Thomson, Christopher (1799–1871) 212
Thomson, John (1778–1840) 212
Tibble, Geoffrey Arthur (1909–1952) 213
Tingle, Roy 267
Tintoretto, Jacopo (1519–1594) 32
Tissot, James (1836–1902) 213
Titcomb, William Holt Yates (1858–1930) 267, 271
Titian (c.1488–1576) 201
Tol, Dominicus van (c.1635–1676) 213
Tollast, Robert (1918–1996) 272
Tom 283
Tommasi, Adolfo (1851–1933) 213
Tonge, Robert (1823–1856) 213
Topham, Francis Williams (1808–1877) 213
Torrance, James (1859–1916) 214
Torre, Raffaelo (1844–1927) 214
Towner, Donald Chisholm (1903–1985) 214
Townley, James Morrison (1917–1995) 214
Townroe, Reuben (1835–1911) 214
Townsend, Ernest (1885–1944) 214
Townsend, William (1909–1973) 214
Tracy, John Martin (1843–1893) 302
Traies, William (1789–1872) 214
Tucker, R. A. 261
Turner, E. M. T. 261
Turner, Joseph Mallord William (1775–1851) 28, 215
Tyzack, Michael (1933–2007) 215
Underhill, Frederick Charles (c.1832–1896) 215
Underhill, Graham (b.1946) 302
Unterberger, Franz Richard (1838–1902) 154, 231
Van Assen, Benedictus Antonio (1788–1817) 231
Van Boskerck, Robert Ward (1855–1932) 232
Van de Tonge, Louis (1871–1937) 232

Van der Hoef, Abraham (1611/1612–1649) 232
Van der Nat, Willem Hendrik (1865–1929) 232
Van Heemskerck van Beest, Jacob Eduard (1828–1894) 232
Vanderbank, John (c.1694–1739) 232
Varkalis, Amrik (b.1949) 303
Varley, John II (1850–1933) 232, 233
Vaughan, John Keith (1912–1977) 233
Vaux, Marc (b.1932) 233
Vawser, George Robert (1815–1893) 233
Velde, Willem van de II (1633–1707) 233
Verheyden, François (1806–1889/1890) 234
Vernet, Claude-Joseph (1714–1789) 234
Vernet, Horace (1789–1863) 234
Vernier, Émile Louis (1829–1887) 234
Verrochio, Andrea del (1435–1488) 6
Veyrassat, Jules Jacques (1828–1893) 234
Vianello, Giovanni (1873–1926) 234
Vickers, Alfred (1786–1868) 236, 237
Vidal, Louis (c.1754–1804) 237
Villamil, Eugenio Lucas (1858–1918) 237
Vincent, George (1796–1831) 237
Vizard, W. (active 1884–1903) 237
Vlaminck, Maurice de (1876–1958) 238
Vollon, Alexis (1865–1945) 238
Vollon, Antoine (1833–1900) 238
Von Gegerfeldt, Wilhelm (1844–1920) 238
Von Löfftz, Ludwig (1845–1910) 238
Vuram, J. 238
Wadsworth, Edward Alexander (1889–1949) 239
Wainewright, Thomas Francis (1794–1883) 239
Waite, Philippa 283
Wakle, J. F. 239
Walker, Ethel (1861–1951) 239
Walker, Robert (1599–1658) 239
Wall, Tom (1941–1992) 304
Waller, Mary Lemon (1852–c.1931) 273, 304
Waller, Samuel Edmund (1850–1903) 239
Wallis, Alfred (1855–1942) 239
Waplington, Paul Anthony (b.1938) 37, 240, 304
Ward, Edward Matthew (1816–1879) 240, 304
Ward, Grace (active 1930–1940s) 240
Ward, James (1769–1859) 240
Ward, Martin Theodore (1799–1874) 241
Ward, T. (active 1819–1865) 241
Warmby, Byron Winston (1902–1978) 241
Warr, George H. (1907–1933) 241
Warren, William White (1832–1915) 241
Warrender, Vera 304
Waterhouse, John William (1849–1917) 241
Watson, William II (active 1866–1921) 241
Watts, George Frederick (1817–1904) 242
Weatherhead, William Harris (1843–1903) 242
Webb, James (1825–1895) 242, 243
Webster, Thomas George (1800–1886) 243
Weekes, Henry I (1807–1877) 245
Weeks, Edwin Lord (1849–1903) 245
Weight, Carel Victor Morlais (1908–1997) 245
Weir, William (d.1865) 245
Weiss, José (1859–1919) 245, 246
Weissenbruch, Jan Hendrik (1824–1903) 246
Wentzel, Niels Gustav (1859–1927) 246
Werff, Adriaen van der (1659–1722) 246
Wheatley, Francis (1747–1801) 246
Wheatley, Grace (1888–1970) 304
Wheatley, John (1892–1955) 246
Wheelwright, Rowland (1870–1955) 246
Whistler, James Abbott McNeill (1834–1903) 246, 247
Whittington, Marjory (active 20th C) 247
Widdop, John 304
Wilkie, David (1785–1841) 81, 247
Wilkinson, Charles A. (b.1830) 247
Willcock, George Burrell (1811–1852) 247
Williams, Edward (1782–1855) 247, 248
Williams, Edward Charles (1807–1881) 248
Williams, Margaret Lindsay (1887–1960) 273
Williams, Terrick John (1860–1936) 248
Wilson, Arthur (1838–1914) 248
Wilson, Graeme (b.1951) 305
Wilson, John H. 'Jock' (1774–1855) 248
Wilson, John James II (1818–1875) 248
Wilson, Richard (1712/1713–1782) 248–250
Wilson, W. 250
Wilson, Winifred (1882–1973) 250
Wilson of Sheffield 250
Wimmer, L. 251
Wimperis, Edmund Morison (1835–1900) 251
Winterbottom, Austin (1860–1919) 251
Witherington, William Frederick (1785–1865) 251
Wohlgarten, Joseph van 251
Wollen, William Barnes (1857–1936) 251
Wolmark, Alfred Aaron (1877–1961) 251
Wood, Christopher (1901–1930) 252
Wood, Tom (b.1955) 264
Woods, Grace Mary (b.1909) 252
Woolhouse, George (1751–1835) 252
Woolmer, Alfred Joseph (1805–1892) 252
Woolner, Thomas (1825–1892) 252
Wopfner, Josef (1843–1927) 252
Wouwerman, Philips (1619–1668) 254
Wright, Joseph of Derby (1734–1797) 254
Wyatt, Houghton (b.1953/1954) 284–288, 290
Wyld, William (1806–1889) 254
Wyllie, William Lionel (1851–1931) 254
Yarnold, Joseph (c.1817–1852) 254
Yeames, William Frederick (1835–1918) 254
Ziem, Félix François Georges Philibert (1821–1911) 254
Zimmermann, Ernst Karl Georg (1852–1901) 255
Zoffany, Johann (1733–1810) 255, 273
Zuccarelli, Franco (1702–1788) 255

Acknowledgements

The Public Catalogue Foundation would like to thank the individual artists and copyright holders for their permission to reproduce for free the paintings in this catalogue. Exhaustive efforts have been made to locate the copyright owners of all the images included within this catalogue and to meet their requirements. Copyright credit lines for copyright owners who have been traced are listed in the Further Information section.

The Public Catalogue Foundation would like to express its great appreciation to the following organisations for their kind assistance in the preparation of this catalogue:

Bridgeman Art Library
Flowers East
Marlborough Fine Art
National Association of Decorative & Fine Arts Societies (NADFAS)
National Gallery, London
National Portrait Gallery, London
Royal Academy of Arts, London
Tate

The Public Catalogue Foundation

The Public Catalogue Foundation is a registered charity. It was launched in 2003 to create a photographic record of the entire national collection of oil, tempera and acrylic paintings in public ownership in the United Kingdom.

Whilst our public galleries and civic buildings hold arguably the greatest collection of oil paintings in the world, over 80 per cent of these are not on view. Few collections have a complete photographic record of their paintings let alone a comprehensive illustrated catalogue. What is publicly owned is not publicly accessible.

The Foundation is publishing a series of fully illustrated, county-by-county catalogues that will cover, eventually, the entire national UK collection. To date, it has published over 30 volumes, presenting over 72,000 paintings.

In partnership with the BBC, the Foundation will make its database of the entire UK collection of 200,000 oil paintings available online through a new website called *Your Paintings*. The website was launched in the summer of 2011.

Your Paintings (*www.bbc.co.uk/arts/yourpaintings*) offers a variety of ways of searching for paintings as well as further information about the paintings and artists, including links to the participating collections' websites. For those interested in paintings and the subjects they portray *Your Paintings* is an unparalleled learning resource.

Collections benefit substantially from the work of the Foundation, not least from the digital images that are given to them for free following photography, and from the increased recognition that the project brings. These substantial benefits come at no financial cost to the collections.

The Foundation is funded by a combination of support from individuals, charitable trusts, companies and the public sector although the latter provides less than 20 per cent of the Foundation's financial support.

Supporters

Master Patrons

The Public Catalogue Foundation is greatly indebted to the following Master Patrons who have helped it in the past or are currently working with it to raise funds for the publication of their county catalogues. All of them have given freely of their time and have made an enormous contribution to the work of the Foundation.

Peter Andreae *(Hampshire)*
Sir Henry Aubrey-Fletcher, Bt, Lord Lieutenant of Buckinghamshire *(Buckinghamshire)*
Sir Nicholas Bacon, DL, High Sheriff of Norfolk *(Norfolk)*
Sir John Bather, Lord Lieutenant of Derbyshire *(Derbyshire)*
The Hon. Mrs Bayliss, JP, Lord Lieutenant of Berkshire *(Berkshire)*
Ian Bonas *(County Durham)*
Peter Bretherton *(West Yorkshire: Leeds)*
Michael Brinton, Lord Lieutenant of Worcestershire *(Worcestershire)*
Sir Hugo Brunner, KCVO, JP *(Oxfordshire)*
Mr John Bush, OBE, Lord-Lieutenant of Wiltshire *(Wiltshire)*
Lady Butler *(Warwickshire)*
Richard Compton *(North Yorkshire)*
George Courtauld, DL, Vice Lord Lieutenant of Essex *(Essex)*

The Countess of Darnley, Lord Lieutenant of Herefordshire *(Herefordshire)*
The Marquess of Downshire *(North Yorkshire)*
Martin Dunne, Lord Lieutenant of Warwickshire *(Warwickshire)*
Sir Henry Elwes, KCVO, Lord-Lieutenant of Gloucestershire *(Gloucestershire)*
Jenny Farr, MBE, DL *(Nottinghamshire)*
John Fenwick *(Tyne & Wear Museums)*
Mark Fisher, MP *(Staffordshire)*
Patricia Grayburn, MBE, DL *(Surrey)*
The Earl of Halifax, KStJ, JP, DL *(East Riding of Yorkshire)*
Lord Roy Hattersley, PC *(South Yorkshire: Sheffield)*
Algy Heber-Percy, Lord Lieutenant of Shropshire *(Shropshire)*
The Lady Mary Holborow, Lord Lieutenant of Cornwall *(Cornwall)*
Sarah Holman *(Warwickshire)*
Tommy Jowitt *(West Yorkshire)*
Alderman Sir David Lewis, The Rt Hon. The Lord Mayor of London, 2007–2008 *(The City of London)*
Sir Michael Lickiss *(Cornwall)*
Magnus Linklater *(Scotland)*
Lord Marlesford, DL *(Suffolk)*
Dr Bridget McConnell *(Glasgow)*
Lady Sarah Nicholson *(County Durham)*
Malcolm V. L. Pearce, MP *(Somerset)*
Sir John Riddell, Lord Lieutenant of Northumberland *(Northumberland)*
Venetia Ross Skinner *(Dorset)*
The Most Hon. The Marquess of Salisbury, PC, DL *(Hertfordshire)*
Julia Somerville *(Government Art Collection)*
Tim Stevenson, OBE, Lord Lieutenant of Oxfordshire *(Oxfordshire)*
Phyllida Stewart-Roberts, OBE *(East Sussex)*
Lady Juliet Townsend, Lord Lieutenant of Northamptonshire *(Northamptonshire)*
Leslie Weller, DL *(West Sussex)*
Sir Samuel C. Whitbread, KCVO, Lord Lieutenant of Bedfordshire *(Bedfordshire)*

Financial support

The Public Catalogue Foundation is particularly grateful to the following organisations and individuals who have given it generous financial support since the project started in 2003.

National Sponsor

Christie's

Benefactors (£10,000–£50,000)

The 29th May 1961 Charitable Trust
Arts Council England
The Barbour Trust
Binks Trust
City of Bradford Metropolitan District Council
Deborah Loeb Brice Foundation
The Bulldog Trust
A. & S. Burton 1960 Charitable Trust
Christie's
City of London Corporation
The John S. Cohen Foundation
Covent Garden London
Creative Scotland
Department for Culture, Media and Sport
Sir Harry Djanogly, CBE
Mr Lloyd Dorfman
Dunard Fund
The Elmley Foundation
Fenwick Ltd
Fidelity UK Foundation
Marc Fitch Fund
The Foyle Foundation
J. Paul Getty Jr Trust
Hampshire County Council
The Charles Hayward Foundation
Peter Harrison Foundation
Mr Robert Hiscox
Hiscox plc
David Hockney, CH, RA
ICAP plc

The Jordan Charitable Foundation
Kent County Council
The Linbury Trust
The Manifold Trust
Paul Mellon Centre for Studies in British Art
The Mercers' Company
Robert Warren Miller
Mr & Mrs A. Mittal
The Monument Trust
Miles Morland
Allan and Carol Murray
National Gallery Trust
Stavros Niarchos Foundation
Norfolk County Council
Northern Rock Foundation
Nottingham City Council
Malcolm V. L. Pearce, MP
P. F. Charitable Trust
The Pilgrim Trust
Provident Financial
RAB Capital plc
The Radcliffe Trust
Renaissance East Midlands
Renaissance West Midlands
Renaissance Yorkshire
Saga Group Ltd
Scottish Government
The Bernard Sunley Charitable Foundation
Townsend Family Trust
University College, London
University of Leeds
The Walker Trust
The Wolfson Foundation
Sir Siegmund Warburg's Voluntary Settlement
Garfield Weston Foundation
Mr & Mrs A. H. Wilkinson
The Wixamtree Trust

Series Patrons (Minimum donation of £2,500)

James & Lindsay Adam
Sir John Bather
Harry Bott
Janey Buchan
Mrs Rhona Callander
Dr Peter Cannon-Brookes
The John S. Cohen Foundation
Bushey Museum in memory of Lavender Watson
Mr Lloyd Dorfman
Lord Douro
Jenny Farr, MBE, DL
Mrs Greta Fenston
The FIRS Trust
Glasgow Museums
Patricia Grayburn, MBE, DL
G. Laurence Harbottle
R. K. Harrison Insurance Services Limited
Paul & Fiona Hart
Paul & Kathrine Haworth
Lord & Lady Heseltine
Patrik Holden & Lin Hinds
Neil Honebon
Michael Jacobson
Grace Jenkins
Dr David Johnson, DL
The Keatley Trust
John Kendall, Esq.
Michael A. Lambert, CBE
David & Amanda Leathers
Miles Morland
Allan & Carol Murray
North East Regional Museums Hub
The University of Northampton
Nottingham Civic Society
Richard & Amika Oldfield
The Roper Family Charitable Trust
Adam Sedgwick
Sir Harry & Lady Soloman
Stuart M. Southall
Simon Still
Chloe Teacher
University of Surrey
David & Cissy Walker
Tony Wilkinson
Mr & Mrs Jo Windsor
Mr & Mrs Charles Wyvill

Catalogue Patrons (£1,000–£10,000)

The 29th May 1961 Charitable Trust
ACE Study Tours
Adams & Remers
Marcus & Kate Agius
The AIM Foundation
D. C. R. Allen
John Alston, CBE
Amberley Castle
The Astor Foundation
The Aylesford Family Charitable Trust
Chairman of Cornwall County Council, Mrs Doris Anson, OBE, JP
Archant Ltd

G. F. Armitage Family Charitable Trust
Mr Ian Askew
Aurelius Charitable Trust
The Bacon Charitable Trust
Lawrence Banks, CBE, DL
Barlow Robbins LLP
Mr James & Lady Emma Barnard
Basingstoke and Deane Borough Council
Bath & North East Somerset District Council Heritage Services
Robert Baxter, DL
Birmingham Common Good Trust
Sir Christopher Bland
Johnnie Boden
The Charlotte Bonham-Carter Charitable Trust
H. R. Pratt Boorman Family Foundation
A. J. H. du Boulay Charitable Trust
The Bowerman Charitable Trust
Viscountess Boyd Charitable Trust
Lord & Lady Bradbury
Bramdean Asset Management LLP
Peter Bretherton
Brewin Dolphin
J. & M. Britton Charitable Trust
Mrs T. Brotherton-Ratcliffe
Janey Buchan
Mr & Mrs Patrick Burgess
Mr & Mrs Mark Burrell
Arnold J. Burton Charitable Trust
Bushey Museum in Memory of Lavender Watson
Mrs Anne Cadbury, OBE, JP, DL
Roger Cadbury
C. J. R. & Mrs C. L. Calderwood
Sir Ralph Carr-Ellison
Mr & Mrs J. Chambers
Chichester District Council
His Honour Richard Cole, DL & Mrs Sheila Cole
The Timothy Colman Charitable Trust
Mr & Mrs Derek Coombs
The Helen Jean Cope Trust
Mr & Mrs Ian Copesteak
Cornwall County Council
Mr S. J. D. Corsan
Graeme Cottam & Gloriana Marks de Chabris
Coutts Charitable Trust
David Crane Trust
Elaine Craven, Earl Street Employment Consultants Ltd
Harriett Cullen
Culture North East
Rt Hon. Viscount Daventry
N. Davie-Thornhill
Brigadier Mike Dauncey, DSO, DL
De La Rue Charitable Trust
Mr Robert Dean
Deborah Gage (Works of Art) Ltd
Derek Johns Ltd, London
Derby City Council
Derby High School Trust Ltd
Derbyshire Building Society
Derbyshire Community Foundation (The Ashby Fund)
J. N. Derbyshire Trust
The Duke of Devonshire's Charitable Trust
S. Dewhirst Charitable Trust
Sir Harry Djanogly, CBE
Dorset County Council
Lord Douro
Professor Patrick & Dr Grace Dowling
Dunn Family Charitable Trust
East Sussex County Council
Eastbourne Borough Council
EEMLAC, through the Association for Suffolk Museums
Lord & Lady Egremont
Sir John & Lady Elliott
Andrew & Lucy Ellis
Peter & Judy Ellwood
Essex County Council
John & Felicity Fairbairn
Fairfield Charitable Trust
Jenny Farr, MBE, DL
John Feeney Charitable Trust
The Trustees of the Finnis Scott Foundation
The Fishmongers' Company
David & Ann FitzWilliam-Lay
Elizabeth & Val Fleming
The Follett Trust
Richard & Elizabeth Fothergill

Christopher & Catherine Foyle
Freemasons of Derbyshire
The Friends of Historic Essex
The Friends of the Laing Art Gallery
The Friends of the Royal Pavilion, Art Gallery & Museums, Brighton
The Friends of Southampton's Museums, Archives and Galleries
The Friends of Sunderland Museums
The Friends of York Art Gallery (E. J. Swift Bequest)
Philip Gibbs
The Hon. H. M. T. Gibson's Charity Trust
Lewis & Jacqueline Golden
The Goldsmiths' Company
Gorringes
Charles Gregson
The Grocers' Company
The Gulland Family
David Gurney
Philip Gwyn
Sir Ernest Hall
The Earl of Halifax, KStJ, JP, DL
The W. A. Handley Charity Trust
The Hartnett Charitable Trust
Hazlitt, Gooden & Fox Ltd
Heartwood Wealth Management Ltd
The Trustees of the King Henry VIII Endowed Trust, Warwick
The Rt Hon. the Lord Heseltine, CH, PC & Lady Heseltine
The Lady Hind Trust
Hobart Charitable Trust
Edward and Anna Hocknell
David Hockney CH, RA
Patrick Holden & Lin Hinds
Mrs Michael Hollingbery
The Holman Family
Mr & Mrs A. Holman-West
The Honourable Company of Gloucestershire
The Hope Scott Trust
David & Prue Hopkinson
Major & Mrs Bill Hutchinson
His Honour Gabriel Hutton
Isle of Wight Council
The J. and S. B. Charitable Trust
Alan & Penny Jerome
James & Lucilla Joll Charitable Trust
Mr & Mrs Peter Jones
Tommy Jowitt
The Keatley Trust
Kent Messenger Group
Garrett Kirk, Jr
Mr John Kirkland, OBE & Mrs Sheila Kirkland
Robert Kirkland
Kirklees Council
The David Laing Foundation
Landau Foundation
Lord Lea of Crondall, OBE
The Leche Trust
Leeds Art Collections Fund
Leeds City Council
Leeds Philosophical and Literary Society
The Hon. David Legh, DL
Lord Leverhulme's Charitable Trust
Mr & Mrs John Lewis
Mark & Sophie Lewisohn
Tom Lugg & the Lane Family
The Orr Mackintosh Foundation
The MacRobert Trust
Maidstone Borough Council
John Manser
Mr & Mrs Derek Mapp
Walter & Barbara Marais
The Marlay Group
Marshall Charitable Trust
Stephen & Carolyn Martin
Tom & Anne Martin
The Medlock Charitable Trust
The Piet Mendels Foundation
MLA East of England
MLA North East of England
Museums Galleries Scotland
Mr Paul Myners
Rupert Nabarro
Nancie Massey Charitable Trust
Newcastle City Council
Bryan Norman
Lord & Lady Northampton
The University of Northampton
NP Aerospace Ltd
Oakmoor Trust
Jasper & Virginia Olivier
The Orr Mackintosh Foundation
Mr Christopher Oughtred
The Owen Family Trust

Sir Idris Pearce
Roger Neville Russ Peers
The Pennycress Trust
Perkins Family
The Lord & Lady Phillimore
Mrs Margaret Pollett
Simon & Ursula Pomeroy
The Portland Family
Portsmouth City Council
George Pragnell Ltd
The Prince Philip Trust Fund for the Royal Borough of Windsor and Maidenhead
Provident Financial plc
Mr John Rank
Rathbone Investment Management Ltd
The Hans and Märit Rausing Charitable Trust
Roger & Jane Reed
Renaissance North East
Renaissance South East
Renaissance South West
Michael Renshall, CBE, MA, FCA
Sir John Riddell
Sir Miles & Lady Rivett-Carnac
Rockley Charitable Trust
Rolls-Royce plc
The Roper Family Charitable Trust
Rothschild Foundation
Royal Cornwall Museum
Graham & Ann Rudd
Sir Nigel Rudd
Russell New
The J. S. & E. C. Rymer Charitable Trust
The Earl St Aldwyn
The Sammermar Trust
Scarfe Charitable Trust
Andrew & Belinda Scott
The Trustees of the Finnis Scott Foundation
Shaftesbury PLC
Mr W. Sharpe
The Shears Foundation
Robert Shields, DL
Smith & Williamson
South West of England Regional Development Agency
Caroline M. Southall
Stuart M. Southall
Southampton City Council
The Jessie Spencer Trust
Hugh & Catherine Stevenson
Mrs Andrew Stewart-Roberts, OBE
Mr Michael Stone
Mr Peter Stormonth Darling
The Stratford-upon-Avon Town Trust
Strutt and Parker
Suffolk County Council, through the Association for Suffolk Museums
Surrey County Council
The John Swire 1989 Charitable Trust
The Tanner Trust
Tennants Auctioneers
Tesco Charity Trust
The Thistle Trust
Prof. Caroline Tisdall
Trusthouse Charitable Foundation
Gladwyn Turbutt
TWM Business Partners
Tyne & Wear Museums
University College Falmouth
University of Derby
University of Essex
David & Grizelda Vermont
Wakefield Metropolitan District Council
Robert & Felicity Waley-Cohen
The Peggy Walker Charitable Trust
The Walland Trust Fund
John Wates Charitable Trust
Leslie Weller, DL
The Welton Foundation
West Sussex County Council
Mr & Mrs David Wigglesworth
Wilkin & Sons Ltd
Mr & Mrs Jo Windsor
Peter Wolton Charitable Trust
Michael J. Woodhall, FRICS
Sir Philip Wroughton
Mrs Angela Yeoman

First published in 2012 by The Public Catalogue Foundation, Printed Catalogue Division,
8 Frederick's Place, London, EC2R 8AB

ISBN 978-1-904931-51-5

South Yorkshire: Sheffield photography: Norman Taylor

Designed by Sally Jeffery

Printed in Hong Kong by Paramount Printing Company Limited

Cover image:

Fry, Roger Eliot 1866–1934
Edith Sitwell (1887–1964), 1918
Museums Sheffield, (see p. 76)

Back cover images (from top to bottom):

Barry, James 1741–1806
Jupiter Beguiled by Juneo on Mount Ida, 1790–1799
Museums Sheffield, (see p. 14)

Blake, Peter b.1932
Footsteps, 1955
Museums Sheffield, (see p. 20)

Underhill, Graham b.1946
Arrangement before a Void, 2008
University of Sheffield, (see p. 302)